The Oxford Spanish Minidictionary

SPANISH–ENGLISH
ENGLISH–SPANISH
ESPAÑOL–INGLÉS
INGLÉS–ESPAÑOL

Christine Lea

Oxford   New York

OXFORD UNIVERSITY PRESS

1997

Oxford University Press, Great Clarendon Street, Oxford OX2 6DP

Oxford New York

Athens Auckland Bangkok Bogota Bombay
Buenos Aires Calcutta Cape Town Dar es Salaam
Delhi Florence Hong Kong Istanbul Karachi
Kuala Lumpur Madras Madrid Melbourne
Mexico City Nairobi Paris Singapore
Taipei Tokyo Toronto

and associated companies in
Berlin Ibadan

Oxford is a trade mark of Oxford University Press

First published 1993
Reissued 1997

British Library Cataloguing in Publication Data
Lea, Christine
The Oxford Spanish minidictionary Spanish-English.
English-Spanish—(Oxford minidictionaries)
1. Spanish language—Dictionaries—English.
2. English language—Dictionaries—Spanish.
I. Title
453cu   PC1640
ISBN 0-19-860141-7

1 3 5 7 9 10 8 6 4 2

Printed in Great Britain by
Charles Letts (Scotland) Ltd., Dalkeith, Scotland

Contents · Índice

Preface

The Oxford Spanish Minidictionary has been written with speakers of both English and Spanish in mind and contains the most useful words and expressions of the English and Spanish languages of today. Wide coverage of culinary and motoring terms has been included to help the tourist.

Common abbreviations, names of countries, and other useful geographical names are included.

English pronunciation is given by means of the International Phonetic Alphabet. It is shown for all headwords and for those derived words whose pronunciation is not easily deduced from that of a headword. The rules for pronunciation of Spanish are given on page viii.

I should like to thank particularly Mary-Carmen Beaven whose comments have been invaluable. I would also like to acknowledge the help given me unwittingly by Dr M. Janes and Mrs J. Andrews whose French and Italian Minidictionaries have served as models for the present work.

C.A.L.

November 1992

Prefacio

Este minidiccionario de Oxford se escribió tanto para los hispanohablantes como para los anglo-parlantes y contiene las palabras y frases más corrientes de ambas lenguas de hoy. Se incluyen muchos términos culinarios y de automovilismo que pueden servir al turista.

Las abreviaturas más corrientes, los nombres de países, y otros términos geográficos figuran en este diccionario.

La pronunciación inglesa sigue el Alfabeto Fonético Internacional. Se incluye para cada palabra clave y todas las derivadas cuya pronunciación no es fácil de deducir a partir de la palabra clave. Las reglas de la pronunciación española se encuentran en la página viii.

Quisiera reconocer la ayuda de Mary-Carmen Beaven cuyas observaciones me han sido muy valiosas. También quiero agradecerles al Dr. M. Janes y a la Sra. J. Andrews cuyos minidiccionarios del francés y del italiano me han servido de modelo para el presente.

C.A.L.

Noviembre 1992

Introduction

The swung dash (∼) is used to replace a headword or that part of a headword preceding the vertical bar (|). In both English and Spanish only irregular plurals are given. Normally Spanish nouns and adjectives ending in an unstressed vowel form the plural by adding *s* (e.g. *libro, libros*). Nouns and adjectives ending in a stressed vowel or a consonant add *es* (e.g. *rubí, rubíes; pared, paredes*). An accent on the final syllable is not required when *es* is added (e.g. *nación, naciones*). Final *z* becomes *ces* (e.g. *vez, veces*). Spanish nouns and adjectives ending in *o* form the feminine by changing the final *o* to *a* (e.g. *hermano, hermana*). Most Spanish nouns and adjectives ending in anything other than final *o* do not have a separate feminine form with the exception of those denoting nationality etc; these add *a* to the masculine singular form (e.g. *español, española*). An accent on the final syllable is then not required (e.g. *inglés, inglesa*). Adjectives ending in *án, ón,* or *or* behave like those denoting nationality with the following exceptions: *inferior, mayor, mejor, menor, peor, superior* where the feminine has the same form as the masculine. Spanish verb tables will be found in the appendix.

The Spanish alphabet

In Spanish *ch, ll* and *ñ* are considered separate letters and in the Spanish-English section, therefore, they will be found after *cu, lu* and *ny* respectively.

Introducción

La tilde ($\sim$) se emplea para substituir a la palabra cabeza de artículo o aquella parte de tal palabra que precede a la barra vertical (|). Tanto en inglés como en español se dan los plurales solamente si son irregulares. Para formar el plural regular en inglés se añade la letra s al sustantivo singular, pero se añade *es* cuando se trata de una palabra que termina en *ch, sh, s, ss, us, x, o z* (p.ej. *sash, sashes*). En el caso de una palabra que termina en *y* precedida por una consonante, la *y* se cambia en *ies* (p.ej. *baby, babies*). Para formar el tiempo pasado y el participio pasado se añade *ed* al infinitivo de los verbos regulares ingleses (p.ej. *last, lasted*). En el caso de los verbos ingleses que terminan en *e* muda se añade sólo la *d* (p.ej. *move, moved*). En el caso de los verbos ingleses que terminan en *y* hay que cambiar la *y* en *ied* (p.ej. *carry, carried*). Los verbos irregulares se encuentran en el diccionario por orden alfabético remitidos al infinitivo, y también en la lista en el apéndice.

Pronunciation of Spanish

Vowels:

a   is between pronunciation of *a* in English *cat* and *arm*

e   is like *e* in English *bed*

i   is like *ee* in English *see* but a little shorter

o   is like *o* in English *hot* but a little longer

u   is like *oo* in English *too*

y   when a vowel is as Spanish **i**

Consonants:

b
1) in initial position or after nasal consonant is like English *b*
2) in other positions is between English *b* and English *v*

c
1) before **e** or **i** is like *th* in English *thin*
2) in other positions is like *c* in English *cat*

ch is like *ch* in English *chip*

d
1) in initial position, after nasal consonants and after **l** is like English *d*
2) in other positions is like *th* in English *this*

f   is like English *f*

g
1) before **e** or **i** is like *ch* in Scottish *loch*
2) in initial position is like *g* in English *get*
3) in other positions is like 2) but a little softer

h   is silent in Spanish but see also **ch**

j   is like *ch* in Scottish *loch*

k   is like English *k*

l   is like English *l* but see also **ll**

ll is like *lli* in English *million*

m is like English *m*

n   is like English *n*

ñ   is like *ni* in English *opinion*

p	is like English *p*
q	is like English *k*
r	is rolled or trilled
s	is like *s* in English *sit*
t	is like English *t*
v	1) in initial position or after nasal consonant is like English *b*
	2) in other positions is between English *b* and English *v*
w	is like Spanish **b** or **v**
x	is like English *x*
y	is like English *y*
z	is like *th* in English *thin*

Proprietary terms

This dictionary includes some words which are, or are asserted to be, proprietary names or trade marks. Their inclusion does not imply that they have acquired for legal purposes a non-proprietary or general significance, nor is any other judgement implied concerning their legal status. In cases where the editor has some evidence that a word is used as a proprietary name or trade mark this is indicated by the letter (P), but no judgement concerning the legal status of such words is made or implied thereby.

Marcas registradas

Este diccionario incluye algunas palabras que son o pretenden ser marcas registradas. No debe atribuirse ningún valor jurídico ni a la presencia ni a la ausencia de tal designación.

Pronunciación Inglesa

Símbolos fonéticos

Vocales y diptongos

iː	s*ee*	ə	*ago*
ɪ	s*i*t	eɪ	p*age*
e	t*e*n	əʊ	h*ome*
æ	h*a*t	aɪ	f*i*ve
ɑː	*ar*m	aɪə	f*ire*
ɒ	g*o*t	aʊ	n*ow*
ɔː	s*aw*	aʊə	fl*our*
ʊ	p*u*t	ɔɪ	j*oi*n
uː	t*oo*	ɪə	n*ear*
ʌ	c*u*p	eə	h*air*
ɜː	f*ur*	ʊə	p*oor*

Consonantes

p	*p*en	s	*s*o
b	*b*ad	z	*z*oo
t	*t*ea	ʃ	*sh*e
d	*d*ip	ʒ	mea*s*ure
k	*c*at	h	*h*ow
g	*g*ot	m	*m*an
tʃ	*ch*in	n	*n*o
dʒ	*J*une	ŋ	si*ng*
f	*f*all	l	*l*eg
v	*v*oice	r	*r*ed
θ	*th*in	j	*y*es
ð	*th*en	w	*w*et

Abbreviations · Abreviaturas

adjective	*a*	adjetivo
abbreviation	*abbr/abrev*	abreviatura
administration	*admin*	administración
adverb	*adv*	adverbio
American	*Amer*	americano
anatomy	*anat*	anatomía
architecture	*archit/arquit*	arquitectura
definite article	*art def*	artículo definido
indefinite article	*art indef*	artículo indefinido
astrology	*astr*	astrología
motoring	*auto*	automóvil
auxiliary	*aux*	auxiliar
aviation	*aviat/aviac*	aviación
biology	*biol*	biología
botany	*bot*	botánica
commerce	*com*	comercio
conjunction	*conj*	conjunción
cookery	*culin*	cocina
electricity	*elec*	electricidad
school	*escol*	enseñanza
Spain	*Esp*	España
feminine	*f*	femenino
familiar	*fam*	familiar
figurative	*fig*	figurado
philosophy	*fil*	filosofía
photography	*foto*	fotografía
geography	*geog*	geografía
geology	*geol*	geología
grammar	*gram*	gramática
humorous	*hum*	humorístico
interjection	*int*	interjección
interrogative	*inter*	interrogativo
invariable	*invar*	invariable
legal, law	*jurid*	jurídico
Latin American	*LAm*	latinoamericano
language	*lang*	lengua(je)
masculine	*m*	masculino
mathematics	*mat(h)*	matemáticas
mechanics	*mec*	mecánica
medicine	*med*	medicina

military	*mil*	militar
music	*mus*	música
mythology	*myth*	mitología
noun	*n*	nombre
nautical	*naut*	náutica
oneself	*o.s.*	uno mismo, se
proprietary term	*P*	marca registrada
pejorative	*pej*	peyorativo
philosophy	*phil*	filosofía
photography	*photo*	fotografía
plural	*pl*	plural
politics	*pol*	política
possessive	*poss*	posesivo
past participle	*pp*	participio de pretérito
prefix	*pref*	prefijo
preposition	*prep*	preposición
present participle	*pres p*	participio de presente
pronoun	*pron*	pronombre
psychology	*psych*	psicología
past tense	*pt*	tiempo pasado
railway	*rail*	ferrocarril
relative	*rel*	relativo
religion	*relig*	religión
school	*schol*	enseñanza
singular	*sing*	singular
slang	*sl*	argot
someone	*s.o.*	alguien
something	*sth*	algo
technical	*tec*	técnico
television	*TV*	televisión
university	*univ*	universidad
auxiliary verb	*v aux*	verbo auxiliar
verb	*vb*	verbo
intransitive verb	*vi*	verbo intransitivo
pronominal verb	*vpr*	verbo pronominal
transitive verb	*vt*	verbo transitivo
transitive & intransitive verb	*vti*	verbo transitivo e intransitivo

ESPAÑOL-INGLÉS
SPANISH—ENGLISH

A

a *prep* in, at; (*dirección*) to; (*tiempo*) at; (*hasta*) to, until; (*fecha*) on; (*más tarde*) later; (*medio*) by; (*precio*) for, at. ~ **5 km** 5 km away. **¿~ cuántos estamos?** what's the date? ~**l día siguiente** the next day. ~ **la francesa** in the French fashion. ~ **las 2** at 2 o'clock. ~ **los 25 años** (*edad*) at the age of 25; (*después de*) after 25 years. ~ **no ser por** but for. ~ **que** I bet. ~ **28 de febrero** on the 28th of February

ábaco *m* abacus

abad *m* abbot

abadejo (*pez*) cod

abad|esa *f* abbess. ~**ía** *f* abbey

abajo *adv* (down) below; (*dirección*) down(wards); (*en casa*) downstairs. —*int* down with. **calle ~** down the street. **el ~ firmante** the undersigned. **escaleras ~** downstairs. **la parte de ~** the bottom part. **los de ~** those at the bottom. **más ~** below.

abalanzarse [10] *vpr* rush towards

abalorio *m* glass bead

abanderado *m* standard-bearer

abandon|ado *adj* abandoned; (*descuidado*) neglected; (*personas*) untidy. ~**ar** *vt* leave (*un lugar*); abandon (*personas, cosas*). —*vi* give up. ~**arse** *vpr* give in; (*descuidarse*) let o.s. go. ~**o** *m* abandonment; (*estado*) abandon

abani|car [7] *vt* fan. ~**co** *m* fan. ~**queo** *m* fanning

abarata|miento *m* reduction in price. ~**r** *vt* reduce. ~**rse** *vpr* (*precios*) come down

abarca *f* sandal

abarcar [7] *vt* put one's arms around, embrace; (*comprender*) embrace; (*LAm, acaparar*) monopolize

abarquillar *vt* warp. ~**se** *vpr* warp

abarrotar *vt* overfill, pack full

abarrotes *mpl* (*LAm*) groceries

abast|ecer [11] *vt* supply. ~**ecimiento** *m* supply; (*acción*) supplying. ~**o** *m* supply. **dar ~o a** supply

abati|do *a* depressed. ~**miento** *m* depression. ~**r** *vt* knock down, demolish; (*fig, humillar*) humiliate. ~**rse** *vpr* swoop (*sobre* on); (*ponerse abatido*) get depressed

abdica|ción *f* abdication. ~**r** [7] *vt vi* abdicate

abdom|en *m* abdomen. ~**inal** *a* abdominal

abec|é *m* (*fam*) alphabet, ABC. ~**edario** *m* alphabet

abedul *m* birch (tree)

abej|a f bee. **~arrón** m bumble-bee. **~ón** m drone. **~orro** m bumble-bee; (insecto coleóptero) cockchafer

aberración f aberration

abertura f opening

abet|al m fir wood. **~o** m fir (tree)

abierto pp véase **abrir**. —a open

abigarra|do a multi-coloured; (fig, mezclado) mixed. **~miento** m variegation

abigeato m (Mex) rustling

abism|al a abysmal; (profundo) deep. **~ar** vt throw into an abyss; (fig, abatir) humble. **~arse** vpr be absorbed (en in), be lost (en in). **~o** m abyss; (fig, diferencia) world of difference

abizcochado a spongy

abjura|ción f abjuration. **~r** vt forswear. —vi. **~r de** forswear

ablanda|miento m softening. **~r** vt soften. **~rse** vpr soften

ablución f ablution

abnega|ción f self-sacrifice. **~do** a self-sacrificing

aboba|do a silly. **~miento** m silliness

aboca|do a (vino) medium. **~r** [7] vt pour out

abocetar vt sketch

abocinado a trumpet-shaped

abochornar vt suffocate; (fig, avergonzar) embarrass; **~se** vpr feel embarrassed; (plantas) wilt

abofetear vt slap

aboga|cía f legal profession. **~do** m lawyer; (notario) solicitor; (en el tribunal) barrister, attorney (Amer). **~r** [12] vi plead

abolengo m ancestry

aboli|ción f abolition. **~cionismo** m abolitionism. **~cionista** m & f abolitionist. **~r** [24] vt abolish

abolsado a baggy

abolla|dura f dent. **~r** vt dent

abomba|do a convex; (Arg, borracho) drunk. **~r** vt make

convex. **~rse** vpr (LAm, corromperse) start to rot, go bad

abomina|ble a abominable. **~ción** f abomination. **~r** vt detest. —vi. **~r de** detest

abona|ble a payable. **~do** a paid. —m subscriber

abonanzar vi (tormenta) abate; (tiempo) improve

abon|ar vt pay; (en agricultura) fertilize. **~aré** m promissory note. **~arse** vpr subscribe. **~o** m payment; (estiércol) fertilizer; (a un periódico) subscription

aborda|ble a reasonable; (persona) approachable. **~je** m boarding. **~r** vt tackle (un asunto); approach (una persona); (naut) come alongside

aborigen a & m native

aborrascarse [7] vpr get stormy

aborrec|er [11] vt hate; (exasperar) annoy. **~ible** a loathsome. **~ido** a hated. **~imiento** m hatred

aborregado a (cielo) mackerel

abort|ar vi have a miscarriage. **~ivo** a abortive. **~o** m miscarriage; (voluntario) abortion; (fig, monstruo) abortion. **hacerse ~ar** have an abortion

abotaga|miento m swelling. **~rse** [12] vpr swell up

abotonar vt button (up)

aboveda|do a vaulted. **~r** vt vault

abra f cove

abracadabra m abracadabra

abrasa|dor a burning. **~r** vt burn; (fig, consumir) consume. **~rse** vpr burn

abrasión f abrasion; (geología) erosion. **~vo** a abrasive

abraz|adera f bracket. **~ar** [10] embrace; (encerrar) enclose. **~arse** vpr embrace. **~o** m hug. **un fuerte ~o de** (en una carta) with best wishes from

abrecartas m paper-knife

ábrego *m* south wind

abrelatas *m invar* tin opener (*Brit*), can opener

abreva|dero *m* watering place. **~r** *vt* water ⟨*animales*⟩. **~rse** *vpr* ⟨*animales*⟩ drink

abrevia|ción *f* abbreviation; ⟨*texto abreviado*⟩ abridged text. **~do** *a* brief; ⟨*texto*⟩ abridged. **~r** *vt* abbreviate; abridge ⟨*texto*⟩; cut short ⟨*viaje etc*⟩. —*vi* be brief. **~tura** *f* abbreviation

abrig|ada *f* shelter. **~adero** *m* shelter. **~ado** *a* ⟨*lugar*⟩ sheltered; ⟨*personas*⟩ well wrapped up. **~ar** [12] *vt* shelter; cherish ⟨*esperanza*⟩; harbour ⟨*duda, sospecha*⟩. **~arse** *vpr* ⟨*take*⟩ shelter; ⟨*con ropa*⟩ wrap up. **~o** *m* (over)coat; ⟨*lugar*⟩ shelter

abril *m* April. **~eño** *a* April

abrillantar *vt* polish

abrir [*pp* **abierto**] *vt/i* open. **~se** *vpr* open; ⟨*extenderse*⟩ open out; ⟨*el tiempo*⟩ clear

abrocha|dor *m* buttonhook. **~r** *vt* do up; ⟨*con botones*⟩ button up

abrojo *m* thistle

abroncar [7] *vt* ⟨*fam*⟩ tell off; ⟨*abuchear*⟩ boo; ⟨*avergonzar*⟩ shame. **~se** *vpr* be ashamed; ⟨*enfadarse*⟩ get annoyed

abroquelarse *vpr* shield o.s.

abruma|dor *a* overwhelming. **~r** *vt* overwhelm

abrupto *a* steep; ⟨*áspero*⟩ harsh

abrutado *a* brutish

absceso *m* abscess

absentismo *m* absenteeism

ábside *m* apse

absintio *m* absinthe

absolu|ción *f* ⟨*relig*⟩ absolution; ⟨*jurid*⟩ acquittal

absolut|amente *adv* absolutely, completely. **~ismo** *m* absolutism. **~ista** *a & m & f* absolutist. **~o** *a* absolute. **~orio** *a* of acquittal. **en ~o** ⟨*de manera*

absoluta⟩ absolutely; ⟨*con sentido negativo*⟩ (not) at all

absolver [2, *pp* **absuelto**] *vt* ⟨*relig*⟩ absolve; ⟨*jurid*⟩ acquit

absor|bente *a* absorbent; ⟨*fig, interesante*⟩ absorbing. **~ber** *vt* absorb. **~ción** *f* absorption. **~to** *a* absorbed

abstemio *a* teetotal. —*m* teetotaller

absten|ción *f* abstention. **~erse** [40] *vpr* abstain, refrain ⟨*de from*⟩

abstinen|cia *f* abstinence. **~te** *a* abstinent

abstra|cción *f* abstraction. **~cto** *a* abstract. **~er** [41] *vt* abstract. **~erse** *vpr* be lost in thought. **~ído** *a* absent-minded

abstruso *a* abstruse

absuelto *a* ⟨*relig*⟩ absolved; ⟨*jurid*⟩ acquitted

absurdo *a* absurd. —*m* absurd thing

abuchear *vt* boo. **~o** *m* booing

abuel|a *f* grandmother. **~o** *m* grandfather. **~os** *mpl* grandparents

ab|ulia *f* lack of willpower. **~úlico** *a* weak-willed

abulta|do *a* bulky. **~miento** *m* bulkiness. **~r** *vt* enlarge; ⟨*hinchar*⟩ swell; ⟨*fig, exagerar*⟩ exaggerate. —*vi* be bulky

abunda|ncia *f* abundance. **~nte** *a* abundant, plentiful. **~r** *vi* be plentiful. **nadar en la ~ncia** *a* be rolling in money

aburguesa|miento *m* conversion to a middle-class way of life. **~rse** *vpr* become middle-class

aburri|do *a* ⟨*con estar*⟩ bored; ⟨*con ser*⟩ boring. **~miento** *m* boredom; ⟨*cosa pesada*⟩ bore. **~r** *vt* bore. **~rse** *vpr* be bored, get bored

abus|ar *vi* take advantage. **~ar de la bebida** drink too much.

~**ivo** a excessive. ~**o** m abuse. ~**ón** a (fam) selfish
abyec|ción f wretchedness. ~**to** a abject

acá adv here; (hasta ahora) until now. ~ **y allá** here and there. de ~ **para allá** to and fro. de ayer ~ since yesterday

acaba|do a finished; (perfecto) perfect; (agotado) worn out. —m finish. ~**miento** m finishing; (fin) end. ~**r** vt/i finish. ~**rse** vpr finish; (agotarse) run out; (morirse) die. ~**r con** put an end to. ~**r de** (+ infinitivo) have just (+ pp). **acabo de llegar** he has just arrived. ~**r por** (+ infinitivo) end up (+ gerundio). **¡se acabó!** that's it!

acabóse m. **ser el** ~ be the end, be the limit

acacia f acacia

acad|emia f academy. ~**émico** a academic

acaec|er [11] vi happen. ~**imiento** m occurrence

acalora|damente adv heatedly. ~**do** a heated. ~**miento** m heat. ~**r** vt warm up; (fig, excitar) excite. ~**rse** vpr get hot; (fig, excitarse) get excited

acallar vt silence

acampanado a bell-shaped

acampar vi camp

acanala|do a grooved. ~**dura** f groove. ~**r** vt groove

acantilado a steep. —m cliff

acanto m acanthus

acapara|r vt hoard; (monopolizar) monopolize. ~**miento** m hoarding; (monopolio) monopolizing

acaracolado a spiral

acaricia|dor a caressing. ~**r** vt caress; (rozar) brush; (proyectos etc) have in mind

ácaro m mite

acarre|ar vt transport; (desgracias etc) cause. ~**o** m transport

acartona|do a (persona) wizened. ~**rse** vpr (ponerse rígido) go stiff; (persona) become wizened

acaso adv maybe, perhaps. —m chance. ~ **llueva mañana** perhaps it will rain tomorrow. **al** ~ at random. **por si** ~ in case

acata|miento m respect (a for). ~**r** vt respect

acatarrarse vpr catch a cold, get a cold

acaudalado a well off

acaudillar vt lead

acceder vi agree; (tener acceso) have access

acces|ibilidad f accessibility. ~**ible** a accessible; (persona) approachable. ~**o** m access, entry; (med, ataque) attack; (llegada) approach

accesorio a & m accessory

accidentado a (terreno) uneven; (agitado) troubled; (persona) injured

accident|al a accidental. ~**arse** vpr have an accident. ~**e** m accident

acci|ón f (incl jurid) action; (hecho) deed. ~**onar** vt work. —vi gesticulate. ~**onista** m & f shareholder

acebo m holly (tree)

acebuche m wild olive tree

acecinar vt cure (carne). ~**se** vpr become wizened

acech|ar vt spy on; (aguardar) lie in wait for. ~**o** m spying. **al** ~**o** on the look-out

acedera f sorrel

acedía f (pez) plaice; (acidez) heartburn

aceit|ar vt oil; (culin) add oil to. ~**e** m oil; (de oliva) olive oil. ~**era** f oil bottle; (para engrasar) oilcan. ~**ero** a oil. ~**oso** a oily

aceituna f olive. ~**ado** a olive. ~**o** m olive tree

acelera|ción f acceleration. **∼damente** adv quickly. **∼dor** m accelerator. **∼r** vt accelerate; (fig) speed up, quicken

acelga f chard

ac|émila f mule; (como insulto) ass (fam). **∼emilero** m muleteer

acendra|do a pure. **∼r** vt purify; refine (metales)

acensuar vt tax

acent|o m accent; (énfasis) stress. **∼uación** f accentuation. **∼uar** [21] vt stress; (fig) emphasize. **∼uarse** vpr become noticeable

aceña f water-mill

acepción f meaning, sense

acepta|ble a acceptable. **∼ción** f acceptance; (aprobación) approval. **∼r** vt accept

acequia f irrigation channel

acera f pavement (Brit), sidewalk (Amer)

acerado a steel; (fig, mordaz) sharp

acerca de prep about

acerca|miento m approach; (fig) reconciliation. **∼r** [7] vt bring near. **∼rse** vpr approach

acería f steelworks

acerico m pincushion

acero m steel. **∼ inoxidable** stainless steel

acérrimo a (fig) staunch

acert|ado a right, correct; (apropiado) appropriate. **∼ar** [1] vt hit (el blanco); (adivinar) get right, guess. —vi get right. **∼ar a** happen to. **∼ar con** hit on. **∼ijo** m riddle

acervo m pile; (bienes) common property

acetato m acetate

acético a acetic

acetileno m acetylene

acetona m acetone

aciago a unlucky

aciano m cornflower

ac|íbar m aloes; (planta) aloe; (fig, amargura) bitterness. **∼ibarar** vt add aloes to; (fig, amargar) embitter

acicala|do a dressed up, overdressed. **∼r** vt dress up. **∼rse** vpr get dressed up

acicate m spur

acid|ez f acidity. **∼ificar** [7] vt acidify. **∼ificarse** vpr acidify

ácido a sour. —m acid

acierto m success; (idea) good idea; (habilidad) skill

aclama|ción f acclaim; (aplausos) applause. **∼r** vt acclaim; (aplaudir) applaud

aclara|ción f explanation. **∼r** vt lighten (colores); (explicar) clarify; (enjuagar) rinse. —vi (el tiempo) brighten up. **∼rse** vpr become clear. **∼torio** a explanatory

aclimata|ción f acclimatization, acclimation (Amer). **∼r** vt acclimatize, acclimate (Amer). **∼rse** vpr become acclimatized, become acclimated (Amer)

acné m acne

acobardar vt intimidate. **∼se** vpr get frightened

acocil m (Mex) freshwater shrimp

acod|ado a bent. **∼ar** vt (doblar) bend; (agricultura) layer. **∼arse** vpr lean on (en on). **∼o** m layer

acog|edor a welcoming; (ambiente) friendly. **∼er** [14] vt welcome; (proteger) shelter; (recibir) receive. **∼erse** vpr take refuge. **∼ida** f welcome; (refugio) refuge

acogollar vi bud. **∼se** vpr bud

acolchado a quilted. **∼r** vt quilt, pad

acólito m acolyte; (monaguillo) altar boy

acomet|edor a aggressive; (emprendedor) enterprising.

~er *vt* attack; (*emprender*) undertake; (*llenar*) fill. **~ida** *f* attack. **~ividad** *f* aggression; (*iniciativa*) enterprise

acomod|able *a* adaptable. **~adizo** *a* accommodating. **~ado** *a* well off. **~ador** *m* usher. **~adora** *f* usherette. **~amiento** *m* suitability. **~ar** *vt* arrange; (*adaptar*) adjust. **~arse** *vpr* settle down; (*adaptarse*) conform. **~aticio** *a* accommodating. **~o** *m* position

acompaña|do *a* accompanied; (*concurrido*) busy. **~miento** *m* accompaniment. **~nta** *f* companion. **~nte** *m* companion; (*mus*) accompanist. **~r** *vt* accompany; (*adjuntar*) enclose. **~rse** *vpr* (*mus*) accompany o.s.

acompasa|do *a* rhythmic. **~r** *vt* keep in time; (*fig, ajustar*) adjust

acondiciona|do *a* equipped. **~miento** *m* conditioning. **~r** *vt* fit out; (*preparar*) prepare

acongojar *vt* distress. **~se** *vpr* get upset

acónito *m* aconite

aconseja|ble *a* advisable. **~do** *a* advised. **~r** *vt* advise. **~rse** *vpr* take advice. **~rse con** consult

aconsonantar *vt/i* rhyme

acontec|er [11] *vi* happen. **~imiento** *m* event

acopi|ar *vt* collect. **~o** *m* store

acopla|do *a* coordinated. **~miento** *m* coupling; (*elec*) connection. **~r** *vt* fit; (*elec*) connect; (*rail*) couple

acoquina|miento *m* intimidation. **~r** *vt* intimidate; **~rse** *vpr* be intimidated

acoraza|do *a* armour-plated. — *m* battleship. **~r** [10] *vt* armour

acorazonado *a* heart-shaped

acorcha|do *a* spongy. **~rse** *vpr* go spongy; (*parte del cuerpo*) go to sleep

acord|ado *a* agreed. **~ar** [2] *vt* agree (upon); (*decidir*) decide; (*recordar*) remind. **~e** *a* in agreement; (*mus*) harmonious. —*m* chord

acorde|ón *m* accordion. **~onista** *m & f* accordionist

acordona|do *a* (*lugar*) cordoned off. **~miento** *m* cordoning off. **~r** *vt* tie, lace; (*rodear*) surround, cordon off

acorrala|miento *m* (*de animales*) rounding up; (*de personas*) cornering. **~r** *vt* round up (*animales*); corner (*personas*)

acorta|miento *m* shortening. **~r** *vt* shorten; (*fig*) cut down

acos|ar *vt* hound; (*fig*) pester. **~o** *m* pursuit; (*fig*) pestering

acostar [2] *vt* put to bed; (*naut*) bring alongside. —*vi* (*naut*) reach land. **~se** *vpr* go to bed; (*echarse*) lie down; (*Mex, parir*) give birth

acostumbra|do *a* (*habitual*) usual. **~do** *a* used to, accustomed to. **~r** *vt* get used. **me ha acostumbrado a levantarme por la noche** he's got me used to getting up at night. —*vi.* **~ (a)** be accustomed to. **acostumbro comer a la una** I usually have lunch at one o'clock. **~rse** *vpr* become accustomed, get used

acota|ción *f* (*nota*) marginal note; (*en el teatro*) stage direction; (*cota*) elevation mark. **~do** *a* enclosed. **~r** *vt* mark out (*terreno*); (*anotar*) annotate

ácrata *a* anarchistic. —*m & f* anarchist

acre *m* acre. —*a* (*olor*) pungent; (*sabor*) sharp, bitter

acrecenta|miento *m* increase. **~r** [1] *vt* increase. **~rse** *vpr* increase

acrecer [11] *vt* increase. **~imiento** *m* increase

acredita|do *a* reputable; (*pol*) accredited. **~r** *vt* prove; accredit ⟨*representante diplomático*⟩; (*garantizar*) guarantee; (*autorizar*) authorize. **~rse** *vpr* make one's name

acreedor *a* worthy (**a** of). **—***m* creditor

acribillar *vt* (*a balazos*) riddle (**a** with); (*a picotazos*) cover (**a** with); (*fig, a preguntas etc*) pester (**a** with)

acrimonia *f* (*de sabor*) sharpness; (*de olor*) pungency; (*fig*) bitterness

acrisola|do *a* pure; (*fig*) proven. **~r** *vt* purify; (*confirmar*) prove

acritud *f* (*de sabor*) sharpness; (*de olor*) pungency; (*fig*) bitterness

acr|obacia *f* acrobatics. **~obacias aéreas** aerobatics. **~óbata** *m* & *f* acrobat. **~obático** *a* acrobatic. **~obatismo** *m* acrobatics

acrónimo *m* acronym

acróstico *a* & *m* acrostic

acta *f* minutes; (*certificado*) certificate

actinia *f* sea anemone

actitud *f* posture, position; (*fig*) attitude, position

activ|ación *f* speed-up. **~amente** *adv* actively. **~ar** *vt* activate; (*acelerar*) speed up. **~idad** *f* activity. **~o** *a* active. **—***m* assets

acto *m* act; (*ceremonia*) ceremony. **en el ~** immediately

act|or *m* actor. **~riz** *f* actress

actuación *f* action; (*conducta*) behaviour; (*theat*) performance

actual *a* present; (*asunto*) topical. **~idad** *f* present. **~idades** *fpl* current affairs. **~ización** *f* modernization. **~izar** [10] *vt* modernize. **~mente** *adv* now,

at the present time. **en la ~idad** nowadays

actuar [21] *vt* work. **—***vi* act. **~ como**, **~ de** act as

actuario *m* clerk of the court. **~ (de seguros)** actuary

acuarel|a *f* watercolour. **~ista** *m* & *f* watercolourist

acuario *m* aquarium. **A~** Aquarius

acuartela|do *a* quartered. **~miento** *m* quartering. **~r** *vt* quarter, billet; (*mantener en cuartel*) confine to barracks

acuático *a* aquatic

acuci|ador *a* pressing. **~ar** *vt* urge on; (*dar prisa a*) hasten. **~oso** *a* keen

acuclillarse *vpr* crouch down, squat down

acuchilla|do *a* slashed; (*persona*) stabbed. **~r** *vt* slash; stab ⟨*persona*⟩; (*alisar*) smooth

acudir *vi*. **~ a** go to, attend; keep ⟨*una cita*⟩; (*en auxilio*) go to help

acueducto *m* aqueduct

acuerdo *m* agreement. **—***vb véase* **acordar. ¡de ~!** OK! **de ~ con** in accordance with. **estar de ~** agree. **ponerse de ~** agree

acuesto *vb véase* **acostar**

acuidad *f* acuity, sharpness

acumula|ción *f* accumulation. **~dor** *a* accumulative. **—***m* accumulator. **~r** *vt* accumulate. **~rse** *vpr* accumulate

acunar *vt* rock

acuña|ción *f* minting, coining. **~r** *vt* mint, coin

acuos|idad *f* wateriness. **~o** *a* watery

acupuntura *f* acupuncture

acurrucarse [7] *vpr* curl up

acusa|ción *f* accusation. **~do** *a* accused; (*destacado*) marked. **—***m* accused. **~dor** *a* accusing. **—***m* accuser. **~r** *vt* accuse; (*mostrar*) show; (*denunciar*) denounce. **~rse** *vpr* confess;

(notarse) become marked. **~to-rio** *m* a accusatory

acuse *m.* **~ de recibo** acknowledgement of receipt

acus|ica *m & f (fam)* telltale. **~ón** *a & m* telltale

acústica *f* acoustics. **~o** *a* acoustic

achacar [7] *vt* attribute

achacoso *a* sickly

achaflanar *vt* bevel

achantar *vt (fam)* intimidate. **~se** *vpr* hide; *(fig)* back down

achaparrado *a* stocky

achaque *m* ailment

achares *mpl (fam).* **dar ~** make jealous

achata|miento *m* flattening. **~r** *vt* flatten

achica|do *a* childish. **~r** [7] *vt* make smaller; *(fig, empequeñecer, fam)* belittle; *(naut)* bale out. **~rse** *vpr* become smaller; *(humillarse)* be humiliated

achicoria *f* chicory

achicharra|dero *m* inferno. **~nte** *a* sweltering. **~r** *vt* burn; *(fig)* pester. **~rse** *vpr* burn

achispa|do *a* tipsy. **~rse** *vpr* get tipsy

achocolatado *a* (chocolate-) brown

achuch|ado *a (fam)* hard. **~ar** *vt* jostle, push. **~ón** *m* shove, push

achulado *a* cocky

adagio *m.* adage, proverb; *(mus)* adagio

adalid *m* leader

adamascado *a* damask

adapta|ble *a* adaptable. **~ción** *f* adaptation. **~dor** *m* adapter. **~r** *vt* adapt; *(ajustar)* fit. **~rse** *vpr* adapt o.s.

adecentar *vt* clean up. **~se** *vpr* tidy o.s. up

adecua|ción *f* suitability. **~damente** *adv* suitably. **~do** *a* suitable. **~r** *vt* adapt, make suitable

adelant|ado *a* advanced; *(niño)* precocious; *(reloj)* fast. **~amiento** *m* advance(ment); *(auto)* overtaking. **~ar** *vt* advance, move forward; *(acelerar)* speed up; put forward *(reloj)*; *(auto)* overtake. **—vi** advance, go forward; *(reloj)* gain, be fast. **~arse** *vpr* advance, move forward; *(reloj)* gain; *(auto)* overtake. **~e** *adv* forward. **—int** come in!; *(¡siga!)* carry on! **~o** *m* advance; *(progreso)* progress. **más ~e** *(lugar)* further on; *(tiempo)* later on. **pagar por ~ado** pay in advance

adelfa *f* oleander

adelgaza|dor *a* slimming. **~miento** *m* slimming. **~r** [10] *vt* make thin. **—vi** lose weight; *(adrede)* slim. **~rse** *vpr* lose weight; *(adrede)* slim

ademán *m* gesture. **ademanes** *mpl (modales)* manners. **en ~ de** as if to

además *adv* besides; *(también)* also. **~ de** besides

adentr|arse *vpr.* **~ en** penetrate into; study thoroughly *(tema etc)*. **~o** *adv* in(side). **mar ~o** out at sea. **tierra ~o** inland

adepto *m* supporter

aderez|ar [10] *vt* flavour *(bebidas)*; *(condimentar)* season; dress *(ensalada)*. **~o** *m* flavouring; *(con condimentos)* seasoning; *(para ensalada)* dressing

adeudar *vt* owe. **~o** *m* debit

adhe|rencia *f* adhesion; *(fig)* adherence. **~rente** *a* adherent. **~rir** [4] *vt* stick on. **—vi** stick. **~rirse** *vpr* stick; *(fig)* follow. **~sión** *f* adhesion; *(fig)* support. **~sivo** *a & m* adhesive

adici|ón *f* addition. **~onal** *a* additional. **~onar** *vt* add

adicto *a* devoted. **—m** follower

adiestra|do *a* trained. ~miento *m* training. ~r *vt* train. ~rse *upr* practise

adinerado *a* wealthy

adiós *int* goodbye!; *(al cruzarse con alguien)* hello!

adit|amento *m* addition; *(accesorio)* accessory. ~ivo *m* additive

adivin|ación *f* divination; *(por conjeturas)* guessing. ~ador *m* fortune-teller. ~anza *f* riddle. ~ar *vt* foretell; *(acertar)* guess. ~o *m* fortune-teller

adjetivo *a* adjectival. —*m* adjective

adjudica|ción *f* award. ~r [7] *vt* award. ~rse *upr* appropriate. ~tario *m* winner of an award

adjunt|ar *vt* enclose. ~o *a* enclosed; *(auxiliar)* assistant. —*m* assistant

adminículo *m* thing, gadget

administra|ción *f* administration; *(gestión)* management. ~dor *m* administrator; *(gerente)* manager. ~dora *f* administrator; manageress. ~r *vt* administer. ~tivo *a* administrative

admira|ble *a* admirable. ~ción *f* admiration. ~dor *m* admirer. ~r *vt* admire; *(asombrar)* astonish. ~rse *upr* be astonished. ~tivo *a* admiring

admi|sibilidad *f* admissibility. ~sible *a* acceptable. ~sión *f* admission; *(aceptación)* acceptance. ~tir *vt* admit; *(aceptar)* accept

adobar *vt* *(culin)* pickle; *(fig)* twist

adobe *m* sun-dried brick. ~ra *f* mould for making (sun-dried) bricks

adobo *m* pickle

adocena|do *a* common. ~rse *upr* become common

adoctrinamiento *m* indoctrination

adolecer [11] *vi* be ill. ~ de suffer with

adolescen|cia *f* adolescent. ~te *a* & *m* & *f* adolescent

adonde *conj* where

adónde *adv* where?

adop|ción *f* adoption. ~tar *vt* adopt. ~tivo *a* adoptive; *(patria)* of adoption

adoquín *m* paving stone; *(imbécil)* idiot. ~inado *m* paving. ~inar *vt* pave

adora|ble *a* adorable. ~ción *f* adoration. ~dor *a* adoring. —*n* worshipper. ~r *vt* adore

adormec|edor *a* soporific; *(droga)* sedative. ~er [11] *vt* send to sleep; *(fig, calmar)* calm, soothe. ~erse *upr* fall asleep; *(un miembro)* go to sleep. ~ido *a* sleepy; *(un miembro)* numb. ~imiento *m* sleepiness; *(de un miembro)* numbness

adormidera *f* opium poppy

adormilarse *upr* doze

adorn|ar *vt* adorn (con, de with). ~o *m* decoration

adosar *vt* lean (a against)

adqui|rido *a* acquired. ~rir [4] *vt* acquire; *(comprar)* buy. ~sición *f* acquisition; *(compra)* purchase. ~sitivo *a* acquisitive. poder ~sitivo purchasing power

adrede *adv* on purpose

adrenalina *f* adrenalin

adscribir [*pp* adscrito] *vt* appoint

aduan|a *f* customs. ~ero *a* customs. —*m* customs officer

aducir [47] *vt* allege

adueñarse *upr* take possession

adul|ación *f* flattery. ~ador *a* flattering. —*m* flatterer. ~ar *vt* flatter

ad|ulteración *f* adulteration. ~ulterar *vt* adulterate. —*ví* commit adultery. **~ulterino** a adulterous. **~ulterio** m adultery. **~última** f adulteress. **~últero** a adulterous. **—**m adulterer

adulto a & m adult, grown-up

adusto a severe, harsh

advenedizo a & m upstart

advenimiento m advent, arrival; (*subida al trono*) accession

adventicio a accidental

adverbial a adverbial. **~o** m adverb

advers|ario m adversary. **~idad** f adversity. **~o** a adverse, unfavourable

advert|encia f warning; (*prólogo*) foreword. **~ido** a informed. **~ir** [4] vt warn; (*notar*) notice

adviento m Advent

advocación f dedication

adyacente a adjacent

aéreo a air; (*photo*) aerial; (*ferrocarril*) overhead; (*fig*) flimsy

aeróbica f aerobics

aerodeslizador m hovercraft

aerodinámic|a f aerodynamics. **~o** a aerodynamic

aeródromo m aerodrome, airdrome (*Amer*)

aero|espacial a aerospace. **~faro** m beacon. **~lito** m meteorite. **~nauta** m & f aeronaut. **~náutica** f aeronautics. **~náutico** a aeronautical. **~nave** f airship. **~puerto** m airport. **~sol** m aerosol

afab|ilidad f affability. **~le** a affable

afamado a famous

afán m hard work; (*deseo*) desire. **~anar** vt (*fam*) pinch. **~anarse** vpr strive (**en, por**) **~anoso** a laborious

afea|miento m disfigurement. **~r** vt disfigure, make ugly; (*censurar*) censure

afección f disease

afecta|ción f affectation. **~do** a affected. **~r** vt affect

afect|ísimo a affectionate. **~ísimo amigo** (*en cartas*) my dear friend. **~ividad** f emotional nature. **~ivo** a sensitive. **~o** m (*cariño*) affection. **—**a. **~o** a attached to. **~uosidad** f affection. **~uoso** a affectionate. **con un ~uoso saludo** (*en cartas*) with kind regards. **suyo ~ísimo** (*en cartas*) yours sincerely

afeita|do m shave. **~dora** f electric razor. **~r** vt shave. **~rse** vpr (have a) shave

afelpado a velvety

afemina|do a effeminate. **—**m effeminate person. **~miento** m effeminacy. **~rse** vpr become effeminate

aferrar [1] vt grasp

afgano a & m Afghan

afianza|miento m (*reforzar*) strengthening; (*garantía*) guarantee. **~rse** [10] vpr become established

afición f liking; (*conjunto de aficionados*) fans. **~onado** a keen (**a** on), fond (**a** of). **—**m fan. **~onar** vt make fond. **~onarse** vpr take a liking to. **por ~ón** as a hobby

afila|do a sharp. **~dor** m knife-grinder. **~dura** f sharpening. **~r** vt sharpen. **~rse** vpr get sharp; (*ponerse flaco*) grow thin

afilia|ción f affiliation. **~do** a affiliated. **~rse** vpr become a member (**a** of)

afiligranado a filigreed; (*fig*) delicate

afín a similar; (*próximo*) adjacent; (*personas*) related

afina|ción f refining; (*auto, mus*) tuning. **~do** a finished; (*mus*) in tune. **~r** vt refine; (*afilar*) sharpen; (*acabar*) finish; (*auto,*

mus) tune. —*vi* be in tune. **~rse**
vpr become more refined

afincarse [7] *vpr* settle

afinidad *f* affinity; (*parentesco*)
relationship

afirma|ción *f* affirmation. **~r** *vt*
make firm; (*asentir*) affirm.
~rse *vpr* steady o.s.; (*confirmar*)
confirm. **~tivo** *a* affirmative

afli|cción *f* affliction. **~tivo** *a*
distressing

afligi|do *a* distressed. —*m* af-
flicted. **~r** [14] *vt* distress. **~rse**
vpr grieve

afloja|miento *m* loosening. **~r**
vt loosen; (*relajar*) ease. —*vi* let
up

aflora|miento *m* outcrop. **~r** *vi*
appear on the surface

aflu|encia *f* flow. **~ente** *a* flow-
ing. —*m* tributary. **~ir** [17] *vi*
flow (a into)

af|onía *f* hoarseness. **~ónico** *a*
hoarse

aforismo *m* aphorism

aforo *m* capacity

afortunado *a* fortunate, lucky

afrancesado *a* francophile

afrent|a *f* insult; (*vergüenza*) dis-
grace. **~ar** *vt* insult. **~oso** *a*
insulting

África *f* Africa. **~ del Sur** South
Africa

africano *a & m* African

afrodisíaco *a & m*, **afrodisiaco**
a & m aphrodisiac

afrontar *vt* bring face to face;
(*enfrentar*) face, confront

afuera *adv* out(side). **¡~!** out of
the way! **~s** *fpl* outskirts.

agachar *vt* lower. **~se** *vpr* bend
over

agalla *f* (*de los peces*) gill. **~s** *fpl*
(*fig*) guts

agarrada *f* row

agarrader|a *f* (*LAm*) handle. **~o**
m handle. **tener ~as** (*LAm*),
tener ~os have influence

agarr|ado *a* (*fig, fam*) mean.
~ador *a* (*Arg*) (*bebida*) strong.
~ar *vt* grasp; (*esp LAm*) take,
catch. —*vi* (*plantas*) take root.
~arse *vpr* hold on; (*reñirse,
fam*) fight. **~ón** *m* tug; (*LAm,
riña*) row

agarrota|miento *m* tightening;
(*auto*) seizing up. **~r** *vt* tie
tightly; (*el frío*) stiffen; garotte
(*un reo*). **~rse** *vpr* go stiff; (*auto*)
seize up

agasaj|ado *m* guest of honour.
~ar *vt* look after well. **~o** *m*
good treatment

ágata *f* agate

agavilla|dora *f* (*máquina*)
binder. **~r** *vt* bind

agazaparse *vpr* hide

agencia *f* agency. **~ de viajes**
travel agency. **~ inmobiliaria**
estate agency (*Brit*), real estate
agency (*Amer*). **~r** *vt* find. **~rse**
vpr find (out) for o.s.

agenda *f* notebook

agente *m* agent; (*de policía*)
policeman. **~ de aduanas** customs officer. **~ de bolsa**
stockbroker

ágil *a* agile

agilidad *f* agility

agita|ción *f* waving; (*de un
líquido*) stirring; (*intran-
quilidad*) agitation. **~do** *a* (*el
mar*) rough; (*fig*) agitated. **~dor**
m (*pol*) agitator

agitanado *a* gypsy-like

agitar *vt* wave; shake (*botellas
etc*); stir (*líquidos*); (*fig*) stir up.
~se *vpr* wave; (*el mar*) get
rough; (*fig*) get excited

aglomera|ción *f* agglomeration;
(*de tráfico*) traffic jam. **~r** *vt*
amass. **~rse** *vpr* form a crowd

agn|osticismo *m* agnosticism.
~óstico *a & m* agnostic

agobi|ador *a* (*trabajo*) exhaust-
ing; (*calor*) oppressive. **~ante** *a*
(*trabajo*) exhausting; (*calor*)

oppressive. **~ar** vt weigh down; (fig, abrumar) overwhelm. **~o** m weight; (cansancio) exhaustion; (opresión) oppression

agolpa|miento m (de gente) crowd; (de cosas) pile. **~rse** vpr crowd together

agon|ía f death throes; (fig) agony. **~izante** a dying; (luz) failing. **~izar** [10] vi be dying

agor|ar [16] vt prophesy. **~ero** a of ill omen. **~m** soothsayer

agostar vt wither

agosto m August. **hacer su ~** feather one's nest

agota|do a exhausted; (libro) out of print. **~dor** a exhausting. **~miento** m exhaustion **~r** vt exhaust; (fig) exhausted; **~rse** vpr be exhausted; (libro) go out of print

agracia|do a attractive; (que tiene suerte) lucky. **~r** make attractive

agrada|ble a pleasant, nice. **~r** vi please. **esto me ~** I like this

agradec|er [11] vt thank (persona); be grateful for (cosa). **~ido** a grateful. **~imiento** m gratitude. ¡**muy ~ido!** thanks a lot!

agrado m pleasure; (amabilidad) friendliness

agrandar vt enlarge; (fig) exaggerate. **~se** vpr get bigger

agrario a agrarian, land; (política) agricultural

agrava|miento m worsening. **~nte** a aggravating. **—f** additional problem. **~r** vt aggravate; (aumentar el peso) make heavier. **~rse** vpr get worse

agravi|ar vt offend; (perjudicar) wrong. **~arse** vpr be offended. **~o** m offence

agraz m. **en ~** prematurely

agredir [24] vt attack. **~ de palabra** insult

agrega|do m aggregate; (funcionario diplomático) attaché.

~r [12] vt add; (unir) join; appoint (persona)

agremiar vt form into a union. **~se** vpr form a union

agres|ión f aggression; (ataque) attack. **~ividad** f aggressiveness. **~ivo** a aggressive. **~or** m aggressor

agreste a country

agria|do a (fig) embittered. **~r** [regular, o raramente 20] vt sour. **~rse** vpr turn sour; (fig) become embittered

agrícola a agricultural. **~icultor** a agricultural. **—m** farmer. **~icultura** f agriculture, farming

agridulce a bitter-sweet; (culin) sweet-and-sour

agriera f (LAm) heartburn

agrietar vt crack. **~se** vpr crack; (piel) chap

agrimens|or m surveyor. **~ura** f surveying

agrio a sour; (fig) sharp. **~s** mpl citrus fruits

agronomía f agronomy

agropecuario a farming

agrupa|ción f group; (acción) grouping. **~r** vt group. **~rse** vpr form a group

agua f water; (lluvia) rain; (marea) tide; (vertiente del tejado) slope. **~ abajo** downstream. **~ arriba** upstream. **~ bendita** holy water. **~ caliente** hot water. **estar entre dos ~s** sit on the fence. **hacer ~** (naut) leak. **nadar entre dos ~s** sit on the fence

aguacate m avocado pear; (árbol) avocado pear tree

aguacero m downpour, heavy shower

agua corriente running water

aguachinarse vpr (Mex) (cultivos) be flooded

aguada f watering place; (naut) drinking water; (acuarela) water-colour

agua *f* **de colonia** eau-de-Cologne

aguad|**o** *a* watery. **~ucho** *m* refreshment kiosk

agua: **~ dulce** fresh water. **~fiestas** *m & f invar* spoil-sport, wet blanket. **~ fría** cold water. **~fuerte** *m* etching

aguaje *m* spring tide

agua: **~mala** *f*, **~mar** *m* jellyfish

aguamarina *f* aquamarine

agua: **~miel** *f* mead. **~ mineral con gas** fizzy mineral water. **~ mineral sin gas** still mineral water. **~nieve** *f* sleet

aguanoso *a* watery; (*tierra*) waterlogged

aguant|**able** *a* bearable. **~aderas** *fpl* patience. **~ar** *vt* put up with, bear; (*sostener*) support. — *vi* hold out. **~arse** *vpr* restrain o.s. **~e** *m* patience; (*resistencia*) endurance

agua: **~pié** *m* watery wine. **~ potable** drinking water. **~r** [15] *vt* water down. **~ salada** salt water.

aguardar *vt* wait for. — *vi* wait

agua: **~rdiente** *m* (*cheap*) brandy. **~rrás** *m* turpentine, turps (*fam*). **~turma** *f* Jerusalem artichoke. **~zal** *m* puddle

agud|**eza** *f* sharpness; (*fig, perspicacia*) insight; (*fig, ingenio*) wit. **~izar** [10] *vt* sharpen. **~izarse** *vpr* (*enfermedad*) get worse. **~o** *a* sharp; (*ángulo, enfermedad*) acute; (*voz*) high-pitched

agüero *m* omen. **ser de buen ~** augur well

aguij|**ada** *f* goad. **~ar** *vt* (*incl fig*) goad. **~ón** *m* point of a goad. **~onazo** *m* prick. **~onear** *vt* goad

águila *f* eagle; (*persona perspicaz*) astute person

aguileña *f* columbine

aguil|**eño** *a* aquiline. **~ucho** *m* eaglet

aguinaldo *m* Christmas box

aguja *f* needle; (*del reloj*) hand; (*arquit*) steeple. **~s** *fpl* (*rail*) points

agujer|**ear** *vt* make holes in. **~o** *m* hole

agujetas *fpl* stiffness. **tener ~** be stiff

agujón *m* hairpin

agusanado *a* full of maggots

agutí *m* (*LAm*) guinea pig

aguz|**ado** *a* sharp. **~amiento** *m* sharpening. **~r** [10] *vt* sharpen

ah *int* ah!, oh!

aherrojar *vt* (*fig*) oppress

ahí *adv* there. **de ~ que** so that. **por ~** over there; (*aproximadamente*) thereabouts

ahija|**da** *f* goddaughter, godchild. **~do** *m* godson, godchild. **~r** *vt* adopt

ahínco *m* enthusiasm; (*empeño*) insistence

ahíto *a* full up

ahog|**ado** *a* (*en el agua*) drowned; (*asfixiado*) suffocated. **~ar** [12] *vt* (*en el agua*) drown; (*asfixiar*) suffocate; put out (*fuego*). **~arse** *vpr* (*en el agua*) drown; (*asfixiarse*) suffocate. **~o** *m* breathlessness; (*fig, angustia*) distress; (*apuro*) financial trouble

ahondar *vt* deepen. — *vi* go deep. **~ en** (*fig*) examine in depth. **~se** *vpr* get deeper

ahora *adv* now; (*hace muy poco*) just now; (*dentro de poco*) very soon. **~ bien** but. **~ mismo** right now. **de ~ en adelante** from now on, in future. **por ~** for the time being

ahorca|**dura** *f* hanging. **~r** [7] *vt* hang. **~rse** *vpr* hang o.s.

ahorita *adv* (*fam*) now. **~ mismo** right now

ahorquillar *vt* shape like a fork

ahorr|ador *a* thrifty. **~ar** *vt* save. **~arse** *vpr* save o.s. **~o** *m* saving; (*cantidad ahorrada*) savings. **~os** *mpl* savings

ahuecar [7] *vt* hollow; fluff up (*colchón*); deepen (*la voz*); (*marcharse, fam*) clear off (*fam*)

ahuizote *m* (*Mex*) bore

ahulado *m* (*LAm*) oilskin

ahuma|do *a* (*culin*) smoked; (*de colores*) smoky. **~r** *vt* (*culin*) smoke; (*llenar de humo*) fill with smoke. *—ví* become. **~rse** *vpr* become smoky; (*comida*) acquire a smoky taste; (*emborracharse, fam*) get drunk

ahusa|do *a* tapering. **~rse** *vpr* taper

ahuyentar *vt* drive away; banish (*pensamientos etc*)

airado *a* annoyed

aire *m* air; (*viento*) breeze; (*corriente*) draught; (*aspecto*) appearance; (*mus*) tune, air. **~ación** *f* ventilation. **~ acondicionado** air-conditioned. **~ar** *vt* air; (*ventilar*) ventilate; (*fig, publicar*) make public. **~arse** *vpr*: **salir para ~arse** go out for some fresh air. **al ~ libre** in the open air. **darse ~s** give o.s. airs

airón *m* heron

airos|amente *adv* gracefully. **~o** *a* draughty; (*fig*) elegant

aisla|do *a* isolated; (*elec*) insulated. **~dor** *a* (*elec*) insulating. *—m* (*elec*) insulator. **~miento** *m* isolation; (*elec*) insulation. **~nte** *a* insulating. **~r** [23] *vt* isolate; (*elec*) insulate

ajajá *int* good! splendid!

ajar *vt* crumple; (*estropear*) spoil

ajedre|cista *m & f* chess-player. **~z** *m* chess. **~zado** *a* chequered, checked

ajenjo *m* absinthe

ajeno *a* (*de otro*) someone else's; (*de otros*) other people's; (*extraño*) alien

ajetre|arse *vpr* be busy. **~o** *m* bustle

ají *m* (*LAm*) chilli; (*salsa*) chilli sauce

aj|iaceite *m* garlic sauce. **~ilimójili** *m* piquant garlic sauce. **~illo** *m* garlic. **al ~illo** cooked with garlic. **~o** *m* garlic. **~o-arriero** *m* cod in garlic sauce

ajorca *f* bracelet

ajuar *m* furnishings; (*de novia*) trousseau

ajuma|do *a* (*fam*) drunk. **~rse** *vpr* (*fam*) get drunk

ajust|ado *a* right; (*vestido*) tight. **~ador** *m* fitter. **~amiento** *m* fitting; (*adaptación*) adjustment; (*acuerdo*) agreement; (*de una cuenta*) settlement. **~ar** *vt* fit; (*adaptar*) adapt; (*acordar*) agree; settle (*una cuenta*); (*apretar*) tighten. *—ví* fit. **~arse** *vpr* fit; (*adaptarse*) adapt o.s.; (*acordarse*) come to an agreement. **~e** *m* fitting; (*adaptación*) *f* adjustment; (*acuerdo*) agreement; (*de una cuenta*) settlement

ajusticiar *vt* execute

al = **a** + **el**

ala *f* wing; (*de sombrero*) brim; (*deportes*) winger

alaba|ncioso *a* boastful. **~nza** *f* praise. **~r** *vt* praise. **~rse** *vpr* boast

alabastro *m* alabaster

álabe *m* (*paleta*) paddle; (*diente*) cog

alabe|ar *vt* warp. **~arse** *vpr* warp. **~o** *m* warping

alacena *f* cupboard (*Brit*), closet (*Amer*)

alacrán *m* scorpion

alacridad *f* alacrity

alado *a* winged

alambi|cado *a* distilled; (*fig*) subtle. **~camiento** *m* distillation; (*fig*) subtlety. **~car** [7] *vt* distil. **~que** *m* still

alambr|ada f wire fence; (de alambre de espinas) barbed wire fence. ~**ar** vt fence. ~**e** m wire. ~**e de espinas** barbed wire. ~**era** f fireguard

alameda f avenue; (plantío de álamos) poplar grove

álamo m poplar. ~ **temblón** aspen

alano m mastiff

alarde m show. ~**ar** vi boast

alarga|dera f extension. ~**do** a long. ~**dor** m extension. ~**miento** m lengthening. ~**r** [12] vt lengthen; stretch out (mano etc); (dar) give, pass. ~**rse** vpr lengthen, get longer

alarido m shriek

alarm|a f alarm. ~**ante** a alarming. ~**ar** vt alarm, frighten. ~**arse** vpr be alarmed. ~**ista** m & f alarmist

alba f dawn

albacea m executor. ~f executrix

albacora (culin) tuna(-fish)

albahaca f basil

albanés a & m Albanian

Albania f Albania

albañal m sewer, drain

albañil m bricklayer. ~**ería** f (arte) bricklaying

albarán m delivery note

albarda f packsaddle; (Mex) saddle. ~**r** vt saddle

albaricoque m apricot. ~**ro** m apricot tree

albatros m albatross

albedrío m will. **libre** ~ free will

albéitar m veterinary surgeon (Brit), veterinarian (Amer), vet (fam)

alberca f tank, reservoir

alberg|ar [12] vt (alojar) put up; (viviendas) house; (dar asilo) shelter. ~**arse** vpr stay; (refugiarse) shelter. ~**ue** m accommodation; (refugio) shelter. ~**ue de juventud** youth hostel

albóndiga f meatball, rissole

albor m dawn. ~**ada** f dawn; (mus) dawn song. ~**ear** vi dawn

albornoz m (de los moros) burnous; (para el baño) bathrobe

alborot|adizo a excitable. ~**ado** a excited; (aturdido) hasty. ~**ador** a rowdy. —m troublemaker. ~**ar** vt disturb, upset. —vi make a racket. ~**arse** vpr get excited; (el mar) get rough. ~**o** m row, uproar

alboroz|ado a overjoyed. ~**ar** [10] vt make laugh; (regocijar) make happy. ~**arse** vpr be overjoyed. ~**o** m joy

álbum m (pl ~es o ~s) album

alcachofa f artichoke

alcald|e m mayor. ~**esa** f mayoress. ~**ía** f mayoralty; (oficina) mayor's office

álcali m alkali

alcalino a alkaline

alcance m reach; (de arma, telescopio etc) range; (déficit) deficit

alcancía f money-box

alcantarilla f sewer; (boca) drain

alcanzar [10] vt (llegar a) catch up; (coger) reach; catch (un autobús); (bala etc) strike, hit. —vi reach; (ser suficiente) be enough. ~ **a** manage

alcaparra f caper

alcaucil m artichoke

alcayata f hook

alcazaba f fortress

alcázar m fortress

alcoba f bedroom

alcoh|ol m alcohol. ~**ol desnaturalizado** methylated spirits, meths (fam). ~**ólico** a & m alcoholic. ~**olímetro** m breathalyser (Brit). ~**olismo** m alcoholism. ~**olizarse** [10] vpr become an alcoholic

Alcorán m Koran

alcornoque *m* cork-oak; *(persona torpe)* idiot

alcuza *f* (olive) oil bottle

aldaba *f* door-knocker. **~da** *f* knock at the door

alde|a *f* village. **~ano** *a* village; *(campesino)* rustic, country. **~huela** *f* hamlet

alea|ción *f* alloy. **~r** *vt* alloy

aleatorio *a* uncertain

aleccciona|dor *a* instructive. **~miento** *m* instruction. **~r** *vt* instruct

aledaños *mpl* outskirts

alega|ción *f* allegation; *(Arg, Mex, disputa)* argument. **~r** [12] *vt* claim; *(jurid)* allege. —*vi* *(LAm)* argue. **~to** *m* plea

aleg|oría *f* allegory. **~órico** *a* allegorical

alegr|ar *vt* make happy; *(avivar)* brighten up. **~arse** *vpr* be happy; *(emborracharse)* get merry. **~e** *a* happy; *(achispado)* merry, tight. **~emente** *adv* happily. **~ía** *f* happiness. **~ón** *m* sudden joy, great happiness

aleja|do *a* distant. **~miento** *m* removal; *(entre personas)* estrangement; *(distancia)* distance. **~r** *vt* remove; *(ahuyentar)* get rid of; *(fig, apartar)* separate. **~rse** *vpr* move away

alela|do *a* stupid. **~r** *vt* stupefy. **~rse** *vpr* be stupefied

aleluya *m* & *f* alleluia

alemán *a* & *m* German

Alemania *f* Germany. **~ Occidental** *(historia)* West Germany. **~ Oriental** *(historia)* East Germany

alenta|dor *a* encouraging. **~r** [1] *vt* encourage. —*vi* breathe

alerce *m* larch

aler|gia *f* allergy. **~érgico** *a* allergic

alero *m* *(del tejado)* eaves

alerón *m* aileron

alerta *adv* alert, on the alert. ¡**~**! look out! **~r** *vt* alert

aleta *f* wing; *(de pez)* fin

aletarga|do *a* lethargic. **~miento** *m* lethargy. **~r** [12] *vt* make lethargic. **~rse** *vpr* become lethargic

alet|azo *m* *(de un ave)* flap of the wings; *(de un pez)* flick of the fin. **~ear** *vi* flap its wings, flutter. **~eo** *m* flapping (of the wings)

aleve *a* treacherous

alevín *m* young fish

alevos|ía *f* treachery. **~o** *a* treacherous

alfab|ético *a* alphabetical. **~etizar** [10] *vt* alphabetize; teach to read and write *(a uno)*. **~eto** *m* alphabet. **~eto Morse** Morse code

alfalfa *f* lucerne *(Brit)*, alfalfa *(Amer)*

alfar *m* pottery. **~ería** *f* pottery. **~ero** *m* potter

alféizar *m* window-sill

alferecía *f* epilepsy

alférez *m* second lieutenant

alfil *m* *(en ajedrez)* bishop

alfil|er *m* pin. **~razo** *m* pinprick. **~tero** *m* pin-case

alfombra *f* *(grande)* carpet; *(pequeña)* rug, mat. **~ar** *vt* carpet. **~illa** *f* rug, mat; *(med)* German measles

alforja *f* saddle-bag

algas *fpl* seaweed

algarabía *f* *(fig, fam)* gibberish, nonsense

algarada *f* uproar

algarrob|a *f* carob bean. **~o** *m* carob tree

algazara *f* uproar

álgebra *f* algebra

algebraico *a* algebraic

álgido *a* *(fig)* decisive

algo *pron* something; *(en frases interrogativas)* anything. —*adv* rather. ¿**~ más**? is there anything else? **¿quieres tomar**

algo? (*de beber*) would you like a drink?; (*de comer*) would you like something to eat?

algodón *m* cotton. **~ón de azúcar** candy floss (*Brit*), cotton candy (*Amer*). **~onero** *a* cotton. **—m** cotton plant. **~ón hidrófilo** cotton wool

alguacil *m* bailiff

alguien *pron* someone, somebody; (*en frases interrogativas*) anyone, anybody

alguno *a* (*delante de nombres masculinos en singular* **algún**) some; (*en frases interrogativas*) any; (*pospuesto al nombre en frases negativas*) at all. **no tiene idea alguna** he hasn't any idea at all. **—pron** one; (*en plural*) some; (*alguien*) someone. **alguna que otra vez** from time to time. **algunas veces, alguna vez** sometimes

alhaja *f* piece of jewellery; (*fig*) treasure. **~r** *vt* deck with jewels; (*amueblar*) furnish

alharaca *f* fuss

alhelí *m* wallflower

alheña *f* privet

alhucema *f* lavender

alia|do *a* allied. **—m** ally. **~nza** *f* alliance; (*anillo*) wedding ring. **~r** [20] *vt* combine. **~rse** *vpr* be combined; (*formar una alianza*) form an alliance

alias *adv* & *m* alias

alicaído *a* (*fig, débil*) weak; (*fig, abatido*) depressed

alicates *mpl* pliers

aliciente *m* incentive; (*de un lugar*) attraction

alien|ado *a* mentally ill. **~ista** *m* & *f* psychiatrist

aliento *m* breath; (*ánimo*) courage

aligera|miento *m* lightening; (*alivio*) alleviation. **~r** *vt* make lighter; (*aliviar*) alleviate, ease; (*apresurar*) quicken

alij|ar *vt* (*descargar*) unload; smuggle ‹*contrabando*›. **~o** *m* unloading; (*contrabando*) contraband

alimaña *f* vicious animal

aliment|ación *f* food; (*acción*) feeding. **~ar** *vt* feed; (*nutrir*) nourish. **—vi** be nourishing. **~arse** *vpr* feed (**con**, **de** on). **~icio** *a* nourishing. **~o** *m* food. **~os** *mpl* (*jurid*) alimony. **productos** *mpl* **~icios** foodstuffs

alimón. al ~ *adv* jointly

alinea|ción *f* alignment; (*en deportes*) line-up. **~r** *vt* align, line up

aliñ|ar *vt* (*culin*) season. **~o** *m* seasoning

alioli *m* garlic sauce

alisar *vt* smooth

alisios *apl*. **vientos** *mpl* **~** trade winds

aliso *m* alder (tree)

alista|miento *m* enrolment. **~r** *vt* put on a list; (*mil*) enlist. **~rse** *vpr* enrol; (*mil*) enlist

aliteración *f* alliteration

alivi|ador *a* comforting. **~ar** *vt* lighten; relieve ‹*dolor, etc*›; (*hurtar, fam*) steal, pinch (*fam*). **~arse** *vpr* ‹*dolor*› diminish; ‹*persona*› get better. **~o** *m* relief

aljibe *m* tank

alma *f* soul; (*habitante*) inhabitant

almac|én *m* warehouse; (*LAm, tienda*) grocer's shop; (*de un arma*) magazine. **~enes** *mpl* department store. **~enaje** *m* storage; (*derechos*) storage charges. **~enamiento** *m* storage; (*mercancías almacenadas*) stock. **~enar** *vt* store; stock up with ‹*provisiones*›. **~enero** *m* (*Arg*) shopkeeper. **~enista** *m* & *f* shopkeeper

almádena *f* sledge-hammer

almanaque *m* almanac

almeja *f* clam

almendr|a f almond. **~ado** a almond-shaped. **~o** m almond tree

almiar m haystack

alm|íbar m syrup. **~ibarado** a syrupy. **~ibarar** vt cover in syrup

almidón m starch. **~onado** a starched; (fig, estirado) starchy

alminar m minaret

almirant|azgo m admiralty. **~e** m admiral

almirez m mortar

almizcle m musk

almohad|a f cushion; (de la cama) pillow; (funda) pillowcase. **~illa** f small cushion; (acerico) pincushion. **~ón** m large pillow, bolster. **consultar con la ~a** sleep on it

almorranas fpl haemorrhoids, piles

alm|orzar [2 & 10] vt (a mediodía) have for lunch; (desayunar) have for breakfast. —vi (a mediodía) have lunch; (desayunar) have breakfast. **~uerzo** m (a mediodía) lunch; (desayuno) breakfast

alocado a scatter-brained

alocución f address, speech

aloja|do m (Mex) lodger, guest. **~miento** m accommodation. **~r** vt put up. **~rse** vpr stay

alondra f lark

alpaca f alpaca

alpargata f canvas shoe, espadrille. **~ería** f shoe shop

Alpes mpl Alps

alpin|ismo m mountaineering, climbing. **~ista** m & f mountaineer, climber. **~o** a Alpine

alpiste m birdseed

alquil|ar vt (tomar en alquiler) hire ⟨vehículo⟩, rent ⟨piso, casa⟩; (dar en alquiler) hire (out) ⟨vehículo⟩, rent (out) ⟨piso, casa⟩. **~arse** vpr ⟨casa⟩ be let; ⟨vehículo⟩ be on hire. **se alquila** to

let (Brit), for rent (Amer). **~er** m (acción de alquilar un piso etc) renting; (acción de alquilar un vehículo) hiring; (precio por el que se alquila un piso etc) rent; (precio por el que se alquila un vehículo) hire charge. **de ~er** for hire

alquimi|a f alchemy. **~sta** m alchemist

alquitara f still. **~r** vt distil

alquitr|án m tar. **~anar** vt tar

alrededor adv around. **~ de** around; (con números) about. **~es** mpl surroundings; (de una ciudad) outskirts

alta f discharge

altamente adv highly

altaner|ía f (orgullo) pride. **~o** a proud, haughty

altar m altar

altavoz m loudspeaker

altera|bilidad f changeability. **~ble** a changeable. **~ción** f change, alteration. **~do** a changed, altered; (perturbado) disturbed. **~r** vt change, alter; (perturbar) disturb; (enfadar) anger, irritate. **~rse** vpr change, alter; (agitarse) get upset; (enfadarse) get angry; (comida) go off

alterca|do m argument. **~r** [7] vi argue

altern|ado a alternate. **~ador** m alternator. **~ante** a alternating. **~ar** vt/i alternate. **~arse** vpr take turns. **~ativa** f alternative. **~ativo** a alternating. **~o** a alternate

alteza f height. **A~** (título) Highness

altibajos mpl (de terreno) unevenness; (fig) ups and downs

altiplanicie f high plateau

altísimo a very high. —m. **el A~** the Almighty

altisonante a, **altísono** a pompous

altitud f height; (aviat, geog) altitude

altivez f arrogance. **∼o** a arrogant

alto a high; (persona) tall; (mus) loud; (fig, elevado) lofty; (mus (nota) high-pitched); (mus (voz, instrumento) alto; (horas) early. **tiene 3 metros de ∼** it is 3 metres high. **—adv** high; (de sonidos) loud(ly). **—m** height; (de un edificio) high floor; (viola) viola; (voz) alto; (parada) stop. **—int** halt!, stop! **en lo ∼ de** on the top of

altoparlante m (esp LAm) loudspeaker

altruismo m altruism. **∼ta** a altruistic. **—m & f** altruist

altura f height; (altitud) altitude; (de agua) depth; (fig, cielo) sky. **a estas ∼s** at this stage. **tiene 3 metros de ∼** it is 3 metres high

alubia f French bean

alucinación f hallucination

alud m avalanche

aludido a in question. **darse por ∼do** take it personally. **no darse por ∼do** turn a deaf ear. **∼r** vi mention

alumbrado a lit; (achispado, fam) tipsy. **—m** lighting. **∼miento** m lighting; (parto) childbirth. **∼r** vt light. **—vi** give birth. **∼rse** vpr (emborracharse) get tipsy

aluminio m aluminium (Brit), aluminum (Amer)

alumno m pupil; (univ) student

alunizaje m landing on the moon. **∼r** [10] vi land on the moon

alusión f allusion. **∼vo** a allusive

alverja f vetch; (LAm, guisante) pea

alza f rise. **∼cuello** m clerical collar, dog-collar (fam). **∼da** f (de caballo) height; (jurid)

appeal. **∼do** a raised; (persona) fraudulently bankrupt; (Mex, soberbio) vain; (precio) fixed. **∼miento** m raising; (aumento) rise, increase; (pol) revolt. **∼r** [10] vt raise, lift (up); raise (precios). **∼rse** vpr rise; (ponerse en pie) stand up; (pol) revolt; (quebrar) go fraudulently bankrupt; (apelar) appeal

allá adv there. **¡∼ él!** that's his business. **∼ fuera** out there. **∼ por el 1970** around about 1970. **el más ∼** the beyond. **más ∼** further on. **más ∼ de** beyond. **por ∼** over there

allanamiento m levelling; (de obstáculos) removal. **∼miento de morada** burglary. **∼r** vt level; remove (obstáculos); (fig) iron out (dificultades etc); burgle (una casa). **∼rse** vpr level off; (hundirse) fall down; (ceder) submit (a to)

allegado a close. **—m** relation. **∼r** [12] vt collect

allí adv there; (tiempo) then. **∼ donde** wherever. **∼ fuera** out there. **por ∼** over there

ama f lady of the house. **∼ de casa** housewife. **∼ de cría** wet-nurse. **∼ de llaves** housekeeper

amabilidad f kindness. **∼le** a kind; (simpático) nice

amado a dear. **∼r** m lover

amaestrado a trained; (en circo) performing. **∼miento** m training. **∼r** vt train

amagar [12] vt (amenazar) threaten; (mostrar intención de) show signs of. **—vi** threaten; (algo bueno) be in the offing. **∼o** m threat; (señal) sign; (med) sympton

amalgama f amalgam. **∼r** vt amalgamate

amamantar vt breast-feed

amancebarse vpr live together

amanecer *m* dawn. —*vi* dawn; ⟨*persona*⟩ wake up. **al ~** at dawn, at daybreak

amanera|do *a* affected. **~miento** *m* affectation. **~rse** *vpr* become affected

amanezca *f* (*Mex*) dawn

amansa|dor *m* tamer. **~miento** *m* taming. **~r** *vt* tame; break in ⟨*un caballo*⟩; soothe ⟨*dolor etc*⟩. **~rse** *vpr* calm down

amante *a* fond. —*m & f* lover

amañ|ar *vt* arrange. **~o** *m* scheme

amapola *f* poppy

amar *vt* love

amara|je *m* landing on the sea; (*de astronave*) splash-down. **~r** *vt* land on the sea; (*astronave*) splash down

amarg|ado *a* embittered. **~ar** [12] *vt* make bitter; embitter (*persona*). **~arse** *vpr* get bitter. **~o** *a* bitter. —*m* bitterness. **~ura** *f* bitterness

amariconado *a* effeminate

amarill|ear *vi* go yellow. **~ento** *a* yellowish; (*tez*) sallow. **~ez** *f* yellow; (*de una persona*) paleness. **~o** *a & m* yellow

amarra *f* mooring rope. **~s** *fpl* (*fig, fam*) influence. **~do** *a* (*LAm*) mean. **~r** *vt* moor; (*atar*) tie. —*vi* (*empollar, fam*) study hard, swot (*fam*)

amartillar *vt* cock (*arma de fuego*)

amas|ar *vt* knead; (*fig, tramar, fam*) concoct, cook up (*fam*). **~ijo** *m* dough; (*acción*) kneading; (*fig, mezcla, fam*) hotchpotch

amate *m* (*Mex*) fig tree

amateur *a & m & f* amateur

amatista *f* amethyst

amazona *f* Amazon; (*mujer varonil*) mannish woman; (*que monta a caballo*) horsewoman

Amazonas *m*. **el río ~** the Amazon

ambages *mpl* circumlocutions. **sin ~** in plain language

ámbar *m* amber

ambarino *a* amber

ambici|ón *f* ambition. **~onar** *vt* strive after. **~onar ser** have an ambition to be. **~oso** *a* ambitious. —*m* ambitious person

ambidextro *a* ambidextrous. —*m* ambidextrous person

ambient|ar *vt* give an atmosphere to. **~arse** *vpr* adapt o.s. **~e** *m* atmosphere; (*medio*) environment

ambig|uamente *adv* ambiguously. **~üedad** *f* ambiguity. **~uo** *a* ambiguous; (*fig, afeminado, fam*) effeminate

ámbito *m* ambit

ambos *a & pron* both. **~ a dos** both (of them)

ambulancia *f* ambulance; (*hospital móvil*) field hospital

ambulante *a* travelling

ambulatorio *m* out-patients' department

amedrentar *vt* frighten, scare. **~se** *vpr* be frightened

amén *m* amen. —*int* amen! **en un decir ~** in an instant

amenaza *f* threat. **~dor** *a*, **~nte** *a* threatening. **~r** [10] *vt* threaten

amen|idad *f* pleasantness. **~izar** [10] *vt* brighten up. **~o** *a* pleasant

América *f* America. **~ Central** Central America. **~ del Norte** North America. **~ del Sur** South America. **~ Latina** Latin America

american|a *f* jacket. **~ismo** *m* Americanism. **~ista** *m & f* Americanist. **~o** *a* American

amerindio *a & m & f* Amerindian, American Indian

amerizaje m landing on the sea; (*de astronave*) splash-down. ∼r [10] vt land on the sea; (*astronave*) splash down

ametralladora f machine-gun. ∼r vt machine-gun

amianto m asbestos

amiga f friend; (*novia*) girlfriend; (*amante*) lover. ∼able a friendly. ∼ablemente adv amicably. ∼rse [12] vpr live together

amígdala f tonsil. ∼igdalitis f tonsillitis

amigo a friendly. —m friend; (*novio*) lover. (*amante*) lover. ser ∼ de be fond of. ser muy ∼s be good friends

amilanar vt frighten, scare. ∼se vpr be frightened

aminorar vt lessen; slow down (*velocidad*)

amistad f friendship. ∼ades mpl friends. ∼osamente adv amicably. ∼oso a friendly

amnesia f amnesia

amnistía f amnesty. ∼iar [20] vt grant an amnesty to

amo m master; (*dueño*) owner; (*jefe*) boss; (*cabeza de familia*) head of the family

amodorramiento m sleepiness. ∼rse vpr get sleepy

amojonar vt mark out

amolador m knife-grinder. ∼r [2] vt sharpen; (*molestar, fam*) annoy

amoldar vt mould; (*acomodar*) fit

amonedar vt coin, mint

amonestación f rebuke, reprimand; (*de una boda*) banns. ∼r vt rebuke, reprimand; (*anunciar la boda*) publish the banns

amoníaco m, **amoniaco** m ammonia

amontillado m Amontillado, pale dry sherry

amontonadamente adv in a heap. ∼miento m piling up. ∼r vt pile up; (*fig, acumular*) accumulate. ∼rse vpr pile up; (*gente*) crowd together; (*amancebarse, fam*) live together

amor m love. ∼es mpl (*relaciones amorosas*) love affairs. con mil ∼es, de mil ∼es with the (greatest of) pleasure. hacer el ∼ make love. por (el) ∼ de Dios for God's sake

amoratado a purple; (*de frío*) blue. ∼rse vpr go black and blue

amorcillo m Cupid

amordazar [10] vt gag; (*fig*) silence

amorfo a amorphous, shapeless

amorío m affair. ∼oso a a loving; (*cartas*) love

amortajar vt shroud

amortiguador a deadening. —m (*auto*) shock absorber. ∼miento m deadening; (*de la luz*) dimming. ∼r [15] vt deaden (*ruido*); dim (*luz*); cushion (*golpe*); tone down (*color*)

amortizable a redeemable. ∼ción f (*de una deuda*) repayment; (*recuperación*) redemption. ∼r [10] vt repay (*una deuda*)

amoscarse [7] vpr (*fam*) get cross, get irritated

amostazarse [10] vpr get cross

amotinado a & m insurgent, rebellious. ∼miento m riot; (*mil*) mutiny. ∼r vt incite to riot. ∼rse vpr rebel; (*mil*) mutiny

amparar vt help; (*proteger*) protect. ∼arse vpr seek protection; (*de la lluvia*) shelter. ∼o m protection; (*de la lluvia*) shelter. al ∼o de under the protection of

amperio m ampere, amp (*fam*)

ampliación f extension; (*photo*) enlargement. ∼r [20] vt enlarge, extend; (*photo*) enlarge

amplifica|ción f amplification. **~dor** m amplifier. **~r** [7] amplify

ampli|o a wide; (*espacioso*) spacious; (*ropa*) loose-fitting. **~tud** f extent; (*espaciosidad*) spaciousness; (*espacio*) space

ampolla f (*med*) blister; (*frasco*) flask; (*de medicamento*) ampoule, phial

ampuloso a pompous

amputa|ción f amputation; (*fig*) deletion. **~r** vt amputate; (*fig*) delete

amueblar vt furnish

amuinar vt (*Mex*) annoy

amuralla|do a walled. **~r** vt build a wall around

anacardo m (*fruto*) cashew nut

anaconda f anaconda

anacr|ónico a anachronistic. **~onismo** m anachronism

ánade m & f duck

anagrama m anagram

anales mpl annals

analfabet|ismo m illiteracy. **~o** a & m illiterate

analgésico a & m analgesic, pain-killer

an|álisis m invar analysis. **~álisis de sangre** blood test. **~alista** m & f analyst. **~alítico** a analytical. **~alizar** [10] vt analyze

an|alogía f analogy. **~álogo** a analogous

ananás m pineapple

anaquel m shelf

anaranjado a orange

an|arquía f anarchy. **~árquico** a anarchic. **~arquismo** m anarchism. **~arquista** a anarchistic. **—m & f** anarchist

anatema m anathema

anat|omía f anatomy. **~ómico** a anatomical

anca f haunch; (*parte superior*) rump; (*nalgas*, *fam*) bottom. **~s** fpl **de rana** frogs' legs

ancestral a ancestral

anciano a elderly, old. **—m** elderly man, old man; (*relig*) elder. **los ~s** old people

ancla f anchor. **~dero** m anchorage. **~r** vi anchor, drop anchor. **echar ~s** anchor. **levar ~s** weigh anchor

áncora f anchor; (*fig*) refuge

ancho a wide; (*ropa*) loose-fitting; (*fig*) relieved; (*demasiado grande*) too big; (*ufano*) smug. **—m** width; (*rail*) gauge. **a mis anchas, a sus anchas** etc comfortable, relaxed. **quedarse tan ancho** behave as if nothing has happened. **tiene 3 metros de ~** it is 3 metres wide

anchoa f anchovy

anchura f width; (*medida*) measurement

andaderas fpl baby-walker

andad|or a good at walking. **—m** baby-walker. **~ura** f walking; (*manera de andar*) walk

Andalucía f Andalusia

andaluz a & m Andalusian

andamio m platform. **~s** mpl scaffolding

andar [25] vt (*recorrer*) cover, go. **—vi** walk; (*máquina*) go, work; (*estar*) be; (*moverse*) move. **—m** walk. **¡anda!** go on! come on! **~iego** a fond of walking; (*itinerante*) wandering. **~por** be about. **~se** vpr (*marcharse*) go away

andén m platform; (*de un muelle*) quayside; (*LAm*, *acera*) pavement (*Brit*), sidewalk (*Amer*)

Andes mpl Andes

andino a Andean

Andorra f Andorra

andrajo m rag. **~so** a ragged

andurriales mpl (*fam*) out-of-the-way place

anduve vb véase **andar**

anécdota f anecdote

anega|dizo a subject to flooding. **~r** [12] vt flood. **~rse** vpr be flooded, flood

anejo a attached. —m annexe; (de libro etc) appendix

an|emia f anaemia. **~émico** a & m anaemic

anest|esia f anaesthesia. **~ésico** a & m anaesthetic. **~esista** m & f anaesthetist

anex|ión f annexation. **~ionar** vt annex. **~o** a attached. —m annexe

anfibio a amphibious. —m amphibian

anfiteatro m amphitheatre; (en un teatro) upper circle

anfitri|ón m host. **~ona** f hostess

ángel m angel; (encanto) charm

angelical a, **angélico** a angelic

angina f. **~ de pecho** angina (pectoris). **tener ~s** have tonsillitis

anglicano a & m Anglican

anglicismo m Anglicism

anglófilo a & m Anglophile

anglo|hispánico a Anglo-Spanish. **~sajón** a & m Anglo-Saxon

angosto a narrow

anguila f eel

angula f elver, baby eel

angular a angular

ángulo m angle; (rincón, esquina) corner; (curva) bend

anguloso a angular

angusti|a f anguish. **~ar** vt distress; (inquietar) worry. **~arse** vpr get distressed; (inquietarse) get worried. **~oso** a anguished; (que causa angustia) distressing

anhel|ante a panting; (deseoso) longing. **~ar** vt (+ nombre) long for; (+ verbo) long to. **—vi** pant. **~o** m (fig) yearning. **~oso** a panting; (fig) eager

anidar vi nest

anill|a f ring. **~o** m ring. **~o de boda** wedding ring

ánima f soul

anima|ción f (de personas) life; (de cosas) liveliness; (bullicio) bustle; (en el cine) animation. **~do** a lively; (sitio etc) busy. **~dor** m compère, host

animadversión f ill will

animal a animal; (fig, torpe, fam) stupid. —m animal; (fig, idiota, fam) idiot; (fig, bruto, fam) brute

animar vt give life to; (dar ánimo) encourage; (dar vivacidad) liven up. **~se** vpr (decidirse) decide; (ponerse alegre) cheer up. **¿te animas a venir al cine?** do you fancy coming to the cinema?

ánimo m soul; (mente) mind; (valor) courage; (intención) intention. **¡~!** come on!, cheer up! **dar ~s** encourage

animosidad f animosity

animoso a brave; (resuelto) determined

aniquila|ción f annihilation. **~miento** m annihilation. **~r** vt annihilate; (acabar con) ruin. **~rse** vpr deteriorate

anís m aniseed; (licor) anisette

aniversario m anniversary

ano m anus

anoche adv last night, yesterday evening

anochecer [11] vi get dark; (persona) be at dusk. **anochecí en Madrid** I was in Madrid at dusk. —m nightfall, dusk. **al ~** at nightfall

anodino a indifferent

an|omalía f anomaly. **~ómalo** a anomalous

an|onimato m anonymity. **~ónimo** a anonymous; (sociedad) limited. —m anonymity; (carta) anonymous letter

anormal a abnormal; (fam) stupid, silly. **~idad** f abnormality

anota|ción f noting; (*acción de poner notas*) annotation; (*nota*) note. **~r** vt (*poner nota*) annotate; (*apuntar*) make a note of

anquilosa|miento m paralysis. **~r** vt paralyze. **~rse** vpr become paralyzed

ansia f anxiety, worry; (*anhelo*) yearning. **~ar** [20 o *regular*] vt long for. **~edad** f anxiety. **~oso** a anxious; (*deseoso*) eager

antag|ónico a antagonistic. **~onismo** m antagonism. **~onista** m & f antagonist

antaño adv in days gone by

antártico a & m Antarctic

ante prep in front of, before; (*en comparación con*) compared with; (*frente a peligro, enemigo*) in the face of; (*en vista de*) in view of. —m (*piel*) suede. **~anoche** adv the night before last. **~ayer** adv the day before yesterday. **~brazo** m forearm

ante... pref ante...

antece|dente a previous. —m antecedent. **~dentes** mpl history, background. **~dentes penales** criminal record. **~der** vt precede. **~sor** m predecessor; (*antepasado*) ancestor

antedicho a aforesaid

antelación f advance. **con ~** in advance

antemano. **de ~** adv. beforehand

antena f antenna; (*radio, TV*) aerial

anteojeras fpl blinkers

anteojo m telescope. **~s** pl (*gemelos*) opera glasses; (*prismáticos*) binoculars; (*LAm, gafas*) glasses, spectacles

ante: **~pasados** mpl forebears, ancestors. **~pecho** m rail; (*de ventana*) sill. **~poner** [34] vt put in front of (a *of*); (*fig*) put before, prefer. **~proyecto** m preliminary sketch; (*fig*) blueprint. **~puesto** a put before

anterior a previous; (*delantero*) front, fore. **~idad** f. **con ~idad** previously. **~mente** adv previously

antes adv before; (*antiguamente*) in days gone by; (*mejor*) rather; (*primero*) first. **~ de** before. **~ de ayer** the day before yesterday. **~ de que** + *subj* before. **~ de que llegue** before he arrives. **~ cuanto ~, lo ~ posible** as soon as possible

antesala f anteroom; (*sala de espera*) waiting-room. **hacer ~** wait (to be received)

anti... pref anti...

anti: **~aéreo** a anti-aircraft. **~biótico** a & m antibiotic. **~ciclón** m anticyclone

anticip|ación f anticipation. **con ~ación** in advance. **con media hora de ~ación** half an hour early. **~adamente** adv in advance. **~ado**. **a. por ~ado** in advance. **~ar** vt bring forward; advance (*dinero*). **~arse** vpr be early. **~o** m (*dinero*) advance; (*fig*) foretaste

anti: **~concepcional** a & m contraceptive. **~conceptivo** a & m contraceptive. **~congelante** m antifreeze

anticua|do a old-fashioned. **~rio** m antique dealer. **~rse** vpr go out of date

anticuerpo m antibody

antídoto m antidote

anti: **~estético** a ugly. **~faz** m mask. **~gás** a invar. **careta ~gás** gas mask

antigualla f old relic. **~amente** adv formerly; (*hace mucho tiempo*) long ago. **~tiedad** f antiquity; (*objeto*) antique; (*en un empleo*) length of service. **~uo** a old, ancient. **chapado a la ~ua** old-fashioned

antílope m antelope

Antillas fpl West Indies

antinatural *a* unnatural

antip|atía *f* dislike; (*cualidad de antipático*) unpleasantness. **~ático** *a* unpleasant, unfriendly

anti: ~semita *m & f* anti-Semite. **~semítico** *a* anti-Semitic. **~semitismo** *m* anti-Semitism. **~séptico** *a & m* antiseptic. **~social** *a* antisocial

antítesis *f invar* antithesis

antoj|adizo *a* capricious. **~arse** *vpr* fancy. **se le ~a un caramelo** he fancies a sweet. **~o** *m* whim; (*de embarazada*) craving

antología *f* anthology

antorcha *f* torch

antro *m* cavern; (*fig*) dump, hole. **~ de perversión** den of iniquity

antropófago *m* cannibal

antrop|ología *f* anthropology. **~ólogo** *m & f* anthropologist

anual *a* annual. **~lidad** *f* annuity. **~lmente** *adv* yearly. **~rio** *m* yearbook

anudar *vt* tie, knot; (*fig, iniciar*) begin; (*fig, continuar*) resume. **~se** *vpr* get into knots. **~se la voz** get a lump in one's throat

anula|ción *f* annulment, cancellation. **~r** *vt* annul, cancel. — *a* (*dedo*) ring. — *m* ring finger

Anunciación *f* Annunciation

anunci|ante *m & f* advertiser. **~ar** *vt* announce; advertise (*producto comercial*); (*presagiar*) be a sign of. **~arse** *vpr* promise to be. **~o** *m* announcement; (*para vender algo*) advertisement, advert (*fam*); (*cartel*) poster

anzuelo *m* (*fish*)hook; (*fig*) bait. **tragar el ~** be taken in, fall for it

añadi|do *a* added. **~dura** *f* addition. **~r** *vt* add. **por ~dura** besides

añejo *a* (*vino*) mature; (*jamón etc*) cured

añicos *mpl* bits. **hacer ~** (*romper*) smash (to pieces); (*dejar cansado*) wear out

añil *m* indigo

año *m* year. **~ bisiesto** leap year. **~ nuevo** new year. **al ~** per year, a year. **¿cuántos ~s tiene? tiene 5 ~s** how old is he? he's 5 (years old). **el ~ pasado** last year. **el ~ que viene** next year. **entrado en ~s** elderly. **los ~s 60** the sixties

añora|nza *f* nostalgia. **~r** *vt* miss. — *vi* pine

apabullar *vt* crush; (*fig*) intimidate

apacentar [1] *vt* graze. **~se** *vpr* graze

apacib|ilidad *f* gentleness; (*calma*) peacefulness. **~le** *a* gentle; (*tiempo*) mild

apacigua|dor *a* pacifying. **~miento** *m* appeasement. **~r** [15] *vt* pacify; (*calmar*) calm; relieve (*dolor etc*). **~rse** *vpr* calm down

apadrina|miento *m* sponsorship. **~r** *vt* sponsor; be godfather to (*a un niño*); (*en una boda*) be best man for

apaga|dizo *a* slow to burn. **~do** *a* extinguished; (*color*) dull; (*aparato eléctrico*) off; (*persona*) lifeless; (*sonido*) muffled. **~r** [12] *vt* put out (*fuego, incendio*); turn off, switch off (*aparato eléctrico*); quench (*sed*); muffle (*sonido*). **~rse** *vpr* (*fuego*) go out; (*luz*) go out; (*sonido*) die away; (*fig*) pass away

apagón *m* blackout

apalabrar *vt* make a verbal agreement; (*contratar*) engage. **~se** *vpr* come to a verbal agreement

apalanca|miento *m* leverage. **~r** [7] *vt* (*levantar*) lever up; (*abrir*) lever open

apalea|miento *m* (*de grano*) winnowing; (*de alfombras,* *frutos, personas*) beating. **~r** *vt* winnow (*grano*); beat (*alfombras, frutos, personas*); (*fig*) be rolling in (*dinero*)

apantallado *a* (*Mex*) stupid

apañ|**ado** *a* handy. **~ar** *vt* (*arreglar*) fix; (*remendar*) mend; (*agarrar*) grasp, take hold of. **~arse** *vpr* get along, manage. **¡estoy ~ado!** that's all I need!

aparador *m* sideboard

aparato *m* apparatus; (*máquina*) machine; (*teléfono*) telephone; (*rad, TV*) set; (*ostentación*) show, pomp. **~samente** *adv* ostentatiously; (*impresionante*) spectacularly. **~sidad** *f* ostentation. **~so** *a* showy, ostentatious; (*caída*) spectacular

aparca|**miento** *m* car park (*Brit*), parking lot (*Amer*). **~r** [7] *vt/i* park

aparea|**miento** *m* pairing off. **~r** *vt* pair off; mate (*animales*). **~rse** *vpr* match; (*animales*) mate

aparecer [11] *vi* appear. **~se** *vpr* appear

aparej|**ado** *a* ready; (*adecuado*) fitting. **llevar ~ado, traer ~ado** mean, entail. **~o** *m* preparation; (*avíos*) equipment

aparent|**ar** *vt* (*afectar*) feign; (*parecer*) look. **—vi** show off. **a 20 años** she looks like she's 20. **~e** *a* apparent; (*adecuado, fam*) suitable

apari|**ción** *f* appearance; (*visión*) apparition. **~encia** *f* appearance; (*fig*) show. **cubrir las ~encias** keep up appearances

apartad|**ero** *m* lay-by; (*rail*) siding. **~o** *a* separated; (*aislado*) isolated. **—m** (*de un texto*) section. **~o** (*de correos*) post-office box, PO box

apartamento *m* flat (*Brit*), apartment

apart|**amiento** *m* separation; (*LAm, piso*) flat (*Brit*), apartment; (*aislamiento*) seclusion. **~ar** *vt* separate; (*quitar*) remove. **~arse** *vpr* leave; abandon (*creencia*); (*quitarse de en medio*) get out of the way; (*aislarse*) cut o.s. off. **~e** *adv* apart; (*por separado*) separately; (*además*) besides. **—m** aside; (*párrafo*) new paragraph. **~e de** apart from. **dejar ~e** leave aside. **eso ~e** apart from that

apasiona|**do** *a* passionate; (*entusiasta*) enthusiastic; (*falto de objetividad*) biassed. **—m** lover (*de* of). **~miento** *m* passion. **~r** *vt* excite. **~rse** *vpr* get excited (*de, por* about), be mad (*de, por* about); (*ser parcial*) become biassed

ap|**atía** *f* apathy. **~ático** *a* apathetic

apea|**dero** *m* (*rail*) halt. **~r** *vt* fell (*árbol*); (*disuadir*) dissuade; overcome (*dificultad*); sort out (*problema*). **~rse** *vpr* (*de un vehículo*) get off

apechugar [12] *vi* push (with one's chest). **~ con** put up with

apedrear *vt* stone

apeg|**ado** *a* attached. **~o** *m* (*fam*) affection. **tener ~o a** be fond of

apela|**ción** *f* appeal. **~r** *vt* appeal; (*recurrir*) resort (*a* to)

apelmazar [10] *vt* compress

apellid|**ar** *vt* call. **~arse** *vpr* be called. **¿cómo te apellidas?** what's your surname? **~o** *m* surname

apenar *vt* pain. **~se** *vpr* grieve

apenas *adv* hardly, scarcely; (*enseguida que*) as soon as. **~ si** (*fam*) hardly

ap|**éndice** *m* (*med*) appendix; (*fig*) appendage; (*de un libro*) appendix. **~endicitis** *f* appendicitis

aperci|miento m warning. **~r** vt warn (**de** of, about); (amenazar) threaten. **~rse** vpr provide pre-pare; (percatarse) provide (**de** with)

apergaminado a (piel) wrinkled

aperitivo m (bebida) aperitif; (comida) appetizer

aperos mpl agricultural equipment

apertura f opening

apesadumbrar vt upset. **~se** vpr be upset

apestar vt stink out; (fastidiar) pester. —vi stink (**a** of)

apet|ecer [11] vt long for; (interesar) appeal to. ¿**te ~ece una copa?** do you fancy a drink? do you feel like a drink?. —vi be welcome. **~ecible** a attractive. **~ito** m appetite; (fig) desire. **~itoso** a tempting

apiadarse vpr feel sorry (**de** for)

ápice m (nada, en frases negativas) anything. **no ceder un ~** not give an inch

apicult|or m bee-keeper. **~ura** f bee-keeping

apilar vt pile up

apiñar vt pack in. **~se** vpr (personas) crowd together; (cosas) be packed tight

apio m celery

apisonadora f steamroller

aplacar [7] vt placate; relieve (dolor)

aplanar vt smooth. **~se** vpr become smooth; (persona) lose heart

aplasta|nte a overwhelming. **~r** vt crush. **~rse** vpr flatten o.s.

aplatanarse vpr become lethargic

aplau|dir vt clap, applaud; (fig) applaud. **~so** m applause; (fig) praise

aplaza|miento m postponement. **~r** [10] vt postpone; defer (pago)

aplebeyarse vpr lower o.s.

aplica|ble a applicable. **~ción** f application. **~do** a (persona) diligent. **~r** [7] vt apply; (fijar) attach. **~rse** vpr apply o.s.

aplom|ado a self-confident; (vertical) vertical. **~o** m (self-) confidence, aplomb; (verticalidad) verticality

apocado a timid

Apocalipsis f Apocalypse

apocalíptico a apocalyptic

apoca|miento m diffidence. **~r** [7] vt belittle (persona). **~rse** vpr feel small

apodar vt nickname

apodera|do m representative. **~r** vt authorize. **~rse** vpr seize

apodo m nickname

apogeo m (fig) height

apolilla|do a moth-eaten. **~rse** vpr get moth-eaten

apolítico a non-political

apología f defence

apoltronarse vpr get lazy

apoplejía f stroke

apoquinar vt/i (fam) fork out

aporrear vt hit, thump; beat up (persona)

aporta|ción f contribution. **~r** vt contribute

aposentar vt put up, lodge. **~o** m room, lodgings

apósito m dressing

aposta adv on purpose

apostar[1] [2] vt/i bet

apostar[2] vt station. **~se** vpr station o.s.

apostilla f note. **~r** vt add notes to

apóstol m apostle

apóstrofo m apostrophe

apoy|ar vt lean (**en** against); (descansar) rest; (asentar) base; (reforzar) support. **~arse** vpr lean, rest. **~o** m support

apreci|able a appreciable; (digno de estima) worthy.

~ación f appreciation; (valoración) appraisal. ~ar vt value; (estimar) appreciate. ~ativo a appreciative. ~o m appraisal; (fig) esteem

aprehensión f capture

apremi|ante a urgent, pressing. ~ar vt urge; (obligar) compel; (dar prisa a) hurry up. —vi be urgent. ~o m urgency; (obligación) obligation

aprender vt/i learn. ~se vpr learn (by heart)

aprendiz m apprentice. ~aje m apprenticeship

aprensi|ón f apprehension; (miedo) fear. ~vo a apprehensive, fearful

apresa|dor m captor. ~miento m capture. ~r vt seize; (prender) capture

aprestar vt prepare. ~se vpr prepare

apresura|damente adv hurriedly, in a hurry. ~do a in a hurry; (hecho con prisa) hurried. ~miento m hurry. ~r vt hurry. ~rse vpr hurry

apret|ado a tight; (difícil) difficult; (tacaño) stingy, mean. ~ar [1] vt tighten; press (botón); squeeze (persona); (comprimir) press down. —vi be too tight. ~arse vpr crowd together. ~ón m squeeze. ~ón de manos handshake

aprieto m difficulty. verse en un ~ be in a tight spot

aprisa adv quickly

aprisionar vt imprison

aproba|ción f approval. ~r [2] vt approve (of); pass (examen). —vi pass

apropia|do a appropriate. ~rse vpr. ~rse de appropriate, take

aprovecha|ble a usable. ~do a (aplicado) diligent; (ingenioso) resourceful; (egoísta) selfish; (económico) thrifty. ~miento m

advantage; (uso) use. ~r vt take advantage of; (utilizar) make use of. —vi be useful. ~rse vpr make the most of it. ~rse de take advantage of. ¡que aproveche! enjoy your meal!

aprovisionar vt supply (con, de with)

aproxima|ción f approximation; (proximidad) closeness; (en la lotería) consolation prize. ~damente adv roughly, approximately. ~do a approximate, rough. ~r vt bring near; (fig) bring together (personas). ~rse vpr come closer, approach

apt|itud f suitability; (capacidad) ability. ~o a (capaz) capable; (adecuado) suitable

apuesta f bet

apuesto a smart. —vb véase **apostar**

apunta|ción f note. ~do a sharp. ~dor m prompter

apuntalar vt shore up

apunt|amiento m aiming (nota) note. ~ar vt aim (arma); (señalar) point at; (anotar) make a note of, note down; (sacar punta) sharpen; (en el teatro) prompt. ~arse vpr put one's name down; score (triunfo, tanto etc). ~e m note; (bosquejo) sketch. tomar ~s take notes

apuñalar vt stab

apur|adamente adv with difficulty. ~ado a difficult; (sin dinero) hard up; (agotado) exhausted; (exacto) precise, carefully done. ~ar vt exhaust; (acabar) finish; drain (vaso etc); (fastidiar) annoy; (causar vergüenza) embarrass. ~arse vpr worry; (esp LAm, apresurarse) hurry up. ~o m tight spot, difficult situation; (vergüenza) embarrassment; (estrechez) hardship, want; (esp LAm, prisa) hurry

aquejar *vt* trouble

aquel *a* (*f* **aquella**, *mpl* **aquellos**, *fpl* **aquellas**) that; (*en plural*) those; (*primero de dos*) former

aquél *pron* (*f* **aquélla**, *mpl* **aquéllos**, *fpl* **aquéllas**) that one; (*en plural*) those; (*primero de dos*) the former

aquello *pron* that; (*asunto*) that business

aquí *adv* here. **de ~** from here. **de ~ a 15 días** in a fortnight's time. **de ~ para allí** to and fro. **de ~ que** so that. **hasta ~** until now. **por ~** around here

aquiescencia *f* acquiescence

aquietar *vt* calm (down)

aquí: ~ fuera out here. **~ mismo** right here

árabe *a* & *m* & *f* Arab; (*lengua*) Arabic

Arabia *f* Arabia. **~ saudita**, **~ saudí** Saudi Arabia

arábigo *a* Arabic

arado *m* plough. **~r** *m* ploughman

Aragón *m* Aragon

aragonés *a* & *m* Aragonese

arancel *m* tariff. **~ario** *a* tariff

arandela *f* washer

araña *f* spider; (*lámpara*) chandelier

arañar *vt* scratch

arar *vt* plough

arbitra|je *m* arbitration; (*en deportes*) refereeing. **~r** *vt/i* arbitrate; (*en fútbol etc*) referee; (*en tenis etc*) umpire

arbitr|ariedad *f* arbitrariness. **~ario** *a* arbitrary. **~io** *m* (*free*) will; (*jurid*) decision, judgement

árbitro *m* arbitrator; (*en fútbol etc*) referee; (*en tenis etc*) umpire

árbol *m* tree; (*eje*) axle; (*palo*) mast

arbol|ado *m* trees. **~adura** *f* rigging. **~eda** *f* wood

árbol: ~ genealógico family tree. **~ de navidad** Christmas tree

arbusto *m* bush

arca *f* (*caja*) chest. **~ de Noé** Noah's ark

arcada *f* arcade; (*de un puente*) arches; (*náuseas*) retching

arc|aico *a* archaic. **~aísmo** *m* archaism

arcángel *m* archangel

arcano *m* mystery. —*a* mysterious, secret

arce *m* maple (tree)

arcén *m* (*de autopista*) hard shoulder; (*de carretera*) verge

arcilla *f* clay

arco *m* arch; (*de curva*) arc; (*arma, mus*) bow. **~ iris** *m* rainbow

archipiélago *m* archipelago

archiv|ador *m* filing cabinet. **~ar** *vt* file (away). **~o** *m* file; (*de documentos históricos*) archives

arder *vt/i* burn; (*fig, de ira*) seethe. **~se** *vpr* burn (up). **estar que arde** be very tense. **y va que arde** and that's enough

ardid *m* trick, scheme

ardiente *a* burning. **~mente** *adv* passionately

ardilla *f* squirrel

ardor *m* heat; (*fig*) ardour. **~ del estómago** *m* heartburn. **~oso** *a* burning

arduo *a* arduous

área *f* area

arena *f* sand; (*en deportes*) arena; (*en los toros*) (bull)ring. **~l** *m* sandy area

arenga *f* harangue. **~r** [12] *vt* harangue

aren|isca *f* sandstone. **~isco** *a*, **~oso** *a* sandy

arenque *m* herring. **~ ahumado** kipper

argamasa *f* mortar

Argel *m* Algiers. **~ia** *f* Algeria

argelino *a* & *m* Algerian

argentado a silver-plated

Argentina f. **la** ~ Argentina

argentin|ismo m Argentinism. ~**o** a silvery; (*de la Argentina*) Argentinian, Argentine. —m Argentinian

argolla f ring

argot m slang

argucia f sophism

argüir [19] vt (*deducir*) deduce; (*probar*) prove, show; (*argumentar*) argue; (*echar en cara*) reproach. —vi argue

argument|ación f argument. ~**ador** a argumentative. ~**ar** vt/i argue. ~**o** m argument; (*de libro, película etc*) story, plot; (*resumen*) synopsis

aria f aria

aridez f aridity, dryness

árido a arid, dry. —m. ~**s** mpl dry goods

Aries m Aries

arisco a (*persona*) unsociable; (*animal*) vicious

arist|ocracia f aristocracy. ~**ócrata** m & f aristocrat. ~**ocrático** a aristocratic

aritmética f arithmetic

arma f arm, weapon; (*sección*) section. ~**da** f navy; (*flota*) fleet. ~ **de fuego** firearm. ~**do** a armed (**de** with). ~**dura** f armour; (*de gafas etc*) frame; (*tec*) framework. ~**mento** m arms, armaments; (*acción de armar*) armament. ~**r** vt arm (**de** with); (*montar*) put together. ~**r un lío** kick up a fuss. **La A~da Invencible** the Armada

armario m cupboard; (*para ropa*) wardrobe. ~ **ropero** wardrobe

armatoste m monstrosity, hulk (*fam*)

armazón m & f frame(work)

armer|ía f gunsmith's shop; (*museo*) war museum. ~**o** m gunsmith

armiño m ermine

armisticio m armistice

armonía f harmony

armónica f harmonica, mouth organ

armoni|oso harmonious. ~**zación** f harmonizing. ~**zar** [10] vt harmonize. —vi harmonize; (*personas*) get on well (**con** with); (*colores*) go well (**con** with)

arnés m armour. **arneses** mpl harness

aro m ring, hoop; (*Arg, pendiente*) ear-ring

arom|a m aroma; (*de vino*) bouquet. ~**ático** a aromatic. ~**atizar** [10] vt perfume; (*culin*) flavour

arpa f harp

arpado a serrated

arpía f harpy; (*fig*) hag

arpillera f sackcloth, sacking

arpista m & f harpist

arp|ón m harpoon. ~**onar** vt, ~**onear** vt harpoon

arque|ar vt arch, bend. ~**arse** vpr arch, bend. ~**o** m arching, bending

arqueo|logía f archaeology. ~**lógico** a archaeological. ~**ólogo** m archaeologist

arquería f arcade

arquero m archer; (*com*) cashier

arqueta f chest

arquetipo m archetype; (*prototipo*) prototype

arquitect|o m architect. ~**ónico** a architectural. ~**ura** f architecture

arrabal m suburb; (*LAm, tugurio*) slum. ~**es** mpl outskirts. ~**ero** a suburban; (*de modales groseros*) common

arracima|do a in a bunch; (*apiñado*) bunched together. ~**rse** vpr bunch together

arraiga|damente adv firmly. ~**r** [12] vi take root. ~**rse** vpr take root; (*fig*) settle

arran|cada *f* sudden start. **~car** [7] *vt* pull up ⟨*planta*⟩; extract ⟨*diente*⟩; ⟨*arrebatar*⟩ snatch; ⟨*auto*⟩ start. —*vi* start. **—carse** *vpr* start. **~que** *m* sudden start. ⟨*auto*⟩ start; ⟨*de emoción*⟩ outburst

arras *fpl* security

arrasa|dor *a* overwhelming, devastating. **~r** *vt* level, smooth; raze to the ground ⟨*edificio etc*⟩; ⟨*llenar*⟩ fill to the brim. —*vi* ⟨*el cielo*⟩ clear. **~rse** *vpr* ⟨*el cielo*⟩ clear; ⟨*los ojos*⟩ fill with tears; ⟨*triunfar*⟩ triumph

arrastr|ado *a* ⟨*penoso*⟩ wretched. **~ar** *vt* pull; ⟨*rozar contra el suelo*⟩ drag along; give rise to ⟨*consecuencias*⟩. —*vi* trail on the ground. **~arse** *vpr* crawl; ⟨*humillarse*⟩ grovel. **~e** *m* dragging; ⟨*transporte*⟩ haulage. **estar para el ~e** ⟨*fam*⟩ have had it, be worn out. **ir ~ado** be hard up

arrayán *m* myrtle

arre *int* gee up! **~ar** *vt* urge on; give ⟨*golpe*⟩

arrebañar *vt* scrape together; scrape clean ⟨*plato etc*⟩

arrebat|ado *a* enraged; ⟨*irreflexivo*⟩ impetuous; ⟨*cara*⟩ flushed. **~ar** *vt* snatch (away); ⟨*el viento*⟩ blow away; ⟨*fig*⟩ win (over); captivate ⟨*corazón etc*⟩. **~arse** *vpr* get carried away. **~o** *m* ⟨*de cólera etc*⟩ fit; ⟨*éxtasis*⟩ extasy

arrebol *m* red glow

arreciar *vi* get worse, increase

arrecife *m* reef

arregl|ado *a* neat; ⟨*bien vestido*⟩ well-dressed; ⟨*moderado*⟩ moderate. **~ar** *vt* arrange; ⟨*poner en orden*⟩ tidy up; sort out ⟨*asunto, problema etc*⟩; ⟨*reparar*⟩ mend. **~arse** *vpr* ⟨*ponerse bien*⟩ improve; ⟨*prepararse*⟩ get ready; ⟨*apañarse*⟩ manage, make do; ⟨*ponerse de acuerdo*⟩ come to an

agreement. **~árselas** manage, get by. **~o** *m* ⟨*incl mus*⟩ arrangement; ⟨*acción de reparar*⟩ repair; ⟨*acuerdo*⟩ agreement; ⟨*orden*⟩ order. **con ~o a** according to

arrellanarse *vpr* lounge, sit back

arremangar [12] *vt* roll up ⟨*mangas*⟩; tuck up ⟨*falda*⟩. **~se** *vpr* roll up one's sleeves

arremeter *vt/i* attack. **~ida** *f* attack

arremolinarse *vpr* mill about

arrenda|dor *m* ⟨*que da en alquiler*⟩ landlord; ⟨*que toma en alquiler*⟩ tenant. **~miento** *m* renting; ⟨*contrato*⟩ lease; ⟨*precio*⟩ rent. **~r** [1] *vt* ⟨*dar casa en alquiler*⟩ let; ⟨*dar cosa en alquiler*⟩ hire out; ⟨*tomar en alquiler*⟩ rent. **~tario** *m* tenant

arreos *mpl* harness

arrepenti|miento *m* repentance, regret. **~rse** [4] *vpr*. **~rse de** be sorry, regret; repent ⟨*pecados*⟩

arrest|ar *vt* arrest, detain; ⟨*encarcelar*⟩ imprison. **~o** *m* arrest; ⟨*encarcelamiento*⟩ imprisonment

arriar [20] *vt* lower ⟨*bandera, vela*⟩; ⟨*aflojar*⟩ loosen; ⟨*inundar*⟩ flood. **~se** *vpr* be flooded

arriba *adv* ⟨*up*⟩ above; ⟨*dirección*⟩ up(wards); ⟨*en casa*⟩ upstairs. —*int* up with; ⟨*¡levántate!*⟩ up you get!; ⟨*¡ánimo!*⟩ come on! **¡~ España!** long live Spain! **~ mencionado** aforementioned. **calle ~** up the street. **de ~ abajo** from top to bottom. **de 100 pesetas para ~** more than 100 pesetas. **escaleras ~** upstairs. **la parte de ~** the top part. **los de ~** those at the top. **más ~** above

arribar *vi* ⟨*barco*⟩ reach port; ⟨*esp LAm, llegar*⟩ arrive

arribista *m & f* self-seeking person, arriviste

arribo *m* (*esp LAm*) arrival

arriero *m* muleteer

arriesga|do *a* risky. **~r** [12] *vt* risk; (*aventurar*) venture. **~se** *vpr* take a risk

arrim|ar *vt* bring close(r); (*apartar*) move out of the way (*cosa*); (*apartar*) push aside (*persona*). **~arse** *vpr* come closer, approach; (*apoyarse*) lean (**a** on). **~o** *m* support. **al ~o de** with the support of

arrincona|do *a* forgotten. **~rse** *vt* put in a corner; (*perseguir*) corner; (*arrumbar*) put aside; (*apartar a uno*) leave out, ignore. **~rse** *vpr* become a recluse

arriscado *a* (*terreno*) uneven

arrobar *vt* entrance. **~se** *vpr* be enraptured

arrocero *a* rice

arrodillarse *vpr* kneel (down)

arrogan|cia *f* arrogance; (*orgullo*) pride. **~te** *a* arrogant; (*orgulloso*) proud

arrogarse [12] *vpr* assume

arroj|ado *a* brave. **~ar** *vt* throw; (*dejar caer*) drop; (*emitir*) give off, throw out; (*producir*) produce. —*vi* (*esp LAm, vomitar*) be sick. **~arse** *vpr* throw o.s. **~o** *m* courage

arrolla|dor *a* overwhelming. **~r** *vt* roll (up); (*atropellar*) run over; (*ejército*) crush; (*agua*) sweep away; (*tratar sin respeto*) have no respect for

arropar *vt* wrap up; (*en la cama*) tuck up; (*fig, amparar*) protect. **~se** *vpr* wrap (o.s.) up

arroy|o *m* stream; (*de una calle*) gutter; (*fig, de lágrimas*) flood; (*fig, de sangre*) pool. **poner en el ~o** throw into the street. **~uelo** *m* small stream

arroz *m* rice. **~al** *m* rice field. **~ con leche** rice pudding

arruga *f* (*en la piel*) wrinkle, line; (*en tela*) crease. **~r** [12] *vt* wrinkle; crumple (*papel*); crease (*tela*). **~rse** *vpr* (*la piel*) wrinkle, get wrinkled; (*tela*) crease, get creased

arruinar *vt* ruin; (*destruir*) destroy. **~se** *vpr* (*persona*) be ruined; (*edificio*) fall into ruins

arrullar *vt* lull to sleep. —*vi* (*palomas*) coo. **~se** *vpr* bill and coo

arrumaco *m* caress; (*zalamería*) flattery

arrumbar *vt* put aside

arsenal *m* (*astillero*) shipyard; (*de armas*) arsenal; (*fig*) store

arsénico *m* arsenic

arte *m in singular, f en plural* art; (*habilidad*) skill; (*astucia*) cunning. **bellas ~s** fine arts. **con ~** skilfully. **malas ~s** trickery. **por amor al ~** for nothing, for love

artefacto *m* device

arter|amente *adv* artfully. **~ia** *f* cunning

arteria *f* artery; (*fig, calle*) main road

artero *a* cunning

artesan|al *a* craft. **~ía** *f* handicrafts. **~o** *m* artisan, craftsman. **objeto** *m* **de ~ía** hand-made article

ártico *a & m* Arctic

articula|ción *f* joint; (*pronunciación*) articulation. **~damente** *adv* articulately. **~do** *a* articulated; (*lenguaje*) articulate. **~r** *vt* articulate

articulista *m & f* columnist

artículo *m* article. **~s** *mpl* (*géneros*) goods. **~ de exportación** export commodity. **~ de fondo** editorial, leader

artificial *a* artificial

artificiero *m* bomb-disposal expert

artificio *m* (*habilidad*) skill; (*dispositivo*) device; (*engaño*) trick. **~so** *a* clever; (*astuto*) artful

artilugio *m* gadget

artillería *f* artillery. **~o** *m* artilleryman, gunner

artimaña *f* trap

art|ista *m* & *f* artist; (*en espectáculos*) artiste. **~ísticamente** *adv* artistically. **~ístico** *a* artistic

artr|ítico *a* arthritic. **~itis** *f* arthritis

arveja *f* vetch; (*LAm, guisante*) pea

arzobispo *m* archbishop

as *m* ace

asa *f* handle

asado *a* roast(ed). **—***m* roast (meat), joint. **~o a la parrilla** grilled. **~o al horno** (*sin grasa*) baked; (*con grasa*) roast. **~or** *m* spit. **~ura** *f* offal

asalariado *a* salaried. **—***m* employee

asalt|ante *m* attacker; (*de un banco*) robber. **~ar** *vt* storm (*fortaleza*); attack (*persona*); raid (*banco etc*); (*duda*) assail; (*fig*) (*idea etc*) cross one's mind. **~o** *m* attack; (*en boxeo*) round

asamble|a *f* assembly; (*reunión*) meeting; (*congreso*) conference. **~ísta** *m* & *f* member of an assembly

asapán *m* (*Mex*) flying squirrel

asar *vt* roast; (*fig, acosar*) pester (**a** with). **~se** *vpr* be very hot. **~ a la parrilla** grill. **~ al horno** (*sin grasa*) bake; (*con grasa*) roast

asbesto *m* asbestos

ascendencia *f* descent

ascend|ente *a* ascending. **~er** [1] *vt* promote. **—***vi* go up, ascend; (*cuenta etc*) come to, amount to; (*ser ascendido*) be promoted. **~iente** *m* & *f* ancestor; (*influencia*) influence

ascens|ión *f* ascent; (*de grado*) promotion. **~ional** *a* upward. **~o** *m* ascent; (*de grado*) promotion. **día m de la A~ión** Ascension Day

ascensor *m* lift (*Brit*), elevator (*Amer*). **~ista** *m* & *f* lift attendant (*Brit*), elevator operator (*Amer*)

asc|eta *m* & *f* ascetic. **~ético** *a* ascetic

asco *m* disgust. **dar ~** be disgusting; (*fig, causar enfado*) be infuriating. **estar hecho un ~** be disgusting. **hacer ~s de algo** turn up one's nose at sth. **me da ~ el ajo** I can't stand garlic. **¡qué ~!** how disgusting! **ser un ~** be a disgrace

ascua *f* ember. **estar en ~s** be on tenterhooks

ase|adamente *adv* cleanly. **~do** *a* clean; (*arreglado*) neat. **~r** *vt* (*lavar*) wash; (*limpiar*) clean; (*arreglar*) tidy up

asedi|ar *vt* besiege; (*fig*) pester. **~o** *m* siege

asegura|do *a* & *m* insured. **~dor** *m* insurer. **~r** *vt* secure, make safe; (*decir*) assure; (*concertar un seguro*) insure; (*preservar*) safeguard. **~rse** *vpr* make sure

asemejarse *vpr* be alike

asenta|da *f. de una ~da* at a sitting. **~do** *a* situated; (*arraigado*) established. **~r** [1] *vt* place; (*asegurar*) settle; (*anotar*) note down. **—***vi* be suitable. **~rse** *vpr* settle; (*estar situado*) be situated

asenti|miento *m* consent. **~r** [4] *vi* agree (**a** to). **~r con la cabeza** nod

aseo *m* cleanliness. **~s** *mpl* toilets

asequible *a* obtainable; (*precio*) reasonable; (*persona*) approachable

asesin|ar vt murder; (pol) assassinate. **~ato** m murder; (pol) assassination. **~o** m murderer; (pol) assassin

asesor m adviser, consultant. **~amiento** m advice. **~ar** vt advise. **~arse** vpr. **~arse con/de** consult. **~ía** f consultancy; (oficina) consultant's office

asestar vt aim (arma); strike (golpe etc); (disparar) fire

asevera|ción f assertion. **~r** vt assert

asfalt|ado a asphalt. **~ar** vt asphalt. **~o** m asphalt

asfixia f suffocation. **~nte** a suffocating. **~r** vt suffocate. **~rse** vpr suffocate

así adv so; (de esta manera) like this, like that. —a such. ~, ~, ~ asá, ~ asado so-so. ~ como just as. ~... como both... and. ~ pues so. ~ que so; (enseguida) as soon as. ~ sea so be it. ~ y todo even so. aun ~ even so. ¿no es ~? isn't that right? y ~ (sucesivamente) and so on

Asia f Asia

asiático a & m Asian

asidero m handle; (fig, pretexto) excuse

asidua|mente adv regularly. **~idad** f regularity. **~o** a & m regular

asiento m seat; (situación) site. ~ **delantero** front seat. ~ **trasero** back seat. **tome Vd** ~ please take a seat

asigna|ción f assignment; (sueldo) salary. **~r** vt assign; allot (porción, tiempo etc)

asignatura f subject. ~ **pendiente** (escol) failed subject; (fig) matter still to be resolved

asil|ado m inmate. **~o** m asylum; (fig) shelter; (de ancianos etc) home. **~o de huérfanos** orphanage. **pedir ~o político** ask for political asylum

asimétrico a asymmetrical

asimila|ción f assimilation. **~r** vt assimilate. **~rse** vpr be assimilated. **~rse a** resemble

asimismo adv in the same way, likewise

asir [45] vt grasp. **~se** vpr grab hold (a, de of)

asist|encia f attendance; (gente) people (present); (en un teatro etc) audience; (ayuda) assistance. **~encia médica** medical care. **~enta** f assistant; (mujer de la limpieza) charwoman. **~ente** m assistant. **~ente social** social worker. **~ido** a assisted. **~ir** vt assist, help; (un médico) treat. —vi. **~ir a** attend, be present at

asma f asthma. **~ático** a & m asthmatic

asn|ada f (fig) silly thing. **~o** m donkey; (fig) ass

asocia|ción f association; (com) partnership. **~do** a associated; (miembro etc) associate. —m associate. **~r** vt associate; (com) take into partnership. **~rse** vpr associate; (com) become a partner

asolador a destructive

asolar[1] [1] vt destroy. **~se** vpr be destroyed

asolar[2] vt dry up (plantas)

asoma|da f brief appearance. **~r** vt show. —vi appear, show. **~rse** vpr (persona) lean out (a, por of); (cosa) appear

asombr|adizo a easily frightened. **~ar** vt (pasmar) amaze; (sorprender) surprise. **~arse** vpr be amazed; (sorprenderse) be surprised. **~o** m amazement, surprise. **~osamente** adv amazingly. **~oso** a amazing, astonishing

asomo m sign. **ni por** ~ by no means

asonada f mob; (motín) riot

aspa f cross, X-shape; (de molino) (windmill) sail. **~do** a X-shaped

aspaviento m show, fuss. **~s** mpl gestures. **hacer ~s** make a big fuss

aspecto m look, appearance; (fig) aspect

aspereza f roughness; (de sabor etc) sourness

áspero a rough; (sabor etc) bitter

aspersión f sprinkling

aspiración f breath; (deseo) ambition

aspirador a suction. **~a** f vacuum cleaner

aspira|nte m candidate. **~r** vt breathe in; (máquina) suck up. **—vi** breathe in; (máquina) suck. **~r a** aspire to

aspirina f aspirin

asquear vt sicken. **—vi** be sickening. **~se** vpr be disgusted

asqueros|amente adv disgustingly. **~idad** f filthiness. **~o** a disgusting

asta f spear; (de la bandera) flagpole; (mango) handle; (cuerno) horn. **a media ~** at half-mast. **~do** a horned

asterisco m asterisk

astilla f splinter. **~s** fpl firewood. **~r** vt splinter. **hacer ~s** smash. **hacerse ~s** shatter

astillero m shipyard

astringente a & m astringent

astro m star

astr|ología f astrology. **~ólogo** m astrologer

astrona|uta m & f astronaut. **~ve** f spaceship

astr|onomía f astronomy. **~onómico** a astronomical. **~ónomo** m astronomer

astu|cia f cleverness; (ardid) cunning. **~to** a astute; (taimado) cunning

asturiano a & m Asturian

Asturias fpl Asturias

asueto m time off, holiday

asumir vt assume

asunción f assumption. **A~** Assumption

asunto m subject; (cuestión) matter; (de una novela) plot; (negocio) business. **~s** mpl exteriores foreign affairs. **el ~ es que** the fact is that

asusta|dizo a easily frightened. **~r** vt frighten. **~rse** vpr be frightened

ataca|nte m & f attacker. **~r** [7] vt attack

atad|ero m rope; (cierre) fastening; (gancho) hook. **~ijo** m bundle. **~o** a tied; (fig) timid. **—** m bundle. **~ura** f tying; (cuerda) string

ataj|ar vi take a short cut. **~o** m short cut; (grupo) bunch. **echar por el ~o** take the easy way out

atalaya f watch-tower; (fig) vantage point

atañer [22] vt concern

ataque m attack; (med) fit, attack. **~ al corazón** heart attack. **~ de nervios** hysterics

atar vt tie (up). **~se** vpr get tied up

atardecer [11] vi get dark. **—m** dusk. **al ~** at dusk

atarea|do a busy. **~rse** vpr work hard

atasc|adero m (fig) stumbling block. **~ar** [7] vt block; (fig) hinder. **~arse** vpr get stuck; (tubo etc) block. **~o** m obstruction; (auto) traffic jam

ataúd m coffin

atavi|ar [20] vt dress up. **~arse** vpr dress up, get dressed up. **~ío** m dress, attire

atemorizar [10] vt frighten. **~se** vpr be frightened

Atenas fpl Athens

atenazar [10] vt (fig) torture; (duda, miedo) grip

atención f attention; (cortesía) courtesy, kindness; (interés) interest. ¡~! look out! **~ a** beware of. **llamar la ~** attract attention, catch the eye. **prestar ~** pay attention

atender [1] *vt* attend to; heed ‹*consejo etc*›; (*cuidar*) look after. —*vi* pay attention

atenerse [40] *vpr* abide (**a** by)

atentado *m* offence; (*ataque*) attack. **~ contra la vida de uno** attempt on s.o.'s life

atentamente *adv* attentively; (*con cortesía*) politely; (*con amabilidad*) kindly. **le saluda ~** (*en cartas*) yours faithfully

atentar *vi* commit an offence. **~ contra la vida de uno** make an attempt on s.o.'s life

atento *a* attentive; (*cortés*) polite; (*amable*) kind

atenua|nte *a* extenuating. —*f* extenuating circumstance. **~r** [21] *vt* attenuate; (*hacer menor*) diminish, lessen. **~rse** *vpr* weaken

ateo *a* atheistic. —*m* atheist

aterciopelado *a* velvety

aterido *a* frozen (stiff), numb (with cold)

aterra|dor *a* terrifying. **~r** *vt* terrify. **~rse** *vpr* be terrified

aterriza|je *m* landing. **~je forzoso** emergency landing. **~r** [10] *vt* land

aterrorizar [10] *vt* terrify

atesorar *vt* hoard

atesta|do *a* packed, full up. —*m* sworn statement. **~r** *vt* fill up, pack; (*jurid*) testify

atestiguar [15] *vt* testify to; (*fig*) prove

atiborrar *vt* fill, stuff. **~se** *vpr* stuff o.s.

ático *m* attic

atilda|do *a* elegant, neat. **~r** *vt* put a tilde over; (*arreglar*) tidy up. **~rse** *vpr* smarten o.s. up

atina|damente *adv* rightly. **~do** *a* right; (*juicioso*) wise, sensible.

~r *vt/i* hit upon; (*acertar*) guess right

atípico *a* exceptional

atiplado *a* high-pitched

atirantar *vt* tighten

atisb|ar *vt* spy on; (*vislumbrar*) make out. **~o** *m* spying; (*indicio*) hint, sign

atizar [10] *vt* poke; give ‹*golpe*›; (*fig*) stir up; arouse, excite ‹*pasión etc*›

atlántico *a* Atlantic. **el (océano) A~** the Atlantic (Ocean)

atlas *m* atlas

atl|eta *m* & *f* athlete. **~ético** *a* athletic. **~etismo** *m* athletics

atm|ósfera *f* atmosphere. **~osférico** *a* atmospheric

atolondra|do *a* scatter-brained; (*aturdido*) bewildered. **~miento** *m* bewilderment; (*irreflexión*) thoughtlessness. **~r** *vt* bewilder; (*pasmar*) stun. **~rse** *vpr* be bewildered

atolladero *m* bog; (*fig*) tight corner

at|ómico *a* atomic. **~omizador** *m* atomizer. **~omizar** [10] *vt* atomize

átomo *m* atom

atónito *m* amazed

atonta|do *a* bewildered; (*tonto*) stupid. **~r** *vt* stun. **~rse** *vpr* get confused

atormenta|dor *a* tormenting. —*m* tormentor. **~r** *vt* torture. **~rse** *vpr* worry, torment o.s.

atornillar *vt* screw on

atosigar [12] *vt* pester

atracador *m* bandit

atracadero *m* quay

atrac|ar [7] *vt* (*amarrar*) tie up; (*arrimar*) bring alongside; rob ‹*banco, persona*›. —*vi* ‹*barco*› tie up; (*astronave*) dock. **~se** *vpr* stuff o.s. (**de** with)

atracción *f* attraction. **~ones** *fpl* entertainment, amusements

atrac|o m hold-up, robbery. **∼ón** m. **darse un ∼ón** stuff o.s.

atractivo a attractive. — m attraction; *(encanto)* charm

atraer [41] vt attract

atragantarse vpr choke **(con** on). **la historia se me atraganta** I can't stand history

atranc|ar [7] vt bolt *(puerta)*; block up *(tubo etc)*. **∼arse** vpr get stuck; *(tubo)* get blocked. **∼o** m difficulty

atrapar vt trap; *(fig)* land *(empleo etc)*; catch *(resfriado)*

atrás adv behind; *(dirección)* back(wards); *(tiempo)* previously, before. —int back! **dar un paso ∼** step backwards. **hacia ∼, para ∼** backwards

atras|ado a behind; *(reloj)* slow; *(con deudas)* in arrears; *(país)* backward. **llegar ∼ado** arrive late. **∼ar** vt slow down; *(retrasar)* put back; *(demorar)* delay, postpone. —vi *(reloj)* be slow. **∼arse** vpr be late; *(reloj)* be slow; *(quedarse atrás)* be behind. **∼o** m delay; *(de un reloj)* slowness; *(de un país)* backwardness. **∼os** mpl arrears

atravesa|do a lying across; *(bizco)* cross-eyed; *(fig, malo)* wicked. **∼r** [1] vt cross; *(traspasar)* go through; *(poner transversalmente)* lay across. **∼rse** vpr lie across; *(en la garganta)* get stuck, stick; *(entrometerse)* interfere

atrayente a attractive

atrev|erse vpr dare. **∼erse con** tackle. **∼ido** a daring, bold; *(insolente)* insolent. **∼imiento** m daring, boldness; *(descaro)* insolence

atribución f attribution. **atribuciones** fpl authority

atribuir [17] vt attribute; confer *(función)*. **∼se** vpr take the credit for

atribular vt afflict. **∼se** vpr be distressed

atribut|ivo a attributive. **∼o** m attribute; *(símbolo)* symbol

atril m lectern; *(mus)* music stand

atrincherar vt fortify with trenches. **∼se** vpr entrench (o.s.)

atrocidad f atrocity. **decir ∼es** make silly remarks. **¡qué ∼!** how terrible!

atrochar vi take a short cut

atrojarse vpr *(Mex)* be cornered

atrona|dor a deafening. **∼r** [2] vt deafen

atropell|adamente adv hurriedly. **∼ado** a hasty. **∼ar** vt knock down, run over; *(empujar)* push aside; *(maltratar)* bully; *(fig)* outrage, insult. **∼arse** vpr rush. **∼o** m *(auto)* accident; *(fig)* outrage

atroz a atrocious; *(fam)* huge. **∼mente** adv atrociously, awfully

atuendo m dress, attire

atufar vt choke; *(fig)* irritate. **∼se** vpr be overcome; *(enfadarse)* get cross

atún m tuna (fish)

aturdi|do a bewildered; *(irreflexivo)* thoughtless. **∼r** vt bewilder, stun; *(ruido)* deafen. **∼rse** vpr be stunned; *(intentar olvidar)* try to forget

atur(r)ullar vt bewilder

atusar vt smooth; trim *(pelo)*

auda|cia f boldness, audacity. **∼z** a bold

audib|ilidad f audibility. **∼le** a audible

audición f hearing; *(concierto)* concert

audiencia f audience; *(tribunal)* court

auditor m judge-advocate; *(de cuentas)* auditor

auditorio *m* audience; (*sala*) auditorium

auge *m* peak; (*com*) boom

augurar *vt* predict; (*cosas*) augur. ~**io** *m* omen. ~**ios** *mpl*. **con nuestros ~ios para** with our best wishes for

augusto *a* august

aula *f* class-room; (*univ*) lecture room

aulaga *f* gorse

aullar [23] *vi* howl. ~**ido** *m* howl

aumentar *vt* increase; put up (*precios*); magnify (*imagen*); step up (*producción, voltaje*). —*vi* increase. ~**arse** *vpr* increase. ~**ativo** *a* & *m* augmentative. ~**o** *m* increase; (*de sueldo*) rise

aun *adv* even. ~ **así** even so. ~ **cuando** although. **más** ~ even more. **ni** ~ not even

aún *adv* still, yet. ~ **no ha llegado** it still hasn't arrived, it hasn't arrived yet

aunar [23] *vt* join. ~**se** *vpr* join together

aunque *conj* although, (even) though

aúpa *int* up! **de** ~ wonderful

aureola *f* halo

auricular *m* (*de teléfono*) receiver. ~**es** *mpl* headphones

aurora *f* dawn

ausencia *f* absence. ~**tarse** *vpr* leave. ~**te** *a* absent. —*m* & *f* absentee; (*jurid*) missing person. **en** ~ **de** in the absence of

auspicio *m* omen. **bajo los** ~**s de** sponsored by

austeridad *f* austerity. ~**o** *a* austere

austral *a* southern. —*m* (*unidad monetaria argentina*) austral

Australia *m* Australia

australiano *a* & *m* Australian

Austria *f* Austria

austriaco, austríaco *a* & *m* Austrian

autenticar [7] authenticate. ~**enticidad** *f* authenticity. ~**éntico** *a* authentic

auto *m* sentence; (*auto, fam*) car. ~**s** *mpl* proceedings

auto... *pref* auto...

autoayuda *f* self-help. ~**biografía** *f* autobiography. ~**biográfico** *a* autobiographical. ~**bombo** *m* self-glorification

autobús *m* bus. **en** ~ by bus

autocar *m* coach (*Brit*), (long-distance) bus (*Amer*)

autocracia *f* autocracy. ~**ócrata** *m* & *f* autocrat. ~**ocrático** *a* autocratic

autóctono *a* autochthonous

auto: ~**determinación** *f* self-determination. ~**defensa** *f* self-defence. ~**didacto** *a* self-taught. —*m* autodidact. ~**escuela** *f* driving school. ~**giro** *m* autogiro

autógrafo *m* autograph

automación *f* automation

autómata *m* robot

automático *a* automatic. —*m* press-stud. ~**atización** *f* automation. ~**atizar** [10] *vt* automate

automotor *a* (*f* **automotriz**) self-propelled. —*m* diesel train

automóvil *a* self-propelled. —*m* car. ~**ovilismo** *m* motoring. ~**ovilista** *m* & *f* driver, motorist

autonomía *f* autonomy. ~**onómico** *a*, ~**ónomo** *a* autonomous

autopista *f* motorway (*Brit*), freeway (*Amer*)

autopsia *f* autopsy

autor *m* author. ~**a** *f* author(ess)

autoridad *f* authority. ~**tario** *a* authoritarian. ~**tarismo** *m* authoritarianism

autorización *f* authorization. ~**damente** *adv* officially. ~**do** *a* authorized, offical; (*opinión etc*) authoritative. **∼r** [10] *vt* authorize

auto: **∼rretrato** *m* self-portrait. **∼servicio** *m* self-service restaurant. **∼stop** *m* hitch-hiking. **hacer ∼stop** hitch-hike

autosuficien|cia *f* self-sufficiency. **∼te** *a* self-sufficient

autovía *f* dual carriageway

auxili|ar *a* assistant; *(servicios)* auxiliary. —*m* assistant. —*vt* help. **∼o** *m* help. **¡∼o!** help! **∼os espirituales** last rites. **en ∼o de** in aid of. **pedir ∼o** shout for help. **primeros ∼os** first aid

Av. *abrev (Avenida)* Ave, Avenue

aval *m* guarantee

avalancha *f* avalanche

avalar *vt* guarantee

avalorar *vt* enhance; *(fig)* encourage

avance *m* advance; *(en el cine)* trailer; *(balance)* balance; *(de noticias)* early news bulletin. **∼ informativo** publicity handout

avante *adv (esp LAm)* forward

avanza|do *a* advanced. **∼r** [10] *vt* move forward. —*vi* advance

avar|icia *f* avarice. **∼icioso** *a*, **∼iento** *a* greedy; *(tacaño)* miserly. **∼o** *a* miserly. —*m* miser

avasalla|dor *a* overwhelming. **∼r** *vt* dominate

Avda. *abrev (Avenida)* Ave, Avenue

ave *f* bird. **∼ de paso** *(incl fig)* bird of passage. **∼ de presa**, **∼ de rapiña** bird of prey

avecinarse *vpr* approach

avecindarse *vpr* settle

avejentarse *vpr* age

avellan|a *f* hazel-nut. **∼o** *m* hazel (tree)

avemaría *f* Hail Mary. **al ∼** at dusk

avena *f* oats

avenar *vt* drain

avenida *f (calle)* avenue; *(de río)* flood

avenir [53] *vt* reconcile. **∼se** *vpr* come to an agreement

aventaja|do *a* outstanding. **∼r** *vt* surpass

aventar [1] *vt* fan; winnow *(grano etc)*; *(viento)* blow away

aventur|a *f* adventure; *(riesgo)* risk. **∼a amorosa** love affair. **∼ado** *a* risky. **∼ar** *vt* risk. **∼arse** *vpr* dare. **∼a sentimental** love affair. **∼ero** *a* adventurous. —*m* adventurer

avergonza|do *a* ashamed; *(embarazado)* embarrassed. **∼r** [10 & 16] *vt* shame; *(embarazar)* embarrass. **∼rse** *vpr* be ashamed; *(embarazarse)* be embarrassed

aver|ía *f (auto)* breakdown; *(daño)* damage. **∼iado** *a* broken down; *(fruta)* damaged, spoilt. **∼iar** [20] *vt* damage. **∼iarse** *vpr* get damaged; *(coche)* break down

averigua|ble *a* verifiable. **∼ción** *f* verification; *(investigación)* investigation; *(Mex, disputa)* argument. **∼dor** *m* investigator. **∼r** [15] *vt* verify; *(enterarse de)* find out; *(investigar)* investigate. —*vi (Mex)* quarrel

aversión *f* aversion (**a**, **hacia**, **por** for)

avestruz *m* ostrich

aviación *f* aviation; *(mil)* air force

aviado *a (Arg)* well off. **estar ∼** be in a mess

aviador *m (aviat)* member of the crew; *(piloto)* pilot; *(Arg, prestamista)* money-lender; *(Arg, de minas)* mining speculator

aviar [20] *vt* get ready, prepare; *(arreglar)* tidy; *(reparar)* repair; *(LAm, prestar dinero)* lend money; *(dar prisa)* hurry up.

~se vpr get ready. ¡**aviate!** hurry up!

avícula f poultry. **~icultor** m poultry farmer. **~icultura** f poultry farming

avidez f eagerness, greed

ávido a eager, greedy

avieso a (maligno) wicked

avinagra|do a sour. **~r** vt sour; (fig) embitter. **~rse** vpr go sour; (fig) become embittered

avío m preparation. **~s** mpl provisions; (utensilios) equipment

avi|ón m aeroplane (Brit), airplane (Amer). **~oneta** f light aircraft

avis|ado a wise. **~ar** vt warn; (informar) notify, inform; call (médico etc). **~o** m warning; (anuncio) notice. **estar sobre ~o** be on the alert. **mal ~ado** ill-advised. **sin previo ~o** without notice

avispa f wasp. **~ado** a sharp. **~ero** m wasps' nest; (fig) mess. **~ón** m hornet

avistar vt catch sight of

avitualla|miento m supplying. **~r** vt provision

avivar vt stoke up (fuego); brighten up (color); arouse (interés, pasión); intensify (dolor). **~se** vpr revive; (animarse) cheer up

axila f axilla, armpit

axioma m axiom. **~ático** a axiomatic

ay int (de dolor) ouch!; (de susto) oh!; (de pena) oh dear! **~ de poor!** ¡**~ de ti!** poor you!

aya f governess, child's nurse

ayer adv yesterday. —m past. **antes de ~** the day before yesterday. **~ por la mañana** yesterday morning. **~ (por la) noche** last night

ayo m tutor

ayote m (Mex) pumpkin

ayuda f help, aid. **~ de cámara** valet. **~nta** f, **~nte** m assistant; (mil) adjutant. **~nte técnico sanitario (ATS)** nurse. **~r** vt help

ayun|ar vi fast. **~as** fpl. **estar en ~as** have had no breakfast; (fig, fam) be in the dark. **~o** m fasting

ayuntamiento m town council, city council; (edificio) town hall

azabache m jet

azada f hoe. **~ón** m (large) hoe

azafata f air hostess

azafrán m saffron

azahar m orange blossom

azar m chance; (desgracia) misfortune. **al ~** at random. **por ~** by chance

azararse vpr go wrong; (fig) get flustered

azaros|amente adv hazardously. **~o** a hazardous, risky; (persona) unlucky

azoga|do a restless. **~rse** [12] vpr be restless

azolve m (Mex) obstruction

azora|do a flustered, excited, alarmed. **~miento** m confusion, embarrassment. **~r** vt embarrass; (aturdir) alarm. **~rse** vpr get flustered, be alarmed

Azores fpl Azores

azot|aina f beating. **~ar** vt whip, beat. **~e** m whip; (golpe) smack; (fig, calamidad) calamity

azotea f flat roof. **estar mal de la ~** be mad

azteca a & m & f Aztec

az|úcar m & f sugar. **~ucarado** a sweet. **~ucarar** vt sweeten. **~ucarero** m sugar bowl

azucena f (white) lily

azufre m sulphur

azul a & m blue. **~ado** a bluish. **~ de lavar** (washing) blue. **~ marino** navy blue

azulejo m tile

azuzar vt urge on, incite

B

bab|**a** *f* spittle. **∼ear** *vi* drool, slobber; *(niño)* dribble. **caerse la ∼a** be delighted

babel *f* bedlam

babe|**o** *m* drooling; *(de un niño)* dribbling. **∼ro** *m* bib

Babia *f.* **estar en ∼** have one's head in the clouds

babieca *a* stupid. —*m & f* simpleton

babor *m* port. **a ∼** to port, on the port side

babosa *f* slug

babosada *f (Mex)* silly remark

babos|**ear** *vt* slobber over; *(niño)* dribble over. **∼eo** *m* drooling; *(de niño)* dribbling. **∼o** *a* slimy; *(LAm, tonto)* silly

babucha *f* slipper

babuino *m* baboon

baca *f* luggage rack

bacaladilla *f* small cod

bacalao *m* cod

bacon *m* bacon

bacteria *f* bacterium

bache *m* hole; *(fig)* bad patch

bachillerato *m* school-leaving examination

badaj|**azo** *m* stroke (of a bell). **∼o** *m* clapper; *(persona)* chatterbox

bagaje *m* baggage; *(animal)* beast of burden; *(fig)* knowledge

bagatela *f* trifle

Bahamas *fpl* Bahamas

bahía *f* bay

bail|**able** *a* dance. **∼ador** *a* dancing. —*m* dancer. **∼aor** *m* Flamenco dancer. **∼ar** *vt/i* dance. **∼arín** dancer. **∼arina** *f* dancer; *(de baile clásico)* ballerina. **∼e** *m* dance. **∼e de etiqueta** ball. **ir a ∼ar** go dancing

baja *f* drop, fall; *(mil)* casualty. **∼ por maternidad** maternity leave. **∼da** *f* slope; *(acto de bajar)* descent. **∼mar** *m* low

tide. **∼r** *vt* lower; *(llevar abajo)* get down; bow *(la cabeza)*. **∼r la escalera** go downstairs. —*vi* go down; *(temperatura, precio)* fall. **∼rse** *vpr* bend down. **∼r(se) de** get out of *(coche)*; get off *(autobús, caballo, tren, bicicleta)*. **dar(se) de ∼** take sick leave

bajeza *f* vile deed

bajío *m* sandbank

bajo *a* low; *(de estatura)* short, small; *(cabeza, ojos)* lowered; *(humilde)* humble, low; *(vil)* vile, low; *(color)* pale; *(voz)* low; *(mus)* deep. —*m* lowland; *(bajío)* sandbank; *(mus)* bass. —*adv* quietly; *(volar)* low. —*prep* under; *(temperatura)* below. **∼ la lluvia** in the rain. **los ∼s fondos** the low district. **por lo ∼** under one's breath; *(fig)* in secret

bajón *m* drop; *(de salud)* decline; *(com)* slump

bala *f* bullet; *(de algodón etc)* bale. **∼ perdida** stray bullet. **como una ∼** like a shot

balada *f* ballad

baladí *a* trivial

baladrón *a* boastful

baladron|**ada** *f* boast. **∼ear** *vi* boast

balanc|**e** *m* swinging; *(de una cuenta)* balance; *(documento)* balance sheet. **∼ear** *vt* balance. —*vi* hesitate. **∼earse** *vpr* swing; *(vacilar)* hesitate. **∼eo** *m* swinging. **∼za** *f* scales; *(com)* balance

balar *vi* bleat

balaustrada *f* balustrade, railing(s); *(de escalera)* banisters

balay *m (LAm)* wicker basket

balazo *m (disparo)* shot; *(herida)* bullet wound

balboa *f (unidad monetaria panameña)* balboa

balbuc|**ear** *vt/i* stammer; *(niño)* babble. **∼eo** *m* stammering; *(de* *niño)* babbling. **~iente** *a* stammering; *(niño)* babbling. **~ir** [24] *vt/i* stammer; *(niño)* babble

balc|ón *m* balcony. **~onada** *f* row of balconies. **~onaje** *m* row of balconies

balda *f* shelf

baldado *a* disabled, crippled; *(rendido)* shattered. —*m* disabled person, cripple

baldaquín *m*, **baldaquino** *m* canopy

baldar *vt* cripple

balde *m* bucket. **de ~** free (of charge). **en ~** in vain. **~ar** *vt* wash down

baldío *a (terreno)* waste; *(fig)* useless

baldosa *f* (floor) tile; *(losa)* flagstone

balduque *m (incl fig)* red tape

balear *a* Balearic. —*m* native of the Balearic Islands. **las Islas** *fpl* **B~es** the Balearics, the Balearic Islands

baleo *m (LAm, tiroteo)* shooting; *(Mex, abanico)* fan

balido *m* bleat; *(varios sonidos)* bleating

bal|ín *m* small bullet. **~ines** *mpl* shot

balística *f* ballistics

baliza *f (naut)* buoy; *(aviat)* beacon

balneario *m* spa; *(con playa)* seaside resort. —*a*. **estación** *f* **balnearia** spa; *(con playa)* seaside resort

balompié *m* football *(Brit)*, soccer

bal|ón *m* ball, football. **~oncesto** *m* basketball. **~onmano** *m* handball. **~volea** *m* volleyball

balotaje *m (LAm)* voting

balsa *f (de agua)* pool; *(plataforma flotante)* raft

bálsamo *m* balsam; *(fig)* balm

balsón *m (Mex)* stagnant water

baluarte *m (incl fig)* bastion

balumba *f* mass, mountain

ballena *f* whale

ballesta *f* crossbow

ballet /ba'le/ *(pl* **ballets** /ba'le/) *m* ballet

bambole|ar *vi* sway; *(mesa etc)* wobble. **~arse** *vpr* sway; *(mesa etc)* wobble. **~o** *m* swaying; *(de mesa etc)* wobbling

bambú *m (pl* **bambúes)** bamboo

banal *a* banal. **~idad** *f* banality

banan|a *f (esp LAm)* banana. **~o** *m (LAm)* banana tree

banast|a *f* large basket. **~o** *m* large round basket

banc|a *f* banking; *(en juegos)* bank; *(LAm, asiento)* bench. **~ario** *a* bank, banking. **~arrota** *f* bankruptcy. **~o** *m (asiento)* bench; *(com)* bank; *(bajío)* sandbank. **hacer ~arrota, ir a la ~arrota** go bankrupt

banda *f (incl mus, radio)* band; *(grupo)* gang, group; *(lado)* side. **~da** *f (de aves)* flock; *(de peces)* shoal. **~ de sonido, ~ sonora** sound-track

bandeja *f* tray; *(LAm, plato)* serving dish. **servir algo en ~ a uno** hand sth to s.o. on a plate

bandera *f* flag; *(estandarte)* banner, standard

banderill|a *f* banderilla. **~ear** *vt* stick the banderillas in. **~ero** *m* banderillero

banderín *m* pennant, small flag, banner

bandido *m* bandit

bando *m* edict, proclamation; *(partido)* faction. **~s** *mpl* banns. **pasarse al otro ~** go over to the other side

bandolero *m* bandit

bandolina *f* mandolin

bandoneón *m* large accordion

banjo *m* banjo

banquero *m* banker

banqueta f stool; (*LAm*, *acera*) pavement (*Brit*), sidewalk (*Amer*)

banquete m banquet; (*de boda*) wedding reception. **~ar** *vt/i* banquet

banquillo m bench; (*jurid*) dock; (*taburete*) footstool

bañ|ado m (*LAm*) swamp. **~ador** m (*de mujer*) swimming costume; (*de hombre*) swimming trunks. **~ar** *vt* bathe, immerse; bath (*niño*); (*culin*, *recubrir*) coat. **~arse** *vpr* go swimming, have a swim; (*en casa*) have a bath. **~era** f bath, bath-tub. **~ero** m life-guard. **~ista** m & f bather. **~o** m bath; (*en piscina*, *mar etc*) swim; (*bañera*) bath, bath-tub; (*capa*) coating

baptisterio m baptistery; (*pila*) font

baquet|a f (*de fusil*) ramrod; (*de tambor*) drumstick. **~ear** *vt* bother. **~eo** m nuisance, bore

bar m bar

barahúnda f uproar

baraja f pack of cards. **~r** *vt* shuffle; juggle, massage (*cifras etc*). **~vi** argue (*con* with); (*enemistarse*) fall out (*con* with). **~s** *fpl* argument. **jugar a la ~** play cards. **jugar a dos ~s**, **jugar con dos ~s** be deceitful, indulge in double-dealing

baranda f, **barandal** m, **barandilla** f handrail; (*de escalera*) banisters

barat|a f (*Mex*) sale. **~ija** f trinket. **~illo** m junk shop; (*géneros*) cheap goods. **~o** a cheap. **—m** sale. **—adv** cheap(ly). **~ura** f cheapness

baraúnda f uproar

barba f chin; (*pelo*) beard. **~do** a bearded

barbacoa f barbecue; (*Mex*, *carne*) barbecued meat

bárbaramente adv savagely; (*fig*) tremendously

barbari|dad f barbarity; (*fig*) outrage; (*mucho*, *fam*) awful lot (*fam*). **¡qué ~dad!** how awful! **~e** f barbarity; (*fig*) ignorance. **~smo** m barbarism

bárbaro a barbaric, cruel; (*bruto*) uncouth; (*estupendo*, *fam*) terrific (*fam*). **—m** barbarian. **¡qué ~!** how marvellous!

barbear *vt* (*afeitar*) shave; (*Mex*, *lisonjear*) fawn on

barbecho m fallow

barber|ía f barber's (shop). **~o** m barber; (*Mex*, *adulador*) flatterer

barbi|lampiño a beardless; (*fig*) inexperienced, green. **~lindo** m dandy

barbilla f chin

barbitúrico m barbiturate

barbo m barbel. **~ de mar** red mullet

barbot|ar *vt/i* mumble. **~ear** *vt/i* mumble. **~eo** m mumbling

barbudo a bearded

barbullar *vi* jabber

barca f (small) boat. **~ de pasaje** ferry. **~je** m fare. **~za** f barge

Barcelona f Barcelona

barcelonés a of Barcelona, from Barcelona. **—m** native of Barcelona

barco m boat; (*navío*) ship. **~ cisterna** tanker. **~ de vapor** steamer. **~ de vela** sailing boat. **ir en ~** go by boat

bario m barium

barítono m baritone

barman m (*pl* **barmans**) barman

barniz m varnish; (*para loza etc*) glaze; (*fig*) veneer. **~ar** [10] *vt* varnish; glaze (*loza etc*)

bar|ométrico a barometric. **~ómetro** m barometer

bar|ón m baron. **~onesa** f baroness

barquero _m_ boatman

barra _f_ bar; _(pan)_ French bread; _(de oro o plata)_ ingot; _(palanca)_ lever. ~ **de labios** lipstick. **no pararse en** ~**s** stop at nothing

barrabasada _f_ mischief, prank

barraca _f_ hut; _(vivienda pobre)_ shack, shanty

barranco _m_ ravine, gully; _(despeñadero)_ cliff, precipice

barre|dera _f_ road-sweeper. ~**dura** _f_ rubbish. ~**minas** _m invar_ mine-sweeper

barren|a _f_ drill, bit. ~**ar** _vt_ drill. ~**o** _m_ large (mechanical) drill. **entrar en** ~**a** _(avión)_ go into a spin

barrer _vt_ sweep; _(quitar)_ sweep aside

barrera _f_ barrier. ~ **del sonido** sound barrier

barriada _f_ district

barrica _f_ barrel

barricada _f_ barricade

barrido _m_ sweeping

barrig|a _f_ (pot-)belly. ~**ón** _a_, ~**udo** _a_ pot-bellied

barril _m_ barrel. ~**ete** _m_ keg, small barrel

barrio _m_ district, area. ~**bajero** _a_ vulgar, common. ~**s bajos** poor quarter, poor area. **el otro** ~ _(fig, fam)_ the other world

barro _m_ mud; _(arcilla)_ clay; _(arcilla cocida)_ earthenware

barroco _a_ Baroque. —_m_ Baroque style

barrote _m_ heavy bar

barrunt|ar _vt_ sense, have a feeling. ~**e** _m_, ~**o** _m_ sign; _(presentimiento)_ feeling

bartola _f_ **tenderse a la** ~, **tumbarse a la** ~ take it easy

bártulos _mpl_ things. **liar los** ~ pack one's bags

barullo _m_ uproar; _(confusión)_ confusion. **a** ~ **galore**

basa _f_, **basamento** _m_ base; _(fig)_ basis

basar _vt_ base. ~**se** _vpr_. ~**se en** be based on

basc|a _f_ crowd. ~**as** _fpl_ nausea. ~**osidad** _f_ filth. **la** ~**a** the gang

báscula _f_ scales

bascular _vi_ tilt

base _f_ base; _(fig)_ basis, foundation. **a** ~ **de** thanks to; _(mediante)_ by means of; _(en una receta)_ as the basic ingredient(s). **a** ~ **de bien** very well. **partiendo de la** ~ **de, tomando como** ~ on the basis of

básico _a_ basic

basílica _f_ basilica

basilisco _m_ basilisk. **hecho un** ~ furious

basta _f_ tack, tacking stitch

bastante _a_ enough; _(varios)_ quite a few, quite a lot of. —_adv_ rather, fairly; _(mucho tiempo)_ long enough; _(suficiente)_ enough; _(Mex, muy)_ very

bastar _vi_ be enough. ¡**basta**! that's enough! **basta decir que** suffice it to say that. **basta y sobra** that's more than enough

bastardilla _f_ italics. **poner en** ~ italicize

bastardo _a_ bastard; _(fig, vil)_ mean, base

bastidor _m_ frame; _(auto)_ chassis. ~**es** _mpl_ _(en el teatro)_ wings. **entre** ~**es** behind the scenes

bastión _m_ _(incl fig)_ bastion

basto _a_ coarse. ~**s** _mpl_ _(naipes)_ clubs

bastón _m_ walking stick. **empuñar el** ~**ón** take command. ~**onazo** _m_ blow with a stick

basur|a _f_ rubbish, garbage _(Amer)_; _(en la calle)_ litter. ~**ero** _m_ dustman _(Brit)_, garbage collector _(Amer)_; _(sitio)_ rubbish dump; _(recipiente)_ dustbin _(Brit)_, garbage can _(Amer)_. **cubo** _m_ **de la** ~**a** dustbin _(Brit)_, garbage can _(Amer)_

bata f dressing-gown; (de médico etc) white coat. ∼ **de cola** Flamenco dress

batall|a f battle. ∼**a campal** pitched battle. ∼**ador** a fighting. —m fighter. ∼**ar** vi battle, fight. ∼**ón** m battalion. —a. **cuestión** f **batallona** vexed question. **de** ∼**a** everyday

batata f sweet potato

bate m bat. ∼**ador** m batter; (cricket) batsman

batería f battery; (mus) percussion. ∼ **de cocina** kitchen utensils, pots and pans

batido a beaten; ⟨nata⟩ whipped. —m batter; (bebida) milk shake. ∼**ra** f beater. ∼**ra eléctrica** mixer

batín m dressing-gown

batir vt beat; ⟨martillar⟩ hammer; mint ⟨monedas⟩; whip ⟨nata⟩; ⟨derribar⟩ knock down. ∼ **el récord** break the record. ∼ **palmas** clap. ∼**se** vpr fight

batuta f baton. **llevar la** ∼ be in command, be the boss

baúl m trunk; (LAm, auto) boot (Brit), trunk (Amer)

bauti|smal a baptismal. ∼**smo** m baptism, christening. ∼**sta** a & m & f Baptist. ∼**zar** [10] vt baptize, christen

baya f berry

bayeta f (floor-)cloth

bayoneta f bayonet. ∼**zo** m (golpe) bayonet thrust; (herida) bayonet wound

baza f (naipes) trick; (fig) advantage. **meter** ∼ interfere

bazar m bazaar

bazofia f leftovers; (basura) rubbish

beat|itud f (fig) bliss. ∼**o** a blessed; (de religiosidad afectada) sanctimonious

bebé m baby

beb|edero m drinking trough; (sitio) watering place. ∼**edizo** a

drinkable. —m potion; (veneno) poison. ∼**edor** a drinking. —m heavy drinker. ∼**er** vt/i drink. **dar de** ∼**er a uno** give s.o. a drink. ∼**ida** f drink. ∼**ido** a tipsy, drunk

beca f grant, scholarship. ∼**rio** m scholarship holder, scholar

becerro m calf

befa f jeer, taunt. ∼**r** vt scoff at. ∼**rse** vpr. ∼**rse de** scoff at. **hacer** ∼ **de** scoff at

beige /beis, bes/ a & m beige

béisbol m baseball

beldad f beauty

belén m crib, nativity scene; (barullo) confusion

belga a & m & f Belgian

Bélgica f Belgium

bélico a, **belicoso** a warlike

beligerante a belligerent

bella|co a wicked. —m rogue. ∼**quear** vi cheat. ∼**quería** f dirty trick

bell|eza f beauty. ∼**o** a beautiful. ∼**as artes** fpl fine arts

bellota f acorn

bemol m flat. **tener (muchos)** ∼**es** be difficult

bencina f (Arg, gasolina) petrol (Brit), gasoline (Amer)

bend|ecir [46 pero imperativo **bendice**, futuro, condicional y pp regulares] vt bless. ∼**ición** f blessing. ∼**ito** a blessed, holy; (que tiene suerte) lucky; (feliz) happy

benefactor m benefactor. ∼**a** f benefactress

benefic|encia f (organización pública) charity. ∼**iar** vt benefit. ∼**iarse** vpr benefit. ∼**iario** m beneficiary; (de un cheque etc) payee. ∼**io** m benefit; (ventaja) advantage; (ganancia) profit, gain. ∼**ioso** a beneficial, advantageous

benéfico a beneficial; (de beneficencia) charitable

benemérito *a* worthy

beneplácito *m* approval

ben|evolencia *f* benevolence. **~évolo** *a* benevolent

bengala *f* flare. **luz** *f* **de B~** flare

benign|idad *f* kindness; (*falta de gravedad*) mildness. **~o** *a* kind; (*moderado*) gentle, mild; (*tumor*) benign

beodo *a* drunk

berberecho *m* cockle

berenjena *f* aubergine (*Brit*), egg-plant. **~l** *m* (*fig*) mess

bermejo *a* red

berr|ear *vi* (*animales*) low, bellow; (*niño*) howl; (*cantar mal*) screech. **~ido** *m* bellow; (*de niño*) howl; (*de cantante*) screech

berrinche *m* temper; (*de un niño*) tantrum

berro *m* watercress

berza *f* cabbage

besamel(a) *f* white sauce

bes|ar *vt* kiss; (*rozar*) brush against. **~arse** *vpr* kiss (each other); (*tocarse*) touch each other. **~o** *m* kiss

bestia *f* beast; (*bruto*) brute; (*idiota*) idiot. **~ de carga** beast of burden. **~l** *a* bestial, animal; (*fig, fam*) terrific. **~lidad** *f* bestiality; (*acción brutal*) horrid thing

besugo *m* sea-bream. **ser un ~** be stupid

besuquear *vt* cover with kisses

betún *m* bitumen; (*para el calzado*) shoe polish

biberón *m* feeding-bottle

Biblia *f* Bible

bíblico *a* biblical

bibliografía *f* bibliography

biblioteca *f* library; (*librería*) bookcase. **~ de consulta** reference library. **~ de préstamo** lending library. **~rio** *m* librarian

bicarbonato *m* bicarbonate. **~ sódico** bicarbonate of soda

bici *f* (*fam*) bicycle, bike (*fam*). **~cleta** *f* bicycle. **ir en ~cleta** go by bicycle, cycle. **montar en ~cleta** ride a bicycle

bicolor *a* two-colour

bicultural *a* bicultural

bicho *m* (*animal*) small animal, creature; (*insecto*) insect. **~ raro** odd sort. **cualquier ~ viviente, todo ~ viviente** everyone

bidé *m*, **bidet** *m* bidet

bidón *m* drum, can

bien *adv* (*mejor*) well; (*muy*) very, quite; (*correctamente*) right; (*de buena gana*) willingly. **—** *m* good; (*efectos*) property; (*provecho*) advantage, benefit. **¡~!** fine!, OK!, good! **~ ... (o) ~** either... or... **~ que** although. **¡está ~!** fine! alright! **más ~** rather. **¡muy ~!** good! **no ~ ...** as soon as. **¡qué ~!** marvellous!, great! (*fam*). **si ~** although

bienal *a* biennial

bien|aventurado *a* fortunate. **~estar** *m* well-being. **~hablado** *a* well-spoken. **~hechor** *m* benefactor. **~hechora** *f* benefactress. **~intencionado** *a* well-meaning

bienio *m* two years, two year-period

bien|quistar *vt* reconcile. **~quistarse** *vpr* become reconciled. **~quisto** *a* well-liked

bienvenid|a *f* welcome. **~o** *a* welcome. **¡~o!** welcome! **dar la ~a a uno** welcome s.o.

bife *m* (*Arg*), **biftek** *m* steak

bifurca|ción *f* fork, junction. **~rse** [7] *vpr* fork

bigamia *f* bigamy. **~ígamo** *a* bigamous. **—** *m & f* bigamist

bigot|e *m* moustache. **~udo** *a* with a big moustache

bikini *m* bikini; (*culin*) toasted cheese and ham sandwich

bilingüe *a* bilingual

billar m billiards

billete m ticket; (de banco) note (Brit), bill (Amer). ~ **de banco** banknote. ~ **de ida y vuelta** return ticket (Brit), round-trip ticket (Amer). ~ **sencillo** single ticket (Brit), one-way ticket (Amer). ~**ro** m, ~**ra** f wallet, billfold (Amer)

billón m billion (Brit), trillion (Amer)

bimbalete m (Mex) swing

bi|mensual a fortnightly, twice-monthly. ~**mestral** a two-monthly. ~**motor** a twin-engined. —m twin-engined plane

binocular a binocular. ~**es** mpl binoculars

biodegradable a biodegradable

bio|grafía f biography. ~**ográfico** a biographical. ~**ógrafo** m biographer

bio|logía f biology. ~**ológico** a biological. ~**ólogo** m biologist

biombo m folding screen

biopsia f biopsy

bioquímic|a f biochemistry; (persona) biochemist. ~**o** m biochemist

bípedo m biped

biplano m biplane

biquini m bikini

birlar vt (fam) steal, pinch (fam)

birlibirloque m. **por arte de** ~ (as if) by magic

Birmania f Burma

birmano a & m Burmese

biromen m (Arg) ball-point pen

bis m encore. —adv twice. ¡~! encore! **vivo en el 3** ~ I live at 3A

bisabuel|a f great-grandmother. ~**o** m great-grandfather. ~**os** mpl great-grandparents

bisagra f hinge

bisar vt encore

bisbis|ear vt whisper. ~**o** m whisper(ing)

bisemanal a twice-weekly

bisiesto a leap. **año** m ~ leap year

bisniet|a f great-granddaughter. ~**o** m great-grandson. ~**os** mpl great-grandchildren

bisonte m bison

bisté m, **bistec** m steak

bisturí m scalpel

bisutería f imitation jewellery, costume jewellery

bizco a cross-eyed. **quedarse** ~ be dumbfounded

bizcocho m sponge (cake); (Mex, galleta) biscuit

bizquear vi squint

blanc|a f white woman; (mus) minim. ~**o** a white; (tez) fair. —m white; (persona) white man; (intervalo) interval; (espacio) blank; (objetivo) target. ~**o de huevo** white of egg, egg-white. **dar en el** ~**o** hit the mark. **dejar en** ~**o** leave blank. **pasar la noche en** ~**o** have a sleepless night. ~**o y negro** black and white. ~**ura** f whiteness. ~**uzco** a whitish

blandir [24] vt brandish

bland|o a soft; (carácter) weak; (cobarde) cowardly; (palabras) gentle, tender. ~**ura** f softness. ~**uzco** a softish

blanque|ar vt whiten; white-wash (paredes); bleach (tela). —vi turn white; (presentarse blanco) look white. ~**cino** a whitish. ~**o** m whitening

blasfem|ador a blasphemous. —m blasphemer. ~**ar** vi blaspheme. ~**ia** f blasphemy. ~**o** a blasphemous. —m blasphemer

blas|ón m coat of arms; (fig,) honour, glory. ~**onar** vt emblazon. —vi boast (**de** of, about)

bledo m nothing. **me importa un** ~, **no se me da un** ~ I couldn't care less

blindaje *m* armour. **~r** *vt* armour

bloc *m* (*pl* **blocs**) pad

bloque *m* block; (*pol*) bloc. **~ar** *vt* block; (*mil*) blockade; (*com*) freeze. **~o** *m* blockade; (*com*) freezing. **en ~** en bloc

blusa *f* blouse

boato *m* show, ostentation

bobada *f* silly thing. **~alicón** *a* stupid. **~ería** *f* silly thing. **decir ~adas** talk nonsense

bobina *f* bobbin, reel; (*foto*) spool; (*elec*) coil

bobo *a* silly, stupid. —*m* idiot, fool

boca *f* mouth; (*fig*, *entrada*) entrance; (*de cañón*) muzzle; (*agujero*) hole. **~ abajo** face down. **~ arriba** face up. **a ~ de jarro** point-blank. **con la ~ abierta** dumbfounded

bocacalle *f* junction. **la primera ~ a la derecha** the first turning on the right

bocadillo *m* sandwich; (*comida ligera, fam*) snack. **~o** *m* mouthful; (*mordisco*) bite; (*de caballo*) bit

boca: ~jarro. a ~jarro point-blank. **~manga** *f* cuff

bocanada *f* puff; (*de vino etc*) mouthful

bocaza *f* invar, **bocazas** *f* invar big-mouth

boceto *m* outline, sketch

bocina *f* horn. **~zo** *m* toot, blast. **tocar la ~** sound one's horn

bock *m* beer mug

bocha *f* bowl. **~s** *fpl* bowls

bochinche *m* uproar

bochorno *m* sultry weather; (*fig*, *vergüenza*) embarrassment. **~so** *a* oppressive; (*fig*) embarrassing. **¡qué ~!** how embarrassing!

boda *f* marriage; (*ceremonia*) wedding

bodega *f* cellar; (*de vino*) wine cellar; (*almacén*) warehouse; (*de un barco*) hold. **~ón** *m* cheap restaurant; (*pintura*) still life

bodoque *m* pellet; (*tonto, fam*) thickhead

bofes *mpl* lights. **echar los ~** slog away

bofetada *f* slap; (*fig*) blow. **dar una ~ada a uno** slap s.o. in the face. **darse de ~adas** clash. **~ón** *m* punch

boga *m & f* rower; (*hombre*) oarsman; (*mujer*) oarswoman; (*moda*) fashion. **estar en ~** be in fashion, be in vogue. **~da** *f* stroke (of the oar). **~dor** rower, oarsman. **~r** [12] *vt* row. **~vante** *m* (*crustáceo*) lobster

Bogotá *f* Bogotá

bogotano *a* from Bogotá. —*m* native of Bogotá

bohemio *a & m* Bohemian

bohío *m* (*LAm*) hut

boicot *m* (*pl* **boicots**) boycott. **~ear** *vt* boycott. **~eo** *m* boycott. **hacer el ~** boycott

boina *f* beret

boîte /bwat/ *m* night-club

bola *f* ball; (*canica*) marble; (*naipes*) slam; (*betún*) shoe polish; (*mentira*) fib; (*Mex, reunión desordenada*) rowdy party. **~ del mundo** (*fam*) globe. **contar ~s** tell fibs. **dejar que ruede la ~** let things take their course. **meter ~s** tell fibs

bolas *fpl* (*LAm*) bolas

boleada *f* (*Mex*) polishing of shoes

boleadoras (*LAm*) *fpl* bolas

bolera *f* bowling alley

bolero *m* (*baile, chaquetilla*) bolero; (*fig, mentiroso, fam*) liar; (*Mex, limpiabotas*) bootblack

boletín *m* bulletin; (*publicación periódica*) journal; (*escolar*) report. **~ de noticias** news bulletin. **~ de precios** price list. **~**

informativo news bulletin. ~
meteorológico weather forecast

boleto m (esp LAm) ticket

boli m (fam) Biro (P), ball-point
pen

boliche m (juego) bowls; (bolera)
bowling alley

bolígrafo m Biro (P), ball-point
pen

bolillo m bobbin; (Mex, panecillo) (bread) roll

bolívar m (unidad monetaria
venezolana) bolívar

Bolivia f Bolivia

boliviano a Bolivian. —m Bolivian; (unidad monetaria de
Bolivia) boliviano

bolo m skittle

bolsa f bag; (monedero) purse;
(LAm, bolsillo) pocket; (com)
stock exchange; (cavidad)
cavity. ~ **de agua caliente** hot-water bottle

bolsillo m pocket; (monedero)
purse. **de** ~ pocket

bolsista m & f stockbroker

bolso m (de mujer) handbag

boll|ería f baker's shop. ~**ero** m
baker. ~**o** m roll; (con azúcar)
bun; (abolladura) dent; (chichón) lump; (fig, jaleo, fam) fuss

bomba f bomb; (máquina) pump;
(noticia) bombshell. ~ **de aceite**
(auto) oil pump. ~ **de agua**
(auto) water pump. ~ **de incendios** fire-engine. **pasarlo** ~
have a marvellous time

bombach|as fpl (LAm) knickers,
pants. ~**o** m (esp Mex) baggy
trousers, baggy pants (Amer)

bombarde|ar vt bombard; (mil)
bomb. ~**o** m bombardment;
(mil) bombing. ~**ro** m (avión)
bomber

bombazo m explosion

bombear vt pump; (mil) bomb

bombero m fireman. **cuerpo** m
de ~**s** fire brigade (Brit), fire
department (Amer)

bombilla f (light) bulb; (LAm,
para maté) pipe for drinking
maté; (Mex, cucharón) ladle

bombín m pump; (sombrero,
fam) bowler (hat) (Brit), derby
(Amer)

bombo m (tambor) bass drum. **a**
~ **y platillos** with a lot of fuss

bombón m chocolate. **ser un**
~**ón** be a peach. ~**ona** f
container. ~**onera** f chocolate
box

bonachón a easygoing; (bueno)
good-natured

bonaerense a from Buenos
Aires. —m native of Buenos
Aires

bonanza f (naut) fair weather;
(prosperidad) prosperity. **ir en**
~ (naut) have fair weather; (fig)
go well

bondad f goodness; (amabilidad)
kindness. **tenga la** ~ **de** would
you be kind enough to. ~**os-
amente** adv kindly. ~**oso** a
kind

bongo m (LAm) canoe

boniato m sweet potato

bonito a nice; (mono) pretty.
¡**muy** ~!, ¡**qué** ~! that's nice!,
very nice!. —m bonito

bono m voucher; (título) bond. ~
del Tesoro government bond

boñiga f dung

boquead|a f gasp. **dar las** ~**s** be
dying

boquerón m anchovy

boquete m hole; (brecha) breach

boquiabierto a open-mouthed;
(fig) amazed, dumbfounded.
quedarse ~ be amazed

boquilla f mouthpiece; (para
cigarrillos) cigarette-holder; (filtro de cigarillo) tip

borbolla|r vi bubble. ~**ón** m
bubble. **hablar a** ~**ones** gabble.
salir a ~**ones** gush out

borbot|ar vi bubble. ~**ón** m
bubble. **hablar a** ~**ones** gabble.
salir a ~**ones** gush out

bordado a embroidered. —m embroidery. **quedar ~, salir ~** come out very well

bordante m (Mex) lodger

bordar vt embroider; (fig, fam) do very well

bord|e m edge; (de carretera) side; (de plato etc) rim; (de un vestido) hem. **~ear** vt go round the edge of; (fig) border on. **~illo** m kerb. **al ~e de** on the edge of; (fig) on the brink of

bordo m board. **a ~** on board

borinqueño a & m Puerto Rican

borla f tassel

borra f flock; (pelusa) fluff; (sedimento) sediment

borrach|era f drunkenness. **~ín** m drunkard. **~o** a drunk. —m drunkard; (temporalmente) drunk. **estar ~o** be drunk. **ni ~o** never in a million years. **ser ~o** be a drunkard

borrador m rough copy; (libro) rough notebook

borradura f crossing-out

borrajear vt/i scribble

borrar vt rub out; (tachar) cross out

borrasc|a f storm. **~oso** a stormy

borreg|o m year-old lamb; (fig) simpleton; (Mex, noticia falsa) hoax. **~uil** a meek

borric|ada f silly thing. **~o** m donkey; (fig, fam) ass

borrón m smudge; (fig, imperfección) blemish; (de una pintura) sketch. **~ y cuenta nueva** let's forget about it!

borroso a blurred; (fig) vague

bos|caje m thicket. **~coso** a wooded. **~que** m wood, forest. **~quecillo** m copse

bosquejar vt sketch. **~o** m sketch

bosta f dung

bostez|ar [10] vi yawn. **~o** m yawn

bota f boot; (recipiente) leather wine bottle

botadero m (Mex) ford

botánic|a f botany. **~o** a botanical. —m botanist. —vi bounce

botar vt launch. —vi bounce. **estar que bota** be hopping mad

botarat|ada f silly thing. **~e** m idiot

bote m bounce; (golpe) blow; (salto) jump; (sacudida) jolt; (lata) tin, can; (vasija) jar; (en un bar) jar for tips; (barca) boat. **~ salvavidas** lifeboat. **de ~ en ~** packed

botell|a f bottle. **~ita** f small bottle

botica f chemist's (shop) (Brit), drugstore (Amer). **~rio** m chemist (Brit), druggist (Amer)

botija f, **botijo** m earthenware jug

botín m half boot; (despojos) booty; (LAm, calcetín) sock

botiquín m medicine chest; (de primeros auxilios) first aid kit

bot|ón m button; (yema) bud. **~onadura** f buttons. **~ón de oro** buttercup. **~ones** m invar bellboy (Brit), bellhop (Amer)

botulismo m botulism

boutique /bu'tik/ m boutique

bóveda f vault

boxe|ador m boxer. **~ar** vi box. **~o** m boxing

boya f buoy; (corcho) float. **~nte** a buoyant

bozal m (de perro etc) muzzle; (de caballo) halter

bracear vi wave one's arms; (nadar) swim, crawl

bracero m labourer. **de ~** (fam) arm in arm

braga f underpants, knickers; (cuerda) rope. **~dura** f crotch. **~s** fpl knickers, pants. **~zas** m invar (fam) henpecked man

bragueta f flies

braille /breil/ m Braille

bram|ar *vi* roar; ⟨*vaca*⟩ moo; ⟨*viento*⟩ howl. **∼ido** *m* roar

branquia *f* gill

bras|a *f* hot coal. **a la ∼a** grilled. **∼ero** *m* brazier; (*LAm, hogar*) hearth

Brasil *m. el* ∼ Brazil

brasile|ño *a & m* Brazilian. **∼ro** *a & m* (*LAm*) Brazilian

bravata *f* boast

bravío *a* wild; ⟨*persona*⟩ coarse, uncouth

brav|o *a* brave; ⟨*animales*⟩ wild; ⟨*mar*⟩ rough. **¡∼!** *int* well done! bravo! **∼ura** *f* ferocity; (*valor*) courage

braz|a *f* fathom. **nadar a ∼a** do the breast-stroke. **∼ada** *f* waving of the arms; (*en natación*) stroke; (*cantidad*) armful. **∼ado** *m* armful. **∼al** *m* arm-band. **∼alete** *m* bracelet; (*brazal*) arm-band. **∼o** *m* arm; (*de animales*) foreleg; (*rama*) branch. **∼o derecho** right-hand man. **a ∼o** by hand. **del ∼o** arm in arm

brea *f* tar, pitch

brear *vt* ill-treat

brécol *m* broccoli

brecha *f* gap; (*mil*) breach; (*med*) gash. **estar en la ∼** be in the thick of it

brega *f* struggle. **∼r** [12] *vi* struggle; (*trabajar mucho*) work hard, slog away. **andar a la ∼** work hard

breña *f*, **breñal** *m* scrub

Bretaña *f* Brittany. **Gran ∼** Great Britain

breve *a* short. **∼dad** *f* shortness. **en ∼** soon, shortly. **en ∼s momentos** soon

brez|al *m* moor. **∼o** *m* heather

brib|ón *m* rogue, rascal. **∼onada** *f*, **∼onería** *f* dirty trick

brida *f* bridle. **a toda ∼** at full speed

bridge /britʃ/ *m* bridge

brigada *f* squad; (*mil*) brigade. **general de ∼** brigadier (*Brit*), brigadier-general (*Amer*)

brill|ante *a* brilliant. —*m* diamond. **∼antez** *f* brilliance. **∼ar** *vi* shine; (*centellear*) sparkle. **∼o** *m* shine; (*brillantez*) brilliance; (*centelleo*) sparkle. **dar ∼o, sacar ∼o** polish

brinc|ar [7] *vi* jump up and down. **∼o** *m* jump. **dar un ∼o** jump. **estar que brinca** be hopping mad. **pegar un ∼o** jump

brind|ar *vt* offer. —*vi.* **∼ar por** toast, drink a toast to. **∼is** *m* toast

br|ío *m* energy; (*decisión*) determination. **∼ioso** *a* spirited; (*garboso*) elegant

brisa *f* breeze

británico *a* British. —*m* Briton, British person

brocado *m* brocade

bróculi *m* broccoli

brocha *f* paintbrush; (*para afeitarse*) shaving-brush

broche *m* clasp, fastener; (*joya*) brooch; (*Arg, sujetapapeles*) paper-clip

brocheta *f* skewer

brom|a *f* joke. **∼a pesada** practical joke. **∼ear** *vi* joke. **∼ista** *a* fun-loving. —*m & f* joker. **de ∼a, en ∼** in a fun. **ni de ∼a** never in a million years

bronca *f* row; (*reprensión*) telling-off

bronce *m* bronze. **∼ado** *a* bronze; (*por el sol*) tanned, sunburnt. **∼ar** *vt* tan ⟨*piel*⟩. **∼arse** *vpr* get a suntan

bronco *a* rough

bronquitis *f* bronchitis

broqueta *f* skewer

brot|ar *vi* ⟨*plantas*⟩ bud, sprout; (*med*) break out; (*líquido*) gush forth; (*lágrimas*) well up. **∼e** *m* bud, shoot; (*med*) outbreak; (*de* *liquido*) gushing; (*de lágrimas*) welling-up

bruces *mpl.* **de** ~ face down-(wards). **caer de** ~ fall flat on one's face

bruj|a *f* witch. —*a* (*Mex*) penniless. ~**ear** *vi* practise witchcraft. ~**ería** *f* witchcraft. ~**o** *m* wizard, magician; (*LAm*) medicine man

brújula *f* compass

brum|a *f* mist; (*fig*) confusion. ~**oso** *a* misty, foggy

bruñi|do *m* polish. ~**r** [22] *vt* polish

brusco *a* (*repentino*) sudden; (*persona*) brusque

Bruselas *fpl* Brussels

brusquedad *f* abruptness

brut|al *a* brutal. ~**alidad** *f* brutality; (*estupidez*) stupidity. ~**o** *a* (*estúpido*) stupid; (*tosco*) rough, uncouth; (*peso, sueldo*) gross

bucal *a* oral

buce|ar *vi* dive; (*fig*) explore. ~**o** *m* diving

bucle *m* curl

budín *m* pudding

budi|smo *m* Buddhism. ~**ta** *a* & *f* Buddhist

buen *véase* **bueno**

buenamente *adv* easily; (*voluntariamente*) willingly

buenaventura *f* good luck; (*adivinación*) fortune. **decir la** ~ **a uno, echar la** ~ **a uno** tell s.o.'s fortune

bueno *a* (*delante de nombre masculino en singular* **buen**) good; (*apropiado*) fit; (*amable*) kind; (*tiempo*) fine. —*int* well!; (*de acuerdo*) OK!, very well! ¡**buena la has hecho!** you've gone and done it now! ¡**buenas noches!** good night! ¡**buenas tardes!** (*antes del atardecer*) good afternoon!; (*después del atardecer*) good evening! ¡~**s días!** good

morning! **estar de buenas** be in a good mood. **por las buenas** willingly

Buenos Aires *m* Buenos Aires

buey *m* ox

búfalo *m* buffalo

bufanda *f* scarf

bufar *vi* snort. **estar que bufa** be hopping mad

bufete *m* (*mesa*) writing-desk; (*despacho*) lawyer's office

bufido *m* snort; (*de ira*) outburst

bufo *a* comic. ~**ón** *a* comical. —*m* buffoon. ~**onada** *f* joke

bugle *m* bugle

buharda *f*, **buhardilla** *f* attic; (*ventana*) dormer window

búho *m* owl

buhoner|ía *f* pedlar's wares. ~**o** *m* pedlar

buitre *m* vulture

bujía *f* candle; (*auto*) spark(ing)-plug

bula *f* bull

bulbo *m* bulb

bulevar *m* avenue, boulevard

Bulgaria *f* Bulgaria

búlgaro *a* & *m* Bulgarian

bulo *m* hoax

bulto *m* (*volumen*) volume; (*tamaño*) size; (*forma*) shape; (*paquete*) package; (*protuberancia*) lump. **a** ~ roughly

bulla *f* uproar; (*muchedumbre*) crowd

bullicio *m* hubbub; (*movimiento*) bustle. ~**so** *a* bustling; (*ruidoso*) noisy

bullir [22] *vt* stir, move. —*vi* boil; (*burbujear*) bubble; (*fig*) bustle

buñuelo *m* doughnut; (*fig*) mess

BUP *abrev* (*Bachillerato Unificado Polivalente*) secondary school education

buque *m* ship, boat

burbuj|a *f* bubble. ~**ear** *vi* bubble; (*vino*) sparkle. ~**eo** *m* bubbling

burdel *m* brothel

burdo *a* rough, coarse; *(excusa)* clumsy

burgu|és *a* middle-class, bourgeois. —*m* middle-class person. **∼esía** *f* middle class, bourgeoisie

burla *f* taunt; *(broma)* joke; *(engaño)* trick. **∼dor** *a* mocking. —*m* seducer. **∼r** *vt* trick, deceive; *(seducir)* seduce. **∼rse** *vpr*. **∼rse de** mock, make fun of

burlesco *a* funny

burlón *a* mocking

bur|ocracia *f* civil service. **∼ócrata** *m & f* civil servant. **∼ocrático** *a* bureaucratic

burro *m* donkey; *(fig)* ass

bursátil *a* stock-exchange

bus *m* *(fam)* bus

busca *f* search. **a la ∼ de** in search of. **en ∼ de** in search of

busca: **∼pié** *m* feeler. **∼pleitos** *m invar* (*LAm*) trouble-maker

buscar [7] *vt* look for. —*vi* look. **buscársela** ask for it. **ir a ∼ a uno** fetch s.o.

buscarruidos *m invar* troublemaker

buscona *f* prostitute

busilis *m* snag

búsqueda *f* search

busto *m* bust

butaca *f* armchair; *(en el teatro etc)* seat

butano *m* butane

buzo *m* diver

buzón *m* postbox (*Brit*), mailbox (*Amer*)

C

C/ *abrev* (Calle) St, Street, Rd, Road

cabal *a* exact; *(completo)* complete. **no estar en sus ∼es** not be in one's right mind

cabalga|dura *f* mount, horse. **∼r** [12] *vt* ride. —*vi* ride, go riding. **∼ta** *f* ride; *(desfile)* procession

cabalmente *adv* completely; *(exactamente)* exactly

caballa *f* mackerel

caballada *f* (*LAm*) stupid thing

caballeresco *a* gentlemanly. **literatura** *f* **caballeresca** books of chivalry

caballer|ía *f* mount, horse. **∼iza** *f* stable. **∼izo** *m* groom

caballero *m* gentleman; *(de orden de caballería)* knight; *(tratamiento)* sir. **∼samente** *adv* like a gentleman. **∼so** *a* gentlemanly

caballete *m* (*del tejado*) ridge; *(de la nariz)* bridge; *(de pintor)* easel

caballito *m* pony. **∼ del diablo** dragonfly. **∼ de mar** sea-horse. **los ∼s** *(tiovivo)* merry-go-round

caballo *m* horse; *(del ajedrez)* knight; *(de la baraja española)* queen. **∼ de vapor** horsepower. **a ∼** on horseback

cabaña *f* hut

cabaret /kaba're/ *m* (*pl* cabarets /kaba're/) night-club

cabece|ar *vi* nod; *(para negar)* shake one's head. **∼o** *m* nodding; nod; *(acción de negar)* shake of the head

cabecera *f* (*de la cama, de la mesa*) head; *(en un impreso)* heading

cabecilla *m* leader

cabell|o *m* hair. **∼os** *mpl* hair. **∼udo** *a* hairy

caber [28] *vi* fit (**en** into). **los libros no caben en la caja** the books won't fit into the box. **no cabe duda** there's no doubt

cabestr|illo *m* sling. **∼o** *m* halter

cabeza *f* head; *(fig, inteligencia)* intelligence. **∼da** *f* butt; *(golpe recibido)* blow; *(saludo, al dormirse)* nod. **∼zo** *m* butt; *(en fútbol)* header. **andar de ∼** have a lot to do. **dar una ∼da** nod off

cabida f capacity; (*extensión*) area. **dar ~ a** leave room for, leave space for

cabina f (*de avión*) cabin, cockpit; (*electoral*) booth; (*de camión*) cab. **~ telefónica** telephone box (*Brit*), telephone booth (*Amer*)

cabizbajo a crestfallen

cable m cable

cabo m end; (*trozo*) bit; (*mil*) corporal; (*mango*) handle; (*geog*) cape; (*naut*) rope. **al ~** eventually. **al ~ de una hora** after an hour. **de ~ a rabo** from beginning to end. **llevar(se) a ~** carry out

cabr|**a** f goat. **~a montesa** f mountain goat. **~iola** f jump, skip. **~itilla** f kid. **~ito** m kid

cabrón m cuckold

cabuya f (*LAm*) pita, agave

cacahuate m (*Mex*), **cacahuete** m peanut

cacao m (*planta y semillas*) cacao; (*polvo*) cocoa; (*fig*) confusion

cacare|**ar** vt boast about. —vi (*gallo*) crow; (*gallina*) cluck. **~o** m (*incl fig*) crowing; (*de gallina*) clucking

cacería f hunt

cacerola f casserole, saucepan

cacique m cacique, Indian chief; (*pol*) cacique, local political boss. **~il** a despotic. **~ismo** m caciquism, despotism

caco m pickpocket, thief

cacof|**onía** f cacophony. **~ónico** a cacophonous

cacto m cactus

cacumen m acumen

cacharro m earthenware pot; (*para flores*) vase; (*coche estropeado*) wreck; (*cosa inútil*) piece of junk; (*chisme*) thing. **~s** mpl pots and pans

cachear vt frisk

cachemir m, **cachemira** f cashmere

cacheo m frisking

cachetada f (*LAm*), **cachete** m slap

cachimba f pipe

cachiporra f club, truncheon. **~zo** m blow with a club

cachivache m thing, piece of junk

cacho m bit, piece; (*LAm, cuerno*) horn; (*miga*) crumb

cachondeo m (*fam*) joking, joke

cachorro m (*perrito*) puppy; (*de otros animales*) young

cada a invar each, every. **~ uno** each one, everyone. **uno de ~ cinco** one in five

cadalso m scaffold

cadáver m corpse. **ingresar ~** be dead on arrival

cadena f chain; (*TV*) channel. **~ de fabricación** production line. **~ de montañas** mountain range. **~ perpetua** life imprisonment

cadencia f cadence, rhythm

cadera f hip

cadete m cadet

caduc|**ar** [7] vi expire. **~idad** f. **fecha** f **de ~idad** sell-by date. **~o** a decrepit

cae|**dizo** a unsteady. **~r** [29] vi fall. **~rse** vpr fall (over). **dejar ~r** drop. **estar al ~r** be about to happen. **este vestido no me ~ bien** this dress doesn't suit me. **hacer ~r** knock over. **Juan me ~ bien** I get on well with Juan. **su cumpleaños cayó en Martes** his birthday fell on a Tuesday

café m coffee; (*cafetería*) café. —a. **color ~** coffee-coloured. **~ con leche** white coffee. **~ cortado** coffee with a little milk. **~ (solo)** black coffee

cafe|**ína** f caffeine. **~tal** m coffee plantation. **~tera** f coffee-pot. **~tería** f café. **~tero** a coffee

caíd|a f fall; (*disminución*) drop; (*pendiente*) slope. **~o** a fallen; (*abatido*) dejected. —m fallen
caigo vb véase **caer**
caimán m cayman, alligator
caj|a f box; (*grande*) case; (*de caudales*) safe; (*donde se efectúan los pagos*) cash desk; (*en supermercado*) check-out. **~a de ahorros** savings bank. **~a de caudales**, **~a fuerte** safe. **~a postal de ahorros** post office savings bank. **~a registradora** till. **~ero** m cashier. **~etilla** f packet. **~ita** f small box. **~ón** m large box; (*de mueble*) drawer; (*puesto de mercado*) stall. **ser de ~ón** be a matter of course
cal m lime
cala f cove
calaba|cín m marrow; (*fig, idiota, fam*) idiot. **~za** f pumpkin; (*fig, idiota, fam*) idiot
calabozo m prison; (*celda*) cell
calado a soaked. —m (*naut*) draught. **estar ~ hasta los huesos** be soaked to the skin
calamar m squid
calambre m cramp
calami|dad f calamity, disaster. **~toso** a calamitous, disastrous
calar vt soak; (*penetrar*) pierce; (*fig, penetrar*) see through; sample (*fruta*). **~se** vpr get soaked; (*zapatos*) leak; (*auto*) stall
calavera f skull
calcar [7] vt trace; (*fig*) copy
calceta f. **hacer ~** knit
calcetín m sock
calcinar vt burn
calcio m calcium
calco m tracing. **~manía** f transfer. **papel m de ~** tracing-paper
calcula|dor a calculating. **~dora** f calculator. **~dora de bolsillo** pocket calculator. **~r** vt calculate; (*suponer*) reckon, think

cálculo m calculation; (*fig*) reckoning
caldea|miento m heating. **~r** vt heat, warm. **~rse** vpr get hot
calder|a f boiler; (*Arg, para café*) coffee-pot; (*Arg, para té*) teapot. **~eta** f small boiler
calderilla f small change, coppers
calder|ón m small boiler. **~ón** m large boiler
caldo m stock; (*sopa*) soup, broth. **poner a ~ a uno** give s.o. a dressing-down
calefacción f heating. **~ central** central heating
caleidoscopio m kaleidoscope
calendario m calendar
caléndula f marigold
calenta|dor m heater. **~miento** m heating; (*en deportes*) warm-up. **~r** [1] vt heat, warm. **~rse** vpr get hot, warm up
calentur|a f fever, (high) temperature. **~iento** a feverish
calibr|ar vt calibrate; (*fig*) measure. **~e** m calibre; (*diámetro*) diameter; (*fig*) importance
calidad f quality; (*función*) capacity. **en ~ de** as
cálido a warm
calidoscopio m kaleidoscope
caliente a hot, warm; (*fig, enfadado*) angry
califica|ción f qualification; (*evaluación*) assessment; (*nota*) mark. **~r** [7] vt qualify; (*evaluar*) assess; mark (*examen etc*). **~r de** describe as, label. **~tivo** a qualifying. —m epithet
caliz|a f limestone. **~o** a lime
calm|a f calm. **¡~a!** calm down! **~ante** a & m sedative. **~ar** vt calm, soothe. —vi (*viento*) abate. **~arse** vpr calm down; (*viento*) abate. **~oso** a calm; (*flemático, fam*) phlegmatic. **en ~a** calm. **perder la ~a** lose one's composure

calor m heat, warmth. **hace ~** it's hot. **tener ~** be hot

caloría f calorie

calorífero m heater

columni|a f calumny; (oral) slander; (escrita) libel. **~ar** vt slander; (por escrito) libel. **~oso** a slanderous; (cosa escrita) libellous

caluros|amente adv warmly. **~o** a warm

calv|a f bald patch. **~ero** m clearing. **~icie** f baldness. **~o** a bald; (terreno) barren

calza f (fam) stocking; (cuña) wedge

calzada f road

calza|do a wearing shoes. —m footwear, shoe. **~dor** m shoehorn. **~r** [10] vt put shoes on; (llevar) wear. —vi wear shoes. —vpr put on. **¿qué número calza Vd?** what shoe size do you take?

calz|ón m shorts; (ropa interior) knickers, pants. **~ones** mpl shorts. **~oncillos** mpl underpants

calla|do a quiet. **~r** vt silence; keep (secreto); hush up (asunto). —vi be quiet, keep quiet, shut up (fam). **~rse** vpr be quiet, keep quiet, shut up (fam). **¡cállate!** be quiet! shut up! (fam)

calle f street, road; (en deportes, en autopista) lane. **~ de dirección única** one-way street. **~ mayor** high street, main street. **abrir ~** make way

callej|a f narrow street. **~ear** vi wander about the streets. **~ero** a street. —m street plan. **~ón** m alley. **~uela** f back street, side street. **~ón sin salida** cul-de-sac

call|ista m & f chiropodist. **~o** m corn, callus. **~os** mpl tripe. **~oso** a hard, rough

cama f bed. **~ de matrimonio** double bed. **~ individual** single bed. **caer en la ~** fall ill. **guardar ~** be confined to bed

camada f litter; (fig, de ladrones) gang

camafeo m cameo

camaleón m chameleon

cámara f room; (de reyes) royal chamber; (fotográfica) camera; (de armas, pol) chamber. **~ fotográfica** camera. **a ~ lenta** in slow motion

camarad|a f colleague; (amigo) companion

camarer|a f chambermaid; (de restaurante etc) waitress; (en casa) maid. **~o** m waiter

camarín m dressing-room; (naut) cabin

camarón m shrimp

camarote m cabin

cambi|able a changeable; (com etc) exchangeable. **~ante** a variable. **~ar** vt change; (trocar) exchange. —vi change. **~ar de idea** change one's mind. **~arse** vpr change. **~o** m change; (com) exchange rate; (moneda menuda) (small) change. **~sta** m & f money-changer. **en ~o** on the other hand

camelia f camellia

camello m camel

camilla f stretcher; (sofá) couch

camina|nte m traveller. **~r** vt cover. —vi travel; (andar) walk; (río, astros etc) move. **~ta** f long walk

camino m road; (sendero) path, track; (dirección, medio) way. **~ de** towards, on the way to. **abrir ~** make way. **a medio ~, a la mitad del ~** half-way. **de ~** on the way. **ponerse en ~** set out

cami|ón m lorry; (Mex, autobús) bus. **~onero** m lorry-driver. **~oneta** f van

camis|a f shirt; (de un fruto) skin. **~a de dormir** nightdress. **~a de fuerza** strait-jacket. **~ería** f shirt shop. ~**eta** f T-shirt; (ropa interior) vest. ~**ón** m nightdress

camorra f (fam) row. **buscar** ~ look for trouble, pick a quarrel

camote m (LAm) sweet potato

campamento m camp

campan|a f bell. ~**ada** f stroke of a bell; (de reloj) striking. ~**ario** m bell tower, belfry. ~**eo** m peal of bells. ~**illa** f bell. ~**udo** a bell-shaped; (estilo) bombastic

campaña f countryside; (mil, pol) campaign. **de** ~ (mil) field

campe|ón a & m champion. ~**onato** m championship

campes|ino a country. —m peasant. ~**tre** a country

camping /'kampin/ m (pl **campings** /'kampin/) camping; (lugar) campsite. **hacer** ~ go camping

campiña f countryside

campo m country; (agricultura, fig) field; (de tenis) court; (de fútbol) pitch; (de golf) course. ~**santo** m cemetery

camufla|do a camouflaged. ~**je** m camouflage. ~**r** vt camouflage

cana f grey hair, white hair. **echar una** ~ **al aire** have a fling. **peinar** ~**s** be getting old

Canadá m. **el** ~ Canada

canadiense a & m Canadian

canal m (incl TV) channel; (artificial) canal; (del tejado) gutter. ~ **de la Mancha** English Channel. ~ **de Panamá** Panama Canal. ~**ón** m (horizontal) gutter; (vertical) drain-pipe

canalla f rabble. —m (fig, fam) swine. ~**da** f dirty trick

canapé m sofa, couch; (culin) canapé

Canarias fpl. (**las islas**) ~ the Canary Islands, the Canaries

canario a of the Canary Islands. —m native of the Canary Islands; (pájaro) canary

canast|a f (large) basket. ~**illa** f small basket; (para un bebé) layette. ~**illo** m small basket. ~**o** m (large) basket

cancela f gate

cancela|ción f cancellation . ~**r** vt cancel; write off (deuda); (fig) forget

cáncer m cancer. **C~** Cancer

canciller m chancellor; (LAm, ministro de asuntos exteriores) Minister of Foreign Affairs

canci|ón f song. ~**ón de cuna** lullaby. ~**onero** m song-book. **¡siempre la misma** ~**ón!** always the same old story!

cancha f (de fútbol) pitch, ground; (de tenis) court

candado m padlock

candel|a f candle. ~**ero** m candlestick. ~**illa** f candle

candente a (rojo) red-hot; (blanco) white-hot; (fig) burning

candidato m candidate

candidez f innocence; (ingenuidad) naïvety

cándido a naïve

candil m oil-lamp; (Mex, araña) chandelier. ~**ejas** fpl footlights

candinga m (Mex) devil

candor m innocence; (ingenuidad) naïvety. ~**oso** a innocent; (ingenuo) naïve

canela f cinnamon. **ser** ~ be beautiful

cangrejo m crab. ~ **de río** crayfish

canguro m kangaroo; (persona) baby-sitter

can|íbal a & m cannibal. ~**ibalismo** m cannibalism

canica f marble

canijo m weak

canino a canine. —m canine (tooth)

canje m exchange. ~**ar** vt exchange

cano a grey-haired

canoa f canoe; (*con motor*) motor boat

canon m canon

canónigo m canon. **~onizar** [10] *vt* canonize

canoso a grey-haired

cansa|do a tired. **~ncio** m tiredness. **~r** *vt* tire; (*aburrir*) bore. —*vi* be tiring; (*aburrir*) get boring. **~rse** *vpr* get tired

cantábrico a Cantabrian. **el mar ~** the Bay of Biscay

canta|nte a singing. —m singer; (*en óperas*) opera singer. **~or** m Flamenco singer. **~r** *vt/i* sing. —m singing; (*canción*) song; (*poema*) poem. **~rlas claras** speak frankly

cántar|a f pitcher. **~o** m pitcher. **llover a ~os** pour down

cante m folk song. **~ flamenco, ~ jondo** Flamenco singing

cantera f quarry

cantidad f quantity; (*número*) number; (*de dinero*) sum. **una ~ de** lots of

cantilena f, **cantinela** f song

cantimplora f water-bottle

cantina f canteen; (*rail*) buffet

canto m singing; (*canción*) song; (*borde*) edge; (*de un cuchillo*) blunt edge; (*esquina*) corner; (*piedra*) pebble. **~ rodado** boulder. **de ~** on edge

cantonés a Cantonese

cantor a singing. —m singer

canturre|ar *vt/i* hum. **~o** m humming

canuto m tube

caña f stalk, stem; (*planta*) reed; (*vaso*) glass; (*de la pierna*) shin. **~ de azúcar** sugar-cane. **~ de pescar** fishing-rod

cañada f ravine; (*camino*) track

cáñamo m hemp. **~ índio** cannabis

cañ|ería f pipe; (*tubería*) piping. **~o** m pipe, tube; (*de fuente*) jet. **~ón** m pipe, tube; (*de órgano*)

pipe; (*de chimenea*) flue; (*arma de fuego*) cannon; (*desfiladero*) canyon. **~onazo** m gunshot. **~onera** f gunboat

caoba f mahogany

ca|os m chaos. **~ótico** a chaotic

capa f cloak; (*de pintura*) coat; (*culin*) coating; (*geol*) stratum, layer

capacidad f capacity; (*fig*) ability

capacitar *vt* qualify, enable; (*instruir*) train

caparazón m shell

capataz m foreman

capaz a capable, able; (*espacioso*) roomy. **~ para** which holds, with a capacity of

capazo m large basket

capcioso a sly, insidious

capellán m chaplain

caperuza f hood; (*de pluma*) cap

capilla f chapel; (*mus*) choir

capita f small cloak, cape

capital a capital, very important. —m (*de dinero*) capital. —f (*ciudad*) capital; (*LAm, letra*) capital (letter). **~ de provincia** county town

capitali|smo m capitalism. **~sta** a & m & f capitalist. **~zar** [10] *vt* capitalize

capit|án m captain. **~anear** *vt* lead, command; (*un equipo*) captain

capitel m (*arqui*) capital

capitulaci|ón f surrender; (*acuerdo*) agreement. **~ones** *fpl* marriage contract

capítulo m chapter. **~s matrimoniales** marriage contract

capó m bonnet (*Brit*), hood (*Amer*)

capón m (*pollo*) capon

caporal m chief, leader

capota f (*de mujer*) capote; (*auto*) folding top, sliding roof

capote m cape

Capricornio m Capricorn

capricho m whim. ∿**so** a capricious, whimsical. **a** ∿ capriciously

cápsula f capsule

captar vt harness ‹agua›; grasp ‹sentido›; hold ‹atención›; win ‹confianza›; (radio) pick up

captura f capture. ∿**r** vt capture

capucha f hood

capullo m bud; (de insecto) cocoon

caqui m khaki

cara f face; (de una moneda) obverse; (de un objeto) side; (aspecto) look, appearance; (descaro) cheek. ∿ a towards; (frente a) facing. ∿ **a** ∿ face to face. ∿ **o cruz** heads or tails. **dar la** ∿ face up to. **hacer** ∿ face. **no volver la** ∿ **atrás** not look back. **tener** ∿ **de** look, seem to be. **tener** ∿ **para** have the face to. **tener mala** ∿ look ill. **volver la** ∿ look the other way

carabela f caravel, small light ship

carabina f rifle; (fig, señora, fam) chaperone

Caracas m Caracas

caracol m snail; (de pelo) curl. **¡∿es!** Good Heavens! **escalera** f **de** ∿ spiral staircase

carácter m (pl **caracteres**) character. **con** ∿ **de**, **por su** ∿ **de** as

característica f characteristic; (LAm, teléfonos) dialling code. ∿**o** a characteristic, typical

caracterizado a characterized; (prestigioso) distinguished. ∿**r** [10] vt characterize

cara: ∿ **dura** cheek, nerve. ∿**dura** m & f cheeky person, rotter (fam)

caramba int good heavens!, goodness me!

carámbano m icicle

caramelo m sweet (Brit), candy (Amer); (azúcar fundido) caramel

carancho m (Arg) vulture

carapacho m shell

caraqueño a from Caracas. —m native of Caracas

carátula f mask; (fig, teatro) theatre; (Mex, esfera del reloj) face

caravana f caravan; (fig, grupo) group; (auto) long line, traffic jam

caray int (fam) good heavens!, goodness me!

carbón m coal; (papel) carbon (paper); (para dibujar) charcoal. ∿**oncillo** m charcoal. ∿**onero** a coal. —m coal-merchant. ∿**onizar** [10] vt (fig) burn (to a cinder). ∿**ono** m carbon

carburador m carburettor

carcajada f burst of laughter. **reírse a** ∿s roar with laughter. **soltar una** ∿ burst out laughing

cárcel m prison, jail; (en carpintería) clamp

carcel|**ario** a prison. ∿**ero** a prison. —m prison officer

carcom|**a** f woodworm. ∿**er** vt eat away; (fig) undermine. ∿**erse** vpr be eaten away; (fig) waste away

cardenal m cardinal; (contusión) bruise

cárdeno a purple

cardiaco, cardíaco a cardiac, heart. —m heart patient

cardinal a cardinal

cardiólogo m cardiologist, heart specialist

cardo m thistle

carear vt bring face to face ‹personas›; compare ‹cosas›

carecer [11] vi. ∿ **de** lack. ∿ **de sentido** not to make sense

caren|**cia** f lack. ∿**te** a lacking

carero a expensive

carestía f (precio elevado) high price; (escasez) shortage

careta f mask

carey *m* tortoiseshell

carga *f* load; *(fig)* burden; *(acción)* loading; *(de barco)* cargo; *(obligación)* obligation. ~**do** *a* loaded; *(fig)* burdened; *(tiempo)* heavy; *(hilo)* live; *(pila)* charged. ~**mento** *m* load; *(acción)* loading; *(de un barco)* cargo. ~**nte** *a* demanding. ~**r** [12] *vt* load; *(fig)* burden; *(mil, elec)* charge; fill *(pluma etc)*; *(fig, molestar, fam)* annoy. —*vi* load. ~**r con** pick up. ~**rse** *vpr* *(llenarse)* fill; *(cielo)* become overcast; *(enfadarse, fam)* get cross. **llevar la ~ de algo** be responsible for sth

cargo *m* load; *(fig)* burden; *(puesto)* post; *(acusación)* accusation, charge; *(responsabilidad)* charge. **a ~ de** in the charge of. **hacerse ~ de** take responsibility for. **tener a su ~** be in charge of

carguero *m* *(Arg)* beast of burden; *(naut)* cargo ship

cari *m* *(LAm)* grey

cariacontecido *a* crestfallen

caria|do *a* decayed. ~**rse** *vpr* decay

caribe *a* Caribbean. **el mar C~** the Caribbean (Sea)

caricatura *f* caricature

caricia *f* caress

caridad *f* charity. **¡por ~!** for goodness sake!

caries *f invar* (dental) decay

carilampiño *a* clean-shaven

cariño *m* affection; *(caricia)* caress. ~ **mío** my darling. ~**samente** *adv* tenderly, lovingly; *(en carta)* with love from. ~**so** *a* affectionate. **con mucho ~** *(en carta)* with love from. **tener ~ a** be fond of. **tomar ~ a** take a liking to. **un ~** *(en carta)* with love from

carism|a *m* charisma. ~**ático** *a* charismatic

caritativo *a* charitable

cariz *m* look

carlinga *f* cockpit

carmesí *a & m* crimson

carmín *m* *(de labios)* lipstick; *(color)* red

carnal *a* carnal; *(pariente)* blood, full. **primo ~** first cousin

carnaval *m* carnival. ~**esco** *a* carnival. **martes de ~** Shrove Tuesday

carne *f* *(incl de frutos)* flesh; *(para comer)* meat. ~ **de cerdo** pork. ~ **de cordero** lamb. ~ **de gallina** goose-flesh. ~ **picada** mince. ~ **de ternera** veal. ~ **de vaca** beef. **me pone la ~ de gallina** it gives me the creeps. **ser de ~ y hueso** be only human

carné *m* card; *(cuaderno)* notebook. ~ **de conducir** driving licence *(Brit)*, driver's license *(Amer)*. ~ **de identidad** identity card.

carnero *m* sheep; *(culin)* lamb

carnet /kar'ne/ *m* card; *(cuaderno)* notebook. ~ **de conducir** driving licence *(Brit)*, driver's license *(Amer)*. ~ **de identidad** identity card

carnicer|ía *f* butcher's (shop); *(fig)* massacre. ~**o** *a* carnivorous; *(fig, cruel)* cruel, savage. —*m* butcher; *(animal)* carnivore

carnívoro *a* carnivorous. —*m* carnivore

carnoso *a* fleshy

caro *a* dear. —*adv* dear, dearly. **costar ~ a uno** cost s.o. dear

carpa *f* carp; *(tienda)* tent

carpeta *f* file, folder. ~**zo** *m*. **dar ~zo a** shelve, put on one side

carpinter|ía *f* carpentry. ~**o** *m* carpenter, joiner

carraspe|ar *vi* clear one's throat. ~**ra** *f*. **tener ~ra** have a frog in one's throat

carrera f run; (*prisa*) rush; (*concurso*) race; (*recorrido, estudios*) course; (*profesión*) profession, career

carreta f cart. ~**da** f cart-load

carrete m reel; (*película*) 35mm film

carretera f road. ~ **de circunvalación** bypass, ring road. ~ **nacional** A road (*Brit*), highway (*Amer*). ~ **secundaria** B road (*Brit*), secondary road (*Amer*)

carret|illa f trolley; (*de una rueda*) wheelbarrow; (*de bebé*) baby-walker. ~**ón** m small cart

carril m rut; (*rail*) rail; (*de autopista etc*) lane

carrillo m cheek; (*polea*) pulley

carrizo m reed

carro m cart; (*LAm, coche*) car. ~ **de asalto**, ~ **de combate** tank

carrocería f (*auto*) bodywork; (*taller*) car repairer's

carroña f carrion

carroza f coach, carriage; (*en desfile de fiesta*) float

carruaje m carriage

carrusel m merry-go-round

carta f letter; (*documento*) document; (*lista de platos*) menu; (*lista de vinos*) list; (*geog*) map; (*naipe*) card. ~ **blanca** free hand. ~ **de crédito** credit card

cartearse vpr correspond

cartel m poster; (*de escuela etc*) wall-chart. ~**era** f hoarding; (*en periódico*) entertainments. ~**ito** m notice. **de** ~ celebrated. **tener** ~ be a hit, be successful

cartera f wallet; (*de colegial*) satchel; (*para documentos*) briefcase

carteria f sorting office

carterista m & f pickpocket

cartero m postman, mailman (*Amer*)

cartílago m cartilage

cartilla f first reading book. ~ **de ahorros** savings book. **leerle la** ~ **a uno** tell s.o. off

cartón m cardboard

cartucho m cartridge

cartulina f thin cardboard

casa f house; (*hogar*) home; (*empresa*) firm; (*edificio*) building. ~ **de correos** post office. ~ **de huéspedes** boarding-house. ~ **de socorro** first aid post. **amigo** m **de la** ~ family friend. **ir a** ~ go home. **salir de** ~ go out

casad|a f married woman. ~**o** a married. —m married man. **los recién** ~**os** the newly-weds

casamentero m matchmaker

casa|miento m marriage; (*ceremonia*) wedding. ~**r** vt marry. —vi get married. ~**rse** vpr get married

cascabel m small bell. ~**eo** m jingling

cascada f waterfall

cascado a broken; (*voz*) harsh

cascanueces m invar nutcrackers

cascar [7] vt break; crack (*frutos secos*); (*pegar*) beat. —vi (*fig, fam*) chatter, natter (*fam*). ~**se** vpr crack

cáscara f (*de huevo, frutos secos*) shell; (*de naranja*) peel; (*de plátano*) skin

casco m helmet; (*de cerámica etc*) piece, fragment; (*cabeza*) head; (*de barco*) hull; (*envase*) empty bottle; (*de caballo*) hoof; (*de una ciudad*) part, area

cascote m rubble

caserío m country house; (*conjunto de casas*) hamlet

casero a home-made; (*doméstico*) domestic, household; (*amante del hogar*) home-loving; (*reunión*) family. —m owner; (*vigilante*) caretaker

caseta f small house, cottage. ~ **de baño** bathing hut

caset(t)e m & f cassette

casi adv almost, nearly; (en frases negativas) hardly. ~ ~ very nearly. ~ **nada** hardly any. ¡~ **nada!** is that all! ~ **nunca** hardly ever

casilla f small house; (cabaña) hut; (de mercado) stall; (en ajedrez etc) square; (departamento de casillero) pigeon-hole

casillero m pigeon-holes

casimir m cashmere

casino m casino; (sociedad) club

caso m case; (atención) notice. ~ **perdido** hopeless case. ~ **urgente** emergency. **darse el (de) que** happen. **el ~ es que** the fact is that. **en ~ de** in the event of. **en cualquier ~** in any case, whatever happens. **en ese ~** in that case. **en todo ~** in any case. **en último ~** as a last resort. **hacer ~ de** take notice of. **poner por ~** suppose

caspa f dandruff

cáspita int good heavens!, goodness me!

casquivano a scatter-brained

cassette m & f cassette

casta f (de animal) breed; (de persona) descent

castaña f chestnut

castañet|a f click of the fingers. ~**ear** vi (dientes) chatter

castaño a chestnut, brown. —m chestnut (tree)

castañuela f castanet

castellano a Castilian. —m (persona) Castilian; (lengua) Castilian, Spanish. ~**parlante** a Castilian-speaking, Spanish-speaking. ¿**habla Vd ~?** do you speak Spanish?

castidad f chastity

castig|ar [12] vt punish; (en deportes) penalize. ~**o** m punishment; (en deportes) penalty

Castilla f Castille. ~ **la Nueva** New Castille. ~ **la Vieja** Old Castille

castillo m castle

cast|izo a true; (lengua) pure. ~**o** a pure

castor m beaver

castra|ción f castration. ~**r** vt castrate

castrense m military

casual a chance, accidental. ~**idad** f chance, coincidence. ~**mente** adv by chance. **dar la ~idad** happen. **de ~idad, por ~idad** by chance. ¡**qué ~idad!** what a coincidence!

cataclismo m cataclysm

catador m taster; (fig) connoisseur

catalán a & m Catalan

catalejo m telescope

catalizador m catalyst

cat|alogar [12] vt catalogue; (fig) classify. ~**álogo** m catalogue

Cataluña f Catalonia

catamarán m catamaran

cataplúm int crash! bang!

catapulta f catapult

catar vt taste, try

catarata f waterfall, falls; (med) cataract

catarro m cold

cat|ástrofe m catastrophe. ~**astrófico** a catastrophic

catecismo m catechism

catedral f cathedral

catedrático m professor; (de instituto) teacher, head of department

categor|ía f category; (clase) class. ~**órico** a categorical. **de ~oría** important. **de primera ~oría** first-class

catinga f (LAm) bad smell

catita f (Arg) parrot

catoche m (Mex) bad mood

cat|olicismo m catholicism. ~**ólico** a (Roman) Catholic. —m (Roman) Catholic

catorce *a & m* fourteen

cauce *m* river bed; (*fig, artificial*) channel

caución *f* caution; (*jurid*) guarantee

caucho *m* rubber

caudal *m* (*de río*) flow; (*riqueza*) wealth. ∼**oso** *a* (*río*) large

caudillo *m* leader, caudillo

causa *f* cause; (*motivo*) reason; (*jurid*) lawsuit. ∼**r** *vt* cause. **a ∼ de, por ∼ de** because of

cáustico *a* caustic

cautel|a *f* caution. ∼**arse** *vpr* guard against. ∼**osamente** *adv* warily, cautiously. ∼**oso** *a* cautious, wary

cauterizar [10] *vt* cauterize; (*fig*) apply drastic measures to

cautiv|ar *vt* capture; (*fig, fascinar*) captivate. ∼**erio** *m*, ∼**idad** *f* captivity. ∼**o** *a & m* captive

cauto *a* cautious

cavar *vt/i* dig

caverna *f* cave, cavern

caviar *m* caviare

cavidad *f* cavity

cavil|ar *vi* ponder, consider. ∼**oso** *a* worried

cayado *m* (*de pastor*) crook; (*de obispo*) crozier

caza *f* hunting; (*una expedición*) hunt; (*animales*) game. —*m* fighter. ∼**dor** *m* hunter. ∼**dora** *f* jacket. ∼ **mayor** big game hunting. ∼ **menor** small game hunting. ∼**r** [10] *vt* hunt; (*fig*) track down; (*obtener*) catch, get. **andar a (la) ∼ de** be in search of. **dar ∼** chase, go after

cazo *m* saucepan; (*cucharón*) ladle. ∼**leta** *f* (small) saucepan

cazuela *f* casserole

cebada *f* barley

ceb|ar *vt* fatten (up); (*con trampa*) bait; prime (*arma de fuego*). ∼**o** *m* bait; (*de arma de fuego*) charge

ceboll|a *f* onion. ∼**ana** *f* chive. ∼**eta** *f* spring onion. ∼**ino** *m* chive

cebra *f* zebra

cece|ar *vi* lisp. ∼**o** *m* lisp

cedazo *m* sieve

ceder *vt* give up. —*vi* give in; (*disminuir*) ease off; (*fallar*) give way, collapse. **ceda el paso** give way

cedilla *f* cedilla

cedro *m* cedar

cédula *f* document; (*ficha*) index card

CE(E) *abrev* (*Comunidad* (*Económica*) *Europea*) E(E)C, European (Economic) Community

cefalea *f* severe headache

ceg|ador *a* blinding. ∼**ar** [1 & 12] *vt* blind; (*tapar*) block up. ∼**arse** *vpr* be blinded (de by). ∼**ato** *a* short-sighted. ∼**uera** *f* blindness

ceja *f* eyebrow

cejar *vi* move back; (*fig*) give way

celada *f* ambush; (*fig*) trap

cela|dor *m* (*de niños*) monitor; (*de cárcel*) prison warder; (*de museo etc*) attendant. ∼**r** *vt* watch

celda *f* cell

celebra|ción *f* celebration. ∼**r** *vt* celebrate; (*alabar*) praise. ∼**rse** *vpr* take place

célebre *a* famous; (*fig, gracioso*) funny

celebridad *f* fame; (*persona*) celebrity

celeridad *f* speed

celeste *a* heavenly. ∼**ial** *a* heavenly. **azul ∼e** sky-blue

celibato *m* celibacy

célibe *a* celibate

celo *m* zeal. ∼**s** *mpl* jealousy. **dar ∼s** make jealous. **papel** *m* ∼ adhesive tape, Sellotape (P). **tener ∼s** be jealous

celofán *m* cellophane

celoso a enthusiastic; (que tiene celos) jealous

celta a Celtic. —m & f Celt

céltico a Celtic

célula f cell

celular a cellular

celuloide m celluloid

celulosa f cellulose

cellisca f sleetstorm

cementerio m cemetery

cemento m cement; (hormigón) concrete; (LAm, cola) glue

cena f dinner; (comida ligera) supper. **~duría** f (Mex) restaurant

cenag|al m marsh, bog; (fig) tight spot. **~oso** a muddy

cenar vt have for dinner; (en cena ligera) have for supper. —vi have dinner; (tomar cena ligera) have supper

cenicero m ashtray

cenit m zenith

ceniz|a f ash. **~o** a ashen. —m jinx

censo m census. **~ electoral** electoral roll

censura f censure; (de prensa etc) censorship. **~r** vt censure; censor (prensa etc)

centavo a & m hundredth; (moneda) centavo

centell|a f flash; (chispa) spark. **~ar** vi, **~ear** vi sparkle. **~eo** m sparkle, sparkling

centena f hundred. **~r** m hundred. a **~res** by the hundred

centenario a centenary; (persona) centenarian. —m centenary; (persona) centenarian

centeno m rye

centésim|a f hundredth. **~o** a hundredth; (moneda) centésimo

cent|ígrado a centigrade, Celsius. **~igramo** m centigram. **~ilitro** m centilitre. **~ímetro** m centimetre

céntimo a hundredth. —m cent

centinela f sentry

centolla f, **centollo** m spider crab

central a central. —f head office. **~ de correos** general post office. **~ eléctrica** power station. **~ nuclear** nuclear power station. **~ telefónica** telephone exchange. **~ismo** m centralism. **~ita** f switchboard

centraliza|ción f centralization. **~r** [10] vt centralize

centrar vt centre

céntrico a central

centrífugo a centrifugal

centro m centre. **~ comercial** shopping centre

Centroamérica f Central America

centroamericano a & m Central American

centuplicar [7] vt increase a hundredfold

ceñi|do a tight. **~r** [5 & 22] vt surround, encircle; (vestido) be a tight fit. **~rse** vpr limit o.s. (a to)

ceñ|o m frown. **~udo** a frowning. **fruncir el ~o** frown

cepill|ar vt brush; (en carpintería) plane. **~o** m brush; (en carpintería) plane. **~o de dientes** toothbrush

cera f wax

cerámica f ceramics; (materia) pottery; (objeto) piece of pottery. **~o** a ceramic

cerca f fence. —adv near, close. **~s** mpl foreground. **~ de** prep near; (con números, con tiempo) nearly. **de ~** from close up, closely

cercado m enclosure

cercan|ía f nearness, proximity. **~ías** fpl outskirts. **tren m de ~ías** local train. **~o** a near, close. **C~o Oriente** m Near East

cercar [7] vt fence in, enclose; (gente) surround, crowd round; (asediar) besiege

cerciorar vt convince. ~**se** vpr make sure, find out

cerco m (grupo) circle; (cercado) enclosure; (asedio) siege

Cerdeña f Sardinia

cerdo m pig; (carne) pork

cereal m cereal

cerebr|al a cerebral. ~**o** m brain; (fig, inteligencia) intelligence, brains

ceremoni|a f ceremony. ~**al** a ceremonial. ~**oso** a ceremonious, stiff

céreo a wax

cerez|a f cherry. ~**o** cherry tree

ceril|la f match. ~**o** m (Mex) match

cern|er [1] vt sieve. ~**erse** vpr hover; (fig, amenazar) hang over. ~**idor** m sieve

cero m nought, zero; (fútbol) nil (Brit), zero (Amer); (tenis) love; (persona) nonentity. **partir de** ~ start from scratch

cerquillo m (LAm, flequillo) fringe

cerquita adv very near

cerra|do a shut, closed; (espacio) shut in, enclosed; (cielo) overcast; (curva) sharp. ~**dura** f lock; (acción de cerrar) shutting, closing. ~**jero** m locksmith. ~**r** [1] vt shut, close; (con llave) lock; (con cerrojo) bolt; (cercar) enclose; turn off (grifo); block up (agujero etc). —vi shut, close. ~**rse** vpr shut, close; (herida) heal. ~**r con llave** lock

cerro m hill. **irse por los** ~**s de Úbeda** ramble on

cerrojo m bolt. **echar el** ~ bolt

certamen m competition, contest

certero a accurate

certeza f, **certidumbre** f certainty

certifica|do a (carta etc) registered. —m certificate;

(carta) registered letter. ~**r** [7] vt certify; register (carta etc)

certitud f certainty

cervato m fawn

cerve|cería f beerhouse, bar; (fábrica) brewery. ~**za** f beer. ~**za de barril** draught beer. ~**za de botella** bottled beer

cesa|ción f cessation, suspension. ~**nte** a out of work. ~**r** vt stop. —vi stop, cease; (dejar un empleo) give up. **sin** ~**r** incessantly

cesáreo a Caesarian. **operación** f **cesárea** Caesarian section

cese m cessation; (de un empleo) dismissal

césped m grass, lawn

cest|a f basket. ~**ada** f basketful. ~**o** m basket. ~**o de los papeles** waste-paper basket

cetro m sceptre; (fig) power

cianuro m cyanide

ciática f sciatica

cibernética f cibernetics

cicatriz f scar. ~**ación** f healing. ~**ar** [10] vt/i heal. ~**arse** vpr heal

ciclamino m cyclamen

cíclico a cyclic(al)

ciclis|mo m cycling. ~**ta** m & f cyclist

ciclo m cycle; (LAm, curso) course

ciclomotor m moped

ciclón m cyclone

ciclostilo m cyclostyle, duplicating machine

ciego a blind. —m blind man, blind person. **a ciegas** in the dark

cielo m sky; (relig) heaven; (persona) darling. ¡~**s!** good heavens!, goodness me!

ciempiés m invar centipede

cien a a hundred. ~ **por** ~ (fam) completely, one hundred per cent. **me pone a** ~ it drives me mad

ciénaga f bog, swamp
ciencia f science; (fig)
knowledge. ~s empresariales business studies. **saber a ~ cierta**
know for a fact, know for certain
cieno m mud
científico a scientific. —m
scientist
ciento a & m (delante de nombres,
y numerales a los que multiplica
cien) a hundred, one hundred.
por ~ per cent
cierne m blossoming. **en ~** in
blossom; (fig) in its infancy
cierre m fastener; (acción de cerrar) shutting, closing. **~ de
cremallera** zip, zipper (Amer)
cierro vb véase **cerrar**
cierto a certain; (verdad) true.
estar en lo ~ be right. **lo ~ es
que** the fact is that. **no es ~**
that's not true. **¿no es ~?** right?
por ~ certainly, by the way. **si
bien es ~ que** although
ciervo m deer
cifra f figure, number; (cantidad)
sum. **~do** a coded. **~r** vt code;
(resumir) summarize. **en ~**
code, in code
cigala f (Norway) lobster
cigarra f cicada
cigarr|illo m cigarette. **~o** m
(cigarillo) cigarette; (puro) cigar
cigüeña f stork
cil|índrico a cylindrical. **~indro** m cylinder; (Mex, organillo)
barrel organ
cima f top; (fig) summit
címbalo m cymbal
cimbrear vt shake. **~se** vpr
sway
cimentar [1] vt lay the foundations of; (fig, reforzar)
strengthen
cimer|a f crest. **~o** a highest
cimiento m foundations; (fig)
source. **desde los ~s** from the
very beginning

cinc m zinc
cincel m chisel. **~ar** vt chisel
cinco a & m five
cincuenta a & m fifty; (quincuagésimo) fiftieth. **~ón** a about
fifty
cine m cinema. **~matografiar**
[20] vt film
cinético a kinetic
cínico a cynical; (desvergonzado)
shameless. —m cynic
cinismo m cynicism; (desvergüenza) shamelessness
cinta f band; (adorno de pelo etc)
ribbon; (película) film; (magnética) tape; (de máquina de
escribir etc) ribbon. **~ aisladora, ~ aislante** insulating
tape. **~ magnetofónica** magnetic tape. **~ métrica** tape
measure
cintur|a f waist. **~ón** m belt.
~ón de seguridad safety belt.
~ón salvavidas lifebelt
ciprés m cypress (tree)
circo m circus
circuito m circuit; (viaje) tour. **~
cerrado** closed circuit. **corto ~**
short circuit
circula|ción f circulation; (vehículos) traffic. **~r** a circular. —vi
circulate. —vi circulate; (líquidos) flow; (conducir) drive; (autobús etc) run
círculo m circle. **~ vicioso**
vicious circle. **en ~** in a circle
circunci|dar vt circumcise.
~sión f circumcision
circunda|nte a surrounding. **~r**
vt surround
circunferencia f circumference
circunflejo m circumflex
circunscri|bir [pp **circunscrito**] vt confine. **~pción** f (distrito) district. **~pción electoral**
constituency
circunspecto a wary, circumspect

circunstan|cia f circumstance. **~te** a surrounding. —m bystander. **los ~tes** those present

circunvalación f. **carretera f de ~** bypass, ring road

cirio m candle

ciruela f plum. **~ claudia** greengage. **~ damascena** damson

ciru|gía f surgery. **~jano** m surgeon

cisne m swan

cisterna f tank, cistern

cita f appointment; (entre chico y chica) date; (referencia) quotation. **~ción** f quotation; (jurid) summons. **~do** a aforementioned. **~r** vt make an appointment with; (mencionar) quote; (jurid) summons. **~rse** vpr arrange to meet

cítara f zither

ciudad f town; (grande) city. **~anía** f citizenship; (habitantes) citizens. **~ano** a civic —m citizen, inhabitant; (habitante de ciudad) city dweller

cívico a civic

civil a civil. —m civil guard. **~idad** f politeness

civiliza|ción f civilization. **~r** [10] vt civilize. **~rse** vpr become civilized

civismo m community spirit

cizaña f (fig) discord

clam|ar vi cry out, clamour. **~ m** cry; (griterío) noise, clamour; (protesta) outcry. **~oroso** a noisy

clandestin|idad f secrecy. **~o** a clandestine, secret

clara f (de huevo) egg white

claraboya f skylight

clarear vi dawn; (aclarar) brighten up. **~se** vpr be transparent

clarete m rosé

claridad f clarity; (luz) light

clarifica|ción f clarification. **~r** [7] vt clarify

clarín m bugle

clarinet|e m clarinet; (músico) clarinettist. **~ista** m & f clarinettist

clarividen|cia f clairvoyance; (fig) far-sightedness. **~te** a clairvoyant; (fig) far-sighted

claro a (con mucha luz) bright; (transparente, evidente) clear; (colores) light; (líquido) thin. —m (en bosque etc) clearing; (espacio) gap. —adv clearly. —int of course! **~ de luna** moonlight. **¡~ que sí!** yes of course! **¡~ que no!** of course not!

clase f class; (aula) classroom. **~ media** middle class. **~ obrera** working class. **~ social** social class. **dar ~s** teach. **toda ~ de** all sorts of

clásico a classical; (fig) classic. —m classic

clasifica|ción f classification; (deportes) league. **~r** [7] vt classify; (seleccionar) sort

claudia f greengage

claudicar [7] (ceder) give in; (cojear) limp

claustro m cloister; (univ) staff

claustrof|obia f claustrophobia. **~óbico** a claustrophobic

cláusula f clause

clausura f closure; (ceremonia) closing ceremony. **~r** vt close

clava|do a fixed; (con clavo) nailed. **~r** vt knock in (clavo); (introducir a mano) stick; (fijar) fix; (juntar) nail together. **es ~do a su padre** he's the spitting image of his father

clave f key; (mus) clef; (clavicémbalo) harpsichord

clavel m carnation

clavicémbalo m harpsichord

clavícula f collar bone, clavicle

clavija f peg; (elec) plug

clavo m nail; (culin) clove

claxon *m* (*pl* **claxons** /'klakson/) horn

clemen|cia *f* clemency, mercy. ~**te** *a* clement, merciful

clementina *f* tangerine

cleptómano *m* kleptomaniac

cler|ecía *f* priesthood. ~**ical** *a* clerical

clérigo *m* priest

clero *m* clergy

cliché *m* cliché; (*foto*) negative

cliente *m & f* client, customer; (*de médico*) patient. ~**la** *f* clientele, customers; (*de médico*) patients, practice

clim|a *m* climate. ~**ático** *a* climatic. ~**atizado** *a* airconditioned. ~**atológico** *a* climatological

clínic|a *f* clinic. ~**o** *a* clinical. —*m* clinician

clip *m* (*pl* **clips**) clip

clo *m* cluck. **hacer** ~ ~ cluck

cloaca *f* drain, sewer

cloque|ar *vi* cluck. ~**o** *m* clucking

cloro *m* chlorine

club *m* (*pl* **clubs** *o* **clubes**) club

coacci|ón *f* coercion, compulsion. ~**onar** *vt* coerce, compel

coagular *vt* coagulate; clot (*sangre*); curdle (*leche*). ~**se** *vpr* coagulate; (*sangre*) clot; (*leche*) curdle

coalición *f* coalition

coartada *f* alibi

coartar *vt* hinder; restrict (*libertad etc*)

cobard|e *a* cowardly. —*m* coward. ~**ía** *f* cowardice

cobaya *f*, **cobayo** *m* guinea pig

cobert|era *f* (*tapadera*) lid. ~**izo** *m* lean-to, shelter. ~**or** *m* bedspread; (*manta*) blanket. ~**ura** *f* covering

cobij|a *f* (*LAm, ropa de cama*) bedclothes; (*Mex, manta*) blanket. ~**ar** *vt* shelter. ~**arse** *vpr*

shelter, take shelter. ~**o** *m* shelter

cobra *f* cobra

cobra|dor *m* conductor. ~**dora** *f* conductress. ~**r** *vt* collect; (*ganar*) earn; charge (*precio*); cash (*cheque*); (*recuperar*) recover. —*vi* be paid. ~**rse** *vpr* recover

cobre *m* copper; (*mus*) brass (instruments)

cobro *m* collection; (*de cheque*) cashing; (*pago*) payment. **ponerse en** ~ go into hiding. **presentar al** ~ cash

cocada *f* (*LAm*) sweet coconut

cocaína *f* cocaine

cocción *f* cooking; (*tec*) baking, firing

cocear *vt/i* kick

coc|er [2 & 9] *vt/i* cook; (*hervir*) boil; (*en horno*) bake. ~**ido** *a* cooked. ~**m** stew

cociente *m* quotient. ~ **intelectual** intelligence quotient, IQ

cocin|a *f* kitchen; (*arte de cocinar*) cookery, cuisine; (*aparato*) cooker. ~**a de gas** gas cooker. ~**a eléctrica** electric cooker. ~**ar** *vt/i* cook. ~**ero** *m* cook

coco *m* coconut; (*árbol*) coconut palm; (*cabeza*) head; (*duende*) bogeyman. **comerse el** ~ think hard

cocodrilo *m* crocodile

cocotero *m* coconut palm

cóctel *m* (*pl* **cócteles** *o* **cócteles**) cocktail; (*reunión*) cocktail party

coche *m* car (*Brit*), motor car (*Brit*), automobile (*Amer*); (*de tren*) coach, carriage. ~**cama** sleeper. ~**fúnebre** hearse. ~**ra** *f* garage; (*de autobuses*) depot. ~ **restaurante** dining-car. ~**s de choque** dodgems

cochin|ada *f* dirty thing. ~**o** *a* dirty, filthy. —*m* pig

cod|azo *m* nudge (with one's elbow); (*Mex, aviso secreto*) tip-off. **~ear** *vt/i* elbow, nudge

codicia *f* greed. **~ado** *a* coveted, sought after. **~ar** *vt* covet. **~oso** *a* greedy (**de** for)

código *m* code. **~ de la circulación** Highway Code

codo *m* elbow; (*dobladura*) bend. **hablar por los ~s** talk too much. **hasta los ~s** up to one's neck

codorniz *m* quail

coeducación *f* coeducation

coerción *f* coercion

coetáneo *a* & *m* contemporary

coexist|encia *f* coexistence. **~ir** *vi* coexist

cofradía *f* brotherhood

cofre *m* chest

coger [14] *vt* (*España*) take; catch (*tren, autobús, pelota, catarro*); (*agarrar*) take hold of; (*del suelo*) pick up; pick (*frutos etc*). **—vi** (*caber*) fit. **~se** *vpr* trap, catch

cogollo *m* (*de lechuga etc*) heart; (*fig, lo mejor*) cream; (*fig, núcleo*) centre

cogote *m* back of the neck

cohech|ar *vt* bribe. **~o** *m* bribery

coherente *a* coherent

cohesión *f* cohesion

cohete *m* rocket; (*Mex, pistola*) pistol

cohibi|ción *f* inhibition. **~r** *vt* restrict; inhibit (*persona*). **~rse** *vpr* feel inhibited; (*contenerse*) restrain o.s.

coincid|encia *f* coincidence. **~ente** *a* coincidental. **~ir** *vi* coincide. **dar la ~encia** happen

coje|ar *vt* limp; (*mueble*) wobble. **~ra** *f* lameness

coj|ín *m* cushion. **~inete** *m* small cushion. **~inete de bolas** ball bearing

cojo *a* lame; (*mueble*) wobbly. **—m** lame person

col *f* cabbage. **~es de Bruselas** Brussel sprouts

cola *f* tail; (*fila*) queue; (*para pegar*) glue. **a la ~** at the end. **hacer ~** queue (up). **tener ~, traer ~** have serious consequences

colabora|ción *f* collaboration. **~dor** *m* collaborator. **~r** *vi* collaborate

colada *f* washing. **hacer la ~** do the washing

colador *m* strainer

colapso *m* collapse; (*fig*) stoppage

colar [2] *vt* strain (*líquidos*); (*lavar*) wash; pass (*moneda falsa etc*). **—vi** (*líquido*) seep through; (*fig*) be believed, wash (*fam*). **~se** *vpr* slip; (*no hacer caso de la cola*) jump the queue; (*en fiesta*) gatecrash; (*meter la pata*) put one's foot in it

colch|a *f* bedspread. **~ón** *m* mattress. **~oneta** *f* mattress

colear *vi* wag its tail; (*asunto*) not be resolved. **vivito y coleando** alive and kicking

colec|ción *f* collection; (*fig, gran número de*) a lot of. **~onar** *vt* collect. **~onista** *m* & *f* collector

colecta *f* collection

colectiv|idad *f* community. **~o** *a* collective. **—m** (*Arg*) minibus

colector *m* (*en las alcantarillas*) main sewer

colega *m* & *f* colleague

colegi|al *m* schoolboy. **~ala** *f* schoolgirl. **~o** *m* private school; (*de ciertas profesiones*) college. **~o mayor** hall of residence

colegir [5 & 14] *vt* gather

cólera *f* cholera; (*ira*) anger, fury. **descargar su ~** vent one's anger. **montar en ~** fly into a rage

colérico *a* furious, irate

colesterol *m* cholesterol

coleta *f* pigtail

colga|nte a hanging. —m pendant. **~r** [2 & 12] vt hang; hang out (colada); hang up (abrigo etc). —vi hang; (teléfono) hang up, ring off. **~rse** vpr hang o.s. **dejar a uno ~do** let s.o. down

cólico m colic

coliflor f cauliflower

colilla f cigarette end

colina f hill

colinda|nte a adjacent. **~r** vt border (con on)

colisión f collision, crash; (fig) clash

colmar vt fill to overflowing; (fig) fulfill. **~ a uno de amabilidad** overwhelm s.o. with kindness

colmena f beehive, hive

colmillo m eye tooth, canine (tooth); (de elefante) tusk; (de otros animales) fang

colmo m height. **ser el ~** be the limit, be the last straw

coloca|ción f positioning; (empleo) job, position. **~r** [7] vt put, place; (buscar empleo) find work for. **~rse** vpr find a job

Colombia f Colombia

colombiano a & m Colombian

colon m colon

colón m (unidad monetaria de Costa Rica y El Salvador) colón

Colonia f Cologne

coloni|a f colony; (agua de colonia) eau-de-Cologne; (LAm, barrio) suburb. **~a de verano** holiday camp. **~al** a colonial. **~ales** mpl imported foodstuffs; (comestibles en general) groceries. **~alista** m & f colonialist. **~zación** f colonization. **~zar** [10] colonize

coloquial a colloquial. **~o** m conversation; (congreso) conference

color m colour. **~ado** a (rojo) red. **~ante** m colouring. **~ar** vt colour. **~ear** vt/i colour. **~ete**

m rouge. **~ido** m colour. **de ~** colour. **en ~** (fotos, película) colour

colosal a colossal; (fig, magnífico, fam) terrific

columna f column; (fig, apoyo) support

columpi|ar vt swing. **~arse** vpr swing. **~o** m swing

collar m necklace; (de perro etc) collar

coma f comma. —m (med) coma

comadre f midwife; (madrina) godmother; (vecina) neighbour. **~ar** vi gossip

comadreja f weasel

comadrona f midwife

comand|ancia f command. **~ante** m commander. **~o** m command; (soldado) commando

comarca f area, region

comba f bend; (juguete) skipping-rope. **~r** vt bend. **~rse** vpr bend. **saltar a la ~** skip

combat|e m fight; (fig) struggle. **~iente** m fighter. **~ir** vt/i fight

combina|ción f combination; (bebida) cocktail; (arreglo) plan, scheme; (prenda) slip. **~r** vt combine; (arreglar) arrange; (armonizar) match, go well with. **~rse** vpr combine; (ponerse de acuerdo) agree (**para** to)

combustible m fuel

comedia f comedy; (cualquier obra de teatro) play. **hacer la ~** pretend

comedi|do a reserved. **~rse** [5] vpr be restrained

comedor m dining-room; (restaurante) restaurant; (persona) glutton. **ser buen ~** have a good appetite

comensal m companion at table, fellow diner

comentar vt comment on; (*anotar*) annotate. ∼**io** m commentary; (*observación*) comment; (*fam*) gossip. ∼**ista** m & f commentator

comenzar [1 & 10] vt/i begin, start

comer vt eat; (*a mediodía*) have for lunch; (*corroer*) eat away; (*en ajedrez*) take. — vi eat; (*a mediodía*) have lunch. ∼**se** vpr eat (up). **dar de** ∼ **a** feed

comercial a commercial. ∼**ante** m trader; (*de tienda*) shopkeeper. ∼**ar** vt trade (con, en in); (*con otra persona*) do business. ∼**o** m commerce; (*actividad*) trade; (*tienda*) shop; (*negocio*) business

comestible a edible. ∼**s** mpl food. **tienda de** ∼**s** grocer's (shop) (*Brit*), grocery (*Amer*)

cometa m comet. — f kite

cometer vt commit; make (*falta*). ∼**ido** m task

comezón m itch

comicastro m poor actor, ham (*fam*)

comicios mpl elections

cómico a comic(al). — m comic actor; (*cualquier actor*) actor

comida f food; (*a mediodía*) lunch. **hacer la** ∼ prepare the meals

comidilla f topic of conversation. **ser la** ∼ **del pueblo** be the talk of the town

comienzo m beginning, start. **a** ∼**s de** at the beginning of

comilón a greedy. ∼**ona** f feast

comillas fpl inverted commas

comino m cumin. **(no) me importa un** ∼ I couldn't care less

comisaría f police station. ∼**io** m commissioner; (*deportes*) steward. ∼**io de policía** police superintendent

comisión f assignment; (*comité*) commission, committee; (*com*) commission

comisura f corner. ∼ **de los labios** corner of the mouth

comité m committee

como adv like, as. — *conj* as; (*en cuanto*) as soon as. ∼ **quieras** as you like. ∼ **sabes** as you know. ∼ **si** as if

cómo a how? ¿∼? I beg your pardon? ¿∼ **está Vd?** how are you? ¡∼ **no!** (*esp LAm*) of course! ¿∼ **son?** what are they like? ¿∼ **te llamas?** what's your name? ¡y ∼! and how!

cómoda f chest of drawers

comodidad f comfort. **a su** ∼ at your convenience

cómodo a comfortable; (*útil*) handy

comoquiera conj. ∼ **que** since. ∼ **que sea** however it may be

compacto a compact; (*denso*) dense; (*líneas etc*) close

compadecer [11] vt feel sorry for. ∼**se** vpr. ∼**se de** feel sorry for

compadre m godfather; (*amigo*) friend

compañero m companion; (*de trabajo*) colleague; (*amigo*) friend. ∼**ía** f company. **en** ∼**ía de** with

comparable a comparable. ∼**ción** f comparison. ∼**r** vt compare. ∼**tivo** a & m comparative. **en** ∼**ción con** in comparison with, compared with

comparecer [11] vi appear

comparsa f group; (*en el teatro*) extra

compartimiento m compartment

compartir vt share

compás m (*instrumento*) (pair of) compasses; (*ritmo*) rhythm; (*división*) bar (*Brit*), measure

(*Amer*); (*naut*) compass. **a ∼ in time**

compasi|**ón** *f* compassion, pity. **tener ∼ón de** feel sorry for. **∼vo** *a* compassionate

compatib|**ilidad** *f* compatibility. **∼le** *a* compatible

compatriota *m & f* compatriot

compeler *vt* compel, force

compendi|**ar** *vt* summarize. **∼o** *m* summary

compenetración *f* mutual understanding

compensa|**ción** *f* compensation. **∼ción por despido** redundancy payment. **∼r** *vt* compensate

competen|**cia** *f* competition; (*capacidad*) competence; (*terreno*) field, scope. **∼te a** competent; (*apropiado*) appropriate, suitable

competi|**ción** *f* competition. **∼dor** *m* competitor. **∼r** [5] *vi* compete

compilar *vt* compile

compinche *m* accomplice; (*amigo, fam*) friend, mate (*fam*)

complac|**encia** *f* pleasure; (*indulgencia*) indulgence. **∼er** [32] *vt* please; (*prestar servicio*) help. **∼erse** *vpr* have pleasure, be pleased. **∼iente** *a* helpful; (*marido*) complaisant

complej|**idad** *f* complexity. **∼o** *a & m* complex

complement|**ario** *a* complementary. **∼o** *m* complement; (*gram*) object, complement

complet|**ar** *vt* complete. **∼o** *a* complete; (*lleno*) full; (*perfecto*) perfect

complexión *f* disposition; (*constitución*) constitution

complica|**ción** *f* complication. **∼r** [7] *vt* complicate; involve (*persona*). **∼rse** *vpr* become complicated

cómplice *m* accomplice

complot *m* (*pl* **complots**) plot

compon|**ente** *a* component. **∼m** component; (*culin*) ingredient; (*miembro*) member. **∼er** [34] *vt* make up; (*mus, literatura* and *música*) write, compose; (*reparar*) mend; (*culin*) prepare; (*arreglar*) restore; settle (*estómago*); reconcile (*diferencias*). **∼erse** *vpr* be made up; (*arreglarse*) get ready. **∼érselas** manage

comporta|**miento** *m* behaviour. **∼r** *vt* involve. **∼rse** *vpr* behave. **∼rse como es debido** behave properly. **∼rse mal** misbehave

composi|**ción** *f* composition. **∼tor** *m* composer

compostelano *a* from Santiago de Compostela. **—m** native of Santiago de Compostela

compostura *f* composition; (*arreglo*) repair; (*culin*) condiment; (*comedimiento*) composure

compota *f* stewed fruit

compra *f* purchase. **∼ a plazos** hire purchase. **∼dor** *m* buyer; (*en una tienda*) customer. **∼r** *vt* buy. **∼venta** *f* dealing. **hacer la ∼, ir a la ∼, ir de ∼s** do the shopping, go shopping. **negocio** *m* **de ∼venta** second-hand shop

comprend|**er** *vt* understand; (*incluir*) include. **∼sible** *a* understandable. **∼sión** *f* understanding. **∼sivo** *a* understanding; (*que incluye*) comprehensive

compresa *f* compress; (*de mujer*) sanitary towel

compr|**esión** *f* compression. **∼imido** *a* compressed. **—m** pill, tablet. **∼imir** *vt* compress; keep back (*lágrimas*); (*fig*) restrain

comproba|**nte** *m* (*recibo*) receipt. **∼r** *vt* check; (*confirmar*) confirm

comprometer *vt* compromise; (*arriesgar*) endager. **∼erse** *vpr* compromise o.s.; (obligarse) agree to. ~ido a (situación) awkward, embarrassing

compromiso m obligation; (apuro) predicament; (cita) appointment; (acuerdo) agreement. sin ~ without obligation

compuesto a compound; (persona) smart. —m compound

compungido a sad, sorry

computador m, **computadora** f computer

computar vt calculate

cómputo m calculation

comulgar [12] vi take Communion

común a common. —m community. en ~ in common. por lo ~ generally

comunal a municipal, communal

comunica|ción f communication. ~do m communiqué. ~do a la prensa press release. ~r [7] vt/i communicate; pass on (enfermedad, información). ~rse vpr communicate; (enfermedad) spread. ~tivo a communicative. está ~ndo (al teléfono) it's engaged, the line's engaged

comunidad f community. ~ de vecinos residents' association. C~ (Económica) Europea European (Economic) Community. en ~ together

comunión f communion; (relig) (Holy) Communion

comunis|mo m communism. ~ta a & m & f communist

comúnmente adv generally, usually

con prep with; (a pesar de) in spite of; (+ infinitivo) by. ~ decir la verdad by telling the truth. ~ que so. ~ tal que as long as

conato m attempt

concatenación f chain, linking

cóncavo a concave

concebir [5] vt/i conceive

conceder vt concede, grant; award (premio); (admitir) admit

concej|al m councillor. ~o m town council

concentra|ción f concentration. ~do m concentrated. ~r vt concentrate. ~rse vpr concentrate

concep|ción f conception. ~to m concept; (opinión) opinion. bajo ningún ~to in no way. en mi ~to in my view. por ningún ~to in no way

concerniente a concerning. en lo ~ a with regard to

concertar [1] vt (mus) harmonize; (coordinar) coordinate; (poner de acuerdo) agree. —vi be in tune; (fig) agree. ~se vpr agree

concertina f concertina

concesión f concession

conciencia f conscience; (conocimiento) consciousness. ~ción f awareness. ~ limpia clear conscience. ~ sucia guilty conscience. a ~ de que fully aware that. en ~ honestly. tener ~ de be aware of. tomar ~ de become aware of

concienzudo a conscientious

concierto m concert; (acuerdo) agreement; (mus, composición) concerto

concilia|ble a reconcilable. ~ción f reconciliation. ~r vt reconcile. ~r el sueño get to sleep. ~rse vpr gain

concilio m council

conciso m concise

conciudadano m fellow citizen

conclu|ir [17] vt finish; (deducir) conclude. —vi finish, end. ~irse vpr finish, end. ~sión f conclusion. ~yente a conclusive

concord|ancia f agreement. ~ar [2] vt reconcile. —vi agree. ~e a in agreement. ~ia f harmony

concret|amente adv specifically, to be exact. ∼ar vt make specific. ∼arse vpr become definite; (limitarse) confine o.s. ∼o a concrete; (determinado) specific, particular. —m (LAm, hormigón) concrete. en ∼o definite; (concretamente) to be exact; (en resumen) in short

concurr|encia f coincidence; (reunión) crowd, audience. ∼ido a crowded, busy. ∼ir vi meet; (asistir) attend; (coincidir) coincide; (contribuir) contribute; (en concurso) compete

concurs|ante m & f competitor, contestant. ∼ar vi compete, take part. ∼o m competition; (concurrencia) crowd; (ayuda) help

concha f shell; (carey) tortoiseshell

condado m county

conde m earl, count

condena f sentence. ∼ción f condemnation. ∼do m convict. ∼r vt condemn; (jurid) convict

condensa|ción f condensation. ∼r vt condense. ∼rse vpr condense

condesa f countess

condescende|ncia f condescension; (tolerancia) indulgence. ∼r [1] vi agree; (dignarse) condescend

condici|ón f condition; (naturaleza) nature. ∼onado a, ∼onal a conditional. ∼onar vt condition. a ∼ón de (que) on the condition that

condiment|ar vt season. ∼o m condiment

condolencia f condolence

condominio m joint ownership

condón m condom

condonar vt (perdonar) reprieve; cancel ⟨deuda⟩

conducir [47] vt drive ⟨vehículo⟩; carry ⟨electricidad, gas, agua

etc.⟩. —vi drive; (fig, llevar) lead. ∼se vpr behave. ¿a qué conduce? what's the point?

conducta f behaviour

conducto m pipe, tube; (anat) duct. por ∼ de through

conductor m driver; (jefe) leader; (elec) conductor

conduzco vb véase conducir

conectar vt/i connect; (enchufar) plug in

conejo m rabbit

conexión f connection

confabularse vpr plot

confecci|ón f making; (prenda) ready-made garment. ∼ones fpl clothing, clothes. ∼onado a ready-made. ∼onar vt make

confederación f confederation

conferencia f conference; (al teléfono) long-distance call; (univ etc) lecture. ∼ cumbre, ∼ en la cima, ∼ en la cumbre summit conference. ∼nte m & f lecturer

conferir [4] vt confer; award ⟨premio⟩

confes|ar [1] vt/i confess. ∼arse vpr confess. ∼ión f confession. ∼ional a confessional. ∼ionario m confessional. ∼or m confessor

confeti m confetti

confia|do a trusting; (seguro de sí mismo) confident. ∼nza f trust; (en sí mismo) confidence; (intimidad) familiarity. ∼r [20] vt entrust. —vi trust. ∼rse vpr put one's trust in

confiden|cia f confidence, secret. ∼cial a confidential. ∼te m & f close friend; (de policía) informer

configuración f configuration, shape

confín m border. ∼inar vt confine; (desterrar) banish. —vi border (con on). ∼ines mpl outermost parts

confirma|ción f confirmation. ~r vt confirm

confiscar [7] vt confiscate

confit|ería f sweet-shop (Brit), candy store (Amer). ~ura f jam

conflagración f conflagration

conflicto m conflict

confluencia f confluence

conforma|ción f conformation, shape. ~r vt (acomodar) adjust. —vi agree. ~rse vpr conform

conforme a in agreement; (contento) happy, satisfied; (según) according (con to). —conj as. —int OK! ~e a in accordance with, according to. ~idad f agreement; (tolerancia) resignation. ~ista m & f conformist

conforta|ble a comfortable. ~nte a comforting. ~r vt comfort

confronta|ción f confrontation; (comparación) comparison. ~r vt confront; (comparar) compare

confu|ndir vt blur; (equivocar) mistake, confuse; (perder) lose; (mezclar) mix up, confuse. ~ndirse vpr become confused; (equivocarse) make a mistake. ~sión f confusion; (vergüenza) embarrassment. ~so a confused; (avergonzado) embarrassed

congela|do a frozen. ~dor m freezer. ~r vt freeze

congeniar vi get on

congesti|ón f congestion. ~onado a congested. ~onar vt congest. ~onarse vpr become congested

congoja f distress

congraciar vt win over. ~se vpr ingratiate o.s.

congratular vt congratulate

congrega|ción f gathering; (relig) congregation. ~rse [12] vpr gather, assemble

congres|ista m & f delegate, member of a congress. ~o m congress, conference. C~o de los Diputados House of Commons

cónico a conical

conifer|a f conifer. ~o a coniferous

conjetura f conjecture, guess. ~r vt conjecture, guess

conjuga|ción f conjugation. ~r [12] vt conjugate

conjunción f conjunction

conjunto a joint. —m collection; (mus) band; (ropa) suit, outfit. en ~ altogether

conjura f, **conjuración** f conspiracy

conjurar vt plot, conspire

conmemora|ción f commemoration. ~r vt commemorate. ~tivo a commemorative

conmigo pron with me

conminar vt threaten; (avisar) warn

conmiseración f commiseration

conmo|ción f shock; (tumulto) upheaval; (terremoto) earthquake. ~cionar vt shock. ~ cerebral concussion. ~ver [2] vt shake; (emocionar) move

conmuta|dor m switch. ~r vt exchange

connivencia f connivance

connota|ción f connotation. ~r vt connote

cono m cone

conoc|edor a & m expert. ~er [11] vt know; (por primera vez) meet; (reconocer) recognize, know. ~erse vpr know o.s.; (dos personas) know each other; (notarse) be obvious. dar a ~er make known. darse a ~er make o.s. known. ~ido a well-known. —m acquaintance. ~imiento m knowledge; (sentido) consciousness; (*conocido*) acquaintance. **perder el ~imiento** faint. **se ~e que** apparently. **tener ~imiento de** know about

conozco *vb véase* **conocer**

conque *conj* so

conquense *a* from Cuenca. —*m* native of Cuenca

conquista *f* conquest. **~dor** *a* conquering. —*m* conqueror; (*de América*) conquistador; (*fig*) lady-killer. **~r** *vt* conquer, win

consabido *a* well-known

consagra|ción *f* consecration. **~r** *vt* consecrate; (*fig*) devote. **~rse** *vpr* devote o.s.

consanguíneo *m* blood relation

consciente *a* conscious

consecución *f* acquisition; (*de un deseo*) realization

consecuen|cia *f* consequence; (*firmeza*) consistency. **~te** *a* consistant. **a ~cia de** as a result of. **en ~cia, por ~cia** consequently

consecutivo *a* consecutive

conseguir [5 & 13] *vt* get, obtain; (*lograr*) manage; achieve (*objetivo*)

conseja *f* story, fable

consej|ero *m* adviser; (*miembro de consejo*) member. **~o** *m* advice; (*pol*) council. **~o de ministros** cabinet

consenso *m* assent, consensus

consenti|do *a* (*niño*) spoilt. **~miento** *m* consent. **~r** [4] *vt* allow. —*vi* consent. **~rse** *vpr* break

conserje *m* porter, caretaker. **~ría** *f* porter's office

conserva *f* preserves; (*mermelada*) jam, preserve; (*en lata*) tinned food. **~ción** *f* conservation; (*de alimentos*) preservation; (*de edificio*) maintenance. **en ~** preserved

conservador *a* & *m* (*pol*) conservative

conservar *vt* keep; preserve (*alimentos*). **~se** *vpr* keep; (*costumbre*) survive

conservatorio *m* conservatory

considera|ble *a* considerable. **~ción** *f* consideration; (*respeto*) respect. **~do** *a* considered; (*amable*) considerate; (*respetado*) respected. **~r** *vt* consider; (*respetar*) respect. **de ~ción** considerable. **de su ~ción** (*en cartas*) yours faithfully. **tomar en ~ción** take into consideration

consigna *f* order; (*rail*) left luggage office (*Brit*), baggage room (*Amer*); (*eslogan*) slogan

consigo *pron* (*él*) with him; (*ella*) with her; (*Ud, Uds*) with you; (*uno mismo*) with o.s.

consiguiente *a* consequent. **por ~** consequently

consist|encia *f* consistency. **~ente** *a* consisting (**en** of); (*firme*) solid. **~ir** *vi* consist (**en** of); (*deberse*) be due (**en** to)

consola|ción *f* consolation. **~r** [2] *vt* console, comfort

consolidar *vt* consolidate. **~se** *vpr* consolidate

consomé *m* clear soup, consommé

consonan|cia *f* consonance. **~te** *a* consonant. —*f* consonant

consorcio *m* consortium

consorte *m & f* consort

conspicuo *a* eminent; (*visible*) visible

conspira|ción *f* conspiracy. **~dor** *m* conspirator. **~r** *vi* conspire

constan|cia *f* constancy. **~te** *a* constant

constar *vi* be clear; (*figurar*) appear, figure; (*componerse*) consist. **hacer ~** point out. **me consta que** I'm sure that. **que conste que** believe me

constatar *vt* check; (*confirmar*) confirm

constelación *f* constellation

consternación *f* consternation

constipa|do *m* cold. —*a.* estar ∼**do** have a cold. ∼**rse** *vpr.* catch a cold

constitu|ción *f* constitution; (*establecimiento*) setting up. ∼**cional** *a* constitutional. ∼**ir** [17] *vt* constitute; (*formar*) form; (*crear*) set up, establish. ∼**irse** *vpr* set o.s. up (**en** as); (*presentarse*) appear. ∼**tivo** *a*, ∼**yente** *a* constituent

constreñir [5 & 22] *vt* force, oblige; (*restringir*) restrain

constricción *f* constriction

constru|cción *f* construction. ∼**ctor** *m* builder. ∼**ir** [17] *vt* construct; build (*edificio*)

consuelo *m* consolation, comfort

consuetudinario *a* customary

cónsul *m* consul

consula|do *m* consulate. ∼**r** *a* consular

consult|a *f* consultation. ∼**ar** *vt* consult. ∼**orio** *m* surgery. ∼**orio** sentimental problem page. horas *fpl* de ∼**a** surgery hours. obra *f* de ∼**a** reference book

consumar *vt* complete; commit (*crimen*); consummate (*matrimonio*)

consum|ición *f* consumption; (*bebida*) drink; (*comida*) food. ∼**ido** *a* (*persona*) skinny, wasted; (*frutas*) shrivelled. ∼**idor** *m* consumer. ∼**ir** *vt* consume. ∼**irse** *vpr* (*persona*) waste away; (*cosa*) wear out; (*quedarse seco*) dry up. ∼**ismo** *m* consumerism. ∼**o** *m* consumption

contab|ilidad *f* book-keeping; (*profesión*) accountancy. ∼**le** *m* & *f* accountant

contacto *m* contact. ponerse en ∼ **con** get in touch with

contado *a* counted. ∼**s** *apl* few. ∼**r** *m* meter; (*LAm, contable*) accountant. al ∼ cash

contagi|ar *vt* infect (*persona*); pass on (*enfermedd*); (*fig*) contaminate. ∼**o** *m* infection. ∼**oso** *a* infectious

contamina|ción *f* contamination, pollution. ∼**r** *vt* contaminate, pollute

contante *a*. dinero *m* ∼ cash

contar [2] *vt* count; tell (*relato*). —*vi* count. ∼ **con** rely on, count on. ∼**se** *vpr* be included (**entre** among); (*decirse*) be said

contempla|ción *f* contemplation. ∼**r** *vt* look at; (*fig*) contemplate. sin ∼**ciones** unceremoniously

contemporáneo *a* & *m* contemporary

contend|er [1] *vi* compete. ∼**iente** *m* & *f* competitor

conten|er [40] *vt* contain; (*restringir*) restrain. ∼**erse** *vpr* restrain o.s. ∼**ido** *a* contained. —*m* contents

content|ar *vt* please. ∼**arse** *vpr*. ∼**arse de** be satisfied with, be pleased with. ∼**o** *a* (*alegre*) happy; (*satisfecho*) pleased

contesta|ción *f* answer. ∼**dor** *m* ∼ automático answering machine. ∼**r** *vt/i* answer; (*replicar*) answer back

contexto *m* context

contienda *f* struggle

contigo *pron* with you

contiguo *a* adjacent

continen|cia *f* continence. ∼**tal** *a* continental. ∼**te** *m* continent

contingen|cia *f* contingency. ∼**te** *a* contingent. —*m* contingent; (*cuota*) quota

continu|ación *f* continuation. ∼**ar** [21] *vt* continue, resume.

—*vi* continue. ~**ará** (*en revista, TV etc*) to be continued. ~**idad** *f* continuity. ~**o** *a* continuous; (*muy frecuente*) continual. **a** ~**ación** immediately after. **corriente** *f* ~**a** direct current

contorno *m* outline; (*geog*) contour. ~**s** *mpl* surrounding area

contorsión *f* contortion

contra *adv* & *prep* against. —*m* cons. **en** ~ against

contraalmirante *m* rear-admiral

contraata|car [7] *vt/i* counterattack. ~**que** *m* counter-attack

contrabajo *m* double-bass; (*persona*) double-bass player

contrabalancear *vt* counterbalance

contraband|ista *m* & *f* smuggler. ~**o** *m* contraband

contracción *f* contraction

contrachapado *m* plywood

contrad|ecir [46] *vt* contradict. ~**icción** *f* contradiction. ~**ictorio** *a* contradictory

contraer [41] *vt* contract. ~ **matrimonio** marry. ~**se** *vpr* contract; (*limitarse*) limit o.s.

contrafuerte *m* buttress

contragolpe *m* backlash

contrahecho *a* fake; (*moneda*) counterfeit; (*persona*) hunchbacked

contraindicación *f* contraindication

contralto *m* alto. —*f* contralto

contramano. a ~ in the wrong direction

contrapartida *f* compensation

contrapelo. a ~ the wrong way

contrapes|ar *vt* counterbalance. ~**o** *m* counterbalance

contraponer [34] oppose; (*comparar*) compare

contraproducente *a* counterproductive

contrari|ar [20] *vt* oppose; (*molestar*) annoy. ~**edad** *f* obstacle; (*disgusto*) annoyance. ~**o**

a contrary; (*dirección*) opposite; (*persona*) opposed. **al** ~**o** on the contrary. **al** ~**o de** contrary to. **de lo** ~**o** otherwise. **en** ~**o** against. **llevar la** ~**a** contradict. **por el** ~**o** on the contrary

contrarrestar *vt* counteract

contrasentido *m* contradiction

contraseña *f* secret mark; (*palabra*) password

contrast|ar *vt* check, verify. —*vi* contrast. ~**e** *m* contrast; (*en oro, plata etc*) hallmark

contratar *vt* sign a contract for; engage (*empleados*)

contratiempo *m* setback; (*accidente*) accident

contrat|ista *m* & *f* contractor. ~**o** *m* contract

contraven|ción *f* contravention. ~**ir** [53] *vi.* ~**ir a** contravene

contraventana *f* shutter

contribu|ción *f* contribution; (*tributo*) tax. ~**ir** [17] *vt/i* contribute. ~**yente** *m* & *f* contributor; (*que paga impuestos*) taxpayer

contrincante *m* rival, opponent

contrito *a* contrite

control *m* control; (*inspección*) check. ~**ar** *vt* control; (*examinar*) check

controversia *f* controversy

contundente *a* (*arma*) blunt; (*argumento etc*) convincing

conturbar *vt* perturb

contusión *f* bruise

convalec|encia *f* convalescence. ~**er** [11] *vi* convalesce. ~**iente** *a* & *m* & *f* convalescent

convalidar *vt* confirm; recognize (*título*)

convenc|er [9] *vt* convince. ~**imiento** *m* conviction

convención *f* convention. ~**onal** *a* conventional

conveni|encia *f* convenience; (*aptitud*) suitability. ~**encias** (*sociales*) conventions. ~**ente**

a suitable; *(aconsejable)* advisable; *(provechoso)* useful, advantageous. ∼r [53] *vt* agree. —*vi* agree; *(ser conveniente)* be convenient for, suit; *(ser aconsejable)* be advisable

convento *m (de monjes)* monastery; *(de monjas)* convent

convergente *a* converging

converger [14] *vi*, **convergir** [14] *vi* converge

conversa|ción *f* conversation. ∼r *vi* converse, talk

conver|sión *f* conversion. ∼**so** *a* converted. —*m* convert. ∼**tible** *a* convertible. ∼**tir** [4] *vt* convert. ∼**tirse** *vpr* be converted

convexo *a* convex

convic|ción *f* conviction. ∼**to** *a* convicted

convida|do *m* guest. ∼r *vt* invite. **te convido a un helado** I'll treat you to an ice-cream

convincente *a* convincing

convite *m* invitation; *(banquete)* banquet

conviv|encia *f* coexistence. ∼**ir** *vi* live together

convocar [7] *vt* convene *(reunión)*; summon *(personas)*

convoy *m* convoy; *(rail)* train; *(vinagrera)* cruet

convulsión *f* convulsion; *(fig)* upheaval

conyugal *a* conjugal; *(vida)* married

cónyuge *m* spouse. ∼**s** *mpl* (married) couple

coñac *m (pl* coñacs*)* brandy

coopera|ción *f* co-operation. ∼r *vi* co-operate. ∼**tiva** *f* co-operative. ∼**tivo** *a* co-operative

coord|enada *f* coordinate. ∼**inación** *f* co-ordination. ∼**inar** *vt* co-ordinate

copa *f* glass; *(deportes, fig)* cup. ∼**s** *fpl (naipes)* hearts. **tomar una** ∼ have a drink

copia *f* copy. ∼ **en limpio** fair copy. ∼r *vt* copy. **sacar una** ∼ make a copy

copioso *a* copious; *(lluvia, nevada etc)* heavy

copla *f* verse; *(canción)* song

copo *m* flake. ∼ **de nieve** snowflake. ∼**s de maíz** cornflakes

coquet|a *f* flirt; *(mueble)* dressing-table. ∼**ear** *vi* flirt. ∼**eo** *m* flirtation. ∼**o** *a* flirtatious

coraje *m* courage; *(rabia)* anger. **dar** ∼ make mad, make furious

coral *a* choral. —*m (materia, animal)* coral

Corán *m* Koran

coraza *f (naut)* armour-plating; *(de tortuga)* shell

corazón *m* heart; *(persona)* darling. ∼**onada** *f* hunch; *(impulso)* impulse. **sin** ∼**ón** heartless. **tener buen** ∼**ón** be good-hearted

corbata *f* tie, necktie *(esp Amer)*. ∼ **de lazo** bow tie

corcova *f* hump. ∼**do** *a* hunchbacked

corchea *f* quaver

corchete *m* fastener, hook and eye; *(gancho)* hook; *(paréntesis)* square bracket

corcho *m* cork

cordel *m* cord, thin rope

cordero *m* lamb

cordial *a* cordial, friendly. —*m* tonic. ∼**idad** *f* cordiality, warmth

cordillera *f* mountain range

córdoba *m (unidad monetaria de Nicaragua)* córdoba

Córdoba *f* Cordova

cordón *m* string; *(de zapatos)* lace; *(cable)* flex; *(fig)* cordon. ∼ **umbilical** umbilical cord

corear *vt* chant

coreografía *f* choreography

corista *m & f* member of the chorus. —*f (bailarina)* chorus girl

corneta *f* bugle. **~ín** *m* cornet
Cornualles *m* Cornwall
cornucopia *f* cornucopia
cornudo *a* horned. —*m* cuckold
coro *m* chorus; (*relig*) choir
corona *f* crown; (*de flores*) wreath, garland. **~ción** *f* coronation. **~r** *vt* crown
coronel *m* colonel
coronilla *f* crown. **estar hasta la ~** be fed up
corporación *f* corporation
corporal *a* corporal
corpulento *a* stout
corpúsculo *m* corpuscle
corral *m* pen. **aves** *fpl* **de ~** poultry
correa *f* strap; (*de perro*) lead; (*cinturón*) belt
corrección *f* correction; (*reprensión*) rebuke; (*cortesía*) good manners. **~to** *a* correct; (*cortés*) polite
corredizo *a* running. **nudo ~dizo** slip knot. **puerta** *f* **~diza** sliding door. **~dor** *m* runner; (*pasillo*) corridor; (*agente*) agent, broker. **~dor** **automovilista** racing driver
corregir [5 & 14] *vt* correct; (*reprender*) rebuke
correlación *f* correlation. **~onar** *vt* correlate
correo *m* courier; (*correos*) post, mail; (*tren*) mail train. **~s** *mpl* post office. **echar al ~** post
correr *vt* run; (*viaje*) travel; **draw** (*cortinas*). —*vi* run; (*agua*, *electricidad etc*) flow; (*tiempo*) pass. **~se** *vpr* (*apartarse*) move along; (*pasarse*) go too far; (*colores*) run. **~se una juerga** have a ball
correspondencia *f* correspondence. **~er** *vi* correspond; (*ser adecuado*) be fitting; (*contestar*) reply; (*pertenecer*) belong; (*incumbir*) fall to. **~erse** *vpr* (*amarse*) love one

another. **~iente** *a* corresponding
corresponsal *m* correspondent
corrida *f* run. **~a de toros** bullfight. **~o** *a* (*peso*) good; (*continuo*) continuous; (*avergonzado*) embarrassed. **de ~a** from memory
corriente *a* (*agua*) running; (*monedas, publicación, cuenta, año etc*) current; (*ordinario*) ordinary. —*f* current; (*de aire*) draught; (*fig*) tendency. —*m* current month. **al ~** (*al día*) up-to-date; (*enterado*) aware
corrillo *m* small group, circle. **~o** *m* circle
corroborar *vt* corroborate
corroer [24 & 37] *vt* corrode; (*geol*) erode; (*fig*) eat away. **~se** *vpr* corrode
corromper *vt* rot (*madera*); turn bad (*alimentos*); (*fig*) corrupt. —*vi* (*fam*) stink. **~se** *vpr* (*madera*) rot; (*alimentos*) go bad; (*fig*) be corrupted
corrosión *f* corrosion. **~vo** *a* corrosive
corrupción *f* (*de madera etc*) rot; (*soborno*) bribery; (*fig*) corruption
corsé *m* corset
cortacésped *m* *invar* lawnmower
cortado *a* cut; (*leche*) sour; (*avergonzado*) embarrassed; (*confuso*) confused. —*m* coffee with a little milk. **~ura** *f* cut
cortante *a* sharp; (*viento*) biting; (*frío*) bitter. **~r** *vt* cut; (*recortar*) cut out; (*aislar, detener*) cut off; (*interrumpir*) cut in. —*vi* cut. **~rse** *vpr* cut o.s.; (*leche etc*) curdle; (*al teléfono*) be cut off; (*fig*) be embarrassed, become tongue-tied. **~rse el pelo** have one's hair cut. **~rse las uñas** cut one's nails
cortauñas *m* *invar* nail-clippers

corte m cutting; (de instrumento cortante) cutting edge; (de corriente) cut; (de prendas de vestir) cut; (de tela) length. —f court. ~ **de luz** power cut. ~ **y confección** dressmaking. **hacer la** ~ court. **las C~s** the Spanish parliament

cortej|**ar** vt court. ~**o** m (de rey etc) entourage. ~**o fúnebre** cortège, funeral procession. ~**o nupcial** wedding procession

cortés a polite

cortesan|**a** f courtesan. ~**o** m courtier

cortesía f courtesy

corteza f bark; (de naranja etc) peel, rind; (de pan) crust

cortijo m farm; (casa) farmhouse

cortina f curtain

corto a short; (escaso) scanty; (apocado) shy. ~**circuito** m short circuit. ~ **de alcances** dim, thick. ~ **de oído** hard of hearing. ~ **de vista** shortsighted. **a la corta o a la larga** sooner or later. **quedarse** ~ fall short; (miscalcular) underestimate

Coruña f. **La** ~ Corunna

corvo a bent

cosa f thing; (asunto) business; (idea) idea. ~ **de about. como si tal** ~ just like that; (como si no hubiera pasado nada) as if nothing had happened. **decirle a uno cuatro** ~**s** tell s.o. a thing or two. **lo que son las** ~**s** much to my surprise

cosaco a & m Cossack

cosech|**a** f harvest; (de vino) vintage. ~**ar** vt harvest. ~**ero** m harvester

coser vt/i sew. ~**se** vpr stick to s.o. **eso es** ~ **y cantar** it's as easy as pie

cosmético a & m cosmetic

cósmico a cosmic

cosmonauta m & f cosmonaut

cosmopolita a & m & f cosmopolitan

cosmos m cosmos

cosquillas fpl ticklishness. **buscar a uno las** ~ provoke s.o. **hacer** ~ tickle. **tener** ~ be ticklish

costa f coast. **a** ~ **de** at the expense of. **a toda** ~ at any cost

costado m side

costal m sack

costar [2] vt/i cost. ~ **caro** be expensive. **cueste lo que cueste** at any cost

Costa Rica f Costa Rica

costarricense a & m, **costarriqueño** a & m Costa Rican

coste m cost. ~**ar** vt pay for; (naut) sail along the coast

costero a coastal

costilla f rib; (chuleta) chop

costo m cost. ~**so** a expensive

costumbre f custom, habit. **de** ~ a usual. —adv usually

costur|**a** f sewing; (línea) seam; (confección) dressmaking. ~**era** f dressmaker. ~**ero** m sewing box

cotejar vt compare

cotidiano a daily

cotill|**ar** vt gossip. ~**o** m gossip

cotiza|**ción** f quotation, price. ~**r** [10] vt (en la bolsa) quote. —vi pay one's subscription. ~**rse** vpr fetch; (en la bolsa) stand at; (fig) be valued

coto m enclosure; (de caza) preserve. ~ **de caza** game preserve

cotorr|**a** f parrot; (urraca) magpie; (fig) chatterbox. ~**ear** vi chatter

coyuntura f joint; (oportunidad) opportunity; (situación) situation; (circunstancia) occasion, juncture

coz f kick

cráneo m skull

cráter m crater

crea|ción f creation. **~dor** a creative. —m creator. **~r** vt create

crec|er [11] vi grow; (aumentar) increase. **~ida** f (de río) flood. **~ido** a (persona) grown-up; (número) large, considerable; (plantas) fully-grown. **~iente** a growing; (luna) crescent. **~imiento** m growth

credencial a credential. **~es** fpl credentials

credibilidad f credibility

crédito m credit. **digno de ~** reliable, trustworthy

credo m creed. **en un ~** in a flash

crédulo a credulous

cre|encia f belief. **~er** [18] believe; (pensar) think. **~o que no** I don't think so, I think not. **~o que sí** I think so. —vi believe. **~erse** upr consider o.s. **no me lo ~o** I don't believe it. **~íble** a credible. **¡ya lo ~o!** I should think so!

crema f cream; (culin) custard. **~ bronceadora** sun-tan cream

cremación f cremation; (de basura) incineration

cremallera f zip, zipper (Amer)

crematorio m crematorium; (de basura) incinerator

crepitar vi crackle

crepúsculo m twilight

crescendo m crescendo

crespo a frizzy. **~ón** m crêpe

cresta f crest; (tupé) toupee; (geog) ridge

Creta f Crete

cretino m cretin

creyente m believer

cría f breeding; (animal) baby animal

cria|da f maid, servant. **~dero** m nursery. **~do** a brought up. —m servant. **~dor** m breeder. **~nza** f breeding. **~r** [20] vt suckle; grow (plantas); breed (animales); (educar) bring up. **~rse** upr grow up

criatura f creature; (niño) baby

crim|en m crime. **~inal** a & m & f criminal

crin m mane; (relleno) horsehair

crinolina f crinoline

crío m child

criollo a & m Creole

cripta f crypt

crisantemo m chrysanthemum

crisis f crisis

crisol m melting-pot

crispar vt twitch; (irritar, fam) annoy. **~ los nervios a uno** get on s.o.'s nerves

cristal m crystal; (vidrio) glass; (de una ventana) pane of glass. **~ de aumento** magnifying glass. **~ino** a crystalline; (fig) crystal-clear. **~izar** [10] crystallize. **limpiar los ~es** clean the windows

cristian|amente adv in a Christian way. **~dad** f Christianity. **~ismo** m Christianity. **~o** a & m Christian

Cristo m Christ

cristo m crucifix

criterio m criterion; (opinión) opinion

crí|tica f criticism; (reseña) review. **~iticar** [7] vt criticize. **~ítico** a critical. —m critic

croar vi croak

crom|ado a chromium-plated. **~o** m chromium, chrome

cromosoma m chromosome

crónic|a f chronicle; (de periódico) news. **~o** a chronic

cronista m & f reporter

cronolog|ía f chronology. **~óg|ico** a chronological

cron|ometraje m timing. **~ometrar** vt time. **~ómetro** m chronometer; (en deportes) stopwatch

croquet /'kroket/ m croquet

croqueta f croquette

cruce m crossing; (de calles, de carreteras) crossroads; (de peatones) (pedestrian) crossing

crucial *a* cross-shaped; *(fig)* crucial

crucifi|car [7] *vt* crucify. **~jo** *m* crucifix. **~xión** *f* crucifiction

crucigrama *m* crossword (puzzle)

crudo *a* raw; *(fig)* crude. **petró-leo** *m* **~** crude oil

cruel *a* cruel. **~dad** *f* cruelty

cruji|do *m* *(de seda, de hojas secas etc)* rustle; *(de muebles etc)* creak. **~r** *vi* *(seda, hojas secas etc)* rustle; *(muebles etc)* creak

cruz *f* cross; *(de moneda)* tails. **~gamada** swastika. **la C~ Roja** the Red Cross

cruzada *f* crusade

cruzar [10] *vt* cross; *(poner de un lado a otro)* lay across. **~se** *vpr* cross; *(pasar en la calle)* pass

cuaderno *m* exercise book; *(para apuntes)* notebook

cuadra *f* *(caballeriza)* stable; *(LAm, manzana)* block

cuadrado *a & m* square

cuadragésimo *a* fortieth

cuadr|ar *vt* square. **~vi** suit; *(estar de acuerdo)* agree. **~arse** *vpr* *(mil)* stand to attention; *(fig)* dig one's heels in. **~ilátero** *a* quadrilateral; *(boxeo)* **~m** quadri-lateral; *(boxeo)* ring

cuadrilla *f* group; *(pandilla)* gang

cuadro *m* square; *(pintura)* painting; *(de obra de teatro, escena)* scene; *(de jardín)* bed; *(de números)* table; *(de mando etc)* panel; *(conjunto del personal)* staff. **~ de distribución** switch-board. **a ~s, de ~s** check. **en ~** in a square. **¡qué ~!, ¡vaya un ~!** what a sight!

cuadrúpedo *m* quadruped

cuádruple *a & m* quadruple

cuajar *vt* thicken; clot *(sangre)*, curdle *(leche)*; *(llenar)* fill up. **—vi** *(nieve)* settle; *(fig, fam)* work out. **cuajado de** full of.

~se *vpr* coagulate; *(sangre)* clot; *(leche)* curdle. **~ón** *m* clot

cual *pron.* **el ~, la ~ etc** *(animales y cosas)* that, which; *(personas, sujeto)* who, that; *(personas, objeto)* whom. **—adv** as, like. **—a** such as. **~ si** as if. **~... tal** like... like. **cada ~** everyone. **por lo ~** because of which

cuál *pron* which

cualidad *f* quality; *(propiedad)* property

cualquiera *a (delante de nom-bres* cualquier, *pl* cua-lesquiera*)* any. **—pron** *(pl* cualesquiera*)* anyone, any-body; *(cosas)* whatever, which-ever. **un ~** a nobody

cuando *adv* when. **—conj** when; *(aunque)* even if. **~ más** at the most. **~ menos** at the least. **~ no** if not. **aun ~** even if. **de ~ en ~** from time to time

cuándo *adv & conj* when. **¿de ~ acá?, ¿desde ~?** since when?

cuant|ía *f* quantity; *(extensión)* extent. **~ioso** *a* abundant

cuanto *a* as much... as, as many... as. **—pron** as much as, as many as. **—adv** as much as. **~ más, mejor** the more the merrier. **en ~** as soon as. **en ~ a** as for. **por ~** since. **unos ~s** a few, some

cuánto *a (interrogativo)* how much?; *(interrogativo en plural)* how many?; *(exclamativo)* what a lot of! **—pron** how much?; *(en plural)* how many? **—adv** how much. **¿~ tiempo?** how long? **¡~ tiempo sin verte!** it's been a long time! **¿a ~?** how much? **¿a ~s estamos?** what's the date today? **un Sr. no sé ~s** Mr So-and-So

cuáquero *m* Quaker

cuarent|a *a & m* forty; *(cua-dragésimo)* fortieth. **~ena** *f* (about) forty; (*med*) quarantine. **∼ón** *a* about forty

cuaresma *f* Lent

cuarta *f* (*palmo*) span

cuartear *vt* quarter, divide into four; (*zigzaguear*) zigzag. **∼se** *vpr* crack

cuartel *m* (*mil*) barracks. **∼ gen-eral** headquarters. **no dar ∼** show no mercy

cuarteto *m* quartet

cuarto *a* fourth. —*m* quarter; (*habitación*) room. **∼ de baño** bathroom. **∼ de estar** living room. **∼ de hora** quarter of an hour. **estar sin un ∼** be broke. **menos ∼** (a) quarter to. **y ∼** (a) quarter past

cuarzo *m* quartz

cuatro *a & m* four. **∼cientos** *a & m* four hundred

Cuba *f* Cuba

cuba: **∼libre** *m* rum and Coke (P). **∼no** *a & m* Cuban

cúbico *a* cubic

cubículo *m* cubicle

cubierta *f* cover, covering; (*de la cama*) bedspread; (*techo*) roof; (*neumático*) tyre; (*naut*) deck. **∼o** *a* covered; (*cielo*) overcast. —*m* place setting, cutlery; (*comida*) meal. **a ∼o** under cover. **a ∼o de** safe from

cubis|mo *m* cubism. **∼ta** *a & m & f* cubist

cubil *m* den, lair. **∼ete** *m* bowl; (*molde*) mould; (*para echar los dados*) cup

cubo *m* bucket; (*en geometría y matemáticas*) cube

cubrecama *m* bedspread

cubrir *vt* (*pp* **cubierto**) cover; (*sonido*) drown; fill (*vacante*). **∼se** *vpr* cover o.s.; (*ponerse el sombrero*) put on one's hat; (*el cielo*) cloud over, become overcast

cucaracha *f* cockroach

cuclillas: **en ∼** *adv* squatting

cuclillo *m* cuckoo

cuco *a* shrewd; (*mono*) pretty, nice. —*m* cuckoo; (*insecto*) grub

cucurucho *m* cornet

cuchar|a *f* spoon. **∼ada** *f* spoon-ful. **∼adita** *f* teaspoonful. **∼illa** *f*, **∼ita** *f* teaspoon. **∼ón** *m* ladle

cuchiche|ar *vi* whisper. **∼o** *m* whispering

cuchill|a *f* large knife; (*de car-nicero*) cleaver; (*hoja de afeitar*) razor blade. **∼ada** *f* slash; (*her-ida*) knife wound. **∼o** *m* knife

cuchitril *m* pigsty; (*fig*) hovel

cuello *m* neck; (*de camisa*) collar. **cortar el ∼ a uno** cut s.o.'s throat

cuenc|a *f* hollow; (*del ojo*) (eye) socket; (*geog*) basin. **∼o** *m* hol-low; (*vasija*) bowl

cuenta *f* count; (*acción de contar*) counting; (*factura*) bill; (*en banco, relato*) account; (*asunto*) affair; (*de collar etc*) bead. **∼ co-rriente** current account, check-ing account (*Amer*). **ajustar las ∼s** settle accounts. **caer en la ∼ de que** realize that. **darse ∼ de** realize. **en resumidas ∼s** in short. **por mi ∼** for myself. **tener en ∼, tomar en ∼** bear in mind

cuentakilómetros *m invar* milometer

cuent|ista *m & f* story-writer; (*de mentiras*) fibber. **∼o** *m* story; (*mentira*) fib, tall story. —*vb* *véase* **contar**

cuerda *f* rope; (*más fina*) string; (*mus*) string. **∼ floja** tightrope. **dar ∼ a** wind up (*un reloj*)

cuerdo *a* (*persona*) sane; (*acción*) sensible

cuern|a *f* horns. **∼o** *m* horn

cuero *m* leather; (*piel*) skin; (*del grifo*) washer. **∼ cabelludo** scalp. **en ∼s** (**vivos**) stark naked

cuerpo *m* body

cuervo *m* crow

cuesta *f* slope, hill. ~ **abajo** downhill. ~ **arriba** uphill. **a** ~ **s** on one's back

cuesti|ón *f* matter; (*altercado*) quarrel; (*dificultad*) trouble. **~onario** *m* questionnaire

cueva *f* cave; (*sótano*) cellar

cuida|do *m* care; (*preocupación*) worry; (*asunto*) affair. ¡~**do!** (be) careful! **~doso** *a* careful. **~dosamente** *adv* carefully. ~r *vt* look after. —*vi*. ~r **de** look after. ~**rse** *vpr* look after o.s. ~**rse de** be careful to. **tener** ~**do** be careful

culata *f* (*de arma de fuego*) butt; (*auto*) cylinder head. ~**zo** *m* recoil

culebra *f* snake

culebrón *m* (*LAm*) soap opera

culinario *a* culinary

culmina|ción *f* culmination. ~r *vi* culminate

culo *m* (*fam*) bottom. **ir de** ~ **go** downhill

culpa *f* fault; (*jurid*) guilt. ~**bilidad** *f* guilt. ~**ble** *a* guilty. — *m* culprit. ~r *vt* blame (**de** for). **echar la** ~ blame. **por** ~ **de** because of. **tener la** ~ **de** be to blame for

cultiv|ar *vt* farm; grow (*plantas*); (*fig*) cultivate. ~**o** *m* farming; (*de plantas*) growing

cult|o *a* (*tierra etc*) cultivated; (*persona*) educated. —*m* cult; (*homenaje*) worship. ~**ura** *f* culture. ~**ural** *a* cultural

culturismo *m* body-building

cumpleaños *m invar* birthday

cumbre *f* summit; (*fig*) height

cumplido *a* perfect; (*grande*) large; (*cortés*) polite. —*m* compliment. ~r *a* reliable. **de** ~ courtesy. **por** ~ out of politeness

cumplim|entar *vt* carry out; (*saludar*) pay a courtesy call to;

(*felicitar*) congratulate. ~**iento** *m* carrying out, execution

cumplir *vt* carry out; observe (*ley*); serve (*condena*); reach (*años*); keep (*promesa*). —*vi* do one's duty. ~**se** *vpr* expire; (*realizarse*) be fulfilled. **hoy cumple 3 años** he's 3 (years old) today. **por** ~ as a mere formality

cumulativo *a* cumulative

cúmulo *m* pile, heap

cuna *f* cradle; (*fig, nacimiento*) birthplace

cundir *vi* spread; (*rendir*) go a long way

cuneta *f* gutter

cuña *f* wedge

cuñad|a *f* sister-in-law. ~**o** *m* brother-in-law

cuño *m* stamp. **de nuevo** ~ new

cuota *f* quota; (*de sociedad etc*) subscription, fees

cupe *vb véase* **caber**

cupé *m* coupé

Cupido *m* Cupid

cupo *m* cuota

cupón *m* coupon

cúpula *f* dome

cura *f* cure; (*tratamiento*) treatment. —*m* priest. ~**ble** *a* curable. ~**ción** *f* healing. ~**ndero** *m* faith-healer. ~r *vt* (*incl culin*) cure; dress (*herida*); (*tratar*) treat; (*fig*) remedy; tan (*pieles*). —*vi* (*persona*) get better; (*herida*) heal; (*fig*) be cured. ~**rse** *vpr* get better

curios|ear *vi* pry; (*mirar*) browse. ~**idad** *f* curiosity; (*limpieza*) cleanliness. ~**o** *a* curious; (*raro*) odd, unusual; (*limpio*) clean

curriculum vitae *m* curriculum vitae

cursar *vt* send; (*estudiar*) study

cursi *a* pretentious, showy. —*m* affected person

cursillo *m* short course

cursiva *f* italics

curso m course; (*univ etc*) year.
en ~ under way; (*año etc*)
current
curtir vt tan; (*fig*) harden. ~**se**
vpr become tanned; (*fig*) become
hardened
curv|a f curve; (*de carretera*)
bend. ~**o** a curved
cúspide f peak
custodi|a f care, safe-keeping.
~**ar** vt take care of. ~**o** a & m
guardian
cutáneo a skin. **enfermedad** f
cutánea skin disease
cutícula f cuticle
cutis m skin, complexion
cuyo pron (*de persona*) whose, of
whom; (*de cosa*) whose, of
which. **en** ~ **caso** in which case

CH

chabacano a common; (*chiste
etc*) vulgar. —m (*Mex, albaricoque*) apricot
chabola f shack. ~**s** fpl shanty
town
chacal m jackal
chacota f fun. **echar a** ~ make
fun of
chacra f (*LAm*) farm
cháchara f chatter
chacharear vt (*Mex*) sell. —vi
chatter
chafar vt crush. **quedar
chafado** be nonplussed
chal m shawl
chalado a (*fam*) crazy
chalé m house (with a garden),
villa
chaleco m waistcoat, vest
(*Amer*). ~ **salvavidas** life-
jacket
chalequear vt (*Arg, Mex*) trick
chalet m (*pl* **chalets**) house
(with a garden), villa
chalón m (*LAm*) shawl

chalote m shallot
chalupa f boat
chamac|o f (*esp Mex*) girl. ~**o** m
(*esp Mex*) boy
chamagoso a (*Mex*) filthy
chamarr|a f sheepskin jacket.
~**o** m (*LAm*) coarse blanket
chamba f (*fam*) fluke; (*Mex,
empleo*) job. **por** ~ by fluke
champán m, **champaña** m
champagne
champiñón m mushroom
champú m (*pl* **champúes** o
champús) shampoo
chamuscar [7] vt scorch; (*Mex,
vender*) sell cheaply
chance m (*esp LAm*) chance
chanclo m clog; (*de caucho*)
rubber overshoe
chancho m (*LAm*) pig
chanchullo m swindle, fiddle
(*fam*)
chandal m tracksuit
chanquete m whitebait
chantaj|e m blackmail. ~**ista** m
& f blackmailer
chanza f joke
chapa f plate, sheet; (*de madera*)
plywood; (*de botella*) metal top.
~**do** a plated. ~**do a la antigua**
old-fashioned. ~**do de oro**
gold-plated
chaparrón m downpour. **llover
a chaparrones** pour (down),
rain cats and dogs
chapotear vi splash
chapuc|ear vt botch; (*Mex,
engañar*) deceive. ~**ro** a (*persona*) careless; (*cosas*)
shoddy. —m careless worker
chapurrar vt, **chapurrear** vt
speak badly, speak a little; mix
(*licores*)
chapuza f botched job, mess; (*de
poca importancia*) odd job
chaqueta f jacket. **cambiar la** ~
change sides
chaquetero m turncoat
charada f charade

charc|a f pond, pool. **~o** m puddle, pool. **cruzar el ~o** cross the water; (ir a América) cross the Atlantic

charla f chat; (conferencia) talk. **~dor** a talkative. **~r** vi (fam) chat

charlatán a talkative. —m chatterbox; (curandero) charlatan

charol m varnish; (cuero) patent leather

chárter a charter

chascar [7] vt crack ⟨látigo⟩; click ⟨lengua⟩; snap ⟨dedos⟩. —vi ⟨látigo⟩ crack; ⟨con la lengua⟩ click one's tongue; ⟨los dedos⟩ snap

chascarrillo m joke, funny story

chasco m disappointment; (broma) joke; (engaño) trick

chasis m (auto) chassis

chasqu|ear vt crack ⟨látigo⟩; click ⟨lengua⟩; snap ⟨dedos⟩. —vi ⟨látigo⟩ crack; ⟨con la lengua⟩ click one's tongue; ⟨los dedos⟩ snap. **~ido** m crack; ⟨de la lengua⟩ click; ⟨de los dedos⟩ snap

chatarra f scrap iron; (fig) scrap

chato a ⟨nariz⟩ snub; ⟨persona⟩ snub-nosed; ⟨objetos⟩ flat. —m wine glass; ⟨niño, mujer, fam⟩ dear, darling; ⟨hombre, fam⟩ mate (fam)

chaval m (fam) boy, lad. **~a** f girl, lass

che int (Arg) listen!, hey!

checo a & m Czech. **la república ~** f **Checa** the Czech Republic

checoslovaco a & m (history) Czechoslovak

Checoslovaquia f (history) Czechoslovakia

chelín m shilling

chelo a (Mex, rubio) fair

cheque m cheque. **~ de viaje** traveller's cheque. **~ra** f cheque-book

chica f girl; (criada) maid, servant

chicano a & m Chicano, Mexican-American

chicle m chewing-gum

chico a (fam) small. —m boy. **~s** mpl children

chicoleo m compliment

chicoria f chicory

chicharra f cicada; (fig) chatterbox

chicharrón m (de cerdo) crackling; (fig) sunburnt person

chichón m bump, lump

chifla|do a (fam) crazy, daft. **~r** vt (fam) drive crazy. **~rse** upr be mad (por about). **le chifla el chocolate** he's mad about chocolate. **le tiene chiflado esa chica** he's crazy about that girl

Chile m Chile

chile m chilli

chileno a & m Chilean

chill|ar vi scream, shriek; ⟨gato⟩ howl; ⟨ratón⟩ squeak; ⟨cerdo⟩ squeal. **~ido** m scream, screech; ⟨de gato etc⟩ howl. **~ón** a noisy; ⟨colores⟩ loud; ⟨sonido⟩ shrill

chimenea f chimney; (hogar) fireplace

chimpancé m chimpanzee

China f China

chinch|ar vt (fam) annoy, pester. **~e** m drawing-pin (Brit), thumbtack (Amer); (insecto) bedbug; (fig) nuisance. **~eta** f drawing-pin (Brit), thumbtack (Amer)

chinela f slipper

chino a & m Chinese

Chipre m Cyprus

chipriota a & m & f Cypriot

chiquillo a childish. —m child, kid (fam)

chiquito a small, tiny. —m child, kid (fam)

chiribita f spark. **estar que echa ~s** be furious

chirimoya f custard apple

chiripa f fluke. **por ~** by fluke
chirivía f parsnip
chirri|ar vi creak; ⟨pájaro⟩ chirp. **~do** m creaking; ⟨al freír⟩ sizzling; ⟨de pájaros⟩ chirping
chis int sh!, hush!; ⟨para llamar a uno, fam⟩ hey!, psst!
chism|e m gadget, thingumajig ⟨fam⟩; ⟨chismorreo⟩ piece of gossip. **~es** mpl things, bits and pieces. **~orreo** m gossip. **~oso** a gossipy. **—m** gossip
chispa f spark; ⟨gota⟩ drop; ⟨gracia⟩ wit; ⟨fig⟩ sparkle. **estar que echa ~(s)** be furious
chispea|nte a sparkling. **~r** vi spark; ⟨lloviznar⟩ drizzle; ⟨fig⟩ sparkle
chisporrotear vt throw out sparks; ⟨fuego⟩ crackle; ⟨aceite⟩ sizzle
chistar vi speak. **sin ~** without saying a word
chiste m joke, funny story. **hacer ~ de** make fun of. **tener ~** be funny
chistera f ⟨fam⟩ top hat, topper ⟨fam⟩
chistoso a funny
chiva|r vi inform ⟨policía⟩; ⟨niño⟩ tell. **~tazo** m tip-off. **~to** m informer; ⟨niño⟩ telltale
chivo m kid, young goat
choca|nte a surprising; ⟨persona⟩ odd. **~r** [7] vt clink ⟨vasos⟩; shake ⟨la mano⟩. **—vi** collide, hit. **~r con, ~r contra** crash into. **lo ~nte es que** the surprising thing is that
chocolate m chocolate. **tableta f de ~** bar of chocolate
choch|ear vi be senile. **~o a** senile; ⟨fig⟩ soft
chófer m chauffeur; ⟨conductor⟩ driver
cholo a & m ⟨LAm⟩ half-breed
chopo m poplar
choque m collision; ⟨fig⟩ clash; ⟨eléctrico⟩ shock; ⟨auto, rail etc⟩ crash, accident; ⟨sacudida⟩ jolt

chorizo m salami
chorr|ear vi gush forth; ⟨fig⟩ be dripping. **—m** jet, stream; ⟨caudal pequeño⟩ trickle; ⟨fig⟩ stream. **a ~os** drip in abundance. **hablar a ~os** jabber
chovinis|mo m chauvinism. **~ta** a chauvinistic. **—m & f** chauvinist
choza f hut
chubas|co m squall, heavy shower; ⟨fig⟩ bad patch. **~quero** m raincoat, anorak
chuchería f trinket; ⟨culin⟩ sweet
chufa f tiger nut
chuleta f chop
chulo a insolent; ⟨vistoso⟩ showy. **—m** ruffian; ⟨rufián⟩ pimp
chumbo m prickly pear; ⟨fam⟩ bump. **higo m ~** prickly pear
chup|ada f suck; ⟨al cigarro etc⟩ puff. **~ado a** skinny; ⟨fácil, fam⟩ very easy. **~ar** vt suck, lick; puff at ⟨cigarro etc⟩; ⟨absorber⟩ absorb. **~arse** vpr lose weight. **~ete** m dummy ⟨Brit⟩, pacifier ⟨Amer⟩
churro m fritter; ⟨fam⟩ mess. **me salió un ~** I made a mess of it
chusco a funny
chusma f riff-raff
chutar vi shoot. **¡va que chuta!** it's going well!

D

dactilógrafo m typist
dado m dice. **~ a** given; ⟨hora⟩ gone. **~ que** since, given that
dalia f dahlia
daltoniano a colour-blind
dama f lady; ⟨en la corte⟩ lady-in-waiting. **~s** fpl draughts ⟨Brit⟩, checkers ⟨Amer⟩
damasco m damask

danés *a* Danish. —*m* Dane; *(idioma)* Danish.

danza *f* dance; *(acción)* dancing; *(enredo)* affair. ~**r** [10] *vt/i* dance

dañ|ado *a* damaged. ~**ar** *vt* damage; harm *(persona)*. ~**ino** *a* harmful. ~**o** *m* damage; *(a una persona)* harm. ~**oso** *a* harmful. ~**os y perjuicios** damages. **hacer** ~**o a** harm; hurt *(persona)*. **hacerse** ~**o** hurt o.s.

dar [26] *vt* give; *(producir)* yield; strike *(la hora)*. —*vi* give. **da igual** it doesn't matter. **¡dale!** go on! **da lo mismo** it doesn't matter. ~ **con** meet *(persona)*; find *(cosa)*; ~ **de cabeza** fall flat on one's face. ~ **por** assume; (+ *infinitivo*) decide. ~**se** *vpr* give o.s. up; *(suceder)* happen. **dárselas de** make o.s. out to be. ~**se por** consider o.s. **¿qué más da?** it doesn't matter!

dardo *m* dart

dársena *f* dock

datar *vt* date. —*vi.* ~ **de** date from

dátil *m* date

dato *m* fact. ~**s** *mpl* data, information

de *prep* of; *(procedencia)* from; *(suposición)* if. ~ **día** by day. ~ **dos en dos** two by two. ~ **haberlo sabido** if I (you, he etc) had known. ~ **niño** as a child. **el libro** ~ **mi amigo** my friend's book. **las 2** ~ **la madrugada** 2 (o'clock) in the morning. **un puente** ~ **hierro** an iron bridge. **soy** ~ **Loughborough** I'm from Loughborough

deambular *vi* stroll

debajo *adv* underneath. ~ **de** underneath, under. **el de** ~ the one underneath. **por** ~ underneath. **por** ~ **de** below

debat|e *m* debate. ~**ir** *vt* debate

deber *vt* owe. —*vi* have to, must. —*m* duty. ~**es** *mpl* homework. ~**se** *vpr.* ~**se a** be due to. **debo marcharme** I must go, I have to go

debido *a* due; *(correcto)* proper. ~ **a** due to. **como es** ~ as is proper. **con el respeto** ~ with due respect

débil *a* weak; *(ruido)* faint; *(luz)* dim

debili|dad *f* weakness. ~**tar** *vt* weaken. ~**tarse** *vpr* weaken, get weak

débito *m* debit; *(deuda)* debt

debutar *vi* make one's debut

década *f* decade

deca|dencia *f* decline. ~**dente** *a* decadent. ~**er** [29] *vi* decline; *(debilitarse)* weaken. ~**ído** *a* depressed. ~**imiento** *m* decline, weakening

decano *m* dean; *(miembro más antiguo)* senior member

decantar *vt* decant *(vino etc)*

decapitar *vt* behead

decena *f* ten; *(aproximadamente)* about ten

decencia *f* decency, honesty

decenio *m* decade

decente *a* *(persona)* respectable, honest; *(cosas)* modest; *(limpio)* clean, tidy

decepción *f* disappointment. ~**onar** *vt* disappoint

decibelio *m* decibel

decidi|do *a* decided; *(persona)* determined, resolute. ~**r** *vt* decide; settle *(cuestión etc)*. —*vi* decide. ~**rse** *vpr* make up one's mind

decimal *a* & *m* decimal

décimo *a* & *m* tenth. —*m* *(de lotería)* tenth part of a lottery ticket

decimo: ~**ctavo** *a* & *m* eighteenth. ~**cuarto** *a* & *m* fourteenth. ~**nono** *a* & *m,* ~**noveno** *a* & *m* nineteenth. ~**quinto** *a* & *m* fifteenth. ~**séptimo** *a* & *m* seventeenth. **~sexto** *a & m* six-teenth. **~tercero** *a & m*, **~ter-cio** *a & m* thirteenth.

decir [46] *vt* say; *(contar)* tell. **—m** saying. **~se** *upr* be said. **~ que no** say no. **~ que sí** say yes. **dicho de otro modo** in other words. **dicho y hecho** no sooner said than done. **¿dígame!** can I help you? **¡dígame!** *(al teléfono)* hello **digamos** let's say. **es ~** that is to say. **mejor dicho** rather. **¡no me digas!** you don't say!, really! **por así ~, por ~lo así** so to speak, as it were. **querer ~** mean. **se dice que** it is said that, they say that

decisión *f* decision. **~vo** *a* decisive

declamar *vt* declaim

declaración *f* statement. **~ción de renta** income tax return. **~r** *vt/i* declare. **~rse** *upr* declare o.s.; *(epidemia etc)* break out

declinación *f* *(gram)* declension. **~r** *vt/i* decline; *(salud)* deteriorate

declive *m* slope; *(fig)* decline. **en ~** sloping

decolorar *vt* discolour, fade. **~se** *upr* become discoloured, fade

decoración *f* decoration. **~do** *m* *(en el teatro)* set. **~dor** *m* decorator. **~r** *vt* decorate. **~tivo** *a* decorative

decoro *m* decorum; *(respeto)* respect. **~so** *a* proper; *(modesto)* modest; *(profesión)* honourable

decrecer [11] *vi* decrease, diminish; *(aguas)* subside

decrépito *a* decrepit

decretar *vt* decree. **~o** *m* decree

dedal *m* thimble

dedicación *f* dedication. **~r** [7] *vt* dedicate; devote *(tiempo)*. **~toria** *f* dedication, inscription

dedil *m* finger-stall. **~illo** *m*. **al ~illo** at one's fingertips. **~o** *m* finger; *(del pie)* toe. **~o anular** ring finger. **~o corazón** middle finger. **~o gordo** thumb. **~o índice** index finger. **~o meñique** little finger. **~o pulgar** thumb

deducción *f* deduction. **~ir** [47] *vt* deduce; *(descontar)* deduct

defecto *m* fault, defect. **~uoso** *a* defective

defender [1] *vt* defend. **~sa** *f* defence. **~sivo** *a* defensive. **~sor** *m* defender. **abogado** *m* **~sor** defence counsel

deferencia *f* deference. **~te** *a* deferential

deficiencia *f* deficiency. **~cia mental** mental handicap. **~te** *a* deficient; *(imperfecto)* defective. **~te mental** mentally handicapped

déficit *m invar* deficit

definición *f* definition. **~do** *a* defined. **~r** *vt* define; *(aclarar)* clarify. **~tivo** *a* definitive. **en ~tiva** *(en resumen)* in short

deflación *f* deflation

deformación *f* deformation; *(TV etc)* distortion. **~ar** *vt* deform; *(TV etc)* distort. **~arse** *upr* go out of shape. **~e** *a* deformed; *(feo)* ugly

defraudar *vt* cheat; *(decepcionar)* disappoint; evade *(impuestos etc)*

defunción *f* death

degeneración *f* degeneration; *(moral)* degeneracy. **~do** *a* degenerate. **~r** *vi* degenerate

deglutir *vt/i* swallow

degollar [16] *vt* cut s.o.'s throat; *(fig, arruinar)* ruin

degradar *vt* degrade. **~se** *upr* lower o.s.

degustación *f* tasting. **~r** *vt* taste

dehesa *f* pasture

dei|dad f deity. **∼ficar** [7] vt deify

deja|ción f surrender. **∼dez** f abandon; (pereza) laziness. **∼do** a negligent. **∼r** vt leave; (abandonar) abandon; (prestar) lend; (permitir) let. **∼r aparte**, **∼r a un lado** leave aside. **∼r de** stop. **no ∼r de** not fail to

dejo m aftertaste; (tonillo) accent

del = **de** + **el**

delantal m apron

delante adv in front; (enfrente) opposite. **∼ de** in front of. **de ∼** front

delanter|a f front; (de teatro etc) front row; (ventaja) advantage. **coger la ∼a** get ahead. **∼o** a front. **∼m** forward. **llevar la ∼a** be ahead

delat|ar vt denounce. **∼or** m informer

delega|ción f delegation; (sucursal) branch. **∼do** m delegate; (com) agent, representative. **∼r** [12] vt delegate

deleit|ar vt delight. **∼e** m delight

deletéreo a deleterious

deletre|ar vt spell (out). **∼o** m spelling

deleznable a brittle, crumbly; (argumento etc) weak

delfín m dolphin

delgad|ez f thinness. **∼o** a thin; (esbelto) slim. **∼ucho** a skinny

delibera|ción f deliberation. **∼r** vt discuss, decide. **∼vi** deliberate

delicad|eza f delicacy; (fragilidad) frailty; (tacto) tact. **∼o** a delicate; (sensible) sensitive; (discreto) tactful, discreet. **falta de ∼eza** tactlessness

delici|a f delight. **∼oso** a delightful; (sabor etc) delicious; (gracioso, fam) funny

delimitar vt delimit

delincuen|cia f delinquency. **∼te** a & m delinquent

delinea|nte m draughtsman. **∼r** vt outline; (dibujar) draw

delinquir [8] vi commit an offence

delir|ante a delirious. **∼ar** vi be delirious; (fig) talk nonsense. **∼io** m delirium; (fig) frenzy

delito m crime, offence

delta f delta

demacrado a emaciated

demagogo m demagogue

demanda f. **en ∼ de** asking for; (en busca de) in search of. **∼nte** m & f (jurid) plaintiff. **∼r** vt (jurid) bring an action against

demarca|ción f demarcation. **∼r** [7] vt demarcate

demás a rest of the other. **—pron** rest, others. **lo ∼** the rest. **por ∼** useless; (muy) very. **por lo ∼** otherwise

demasía f excess; (abuso) outrage; (atrevimiento) insolence. **en ∼** too much

demasiado a too much; (en plural) too many. **—adv** too much; (con adjetivo) too

demen|cia f madness. **∼te** a demented, mad

democra|cia f democracy. **∼ócrata** m & f democrat. **∼ocrático** a democratic

demol|er [2] vt demolish. **∼ición** f demolition

demonio m devil, demon. **¡∼s!** hell! **¿cómo ∼s?** how the hell? **¡qué ∼s!** what the hell!

demora f delay. **∼r** vt delay. **—vi** stay on. **∼rse** upr be a long time

demostra|ción f demonstration, show. **∼r** [2] vt demonstrate; (mostrar) show; (probar) prove. **∼tivo** a demonstrative

denegar [1 & 12] vt refuse

dengoso a affected, finicky. **∼ue** m affectation

denigrar vt denigrate

denomina|ción f denomination. **∼do** a called. **∼dor** m denominator. **∼r** vt name

denotar *vt* denote

dens|idad *f* density. **~o** *a* dense, thick

denta|dura *f* teeth. **~dura post-iza** denture, false teeth. **~l** *a* dental

dentera *f*. **dar ~ a uno** set s.o.'s teeth on edge; *(dar envidia)* make s.o. green with envy

dentífrico *m* toothpaste

dentista *m & f* dentist

dentro *adv* inside; *(de un edificio)* indoors. **~ de** in. **~ de poco** soon. **por ~** inside

denuncia *f* report; *(acusación)* accusation. **~r** *vt* report (a crime); *(periódico etc)* denounce; *(indicar)* indicate

departamento *m* department; *(Arg, piso)* flat *(Brit)*, apartment *(Amer)*

dependencia *f* dependence; *(sección)* section; *(sucursal)* branch

depender *vi* depend *(de on)*

dependient|a *f* shop assistant. **~e** *a* dependent *(de on)*. **—m** employee; *(de oficina)* clerk; *(de tienda)* shop assistant

depila|ción *f* depilation. **~r** *vt* depilate. **~torio** *a* depilatory

deplora|ble *a* deplorable. **~r** *vt* deplore, regret

deponer [34] *vt* remove from office. **—vi** give evidence

deporta|ción *f* deportation. **~r** *vt* deport

deporte *m* sport. **~ista** *m* sportsman. **—f** sportswoman. **~ivo** *a* sports. **—m** sports car. **hacer ~e** take part in sports

deposición *f* deposition; *(de un empleo)* removal from office

dep|ositador *m* depositor. **~os-itante** *m & f* depositor. **~ositar** *vt* deposit; *(poner)* put, place. **~ósito** *m* deposit; *(conjunto de cosas)* store; *(almacén)* ware-house; *(mil)* depot; *(de líquidos)* tank

deprava|ción *f* depravity. **~do** *a* depraved. **~r** *vt* deprave. **~rse** *vpr* become depraved

deprecia|ción *f* depreciation. **~r** *vt* depreciate. **~rse** *vpr* depreciate

depresión *f* depression

deprim|ente *a* depressing. **~ido** *a* depressed. **~ir** *vt* depress. **~irse** *vpr* get depressed

depura|ción *f* purification; *(pol)* purging. **~r** *vt* purify; *(pol)* purge

derech|a *f* *(mano)* right hand; *(lado)* right. **~ista** *a* right-wing. **—m & f** right-winger. **~o** *a* right; *(vertical)* upright; *(recto)* straight. **—adv** straight. **—m** right; *(ley)* law; *(lado)* right side. **~os** *mpl* dues. **~os de autor** royalties. **a la ~a** on the right; *(hacia el lado derecho)* to the right. **todo ~o** straight on

deriva *f* drift. **a la ~** drifting, adrift

deriva|ción *f* derivation; *(cam-bio)* diversion. **~do** *a* derived. **—m** derivative, by-product. **~r** *vt* derive; *(cambiar la dirección de)* divert. **—vi. ~r de** derive from, be derived from. **~rse** *vpr* be derived

derram|amiento *m* spilling. **~amiento de sangre** blood-shed. **~ar** *vt* spill *(verter)* pour; shed *(lágrimas)*. **~arse** *vpr* spill. **~e** *m* spilling; *(pérdida)* leakage; *(cantidad perdida)* spillage; *(med)* discharge; *(med, de sangre)* haemorrhage

derretir [5] *vt* melt. **~se** *vpr* melt; *(enamorarse)* fall in love *(por* with*)*

derriba|do *a* fallen down. **~r** *vt* knock down; bring down, over-throw *(gobierno etc)*. **~rse** *vpr* fall down

derrocar [7] *vt* bring down, over-throw *(gobierno etc)*

derroch|ar *vt* squander. **∼e** *m* waste

derrot|a *f* defeat; *(rumbo)* course. **∼ar** *vt* defeat. **∼ado** *a* defeated; *(vestido)* shabby. **∼ero** *m* course

derrumba|miento *m* collapse. **∼r** *vt (derribar)* knock down. **∼rse** *vpr* collapse

desaborido *a* tasteless; *(persona)* dull

desabotonar *vt* unbutton, undo. —*vi* bloom. **∼se** *vpr* come undone

desabrido *a* tasteless; *(tiempo)* unpleasant; *(persona)* surly

desabrochar *vt* undo. **∼se** *vpr* come undone

desacat|ar *vt* have no respect for. **∼o** *m* disrespect

desac|ertado *a* ill-advised; *(erróneo)* wrong. **∼ertar** [1] *vt* be wrong. **∼ierto** *m* mistake

desaconseja|ble *a* inadvisable. **∼do** *a* unwise, ill-advised. **∼r** *vt* advise against, dissuade

desacorde *a* discordant

desacostumbra|do *a* unusual. **∼r** *vt* give up

desacreditar *vt* discredit

desactivar *vt* defuse

desacuerdo *m* disagreement

desafiar [20] *vt* challenge; *(afrontar)* defy

desafilado *a* blunt

desafina|do *a* out of tune. **∼r** *vi* be out of tune. **∼rse** *vpr* go out of tune

desafío *m* challenge; *(combate)* duel

desaforado *a (comportamiento)* outrageous; *(desmedido)* excessive; *(sonido)* loud; *(enorme)* huge

desafortunad|amente *adv* unfortunately. **∼o** *a* unfortunate

desagrada|ble *a* unpleasant. **∼r** *vt* displease. —*vi* be unpleasant.

me ∼ el sabor I don't like the taste

desagradecido *a* ungrateful

desagrado *m* displeasure. **con ∼** unwillingly

desagravi|ar *vt* make amends to. **∼o** *m* amends; *(expiación)* atonement

desagregar [12] *vt* break up. **∼se** *vpr* disintegrate

desagüe *m* drain; *(acción)* drainage. **tubo** *m* **de ∼** drain-pipe

desaguisado *a* illegal. —*m* offence; *(fam)* disaster

desahog|ado *a* roomy; *(adinerado)* well-off; *(fig, descarado, fam)* impudent. **∼ar** [12] *vt* relieve; vent *(ira)*. **∼arse** *vpr (desfogarse)* let off steam. **∼o** *m* comfort; *(alivio)* relief

desahuci|ar *vt* deprive of hope; give up hope for *(enfermo)*; evict *(inquilino)*. **∼o** *m* eviction

desair|ado *a* humiliating; *(persona)* humiliated, spurned. **∼ar** *vt* snub *(persona)*; disregard *(cosa)*. **∼e** *m* rebuff

desajuste *m* maladjustment; *(avería)* breakdown

desal|entador *a* disheartening. **∼entar** [1] *vt (fig)* discourage. **∼iento** *m* discouragement

desaliño *m* untidiness, scruffiness

desalmado *a* wicked

desalojar *vt* eject *(persona)*; evacuate *(sitio)*. —*vi* move (house)

desampar|ado *a* helpless; *(abandonado)* abandoned. **∼ar** *vt* abandon. **∼o** *m* helplessness; *(abandono)* abandonment

desangelado *a* insipid, dull

desangrar *vt* bleed. **∼se** *vpr* bleed

desanima|do *a* down-hearted. **∼r** *vt* discourage. **∼rse** *vpr* lose heart

desánimo *m* discouragement

desanudar *vt* untie

desapacible *a* unpleasant; ⟨sonido⟩ harsh

desapar|ecer [11] *vi* disappear; ⟨efecto⟩ wear off. **~ecido** *a* disappeared. *—m* missing person. **~ecidos** *mpl* missing. **~ición** *f* disappearance

desapasionado *a* dispassionate

desapego *m* indifference

desapercebido *a* unnoticed

desaplicado *a* lazy

desaprensi|ón *f* unscrupulousness. **~vo** *a* unscrupulous

desaproba|ción *f* disapproval. **~r** [2] *vt* disapprove of; ⟨rechazar⟩ reject.

desaprovecha|do *a* wasted; ⟨alumno⟩ lazy. **~r** *vt* waste

desarm|ar *vt* disarm; ⟨desmontar⟩ take to pieces. **~e** *m* disarmament

desarraig|ado *a* rootless. **~ar** [12] *vt* uproot; ⟨fig, erradicar⟩ wipe out. **~o** *m* uprooting; ⟨fig⟩ eradication

desarregl|ado *a* untidy; ⟨desordenado⟩ disorderly. **~ar** *vt* mess up; ⟨deshacer el orden⟩ make untidy. **~o** *m* disorder; ⟨de persona⟩ untidiness

desarroll|ado *a* (well-) developed. **~ar** *vt* develop; ⟨desenrollar⟩ unroll, unfold. **~arse** *vpr* ⟨incl foto⟩ develop; ⟨desenrollarse⟩ unroll; ⟨suceso⟩ take place. **~o** *m* development

desarrugar [12] *vt* smooth out

desarticular *vt* dislocate ⟨hueso⟩; ⟨fig⟩ break up

desaseado *a* dirty; ⟨desordenado⟩ untidy

desasirse [45] *vpr* let go ⟨de of⟩

desasos|egar [1 & 12] *vt* disturb. **~egarse** *vpr* get uneasy. **~iego** *m* anxiety; ⟨intranquilidad⟩ restlessness

desastr|ado *a* scruffy. **~e** *m* disaster. **~oso** *a* disastrous

desata|do *a* untied; ⟨fig⟩ wild. **~r** *vt* untie; ⟨fig, soltar⟩ unleash. **~rse** *vpr* come undone

desatascar [7] *vt* pull out of the mud; unblock ⟨tubo etc⟩

desaten|ción *f* inattention; ⟨descortesía⟩ discourtesy. **~der** [1] *vt* not pay attention to; neglect ⟨deber etc⟩. **~to** *a* inattentive; ⟨descortés⟩ discourteous

desatin|ado *a* silly. **~o** *m* silliness; ⟨error⟩ mistake

desatornillar *vt* unscrew

desatracar [7] *vt/i* cast off

desautorizar [10] *vt* declare unauthorized; ⟨desmentir⟩ deny

desavenencia *f* disagreement

desayun|ar *vt* have for breakfast. *—vi* have breakfast. **~o** *m* breakfast

desazón *m* ⟨fig⟩ anxiety

desbandarse *vpr* ⟨mil⟩ disband; ⟨dispersarse⟩ disperse

desbarajust|ar *vt* throw into confusion. **~e** *m* confusion

desbaratar *vt* spoil

desbloquear *vt* unfreeze

desboca|do *a* ⟨vasija etc⟩ chipped; ⟨caballo⟩ runaway; ⟨persona⟩ foul-mouthed

desborda|nte *a* overflowing. **~r** *vt* go beyond; ⟨exceder⟩ exceed. *—vi* overflow. **~rse** *vpr* overflow

descabalgar [12] *vi* dismount

descabellado *a* crazy

descabezar [10] *vt* behead

descafeinado *a* decaffeinated. *—m* decaffeinated coffee

descalabr|ar *vt* injure in the head; ⟨fig⟩ damage. **~o** *m* disaster

descalificar [7] *vt* disqualify; ⟨desacreditar⟩ discredit

descalz|ar [10] *vt* take off ⟨zapato⟩. **~o** *a* barefoot

descaminar *vt* misdirect; ⟨fig⟩ lead astray

descamisado a shirtless; (fig) shabby

descampado a open. —m open ground

descans\|ado a rested; ⟨trabajo⟩ easy. ∼**apiés** m footrest. ∼**ar** vt/i rest. ∼**illo** m landing. ∼o m rest; (descansillo) landing; (en deportes) half-time; (en el teatro etc) interval

descapotable a convertible

descarado a insolent, cheeky; (sin vergüenza) shameless

descarg\|a f unloading; (mil, elec) discharge. ∼**ar** [12] vt unload; (mil, elec) discharge, shock; deal (golpe etc). —vi flow into. ∼o m unloading; (recibo) receipt; (jurid) evidence

descarnado a scrawny, lean; (fig) bare

descaro m insolence, cheek; (cinismo) nerve, effrontery

descarriar [20] vt misdirect; (fig) lead astray. ∼**se** vpr go the wrong way; ⟨res⟩ stray; (fig) go astray

descarrila\|miento m derailment. ∼r vi be derailed. ∼**se** vpr be derailed

descartar vt discard; (rechazar) reject. ∼**se** vpr discard

descascarar vt shell

descen\|dencia f descent; (personas) descendants. ∼**dente** a descending. ∼**der** [1] vt lower, get down; go down ⟨escalera etc⟩. —vi go down; (provenir) be descended (de from). ∼**diente** m & f descendent. ∼**so** m descent; (de temperatura, fiebre etc) fall, drop

descentralizar [10] vt decentralize

descifrar vt decipher; decode ⟨clave⟩

descolgar [2 & 12] vt take down; pick up ⟨el teléfono⟩. ∼**se** vpr let o.s. down; (fig, fam) turn up

descolorar vt discolour, fade

descolori\|do a discoloured, faded; ⟨persona⟩ pale. ∼r vt discolour, fade

descomedido a rude; (excesivo) excessive, extreme

descomp\|ás m disproportion. ∼**asado** a disproportionate

descomp\|oner [34] vt break down; decompose ⟨substancia⟩; distort ⟨rasgos⟩; (estropear) break; (desarreglar) disturb, spoil. ∼**onerse** vpr decompose; ⟨persona⟩ lose one's temper. ∼**osición** f decomposition; (med) diarrhoea. ∼**ostura** f breaking; (de un motor) breakdown; (desorden) disorder. ∼**uesto** a broken; (podrido) decomposed; (encolerizado) angry. **estar** ∼**uesto** have diarrhoea

descomunal a (fam) enormous

descon\|certante a disconcerting. ∼**ertar** [1] vt disconcert; (dejar perplejo) puzzle. ∼**ertarse** vpr be put out, be disconcerted; ⟨mecanismo⟩ break down. ∼**ierto** m confusion

desconectar vt disconnect

desconfia\|do a distrustful. ∼**nza** f distrust, suspicion. ∼r [20] vi. ∼r de not trust; (no creer) doubt

descongelar vt defrost; (com) unfreeze

desconoc\|er [11] vt not know, not recognize. ∼**ido** a unknown; (cambiado) unrecognizable. —m stranger. ∼**imiento** m ignorance

desconsidera\|ción f lack of consideration. ∼**do** a inconsiderate

descons\|olado a distressed. ∼**olar** [2] vt distress. ∼**olarse** vpr despair. ∼**uelo** m distress; (tristeza) sadness

descontado a. **dar por** ∼**do** take for granted. **por** ∼**do** of course. ∼r [2] vt discount

descontent|adizo a hard to please. **~ar** vt displease. **~o** a unhappy (**de** about), discontented (**de** with). **—m** discontent

descontrolado a uncontrolled

descorazonar vt discourage. **~se** vpr lose heart

descorchar vt uncork

descorrer vt draw ⟨cortina⟩. **~ el cerrojo** unbolt the door

descort|és a rude, discourteous. **~esía** f rudeness

descos|er vt unpick. **~erse** vpr come undone. **~ido** a unstitched; (fig) disjointed. **como un ~ido** a lot

descoyuntar vt dislocate

descrédito m disrepute. **ir en ~ de** damage the reputation of

descreído a unbelieving

descremar vt skim

descri|bir [pp **descrito**] vt describe. **~pción** f description. **~ptivo** a descriptive

descuartizar [10] vt cut up

descubierto a disvovered; (no cubierto) uncovered; (expuesto) exposed; (cielo) clear; (sin sombrero) bareheaded. **—m** overdraft; (déficit) deficit. **poner al ~** expose

descubri|miento m discovery. **~r** [pp **descubierto**] vt discover; (quitar lo que cubre) uncover; (revelar) reveal; unveil ⟨estatua⟩. **~rse** vpr be discovered; (cielo) clear; (quitarse el sombrero) take off one's hat

descuento m discount

descuid|ado a careless; (aspecto etc) untidy; (desprevenido) unprepared. **~ar** vt neglect. **—vi** not worry. **~arse** vpr be careless; (no preocuparse) not worry. **¡~a!** don't worry! **~o** m carelessness; (negligencia) negligence. **al ~o** nonchalantly.

estar ~ado not worry, rest assured

desde prep (lugar etc) from; (tiempo) since, from. **~ hace poco** for a short time. **~ hace un mes** for a month. **~ luego** of course. **~ Madrid hasta Barcelona** from Madrid to Barcelona. **~ niño** since childhood

desdecir [46, pero imperativo **desdice**, futuro y condicional regulares] vi. **~ de** be unworthy of; (no armonizar) not match. **~se** vpr. **~ de** take back ⟨palabras etc⟩; go back on ⟨promesa⟩

desd|én m scorn. **~eñable** a contemptible. **~eñar** vt scorn. **~eñoso** a scornful

desdicha f misfortune. **~do** a unfortunate. **por ~** unfortunately

desdoblar vt straighten; (desplegar) unfold

desea|ble a desirable. **~r** vt want; wish ⟨algo a uno⟩. **de ~r** desirable. **le deseo un buen viaje** I hope you have a good journey. **¿qué desea Vd?** can I help you?

desecar [7] vt dry up

desech|ar vt throw out. **~o** m rubbish

desembalar vt unpack

desembarazar [10] vt clear. **~se** vpr free o.s.

desembarca|dero m landing stage. **~r** [7] vt unload. **—vi** disembark

desemboca|dura f (de río) mouth; (de calle) opening. **~r** [7] vi. **~r en** ⟨río⟩ flow into; ⟨calle⟩ join; (fig) lead to, end in

desembols|ar vt pay. **~o** m payment

desembragar [12] vi declutch

desembrollar vt unravel

desembuchar vi tell, reveal a secret

desemejan|te *a* unlike, dissimilar. **~za** *f* dissimilarity

desempapelar *vt* unwrap

desempaquetar *vt* unpack, unwrap

desempat|ar *vi* break a tie. **~e** *m* tie-breaker

desempeñ|ar *vt* redeem; play ⟨*papel*⟩; hold ⟨*cargo*⟩; perform, carry out ⟨*deber etc*⟩. **~arse** *vpr* get out of debt. **~o** *m* redemption; (*de un papel, de un cargo*) performance

desemple|ado *a* unemployed. —*m* unemployed person. **~o** *m* unemployment. **los ~ados** *mpl* the unemployed

desempolvar *vt* dust; (*fig*) unearth

desencadenar *vt* unchain; (*fig*) unleash. **~se** *vpr* break loose; ⟨*guerra etc*⟩ break out

desencaj|ar *vt* dislocate; (*desconectar*) disconnect. **~se** *vpr* become distorted

desencant|ar *vt* disillusion. **~o** *m* disillusionment

desenchufar *vt* unplug

desenfad|ado *a* uninhibited. **~ar** *vt* calm down. **~arse** *vpr* calm down. **~o** *m* openness; (*desenvoltura*) assurance

desenfocado *a* out of focus

desenfren|ado *a* unrestrained. **~arse** *vpr* rage. **~o** *m* licentiousness

desenganchar *vt* unhook

desengañ|ar *vt* disillusion. **~arse** *vpr* be disillusioned; (*darse cuenta*) realize. **~o** *m* disillusionment, disappointment

desengrasar *vt* remove the grease from. —*vi* lose weight

desenlace *m* outcome. **~zar** [10] *vt* undo; solve ⟨*problema*⟩

desenmarañar *vt* unravel

desenmascarar *vt* unmask

desenojar *vt* calm down. **~se** *vpr* calm down

desenred|ar *vt* unravel. **~arse** *vpr* extricate o.s. **~o** *m* denoument

desenrollar *vt* unroll, unwind

desenroscar [7] *vt* unscrew

desentenderse [1] *vpr* want nothing to do with; (*afectar ignorancia*) pretend not to know. **hacerse el desentendido** (*fingir no oir*) pretend not to hear

desenterrar [1] *vt* exhume; (*fig*) unearth

desenton|ar *vi* be out of tune; ⟨*colores*⟩ clash. **~o** *m* rudeness

desentrañar *vt* work out

desenvoltura *f* ease; (*falta de timidez*) confidence; (*descaro*) insolence

desenvolver [2, *pp* **desenvuelto**] *vt* unwrap; expound ⟨*idea etc*⟩. **~se** *vpr* act with confidence

deseo *m* wish, desire. **~so** *a* desirous. **arder en ~s de** long for. **buen ~** good intentions. **estar ~so de** be eager to

desequilibr|ado *a* unbalanced. **~io** *m* imbalance

des|erción *f* desertion; (*pol*) defection. **~ertar** *vt* desert. **~értico** *a* desert-like. **~ertor** *m* deserter

desespera|ción *f* despair. **~do** *a* desperate. **~nte** *a* infuriating. **~r** *vt* drive to despair. —*vi* despair (be of). **~rse** *vpr* despair

desestimar *vt* (*rechazar*) reject

desfachat|ado *a* brazen, impudent. **~ez** *f* impudence

desfalc|ar [7] *vt* embezzle. **~o** *m* embezzlement

desfallec|er [11] *vt* weaken. —*vi* get weak; (*desmayarse*) faint. **~imiento** *m* weakness

desfas|ado *a* ⟨*persona*⟩ out of place, out of step; ⟨*máquina etc*⟩ out of phase. **~e** *m* jet-lag. **estar ~ado** have jet-lag

desfavor|able a unfavourable.
~ecer [11] vt ‹ropa› not suit

desfigurar vt disfigure; ‹desdibujar› blur; ‹fig› distort

desfiladero m pass

desfil|ar vi march (past). **~e** m procession, parade. **~e de modelos** fashion show

desfogar [12] vt vent ⟨en, con on⟩. **~se** vpr let off steam

desgajar vt tear off; ‹fig› uproot ‹persona›. **~se** vpr come off

desgana f ‹falta de apetito› lack of appetite; ‹med› weakness, faintness; ‹fig› unwillingness

desgarr|ador a heart-rending. **~ar** vt tear; ‹fig› break ‹corazón›. **~o** m tear, rip; ‹descaro› insolence. **~ón** m tear

desgast|ar vt wear away; wear out ‹ropa›. **~arse** vpr wear away; ‹ropa› be worn out; ‹persona› wear o.s. out. **~e** m wear

desgracia f misfortune; ‹accidente› accident; ‹mala suerte› bad luck. **~damente** adv unfortunately. **~do** a unlucky; ‹pobre› poor; ‹desagradable› unpleasant. —m unfortunate person, poor devil ⟨fam⟩. **~r** vt spoil. **caer en ~** fall from favour. **estar en ~** be unfortunate. **por ~** unfortunately. **¡qué ~!** what a shame!

desgranar vt shell ‹guisantes etc›

desgreñado a ruffled, dishevelled

desgua|ce m scrapyard. **~zar** [10] vt scrap

deshabitado a uninhabited

deshabituarse [21] vpr get out of the habit

deshacer [31] vt undo; strip ‹cama›; unpack ‹maleta›; ‹desmontar› take to pieces; break ‹trato›; ‹derretir› melt; ‹en agua› dissolve; ‹destruir› destroy; ‹estropear› spoil; ‹derrotar› defeat.

~se vpr come undone; ‹descomponerse› fall to pieces; ‹derretirse› melt. **~se de algo** get rid of sth. **~se en lágrimas** burst into tears. **~se por hacer algo** go out of one's way to do sth

deshelar [1] vt thaw. **~se** vpr thaw

desheredar vt disinherit

deshidratar vt dehydrate. **~se** vpr become dehydrated

deshielo m thaw

deshilachado a frayed

deshincha|do a ‹neumático› flat. **~r** vt deflate. **~rse** vpr go down

deshollina|dor m ‹chimney-› sweep. **~r** vt sweep ‹chimenea›

deshon|esto a dishonest; ‹obsceno› indecent. **~or** m, **~ra** f disgrace. **~rar** vt dishonour

deshora f. **a ~** ‹a hora desacostumbrada› at an unusual time; ‹a hora inoportuna› at an inconvenient time; ‹a hora avanzada› very late

deshuesar vt bone ‹carne›; stone ‹fruta›

desidia f laziness

desierto a deserted. —m desert

designa|ción f designation. **~r** vt designate; ‹fijar› fix

desigual a unequal; ‹terreno› uneven; ‹distinto› different. **~dad** f inequality

desilusi|ón f disappointment; ‹pérdida de ilusiones› disillusionment. **~onar** vt disappoint; ‹quitar las ilusiones› disillusion. **~onarse** vpr become disillusioned

desinfecta|nte m disinfectant. **~r** vt disinfect

desinfestar vt decontaminate

desinflar vt deflate. **~se** vpr go down

desinhibido a uninhibited

desintegra|ción f disintegration. **~r** vt disintegrate. **~rse** vpr disintegrate

desinter|és *m* impartiality; (*generosidad*) generosity. **~esado** *a* impartial; (*liberal*) generous

desistir *vi*. **~ de** give up

desleal *a* disloyal. **~tad** *f* disloyalty

desleír [51] *vt* thin down, dilute

deslenguado *a* foul-mouthed

desligar [12] *vt* untie; (*separar*) separate; (*fig, librar*) free. **~se** *vpr* break away; (*de un compromiso*) free o.s.

deslizar [10] *vt* slide, slip. **~se** *vpr* slide, slip; (*tiempo*) slide by, pass; (*fluir*) flow

deslucido *a* tarnished; (*gastado*) worn out; (*fig*) undistinguished

deslumbrar *vt* dazzle

deslustrar *vt* tarnish

desmadr|ado *a* unruly. **~arse** *vpr* get out of control. **~e** *m* excess

desmán *m* outrage

desmandarse *vpr* get out of control

desmantelar *vt* dismantle; (*despojar*) strip

desmañado *a* clumsy

desmaquillador *m* make-up remover

desmay|ado *a* unconscious. **~ar** *vi* lose heart. **~arse** *vpr* faint. **~o** *m* faint; (*estado*) unconsciousness; (*fig*) depression

desmedido *a* excessive

desmedrarse *vpr* waste away

desmejorarse *vpr* deteriorate

desmelenado *a* dishevelled

desmembrar *vt* (*fig*) divide up

desmemoriado *a* forgetful

desmentir [4] *vt* deny. **~se** *vpr* contradict o.s.; (*desdecirse*) go back on one's word

desmenuzar [10] *vt* crumble; chop (*carne etc*)

desmerecer [11] *vt* be unworthy of. **—vi** deteriorate

desmesurado *a* excessive; (*enorme*) enormous

desmigajar *vt*, **desmigar** [12] *vt* crumble

desmonta|ble *a* collapsible. **~r** *vt* (*quitar*) remove; (*desarmar*) take to pieces; (*derribar*) knock down; (*allanar*) level. **—vi** dismount

desmoralizar [10] *vt* demoralize

desmoronar (*fig*) make inroads into. **~se** *vpr* crumble

desmovilizar [10] *vt/i* demobilize

desnatar *vt* skim

desnivel *m* unevenness; (*fig*) difference, inequality

desnud|ar *vt* strip; undress, strip (*persona*). **~arse** *vpr* get undressed. **~ez** *f* nudity. **~o** *a* naked; (*fig*) bare. **—m** nude

desnutri|ción *f* malnutrition. **~do** *a* undernourished

desobed|ecer [11] *vt* disobey. **~iencia** *f* disobedience. **~iente** *a* disobedient

desocupa|do *a* (*asiento etc*) vacant, free; (*sin trabajo*) unemployed; (*ocioso*) idle. **~r** *vt* vacate

desodorante *m* deodorant

desoír [50] *vt* take no notice of

desola|ción *f* desolation; (*fig*) distress. **~do** *a* desolate; (*persona*) sorry, sad. **~r** *vt* ruin; (*desconsolar*) distress

desollar *vt* skin; (*fig, criticar*) criticize; (*fig, hacer pagar demasiado, fam*) fleece

desorbitante *a* excessive

desorden *m* disorder, untidiness; (*confusión*) confusion. **~ado** *a* untidy. **~ar** *vt* disarrange, make a mess of

desorganizar [10] *vt* disorganize; (*trastornar*) disturb

desorienta|do *a* confused. **~r** *vt* disorientate. **~rse** *vpr* lose one's bearings

desovar *vi* ⟨*pez*⟩ spawn; ⟨*insecto*⟩ lay eggs

despabila|do *a* wide awake; ⟨*listo*⟩ quick. **~r** *vt* ⟨*despertar*⟩ wake up; ⟨*avivar*⟩ brighten up. **~rse** *vpr* wake up; ⟨*avivarse*⟩ brighten up. **¡despabílate!** get a move on!

despacio *adv* slowly. **~int** easy does it! **~to** *adv* slowly

despach|ar *vt* finish; ⟨*tratar con*⟩ deal with; ⟨*vender*⟩ sell; ⟨*enviar*⟩ send; ⟨*despedir*⟩ send away; issue ⟨*billete*⟩. **~vi** hurry up. **~arse** *vpr* get rid; ⟨*terminar*⟩ finish. **~o** *m* dispatch; ⟨*oficina*⟩ office; ⟨*venta*⟩ sale; ⟨*del teatro*⟩ box office

despampanante *a* stunning

desparejado *a* odd

desparpajo *m* confidence; ⟨*descaro*⟩ impudence

desparramar *vt* scatter; spill ⟨*líquidos*⟩; squander ⟨*fortuna*⟩

despavorido *a* terrified

despectivo *a* disparaging; ⟨*sentido etc*⟩ pejorative

despecho *m* spite. **a ~ de** in spite of. **por ~** out of spite

despedazar [10] *vt* tear to pieces

despedi|da *f* goodbye, farewell. **~da de soltero** stag-party. **~r** [5] *vt* say goodbye, see off; dismiss ⟨*empleado*⟩; evict ⟨*inquilino*⟩; ⟨*arrojar*⟩ throw; give off ⟨*olor etc*⟩. **~rse** *vpr.* **~rse de** say goodbye to

despeg|ado *a* cold, indifferent. **~ar** [12] *vt* unstick. **~vi** ⟨*avión*⟩ take off. **~o** *m* indifference. **~ue** *m* take-off

despeinar *vt* ruffle the hair of

despeja|do *a* clear; ⟨*persona*⟩ wide awake. **~r** *vt* clear; ⟨*aclarar*⟩ clarify. **~vi** clear. **~rse** *vpr* ⟨*aclararse*⟩ become clear; ⟨*cielo*⟩ clear; ⟨*tiempo*⟩ clear up; ⟨*persona*⟩ liven up

despellejar *vt* skin

despensa *f* pantry, larder

despeñadero *m* cliff

desperdici|ar *vt* waste. **~o** *m* waste. **~os** *mpl* rubbish. **no tener ~o** be good all the way through

desperezarse [10] *vpr* stretch

desperfecto *m* flaw

desperta|dor *m* alarm clock. **~r** [1] *vt* wake up; ⟨*fig*⟩ awaken. **~rse** *vpr* wake up

despiadado *a* merciless

despido *m* dismissal

despierto *a* awake; ⟨*listo*⟩ bright

despilfarr|ar *vt* waste. **~o** *m* squandering; ⟨*gasto innecesario*⟩ extravagance

despista|do *a* ⟨*con estar*⟩ confused; ⟨*con ser*⟩ absent-minded. **~r** *vt* throw off the scent; ⟨*fig*⟩ mislead. **~rse** *vpr* go wrong; ⟨*fig*⟩ get confused

despiste *m* swerve; ⟨*error*⟩ mistake; ⟨*confusión*⟩ muddle

desplaza|do *a* out of place. **~miento** *m* displacement; ⟨*de opinión etc*⟩ swing, shift. **~r** [10] *vt* displace. **~rse** *vpr* travel

despl|egar [1 & 12] *vt* open out; spread ⟨*alas*⟩; ⟨*fig*⟩ show. **~iegue** *m* opening; ⟨*fig*⟩ show

desplomarse *vpr* lean; ⟨*caerse*⟩ collapse

desplumar *vt* pluck; ⟨*fig, fam*⟩ fleece

despobla|do *m* deserted area. **~r** [2] *vt* depopulate

despoj|ar *vt* deprive ⟨*persona*⟩; strip ⟨*cosa*⟩. **~o** *m* plundering; ⟨*botín*⟩ booty. **~os** *mpl* leftovers; ⟨*de res*⟩ offal; ⟨*de ave*⟩ giblets

desposado *a & m* newly-wed

déspota *m & f* despot

despreci|able *a* despicable; ⟨*cantidad*⟩ negligible. **~ar** *vt* despise; ⟨*rechazar*⟩ scorn. **~o** *m* contempt

desprend|er vt remove; give off ⟨olor⟩. ~**erse** vpr fall off; (fig) part with; (deducirse) follow. ~**imiento** m loosening; (generosidad) generosity

despreocupa|ción f carelessness. ~**do** a unconcerned; (descuidado) careless. ~**rse** vpr not worry

desprestigiar vt discredit

desprevenido a unprepared. **coger a uno** ~ catch s.o. unawares

desproporci|ón f disproportion. ~**onado** a disproportionate

despropósito m irrelevant remark

desprovisto a. ~ **de** lacking, without

después adv after, afterwards; (más tarde) later; (a continuación) then. ~ **de** after. ~ **de comer** after eating. ~ **de todo** after all. ~ **que** after. **poco** ~ soon after. **una semana** ~ a week later

desquiciar vt disturb

desquit|ar vt compensate. ~**arse** vpr make up for; (vengarse) take revenge. ~**e** m compensation; (venganza) revenge

destaca|do a outstanding. ~**r** [7] vt emphasize. —vi stand out. ~**rse** vpr stand out

destajo m piece-work. **hablar a** ~ talk nineteen to the dozen

destap|ar vt uncover; open ⟨botella⟩. ~**arse** vpr reveal one's true self. ~**e** m (fig) permissiveness

destartalado a ⟨habitación⟩ untidy; ⟨casa⟩ rambling

destell|ar vi sparkle. ~**o** m sparkle; (de estrella) twinkle; (fig) glimmer

destemplado a out of tune; (agrio) harsh; ⟨tiempo⟩ unsettled; ⟨persona⟩ out of sorts

desteñir [5 & 22] vt fade; (manchar) discolour. —vi fade. ~**se** vpr fade; ⟨color⟩ run

desterra|do m exile. ~**r** [1] vt banish

destetar vt wean

destiempo m. **a** ~ at the wrong moment

destierro m exile

destil|ación f distillation. ~**ar** vt distil. ~**ería** f distillery

destin|ar vt destine; (nombrar) appoint. ~**atario** m addressee. ~**o** m (uso) use, function; (lugar) destination; (empleo) position; (suerte) destiny. **con** ~**o a** going to, bound for. **dar** ~**o a** find a use for

destitu|ción f dismissal. ~**ir** [17] vt dismiss

destornilla|dor m screwdriver. ~**r** vt unscrew

destreza f skill

destripar vt rip open

destroz|ar [10] vt ruin; (fig) shatter. ~**o** m destruction. **causar** ~**os, hacer** ~**os** ruin

destru|cción f destruction. ~**ctivo** a destructive. ~**ir** [17] vt destroy; demolish ⟨edificio⟩

desunir vt separate

desus|ado a old-fashioned; (insólito) unusual. ~**o** m disuse. **caer en** ~**o** become obsolete

desvaído a pale; (borroso) blurred; ⟨persona⟩ dull

desvalido a needy, destitute

desvalijar vt rob; burgle ⟨casa⟩

desvalorizar [10] vt devalue

desván m loft

desvanec|er [11] vt make disappear; tone down ⟨colores⟩; (borrar) blur; (fig) dispel. ~**erse** vpr disappear; (desmayarse) faint. ~**imiento** m (med) fainting fit

desvariar [20] vi be delirious; (fig) talk nonsense

desvelar vt keep awake. ∼arse vpr stay awake, have a sleepless night. ∼o m insomnia, sleeplessness

desvencijar vt break; (agotar) exhaust

desventaja f disadvantage

desventura f misfortune. ∼do a unfortunate

desvergonzado a impudent, cheeky. ∼üenza f impudence, cheek

desvestirse [5] vpr undress

desviación f deviation; (auto) diversion. ∼iar [20] vt deflect, turn aside. ∼iarse vpr be deflected; (del camino) make a detour; (del tema) stray. ∼ío m diversion; (frialdad) f indifference

desvivirse vpr long (por for); (afanarse) strive, do one's utmost

detallar vt relate in detail. ∼e m detail; (fig) gesture. ∼ista m & f retailer. al ∼e in detail; (al por menor) retail. con todo ∼e in great detail. en ∼es in detail. ¡qué ∼e! how thoughtful!

detectar vt detect. ∼ive m detective

detención f stopping; (jurid) arrest; (en la cárcel) detention. ∼er [40] vt stop; (jurid) arrest; (encarcelar) detain; (retrasar) delay. ∼erse vpr stop; (entretenerse) spend a lot of time. ∼idamente adv carefully. ∼ido a (jurid) under arrest; (minucioso) detailed. —m prisoner

detergente a & m detergent

deteriorar vt damage, spoil. ∼arse vpr deteriorate. ∼o m damage

determinación f determination; (decisión) decison. ∼nte a decisive. ∼r vt determine; (decidir) decide; (fijar) fix. tomar una ∼ción make a decision

detestar vt detest

detonar vi explode

detrás adv behind; (en la parte posterior) on the back. ∼ de behind. por ∼ on the back; (detrás de) behind

detrimento m detriment. en ∼ de to the detriment of

detrito m debris

deuda f debt. ∼or m debtor

devaluación f devaluation. ∼r [21] vt devalue

devanar vt wind

devastador a devastating. ∼r vt devastate

devoción f devotion

devolución f return; (com) repayment, refund. ∼ver [5] (pp **devuelto**) vt return; (com) repay, refund; restore (edificio etc). —vi be sick

devorar vt devour

devoto a devout; (amigo etc) devoted. —m enthusiast

di vb véase **dar**

día m day. ∼ de fiesta (public) holiday. ∼ del santo saint's day. ∼ festivo (public) holiday. ∼ hábil, ∼ laborable working day. al ∼ up to date. al ∼ siguiente (on) the following day. ¡buenos ∼s! good morning! dar los buenos ∼s say good morning. de ∼ by day. de ∼ hoy today. el ∼ de mañana tomorrow. en pleno ∼ in broad daylight. en su ∼ in due course. todo el santo ∼ all day long. un ∼ de estos one of these days. un ∼ sí y otro no every other day. vivir al ∼ live from hand to mouth

diabetes f diabetes. ∼ético a diabetic

diablo m devil. ∼lura f mischief. ∼ólico a diabolical

diácono m deacon

diadema f diadem

diáfano a diaphanous

diafragma m diaphragm

diagn|osis f diagnosis. **~osticar** [7] vt diagnose. **~óstico** a diagnostic

diagonal a & f diagonal

diagrama m diagram

dialecto m dialect

diálisis f dialysis

di|alogar [12] vi talk. **~álogo** m dialogue

diamante m diamond

diámetro m diameter

diana f reveille; (blanco) bull's-eye

diapasón m (para afinar) tuning fork

diapositiva f slide, transparency

diari|amente adv every day. **~o** a daily. —m newspaper; (libro) diary. **a ~o** daily. **~o hablado** (en la radio) news bulletin. **de ~o** everyday, ordinary

diarrea f diarrhoea

diatriba f diatribe

dibuj|ar vt draw. **~o** m drawing. **~os animados** cartoon (film)

diccionario m dictionary

diciembre m December

dictado m dictation

dictad|or m dictator. **~ura** f dictatorship

dictamen m opinion; (informe) report

dictar vt dictate; pronounce (sentencia etc)

dich|a f happiness. **~o** a said; (susodicho) aforementioned. —m saying. **~oso** a happy; (afortunado) fortunate. **~o y hecho** no sooner said than done. **mejor ~o** rather. **por ~a** fortunately

didáctico a didactic

dieci|nueve a & m nineteen. **~ocho** a & m eighteen. **~séis** a & m sixteen. **~siete** a & m seventeen

diente m tooth; (de tenedor) prong; (de ajo) clove. **~ de león**

dandelion. **hablar entre ~s** mumble

diesel /'disel/ a diesel

diestr|a f right hand. **~o** a (derecho) right; (hábil) skillful

dieta f diet

diez a & m ten

diezmar vt decimate

difama|ción f (con palabras) slander; (por escrito) libel. **~r** vt (hablando) slander; (por escrito) libel

diferen|cia f difference; (desacuerdo) disagreement. **~ciar** vt differentiate between. —vi differ. **~ciarse** vpr differ. **~te** a different

difer|ido a (TV etc) recorded. **~ir** [4] vt postpone, defer. —vi differ

difícil a difficult. **~ultad** f difficulty; (problema) problem. **~ultar** vt make difficult

difteria f diphtheria

difundir vt spread; (TV etc) broadcast. **~se** vpr spread

difunto a late, deceased. —m deceased

difusión f spreading

dige|rir [4] vt digest. **~stión** f digestion. **~stivo** a digestive

digital a digital; (de los dedos) finger

dignarse vpr deign. **dígnese Vd** be so kind as

dign|atario m dignitary. **~idad** f dignity; (empleo) office. **~o** a worthy; (apropiado) appropriate

digo vb véase **decir**

digresión f digression

dije vb véase **decir**

dila|ción f delay. **~tación** f dilation, expansion. **~tado** a extensive; (tiempo) long. **~tar** vt expand; (med) dilate; (prolongar) prolong. **~tarse** vpr expand; (med) dilate; (extenderse) extend. **sin ~ción** immediately

dilema *m* dilemma
diligen|cia *f* diligence; (*gestión*) job; (*historia*) stagecoach. ~**te** *a* diligent
dilucidar *vt* explain; solve (*misterio*)
diluir [17] *vt* dilute
diluvio *m* flood
dimensión *f* dimension; (*tamaño*) size
diminut|ivo *a* & *m* diminutive. ~**o** *a* minute
dimi|sión *f* resignation. ~**tir** *vt/i* resign
Dinamarca *f* Denmark
dinamarqués *a* Danish. —*m* Dane
din|ámica *f* dynamics. ~**ámico** *a* dynamic. ~**amismo** *m* dynamism
dinamita *f* dynamite
dínamo *m*, **dinamo** *m* dynamo
dinastía *f* dynasty
dineral *m* fortune
dinero *m* money. ~ **efectivo** cash. ~ **suelto** change
dinosaurio *m* dinosaur
diócesis *f* diocese
dios *m* god. ~**a** *f* goddess. ¡**D**~ **mío!** good heavens! ¡**gracias a D**~! thank God! ¡**válgame D**~! bless my soul!
diploma *m* diploma
diplomacia *f* diplomacy
diplomado *a* qualified
diplomático *a* diplomatic. —*m* diplomat
diptongo *m* diphthong
diputa|ción *f* delegation. ~**ción provincial** county council. ~**do** *m* delegate; (*pol, en España*) member of the Cortes; (*pol, en Inglaterra*) Member of Parliament; (*pol, en Estados Unidos*) congressman
dique *m* dike
direc|ción *f* direction; (*señas*) address; (*los que dirigen*) management; (*pol*) leadership.

~**ción prohibida** no entry. ~**ción única** one-way. ~**ta** *f* (*auto*) top gear. ~**tiva** *f* directive, guideline. ~**tivo** *m* executive. ~**to** *a* direct; (*línea*) straight; (*tren*) through. ~**tor** *m* director; (*mus*) conductor; (*de escuela etc*) headmaster; (*de periódico*) editor; (*gerente*) manager. ~**tora** *f* (*de escuela etc*) headmistress. **en** ~**to** (*TV etc*) live. **llevar la** ~**ción de** direct
dirig|ente *a* ruling. —*m* & *f* leader; (*de empresa*) manager. ~**ible** *a* & *m* dirigible. ~**ir** [14] *vt* direct; (*mus*) conduct; run (*empresa etc*); address (*carta etc*). ~**irse** *vpr* make one's way; (*hablar*) address
discernir [1] *vt* distinguish
disciplina *f* discipline. ~**r** *vt* discipline. ~**rio** *a* disciplinary
discípulo *m* disciple; (*alumno*) pupil
disco *m* disc; (*mus*) record; (*deportes*) discus; (*de teléfono*) dial; (*auto*) lights; (*rail*) signal
disconforme *a* not in agreement
discontinuo *a* discontinuous
discord|ante *a* discordant. ~**e** *a* discordant. ~**ia** *f* discord
discoteca *f* discothèque, disco (*fam*); (*colección de discos*) record library
discreción *f* discretion
discrepa|ncia *f* discrepancy; (*desacuerdo*) disagreement. ~**r** *vi* differ
discreto *a* discreet; (*moderado*) moderate; (*color*) subdued
discrimina|ción *f* discrimination. ~**r** *vt* (*distinguir*) discriminate between; (*tratar injustamente*) discriminate against
disculpa *f* apology; (*excusa*) excuse. ~**r** *vt* excuse, forgive. ~**rse** *vpr* apologize. **dar** ~**s**

make excuses. **pedir** ∼s apologize

discurrir *vt* think up. —*vi* think (en about); ⟨*tiempo*⟩ pass

discursⓐante *m* speaker. ∼**ar** *vi* speak (sobre about). ∼**o** *m* speech

discusión *f* discussion; (riña) argument. **eso no admite** ∼ there can be no argument about that

discutiⓑle *a* debatable. ∼**r** *vt* discuss; (argumentar) argue about; (contradecir) contradict. —*vi* discuss; (argumentar) argue

disecⓐar [7] *vt* dissect; stuff ⟨*animal muerto*⟩. ∼**ción** *f* dissection

diseminaⓒción *f* dissemination. ∼**r** *vt* disseminate, spread

disentería *f* dysentery

disentiⓜmiento *m* dissent, disagreement. ∼**r** [4] *vi* disagree (de with) (en on)

diseñⓐador *m* designer. ∼**ar** *vt* design. ∼**o** *m* design; (fig) sketch

disertación *f* dissertation

disfraz *m* disguise; (vestido) fancy dress. ∼**ar** [10] *vt* disguise. ∼**arse** *vpr*. ∼**arse de** disguise o.s. as

disfrutar *vt* enjoy. —*vi* enjoy o.s. ∼ **de** enjoy

disgregar [12] *vt* disintegrate

disgustⓐar *vt* displease; (molestar) annoy. ∼**arse** *vpr* get annoyed, get upset; ⟨*dos personas*⟩ fall out. ∼**o** *m* annoyance; (problema) trouble; (repugnancia) disgust; (riña) quarrel; (dolor) sorrow, grief

disidenⓒcia *f* disagreement, dissent. ∼**te** *a* & *m* & *f* dissident

disímil *a* (*LAm*) dissimilar

disimulⓐar *vt* conceal. —*vi* pretend

disipaⓒción *f* dissipation; (de dinero) squandering. ∼**r** *vt* dissipate; (derrochar) squander

diskette *m* floppy disk

dislocarse [7] *vpr* dislocate

disminuⓒción *f* decrease. ∼**ir** [17] *vi* diminish

disociar *vt* dissociate

disol|ver [2, *pp* **disuelto**] *vt* dissolve. ∼**se** *vpr* dissolve

disonante *a* dissonant

dispar *a* different

disparar *vt* fire. —*vi* shoot (contra at)

disparatⓐado *a* absurd. ∼**ar** *vi* talk nonsense. ∼**e** *m* silly thing; (error) mistake. **decir** ∼**es** talk nonsense. **¡qué** ∼**e!** how ridiculous! **un** ∼**e** (mucho, fam) a lot, an awful lot (fam)

disparidad *f* disparity

disparo *m* (acción) firing; (tiro) shot

dispensar *vt* distribute; (disculpar) excuse. **¡Vd dispense!** forgive me

dispersⓐar *vt* scatter, disperse. ∼**arse** *vpr* scatter, disperse. ∼**ión** *f* dispersion. ∼**o** *a* scattered

disponⓔer [34] *vt* arrange; (preparar) prepare. —*vi*. ∼**er de** have; (vender etc) dispose of. ∼**erse** *vpr* get ready. ∼**ibilidad** *f* availability. ∼**ible** *a* available

disposición *f* arrangement; (aptitud) talent; (disponibilidad) disposal; (jurid) order, decree. ∼ **de ánimo** frame of mind. **a la** ∼ **de** at the disposal of. **a su** ∼ at your service

dispositivo *m* device

dispuesto *a* ready; (hábil) clever; (inclinado) disposed; (servicial) helpful

disputⓐa *f* dispute. —*vi*. ∼**r** dispute about; (competir para) compete for. **sin** ∼ undoubtedly

distanⓒcia *f* distance. ∼**ciar** *vt* space out; (en deportes) outdistance. ∼**ciarse** *vpr* ⟨*dos personas*⟩ fall out. ∼**te** *a* distant. **a**

~**cia** from a distance. **guardar las ~cias** keep one's distance

distar vi be away; (fig) be far. **dista 5 kilómetros** it's 5 kilometres away

distin|ción f distinction. ~**guido** a distinguished; (en cartas) Honoured. ~**guir** [13] vt/i distinguish. ~**guirse** vpr distinguish o.s.; (diferenciarse) differ; (verse) be visible. ~**tivo** a distinctive. —m badge. ~**to** a different; (claro) distinct

distorsión f distortion; (med) sprain

distra|cción f amusement; (descuido) absent-mindedness, inattention. ~**er** [41] vt distract; (divertir) amuse; embezzle (fondos). ~**vi** be entertaining. —**vi** vpr amuse o.s.; (descuidarse) not pay attention. ~**ido** a amusing; (desatento) absent-minded

distribu|ción f distribution. ~**idor** m distributor, agent. ~**idor automático** vending machine. ~**ir** [17] vt distribute

distrito m district

disturbio m disturbance

disuadir vt dissuade

diurético a & m diuretic

diurno a daytime

divagar [12] vi (al hablar) digress

diván m settee, sofa

diverg|encia f divergence. ~**ente** a divergent. ~**ir** [14] vi diverge

diversidad f diversity

diversificar [7] vt diversify

diversión f amusement, entertainment; (pasatiempo) pastime

diverso a different

diverti|do a amusing; (que tiene gracia) funny; (agradable) enjoyable. ~**r** [4] vt amuse, entertain. ~**rse** vpr enjoy o.s.

dividir vt divide; (repartir) share out

divin|idad f divinity. ~**o** a divine

divisa f emblem. ~**s** fpl foreign exchange

divisar vt make out

divis|ión f division. ~**or** m divisor. ~**orio** a dividing

divorci|ado a divorced. —m divorcee. ~**ar** vt divorce. ~**arse** vpr get divorced. ~**o** m divorce

divulgar [12] vt divulge; (propagar) spread. ~**se** vpr become known

do m C; (solfa) doh

dobl|adillo m hem; (de pantalón) turn-up (Brit), cuff (Amer). ~**ado** a double; (plegado) folded; (película) dubbed. ~**ar** vt double; (plegar) fold; (torcer) bend; turn (esquina); dub (película). —**vi** turn; (campana) toll. ~**arse** vpr double; (encorvarse) bend; (ceder) give in. ~**e** a double. —m double; (pliegue) fold. ~**egar** [12] vt (fig) force to give in. ~**egarse** vpr give in. **el ~e** twice as much

doce a & m twelve. ~**na** f dozen. ~**no** a twelfth

docente a teaching. —m & f teacher

dócil a obedient

doct|o a learned. ~**or** m doctor. ~**orado** m doctorate. ~**rina** f doctrine

document|ación f documentation, papers. ~**al** a & m documentary. ~**ar** vt document. ~**arse** vpr gather information. ~**o** m document. **D~o Nacional de Identidad** national identity card

dogma m dogma. ~**ático** a dogmatic

dólar m dollar

dol|er [2] vi hurt, ache; (fig) grieve. **me duele la cabeza** my head hurts. **le duele el estómago** he has a pain in his stomach. ~**erse** vpr regret; (quejarse) complain. ~or *m* pain; (*sordo*) ache; (*fig*) sorrow. ~oroso *a* painful. ~or de cabeza headache. ~or de muelas toothache

domar *vt* tame; break in (*caballo*)

dom|esticar [7] *vt* domesticate. ~éstico *a* domestic. —*m* servant

domicilio *m* home. **a** ~ at home. **servicio a** ~ home delivery service

domina|ción *f* domination. ~nte *a* dominant; (*persona*) domineering. ~r *vt* dominate; (*contener*) control; (*conocer*) have a good knowledge of. —*vi* dominate; (*destacarse*) stand out. ~rse *vpr* control o.s.

domin|go *m* Sunday. ~guero *a* Sunday. ~ical *a* Sunday

dominio *m* authority; (*territorio*) domain; (*fig*) good knowledge

dominó *m* (*juego*) dominoes

don *m* talent, gift; (*en un sobre*) Mr. ~ **Pedro** Pedro. **tener** ~ **de lenguas** have a gift for languages. **tener** ~ **de gentes** have a way with people

donación *f* donation

donaire *m* grace, charm

dona|nte *m* (*de sangre*) donor. ~r *vt* donate

doncella *f* (*criada*) maid

donde *adv* where

dónde *adv* where? ¿hasta ~? how far? ¿por ~? whereabouts?; (¿*por qué camino?*) which way? ¿a ~ **vas**? where are you going? ¿de ~ **eres**? where are you from?

dondequiera *adv* anywhere; (*en todas partes*) everywhere. ~ **que** wherever. **por** ~ everywhere

doña *f* (*en un sobre*) Mrs. ~ **María**

dora|do *a* golden; (*cubierto de oro*) gilt. ~**dura** *f* gilding. ~r *vt* gilt; (*culin*) brown

dormi|lón *m* sleepyhead. —*a* lazy. ~r [6] *vt* send to sleep. —*vi* sleep. ~rse *vpr* go to sleep. ~tar *vi* doze. ~torio *m* bedroom. ~r **la siesta** have an afternoon nap, have a siesta. **echarse a dormir** go to bed

dors|al *a* back. —*m* (*en deportes*) number. ~o *m* back

dos *a & m* two. ~**cientos** *a & m* two hundred. **cada** ~ **por tres** every five minutes. **de** ~ **en** ~ in twos, in pairs. **en un** ~ **por tres** in no time. **los dos, las dos** both (of them)

dosi|ficar [7] *vt* dose; (*fig*) measure out. ~**s** *f* dose

dota|do *a* gifted. ~r *vt* give a dowry; (*proveer*) endow (**de** with). ~**e** *m* dowry

doy *vb véase* **dar**

dragar [12] *vt* dredge

drago *m* dragon tree

dragón *m* dragon

dram|a *m* drama; (*obra de teatro*) play. ~**ático** *a* dramatic. ~**atizar** [10] *vt* dramatize. ~**aturgo** *m* playwright

drástico *a* drastic

droga *f* drug. ~**dicto** *m* drug addict. ~**do** *a* drugged. —*m* drug addict. ~r [12] *vt* drug. ~**rse** *vpr* take drugs. ~**ta** *m & f* (*fam*) drug addict

droguería *f* hardware shop (*Brit*), hardware store (*Amer*)

dromedario *m* dromedary

ducha *f* shower. ~**rse** *vpr* have a shower

dud|a *f* doubt. ~**ar** *vt/i* doubt. ~**oso** *a* doubtful; (*sospechoso*) dubious. **poner en** ~**a** question. **sin** ~**a (alguna)** without a doubt

duelo *m* duel; (*luto*) mourning

duende *m* imp

dueña *f* owner, proprietress; (*de una pensión*) landlady. ~**o** *m* owner, proprietor; (de una pensión) landlord

duermo vb véase **dormir**

dul|ce a sweet; (agua) fresh; (suave) soft, gentle. —m sweet. ~**zura** f sweetness; (fig) gentleness

duna f dune

dúo m duet, duo

duodécimo a & m twelfth

duplica|do a in duplicate. —m duplicate. ~**r** [7] vt duplicate. ~**rse** vpr double

duque m duke. ~**sa** f duchess

dura|ción f duration, length. ~**dero** a lasting

durante prep during, in; (medida de tiempo) for. ~ **todo el año** all year round

durar vi last

durazno m (LAm, fruta) peach

dureza f hardness, toughness; (med) hard patch

durmiente a sleeping

duro a hard; (culin) tough; (fig) harsh. —adv hard. —m five-peseta coin. **ser ~ de oído** be hard of hearing

E

e conj and

ebanista m & f cabinet-maker

ébano m ebony

ebri|edad f drunkenness. ~**o** a drunk

ebullición f boiling

eccema m eczema

eclesiástico a ecclesiastical. —m clergyman

eclipse m eclipse

eco m echo. **hacer(se)** ~ echo

ecolog|ía f ecology. ~**ista** m & f ecologist

economato m cooperative store

econom|ía f economy; (ciencia) economics. ~**ómicamente** adv

economically. ~**ómico** a economic(al); (no caro) inexpensive. ~**omista** m & f economist. ~**omizar** [10] vt/i economize

ecuación f equation

ecuador m equator. **el E~** Ecuador

ecuánime a level-headed; (imparcial) impartial

ecuanimidad f equanimity

ecuatoriano a & m Ecuadorian

ecuestre a equestrian

echar vt throw; post (carta); give off (olor); pour (líquido); sprout (hojas etc); (despedir) throw out; dismiss (empleado); (poner) put on; put out (raíces); show (película). ~**se** vpr throw o.s.; (tumbarse) lie down. ~ **a** start. ~ **a perder** spoil. ~ **de menos** miss. ~**se** atrás (fig) back down. **echárselas de** feign

edad f age. ~ **avanzada** old age. **E~ de Piedra** Stone Age. **E~ Media** Middle Ages. ¿**qué** ~ **tiene?** how old is he?

edición f edition; (publicación) publication

edicto m edict

edifica|ción f building. ~**ante** a edifying. ~**ar** [7] vt build; (fig) edify. ~**io** m building; (fig) structure

Edimburgo m Edinburgh

edit|ar vt publish. ~**or** a publishing. —m publisher. ~**orial** a editorial. —m leading article. —f publishing house

edredón m eiderdown

educa|ción f upbringing; (modales) (good) manners; (enseñanza) education. ~**do** a polite. ~**dor** m teacher. ~**r** [7] vt bring up; (enseñar) educate. ~**tivo** a educational. **falta de** ~**ción** rudeness, bad manners. **mal** ~**do** rude

edulcorante m sweetener

EE.UU. *abrev* (*Estados Unidos*) USA, United States (of America)

efect|**ivamente** *adv* really; (*por supuesto*) indeed. ~**ivo** *a* effective; (*auténtico*) real; (*empleo*) permanent. —*m* cash. ~**o** *m* effect; (*impresión*) impression. ~**os** *mpl* belongings; (*com*) goods. ~**uar** [21] *vt* carry out, effect; make (*viaje, compras etc*). **en** ~**o** in fact; (*por supuesto*) indeed

efervescente *a* effervescent; (*bebidas*) fizzy

efica|**cia** *f* effectiveness; (*de persona*) efficiency. ~**z** *a* effective; (*persona*) efficient

eficien|**cia** *f* efficiency. ~**te** *a* efficient

efigie *f* effigy

efímero *a* ephemeral

efluvio *m* outflow

efusi|**ón** *n* effusion. ~**vo** *a* effusive; (*gracias*) warm

Egeo *m. mar* ~ Aegean Sea

égida *f* aegis

egipcio *a & m* Egyptian

Egipto *m* Egypt

ego|**céntrico** *a* egocentric. —*m* egocentric person. ~**ísmo** *m* selfishness. ~**ísta** *a* selfish. —*m* selfish person

egregio *a* eminent

egresar *vi* (*LAm*) leave; (*univ*) graduate

eje *m* axis; (*tec*) axle

ejecu|**ción** *f* execution; (*mus etc*) performance. ~**tante** *m & f* executor; (*mus etc*) performer. ~**tar** *vt* carry out; (*mus etc*) perform; (*matar*) execute

ejecutivo *m* director, manager

ejempl|**ar** *a* exemplary. —*m* (*ejemplo*) example, specimen; (*libro*) copy; (*revista*) issue, number. ~**ificar** [7] *vt* exemplify. ~**o** *m* example. **dar** ~ set an example. **por** ~**o** for example. **sin** ~ unprecedented

ejerc|**er** [9] *vt* exercise; practise (*profesión*); exert (*influencia*). —*vi* practise. ~**icio** *m* exercise; (*de una profesión*) practice. ~**itar** *vt* exercise. ~**itarse** *upr* exercise. **hacer** ~**icios** take exercise

ejército *m* army

el *art def m* (*pl* **los**) the. —*pron* (*pl* **los**) the one. ~ **de Antonio** Antonio's. ~ **que** whoever, the one

él *pron* (*persona*) he; (*persona con prep*) him; (*cosa*) it. **el libro de** ~ his book

elabora|**ción** *f* processing; (*fabricación*) manufacture. ~**r** *vt* process; manufacture (*producto*); (*producir*) produce

el|**asticidad** *f* elasticity. ~**ástico** *a & m* elastic

elec|**ción** *f* choice; (*de político etc*) election. ~**ciones** *fpl* (*pol*) election. ~**tor** *m* voter. ~**torado** *m* electorate. ~**toral** *a* electoral

electrici|**dad** *f* electricity. ~**sta** *m & f* electrician

eléctrico *a* electric; (*de la electricidad*) electrical

electrificar [7] *vt*, **electrizar** [10] *vt* electrify

electrocutar *vt* electrocute

electrodo *m* electrode

electrodoméstico *a* electrical household. ~**s** *mpl* electrical household appliances

electrólisis *f* electrolysis

electrón *m* electron

electrónic|**a** *f* electronics. ~**o** *a* electronic

elefante *m* elephant

elegan|**cia** *f* elegance. ~**te** *a* elegant

elegía *f* elegy

elegi|**ble** *a* eligible. ~**do** *a* chosen. ~**r** [5 & 14] *vt* choose; (*por votación*) elect

element|**al** *a* elementary. ~**o** *m* element; (*persona*) person, bloke *(fam).* **~os** *mpl (nociones)* basic principles

elenco *m (en el teatro)* cast
eleva|ción *f* elevation; *(de precios)* rise, increase; *(acción)* raising. **~dor** *m (LAm)* lift. **~r** *vt* raise; *(promover)* promote
elimina|ción *f* elimination. **~r** *vt* eliminate. **~toria** *f* preliminary heat
el|ipse *f* ellipse. **~íptico** *a* elliptical
élite /e'lit, e'lite/ *f* elite
elixir *m* elixir
elocución *f* elocution
elocuen|cia *f* eloquence. **~te** *a* eloquent
elogi|ar *vt* praise. **~o** *m* praise
elote *m (Mex)* corn on the cob
eludir *vt* avoid, elude
ella *pron (persona)* she; *(persona con prep)* her; *(cosa)* it. **~s** *pron pl* they; *(con prep)* them. **el libro de ~** her book. **el libro de ~s** their book
ello *pron* it
ellos *pron pl* they; *(con prep)* them. **el libro de ~** their book
emaciado *a* emaciated
emana|ción *f* emanation. **~r** *vi* emanate *(de* from*)*; *(originarse)* originate *(de* from, in*)*
emancipa|ción *f* emancipation. **~do** *a* emancipated. **~r** *vt* emancipate. **~rse** *vpr* become emancipated
embadurnar *vt* smear
embaja|da *f* embassy. **~or** *m* ambassador
embalar *vt* pack
embaldosar *vt* tile
embalsamar *vt* embalm
embalse *m* dam; *(pantano)* reservoir
embaraz|ada *a* pregnant. *—f* pregnant woman. **~ar** [10] *vt* hinder. **~o** *m* hindrance; *(de mujer)* pregnancy. **~oso** *a* awkward, embarrassing

embar|cación *f* boat. **~cadero** *m* jetty, pier. **~car** [7] *vt* embark *(personas)*; ship *(mercancías)*. **~carse** *vpr* embark. **~carse en** *(fig)* embark upon
embargo *m* embargo; *(jurid)* seizure. **sin ~** however
embarque *m* loading
embarullar *vt* muddle
embaucar [7] *vt* deceive
embeber *vt* absorb; *(empapar)* soak. *—vi* shrink. **~se** *vpr* be absorbed
embelesar *vt* delight. **~se** *vpr* be delighted
embellecer [11] *vt* embellish
embesti|da *f* attack. **~r** [5] *vt/i* attack
emblema *m* emblem
embobar *vt* amaze
embobecer [11] *vt* make silly. **~se** *vpr* get silly
embocadura *f (de un río)* mouth
emboquillado *a* tipped
embolsar *vt* pocket
emborrachar *vt* get drunk. **~se** *vpr* get drunk
emborrascarse [7] *vpr* get stormy
emborronar *vt* blot
embosca|da *f* ambush. **~rse** [7] *vpr* lie in wait
embotar *vt* blunt; *(fig)* dull
embotella|miento *m (de vehículos)* traffic jam. **~r** *vt* bottle
embrague *m* clutch
embriag|ar [12] *vt* get drunk; *(fig)* intoxicate; *(fig, enajenar)* enrapture. **~arse** *vpr* get drunk. **~uez** *f* drunkenness; *(fig)* intoxication
embrión *m* embryo
embroll|ar *vt* mix up; involve *(personas)*. **~arse** *vpr* get into a muddle; *(en un asunto)* get involved. **~o** *m* tangle; *(fig)* muddle. **~ón** *m* troublemaker
embromar *vt* make fun of; *(engañar)* fool

embruja|do a bewitched; ⟨casa etc⟩ haunted. **~r** vt bewitch

embrutecer [11] vt brutalize

embuchar vt wolf ⟨comida⟩

embudo m funnel

embuste m lie. **~ro** a deceitful. **—m** liar

embuti|do m ⟨culin⟩ sausage. **~r** vt stuff

emergencia f emergency; ⟨acción de emerger⟩ emergence. **en caso de ~** in case of emergency

emerger [14] vi appear, emerge; ⟨submarino⟩ surface

emigra|ción f emigration. **~nte** m & f emigrant. **~r** vi emigrate

eminen|cia f eminence. **~te** a eminent

emisario m emissary

emis|ión f emission; ⟨de dinero⟩ issue; ⟨TV etc⟩ broadcast. **~or** a issuing; ⟨TV etc⟩ broadcasting. **~ora** f radio station

emitir vt emit; let out ⟨grito⟩; ⟨TV etc⟩ broadcast; ⟨expresar⟩ express; ⟨poner en circulación⟩ issue

emoci|ón f emotion; ⟨excitación⟩ excitement. **~onado** a moved. **~onante** a exciting; ⟨conmovedor⟩ moving. **~onar** vt excite; ⟨conmover⟩ move. **~onarse** vpr get excited; ⟨conmoverse⟩ be moved. **¡qué ~ón!** how exciting!

emotivo a emotional; ⟨conmovedor⟩ moving

empacar [7] vt ⟨LAm⟩ pack

empacho m indigestion; ⟨vergüenza⟩ embarrassment

empadronar vt register. **~se** vpr register

empalagoso a sickly; ⟨demasiado amable⟩ ingratiating; ⟨demasiado sentimental⟩ mawkish

empalizada f fence

empalm|ar vt connect, join. **—vi** meet. **~e** m junction; ⟨de trenes⟩ connection

empanad|a f ⟨savoury⟩ pie. **~illa** f ⟨small⟩ pie. **~o** a fried in breadcrumbs

empanizado a ⟨Mex⟩ fried in breadcrumbs

empantanar vt flood. **~se** vpr become flooded; ⟨fig⟩ get bogged down

empañar vt mist; dull ⟨metales etc⟩; ⟨fig⟩ tarnish. **~se** vpr ⟨cristales⟩ steam up

empapar vt soak; ⟨absorber⟩ soak up. **~se** vpr be soaked

empapela|do m wallpaper. **~r** vt paper; ⟨envolver⟩ wrap (in paper)

empaquetar vt package; pack ⟨personas⟩

emparedado m sandwich

emparejar vt match; ⟨nivelar⟩ make level. **~se** vpr pair off

empast|ar vt fill ⟨muela⟩. **~e** m filling

empat|ar vi draw. **~e** m draw

empedernido a inveterate; ⟨insensible⟩ hard

empedrar [1] vt pave

empeine m instep

empeñ|ado a in debt; ⟨decidido⟩ determined; ⟨acalorado⟩ heated. **~ar** vt pawn; pledge ⟨palabras⟩; ⟨principiar⟩ start. **~arse** vpr ⟨endeudarse⟩ get into debt; ⟨meterse⟩ get involved; ⟨estar decidido a⟩ insist (en on). **~o** m pledge; ⟨resolución⟩ determination. **casa de ~s** pawnshop

empeorar vt make worse. **—vi** get worse. **~se** vpr get worse

empequeñecer [11] vt dwarf; ⟨fig⟩ belittle

empera|dor m emperor. **~triz** f empress

empezar [1 & 10] vt/i start, begin. **para ~** to begin with

empina|do *a* upright; ⟨*cuesta*⟩ steep. ~**r** *vt* raise. ~**rse** *vpr* ⟨*persona*⟩ stand on tiptoe; ⟨*animal*⟩ rear

empírico *a* empirical

emplasto *m* plaster

emplaza|miento *m* ⟨*jurid*⟩ summons; ⟨*lugar*⟩ site. ~**r** [10] *vt* summon; ⟨*situar*⟩ site

emple|ado *m* employee. ~**ar** *vt* use; employ ⟨*persona*⟩; spend ⟨*tiempo*⟩. ~**arse** *vpr* be used; ⟨*persona*⟩ be employed. ~**o** *m* use; ⟨*trabajo*⟩ employment; ⟨*puesto*⟩ job

empobrecer [11] *vt* impoverish. ~**se** *vpr* become poor

empolvar *vt* powder

empoll|ar *vt* incubate ⟨*huevos*⟩; ⟨*estudiar, fam*⟩ swot up ⟨*Brit*⟩, grind away at ⟨*Amer*⟩. —*vi* ⟨*ave*⟩ sit; ⟨*estudiante*⟩ swot ⟨*Brit*⟩, grind away ⟨*Amer*⟩. ~**ón** *m* swot

emponzoñar *vt* poison

emporio *m* emporium; ⟨*LAm, almacén*⟩ department store

empotra|do *a* built-in, fitted. ~**r** *vt* fit

emprendedor *a* enterprising

emprender *vt* undertake; set out on ⟨*viaje etc*⟩. ~**la con uno** pick a fight with s.o.

empresa *f* undertaking; ⟨*com*⟩ company, firm. ~**rio** *m* impresario; ⟨*com*⟩ contractor

empréstito *m* loan

empuj|ar *vt* push; press ⟨*botón*⟩. ~**e** *m* push, shove; ⟨*fig*⟩ drive. ~**ón** *m* push, shove

empuñar *vt* grasp; take up ⟨*pluma, espada*⟩

emular *vt* emulate

emulsión *f* emulsion

en *prep* in; ⟨*sobre*⟩ on; ⟨*dentro*⟩ inside, in; ⟨*con dirección*⟩ into; ⟨*medio de transporte*⟩ by. ~ **casa** at home. ~ **coche** by car. ~ **10 días** in 10 days. **de pueblo** ~ **pueblo** from town to town

enagua *f* petticoat

enajena|ción *f* alienation; ⟨*éxtasis*⟩ rapture. ~**r** *vt* alienate; ⟨*volver loco*⟩ drive mad; ⟨*fig, extasiar*⟩ enrapture. ~**ción mental** insanity

enamora|do *a* in love. —*m* lover. ~**r** *vt* win the love of. ~**rse** *vpr* fall in love (**de** with)

enan|ito *m* dwarf. ~**o** *a* & *m* dwarf

enardecer [11] *vt* inflame. ~**se** *vpr* get excited (**por** about)

encabeza|miento *m* heading; ⟨*de periódico*⟩ headline. ~**r** [10] *vt* introduce ⟨*escrito*⟩; ⟨*poner título a*⟩ entitle; head ⟨*una lista*⟩; lead ⟨*revolución etc*⟩; ⟨*empadronar*⟩ register

encadenar *vt* chain; ⟨*fig*⟩ tie down

encaj|ar *vt* fit; fit together ⟨*varias piezas*⟩. —*vi* fit; ⟨*estar de acuerdo*⟩ tally. ~**arse** *vpr* squeeze into. ~**e** *m* lace; ⟨*acción de encajar*⟩ fitting

encajonar *vt* box; ⟨*en sitio estrecho*⟩ squeeze in

encalar *vt* whitewash

encallar *vt* run aground; ⟨*fig*⟩ get bogged down

encamina|r *vt* direct. ~**se** *vpr* make one's way

encandilar *vt* ⟨*pasmar*⟩ bewilder; ⟨*estimular*⟩ stimulate

encanecer [11] *vi* go grey

encant|ado *a* enchanted; ⟨*hechizado*⟩ bewitched; ⟨*casa etc*⟩ haunted. ~**ador** *a* charming. —*m* magician. ~**amiento** *m* magic. ~**ar** *vt* bewitch; ⟨*fig*⟩ charm, delight. ~**o** *m* magic; ⟨*fig*⟩ delight. **¡~ado!** pleased to meet you! **me** ~**a la leche** I love milk

encapotado *a* ⟨*cielo*⟩ overcast

encapricharse *vpr*. ~ **con** take a fancy to

encarar vt face. ~se vpr. ~se con face

encarcelar vt imprison

encarecer [11] vt put up the price of; (alabar) praise. —vi go up

encarg|ado a in charge. —m manager, attendant, person in charge. ~ar [12] vt entrust; (pedir) order. ~arse vpr take charge (de of). ~o m job; (com) order; (recado) errand. hecho de ~o made to measure

encariñarse vpr. ~ con take to, become fond of

encarna|ción f incarnation. ~do a incarnate; (rojo) red. —m red

encarnizado a bitter

encarpetar vt file; (LAm, dar carpetazo) shelve

encarrilar vt put back on the rails; (fig) direct, put on the right road

encasillar vt pigeonhole

encastillarse vpr. ~ en (fig) stick to

encauzar [10] vt channel

encend|edor m lighter. ~er [1] vt light; (pegar fuego a) set fire to; switch on, turn on (aparato eléctrico); (fig) arouse. ~erse vpr light; (prender fuego) catch fire; (excitarse) get excited; (ruborizarse) blush. ~ido a lit; (aparato eléctrico) on; (rojo) bright red. —m (auto) ignition

encera|do a waxed. —m (pizarra) blackboard. ~r vt wax

encerr|ar [1] vt shut in; (con llave) lock up; (fig, contener) contain. ~ona f trap

encía f gum

encíclica f encyclical

enciclop|edia f encyclopaedia. ~édico a encyclopaedic

encierro m confinement; (cárcel) prison

encima adv on top; (arriba) above. ~ de on, on top of; (sobre) over; (además de) besides, as well as. por ~ on top; (a la ligera) superficially. por ~ de todo above all

encina f holm oak

encinta a pregnant

enclave m enclave

enclenque a weak; (enfermizo) sickly

encog|er [14] vt shrink; (contraer) contract. ~erse vpr shrink. ~erse de hombros shrug one's shoulders. ~ido a shrunk; (fig, tímido) timid

encolar vt glue; (pegar) stick

encolerizar [10] vt make angry. ~se vpr get angry, lose one's temper

encomendar [1] vt entrust

encomi|ar vt praise. ~o m praise

encono m bitterness, ill will

encontra|do a contrary, conflicting. ~r [2] vt find; (tropezar con) meet. ~rse vpr meet; (hallarse) be. no ~rse feel uncomfortable

encorvar vt bend, curve. ~se vpr stoop

encrespado a (pelo) curly; (mar) rough

encrucijada f crossroads

encuaderna|ción f binding. ~dor m bookbinder. ~r vt bind

encuadrar vt frame

encub|ierto a hidden. ~rir [pp encubierto] vt hide, conceal; shelter (delincuente)

encuentro m meeting; (colisión) crash; (en deportes) match; (mil) skirmish

encuesta f survey; (investigación) inquiry

encumbra|do a eminent. ~r vt (fig, elevar) exalt. ~rse vpr rise

encurtidos mpl pickles

encharcar [7] vt flood. ~se vpr be flooded

enchufa|do a switched on. ~ar vt plug in; fit together (tubos etc).

~e *m* socket; (*clavija*) plug; (*de tubos etc*) joint; (*fig, empleo, fam*) cushy job; (*influencia, fam*) influence. **tener ~e** have friends in the right places

endeble *a* weak

endemoniado *a* possessed; (*malo*) wicked

enderezar [10] *vt* straighten out; (*poner vertical*) put upright (again); (*fig, arreglar*) put right, sort out; (*dirigir*) direct. **~se** *vpr* straighten out

endeudarse *vpr* get into debt

endiablado *a* possessed; (*malo*) wicked

endomingarse [12] *vpr* dress up

endosar *vt* endorse (*cheque etc*); (*fig, fam*) lumber

endrogarse [12] *vpr* (*Mex*) get into debt

endulzar [10] *vt* sweeten; (*fig*) soften

endurecer [11] *vt* harden. **~se** *vpr* harden; (*fig*) become hardened

enema *m* enema

enemi|go *a* hostile. —*m* enemy. **~stad** *f* enmity. **~star** *vt* make an enemy of. **~starse** *vpr* fall out (**con** with)

en|ergía *f* energy. **~érgico** *a* (*persona*) lively; (*decisión*) forceful

energúmeno *m* madman

enero *m* January

enervar *vt* enervate

enésimo *a* nth, umpteenth (*fam*)

enfad|adizo *a* irritable. **~ado** *a* cross, angry. **~ar** *vt* make cross, anger; (*molestar*) annoy. **~arse** *vpr* get cross. **~o** *m* anger; (*molestia*) annoyance

énfasis *m invar* emphasis, stress. **poner ~** stress, emphasize

enfático *a* emphatic

enferm|ar *vi* fall ill. **~edad** *f* illness. **~era** *f* nurse. **~ería** *f* sick

bay. **~ero** *m* (male) nurse. **~izo** *a* sickly. **~o** *a* ill. —*m* patient

enflaquecer [11] *vt* make thin. —*vi* lose weight

enfo|car [7] *vt* shine on; focus (*lente etc*); (*fig*) consider. **~que** *m* focus; (*fig*) point of view

enfrascarse [7] *vpr* (*fig*) be absorbed

enfrentar *vt* face, confront; (*poner frente a frente*) bring face to face. **~se** *vpr*. **~se con** confront; (*en deportes*) meet

enfrente *adv* opposite. **~ de** opposite. **de ~** opposite

enfria|miento *m* cooling; (*catarro*) cold. **~r** [20] *vt* cool (down); (*fig*) cool down. **~rse** *vpr* go cold; (*fig*) cool off

enfurecer [11] *vt* infuriate. **~se** *vpr* lose one's temper; (*mar*) get rough

enfurruñarse *vpr* sulk

engalanar *vt* adorn. **~se** *vpr* dress up

enganchar *vt* hook; hang up (*ropa*). **~se** *vpr* get caught; (*mil*) enlist

engañ|ar *vt* deceive, trick; (*ser infiel*) be unfaithful. **~arse** *vpr* be wrong, be mistaken; (*no admitir la verdad*) deceive o.s. **~o** *m* deceit, trickery; (*error*) mistake. **~oso** *a* deceptive; (*persona*) deceitful

engarzar [10] *vt* string (*cuentas*); set (*joyas*); (*fig*) link

engatusar *vt* (*fam*) coax

engendr|ar *vt* breed; (*fig*) produce. **~o** *m* (*monstruo*) monster; (*fig*) brainchild

englobar *vt* include

engomar *vt* glue

engordar *vt* fatten. —*vi* get fatter, put on weight

engorro *m* nuisance

engranaje *m* (*auto*) gear

engrandecer [11] *vt* (*enaltecer*) exalt, raise

engrasar vt grease; (con aceite) oil; (ensuciar) make greasy

engreído a arrogant

engrosar [2] vt swell. —vi (persona) get fatter; (río) swell

engullir [22] vt gulp down

enharinar vt sprinkle with flour

enhebrar vt thread

enhorabuena f congratulations. **dar la ~** congratulate

enigm|a m enigma. **~ático** a enigmatic

enjabonar vt soap; (fig, fam) butter up

enjalbegar [12] vt whitewash

enjambre m swarm

enjaular vt put in a cage

enjuag|ar [12] vt rinse (out). **~atorio** m mouthwash. **~ue** m rinsing; (para la boca) mouthwash

enjugar [12] vt dry; (limpiar) wipe; cancel (deuda)

enjuiciar vt pass judgement on

enjuto a (persona) skinny

enlace m connection; (matrimonial) wedding

enlatar vt tin, can

enlazar [10] vt tie together; (fig) relate, connect

enlodar vt, **enlodazar** [10] vt cover in mud

enloquecer [11] vt drive mad. —vi go mad. **~se** vpr go mad

enlosar vt (con losas) pave; (con baldosas) tile

enlucir [11] vt plaster

enluta|do a in mourning. **~r** vt dress in mourning; (fig) sadden

enmarañar vt tangle (up), entangle; (confundir) confuse. **~se** vpr get into a tangle; (confundirse) get confused

enmarcar [7] vt frame

enmascarar vt mask. **~se de** masquerade as

enm|endar vt correct. **~endarse** vpr mend one's way.

~ienda f correction; (de ley etc) amendment

enmohecerse [11] vpr (con óxido) go rusty; (con hongos) go mouldy

enmudecer [11] vi be dumbstruck; (callar) say nothing

ennegrecer [11] vt blacken

ennoblecer [11] vt ennoble; (fig) add style to

enoj|adizo a irritable. **~ado** a angry, cross. **~ar** vt make cross, anger; (molestar) annoy. **~arse** vpr get cross. **~o** m anger; (molestia) annoyance. **~oso** a annoying

enorgullecerse [11] vpr be proud

enorm|e a enormous; (malo) wicked. **~emente** adv enormously. **~idad** f immensity; (atrocidad) enormity. **me gusta una ~idad** I like it enormously

enrabiar vt infuriate

enraizar [10 & 20] vi take root

enrarecido a rarefied

enrasar vt make level

enred|adera f creeper. **~adero** a climbing. **~ar** vt tangle (up), entangle; (confundir) confuse; (comprometer a uno) involve, implicate; (sembrar la discordia) cause trouble between. —vi get up to mischief. **~ar con** fiddle with, play with. **~arse** vpr get into a tangle; (confundirse) get confused; (persona) get involved. **~o** m tangle; (fig) muddle, mess

enrejado m bars

enrevesado a complicated

enriquecer [11] vt make rich; (fig) enrich. **~se** vpr get rich

enrojecer [11] vt turn red, redden. **~se** vpr (persona) go red, blush

enrolar vt enlist

enrollar vt roll (up); wind (hilo etc)

enroscar [7] vt coil; (atornillar) screw in

ensalada f salad. ~**era** f salad bowl. ~**illa** f Russian salad. **armar una** ~**a** make a mess

ensalzar [10] vt praise; (enaltecer) exalt

ensambladura f, **ensamblaje** m (acción) assembling; (efecto) joint

ensamblar vt join

ensanch|ar vt widen; (agrandar) enlarge. ~**arse** vpr get wider. ~**e** m widening; (de ciudad) new district

ensangrentar [1] vt stain with blood

ensañarse vpr. ~ **con** treat cruelly

ensartar vt string (cuentas etc)

ensay|ar vt test; rehearse (obra de teatro etc). ~**arse** vpr rehearse. ~**o** m test, trial; (composición literaria) essay

ensenada f inlet, cove

enseña|nza f education; (acción de enseñar) teaching. ~**nza media** secondary education. ~**r** vt teach; (mostrar) show

enseñorearse vpr take over

enseres mpl equipment

ensillar vt saddle

ensimismarse vpr be lost in thought

ensoberbecerse [11] vpr become conceited

ensombrecer [11] vt darken

ensordecer [11] vt deafen. —vi go deaf

ensortijar vt curl (pelo etc)

ensuciar vt dirty. ~**se** vpr get dirty

ensueño m dream

entablar vt (empezar) start

entablillar vt put in a splint

entalegar [12] vt put into a bag; (fig) hoard

entallar vt fit (un vestido). —vi fit

entarimado m parquet

ente m entity, being; (persona rara, fam) odd person; (com) firm, company

entend|er [1] vt understand; (opinar) believe, think; (querer decir) mean. —vi understand. ~**erse** vpr make o.s. understood; (comprenderse) be understood. ~**er de** know all about. ~**erse con** get on with. ~**ido** a understood; (enterado) wellinformed. —interj agreed!, OK! (fam). ~**imiento** m understanding. **a mi** ~**er** in my opinion. **dar a** ~**er** hint. **no darse por** ~**ido** pretend not to understand, turn a deaf ear

entenebrecer [11] vt darken. ~**se** vpr get dark

enterado a well-informed; (que sabe) aware. **no darse por** ~ pretend not to understand, turn a deaf ear

enteramente adv entirely, completely

enterar vt inform. ~**se** vpr. ~**se de** find out about, hear of. ¡**entérate!** listen! ¿**te enteras?** do you understand?

entereza f (carácter) strength of character

enternecer [11] vt (fig) move, touch. ~**se** vpr be moved, be touched

entero a entire, whole; (firme) firm. **por** ~ entirely, completely

enterra|dor m gravedigger. ~**r** [1] vt bury

entibiar vt cool. ~**se** vpr cool down; (fig) cool off

entidad f entity; (organización) organization; (com) company

entierro m burial; (ceremonia) funeral

entona|ción f intonation; (fig) arrogance. ~**r** vt intone. —vi (mus) be in tune; (colores) match. ~**rse** vpr (fortalecerse) tone o.s. up; ⟨*engreírse*⟩ be arrogant

entonces *adv* then. **en aquel ∼, por aquel ∼** at that time, then

entontecer [11] *vt* make silly. **∼se** *vpr* get silly

entornar *vt* half close; leave ajar ⟨*puerta*⟩

entorpecer [11] *vt* ⟨*frío etc*⟩ numb; ⟨*dificultar*⟩ hinder

entrada *f* entrance; ⟨*acceso*⟩ admission, entry; ⟨*billete*⟩ ticket; ⟨*de datos, tec*⟩ input. **∼do** *a*. **∼do en años** elderly. **ya ∼da la noche** late at night. **∼nte** *a* next, coming. **dar ∼da** *a* ⟨*admitir*⟩ admit. **de ∼da** right away.

entraña *f* ⟨*fig*⟩ heart. **∼s** *fpl* entrails; ⟨*fig*⟩ heart. **∼ble** *a* ⟨*cariño etc*⟩ deep; ⟨*amigo*⟩ close. **∼r** *vt* involve

entrar *vt* put; ⟨*traer*⟩ bring. −*vi* go in, enter; ⟨*venir*⟩ come in, enter; ⟨*empezar*⟩ start, begin. **no ∼ ni salir en** have nothing to do with

entre *prep* ⟨*de dos personas o cosas*⟩ between; ⟨*más de dos*⟩ among(st)

entreabierto *a* half-open. **∼rir** [*pp* **entreabierto**] *vt* half open

entreacto *m* interval

entrecano *a* ⟨*pelo*⟩ greying; ⟨*persona*⟩ who is going grey

entrecejo *m* forehead. **arrugar el ∼, fruncir el ∼** frown

entrecerrar [1] *vt* ⟨*Amer*⟩ half close

entrecortado *a* ⟨*voz*⟩ faltering; ⟨*respiración*⟩ laboured

entrecruzar [10] *vt* intertwine

entrega *f* handing over; ⟨*de mercancías etc*⟩ delivery; ⟨*de novela etc*⟩ instalment; ⟨*dedicación*⟩ commitment. **∼r** [12] *vt* hand over, deliver, give. **∼rse** *vpr* surrender, give o.s. up; ⟨*dedicarse*⟩ devote o.s. (**a** to)

entrelazar [10] *vt* intertwine

entremés *m* hors-d'oeuvre; ⟨*en el teatro*⟩ short comedy

entremeter *vt* insert. **∼erse** *vpr* interfere. **∼ido** *a* interfering

entremezclar *vt* mix

entrenador *m* trainer. **∼miento** *m* training. **∼r** *vt* train. **∼rse** *vpr* train

entrepierna *f* crotch

entresacar [7] *vt* pick out

entresuelo *m* mezzanine

entretanto *adv* meanwhile

entretejer *vt* interweave

entretener [40] *vt* entertain, amuse; ⟨*detener*⟩ delay, keep; ⟨*mantener*⟩ keep alive, keep going. **∼erse** *vpr* amuse o.s.; ⟨*tardar*⟩ delay, linger. **∼ido** *a* entertaining. **∼imiento** *m* entertainment; ⟨*mantenimiento*⟩ upkeep

entrever [43] *vt* make out, glimpse

entrevista *f* interview; ⟨*reunión*⟩ meeting. **∼rse** *vpr* have an interview

entristecer [11] *vt* sadden, make sad. **∼se** *vpr* be sad

entrometerse *vpr* interfere. **∼ido** *a* interfering

entroncar [7] *vi* be related

entruchada *f*, **entruchado** *m* ⟨*fam*⟩ plot

entumecerse [11] *vpr* go numb. **∼ido** *a* numb

enturbiar *vt* cloud

entusiasmar *vt* fill with enthusiasm; ⟨*gustar mucho*⟩ delight. **∼asmarse** *vpr*. **∼asmarse con** get enthusiastic about; ⟨*ser aficionado a*⟩ be mad about, love. **∼asmo** *m* enthusiasm. **∼asta** *a* enthusiastic. **−m & f** enthusiast. **∼ástico** *a* enthusiastic

enumeración *f* count, reckoning. **∼r** *vt* enumerate

enunciación *f* enunciation. **∼r** *vt* enunciate

envainar vt sheathe

envalentonar vt encourage. **~se** vpr be brave, pluck up courage

envanecer [11] vt make conceited. **~se** vpr be conceited

envas|ado a tinned. —m packaging. **~ar** vt package; (en latas) tin, can; (en botellas) bottle. **~e** m packing; (lata) tin, can; (botella) bottle

envejec|er [11] vt make old. —vi get old, grow old. **~erse** vpr get old, grow old. **~ido** a aged, old

envenenar vt poison

envergadura f (alcance) scope

envés m wrong side

envia|do a sent. —m representative; (de la prensa) correspondent. **~r** vt send

enviciar vt corrupt

envidi|a f envy; (celos) jealousy. **~able** a enviable. **~ar** vt envy, be envious of. **~oso** a envious. **tener ~a a** envy

envilecer [11] vt degrade

envío m sending, dispatch; (de mercancías) consignment; (de dinero) remittance. **~ contra reembolso** cash on delivery. **gastos mpl de envío** postage and packing (costs)

enviudar vi (mujer) become a widow, be widowed; (hombre) become a widower, be widowed

env|oltura f wrapping. **~olver** [2, pp envuelto] vt wrap; (cubrir) cover; (fig, acorralar) corner; (fig, enredar) involve; (mil) surround. **~olvimiento** m involvement. **~uelto** a wrapped (up)

enyesar vt plaster; (med) put in plaster

enzima f enzyme

épica f epic

epicentro m epicentre

épico a epic

epid|emia f epidemic. **~émico** a epidemic

epil|epsia f epilepsy. **~éptico** a epileptic

epílogo m epilogue

episodio m episode

epístola f epistle

epitafio m epitaph

epíteto m epithet

epítome m epitome

época f age; (período) period. **hacer ~** make history, be epoch-making

equidad f equity

equilátero a equilateral

equilibr|ar vt balance. **~io** m balance; (de balanza) equilibrium. **~ista** m & f tightrope walker

equino a horse, equine

equinoccio m equinox

equipaje m luggage (esp Brit), baggage (esp Amer); (de barco) crew

equipar vt equip; (de ropa) fit out

equiparar vt make equal; (comparar) compare

equipo m equipment; (en deportes) team

equitación f riding

equivale|ncia f equivalence. **~nte** a equivalent. **~r** [42] vi be equivalent; (significar) mean

equivoca|ción f mistake, error. **~do** a wrong. **~r** [7] vt mistake. **~rse** vpr be mistaken, be wrong, make a mistake. **~rse de** be wrong about. **~rse de número** dial the wrong number. **si no me equivoco** if I'm not mistaken

equívoco a equivocal; (sospechoso) suspicious. —m ambiguity; (juego de palabras) pun; (doble sentido) double meaning

era f era. —vb véase **ser**

erario m treasury

erección f erection; (fig) establishment

eremita *m* hermit
eres *vb véase* ser
erguir [48] *vt* raise. ~ **la cabeza** hold one's head high. ~**se** *vpr* straighten up
erigir [14] *vt* erect. ~**se** *vpr* set o.s. up (**en** as)
eriza|**do** *a* prickly. ~**rse** [10] *vpr* stand on end
erizo *m* hedgehog; (*de mar*) sea urchin. ~ **de mar**, ~ **marino** sea urchin
ermita *f* hermitage. ~**ño** *m* hermit
erosi|**ón** *f* erosion. ~**onar** *vt* erode
er|**ótico** *a* erotic. ~**otismo** *m* eroticism
errar [1, la i inicial se escribe **y**] *vt* miss. —*vi* wander; (*equivocarse*) make a mistake, be wrong
errata *f* misprint
erróneo *a* erroneous, wrong
error *m* error, mistake. **estar en un** ~ be wrong, be mistaken
eructar *vi* belch
erudi|**ción** *f* learning, erudition. ~**to** *a* learned
erupción *f* eruption; (*med*) rash
es *vb véase* ser
esa *a véase* ese
ésa *pron véase* **ése**
esbelto *a* slender, slim
esboz|**ar** [10] *vt* sketch, outline. ~**o** *m* sketch, outline
escabeche *m* pickle. **en** ~ pickled
escabroso *a* ⟨*terreno*⟩ rough; ⟨*asunto*⟩ difficult; (*atrevido*) crude
escabullirse [22] *vpr* slip away
escafandra *f*, **escafandro** *m* diving-suit
escala *f* scale; (*escalera de mano*) ladder; (*de avión*) stopover. ~**da** *f* climbing; (*pol*) escalation. ~**r** *vt* scale; break into ⟨*una casa*⟩. —*vi* (*pol*) escalate. **hacer** ~ **en**

stop at. **vuelo sin** ~**s** non-stop flight
escaldar *vt* scald
escalera *f* staircase, stairs; (*de mano*) ladder. ~ **de caracol** spiral staircase. ~ **de incendios** fire escape. ~ **mecánica** escalator. ~ **plegable** stepladder
escalfa|**do** *a* poached. ~**r** *vt* poach
escalinata *f* flight of steps
escalofrío *m* shiver
escal|**ón** *m* step; (*de escalera interior*) stair; (*de escala*) rung. ~**onar** *vt* spread out
escalope *m* escalope
escam|**a** *f* scale; (*de jabón*) flake; (*fig*) suspicion. ~**oso** *a* scaly
escamotear *vt* make disappear; (*robar*) steal, pinch (*fam*); disregard ⟨*dificultad*⟩
escampar *vi* stop raining
esc|**andalizar** [10] *vt* scandalize, shock. ~**andalizarse** *vpr* be shocked. ~**ándalo** *m* scandal; (*alboroto*) uproar. ~**andaloso** *a* scandalous; (*alborotador*) noisy
Escandinavia *f* Scandinavia
escandinavo *a* & *m* Scandinavian
escaño *m* bench; (*pol*) seat
escapa|**da** *f* escape; (*visita*) flying visit. ~**do** *a* in a hurry. ~**r** *vi* escape. ~**rse** *vpr* escape; (*líquido, gas*) leak. **dejar** ~**r** let out
escaparate *m* (shop) window. **ir de** ~**s** go window-shopping
escapatoria *f* (*fig, fam*) way out
escape *m* (*de gas, de líquido*) leak; (*fuga*) escape; (*auto*) exhaust
escarabajo *m* beetle
escaramuza *f* skirmish
escarbar *vt* scratch; pick ⟨*dientes, herida etc*⟩; (*fig, escudriñar*) delve (**en** into)
escarcha *f* frost. ~**do** *a* ⟨*fruta*⟩ crystallized

escarlat|a *a invar* scarlet. **~ina** *f* scarlet fever

escarm|entar [1] *vt* punish severely. —*vi* learn one's lesson. **~iento** *m* punishment; (*lección*) lesson

escarn|ecer [11] *vt* mock. **~io** *m* ridicule

escarola *f* endive

escarpa *f* slope. **~do** *a* steep

escas|ear *vi* be scarce. **~ez** *f* scarcity, shortage; (*pobreza*) poverty. **~o** *a* scarce; (*poco*) little; (*insuficiente*) short; (*muy justo*) barely

escatimar *vt* be sparing with

escayola *f* plaster. **~r** *vt* put in plaster

escena *f* scene; (*escenario*) stage. **~rio** *m* stage; (*en el cine*) scenario; (*fig*) scene

escénico *a* scenic

escenografía *f* scenery

esc|epticismo *m* scepticism. **~éptico** *a* sceptical. —*m* sceptic

esclarecer [11] *vt* (*fig*) throw light on, clarify

esclavina *f* cape

esclav|itud *f* slavery. **~izar** [10] *vt* enslave. **~o** *m* slave

esclerosis *f* sclerosis

esclusa *f* lock

escoba *f* broom

escocer [2 & 9] *vt* hurt. —*vi* sting

escocés *a* Scottish. —*m* Scotsman

Escocia *f* Scotland

escog|er [14] *vt* choose, select. **~ido** *a* chosen; (*de buena calidad*) choice

escolar *a* school. —*m* schoolboy. —*f* schoolgirl. **~idad** *f* schooling

escolta *f* escort

escombros *mpl* rubble

escond|er *vt* hide. **~erse** *vpr* hide. **~idas. a ~idas** secretly. **~ite** *m* hiding place; (*juego*) hide-and-seek. **~rijo** *m* hiding place

escopeta *f* shotgun. **~zo** *m* shot

escoplo *m* chisel

escoria *f* slag; (*fig*) dregs

Escorpión *m* Scorpio

escorpión *m* scorpion

escot|ado *a* low-cut. **~adura** *f* low neckline. **~ar** *vt* cut out. —*vi* pay one's share. **~e** *m* low neckline. **ir a ~e, pagar a ~e** share the expenses

escozor *m* pain

escri|bano *m* clerk. **~biente** *m* clerk. **~bir** [*pp* escrito] *vt/i* write. **~bir a máquina** type. **~birse** *vpr* write to each other; (*deletrearse*) be spelt. **~to** *a* written. —*m* writing; (*documento*) document. **~tor** *m* writer. **~torio** *m* desk; (*oficina*) office. **~tura** *f* (hand)writing; (*documento*) document; (*jurid*) deed. **¿cómo se escribe...?** how do you spell...? **poner por ~to** put into writing

escr|úpulo *m* scruple; (*escrupulosidad*) care, scrupulousness. **~uloso** *a* scrupulous

escrut|ar *vt* scrutinize; count (*votos*). **~inio** *m* count. **hacer el ~inio** count the votes

escuadr|a *f* (*instrumento*) square; (*mil*) squad; (*naut*) fleet. **~ón** *m* squadron

escuálido *a* skinny; (*sucio*) squalid

escuchar *vt* listen to. —*vi* listen

escudilla *f* bowl

escudo *m* shield. **~ de armas** coat of arms

escudriñar *vt* examine

escuela *f* school. **~ normal** teachers' training college

escueto *a* simple

escuincle *m* (*Mex, perro*) stray dog; (*Mex, muchacho, fam*) child, kid (*fam*)

esculpir vt sculpture. ~**tor** m sculptor. ~**tora** f sculptress. ~**tura** f sculpture; (en madera) carving

escupir vt/i spit

escurr|eplatos m invar plate-rack. ~**idizo** a slippery. ~**ir** vt drain; wring out ⟨ropa⟩. —vi drip; (ser resbaladizo) be slippery. ~**irse** vpr slip

ese a (f **esa**, mpl **esos**, fpl **esas**) that; (en plural) those

ése pron (f **ésa**, mpl **ésos**, fpl **ésas**) that one; (en plural) those; (primero de dos) the former. **ni por ésas** on no account

esencia f essence. ~**l** a essential. **lo** ~**l** the main thing

esfera f sphere; (de reloj) face. ~**érico** a spherical

esfinge f sphinx

esf|orzarse [2 & 10] vpr make an effort. ~**uerzo** m effort

esfumarse vpr fade away; ⟨persona⟩ vanish

esgrim|a f fencing. ~**ir** vt brandish; (fig) use

esguince m swerve; (med) sprain

eslab|ón m link. ~**onar** vt link (together)

eslavo a Slav, Slavonic

eslogan m slogan

esmalt|ar vt enamel; varnish ⟨uñas⟩; (fig) adorn. ~**e** m enamel. ~**e de uñas**, ~**e para las uñas** nail varnish (Brit), nail polish (Amer)

esmerado a careful

esmeralda f emerald

esmerarse vpr take care (**en** over)

esmeril m emery

esmero m care

esmoquin m dinner jacket, tuxedo (Amer)

esnob a invar snobbish. —m & f (pl **esnobs**) snob. ~**ismo** m snobbery

esnórkel m snorkel

eso pron that. **¡**~ **es!** that's it! ~ **mismo** exactly. **¡**~ **no!** certainly not! ⟨por⟩ ~ **sí!** of course. **a** ~ **de** about. **en** ~ at that moment. **¿no es** ~**?** isn't that right? **por** ~ therefore. **y** ~ **que** although

esos a pl véase **ese**

ésos pron pl véase **ése**

espabila|do a bright. ~**r** vt snuff ⟨vela⟩; (avivar) brighten up; (despertar) wake up. ~**rse** vpr wake up; (apresurarse) hurry up

espaci|al a space. ~**ar** vt space out. ~**o** m space. ~**oso** a spacious

espada f sword. ~**s** fpl (en naipes) spades

espagueti m spaghetti

espald|a f back. ~**illa** f shoulder-blade. **a** ~**as de uno** behind s.o.'s back. **a** ~**as de uno** on one's back. **tener las** ~**as anchas** be broad-shouldered. **volver la** ~**a a uno, volver las** ~**as a uno** give s.o. the cold shoulder

espant|ada f stampede. ~**adizo** a timid, timorous. ~**ajo** m, ~**apájaros** m invar scarecrow. ~**ar** vt frighten; (ahuyentar) frighten away. ~**arse** vpr be frightened; (ahuyentarse) be frightened away. ~**o** m terror; (horror) horror. ~**oso** a frightening; (muy grande) terrible. **¡qué** ~**ajo!** what a sight!

España f Spain

español a Spanish. —m (persona) Spaniard; (lengua) Spanish. **los** ~**es** the Spanish. ~**izado** a Hispanicized

esparadrapo m sticking-plaster, plaster (Brit)

esparci|do a scattered; (fig) widespread. ~**r** [9] vt scatter; (difundir) spread. ~**rse** vpr be scattered; (difundirse) spread; (divertirse) enjoy o.s.

espárrago m asparagus

esparto *m* esparto (grass)

espasm|o *m* spasm. **~ódico** *a* spasmodic

espátula *f* spatula; (*en pintura*) palette knife

especia *f* spice

especial *a* special. **~idad** *f* speciality (*Brit*), specialty (*Amer*). **~ista** *a* & *m* & *f* specialist. **~ización** *f* specialization. **~izar** [10] *vt* specialize. **~izarse** *vpr* specialize. **~mente** *adv* especially. **en ~** especially

especie *f* kind, sort; (*en biología*) species; (*noticia*) piece of news. **en ~** in kind

especifica|ción *f* specification. **~r** [7] *vt* specify

específico *a* a specific

espect|áculo *m* sight; (*diversión*) entertainment, show. **~ador** *m* & *f* spectator. **~acular** *a* spectacular

espectro *m* spectre; (*en física*) spectrum

especula|ción *f* speculation. **~dor** *m* speculator. **~r** *vi* speculate. **~tivo** *a* speculative

espej|ismo *m* mirage. **~o** *m* mirror. **~o retrovisor** (*auto*) rearview mirror

espeleólogo *m* potholer

espeluznante *a* horrifying

espera *f* wait. **sala** *f* **de ~** waiting room

espera|nza *f* hope. **~r** *vt* hope; (*aguardar*) wait for; (*creer*) expect. —*vi* hope; (*aguardar*) wait. **~r en uno** trust in s.o. **en ~ de** awaiting. **espero que no** I hope not. **espero que sí** I hope so

esperma *f* sperm

esperpento *m* fright; (*disparate*) nonsense

espes|ar *vt* thicken. **~arse** *vpr* thicken. **~o** *a* thick; (*pasta etc*) stiff. **~or** *m*, **~ura** *f* thickness; (*bot*) thicket

espetón *m* spit

esp|ía *f* spy. **~iar** [20] *vt* spy on. —*vi* spy

espiga *f* (*de trigo etc*) ear

espina *f* thorn; (*de pez*) bone; (*dorsal*) spine; (*astilla*) splinter; (*fig, dificultad*) difficulty. **~ dorsal** spine

espinaca *f* spinach

espinazo *m* spine

espinilla *f* shin; (*med*) blackhead

espino *m* hawthorn. **~ artificial** barbed wire. **~so** *a* thorny; (*pez*) bony; (*fig*) difficult

espionaje *m* espionage

espiral *a* & *f* spiral

espirar *vt/i* breathe out

esp|iritismo *m* spiritualism. **~iritoso** *a* spirited. **~iritista** *m* & *f* spiritualist. **~íritu** *m* spirit; (*mente*) mind; (*inteligencia*) intelligence. **~iritual** *a* spiritual. **~iritualismo** *m* spiritualism

espita *f* tap, faucet (*Amer*)

espl|éndido *a* splendid; (*persona*) generous. **~endor** *m* splendour

espliego *m* lavender

espolear *vt* (*fig*) spur on

espoleta *f* fuse

espolvorear *vt* sprinkle

esponj|a *f* sponge; (*tejido*) towelling. **~oso** *a* spongy. **pasar la ~a** forget about it

espont|aneidad *f* spontaneity. **~áneo** *a* spontaneous

esporádico *a* sporadic

espos|a *f* wife. **~as** *fpl* handcuffs. **~ar** *vt* handcuff. **~o** *m* husband. **los ~os** the couple

espuela *f* spur; (*fig*) incentive. **dar de ~s** spur on

espum|a *f* foam; (*en bebidas*) froth; (*de jabón*) lather. **~ar** *vt* skim. —*vi* foam; (*bebidas*) froth; (*jabón*) lather. **~oso** *a* (*vino*) sparkling. **echar ~a** foam, froth

esqueleto *m* skeleton

esquem|a *m* outline. **∼ático** *a* sketchy

esqu|í *m* (*pl* **esquís**) ski; (*el deporte*) skiing. **∼iador** *m* skier. **∼iar** [20] *vi* ski

esquilar *vt* shear

esquimal *a* & *m* Eskimo

esquina *f* corner

esquirol *m* blackleg

esquiv|ar *vt* avoid. **∼o** *a* aloof

esquizofrénico *a* & *m* schizophrenic

esta *a véase* **este**

ésta *pron véase* **éste**

estab|ilidad *f* stability. **∼ilizador** *m* stabilizer. **∼ilizar** [10] *vt* stabilize. **∼le** *a* stable

establec|er [11] *vt* establish. **∼erse** *vpr* settle; (*com*) start a business. **∼imiento** *m* establishment

establo *m* cowshed

estaca *f* stake; (*para apalear*) stick. **∼da** *f* (*cerca*) fence

estación *f* station; (*del año*) season; (*de vacaciones*) resort. **∼ de servicio** service station

estaciona|miento *m* parking. **∼r** *vt* station; (*auto*) park. **∼rio** *a* stationary

estadio *m* stadium; (*fase*) stage

estadista *m* statesman. **–f** stateswoman

estadístic|a *f* statistics. **∼o** *a* statistical

estado *m* state. **∼ civil** marital status. **∼ de ánimo** frame of mind. **∼ de cuenta** bank statement. **∼ mayor** (*mil*) staff. **en buen ∼** in good condition. **en ∼ (interesante)** pregnant

Estados Unidos *mpl* United States

estadounidense *a* American, United States. **–m & f** American

estafa *f* swindle. **∼r** *vt* swindle

estafeta *f* (*oficina de correos*) (sub-)post office

estala|ctita *f* stalactite. **∼gmita** *f* stalagmite

estall|ar *vi* explode; (*olas*) break; (*guerra, epidemia etc*) break out; (*fig*) burst. **∼ar en llanto** burst into tears. **∼ar de risa** burst out laughing. **∼ido** *m* explosion; (*de guerra, epidemia etc*) outbreak; (*de risa etc*) outburst

estampa *f* print; (*aspecto*) appearance. **∼ado** *a* printed. **–m** printing; (*tela*) cotton print. **∼ar** *vt* stamp; (*imprimir*) print. **dar a la ∼a** (*imprimir*) print; (*publicar*) publish. **la viva ∼a** the image

estampía. de ∼ía suddenly

estampido *m* explosion

estampilla *f* stamp; (*Mex*) (postage) stamp

estanca|do *a* stagnant. **∼miento** *m* stagnation. **∼r** [7] *vt* stem; (*com*) turn into a monopoly

estanci|a *f* stay; (*Arg, finca*) ranch, farm; (*cuarto*) room. **∼ero** *m* (*Arg*) farmer

estanco *a* watertight. **–m** tobacconist's (shop)

estandarte *m* standard, banner

estanque *m* lake; (*depósito de agua*) reservoir

estanquero *m* tobacconist

estante *m* shelf. **∼ría** *f* shelves; (*para libros*) bookcase

estaño *m* tin. **∼adura** *f* tinplating

estar [27] *vi* be; (*quedarse*) stay; (*estar en casa*) be in. **¿estamos?** alright? **estamos a 29 de noviembre** it's the 29th of November. **∼ para** be about to. **∼ por** remain to be; (*con ganas de*) be tempted to; (*ser partidario de*) be in favour of. **∼se** *vpr* stay. **¿cómo está Vd?, ¿cómo estás?** how are you?

estarcir [9] *vt* stencil

estatal *a* state

estático a static; (pasmado) dumbfounded

estatua f statue

estatura f height

estatutario a statutory. **~o** m statute

este m east; (viento) east wind. **—** a (f **esta**, mpl **estos**, fpl **estas**) this; (en plural) these. **—int** (LAm) well, er

éste pron (f **ésta**, mpl **éstos**, fpl **éstas**) this one, (en plural) these; (segundo de dos) the latter

estela f wake; (arquit) carved stone

estera f mat; (tejido) matting

estéreo a stereo. **~reofónico** a stereo, stereophonic

esterilla f mat

estereotipado a stereotyped. **~o** m stereotype

estéril a sterile; (mujer) infertile; (terreno) barren. **~erilidad** f sterility; (de mujer) infertility; (de terreno) barrenness

esterlina a sterling. **libra** f **~** pound sterling

estético a aesthetic

estevado a bow-legged

estiércol m dung; (abono) manure

estigma m stigma. **~s** mpl (relig) stigmata

estilarse vpr be used

estilista m & f stylist. **~izar** [10] vt stylize. **~o** m style. **por el ~** of that sort

estilográfica f fountain pen

estima f esteem. **~do** a esteemed. **~do señor** (en cartas) Dear Sir. **~r** vt esteem; have great respect for (persona); (valorar) value; (juzgar) think

estimulante a stimulating. **—m** stimulant. **~imular** vt stimulate; (incitar) incite. **~ímulo** m stimulus

estipular vt stipulate

estirado a stretched; (persona) haughty. **~ar** vt stretch; (fig) stretch out. **~ón** m pull, tug; (crecimiento) sudden growth

estival a summer

esto pron neutro this; (este asunto) this business. **en ~** at this point. **en ~ de** in this business of. **por ~** therefore

estofa f class. **de baja ~** (gente) low-class

estofado a stewed. **—m** stew. **~r** vt stew

estoicismo m stoicism. **~o** a stoical. **—m** stoic

estómago m stomach. **dolor** m **de ~** stomach-ache

estorbar vt hinder, obstruct; (molestar) bother, annoy. **—vi** be in the way. **~o** m hindrance; (molestia) nuisance

estornino m starling

estornudar vi sneeze. **~o** m sneeze

estos a mpl véase **este**

éstos pron mpl véase **éste**

estoy vb véase **estar**

estrabismo m squint

estrado m stage; (mus) band-stand

estrafalario a outlandish

estragar [12] vt devastate. **~o** m devastation. **hacer ~os** devastate

estragón m tarragon

estrambótico a outlandish

estrangulación f strangulation. **~dor** m strangler; (auto) choke. **~miento** m blockage; (auto) bottleneck. **~r** vt strangle

estraperlo m black market. **comprar algo de ~** buy sth on the black market

estratagema f stratagem

estratega m & f strategist. **~ia** f strategy

estratégic|amente *adv* strategically. **~o** *a* strategic

estrato *m* stratum

estratosfera *f* stratosphere

estrech|ar *vt* make narrower; take in *(vestido)*; *(apretar)* squeeze; hug *(persona)*. **~ar la mano a uno** shake hands with s.o. **~arse** *vpr* become narrower; *(apretarse)* squeeze up. **~ez** *f* narrowness; *(apuro)* tight spot; *(falta de dinero)* want. **~o** *a* narrow; *(vestido etc)* tight; *(fig, íntimo)* close. —*m* straits. **~o de miras, de miras ~as** narrow-minded

estregar [1 & 12] *vt* rub

estrella *f* star. **~ de mar, ~mar** *m* starfish

estrellar *vt* smash; fry *(huevos)*. **~se** *vpr* smash; *(fracasar)* fail. **~se contra** crash into

estremec|er [11] *vt* shake. **~erse** *vpr* tremble (**de** with). **~imiento** *m* shaking

estren|ar *vt* use for the first time; wear for the first time *(vestido etc)*; show for the first time *(película)*. **~arse** *vpr* make one's début; *(película)* have its première; *(obra de teatro)* open. **~o** *m* first use; *(de película)* première; *(de obra de teatro)* first night

estreñi|do *a* constipated. **~miento** *m* constipation

estré|pito *m* din. **~epitoso** *a* noisy; *(fig)* resounding

estreptomicina *f* streptomycin

estrés *m* stress

estría *f* groove

estribar *vt* rest (**en** on); *(consistir)* lie (**en** in)

estribillo *m* refrain; *(muletilla)* catchphrase

estribo *m* stirrup; *(de vehículo)* step; *(contrafuerte)* buttress. **perder los ~** lose one's temper

estribor *m* starboard

estricto *a* strict

estridente *a* strident, raucous

estrofa *f* strophe

estropajo *m* scourer. **~so** *a* *(carne etc)* tough; *(persona)* slovenly

estropear *vt* spoil; *(romper)* break. **~se** *vpr* be damaged; *(fruta etc)* go bad; *(fracasar)* fail

estructura *f* structure. **~l** *a* structural

estruendo *m* din; *(de mucha gente)* uproar. **~so** *a* deafening

estrujar *vt* squeeze; *(fig)* drain

estuario *m* estuary

estuco *m* stucco

estuche *m* case

estudi|ante *m & f* student. **~antil** *a* student. **~ar** *vt* study. **~o** *m* study; *(de artista)* studio. **~oso** *a* studious

estufa *f* heater; *(LAm)* cooker

estupefac|ción *f* astonishment. **~iente** *a* astonishing. —*m* narcotic. **~to** *a* astonished

estupendo *a* marvellous; *(hermoso)* beautiful

estup|idez *f* stupidity; *(acto)* stupid thing. **~úpido** *a* stupid

estupor *m* amazement

esturión *m* sturgeon

estuve *vb véase* **estar**

etapa *f* stage. **hacer ~ en** break the journey at. **por ~s** in stages

etc *abrev* *(etcétera)* etc

etcétera *adv* et cetera

éter *m* ether

etéreo *a* ethereal

etern|amente *adv* eternally. **~idad** *f* eternity. **~izar** [10] *vt* drag out. **~izarse** *vpr* be interminable. **~o** *a* eternal

étic|a *f* ethics. **~o** *a* ethical

etimología *f* etymology

etiqueta *f* ticket, tag; *(ceremonial)* etiquette. **de ~** formal

étnico *a* ethnic

eucalipto *m* eucalyptus

eufemismo *m* euphemism

euforia *f* euphoria

Europa f Europe

europeo a & m European. **~izar** [10] vt Europeanize

eutanasia f euthanasia

evacuación f evacuation. **~r** [21 o regular] vt evacuate

evadir vt avoid. **~se** vpr escape

evaluar [21] vt evaluate

evangélico a evangelical. **~elio** m gospel. **~elista** m & f evangelist

evaporación f evaporation. **~r** vi evaporate. **~rse** vpr evaporate; (fig) disappear

evasión f evasion; (fuga) escape. **~vo** a evasive

evento m event. **a todo ~** at all events

eventual a possible. **~idad** f eventuality

evidencia f evidence. **~ciar** vt show. **~ciarse** vpr be obvious. **~te** a obvious. **~temente** adv obviously. **poner en ~cia** show; (fig) make a fool of

evitar vt avoid; (ahorrar) spare

evocar [7] vt evoke

evolución f evolution. **~onado** a fully-developed. **~onar** vi evolve; (mil) manoeuvre

ex pref ex-, former

exacerbar vt exacerbate

exactamente adv exactly. **~itud** f exactness. **~o** a exact; (preciso) accurate; (puntual) punctual. **¡~!** exactly!. **con ~itud** exactly

exageración f exaggeration. **~do** a exaggerated. **~r** vt/i exaggerate

exaltado a exalted; (fanático) fanatical. **~r** vt exalt. **~rse** vpr get excited

examen m examination; (escol, univ) exam(ination). **~inador** m examiner. **~inar** vt examine. **~inarse** vpr take an exam

exánime a lifeless

exasperación f exasperation. **~r** vt exasperate. **~rse** vpr get exasperated

excavación f excavation. **~dora** f digger. **~r** vt excavate

excedencia f leave of absence. **~nte** a & m surplus. **~r** vi exceed. **~rse** vpr go too far. **~rse a sí mismo** excel o.s.

excelencia f excellence; (tratamiento) Excellency. **~te** a excellent

excentricidad f eccentricity. **~éntrico** a & m eccentric

excepción f exception. **~onal** a exceptional. **a ~ón de, con ~ón de** except (for)

excepto prep except (for). **~uar** [21] vt except

excesivo a excessive. **~o** m excess. **~o de equipaje** excess luggage (esp Brit), excess baggage (esp Amer)

excitable a excitable. **~ción** f excitement. **~nte** a exciting. —m stimulant. **~r** vt excite; (incitar) incite. **~rse** vpr get excited

exclamación f exclamation. **~r** vi exclaim

excluir [17] vt exclude. **~sión** f exclusion. **~siva** f sole right; (en la prensa) exclusive (story). **~sive** adv exclusive; (exclusivamente) exclusively. **~sivo** a exclusive

excomulgar [12] vt excommunicate. **~nión** f excommunication

excremento m excrement

exculpar vt exonerate; (jurid) acquit

excursión f excursion, trip. **~onista** m & f day-tripper. **ir de ~** go on an excursion

excusa f excuse; (disculpa) apology. **~r** vt excuse. **presentar sus ~s** apologize

execra|ble a loathsome. ~r vt loathe

exento a exempt; (libre) free

exequias fpl funeral rites

exhala|ción f shooting star. ~r vt exhale, breath out; give off ⟨olor etc⟩. ~rse vpr hurry. **como una ~ción** at top speed

exhaust|ivo a exhaustive. ~o a exhausted

exhibi|ción f exhibition. ~cionista m & f exhibitionist. ~r vt exhibit

exhortar vt exhort (a to)

exhumar vt exhume; (fig) dig up

exigen|cia f demand. ~ente a demanding. ~ir [14] vt demand. **tener muchas ~encias** be very demanding

exiguo a meagre

exil|(i)ado a exiled. —m exile. ~(i)arse vpr go into exile. ~io m exile

eximio a distinguished

eximir vt exempt; (liberar) free

existen|cia f existence. ~s fpl stock

existencial a existential. ~ismo m existentialism

exist|ente a existing. ~ir vi exist

éxito m success. **no tener ~** fail. **tener ~** be successful

exitoso a successful

éxodo m exodus

exonerar vt (de un empleo) dismiss; (de un honor etc) strip

exorbitante a exorbitant

exorci|smo m exorcism. ~zar [10] vt exorcise

exótico a exotic

expan|dir vt expand; (fig) spread. ~dirse vpr expand. ~sión f expansion. ~sivo a expansive

expatria|do a & m expatriate. ~r vt banish. ~rse vpr emigrate; (exiliarse) go into exile

expectativa f. **estar a la ~** be on the lookout

expedi|ción f dispatch; (cosa expedida) shipment; (mil, científico etc) expedition

expediente m expedient; (jurid) proceedings; (documentos) record, file

expedi|r [5] vt dispatch, send; issue ⟨documento⟩. ~to a clear

expeler vt expel

expende|dor m dealer. ~dor automático vending machine. ~duría f shop; (de billetes) ticket office. ~r vt sell

expensas fpl. **a ~ de** at the expense of. **a mis ~** at my expense

experiencia f experience

experiment|al a experimental. ~ar vt test, experiment with; (sentir) experience. ~o m experiment

experto a & m expert

expiar [20] vt atone for

expirar vi expire; (morir) die

explana|da f levelled area; (paseo) esplanade. ~r vt level

explayar vt extend. ~se vpr spread out, extend; (hablar) be long-winded; (confiarse) confide (a in)

expletivo m expletive

explica|ción f explanation. ~r [7] vt explain. ~rse vpr understand; (hacerse comprender) explain o.s. **no me lo explico** I can't understand it

explícito a explicit

explora|ción f exploration. ~dor m explorer; (muchacho) boy scout. ~r vt explore. ~torio a exploratory

explosi|ón f explosion; (fig) outburst. ~onar vt blow up. ~vo a & m explosive

explota|ción f working; (abuso) exploitation. ~r vt work ⟨mina⟩; farm ⟨tierra⟩; (abusar) exploit. —vi explode.

expone|nte m exponent. **∼r** [34] vt expose; display ⟨mercancías⟩; ⟨explicar⟩ expound; exhibit ⟨cuadros etc⟩; ⟨arriesgar⟩ risk. —vi hold an exhibition. **∼rse** upr run the risk (**a** of)

exporta|ción f export. **∼dor** m exporter. **∼r** vt export

exposición f exposure; ⟨de cuadros etc⟩ exhibition; ⟨en escaparate etc⟩ display; ⟨explicación⟩ exposition, explanation

expresamente adv specifically

expres|ar vt express. **∼arse** upr express o.s. **∼ión** f expression. **∼ivo** a expressive; ⟨cariñoso⟩ affectionate

expreso a express. —m express messenger; ⟨tren⟩ express

exprimi|dor m squeezer. **∼r** vt squeeze; ⟨explotar⟩ exploit

expropiar vt expropriate

expuesto a on display; ⟨lugar etc⟩ exposed; ⟨peligroso⟩ dangerous. **estar ∼ a** be liable to

expuls|ar vt expel; throw out ⟨persona⟩; send off ⟨jugador⟩. **∼ión** f expulsion

expurgar [12] vt expurgate

exquisito a exquisite. **∼amente** adv exquisitely

extasiar [20] vt enrapture

éxtasis m invar ecstasy

extático a ecstatic

extend|er [1] vt spread (out); draw up ⟨documento⟩. **∼erse** upr spread; ⟨paisaje etc⟩ extend, stretch; ⟨tenderse⟩ stretch out. **∼ido** a spread out; ⟨generalizado⟩ widespread; ⟨brazos⟩ outstretched

extens|amente adv widely; ⟨detalladamente⟩ in full. **∼ión** f extension; ⟨amplitud⟩ expanse; ⟨mus⟩ range. **∼o** a extensive

extenuar [21] vt exhaust

exterior a external, exterior; ⟨del extranjero⟩ foreign; ⟨aspecto etc⟩ outward. —m exterior;

⟨países extranjeros⟩ abroad. **∼izar** [10] vt show

extermin|ación f extermination. **∼ar** vt exterminate. **∼io** m extermination

externo a external; ⟨signo etc⟩ outward. —m day pupil

extin|ción f extinction. **∼guir** [13] vt extinguish. **∼guirse** upr die out; ⟨fuego⟩ go out. **∼to** a extinguished; ⟨raza etc⟩ extinct. **∼tor** m fire extinguisher

extirpa|r vt uproot; extract ⟨muela etc⟩; remove ⟨tumor⟩. **∼ción** f (fig) eradication

extorsi|ón f (fig) inconvenience. **∼onar** vt inconvenience

extra a invar extra; ⟨de buena calidad⟩ good-quality; ⟨huevos⟩ large. **paga f ∼** bonus

extrac|ción f extraction; ⟨de lotería⟩ draw. **∼to** m extract

extradición f extradition

extraer [41] vt extract

extranjero a foreign. —m foreigner; ⟨países⟩ foreign countries. **del ∼** from abroad. **en el ∼, por el ∼** abroad

extrañ|ar vt surprise; ⟨encontrar extraño⟩ find strange; ⟨LAm, echar de menos⟩ miss; ⟨desterrar⟩ banish. **∼arse** upr be surprised (**de** at); ⟨2 personas⟩ grow apart. **∼eza** f strangeness; ⟨asombro⟩ surprise. **∼o** a strange. —m stranger

extraoficial a unofficial

extraordinario a extraordinary. —m ⟨correo⟩ special delivery; ⟨plato⟩ extra dish; ⟨de periódico etc⟩ special edition. **horas fpl extraordinarias** overtime

extrarradio m suburbs

extrasensible a extra-sensory

extraterrestre a extraterrestrial. —m alien

extravagan|cia f oddness, eccentricity. **∼te** a odd, eccentric

extravertido *a* & *m* extrovert

extrav|iado *a* lost; *(lugar)* isolated. ~**iar** [20] *vt* lose. ~**iarse** *vpr* get lost; *(objetos)* be missing. ~**ío** *m* loss

extremar *vt* overdo. ~**se** *vpr* make every effort

extremeño *a* from Extremadura. —*m* person from Extremadura

extrem|idad *f* extremity. ~**id-ades** *fpl* extremities. ~**ista** *a* & *m* & *f* extremist. ~**o** *a* extreme. —*m* end; *(colmo)* extreme. **en** ~**o** extremely. **en** *último* ~**o** as a last resort

extrovertido *a* & *m* extrovert

exuberan|cia *f* exuberance. ~**te** *a* exuberant

exulta|ción *f* exultation. ~**r** *vi* exult

eyacular *vt/i* ejaculate

F

fa *m* F; *(solfa)* fah

fabada *f* Asturian stew

fábrica *f* factory. **marca** *f* **de** ~ trade mark

fabrica|ción *f* manufacture. ~**ción en serie** mass production. ~**nte** *m* & *f* manufacturer. ~**r** [7] *vt* manufacture; *(inventar)* fabricate

fábula *f* fable; *(mentira)* story, lie; *(chisme)* gossip

fabuloso *a* fabulous

facci|ón *f* faction. ~**ones** *fpl* *(de la cara)* features

faceta *f* facet

fácil *a* easy; *(probable)* likely; *(persona)* easygoing

facili|dad *f* ease; *(disposición)* aptitude. ~**dades** *fpl* facilities. ~**tar** *vt* facilitate; *(proporcionar)* provide

fácilmente *adv* easily

facistol *m* lectern

facón *m* *(Arg)* gaucho knife

facsímil(e) *m* facsimile

factible *a* feasible

factor *m* factor

factoría *f* agency; *(esp LAm, fábrica)* factory

factura *f* bill, invoice; *(hechura)* manufacture. ~**r** *vt* *(hacer la factura)* invoice; *(cobrar)* charge; *(en ferrocarril)* register *(Brit)*, check *(Amer)*

faculta|d *f* faculty; *(capacidad)* ability; *(poder)* power. ~**tivo** *a* optional

facha *f* *(aspecto, fam)* look

fachada *f* façade; *(fig, apariencia)* show

faena *f* job. ~**s domésticas** housework

fagot *m* bassoon; *(músico)* bassoonist

faisán *m* pheasant

faja *f* *(de tierra)* strip; *(corsé)* corset; *(mil etc)* sash

fajo *m* bundle; *(de billetes)* wad

falang|e *f* *(política española)* Falange. ~**ista** *m* & *f* Falangist

falda *f* skirt; *(de montaña)* side

fálico *a* phallic

fals|ear *vt* falsify, distort. ~**edad** *f* falseness; *(mentira)* lie, falsehood. ~**ificación** *f* forgery. ~**ificador** *m* forger. ~**ificar** [7] *vt* forge. ~**o** *a* false; *(equivocado)* wrong; *(falsificado)* fake

falt|a *f* lack; *(ausencia)* absence; *(escasez)* shortage; *(defecto)* fault, defect; *(culpa)* fault; *(error)* mistake; *(en fútbol etc)* foul; *(en tenis)* fault. ~**ar** *vi* be lacking; *(estar ausente)* be absent. ~**o** *a* lacking **(de** in). **a** ~**a de** for lack of. **echar en** ~**a** miss. **hacer** ~**a** be necessary. **me hace** ~**a** I need. **¡no** ~**aba más!** don't mention it! *(naturalmente)* of course! **sacar** ~**as** find fault

falla f (incl geol) fault. ~r vi fail; (romperse) break, give way; (motor, tiro etc) miss. **sin ~r** without fail

fallec|er [11] vi die. **~ido** a late. **—m** deceased

fallido a vain; (fracasado) unsuccessful

fallo m failure; (defecto) fault; (jurid) sentence

fama f fame; (reputación) reputation. **de mala ~** of ill repute. **tener ~ de** have the reputation of

famélico a starving

familia f family. **~ numerosa** large family. **~r** a familiar; (de la familia) family; (sin ceremonia) informal. **~ridad** f familiarity. **~rizarse** [10] vpr become familiar (con with)

famoso a famous

fanático a fanatical. **—m** fanatic

fanfarr|ón a boastful. **—m** braggart. **~onada** f boasting; (dicho) boast. **~onear** vi show off

fango m mud. **~so** a muddy

fantase|ar vi daydream; (imaginar) fantasize. **~ía** f fantasy. **de ~** fancy

fantasma m ghost

fantástico a fantastic

fantoche m puppet

faringe f pharynx

fardo m bundle

farfullar vi jabber, gabble

farmac|éutico a pharmaceutical. **—m** chemist (Brit), pharmacist, druggist (Amer). **~ia** f (ciencia) pharmacy; (tienda) chemist's (shop) (Brit), pharmacy, drugstore (Amer)

faro m lighthouse; (aviac) beacon; (auto) headlight

farol m lantern; (de la calle) street lamp. **~a** f street lamp. **~ita** f small street lamp

farsa f farce

fas adv. **por ~ o por nefas** rightly or wrongly

fascículo m instalment

fascina|ción f fascination. **~r** vt fascinate

fascis|mo m fascism. **~ta** a & m & f fascist

fase f phase

fastidi|ar vt annoy; (estropear) spoil. **~arse** vpr (aguantarse) put up with it; (hacerse daño) hurt o.s. **~o** m nuisance; (aburrimiento) boredom. **~oso** a annoying. **¡para que te ~es!** so there! **¡qué ~o!** what a nuisance!

fatal a fateful; (mortal) fatal; (pésimo, fam) terrible. **~idad** f fate; (desgracia) misfortune. **~ista** m & f fatalist

fatig|a f fatigue. **~as** fpl troubles. **~ar** [12] vt tire. **~arse** vpr get tired. **~oso** a tiring

fatuo a fatuous

fauna f fauna

fausto a lucky

favor m favour. **~able** a favourable. **a ~ de, en ~ de** in favour of. **haga el ~ de** would you be so kind as to, please. **por ~** please

favorec|edor a flattering. **~er** [11] vt favour; (vestido, peinado etc) suit. **~ido** a favoured

favorit|ismo m favouritism. **~o** a & m favourite

faz f face

fe f faith. **dar ~ de** certify. **de buena ~** in good faith

fealdad f ugliness

febrero m February

febril a feverish

fecund|ación f fertilization. **~ación artificial** artificial insemination. **~ar** vt fertilize. **~o** a fertile; (fig) prolific

fecha f date. **~r** vt date. **a estas ~s** now; (todavía) still. **hasta la ~** so far. **poner la ~** date

fechoría f misdeed

federa|ción f federation. **~l** a federal

feísimo a hideous

felici|dad f happiness. **~dades** fpl best wishes; (congratulaciones) congratulations. **~tación** f congratulation. **~tar** vt congratulate. **~tarse** upr be glad

feligr|és m parishioner. **~esía** f parish

felino a & m feline

feliz a happy; (afortunado) lucky. **¡Felices Pascuas!** Happy Christmas! **¡F~ Año Nuevo!** Happy New Year!

felpudo a plush. —m doormat

femen|il a feminine. **~no** a feminine; (biol, bot) female. —m feminine. **~nidad** f femeninity. **~sta** a & m & f feminist

fen|omenal a phenomenal. **~ómeno** m phenomenon; (monstruo) freak

feo a ugly; (desagradable) nasty; (malo) bad

féretro m coffin

feria f fair; (verbena) carnival; (descanso) holiday; (Mex, cambio) change. **~do** a. **día ~do** holiday

ferment|ación f fermentation. **~ar** vt/i ferment. **~o** m ferment

fero|cidad f ferocity. **~z** a fierce; (persona) savage

férreo a iron. **vía férrea** railway (Brit), railroad (Amer)

ferreter|ía f ironmonger's (shop) (Brit), hardware store (Amer). **~o** m ironmonger (Brit), hardware dealer (Amer)

ferro|bús m local train. **~carril** m railway (Brit), railroad (Amer). **~viario** a rail. —m railwayman (Brit), railroad worker (Amer)

fértil a fertile

fertili|dad f fertility. **~zante** m fertilizer. **~zar** [10] vt fertilize

férvido a fervent

ferv|iente a fervent. **~or** m fervour

festej|ar vt celebrate; entertain (persona); court (novia etc); (Mex, golpear) beat. **~o** m entertainment; (celebración) celebration

festival m festival. **~idad** f festivity. **~o** a festive; (humorístico) humorous. **día ~o** feast day, holiday

festonear vt festoon

fétido a stinking

feto m foetus

feudal a feudal

fiado m. **al ~** on credit. **~r** m fastener; (jurid) guarantor

fiambre m cold meat

fianza f (dinero) deposit; (objeto) surety. **bajo ~** on bail. **dar ~** pay a deposit

fiar [20] vt guarantee; (vender) sell on credit; (confiar) confide. —vi trust. **~se** upr. **~se de** trust

fiasco m fiasco

fibra f fibre; (fig) energy. **~ de vidrio** fibreglass

ficci|ón f fiction. **~ticio** a fictitious; (falso) false

fich|a f token; (tarjeta) index card; (en los juegos) counter. **~ar** vt file. **~ero** m card index. **estar ~ado** have a (police) record

fidedigno a reliable

fidelidad f faithfulness. **alta ~** hi-fi (fam), high fidelity

fideos mpl noodles

fiebre f fever. **~ del heno** hay fever. **tener ~** have a temperature

fiel a faithful; (memoria, relato etc) reliable. —m believer; (de balanza) needle. **los ~es** the faithful

fieltro m felt

fiera f wild animal; (*persona*) brute. **~o** a fierce; (*cruel*) cruel. **estar hecho una ~a** be furious

fierro m (*LAm*) iron

fiesta f party; (*día festivo*) holiday. **~s** fpl celebrations. **~ nacional** bank holiday (*Brit*), national holiday

figura f figure; (*forma*) shape; (*en obra de teatro*) character; (*en naipes*) court-card. **~r** vt feign; (*representar*) represent. *—vi* figure; (*ser importante*) be important. **~rse** vpr imagine. ¡**figúrate**! just imagine! **~tivo** a figurative

fij|ación f fixing. **~ar** vt fix; stick (*sello*); post (*cartel*). **~arse** vpr settle; (*fig, poner atención*) notice. ¡**fíjate**! just imagine! **~o** a fixed; (*firme*) stable; (*persona*) settled. **de ~o** certainly

fila f line; (*de soldados etc*) file; (*en el teatro, cine etc*) row; (*cola*) queue. **ponerse en ~** line up

filamento m filament

fil|antropía f philanthropy. **~antrópico** a philanthropic. **~ántropo** m philanthropist

filarmónico a philharmonic

filat|elia f stamp collecting, philately. **~élico** a philatelic. *—m* stamp collector, philatelist

filete m fillet

filfa f (*fam*) hoax

filial a filial. *—f* subsidiary

filigrana f filigree (work); (*en papel*) watermark

Filipinas fpl. **las (islas) ~** the Philippines

filipino a Philippine, Filipino

filmar vt film

filo m edge; (*de hoja*) cutting edge; (*Mex, hambre*) hunger. **al ~ de las doce** at exactly twelve o'clock. **dar ~ a, sacar ~ a** sharpen

filología f philology

filón m vein; (*fig*) gold-mine

fil|osofía f philosophy. **~osófico** a philosophical. **~ósofo** m philosopher

filtr|ar vt filter. **~arse** vpr filter; (*dinero*) disappear. **~o** m filter; (*bebida*) philtre

fin m end; (*objetivo*) aim. **~ de semana** weekend. **a ~ de** in order to. **a ~ de cuentas** all things considered. **a ~ de que** in order that. **a ~es de** at the end of. **al ~** finally. **al ~ y al cabo** after all. **dar ~ a** end. **en ~** in short. **poner ~ a** end. **por ~** finally. **sin ~** endless

final a final, last. *—m* end. *—f* final. **~idad** f aim. **~ista** m & f finalist. **~izar** [10] vt/i end. **~mente** adv finally

financi|ar vt finance. **~ero** a financial. *—m* financier

finca f property; (*tierras*) estate; (*LAm, granja*) farm

finés a Finnish. *—m* Finn; (*lengua*) Finnish

fingi|do a false. **~r** [14] vt feign; (*simular*) simulate. *—vi* pretend. **~rse** vpr pretend to be

finito a finite

finlandés a Finnish. *—m* (*persona*) Finn; (*lengua*) Finnish

Finlandia f Finland

fin|o a fine; (*delgado*) slender; (*astuto*) shrewd; (*sentido*) keen; (*cortés*) polite; (*jerez*) dry. **~ura** f fineness; (*astucia*) shrewdness; (*de sentido*) keenness; (*cortesía*) politeness

fiordo m fiord

firma f signature; (*empresa*) firm

firmamento m firmament

firmar vt sign

firme a firm; (*estable*) stable, steady; (*persona*) steadfast. *—m* (*pavimento*) road) surface. *—adv* hard. **~za** f firmness. **de ~** hard. **en ~** firm, definite

fiscal a fiscal. *—m & f* public prosecutor. **~o** m treasury

fisg|ar [12] vt pry into ⟨asunto⟩; spy on ⟨persona⟩. —vi pry. ~**ón** a prying. —m busybody

físic|a f physics. ~**o** a physical. —m physique; ⟨persona⟩ physicist

fisi|ología f physiology. ~**ológico** a physiological. ~**ólogo** m physiologist

fisioterap|euta m & f physiotherapist. ~**ia** f physiotherapy. ~**ista** m & f ⟨fam⟩ physiotherapist

fisonom|ía f physiognomy, face. ~**ista** m & f. **ser buen** ~**ista** be good at remembering faces

fisura f ⟨Med⟩ fracture

fláccido a flabby

flaco a thin, skinny; ⟨débil⟩ weak

flagelo m scourge

flagrante a flagrant. **en** ~ red-handed

flamante a splendid; ⟨nuevo⟩ brand-new

flamenco a flamenco; ⟨de Flandes⟩ Flemish. —m ⟨música etc⟩ flamenco

flan m crème caramel

flaqueza f thinness; ⟨debilidad⟩ weakness

flash m flash

flato m, **flatulencia** f flatulence

flaut|a f flute. —m & f ⟨músico⟩ flautist, flutist ⟨Amer⟩. ~**ín** m piccolo. ~**ista** m & f flautist, flutist ⟨Amer⟩

fleco m fringe

flecha f arrow

flem|a f phlegm. ~**ático** a phlegmatic

flequillo m fringe

fletar vt charter

flexib|ilidad f flexibility. ~**le** a flexible. —m flex, cable

flirt|ear vi flirt. ~**eo** m flirting

floj|ear vi ease up. ~**o** a loose; ⟨poco fuerte⟩ weak; ⟨viento⟩ light; ⟨perezoso⟩ lazy

flor f flower; ⟨fig⟩ cream. ~**a** f flora. ~**al** a floral. ~**ecer** [11] vi

flower, bloom; ⟨fig⟩ flourish. ~**eciente** a ⟨fig⟩ flourishing. ~**ero** m flower vase. ~**ido** a flowery; ⟨selecto⟩ select; ⟨lenguaje⟩ florid. ~**ista** m & f florist

flota f fleet

flot|ador m float. ~**ar** vi float. ~**e**. **a** ~**e** afloat

flotilla f flotilla

fluctua|ción f fluctuation. ~**r** [21] vi fluctuate

flu|idez f fluidity; ⟨fig⟩ fluency. ~**ido** a fluid; ⟨fig⟩ fluent. —m fluid. ~**ir** [17] vi flow. ~**jo** m flow. ~**o y reflujo** ebb and flow

fluorescente a fluorescent

fluoruro m fluoride

fluvial a river

fobia f phobia

foca f seal

foc|al a focal. ~**o** m focus; ⟨lámpara⟩ floodlight; ⟨LAm, bombilla⟩ light bulb

fogón m ⟨cocina⟩ cooker

fogoso a spirited

folio m leaf

folkl|ore m folklore. ~**órico** a folk

follaje m foliage

follet|ín m newspaper serial. ~**o** m pamphlet

follón m ⟨lío⟩ mess; ⟨alboroto⟩ row

fomentar vt foment, stir up

fonda f ⟨pensión⟩ boarding-house

fondo m bottom; ⟨parte más lejana⟩ bottom, end; ⟨de escenario, pintura etc⟩ background; ⟨profundidad⟩ depth. ~**s** mpl funds, money. **a** ~ thoroughly. **en el** ~ deep down

fonética f phonetics. ~**o** a phonetic

fono m ⟨LAm, del teléfono⟩ earpiece

fontaner|ía f plumbing. ~**o** m plumber

footing /ˈfutin/ m jogging

forastero a alien. —m stranger

forceje|ar *vi* struggle. **~o** *m* struggle

fórceps *m invar* forceps

forense *a* forensic

forjar *vt* forge

forma *f* form, shape; (*horma*) mould; (*modo*) way; (*de zapatero*) last. **~s** *fpl* conventions. **~ción** *f* formation; (*educación*) training. **dar ~** a shape; (*expresar*) formulate. **de ~ que** so (that). **de todas ~s** anyway. **estar en ~** be in good form. **guardar ~s** keep up appearances

formal *a* formal; (*de fiar*) reliable; (*serio*) serious. **~idad** *f* formality; (*fiabilidad*) reliability; (*seriedad*) seriousness

formar *vt* form; (*hacer*) make; (*enseñar*) train. **~se** *vpr* form; (*desarrollarse*) develop

formato *m* format

formidable *a* formidable; (*muy grande*) enormous; (*muy bueno*, *fam*) marvellous

fórmula *f* formula; (*receta*) recipe

formular *vt* formulate; make (*queja etc*); (*expresar*) express

fornido *a* well-built

forraje *m* fodder. **~ar** *vt/i* forage

forr|ar *vt* (*en el interior*) line; (*en el exterior*) cover. **~o** *m* lining; (*cubierta*) cover. **~o del freno** brake lining

fortale|cer [11] *vt* strengthen. **~za** *f* strength; (*mil*) fortress; (*fuerza moral*) fortitude

fortificar [7] *vt* fortify

fortuito *a* fortuitous. **encuentro ~** chance meeting

fortuna *f* fortune; (*suerte*) luck. **por ~** fortunately

forz|ado *a* hard. **~ar** [2 & 10] *vt* force. **~osamente** *adv* necessarily. **~oso** *a* inevitable; (*necesario*) necessary

fosa *f* grave

fosfato *m* phosphate

fósforo *m* phosphorus; (*cerilla*) match

fósil *a & m* fossil

fosilizarse [10] *vpr* fossilize

foso *m* ditch

foto *f* photo, photograph. **sacar ~s** take photographs

fotocopia *f* photocopy. **~dora** *f* photocopier. **~r** *vt* photocopy

fotogénico *a* photogenic

fot|ografía *f* photography; (*foto*) photograph. **~ografiar** [20] *vt* photograph. **~ográfico** *a* photographic. **~ógrafo** *m* photographer. **sacar ~ografías** take photographs

foyer *m* foyer

frac *m* (*pl* **fraques** *o* **fracs**) tails

fracas|ar *vi* fail. **~o** *m* failure

fracción *f* fraction; (*pol*) faction

fractura *f* fracture. **~r** *vt* fracture, break. **~rse** *vpr* fracture, break

fragan|cia *f* fragrance. **~te** *a* fragrant

fragata *f* frigate

frág|il *a* fragile; (*débil*) weak. **~agilidad** *f* fragility; (*debilidad*) weakness

fragment|ario *a* fragmentary. **~o** *m* fragment

fragor *m* din

fragoso *a* rough

fragua *f* forge. **~r** [15] *vt* forge; (*fig*) concoct. **—*vi*** harden

fraile *m* friar; (*monje*) monk

frambuesa *f* raspberry

francés *a* French. **—*m*** (*persona*) Frenchman; (*lengua*) French

Francia *f* France

franco *a* frank; (*com*) free. **—*m*** (*moneda*) franc

francotirador *m* sniper

franela *f* flannel

franja *f* border; (*fleco*) fringe

franque|ar *vt* clear; stamp (*carta*); overcome (*obstáculo*). **~o** *m* stamping; (*cantidad*) postage

franqueza f frankness; (*familiaridad*) familiarity

franquismo m General Franco's regime; (*política*) Franco's policy. ~**ta** a pro-Franco

frasco m small bottle

frase f phrase; (*oración*) sentence. ~ **hecha** set phrase

fraternal a fraternal. ~**idad** f fraternity

fraude m fraud. ~**ulento** a fraudulent

fray m brother, friar

frecuencia f frequency. ~**tar** vt frequent. ~**te** a frequent. con ~**cia** frequently

fregadero m sink. ~**r** [1 & 12] vt scrub; wash up (*los platos*); mop (*el suelo*); (*LAm, fig, molestar, fam*) annoy

freír [51, pp **frito**] vt fry; (*fig, molestar, fam*) annoy. ~**se** vpr fry; (*persona*) be very hot, be boiling (*fam*)

frenar vt brake; (*fig*) check

frenesí m frenzy. ~**ético** a frenzied

freno m (*de caballería*) bit; (*auto*) brake; (*fig*) check

frente m front. ~f forehead. ~ a opposite; (*en contra de*) opposed to. ~ **por** ~ opposite; (*en un choque*) head-on. **al** ~ at the head; (*hacia delante*) forward. **arrugar la** ~ frown. **de** ~ forward. **hacer** ~ **a** face (*cosa*); stand up to (*persona*)

fresa f strawberry

fresca f fresh air. ~**o** a (*frío*) cool; (*nuevo*) fresh; (*descarado*) cheeky. ~m fresh air; (*frescor*) coolness; (*mural*) fresco; (*persona*) impudent person. ~**or** m coolness. ~**ura** f freshness; (*frío*) coolness; (*descaro*) cheek. **al** ~**o** in the open air. **hacer** ~**o** be cool. **tomar el** ~**o** get some fresh air

fresno m ash (tree)

friable a friable

frialdad f coldness; (*fig*) indifference

fricción f rubbing; (*fig, tec*) friction; (*masaje*) massage. ~**onar** vt rub

frigidez f coldness; (*fig*) frigidity

frígido a frigid

frigorífico m refrigerator, fridge (*fam*)

frijol m bean. ~**es refritos** (*Mex*) purée of black beans

frío a & m cold. **coger** ~ catch cold. **hacer** ~ be cold

frisar vi. ~ **en** be getting on for, be about

frito a fried; (*exasperado*) exasperated. **me tiene** ~ I'm sick of him

frivolidad f frivolity. ~**ívolo** a frivolous

fronda f foliage

frontera f frontier; (*fig*) limit. ~**izo** a frontier. ~**o** a opposite

frontón m pelota court

frotar vt rub; strike (*cerilla*)

fructífero a fruitful

frugal a frugal

fruncir [9] vt gather (*tela*), wrinkle (*piel*)

fruslería f trifle

frustración f frustration. ~**r** vt frustrate. ~**rse** vpr (*fracasar*) fail. **quedar** ~**do** be disappointed

fruta f fruit. ~**ería** f fruit shop. ~**ero** a fruit. ~m fruiterer; (*recipiente*) fruit bowl. ~**icultura** f fruit-growing. ~**illa** f (*LAm*) strawberry. ~**o** m fruit

fucsia f fuchsia

fuego m fire. ~**s artificiales** fireworks. **a** ~ **lento** on a low heat. **tener** ~ have a light

fuente f fountain; (*manantial*) spring; (*plato*) serving dish; (*fig*) source

fuera *adv* out; (*al exterior*) outside; (*en otra parte*) away; (*en el extranjero*) abroad. —*vb véase* **ir** *y* **ser**. ~ **de** outside; (*excepto*) except for, besides. **por** ~ on the outside

fuerte *a* strong; (*color*) bright; (*sonido*) loud; (*dolor*) severe; (*duro*) hard; (*grande*) large; (*lluvia, nevada*) heavy. —*m* fort; (*fig*) strong point. —*adv* hard; (*con hablar etc*) loudly; (*mucho*) a lot

fuerza *f* strength; (*poder*) power; (*en física*) force; (*mil*) forces. ~ **de voluntad** will-power. **a** ~ **de** by dint of, by means of. **a la** ~ by necessity. **por** ~ by force; (*por necesidad*) by necessity. **tener** ~**s** have the strength to

fuese *vb véase* **ir** *y* **ser**

fuga *f* flight, escape; (*de gas etc*) leak; (*mus*) fugue. ~**arse** [12] *vpr* flee, escape. ~**az** *a* fleeting. ~**itivo** *a* & *m* fugitive. **ponerse en** ~**a** take to flight

fui *vb véase* **ir** *y* **ser**

fulano *m* so-and-so. ~, **mengano y zutano** Tom, Dick and Harry

fulgor *m* brilliance; (*fig*) splendour

fulminar *vt* strike by lightning; (*fig, mirar*) look daggers at

fuma|dor *a* smoking. —*m* smoker. ~**r** *vt/i* smoke. ~**rse** *vpr* smoke; (*fig, gastar*) squander. ~**rada** *f* puff of smoke. ~**r en pipa** smoke a pipe. **prohibido** ~**r** no smoking

funámbulo *m* tightrope walker

funci|ón *f* function; (*de un cargo etc*) duties; (*de teatro*) show, performance. ~**onal** *a* functional. ~**onar** *vi* work, function. ~**onario** *m* civil servant. **no** ~**ona** out of order

funda *f* cover. ~ **de almohada** pillowcase

funda|ción *f* foundation. ~**mental** *a* fundamental. ~**mentar** *vt* lay the foundations of; (*fig*) base. ~**mento** *m* foundation. ~**r** *vt* found; (*fig*) base. ~**rse** *vpr* be based

fundi|ción *f* melting; (*de metales*) smelting; (*taller*) foundry. ~**r** *vt* melt; smelt (*metales*); cast (*objeto*); blend (*colores*); (*fusionar*) merge. ~**rse** *vpr* melt; (*unirse*) merge

fúnebre *a* funeral; (*sombrío*) gloomy

funeral *a* funeral. —*m* funeral. ~**es** *mpl* funeral

funicular *a* & *m* funicular

furgón *m* van. ~**oneta** *f* van

fur|ia *f* fury; (*violencia*) violence. ~**ibundo** *a* furious. ~**ioso** *a* furious. ~**or** *m* fury

furtivo *a* furtive

furúnculo *m* boil

fuselaje *m* fuselage

fusible *m* fuse

fusil *m* gun. ~**ar** *vt* shoot

fusión *f* melting; (*unión*) fusion; (*com*) merger

fútbol *m* football

futbolista *m* footballer

fútil *a* futile

futur|ista *a* futuristic. —*m* & *f* futurist. ~**o** *a* & *m* future

G

gabán *m* overcoat

gabardina *f* raincoat; (*tela*) gabardine

gabinete *m* (*pol*) cabinet; (*en museo etc*) room; (*de dentista, médico etc*) consulting room

gacela *f* gazelle

gaceta *f* gazette

gachas *fpl* porridge

gacho *a* drooping

gaélico *a* Gaelic

gafa f hook. ~s fpl glasses, spectacles. ~s de sol sun-glasses

gafar vt hook; (fam) bring bad luck to. ~e m jinx

gaita f bagpipes

gajo m (de naranja, nuez etc) segment

gala|s fpl finery, best clothes. **estar de** ~ be dressed up. **hacer** ~ **de** show off

galán m (en el teatro) male lead; (enamorado) lover

galante a gallant. ~**ar** vt court. ~**ría** f gallantry

galápago m turtle

galardón m reward

galaxia f galaxy

galeón m galleon

galera f galley

galería f gallery

Gales m Wales. **país de** ~ Wales

gal|és a Welsh. —m Welshman; (lengua) Welsh. ~**esa** f Welshwoman

galgo m greyhound

Galicia f Galicia

galimatías m invar (fam) gibberish

galón m gallon; (cinta) braid; (mil) stripe

galop|ar vi gallop. ~**e** m gallop

galvanizar [10] vt galvanize

gallard|ía f elegance. ~**o** a elegant

gallego a & m Galician

galleta f biscuit (Brit), cookie (Amer)

gall|ina f hen, chicken; (fig, fam) coward. ~**o** m cock

gama f scale; (fig) range

gamba f prawn (Brit), shrimp (Amer)

gamberro m hooligan

gamuza f (piel) chamois leather

gana f wish, desire; (apetito) appetite. **de buena** ~ willingly. **de mala** ~ reluctantly. **no me da la** ~ I don't feel like it. **tener**

~s **de** (+ infinitivo) feel like (+ gerundio)

ganad|ería f cattle raising; (ganado) livestock. ~**o** m livestock. ~**o de cerda** pigs. ~**o lanar** sheep. ~**o vacuno** cattle

ganar vt earn; (en concurso, juego etc) win; (alcanzar) reach; (aventajar) beat. —vi (vencer) win; (mejorar) improve. ~**se la vida** earn a living. **salir ganando** come out better off

ganch|illo m crochet. ~**o** m hook. ~**oso** a, ~**udo** a hooked. **echar el** ~**o** a hook. **hacer** ~**illo** crochet. **tener** ~**o** be very attractive

gandul a & m & f good-for-nothing

ganga f bargain; (buena situación) easy job, cushy job (fam)

gangrena f gangrene

gans|ada f silly thing. ~**o** m goose

gañi|do m yelping. ~**r** [22] vi yelp

garabat|ear vt/i (garrapatear) scribble. ~**o** m (garrapato) scribble

garaje m garage. ~**ista** m & f garage attendant

garant|e m & f guarantor. ~**ía** f guarantee. ~**ir** [24] vt (esp LAm) guarantee. ~**izar** [10] vt guarantee

garapiñado a. **almendras** fpl **garapiñadas** sugared almonds

garbanzo m chick-pea

garbo m poise; (de escrito) style. ~**so** a elegant

garfio m hook

garganta f throat; (desfiladero) gorge; (de botella) neck

gárgaras fpl. **hacer** ~ gargle

gargarismo m gargle

gárgola f gargoyle

garita f hut; (de centinela) sentry box

garito m gambling den

garra f (de animal) claw; (de ave) talon

garrafa *f* carafe

garrapata *f* tick

garrapat|ear *vi* scribble. **~o** *m* scribble

garrote *m* club, cudgel; *(tormento)* garrotte

gárrulo *a* garrulous

garúa *f (LAm)* drizzle

garza *f* heron

gas *m* gas. **con ~** fizzy. **sin ~** still

gasa *f* gauze

gaseosa *f* lemonade

gasfitero *m (Arg)* plumber

gas|óleo *m* diesel. **~olina** *f* petrol *(Brit)*, gasoline *(Amer)*, gas *(Amer)*. **~olinera** *f* petrol station *(Brit)*, gas station *(Amer)*; *(lancha)* motor boat. **~ómetro** *m* gasometer

gast|ado *a* spent; *(vestido etc)* worn out. **~ador** *m* spendthrift. **~ar** *vt* spend; *(consumir)* use; *(malgastar)* waste; wear *(vestido etc)*; crack *(broma)*. —*vi* spend. **~arse** *vpr* wear out. **~o** *m* expense; *(acción de gastar)* spending

gástrico *a* gastric

gastronomía *f* gastronomy

gat|a *f* cat. **a ~as** on all fours. **~ear** *vi* crawl

gatillo *m* trigger; *(de dentista)* (dental) forceps

gat|ito *m* kitten. **~o** *m* cat. **dar ~o por liebre** take s.o. in

gaucho *a & m* Gaucho

gaveta *f* drawer

gavilla *f* sheaf; *(de personas)* band, gang

gaviota *f* seagull

gazpacho *m* gazpacho, cold soup

géiser *m* geyser

gelatina *f* gelatine; *(jalea)* jelly

gelignita *f* gelignite

gema *f* gem

gemelo *m* twin. **~s** *mpl (anteojos)* binoculars; *(de camisa)* cuff-links. **G~s** Gemini

gemido *m* groan

Géminis *mpl* Gemini

gemir [5] *vi* groan; *(animal)* whine, howl

gen *m*, **gene** *m* gene

geneal|ogía *f* genealogy. **~ógico** *a* genealogical. **árbol** *m* **~ógico** family tree

generación *f* generation

general *a* general; *(corriente)* common. —*m* general. **~ísimo** *m* generalissimo, supreme commander. **~ización** *f* generalization. **~izar** [10] *vt/i* generalize. **~mente** *adv* generally. **en ~** in general. **por lo ~** generally

generar *vt* generate

género *m* type, sort; *(biol)* genus; *(gram)* gender; *(producto)* product. **~s de punto** knitwear. **~ humano** mankind

generos|idad *f* generosity. **~o** *a* generous; *(vino)* full-bodied

génesis *f* genesis

genétic|a *f* genetics. **~o** *a* genetic

genial *a* brilliant; *(agradable)* pleasant

genio *m* temper; *(carácter)* nature; *(talento, persona)* genius; *(gram)* genital. **~es** *mpl* genitals

gente *f* people; *(nación)* nation; *(familia, fam)* family; *(Mex, persona)* person

gentil *a* charming; *(pagano)* pagan. **~eza** *f* elegance; *(encanto)* charm; *(amabilidad)* kindness

gentío *m* crowd

genuflexión *f* genuflection

genuino *a* genuine

geo|grafía *f* geography. **~ográfico** *a* geographical. **~ógrafo** *m* geographer

geo|logía *f* geology. **~ólogo** *m* geologist

geo|metría *f* geometry. **~étrico** *a* geometrical

geranio *m* geranium

geren|cia f management. ~**te** m manager

geriatría f geriatrics

germánico a & m Germanic

germen m germ

germicida f germicide

germinar vi germinate

gestación f gestation

gesticula|ción f gesticulation. ~**r** vi gesticulate; (hacer muecas) grimace

gesti|ón f step; (administración) management. ~**onar** vt take steps to arrange; (dirigir) manage

gesto m expression; (ademán) gesture; (mueca) grimace

Gibraltar m Gibraltar

gibraltareño a & m Gibraltarian

gigante a gigantic. —m giant. ~**sco** a gigantic

gimn|asia f gymnastics. ~**asio** m gymnasium, gym (fam). ~**asta** m & f gymnast. ~**ástica** f gymnastics

gimotear vi whine

ginebra f gin

Ginebra f Geneva

ginec|ología f gynaecology. ~**ólogo** m gynaecologist

gira f excursion; (a varios sitios) tour

girar vt spin; (por giro postal) transfer. —vi rotate, go round; ‹camino etc› turn

girasol m sunflower

gir|atorio a revolving. ~**o** m turn; (com) draft; (locución) expression. ~**o postal** postal order

giroscopio m gyroscope

gis m chalk

gitano a & m gypsy

glacial a icy. ~**r** m glacier

gladiador m gladiator

glándula f gland

glasear vt glaze; (culin) ice

glicerina f glycerine

glicina f wisteria

global a global; (fig) overall. ~**o** m globe; (aeróstato, juguete) balloon

glóbulo m globule; (med) corpuscle

gloria f glory. ~**rse** vpr boast (de about)

glorieta f bower; (auto) roundabout (Brit), ⟨traffic⟩ circle (Amer)

glorificar [7] vt glorify

glorioso a glorious

glosario m glossary

glot|ón a gluttonous. —m glutton. ~**onería** f gluttony

glucosa f glucose

gnomo /'nomo/ m gnome

gob|ernación f government. ~**ernador** a governing. —m governor. ~**ernante** a governing. ~**ernar** [1] vt govern; (dirigir) manage, direct. ~**ierno** m government; (dirección) management, direction. ~**ierno de la casa** housekeeping. **Ministerio** m **de la G~ernación** Home Office (Brit), Department of the Interior (Amer)

goce m enjoyment

gol m goal

golf m golf

golfo m gulf; (niño) urchin; (holgazán) layabout

golondrina f swallow

golos|ina f titbit; (dulce) sweet. ~**o** a fond of sweets

golpe m blow; (puñetazo) punch; (choque) bump; (de emoción) shock; (acceso) fit; (en fútbol) shot; (en golf, en tenis, de remo) stroke. ~**ar** vt hit; (dar varios golpes) beat; (con mucho ruido) bang; (con el puño) punch. —vi knock. ~ **de estado** coup d'etat. ~ **de fortuna** stroke of luck. ~ **de mano** raid. ~ **de vista** glance. ~ **militar** military coup. **de ~** suddenly. **de un ~** at one go

goma f rubber; (*para pegar*) glue; (*anillo*) rubber band; (*elástico*) elastic. **~a de borrar** rubber. **~a de pegar** glue. **~a espuma** foam rubber. **~ita** f rubber band

gongo m gong

gord|a f (*Mex*) thick tortilla. **~iflón** m (*fam*), **~inflón** m (*fam*) fatty. **~o** a (*persona*) fat; (*carne*) fatty; (*grande*) large, big. **—m** first prize. **~ura** f fatness; (*grasa*) fat

gorila f gorilla

gorje|ar vi chirp. **~o** m chirping

gorra f cap

gorrión m sparrow

gorro m cap; (*de niño*) bonnet

got|a f drop; (*med*) gout. **~ear** vi drip. **~eo** m dripping. **~era** f leak. **ni ~a** nothing

gótico a Gothic

gozar [10] vt enjoy. **—vi. ~ de** enjoy. **~se** vpr enjoy

gozne m hinge

gozo m pleasure; (*alegría*) joy. **~so** a delighted

graba|ción f recording. **~do** m engraving, print; (*en libro*) illustration. **~r** vt engrave; record (*discos etc*)

gracejo m wit

graci|a f grace; (*favor*) favour; (*humor*) wit. **~as** fpl thanks. **¡~as!** thank you!, thanks! **~oso** a funny. **—m** fool, comic character. **dar las ~as** thank. **hacer ~a** amuse; (*gustar*) please. **¡muchas ~as!** thank you very much! **tener ~a** be funny

grad|a f step; (*línea*) row; (*de anfiteatro*) tier. **~ación** f gradation. **~o** m degree; (*escol*) year (*Brit*), grade (*Amer*); (*voluntad*) willingness

gradua|ción f graduation; (*de alcohol*) proof. **~do** m graduate.

~l a gradual. **~r** [21] vt graduate; (*medir*) measure; (*univ*) confer a degree on. **~rse** vpr graduate

gráfic|a f graph. **~o** a graphic. **—m** graph

gram|ática f grammar. **~atical** a grammatical

gramo m gram, gramme (*Brit*)

gramófono m record-player, gramophone (*Brit*), phonograph (*Amer*)

gran a véase **grande**

grana f (*color*) scarlet

granada f pomegranate; (*mil*) grenade

granate m garnet

Gran Bretaña f Great Britain

grande a (*delante de nombre en singular* **gran**) big, large; (*alto*) tall; (*fig*) great. **—m** grandee. **~za** f greatness

grandioso a magnificent

granel m. a ~ in bulk; (*suelto*) loose; (*fig*) in abundance

granero m barn

granito m granite; (*grano*) small grain

graniz|ado m iced drink. **~ar** [10] vi hail. **~o** m hail

granj|a f farm. **~ero** m farmer

grano m grain; (*semilla*) seed; (*de café*) bean; (*med*) spot. **~s** mpl cereals

granuja m & f rogue

gránulo m granule

grapa f staple

gras|a f grease; (*culin*) fat. **~iento** a greasy

gratifica|ción f (*propina*) tip; (*de sueldo*) bonus. **~r** [7] vt (*dar propina*) tip

gratis adv free

gratitud f gratitude

grato a pleasant; (*bienvenido*) welcome

gratuito a free; (*fig*) uncalled for

grava f gravel

grava|men *m* obligation. **~r** *vt* tax; ⟨*cargar*⟩ burden

grave *a* serious; ⟨*pesado*⟩ heavy; ⟨*sonido*⟩ low; ⟨*acento*⟩ grave. **~dad** *f* gravity

gravilla *f* gravel

gravita|ción *f* gravitation. **~r** *vi* gravitate; ⟨*apoyarse*⟩ rest ⟨**sobre** on⟩; ⟨*fig, pesar*⟩ weigh ⟨**sobre** on⟩

gravoso *a* onerous; ⟨*costoso*⟩ expensive

graznar *vi* ⟨*cuervo*⟩ caw; ⟨*pato*⟩ quack

Grecia *f* Greece

gregario *a* gregarious

greguería *f* uproar

gremio *m* union

greña *f* mop of hair. **~udo** *a* unkempt

gresca *f* uproar; ⟨*riña*⟩ quarrel

griego *a & m* Greek

grieta *f* crack

grifo *m* tap, faucet (*Amer*); ⟨*animal fantástico*⟩ griffin

grilletes *mpl* shackles

grillo *m* cricket; ⟨*bot*⟩ shoot. **~s** *mpl* shackles

grima *f*. **dar ~** annoy

gringo *m* (*LAm*) Yankee (*fam*), American

gripe *f* (*fam*), influenza

gris *a* grey. **—***m* grey; ⟨*policía, fam*⟩ policeman

grit|ar *vt* shout (for); ⟨*como protesta*⟩ boo. **—***vi* shout. **~ería** *f*, **~erío** *m* uproar. **~o** *m* shout; ⟨*de dolor, sorpresa*⟩ cry; ⟨*chillido*⟩ scream. **dar ~s** shout

grosella *f* redcurrant. **~ negra** blackcurrant

groser|ía *f* coarseness; ⟨*palabras etc*⟩ coarse remark. **~o** *a* coarse; ⟨*descortés*⟩ rude

grosor *m* thickness

grotesco *a* grotesque

grúa *f* crane

grues|a *f* gross. **~o** *a* thick; ⟨*persona*⟩ fat, stout. **—***m* thickness; ⟨*fig*⟩ main body

grulla *f* crane

grumo *m* clot; ⟨*de leche*⟩ curd

gruñi|do *m* grunt; ⟨*fig*⟩ grumble. **~r** [22] *vi* grunt; ⟨*perro*⟩ growl; ⟨*refunfuñar*⟩ grumble

grupa *f* hindquarters

grupo *m* group

gruta *f* grotto

guacamole *m* (*Mex*) avocado purée

guadaña *f* scythe

guagua *f* trifle; ⟨*esp LAm, autobús, fam*⟩ bus

guante *m* glove

guapo *a* good-looking; ⟨*chica*⟩ pretty; ⟨*elegante*⟩ smart

guarapo *m* (*LAm*) sugar cane liquor

guarda *m & f* guard; ⟨*de parque etc*⟩ keeper. **—***f* protection. **~barros** *m invar* mudguard. **~bosque** *m* gamekeeper. **~costas** *m invar* coastguard vessel. **~dor** *a* careful. **—***m* keeper. **~espaldas** *m invar* bodyguard. **~meta** *m invar* goalkeeper. **~r** *vt* keep; ⟨*vigilar*⟩ guard; ⟨*proteger*⟩ protect; ⟨*reservar*⟩ save, keep. **~rse** *vpr* be on one's guard. **~rse de** (+ *infinitivo*) avoid (+ *gerundio*). **~rropa** *m* wardrobe; ⟨*en local público*⟩ cloakroom. **~vallas** *m invar* (*LAm*) goalkeeper

guardería *f* nursery

guardia *f* guard; ⟨*custodia*⟩ care. **—***f* guard. **G~ Civil** Civil Guard. **~ municipal** policeman. **~ de tráfico** traffic policeman. **estar de ~** be on duty. **estar en ~** be on one's guard. **montar la ~** mount guard

guardián *m* guardian; ⟨*de parque etc*⟩ keeper; ⟨*de edificio*⟩ caretaker

guardilla *f* attic

guar|ecer [11] ⟨*albergar*⟩ give shelter to. **~ecerse** *vpr* take shelter. ~ida *f* den, lair; (*de personas*) hideout

guarn|ecer [11] *vt* provide; (*adornar*) decorate; (*culin*) garnish. ~ición *m* decoration; (*de caballo*) harness; (*culin*) garnish; (*mil*) garrison; (*de piedra preciosa*) setting

guarro *m* pig

guasa *f* joke; (*ironía*) irony

guaso *a* (*Arg*) coarse

guasón *a* humorous. —*m* joker

Guatemala *f* Guatemala

guatemalteco *a* from Guatemala. —*m* person from Guatemala

guateque *m* party

guayaba *f* guava; (*dulce*) guava jelly

guayabera *f* (*Mex*) shirt

gubernamental *a*, **gubernativo** *a* governmental

güero *a* (*Mex*) fair

guerr|a *f* war; (*método*) warfare. ~a civil civil war. ~ear *vi* wage war. ~ero *a* war; (*belicoso*) fighting. —*m* warrior. ~illa *f* band of guerillas. ~illero *m* guerilla. dar ~a annoy

guía *m* & *f* guide. —*f* guidebook; (*de teléfonos*) directory; (*de ferrocarriles*) timetable

guiar [20] *vt* guide; (*llevar*) lead; (*auto*) drive. ~se *vpr* be guided (*por* by)

guij|arro *m* pebble. ~o *m* gravel

guillotina *f* guillotine

guind|a *f* morello cherry. ~illa *f* chilli

guiñapo *m* rag; (*fig, persona*) reprobate

guiñ|ar *vt/i* wink. ~o *m* wink. **hacer** ~os wink

gui|ón *m* hyphen, dash; (*de película etc*) script. ~onista *m* & *f* scriptwriter

guirnalda *f* garland

güiro *m* (*LAm*) gourd

guisa *f* manner, way. **a ~ de** as. **de tal ~** in such a way

guisado *m* stew

guisante *m* pea. **~ de olor** sweet pea

guis|ar *vt/i* cook. ~o *m* dish

güisqui *m* whisky

guitarr|a *f* guitar. ~ista *m* & *f* guitarist

gula *f* gluttony

gusano *m* worm; (*larva de mosca*) maggot

gustar *vt* taste. —*vi* please. ¿**te gusta?** do you like it? **me gusta el vino** I like wine

gusto *m* taste; (*placer*) pleasure. **~so** *a* tasty; (*agradable*) pleasant. **a mi ~** to my liking. **buen ~** (good) taste. **con mucho ~** with pleasure. **dar ~** please. **mucho ~** pleased to meet you

gutural *a* guttural

H

ha *vb* *véase* **haber**

haba *f* broad bean; (*de café etc*) bean

Habana *f*. **la ~** Havana

haban|era *f* habanera, Cuban dance. ~ero *a* from Havana. —*m* person from Havana. ~o *m* (*puro*) Havana

haber *v aux* [30] have. —*v impersonal* (*presente s* & *pl* **hay**, *imperfecto s* & *pl* **había**, *pretérito s* & *pl* **hubo**) be. **hay 5 bancos en la plaza** there are 5 banks in the square. **hay que hacerlo** it must be done, you have to do it. **he aquí** here is, here are. **no hay de qué** don't mention it, not at all. ¿**qué hay?** (¿*qué pasa?*) what's the matter?; (¿*qué tal?*) how are you?

habichuela *f* bean

hábil a skilful; (*listo*) clever; (*adecuado*) suitable

habilidad f skill; (*astucia*) cleverness

habilita|ción f qualification. ~r vt qualify

habita|ble a habitable. ~ción f room; (*casa etc*) dwelling; (*cuarto de dormir*) bedroom; (*en biología*) habitat. ~ción de matrimonio, ~ción doble double room. ~ción individual , ~ción sencilla single room. ~do a inhabited. ~nte m inhabitant. ~r vt live in. —vi live

hábito m habit

habitual a usual, habitual; (*cliente*) regular. ~mente adv usually

habituar [21] vt accustom. ~se vpr. ~se a get used to

habla f speech; (*idioma*) language; (*dialecto*) dialect. al ~ (*al teléfono*) speaking. ponerse al ~ con get in touch with. ~dor a talkative. —m chatterbox. ~duría f rumour. ~durías fpl gossip. ~nte a speaking. —m & f speaker. ~r vt speak. —vi speak, talk (con to). ~rse vpr speak. ¡ni ~r! out of the question! se ~ español Spanish spoken

hacedor m creator, maker

hacendado m landowner; (*LAm*) farmer

hacendoso a hard-working

hacer [31] vt do; (*fabricar, producir etc*) make; (*en matemáticas*) make, be. —v impersonal (*con expresiones meteorológicas*) be; (*con determinado periodo de tiempo*) ago. ~se vpr become; (*acostumbrarse*) get used (a to); (*estar hecho*) be made. ~ de act as. ~se a la mar put to sea. ~se el sordo pretend to be deaf. hace buen tiempo it's fine weather.

hace calor it's hot. hace frío it's cold. hace poco recently. hace 7 años 7 years ago. hace sol it's sunny. hace viento it's windy. ¿qué le vamos a ~? what are we going to do?

hacia prep towards; (*cerca de*) near; (*con tiempo*) at about. ~ abajo down(wards). ~ arriba up(wards). ~ las dos at about two o'clock

hacienda f country estate; (*en LAm*) ranch; (*LAm, ganado*) livestock; (*pública*) treasury. Ministerio m de H~ Ministry of Finance; (*en Gran Bretaña*) Exchequer; (*en Estados Unidos*) Treasury. mi:nistro m de H~ Minister of Finance; (*en Gran Bretaña*) Chancellor of the Exchequer; (*en Estados Unidos*) Secretary of the Treasury

hacinar vt stack

hacha f axe; (*antorcha*) torch

hachís m hashish

hada f fairy. cuento m de ~s fairy tale

hado m fate

hago vb véase **hacer**

Haití m Haiti

halag|ar [12] vt flatter. ~üeño a flattering

halcón m falcon

hálito m breath

halo m halo

hall /xol/ m hall

halla|r vt find; (*descubrir*) discover. ~rse vpr be. ~zgo m discovery

hamaca f hammock; (*asiento*) deck-chair

hambr|e f hunger; (*de muchos*) famine. ~iento a starving. tener ~e be hungry

Hamburgo m Hamburg

hamburguesa f hamburger

hampa f underworld. ~ón m thug

handicap /'xandikap/ *m* handicap

hangar *m* hangar

haragán *a* lazy, idle. —*m* layabout

harapiento *a* in rags. ∼o *m* rag

harina *f* flour

harpa *m* harp

hartar *vt* satisfy; (*fastidiar*) annoy. ∼arse *vpr* (*comer*) eat one's fill; (*cansarse*) get fed up (**de** with). ∼azgo *m* surfeit. ∼o *a* full; (*cansado*) tired; (*fastidiado*) fed up (**de** with). —*adv* enough; (*muy*) very. ∼ura *f* surfeit; (*abundancia*) plenty; (*de deseo*) satisfaction

hasta *prep* as far as; (*con tiempo*) until, till; (*Mex*) not until. —*adv* even. **¡∼ la vista!** goodbye!, see you! (*fam*). **¡∼ luego!** see you later! **¡∼ mañana!** see you tomorrow! **¡∼ pronto!** see you soon!

hastiar [20] *vt* annoy; (*cansar*) weary, tire; (*aburrir*) bore. ∼arse *vpr* get fed up (**de** with). ∼io *m* weariness; (*aburrimiento*) boredom; (*asco*) disgust

hatillo *m* bundle (of belongings); (*ganado*) small flock. ∼o *m* belongings; (*ganado*) flock, herd

haya *f* beech (tree). —*vb véase* **haber**

Haya *f*. **la** ∼ the Hague

haz *m* bundle; (*de trigo*) sheaf; (*de rayos*) beam

hazaña *f* exploit

hazmerreír *m* laughing-stock

he *vb véase* **haber**

hebdomadario *a* weekly

hebilla *f* buckle

hebra *f* thread; (*fibra*) fibre

hebreo *a* Hebrew; (*actualmente*) Jewish. —*m* Hebrew; (*actualmente*) Jew; (*lengua*) Hebrew

hecatombe *m* (*fig*) disaster

hechicera *f* witch. ∼cería *f* witchcraft. ∼cero *a* magic. —*m* wizard. ∼zar [10] *vt* cast a spell on; (*fig*) fascinate. ∼zo *m* witchcraft; (*un acto de brujería*) spell; (*fig*) fascination

hecho *pp de* **hacer**. —*a* mature; (*terminado*) finished; (*vestidos etc*) ready-made; (*culin*) done. —*m* fact; (*acto*) deed; (*cuestión*) matter; (*suceso*) event. ∼ura *f* making; (*forma*) form; (*del cuerpo*) build; (*calidad de fabricación*) workmanship. **de** ∼**o** in fact

heder [1] *vi* stink. ∼iondez *f* stench. ∼iondo *a* stinking, smelly. ∼or *m* stench

helada *f* freeze; (*escarcha*) frost. ∼dera *f* (*LAm*) refrigerator, fridge (*Brit, fam*). ∼dería *f* ice-cream shop. ∼do *a* frozen; (*muy frío*) very cold. —*m* ice-cream. ∼dora *f* freezer. ∼r [1] *vt* freeze. ∼rse *vpr* freeze

helecho *m* fern

hélice *f* spiral; (*propulsor*) propeller

helicóptero *m* helicopter. ∼puerto *m* heliport

hembra *f* female; (*mujer*) woman

hemisferio *m* hemisphere

hemorragia *f* haemorrhage

hemorroides *fpl* haemorrhoids, piles

henchir [5] *vt* fill. ∼se *vpr* stuff o.s.

hender [1] *vt* split. ∼idura *f* crack, split; (*geol*) fissure

heno *m* hay

heráldica *f* heraldry

herbáceo *a* herbaceous. ∼olario *m* herbalist. ∼oso *a* grassy

heredad *f* country estate. ∼ar *vt/i* inherit. ∼era *f* heiress. ∼ero *m* heir. ∼itario *a* hereditary

hereje *m* heretic. ∼ía *f* heresy

herencia f inheritance; (fig) heritage

heri|da f injury. **~do** a injured, wounded. —m injured person. **~r** [4] vt injure, wound; (fig) hurt. **~rse** vpr hurt o.s. **los ~dos** the injured; (cantidad) the number of injured

herman|a f sister. **~a política** sister-in-law. **~astra** f stepsister. **~astro** m stepbrother. **~dad** f brotherhood. **~o** m brother. **~o político** brother-in-law. **~os gemelos** twins

hermético a hermetic; (fig) watertight

hermos|o a beautiful; (espléndido) splendid; (hombre) handsome. **~ura** f beauty

hernia f hernia

héroe m hero

hero|ico a heroic. **~ína** f heroine; (droga) heroin. **~ísmo** m heroism

herr|adura f horseshoe. **~amienta** f tool. **~ería** f smithy. **~ero** m blacksmith. **~umbre** f rust

herv|idero m (manantial) spring; (fig) hotbed; (multitud) throng. **~ir** [4] vt/i boil. **~or** m boiling; (fig) ardour

heterogéneo a heterogeneous

heterosexual a & m & f heterosexual

hex|agonal a hexagonal. **~ágono** m hexagon

hiato m hiatus

hiberna|ción f hibernation. **~r** vi hibernate

hibisco m hibiscus

híbrido a & m hybrid

hice vb véase **hacer**

hidalgo m nobleman

hidrata|nte a moisturizing. **~r** vt hydrate; (crema etc) moisturize. **crema** f **~nte** moisturizing cream

hidráulico a hydraulic

hidroavión m seaplane

hidroeléctrico a hydroelectric

hidrófilo a absorbent

hidr|ofobia f rabies. **~ófobo** a rabid

hidrógeno m hydrogen

hidroplano m seaplane

hiedra f ivy

hiel f (fig) bitterness

hielo m ice; (escarcha) frost; (fig) coldness

hiena f hyena; (fig) brute

hierba f grass; (culin, med) herb. **~buena** f mint. **mala ~** weed; (gente) bad people, evil people

hierro m iron

hígado m liver

higi|ene f hygiene. **~énico** a hygienic

hig|o m fig. **~uera** f fig tree

hij|a f daughter. **~a política** daughter-in-law. **~astra** f stepdaughter. **~astro** m stepson. **~o** m son. **~o político** son-in-law. **~s** mpl sons; (chicos y chicas) children

hilar vt spin. **~ delgado** split hairs

hilaridad f laughter, hilarity

hilera f row; (mil) file

hilo m thread; (elec) wire; (de líquido) trickle; (lino) linen

hilv|án m tacking. **~anar** vt tack; (fig, bosquejar) outline

himno m hymn. **~ nacional** anthem

hincapié m. **hacer ~ en** stress, insist on

hincar [7] vt drive in. **~se** vpr sink into. **~se de rodillas** kneel down

hincha f (fam) grudge; (aficionado, fam) fan

hincha|do a inflated; (med) swollen; (persona) arrogant. **~r** vt inflate, blow up. **~rse** vpr swell up; (fig, comer mucho, fam) gorge o.s. **~zón** f swelling; (fig) arrogance

hindi *m* Hindi

hindú *a* Hindu

hiniesta *f (bot)* broom

hinojo *m* fennel

hiper... *pref* hyper...

hiper|mercado *m* hypermarket. **~sensible** *a* hypersensitive. **~tensión** *f* high blood pressure

hípico *a* horse

hipn|osis *f* hypnosis. **~ótico** *a* hypnotic. **~otismo** *m* hypnotism. **~otizador** *m* hypnotist. **~otizar** [10] *vt* hypnotize

hipo *m* hiccup. **tener ~** have hiccups

hipocondríaco *a & m* hypochondriac

hip|ocresía *f* hypocrisy. **~ócrita** *a* hypocritical. —*m & f* hypocrite

hipodérmico *a* hypodermic

hipódromo *m* racecourse

hipopótamo *m* hippopotamus

hipoteca *f* mortgage. **~r** [7] *vt* mortgage

hip|ótesis *f invar* hypothesis. **~otético** *a* hypothetical

hiriente *a* offensive, wounding

hirsuto *a* shaggy

hirviente *a* boiling

hispánico *a* Hispanic

hispano *pref* Spanish

Hispanoamérica *f* Spanish America

hispano|americano *a* Spanish American. **~hablante** *a*, **~parlante** *a* Spanish-speaking

hist|eria *f* hysteria. **~érico** *a* hysterical. **~erismo** *m* hysteria

hist|oria *f* history; *(cuento)* story. **~oriador** *m* historian. **~órico** *a* historical. **~orieta** *f* tale; *(con dibujos)* strip cartoon. **pasar a la ~oria** go down in history

hito *m* milestone

hizo *vb véase* **hacer**

hocico *m* snout; *(fig, de enfado)* grimace

hockey *m* hockey. **~ sobre hielo** ice hockey

hogar *m* hearth; *(fig)* home. **~eño** *a* home; *(persona)* home-loving

hogaza *f* large loaf

hoguera *f* bonfire

hoja *f* leaf; *(de papel, metal etc)* sheet; *(de cuchillo, espada etc)* blade. **~ de afeitar** razor blade. **~lata** *f* tin. **~latería** *f* tinware. **~latero** *m* tinsmith

hojaldre *m* puff pastry, flaky pastry

hojear *vt* leaf through; *(leer superficialmente)* glance through

hola *int* hello!

Holanda *f* Holland

holand|és *a* Dutch. —*m* Dutchman; *(lengua)* Dutch. **~esa** *f* Dutchwoman

holg|ado *a* loose; *(fig)* comfortable. **~ar** [2 & 12] *vt (no trabajar)* not work, have a day off; *(sobrar)* be unnecessary. **~azán** *a* lazy. —*m* idler. **~ura** *f* looseness; *(fig)* comfort; *(en mecánica)* play. **huelga decir que** needless to say

holocausto *m* holocaust

hollín *m* soot

hombre *m* man; *(especie humana)* man(kind). —*int* Good Heavens!; *(de duda)* well. **~ de estado** statesman. **~ de negocios** businessman. **~ rana** frogman. **el ~ de la calle** the man in the street

hombr|era *f* epaulette; *(almohadilla)* shoulder pad. **~o** *m* shoulder

hombruno *a* masculine

homenaje *m* homage; *(fig)* tribute. **rendir ~ a** pay tribute to

home|ópata *m* homoeopath. **~opatía** *f* homoeopathy. **~opático** *a* homoeopathic

homicid|a *a* murderous. —*m & f* murderer. **~io** *m* murder

homogéneo *a* homogeneous

homosexual *a & m & f* homosexual. **~idad** *f* homosexuality

hond|o *a* deep. **~onada** *f* hollow. **~ura** *f* depth

Honduras *fpl* Honduras

hondureño *a & m* Honduran

honest|idad *f* decency. **~o** *a* proper

hongo *m* fungus; (*culin*) mushroom; (*venenoso*) toadstool

hon|or *m* honour. **~orable** *a* honourable. **~orario** *a* honorary. **~orarios** *mpl* fees. **~ra** *f* honour; (*buena fama*) good name. **~radez** *f* honesty. **~rado** *a* honest. **~rar** *vt* honour. **~rarse** *vpr* be honoured

hora *f* hour; (*momento determinado, momento oportuno*) time. **~ avanzada** late hour. **~ punta** rush hour. **~s** *fpl* **de trabajo** working hours. **~s** *fpl* **extraordinarias** overtime. **a estas ~s** now. **¿a qué ~?** at what time? when? **de ~ en ~** hourly. **de última ~** last-minute. **en buena ~** at the right time. **media ~** half an hour. **¿qué ~ es?** what time is it? **¿tiene Vd ~?** can you tell me the time?

horario *a* time; (*cada hora*) hourly. —*m* timetable. **a ~** (*LAm*) on time

horca *f* gallows

horcajadas, **a ~** astride

horchata *f* tiger-nut milk

horda *f* horde

horizont|al *a & f* horizontal. **~e** *m* horizon

horma *f* mould; (*para fabricar calzado*) last; (*para conservar forma del calzado*) shoe-tree

hormiga *f* ant

hormigón *m* concrete

hormigue|ar *vt* tingle; (*bullir*) swarm. **me ~a la mano** I've got pins and needles in my hand. **~o** *m* tingling; (*fig*) anxiety

hormiguero *m* anthill; (*de gente*) swarm

hormona *f* hormone

horn|ada *f* batch. **~ero** *m* baker. **~illo** *m* cooker. **~o** *m* oven; (*para ladrillos, cerámica etc*) kiln; (*tec*) furnace

horóscopo *m* horoscope

horquilla *f* pitchfork; (*para el pelo*) hairpin

horr|endo *a* awful. **~ible** *a* horrible. **~ipilante** *a* terrifying. **~or** *m* horror; (*atrocidad*) atrocity. **~orizar** [10] *vt* horrify. **~orizarse** *vpr* be horrified. **~oroso** *a* horrifying. **¡qué ~or!** how awful!

hort|aliza *f* vegetable. **~elano** *m* market gardener. **~icultura** *f* horticulture

hosco *a* surly; (*lugar*) gloomy

hospeda|je *m* lodging. **~r** *vt* put up. **~rse** *vpr* lodge

hospital *m* hospital

hospital|ario *m* hospitable. **~idad** *f* hospitality

hostal *m* boarding-house

hostería *f* inn

hostia *f* (*relig*) host; (*golpe, fam*) punch

hostigar [12] *vt* whip; (*fig, excitar*) urge; (*fig, molestar*) pester

hostil *a* hostile. **~idad** *f* hostility

hotel *m* hotel. **~ero** *a* hotel. —*m* hotelier

hoy *adv* today. **~ (en) día** nowadays. **~ mismo** this very day. **~ por ~** for the time being. **de ~ en adelante** from now on

hoy|a *f* hole; (*sepultura*) grave. **~o** *m* hole; (*sepultura*) grave. **~uelo** *m* dimple

hoz *f* sickle; (*desfiladero*) pass

hube *vb véase* **haber**

hucha *f* money box

hueco *a* hollow; *(vacío)* empty; *(esponjoso)* spongy; *(resonante)* resonant. —*m* hollow

huelga *f* strike. ~**a de brazos caídos** sit-down strike. ~**a de celo** work-to-rule. ~**a de hambre** hunger strike. ~**uista** *m & f* striker. **declarar la** ~**a, declararse en** ~**a** come out on strike

huelo *vb véase* **oler**

huella *f* footprint; *(de animal, vehículo etc)* track. ~ **dactilar**, ~ **digital** fingerprint

huérfano *a* orphaned. —*m* orphan. ~ **de** without

huero *a* empty

huert|a *f* market garden *(Brit)*, truck farm *(Amer)*; *(terreno de regadío)* irrigated plain. ~**o** *m* vegetable garden; *(de árboles frutales)* orchard

huesa *f* grave

hueso *m* bone; *(de fruta)* stone. ~**so** *a* bony

huésped *m* guest; *(que paga)* lodger; *(animal)* host

huesudo *a* bony

huev|a *f* roe. ~**era** *f* eggcup. ~**o** *m* egg. ~**o duro** hard-boiled egg. ~**o escalfado** poached egg. ~**o estrellado**, ~**o frito** fried egg. ~**o pasado por agua** boiled egg. ~**os revueltos** scrambled eggs

hui|da *f* flight, escape. ~**dizo** *a (tímido)* shy; *(fugaz)* fleeting. ~**r** [17] *vt/i* flee, run away; *(evitar)* avoid

huipil *m (Mex)* embroidered smock

huitlacoche *m (Mex)* edible black fungus

hule *m* oilcloth, oilskin

human|idad *f* mankind; *(fig)* humanity. ~**idades** *fpl* humanities. ~**ismo** *m* humanism. ~**ista** *m & f* humanist. ~**itario** *a* humanitarian. ~**o** *a* human;

(benévolo) humane. —*m* human (being)

hum|areda *f* cloud of smoke. ~**ear** *vi* smoke; *(echar vapor)* steam

humed|ad *f* dampness *(en meteorología)* humidity. ~**ecer** [11] *vt* moisten. ~**ecerse** *vpr* become moist

húmedo *a* damp; *(clima)* humid; *(mojado)* wet

humi|ldad *f* humility. ~**lde** *a* humble. ~**llación** *f* humiliation. ~**llar** *vt* humiliate. ~**llarse** *vpr* humble o.s.

humo *m* smoke; *(vapor)* steam; *(gas nocivo)* fumes. ~**s** *mpl* conceit

humor *m* mood, temper; *(gracia)* humour. ~**ismo** *m* humour. ~**ista** *m & f* humorist. ~**ístico** *a* humorous. **estar de mal** ~ be in a bad mood

hundi|do *a* sunken. ~**miento** *m* sinking. ~**r** *vt* sink; destroy *(edificio)*. ~**rse** *vpr* sink; *(edificio)* collapse

húngaro *a & m* Hungarian

Hungría *f* Hungary

huracán *m* hurricane

huraño *a* unsociable

hurg|ar [12] *vt* poke; *(fig)* stir up. ~**ón** *m* poker

hurón *m* ferret. —*a* unsociable

hurra *int* hurray!

hurraca *f* magpie

hurtadillas. a ~ stealthily

hurt|ar *vt* steal. ~**o** *m* theft; *(cosa robada)* stolen object

husmear *vt* sniff out; *(fig)* pry into

huyo *vb véase* **huir**

I

Iberia *f* Iberia

ibérico *a* Iberian

ibero a & m Iberian

ibice m ibex, mountain goat

Ibiza f Ibiza

iceberg /i0'ber/ m iceberg

icono m icon

ictericia f jaundice

ida f outward journey; (*salida*) departure. **de ∼ y vuelta** return (*Brit*), round-trip (*Amer*)

idea f idea; (*opinión*) opinion. **cambiar de ∼** change one's mind. **no tener la más remota ∼, no tener la menor ∼** not have the slightest idea, not have a clue (*fam*)

ideal a ideal; (*imaginario*) imaginary. —m ideal. **∼ista** m & f idealist. **∼izar** [10] vt idealize

idear vt think up, conceive; (*inventar*) invent

ídem pron & adv the same

idéntico a identical

identi|dad f identity. **∼ficación** f identification. **∼ficar** [7] vt identify. **∼ficarse** vpr. **∼ficarse con** identify with

ideolog|ía f ideology. **∼ógico** a ideological

idílico a idyllic

idilio m idyll

idioma m language. **∼ático** a idiomatic

idiosincrasia f idiosyncrasy

idiot|a a idiotic. —m & f idiot. **∼ez** f idiocy

idiotismo m idiom

idolatrar vt worship; (*fig*) idolize

ídolo m idol

idóneo a suitable (**para** for)

iglesia f church

iglú m igloo

ignición f ignition

ignomini|a f ignominy, disgrace. **∼oso** a ignominious

ignora|ncia f ignorance. **∼nte** a ignorant. —m ignoramus. **∼r** vt not know, be unaware of

igual a equal; (*mismo*) the same; (*similar*) like; (*llano*) even; (*liso*)

smooth. —adv easily. —m equal. **∼ que** (the same) as. **al ∼ que** the same as. **da ∼, es ∼** it doesn't matter

igual|ar vt make equal; (*ser igual*) equal; (*allanar*) level. **∼arse** vpr be equal. **∼dad** f equality. **∼mente** adv equally; (*también*) also, likewise; (*respuesta de cortesía*) the same to you

ijada f flank

ilegal a illegal

ilegible a illegible

ilegítimo a illegitimate

ileso a unhurt

ilícito a illicit

ilimitado a unlimited

ilógico a illogical

ilumina|ción f illumination; (*alumbrado*) lighting; (*fig*) enlightenment. **∼r** vt light (up); (*fig*) enlighten. **∼rse** vpr light up

ilusi|ón f illusion; (*sueño*) dream; (*alegría*) joy. **∼onado** a excited. **∼onar** vt give false hope. **∼onarse** vpr have false hopes. **hacerse ∼ones** build up one's hopes. **me hace ∼ón** I'm thrilled; I'm looking forward to (*algo en el futuro*)

ilusionis|mo m conjuring. **∼ta** m & f conjurer

iluso a easily deceived. —m dreamer. **∼rio** a illusory

ilustra|ción f learning; (*dibujo*) illustration. **∼do** a learned; (*con dibujos*) illustrated. **∼r** vt explain; (*instruir*) instruct; (*añadir dibujos etc*) illustrate. **∼rse** vpr acquire knowledge. **∼tivo** a illustrative

ilustre a illustrious

imagen f image; (*TV etc*) picture

imagina|ble a imaginable. **∼ción** f imagination. **∼r** vt imagine. **∼rse** vpr imagine. **∼rio** m imaginary. **∼tivo** a imaginative

imán m magnet

imantar *vt* magnetize

imbécil *a* stupid. —*m* & *f* imbecile, idiot

imborrable *a* indelible; ⟨recuerdo *etc*⟩ unforgettable

imbuir [17] *vt* imbue (**de** with)

imita|ción *f* imitation. **∼r** *vt* imitate

impacien|cia *f* impatience. **∼tarse** *vpr* lose one's patience. **∼te** *a* impatient; ⟨intranquilo⟩ anxious

impacto *m* impact

impar *a* odd

imparcial *a* impartial. **∼idad** *f* impartiality

impartir *vt* impart

impasible *a* impassive

impávido *a* fearless; ⟨impasible⟩ impassive

impecable *a* impeccable

impedi|do *a* disabled. **∼menta** *f* (*esp mil*) baggage. **∼mento** *m* hindrance. **∼r** [5] *vt* prevent; ⟨obstruir⟩ hinder

impeler *vt* drive

impenetrable *a* impenetrable

impenitente *a* unrepentant

impensa|ble *a* unthinkable. **∼do** *a* unexpected

imperar *vi* reign

imperativo *a* imperative; ⟨persona⟩ imperious

imperceptible *a* imperceptible

imperdible *m* safety pin

imperdonable *a* unforgivable

imperfec|ción *f* imperfection. **∼to** *a* imperfect

imperial *a* imperial. —*f* upper deck. **∼ismo** *m* imperialism

imperio *m* empire; ⟨poder⟩ rule; (*fig*) pride. **∼so** *a* imperious

impermeable *a* waterproof. —*m* raincoat

impersonal *a* impersonal

impertérrito *a* undaunted

impertinen|cia *f* impertinence. **∼te** *a* impertinent

imperturbable *a* imperturbable

ímpetu *m* impetus; ⟨impulso⟩ impulse; ⟨impetuosidad⟩ impetuosity

impetuos|idad *f* impetuosity; ⟨violencia⟩ violence. **∼o** *a* impetuous; ⟨violento⟩ violent

impío *a* ungodly; ⟨acción⟩ irreverent

implacable *a* implacable

implantar *vt* introduce

implica|ción *f* implication. **∼r** [7] *vt* implicate; ⟨significar⟩ imply

implícito *a* implicit

implora|ción *f* entreaty. **∼r** *vt* implore

imponderable *a* imponderable; ⟨inapreciable⟩ invaluable

impon|ente *a* imposing; (*fam*) terrific. **∼er** [34] *vt* impose; ⟨requerir⟩ demand; deposit ⟨dinero⟩. **∼erse** *vpr* be imposed; ⟨hacerse obedecer⟩ assert o.s.; ⟨hacerse respetar⟩ command respect. **∼ible** *a* taxable

impopular *a* unpopular. **∼idad** *f* unpopularity

importa|ción *f* import; ⟨artículo⟩ import. **∼dor** *a* importing. —*m* importer

importa|ncia *f* importance; ⟨tamaño⟩ size. **∼nte** *a* important; ⟨en cantidad⟩ considerable. **∼r** *vt* import; ⟨valer⟩ cost. —*vi* be important, matter. **¡le importa...?** would you mind...? **no ∼** it doesn't matter

importe *m* price; ⟨total⟩ amount

importun|ar *vt* bother. **∼o** *a* troublesome; ⟨inoportuno⟩ inopportune

imposib|ilidad *f* impossibility. **∼le** *a* impossible. **hacer lo ∼le** do all one can

imposición *f* imposition; ⟨impuesto⟩ tax

impostor *m* & *f* impostor

impotable *a* undrinkable

impoten|cia f impotence. ~**te** a powerless, impotent

impracticable a impracticable; (*intransitable*) unpassable

impreca|ción f curse. ~**r** [7] vt curse

imprecis|ión f vagueness. ~**o** a imprecise

impregnar vt impregnate; (*empapar*) soak; (*fig*) cover

imprenta f printing; (*taller*) printing house, printer's

imprescindible a indispensable, essential

impresi|ón f impression; (*acción de imprimir*) printing; (*tirada*) edition; (*huella*) imprint. ~**onable** a impressionable. ~**onante** a impressive; (*espantoso*) frightening. ~**onar** vt impress; (*foto*) expose. ~**onarse** vpr be impressed; (*conmover*) be moved

impresionis|mo m impressionism. ~**ta** a & m & f impressionist

impreso a printed. —m printed paper, printed matter. ~**ra** f printer

imprevis|ible a unforeseeable. ~**to** a unforeseen

imprimir [*pp* **impreso**] vt impress; print ‹*libro etc*›

improbab|ilidad f improbability. ~**le** a unlikely, improbable

improcedente a unsuitable

improductivo a unproductive

improperio m insult. ~**s** mpl abuse

impropio a improper

improvis|ación f improvisation. ~**adamente** adv suddenly. ~**ado** a improvised. ~**ar** vt improvise. ~**o** a. **de** ~**o** suddenly

impruden|cia f imprudence. ~**te** a imprudent

impuden|cia f impudence. ~**te** a impudent

imp|údico a immodest; (*desvergonzado*) shameless. ~**udor** m immodesty; (*desvergüenza*) shamelessness

impuesto a imposed. —m tax. ~ **sobre el valor añadido** VAT, value added tax

impugnar vt contest; (*refutar*) refute

impulsar vt impel

impuls|ividad f impulsiveness. ~**ivo** a impulsive. ~**o** m impulse

impune a unpunished. ~**idad** f impunity

impur|eza f impurity. ~**o** a impure

imputa|ción f charge. ~**r** vt attribute; (*acusar*) charge

inacabable a interminable

inaccesible a inaccessible

inaceptable a unacceptable

inacostumbrado a unaccustomed

inactiv|idad f inactivity. ~**o** a inactive

inadaptado a maladjusted

inadecuado a inadequate; (*inapropiado*) unsuitable

inadmisible a inadmissible; (*intolerable*) intolerable

inadvert|ido a unnoticed. ~**encia** f inadvertence

inagotable a inexhaustible

inaguantable a unbearable; (*persona*) insufferable

inalterable a unchangeable; (*color*) fast; (*carácter*) calm. ~**do** a unchanged

inanimado a inanimate

inaplicable a inapplicable

inapreciable a imperceptible

inapropiado a inappropriate

inarticulado a inarticulate

inasequible a out of reach

inaudito a unheard-of

inaugura|ción f inauguration. ~**l** a inaugural. ~**r** vt inaugurate

inca *a* Incan. —*m & f* Inca. ~**ico** *a* Incan

incalculable *a* incalculable

incandescen|cia *f* incandescence. ~**te** *a* incandescent

incansable *a* tireless

incapa|cidad *f* incapacity. ~**ci-tar** *vt* incapacitate. ~**z** *a* incapable

incauto *a* unwary; (*fácil de engañar*) gullible

incendi|ar *vt* set fire to. ~**arse** *vpr* catch fire. ~**ario** *a* incendiary. —*m* arsonist. ~**o** *m* fire

incentivo *m* incentive

incertidumbre *f* uncertainty

incesante *a* incessant

incest|o *m* incest. ~**uoso** *a* incestuous

inciden|cia *f* incidence; (*incidente*) incident. ~**tal** *a* incidental. ~**te** *m* incident

incidir *vi* fall; (*influir*) influence

incienso *m* incense

incierto *a* uncertain

incinera|ción *f* incineration; (*de cadáveres*) cremation. ~**dor** *m* incinerator. ~**r** *vt* incinerate; cremate (*cadáver*)

incipiente *a* incipient

incisión *f* incision

incisivo *a* incisive. —*m* incisor

incitar *vt* incite

incivil *a* rude

inclemen|cia *f* harshness. ~**te** *a* harsh

inclina|ción *f* slope; (*de la cabeza*) nod; (*fig*) inclination. ~**r** *vt* incline. ~**rse** *vpr* lean; (*encorvarse*) stoop; (*en saludo*) bow; (*fig*) be inclined. ~**rse a** (*parecerse*) resemble

inclu|ido *a* included; (*precio*) inclusive; (*en cartas*) enclosed. ~**ir** [17] *vt* include; (*en cartas*) enclose. ~**sión** *f* inclusion. ~**sive** *adv* inclusive. **hasta el lunes** ~**sive** up to and including Monday. ~**so** *a* included; (*en*

cartas) enclosed. —*adv* including; (*hasta*) even

incógnito *a* unknown. **de** ~ incognito

incoheren|cia *f* incoherence. ~**te** *a* incoherent

incoloro *a* colourless

incólume *a* unharmed

incomestible *a*, **incomible** *a* uneatable, inedible

incomodar *vt* inconvenience; (*molestar*) bother. ~**se** *vpr* trouble o.s.; (*enfadarse*) get angry

incómodo *a* uncomfortable; (*inoportuno*) inconvenient

incomparable *a* imcomparable

incompatib|ilidad *f* incompatibility. ~**le** *a* incompatible

incompeten|cia *f* incompetence. ~**te** *a* incompetent

incompleto *a* incomplete

incompren|dido *a* misunderstood. ~**sible** *a* incomprehensible. ~**sión** *f* incomprehension

incomunicado *a* isolated; (*preso*) in solitary confinement

inconcebible *a* inconceivable

inconciliable *a* irreconcilable

inconcluso *a* unfinished

incondicional *a* unconditional

inconfundible *a* unmistakable

incongruente *a* incongruous

inconmensurable *a* (*fam*) enormous

inconscien|cia *f* unconsciousness; (*irreflexión*) recklessness. ~**te** *a* unconscious; (*irreflexivo*) reckless

inconsecuente *a* inconsistent

inconsiderado *a* inconsiderate

inconsistente *a* insubstantial

inconsolable *a* unconsolable

inconstan|cia *f* inconstancy. ~**te** *a* changeable; (*persona*) fickle

incontable *a* countless

incontaminado *a* uncontaminated

incontenible *a* irrepressible

incontestable *a* indisputable

incontinencia *f* incontinence. ~**te** *a* incontinent

inconveniencia *f* disadvantage. ~**te** *a* inconvenient; (*inapropiado*) inappropriate; (*incorrecto*) improper. —*m* difficulty; (*desventaja*) drawback

incorporación *f* incorporation. ~**r** *vt* incorporate; (*culin*) mix. ~**rse** *vpr* sit up; join (*sociedad, regimiento etc*)

incorrecto *a* incorrect; (*acción*) improper; (*descortés*) discourteous

incorregible *a* incorrigible

incorruptible *a* incorruptible

incrédulo *a* incredulous

increíble *a* incredible

incrementar *vt* increase. ~**o** *m* increase

incriminar *vt* incriminate

incrustar *vt* encrust

incubación *f* incubation. ~**dora** *f* incubator. ~**r** *vt* incubate; (*fig*) hatch

incuestionable *a* unquestionable

inculcar [7] *vt* inculcate

inculpar *vt* accuse; (*culpar*) blame

inculto *a* uncultivated; (*persona*) uneducated

incumplimiento *m* non-fulfilment; (*de un contrato*) breach

incurable *a* incurable

incurrir *vi*. ~ **en** incur; fall into (*error*); commit (*crimen*)

incursión *f* raid

indagación *f* investigation. ~**r** [12] *vt* investigate

indebido *a* undue

indecencia *f* indecency. ~**te** *a* indecent

indecible *a* inexpressible

indecisión *f* indecision. ~**o** *a* undecided

indefenso *a* defenceless

indefinible *a* indefinable. ~**do** *a* indefinite

indeleble *a* indelible

indelicadeza *f* indelicacy. ~**o** *a* indelicate; (*falto de escrúpulo*) unscrupulous

indemne *a* undamaged; (*persona*) unhurt. ~**idad** *f* indemnity. ~**izar** [10] *vt* indemnify, compensate

independencia *f* independence. ~**iente** *a* independent

independizarse [10] *vpr* become independent

indescifrable *a* indecipherable, incomprehensible

indescriptible *a* indescribable

indeseable *a* undesirable

indestructible *a* indestructible

indeterminable *a* indeterminable. ~**do** *a* indeterminate

India *f*. la ~ India. **las** ~**s** *fpl* the Indies

indicación *f* indication; (*sugerencia*) suggestion. ~**ciones** *fpl* directions. ~**dor** *m* indicator; (*tec*) gauge. ~**r** [7] *vt* show, indicate; (*apuntar*) point at; (*hacer saber*) point out; (*aconsejar*) advise. ~**tivo** *a* indicative. —*m* indicative; (*al teléfono*) dialling code

índice *m* indication; (*dedo*) index finger; (*de libro*) index; (*catálogo*) catalogue; (*aguja*) pointer

indicio *m* indication, sign; (*vestigio*) trace

indiferencia *f* indifference. ~**te** *a* indifferent. **me es** ~**te** it's all the same to me

indígena *a* indigenous. —*m* & *f* native

indigencia *f* poverty. ~**te** *a* needy

indigest|**ión** f indigestion. **~o** a undigested; (difícil de digerir) indigestible

indign|**ación** f indignation. **~ado** a indignant. **~ar** vt make indignant. **~arse** vpr be indignant. **~o** a unworthy; (despreciable) contemptible

indio a & m Indian

indirect|**a** f hint. **~o** a indirect

indisciplina f lack of discipline. **~do** a undisciplined

indiscre|**ción** f indiscretion. **~to** a indiscreet

indiscutible a unquestionable

indisoluble a indissoluble

indispensable a indispensable

indisp|**oner** [34] vt (enemistar) set against. **~onerse** vpr fall out; (ponerse enfermo) fall ill. **~osición** f indisposition. **~uesto** a indisposed

indistinto a indistinct

individu|**al** a individual; (cama) single. **~alidad** f individuality. **~alista** m & f individualist. **~alizar** [10] vt individualize. **~o** a & m individual

índole f nature; (clase) type

indolen|**cia** f indolence. **~te** a indolent

indoloro a painless

indomable a untameable

indómito a indomitable

Indonesia f Indonesia

induc|**ir** [47] vt induce; (deducir) infer

indudable a undoubted. **~mente** adv undoubtedly

indulgen|**cia** f indulgence. **~te** a indulgent

indult|**ar** vt pardon; exempt (de un pago etc). **~o** m pardon

industria f industry. **~l** a industrial. **—m** industrialist. **~lización** f industrialization. **~lizar** [10] vt industrialize

industriarse vpr do one's best

industrioso a industrious

inédito a unpublished; (fig) unknown

ineducado a impolite

inefable a inexpressible

ineficaz a ineffective

ineficiente a inefficient

inelegible a ineligible

ineludible a inescapable, unavoidable

inept|**itud** f ineptitude. **~o** a inept

inequívoco a unequivocal

iner|**cia** f inertia

inerme a unarmed; (fig) defenceless

inerte a inert

inesperado a unexpected

inestable a unstable

inestimable a inestimable

inevitable a inevitable

inexacto a inaccurate; (incorrecto) incorrect; (falso) untrue

inexistente a non-existent

inexorable a inexorable

inexperi|**encia** f inexperience. **~to** a inexperienced

inexplicable a inexplicable

infalible a infallible

infam|**ar** vt defame. **~atorio** a defamatory. **~e** a infamous; (fig, muy malo, fam) awful. **~ia** f infamy

infancia f infancy

infant|**a** f infanta, princess. **~e** m infante, prince; (mil) infantryman. **~ería** f infantry. **~il** a (de niño) child's; (como un niño) infantile

infarto m coronary (thrombosis)

infatigable a untiring

infatua|**ción** f conceit. **~rse** vpr get conceited

infausto a unlucky

infec|**ción** f infection. **~cioso** a infectious. **~tar** vt infect. **~tarse** vpr become infected. **~to** a infected; (fam) disgusting

infecundo a infertile

infeli|cidad f unhappiness. **∼z** a unhappy

inferior a inferior. —m & f inferior. **∼idad** f lower; (*calidad*) inferiority

inferir [4] vt infer; (*causar*) cause

infernal a infernal, hellish

infestar vt infest; (*fig*) inundate

infi|delidad f unfaithfulness. **∼el** a unfaithful

infierno m hell

infiltra|ción f infiltration. **∼rse** vpr infiltrate

ínfimo a lowest

infini|dad f infinity. **∼tivo** m infinitive. **∼to** a infinite. —m infinite; (*en matemáticas*) infinity. **una ∼dad de** countless

inflación f inflation; (*fig*) conceit

inflama|ble a (in)flammable. **∼ción** f inflammation. —vt set on fire; (*fig, med*) inflame. **∼rse** vpr catch fire; (*med*) become inflamed

inflar vt inflate; (*fig, exagerar*) exaggerate

inflexi|ble a inflexible. **∼ón** f inflexion

infligir [14] vt inflict

influ|encia f influence. **∼enza** f flu (*fam*), influenza. **∼ir** [17] vt/i influence. **∼jo** m influence. **∼yente** a influential

informa|ción f information. **∼ciones** fpl (*noticias*) news; (*de teléfonos*) directory enquiries. **∼dor** m informant

informal a informal; (*incorrecto*) incorrect

inform|ante m & f informant. **∼ar** vt/i inform. **∼arse** vpr find out. **∼ática** f information technology. **∼ativo** a informative

informe a shapeless. —m report; (*información*) information

infortun|ado a unfortunate. **∼io** m misfortune

infracción f infringement

infraestructura f infrastructure

infranqueable a impassable; (*fig*) insuperable

infrarrojo a infrared

infrecuente a infrequent

infringir [14] vt infringe

infructuoso a fruitless

infundado a unfounded

infu|ndir vt instil. **∼sión** f infusion

ingeniar vt invent

ingenier|ía f engineering. **∼o** m engineer

ingenio m ingenuity; (*agudeza*) wit; (*LAm, de azúcar*) refinery. **∼so** a ingenious

ingenu|idad f ingenuousness. **∼o** a ingenuous

ingerir [4] vt swallow

Inglaterra f England

ingle f groin

ingl|és a English. —m Englishman; (*lengua*) English. **∼esa** f Englishwoman

ingrat|itud f ingratitude. **∼o** a ungrateful; (*desagradable*) thankless

ingrediente m ingredient

ingres|ar vt deposit. —vi. **∼ar en** come in, enter; join (*sociedad*). **∼o** m entry; (*en sociedad, hospital etc*) admission. **∼os** mpl income

inh|ábil a unskillful; (*no apto*) unfit. **∼abilidad** f unskillfulness

inhabitable a uninhabitable

inhala|ción f inhalation. **∼dor** m inhaler. **∼r** vt inhale

inherente a inherent

inhibi|ción f inhibition. **∼r** vt inhibit

inhospitalario a, **inhóspito** a inhospitable

inhumano a inhuman

inicia|ción f beginning. **∼l** a & f initial. **∼r** vt initiate; (*comenzar*) begin, start. **∼tiva** f initiative

inicio *m* beginning

inicuo *a* iniquitous

inigualado *a* unequalled

ininterrumpido *a* continuous

injer|encia *f* interference. ∼ir [4] *vt* insert. ∼irse *vpr* interfere

injert|ar *vt* graft. ∼to *m* graft

injuri|a *f* insult; (*ofensa*) offence. ∼ar *vt* insult. ∼oso *a* offensive

injust|icia *f* injustice. ∼o *a* unjust

inmaculado *a* immaculate

inmaduro *a* unripe; (*persona*) immature

inmediaciones *fpl* neighbourhood

inmediat|amente *adv* immediately. ∼o *a* immediate; (*contiguo*) next

inmejorable *a* excellent

inmemorable *a* immemorial

inmens|idad *f* immensity. ∼a *a* immense

inmerecido *a* undeserved

inmersión *f* immersion

inmigra|ción *f* immigration. ∼nte *a & m* immigrant. ∼r *vt* immigrate

inminen|cia *f* imminence. ∼te *a* imminent

inmiscuirse [17] *vpr* interfere

inmobiliario *a* property

inmoderado *a* immoderate

inmodesto *a* immodest

inmolar *vt* sacrifice

inmoral *a* immoral. ∼idad *f* immorality

inmortal *a* immortal. ∼izar [10] *vt* immortalize

inmóvil *a* immobile

inmueble *a*. bienes ∼s property

inmund|icia *f* filth. ∼icias *fpl* rubbish. ∼o *a* filthy

inmun|e *a* immune. ∼idad *f* immunity. ∼ización *f* immunization. ∼izar [10] *vt* immunize

inmuta|ble *a* unchangeable. ∼rse *vpr* turn pale

innato *a* innate

innecesario *a* unnecessary

innegable *a* undeniable

innoble *a* ignoble

innova|ción *f* innovation. ∼r *vt/i* innovate

innumerable *a* innumerable

inocen|cia *f* innocence. ∼tada *f* practical joke. ∼te *a* innocent. ∼tón *a* naïve

inocuo *a* innocuous

inodoro *a* odourless. —*m* toilet

inofensivo *a* inoffensive

inolvidable *a* unforgettable

inoperable *a* inoperable

inopinado *a* unexpected

inoportuno *a* untimely; (*incómodo*) inconvenient

inorgánico *a* inorganic

inoxidable *a* stainless

inquebrantable *a* unbreakable

inquiet|ar *vt* worry. ∼arse *vpr* get worried. ∼o *a* worried; (*agitado*) restless. ∼ud *f* anxiety

inquilino *m* tenant

inquirir [4] *vt* enquire into, investigate

insaciable *a* insatiable

insalubre *a* unhealthy

insanable *a* incurable

insatisfecho *a* unsatisfied; (*descontento*) dissatisfied

inscri|bir [*pp* inscrito] *vt* inscribe; (*en registro etc*) enrol, register. ∼birse *vpr* register. ∼pción *f* inscription; (*registro*) registration

insect|icida *m* insecticide. ∼o *m* insect

insegur|idad *f* insecurity. ∼o *a* insecure; (*dudoso*) uncertain

insemina|ción *f* insemination. ∼r *vt* inseminate

insensato *a* senseless

insensible *a* insensitive; (*med*) insensible; (*imperceptible*) imperceptible

inseparable *a* inseparable

insertar *vt* insert

insidi|a *f* trap. ∼oso *a* insidious

insigne *a* famous

insignia *f* badge; (*bandera*) flag

insignificante *a* insignificant

insincero *a* insincere

insinua|**ción** *f* insinuation. **~nte** *a* insinuating. **~r** [21] *vt* insinuate. **~rse** *upr* ingratiate o.s. **~rse en** creep into

insípido *a* insipid

insist|**encia** *f* insistence. **~ente** *a* insistent. **~ir** *vi* insist; (*hacer hincapié*) stress

insolación *f* sunstroke

insolen|**cia** *f* rudeness, insolence. **~te** *a* rude, insolent

insólito *a* unusual

insoluble *a* insoluble

insolven|**cia** *f* insolvency. **~te** *a* & *m & f* insolvent

insomne *a* sleepless. **~io** *m* insomnia

insondable *a* unfathomable

insoportable *a* unbearable

insospechado *a* unexpected

insostenible *a* untenable

inspec|**ción** *f* inspection. **~cionar** *vt* inspect. **~tor** *m* inspector

inspira|**ción** *f* inspiration. **~r** *vt* inspire. **~rse** *upr* be inspired

instala|**ción** *f* installation. **~r** *vt* install. **~rse** *upr* settle

instancia *f* request

instant|**ánea** *f* snapshot. **~áneo** *a* instantaneous; (*café etc*) instant. **~e** *m* instant. **a cada ~e** constantly. **al ~e** immediately

instar *vt* urge

instaura|**ción** *f* establishment. **~r** *vt* establish

instiga|**ción** *f* instigation. **~dor** *m* instigator. **~r** [12] *vt* instigate; (*incitar*) incite

instint|**ivo** *a* instinctive. **~o** *m* instinct

institu|**ción** *f* institution. **~cional** *a* institutional. **~ir** [17] *vt* establish. **~to** *m* institute;

(*escol*) (secondary) school. **~triz** *f* governess

instruc|**ción** *f* instruction. **~ctivo** *a* instructive. **~ctor** *m* instructor. **~ir** [17] *vt* instruct; (*enseñar*) teach

instrument|**ación** *f* instrumentation. **~al** *a* instrumental. **~o** *m* instrument; (*herramienta*) tool

insubordina|**ción** *f* insubordination. **~r** *vt* stir up. **~rse** *upr* rebel

insuficien|**cia** *f* insufficiency; (*inadecuación*) inadequacy. **~te** *a* insufficient

insufrible *a* insufferable

insular *a* insular

insulina *f* insulin

insulso *a* tasteless; (*fig*) insipid

insult|**ar** *vt* insult. **~o** *m* insult

insuperable *a* insuperable; (*excelente*) excellent

insurgente *a* insurgent

insurrec|**ción** *f* insurrection. **~to** *a* insurgent

intacto *a* intact

intachable *a* irreproachable

intangible *a* intangible

integra|**ción** *f* integration. **~l** *a* integral; (*completo*) complete; (*pan*) wholemeal (*Brit*), wholewheat (*Amer*). **~r** *vt* make up

integridad *f* integrity; (*entereza*) wholeness

íntegro *a* complete; (*fig*) upright

intelec|**to** *m* intellect. **~ual** *a* & *m & f* intellectual

inteligen|**cia** *f* intelligence. **~te** *a* intelligent

inteligible *a* intelligible

intemperancia *f* intemperance

intemperie *f* bad weather. **a la ~** in the open

intempestivo *a* untimely

intención *f* intention. **~onado** *a* deliberate. **~onal** *a* intentional. **bien ~onado** well-meaning. **mal ~onado** malicious. **segunda ~ón** duplicity

intens|idad *f* intensity. **~ificar**
[7] *vt* intensify. **~ivo** *a* intensive. **~o** *a* intense

intent|ar *vt* try. **~o** *m* intent;
(*tentativa*) attempt. **de ~o** intentionally

intercalar *vt* insert

intercambio *m* exchange

interceder *vt* intercede

interceptar *vt* intercept

intercesión *f* intercession

interdicto *m* ban

inter|és *m* interest; (*egoísmo*)
self-interest. **~esado** *a* interested; (*parcial*) biassed; (*egoísta*)
selfish. **~esante** *a* interesting.
~esar *vt* interest; (*afectar*) concern. *—vi* be of interest. **~esarse** *vpr* take an interest (**por**
in)

interferencia *f* interference.
~ir [4] *vi* interfere

interino *a* temporary; (*persona*)
acting. *—m* stand-in; (*médico*)
locum

interior *a* interior. *—m* inside.
Ministerio *m* del I~ Home
Office (*Brit*), Department of the
Interior (*Amer*)

interjección *f* interjection

interlocutor *m* speaker

interludio *m* interlude

intermediario *a & m* intermediary

intermedio *a* intermediate. *—m*
interval

interminable *a* interminable

intermitente *a* intermittent.
—m indicator

internacional *a* international

intern|ado *m* (*escol*) boarding-school. **~ar** *vt* intern; (*en manicomio*) commit. **~arse** *vpr* penetrate. **~o** *a* internal; (*escol*)
boarding. *—m* (*escol*) boarder

interpelar *vt* appeal

interponer [34] *vt* interpose. **~se**
vpr intervene

inter|pretación *f* interpretation. **~erpretar** *vt* interpret.
~érprete *m* interpreter; (*mus*)
performer

interroga|ción *f* question;
(*acción*) interrogation; (*signo*)
question mark. **~r** [12] *vt* question. **~tivo** *a* interrogative

interru|mpir *vt* interrupt; (*suspender*) stop. **~pción** *f* interruption. **~ptor** *m* switch

intersección *f* intersection

interurbano *a* inter-city; (*conferencia*) long-distance

intervalo *m* interval; (*espacio*)
space. **a ~s** at intervals

interven|ir [53] *vt* control; (*med*)
operate on. *—vi* intervene;
(*participar*) take part. **~tor** *m*
inspector; (*com*) auditor

intestino *m* intestine

intim|ar *vi* become friendly.
~idad *f* intimacy

intimidar *vt* intimidate

íntimo *a* intimate. *—m* close
friend

intitular *vt* entitle

intolera|ble *a* intolerable. **~nte**
a intolerant

intoxicar [7] *vt* poison

intranquil|izar [10] *vt* worry.
~o *a* worried

intransigente *a* intransigent

intransitable *a* impassable

intransitivo *a* intransitive

intratable *a* intractable

intrépido *a* intrepid

intriga *f* intrigue. **~nte** *a* intriguing. **~r** [12] *vt/i* intrigue

intrincado *a* intricate

intrínseco *a* intrinsic

introduc|ción *f* introduction.
~ir [47] *vt* introduce; (*meter*)
insert. **~irse** *vpr* get into; (*entrometerse*) interfere

intromisión *f* interference

introvertido *a & m* introvert

intrus|ión *f* intrusion. **~o** *a*
intrusive. *—m* intruder

intui|ción f intuition. **~r** [17] vt sense. **~tivo** a intuitive

inunda|ción f flooding. **~r** vt flood

inusitado a unusual

in|útil a useless; (vano) futile. **~utilidad** f uselessness

invadir vt invade

inv|alidez f invalidity; (med) disability. **~álido** a & m invalid

invaria|ble a invariable. **~do** a unchanged

inva|sión f invasion. **~or** a invading. —m invader

invectiva f invective

invencible a invincible

inven|ción f invention. **~tar** vt invent

inventario m inventory

invent|iva f inventiveness. **~ivo** a inventive. **~or** m inventor

invernadero m greenhouse

invernal a winter

inverosímil a improbable

inversión f inversion; (com) investment

inverso a inverse; (contrario) opposite. **a la inversa** the other way round

invertebrado a & m invertebrate

inverti|do a inverted; (homosexual) homosexual. —m homosexual. **~r** [4] vt reverse; (volcar) turn upside down; (com) invest; spend (tiempo)

investidura f investiture

investiga|ción f investigation; (univ) research. **~dor** m investigator. **~r** [12] vt investigate

investir [5] vt invest

inveterado a inveterate

invicto a unbeaten

invierno m winter

inviolable a inviolate

invisib|ilidad f invisibility. **~le** a invisible

invita|ción f invitation. **~do** m guest. **~r** vt invite. **te invito a una copa** I'll buy you a drink

invoca|ción f invocation. **~r** [7] vt invoke

involuntario a involuntary

invulnerable a invulnerable

inyec|ción f injection. **~tar** vt inject

ion m ion

ir [49] vi go; (ropa) (convenir) suit. —m going. **~se** vpr go away. **~ a hacer** to be going to do. **~ a pie** walk. **~ de paseo** go for a walk. **~ en coche** go by car. **no me va ni me viene** it's all the same to me. **no vaya a ser que** in case. **¡qué va!** nonsense! **va mejorando** it's gradually getting better. **¡vamos!, ¡vámonos!** come on! let's go! **¡vaya** fancy that! **¡vete a saber!** who knows? **¡ya voy!** I'm coming!

ira f anger. **~cundo** a irascible

Irak m Iraq

Irán m Iran

iraní a & m & f Iranian

iraquí a & m & f Iraqi

iris m (anat) iris; (arco iris) rainbow

Irlanda f Ireland

irland|és a Irish. —m Irishman; (lengua) Irish. **~esa** f Irishwoman

ir|onía f irony. **~ónico** a ironic

irracional a irrational

irradiar vt/i radiate

irrazonable a unreasonable

irreal a unreal. **~idad** f unreality

irrealizable a unattainable

irreconciliable a irreconcilable

irreconocible a unrecognizable

irrecuperable a irretrievable

irreducible a irreducible

irreflexión f impetuosity

irrefutable a irrefutable

irregular a irregular. **~idad** f irregularity

irreparable a irreparable

irreprimible a irrepressible

irreprochable a irreproachable

irresistible *a* irresistible
irresoluto *a* irresolute
irrespetuoso *a* disrespectful
irresponsable *a* irresponsible
irrevocable *a* irrevocable
irriga|ción *f* irrigation. **~r** [12] *vt* irrigate
irrisorio *a* derisive; (*insignificante*) ridiculous
irrita|ble *a* irritable. **~ción** *f* irritation. **~r** *vt* irritate. **~rse** *upr* get annoyed
irrumpir *vi* burst (**en** in)
irrupción *f* irruption
isla *f* island. **las I~s Británicas** the British Isles
Islam *m* Islam
islámico *a* Islamic
islandés *a* Icelandic. *—m* Icelander; (*lengua*) Icelandic
Islandia *f* Iceland
isleño *a* island. *—m* islander
Israel *m* Israel
israelí *a* & *m* Israeli
istmo /'ismo/ *m* isthmus
Italia *f* Italy
italiano *a* & *m* Italian
itinerario *m* itinerary
IVA *abrev* (*impuesto sobre el valor añadido*) VAT, value added tax
izar [10] *vt* hoist
izquierd|a *f* left(-hand); (*pol*) left(-wing). **~ista** *m* & *f* leftist. **~o** *a* left. **a la ~a** on the left; (*con movimiento*) to the left

J

ja *int* ha!
jabalí *m* wild boar
jabalina *f* javelin
jab|ón *m* soap. **~onar** *vt* soap. **~onoso** *a* soapy
jaca *f* pony
jacinto *m* hyacinth

jacta|ncia *f* boastfulness; (*acción*) boasting. **~rse** *upr* boast
jadea|nte *a* panting. **~r** *vi* pant
jaez *m* harness
jaguar *m* jaguar
jalea *f* jelly
jaleo *m* row, uproar. **armar un ~** kick up a fuss
jalón *m* (*LAm, tirón*) pull; (*Mex, trago*) drink
Jamaica *f* Jamaica
jamás *adv* never; (*en frases afirmativas*) ever
jamelgo *m* nag
jamón *m* ham. **~ de York** boiled ham. **~ serrano** cured ham
Japón *m.* **el ~** Japan
japonés *a* & *m* Japanese
jaque *m* check. **~ mate** checkmate
jaqueca *f* migraine. **dar ~** bother
jarabe *m* syrup
jardín *m* garden. **~ de la infancia** kindergarten, nursery school
jardiner|ía *f* gardening. **~o** *m* gardener
jarocho *a* (*Mex*) from Veracruz
jarr|a *f* jug. **~o** *m* jug. **echar un ~o de agua fría** a throw cold water on. **en ~as** with hands on hips
jaula *f* cage
jauría *f* pack of hounds
jazmín *m* jasmine
jef|a *f* boss. **~atura** *f* leadership; (*sede*) headquarters. **~e** *m* boss; (*pol etc*) leader. **~e de camareros** head waiter. **~e de estación** stationmaster. **~e de ventas** sales manager
jengibre *m* ginger
jeque *m* sheikh
jer|arquía *f* hierarchy. **~árquico** *a* hierarchical
jerez *m* sherry. **al ~** with sherry

jerga f coarse cloth; (argot) jargon

jerigonza f jargon; (galimatías) gibberish

jeringa f syringe; (Am, molestia) nuisance. ~r [12] vt (fig, molestar, fam) annoy

jeroglífico m hieroglyph(ic)

jersey m (pl jerseys) jersey

Jerusalén m Jerusalem

Jesucristo m Jesus Christ. **antes de** ~ BC, before Christ

jesuita a & m & f Jesuit

Jesús m Jesus. —int good heavens!; (al estornudar) bless you!

jícara f small cup

jilguero m goldfinch

jinete m rider, horseman

jipijapa f straw hat

jirafa f giraffe

jirón m shred, tatter

jocoso a funny, humorous

jornada f working day; (viaje) journey; (etapa) stage. ~l m day's wage; (trabajo) day's work. ~lero m day labourer

joroba f hump. ~do a hunchbacked. —m hunchback. ~r vt annoy

jota f letter J; (danza) jota, popular dance; (fig) iota. **ni** ~ nothing

joven (pl jóvenes) a young. —m young man, youth. —f young woman, girl

jovial a jovial

joya f jewel. ~as fpl jewellery. ~ería f jeweller's (shop). ~ero m jeweller; (estuche) jewellery box

juanete m bunion

jubilación f retirement. ~ado a retired. ~ar vt pension off. ~arse vpr retire. ~eo m jubilee

júbilo m joy

jubiloso a jubilant

judaísmo m Judaism

judía f Jewish woman; (alubia) bean. ~ **blanca** haricot bean. ~ **escarlata** runner bean. ~ **verde** French bean

judicial a judicial

judío a Jewish. —m Jewish man

judo m judo

juego m game; (de niños, tec) play; (de azar) gambling; (conjunto) set. —vb véase **jugar**. **estar en** ~ be at stake. **estar fuera de** ~ be offside. **hacer** ~ match

juerga f spree

jueves m Thursday

juez m judge. ~ **de instrucción** examining magistrate. ~ **de línea** linesman

jugador m player; (en juegos de azar) gambler. ~r [3] vt play. —vi play; (a juegos de azar) gamble; (apostar) bet. ~rse vpr risk. ~r al fútbol play football

juglar m minstrel

jugo m juice; (de carne) gravy; (fig) substance. ~so a juicy; (fig) substantial

juguete m toy. ~ear vi play. ~ón a playful

juicio m judgement; (opinión) opinion; (razón) reason. ~so a wise. **a mi** ~ in my opinion

juliana f vegetable soup

julio m July

junco m rush, reed

jungla f jungle

junio m June

junta f meeting; (consejo) board, committee; (pol) junta; (tec) joint. ~ar vt join; (reunir) collect. ~arse vpr join; (gente) meet. ~o a joined; (en plural) together. ~o a next to. ~ura f joint. **por** ~o all together

jurado a sworn. —m jury; (miembro de jurado) juror. ~mento m oath. ~r vt/i swear. ~r en falso commit perjury. **jurárselas a uno** have it in for s.o. **prestar** ~**mento** take the oath

jurel m (type of) mackerel

jurídico a legal

juris|dicción f jurisdiction. ~**prudencia** f jurisprudence

justamente a exactly; ⟨con justicia⟩ fairly

justicia f justice

justifica|ción f justification. ~**r** [7] vt justify

justo a fair, just; ⟨exacto⟩ exact; ⟨ropa⟩ tight. —adv just. ~ **a tiempo** just in time

juven|il a youthful. ~**tud** f youth; ⟨gente joven⟩ young people

juzga|do m ⟨tribunal⟩ court. ~**r** [12] vt judge. **a** ~**r por** judging by

K

kilo m, **kilogramo** m kilo, kilogram

kil|ometraje m distance in kilometres, mileage. ~**ométrico** a ⟨fam⟩ endless. ~**ómetro** m kilometre. ~**ómetro cuadrado** square kilometre

kilovatio m kilowatt

kiosco m kiosk

L

la m A; ⟨solfa⟩ lah. —art def f the. —pron ⟨ella⟩ her; ⟨Vd⟩ you; ⟨ello⟩ it. ~ **de** the one. ~ **de Vd** your one, yours. ~ **que** whoever, the one

laberinto m labyrinth, maze

labia f glibness

labio m lip

labor f work; ⟨tarea⟩ job. ~**able** a working. ~**ar** vi work. ~**es** fpl

de aguja needlework. ~**es** fpl **de ganchillo** crochet. ~**es** fpl **de punto** knitting. ~**es** fpl **domésticas** housework

laboratorio m laboratory

laborioso a laborious

laborista a Labour. —m & f member of the Labour Party

labra|do a worked; ⟨madera⟩ carved; ⟨metal⟩ wrought; ⟨tierra⟩ ploughed. ~**dor** m farmer; ⟨obrero⟩ labourer. ~**nza** f farming. ~**r** vt work; carve ⟨madera⟩; cut ⟨piedra⟩; till ⟨la tierra⟩; ⟨fig, causar⟩ cause

labriego m peasant

laca f lacquer

lacayo m lackey

lacerar vt lacerate

lacero m lassoer; ⟨cazador⟩ poacher

lacio a straight; ⟨flojo⟩ limp

lacón m shoulder of pork

lacónico a laconic

lacra f scar

lacr|ar vt seal. ~**e** m sealing wax

lactante a breast-fed

lácteo a milky. **productos** mpl ~**s** dairy products

ladear vt/i tilt. ~**se** vpr lean

ladera f slope

ladino a astute

lado m side. **al** ~ near. **al** ~ **de** at the side of, beside. **los de al** ~ the next door neighbours. **por otro** ~ on the other hand. **por todos** ~**s** on all sides. **por un** ~ on the one hand

ladr|ar vi bark. ~**ido** m bark

ladrillo m brick; ⟨de chocolate⟩ block

ladrón a thieving. ~m thief

lagart|ija f ⟨small⟩ lizard. ~**o** m lizard

lago m lake

lágrima f tear

lagrimoso a tearful

laguna f small lake; ⟨fig, omisión⟩ gap

laico *a* lay

lamé *m* lamé

lamedura *f* lick

lament|able *a* lamentable, pitiful. **~ar** *vt* be sorry about. **~arse** *vpr* lament; (*quejarse*) complain. **~o** *m* moan

lamer *vt* lick; (*olas etc*) lap

lámina *f* sheet; (*foto*) plate; (*dibujo*) picture

lamina|do *a* laminated. **~r** *vt* laminate

lámpara *f* lamp; (*bombilla*) bulb; (*lamparón*) grease stain. **~ de pie** standard lamp

lamparón *m* grease stain

lampiño *a* clean-shaven, beardless

lana *f* wool. **~r** *a*. **ganado** *m* **~r** sheep. **de ~** wool(len)

lanceta *f* lancet

lancha *f* boat. **~ motora** *f* motor boat. **~ salvavidas** lifeboat

lanero *a* wool(len)

langost|a *f* (*crustáceo marino*) lobster; (*insecto*) locust. **~ino** *m* prawn

languide|cer [11] *vi* languish. **~z** *f* languor

lánguido *a* languid; (*decaído*) listless

lanilla *f* nap; (*tela fina*) flannel

lanudo *a* woolly

lanza *f* lance, spear

lanza|llamas *m invar* flamethrower. **~miento** *m* throw; (*acción de lanzar*) throwing; (*de proyectil, de producto*) launch. **~r** [10] *vt* throw; (*de un avión*) drop; launch (*proyectil, producto*). **~rse** *vpr* fling o.s.

lapicero *m* (propelling) pencil

lápida *f* memorial tablet. **~ sepulcral** tombstone

lapidar *vt* stone

lápiz *m* pencil; (*grafito*) lead. **~ de labios** lipstick

Laponia *f* Lapland

lapso *m* lapse

larg|a *f*. **a la ~a** in the long run. **dar ~as** put off. **~ar** [12] *vt* slacken; (*dar, fam*) give; (*fam*) deal (*bofetada etc*). **~arse** *vpr* (*fam*) go away, clear off (*fam*). **~o** *a* long; (*demasiado*) too long. **—m** length. **¡~o!** go away! **~ueza** *f* generosity. **a lo ~o** lengthwise. **a lo ~o de** along. **tener 100 metros de ~o** be 100 metres long

laring|e *f* larynx. **~itis** *f* laryngitis

larva *f* larva

las *art def fpl* the. **—pron** them. **~ de** those, the ones. **~ de Vd** your ones, yours. **~ que** whoever, the ones

lascivo *a* lascivious

láser *m* laser

lástima *f* pity; (*queja*) complaint. **dar ~** be pitiful. **ella me da ~** I feel sorry for her. **¡qué ~!** what a pity!

lastim|ado *a* hurt. **~ar** *vt* hurt. **~arse** *vpr* hurt o.s. **~ero** *a* doleful. **~oso** *a* pitiful

lastre *m* ballast

lata *f* tinplate; (*envase*) tin (*esp Brit*), can; (*molestia, fam*) nuisance. **dar la ~** be a nuisance. **¡qué ~!** what a nuisance!

latente *a* latent

lateral *a* side, lateral

latido *m* beating; (*cada golpe*) beat

latifundio *m* large estate

latigazo *m* (*golpe*) lash; (*chasquido*) crack

látigo *m* whip

latín *m* Latin. **saber ~** (*fam*) not be stupid

latino *a* Latin. **L~américa** *f* Latin America. **~americano** *a* & *m* Latin American

latir *vi* beat; (*herida*) throb

latitud *f* latitude

latón *m* brass

latoso *a* annoying; (*pesado*) boring

laucha *f* (*Arg*) mouse

laúd *m* lute

laudable *a* laudable

laureado *a* honoured; (*premiado*) prize-winning

laurel *m* laurel; (*culin*) bay

lava *f* lava

lava|ble *a* washable. ∼**bo** *m* wash-basin; (*retrete*) toilet. ∼**dero** *m* sink, wash-basin. ∼**do** *m* washing. ∼**do de cerebro** brainwashing. ∼**do en seco** dry-cleaning. ∼**dora** *f* washing machine. ∼**ndería** *f* laundry. ∼**ndería automática** launderette, laundromat (*esp Amer*). ∼**parabrisas** *m invar* windscreen washer (*Brit*), windshield washer (*Amer*). ∼**platos** *m* & *f invar* dishwasher (*Mex, fregadero*) sink. ∼**r** *vt* wash. ∼**r en seco** dry-clean. ∼**rse** *vpr* have a wash. ∼**rse las manos** (*incl fig*) wash one's hands. ∼**tiva** *f* enema. ∼**vajillas** *m* & *f inv* dishwasher

laxante *a* & *m* laxative. ∼**o** *a* loose

laz|ada *f* bow. ∼**o** *m* knot; (*lazada*) bow; (*fig, vínculo*) tie; (*cuerda con nudo corredizo*) lasso; (*trampa*) trap

le *pron* (*acusativo, él*) him; (*acusativo, Vd*) you; (*dativo, él*) (to) him; (*dativo, ella*) (to) her; (*dativo, ello*) (to) it; (*dativo, Vd*) (to) you

leal *a* loyal; (*fiel*) faithful. ∼**tad** *f* loyalty; (*fidelidad*) faithfulness

lebrel *m* greyhound

lección *f* lesson; (*univ*) lecture

lect|or *m* reader; (*univ*) language assistant. ∼**ura** *f* reading

leche *f* milk; (*golpe*) bash. ∼ **condensada** condensed milk. ∼ **desnatada** skimmed milk. ∼ **en polvo** powdered milk. ∼**ra** *f*

(*vasija*) milk jug. ∼**ría** *f* dairy. ∼**ro** *a* milk, dairy. —*m* milkman. ∼ **sin desnatar** whole milk. **tener mala** ∼ be spiteful

lecho *m* bed

lechoso *a* milky

lechuga *f* lettuce

lechuza *f* owl

leer [18] *vt/i* read

legación *f* legation

legado *m* legacy; (*enviado*) legate

legajo *m* bundle, file

legal *a* legal. ∼**idad** *f* legality. ∼**izar** [10] *vt* legalize; (*certificar*) authenticate. ∼**mente** *adv* legally

legar [12] *vt* bequeath

legendario *a* legendary

legible *a* legible

legión *f* legion. ∼**onario** *m* legionary

legisla|ción *f* legislation. ∼**dor** *m* legislator. ∼**r** *vi* legislate. ∼**tura** *f* legislature

leg|itimidad *f* legitimacy. ∼**ítimo** *a* legitimate; (*verdadero*) real

lego *a* lay; (*ignorante*) ignorant. —*m* layman

legua *f* league

legumbre *f* vegetable

lejan|ía *f* distance. ∼**o** *a* distant

lejía *f* bleach

lejos *adv* far. ∼ **de** far from. **a lo** ∼ in the distance. **desde** ∼ from a distance, from afar

lelo *a* stupid

lema *m* motto

lencería *f* linen; (*de mujer*) lingerie

lengua *f* tongue; (*idioma*) language. **irse de la** ∼ talk too much. **morderse la** ∼ hold one's tongue. **tener mala** ∼ have a vicious tongue

lenguado *m* sole

lenguaje *m* language

lengüeta *f* (*de zapato*) tongue

lengüetada f, **lengüetazo** m lick

lente f lens; **~s** mpl glasses. **~s de contacto** contact lenses

lenteja f lentil. **~uela** f sequin

lentilla f contact lens

lentitud f slowness. **~o** a slow

leña f firewood. **~ador** m woodcutter. **~o** m log

Leo m Leo

león m lion. **León** Leo. **~ona** f lioness

leopardo m leopard

leotardo m thick tights

lepra f leprosy. **~oso** m leper

lerdo a dim; (torpe) clumsy

les pron (acusativo) them; (acusativo, Vds) you; (dativo) (to) them; (dativo, Vds) (to) you

lesbia(na) f lesbian

lesbiano a, **lesbio** a lesbian

lesión f wound. **~onado** a injured; **~onar** vt injure; (dañar) damage

letal a lethal

letanía f litany

letárgico a lethargic. **~argo** m lethargy

letra f letter; (escritura) handwriting; (de una canción) words, lyrics. **~a de cambio** bill of exchange. **~a de imprenta** print. **~ado** a learned. **~ero** m notice; (cartel) poster

letrina f latrine

leucemia f leukaemia

levadizo a. **puente** m **~** drawbridge

levadura f yeast. **~ en polvo** baking powder

levantamiento m lifting; (sublevación) uprising. **~r** vt raise, lift; (construir) build; (recoger) pick up; (separar) take off. **~rse** vpr get up; (ponerse de pie) stand up; (erguirse, sublevarse) rise up

levante m east; (viento) east wind. **L~** Levant

levar vt weigh (ancla). **—vi** set sail

leve a light; (enfermedad etc) slight; (de poca importancia) trivial. **~dad** f lightness; (fig) slightness

léxico m vocabulary

lexicografía f lexicography

ley f law; (parlamentaria) act. **plata** f **de ~** sterling silver

leyenda f legend

liar [20] vt tie; (envolver) wrap up; roll (cigarrillo); (fig, confundir) confuse; (fig, enredar) involve. **~se** vpr get involved

libanés a & m Lebanese

Líbano m. **el ~** Lebanon

libelista m & f satirist. **~o** m satire

libélula f dragonfly

liberación f liberation. **~dor** a liberating. **—m** liberator

liberal a & m & f liberal. **~idad** f liberality. **~mente** adv liberally

liberar vt free. **~tad** f freedom. **~tad de cultos** freedom of worship. **~tad de imprenta** freedom of the press. **~tad provisional** bail. **~tar** vt free. **en ~tad** free

libertino m libertine

Libia f Libya

libido m libido

libio a & m Libyan

libra f pound. **~ esterlina** pound sterling

Libra f Libra

librador m (com) drawer. **~r** vt free; (de un peligro) rescue. **~rse** vpr free o.s. **~rse de** get rid of

libre a free; (aire) open; (en natación) freestyle. **~ de impuestos** tax-free. **—m** (Mex) taxi

librea f livery

librería f bookshop (Brit), bookstore (Amer); (mueble) bookcase. **~ero** m bookseller. **~eta** f notebook. **~o** m book. **~o de a bordo** logbook. **~o de bolsillo** paperback. **~o de ejercicios**

exercise book. ∼o de reclamaciones complaints book
licencia f permission; (documento) licence. ∼do m graduate. ∼ para manejar (LAm) driving licence. ∼r vt (mil) discharge; (echar) dismiss. ∼tura f degree
licencioso a licentious
liceo m (esp LAm) (secondary) school
licita|dor m bidder. ∼r vt bid for
lícito a legal; (permisible) permissible
licor m liquid; (alcohólico) liqueur
licua|dora f liquidizer. ∼r [21] liquefy
lid f hare. en buena ∼ by fair means
líder m leader
liderato m, liderazgo m leadership
lidia f bullfighting; (lucha) fight; (LAm, molestia) nuisance. ∼r vt/i fight
liebre f hare
lienzo m linen; (del pintor) canvas; (muro, pared) wall
liga f garter; (alianza) league; (mezcla) mixture. ∼dura f bond; (mus) slur; (med) ligature. ∼mento m ligament. ∼r [12] vt tie; (fig) join; (mus) slur. —vi mix. ∼r con (fig) pick up. ∼rse vpr (fig) commit o.s.
liger|eza f lightness; (agilidad) agility; (rapidez) swiftness; (de carácter) fickleness. ∼o a light; (rápido) quick; (ágil) agile; (superficial) superficial; (de poca importancia) slight. —adv quickly. a la ∼a lightly, superficially
liguero m suspender belt
lija f dogfish; (papel de lija) sandpaper. ∼r vt sand
lila f lilac
Lima f Lima

lima f file; (fruta) lime. ∼duras fpl filings. ∼r vt file (down)
limbo m limbo
limita|ción f limitation. ∼do a limited. ∼r vt limit. ∼r con border on. ∼tivo a limiting
límite m limit. ∼ de velocidad speed limit
limítrofe a bordering
limo m mud
lim|ón m lemon. ∼onada f lemonade
limosn|a f alms. ∼ear vi beg. pedir ∼a beg
limpia f cleaning. ∼botas m invar bootblack. ∼parabrisas m inv windscreen wiper (Brit), windshield wiper (Amer). ∼pipas m invar pipe-cleaner. ∼r vt clean; (enjugar) wipe
limpi|eza f cleanliness; (acción de limpiar) cleaning. ∼eza en seco dry-cleaning. ∼o a clean; (cielo) clear; (fig, honrado) honest. —adv fairly. en ∼o (com) net. jugar ∼o play fair
linaje m lineage; (fig, clase) kind
lince m lynx
linchar vt lynch
lind|ante a bordering (con on). ∼ar vi border (con on). ∼e f boundary. ∼ero m border
lindo a pretty, lovely. de lo ∼ (fam) a lot
línea f line. en ∼s generales in broad outline. guardar la ∼ watch one's figure
lingote m ingot
lingü|ista m & f linguist. ∼ística f linguistics. ∼ístico a linguistic
lino m flax; (tela) linen
linóleo m, linóeum m lino, linoleum
linterna f lantern; (de bolsillo) torch, flashlight (Amer)
lío m bundle; (jaleo) fuss; (embrollo) muddle; (amorío) affair
liquen m lichen

liquida|ción f liquidation; (*venta especial*) (clearance) sale. **~r** vt liquify; (*com*) liquidate; settle (*cuenta*)

líquido a liquid; (*com*) net. **—m** liquid

lira f lyre; (*moneda italiana*) lira

líric|a f lyric poetry. **~o** a lyric(al)

lirio m iris. **~ de los valles** lily of the valley

lirón m dormouse; (*fig*) sleepy-head. **dormir como un ~** sleep like a log

Lisboa f Lisbon

lisia|do a disabled. **~r** vt disable; (*herir*) injure

liso a smooth; (*pelo*) straight; (*tierra*) flat; (*sencillo*) plain

lisonj|a f flattery. **~eador** a flattering. **—m** flatterer. **~ear** vt flatter. **~ero** a flattering

lista f stripe; (*enumeración*) list; (*de platos*) menu. **~ de correos** poste restante. **~do** a striped. **a ~s** striped

listo a clever; (*preparado*) ready

listón m ribbon; (*de madera*) strip

lisura f smoothness

litera f (*en barco*) berth; (*en tren*) sleeper; (*en habitación*) bunk bed

literal a literal

litera|rio a literary. **~tura** f literature

litig|ar [12] vi dispute; (*jurid*) litigate. **~io** m dispute; (*jurid*) litigation

litografía f (*arte*) lithography; (*cuadro*) lithograph

litoral a coastal. **—m** coast

litro m litre

lituano a & m Lithuanian

liturgia f liturgy

liviano a fickle, inconstant

lívido a livid

lizo m warp thread

lo art def neutro. **~ importante** what is important, the important thing. **—pron** (*él*) him; (*ello*) it. **~ que** what(ever), that which

loa f praise. **~ble** a praise-worthy. **~r** vt praise

lobo m wolf

lóbrego a gloomy

lóbulo m lobe

local a local. **—m** premises; (*lugar*) place. **~idad** f locality; (*de un espectáculo*) seat; (*entrada*) ticket. **~izar** [10] vt localize; (*encontrar*) find, locate

loción f lotion

loco a mad; (*fig*) foolish. **—m** lunatic. **~ de alegría** mad with joy. **estar ~ por** be crazy about. **volverse ~** go mad

locomo|ción f locomotion. **~tora** f locomotive

locuaz a talkative

locución f expression

locura f madness; (*acto*) crazy thing. **con ~** madly

locutor m announcer

locutorio m (*de teléfono*) telephone booth

lodazal m quagmire. **~o** m mud

logaritmo m logarithm, log

lógic|a f logic. **~o** a logical

logística f logistics

logr|ar vt get; win (*premio*). **~ hacer** manage to do. **~o** m achievement; (*de premio*) winning; (*éxito*) success

loma f small hill

lombriz f worm

lomo m back; (*de libro*) spine; (*doblez*) fold. **~ de cerdo** loin of pork

lona f canvas

loncha f slice; (*de tocino*) rasher

londinense a from London. **—m** Londoner

Londres m London

loneta f thin canvas

longánimo a magnanimous

longaniza f sausage

longev|idad f longevity. **~o** a long-lived

longitud f length; (geog) longitude

lonja f slice; (de tocino) rasher; (com) market

lord m (pl **lores**) lord

loro m parrot

los art def mpl the. **—pron** them. **~ de Antonio** Antonio's. **~ que** whoever, the ones

losa f slab; (baldosa) flagstone. **~ sepulcral** tombstone

lote m share

lotería f lottery

loto m lotus

loza f crockery

lozano a fresh; (vegetación) lush; (persona) lively

lubri(fi)ca|nte a lubricating. **—m** lubricant. **~r** [7] vt lubricate

lucero m (estrella) bright star; (planeta) Venus

lucid|ez f lucidity. **~o** a splendid

lúcido a lucid

luciérnaga f glow-worm

lucimiento m brilliance

lucir [11] vt (fig) show off. **—vi** shine; (lámpara) give off light; (joya) sparkle. **~se** vpr (fig) shine, excel

lucr|ativo a lucrative. **~o** m gain

lucha f fight. **~dor** m fighter. **~r** vi fight

luego adv then; (más tarde) later. **—conj** therefore. **~ que** as soon as. **desde ~** of course

lugar m place. **~ común** cliché. **~eño** a village. **dar ~ a** give rise to. **en ~ de** instead of. **en primer ~** in the first place. **hacer ~** make room. **tener ~** take place

lugarteniente m deputy

lúgubre a gloomy

lujo m luxury. **~so** a luxurious. **de ~** de luxe

lujuria f lust

lumbago m lumbago

lumbre f fire; (luz) light. **¿tienes ~?** have you got a light?

luminoso a luminous; (fig) brilliant

luna f moon; (de escaparate) window; (espejo) mirror. **~ de miel** honeymoon. **~r** a lunar. **—m** mole. **claro de ~** moonlight. **estar en la ~** be miles away

lunes m Monday. **cada ~ y cada martes** day in, day out

lupa f magnifying glass

lúpulo m hop

lustr|abotas m inv (LAm) boot-black. **~ar** vt shine, polish. **~e** m shine; (fig, esplendor) splendour. **~oso** a shining. **dar ~e a, sacar ~e a** polish

luto m mourning. **estar de ~** be in mourning

luxación f dislocation

Luxemburgo m Luxemburg

luz f light; (electricidad) electricity. **luces** fpl intelligence. **~ antiniebla** (auto) fog light. **a la ~ de** in the light of. **a todas luces** obviously. **dar a ~** give birth. **hacer la ~ sobre** shed light on. **sacar a la ~** bring to light

LL

llaga f wound; (úlcera) ulcer

llama f flame; (animal) llama

llamada f call; (golpe) knock; (señal) sign

llama|do a known as. **~miento** m call. **~r** vt call; (por teléfono) ring (up). **—vi** call; (golpear en la puerta) knock; (tocar el timbre) ring. **~rse** vpr be called. **~r por teléfono** ring (up), telephone. **¿cómo te ~s?** what's your name?

llamarada f blaze; (fig) blush; (fig, de pasión etc) outburst

llamativo *a* loud, gaudy

llamear *vi* blaze

llan|eza *f* simplicity. **~o** *a* flat, level; ⟨persona⟩ natural; ⟨sencillo⟩ plain. **—m** plain

llanta *f* (auto) (wheel) rim; (LAm, neumático) tyre

llanto *m* weeping

llanura *f* plain

llave *f* key; (para tuercas) spanner; (grifo) tap (Brit), faucet (Amer); (elec) switch. **~ inglesa** monkey wrench. **~ro** *m* key-ring. **cerrar con ~** lock. **echar la ~** lock up

llega|da *f* arrival. **~r** [12] *vi* arrive, come; (alcanzar) reach; (bastar) be enough. **~rse** *vpr* come near; (ir) go (round). **~r a** (conseguir) manage to. **~r a saber** find out. **~r a ser** become

llen|ar *vt* fill (up); (rellenar) fill in. **~o** *a* full. **—m** (en el teatro etc) full house. **de ~** completely

lleva|dero *a* tolerable. **~r** *vt* carry; (inducir, conducir) lead; (acompañar) take; wear (ropa); (traer) bring. **~rse** *vpr* run off with (cosa). **~rse bien** get on well together. **¿cuánto tiempo ~s aquí?** how long have you been here? **llevo 3 años estudiando inglés** I've been studying English for 3 years

llor|ar *vi* cry; (ojos) water. **~iquear** *vi* whine. **~iqueo** *m* whining. **~o** *m* crying. **~ón** *a* whining. **—m** cry-baby. **~oso** *a* tearful

llov|er [2] *vi* rain. **~izna** *f* drizzle. **~iznar** *vi* drizzle

llueve *vb véase* **llover**

lluvi|a *f* rain; (fig) shower. **~oso** *a* rainy; ⟨clima⟩ wet

M

maca *f* defect; (en fruta) bruise

macabro *a* macabre

macaco *a* (LAm) ugly. **—m** macaque (monkey)

macadam *m*, **macadán** *m* Tarmac (P)

macanudo *a* (fam) great

macarrón *m* macaroon. **~es** *mpl* macaroni

macerar *vt* macerate

maceta *f* mallet; (tiesto) flowerpot

macilento *a* wan

macizo *a* solid. **—m** mass; (de plantas) bed

macrobiótico *a* macrobiotic

mácula *f* stain

macuto *m* knapsack

mach /mak/ *m.* **(número de) ~** Mach (number)

machac|ar [7] *vt* crush. **—vi** go on (about). **~ón** *a* boring. **—m** bore

machamartillo. a ~ *adv* firmly

machaqueo *m* crushing

machet|azo *m* blow with a machete; (herida) wound from a machete. **~e** *m* machete

mach|ista *m* male chauvinist. **~o** *a* male; (varonil) macho

machón *m* buttress

machucar [7] *vt* crush; (estropear) damage

madeja *f* skein

madera *f* (vino) Madeira. **—f** wood; (naturaleza) nature. **~ble** *a* yielding timber. **~je** *m*, **~men** *m* woodwork

madero *m* log; (de construcción) timber

madona *f* Madonna

madr|astra *f* stepmother. **~e** *f* mother. **~eperla** *f* mother-of-pearl. **~eselva** *f* honeysuckle

madrigal *m* madrigal

madrigu|era *f* den; (de liebre) burrow

madrileño *a* of Madrid. **—m** person from Madrid

madrina f godmother; (en una boda) chief bridesmaid

madroño m strawberry-tree

madrug|ada f dawn. **∼ador** a who gets up early. **—m** early riser. **∼ar** [12] vi get up early. **∼ón** m. darse un **∼ón** get up very early

madur|ación f maturing; (de fruta) ripening. **∼ar** vt/i mature; (fruta) ripen. **∼ez** f maturity; (de fruta) ripeness. **∼o** a mature; (fruta) ripe

maestr|ía f teacher. **∼ía** f skill. **∼o** m master. **∼a, ∼o** (de escuela) schoolteacher

mafia f Mafia

magdalena f madeleine, small sponge cake

magia f magic

mágico a magic; (maravilloso) magical

magín m (fam) imagination

magisterio m teaching (profession); (conjunto de maestros) teachers

magistrado m magistrate; (juez) judge

magistral a teaching; (bien hecho) masterly; (lenguaje) pedantic

magistratura f magistracy

magn|animidad f magnanimity. **∼ánimo** a magnanimous

magnate m magnate

magnesia f magnesia. **∼ efervescente** milk of magnesia

magnético a magnetic

magneti|smo m magnetism. **∼zar** [10] vt magnetize

magnetofón m, **magnetófono** m tape recorder

magnificencia f magnificence

magnífico a magnificent

magnitud f magnitude

magnolia f magnolia

mago m magician. los (tres) reyes **∼s** the Magi

magr|a f slice of ham. **∼o** a lean; (tierra) poor; (persona) thin

magulla|dura f bruise. **∼r** vt bruise

mahometano a & m Muhammadan

maíz m maize, corn (Amer)

maj|ada f sheepfold; (estiércol) manure; (LAm) flock of sheep

majader|ía f silly thing. **∼o** m idiot; (mano del mortero) pestle. —a stupid

majador m crusher

majagranzas m idiot

majar vt crush; (molestar) bother

majest|ad f majesty. **∼uoso** a majestic

majo a nice

mal adv badly; (poco) poorly; (difícilmente) hardly; (equivocadamente) wrongly. —a see **malo**. —m evil; (daño) harm; (enfermedad) illness. **∼ que bien** somehow or other). de **∼ en peor** worse and worse. hacer **∼ en** be wrong to. ¡menos **∼**! thank goodness!

malabar a. juegos **∼es** juggling. **∼ismo** m juggling. **∼ista** m & f juggler

malaconsejado a ill-advised

malacostumbrado a with bad habits

malagueño a of Málaga. —m person from Málaga

malamente adv badly; (fam) hardly enough

malandanza f misfortune

malapata m & f nuisance

malaria f malaria

Malasia f Malaysia

malasombra m & f clumsy person

malavenido a incompatible

malaventura f misfortune. **∼do** a unfortunate

malayo a Malay(an)

malbaratar vt sell off cheap; (malgastar) squander

malcarado *a* ugly

malcasado *a* unhappily married; (*infiel*) unfaithful

malcomer *vi* eat poorly

malcriad|eza *f* (*LAm*) bad manners. ~o *a* (*niño*) spoilt

maldad *f* evil; (*acción*) wicked thing

maldecir [46 *pero imperativo* **maldice**, *futuro y condicional regulares*, pp **maldecido** *o* **maldito**] *vt* curse. —*vi* speak ill (**de** of); (*quejarse*) complain (**de** about)

maldici|ente *a* backbiting; (*que blasfema*) foul-mouthed. ~ón *f* curse

maldit|a *f* tongue. ¡~a sea! damn it! ~o *a* damned. —*m* (*en el teatro*) extra

maleab|ilidad *f* malleability. ~le *a* malleable

malea|nte *a* wicked. —*m* vagrant. ~r *vt* damage; (*pervertir*) corrupt. ~rse *vpr* be spoilt; (*pervertirse*) be corrupted

malecón *m* breakwater; (*rail*) embankment; (*para atracar*) jetty

maledicencia *f* slander

maleficio *m* curse

maléfico *a* evil

malestar *m* indisposition; (*fig*) uneasiness

malet|a *f* (suit)case; (*auto*) boot, trunk (*Amer*); (*LAm, lío de ropa*) bundle; (*LAm, de bicicleta*) saddlebag. **hacer la ~a** pack one's bags. —*m* & *f* (*fam*) bungler. ~ero *m* porter; (*auto*) boot, trunk (*Amer*). ~ín *m* small case

malevolencia *f* malevolence

malévolo *a* malevolent

maleza *f* weeds; (*matorral*) undergrowth

malgasta|dor *a* wasteful. —*m* spendthrift. ~r *vt* waste

malgeniado *a* (*LAm*) bad-tempered

malhablado *a* foul-mouthed

malhadado *a* unfortunate

malhechor *m* criminal

malhumorado *a* bad-tempered

malici|a *f* malice; (*astucia*) suspect. ~as *fpl* (*fam*) suspicions. ~oso *a* malicious

malign|idad *f* malice; (*med*) malignancy. ~o *a* malignant; (*persona*) malicious

malintencionado *a* malicious

malmandado *a* disobedient

malmirado *a* (*con estar*) disliked; (*con ser*) inconsiderate

malo *a* (*delante de nombre masculino en singular* **mal**) bad; (*enfermo*) ill. ~ **de** difficult. **estar de malas** be out of luck; (*malhumorado*) be in a bad mood. **lo ~ es que** the trouble is that. **ponerse a malas con uno** fall out with s.o. **por las malas** by force

malogr|ar *vt* waste; (*estropear*) spoil. ~arse *vpr* fall through. ~o *m* failure

maloliente *a* smelly

malparto *m* miscarriage

malpensado *a* nasty, malicious

malquerencia *f* dislike

malquist|ar *vt* set against. ~arse *vpr* fall out. ~o *a* disliked

malsano *a* unhealthy; (*enfermizo*) sickly

malsonante *a* ill-sounding; (*grosero*) offensive

malta *f* malt; (*cerveza*) beer

maltés *a & m* Maltese

maltratar *vt* ill-treat

maltrecho *a* battered

malucho *a* (*fam*) poorly

malva *f* mallow. (**color de**) ~ *a invar* mauve

malvado *a* wicked

malvavisco *m* marshmallow

malvender *vt* sell off cheap

malversa|ción f embezzlement. **∼dor** a embezzling. —m embezzler. **∼r** vt embezzle.

Malvinas fpl. **las islas ∼** the Falkland Islands

malla f mesh. **cota de ∼** coat of mail

mallo m mallet

Mallor|ca f Majorca. **∼quín** a & m Majorcan

mama f teat; (de mujer) breast

mamá f mum(my)

mama|da f sucking. **∼r** vt suck; (fig) grow up with; (engullir) gobble

mamario a mammary

mamarrach|adas fpl nonsense. **∼o** m clown; (cosa ridícula) (ridiculous) sight

mameluco a Brazilian halfbreed; (necio) idiot

mamífero a mammalian. —m mammal

mamola f. **hacer la ∼** chuck (under the chin); (fig) make fun of

mamotreto m notebook; (libro voluminoso) big book

mampara f screen

mamporro m blow

mampostería f masonry

mamut m mammoth

maná f manna

manada f herd; (de lobos) pack. **en ∼** in crowds

manager /manaʒer/ m manager

mana|ntial m spring; (fig) source. **∼r** vi flow; (fig) abound. —vt run with

manaza f big hand; (sucia) dirty hand. **ser un ∼s** be clumsy

manceb|a f concubine. **∼ía** f brothel. **∼o** m youth; (soltero) bachelor

mancera f plough handle

mancilla f stain. **∼r** vt stain

manco a (de una mano) onehanded; (de las dos manos) handless; (de un brazo) one-armed; (de los dos brazos) armless

mancomún adv. **de ∼** jointly

mancomun|adamente adv jointly. **∼ar** vt unite; (jurid) make jointly liable. **∼arse** vpr unite. **∼idad** f union

mancha f stain

Mancha f. **la ∼** la Mancha (region of Spain). **el canal de la ∼** the English Channel

mancha|do a dirty; (animal) spotted. **∼r** vt stain. **∼rse** vpr get dirty

manchego a of la Mancha. —m person from la Mancha

manchón m large stain

manda f legacy

manda|dero m messenger. **∼miento** m order; (relig) commandment. **∼r** vt order; (enviar) send; (gobernar) rule. —vi be in command. **¿mande?** (esp LAm) pardon?

mandarín m mandarin

mandarin|a f (naranja) mandarin; (lengua) Mandarin. **∼o** m mandarin tree

mandat|ario m attorney. **∼o** m order; (jurid) power of attorney

mandíbula f jaw

mandil m apron

mandioca f cassava

mando m command; (pol) term of office. **∼ a distancia** remote control. **los ∼s** the leaders

mandolina f mandolin

mandón a bossy

manducar [7] vt (fam) stuff oneself with

manecilla f needle; (de reloj) hand

manej|able a manageable. **∼ar** vt handle; (fig) manage; (LAm, conducir) drive. **∼arse** vpr behave. **∼o** m handling; (intriga) intrigue

manera f way. **∼s** fpl manners. **de ∼ que** so (that). **de ninguna ∼** not at all. **de otra ∼** otherwise. **de todas ∼s** anyway

manga f sleeve; (tubo de goma) hose(pipe); (red) net; (para colar) filter

mangante m beggar; (fam) scrounger

mangle m mangrove

mango m handle; (fruta) mango

mangonear vt boss about. —vi (entrometerse) interfere

manguera f hose(pipe)

manguito m muff

manía f mania; (antipatía) dislike

maníaco a, **maniaco** a maniac(al). —m maniac

maniatar vt tie s.o.'s hands

maniático a maniac(al); (fig) crazy

manicomio m lunatic asylum

manicura f manicure; (mujer) manicurist

manido a stale; (carne) high

manifesta|ción f manifestation; (pol) demonstration. ~nte m demonstrator. ~r [1] vi manifest; (pol) state. ~rse vpr show; (pol) demonstrate

manifiesto a clear; (error) obvious; (verdad) manifest. —m manifesto

manilargo a light-fingered

manilla f bracelet; (de hierro) handcuffs

manillar m handlebar(s)

maniobra f manoeuvring; (rail) shunting; (fig) manoeuvre. ~r vt operate; (rail) shunt. —vi manoeuvre. ~s fpl (mil) manoeuvres

manipula|ción f manipulation. ~r vt manipulate

maniquí m dummy. —f model

manirroto a extravagant. —m spendthrift

manita f little hand

manivela f crank

manjar m (special) dish

mano f hand; (de animales) front foot; (de perros, gatos) front paw. ~ de obra work force. ¡~s

arriba! hands up! **a ~** by hand; (próximo) handy. **de segunda ~** second hand. **echar una ~** lend a hand. **tener buena ~ para** be good at

manojo m bunch

manose|ar vt handle; (fig) overwork. ~o m handling

manotada f, **manotazo** m slap

manote|ar vi gesticulate. ~o m gesticulation

mansalva. **a ~** adv without risk

mansarda f attic

mansedumbre f gentleness; (de animal) tameness

mansión f stately home

manso a gentle; (animal) tame

manta f blanket. ~ eléctrica electric blanket. **a ~ (de Dios)** a lot

manteca f fat; (LAm) butter. ~ado m bun; (helado) ice-cream. ~oso a greasy

mantel m tablecloth; (del altar) altar cloth. ~ería f table linen

mante|ner [40] vt support; (conservar) keep; (sostener) maintain. ~erse vpr remain. ~ de/con live off. ~imiento m maintenance

manteque|ra f butter churn. ~ería f dairy. ~illa f butter

mantilla f mantilla

manto m cloak

mantón m shawl

manual a & m manual

manubrio m crank

manufactura f manufacture; (fábrica) factory

manuscrito a handwritten. —m manuscript

manutención f maintenance

manzana f apple. ~r m (apple) orchard

manzanilla f camomile tea; (vino) manzanilla, pale dry sherry

manzano m apple tree

maña f skill. ~s fpl cunning

mañana f morning; (el día siguiente) tomorrow. —m future. —adv tomorrow. ~ero a who gets up early. —m early riser. ~a por la ~a tomorrow morning. pasado ~a the day after tomorrow. por la ~a in the morning

mañoso a clever; (astuto) crafty

mapa m map. ~mundi m map of the world

mapache m racoon

mapurite m skunk

maqueta f scale model

maquiavélico a machiavellian

maquillaje m make-up. ~r vt make up. ~rse vpr make up

máquina f machine; (rail) engine. ~ de escribir typewriter. ~ fotográfica camera

maquin|ación f machination. ~al a mechanical. ~aria f machinery. ~ista m & f operator; (rail) engine driver

mar m & f sea. alta ~ high seas. la ~ de (fam) lots of

maraña f thicket; (enredo) tangle; (embrollo) muddle

maravedí m (pl maravedís, maravedises) maravedi, old Spanish coin

maravill|a f wonder. ~ar vt astonish. ~arse vpr be astonished (con at). ~oso a marvellous, wonderful. a ~a, a las mil ~as marvellously. contar/decir ~as de speak wonderfully of. hacer ~as work wonders

marbete m label

marca f mark; (de fábrica) trademark; (deportes) record. ~da a marked. ~dor m marker; (deportes) scoreboard. ~r [7] vt mark; (señalar) show; (anotar) note down; score (un gol); dial (número de teléfono). —vi score. de ~ brand name; (fig) excellent. de ~ mayor (fam) first-class

marcial a martial

marciano a & m Martian

marco m frame; (moneda alemana) mark; (deportes) goalposts

marcha f (incl mus) march; (auto) gear; (curso) course. a toda ~ at full speed. dar/hacer ~ atrás put into reverse. poner en ~ start; (fig) set in motion

marchante m (f marchanta) dealer; (LAm, parroquiano) client

marchar vi go; (funcionar) work, go. ~se vpr go away, leave

marchit|ar vt wither. ~arse vpr wither. ~o a withered

marea f tide. ~do a sick; (en el mar) seasick; (aturdido) dizzy; (borracho) drunk. ~r vt sail, navigate; (baquetear) annoy. ~rse vpr feel sick; (en un barco) be seasick; (estar aturdido) feel dizzy; (irse la cabeza) feel faint; (emborracharse) get slightly drunk

marejada f swell; (fig) wave

maremagno m (de cosas) sea; (de gente) (noisy) crowd

mareo m sickness; (en el mar) seasickness; (aturdimiento) dizziness; (fig, molestia) nuisance

marfil m ivory. ~eño a ivory. torre de ~ ivory tower

margarina f margarine

margarita f pearl; (bot) daisy

marg|en m margin; (borde) edge, border; (de un río) bank; (de un camino) side; (nota marginal) marginal note. —m outcast. ~inado a on the edge. —m outcast. ~inal a marginal. ~inar vt (excluir) exclude; (dejar márgenes) leave margins; (poner notas) write notes in the margin. al ~en (fig) outside

mariachi (Mex) m (música popular de Jalisco) Mariachi; (conjunto popular) Mariachi band

mariano a Marian

marica f (hombre afeminado) sissy; (urraca) magpie

maricón m homosexual, queer (sl)

marid|**aje** m married life; (fig) harmony. **~o** m husband

mariguana f, **marihuana** f marijuana

marimacho m mannish woman

marimandona f bossy woman

marimba f (type of) drum; (LAm, especie de xilofón) marimba

marimorena f (fam) row

marin|**a** f coast; (cuadro) seascape; (conjunto de barcos) navy; (arte de navegar) seamanship. **~era** f seamanship; (conjunto de marineros) crew. **~ero** a marine; (barco) seaworthy. **~m** sailor. **~a** a marine. **~a de guerra** navy. **~a mercante** merchant navy. **a la ~era** in tomato and garlic sauce. **azul ~o** navy blue

marioneta f puppet. **~s** fpl puppet show

maripos|**a** f butterfly. **~ear** vi be fickle; (galantear) flirt. **~n** m flirt. **~a nocturna** moth

mariquita f ladybird, ladybug (Amer)

marisabidilla f know-all

mariscador m shell-fisher

mariscal m marshal

maris|**co** m seafood, shellfish. **~quero** m (persona que pesca mariscos) seafood fisherman; (persona que vende mariscos) seafood seller

marital a marital

marítimo a maritime; (ciudad etc) coastal, seaside

maritornes f uncouth servant

marmit|**a** f pot. **~ón** m kitchen boy

mármol m marble

marmol|**era** f marblework, marbles. **~ista** m & f marble worker

marmóreo a marble

marmota f marmot

maroma f rope; (LAm, función de volatines) tightrope walking

marqués m marquess. **~esa** f marchioness. **~esina** f glass canopy

marquetería f marquetry

marrajo a (toro) vicious; (persona) cunning. **~m** shark

marran|**a** f sow. **~ada** f filthy thing; (cochinada) dirty trick. **~o** a filthy. **~m** hog

marrar vt (errar) miss; (fallar) fail

marrón a & m brown

marroquí a & m & f Moroccan. **~m** (tafilete) morocco

marrubio m (bot) horehound

Marruecos m Morocco

marruller|**ía** f cajolery. **~o** a cajoling. **~m** cajoler

marsopa f porpoise

marsupial a & m marsupial

marta f marten

martajar vt (Mex) grind (maíz)

Marte m Mars

martes m Tuesday

martill|**ada** f blow with a hammer. **~ar** vt hammer. **~azo** m blow with a hammer. **~ear** vt hammer. **~eo** m hammering. **~o** m hammer

martín m **pescador** kingfisher

martinete m (macillo del piano) hammer; (mazo) drop hammer

martingala f (ardid) trick

mártir m & f martyr

martir|**io** m martyrdom. **~izar** [10] vt martyr; (fig) torment, torture. **~ologio** m martyrology

marxis|**mo** m Marxism. **~ta** a & m & f Marxist

marzo m March

más adv & a (comparativo) more; (superlativo) most. **~ caro** dearer. **~ curioso** more curious. **el ~ caro** the dearest; (de dos) the dearer. **el ~ curioso**

the most curious; (*de dos*) the more curious. —*conj* and, plus. —*m* plus (sign). ~ **bien** rather. ~ **de** (*cantidad indeterminada*) more than. ~ **menos** more or less. ~ **que** more than. ~ **y** ~ more and more. **a lo** ~ **de** (*the*) most. **de** ~ too many. **es** ~ moreover. **no** ~ no more

masa *f* dough; (*cantidad*) mass; (*física*) mass. **en** ~ **en masse**

masacre *f* massacre

masaje *m* massage. ~**ista** *m* masseur. —*f* masseuse

mascada (*LAm*) plug of tobacco. ~**dura** *f* chewing. ~**r** [7] *vt* chew

máscara *f* mask; (*persona*) masked figure/person

mascarada *f* masquerade. ~**illa** *f* mask. ~**ón** *m* (large) mask

mascota *f* mascot

masculinidad *f* masculinity. ~**o** *a* masculine; (*sexo*) male. —*m* masculine

mascullar [3] *vt* mumble

masilla *f* putty

masivo *a* massive, large-scale

masón *m* (free)mason. ~**onería** *f* (free)masonry. ~**ónico** *a* masonic

masoquismo *m* masochism. ~**ta** *a* masochistic. —*m* & *f* masochist

mastate *m* (*Mex*) loincloth

mastelero *m* topmast

masticación *f* chewing. ~**r** [7] *vt* chew; (*fig*) chew over

mástil *m* mast; (*palo*) pole; (*en instrumentos de cuerda*) neck

mastín *m* mastiff

mastitis *f* mastitis

mastodonte *a* mastodon

mastoides *a* & *f* mastoid

mastuerzo *m* cress

masturbación *f* masturbation. ~**rse** *vpr* masturbate

mata *f* grove; (*arbusto*) bush

matadero *m* slaughterhouse. ~**or** *a* killing. —*m* killer; (*torero*) matador

matadura *f* sore

matamoscas *m invar* fly swatter

matanza *f* killing. ~**r** *vt* kill (*personas*); slaughter (*reses*). ~**rife** *m* butcher. ~**rse** *vpr* commit suicide; (*en un accidente*) be killed. **estar a** ~**r con uno** be deadly enemies with s.o.

matarratas *m invar* cheap liquor

matasanos *m invar* quack

matasellos *m invar* postmark

match *m* match

mate *a* matt, dull; (*sonido*) dull. —*m* (*ajedrez*) (check)mate; (*LAm, bebida*) maté

matemáticas *fpl* mathematics, maths (*fam*), math (*Amer, fam*). ~**o** *a* mathematical. —*m* mathematician

materia *f* matter; (*material*) material. ~ **prima** raw material. **en** ~ **de** on the question of

material *a* & *m* material. ~**idad** *f* material nature. ~**ismo** *m* materialism. ~**ista** *a* materialistic. —*m* & *f* materialist. ~**izar** [10] *vt* materialize. ~**izarse** *vpr* materialize. ~**mente** *adv* materially; (*absolutamente*) absolutely

maternal *a* maternal; (*como de madre*) motherly. ~**idad** *f* motherhood; (*casa de maternidad*) maternity home. ~**o** *a* motherly; (*lengua*) mother

matinal *a* morning. ~**ée** *m* matinée

matiz *m* shade. ~**ación** *f* combination of colours. ~**ar** [10] *vt* blend (*colores*); (*introducir variedad*) vary; (*teñir*) tinge (**de** with)

matojo *m* bush

matón *m* bully. ~**onismo** *m* bullying

matorral m scrub; (*conjunto de matas*) thicket

matra|ca f rattle. **~quear** vi rattle; (*dar matraca*) pester. **dar ~ca** pester. **ser un(a) ~ca** be a nuisance

matraz m flask

matriarca|do m matriarchy. **~l** a matriarchal

matr|ícula f (*lista*) register, list; (*acto de matricularse*) registration; (*auto*) registration number. **~icular** vt register. **~icularse** vpr enrol, register

matrimoni|al a matrimonial. **~o** m marriage; (*pareja*) married couple

matritense a from Madrid

matriz f matrix; (*anat*) womb, uterus

matrona f matron; (*partera*) midwife

Matusalén m Methuselah. **más viejo que ~** as old as Methuselah

matute m smuggling. **~ro** m smuggler

matutino a morning

maula f piece of junk

maull|ar vi miaow. **~ido** m miaow

mauritano a & m Mauritanian

mausoleo m mausoleum

maxilar a maxillary. **hueso ~** jaw(bone)

máxima f maxim

máxime adv especially

máximo a maximum; (*más alto*) highest. **—m** maximum

maya f daisy; (*persona*) Maya Indian

mayestático a majestic

mayo m May; (*palo*) maypole

mayólica f majolica

mayonesa f mayonnaise

mayor a (*más grande, comparativo*) bigger; (*más grande, superlativo*) biggest; (*de edad, comparativo*) older; (*de edad,*

superlativo) oldest; (*adulto*) grown-up; (*principal*) main, major; (*mus*) major. **—m & f** boss; (*adulto*) adult. **~al** m foreman; (*pastor*) head shepherd. **~azgo** m entailed estate. **al por ~** wholesale

mayordomo m butler

mayor|ía f majority. **~ista** m & f wholesaler. **~mente** adv especially

mayúscul|a f capital (letter). **~o** a capital; (*fig, grande*) big

maza f mace

mazacote m hard mass

mazapán m marzipan

mazmorra f dungeon

mazo m mallet; (*manojo*) bunch

mazorca f. **~ de maíz** corn on the cob

me pron (*acusativo*) me; (*dativo*) (to) me; (*reflexivo*) (to) myself

meandro m meander

mecánic|a f mechanics. **~o** a mechanical. **—m** mechanic

mecani|smo m mechanism. **~zación** f mechanization. **~zar** [10] vt mechanize

mecanograf|ía f typing. **~iado** a typed, typewritten. **~iar** [20] vt type

mecanógrafo m typist

mecate m (*LAm*) (*pita*) rope

mecedora f rocking chair

mecenazgo m patronage

mecer [9] vt rock; swing (*columpio*). **~se** vpr rock; (*en un columpio*) swing

mecha f (*de vela*) wick; (*de mina*) fuse

mechar vt stuff, lard

mechero m (*cigarette*) lighter

mechón m (*de pelo*) lock

medall|a f medal. **~ón** m medallion; (*relicario*) locket

media f stocking; (*promedio*) average

mediación f mediation

mediado *a* half full; ⟨*trabajo etc*⟩ halfway through. **a ~s de marzo** in the middle of March

mediador *m* mediator

medialuna *f* croissant

median|amente *adv* fairly. **~era** *f* party wall. **~ero** *a* ⟨*muro*⟩ party. **~a** *f* average circumstances. **~o** *a* average, medium; ⟨*mediocre*⟩ mediocre

medianoche *f* midnight; ⟨*culin*⟩ small sandwich

mediante *prep* through, by means of

mediar *vi* mediate; ⟨*llegar a la mitad*⟩ be halfway (**en** through)

mediatizar [10] *vt* annex

medic|ación *f* medication. **~amento** *m* medicine. **~ina** *f* medicine. **~inal** *a* medicinal. **~inar** *vt* administer medicine

medición *f* measurement

médico *a* medical. —*m* doctor. **~ de cabecera** GP, general practitioner

medid|a *f* measurement; ⟨*unidad*⟩ measure; ⟨*disposición*⟩ measure, step; ⟨*prudencia*⟩ moderation. **~or** *m* (*LAm*) meter. **a la ~a** made to measure. **a ~a que** as. **en cierta ~a** to a certain point

mediero *m* share-cropper

medieval *a* medieval. **~ista** *m & f* medievalist

medio *a* half (a); ⟨*mediano*⟩ average. **~ litro** half a litre. —*m* middle; ⟨*manera*⟩ means; ⟨*en deportes*⟩ half(-back). **en ~** in the middle (**de** of). **por ~ de** through

mediocr|e *a* ⟨*mediano*⟩ average; ⟨*de escaso mérito*⟩ mediocre. **~idad** *f* mediocrity

mediodía *m* midday, noon; ⟨*sur*⟩ south

medioevo *m* Middle Ages

Medio Oriente *m* Middle East

medir [5] *vt* medir; weigh up ⟨*palabras etc*⟩. —*vi* measure, be. **~se** *vpr* ⟨*moderarse*⟩ be moderate

medita|bundo *a* thoughtful. **~ción** *f* meditation. **~r** *vt* think about. —*vi* meditate

Mediterráneo *m* Mediterranean

mediterráneo *a* Mediterranean

médium *m & f* medium

medrar *vi* thrive

medroso *a* ⟨*con estar*⟩ frightened; ⟨*con ser*⟩ fearful

médula *f* marrow

medusa *f* jellyfish

mefítico *a* noxious

mega... *pref* mega...

megáfono *m* megaphone

megal|ítico *a* megalithic. **~ito** *m* megalith

megal|omanía *f* megalomania. **~ómano** *m* megalomaniac

mejicano *a & m* Mexican

Méjico *m* Mexico

mejido *a* ⟨*huevo*⟩ beaten

mejilla *f* cheek

mejillón *m* mussel

mejor *a & adv* ⟨*comparativo*⟩ better; ⟨*superlativo*⟩ best. **~a** *f* improvement. **~able** *a* improvable. **~amiento** *m* improvement. **~ dicho** rather. **a lo ~** perhaps. **tanto ~** so much the better

mejorana *f* marjoram

mejorar *vt* improve, better. —*vi* get better

mejunje *m* mixture

melanc|olía *f* melancholy. **~ólico** *a* melancholic

melaza *f* molasses, treacle (*Amer*)

melen|a *f* long hair; ⟨*de león*⟩ mane. **~udo** *a* long-haired

melifluo *a* mellifluous

melillense *a* of/from Melilla. —*m* person from Melilla

melindr|**e** *m* (*mazapán*) sugared marzipan cake; (*masa frita con miel*) honey fritter. ~**oso** *a* affected

melocot|**ón** *m* peach. ~**onero** *m* peach tree

mel|**odía** *f* melody. ~**ódico** *a* melodic. ~**odioso** *a* melodious

melodram|**a** *m* melodrama. ~**áticamente** *adv* melodramatically. ~**ático** *a* melodramatic

melómano *m* music lover

mel|**ón** *m* melon; (*bobo*) fool. ~**onada** *f* something stupid

meloncillo *m* (*animal*) mongoose

melos|**idad** *f* sweetness. ~**o** *a* sweet

mella *f* notch. ~**do** *a* jagged. ~**r** *vt* notch

mellizo *a* & *m* twin

membran|**a** *f* membrane. ~**oso** *a* membranous

membrete *m* letterhead

membrill|**ero** *m* quince tree. ~**o** *m* quince

membrudo *a* burly

memez *f* something silly

memo *a* stupid. —*m* idiot

memorable *a* memorable

memorando *m*, **memorándum** *m* notebook; (*nota*) memorandum

memoria *f* memory; (*informe*) report; (*tesis*) thesis. ~**s** *fpl* (*recuerdos personales*) memoirs. **de** ~ from memory

memorial *m* memorial. ~**ista** *m* amanuensis

memor|**ión** *m* good memory. ~**ista** *a* having a good memory. ~**ístico** *a* memory

mena *f* ore

menaje *m* furnishings

menci|**ón** *f* mention. ~**onado** *a* aforementioned. ~**onar** *vt* mention

menda|**cidad** *f* mendacity. ~**z** *a* lying

mendi|**cante** *a* & *m* mendicant. ~**cidad** *f* begging. ~**gar** [12] *vt* beg (for). —*vi* beg. ~**go** *m* beggar

mendrugo *m* (*pan*) hard crust; (*zoquete*) blockhead

mene|**ar** *vt* move, shake. ~**arse** *upr* move, shake. ~**o** *m* movement, shake

menester *m* need. ~**oso** *a* needy. **ser** ~ be necessary

menestra *f* stew

menestral *m* artesan

mengua *f* decrease; (*falta*) lack; (*descrédito*) discredit. ~**do** *a* miserable; (*falto de carácter*) spineless. ~**nte** *a* decreasing; (*luna*) waning; (*marea*) ebb. —*f* (*del mar*) ebb tide; (*de un río*) low water. ~**r** [15] *vt/i* decrease, diminish

meningitis *f* meningitis

menisco *m* meniscus

menjurje *m* mixture

menopausia *f* menopause

menor *a* (*más pequeño, comparativo*) smaller; (*más pequeño, superlativo*) smallest; (*más joven, comparativo*) younger; (*más joven*) youngest; (*mus*) minor. —*m* & *f* (*menor de edad*) minor. **al por** ~ retail

Menorca *f* Minorca

menorquín *a* & *m* Minorcan

menos *a* (*comparativo*) less; (*comparativo, con plural*) fewer; (*superlativo*) least; (*superlativo, con plural*) fewest. —*adv* (*comparativo*) less; (*superlativo*) least. —*prep* except. ~**cabar** *vt* lessen; (*fig, estropear*) damage. ~**cabo** *m* lessening. ~**preciable** *a* contemptible. ~**preciar** *vt* despise. ~**precio** *m* contempt. **a** ~ **que** unless. **al** ~ at least. **ni mucho** ~ far from it. **por lo** ~ at least

mensaje *m* message. **~ro** *m* messenger

menso *a* (*Mex*) stupid

menstruación *f* menstruation. **~al** *a* menstrual. **~ar** [21] *vi* menstruate. **~o** *m* menstruation

mensual *a* monthly. **~idad** *f* monthly pay

ménsula *f* bracket

mensurable *a* measurable

menta *f* mint

mental *a* mental. **~idad** *f* mentality. **~mente** *adv* mentally

mentar [1] *vt* mention, name

mente *f* mind

mentecato *a* stupid. *—m* idiot

mentir [4] *vi* lie. **~a** *f* lie. **~oso** *a* lying. *—m* liar. **de ~ijillas** for a joke

mentís *m* invar denial

mentol *m* menthol

mentor *m* mentor

menú *m* menu

menudear *vi* happen frequently

menudencia *f* trifle

menudeo *m* retail trade

menudillos *mpl* giblets

menudo *a* tiny; (*lluvia*) fine; (*insignificante*) insignificant. **~s** *mpl* giblets. **a ~** often

meñique *a* (*dedo*) little. *—m* little finger

meollo *m* brain; (*médula*) marrow; (*parte blanda*) soft part; (*fig, inteligencia*) brains

meramente *adv* merely

mercachifle *m* hawker; (*fig*) profiteer

mercader *m* (*LAm*) merchant

mercado *m* market. **M~ Común** Common Market. **~ negro** black market

mercancía *f* article. **~cías** *fpl* goods, merchandise. **~te** *a* & *m* merchant. **~til** *a* mercantile, commercial. **~tilismo** *m* mercantilism

mercar [7] *vt* buy

merced *f* favour. **su/vuestra ~** your honour

mercenario *a* & *m* mercenary

mercería *f* haberdashery, notions (*Amer*). **~o** *m* haberdasher

mercurial *a* mercurial

Mercurio *m* Mercury

mercurio *m* mercury

merecedor *a* deserving. **~er** [11] *vt* deserve. *—vi* be deserving. **~idamente** *adv* deservedly. **~ido** *a* well deserved. **~imiento** *m* (*mérito*) merit

merendar [1] vt have as an afternoon snack. *—vi* have an afternoon snack. **~ero** *m* snack bar; (*lugar*) picnic area

merengue *m* meringue

meretriz *f* prostitute

mergo *m* cormorant

meridiana *f* (*diván*) couch. **~o** *a* midday; (*fig*) dazzling. *—m* meridian

meridional *a* southern. *—m* southerner

merienda *f* afternoon snack

merino *a* merino

mérito *m* merit; (*valor*) worth

meritorio *a* meritorious. *—m* unpaid trainee

merlo *m* black wrasse

merluza *f* hake

merma *f* decrease. **~r** *vt/i* decrease, reduce

mermelada *f* jam

mero *a* mere; (*Mex, verdadero*) real. *—adv* (*Mex, precisamente*) exactly; (*Mex, verdaderamente*) really. *—m* grouper

merodeador *a* marauding. *—m* marauder. **~ar** *vi* maraud. **~o** *m* marauding

merovingio *a* & *m* Merovingian

mes *m* month; (*mensualidad*) monthly pay

mesa *f* table; (*para escribir o estudiar*) desk. **poner la ~** lay the table mesana f (palo) mizen-mast

mesarse vpr tear at one's hair

mesenterio m mesentery

meseta f plateau; (descansillo) landing

mesiánico a Messianic

Mesías m Messiah

mesilla f small table. ~ de noche bedside table

mesón m inn

mesoner|a f landlady. ~o m landlord

mestiz|aje m crossbreeding. ~o a (persona) half-caste; (animal) cross-bred. —m (persona) half-caste; (animal) cross-breed

mesura f moderation. ~do a moderate

meta f goal; (de una carrera) finish

metabolismo m metabolism

metacarpiano m metacarpal

metafísic|a f metaphysics. ~o a metaphysical

met|áfora f metaphor. ~afórico a metaphorical

met|al m metal; (instrumentos de latón) brass; (de la voz) timbre. ~álico a (objeto) metal; (sonido) metallic. ~alizarse [10] vpr (fig) become mercenary

metal|urgia f metallurgy. ~úrgico a metallurgical

metam|órfico a metamorphic. ~orfosear vt transform. ~orfosis f metamorphosis

metano m methane

metatarsiano m metatarsal

metátesis f invar metathesis

metedura f. ~ de pata blunder

mete|órico a meteoric. ~orito m meteorite. ~oro m meteor. ~orología f meteorology. ~orológico meteorological. ~oró-logo m meteorologist

meter vt put, place; (ingresar) deposit; score (un gol); (enredar) involve; (causar) make. ~se vpr

get; (entrometerse) meddle. ~se con uno pick a quarrel with s.o.

meticulos|idad f meticulousness. ~o a meticulous

metido m reprimand. —a. ~ en años getting on. estar muy ~ con uno be well in with s.o.

metilo m methyl

metódico a methodical

metodis|mo m Methodism. ~ta a & m & f Methodist

método m method

metodología f methodology

metomentodo m busybody

metraje m length. de largo ~ (película) feature

metrall|a f shrapnel. ~eta f sub-machine gun

métric|a f metrics. ~o a metric; (verso) metrical

metro m metre; (tren) under-ground, subway (Amer). ~ cua-drado cubic metre

metrónomo m metronome

metr|ópoli f metropolis. ~opo-litano a metropolitan. —m met-ropolitan; (tren) underground, subway (Amer)

mexicano a & m (LAm) Mexican

México m (LAm) Mexico. ~ D. F. Mexico City

mezcal m (Mex) (type of) brandy

mezc|la f (acción) mixing; (sub-stancia) mixture; (argamasa) mortar. ~lador m mixer. ~lar vt mix; shuffle (los naipes). ~larse vpr mix; (intervenir) interfere. ~olanza f mixture

mezquin|dad f meanness. ~o a mean; (escaso) meagre. —m mean person

mezquita f mosque

mi a my. —m (mus) E; (solfa) mi

mi pron me

miaja f crumb

miasma m miasma

miau m miaow

mica f (silicato) mica; (Mex, embriaguez) drunkenness

mico *m* (long-tailed) monkey
micro... *pref* micro...
microbio *m* microbe
micro: ~**biología** *f* microbiology. ~**cosmo** *m* microcosm. ~**film(e)** *m* microfilm
micrófono *m* microphone
micrómetro *m* micrometer
microonda *f* microwave. **horno de** ~**s** microwave oven
microordenador *m* microcomputer
microsc|ópico *a* microscopic. ~**opio** *m* microscope
micro: ~**surco** *m* long-playing record. ~**taxi** *m* minicab
miedo *m* fear. ~**so** *a* a fearful. **dar** ~ frighten. **morirse de** ~ be scared to death. **tener** ~ be frightened
miel *f* honey
mielga *f* lucerne, alfalfa (*Amer*)
miembro *m* limb; (*persona*) member
mientras *conj* while. —*adv* meanwhile. ~ **que** whereas. ~ **tanto** in the meantime
miércoles *m* Wednesday. ~ **de ceniza** Ash Wednesday
mierda *f* (*vulgar*) shit
mies *f* corn, grain (*Amer*)
miga *f* crumb; (*fig, meollo*) essence. ~**jas** *fpl* crumbs. ~**r** [12] *vt* crumble
migra|ción *f* migration. ~**torio** *a* migratory
mijo *m* millet
mil *a* & *m* a/one thousand. ~**es de** thousands of. ~ **novecientos noventa y dos** nineteen ninety-two. ~ **pesetas** a thousand pesetas
milagro *m* miracle. ~**so** *a* miraculous
milano *m* kite
mildeu *m*, **mildiu** *m* mildew
milen|ario *a* millenial. ~**io** *m* millennium
milenrama *f* milfoil

milésimo *a* & *m* thousandth
mili *f* (*fam*) military service
milicia *f* soldiering; (*gente armada*) militia
mili|gramo *m* milligram. ~**litro** *m* millilitre
milímetro *m* millimetre
militante *a* militant
militar *a* military. —*m* soldier. ~**ismo** *m* militarism. ~**ista** *a* militaristic. —*m* & *f* militarist. ~**izar** [10] *vt* militarize
milonga *f* (*Arg, canción*) popular song; (*Arg, baile*) popular dance
milord *m*. **vivir como un** ~ live like a lord
milpies *m invar* woodlouse
milla *f* mile
millar *m* thousand. **a** ~**es** by the thousand
mill|ón *m* million. ~**onada** *f* fortune. ~**onario** *m* millionaire. ~**onésimo** *a* & *m* millionth. **un** ~**n de libros** a million books
mimar *vt* spoil
mimbre *m* & *f* wicker. ~**arse** *vpr* sway. ~**ra** *f* osier. ~**ral** *m* osier-bed
mimetismo *m* mimicry
mímic|a *f* mime. ~**o** *a* mimic
mimo *m* mime; (*a un niño*) spoiling; (*caricia*) caress
mimosa *f* mimosa
mina *f* mine. ~**r** *vt* mine; (*fig*) undermine
minarete *m* minaret
mineral *m* mineral; (*mena*) ore. ~**ogía** *f* mineralogy. ~**ogista** *m* & *f* mineralogist
miner|ía *f* mining. ~**o** *a* mining. —*m* miner
mini... *pref* mini...
miniar *vt* paint in miniature
miniatura *f* miniature
minifundio *m* smallholding
minimizar [10] *vt* minimize
mínim|o *a* & *m* minimum. ~**um** *m* minimum
minino *m* (*fam*) cat, puss (*fam*)

minio *m* red lead

minist|erial *a* ministerial. **∼erio** *m* ministry. **∼ro** *m* minister

minor|ación *f* diminution. **∼a** *f* minority. **∼idad** *f* minority. **∼ista** *m* & *f* retailer

minuci|a *f* trifle. **∼osidad** *f* thoroughness. **∼oso** *a* thorough; *(con muchos detalles)* detailed

minué *m* minuet

minúscul|a *f* small letter, lower case letter. **∼o** *a* tiny

minuta *f* draft; *(menú)* menu

minut|ero *m* minute hand. **∼o** *m* minute

mío *a* & *pron* mine. **un amigo ∼** a friend of mine

miop|e *a* short-sighted. — *m* & *f* short-sighted person. **∼ía** *f* short-sightedness

mira *f* sight; *(fig, intención)* aim. **∼da** *f* look. **∼do** *a* thought of; *(comedido)* considerate; *(circunspecto)* circumspect. **∼dor** *m* windowed balcony; *(lugar)* viewpoint. **∼miento** *m* consideration. **∼r** *vt* look at; *(observar)* watch; *(considerar)* consider. **∼r fijamente a** stare at. — *vi* look; *(edificio etc)* face. **∼rse** *vpr* *(personas)* look at each other. **a la ∼** on the lookout for. **con ∼s a** with a view to. **echar una ∼da a** glance at

mirilla *f* peephole

miriñaque *m* crinoline

mirlo *m* blackbird

mirón *a* nosey. — *m* nosey-parker; *(espectador)* onlooker

mirra *f* myrrh

mirto *m* myrtle

misa *f* mass

misal *m* missal

mis|antropía *f* misanthropy. **∼antrópico** *a* misanthropic. **∼ántropo** *m* misanthropist

miscelánea *f* miscellany; *(Mex, tienda)* corner shop

miser|able *a* very poor; *(lastimoso)* miserable; *(tacaño)* mean. **∼ia** *f* extreme poverty; *(suciedad)* squalor

misericordi|a *f* pity; *(piedad)* mercy. **∼oso** *a* merciful

mísero *a* very poor; *(lastimoso)* miserable; *(tacaño)* mean

misil *m* missile

mis|ión *f* mission. **∼onal** *a* missionary. **∼onero** *m* missionary

misiva *f* missive

mism|amente *adv* just. **∼ísimo** *a* very same. **∼o** *a* same; *(después de pronombre personal)* myself, yourself, himself, herself, itself, ourselves, yourselves, themselves; *(enfático)* very. —*adv* right. **ahora ∼** right now. **aquí ∼** right here

mis|oginia *f* misogyny. **∼ógino** *m* misogynist

misterio *m* mystery. **∼so** *a* mysterious

mística *f* mysticism. **∼o** *a* mystical

mistifica|ción *f* falsification; *(engaño)* trick. **∼r** [7] *vt* falsify; *(engañar)* deceive

mitad *f* half; *(centro)* middle

mítico *a* mythical

mitiga|ción *f* mitigation. **∼r** [12] *vt* mitigate; quench *(sed)*; relieve *(dolor etc)*

mitin *m* meeting

mito *m* myth. **∼logía** *f* mythology. **∼lógico** *a* mythological

mitón *m* mitten

mitote *m* *(LAm)* Indian dance

mitra *f* mitre. **∼do** *m* prelate

mixteca *f* *(Mex)* southern Mexico

mixt|o *a* mixed. —*m* passenger and goods train; *(cerilla)* match. **∼ura** *f* mixture

mnemotécnic|a *f* mnemonics. **∼o** *a* mnemonic

moaré *m* moiré

mobiliario *m* furniture

moblaje *m* furniture

moca *m* mocha

mocedad *f* youth. **~ro** *m* young people. **~tón** *m* strapping lad

moción *f* motion

moco *m* mucus

mochales *a invar.* **estar ~** be round the bend

mochila *f* rucksack

mocho *a* blunt. —*m* butt end

mochuelo *m* little owl

moda *f* fashion. **~l** *a* modal. **~les** *mpl* manners. **~lidad** *f* kind. **de ~** in fashion

modelado *m* modelling. **~ador** *m* modeller. **~ar** *vt* model; (*fig, configurar*) form. **~o** *m* model

moderación *f* moderation. **~do** *a* moderate. **~r** *vt* moderate; reduce (*velocidad*). **~rse** *vpr* control oneself

moderno | **amente** *adv* recently. **~idad** *f* modernity. **~ismo** *m* modernism. **~ista** *m & f* modernist. **~izar** [10] *vt* modernize. **~o** *a* modern

modest | **ia** *f* modesty. **~o** *a* modest

modicidad *f* reasonableness

módico *a* moderate

modificación *f* modification. **~r** [7] *vt* modify

modismo *m* idiom

modist | **a** *f* dressmaker. **~o** *m & f* designer

modo *m* manner, way; (*gram*) mood; (*mus*) mode. **~ de ser** character. **de ~ que** so that. **de ningún ~** certainly not. **de todos ~s** anyhow

modorra *f* drowsiness. **~o** *a* drowsy

modoso *a* well-behaved

modulación *f* modulation. **~dor** *m* modulator. **~r** *vt* modulate

módulo *m* module

mofa *f* mockery. **~rse** *vpr*. **~rse de** make fun of

mofeta *f* skunk

moflet | **e** *m* chubby cheek. **~udo** *a* with chubby cheeks

mogol *m* Mongol. **el Gran M~** the Great Mogul

mohín *m* grimace. **~ino** *a* sulky. **hacer un ~ín** pull a face

moho *m* mould; (*óxido*) rust. **~so** *a* mouldy; (*metales*) rusty

moisés *m* Moses basket

mojado *a* damp, wet

mojama *f* salted tuna

mojar *vt* wet; (*empapar*) soak; (*humedecer*) moisten, dampen. —*vi.* **~ en** get involved in

mojicón *m* blow in the face; (*bizcocho*) sponge cake

mojiganga *f* masked ball; (*en el teatro*) farce

mojigat | **ería** *f* hypocrisy. **~o** *m* hypocrite

mojón *m* boundary post; (*señal*) signpost

molar *m* molar

molde | *m* mould; (*aguja*) knitting needle. **~ar** *vt* mould, shape; (*fig*) form. **~ura** *f* moulding

mole *f* mass, bulk. —*m* (*Mex, guisado*) (Mexican) stew with chili sauce

molécula *f* molecule. **~ecular** *a* molecular

mole | **dor** *a* grinding. —*m* grinder; (*persona*) bore. **~r** [2] grind; (*hacer polvo*) pulverize

molest | **ar** *vt* annoy; (*incomodar*) bother. **¿le ~a que fume?** do you mind if I smoke? **no ~ar** do not disturb. —*vi* be a nuisance. **~arse** *vpr* bother; (*ofenderse*) take offence. **~ia** *f* bother, nuisance; (*inconveniente*) inconvenience; (*incomodidad*) discomfort. **~o** *a* annoying; (*inconveniente*) inconvenient; (*ofendido*) offended

molicie *f* softness; (*excesiva comodidad*) easy life

molido *a* ground; (*fig, muy cansado*) worn out

molienda *f* grinding

molin|ero *m* miller. ~**ete** *m* toy windmill. ~**illo** *m* mill; (*juguete*) toy windmill. ~**o** *m* (water) mill. ~**o de viento** windmill

molusco *m* mollusc

mollar *a* soft

molleja *f* gizzard

mollera *f* (*de la cabeza*) crown; (*fig, sesera*) brains

moment|áneamente *adv* momentarily; (*por el momento*) right now. ~**áneo** *a* momentary. ~**o** *m* moment; (*mecánica*) momentum

momi|a *f* mummy. ~**ficación** *f* mummification. ~**ficar** [7] *vt* mummify. ~**ficarse** *vpr* become mummified

momio *a* lean. —*m* bargain; (*trabajo*) cushy job

monaca|l *a* monastic. ~**to** *m* monasticism

monada *f* beautiful thing; (*de un niño*) charming way; (*acción tonta*) silliness

monaguillo *m* altar boy

mon|arca *m & f* monarch. ~**arquía** *f* monarchy. ~**árquico** *a* monarchic(al). ~**arquismo** *m* monarchism

mon|asterio *m* monastery. ~**ástico** *a* monastic

monda *f* pruning; (*peladura*) peel

mond|adientes *m invar* toothpick. ~**adura** *f* pruning; (*peladura*) peel. ~**ar** *vt* peel (*fruta etc*); dredge (*un río*). ~**o** *a* (*sin pelo*) bald; (*sin dinero*) broke; (*sencillo*) plain

mondongo *m* innards

moned|a *f* coin; (*de un país*) currency. ~**ero** *m* minter; (*portamonedas*) purse

monetario *a* monetary

mongol *a & m* Mongolian

mongolismo *m* Down's syndrome

monigote *m* weak character; (*muñeca*) rag doll; (*dibujo*) doodle

monises *mpl* money, dough (*fam*)

monitor *m* monitor

monj|a *f* nun. ~**e** *m* monk. ~**il** *a* nun's; (*como de monja*) like a nun

mono *m* monkey; (*sobretodo*) overalls. —*a* pretty

mono... *pref* mono...

monocromo *a & m* monochrome

monóculo *m* monocle

mon|ogamia *f* monogamy. ~**ógamo** *a* monogamous

monografía *f* monograph

monograma *m* monogram

monol|ítico *a* monolithic. ~**ito** *m* monolith

mon|ologar [12] *vi* soliloquize. ~**ólogo** *m* monologue

monoman|ía *f* monomania. ~**íaco** *m* monomaniac

monoplano *m* monoplane

monopoli|o *m* monopoly. ~**zar** [10] *vt* monopolize

monos|ilábico *a* monosyllabic. ~**ílabo** *m* monosyllable

monoteís|mo *m* monotheism. ~**ta** *a* monotheistic. —*m & f* monotheist

mon|otonía *f* monotony. ~**ótono** *a* monotonous

monseñor *m* monsignor

monserga *f* boring talk

monstruo *m* monster. ~**sidad** *f* monstrosity. ~**so** *a* monstrous

monta *f* mounting; (*valor*) value

montacargas *m invar* service lift

monta|do *a* mounted. ~**dor** *m* fitter. ~**je** *m* assembly; (*cine*) montage; (*teatro*) staging, production

montañ|a *f* mountain. ~**ero** *a* mountaineer. ~**és** *a* mountain. —*m* highlander. ~**ismo** *m* mountaineering. ~**oso** *a* mountainous. ~**a rusa** big dipper

montaplatos *m invar* service lift

montar *vt* ride; (*subirse*) get on; (*ensamblar*) assemble; cock (*arma*); set up (*una casa, un negocio*). —*vi* ride; (*subirse a*) mount. ~ **a caballo** ride a horse

montaraz *a* (*animales*) wild; (*personas*) mountain

monte *m* (*montaña*) mountain; (*terreno inculto*) scrub; (*bosque*) forest. ~ **de piedad** pawn-shop. **ingeniero** *m* **de** ~**s** forestry expert

montepío *m* charitable fund for dependents

monter|a *f* cloth cap. ~**o** *m* hunter

montés *a* wild

Montevideo *m* Montevideo

montevideano *a* & *m* Montevidean

montículo *m* hillock

montón *m* heap, pile. **a montones** in abundance, lots of

montuoso *a* hilly

montura *f* mount; (*silla*) saddle

monument|al *a* monumental; (*fig, muy grande*) enormous. ~**o** *m* monument

monzón *m* & *f* monsoon

moñ|a *f* hair ribbon. ~**o** *m* bun

moque|a *f* runny nose. ~**ro** *m* handkerchief

moqueta *f* fitted carpet

moquillo *m* distemper

mora *f* mulberry; (*zarzamora*) blackberry

morada *f* dwelling

morado *a* purple

morador *m* inhabitant

moral *m* mulberry tree. —*f* morals. —*a* moral. ~**eja** *f* moral. ~**idad** *f* morality. ~**ista** *m* & *f* moralist. ~**izador** *a* moralizing. —*m* moralist. ~**izar** [10] *vt* moralize

morapio *m* (*fam*) cheap red wine

morar *vi* live

moratoria *f* moratorium

morbidez *f* softness

mórbido *a* soft; (*malsano*) morbid

morbo *m* illness. ~**sidad** *f* morbidity. ~**so** *a* unhealthy

morcilla *f* black pudding

morda|cidad *f* bite. ~**z** *a* biting

mordaza *f* gag

mordazmente *adv* bitingly

morde|dura *f* bite. ~**r** [2] *vt* bite; (*fig, quitar porciones a*) eat into; (*denigrar*) gossip about. —*vi* bite

mordis|car [7] *vt* nibble (at). —*vi* nibble. ~**co** *m* bite. ~**quear** *vt* nibble (at)

morelense *a* (*Mex*) from Morelos. —*m* & *f* person from Morelos

morena *f* (*geol*) moraine

moreno *a* dark; (*de pelo obscuro*) dark-haired; (*de raza negra*) negro

morera *f* mulberry tree

morería *f* Moorish lands; (*barrio*) Moorish quarter

moretón *m* bruise

morfema *m* morpheme

morfin|a *f* morphine. ~**ómano** *a* morphine. —*m* morphine addict

morfolog|ía *f* morphology. ~**ógico** *a* morphological

moribundo *a* moribund

morillo *m* andiron

morir [6] (*pp* **muerto**) *vi* die; (*fig, extinguirse*) die away; (*fig, terminar*) end. ~**se** *vpr* die. ~**se de hambre** starve to death; (*fig*) be starving. **se muere por una flauta** she's dying to have a flute

moris|co *a* Moorish. —*m* Moor. ~**ma** *f* Moors

morm|ón *m* & *f* Mormon. ~**ónico** *a* Mormon. ~**onismo** *m* Mormonism

moro *a* Moorish. —*m* Moor

moros|idad *f* dilatoriness. ~**o** *a* dilatory

morrada *f* butt; *(puñetazo)* punch

morral *m* *(mochila)* rucksack; *(del cazador)* gamebag; *(para caballos)* nosebag

morralla *f* rubbish

morrillo *m* nape of the neck

morriña *f* homesickness

morro *m* snout

morrocotudo *a* *(esp Mex)* *(fam)* terrific *(fam)*

morsa *f* walrus

mortaja *f* shroud

mortal *a & m & f* mortal. **~idad** *f* mortality. **~mente** *adv* mortally

mortandad *f* death toll

mortecino *a* failing; *(color)* faded

mortero *m* mortar

mortífero *a* deadly

mortifica|ción *f* mortification. **~r** [7] *vt* *(med)* damage; *(atormentar)* plague; *(humillar)* humiliate. **~rse** *vpr* *(Mex)* feel embarassed

mortuorio *a* death

morueco *m* ram

moruno *a* Moorish

mosaico *a* of Moses, Mosaic. *—m* mosaic

mosca *f* fly. **~rda** *f* blowfly. **~rdón** *m* botfly; *(mosca de cuerpo azul)* bluebottle

moscatel *a* muscatel

moscón *m* botfly; *(mosca de cuerpo azul)* bluebottle

moscovita *a & m & f* Muscovite

Moscú *m* Moscow

mosque|arse *vpr* get cross. **~o** *m* resentment

mosquete *m* musket. **~ro** *m* musketeer

mosquit|ero *m* mosquito net. **~o** *m* mosquito; *(mosca pequeña)* fly, gnat

mostacho *m* moustache

mostachón *m* macaroon

mostaza *f* mustard

mosto *m* must

mostrador *m* counter

mostrar [2] *vt* show. **~se** *vpr* (show oneself to) be. **se mostró muy amable** he was very kind

mostrenco *a* ownerless; *(animal)* stray; *(torpe)* thick; *(gordo)* fat

mota *f* spot, speck

mote *m* nickname; *(lema)* motto

motea|do *a* speckled. **~r** *vt* speckle

motejar *vt* call

motel *m* motel

motete *m* motet

motín *m* riot; *(rebelión)* uprising; *(de tropas)* mutiny

motiv|ación *f* motivation. **~ar** *vt* motivate; *(explicar)* explain. **~o** *m* reason. **con ~o de** because of

motocicl|eta *f* motor cycle, motor bike *(fam)*. **~ista** *m & f* motor-cyclist

motón *m* pulley

motonave *f* motor boat

motor *a* motor. *—m* motor, engine. **~a** *f* motor boat. **~ de arranque** starter motor

motoris|mo *m* motorcycling. **~ta** *m & f* motorist; *(de una moto)* motorcyclist

motorizar [10] *vt* motorize

motriz *af* motive, driving

move|dizo *a* movable; *(poco firme)* unstable; *(persona)* fickle. **~r** [2] *vt* move; shake *(la cabeza)*; *(provocar)* cause. **~rse** *vpr* move; *(darse prisa)* hurry up. **arenas** *fpl* **~dizas** quicksand

movi|ble *a* movable. **~do** *a* moved; *(foto)* blurred; *(inquieto)* fidgety

móvil *a* movable. *—m* motive

movili|dad *f* mobility. **~zación** *f* mobilization. **~zar** [10] *vt* mobilize

movimiento *m* movement, motion; *(agitación)* bustle

moza f girl; (*sirvienta*) servant, maid. **~lbete** m young lad

mozárabe a Mozarabic. —m & f Mozarab

mozo m boy, lad. **~uela** f young girl. **~uelo** m young boy/lad

muaré m moiré

mucama f (*Arg*) servant. **~o** m (*Arg*) servant

mucosidad f mucus. **~o** a mucous

muchacha f girl; (*sirvienta*) servant, maid. **~o** m boy, lad; (*criado*) servant

muchedumbre f crowd

muchísimo a very much. —adv a lot

mucho a much (pl many), a lot of. —pron a lot; (*personas*) many (people). —adv a lot, very much; (*de tiempo*) long, a long time. **ni ~ menos** by no means. **por ~ que** however much

muda f change of clothing; (*de animales*) moult. **~ble** a changeable; (*personas*) fickle. **~nza** f change; (*de casa*) removal. **~r** vt/i change. **~rse** (*de ropa*) change one's clothes; (*de casa*) move (house)

mudéjar a & m & f Mudéjar

mudez f dumbness. **~o** a dumb; (*callado*) silent

mueble a movable. —m piece of furniture

mueca f grimace, face. **hacer una ~** pull a face

muela f (*diente*) tooth; (*diente molar*) molar; (*piedra de afilar*) grindstone; (*piedra de molino*) millstone

muelle a soft. —m spring; (*naut*) wharf; (*malecón*) jetty

muérdago m mistletoe

muero vb véase **morir**

muerte f death; (*homicidio*) murder. **~o** a dead; (*matado*, *fam*) killed; (*colores*) pale. —m

dead person; (*cadáver*) body, corpse

muesca f nick; (*ranura*) slot

muestra f sample; (*prueba*) proof; (*modelo*) model; (*seal*) sign. **~rio** m collection of samples

muestro vb véase **mostrar**

muevo vb véase **mover**

mugido m moo. **~r** [14] vi moo; (*fig*) roar

mugre m dirt. **~iento** a dirty, filthy

mugrón m sucker

muguete m lily of the valley

mujer f woman; (*esposa*) wife. —int my dear! **~iego** a ⟨*hombre*⟩ fond of the women. **~il** a womanly. **~ío** m (crowd of) women. **~zuela** f prostitute

mújol m mullet

mula f mule; (*Mex*) unsaleable goods. **~da** f drove of mules

mulato a & m mulatto

mulero m muleteer

muleta f crutch; (*fig*) support; (*toreo*) stick with a red flag

mulo m mule

multa f fine. **~r** vt fine

multi... pref multi...

multicolor a multicolour(ed)

multicopista m copying machine

multiforme a multiform

multilateral a multilateral

multilingüe a multilingual

multimillonario m multimillionaire

múltiple a multiple

multiplicación f multiplication. **~ar** [7] vt multiply. **~arse** vpr multiply; (*fig*) go out of one's way. **~idad** f multiplicity

múltiplo a & m multiple

multitud f multitude, crowd. **~inario** a multitudinous

mullido a soft. —m stuffing. **~r** [22] vt soften

mund|ano *a* wordly; (*de la sociedad elegante*) society. —*m* socialite. ~**ial** *a* world-wide. la **segunda guerra** ~**ial** the Second World War. ~**illo** *m* world, circles. ~**o** *m* world. ~**ología** *f* worldly wisdom. **todo el** ~ everybody

munición *f* ammunition. (*provisiones*) supplies

municip|al *a* municipal. ~**al-idad** *f* municipality. ~**io** *m* municipality; (*ayuntamiento*) town council

munificencia *f* munificence. ~**ífico** *a* munificent

muñe|ca *f* (*anat*) wrist; (*juguete*) doll; (*maniquí*) dummy. ~**co** *m* boy doll. ~**quera** *f* wristband

muñón *m* stump

mural|a a mural, wall. —*m* mural. ~**lla** *f* (*city*) wall. ~**r** *vt* wall

murciélago *m* bat

murga *f* street band; (*lata*) bore, nuisance. **dar la** ~ bother, be a pain (*fam*)

murmullo *m* (*de personas*) whisper(ing), murmur(ing); (*del agua*) rippling; (*del viento*) sighing, rustle

murmura|ción *f* gossip. ~**dor** *a* gossiping. —*m* gossip. ~**r** *vi* murmur; (*hablar en voz baja*) whisper; (*quejarse en voz baja*) mutter; (*criticar*) gossip

muro *m* wall

murri|a *f* depression. ~**o** *a* depressed

mus *m* card game

musa *f* muse

musaraña *f* shrew

muscular *a* muscular. ~**tura** *f* muscles

músculo *m* muscle

musculoso *a* muscular

muselina *f* muslin

museo *m* museum. ~ **de arte** art gallery

musgaño *m* shrew

musgo *m* moss. ~**so** *a* mossy

música *f* music

musical *a* & *m* musical

músico *a* musical. —*m* musician

music|ología *f* musicology. ~**ólogo** *m* musicologist

musitar *vt/i* mumble

muslímico *a* Muslim

muslo *m* thigh

mustela *a* weasel

musti|arse *vpr* wither, wilt. ~**o** *a* (*plantas*) withered; (*cosas*) faded; (*personas*) gloomy; (*Mex, hipócrita*) hypocritical

musulmán *a* & *m* Muslim

muta|bilidad *f* mutability. ~**ción** *f* change; (*en biología*) mutation

mutila|ción *f* mutilation. ~**do** *a* crippled. —*m* cripple. ~**r** *vt* mutilate; cripple, maim (*persona*)

mutis *m* (*en el teatro*) exit. ~**mo** *m* silence

mutu|alidad *f* mutuality; (*asociación*) friendly society. ~**a-mente** *adv* mutually. ~**o** *a* mutual

muy *adv* very; (*demasiado*) too

N

nab|a *f* swede. ~**o** *m* turnip

nácar *m* mother-of-pearl

nac|er [11] *vi* be born; (*huevo*) hatch; (*planta*) sprout. ~**ido** *a* born. ~**iente** *a* (*sol*) rising. ~**imiento** *m* birth; (*de río*) source; (*belén*) crib. **dar** ~**imiento a** give rise to. **lugar de** ~**imiento** place of birth. **recien** ~**ido** newborn. **volver a** ~**er** have a narrow escape

nación *f* nation. ~**onal** *a* national. ~**onalidad** *f* nationality. ~**onalismo** *m* nationalism. ~**onalista** *m* & *f* nationalist. **~onalizar** [10] *vt* nationalize. **~onalizarse** *vpr* become naturalized

nada *pron* nothing, not anything. —*adv* not at all. **¡~ de eso!** nothing of the sort! **antes de ~** first of all. **¡de ~!** (*después de 'gracias'*) don't mention it! **para ~** (not) at all. **por ~ del mundo** not for anything in the world

nada|dor *m* swimmer. **~r** *vi* swim

nadería *f* trifle

nadie *pron* no one, nobody

nado *adv.* **a ~** swimming

nafta *f* (*LAm, gasolina*) petrol, (*Brit*), gas (*Amer*)

nailon *m* nylon

naipe *m* (playing) card. **juegos** *mpl* **de ~s** card games

nalga *f* buttock. **~s** *fpl* bottom

nana *f* lullaby

Nápoles *m* Naples

naranj|a *f* orange. **~ada** *f* orangeade. **~al** *m* orange grove. **~o** *m* orange tree

narcótico *a & m* narcotic

nariz *f* nose; (*orificio de la nariz*) nostril. **¡narices!** rubbish!

narra|ción *f* narration. **~dor** *m* narrator. **~r** *vt* tell. **~tivo** *a* narrative

nasal *a* nasal

nata *f* cream

natación *f* swimming

natal *a* (*pueblo etc*) home. **~idad** *f* birth rate

natillas *fpl* custard

natividad *f* nativity

nativo *a & m* native

nato *a* born

natural *a* natural. —*m* native. **~eza** *f* nature; (*nacionalidad*) nationality; (*ciudadanía*) naturalization. **~eza muerta** still life. **~idad** *f* naturalness. **~ista** *m & f* naturalist. **~izar** [10] *vt* naturalize. **~izarse** *vpr* become

naturalized. **~mente** *adv* naturally. —*int* of course!

naufrag|ar [12] *vi* (*barco*) sink; (*persona*) be shipwrecked; (*fig*) fail. **~io** *m* shipwreck

náufrago *a* shipwrecked. —*m* shipwrecked person

náusea *f* nausea. **dar ~s a uno** make s.o. feel sick. **sentir ~s** feel sick

nauseabundo *a* sickening

náutico *a* nautical

navaja *f* penknife; (*de afeitar*) razor. **~zo** *m* slash

naval *a* naval

Navarra *f* Navarre

nave *f* ship; (*de iglesia*) nave. **~ espacial** spaceship. **quemar las ~s** burn one's boats

navega|ble *a* navigable; (*barco*) seaworthy. **~ción** *f* navigation. **~nte** *m & f* navigator. **~r** [12] *vi* sail; (*avión*) fly

Navid|ad *f* Christmas. **~eño** *a* Christmas. **en ~ades** at Christmas. **¡feliz ~ad!** Happy Christmas! **por ~ad** at Christmas

navío *m* ship

nazi *a & m & f* Nazi

neblina *f* mist

nebuloso *a* misty; (*fig*) vague

necedad *f* foolishness. **decir ~es** talk nonsense. **hacer una ~** do sth stupid

necesari|amente *adv* necessarily. **~o** *a* necessary

necesi|dad *f* necessity; (*pobreza*) poverty. **~dades** *fpl* hardships. **por ~dad** (out) of necessity. **~tado** *a* in need (**de** of); (*pobre*) needy. **~tar** *vt* need. —*vi.* **~tar de** need

necio *a* silly. —*m* idiot

necrología *f* obituary column

néctar *m* nectar

nectarina *f* nectarine

nefasto *a* unfortunate, ominous

nega|ción *f* negation; (*desmentimiento*) denial; (*gram*) negative. **~do** *a* incompetent. **~r** [1 &

12] *vt* deny; (*rehusar*) refuse. ~**rse** *vpr*. ~**rse a** refuse. ~**tiva** *f* negative; (*acción*) denial; (*acción de rehusar*) refusal. ~**tivo** *a* & *m* negative

negligen|cia *f* negligence. ~**te** *a* negligent

negoci|able *a* negotiable. ~**ación** *f* negotiation. ~**ante** *a* & *f* dealer. ~**ar** *vt/i* negotiate. ~**ar en** trade in. ~**o** *m* business; (*com, trato*) deal. ~**os** *mpl* business. **hombre** *m* **de** ~**os** businessman

negr|a *f* Negress; (*mus*) crotchet. ~**o** *a* black; (*persona*) Negro. —*m* (*color*) black; (*persona*) Negro. ~**ura** *f* blackness. ~**uzco** *a* blackish

nene *m* & *f* baby, child

nenúfar *m* water lily

neo... *pref* neo...

neocelandés *a* from New Zealand. —*m* New Zealander

neolítico *a* Neolithic

neón *m* neon

nepotismo *m* nepotism

nervio *m* nerve; (*tendón*) sinew; (*bot*) vein. ~**sidad** *f*, ~**sismo** *m* nervousness; (*impaciencia*) impatience. ~**so** *a* nervous; (*de temperamento*) highly-strung. **crispar los** ~**s a uno** (*fam*) get on s.o.'s nerves. **ponerse** ~**so** get excited

neto *a* clear; (*verdad*) simple; (*com*) net

neumático *a* pneumatic. —*m* tyre

neumonía *f* pneumonia

neuralgia *f* neuralgia

neur|ología *f* neurology. ~**ólogo** *m* neurologist

neur|osis *f* neurosis. ~**ótico** *a* neurotic

neutr|al *a* neutral. ~**alidad** *f* neutrality. ~**alizar** [10] *vt* neutralize. ~**o** *a* neutral; (*gram*) neuter

neutrón *m* neutron

neva|da *f* snowfall. ~**r** [1] *vi* snow. ~**sca** *f* blizzard

nevera *f* fridge (*Brit, fam*), refrigerator

nevisca *f* light snowfall. ~**r** [7] *vi* snow lightly

nexo *m* link

ni *conj* nor, neither; (*ni siquiera*) not even. ~... ~ neither... nor. ~ **que** **as if.** ~ **siquiera** not even

Nicaragua *f* Nicaragua

nicaragüense *a* & *m* & *f* Nicaraguan

nicotina *f* nicotine

nicho *m* niche

nido *m* nest; (*de ladrones*) den; (*escondrijo*) hiding-place

niebla *f* fog; (*neblina*) mist. **hay** ~ it's foggy

niet|a *f* granddaughter. ~**o** *m* grandson. ~**os** *mpl* grandchildren

nieve *f* snow; (*LAm, helado*) ice-cream

Nigeria *f* Nigeria. ~**no** *a* Nigerian

niki *m* T-shirt

nilón *m* nylon

nimbo *m* halo

nimi|edad *f* triviality. ~**o** *a* insignificant

ninfa *f* nymph

ninfea *f* water lily

ningún *véase* **ninguno**

ninguno *a* (*delante de nombre masculino en singular* **ningún**) no, not any. —*pron* none; (*persona*) no-one, nobody; (*de dos*) neither. **de ninguna manera**, **de ningún modo** by no means. **en ninguna parte** nowhere

niñ|a *f* (little) girl. ~**ada** *f* childish thing. ~**era** *f* nanny. ~**ería** *f* childish thing. ~**ez** *f* childhood. ~**o** *a* childish. —*m* (little) boy. **de** ~**o** as a child. **desde** ~**o** from childhood

níquel *m* nickel

níspero m medlar

nitidez f clearness

nítido a clear; (foto) sharp

nitrato m nitrate

nítrico a nitric

nitrógeno m nitrogen

nivel m level; (fig) standard. **~ar** vt level. **~arse** vpr become level. **~ de vida** standard of living

no adv not; (como respuesta) no. ¿**~**? isn't it? **~ más** only. ¡a que **~**! I bet you don't! ¡cómo **~**! of course! **Felipe ~ tiene hijos** Felipe has no children. ¡que **~**! certainly not!

nob|iliario a noble. **~le** a & m & f noble. **~leza** f nobility

noción f notion. **nociones** fpl rudiments

nocivo a harmful

nocturno a nocturnal; (clase) evening; (tren etc) night. **—m** nocturne

noche f night. **~ vieja** New Year's Eve. **de ~** at night. **hacer ~** spend the night. **media ~** midnight. **por la ~** at night

Nochebuena f Christmas Eve

nodo m (Esp, película) newsreel

nodriza f nanny

nódulo m nodule

nogal m walnut(-tree)

nómada a nomadic. **—m & f** nomad

nombr|adía f fame. **~ado** a famous; (susodicho) aforementioned. **~amiento** m appointment. **~ar** vt appoint; (citar) mention. **~e** m name; (gram) noun; (fama) renown. **~e de pila** Christian name. **en ~e de** in the name of. **no tener ~e** be unspeakable. **poner de ~e** call

nomeolvides m invar forget-me-not

nómina f payroll

nominal a nominal. **~tivo** a & m nominative. **~tivo a** (cheque etc) made out to

non a odd. **—m** odd number

nonada f trifle

nono a ninth

nordeste a (región) northeastern; (viento) northeasterly. **—m** north-east

nórdico a northern. **—m** northerner

noria f water-wheel; (en una feria) ferris wheel

norma f rule

normal a normal. **—f** teachers' training college. **~idad** normality (Brit), normalcy (Amer). **~izar** [10] vt normalize. **~mente** adv normally, usually

Normandía f Normandy

noroeste a (región) northwestern; (viento) northwesterly. **—m** north-west

norte m north; (viento) north wind; (fig, meta) aim

Norteamérica f (North) America

norteamericano a & m (North) American

norteño a northern. **—m** northerner

Noruega f Norway

noruego a & m Norwegian

nos pron (acusativo) us; (dativo) (to) us; (reflexivo) (to) ourselves; (recíproco) (to) each other

nosotros pron we; (con prep) us

nost|algia f nostalgia; (de casa, de patria) homesickness. **~álgico** a nostalgic

nota f note; (de examen etc) mark. **~ble** a notable. **~ción** f notation. **~r** vt notice; (apuntar) note down. **de mala ~** notorious. **de ~** famous. **digno de ~** notable. **es de ~r** it should be noted. **hacerse ~r** stand out

notario m notary

notici|a f (piece of) news. **~as** fpl news. **~ario** m news. **~ero** a news. **atrasado de ~as** behind

the times. **tener ~as de** hear from

notifica|ción f notification. **~r** [7] vt notify

notori|edad f notoriety. **~o** a well-known; (*evidente*) obvious

novato m novice

novecientos a & m nine hundred

noved|ad f newness; (*noticia*) news; (*cambio*) change; (*moda*) latest fashion. **~oso** a (*LAm*) novel. **sin ~ad** no news

novel|a f novel. **~ista** m & f novelist

noveno a ninth

novent|a a & m ninety; (*nonagésimo*) ninetieth. **~ón** a & m ninety-year-old

novia f girlfriend; (*prometida*) fiancée; (*en boda*) bride. **~zgo** m engagement

novicio m novice

noviembre m November

novilunio m new moon

novill|a f heifer. **~o** m bullock. **hacer ~os** play truant

novio m boyfriend; (*prometido*) fiancé; (*en boda*) bridegroom. **los ~s** the bride and groom

novísimo a very new

nub|arrón m large dark cloud. **~e** f cloud; (*de insectos etc*) swarm. **~lado** a cloudy, overcast. **—m** cloud. **~lar** vt cloud. **~larse** vpr become cloudy. **~loso** a cloudy

nuca f back of the neck

nuclear a nuclear

núcleo m nucleus

nudillo m knuckle

nudis|mo m nudism. **~ta** m & f nudist

nudo m knot; (*de asunto etc*) crux. **~so** a knotty. **tener un ~ en la garganta** have a lump in one's throat

nuera f daughter-in-law

nuestro a our; (*pospuesto al sustantivo*) of ours. **—pron** ours. **~ coche** our car. **un coche ~** a car of ours

nueva f (*piece of*) news. **~s** fpl news. **~mente** adv newly; (*de nuevo*) again

Nueva York f New York

Nueva Zelanda f, **Nueva Zelandia** f (*LAm*) New Zealand

nueve a & m nine

nuevo a new. **de ~** again

nuez f nut; (*del nogal*) walnut; (*anat*) Adam's apple. **~ de Adán** Adam's apple. **~ moscada** nutmeg

nul|idad f incompetence; (*persona, fam*) nonentity. **~o** a useless; (*jurid*) null and void

numer|ación f numbering. **~al** a & m numeral. **~ar** vt number. **~érico** a numerical

número m number; (*arábigo, romano*) numeral; (*de zapatos etc*) size. **sin ~** countless

numeroso a numerous

nunca adv never, not ever. **~ (ja)más** never again. **casi ~** hardly ever. **más que ~** more than ever

nupcia|l a nuptial. **~s** fpl wedding. **banquete ~l** wedding breakfast

nutria f otter

nutri|ción f nutrition. **~do** a nourished, fed; (*fig*) large; (*aplausos*) loud; (*fuego*) heavy. **~r** vt nourish, feed; (*fig*) feed. **~tivo** a nutritious. **valor m ~tivo** nutritional value

nylon m nylon

Ñ

ña f (*LAm, fam*) Mrs

ñacanina f (*Arg*) poisonous snake

ñame m yam

ñapindá m (Arg) mimosa

ñato (LAm) snub-nosed

ño m (LAm, fam) Mr

ñoñ|ería f, **~ez** f insipidity. **~o** a insipid; (tímido) bashful; (quisquilloso) prudish

ñu m gnu

O

o conj or. **~ bien** rather. **~...** ~ either... or. **~ sea** in other words

oasis m invar oasis

obcecar [7] vt blind

obed|ecer [11] vt/i obey. **~iencia** f obedience. **~iente** a obedient

obelisco m obelisk

obertura f overture

obes|idad f obesity. **~o** a obese

obispo m bishop

obje|ción f objection. **~tar** vt/i object

objetiv|idad f objectivity. **~o** a objective. —m objective; (foto etc) lens

objeto m object

objetor m objector. **~ de conciencia** conscientious objector

oblicuo a oblique; (mirada) sidelong

obliga|ción f obligation; (com) bond. **~do** a obliged; (forzoso) obligatory; **~r** [12] vt force, oblige. **~rse** vpr. **~rse a** undertake to. **~torio** a obligatory

oboe m oboe; (músico) oboist

obra f work; (de teatro) play; (construcción) building. **~ maestra** masterpiece. **en ~** under construction. **por ~ de** thanks to. **~r** vt do; (construir) build

obrero a labour; (clase) working. —m workman; (en fábrica) worker

obscen|idad f obscenity. **~o** a obscene

obscu... véase **oscu...**

obsequi|ar vt lavish attention on. **~ar con** give, present with. **~o** m gift, present; (agasajo) attention. **~oso** a obliging. **en ~o de** in honour of

observa|ción f observation; (objeción) objection. **~dor** m observer. **~ncia** f observance. **~nte** a observant. **~r** vt observe; (notar) notice. **~rse** vpr be noted. **~torio** m observatory. **hacer una ~ción** make a remark

obses|ión f obsession. **~ionar** vt obsess. **~ivo** a obsessive. **~o** a obsessed

obst|aculizar [10] vt hinder. **~áculo** m obstacle

obstante, **no ~** adv however, nevertheless. —prep in spite of

obstar vi. **~ para** prevent

obstétrico a obstetric

obstina|ción f obstinacy. **~do** a obstinate. **~rse** vpr be obstinate. **~rse en** (+ infinitivo) persist in (+ gerundio)

obstru|cción f obstruction. **~ir** [17] vt obstruct

obtener [40] vt get, obtain

obtura|dor m (foto) shutter. **~r** vt plug; fill (muela etc)

obtuso a obtuse

obviar vt remove

obvio a obvious

oca f goose

ocasi|ón f occasion; (oportunidad) opportunity; (motivo) cause. **~onal** a chance. **~onar** vt cause. **aprovechar la ~ón** take the opportunity. **con ~ón de** on the occasion of. **de ~ón** bargain; (usado) second-hand. **en ~ones** sometimes. **perder una ~ón** miss a chance

ocaso m sunset; (fig) decline

occident|al a western. —m & f westerner. **~e** m west

océano m ocean

ocio *m* idleness; *(tiempo libre)* leisure time. **~sidad** *f* idleness. **~so** *a* idle; *(inútil)* pointless

oclusión *f* occlusion

octano *m* octane. **índice** *m* de **~** octane number, octane rating

octava *f* octave. **~o** *a* & *m* eighth

octogenario *a* & *m* octogenarian, eighty-year-old

octogonal *a* octagonal. **~ógono** *m* octagon

octubre *m* October

oculista *m* & *f* oculist, optician

ocular *a* eye

ocultar *vt* hide. **~arse** *vpr* hide. **~o** *a* hidden; *(secreto)* secret

ocupación *f* occupation. **~do** *a* occupied; *(persona)* busy. **~nte** *m* occupant. **~r** *vt* occupy. **~rse** *vpr* look after

ocurrencia *f* occurrence, event; *(idea)* idea; *(que tiene gracia)* witty remark. **~ir** *vi* happen. **~irse** *vpr* occur. **¿qué ~e?** what's the matter? **se me ~e que** it occurs to me that

ochenta *a* & *m* eighty. **~ón** *a* & *m* eighty-year-old

ocho *a* & *m* eight. **~cientos** *a* & *m* eight hundred

oda *f* ode

odiar *vt* hate. **~o** *m* hatred. **~oso** *a* hateful

odisea *f* odyssey

oeste *m* west; *(viento)* west wind

ofender *vt* offend; *(insultar)* insult. **~derse** *vpr* take offence. **~sa** *f* offence. **~siva** *f* offensive. **~sivo** *a* offensive

oferta *f* offer; *(en subasta)* bid; *(regalo)* gift. **~s de empleo** situations vacant. **en ~** on (special) offer

oficial *a* official. **—m** *m* skilled worker; *(funcionario)* civil servant; *(mil)* officer. **~a** *f* skilled (woman) worker

oficina *f* office. **~a de colocación** employment office. **~a**

de Estado government office. **~a de turismo** tourist office. **~ista** *m* & *f* office worker. **horas** *fpl* de **~a** business hours

oficio *m* job; *(profesión)* profession; *(puesto)* post. **~so** *a* (*no oficial*) unofficial

ofrecer [11] *vt* offer; give *(fiesta, banquete etc)*; *(prometer)* promise. **~erse** *vpr* *(persona)* volunteer; *(cosa)* occur. **~imiento** *m* offer

ofrenda *f* offering. **~r** *vt* offer

ofuscación *f* blindness; *(confusión)* confusion. **~r** [7] *vt* blind; *(confundir)* confuse. **~rse** *vpr* be dazzled

ogro *m* ogre

oíble *a* audible. **~da** *f* hearing. **~do** *m* hearing; *(anat)* ear. **al ~do** in one's ear. **de ~das** by hearsay. **de ~do** by ear. **duro de ~do** hard of hearing

oigo *vb* véase **oír**

oír [50] *vt* hear. **~ misa** go to mass. **¡oiga!** listen!; *(al teléfono)* hello!

ojal *m* buttonhole

ojalá *int* I hope so! —*conj* if only

ojeada *f* glance. **~r** *vt* eye; *(para inspeccionar)* see; *(ahuyentar)* scare away. **dar una ~da a**, **echar una ~da a** glance at

ojeras *fpl* *(del ojo)* bags

ojeriza *f* ill will. **tener ~ a** have a grudge against

ojete *m* eyelet

ojo *m* eye; *(de cerradura)* keyhole; *(de un puente)* span. **¡~!** careful!

ola *f* wave

olé *int* bravo!

oleada *f* wave. **~je** *m* swell

óleo *m* oil; *(cuadro)* oil painting

oleoducto *m* oil pipeline

oler [2, *las formas que empezarían por* ue *se escriben* **hue**] *vt* smell; *(curiosear)* pry into;

(*descubrir*) discover. —*vi* smell
(**a** of)

olfat|ear *vt* smell, sniff; (*fig*) sniff
out. ~o *m* (sense of) smell; (*fig*)
intuition

olimpiada *f*, olimpíada *f* Olympic games, Olympics

olímpico *a* (*juegos*) Olympic

oliv|a *f* olive; (*olivo*) olive tree.
~ar *m* olive grove. ~o *m* olive
tree

olmo *m* elm (tree)

olor *m* smell. ~oso *a*
sweet-smelling

olvid|adizo *a* forgetful. ~ar *vt*
forget. ~arse *upr* forget; (*estar
olvidado*) be forgotten. ~o *m*
oblivion; (*acción de olvidar*) for-
getfulness. se me ~ó I forgot

olla *f* pot, casserole; (*guisado*)
stew. ~ a|de presión, ~
exprés pressure cooker. ~ pod-
rida Spanish stew

ombligo *m* navel

ominoso *a* awful, abominable

omi|sión *f* omission; (*olvido*) for-
getfulness. ~tir *vt* omit

ómnibus *m* omnibus

omnipotente *a* omnipotent

omóplato *m*, omoplato *m*
shoulder blade

once *a & m* eleven

ond|a *f* wave. ~a corta short
wave. ~a larga long wave.
~ear *vi* wave; (*agua*) ripple.
~ulación *f* undulation; (*del
pelo*) wave. ~ular *vi* wave. longitud *f* de ~a wavelength

oneroso *a* onerous

ónice *m* onyx

onomástico *a*. día ~, fiesta
onomástica name-day

ONU *abrev* (*Organización de las
Naciones Unidas*) UN, United
Nations

onza *f* ounce

opa *a* (*LAm*) stupid

opaco *a* opaque; (*fig*) dull

ópalo *m* opal

opción *f* option

ópera *f* opera

opera|ción *f* operation; (*com*)
transaction. ~dor *m* operator;
(*cirujano*) surgeon; (*TV*) cam-
eraman. ~r *vt* operate on; work
(*milagro etc*). —*vi* operate; (*com*)
deal. ~rse *upr* occur; (*med*) have
an operation. ~torio *a* operative

opereta *f* operetta

opin|ar *vi* think. ~ión *f* opinion.
la ~ión pública public opinion

opio *m* opium

opone|nte *a* opposing. —*m & f*
opponent. ~r *vt* oppose; offer (*resistencia*); raise (*objeción*). ~rse
upr be opposed; (*dos personas*)
oppose each other

oporto *m* port (wine)

oportun|idad *f* opportunity;
(*cualidad de oportuno*) time-
liness. ~ista *m & f* opportunist.
~o *a* opportune; (*apropiado*)
suitable

oposi|ción *f* opposition. ~ciones
fpl competition, public examination. ~tor *m* candidate

opres|ión *f* oppression; (*ahogo*)
difficulty in breathing. ~ivo *a*
oppressive. ~o *a* oppressed.
~or *m* oppressor

oprimir *vt* squeeze; press (*botón
etc*); (*ropa*) be too tight for; (*fig*)
oppress

oprobio *m* disgrace

optar *vi* choose. ~ por opt for

ópti|ca *f* optics; (*tienda*)
optician's (shop). ~o *a*
optic(al). —*m* optician

optimis|mo *m* optimism. ~ta *a*
optimistic. —*m & f* optimist

opuesto *a* opposite; (*enemigo*)
opposed

opulen|cia *f* opulence. ~to *a*
opulent

oración *f* prayer; (*discurso*)
speech; (*gram*) sentence

oráculo *m* oracle

orador *m* speaker

oral *a* oral

orar *vi* pray

oratori|**a** *f* oratory. **~o** *a* oratorical. **—** *m* (*mus*) oratorio

orbe *m* orb

órbita *f* orbit

orden *m* & *f* order; (*Mex, porción*) portion. **~ado** *a* tidy. **~ del día** agenda. **órdenes** *fpl* **sagradas** Holy Orders. **en ~** in order. **por ~** in turn

ordenador *m* computer

ordena|**nza** *f* order. **—** *m* (*mil*) orderly. **~r** *vt* put in order; (*mandar*) order; (*relig*) ordain

ordeñar *vt* milk

ordinal *a* & *m* ordinal

ordinari|**a** *a* ordinary; (*grosero*) common

orear *vt* air

orégano *m* oregano

oreja *f* ear

orfanato *m* orphanage

orfebre *m* goldsmith, silversmith

orfeón *m* choral society

orgánico *a* organic

organigrama *m* flow chart

organillo *m* barrel-organ

organismo *m* organism

organista *m* & *f* organist

organiza|**ción** *f* organization. **~dor** *m* organizer. **~r** [10] *vt* organize. **~rse** *vpr* get organized

órgano *m* organ

orgasmo *m* orgasm

orgía *f* orgy

orgullo *m* pride. **~so** *a* proud

orientación *f* direction

oriental *a* & *m* & *f* oriental

orientar *vt* position. **~se** *vpr* point; (*persona*) find one's bearings

oriente *m* east. **O~ Medio** Middle East

orificio *m* hole

orig|**en** *m* origin. **~inal** *a* original; (*excéntrico*) odd. **~inalidad** *f* originality. **~inar** *vt* give rise to. **~inario** *a* original; (*nativo*) native. **dar ~ a** give rise to. **ser ~inario de** come from

orilla *f* (*del mar*) shore; (*de río*) bank; (*borde*) edge

orín *m* rust

orina *f* urine. **~l** *m* chamber-pot. **~r** *vi* urinate

oriundo *a.* **~ de** (*persona*) (originating) from; (*animal etc*) native to

orla *f* border

ornamental *a* ornamental

ornitología *f* ornithology

oro *m* gold. **~s** *mpl* Spanish card suit. **~ de ley** 9 carat gold. **hacerse de ~** make a fortune. **prometer el ~ y el moro** promise the moon

oropel *m* tinsel

orquesta *f* orchestra. **~l** *a* orchestral. **~r** *vt* orchestrate

orquídea *f* orchid

ortiga *f* nettle

ortodox|**ia** *f* orthodoxy. **~o** *a* orthodox

ortografía *f* spelling

ortop|**edia** *f* orthopaedics. **~édico** *a* orthopaedic

oruga *f* caterpillar

orzuelo *m* sty

os *pron* (*acusativo*) you; (*dativo*) (to) you; (*reflexivo*) (to) yourselves; (*recíproco*) (to) each other

osad|**ía** *f* boldness. **~o** *a* bold

oscila|**ción** *f* swinging; (*de precios*) fluctuation; (*tec*) oscillation. **~r** *vi* swing; (*precio*) fluctuate; (*tec*) oscillate; (*fig, vacilar*) hesitate

oscur|**ecer** [11] *vi* darken; (*fig*) obscure. **~ecerse** *vpr* grow dark; (*nublarse*) cloud over. **~idad** *f* darkness; (*fig*) obscurity. **~o** *a* dark; (*fig*) obscure. **a ~as** in the dark

óseo *a* bony

oso *m* bear. **∼ de felpa**, **∼ de peluche** teddy bear

ostensible *a* obvious

ostent|ación *f* ostentation. **∼ar** *vt* show off; *(mostrar)* show. **∼oso** *a* ostentatious

osteoartritis *f* osteoarthritis

oste|ópata *m* & *f* osteopath. **∼opatía** *f* osteopathy

ostión *m* *(esp Mex)* oyster

ostra *f* oyster

ostracismo *m* ostracism

Otan *abrev* *(Organización del Tratado del Atlántico Norte)* NATO, North Atlantic Treaty Organization

otear *vt* observe; *(escudriñar)* scan, survey

otitis *f* inflammation of the ear

otoño *m* autumn *(Brit)*, fall *(Amer)*

otorga|miento *m* granting; *(documento)* authorization. **∼r** [12] *vt* give; *(jurid)* draw up

otorrinolaringólogo *m* ear, nose and throat specialist

otro *a* other; *(uno más)* another. —*pron* another (one); *(en plural)* others; *(otra persona)* someone else. **el ∼** the other. **el uno al ∼** one another, each other

ovación *f* ovation

oval *a* oval

óvalo *m* oval

ovario *m* ovary

oveja *f* sheep; *(hembra)* ewe

overol *m* *(LAm)* overalls

ovino *a* sheep

ovillo *m* ball. **hacerse un ∼** curl up

OVNI *abrev* *(objeto volante no identificado)* UFO, unidentified flying object

ovulación *f* ovulation

oxida|ción *f* rusting. **∼r** *vi* rust. **∼rse** *vpr* go rusty

óxido *m* oxide

oxígeno *m* oxygen

oye *vb* *véase* **oir**

oyente *a* listening. —*m* & *f* listener

ozono *m* ozone

P

pabellón *m* bell tent; *(edificio)* building; *(de instrumento)* bell; *(bandera)* flag

pabilo *m* wick

paceño *a* from La Paz. —*m* person from La Paz

pacer [11] *vi* graze

pacien|cia *f* patience. **∼te** *a* & *m* & *f* patient

pacificar [7] *vt* pacify; reconcile *(dos personas)*. **∼se** *vpr* calm down

pacífico *a* peaceful. **el (Océano** *m* **)P∼** the Pacific (Ocean)

pacifis|mo *m* pacifism. **∼ta** *a* & *m* & *f* pacifist

pact|ar *vi* agree, make a pact. **∼o** *m* pact, agreement

pachucho *a* *(fruta)* overripe; *(persona)* poorly

padec|er [11] *vt/i* suffer *(de* from); *(soportar)* bear. **∼imiento** *m* suffering; *(enfermedad)* ailment

padrastro *m* stepfather

padre *a* *(fam)* great. —*m* father. **∼s** *mpl* parents

padrino *m* godfather; *(en boda)* best man

padrón *m* census

paella *f* paella

paga *f* pay, wages. **∼ble** *a*, **∼dero** *a* payable

pagano *a* & *m* pagan

pagar [12] *vt* pay; pay for *(compras)*. —*vi* pay. **∼é** *m* IOU

página *f* page

pago *m* payment

pagoda *f* pagoda

país m country; (*región*) region. ~ **natal** native land. **el P~ Vasco** the Basque Country. **los P~es Bajos** the Low Countries

paisaje m countryside. **~no a** of the same country. **—m** compatriot

paja f straw; (*fig*) nonsense

pajarera f aviary

pájaro m bird. ~ **carpintero** woodpecker

paje m page

Pakistán m. **el** ~ Pakistan

pala f shovel; (*laya*) spade; (*en deportes*) bat; (*de tenis*) racquet

palabr a f word; (*habla*) speech. **~ota** f swear-word. **decir ~otas** swear. **pedir la** ~ **a** ask to speak. **soltar ~otas** swear. **tomar la** ~**a** (begin to) speak

palacio m palace; (*casa grande*) mansion

paladar m palate

paladino a clear; (*público*) public

palanca f lever; (*fig*) influence. ~ **de cambio** (**de velocidades**) gear lever (*Brit*), gear shift (*Amer*)

palangana f wash-basin

palco m (*en el teatro*) box

Palestina f Palestine

palestino a & m Palestinian

palestra f (*fig*) arena

paleta f (*de pintor*) palette; (*de albañil*) trowel

paleto m yokel

paliativo a & m palliative

palide cer [11] *vi* turn pale. **~z** f paleness

pálido a pale

palillo m small stick; (*de dientes*) toothpick

palique m. **estar de** ~ be chatting

paliza f beating

palizada f fence; (*recinto*) enclosure

palma f (*de la mano*) palm; (*árbol*) palm (tree); (*de dátiles*) date palm. **~s** fpl applause. **~da** f slap. **~das** fpl applause. **dar ~(da)s** clap. **tocar las** ~**s** clap

palmera f date palm

palmo m span; (*fig, pequeña cantidad*) small amount. ~ **a** ~ inch by inch

palmote ar *vi* clap, applaud. **~o** m clapping, applause

palo m stick; (*del teléfono etc*) pole; (*mango*) handle; (*de golf*) club; (*golpe*) blow; (*de naipes*) suit; (*mástil*) mast

paloma f pigeon, dove

palomitas fpl popcorn

palpa ble a palpable. **~r** *vt* feel

palpita ción f palpitation. **~nte** a throbbing. **~r** *vi* throb; (*latir*) beat

palta f (*LAm*) avocado pear

pal údico a marshy; (*de paludismo*) malarial. **~udismo** m malaria

pamp a f pampas. **~ear** *vi* (*LAm*) travel across the pampas. **~ero** a of the pampas

pan m bread; (*barra*) loaf. ~ **integral** wholemeal bread (*Brit*), wholewheat bread (*Amer*). ~ **tostado** toast. ~ **rallado** breadcrumbs. **ganarse el** ~ earn one's living

pana f corduroy

panacea f panacea

panader ía f bakery; (*tienda*) baker's (shop). **~o** m baker

panal m honeycomb

Panamá f Panama

panameño a & m Panamanian

pancarta f placard

panda m panda; (*pandilla*) gang

pander eta f (small) tambourine. **~o** m tambourine

pandilla f gang

panecillo m (bread) roll

panel m panel

panfleto m pamphlet

pánico *m* panic

panor|ama *m* panorama. ~ámico *a* panoramic

panqué *m* (*LAm*) pancake

pantaletas *fpl* (*LAm*) underpants, knickers

pantal|ón *m* trousers. ~ones *mpl* trousers. ~ón corto shorts. ~ón tejano, ~ón vaquero jeans

pantalla *f* screen; (*de lámpara*) (lamp)shade

pantano *m* marsh; (*embalse*) reservoir. ~so *a* boggy

pantera *f* panther

pantomima *f* pantomime

pantorrilla *f* calf

pantufla *f* slipper

panucho *m* (*Mex*) stuffed tortilla

panz|a *f* belly. ~ada *f* (*hartazgo, fam*) bellyful; (*golpe, fam*) blow in the belly. ~udo *a* fat, pot-bellied

pañal *m* nappy (*Brit*), diaper (*Amer*)

pañ|ería *f* draper's (shop). ~o *m* material; (*de lana*) woollen cloth; (*trapo*) cloth. ~o de cocina dishcloth; (*para secar*) tea towel. ~o higiénico sanitary towel. en ~os menores in one's underclothes

pañuelo *m* handkerchief; (*de cabeza*) scarf

papa *m* pope. ~*f* (*esp LAm*) potato. ~s francesas (*LAm*) chips

papá *m* dad(dy). ~s *mpl* parents. P~ Noel Father Christmas

papada *f* (*de persona*) double chin

papado *m* papacy

papagayo *m* parrot

papal *a* papal

papanatas *m inv* simpleton

paparrucha *f* (*tontería*) silly thing

papaya *f* pawpaw

papel *m* paper; (*en el teatro etc*) role. ~ carbón carbon paper. ~ celofán cellophane paper. ~ de calcar carbon paper. ~ de embalar, ~ de envolver wrapping paper. ~ de plata silver paper. ~ de seda tissue paper. ~era *f* waste-paper basket. ~ería *f* stationer's (shop). ~eta *f* ticket; (*para votar*) paper. ~ higiénico toilet paper. ~ pintado wallpaper. ~ secante blotting paper. blanco como el ~ as white as a sheet. desempeñar un ~, hacer un ~ play a role

paperas *fpl* mumps

paquebote *m* packet (boat)

paquete *m* packet; (*paquebote*) packet (boat); (*Mex, asunto difícil*) difficult job. ~ postal parcel

paquistaní *a & m* Pakistani

par *a* equal; (*número*) even. ~ *m* couple; (*dos cosas iguales*) pair; (*igual*) equal; (*título*) peer. a la ~ at the same time; (*monedas*) at par. al ~ que at the same time. a ~es two by two. de ~ en ~ wide open. sin ~ without equal

para *prep* for; (*hacia*) towards; (*antes del infinitivo*) (in order) to. ~ que so that. ¿~ qué? why? ~ que so that

parabienes *mpl* congratulations

parábola *f* (*narración*) parable

parabrisas *m inv* windscreen (*Brit*), windshield (*Amer*)

paraca *f* (*LAm*) strong wind (from the Pacific)

paraca|ídas *m inv* parachute. ~idista *m & f* parachutist; (*mil*) paratrooper

parachoques *m inv* bumper (*Brit*), fender (*Amer*); (*rail*) buffer

parad|a *f* (*acción*) stopping; (*sitio*) stop; (*de taxis*) rank; (*mil*) parade. ~ero *m* whereabouts:

(*alojamiento*) lodging. ~o a stationary; (*obrero*) unemployed; (*lento*) slow. **dejar** ~o confuse. **tener mal** ~**ero** come to a sticky end

paradoja f paradox

parador m state-owned hotel

parafina f paraffin

par|afrasear vt paraphrase. ~**áfrasis** f inv paraphrase

paraguas m inv umbrella

Paraguay m Paraguay

paraguayo a & m Paraguayan

paraíso m paradise; (*en el teatro*) gallery

paralel|a f parallel (line). ~**as** fpl parallel bars. ~**o** a & m parallel

par|álisis f inv paralysis. ~**alítico** a paralytic. ~**alizar** [10] vt paralyse

paramilitar a paramilitary

páramo m barren plain

parang|ón m comparison. ~**onar** vt compare

paraninfo m hall

paranoi|a f paranoia. ~**co** a paranoiac

parapeto m parapet; (*fig*) barricade

parapléjico a & m paraplegic

parar vt/i stop. ~**se** vpr stop. **sin** ~ continuously

pararrayos m inv lightning conductor

parásito a parasitic. —m parasite

parasol m parasol

parcela f plot. ~**r** vt divide into plots

parcial a partial. ~**idad** f prejudice; (*pol*) faction. **a tiempo** ~ part-time

parco a sparing, frugal

parche m patch

pardo a brown

parear vt pair off

parec|er m opinion; (*aspecto*) appearance. —vi [11] seem; (*asemejarse*) look like; (*aparecer*)

appear. ~**erse** vpr resemble, look like. ~**ido** a similar. —m similarity. **al** ~**er** apparently. **a mi** ~**er** in my opinion. **bien** ~**ido** good-looking. **me** ~**e** I think. **¿qué te parece?** what do you think? **según** ~**e** apparently

pared f wall. ~**ón** m thick wall; (*de ruinas*) standing wall. ~ **por medio** next door. **llevar al** ~**ón** shoot

parej|a f pair; (*hombre y mujer*) couple; (*la otra persona*) partner. ~**o** a alike, the same; (*liso*) smooth

parentela f relations. ~**sco** m relationship

paréntesis m inv parenthesis; (*signo ortográfico*) bracket. **entre** ~ (*fig*) by the way

paria m & f outcast

paridad f equality

pariente m & f relation, relative

parihuela f, **parihuelas** fpl stretcher

parir vt give birth to. —vi have a baby, give birth

París m Paris

parisiense a & m & f, **parisino** a & m Parisian

parking /'parkin/ m car park (*Brit*), parking lot (*Amer*)

parlament|ar vi discuss. ~**ario** a parliamentary. —m member of parliament (*Brit*), congressman (*Amer*). ~**o** m parliament

parlanchín a talkative. —m chatterbox

parmesano a Parmesan

paro m stoppage; (*desempleo*) unemployment; (*pájaro*) tit

parodia f parody. ~**r** vt parody

parpadear vi blink; (*luz*) flicker; (*estrella*) twinkle

párpado m eyelid

parque m park. ~ **de atracciones** funfair. ~ **infantil** children's playground. ~ **zoológico** zoo, zoological gardens

parqué m parquet

parquedad f frugality; (*moderación*) moderation

parra f grapevine

párrafo m paragraph

parrilla f grill; (*LAm*, *auto*) radiator grill. ~**da** f grill. **a la** ~ grilled

párroco m parish priest

parroquia f parish; (*iglesia*) parish church. ~**no** m parishioner; (*cliente*) customer

parsimoni|a f thrift. ~**oso** a thrifty

parte m message; (*informe*) report. — f part; (*porción*) share; (*lado*) side; (*jurid*) party. **dar** ~ report. **de mi** ~ for me. **de** ~ **de** from. **¿de** ~ **de quién?** (*al teléfono*) who's speaking? **en cualquier** ~ anywhere. **en gran** ~ largely. **en** ~ partly. **en todas** ~**s** everywhere. **la mayor** ~ the majority. **ninguna** ~ nowhere. **por otra** ~ on the other hand. **por todas** ~**s** everywhere

partera f midwife

partición f sharing out

participa|ción f participation; (*noticia*) notice; (*de lotería*) lottery ticket. ~**nte** a & participant. ~**r** vt notify. — vi take part

participio m participle

partícula f particle

particular a particular; (*clase*) private. — m matter. ~**idad** f peculiarity. ~**izar** [10] vt distinguish; (*detallar*) give details about. **en** ~ in particular. **nada de** ~ nothing special

partida f departure; (*en registro*) entry; (*documento*) certificate;

(*juego*) game; (*de gente*) group. **mala** ~ dirty trick

partidario a & m partisan. ~ **de** keen on

parti|do a divided. — m (*pol*) party; (*encuentro*) match, game; (*equipo*) team. — **r** vt divide. — vi leave; (*empezar*) start. ~**rse** vpr (*romperse*) break; (*dividirse*) split. **a** ~**r de** (*starting from*)

partitura f (*mus*) score

parto m birth; (*fig*) creation. **estar de** ~ be in labour

párvulo m. **colegio de** ~**s** nursery school

pasa f raisin. ~ **de Corinto** currant. ~ **de Esmirna** sultana

pasa|ble a passable. ~**da** f passing; (*de puntos*) row. ~**dero** a passable. ~**dizo** m passage. — **o** a past; (*día*, *mes* etc) last; (*anticuado*) old-fashioned; (*comida*) bad, off. ~**do mañana** the day after tomorrow. ~**dor** m bolt; (*de pelo*) hair-slide; (*culin*) strainer. **de** ~**da** in passing. **el lunes** ~**do** last Monday

pasaje m passage; (*naut*) crossing; (*viajeros*) passengers. ~**ro** a passing. — m passenger

pasamano(s) m handrail; (*barandilla de escalera*) banister(s)

pasamontañas m inv Balaclava (helmet)

pasaporte m passport

pasar vt pass; (*poner*) put; (*filtrar*) strain; spend (*tiempo*); (*tragar*) swallow; show (*película*); (*tolerar*) tolerate, overlook; give (*mensaje*, *enfermedad*). — vi pass; (*suceder*) happen; (*ir*) go; (*venir*) come; (*tiempo*) go by. ~ **de** have no interest in. ~**se** vpr pass; (*terminarse*) be over; (*flores*) wither; (*comida*) go bad; spend (*tiempo*); (*excederse*) go too far. ~**lo bien** have a good time. ~ **por alto** leave out. **como si no hubiese pasado nada** as if nothing had happened. **lo que pasa es que** the fact is that. **pase lo que pase** whatever happens. **¡pase Vd!** come in!, go in! **¡que lo pases bien!** have a good time! **¿qué pasa?** what's the matter?, what's happening?

pasarela *f* footbridge; *(naut)* gangway

pasatiempo *m* hobby, pastime

pascua *f (fiesta de los hebreos)* Passover; *(de Resurrección)* Easter; *(Navidad)* Christmas. ~**s** *fpl* Christmas. **hacer la ~ a uno** mess things up for s.o. **¡y santas ~s!** and that's that!

pase *m* pass

pase|ante *m & f* passer-by. ~**ar** *vt* take for a walk; *(exhibir)* show off. —*vi* go for a walk; *(en coche etc)* go for a ride. ~**arse** *vpr* go for a walk; *(en coche etc)* go for a ride. ~**o** *m* walk; *(en coche etc)* ride; *(calle)* avenue. ~**o marítimo** promenade. **dar un ~o** go for a walk. **¡vete a ~o!** *(fam)* go away!, get lost! *(fam)*

pasillo *m* passage

pasión *f* passion

pasiv|idad *f* passiveness. ~**o** *a* passive

pasm|ar *vt* astonish. ~**arse** *vpr* be astonished. ~**o** *m* astonishment. ~**oso** *a* astonishing

paso *a (fruta)* dried —*m* step; *(acción de pasar)* passing; *(huella)* footprint; *(manera de andar)* walk; *(camino)* way through; *(entre montañas)* pass; *(estrecho)* strait(s). ~ **a nivel** level crossing *(Brit)*, grade crossing *(Amer)*. ~ **de cebra** Zebra crossing. ~ **de peatones** pedestrian crossing. ~ **elevado** flyover. **a cada ~** at every turn. **a dos ~s** very near. **al ~ que**

at the same time as. **a ~ lento** slowly. **ceda el ~** give way. **de ~ in passing. **de ~ por** on the way through. **prohibido el ~** no entry

pasodoble *m (baile)* pasodoble

pasota *m & f* drop-out

pasta *f* paste; *(masa)* dough; *(dinero, fam)* money. ~**s** *fpl* pasta; *(pasteles)* pastries. ~ **de dientes**, ~ **dentífrica** toothpaste

pastar *vt/i* graze

pastel *m* cake; *(empanada)* pie; *(lápiz)* pastel. ~**ería** *f* cakes; *(tienda)* cake shop, confectioner's

paste(u)rizar [10] *vt* pasteurize

pastiche *m* pastiche

pastilla *f* pastille; *(de jabón)* bar; *(de chocolate)* piece

pastinaca *f* parsnip

pasto *m* pasture; *(hierba)* grass; *(Mex, césped)* lawn. ~**r** *m* shepherd; *(relig)* minister. ~**ral** *a* pastoral

pata *f* leg; *(pie)* paw, foot. ~**s arriba** upside down. **a cuatro ~s** on all fours. **meter la ~** put one's foot in it. **tener mala ~** have bad luck

pataca *f* Jerusalem artichoke

patad|a *f* kick. ~**lear** *vt* stamp; *(niño pequeño)* kick

pataplum *int* crash!

patata *f* potato. ~**s fritas** chips *(Brit)*, French fries *(Amer)*. ~**s fritas (a la inglesa)** *(potato)* crisps *(Brit)*, potato chips *(Amer)*

patent|ar *vt* patent. ~**e** *a* obvious. —*f* licence. ~ **de invención** patent

patern|al *a* paternal; *(cariño etc)* fatherly. ~**idad** *f* paternity. ~**o** *a* paternal; *(cariño etc)* fatherly

patético *a* moving

patillas *fpl* sideburns

patín *m* skate; *(juguete)* scooter

pátina f patina
patina|dero m skating rink.
 ~dor m skater. **~je** m skating.
 ~r vi skate; (deslizarse) slide.
 ~zo m skid; (fig, fam) blunder
patio m patio. **~ de butacas**
 stalls (Brit), orchestra (Amer)
pato m duck
patolog|ía f pathology. **~ógico** a
 pathological
patoso a clumsy
patraña f hoax
patria f native land
patriarca m patriarch
patrimonio m inheritance; (fig)
 heritage
patri|ota a patriotic. —m & f pat-
 riot. **~ótico** a patriotic. **~ot-**
 ismo m patriotism
patrocin|ar vt sponsor. **~io** m
 sponsorship
patr|ón m patron; (jefe) boss; (de
 pensión etc) landlord; (modelo)
 pattern. **~onato** m patronage;
 (fundación) trust, foundation
patrulla f patrol; (fig, cuadrilla)
 group. **~r** vt/i patrol
paulatinamente adv slowly
pausa f pause. **~do** a slow
pauta f guideline
pavimentar vt pave. **~o** m
 pavement
pavo m turkey. **~ real** peacock
pavor m terror. **~oso** a
 terrifying
payas|ada f buffoonery. **~o** m
 clown
paz f peace. **La P~** La Paz
peaje m toll
peatón m pedestrian
pebet|a f (LAm) little girl. **~e** m
 little boy
peca f freckle
peca|do m sin; (defecto) fault.
 ~dor m sinner. **~minoso** a sinful. **~r** [7] vi sin
pecoso a freckled
pectoral a pectoral; (para la tos)
 cough

peculiar a peculiar, particular.
 ~idad f peculiarity
pech|era f front. **~ero** m bib. **~o**
 m chest; (de mujer) breast; (fig,
 corazón) heart. **~uga** f breast.
 dar el ~o breast-feed (a un
 niño); (afrontar) confront.
 tomar a ~o take to heart
pedagogo m teacher
pedal m pedal. **~ear** vi pedal
pedante a pedantic
pedazo m piece, bit. **a ~s** in
 pieces. **hacer ~s** break to
 pieces. **hacerse ~s** fall to pieces
pedernal m flint
pedestal m pedestal
pedestre a pedestrian
pediatra m & f paediatrician
pedicuro m chiropodist
pedi|do m order. **~r** [5] vt ask
 (for); (com, en restaurante)
 order. —vi ask. **~r prestado**
 borrow
pegadizo a sticky; (mus) catchy
pegajoso a sticky
pegar [12] vt stick (on); (coser)
 sew on; give (enfermedad etc);
 (juntar) join; (golpear) hit; (dar)
 give. —vi stick. **~rse** vpr stick;
 (pelearse) hit each other. **~r**
 fuego a set fire to. **~tina** f
 sticker
pein|ado m hairstyle. **~ar** vt
 comb. **~arse** vpr comb one's
 hair. **~e** m comb. **~eta** f ornamental comb
p.ej. abrev (por ejemplo) e.g., for
 example
pela|do a (fruta) peeled; (cabeza)
 bald; (número) exactly; (terreno)
 barren. —m bare patch. **~dura**
 f (acción) peeling; (mondadura)
 peelings
pela|je m (de animal) fur; (fig,
 aspecto) appearance. **~mbre** m
 (de animal) fur; (de persona)
 thick hair
pelar vt cut the hair; (mondar)
 peel; (quitar el pellejo) skin

peldaño m step; (de escalera de mano) rung

pelea f fight; (discusión) quarrel. ~r vi fight. ~rse vpr fight

peletería f fur shop

peliagudo a difficult, tricky

pelícano m, **pelicano** m pelican

película f film (esp Brit), movie (Amer). ~ de dibujos (animados) cartoon (film). ~ en colores colour film

peligro m danger; (riesgo) risk. ~so a dangerous. poner en ~ endanger

pelirrojo a red-haired

pelma m & f, **pelmazo** m bore, nuisance

pel|o m hair; (de barba o bigote) whisker. ~ón a bald; (rapado) with very short hair. no tener ~os en la lengua be outspoken. tomar el ~o a uno pull s.o.'s leg

pelota f ball; (juego vasco) pelota. ~ vasca pelota. en ~(s) naked

pelotera f squabble

pelotilla f. hacer la ~ a ingratiate o.s. with

peluca f wig

peludo a hairy

peluquer|ía f (de mujer) hairdresser's; (de hombre) barber's. ~o m (de mujer) hairdresser; (de hombre) barber

pelusa f down; (celos, fam) jealousy

pelvis f pelvis

pella f lump

pelleja f, **pellejo** m skin

pellizc|ar [7] vt pinch. ~o m pinch

pena f sadness; (dificultad) difficulty. ~ de muerte death penalty. a duras ~s with difficulty. da ~ que it's a pity that. me da ~ que I'm sorry that. merecer la ~ be worthwhile. ¡qué ~! what a pity! valer la ~ be worthwhile

penacho m tuft; (fig) plume

pen|al a penal; (criminal) criminal. —m prison. ~idad f suffering; (jurid) penalty. ~izar [10] vt penalize

penalty m penalty

penar vt punish. —vi suffer. ~ por long for

pend|er vi hang. ~iente a hanging; (terreno) sloping; (cuenta) outstanding; (fig) (asunto etc) pending. —m earring. —f slope

pendón m banner

péndulo a hanging. —m pendulum

pene m penis

penetra|nte a penetrating; (sonido) piercing; (herida) deep. ~r vt penetrate; (fig) pierce; (entender) understand. —vi penetrate; (entrar) go into

penicilina f penicillin

pen|ínsula f peninsula. ~ínsula Ibérica Iberian Peninsula. ~insular a peninsular

penique m penny

peniten|cia f penitence; (castigo) penance. ~te a & m & f penitent

penoso a painful; (difícil) difficult

pensa|do a thought. ~dor m thinker. ~miento m thought. ~r [1] vt think; (considerar) consider. —vi think. ~r en think about. ~tivo a thoughtful. bien ~do all things considered. cuando menos se piensa when least expected. menos ~do least expected. ¡ni ~rlo! certainly not! pienso que sí I think so

pensi|ón f pension; (casa de huéspedes) guest-house. ~ón completa full board. ~onista m & f pensioner; (huésped) lodger; (escol) boarder

pentágono m pentagon

pentagrama m stave

Pentecostés *m* Whitsun; *(fiesta judía)* Pentecost

penúltimo *a* & *m* penultimate, last but one

penumbra *f* half-light

penuria *f* shortage

peña *f* rock; *(de amigos)* group; *(club)* club. **~ón** *m* rock. **el peñón de Gibraltar** The Rock (of Gibraltar)

peón *m* labourer; *(en ajedrez)* pawn; *(en damas)* piece; *(juguete)* (spinning) top

peonía *f* peony

peonza *f* (spinning) top

peor *a* *(comparativo)* worse; *(superlativo)* worst. **—adv** worse. **~ que** ~ worse and worse. **lo ~** the worst thing. **tanto** ~ so much the worse

pepin|illo *m* gherkin. **~o** *m* cucumber. **(no) me importa un ~o** I couldn't care less

pepita *f* pip

pepitoria *f* fricassee

pequeñ|ez *f* smallness; *(minucia)* trifle. **~ito** *a* very small, tiny. **~o** *a* small, little. **de ~o** as a child. **en ~o** in miniature

pequinés *m (perro)* Pekingese

pera *f (fruta)* pear. **~l** *m* pear (tree)

percance *m* setback

percatarse *vpr.* ~ **de** notice

perc|epción *f* perception. **~eptible** *a* perceptible. **~eptivo** *a* perceptive. **~ibir** *vt* perceive; earn *(dinero)*

percusión *f* percussion

percutir *vt* tap

percha *f* hanger; *(de aves)* perch. **de ~** off the peg

perde|dor *a* losing. **—m** loser. **~r** [1] *vt* lose; *(malgastar)* waste; miss *(tren etc)*. **—vi** lose; *(tela)* fade. **~rse** *vpr* get lost; *(desaparecer)* disappear; *(desperdiciarse)* be wasted; *(estropearse)* be spoilt. **echar(se) a ~r** spoil

pérdida *f* loss; *(de líquido)* leak; *(de tiempo)* waste

perdido *a* lost

perdiz *f* partridge

perdón *m* pardon, forgiveness. **—int** sorry! **~onar** *vt* excuse, forgive; *(jurid)* pardon. **¡~one (Vd)!** sorry! **pedir ~ón** apologize

perdura|ble *a* lasting. **~r** *vi* last

perece|dero *a* perishable. **~r** [11] *vi* perish

peregrin|ación *f* pilgrimage. **~ar** *vi* go on a pilgrimage; *(fig, fam)* travel. **~o** *a* strange. **—m** pilgrim

perejil *m* parsley

perengano *m* so-and-so

perenne *a* everlasting; *(bot)* perennial

perentorio *a* peremptory

perez|a *f* laziness. **~oso** *a* lazy

perfec|ción *f* perfection. **~cionamiento** *m* perfection; *(mejora)* improvement. **~cionar** *vt* perfect; *(mejorar)* improve. **~cionista** *m* & *f* perfectionist. **~tamente** *adv* perfectly. **—int** of course! **~to** *a* perfect; *(completo)* complete. **a la ~ción** perfectly, to perfection

perfidia *f* treachery

pérfido *a* treacherous

perfil *m* profile; *(contorno)* outline; **~es** *mpl (fig, rasgos)* features. **~ado** *a (bien terminado)* well-finished. **~ar** *vt* draw in profile; *(fig)* put the finishing touches to

perfora|ción *f* perforation. **~do** *m* perforation. **~dora** *f* punch. **~r** *vt* pierce, perforate; punch *(papel, tarjeta etc)*

perfum|ar *vt* perfume. **~arse** *vpr* put perfume on. **~e** *m* perfume, scent. **~ería** *f* perfumery

pergamino *m* parchment

pericia *f* expertise

pericón m popular Argentinian dance

perif|eria f (de población) outskirts. **~érico** a peripheral

perilla f (barba) goatee

perímetro m perimeter

periódi|co a periodic(al). —m newspaper

periodis|mo m journalism. **~ta** m & f journalist

período m, **periodo** m period

periquito m budgerigar

periscopio m periscope

perito a & m expert

perju|dicar [7] vt harm; (desfavorecer) not suit. **~dicial** a harmful. **~icio** m harm. **en ~icio de** to the detriment of

perjur|ar vi perjure o.s. **~io** m perjury

perla f pearl. **de ~s** adv very well. **~a** excellent

permane|cer [11] vi remain. **~ncia** f permanence; (estancia) stay. **~nte** a permanent. —f perm

permeable a permeable

permi|sible a permissible. **~sivo** a permissive. **~so** m permission; (documento) licence; (mil etc) leave. **~so de conducción**, **~so de conducir** driving licence (Brit), driver's license (Amer). **~tir** vt allow, permit. **~tirse** vpr be allowed. **con ~so** excuse me. **¿me ~te?** may I?

permutación f exchange; (math) permutation

pernicioso a pernicious; (persona) wicked

pernio m hinge

perno m bolt

pero conj but. —m fault; (objeción) objection

perogrullada f platitude

perol m pan

peronista m & f follower of Juan Perón

perorar vi make a speech

perpendicular a & f perpendicular

perpetrar vt perpetrate

perpetu|ar [21] vt perpetuate. **~o** a perpetual

perplej|idad f perplexity. **~o** a perplexed

perr|a f (animal) bitch; (moneda) coin, penny (Brit), cent (Amer); (rabieta) tantrum. **~era** f kennel. **~ería** f (mala jugada) dirty trick; (palabra) harsh word. **~o** a awful. —m dog. **~o corredor** hound. **~o de aguas** spaniel. **~o del hortelano** dog in the manger. **~o galgo** greyhound. **de ~os** awful. **estar sin una ~a** be broke

persa a & m & f Persian

perse|cución f pursuit; (tormento) persecution. **~guir** [5 & 13] vt pursue; (atormentar) persecute

persevera|ncia f perseverance. **~nte** a persevering. **~r** vi persevere

persiana f (Venetian) blind

persist|encia f persistence. **~ente** a persistent. **~ir** vi persist

person|a f person. **~as** fpl people. **~aje** m (persona importante) important person; (de obra literaria) character. **~al** a personal; (para una persona) single. —m staff. **~alidad** f personality. **~arse** vpr appear in person. **~ificar** [7] vt personify. **~ificación** f personification

perspectiva f perspective

perspicac|ia f shrewdness; (de vista) keen eye-sight. **~z** a shrewd; (vista) keen

persua|dir vt persuade. **~sión** f persuasion. **~sivo** a persuasive

pertenecer [11] vi belong

pertinaz a persistent

pertinente a relevant

perturba|ción f disturbance. **~r** vt perturb

Perú m. **el ~** Peru

peruano a & m Peruvian

perver|sión f perversion. **~so** a perverse. **—m** pervert. **~tir** [4] vt pervert

pervivir vi live on

pesa f weight. **~dez** f weight; (de cabeza etc) heaviness; (lentitud) sluggishness; (cualidad de fastidioso) tediousness; (cosa fastidiosa) bore, nuisance

pesadilla f nightmare

pesad|o a heavy; (lento) slow; (duro) hard; (aburrido) boring, tedious. **~umbre** f (pena) sorrow

pésame m sympathy, condolences

pesar vt/i weigh. **—m** sorrow; (remordimiento) regret. **a ~ de (que)** in spite of. **me pesa que** I'm sorry that. **pese a (que)** in spite of

pesario m pessary

pesca f fishing; (peces) fish; (pescado) catch. **~da** f hake. **~dería** f fish shop. **~dilla** f whiting. **~do** m fish. **~dor** a fishing. **—m** fisherman. **~r** [7] vt catch. **—vi** fish. **ir de ~** go fishing

pescuezo m neck

pesebre m manger

pesero m (Mex) minibus taxi

peseta f peseta; (Mex) twenty-five centavos

pesimis|mo m pessimism. **~ta** a pessimistic. **—m & f** pessimist

pésimo a very bad, awful

peso m weight; (moneda) peso. **~ bruto** gross weight. **~ neto** net weight. **a ~** by weight. **de ~** influential

pesquero a fishing

pesquisa f inquiry

pestaña f eyelash. **~ear** vi blink. **sin ~ear** without batting an eyelid

peste f plague; (hedor) stench. **~icida** m pesticide. **~ilencia** f pestilence; (hedor) stench

pestillo m bolt

pestiño m pancake with honey

petaca f tobacco case; (LAm, maleta) suitcase

pétalo m petal

petardo m firework

petición f request; (escrito) petition. **a ~ de** at the request of

petirrojo m robin

petrificar [7] vt petrify

petró|leo m oil. **~olero** a oil. **—m** oil tanker. **~olífero** a oil-bearing

petulante a arrogant

peyorativo a pejorative

pez f fish; (substancia negruzca) pitch. **~ espada** swordfish

pezón m nipple; (bot) stalk

pezuña f hoof

piada f chirp

piadoso a compassionate; (devoto) devout

pian|ista m & f pianist. **~o** m piano. **~o de cola** grand piano

piar [20] vi chirp

pib|a f (LAm) little girl. **~e** m (LAm) little boy

picad|illo m mince; (guiso) stew. **~o** a perforated; (carne) minced; (ofendido) offended; (mar) choppy; (diente) bad. **~ura** f bite, sting; (de polilla) moth hole

picante a hot; (palabras etc) cutting

picaporte m door-handle; (aldaba) knocker

picar [7] vt prick, pierce; (ave) peck; (insecto, pez) bite; (avispa) sting; (comer poco) pick at; mince (carne). **—vi** prick; (ave) peck; (insecto, pez) bite; (sol) scorch; (sabor fuerte) be hot. **~ alto** aim high

picard|ear vt corrupt. **~ía** f wickedness; (travesura) naughty thing

picaresco *a* roguish; ⟨*literatura*⟩ picaresque

pícaro *a* villainous; ⟨*niño*⟩ mischievous. —*m* rogue

picatoste *m* toast; ⟨*frito*⟩ fried bread

picazón *f* itch

pico *m* beak; ⟨*punta*⟩ corner; ⟨*herramienta*⟩ pickaxe; ⟨*cima*⟩ peak. ~**tear** *vt* peck; ⟨*comer, fam*⟩ pick at. **y** ~ ⟨*con tiempo*⟩ a little after; ⟨*con cantidad*⟩ a little more than

picudo *a* pointed

pich|ona *f* ⟨*fig*⟩ darling; ~**ón** *m* pigeon

pido *vb véase* **pedir**

pie *m* foot; ⟨*bot, de vaso*⟩ stem. ~ **cuadrado** square foot. **a** ~**s** on all fours. **al** ~ **de la letra** literally. **a** ~ on foot. **a** ~**(s) juntillas** ⟨*fig*⟩ firmly. **buscarle tres** ~**s al gato** split hairs. **de** ~ standing (up). **de** ~ **a cabeza** from head to foot. **en** ~ standing (up). **ponerse de/en** ~ stand up

piedad *f* pity; ⟨*relig*⟩ piety

piedra *f* stone; ⟨*de mechero*⟩ flint; ⟨*granizo*⟩ hailstone

piel *f* skin; ⟨*cuero*⟩ leather. **artículos de** ~ leather goods

pienso *vb véase* **pensar**

pierdo *vb véase* **perder**

pierna *f* leg. **estirar las** ~**s** stretch one's legs

pieza *f* piece; ⟨*parte*⟩ part; ⟨*obra teatral*⟩ play; ⟨*moneda*⟩ coin; ⟨*habitación*⟩ room. ~ **de recambio** spare part

pífano *m* fife

pigment|ación *f* pigmentation. ~**o** *m* pigment

pigmeo *a* & *m* pygmy

pijama *m* pyjamas

pila *f* ⟨*montón*⟩ pile; ⟨*recipiente*⟩ basin; ⟨*eléctrica*⟩ battery. ~ **bautismal** font

píldora *f* pill

pilot|ar *vt* pilot. ~**o** *m* pilot

pilla|je *m* pillage. ~**r** *vt* pillage; ⟨*alcanzar, agarrar*⟩ catch; ⟨*atropellar*⟩ run over

pillo *a* wicked. —*m* rogue

pim|entero *m* ⟨*vasija*⟩ pepperpot. ~**entón** *m* paprika, cayenne pepper. ~**ienta** *f* pepper. ~**iento** *m* pepper. **grano** *m* **de** ~**ienta** peppercorn

pináculo *m* pinnacle

pinar *m* pine forest

pincel *m* paintbrush. ~**ada** *f* brush-stroke. **la última** ~**ada** ⟨*fig*⟩ the finishing touch

pinch|ar *vt* pierce, prick; puncture ⟨*neumático*⟩; ⟨*fig, incitar*⟩ push; ⟨*med, fam*⟩ give an injection to. ~**azo** *m* prick; ⟨*en neumático*⟩ puncture. ~**itos** *mpl* kebab(s); ⟨*tapas*⟩ savoury snacks. ~**o** *m* point

pingajo *m* rag. ~**o** *m* rag

ping-pong *m* table tennis, ping-pong

pingüino *m* penguin

pino *m* pine (tree)

pint|a *f* spot; ⟨*fig, aspecto*⟩ appearance. ~**ada** *f* graffiti. ~**ar** *vt* paint. ~**arse** *vpr* put on make-up. ~**or** *m* painter. ~**or de brocha gorda** painter and decorator. ~**oresco** *a* picturesque. ~**ura** *f* painting. **no** ~**a nada** ⟨*fig*⟩ it doesn't count. **tener** ~**a de** look like

pinza *f* ⟨*clothes-*⟩**peg** ⟨*Brit*⟩, ⟨*clothes-*⟩**pin** ⟨*Amer*⟩; ⟨*de cangrejo etc*⟩ claw. ~**s** *fpl* tweezers

pinzón *m* chaffinch

piña *f* pine cone; ⟨*ananás*⟩ pineapple; ⟨*fig, grupo*⟩ group. ~**ón** *m* ⟨*semilla*⟩ pine nut

pío *a* pious; ⟨*caballo*⟩ piebald. —*m* chirp. **no decir (ni)** ~ not say a word

piocha *f* pickaxe

piojo *m* louse

pionero *m* pioneer

pipa f pipe; (semilla) seed; (de girasol) sunflower seed

pipián m (LAm) stew

pique m resentment; (rivalidad) rivalry. irse a ~ sink

piqueta f pickaxe

piquete m picket

piragua f canoe

pirámide f pyramid

pirata m & f pirate

Pirineos mpl Pyrenees

piropo m (fam) compliment

pirueta f pirouette. ~ear vi pirouette

piruli m lollipop

pisa|da f footstep; (huella) footprint. ~papeles m invar paperweight. ~r vt tread on; (apretar) press; (fig) walk over. —vi tread. no ~r el césped keep off the grass

piscina f swimming pool; (para peces) fish-pond

Piscis m Pisces

piso m floor; (vivienda) flat (Brit), apartment (Amer); (de zapato) sole

pisotear vt trample (on)

pista f track; (fig, indicio) clue. ~ de aterrizaje runway. ~ de baile dance floor. ~ de hielo skating-rink. ~ de tenis tennis court

pistacho m pistachio (nut)

pisto m fried vegetables

pistol|a f pistol. ~era f holster. ~ero m gunman

pistón m piston

pit|ar vt whistle at. —vi blow a whistle; (auto) sound one's horn. ~ido m whistle

pitillera f cigarette case. ~o m cigarette

pito m whistle; (auto) horn

pitón m python

pitorre|arse upr. ~arse de make fun of. ~o m teasing

pitorro m spout

pivote m pivot

pizarr|a f slate; (encerrado) blackboard. ~ón m (LAm) blackboard

pizca f (fam) tiny piece; (de sal) pinch. ni ~ not at all

pizz|a f pizza. ~ería f pizzeria

placa f plate; (conmemorativa) plaque; (distintivo) badge

pláceme m congratulations

place|ntero a pleasant. ~r [32] vt please. me ~ I like. —m pleasure

plácido a placid

plaga f plague; (fig, calamidad) disaster; (fig, abundancia) glut. ~r [12] vt fill

plagi|ar vt plagiarize. ~o m plagiarism

plan m plan; (med) course of treatment. a todo ~ on a grand scale. en ~ de as

plana f (llanura) plain; (página) page. en primera ~ on the front page

plancha f iron; (lámina) sheet. ~do m ironing. ~r vt/i iron. a la ~ grilled. tirarse una ~ put one's foot in it

planeador m glider

planear vt plan. —vi glide

planeta m planet. ~rio a planetary. —m planetarium

planicie f plain

planifica|ción f planning. ~r [7] vt plan

planilla f (LAm) list

plano a flat. —m plane; (de ciudad) plan. primer ~ foreground; (foto) close-up

planta f (anat) sole; (bot, fábrica) plant; (plano) ground plan; (piso) floor. ~ baja ground floor (Brit), first floor (Amer)

planta|ción f plantation. ~do a planted. ~r vt plant; deal (golpe). ~r en la calle throw out. ~rse vpr stand; (fig) stand firm. bien ~do good-looking

plantear vt (exponer) expound; (causar) create; raise (cuestión)

plantilla f insole; (*modelo*) pattern; (*personal*) personnel

plaqué m plate

plasma m plasma

plástico a & m plastic

plata f silver; (*fig*, *dinero*, *fam*) money. ~ **de ley** sterling silver. ~ **alemana** nickel silver

plataforma f platform

plátano m plane (tree); (*fruta*) banana; (*platanero*) banana tree

platea f stalls (*Brit*), orchestra (*Amer*)

plateado a silver-plated; (*color de plata*) silver

pl|**ática** f chat, talk. ~**aticar** [7] vi chat, talk

platija f plaice

platillo m saucer; (*mus*) cymbal. ~ **volante** flying saucer

platino m platinum. ~**s** mpl (*auto*) points

plato m plate; (*comida*) dish; (*parte de una comida*) course

platónico a platonic

plausible a plausible; (*loable*) praiseworthy

playa f beach; (*fig*) seaside

plaza f square; (*mercado*) market; (*sitio*) place; (*empleo*) job. ~ **de toros** bullring

plazco vb véase **placer**

plazo m period; (*pago*) instalment; (*fecha*) date. **comprar a** ~**s** buy on hire purchase (*Brit*), buy on the installment plan (*Amer*)

plazuela f little square

pleamar f high tide

plebe f common people. ~**yo** a & m plebeian

plebiscito m plebiscite

plectro m plectrum

plega|**ble** a pliable; ‹*silla etc*› folding. ~**r** [1 & 12] vt fold. ~**rse** vpr bend; (*fig*) give way

pleito m (court) case; (*fig*) dispute

plenilunio m full moon

plen|**itud** f fullness; (*fig*) height. ~**o** a full. **en** ~**o día** in broad daylight. **en** ~**o verano** at the height of the summer

pleuresía f pleurisy

plieg|**o** m sheet. ~**ue** m fold; (*en ropa*) pleat

plinto m plinth

plisar vt pleat

plom|**ero** m (*esp LAm*) plumber. ~**o** m lead; (*elec*) fuse. **de** ~**o** lead

pluma f feather; (*para escribir*) pen. ~ **estilográfica** fountain pen. ~**je** m plumage

plúmbeo a leaden

plum|**ero** m feather duster; (*para plumas, lapices etc*) pencil-case. ~**ón** m down

plural a & m plural. ~**idad** f plurality; (*mayoría*) majority. **en** ~ in the plural

pluriempleo m having more than one job

plus m bonus

pluscuamperfecto m pluperfect

plusvalía f appreciation

plut|**ocracia** f plutocracy. ~**óc**-**rata** m & f plutocrat. ~**ocrático** a plutocratic

plutonio m plutonium

pluvial a rain

pobla|**ción** f population; (*ciudad*) city, town; (*pueblo*) village. ~**do** a populated. —m village. ~**r** [2] vt populate; (*habitar*) inhabit. ~**rse** vpr get crowded

pobre a poor. —m & f poor person; (*fig*) poor thing. ¡~**cito**! poor (little) thing! ¡~ **de mí**! poor (old) me! ~**za** f poverty

pocilga f pigsty

poción f potion

poco a not much, little; (*en plural*) few; (*unos*) a few. —m (a) little. —adv little, not much; (*con adjetivo*) not very; (*poco tiempo*) not long. ~ **a** ~ little by little, gradually. **a** ~ **de** soon after.

dentro de ~ soon. hace ~ not long ago. poca cosa nothing much. por ~ (fam) nearly

podar vt prune

poder [33] vt be able. no pudo venir he couldn't come. ¿puedo hacer algo? can I do anything? ¿puedo pasar? may I come in? —m power. ~es mpl públicos authorities. ~oso a powerful. en el ~ in power. no ~ con not be able to cope with; (no aguantar) not be able to stand. no ~ más be exhausted; (estar harto de algo) not be able to manage any more. no ~ menos que not be able to help. puede que it is possible that. puede ser it is possible. ¿se puede ...? may I ...?

podrido a rotten

po|ema m poem. ~esía f poetry; (poema) poem. ~eta m poet. ~ético a poetic

polaco a Polish. —m Pole; (lengua) Polish

polar a polar. estrella ~ polestar

polarizar [10] vt polarize

polca f polka

polea f pulley

pol|émica f controversy. ~émico a polemic(al). ~emizar [10] vi argue

polen m pollen

policía f police (force); (persona) policewoman. —m policeman. ~co a police; (novela etc) detective

policlínica f clinic, hospital

policromo, polícromo a polychrome

polideportivo m sports centre

poliéster m polyester

poliestireno m polystyrene

polietileno m polythene

pol|igamia f polygamy. ~ígamo a polygamous

políglota m & f polyglot

polígono m polygon

polilla f moth

polio(mielitis) f polio(myelitis)

pólipo m polyp

politécnic|a f polytechnic. ~o a polytechnic

polític|a f politics. ~o a political; (pariente) -in-law. —m politician. padre m ~o father-in-law

póliza f document; (de seguros) policy

polo m pole; (helado) ice lolly (Brit); (juego) polo. ~ helado ice lolly (Brit). ~ norte North Pole

Polonia f Poland

poltrona f armchair

polución f (contaminación) pollution

polv|areda f cloud of dust; (fig, escándalo) scandal. ~era f compact. ~o m powder; (suciedad) dust. ~os mpl powder. en ~o powdered. estar hecho ~o be exhausted. quitar el ~ dust

pólvora f gunpowder; (fuegos artificiales) fireworks

polvor|iento a dusty. ~ón m Spanish Christmas shortcake

poll|ada f brood. ~era f (para niños) baby-walker; (LAm, falda) skirt. ~ería f poultry shop. ~o m chicken; (gallo joven) chick

pomada f ointment

pomelo m grapefruit

pómez a. piedra f ~ pumice stone

pomp|a f bubble; (esplendor) pomp. ~as fúnebres funeral. ~oso a pompous; (espléndido) splendid

pómulo m cheek; (hueso) cheekbone

poncha|do a (Mex) punctured, flat. ~r vt (Mex) puncture

ponche m punch

poncho m poncho

ponderar vt (alabar) speak highly of

poner [34] vt put; put on (ropa, obra de teatro, TV etc); (suponer) suppose; lay (la mesa, un huevo); (hacer) make; (contribuir) contribute; give (nombre); show (película, interés); open (una tienda); equip (una casa). —vi lay. ~se upr put o.s.; (volverse) get; put on (ropa); (sol) set. ~ con (al teléfono) put through to. ~ en claro clarify. ~ por escrito put into writing. ~ una multa fine. ~se a start to. ~se a mal con uno fall out with s.o. pongamos let's suppose

pongo vb véase **poner**

poniente m west; (viento) west wind

pont|ificado m pontificate. ~ifical a pontifical. ~ificar [7] vi pontificate. ~ifice m pontiff

pontón m pontoon

popa f stern

popelín m poplin

popul|acho m masses. ~ar a popular; (lenguaje) colloquial. ~aridad f popularity. ~arizar [10] vt popularize. ~oso a populous

póquer m poker

poquito m a little bit. —adv a little

por prep for; (para) (in order) to; (a través de) through; (a causa de) because of; (como agente) by; (en matemática) times; (como función) as; (en lugar de) instead of. ~ la calle along the street. ~ mí as for me, for my part. ~ si in case. ~ todo el país throughout the country. **50 kilómetros ~ hora** 50 kilometres per hour

porcelana f china

porcentaje m percentage

porcino a pig. —m small pig

porción f portion; (de chocolate) piece

pordiosero m beggar

porf|ía f persistence; (disputa) dispute. ~iado a persistent. ~iar [20] vi insist. ~ía in competition

pormenor m detail

pornogr|afía f pornography. ~áfico a pornographic

poro m pore. ~so a porous

poroto m (LAm, judía) bean

porque conj because; (para que) so that

porqué m reason

porquería f filth; (basura) rubbish; (grosería) dirty trick

porra f club; (culin) fritter

porrón m wine jug (with a long spout)

portaaviones m invar aircraft-carrier

portada f façade; (de libro) title page

portador m bearer

porta|equipaje(s) m invar boot (Brit), trunk (Amer); (encima del coche) roof-rack. ~estandarte m standard-bearer

portal m hall; (puerta principal) main entrance; (soportal) porch

porta|lámparas m invar socket. ~ligas m invar suspender belt. ~monedas m invar purse

portarse upr behave

portátil a portable

portavoz m megaphone; (fig, persona) spokesman

portazgo m toll

portazo m bang. **dar un ~** slam the door

porte m transport; (precio) carriage. ~ador m carrier

portento m marvel

porteño a (de Buenos Aires) from Buenos Aires. —m person from Buenos Aires

porter|ía f caretaker's lodge, porter's lodge; (en deportes) goal. ~o m caretaker; porter; (en deportes) goalkeeper. ~o automático intercom (fam)

portezuela f small door; (auto) door

pórtico m portico

portilla f gate; (en barco) porthole. ~o m opening

portorriqueño a Puerto Rican

Portugal m Portugal

portugués a & m Portuguese

porvenir m future

posada f guest house; (mesón) inn

posaderas fpl (fam) bottom

posar vt put. —vi (pájaro) perch; (modelo) sit. ~se vpr settle

posdata f postscript

pose|edor m owner. ~er [18] vt have, own; (saber) know well. ~ído a possessed. ~sión f possession. ~sionar vt. ~sionar de hand over. ~sionarse vpr. ~sionarse de take possession of. ~sivo a possessive

posfechar vt postdate

posguerra f post-war years

posib|ilidad f possibility. ~le a possible. de ser ~le if possible. en lo ~le as far as possible. hacer todo lo ~le para do everything possible to. si es ~le if possible

posición f position

positivo a positive

poso m sediment

posponer [34] vt put after; (diferir) postpone

posta f. a ~ on purpose

postal a postal. —f postcard

poste m pole

postergar [12] vt pass over; (diferir) postpone

posteri|dad f posterity. ~or a back; (ulterior) later. ~ormente adv later

postigo m door; (contraventana) shutter

postizo a false, artificial. —m hairpiece

postra|do a prostrate. ~r vt prostrate. ~rse vpr prostrate o.s.

postre m dessert, sweet (Brit). de ~ for dessert

postular vt postulate; collect (dinero)

póstumo a posthumous

postura f position, stance

potable a drinkable; (agua) drinking

potaje m vegetable stew

potasio m potassium

pote m jar

poten|cia f power. ~cial a & m potential. ~te a powerful. en ~cia potential

potingue m (fam) concoction

potr|a f filly. ~o m colt; (en gimnasia) horse. tener ~a be lucky

pozo m well; (hoyo seco) pit; (de mina) shaft

pozole m (Mex) stew

prácti|ca f practice; (destreza) skill. en la ~ca in practice. poner en ~ca put into practice

practicable a practicable. ~nte m &f nurse. ~r [7] vt practise; play (deportes); (ejecutar) carry out

práctico a practical; (diestro) skilled. —m practitioner

prad|era f meadow; (terreno grande) prairie. ~o m meadow

pragmático a pragmatic

preámbulo m preamble

precario a precarious

precaución f precaution; (cautela) caution. con ~ cautiously

precaver vt guard against

precede|ncia f precedence; (prioridad) priority. ~nte a preceding. —m precedent. ~r vt/i precede

precepto m precept. ~r m tutor

precia|do a valuable; (estimado) esteemed. ~rse vpr boast

precinto m seal

precio m price. ~ de venta al público retail price. al ~ de at the cost of. no tener ~ be priceless. ¿qué ~ tiene? how much is it?

precios|idad _f_ value; (_cosa preciosa_) beautiful thing. **~o** _a_ precious; (_bonito_) beautiful. **¡es una ~idad!** it's beautiful!

precipicio _m_ precipice

precipita|ción _f_ precipitation. **~damente** _adv_ hastily. **~do** _a_ hasty. **~r** _vt_ hurl; (_acelerar_) accelerate; (_apresurar_) hasten. **~rse** _vpr_ throw o.s.; (_correr_) rush; (_actuar sin reflexionar_) act rashly

precis|amente _a_ exactly. **~ar** _vt_ require; (_determinar_) determine. **~ión** _f_ precision; (_necesidad_) need. **~o** _a_ precise; (_necesario_) necessary

preconcebido _a_ preconceived

precoz _a_ early; (_niño_) precocious

precursor _m_ forerunner

predecesor _m_ predecessor

predecir [46]; _o_ [46, _pero imperativo_ **predice**, _futuro y condicional regulares_] _vt_ foretell

predestina|ción _f_ predestination. **~r** _vt_ predestine

prédica _f_ sermon

predicamento _m_ influence

predicar [7] _vt/i_ preach

predicción _f_ prediction; (_del tiempo_) forecast

predilec|ción _f_ predilection. **~to** _a_ favourite

predisponer [34] _vt_ predispose

predomin|ante _a_ predominant. **~ar** _vt_ dominate. **—vi** dominate. **~io** _m_ predominance

preeminente _a_ pre-eminent

prefabricado _a_ prefabricated

prefacio _m_ preface

prefec|to _m_ prefect. **~ura** _f_ prefecture

prefer|encia _f_ preference. **~ente** _a_ preferential. **~ible** _a_ preferable. **~ido** _a_ favourite. **~ir** [4] _vt_ prefer. **de ~encia** preferably

prefigurar _vt_ foreshadow

prefij|ar _vt_ fix beforehand; (_gram_) prefix. **~o** _m_ prefix; (_telefónico_) dialling code

preg|ón _m_ announcement. **~onar** _vt_ announce

pregunta _f_ question. **~r** _vt/i_ ask. **~rse** _vpr_ wonder. **hacer ~s** ask questions

prehistórico _a_ prehistoric

preju|icio _m_ prejudice. **~zgar** [12] _vt_ prejudge

prelado _m_ prelate

preliminar _a & m_ preliminary

preludio _m_ prelude

premarital _a_, **prematrimonial** _a_ premarital

prematuro _a_ premature

premedita|ción _f_ premeditation. **~r** _vt_ premeditate

premi|ar _vt_ give a prize to; (_recompensar_) reward. **~o** _m_ prize; (_recompensa_) reward; (_com_) premium. **~o gordo** first prize

premonición _f_ premonition

premura _f_ urgency; (_falta_) lack

prenatal _a_ antenatal

prenda _f_ pledge; (_de vestir_) article of clothing, garment; (_de cama etc_) linen. **~s** _fpl_ (_cualidades_) talents; (_juego_) forfeits. **~r** _vt_ captivate. **~rse** _vpr_ be captivated (**de** by); (_enamorarse_) fall in love (**de** with)

prender _vt_ capture; (_sujetar_) fasten. **—vi** catch; (_arraigar_) take root. **~se** _vpr_ (_encenderse_) catch fire

prensa _f_ press. **~r** _vt_ press

preñado _a_ pregnant; (_fig_) full

preocupa|ción _f_ worry. **~do** _a_ worried. **~r** _vt_ worry. **~rse** _vpr_ worry. **~rse de** look after. **¡no te preocupes!** don't worry!

prepara|ción _f_ preparation. **~do** _a_ prepared. **—m** preparation. **~r** _vt_ prepare. **~rse** _vpr_ get ready. **~tivo** _a_ preparatory. **—**

m preparation. ∼**torio** *a* preparatory

preponderancia *f* preponderance

preposición *f* preposition

prepotente *a* powerful; *(fig)* presumptuous

prerrogativa *f* prerogative

presa *f* *(acción)* capture; *(cosa)* catch; *(embalse)* dam

presagi|ar *vt* presage. ∼**o** *m* omen; *(premonición)* premonition

présbita *a* long-sighted

presb|iteriano *a* & *m* Presbyterian. ∼**iterio** *m* presbytery. ∼**ítero** *m* priest

prescindir *vi.* ∼ **de** do without; *(deshacerse de)* dispense with

prescri|bir *(pp* prescrito*)* *vt* prescribe. ∼**pción** *f* prescription

presencia *f* presence; *(aspecto)* appearance. ∼**r** *vt* be present at; *(ver)* witness. **en** ∼ **de** in the presence of

presenta|ble *a* presentable. ∼**ción** *f* presentation; *(aspecto)* appearance; *(de una persona a otra)* introduction. ∼**dor** *m* presenter. ∼**r** *vt* present; *(ofrecer)* offer; *(hacer conocer)* introduce; show *(película).* ∼**rse** *vpr* present o.s.; *(hacerse conocer)* introduce o.s.; *(aparecer)* turn up

presente *a* present; *(este)* this. —*m* present. **los** ∼**s** those present. **tener** ∼ remember

presenti|miento *m* presentiment; *(de algo malo)* foreboding. ∼**r** [4] *vt* have a presentiment of

preserva|ción *f* preservation. ∼**r** *vt* preserve. ∼**tivo** *m* condom

presiden|cia *f* presidency; *(de asamblea)* chairmanship. ∼**cial** *a* presidential. ∼**ta** *f* (woman) president. ∼**te** *m* president; *(de*

asamblea) chairman. ∼**te del gobierno** leader of the government, prime minister

presidi|ario *m* convict. ∼**o** *m* prison

presidir *vt* preside over

presilla *f* fastener

presi|ón *f* pressure. ∼**onar** *vt* press; *(fig)* put pressure on. **a** ∼**ón** under pressure. **hacer** ∼**ón** press

preso *a* under arrest; *(fig)* stricken. —*m* prisoner

presta|do *a* *(a uno)* lent; *(de uno)* borrowed. ∼**mista** *m* & *f* moneylender. **pedir** ∼**do** borrow

préstamo *m* loan; *(acción de pedir prestado)* borrowing

prestar *vt* lend; give *(ayuda etc)*; pay *(atención).* ∼**i** lend

prestidigita|ción *f* conjuring. ∼**dor** *m* magician

prestigio *m* prestige. ∼**so** *a* prestigious

presu|mido *a* presumptuous. ∼**mir** *vi* presume. —*vi* be conceited. ∼**nción** *f* presumption. ∼**nto** *a* presumed. ∼**ntuoso** *a* presumptuous

presup|oner [34] *vt* presuppose. ∼**uesto** *m* budget

presuroso *a* quick

preten|cioso *a* pretentious. ∼**der** *vt* try to; *(afirmar)* claim; *(solicitar)* apply for; *(cortejar)* court. ∼**dido** *a* so-called. ∼**diente** *m* pretender; *(a una mujer)* suitor. ∼**sión** *f* pretension; *(aspiración)* aspiration

pretérito *m* preterite, past

pretexto *m* pretext. **a** ∼ **de** on the pretext of

prevalec|er [11] *vi* prevail. ∼**iente** *a* prevalent

prevalerse [42] *vpr* take advantage

preven|ción *f* prevention; *(prejuicio)* prejudice. ∼**ido** *a* ready;

(*precavido*) cautious. ~**ir** [53] *vt* prepare; (*proveer*) provide; (*precaver*) prevent; (*advertir*) warn. ~**tivo** *a* preventive

prever [43] *vt* foresee; (*prepararse*) plan

previo *a* previous

previs|ible *a* predictable. ~**ión** *f* forecast; (*prudencia*) prudence. ~**ión de tiempo** weather forecast. ~**to** *a* foreseen

prima *f* (*pariente*) cousin; (*cantidad*) bonus

primario *a* primary

primate *m* primate; (*fig, persona*) important person

primavera *f* spring. ~**l** *a* spring

primer *a véase* **primero**

primer|a *f* (*auto*) first (gear); (*en tren etc*) first class. ~**o** *a* (*delante de nombre masculino en singular* **primer**) first; (*principal*) main; (*anterior*) former; (*mejor*) best. —*n* (the) first. —*adv* first. ~**a enseñanza** primary education. **a** ~**os de** at the beginning of. **de** ~**a** first-class

primitivo *a* primitive

primo *m* cousin; (*fam*) fool. **hacer el** ~ be taken for a ride

primogénito *a* & *m* first-born, eldest

primor *m* delicacy; (*cosa*) beautiful thing

primordial *a* basic

princesa *f* princess

principado *m* principality

principal *a* principal. —*m* (*jefe*) head, boss (*fam*)

príncipe *m* prince

principi|ante *m* & *f* beginner. ~**ar** *vt/i* begin, start. ~**o** *m* beginning; (*moral, idea*) principle; (*origen*) origin. **al** ~**o** at first. **a** ~**o(s) de** at the beginning of. **dar** ~**o a** a start. **desde el** ~**o** from the outset. **en** ~ in principle. ~**os** *mpl* (*nociones*) rudiments

pring|oso *a* greasy. ~**ue** *m* dripping; (*mancha*) grease mark

prior *m* prior. ~**ato** *m* priory

prioridad *f* priority

prisa *f* hurry, haste. **a** ~ quickly. **a toda** ~ (*fam*) as quickly as possible. **correr** ~ be urgent. **darse** ~ hurry (up). **de** ~ quickly. **tener** ~ be in a hurry

prisi|ón *f* prison; (*encarcelamiento*) imprisonment. ~**onero** *m* prisoner

prisma *m* prism. ~**áticos** *mpl* binoculars

privaci|ón *f* deprivation. ~**do** *a* (*particular*) private. ~**r** *vt* deprive (**de** of); (*prohibir*) prevent (**de** from). —*vi* be popular. ~**tivo** *a* exclusive (**de** to)

privilegi|ado *a* privileged; (*muy bueno*) exceptional. ~**o** *m* privilege

pro *prep* for. —*m* advantage. —*pref* pro-. **el** ~ **y el contra** the pros and cons. **en** ~ **de** on behalf of. **los** ~**s y los contras** the pros and cons

proa *f* bows

probab|ilidad *f* probability. ~**le** *a* probable, likely. ~**lemente** *adv* probably

proba|dor *m* fitting-room. ~**r** [2] *vt* try; try on (*ropa*); (*demostrar*) prove. —*vi* try. ~**rse** *vpr* try on

probeta *f* test-tube

problem|a *m* problem. ~**ático** *a* problematic

procaz *a* insolent

proced|encia *f* origin. ~**ente** *a* (*razonable*) reasonable. ~**ente de** (coming) from. ~**er** *m* conduct. —*vi* proceed. ~**er con tra** start legal proceedings against. ~**er de** come from. ~**imiento** *m* procedure; (*sistema*) process; (*jurid*) proceedings

procesador *m*. ~ **de textos** word processor

procesal *a.* costas ~es legal costs

procesamiento *m* processing. ~ **de textos** word-processing

procesar *vt* prosecute

procesión *f* procession

proceso *m* process; *(jurid)* trial; *(transcurso)* course

proclama *f* proclamation. ~**ción** *f* proclamation. ~**r** *vt* proclaim

procreación *f* procreation. ~**r** *vt* procreate

procurador *m* attorney, solicitor. ~**r** *vt* try; *(obtener)* get; *(dar)* give

prodigar [12] *vt* lavish. ~**se** *vpr* do one's best

prodigio *m* prodigy; *(milagro)* miracle. ~**ioso** *a* prodigious

pródigo *a* prodigal

producción *f* production. ~**ir** [47] *vt* produce; *(causar)* cause. ~**irse** *vpr* *(aparecer)* appear; *(suceder)* happen. ~**tivo** *a* productive. ~**to** *m* product. ~**tor** *m* producer. ~**to** ~**derivado** by-product. ~**tos agrícolas** farm produce. ~**tos de belleza** cosmetics. ~**tos de consumo** consumer goods

proeza *f* exploit

profanación *f* desecration. ~**ar** *vt* desecrate. ~**o** *a* profane

profecía *f* prophecy

proferir [4] *vt* utter; hurl *(insultos etc)*

profesar *vt* profess; practise *(profesión)*. ~**ión** *f* profession. ~**ional** *a* professional. ~**or** *m* teacher; *(en universidad etc)* lecturer. ~**orado** *m* teaching profession; *(conjunto de profesores)* staff

profeta *m* prophet. ~**ético** *a* prophetic. ~**etizar** [10] *vt/i* prophesize

prófugo *a* & *m* fugitive

profundidad *f* depth. ~**o** *a* deep; *(fig)* profound

profusión *f* profusion. ~**o** *a* profuse. con ~**ión** profusely

progenie *f* progeny

programa *m* programme; *(de ordenador)* program; *(de estudios)* curriculum. ~**ción** *f* programming; *(TV etc)* programmes; *(en periódico)* TV guide. ~**r** *vt* programme; program *(ordenador)*. ~**dor** *m* computer programmer

progresar *vi* (make) progress. ~**ión** *f* progression. ~**ista** *a* progressive. ~**ivo** *a* progressive. ~**o** *m* progress. hacer ~**os** make progress

prohibición *f* prohibition. ~**do** *a* forbidden. ~**r** *vt* forbid. ~**tivo** *a* prohibitive

prójimo *m* fellow man

prole *f* offspring

proletariado *m* proletariat. ~**o** *a* & *m* proletarian

proliferación *f* proliferation. ~**iferar** *vi* proliferate. ~**ífico** *a* prolific

prolijo *a* long-winded, extensive

prólogo *m* prologue

prolongar [12] *vt* prolong; *(alargar)* lengthen. ~**se** *vpr* go on

promedio *m* average

promesa *f* promise. ~**ter** *vt/i* promise. ~**terse** *vpr* *(novios)* get engaged. ~**térselas muy felices** have high hopes. ~**tida** *f* fiancée. ~**tido** *a* promised; *(novios)* engaged. —*m* fiancé

prominencia *f* prominence. ~**te** *a* prominent

promiscuidad *f* promiscuity. ~**o** *a* promiscuous

promoción *f* promotion

promontorio *m* promontory

promotor *m* promoter. ~**ver** [2] *vt* promote; *(causar)* cause

promulgar [12] *vt* promulgate

pronombre *m* pronoun

pron|osticar [7] *vt* predict. ~**óstico** *m* prediction; (*del tiempo*) forecast; (*med*) prognosis

pront|itud *f* quickness. ~**o** *a* quick; (*preparado*) ready. —*adv* quickly; (*dentro de poco*) soon; (*temprano*) early. —*m* urge. **al** ~**o** at first. **de** ~**o** suddenly. **por lo** ~**o** for the time being; (*al menos*) anyway. **tan** ~**o como** as soon as

pronuncia|ción *f* pronunciation. ~**miento** *m* revolt. ~**r** *vt* pronounce; deliver (*discurso*). ~**rse** *vpr* be pronounced; (*declarase*) declare o.s.; (*sublevarse*) rise up

propagación *f* propagation

propaganda *f* propaganda; (*anuncios*) advertising

propagar [12] *vt/i* propagate. ~**se** *vpr* spread

propano *m* propane

propasarse *vpr* go too far

propens|ión *f* inclination. ~**o** *a* inclined

propiamente *adv* exactly

propici|ar *vt* (*provocar*) cause, bring about. ~**o** *a* favourable

propie|dad *f* property; (*posesión*) possession. ~**tario** *m* owner

propina *f* tip

propio *a* own; (*característico*) typical; (*natural*) natural; (*apropiado*) proper. **de** ~ on purpose. **el médico** ~ the doctor himself

proponer [34] *vt* propose. ~**se** *vpr* propose

proporci|ón *f* proportion. ~**onado** *a* proportioned. ~**onal** *a* proportional. ~**onar** *vt* proportion; (*facilitar*) provide

proposición *f* proposition

propósito *m* intention. **a** ~ (*adrede*) on purpose; (*de paso*) incidentally. **a** ~ **de** with regard to. **de** ~ on purpose

propuesta *f* proposal

propuls|ar *vt* propel; (*fig*) promote. ~**ión** *f* propulsion. ~**ión a chorro** jet propulsion

prórroga *f* extension

prorrogar [12] *vt* extend

prorrumpir *vi* burst out

prosa *f* prose. ~**ico** *a* prosaic

proscri|bir (*pp* **proscrito**) *vt* banish; (*prohibido*) ban. ~**to a** banned. —*m* exile; (*persona*) outlaw

prosecución *f* continuation

proseguir [5 & 13] *vt/i* continue

prospección *f* prospecting

prospecto *m* prospectus

prosper|ar *vi* prosper. ~**idad** *f* prosperity; (*éxito*) success

próspero *a* prosperous. **¡P~ Año Nuevo!** Happy New Year!

prostit|ución *f* prostitution. ~**uta** *f* prostitute

protagonista *m & f* protagonist

prote|cción *f* protection. ~**ctor** *a* protective. —*m* protector; (*patrocinador*) patron. ~**ger** [14] *vt* protect. ~**gida** *f* protegée. ~**gido** *a* protected. —*m* protegé

proteína *f* protein

protesta *f* protest; (*declaración*) protestation

protestante *a & m & f* (*relig*) Protestant

protestar *vt/i* protest

protocolo *m* protocol

protuberan|cia *f* protuberance. ~**te** *a* protuberant

provecho *m* benefit. **¡buen** ~**!** enjoy your meal! **de** ~ useful. **en** ~ **de** to the benefit of. **sacar** ~ **de** benefit from

proveer [18] (*pp* **proveído** *y* **provisto**) *vt* supply, provide

provenir [53] *vi* come (**de** from)

proverbi|al *a* proverbial. ~**o** *m* proverb

providencia *f* providence. ~**l** *a* providential

provincia *f* province. ~**l** *a*, ~**no a** provincial

provisión f provision; (*medida*) measure. **~onal** a provisional

provisto a provided (**de** with)

provocación f provocation. **~r** [7] vt provoke; (*causar*) cause. **~tivo** a provocative

próximamente adv soon

proximidad f proximity

próximo a next; (*cerca*) near

proyección f projection. **~tar** vt hurl; cast (*luz*); show (*película*). **~til** m missile. **~to** m plan. **~to de ley** bill. **~tor** m projector. **en ~to** planned

prudencia f prudence. **~nte** a prudent, sensible

prueba f proof; (*examen*) test; (*de ropa*) fitting. **a ~** on trial. **a ~ de proof** against. **a ~ de agua** waterproof. **en ~ de** in proof of. **poner a ~** test

pruebo vb véase **probar**

psicoanálisis f psychoanalysis. **~alista** m & f psychoanalyst. **~alizar** [10] vt psychoanalyse

psicodélico a psychedelic

psicología f psychology. **~ológico** a psychological. **~ólogo** m psychologist

psicópata m & f psychopath

psicosis f psychosis

psique f psyche

psiquiatra m & f psychiatrist. **~atría** f psychiatry. **~átrico** a psychiatric

psíquico a psychic

ptas, pts abrev (*pesetas*) pesetas

púa f sharp point; (*bot*) thorn; (*de erizo*) quill; (*de peine*) tooth; (*mus*) plectrum

pubertad f puberty

publicación f publication. **~r** [7] vt publish; (*anunciar*) announce

publicidad f publicity; (*com*) advertising. **~tario** a advertising

público a public. —m public; (*de espectáculo etc*) audience. **dar al ~** publish

puchero m cooking pot; (*guisado*) stew. **hacer ~s** (*fig, fam*) pout

pude vb véase **poder**

púdico a modest

pudiente a rich

pudín m pudding

pudor m modesty. **~oso** a modest

pudrir (*pp* **podrido**) vt rot; (*fig, molestar*) annoy. **~se** vpr rot

pueblecito m small village. **~o** m town; (*aldea*) village; (*nación*) nation, people

puedo vb véase **poder**

puente m bridge; (*fig, fam*) long weekend. **~ colgante** suspension bridge. **~ levadizo** drawbridge. **hacer ~** (*fam*) have a long weekend

puerco a filthy; (*grosero*) coarse. —m pig. **~ espín** porcupine

pueril a childish

puerro m leek

puerta f door; (*en deportes*) goal; (*de ciudad*) gate. **~ principal** main entrance. **a ~ cerrada** behind closed doors

puerto m port; (*fig, refugio*) refuge; (*entre montañas*) pass. **~ franco** free port

Puerto Rico m Puerto Rico

puertorriqueño a & m Puerto Rican

pues adv (*entonces*) then; (*bueno*) well. —conj since

puesta f setting; (*en juegos*) bet. **~a de sol** sunset. **~a en escena** staging. **~a en marcha** starting. **~o** a put; (*vestido*) dressed. —m place; (*empleo*) position, job; (*en mercado etc*) stall. —conj. **~o que** since. **~o de socorro** first aid post

pugna f fight. **~r** vt fight

puja f effort; (*en subasta*) bid. **~r** vt struggle; (*en subasta*) bid

pulcro a neat

pulga f flea; (de juego) tiddly-wink. **tener malas ∼s** be bad-tempered

pulga|da f inch. **∼r** m thumb; (del pie) big toe

puli|do a neat. **∼mentar** vt polish. **∼mento** m polishing; (substancia) polish. **∼r** vt polish; (suavizar) smooth

pulm|ón m lung. **∼onar** a pulmonary. **∼onía** f pneumonia

pulpa f pulp

pulpería f (LAm) grocer's shop (Brit), grocery store (Amer)

púlpito m pulpit

pulpo m octopus

pulque m (Mex) pulque, alcoholic Mexican drink

pulsa|ción f pulsation. **∼dor** a pulsating. **—m** button. **∼r** vt (mus) play

pulsera f bracelet; (de reloj) strap

pulso m pulse; (muñeca) wrist; (firmeza) steady hand; (fuerza) strength; (fig, tacto) tact. **tomar el ∼ a uno** take s.o.'s pulse

pulular vi teem with

pulveriza|dor m (de perfume) atomizer. **∼r** [10] vt pulverize; atomize (líquido)

pulla f cutting remark

pum int bang!

puma m puma

puna f puna, high plateau

punitivo a punitive

punta f point; (extremo) tip; (clavo) (small) nail. **estar de ∼** be in a bad mood. **estar de ∼ con uno** be at odds with s.o. **ponerse de ∼ con uno** fall out with s.o. **sacar ∼ a** sharpen; (fig) find fault with

puntada f stitch

puntal m prop, support

puntapié m kick

puntear vt mark; (mus) pluck

puntera f toe

puntería f aim; (destreza) marksmanship

puntiagudo a sharp, pointed

puntilla f (encaje) lace. **de ∼s** on tiptoe

punto m point; (señal) dot; (de examen) mark; (lugar) spot, place; (de taxis) stand; (momento) moment; (punto final) full stop (Brit), period (Amer); (puntada) stitch; (de tela) mesh. **∼ de admiración** exclamation mark. **∼ de arranque** starting point. **∼ de exclamación** exclamation mark. **∼ de interrogación** question mark. **∼ de vista** point of view. **∼ final** full stop. **∼ muerto** (auto) neutral (gear). **∼ y aparte** full stop, new paragraph (Brit), period, new paragraph (Amer). **∼ y coma** semicolon. a **∼** on time; (listo) ready. a **∼ de** on the point of. **dos ∼s** colon. **en ∼** exactly. **hacer ∼** knit. **hasta cierto ∼** to a certain extent

puntuación f punctuation; (en deportes, acción) scoring; (en deportes, número de puntos) score

puntual a punctual; (exacto) accurate. **∼idad** f punctuality; (exactitud) accuracy

puntuar [21] vt punctuate. **—vi** score

punza|da f prick; (dolor) pain; (fig) pang. **∼nte** a sharp. **∼r** [10] vt prick

puñado m handful. a **∼s** by the handful

puñal m dagger. **∼ada** f stab

puñ|etazo m punch. **∼o** m fist; (de ropa) cuff; (mango) handle. **de su ∼o (y letra)** in his own handwriting

pupa f spot; (en los labios) cold sore. **hacer ∼** hurt. **hacerse ∼** hurt o.s.

pupila f pupil

pupitre m desk

puquío m (*Arg*) spring

puré m purée; (*sopa*) thick soup. **~ de patatas** mashed potato

pureza f purity

purga f purge. **~r** [12] vt purge. **~torio** m purgatory

purifica|ción f purification. **~r** [7] vt purify

purista m & f purist

puritano a puritanical. —m puritan

puro a pure; ⟨cielo⟩ clear; (*fig*) simple. —m cigar. **~ so. de pura casualidad** by sheer chance

púrpura f purple

purpúreo a purple

pus m pus

puse vb véase **poner**

pusilánime a cowardly

pústula f spot

puta f whore

putrefacción f putrefaction

pútrido a rotten, putrid

Q

que pron rel (*personas, sujeto*) who; (*personas, complemento*) whom; (*cosas*) which, that. —conj that. **¡~ tengan Vds buen viaje!** have a good journey! **¡que venga!** let him come! **¡~ venga o no venga** whether he comes or not. **a ~ I bet. creo que tiene razón** I think (that) he is right. **de ~** from which. **yo ~ tú** if I were you

qué a (*con sustantivo*) what; (*con a o adv*) how. —pron what. **¡~ bonito!** how nice. **¿en ~ piensas?** what are you thinking about?

quebra|da f gorge; (*paso*) pass. **~dizo** a fragile. **~do** a broken; (*com*) bankrupt. —m (*math*) fraction. **~dura** f fracture;

(*hondonada*) gorge. **~ntar** vt break; (*debilitar*) weaken. **~nto** m (*pérdida*) loss; (*daño*) damage. **~r** [1] vt break. —vi break; (*com*) go bankrupt. **~rse** vpr break

quechua a & m & f Quechuan

queda f curfew

quedar vi stay, remain; (*estar*) be; (*faltar, sobrar*) be left. **~ bien** come off well. **~se** vpr stay. **~ con** arrange to meet. **~ en** agree to. **~ en nada** come to nothing. **~ por** (+ *infinitivo*) remain to be (+ *pp*)

quehacer m job. **~es domésticos** household chores

queja f complaint; (*de dolor*) moan. **~arse** vpr complain (*de about*); (*gemir*) moan. **~ido** m moan. **~oso** a complaining

quema|do a burnt; (*fig, fam*) bitter. **~dor** m burner. **~dura** f burn. **~r** vt burn; (*prender fuego a*) set fire to. —vi burn. **~rse** vpr burn o.s.; (*consumirse*) burn up; (*con el sol*) get sunburnt. **~rropa** adv. **a ~rropa** point-blank

quena f Indian flute

quepo vb véase **caber**

queque m (*Mex*) cake

querella f (*riña*) quarrel, dispute; (*jurid*) charge

quer|er [35] vt want; (*amar*) love; (*necesitar*) need. **~er decir** mean. **~ido** a dear; (*amado*) loved. —m darling; (*amante*) lover. **como quiera** que since; (*de cualquier modo*) however. **cuando quiera que** whenever. **donde quiera** wherever. **¿quieres darme ese libro?** would you pass me that book? **quiere llover** it's trying to rain. **¿quieres un helado?** would you like an ice-cream? **quisiera ir a la playa** I'd like to go to the beach. **sin ~er** without meaning to

queroseno *m* kerosene

querubín *m* cherub

ques|**adilla** *f* cheesecake; (*Mex, empanadilla*) pie. **~o** *m* cheese. **~o de bola** Edam cheese

quiá *int* never!, surely not!

quicio *m* frame. **sacar de ~ a uno** infuriate s.o.

quiebra *f* break; (*fig*) collapse; (*com*) bankruptcy

quiebro *m* dodge

quien *pron rel* (*sujeto*) who; (*complemento*) whom

quién *pron interrogativo* (*sujeto*) who; (*tras preposición*) whom. **¿de ~?** whose. **¿de ~ son estos libros?** whose are these books?

quienquiera *pron* whoever

quiero *vb véase* querer

quiet|**o** *a* still; (*inmóvil*) motionless; (*carácter etc*) calm. **~ud** *f* stillness

quijada *f* jaw

quilate *m* carat

quilla *f* keel

quimera *f* (*fig*) illusion

químic|**a** *f* chemistry. **~o** *a* chemical. —*m* chemist

quincalla *f* hardware; (*de adorno*) trinket

quince *a & m* fifteen. **~ días** *a* fortnight. **~na** *f* fortnight. **~nal** *a* fortnightly

quincuagésimo *a* fiftieth

quiniela *f* pools coupon. **~s** *fpl* (football) pools

quinientos *a & m* five hundred

quinino *m* quinine

quinqué *m* oil-lamp; (*fig, fam*) shrewdness

quinquenio *m* (period of) five years

quinta *f* (*casa*) villa

quintaesencia *f* quintessence

quintal *m* a hundred kilograms

quinteto *m* quintet

quinto *a & m* fifth

quiosco *m* kiosk; (*en jardín*) summerhouse; (*en parque etc*) bandstand

quirúrgico *a* surgical

quise *vb véase* querer

quisque *pron*. **cada ~** (*fam*) (absolutely) everybody

quisquilla *f* trifle; (*camarón*) shrimp. **~oso** *a* irritable; (*chinchorrero*) fussy

quita|**manchas** *m invar* stain remover. **~nieves** *m invar* snow plough. **~r** *vt* remove, take away; take off (*ropa*); (*robar*) steal. **~ndo** (*a excepción de, fam*) apart from. **~rse** *vpr* be removed; take off (*ropa*). **~rse de** (*no hacerlo más*) stop. **~rse de en medio** get out of the way. **~sol** *m invar* sunshade

Quito *m* Quito

quizá(s) *adv* perhaps

quórum *m* quorum

R

rábano *m* radish. **~ picante** horseradish. **me importa un ~** I couldn't care less

rabi|**a** *f* rabies; (*fig*) rage. **~ar** *vi* (*de dolor*) be in great pain; (*estar enfadado*) be furious; (*fig, tener ganas, fam*) long. **~ar por algo** long for sth. **~ar por hacer algo** long to do sth. **~eta** *f* tantrum. **dar ~a** infuriate

rabino *m* Rabbi

rabioso *a* rabid; (*furioso*) furious; (*dolor etc*) violent

rabo *m* tail

racial *a* racial

racimo *m* bunch

raciocinio *m* reason; (*razonamiento*) reasoning

ración *f* share, ration; (*de comida*) portion

racional *a* rational. **~izar** [10] *vt* rationalize

racionar *vt* (*limitar*) ration; (*repartir*) ration out

racis|mo m racism. **~ta** a racist

racha f gust of wind; (fig) spate

radar m radar

radiación f radiation

radiactivi|dad f radioactivity. **~o** a radioactive

radiador m radiator

radial a radial

radiante a radiant

radical a & m & f radical

radicar [7] vi (estar) be. **~ en** (fig) lie in

radio m radius; (de rueda) spoke; (elemento metálico) radium. —f radio

radioactivi|dad f radioactivity. **~o** a radioactive

radio|difusión f broadcasting. **~emisora** f radio station. **~escucha** m & f listener

radiografía f radiography

radio|logía f radiology. **~ólogo** m radiologist

radioterapia f radiotherapy

radioyente m & f listener

raer [36] vt scrape off

ráfaga f (de viento) gust; (de luz) flash; (de ametralladora) burst

rafia f raffia

raído a threadbare

raigambre f roots; (fig) tradition

raíz f root. a **~ de** immediately after. **echar raíces** (fig) settle

raja f split; (culin) slice. **~r** vt split. **~rse** vpr split; (fig) back out

rajatabla. a ~ vigorously

ralea f sort

ralo a sparse

ralla|dor m grater. **~r** vt grate

rama f branch. **~s** branches. **~l** m branch. **en ~** raw

rambla f gully; (avenida) avenue

ramera f prostitute

ramifica|ción f ramification. **~rse** [7] upr branch out

ramilla f twig

ramillete m bunch

ramo m branch; (de flores) bouquet

rampa f ramp, slope

ramplón a vulgar

rana f frog. **ancas** fpl **de ~** frogs' legs. **no ser ~** not be stupid

rancio a rancid; (vino) old; (fig) ancient

ranch|ero m cook; (LAm, jefe de rancho) farmer. **~o** m (LAm) ranch, farm

rango m rank

ranúnculo m buttercup

ranura f groove; (para moneda) slot

rapar vt shave; crop (pelo)

rapaz a rapacious; (ave) of prey. —m bird of prey

rapidez f speed

rápido a fast, quick. —adv quickly. —m (tren) express. **~s** mpl rapids

rapiña f robbery. **ave** f **de ~** bird of prey

rapsodia f rhapsody

rapt|ar vt kidnap. **~o** m kidnapping; (de ira etc) fit; (éxtasis) ecstasy

raqueta f racquet

raramente adv seldom, rarely

rarefacción f rarefaction

rar|eza f rarity; (cosa rara) oddity. **~o** a rare; (extraño) odd. **es ~o que** it is strange that. **¡qué ~o!** how strange!

ras. a ~ de level with

rasar vt level; (rozar) graze

rasca|cielos m invar skyscraper. **~dura** f scratch. **~r** [7] vt scratch; (raspar) scrape

rasgar [12] vt tear

rasgo m stroke. **~s** mpl (facciones) features

rasguear vt strum; (fig, escribir) write

rasguñ|ar vt scratch. **~o** m scratch

raso a (llano) flat; (liso) smooth; (cielo) clear; (cucharada etc)

level; (*vuelo etc*) low. —*m* satin.
al ~ in the open air. **soldado** *m*
~ private
raspa *f* (*de pescado*) backbone
raspa|dura *f* scratch; (*acción*)
scratching. **~r** *vt* scratch;
(*rozar*) scrape
rastr|a *f* rake. **a ~as** dragging.
~ear *vt* track. **~eo** *m* dragging.
~ero *a* creeping; (*vuelo*) low.
~illar *vt* rake. **~illo** *m* rake. **~o**
m rake; (*huella*) track; (*señal*)
sign. **el R~o** the flea market in
Madrid. **ni ~o** not a trace
rata *f* rat
rate|ar *vt* steal. **~ría** *f* pilfering.
~ro *m* petty thief
ratifica|ción *f* ratification. **~r** [7]
vt ratify
rato *m* moment, short time. **~s**
libres spare time. **a ~s** at times.
hace un ~ a moment ago.
¡hasta otro ~! (*fam*) see you
soon! **pasar mal ~** have a rough
time
rat|ón *m* mouse. **~onera** *f*
mousetrap; (*madriguera*)
mouse hole
raud|al *m* torrent; (*fig*) floods.
~o *a* swift
raya *f* line; (*lista*) stripe; (*de pelo*)
parting. **~r** *vt* rule. —*vi* border
(**con** on). **a ~s** striped. **pasar de
la ~** go too far
rayo *m* ray; (*descarga eléctrica*)
lightning. **~s X** X-rays
raza *f* race; (*de animal*) breed. **de
~** (*caballo*) thoroughbred; (*perro*) pedigree
raz|ón *f* reason. **a ~ón de** at the
rate of. **perder la ~ón** go out of
one's mind. **tener ~ón** be right.
~onable *a* reasonable. **~on-
amiento** *m* reasoning. **~onar**
vt reason out. —*vi* reason
re *m* D; (*solfa*) re
reac|ción *f* reaction. **~cionario**
a & **~ción en** reactionary. **~ción en**

cadena chain reaction. **~tor** *m*
reactor; (*avión*) jet
real *a* (*de rey etc*) royal. —*m*
real, old Spanish coin
realce *m* relief; (*fig*) splendour
realidad *f* reality; (*verdad*) truth.
en ~ in fact
realis|mo *m* realism. **~ta** *a* real-
istic. —*m* & *f* realist; (*monárquico*) royalist
realiza|ción *f* fulfilment. **~r** [10]
vt carry out; make (*viaje*);
achieve (*meta*); (*vender*) sell.
~rse *vpr* (*plan etc*) be carried
out; (*sueño, predicción etc*) come
true; (*persona*) fulfil o.s.
realzar [10] *vt* (*fig*) enhance
reanima|ción *f* revival. **~r** *vt*
revive. **~rse** *vpr* revive
reanudar *vt* resume; renew
(*amistad*)
reaparecer [11] *vi* reappear
rearm|ar *vt* rearm. **~e** *m*
rearmament
reavivar *vt* revive
rebaja *f* reduction. **~do** *a* (*precio*) reduced. **~r** *vt* lower. **en ~s**
in the sale
rebanada *f* slice
rebaño *m* herd; (*de ovejas*) flock
rebasar *vt* exceed; (*dejar atrás*)
leave behind
rebatir *vt* refute
rebel|arse *vpr* rebel. **~de** *a*
rebellious. —*m* rebel. **~día** *f*
rebelliousness. **~ión** *f* rebellion
reblandecer [11] *vt* soften
rebosa|nte *a* overflowing. **~r** *vi*
overflow; (*abundar*) abound
rebot|ar *vt* bounce; (*rechazar*)
repel. —*vi* bounce; (*bala*) ricochet. **~e** *m* bounce, rebound. **de
~e** on the rebound
rebozar [10] *vt* wrap up; (*culin*)
coat in batter
rebullir [22] *vi* stir
rebusca|do *a* affected. **~r** [7] *vt*
search thoroughly
rebuznar *vi* bray

recabar vt claim

recado m errand; (*mensaje*) message. **dejar** ~ leave a message

reca|er [29] vi fall back; (*med*) relapse; (*fig*) fall. ~**ida** f relapse

recalcar [7] vt squeeze; (*fig*) stress

recalcitrante a recalcitrant

recalentar [1] vt (*de nuevo*) reheat; (*demasiado*) overheat

recamar vt embroider

recámara f small room; (*de arma de fuego*) chamber; (*LAm, dormitorio*) bedroom

recambio m change; (*de pluma etc*) refill. ~**s** mpl spare parts. **de** ~ spare

recapitula|ción f summing up. ~**r** vt sum up

recarg|ar [12] vt overload; (*aumentar*) increase; recharge (*batería*). ~**o** m increase

recat|ado a modest. ~**ar** vt hide. ~**arse** vpr make o.s. away; (*actuar discretamente*) act discreetly. ~**o** m prudence; (*modestia*) modesty. **sin** ~**arse**, **sin** ~**o** openly

recauda|ción f (*cantidad*) takings. ~**dor** m tax collector. ~**r** vt collect

recel|ar vt/i suspect. ~**o** m distrust; (*temor*) fear. ~**oso** a suspicious

recepción f reception. ~**onista** m & f receptionist

receptáculo m receptacle

recept|ivo a receptive. ~**or** m receiver

recesión f recession

receta f recipe; (*med*) prescription

recib|imiento m (*acogida*) welcome. ~**ir** vt receive; (*acoger*) welcome. —vi entertain. ~**irse** vpr graduate. ~**o** m receipt. **acusar** ~**o** acknowledge receipt

recién adv recently; (*casado, nacido etc*) newly. ~**ente** a recent; (*culin*) fresh

recinto m enclosure

recio a strong; (*voz*) loud. —adv hard; (*en voz alta*) loudly

recipiente m (*persona*) recipient; (*cosa*) receptacle

recíproco a reciprocal. **a la recíproca** vice versa

recital m recital; (*de poesías*) reading. ~**r** vt recite

reclama|ción f claim; (*queja*) complaint. ~**r** vt claim. —vi appeal

reclinar vi lean. ~**se** vpr lean

reclu|ir [17] vt shut away. ~**sión** f seclusion; (*cárcel*) prison. ~**so** m prisoner

recluta m recruit. —f recruitment. ~**miento** m recruitment; (*conjunto de reclutas*) recruits. ~**r** vt recruit

recobrar vt recover. ~**se** vpr recover

recodo m bend

recog|er [14] vt collect; pick up (*cosa caída*); (*cosechar*) harvest; (*dar asilo*) shelter. ~**erse** vpr withdraw; (*ir a casa*) go home; (*acostarse*) go to bed. ~**ida** f collection; (*cosecha*) harvest. ~**ido** a withdrawn; (*pequeño*) small

recolección f harvest

recomenda|ción f recommendation. ~**r** [1] vt recommend; (*encomendar*) entrust

recomenzar [1 & 10] vt/i start again

recompensa f reward. ~**r** vt reward

recomponer [34] vt mend

reconcilia|ción f reconciliation. ~**r** vt reconcile. ~**rse** vpr reconciled

recóndito a hidden

reconoc|er [11] vt recognize; (*admitir*) acknowledge; (*examinar*) examine. ~**imiento** m recognition; (*admisión*) acknowledgement; (*agradecimiento*) gratitude; (*examen*) examination

reconozco *vb véase* **reconocer**

reconquista *f* reconquest. ~r *vt* reconquer; (*fig*) win back

reconsiderar *vt* reconsider

reconstituir [17] *vt* reconstitute. ~yente *m* tonic

reconstru|cción *f* reconstruction. ~ir [17] *vt* reconstruct

récord /'rekor/ *m* record. **batir un** ~ break a record

recordar [2] *vt* remember; (*hacer acordar*) remind; (*Lam, despertar*) wake up. —*vi* remember. **que yo recuerde** as far as I remember. **si mal no recuerdo** if I remember rightly

recorr|er *vt* tour (*país*); (*pasar por*) travel through; cover (*distancia*); (*registrar*) look over. ~ido *m* journey; (*itinerario*) route

recort|ado *a* jagged. ~ar *vt* cut (out). ~e *m* cutting (out); (*de periódico etc*) cutting

recoser *vt* mend

recostar [2] *vt* lean. ~se *vpr* lie back

recoveco *m* bend; (*rincón*) nook

recre|ación *f* recreation. ~ar *vt* re-create; (*divertir*) entertain. ~arse *vpr* amuse o.s. ~ativo *a* recreational. ~o *m* recreation; (*escol*) break

recriminación *f* recrimination. ~r *vt* reproach

recrudecer [11] *vi* increase, worsen, get worse

recta *f* straight line

rect|angular *a* rectangular; (*triángulo*) right-angled. ~ángulo *a* rectangular; (*triángulo*) right-angled. —*m* rectangle

rectifica|ción *f* rectification. ~r [7] *vt* rectify

rect|itud *f* straightness; (*fig*) honesty. ~o *a* straight; (*fig,*

justo) fair; (*fig, honrado*) honest. —*m* rectum. **todo** ~o straight on

rector *a* governing. —*m* rector

recuadro *m* (*en periódico*) box

recubrir [*pp* **recubierto**] *vt* cover

recuerdo *m* memory; (*regalo*) souvenir. —*vb véase* **recordar**. ~s *mpl* (*saludos*) regards

recupera|ción *f* recovery. ~r *vt* recover. ~rse *vpr* recover. ~r **el tiempo perdido** make up for lost time

recur|rir *vi*. ~rir a resort to (*cosa*); turn to (*persona*). ~so *m* resort; (*medio*) resource; (*jurid*) appeal. ~sos *mpl* resources

recusar *vt* refuse

rechaz|ar [10] *vt* repel; reflect (*luz*); (*no aceptar*) refuse; (*negar*) deny. ~o *m*. **de** ~o on the rebound; (*fig*) consequently

rechifla *f* booing; (*burla*) derision

rechinar *vi* squeak; (*madera etc*) creak; (*dientes*) grind

rechistar *vi* murmur. **sin** ~ without saying a word

rechoncho *a* stout

red *f* network; (*malla*) net; (*para equipaje*) luggage rack; (*fig, engaño*) trap

redac|ción *f* editing; (*conjunto de redactores*) editorial staff; (*oficina*) editorial office; (*escol, univ*) essay. ~tar *vt* write. ~tor *m* writer; (*de periódico*) editor

redada *f* casting; (*de policía*) raid

redecilla *f* small net; (*para el pelo*) hairnet

rededor *m*. **al** ~, **en** ~ around

reden|ción *f* redemption. ~tor *a* redeeming

redil *f* sheepfold

redimir *vt* redeem

rédito *m* interest

redoblar *vt* redouble; (*doblar*) bend back

redoma f flask
redomado a sly
redond|a f (de imprenta) roman (type); (mus) semibreve (Brit), whole note (Amer). **~amente** adv (categóricamente) flatly. **~ear** vt round off. **~el** m circle; (de plaza de toros) arena. **~o** a round; (completo) complete. **—m** circle. **a la ~a** around; **en ~o** round; (categóricamente) flatly
reduc|ción f reduction. **~ido** a reduced; (limitado) limited; (pequeño) small; (precio) low. **~ir** [47] vt reduce. **~irse** vpr be reduced; (fig) amount
reduje vb véase **reducir**
redundan|cia f redundancy. **~te** a redundant
reduplicar [7] vt (aumentar) redouble
reduzco vb véase **reducir**
reedificar [7] vt reconstruct
reembols|ar vt reimburse. **~o** m repayment. **contra ~o** cash on delivery
reemplaz|ar [10] vt replace. **~o** m replacement
reemprender vt start again
reenviar [20] vt, **reexpedir** [5] vt forward
referencia f reference; (información) report. **con ~a** with reference to. **hacer ~a** refer to
referéndum m (pl referéndums) referendum
referir [4] vt tell; (remitir) refer. **~se** vpr refer. **por lo que se refiere a** as regards
refiero vb véase **referir**
refilón. de ~ obliquely
refin|amiento m refinement. **~ar** vt refine. **~ería** f refinery
reflector m reflector; (proyector) searchlight
reflej|ar vt reflect. **~o** a reflected; (med) reflex. **—m** reflection; (med) reflex; (en el pelo) highlights

reflexi|ón f reflection. **~onar** vi reflect. **~vo** a (persona) thoughtful; (gram) reflexive. **con ~ón** on reflection. **sin ~ón** without thinking
reflujo m ebb
reforma f reform. **~s** fpl (reparaciones) repairs. **~r** vt reform. **~rse** vpr reform
reforzar [2 & 10] vt reinforce
refrac|ción f refraction. **~tar** vt refract. **~tario** a heat-resistant
refrán m saying
refregar [1 & 12] vt rub
refrenar vt rein in (caballo); (fig) restrain
refrendar vt endorse
refresc|ar [7] vt refresh; (enfriar) cool. **—vi** get cooler. **~arse** vpr refresh o.s.; (salir) go out for a walk. **~o** m cold drink. **~os** mpl refreshments
refrigera|ción f refrigeration; (aire acondicionado) air-conditioning. **~r** vt refrigerate. **~dor** m, **~dora** f refrigerator
refuerzo m reinforcement
refugi|ado m refugee. **~arse** vpr take refuge. **~o** m refuge, shelter
refulgir [14] vi shine
refundir vt (fig) revise, rehash
refunfuñar vi grumble
refutar vt refute
regadera f watering-can; (Mex, ducha) shower
regala|damente adv very well. **~do** a as a present; free; (cómodo) comfortable. **~r** vt give; (agasajar) treat very well. **~rse** vpr indulge o.s.
regaliz m liquorice
regalo m present, gift; (placer) joy; (comodidad) comfort
regañ|adientes. a ~adientes reluctantly. **~ar** vt scold. **—vi** moan; (dos personas) quarrel. **~o** m (reprensión) scolding
regar [1 & 12] vt water

regata f regatta

regate m dodge; (en deportes) dribbling. **~ar** vt haggle over; (economizar) economize on. —vi haggle; (en deportes) dribble. **~o** m haggling; (en deportes) dribbling

regazo m lap

regencia f regency

regenerar vt regenerate

regente m & f regent; (director) manager

régimen m (pl regímenes) rule; (pol) regime; (med) diet. — **alimenticio** diet

regimiento m regiment

regio a royal

regi|ón f region. **~onal** a regional

regir [5 & 14] vt rule; govern (país); run (colegio, empresa). —vi apply, be in force

registr|ado a registered. **~ador** m recorder; (persona) registrar. **~ar** vt register; (grabar) record; (examinar) search. **~arse** vpr register; (darse) be reported. **~o** m (acción de registrar) registration; (libro) register; (cosa anotada) entry; (inspección) search. **~o civil** (oficina) register office

regla f ruler; (norma) rule; (menstruación) period, menstruation. **~mentación** f regulation. **~mentar** vt regulate. **~mentario** a obligatory. **~mento** m regulations. **en ~** in order. **por ~ general** as a rule

regocij|ar vt delight. **~arse** vpr be delighted. **~o** m delight. **~os** mpl festivities

regode|arse vpr be delighted. **~o** m delight

regordete a chubby

regres|ar vi return. **~ión** f regression. **~ivo** a backward. **~o** m return

reguer|a f irrigation ditch. **~o** m irrigation ditch; (señal) trail

regula|dor m control. **~r** a regular; (mediano) average; (no bueno) so-so. —vt regulate; (controlar) control. **~ridad** f regularity. **con ~ridad** regularly. **por lo ~r** as a rule

rehabilita|ción f rehabilitation; (en un empleo etc) reinstatement. **~r** vt rehabilitate; (al empleo etc) reinstate

rehacer [31] vt redo; (repetir) repeat; (reparar) repair. **~se** vpr recover

rehén m hostage

rehogar [12] vt sauté

rehuir [17] vt avoid

rehusar vt/i refuse

reimpr|esión f reprinting. **~imir** (pp **reimpreso**) vt reprint

reina f queen. **~do** m reign. **~nte** a ruling; (fig) prevailing. **~r** vi reign; (fig) prevail

reincidir vi relapse, repeat an offence

reino m kingdom. **R~ Unido** United Kingdom

reinstaurar vt restore

reintegr|ar vt reinstate (persona); refund (cantidad). **~arse** vpr return. **~o** m refund

reír [51] vi laugh. **~se** vpr laugh. **~se de** laugh at. **echarse a ~** burst out laughing

reivindica|ción f claim. **~r** [7] vt claim; (restaurar) restore

rej|a f grille, grating. **~illa** f grille, grating; (red) luggage rack; (de mimbre) wickerwork. **entre ~as** behind bars

rejuvenecer [11] vt/i rejuvenate. **~se** vpr be rejuvenated

relaci|ón f relation(ship); (relato) tale; (lista) list. **~onado** a concerning. **~onar** vt relate (con to). **~onarse** vpr be connected. **bien ~onado** well-connected. **con ~ón a, en ~ón**

a in relation to. **hacer ~ón a**
refer to

relaja|ción f relaxation; (*aflo-
jamiento*) slackening. **~do** a
loose. **~r** vt relax; (*aflojar*)
slacken. **~rse** vpr relax

relamerse vt lick one's lips

relamido a overdressed

rel|ámpago m (flash of) light-
ning. **~ampaguear** vi thunder;
(*fig*) sparkle

relatar vt tell, relate

relativ|idad f relativity. **~o** a
relative. **en lo ~o a** in relation
to

relato m tale; (*informe*) report

relegar [12] vt relegate. **~ al
olvido** forget about

relev|ante a outstanding. **~ar** vt
relieve; (*substituir*) replace. **~o**
m relief. **carrera f de ~os** relay
race

relieve m relief; (*fig*) importance. **de ~** important. **poner de
~** emphasize

religi|ón f religion. **~osa** f nun.
~oso a religious. —m monk

relinchar vi neigh. **~o** m neigh

reliquia f relic

reloj m clock; (*de bolsillo o
pulsera*) watch. **~ de caja**
grandfather clock. **~ de
pulsera** wrist-watch. **~ de sol**
sundial. **~ despertador** alarm
clock. **~ería** f watchmaker's
(shop). **~ero** m watchmaker

reluci|ente a shining. **~r** [11] vi
shine; (*destellar*) sparkle

relumbrar vi shine

rellano m landing

rellen|ar vt refill; (*culin*) stuff;
fill in (*formulario*). **~o** a full up;
(*culin*) stuffed. —m filling;
(*culin*) stuffing

remach|ar vt rivet; (*fig*) drive
home. **~e** m rivet

remangar [12] vt roll up

remanso m pool; (*fig*) haven

remar vi row

remat|ado a (*total*) complete;
(*niño*) very naughty. **~ar** vt finish off; (*agotar*) use up; (*com*) sell
off cheap. **~e** m end; (*fig*) finishing touch. **de ~e** completely

remedar vt imitate

remedi|ar vt remedy; (*ayudar*)
help; (*poner fin a*) put a stop to;
(*fig, resolver*) solve. **~o** m remedy; (*fig*) solution. **como último
~o** as a last resort. **no hay más
~o** there's no other way. **no
tener más ~o** have no choice

remedo m imitation

remendar [1] vt repair. **~iendo**
m patch; (*fig, mejora*)
improvement

remilg|ado a fussy; (*afectado*)
affected. **~o** m fussiness; (*afectación*) affectation

reminiscencia f reminiscence

remirar vt look again at

remisi|ón f sending; (*referencia*)
reference; (*perdón*) forgiveness

remiso a remiss

remit|e m sender's name and
address. **~ente** m sender. **~ir** vt
send; (*referir*) refer. —vi
diminish

remo m oar

remoj|ar vt soak; (*fig, fam*) cel-
ebrate. **~o** m soaking. **poner a
~o** soak

remolacha f beetroot. **~ azuca-
rera** sugar beet

remolcar [7] vt tow

remolino m swirl; (*de aire etc*)
whirl; (*de gente*) throng

remolque m towing; (*cabo*) tow-
rope; (*vehículo*) trailer. **a ~** on
tow. **dar ~ a** tow

remontar vt mend. **~se** vpr soar;
(*con tiempo*) go back to

rémora f (*fig*) hindrance

remord|er [2] (*fig*) worry. **~imi-
ento** m remorse. **tener ~imi-
entos** feel remorse

remoto a remote

remover [2] *vt* move; stir ‹líquido›; turn over ‹tierra›; (quitar) remove; (fig, activar) revive

remozar [10] *vt* rejuvenate ‹persona›; renovate ‹edificio etc›

remunera|ción *f* remuneration. ~**r** *vt* remunerate

renac|er [11] *vi* be reborn; (fig) revive. ~**imiento** *m* rebirth. **R~** Renaissance

renacuajo *m* tadpole; (fig) tiddler

rencilla *f* quarrel

rencor *m* bitterness. ~**oso** *a* (estar) resentful; (ser) spiteful. **guardar** ~ **a** have a grudge against

rendi|ción *f* surrender. ~**do** *a* submissive; (agotado) exhausted

rendija *f* crack

rendi|miento *m* efficiency; (com) yield. ~**r** [5] *vt* yield; (vencer) defeat; (agotar) exhaust; pay ‹homenaje›. ~**vi** pay; (producir) produce. ~**rse** *vpr* surrender

renega|do *a & m* renegade. ~**r** [1 & 12] *vt* deny. ~**vi** grumble. ~**r de** renounce ‹fe etc›; disown ‹personas›

RENFE *abrev* (Red Nacional de los Ferrocarriles Españoles) Spanish National Railways

renglón *m* line; (com) item. **a** ~ **seguido** straight away

reno *m* reindeer

renombr|ado *a* renowned. ~**e** *m* renown

renova|ción *f* renewal; (de edificio) renovation; (de cuarto) decorating. ~**r** *vt* renew; renovate ‹edificio›; decorate ‹cuarto›

rent|a *f* income; (alquiler) rent; (deuda) national debt. ~**able** *a* profitable. ~**ar** *vt* produce, yield; (LAm, alquilar) rent, hire. ~**a vitalicia** (life) annuity. ~**ista** *m & f* person of independent means

renuncia *f* renunciation. ~**r** *vi*. ~**r a** renounce, give up

reñi|do *a* hard-fought. ~**r** [5 & 22] *vt* tell off. ~ quarrel. **estar** ~**do con** be incompatible with ‹cosas›; be on bad terms with ‹personas›

reo *m & f* culprit; (jurid) accused. ~ **de Estado** person accused of treason. ~ **de muerte** prisoner sentenced to death

reojo. mirar de ~ look out of the corner of one's eye at; (fig) look askance at

reorganizar [10] *vt* reorganize

repanchigarse [12] *vpr*, **repantigarse** [12] *vpr* sprawl out

repar|ación *f* repair; (acción) repairing; (fig, compensación) reparation. ~**ar** *vt* repair; (fig) make amends for; (notar) notice. ~**vi**. ~**ar en** notice; (hacer caso de) pay attention to. ~**o** *m* fault; (objeción) objection. **poner** ~**os** raise objections

repart|ición *f* division. ~**idor** *m* delivery man. ~**imiento** *m* distribution. ~**ir** *vt* distribute, share out; deliver ‹cartas, leche etc›; hand out ‹folleto, premio›. ~**o** *m* distribution; (de cartas, leche etc) delivery; (actores) cast

repas|ar *vt* go over; check ‹cuenta›; revise ‹texto›; (leer a la ligera) glance through; (coser) mend. ~**vi** go back. ~**o** *m* revision; (de ropa) mending. **dar un** ~ look through

repatria|ción *f* repatriation. ~**r** *vt* repatriate

repecho *m* steep slope

repele|nte *a* repulsive. ~**r** *vt* repel

repensar [1] *vt* reconsider

repente. de ~ suddenly. ~**ino** *a* sudden

repercu|sión *f* repercussion. ~**tir** *vi* reverberate; (fig) have repercussions (**en** on)

repertorio *m* repertoire; (*lista*) index

repeti|ción *f* repetition; (*mus*) repeat. ~**damente** *adv* repeatedly. ~**r** [5] *vt* repeat; (*imitar*) copy; —*vi.* ~**r de** have a second helping of. ¡**que se repita!** encore!

repi|car [7] *vt* ring (*campanas*). ~**que** *m* peal

repisa *f* shelf. ~ **de chimenea** mantlepiece

repito *vb véase* **repetir**

replegarse [1 & 12] *vpr* withdraw

repleto *a* full up

réplica *a* answer; (*copia*) replica

replicar [7] *vi* answer

repliegue *m* crease; (*mil*) withdrawal

repollo *m* cabbage

reponer [34] *vt* replace; revive ⟨*obra de teatro*⟩; (*contestar*) reply. ~**se** *vpr* recover

report|aje *m* report. ~**ero** *m* reporter

repos|ado *a* quiet; (*sin prisa*) unhurried. ~**ar** *vi* rest. ~**arse** *vpr* settle. ~**o** *m* rest

repost|ar *vt* replenish; refuel ⟨*avión*⟩; fill up ⟨*coche etc*⟩. ~**ería** *f* cake shop

repren|der *vt* reprimand. ~**sible** *a* reprehensible

represalia *f* reprisal. **tomar** ~**s** retaliate

representa|ción *f* representation; (*en el teatro*) performance. **en** ~**ción de** representing. ~**nte** *m* representative; (*actor*) actor. —*f* representative; (*actriz*) actress. ~**r** *vt* represent; perform ⟨*obra de teatro*⟩; play ⟨*papel*⟩; (*aparentar*) look. ~**rse** *vpr* imagine. ~**tivo** *a* representative

represi|ón *f* repression. ~**vo** *a* repressive

reprimenda *f* reprimand

reprimir *vt* supress. ~**se** *vpr* stop o.s.

reprobar [2] *vt* condemn; reproach ⟨*persona*⟩

réprobo *a* & *m* reprobate

reproch|ar *vt* reproach. ~**e** *m* reproach

reproduc|ción *f* reproduction. ~**ir** [47] *vt* reproduce. ~**tor** *a* reproductive

reptil *m* reptile

repúblic|a *f* republic. ~**ublicano** *a* & *m* republican

repudiar *vt* repudiate

repuesto *m* store; (*auto*) spare (part). **de** ~ in reserve

repugna|ncia *f* disgust. ~**nte** *a* repugnant. ~**r** *vt* disgust

repujar *vt* emboss

repuls|a *f* rebuff. ~**ión** *f* repulsion. ~**ivo** *a* repulsive

reputa|ción *f* reputation. ~**do** *a* reputable. ~**r** *vt* consider

requebrar [1] *vt* flatter

requemar *vt* scorch; (*culin*) burn; tan ⟨*piel*⟩

requeri|miento *m* request; (*jurid*) summons. ~**r** [4] *vt* need; (*pedir*) ask

requesón *m* cottage cheese

requete... *pref* extremely

requiebro *m* compliment

réquiem *m* (*pl* **réquiems**) *m* requiem

requis|a *f* inspection; (*mil*) requisition. ~**ar** *vt* requisition. ~**ito** *m* requirement

res *f* animal. ~ **lanar** sheep. ~ **vacuna** (*vaca*) cow; (*toro*) bull; (*buey*) ox. **carne de** ~ (*Mex*) beef

resabi|ado *a* well-known; ⟨*persona*⟩ pedantic

resabio *m* (unpleasant) aftertaste; (*vicio*) bad habit

resaca *f* undercurrent; (*después de beber alcohol*) hangover

resaltar *vi* stand out. **hacer** ~ emphasize

resarcir [9] *vt* repay; (*compensar*) compensate. **~se** *vpr* make up for

resbal|adizo *a* slippery. **~ar** *vi* slip; (*auto*) skid; (*líquido*) trickle. **~arse** *vpr* slip; (*auto*) skid; (*líquido*) trickle. **~ón** *m* slip; (*de vehículo*) skid

rescat|ar *vt* ransom; (*recuperar*) recapture; (*fig*) recover. **~e** *m* ransom; (*recuperación*) recapture; (*salvamento*) rescue

rescindir *vt* cancel

rescoldo *m* embers

resec|ar [7] *vt* dry up; (*med*) remove. **~se** *vpr* dry up

resenti|do *a* resentful. **~miento** *m* resentment. **~rse** *vpr* feel the effects; (*debilitarse*) be weakened; (*ofenderse*) take offence (**de** at)

reseña *f* account; (*en periódico*) report, review. **~r** *vt* describe; (*en periódico*) report on, review

resero *m* (*Arg*) herdsman

reserva *f* reservation; (*provisión*) reserve(s). **~ción** *f* reservation. **~do** *a* reserved. **~r** *vt* reserve; (*guardar*) keep, save. **~rse** *vpr* save o.s. **a ~ de** except for. **a ~ de que** unless. **de ~** in reserve

resfria|do *m* cold; (*enfriamiento*) chill. **~r** *vt*. **~r a uno** give s.o. a cold. **~rse** *vpr* catch a cold; (*fig*) cool off

resguard|ar *vt* protect. **~arse** *vpr* protect o.s.; (*fig*) take care. **~o** *m* protection; (*garantía*) guarantee; (*recibo*) receipt

resid|encia *f* residence; (*univ*) hall of residence, dormitory (*Amer*); (*de ancianos etc*) home. **~encial** *a* residential. **~ente** *a & m & f* resident. **~ir** *vi* reside; (*fig*) lie

residu|al *a* residual. **~o** *m* remainder. **~os** *mpl* waste

resigna|ción *f* resignation. **~damente** *adv* with resignation. **~r** *vt* resign. **~rse** *vpr* resign o.s. (**a**, **con** to)

resina *f* resin

resist|encia *f* resistence. **~ente** *a* resistent. **~ir** *vt* resist; (*soportar*) bear. **—vi** resist. **oponer ~encia a** resist

resma *f* ream

resobado *a* trite

resol|ución *f* resolution; (*solución*) solution; (*decisión*) decision. **~ver** [2] *vt* resolve; solve (*problema etc*). **~verse** *vpr* be solved; (*resultar bien*) work out; (*decidirse*) make up one's mind

resollar [2] *vi* breathe heavily. **sin ~** without saying a word

resona|ncia *f* resonance. **~nte** *a* resonant; (*fig*) resounding. **~r** [2] *vi* resound. **tener ~ncia** cause a stir

resopl|ar *vi* puff; (*por enfado*) snort; (*por cansancio*) pant. **~ido** *m* heavy breathing; (*de enfado*) snort; (*de cansancio*) panting

resorte *m* spring. **tocar (todos los) ~s** (*fig*) pull strings

respald|ar *vt* back; (*escribir*) endorse. **~arse** *vpr* lean back. **~o** *m* back

respect|ar *vi* concern. **~ivo** *a* respective. **~o** *m* respect. **al ~o** on the matter. (**con**) **~o a** as regards. **en/por lo que ~a** as regards

respet|able *a* respectable. **—m** audience. **~ar** *vt* respect. **~o** *m* respect. **~uoso** *a* respectful. **de ~o** best. **faltar al ~o a** be disrespectful to. **hacerse ~ar** command respect

respingo *m* start

respir|ación *f* breathing; (*med*) respiration; (*ventilación*) ventilation. **~ador** *a* respiratory.

~**ar** *vi* breathe; (*fig*) breathe a sigh of relief. **no** ~**ar** (*no hablar*) not say a word. ~**o** *m* breathing; (*fig*) rest

resplandecer [11] *vi* shine. ~**eciente** *a* shining. ~**or** *m* brilliance; (*de llamas*) glow

responder *vi* answer; (*replicar*) answer back; (*fig*) reply, respond. ~ **de** answer for

responsab|ilidad *f* responsibility. ~**le** *a* responsible. **hacerse** ~**le de** assume responsibility for

respuesta *f* reply, answer

resquebra|dura *f* crack. ~**jar** *vt* crack. ~**jarse** *upr* crack

resquemor *m* (*fig*) uneasiness

resquicio *m* crack; (*fig*) possibility

resta *f* subtraction

restablecer [11] *vt* restore. ~**se** *upr* recover

restallar *vi* crack

restante *a* remaining. **lo** ~ the rest

restar *vt* take away; (*substraer*) subtract. —*vi* be left

restaura|ción *f* restoration. ~**nte** *m* restaurant. ~**r** *vt* restore

restitu|ción *f* restitution. ~**ir** [17] *vt* return; (*restaurar*) restore

resto *m* rest, remainder; (*en matemática*) remainder. ~**s** *mpl* remains; (*de comida*) leftovers

restorán *m* restaurant

restregar [1 & 12] *vt* rub

restri|cción *f* restriction. ~**ngir** [14] *vt* restrict, limit

resucitar *vt* resuscitate; (*fig*) revive. —*vi* return to life

resuelto *a* resolute

resuello *m* breath; (*respiración*) breathing

resulta|do *m* result. ~**r** *vi* result; (*salir*) turn out; (*ser*) be; (*ocurrir*) happen; (*costar*) come to

resum|en *m* summary. ~**ir** *vt* summarize; (*recapitular*) sum up; (*abreviar*) abridge. **en** ~**en** in short

resur|gir [14] *vi* reappear; (*fig*) revive. ~**gimiento** *m* resurgence. ~**rección** *f* resurrection

retaguardia *f* (*mil*) rearguard

retahíla *f* string

retal *m* remnant

retama *f*, **retamo** *m* (*LAm*) broom

retar *vt* challenge

retardar *vt* slow down; (*demorar*) delay

retazo *m* remnant; (*fig*) piece, bit

retemblar [1] *vi* shake

rete... *pref* extremely

reten|ción *f* retention. ~**er** [40] *vt* keep; (*en la memoria*) retain; (*no dar*) withhold

reticencia *f* insinuation; (*reserva*) reticence, reluctance

retina *f* retina

retintín *m* ringing. **con** ~ (*fig*) sarcastically

retir|ada *f* withdrawal. ~**ado** *a* secluded; (*jubilado*) retired. ~**ar** *vt* move away; (*quitar*) remove; withdraw (*dinero*); (*jubilar*) pension off. ~**arse** *upr* draw back; (*mil*) withdraw; (*jubilarse*) retire; (*acostarse*) go to bed. ~**o** *m* retirement; (*pensión*) pension; (*lugar apartado*) retreat

reto *m* challenge

retocar [7] *vt* retouch

retoño *m* shoot

retoque *m* (*acción*) retouching; (*efecto*) finishing touch

retorc|er [2 & 9] *vt* twist; wring (*ropa*). ~**erse** *upr* get twisted up; (*de dolor*) writhe. ~**imiento** *m* twisting; (*de ropa*) wringing

retórica *f* rhetoric; (*grandilocuencia*) grandiloquence. ~**o** *m* rhetorical

retorn|ar *vt/i* return. ~**o** *m* return

retortijón *m* twist; (*de tripas*) stomach cramp

retoz|ar [10] *vi* romp, frolic. ~**ón** *a* playful

retractar *vt* retract. ~**se** *vpr* retract

retra|er [41] *vt* retract. ~**erse** *vpr* withdraw. ~**ído** *a* retiring

retransmitir *vt* relay

retras|ado *a* behind; (*reloj*) slow; (*poco desarrollado*) backward; (*anticuado*) old-fashioned; (*med*) mentally retarded. ~**ar** *vt* delay; put back (*reloj*); (*retardar*) slow down. —*vi* fall behind; (*reloj*) be slow. ~**arse** *vpr* be behind; (*reloj*) be slow. ~**o** *m* delay; (*poco desarrollo*) backwardness; (*de reloj*) slowness. ~**os** *mpl* arrears. **con 5 minutos de** ~**o** 5 minutes late. **traer** ~**o** be late

retrat|ar *vt* paint a portrait of; (*foto*) photograph; (*fig*) protray. ~**ista** *m & f* portrait painter. ~**o** *m* portrait; (*fig, descripción*) description. **ser el vivo** ~**o de** be the living image of

retreparse *vpr* lean back

retreta *f* retreat

retrete *m* toilet

retribu|ción *f* payment. ~**ir** [17] *vt* pay

retroce|der *vi* move back; (*fig*) back down. ~**so** *m* backward movement; (*de arma de fuego*) recoil; (*med*) relapse

retrógrado *a & m* (*pol*) reactionary

retropropulsión *f* jet propulsion

retrospectivo *a* retrospective

retrovisor *m* rear-view mirror

retumbar *vt* echo; (*trueno etc*) boom

reuma *m*, **reúma** *m* rheumatism

reum|ático *a* rheumatic. ~**atismo** *m* rheumatism

reuni|ón *f* meeting; (*entre amigos*) reunion. ~**r** [23] *vt* join together; (*recoger*) gather (together). ~**rse** *vpr* join together; (*personas*) meet

rev|álida *f* final exam. ~**alidar** *vt* confirm; (*escol*) take an exam in

revancha *f* revenge. **tomar la** ~ get one's own back

revela|ción *f* revelation. ~**do** *m* developing. ~**dor** *a* revealing. ~**r** *vt* reveal; (*foto*) develop

revent|ar [1] *vi* burst; (*tener ganas*) be dying to. ~**arse** *vpr* burst. ~**ón** *m* burst; (*auto*) puncture

reverbera|ción *f* (*de luz*) reflection; (*de sonido*) reverberation. ~**r** *vi* (*luz*) be reflected; (*sonido*) reverberate

reveren|cia *f* reverence; (*muestra de respeto*) bow; (*muestra de respeto de mujer*) curtsy. ~**ciar** *vt* revere. ~**do** *a* respected; (*relig*) reverend. ~**te** *a* reverent

revers|ible *a* reversible. ~**o** *m* reverse

revertir [4] *vi* revert

revés *m* wrong side; (*desgracia*) misfortune; (*en deportes*) backhand. **al** ~ the other way round; (*con lo de arriba abajo*) upside down; (*con lo de dentro fuera*) inside out

revesti|miento *m* coating. ~**r** [5] *vt* cover; put on (*ropa*); (*fig*) take on

revis|ar *vt* check; overhaul (*mecanismo*); service (*coche etc*). ~**ión** *f* check(ing); (*inspección*) inspection; (*de coche etc*) service. ~**or** *m* inspector

revist|a *f* magazine; (*inspección*) inspection; (*artículo*) review; (*espectáculo*) revue. ~**ero** *m* critic; (*mueble*) magazine rack. **pasar** ~**a** a inspect

revivir *vi* come to life again

revocar [7] *vt* revoke; whitewash ⟨*pared*⟩

revolcar [2 & 7] *vt* knock over. **~se** *vpr* roll

revolotear *vi* flutter

revoltijo *m*, **revoltillo** *m* mess. **~ de huevos** scrambled eggs

revoltoso *a* rebellious; ⟨*niño*⟩ naughty

revolución *f* revolution. **~onar** *vt* revolutionize. **~onario** *a & m* revolutionary

revolver [2, *pp* **revuelto**] *vt* mix; stir ⟨*líquido*⟩; ⟨*desordenar*⟩ mess up; ⟨*pol*⟩ stir up. **~se** *vpr* turn round. **~se contra** turn on

revólver *m* revolver

revoque *m* ⟨*con cal*⟩ white-washing

revuelo *m* fluttering; ⟨*fig*⟩ stir

revuelta *f* turn; ⟨*de calle etc*⟩ bend; ⟨*motín*⟩ revolt; ⟨*con-moción*⟩ disturbance. **~o** *a* mixed up; ⟨*líquido*⟩ cloudy; ⟨*mar*⟩ rough; ⟨*tiempo*⟩ unsettled; ⟨*huevos*⟩ scrambled

rey *m* king. **~es** *mpl* king and queen

reyerta *f* quarrel

rezagarse [12] *vpr* fall behind

rezar [10] *vt* say. *—vi* pray; ⟨*decir*⟩ say. **~o** *m* praying; ⟨*oración*⟩ prayer

rezongar [12] *vi* grumble

rezumar *vt/i* ooze

ría *f* estuary

riachuelo *m* stream

riada *f* flood

ribera *f* bank

ribete *m* border; ⟨*fig*⟩ em-bellishment

ricino *m*. **aceite de ~** castor oil

rico *a* rich; ⟨*culin*, *fam*⟩ delicious. *—m* rich person

ridículo *a* ridiculous. **~ic-ulizar** [10] *vt* ridicule

riego *m* watering; ⟨*irrigación*⟩ irrigation

riel *m* rail

rienda *f* rein

riesgo *m* risk. **a ~ de** at the risk of. **correr (el) ~ de** run the risk of

rifa *f* raffle. **~r** *vt* raffle. **~rse** *vpr* ⟨*fam*⟩ quarrel over

rifle *m* rifle

rigidez *f* rigidity; ⟨*fig*⟩ in-flexibility

rígido *a* rigid; ⟨*fig*⟩ inflexible

rigor *m* strictness; ⟨*exactitud*⟩ exactness; ⟨*de clima*⟩ severity. **~uroso** *a* rigorous. **de ~** compulsory. **en ~** strictly speaking

rima *f* rhyme. **~r** *vt/i* rhyme

rimbombante *a* resounding; ⟨*lenguaje*⟩ pompous; ⟨*fig*, *ostentoso*⟩ showy

rimel *m* mascara

rincón *m* corner

rinoceronte *m* rhinoceros

riña *f* quarrel; ⟨*pelea*⟩ fight

riñón *m* kidney. **~onada** *f* loin; ⟨*guiso*⟩ kidney stew

río *m* river; ⟨*fig*⟩ stream. *—vb* véase **reír**. **~ abajo** down-stream. **~ arriba** upstream

rioja *m* Rioja wine

riqueza *f* wealth; ⟨*fig*⟩ richness. **~s** *fpl* riches

riquísimo *a* delicious

risa *f* laugh. **desternillarse de ~** split one's sides laughing. **la ~** laughter

risco *m* cliff

risible *a* laughable. **~otada** *f* guffaw

ristra *f* string

risueño *a* smiling; ⟨*fig*⟩ happy

rítmico *a* rhythmic(al)

ritmo *m* rhythm; ⟨*fig*⟩ rate

rito *m* rite; ⟨*fig*⟩ ritual. **~ual** *a & m* ritual. **de ~ual** customary

rival *a & m & f* rival. **~idad** *f* rivalry. **~izar** [10] *vi* rival

rizado *a* curly. **~ar** [10] *vt* curl; ripple ⟨*agua*⟩. **~o** *m* curl; ⟨*en agua*⟩ ripple. **~oso** *a* curly

róbalo *m* bass

robar *vt* steal ‹*cosa*›; rob ‹*persona*›; (*raptar*) kidnap

roble *m* oak (tree)

roblón *m* rivet

robo *m* theft; (*fig, estafa*) robbery

robot (*pl* **robots**) *m* robot

robust|ez *f* strength. ~**o** *a* strong

roca *f* rock

roce *m* rubbing; (*toque ligero*) touch; (*señal*) mark; (*fig, entre personas*) contact

rociar [20] *vt* spray

rocín *m* nag

rocío *m* dew

rodaballo *m* turbot

rodado *m* (*Arg, vehículo*) vehicle

rodaja *f* disc; (*culin*) slice

rodaje *m* (*de película*) shooting; (*de coche*) running in. ~**r** [2] *vt* shoot ‹*película*›; run in ‹*coche*›; (*recorrer*) travel. —*vi* roll; ‹*coche*› run; (*hacer una película*) shoot

rode|ar *vt* surround. ~**arse** *vpr* surround o.s. (**de** with). ~**o** *m* long way round; (*de ganado*) round-up. **andar con** ~**os** beat about the bush. **sin** ~**os** plainly

rodill|a *f* knee. ~**era** *f* knee-pad. **de** ~**as** kneeling

rodillo *m* roller; (*culin*) rolling-pin

rododendro *m* rhododendron

rodrigón *m* stake

roe|dor *m* rodent. ~**r** [37] *vt* gnaw

rogar [2 & 12] *vt/i* ask; (*relig*) pray. **se ruega a los Sres pasajeros...** passengers are requested.... **se ruega no fumar** please do not smoke

roj|ete *m* rouge. ~**ez** *f* redness. ~**izo** *a* reddish. ~**o** *a* & *m* red. **ponerse** ~**o** blush

roll|izo *a* round; (*persona*) plump. ~**o** *m* roll; (*de cuerda*) coil; (*culin, rodillo*) rolling-pin; (*fig, pesadez, fam*) bore

romance *a* Romance. —*m* Romance language; (*poema*) romance. **hablar en** ~ speak plainly

rom|ánico *a* Romanesque; (*lengua*) Romance. ~**ano** *a* & *m* Roman. **a la** ~**ana** (*culin*) (deep-)fried in batter

rom|anticismo *m* romanticism. ~**ántico** *a* romantic

romería *f* pilgrimage

romero *m* rosemary

romo *a* blunt; ‹*nariz*› snub; (*fig, torpe*) dull

rompe|cabezas *m invar* puzzle; (*con tacos de madera*) jigsaw (puzzle). ~**nueces** *m invar* nutcrackers. ~**olas** *m invar* breakwater

romper (*pp* **roto**) *vt* break; break off ‹*relaciones etc*›. —*vi* break; (*sol*) break through. ~**erse** *vpr* break. ~**er** *a* burst out. ~**imiento** *m* (*de relaciones etc*) breaking off

ron *m* rum

roncar [7] *vi* snore. ~**o** *a* hoarse

roncha *f* lump; (*culin*) slice

ronda *f* round; (*patrulla*) patrol; (*carretera*) ring road. ~**lla** *f* group of serenaders; (*invención*) story. ~**r** *vt/i* patrol

rondón. de ~ unannounced

ronquedad *f*, **ronquera** *f* hoarseness

ronquido *m* snore

ronronear *vi* purr

ronzal *m* halter

roñ|a *f* (*suciedad*) grime. ~**oso** *a* dirty; (*oxidado*) rusty; (*tacaño*) mean

rop|a *f* clothes, clothing. ~**a blanca** linen; (*ropa interior*) underwear. ~**a de cama** bedclothes. ~**a hecha** ready-made clothes. ~**a interior** underwear. ~**aje** *m* robes; (*excesivo*) heavy clothing. ~**ero** *m* wardrobe

rosa *a invar* pink. —*f* rose; (*color*) pink. ∼**áceo** *a* pink. ∼**ado** *a* rosy. —*m* (*vino*) rosé. ∼**al** *m* rose-bush

rosario *m* rosary; (*fig*) series

rosbif *m* roast beef

rosc|**a** *f* coil; (*de tornillo*) thread; (*de pan*) roll. ∼**o** *m* roll

rosetón *m* rosette

rosquilla *f* doughnut; (*oruga*) grub

rostro *m* face

rota|**ción** *f* rotation. ∼**tivo** *a* rotary

roto *a* broken

rótula *f* kneecap

rotulador *m* felt-tip pen

rótulo *m* sign; (*etiqueta*) label

rotundo *a* emphatic

rotura *f* break

roturar *vt* plough

roza *f* groove. ∼**dura** *f* scratch

rozagante *a* showy

rozar [10] *vt* rub against; (*ligeramente*) brush against; (*ensuciar*) dirty; (*fig*) touch on. ∼**se** *vpr* rub; (*con otras personas*) mix

Rte. *abrev* (*Remite(nte)*) sender

rúa *f* (small) street

rubéola *f* German measles

rubí *m* ruby

rubicundo *a* ruddy

rubio *a* (*pelo*) fair; (*persona*) fair-haired; (*tabaco*) Virginian

rubor *m* blush; (*fig*) shame. ∼**izado** *a* blushing; (*fig*) ashamed. ∼**izar** [10] *vt* make blush. ∼**izarse** *vpr* blush

rúbrica *f* red mark; (*de firma*) flourish; (*título*) heading

rudeza *f* roughness

rudiment|**al** *a* rudimentary. ∼**os** *mpl* rudiments

rudo *a* rough; (*sencillo*) simple

rueda *f* wheel; (*de mueble*) castor; (*de personas*) ring; (*culin*) slice. ∼ **de prensa** press conference

ruedo *m* edge; (*redondel*) arena

ruego *m* request; (*súplica*) entreaty. —*vb véase* **rogar**

rufián *m* pimp; (*granuja*) villain. ∼**anesco** *a* roguish

rugby *m* Rugby

rugi|**do** *m* roar. ∼**r** [14] *vi* roar

ruibarbo *m* rhubarb

ruido *m* noise; (*alboroto*) din; (*escándalo*) commotion. ∼**so** *a* noisy; (*fig*) sensational

ruin *a* despicable; (*tacaño*) mean

ruina *f* ruin; (*colapso*) collapse

ruindad *f* meanness

ruinoso *a* ruinous

ruiseñor *m* nightingale

ruleta *f* roulette

rulo *m* (*culin*) rolling-pin; (*del pelo*) curler

Rumania *f* Romania

rumano *a & m* Romanian

rumba *f* rumba

rumbo *m* direction; (*fig*) course; (*fig, generosidad*) lavishness. ∼**so** *a* lavish. **con** ∼ **a** in the direction of. **hacer** ∼ **a** a head for

rumia|**nte** *a & m* ruminant. ∼**r** *vt* chew; (*fig*) chew over. —*vi* ruminate

rumor *m* rumour; (*ruido*) murmur. ∼**earse** *vpr* be rumoured. ∼**oso** *a* murmuring

runr|**ún** *m* rumour; (*ruido*) murmur. ∼**unearse** *vpr* be rumoured

ruptura *f* break; (*de relaciones etc*) breaking off

rural *a* rural

Rusia *f* Russia

ruso *a & m* Russian

rústico *a* rural; (*de carácter*) coarse. **en rústica** paperback

ruta *f* route; (*camino*) road; (*fig*) course

rutilante *a* shining

rutina *f* routine. ∼**rio** *a* routine

S

S.A. *abrev* (*Sociedad Anónima*)

Ltd, Limited, plc, Public Limited Company

sábado m Saturday

sabana f (esp LAm) savannah

sábana f sheet

sabandija f bug

sabañón m chilblain

sabático a sabbatical

sabelotodo m & f invar know-all (fam). **~er** [38] vt know; (ser capaz de) be able to, know how to; (enterarse de) learn. —vi. **~er** a taste of. **~er** m knowledge. **~ido** a well-known. **~iduría** f wisdom; (conocimientos) knowledge. **a ~er** si I wonder if. ¡**haberlo ~ido**! if only I'd known! **hacer ~er** let know. **no sé cuántos** what's-his-name. **para que lo sepas** let me tell you. ¡**qué sé yo!** how should I know? **que yo sepa** as far as I know. ¿**~es nadar?** can you swim? **un no sé qué** a certain sth. ¡**yo qué sé!** how should I know?

sabiendas. a ~ knowingly; (a propósito) on purpose

sabio a learned; (prudente) wise

sabor m taste, flavour; (fig) flavour. **~ear** vt taste; (fig) savour

sabotaje m sabotage. **~eador** m saboteur. **~ear** vt sabotage

sabroso a tasty; (fig, substancioso) meaty

sabueso m (perro) bloodhound; (fig, detective) detective

sacacorchos m invar corkscrew. **~puntas** m invar pencil-sharpener

sacar [7] vt take out; put out (parte del cuerpo); (quitar) remove; take (foto); win (premio); get (billete, entrada etc); withdraw (dinero); reach (solución); draw (conclusión); make (copia). **~ adelante** bring up (niño); carry on (negocio)

sacarina f saccharin

sacerdocio m priesthood. **~tal** a priestly. **~te** m priest

saciar vt satisfy

saco m bag; (anat) sac; (LAm, chaqueta) jacket; (de mentiras) pack. **~ de dormir** sleeping-bag

sacramento m sacrament

sacrificar [7] vt sacrifice. **~arse** vpr sacrifice o.s. **~io** m sacrifice

sacrilegio m sacrilege. **~ílego** a sacrilegious

sacro a sacred, holy. **~santo** a sacrosanct

sacudida f shake; (movimiento brusco) jolt, jerk; (fig) shock. **~da eléctrica** electric shock. **~r** vt shake; (golpear) beat; (ahuyentar) chase away. **~rse** vpr shake off; (fig) get rid of

sádico a sadistic. —m sadist

sadismo m sadism

saeta f arrow; (de reloj) hand

safari m safari

sagaz a shrewd

Sagitario m Sagittarius

sagrado a sacred, holy. —m sanctuary

Sahara m, **Sáhara** /'saxara/ m Sahara

sainete m short comedy

sal f salt

sala f room; (en teatro) house. **~ de espectáculos** concert hall, auditorium. **~ de espera** waiting-room. **~ de estar** living-room. **~ de fiestas** nightclub

salado a salty; (agua del mar) salt; (vivo) lively; (encantador) cute; (fig) witty. **~r** vt salt

salario m wages

salazón f (carne) salted meat; (pescado) salted fish

salchicha f (pork) sausage. **~ón** m salami

saldar vt pay (cuenta); (vender) sell off; (fig) settle. **~o** m balance; (venta) sale; (lo que queda) remnant

salero m salt-cellar

salgo vb véase **salir**

sali|da f departure; (puerta) exit, way out; (de gas, de líquido) leak; (de astro) rising; (com, posibilidad de venta) opening; (chiste) witty remark; (fig) way out. **~da de emergencia** emergency exit. **~ente** a projecting; (fig) outstanding. **~r** [52] vi leave; (de casa etc) go out; (revista etc) be published; (resultar) turn out; (astro) rise; (aparecer) appear. **~rse** vpr leave; (recipiente, líquido etc) leak. **~r adelante** get by. **~rse con la suya** get one's own way

saliva f saliva

salmo m psalm

salm|ón m salmon. **~onete** m red mullet

salmuera f brine

sal|ón m lounge, sitting-room. **~ de actos** assembly hall. **~ de fiestas** dancehall

salpica|dero m (auto) dashboard. **~dura** f splash; (acción) splashing. **~r** [7] vt splash; (fig) sprinkle

sals|a f sauce; (para carne asada) gravy; (fig) spice. **~a verde** parsley sauce. **~era** f sauce-boat

salt|amontes m invar grasshopper. **~ar** vt jump (over); (fig) miss out. **—vi** jump; (romperse) break; (líquido) spurt out; (desprenderse) come off; (pelota) bounce; (estallar) explode. **~eador** m highwayman. **~ear** vt rob; (culin) sauté. **—vi** skip through

saltimbanqui m acrobat

salt|o m jump; (al agua) dive. **~o de agua** waterfall. **~ón** a (ojos) bulging. **—m** grasshopper. **a ~os** by jumping; (fig) by leaps and bounds. **de un ~o** with one jump

salud f health; (fig) welfare. **—int** cheers! **~able** a healthy

salud|ar vt greet, say hello to; (mil) salute. **~o** m greeting; (mil) salute. **~os** mpl best wishes. **le ~a atentamente** (en cartas) yours faithfully

salva f salvo; (de aplausos) thunders

salvación f salvation

salvado m bran

Salvador m. **El ~** El Salvador

salvaguardia f safeguard

salvaje a (planta, animal) wild; (primitivo) savage. **—m & f** savage

salvamanteles m invar table-mat

salva|mento m rescue. **~r** vt save, rescue; (atravesar) cross; (recorrer) travel; (fig) overcome. **~rse** vpr save o.s. **~vidas** m invar lifebelt. **chaleco** m **~vidas** life-jacket

salvia f sage

salvo a safe. **—adv & prep** except (for). **~ que** unless. **~conducto** m safe-conduct. **a ~** out of danger. **poner a ~** put in a safe place

samba f samba

San a Saint, St. **~ Miguel** St Michael

sana|r vt cure. **—vi** recover. **~torio** m sanatorium

sanción f sanction. **~onar** vt sanction

sancocho m (LAm) stew

sandalia f sandal

sándalo m sandalwood

sandía f water melon

sandwich /'sambitʃ/ m (pl **sandwichs**, **sandwiches**) sandwich

sanear vt drain

sangr|ante a bleeding; (fig) flagrant. **~ar** vt/i bleed. **~e** f blood. **a ~e fría** in cold blood

sangría f (bebida) sangria

sangriento a bloody

sangu|ijuela f leech. **∼íneo** a blood

san|idad f health. **∼itario** a sanitary. **∼o** a healthy; (*seguro*) sound. **∼o y salvo** safe and sound. **cortar por lo ∼o** settle things once and for all

santiamén m. **en un ∼** in an instant

sant|idad f sanctity. **∼ificar** [7] vt sanctify. **∼iguar** [15] vt make the sign of the cross over. **∼iguarse** vpr cross o.s. **∼o** a holy; (*delante de nombre*) Saint, St. —m saint; (*día*) saint's day, name day. **∼uario** m sanctuary. **∼urrón** a sanctimonious, hypocritical

saña f fury; (*crueldad*) cruelty. **∼oso** a, **∼udo** a furious

sapo m toad; (*bicho, fam*) small animal, creature

saque m (*en tenis*) service; (*en fútbol*) throw-in; (*inicial en fútbol*) kick-off

saque|ar vt loot. **∼o** m looting

sarampión m measles

sarape m (*Mex*) blanket

sarc|asmo m sarcasm. **∼ástico** a sarcastic

sardana f Catalonian dance

sardina f sardine

sardo a & m Sardinian

sardónico a sardonic

sargento m sergeant

sarmiento m vine shoot

sarpullido m rash

sarta f string

sartén f frying-pan (*Brit*), fry-pan (*Amer*)

sastre m tailor. **∼ría** f tailoring; (*tienda*) tailor's (shop)

Satanás m Satan

satánico a satanic

satélite m satellite

satinado a shiny

sátira f satire

satírico a satirical. —m satirist

satisf|acción f satisfaction. **∼acer** [31] vt satisfy; (*pagar*) pay; (*gustar*) please; meet (*gastos, requisitos*). **∼acerse** vpr satisfy o.s.; (*vengarse*) take revenge. **∼actorio** a satisfactory. **∼echo** a satisfied. **∼echo de sí mismo** smug

satura|ción f saturation. **∼r** vt saturate

Saturno m Saturn

sauce m willow. **∼ llorón** weeping willow

saúco m elder

savia f sap

sauna f sauna

saxofón m, **saxófono** m saxophone

saz|ón f ripeness; (*culin*) seasoning. **∼onado** a ripe; (*culin*) seasoned. **∼onar** vt ripen; (*culin*) season. **en ∼ón** in season

se pron (*él*) him; (*ella*) her; (*Vd*) you; (*reflexivo, él*) himself; (*reflexivo, ella*) herself; (*reflexivo, ello*) itself; (*reflexivo, uno*) oneself; (*reflexivo, Vd*) yourself; (*reflexivo, ellos, ellas*) themselves; (*reflexivo, Vds*) yourselves; (*recíproco*) (to) each other. **∼ dice** people say, they say, it is said (**que** that). **∼ habla español** Spanish spoken

sé vb *véase* **saber** y **ser**

sea vb *véase* **ser**

sebo m tallow; (*culin*) suet

seca|dor m drier; (*de pelo*) hairdrier. **∼nte** a drying. —m blotting-paper. **∼r** [7] vt dry. **∼rse** vpr dry; (*río etc*) dry up; (*persona*) dry o.s.

sección f section

seco a dry; (*frutos, flores*) dried; (*flaco*) thin; (*respuesta*) curt; (*escueto*) plain. **a secas** just. **en ∼** (*bruscamente*) suddenly. **lavar en ∼** dry-clean

secre|ción f secretion. **∼tar** vt secrete

secretar|ía f secretariat. **~io** m secretary

secreto a & m secret

secta f sect. **~rio** a sectarian

sector m sector

secuela f consequence

secuencia f sequence

secuestr|ar vt confiscate; kidnap (persona); hijack (avión). **~o** m seizure; (de persona) kidnapping; (de avión) hijack(ing)

secular a secular

secundar vt second, help. **~io** a secondary

sed f thirst. —vb véase ser. **tener ~** be thirsty. **tener ~ de** (fig) be hungry for

seda f silk

sedante a & m, **sedativo** a & m sedative

sede f seat; (relig) see

sedentario a sedentary

sedici|ón f sedition. **~oso** a seditious

sediento a thirsty

sediment|ar vi deposit. **~arse** vpr settle. **~o** m sediment

seducición f seduction. **~ir** [47] vt seduce; (atraer) attract. **~tor** a seductive. —m seducer

sega|dor m harvester. **~dora** f harvester; (máquina) mower. **~r** [1 & 12] vt reap

seglar a secular. —m layman

segmento m segment

segoviano m person from Segovia

segrega|ción f segregation. **~r** [12] vt segregate

segui|da f. **en ~da** immediately. **~do** a continuous; (en plural) consecutive. —adv straight; (después) after. **todo ~do** straight ahead. **~dor** a following. —m follower. **~r** [5 & 13] vt follow (continuar) continue

según prep according to. —adv it depends; (a medida que) as

segundo a second. —m second; (culin) second course

segur|amente adv certainly; (muy probablemente) surely. **~idad** f safety; (certeza) certainty; (aplomo) confidence. **~idad en sí mismo** self-confidence. **~idad social** social security. **~o** a safe; (cierto) certain, sure; (firme) secure; (de fiar) reliable. —adv for certain. —m insurance; (dispositivo de seguridad) safety device. **~o de sí mismo** self-confident. **~o de terceros** third-party insurance

seis a & m six. **~cientos** a & m six hundred

seísmo m earthquake

selec|ción f selection. **~cionar** vt select, choose. **~tivo** a selective. **~to** a selected; (fig) choice

selva f forest; (jungla) jungle

sell|ar vt stamp; (cerrar) seal. **~o** m stamp; (en documento oficial) seal; (fig, distintivo) hallmark

semáforo m semaphore; (auto) traffic lights; (rail) signal

semana f week. **~l** a weekly. **~rio** a & m weekly. **S~ Santa** Holy Week

semántic|a f semantics. **~o** a semantic

semblante m face; (fig) look

sembrar [1] vt sow; (fig) scatter

semeja|nte a similar; (tal) such. —m fellow man; (cosa) equal. **~nza** f similarity. **~r** vi seem. **~rse** vpr look alike. a **~nza de** like. **tener ~nza con** resemble

semen m semen. **~tal** a stud. —m stud animal

semestral a half-yearly. —m six months

semibreve f semibreve (Brit), whole note (Amer)

semicircular a semicircular. **~írculo** m semicircle

semicorchea *f* semiquaver (*Brit*), sixteenth note (*Amer*)

semifinal *f* semifinal

semill|a *f* seed. ~**ero** *m* nursery; (*fig*) hotbed

seminario *m* (*univ*) seminar; (*relig*) seminary

sem|ita *a* Semitic. —*m* Semite. ~**ítico** *a* Semitic

sémola *f* semolina

senado *m* senate; (*fig*) assembly. ~**r** *m* senator

sencill|ez *f* simplicity. ~**o** *a* simple; (*uno solo*) single

senda *f*, **sendero** *m* path

sendos *apl* each

seno *m* bosom. ~ **materno** womb

sensaci|ón *f* sensation. ~**onal** *a* sensational

sensat|ez *f* good sense. ~**o** *a* sensible

sensi|bilidad *f* sensibility. ~**ble** *a* sensitive; (*notable*) notable; (*lamentable*) lamentable. ~**tivo** *a* (*órgano*) sense

sensual *a* sensual. ~**idad** *f* sensuality

senta|do *a* sitting (down). **dar algo por** ~**do** take something for granted. ~**r** [1] *vt* place; (*establecer*) establish. —*vi* suit; (*de medidas*) fit; (*comida*) agree with. ~**rse** *vpr* sit (down); (*sedimento*) settle

sentencia *f* saying; (*jurid*) sentence. ~**r** *vt* sentence

sentido *a* deeply felt; (*sincero*) sincere; (*sensible*) sensitive. —*m* sense; (*dirección*) direction. ~ **común** common sense. ~ **del humor** sense of humour. ~ **único** one-way. **doble** ~ double meaning. **no tener** ~ not make sense. **perder el** ~ faint. **sin** ~ unconscious; (*cosa*) senseless

sentim|ental *a* sentimental. ~**iento** *m* feeling; (*sentido*) sense; (*pesar*) regret

sentir [4] *vt* feel; (*oír*) hear; (*lamentar*) be sorry for. —*vi* feel; (*lamentarse*) be sorry. —*m* (*opinión*) opinion. ~**se** *vpr* feel. **lo siento** I'm sorry

seña *f* sign. ~**s** *fpl* (*dirección*) address; (*descripción*) description

señal *f* sign; (*rail etc*) signal; (*telefónico*) tone; (*com*) deposit. ~**ado** *a* notable. ~**ar** *vt* signal; (*poner señales en*) mark; (*apuntar*) point out; (*manecilla, aguja*) point to; (*determinar*) fix. ~**arse** *vpr* stand out. **dar** ~**es de** show signs of. **en** ~ **de** as a token of

señero *a* alone; (*sin par*) unique

señor *m* man; (*caballero*) gentleman; (*delante de nombre propio*) Mr; (*tratamiento directo*) sir. ~**a** *f* lady, woman; (*delante de nombre propio*) Mrs; (*esposa*) wife; (*tratamiento directo*) madam. ~**ial** *a* (*casa*) stately. ~**ita** *f* young lady; (*delante de nombre propio*) Miss; (*tratamiento directo*) miss. ~**ito** *m* young gentleman. **el** ~ **alcalde** the mayor. **el** ~ Mr. **muy** ~ **mío** Dear Sir. **¡no** ~! certainly not! **ser** ~ **de** be master of, control

señuelo *m* lure

sepa *vb* *véase* **saber**

separa|ción *f* separation. ~**do** *a* separate. ~**r** *vt* separate; (*apartar*) move away; (*de empleo*) dismiss. ~**rse** *vpr* separate; (*amigos*) part. ~**tista** *a* & *m* & *f* separatist. **por** ~**do** separately

septentrional *a* north(ern)

séptico *a* septic

septiembre *m* September

séptimo *a* seventh

sepulcro *m* sepulchre

sepult|ar *vt* bury. ~**ura** *f* burial; (*tumba*) grave. ~**urero** *m* gravedigger

sequ|edad f dryness. **~ía** f drought

séquito m entourage; (fig) aftermath

ser [39] vi be. —m being. **~ de** be made of; (provenir de) come from; (pertenecer a) belong to. **~ humano** human being. **a no ~ que** unless. **¡así sea!** so be it! **es más** what is more. **lo que sea** anything. **no sea que, no vaya a ~ que** in case. **o sea** in other words. **sea lo que fuere** be that as it may. **sea... sea** either... or. **siendo así que** since. **soy yo** it's me

seren|ar vt calm down. **~arse** vpr calm down; (tiempo) clear up. **~ata** f serenade. **~idad** f serenity. **~o** a ⟨cielo⟩ clear; ⟨tiempo⟩ fine; (fig) calm. —m night watchman. **al ~o** in the open

seri|al m serial. **~e** f series. **fuera de ~e** (fig, extraordinario) special. **producción f en ~e** mass production

seri|edad f seriousness. **~o** a serious; (confiable) reliable. **en ~o** seriously. **poco ~o** frivolous

sermón m sermon

serp|enteante a winding. **~entear** vi wind. **~iente** f snake. **~iente de cascabel** rattlesnake

serrano a mountain; ⟨jamón⟩ cured

serr|ar [1] vt saw. **~ín** m sawdust. **~ucho** m (hand)saw

servi|cial a helpful. **~cio** m service; (conjunto) set; (aseo) toilet. **~cio a domicilio** delivery service. **~dor** m servant. **~dumbre** f servitude; (criados) servants, staff. **~l** a servile. **su (seguro) ~dor** (en cartas) yours faithfully

servilleta f serviette, (table) napkin

servir [5] vt serve; (ayudar) help; (en restaurante) wait on. —vi serve; (ser útil) be of use. **~se** vpr help o.s. **~se de** use. **no ~ de nada** be useless. **para ~le** at your service. **sírvase sentarse** please sit down

sesear vi pronounce the Spanish c as an s

sesent|a a & m sixty. **~ón** a & m sixty-year-old

seseo m pronunciation of the Spanish c as an s

sesg|ado a slanting. **~o** m slant; (fig, rumbo) turn

sesión f session; (en el cine) showing; (en el teatro) performance

seso m brain; (fig) brains. **~udo** a inteligent; (sensato) sensible

seta f mushroom

sete|cientos a & m seven hundred. **~nta** a & m seventy. **~ntón** a & m seventy-year-old

setiembre m September

seto m fence; (de plantas) hedge. **~ vivo** hedge

seudo... pref pseudo...

seudónimo m pseudonym

sever|idad f severity. **~o** a severe; (disciplina, profesor etc) strict

Sevilla f Seville

sevillan|as fpl popular dance from Seville. **~o** m person from Seville

sexo m sex

sext|eto m sextet. **~o** a sixth

sexual a sexual. **~idad** f sexuality

si m (mus) B; (solfa) te. —conj if; (dubitativo) whether. **~ no** or else. **por ~ (acaso)** in case

sí pron reflexivo ⟨él⟩ himself; ⟨ella⟩ herself; ⟨ello⟩ itself; (uno) oneself; ⟨Vd⟩ yourself; ⟨ellos, ellas⟩ themselves; ⟨Vds⟩ yourselves; (recíproco) each other

sí adv yes. —m consent

Siamés a & m Siamese

Sicilia f Sicily
sida m Aids
siderurgia f iron and steel industry
sidra f cider
siega f harvesting; (época) harvest time
siembra f sowing; (época) sowing time
siempre adv always. ∼ que if. **como** ∼ as usual. **de** ∼ (acostumbrado) usual. **lo de** ∼ the same old story. **para** ∼ for ever
sien f temple
siento vb véase **sentar** y **sentir**
sierra f saw; (cordillera) mountain range
siervo m slave
siesta f siesta
siete a & m seven
sífilis f syphilis
sifón m U-bend; (de soda) syphon
sigilo m secrecy
sigla f initials, abbreviation
siglo m century; (época) time, age; (fig, mucho tiempo, fam) ages; (fig, mundo) world
significa|ción f meaning; (importancia) significance. ∼**do** a (conocido) well-known. —m meaning. ∼**r** [7] vt mean; (expresar) express. ∼**rse** vpr stand out. ∼**tivo** a significant
signo m sign. ∼ **de admiración** exclamation mark. ∼ **de interrogación** question mark
sigo vb véase **seguir**
siguiente a following, next. **lo** ∼ the following
sílaba f syllable
silb|ar vt/i whistle. ∼**ato** m, ∼**ido** m whistle
silenci|ador m silencer. ∼**ar** vt hush up. ∼**o** m silence. ∼**oso** a silent
sílfide f sylph
silicio m silicon
silo m silo

silueta f silhouette; (dibujo) outline
silvestre a wild
silla f chair; (de montar) saddle; (relig) see. ∼**a de ruedas** wheelchair. ∼**ín** m saddle. ∼**ón** m armchair
simb|ólico a symbolic(al). ∼**olismo** m symbolism. ∼**olizar** [10] vt symbolize
símbolo m symbol
sim|etría f symmetry. ∼**étrico** a symmetric(al)
simiente f seed
similar a similar
simp|atía f liking; (cariño) affection; (fig, amigo) friend. ∼**ático** a nice, likeable; (amable) kind. ∼**atizante** m & f sympathizer. ∼**atizar** [10] vi get on (well together). **me es** ∼**ático** I like
simple a simple; (mero) mere. ∼**eza** f simplicity; (tontería) stupid thing; (insignificancia) trifle. ∼**icidad** f simplicity. ∼**ificar** [7] vt simplify. ∼**ón** m simpleton
simposio m symposium
simula|ción f simulation. ∼**r** vt feign
simultáneo a simultaneous
sin prep without. ∼ **que** without
sinagoga f synagogue
sincer|idad f sincerity. ∼**o** a sincere
síncopa f (mus) syncopation
sincopar vt syncopate
sincronizar [10] vt synchronize
sindica|l a (trade-)union. ∼**lista** m & f trade-unionist. ∼**to** m trade union
síndrome m syndrome
sinfín m endless number
sinf|onía f symphony. ∼**ónico** a symphonic
singular a singular; (excepcional) exceptional. ∼**izar** [10] vt single out. ∼**izarse** vpr stand out

siniestro *a* sinister; *(desgraciado)* unlucky. —*m* disaster

sinnúmero *m* endless number

sino *m* fate. —*conj* but; *(salvo)* except

sínodo *m* synod

sinónimo *a* synoymous. —*m* synonym

sinrazón *f* wrong

sintaxis *f* syntax

síntesis *f invar* synthesis

sint ético *a* synthetic. **~etizar** [10] *vt* synthesize; *(resumir)* summarize

síntoma *f* sympton

sintomático *a* symptomatic

sinton ia *f (en la radio)* signature tune. **~izar** [10] *vt (con la radio)* tune (in)

sinuoso *a* winding

sinvergüenza *m & f* scoundrel

sionis mo *m* Zionism. **~ta** *m & f* Zionist

siquiera *conj* even if. —*adv* at least. **ni ~** not even

sirena *f* siren

Siria *f* Syria

sirio *a & m* Syrian

siroco *m* sirocco

sirvienta *f*, **sirviente** *m* servant

sirvo *vb véase* servir

sise ar *vt/i* hiss. **~o** *m* hissing

sísmico *a* seismic

sismo *m* earthquake

sistem a *m* system. **~ático** *a* systematic. **por ~a** as a rule

sitiar *vt* besiege; *(fig)* surround

sitio *m* place; *(espacio)* space; *(mil)* siege. **en cualquier ~** anywhere

situa ción *f* position. **~r** [21] *vt* situate; *(poner)* put; *(depositar)* deposit. **~rse** *vpr* be successful, establish o.s.

slip /es'lip/ *m (pl* slips /es'lip/) underpants, briefs

slogan /es'logan/ *m (pl* slogans /es'logan/) slogan

smoking /es'mokin/ *m (pl* smokings /es'mokin/) dinner jacket *(Brit)*, tuxedo *(Amer)*

sobaco *m* armpit

sobar *vt* handle; knead *(masa)*

soberan ia *f* sovereignty. **~o** *a* sovereign; *(fig)* supreme. —*m* sovereign

soberbi a *f* pride; *(altanería)* arrogance. **~o** *a* proud; *(altivo)* arrogant

soborn ar *vt* bribe. **~o** *m* bribe

sobra *f* surplus. **~s** *fpl* leftovers. **~do** *a* more than enough. **~nte** *a* surplus. **~r** *vi* be left over; *(estorbar)* be in the way. **de ~** more than enough

sobrasada *f* Majorcan sausage

sobre *prep* on; *(encima de)* on top of; *(más o menos)* about; *(por encima de)* above; *(sin tocar)* over; *(además de)* on top of. —*m* envelope. **~cargar** [12] *vt* overload. **~coger** [14] *vt* startle. **~cogerse** *vpr* be startled. **~cubierta** *f* dust cover. **~dicho** *a* aforementioned. **~entender** [1] *vt* understand, infer. **~entendido** *a* implicit. **~humano** *a* superhuman. **~llevar** *vt* bear. **~mesa** *f*. **de ~mesa** after-dinner. **~natural** *a* supernatural. **~nombre** *m* nickname. **~pasar** *vt* exceed. **~poner** [34] *vt* superimpose; *(fig, anteponer)* put before. **~ponerse** *vpr* overcome. **~pujar** *vt* surpass. **~saliente** *a (fig)* outstanding. —*m* excellent mark. **~salir** [52] *vi* stick out; *(fig)* stand out. **~saltar** *vt* startle. **~salto** *m* fright. **~sueldo** *m* bonus. **~todo** *m* overall; *(abrigo)* overcoat. **~ todo** above all, especially. **~venir** [53] *vi* happen. **~viviente** *a* surviving. —*m & f* survivor. **~vivir** *vi* survive. **~volar** *vt* fly over

sobriedad *f* restraint
sobrin|a *f* niece. **~o** *m* nephew
sobrio *a* moderate, sober
socarr|ón *a* sarcastic; *(taimado)* sly. **~onería** *f* sarcasm
socavar *vt* undermine
soci|able *a* sociable. **~al** *a* social. **~aldemocracia** *f* social democracy. **~aldemócrata** *m & f* social democrat. **~alismo** *m* socialsim. **~alista** *a & m & f* socialist. **~alizar** [10] *vt* nationalize. **~edad** *f* society; *(com)* company. **~edad anónima** limited company. **~o** *m* member; *(com)* partner. **~ología** *f* sociology. **~ólogo** *m* sociologist
socorr|er *vt* help. **~o** *m* help
soda *f (bebida)* soda (water)
sodio *m* sodium
sofá *m* sofa, settee
sofistica|ción *f* sophistication. **~do** *a* sophisticated. **~r** [7] *vt* adulterate
sofoca|ción *f* suffocation. **~nte** *a (fig)* stifling. **~r** [7] *vt* suffocate; *(fig)* stifle. **~rse** *vpr* suffocate; *(ruborizarse)* blush
soga *f* rope
soja *f* soya (bean)
sojuzgar [12] *vt* subdue
sol *m* sun; *(luz solar)* sunlight; *(mus)* G; *(solfa)* soh. **al ~** in the sun. **día** *m* **de ~** sunny day. **hace ~, hay ~** it is sunny. **tomar el ~** sunbathe
solamente *adv* only
solapa *f* lapel; *(de bolsillo etc)* flap. **~do** *a* sly. **~r** *vt/i* overlap
solar *a* solar. **~** *m* plot
solariego *a (casa)* ancestral
solaz *m* relaxation
soldado *m* soldier. **~ raso** private
solda|dor *m* welder; *(utensilio)* soldering iron. **~r** [2] *vt* weld, solder
solea|do *a* sunny. **~r** *vt* put in the sun

soledad *f* solitude; *(aislamiento)* loneliness
solemn|e *a* solemn. **~idad** *f* solemnity; *(ceremonia)* ceremony
soler [2] *vi* be in the habit of. **suele despertarse a las 6** he usually wakes up at 6 o'clock
sol|icitar *vt* request; apply for *(empleo)*; attract *(atención)*. **~ícito** *a* solicitous. **~icitud** *f (atención)* concern; *(petición)* request; *(para un puesto)* application
solidaridad *f* solidarity
solid|ez *f* solidity; *(de color)* fastness. **~ificar** [7] *vt* solidify. **~ificarse** *vpr* solidify
sólido *a* solid; *(color)* fast; *(robusto)* strong. **—** *m* solid
soliloquio *m* soliloquy
solista *m & f* soloist
solitario *a* solitary; *(aislado)* lonely. **—** *m* recluse; *(juego, diamante)* solitaire
solo *a (sin compañía)* alone; *(aislado)* lonely; *(único)* only; *(mus)* solo; *(café)* black. **—** *m* solo; *(juego)* solitaire. **a solas** alone
sólo *adv* only. **~ que** only. **aunque ~ sea** even if it is only. **con ~ que** if; *(con tal que)* as long as. **no ~... sino también** not only... but also... **tan ~** only
solomillo *m* sirloin
solsticio *m* solstice
soltar [2] *vt* let go of; *(dejar caer)* drop; *(dejar salir, decir)* let out; give *(golpe etc)*. **~se** *vpr* come undone; *(librarse)* break loose
solter|a *f* single woman. **~o** *a* single. **—** *m* bachelor. **apellido** *m* **de ~a** maiden name
soltura *f* looseness; *(agilidad)* agility; *(en hablar)* ease, fluency
solu|ble *a* soluble. **~ción** *f* solution. **~cionar** *vt* solve; settle *(huelga, asunto)*

solvent|ar vt resolve; settle ⟨deuda⟩. **~e a** & m solvent

sollo m sturgeon

solloz|ar [10] vi sob. **~o** m sob

sombr|a f shade; ⟨imagen oscura⟩ shadow. **~eado** a shady. **a la ~a** in the shade

sombrero m hat. **~ hongo** bowler hat

sombrío a sombre

somero a shallow

someter vt subdue; subject ⟨persona⟩; ⟨presentar⟩ submit. **~se** vpr give in

somn|oliento a sleepy. **~ífero** m sleeping-pill

somos vb véase **ser**

son m sound. —vb véase **ser**

sonámbulo m sleepwalker

sonar [2] vt blow; ring ⟨timbre⟩. —vi sound; ⟨timbre, teléfono etc⟩ ring; ⟨reloj⟩ strike; ⟨pronunciarse⟩ be pronounced; ⟨mus⟩ play; ⟨fig, ser conocido⟩ be familiar. **~se** vpr blow one's nose. **~ a** sound like

sonata f sonata

sonde|ar vt sound; ⟨fig⟩ sound out. **~o** m sounding; ⟨fig⟩ poll

soneto m sonnet

sónico a sonic

sonido m sound

sonoro a sonorous; ⟨ruidoso⟩ loud

sonr|eír [51] vi smile. **~eírse** vpr smile. **~iente** a smiling. **~isa** f smile

sonroj|ar vt make blush. **~arse** vpr blush. **~o** m blush

sonrosado a rosy, pink

sonsacar [7] vt wheedle out

soñ|ado a dream. **~ar** [2] vi dream ⟨con of⟩. **¡ni ~arlo!** not likely! ⟨que⟩ **ni ~ado** marvellous

sopa f soup

sopesar vt ⟨fig⟩ weigh up

sopl|ar vt blow; blow out ⟨vela⟩; blow off ⟨polvo⟩; ⟨inflar⟩ blow up. —vi blow. **~ete** m blowlamp. **~o** m puff; ⟨fig, momento⟩ moment

soporífero a soporific. —m sleeping-pill

soport|al m porch. **~ales** mpl arcade. **~ar** vt support; ⟨fig⟩ bear. **~e** m support

soprano f soprano

sor f sister

sorb|er vt suck; sip ⟨bebida⟩; ⟨absorber⟩ absorb. **~ete** m sorbet, water-ice. **~o** m swallow; ⟨pequeña cantidad⟩ sip

sord|amente adv silently, dully. **~era** f deafness

sórdido a squalid; ⟨tacaño⟩ mean

sordo a deaf; ⟨silencioso⟩ quiet. —m deaf person. **~mudo** a deaf and dumb. **a la sorda, a sordas** on the quiet. **hacerse el ~** turn a deaf ear

sorna f sarcasm. **con ~** sarcastically

soroche m ⟨LAm⟩ mountain sickness

sorpre|ndente a surprising. **~nder** vt surprise; ⟨coger desprevenido⟩ catch. **~sa** f surprise

sorte|ar vt draw lots for; ⟨rifar⟩ raffle; ⟨fig⟩ avoid. —vi draw lots; ⟨con moneda⟩ toss up. **~o** m draw; ⟨rifa⟩ raffle; ⟨fig⟩ avoidance

sortija f ring; ⟨de pelo⟩ ringlet

sortilegio m witchcraft; ⟨fig⟩ spell

sos|egado a calm. **~egar** [1 & 12] vt calm. —vi rest. **~iego** m calmness. **con ~iego** calmly

soslayo. al ~, de ~ sideways

soso a tasteless; ⟨fig⟩ dull

sospech|a f suspicion. **~ar** vt/i suspect. **~oso** a suspicious. —m suspect

sostén m support; ⟨prenda femenina⟩ bra ⟨fam⟩, brassière. **~ener** [40] vt support; ⟨sujetar⟩

hold; (*mantener*) maintain; (*alimentar*) sustain. **~enerse** *vpr* support o.s.; (*continuar*) remain. **~enido** *a* sustained; (*mus*) sharp. —*m* (*mus*) sharp

sota *f* (*de naipes*) jack

sótano *m* basement

sotavento *m* lee

soto *m* grove; (*matorral*) thicket

soviético *a* (*historia*) Soviet

soy *vb véase* **ser**

Sr *abrev* (*Señor*) Mr. **~a** *abrev* (*Señora*) Mrs. **~ta** *abrev* (*Señorita*) Miss

su *a* (*de él*) his; (*de ella*) her; (*de ello*) its; (*de uno*) one's; (*de Vd*) your; (*de ellos, de ellas*) their; (*de Vds*) your

suav|e *a* smooth; (*fig*) gentle; (*color, sonido*) soft. **~idad** *f* smoothness, softness. **~izar** [10] *vt* smooth, soften

subalimentado *a* underfed

subalterno *a* secondary; (*persona*) auxiliary

subarrendar [1] *vt* sublet

subasta *f* auction; (*oferta*) tender. **~r** *vt* auction

sub|campeón *m* runner-up. **~consciencia** *f* subconscious. **~consciente** *a & m* subconscious. **~continente** *m* subcontinent. **~desarrollado** *a* under-developed. **~director** *m* assistant manager

súbdito *m* subject

sub|dividir *vt* subdivide. **~estimar** *vt* underestimate. **~gerente** *m & f* assistant manager

subi|da *f* ascent; (*aumento*) rise; (*pendiente*) slope. **~do** *a* (*precio*) high; (*color*) bright; (*olor*) strong. **~r** *vt* go up; (*poner*) put; (*llevar*) take up; (*aumentar*) increase. —*vi* go up. **~r a** get into (*coche*); get on (*autobús, avión, barco, tren*); (*aumentar*) increase. **~rse** *vpr* climb up. **~rse a** get on (*tren etc*)

súbito *a* sudden. —*adv* suddenly. **de ~** suddenly

subjetivo *a* subjective

subjuntivo *a & m* subjunctive

subleva|ción *f* uprising. **~r** *vt* incite to rebellion. **~rse** *vpr* rebel

sublim|ar *vt* sublimate. **~e** *a* sublime

submarino *a* underwater. —*m* submarine

subordinado *a & m* subordinate

subrayar *vt* underline

subrepticio *a* surreptitious

subsanar *vt* remedy; overcome (*dificultad*)

subscri|bir *vt* (*pp* **subscrito**) sign. **~birse** *vpr* subscribe. **~pción** *f* subscription

subsidi|ario *a* subsidiary. **~o** *m* subsidy. **~o de paro** unemployment benefit

subsiguiente *a* subsequent

subsist|encia *f* subsistence. **~ir** *vi* subsist; (*perdurar*) survive

substanci|a *f* substance. **~al** *a* important. **~oso** *a* substantial

substantivo *m* noun

substitu|ción *f* substitution. **~ir** [17] *vt/i* substitute. **~to** *a & m* substitute

substraer [41] *vt* take away

subterfugio *m* subterfuge

subterráneo *a* underground. —*m* (*bodega*) cellar; (*conducto*) underground passage

subtítulo *m* subtitle

suburb|ano *a* suburban. —*m* suburban train. **~io** *m* suburb; (*en barrio pobre*) slum

subvenci|ón *f* grant. **~onar** *vt* subsidize

subver|sión *f* subversion. **~sivo** *a* subversive. **~tir** [4] *vt* subvert

subyugar [12] *vt* subjugate; (*fig*) subdue

succión *f* suction

suce|der *vi* happen; (*seguir*) follow; (*substituir*) succeed. **~dido**

m event. **lo** ~**dido** what happened. ~**sión** *f* succession. ~**sivo** *a* successive; (*consecutivo*) consecutive. ~**so** *m* event; (*incidente*) incident. ~**sor** *m* successor. **en lo** ~**sivo** in future. **lo que** ~**de es que** the trouble is that. **¿qué** ~**de?** what's the matter?

suciedad *f* dirt; (*estado*) dirtiness

sucinto *a* concise; (*prenda*) scanty

sucio *a* dirty; (*vil*) mean; (*conciencia*) guilty. **en** ~ in rough

sucre *m* (*unidad monetaria del Ecuador*) sucre

suculento *a* succulent

sucumbir *vi* succumb

sucursal *f* branch (office)

Sudáfrica *m* & *f* South Africa

sudafricano *a* & *m* South African

Sudamérica *f* South America

sudamericano *a* & *m* South American

sudar *vt* work hard for. —*vi* sweat

sudeste *m* south-east; (*viento*) south-east wind. ~**oeste** *m* south-west; (*viento*) south-west wind

sudor *m* sweat

Suecia *f* Sweden

sueco *a* Swedish. —*m* (*persona*) Swede; (*lengua*) Swedish. **hacerse el** ~ pretend not to hear

suegr|**a** *f* mother-in-law. ~**o** *m* father-in-law. **mis** ~**os** my in-laws

suela *f* sole

sueldo *m* salary

suelo *m* ground; (*dentro de edificio*) floor; (*tierra*) land. —*vb véase* **soler**

suelto *a* loose; (*libre*) free; (*sin pareja*) odd; (*lenguaje*) fluent. —*m* (*en periódico*) item; (*dinero*) change

sueño *m* sleep; (*ilusión*) dream. **tener** ~ be sleepy

suero *m* serum; (*de leche*) whey

suerte *f* luck; (*destino*) fate; (*azar*) chance. **de otra** ~ otherwise. **de** ~ **que** so. **echar** ~**s** draw lots. **por** ~ fortunately. **tener** ~ be lucky

suéter *m* jersey

suficien|**cia** *f* sufficiency; (*presunción*) smugness; (*aptitud*) suitability. ~**te** *a* sufficient; (*presumido*) smug. ~**temente** *adv* enough

sufijo *m* suffix

sufragio *m* (*voto*) vote

sufri|**do** *a* (*persona*) long-suffering; (*tela*) hard-wearing. ~**miento** *m* suffering. ~**r** *vt* suffer; (*experimentar*) undergo; (*soportar*) bear. —*vi* suffer

suge|**rencia** *f* suggestion. ~**rir** [4] *vt* suggest. ~**stión** *f* suggestion. ~**stionable** *a* impressionable. ~**stionar** *vt* influence. ~**stivo** *a* (*estimulante*) stimulating; (*atractivo*) attractive

suicid|**a** *a* suicidal. —*m* & *f* suicide; (*fig*) maniac. ~**arse** *vpr* commit suicide. ~**io** *m* suicide

Suiza *f* Switzerland

suizo *a* Swiss. —*m* Swiss; (*bollo*) bun

suje|**ción** *f* subjection. ~**tador** *m* fastener; (*de pelo, papeles etc*) clip; (*prenda femenina*) bra (*fam*), brassière. ~**tapapeles** *m invar* paper-clip. ~**tar** *vt* fasten; (*agarrar*) hold; (*fig*) restrain. ~**tarse** *vr* subject o.s.; (*ajustarse*) conform. ~**to** *a* fastened; (*susceptible*) subject. —*m* individual

sulfamida *f* sulpha (drug)

sulfúrico *a* sulphuric

sult|**án** *m* sultan. ~**ana** *f* sultana

suma *f* sum; (*total*) total. **en** ~ in short. ~**mente** *adv* extremely.

~r *vt* add (up); (*fig*) gather. —*vi* add up. **~rse** *vpr*. **~rse a** join in

sumario *a* brief. —*m* summary; (*jurid*) indictment

sumergi|ble *m* submarine. —*a* submersible. **~r** [14] *vt* submerge

sumidero *m* drain

suministr|ar *vt* supply. **~o** *m* supply; (*acción*) supplying

sumir *vt* sink; (*fig*) plunge

sumis|ión *f* submission. **~o** *a* submissive

sumo *a* greatest; (*supremo*) supreme. **a lo ~** at the most

suntuoso *a* sumptuous

supe *vb véase* **saber**

superar *vt* surpass; (*vencer*) overcome; (*dejar atrás*) get past. **~se** *vpr* excel o.s.

superchería *f* swindle

superestructura *f* superstructure

superfici|al *a* superficial. **~e** *f* surface; (*extensión*) area. **de ~e** surface

superfluo *a* superfluous

superhombre *m* superman

superintendente *m* superintendent

superior *a* superior; (*más alto*) higher; (*mejor*) better; (*piso*) upper. —*m* superior. **~idad** *f* superiority

superlativo *a & m* superlative

supermercado *m* supermarket

supersónico *a* supersonic

superstici|ón *f* superstition. **~oso** *a* superstitious

supervis|ión *f* supervision. **~or** *m* supervisor

superviviente *a* surviving. —*m & f* survivor

suplantar *vt* supplant

suplement|ario *a* supplementary. **~o** *m* supplement

suplente *a & m & f* substitute

súplica *f* entreaty; (*petición*) request

suplicar [7] *vt* beg

suplicio *m* torture

suplir *vt* make up for; (*reemplazar*) replace

supo|ner [34] *vt* suppose; (*significar*) mean; (*costar*) cost. **~sición** *f* supposition

supositorio *m* suppository

suprem|acía *f* supremacy. **~o** *a* supreme; (*momento etc*) critical

supr|esión *f* suppression. **~imir** *vt* suppress; (*omitir*) omit

supuesto *a* supposed. —*m* assumption. **~ que** if. **¡por ~!** of course!

sur *m* south; (*viento*) south wind

surc|ar [7] *vt* plough. **~o** *m* furrow; (*de rueda*) rut; (*en la piel*) wrinkle

surgir [14] *vi* spring up; (*elevarse*) loom up; (*aparecer*) appear; (*dificultad, oportunidad*) arise, crop up

surrealis|mo *m* surrealism. **~ta** *a & m & f* surrealist

surti|do *a* well-stocked; (*variado*) assorted. —*m* assortment, selection. **~dor** *m* (*de gasolina*) petrol pump (*Brit*), gas pump (*Amer*). **~r** *vt* supply; have (*efecto*). **~rse** *vpr* provide o.s. (**de** with)

susceptib|ilidad *f* susceptibility; (*sensibilidad*) sensitivity. **~le** *a* susceptible; (*sensible*) sensitive

suscitar *vt* provoke; arouse (*curiosidad, interés, sospechas*)

suscr... *véase* **subscr...**

susodicho *a* aforementioned

suspen|der *vt* hang (up); (*interrumpir*) suspend; (*univ etc*) fail. **~derse** *vpr* stop. **~sión** *f* suspension. **~so** *a* hanging; (*pasmado*) amazed; (*univ etc*) failed. —*m* fail. **en ~so** pending

suspicaz *a* suspicious

suspir|ar *vi* sigh. **~o** *m* sigh

sust... *véase* **subst...**

sustent|ación f support. **∼ar** vt support; (alimentar) sustain; (mantener) maintain. **∼o** m support; (alimento) sustenance

susto m fright. **caerse del ∼** be frightened to death

susurr|ar vi (persona) whisper; (agua) murmur; (hojas) rustle **∼o** m (de persona) whisper; (de agua) murmur; (de hojas) rustle

sutil a fine; (fig) subtle. **∼eza** f fineness; (fig) subtlety

suyo a & pron (de él) his; (de ella) hers; (de ello) its; (de uno) one's; (de Vd) yours; (de ellos, de ellas) theirs; (de Vds) yours. **un amigo ∼** a friend of his, a friend of theirs, etc

T

taba f (anat) ankle-bone; (juego) jacks

tabac|alera f (state) tobacconist. **∼alero** a tobacco. **∼o** m tobacco; (cigarrillos) cigarettes; (rapé) snuff

tabalear vi drum (with one's fingers)

Tabasco m Tabasco (P)

tabern|a f bar. **∼ero** m barman; (dueño) landlord

tabernáculo m tabernacle

tabique m (thin) wall

tabl|a f plank; (de piedra etc) slab; (estante) shelf; (de vestido) pleat; (lista) list; (índice) index; (en matemática etc) table. **∼ado** m platform; (en el teatro) stage. **∼ao** m place where flamenco shows are held. **∼as reales** backgammon. **∼ero** m board. **∼ero de mandos** dashboard. **hacer ∼a rasa de** disregard

tableta f tablet; (de chocolate) bar

tabl|illa f small board. **∼ón** m plank. **∼ón de anuncios** notice

board (esp Brit), bulletin board (Amer)

tabú m taboo

tabular vt tabulate

taburete m stool

tacaño a mean

tacita f small cup

tácito a tacit

taciturno a taciturn; (triste) miserable

taco m plug; (LAm, tacón) heel; (de billar) cue; (de billetes) book; (fig, lío, fam) mess; (Mex, culin) filled tortilla

tacógrafo m tachograph

tacón m heel

táctic|a f tactics. **∼o** a tactical

táctil a tactile

tacto m touch; (fig) tact

tacuara f (Arg) bamboo

tacurú m (small) ant

tacha f fault; (clavo) tack. **poner ∼s a** find fault with. **sin ∼** flawless

tachar vt (borrar) rub out; (con raya) cross out. **∼ de** accuse of

tafia f (LAm) rum

tafilete m morocco

tahúr m card-sharp

Tailandia f Thailand

tailandés a & m Thai

taimado a sly

taj|ada f slice. **∼ante** a sharp. **∼o** m slash; (fig, trabajo, fam) job; (culin) chopping block. **sacar ∼ada** profit

Tajo m Tagus

tal a such; (ante sustantivo en singular) such a. **∼pron** (persona) someone; (cosa) such a thing. **∼adv** so; (de tal manera) in such a way. **∼ como** the way. **∼ cual** (tal como) the way; (regular) fair. **∼ para cual** (fam) two of a kind. **con ∼ que** as long as. **¿qué ∼?** how are you? **un ∼** a certain

taladr|ar vt drill. **∼o** m drill; (agujero) drill hole

talante *m* mood. **de buen ∼** willingly

talar *vt* fell; *(fig)* destroy

talco *m* talcum powder

talcualillo *a (fam)* so so

talega *f*, **talego** *m* sack

talento *m* talent

TALGO *m* high-speed train

talismán *m* talisman

tal|ón *m* heel; *(recibo)* counterfoil; *(cheque)* cheque. **∼onario** *m* receipt book; *(de cheques)* cheque book

talla *f* carving; *(grabado)* engraving; *(de piedra preciosa)* cutting; *(estatura)* height; *(medida)* size; *(palo)* measuring stick; *(Arg, charla)* gossip. **∼do** *a* carved. **—***m* carving. **∼dor** *m* engraver

tallarín *m* noodle

talle *m* waist; *(figura)* figure; *(medida)* size

taller *m* workshop; *(de pintor etc)* studio

tallo *m* stem, stalk

tamal *m (LAm)* tamale

tamaño *a (tan grande)* so big a; *(tan pequeño)* so small a. **—***m* size. **de ∼ natural** life-size

tambalearse *vpr ⟨persona⟩* stagger; *⟨cosa⟩* wobble

también *adv* also, too

tambor *m* drum. **∼ del freno** brake drum. **∼ilear** *vi* drum

Támesis *m* Thames

tamiz *m* sieve. **∼ar** [10] *vt* sieve

tampoco *adv* nor, neither, not either

tampón *m* tampon; *(para entintar)* ink-pad

tan *adv* so. **tan... ∼** as... as

tanda *f* group; *(capa)* layer; *(de obreros)* shift

tangente *a & f* tangent

Tánger *m* Tangier

tangible *a* tangible

tango *m* tango

tanque *m* tank; *(camión, barco)* tanker

tante|ar *vt* estimate; *(ensayar)* test; *(fig)* weigh up. **—***vi* score. **∼o** *m* estimate; *(prueba)* test; *(en deportes)* score

tanto *a (en singular)* so much; *(en plural)* so many; *(comparación en singular)* as much; *(comparación en plural)* as many. **—***pron* so much; *(en plural)* so many. **—***adv* so much; *(tiempo)* so long. **—***m* certain amount; *(punto)* point; *(gol)* goal. **∼ como** as well as; *(cantidad)* as much as. **∼ más... cuanto que** all the more... because. **∼ si... como si** whether... or. **a ∼s de** sometime in. **en ∼, entre ∼** meanwhile. **en ∼ que** while. **entre ∼** meanwhile. **estar al ∼ de** be up to date with. **hasta ∼ que** until. **no es para ∼** it's not as bad as all that. **otro ∼** the same; *(el doble)* as much again. **por (lo) ∼** so. **un ∼ adv** somewhat

tañer [22] *vt* play

tapa *f* lid; *(de botella)* top; *(de libro)* cover. **∼s** *fpl* savoury snacks

tapacubos *m invar* hub-cap

tapa|dera *f* cover, lid; *(fig)* cover. **∼r** *vt* cover; *(abrigar)* wrap up; *(obturar)* plug; put the top on *⟨botella⟩*

taparrabo(s) *m invar* loincloth; *(bañador)* swimming-trunks

tapete *m (de mesa)* table cover; *(alfombra)* rug

tapia *f* wall. **∼r** *vt* enclose

tapicería *f* tapestry; *(de muebles)* upholstery

tapioca *f* tapioca

tapiz *m* tapestry. **∼ar** [10] *vt* hang with tapestries; upholster *⟨muebles⟩*

tap|ón *m* stopper; *(corcho)* cork; *(med)* tampon; *(tec)* plug. **∼onazo** *m* pop

taqui|igrafía *f* shorthand. **~í-grafo** *m* shorthand writer

taquilla *f* ticket office; (*archivador*) filing cabinet; (*fig, dinero*) takings. **~ero** *m* clerk, ticket seller. —*a* box-office

tara *f* (*peso*) tare; (*defecto*) defect

taracea *f* marquetry

tarántula *f* tarantula

tararear *vt/i* hum

tarda|nza *f* delay. **~r** *vi* take; (*mucho tiempo*) take a long time. **a más ~r** at the latest. **sin ~r** without delay

tard|e *adv* late. —*f* (*antes del atardecer*) afternoon; (*después del atardecer*) evening. **~e o temprano** sooner or later. **~ío** *a* late. **de ~e en ~e** from time to time. **por la ~e** in the afternoon

tardo *a* (*torpe*) slow

tarea *f* task, job

tarifa *f* rate, tariff

tarima *f* platform

tarjeta *f* card. **~ de crédito** credit card. **~ postal** postcard

tarro *m* jar

tarta *f* cake; (*torta*) tart. **~ helada** ice-cream cake

tartamud|ear *vi* stammer. **~o** *a* stammering. —*m* stammerer. **es ~o** he stammers

tártaro *m* tartar

tarugo *m* chunk

tasa *f* valuation; (*precio*) fixed price; (*índice*) rate. **~r** *vt* fix a price for; (*limitar*) ration; (*evaluar*) value

tasca *f* bar

tatarabuel|a *f* great-great-grandmother. **~o** *m* great-great-gandfather

tatua|je *m* (*acción*) tattooing; (*dibujo*) tattoo. **~r** [21] *vt* tattoo

taurino *a* bullfighting

Tauro *m* Taurus

tauromaquia *f* bullfighting

taxi| *m* taxi. **~ímetro** *m* taxi meter. **~ista** *m & f* taxi-driver

tayuyá *m* (*Arg*) water melon

taz|a *f* cup. **~ón** *m* bowl

te *pron* (*acusativo*) you; (*dativo*) (to) you; (*reflexivo*) (to) yourself

té *m* tea. **dar el ~** bore

tea *f* torch

teatr|al *a* theatre; (*exagerado*) theatrical. **~alizar** [10] *vt* dramatize. **~o** *m* theatre; (*literatura*) drama. **obra** *f* **~al** play

tebeo *m* comic

teca *f* teak

tecla *f* key. **~do** *m* keyboard. **tocar la ~, tocar una ~** pull strings

técnica *f* technique

tecn|icismo *m* technicality

técnico *a* technical. —*m* technician

tecnolog|ía *f* technology. **~óg-ico** *a* technological

tecolote *m* (*Mex*) owl

tecomate *m* (*Mex*) earthenware cup

tech|ado *m* roof. **~ar** *vt* roof. **~o** *m* (*interior*) ceiling; (*exterior*) roof. **~umbre** *f* roofing. **bajo ~ado** indoors

teja *f* tile. **~do** *m* roof. **a toca ~** cash

teje|dor *m* weaver. **~r** *vt* weave; (*hacer punto*) knit

tejemaneje *m* (*fam*) fuss; (*intriga*) scheming

tejido *m* material; (*anat, fig*) tissue. **~s** *mpl* textiles

tejón *m* badger

tela *f* material; (*de araña*) web; (*en líquido*) skin

telar *m* loom. **~es** *mpl* textile mill

telaraña *f* spider's web, cobweb

tele *f* (*fam*) television

tele|comunicación *f* telecommunication. **~diario** *m* television news. **~dirigido** *a* remote-controlled. **~férico** *m* cable-car; (*tren*) cable-railway

tel|efonear *vt/i* telephone.
~efónico *a* telephone. **~efonista** *m & f* telephonist. **~efono** *m* telephone. **al ~éfono** on the phone

tel|egrafía *f* telegraphy. **~egrafiar** [20] *vt* telegraph. **~egráfico** *a* telegraphic. **~égrafo** *m* telegraph

telegrama *m* telegram

telenovela *f* television soap opera

teleobjetivo *m* telephoto lens

telepatía *f* telepathy. **~ático** *a* telepathic

telesc|ópico *a* telescopic. **~opio** *m* telescope

telesilla *f* ski-lift, chair-lift

telespectador *m* viewer

telesquí *m* ski-lift

televi|dente *m & f* viewer. **~sar** *vt* televise. **~sión** *f* television. **~sor** *m* television (set)

télex *m* telex

telón *m* curtain. **~ de acero** (*historia*) Iron Curtain

tema *m* subject; (*mus*) theme

templ|ar [1] *vi* shake; (*de miedo*) tremble; (*de frío*) shiver; (*fig*) shudder. **~or** *m* shaking; (*de miedo*) trembling; (*de frío*) shivering. **~or de tierra** earthquake. **~oroso** *a* trembling

temer *vt* be afraid (of). **~vi** be afraid. **~se** *vpr* be afraid

temerario *a* reckless

tem|eroso *a* frightened. **~ible** *a* fearsome. **~or** *m* fear

témpano *m* floe

temperamento *m* temperament

temperatura *f* temperature

temperie *f* weather

tempest|ad *f* storm. **~uoso** *a* stormy. **levantar ~ades** (*fig*) cause a storm

templ|ado *a* moderate; (*tibio*) warm; (*clima, tiempo*) mild; (*valiente*) courageous; (*listo*) bright. **~anza** *f* moderation; (*de clima o*

tiempo) mildness. **~ar** *vt* temper; (*calentar*) warm; (*mus*) tune. **~e** *m* tempering; (*temperatura*) temperature; (*humor*) mood

templ|ete *m* niche; (*pabellón*) pavillion. **~o** *m* temple

tempora|da *f* time; (*época*) season. **~l** *a* temporary. **—m** (*tempestad*) storm; (*período de lluvia*) rainy spell

tempran|ero *a* (*frutos*) early. **~o** *a & adv* early. **ser ~ero** be an early riser

tena|cidad *f* tenacity

tenacillas *fpl* tongs

tenaz *a* tenacious

tenaza *f*, **tenazas** *fpl* pliers; (*para arrancar clavos*) pincers; (*para el fuego, culin*) tongs

tende|ncia *f* tendency. **~nte** *a*. **~nte a** aimed at. **~r** [1] *vt* spread (out); hang out (*ropa a secar*); (*colocar*) lay. **—vi** have a tendency (a to). **~rse** *vpr* stretch out

tender|ete *m* stall. **~o** *m* shopkeeper

tendido *a* spread out; (*ropa*) hung out; (*persona*) stretched out. **—m** (*en plaza de toros*) front rows. **~s** *mpl* (*ropa lavada*) washing

tendón *m* tendon

tenebroso *a* gloomy; (*turbio*) shady

tenedor *m* fork; (*poseedor*) holder

tener [40] *vt* have (got); (*agarrar*) hold; be (*años, calor, celos, cuidado, frío, ganas, hambre, miedo, razón, sed etc*). **¡ten cuidado!** be careful! **tengo calor** I'm hot. **tiene 3 años** he's 3 (years old). **~se** *vpr* stand up; (*considerarse*) consider o.s.; think o.s. **~ al corriente**, **~ al día** keep up to date. **~ 2 cm de largo** be 2 cms long. **~ a uno**

por consider s.o. ~ **que** have (got) to. **tenemos que comprar pan** we've got to buy some bread. **¡ahí tienes!** there you are! **no** ~ **nada que ver con** have nothing to do with. **¿qué tienes?** what's the matter (with you)? **¡tenga!** here you are!

tengo *vb véase* **tener**

teniente *m* lieutenant. ~ **de alcalde** deputy mayor

tenis *m* tennis. ~**ta** *m & f* tennis player

tenor *m* sense; (*mus*) tenor. **a este** ~ in this fashion

tensión *f* tension; (*presión*) pressure; (*arterial*) blood pressure; (*elec*) voltage; (*de persona*) tenseness. ~**o** *a* tense

tentación *f* temptation

tentáculo *m* tentacle

tenta|dor *a* tempting. ~**r** [1] *vt* feel; (*seducir*) tempt

tentativa *f* attempt

tenue *a* thin; (*luz, voz*) faint

teñi|do *m* dye. ~**r** [5 & 22] *vt* dye; (*fig*) tinge (**de** with). ~**rse** *vpr* dye one's hair

te|ología *f* theology. ~**ológico** *a* theological. ~**ólogo** *m* theologian

teorema *m* theorem

teo|ría *f* theory. ~**órico** *a* theoretical

tepache *m* (*Mex*) (alcoholic) drink

tequila *f* tequila

TER *m* high-speed train

terap|éutico *a* therapeutic. ~**ia** *f* therapy

tercer *a véase* **tercero**. ~**a** *f* (*auto*) third (gear). ~**o** *a* (*delante de nombre masculino en singular* **tercer**) third. —*m* third party

terceto *m* trio

terciar *vi* mediate. ~ **en** join in. ~**se** *vpr* occur

tercio *m* third

terciopelo *m* velvet

terco *a* obstinate

tergiversar *vt* distort

termal *a* thermal. ~**s** *fpl* thermal baths

termes *m invar* termite

térmico *a* thermal

termina|ción *f* ending; (*conclusión*) conclusion. ~**l** *a & m* terminal. ~**nte** *a* categorical. ~**r** *vt* finish, end. ~**rse** *vpr* come to an end. ~**r por** end up

término *m* end; (*palabra*) term; (*plazo*) period. ~ **medio** average. ~ **municipal** municipal district. **dar** ~ **a** finish off. **en último** ~ as a last resort. **estar en buenos** ~**s con** be on good terms with. **llevar a** ~ carry out. **poner** ~ **a** put an end to. **primer** ~ foreground

terminología *f* terminology

termita *f* termite

termo *m* Thermos flask (P), flask

termómetro *m* thermometer

termo|nuclear *a* thermonuclear. ~**sifón** *m* boiler. ~**stato** *m* thermostat

terner|a *f* (*carne*) veal. ~**o** *m* calf

ternura *f* tenderness

terquedad *f* stubbornness

terracota *f* terracotta

terrado *m* flat roof

terraplén *m* embankment

terrateniente *m & f* landowner

terraza *f* terrace; (*terrado*) flat roof

terremoto *m* earthquake

terre|no *a* earthly. —*m* land; (*solar*) plot; (*fig*) field. ~**stre** *a* earthly; (*mil*) ground

terr|ible *a* terrible. ~**iblemente** *adv* awfully. ~**ífico** *a* terrifying

territori|al *a* territorial. ~**o** *m* territory

terrón *m* (*de tierra*) clod; (*culin*) lump

terror *m* terror. ~**ífico** *a* terrifying. ~**ismo** *m* terrorism. ~**ista** *m & f* terrorist

terr|oso *a* earthy; (*color*) brown. **~uño** *m* land; (*patria*) native land

terso *a* polished; (*piel*) smooth

tertulia *f* social gathering, get-together (*fam*). **~r** *vi* (*LAm*) get together. **estar de ~** chat. **hacer ~** get together

tesina *f* dissertation. **~s** *f inv* thesis; (*opinión*) theory

tesón *m* perseverance

tesor|ería *f* treasury. **~ero** *m* treasurer. **~o** *m* treasure; (*tesorería*) treasury; (*libro*) thesaurus

testa *f* (*fam*) head. **~ferro** *m* figurehead

testa|mento *m* will. **T~mento** (*relig*) Testament. **~r** *vi* make a will

testarudo *a* stubborn

testículo *m* testicle

testi|ficar [7] *vt/i* testify. **~go** *m* witness. **~go de vista**, **~go ocular**, **~go presencial** eye-witness. **~monio** *m* testimony

teta *f* nipple; (*de biberón*) teat

tétanos *m* tetanus

tetera *f* (*para el té*) teapot; (*Mex*, *biberón*) feeding-bottle

tetilla *f* nipple; (*de biberón*) teat

tétrico *a* gloomy

textil *a* & *m* textile

text|o *m* text. **~ual** *a* textual

textura *f* texture

teyú *m* (*Arg*) iguana

tez *f* complexion

ti *pron* you

tía *f* aunt; (*fam*) woman

tiara *f* tiara

tibio *a* lukewarm. **ponerle ~ a uno** insult s.o.

tiburón *m* shark

tic *m* tic

tiempo *m* time; (*atmosférico*) weather; (*mus*) tempo; (*gram*) tense; (*en deportes*) half. **a su ~** in due course. **a ~** in time. **¿cuánto ~?** how long? **hace**

buen ~ the weather is fine. **hace ~** some time ago. **mucho ~** a long time. **perder el ~** waste time. **¿qué ~ hace?** what is the weather like?

tienda *f* shop; (*de campaña*) tent. **~ de comestibles**, **~ de ultramarinos** grocer's (shop) (*Brit*), grocery store (*Amer*)

tiene *vb véase* **tener**

tienta. **a ~s** gropingly. **andar a ~s** grope one's way

tiento *m* touch; (*de ciego*) blind person's stick; (*fig*) tact

tierno *a* tender; (*joven*) young

tierra *f* land; (*planeta*, *elec*) earth; (*suelo*) ground; (*geol*) soil, earth. **caer por ~** (*fig*) crumble. **por ~** overland, by land

tieso *a* stiff; (*firme*) firm; (*engreído*) conceited; (*orgulloso*) proud

tiesto *m* flowerpot

tifoideo *a* typhoid

tifón *m* typhoon

tifus *m* typhus; (*fiebre tifoidea*) typhoid (fever); (*en el teatro*) people with complimentary tickets

tigre *m* tiger

tijera *f*, **tijeras** *fpl* scissors; (*de jardín*) shears

tijeret|a *f* (*insecto*) earwig; (*bot*) tendril. **~ear** *vt* snip

tila *f* lime(-tree); (*infusión*) lime tea

tild|ar *vt*. **~ar de** (*fig*) call. **~e** *m* tilde

tilín *m* tinkle. **hacer ~** appeal

tilingo *a* (*Arg*, *Mex*) silly

tilma *f* (*Mex*) poncho

tilo *m* lime(-tree)

timar *vt* swindle

timbal *m* drum; (*culin*) timbale, meat pie

timbiriche *m* (*Mex*) (alcoholic) drink

timbr|ar *vt* stamp. **~e** *m* (*sello*) stamp; (*elec*) bell; (*sonido*) timbre. **tocar el ~e** ring the bell

timidez *f* shyness

tímido *a* shy

timo *m* swindle

timón *m* rudder; *(fig)* helm

tímpano *m* kettledrum; *(anat)* eardrum. **~s** *mpl (mus)* timpani

tina *f* tub. **~ja** *f* large earthenware jar

tinglado *m (fig)* intrigue

tinieblas *fpl* darkness; *(fig)* confusion

tino *f (habilidad)* skill; *(moderación)* moderation; *(tacto)* tact

tint|**a** *f* ink. **~e** *m* dyeing; *(color)* dye; *(fig)* tinge. **~ero** *m* ink-well. **de buena ~a** on good authority

tint|**ín** *m* tinkle; *(de vasos)* chink, clink. **~inear** *vi* tinkle; *(vasos)* chink, clink

tinto *a (vino)* red

tintorería *f* dyeing; *(tienda)* dry cleaner's

tintura *f* dyeing; *(color)* dye; *(noción superficial)* smattering

tío *m* uncle; *(fam)* man. **~s** *mpl* uncle and aunt

tiovivo *m* merry-go-round

típico *a* typical

tipo *m* type; *(persona, fam)* person; *(figura de mujer)* figure; *(figura de hombre)* build; *(com)* rate

tip|**ografía** *f* typography. **~ográfico** *a* typographic(al). **~ógrafo** *m* printer

típula *f* crane-fly, daddy-long-legs

tique *m*, **tiquet** *m* ticket

tiquete *m (LAm)* ticket

tira *f* strip. **la ~ de** lots of

tirabuzón *m* corkscrew; *(de pelo)* ringlet

tirad|**a** *f* distance; *(serie)* series; *(de libros etc)* edition. **~o** *a (barato)* very cheap; *(fácil, fam)* very easy. **~or** *m (asa)* handle; *(juguete)* catapult *(Brit)*, slingshot *(Amer)*. **de una ~a** at one go

tiran|**ía** *f* tyranny. **~izar** [10] *vt* tyrannize. **~o** *a* tyrannical. —*m* tyrant

tirante *a* tight; *(fig)* tense; *(relaciones)* strained. —*m* shoulder strap. **~s** *mpl* braces *(esp Brit)*, suspenders *(Amer)*

tirar *vt* throw; *(desechar)* throw away; *(derribar)* knock over; give *(golpe, coz etc)*; *(imprimir)* print. —*vi (disparar)* shoot. **~se** *vpr* throw o.s.; *(tumbarse)* lie down. **~ a** tend to (be); *(parecerse a)* resemble. **~ de** pull; *(atraer)* attract. **a todo ~** at the most. **ir tirando** get by

tirita *f* sticking-plaster, plaster *(Brit)*

tirit|**ar** *vi* shiver. **~ón** *m* shiver

tiro *m* throw; *(disparo)* shot; *(alcance)* range. **~ a gol** shot at goal. **a ~** within range. **errar el ~** miss. **pegarse un ~** shoot o.s.

tiroides *m* thyroid (gland)

tirón *m* tug. **de un ~** in one go

tirote|**ar** *vt* shoot at. **~o** *m* shooting

tisana *f* herb tea

tisis *f* tuberculosis

tisú *m (pl tisus)* tissue

títere *m* puppet. **~ de guante** glove puppet. **~s** *mpl* puppet show

titilar *vi* quiver; *(estrella)* twinkle

titiritero *m* puppeteer; *(acróbata)* acrobat; *(malabarista)* juggler

titube|**ante** *a* shaky; *(fig)* hesitant. **~ar** *vi* stagger; *(cosa)* be unstable; *(fig)* hesitate. **~o** *m* hesitation

titula|**do** *a (libro)* entitled; *(persona)* qualified. **~r** *m* heading; *(persona)* holder. —*vt* call. **~rse** *vpr* be called

título *m* title; *(persona)* titled person; *(académico)* qualification; *(univ)* degree; *(de periódico etc)* headline; (*derecho*) right. **a ~ de** as, by way of

tiza *f* chalk

tiznar *vt* dirty. **~ne** *m* soot. **~ón** *m* half-burnt stick; (*fig*) stain

toalla *f* towel. **~ero** *m* towel-rail

tobillo *m* ankle

tobogán *m* slide; (*para la nieve*) toboggan

tocadiscos *m invar* record-player

tocado *a* (*con sombrero*) wearing. —*m* hat. **~dor** *m* dressing-table. **~dor de señoras** ladies' room. **~nte** *a* touching. **en lo que ~ a,** en lo **~nte a** as for. **estar ~do** (**de la cabeza**) be mad. **te ~ a ti** it's your turn

tocateja. a ~ cash

tocayo *m* namesake

tocino *m* bacon

tocólogo *m* obstetrician

todavía *adv* still, yet. **~ no** not yet

todo *a* all; (*entero*) the whole; (*cada*) every. —*adv* completely, all. —*m* whole. —*pron* everything, all; (*en plural*) everyone. **~ el día** all day. **~ el mundo** everyone. **~ el que** anyone who. **~ incluido** all in. **~ lo contrario** quite the opposite. **~ lo que** anything which. **~s los días** every day. **~s los dos** both (of them). **~s los tres** all three. **ante ~** above all. **a ~ esto** meanwhile. **con ~** still, however. **del ~** completely. **en ~ el mundo** anywhere. **estar en ~** be on the ball. **es ~ uno** it's all the same. **nosotros ~s** all of us. **sobre ~** above all

toldo *m* sunshade

tolerancia *f* tolerance. **~nte** *a* tolerant. **~r** *vt* tolerate

tolondro *m* (*chichón*) lump

toma *f* taking; (*med*) dose; (*de agua*) outlet; (*elec*) socket; (*elec, clavija*) plug. —*int* well!, fancy that! **~ de corriente** power point. **~dura** *f.* **~dura de pelo** hoax. **~r** *vt* take; catch (*autobús, tren etc*); (*beber*) drink, have; (*comer*) eat, have. —*vi* take; (*dirigirse*) go. **~rse** *vpr* take; (*beber*) drink, have; (*comer*) eat, have. **~r a bien** take well. **~r a mal** take badly. **~r en serio** take seriously. **~rla con uno** pick on s.o. **~r nota** take note. **~r por** take for for. **~ y daca** give and take. **¿qué va a ~r?** what would you like?

tomate *m* tomato

tomavistas *m invar* cine-camera

tómbola *f* tombola

tomillo *m* thyme

tomo *m* volume

ton. sin ~ ni son without rhyme or reason

tonada *f,* **tonadilla** *f* tune

tonel *m* barrel. **~ada** *f* ton. **~aje** *m* tonnage

tónica *f* tonic water; (*mus*) tonic. **~o** *a* tonic; (*sílaba*) stressed. **—*m* tonic

tonificar [7] *vt* invigorate

tono *m* tone; (*mus, modo*) key; (*color*) shade

tontería *f* silliness; (*cosa*) silly thing; (*dicho*) silly remark. **~o** *a* silly. —*m* fool, idiot; (*payaso*) clown. **dejarse de ~erías** stop wasting time. **hacer el ~o** act the fool. **hacerse el ~o** feign ignorance

topacio *m* topaz

topar *vt* (*animal*) butt; (*persona*) bump into; (*fig*) run into. —*vi.* **~ con** run into

tope _a_ maximum. —_m_ end; (_de tren_) buffer. **hasta los ~s** crammed full. **ir a ~** go flat out

tópico _a_ topical. —_m_ cliché

topo _m_ mole

topografía _f_ topography. **~áfico** _a_ topographical

toque _m_ touch; (_sonido_) sound; (_de campana_) peal; (_de reloj_) stroke; (_fig_) crux. **~ de queda** curfew. **~tear** _vt_ keep fingering, fiddle with. **dar el último ~** put the finishing touches

toquilla _f_ shawl

tórax _m_ thorax

torbellino _m_ whirlwind; (_de polvo_) cloud of dust; (_fig_) whirl

torcer [2 & 9] _vt_ twist; (_doblar_) bend; wring out (_ropa_). —_vi_ turn. **~se** _vpr_ twist; (_fig, desviarse_) go astray; (_fig, frustrarse_) go wrong

tordo _a_ dapple grey. —_m_ thrush

torear _vt_ fight; (_evitar_) dodge; (_entretener_) put off. —_vi_ fight (bulls). **~o** _m_ bullfighting. **~ro** _m_ bullfighter

tormenta _f_ storm. **~o** _m_ torture. **~oso** _a_ stormy

tornado _m_ tornado

tornar _vt_ return

tornasolado _a_ irridescent

torneo _m_ tournament

tornillo _m_ screw

torniquete _m_ (_entrada_) turnstile

torno _m_ lathe; (_de alfarero_) wheel. **en ~** a around

toro _m_ bull. **~s** _mpl_ bullfighting. **ir a los ~s** go to a bullfight

toronja _f_ grapefruit

torpe _a_ clumsy; (_estúpido_) stupid

torpedero _m_ torpedo-boat. **~o** _m_ torpedo

torpeza _f_ clumsiness; (_de inteligencia_) slowness

torpor _m_ torpor

torrado _m_ toasted chick-pea

torre _f_ tower; (_en ajedrez_) castle, rook

torrefacción _f_ roasting. **~to** _a_ roasted

torrencial _a_ torrential. **~te** _m_ torrent; (_circulatorio_) bloodstream; (_fig_) flood

tórrido _a_ torrid

torrija _f_ French toast

torsión _f_ twisting

torso _m_ torso

torta _f_ tart; (_bollo, fam_) cake; (_golpe_) slap, punch; (_Mex, bocadillo_) sandwich. **~zo** _m_ slap, punch. **no entender ni ~** not understand a word of it. **pegarse un ~zo** have a bad accident

tortícolis _f_ stiff neck

tortilla _f_ omelette; (_Mex, de maíz_) tortilla, maize cake. **~ francesa** plain omelette

tórtola _f_ turtle-dove

tortuga _f_ tortoise; (_de mar_) turtle

tortuoso _a_ winding; (_fig_) devious

tortura _f_ torture. **~r** _vt_ torture

torvo _a_ grim

tos _f_ cough. **~ ferina** whooping cough

tosco _a_ crude; (_persona_) coarse

toser _vi_ cough

tósigo _m_ poison

tosquedad _f_ crudeness; (_de persona_) coarseness

tostada _f_ toast. **~ado** _a_ (_persona_) tanned; (_marrón_) brown. **~ar** _vt_ toast (_pan_); roast (_café_); tan (_piel_). **~ón** _m_ (_pan_) crouton; (_lata_) bore

total _a_ total. —_adv_ after all. —_m_ total; (_totalidad_) whole. **~idad** _f_ whole. **~itario** _a_ totalitarian. **~izar** [10] _vt_ total. **~ que** so, to cut a long story short

tóxico _a_ toxic

toxicómano _m_ drug addict

toxina _f_ toxin

tozudo _a_ stubborn

traba _f_ bond; (_fig, obstáculo_) obstacle. **poner ~s a** hinder

trabaj|ador a hard-working. —m worker. **~ar** vt work (**de** as); knead (*masa*); (*estudiar*) work at; (*actor*) act. —vi work. **~o** m work. **~os** mpl hardships. **~o forzados** hard labour. **~oso** a hard. **costar ~o** be difficult. **¿en qué ~as?** what work do you do?

trabalenguas m invar tongue-twister

traba|r vt (*sujetar*) fasten; (*unir*) join; (*empezar*) start; (*culin*) thicken. **~rse** vpr get tangled up. **trabársele la lengua** get tongue-tied. **~zón** f joining; (*fig*) connection

trabucar [7] vt mix up

trácala f (*Mex*) trick

tracción f traction

tractor m tractor

tradici|ón f tradition. **~onal** a traditional. **~onalista** m & f traditionalist

traduc|ción f translation. **~ir** [47] vt translate (**al** into). **~tor** m translator

traer [41] vt bring; (*llevar*) carry; (*atraer*) attract. **traérselas** be difficil

trafica|nte m & f dealer. **~r** [7] vi deal

tráfico m traffic; (*com*) trade

traga|deras fpl (*fam*) throat. **tener buenas ~deras** (*ser crédulo*) swallow anything; (*ser tolerante*) be easygoing. **~luz** m skylight. **~perras** f invar slot-machine. **~r** [12] vt swallow; (*comer mucho*) devour; (*absorber*) absorb; (*fig*) swallow up. **no (poder) ~r** not be able to stand. **~rse** vpr swallow; (*fig*) swallow up

tragedia f tragedy

trágico a tragic. —m tragedian

trag|o m swallow, gulp; (*pequeña porción*) sip; (*fig, disgusto*) blow. **~ón** a greedy. —m glutton. **ech-ar(se) un ~o** have a drink

trai|ción f treachery; (*pol*) treason. **~cionar** vt betray. **~cionero** a treacherous. **~dor** a treacherous. —m traitor

traigo vb *véase* **traer**

traje m dress; (*de hombre*) suit. —vb *véase* **traer**. **~ de baño** swimming-costume. **~ de ceremonia**, **~ de etiqueta**, **~ de noche** evening dress

traj|ín m (*transporte*) haulage; (*jaleo, fam*) bustle. **~inar** vt transport. —vi bustle about

trama f weft; (*fig*) link; (*fig, argumento*) plot. **~r** vt weave; (*fig*) plot

tramitar vt negotiate

trámite m step. **~s** mpl procedure. **en ~** in hand

tramo m (*parte*) section; (*de escalera*) flight

tramp|a f trap; (*puerta*) trapdoor; (*fig*) trick. **~illa** f trapdoor. **hacer ~a** cheat

trampolín m trampoline; (*fig, de piscina*) springboard

tramposo a cheating. —m cheat

tranca f stick; (*de puerta*) bar

trance m moment; (*hipnótico etc*) trance. **a todo ~** at all costs

tranco m stride

tranquil|idad f (*peace and*) quiet; (*de espíritu*) peace of mind. **~izar** [10] vt reassure. **~o** a quiet; (*conciencia*) clear; (*mar*) calm; (*despreocupado*) thoughtless. **estáte ~o** don't worry

trans... pref (*véase también* **tras...**) trans...

transacción f transaction; (*acuerdo*) compromise

transatlántico a transatlantic. —m (*ocean*) liner

transbord|ador m ferry. **~ar** vt transfer. **~arse** vpr change. —o m transfer. **hacer ~o** change (**en** at)

transcri|bir (pp **transcrito**) vt transcribe. **~pción** f transcription

transcurrir *vi* pass. **~so** *m* course

transeúnte *a* temporary. —*m &* *f* passer-by

transferencia *f* transfer. **~ir** [4] *vt* transfer

transfigurar *vt* transfigure

transformación *f* transformation. **~dor** *m* transformer. **~r** *vt* transform

transfusión *f* transfusion. **hacer una ~** give a blood transfusion

transgredir *vt* transgress. **~sión** *f* transgression

transición *f* transition

transido *a* overcome

transigir [14] *vi* give in, compromise

transistor *m* transistor; *(radio)* radio

transitable *a* passable. **~r** *vi* go

transitivo *a* transitive

tránsito *m* transit; *(tráfico)* traffic

transitorio *a* transitory

translúcido *a* translucent

transmisión *f* transmission; *(radio, TV)* broadcast. **~sor** *m* transmitter. **~sora** *f* broadcasting station. **~tir** *vt* transmit; *(radio, TV)* broadcast; *(fig)* pass on

transparencia *f* transparency. **~tar** *vt* show. **~te** *a* transparent

transpiración *f* perspiration. **~r** *vi* transpire; *(sudar)* sweat

transponer [34] *vt* move. —*vi* disappear round *(esquina etc)*; disappear behind *(montaña etc)*. **~se** *vpr* disappear

transportar *vt* transport. **~e** *m* transport. **empresa** *f* **de ~es** removals company

transversal *a* transverse; *(calle)* side

tranvía *m* tram

trapacería *f* swindle

trapear *vt (LAm)* mop

trapecio *m* trapeze; *(math)* trapezium

trapiche *m (para azúcar)* mill; *(para aceitunas)* press

trapicheo *m* fiddle

trapisonda *f (jaleo, fam)* row; *(enredo, fam)* plot

trapo *m* rag; *(para limpiar)* cloth. **~s** *mpl (fam)* clothes. **a todo ~** out of control

tráquea *f* windpipe, trachea

traquetear *vt* bang, rattle. **~o** *m* banging, rattle

tras *prep* after; *(detrás)* behind; *(encima de)* as well as

tras... *pref (véase también* **trans...)** trans...

trascendencia *f* importance. **~ntal** *a* transcendental; *(importante)* important. **~r** [1] *vi (oler)* smell (**a** of); *(saberse)* become known; *(extenderse)* spread

trasegar [1 & 12] *vt* move around

trasero *a* back, rear. —*m (anat)* bottom

trasgo *m* goblin

trasladar *vt* move; *(aplazar)* postpone; *(traducir)* translate; *(copiar)* copy. **~o** *m* transfer; *(copia)* copy; *(mudanza)* removal. **dar ~o** send a copy

traslúcido *a* translucent. **~ucirse** [11] *vpr* be translucent; *(dejarse ver)* show through; *(fig, revelarse)* be revealed. **~uz** *m.* **al ~uz** against the light

trasmano *m.* **a ~** out of reach; *(fig)* out of the way

trasnochar *vt (acostarse tarde)* go to bed late; *(no acostarse)* stay up all night; *(no dormir)* be unable to sleep; *(pernoctar)* spend the night

traspasar *vt* pierce; *(transferir)* transfer; *(pasar el límite)* go beyond. **~o** *m* transfer. **se ~a** for sale

traspié *m* trip; *(fig)* slip. **dar un ~** stumble; *(fig)* slip up

trasplant|ar vt transplant. **~e** m transplanting; (med) transplant

trastada f stupid thing; (jugada) dirty trick, practical joke

traste m fret. **dar al ~ con** ruin. **ir al ~** fall through

trastero m storeroom

trastienda f back room; (fig) shrewdness

trasto m piece of furniture; (cosa inútil) piece of junk; (persona) useless person, dead loss (fam)

trastorn|ado a mad. **~ar** vt upset; (volver loco) drive mad; (fig, gustar mucho, fam) delight. **~arse** vpr get upset; (volverse loco) go mad. **~o** m (incl med) upset; (pol) disturbance; (fig) confusion

trastrocar [2 & 7] vt change round

trat|able a friendly. **~ado** m treatise; (acuerdo) treaty. **~amiento** m treatment; (título) title. **~ante** m & f dealer. **~ar** vt (incl med) treat; deal with (asunto etc); (com) deal; (manejar) handle; (de tú, de Vd) address (de as); (llamar) call. —vi deal (with). **~ar con** have to do with; know (persona); (com) deal in. **~ar de** be about; (intentar) try. **~o** m treatment; (acuerdo) agreement; (título) title; (relación) relationship. **¡~o hecho!** agreed! **~os** mpl dealings. **¿de qué se ~a?** what's it about?

traum|a m trauma. **~ático** a traumatic

través m (inclinación) slant. **a ~ de** through; (de un lado a otro) across. **de ~** across; (de lado) sideways. **mirar de ~** look askance at

travesaño m crosspiece

travesía f crossing; (calle) side-street

trav|esura f prank. **~ieso** a (niño) mischievous, naughty

trayecto m road; (tramo) stretch; (ruta) route; (viaje) journey. **~ria** f trajectory; (fig) course

traz|a f plan; (aspecto) look, appearance; (habilidad) skill. **~ado** a. **bien ~ado** good-looking. **mal ~ado** unattractive. —m plan. **~ar** [10] vt draw; (bosquejar) sketch. **~o** m line

trébol m clover. **~es** mpl (en naipes) clubs

trece a & m thirteen

trecho m stretch; (distancia) distance; (tiempo) while. **a ~s** in places. **de ~ en ~** at intervals

tregua f truce; (fig) respite

treinta a & m thirty

tremendo a terrible; (extraordinario) terrific

trementina f turpentine

tren m train; (equipaje) luggage. **~ de aterrizaje** landing gear. **~ de vida** lifestyle

tren|cilla f braid. **~za** f braid; (de pelo) plait. **~zar** [10] vt plait

trepa|dor a climbing. **~r** vt/i climb

tres a & m three. **~cientos** a & m three hundred. **~illo** m three-piece suite; (mus) triplet

treta f trick

tri|angular a triangular. **~ángulo** m triangle

tribal a tribal. **~u** f tribe

tribulación f tribulation

tribuna f platform; (de espectadores) stand

tribunal m court; (de examen etc) board; (fig) tribunal

tribut|ar vt pay. **~o** m tribute; (impuesto) tax

triciclo m tricycle

tricolor a three-coloured

tricornio a three-cornered. —m three-cornered hat

tricotar vt/i knit

tridimensional a three-dimensional

tridente m trident

trigésimo a thirtieth

trig|al m wheat field. **~o** m wheat

trigonometría f trigonometry

trigueño a olive-skinned; ⟨pelo⟩ dark blonde

trilogía f trilogy

trilla|do a (fig, manoseado) trite; (fig, conocido) well-known. **~r** vt thresh

trimestr|al a quarterly. **~e** m quarter; (escol, univ) term

trin|ar vi warble. **estar que trina** be furious

trinchar vt carve

trinchera f ditch; (mil) trench; (rail) cutting; (abrigo) trench coat

trineo m sledge

trinidad f trinity

Trinidad f Trinidad

trino m warble

trío m trio

tripa f intestine; (culin) tripe; (fig, vientre) tummy, belly. **~s** fpl (de máquina etc) parts, workings. **me duele la ~** I've got tummy-ache. **revolver las ~s** turn one's stomach

tripicallos mpl tripe

triple a triple. **—m. el ~e (de)** three times as much (as). **~icado** a. **por ~icado** in triplicate. **~icar** [7] vt treble

trípode m tripod

tríptico m triptych

tripula|ción f crew. **~nte** m & f member of the crew. **~r** vt man

triquitraque m (ruido) clatter

tris m crack; (de papel etc) ripping noise. **estar en un ~** be on the point of

triste a sad; ⟨paisaje, tiempo etc⟩ gloomy; (fig, insignificante) miserable. **~za** f sadness

tritón m newt

triturar vt crush

triunf|al a triumphal. **~ante** a triumphant. **~ar** vi triumph (de, sobre over). **~o** m triumph

triunvirato m triumvirate

trivial a trivial

triza f piece. **hacer algo ~s** smash sth to pieces

trocar [2 & 7] vt (ex)change

trocear vt cut up, chop

trocito m small piece

trocha f narrow path; (atajo) short cut

trofeo m trophy

tromba f waterspout. **~ de agua** heavy downpour

trombón m trombone; (músico) trombonist

trombosis f invar thrombosis

trompa f horn; (de orquesta) French horn; (de elefante) trunk; (hocico) snout; (juguete) spinning top; (anat) tube. **—m** horn player. **coger una ~** (fam) get drunk

trompada f, **trompazo** m bump

trompet|a f trumpet; (músico) trumpeter, trumpet player; (clarín) bugle. **~illa** f ear-trumpet

trompicar [7] vi trip

trompo m (juguete) (spinning) top

trona|da f thunder storm. **~r** vt (Mex) shoot. **—vi** thunder

tronco m trunk. **dormir como un ~** sleep like a log

tronchar vt bring down; (fig) cut short. **~se de risa** laugh a lot

trono m throne

trop|a f troops. **~el** m mob. **ser de ~a** be in the army

tropero m (Arg, vaquero) cowboy

tropez|ar [1 & 10] vi trip; (fig) slip up. **~ar con** run into. **~ón** m stumble; (fig) slip

tropical a tropical

trópico a tropical. **—m** tropic

tropiezo m slip; (desgracia) mishap

trotar vi trot. **~e** m trot; (fig) toing and froing. **al ~e** trotting;

(de prisa) in a rush. **de mucho** ~e hard-wearing

trozo *m* piece, bit. **a** ~**s** in bits

truco *m* knack; *(ardid)* trick. **coger el** ~ get the knack

trucha *f* trout

trueno *m* thunder; *(estampido)* bang

trueque *m* exchange. **aun a** ~ **de** even at the expense of

trufa *f* truffle. ~**r** *vt* stuff with truffles

truhán *m* rogue; *(gracioso)* jester

truncar [7] *vt* truncate; *(fig)* cut short

tu *a* your

tú *pron* you

tuba *f* tuba

tubérculo *m* tuber

tuberculosis *f* tuberculosis

tub|ería *f* pipes; *(oleoducto etc)* pipeline. ~**o** *m* tube. ~**o de ensayo** test tube. ~**o de escape** *(auto)* exhaust (pipe). ~**ular** *a* tubular

tuerca *f* nut

tuerto *a* one-eyed, blind in one eye. —*m* one-eyed person

tuétano *m* marrow; *(fig)* heart. **hasta los** ~**s** completely

tufo *m* fumes; *(olor)* bad smell

tugurio *m* hovel, slum

tul *m* tulle

tulipán *m* tulip

tulli|do *a* paralysed. ~**r** [22] *vt* cripple

tumba *f* grave, tomb

tumb|ar *vt* knock down, knock over; *(fig, en examen, fam)* fail; *(pasmar, fam)* overwhelm. ~**arse** *vpr* lie down. ~**o** *m* jolt. **dar un** ~**o** tumble. ~**ona** *f* settee; *(sillón)* armchair; *(de lona)* deckchair

tumefacción *f* swelling

tumido *a* swollen

tumor *m* tumour

tumulto *m* turmoil; *(pol)* riot

tuna *f* prickly pear; *(de estudiantes)* student band

tunante *m & f* rogue

túnel *m* tunnel

Túnez *m (ciudad)* Tunis; *(país)* Tunisia

túnica *f* tunic

Tunicia *f* Tunisia

tupé *m* toupee; *(fig)* nerve

tupido *a* thick

turba *f* peat; *(muchedumbre)* mob

turba|ción *f* disturbance, upset; *(confusión)* confusion. ~**do** *a* upset

turbante *m* turban

turbar *vt* upset; *(molestar)* disturb. ~**se** *vpr* be upset

turbina *f* turbine

turbio *a* cloudy; *(vista)* blurred; *(asunto etc)* unclear. ~**ón** *m* squall

turbulen|cia *f* turbulence; *(disturbio)* disturbance. ~**te** *a* turbulent; *(persona)* restless

turco *a* Turkish. —*m* Turk; *(lengua)* Turkish

tur|ismo *m* tourism; *(coche)* car. ~**ista** *m & f* tourist. ~**ístico** *a* tourist. **oficina** *f* **de** ~**ismo** tourist office

turn|arse *vpr* take turns (**para** to). ~**o** *m* turn; *(de trabajo)* shift. **por** ~**o** in turn

turquesa *f* turquoise

Turquía *f* Turkey

turrón *m* nougat

turulato *a (fam)* stunned

tutear *vt* address as *tú*. ~**se** *vpr* be on familiar terms

tutela *f (jurid)* guardianship; *(fig)* protection

tuteo *m* use of the familiar *tú*

tutor *m* guardian; *(escol)* form master

tuve *vb véase* **tener**

tuyo *a & pron* yours. **un amigo** ~ a friend of yours

U

u *conj* or
ubicuidad *f* ubiquity
ubre *f* udder
ucraniano *a* & *m* Ukrainian
Ud *abrev* (*Usted*) you
uf *int* phew!; (*de repugnancia*) ugh!
ufan arse *vpr* be proud (**con**, **de** of); (*jactarse*) boast (**con**, **de** about). **~o** *a* proud
ujier *m* usher
úlcera *f* ulcer
ulterior *a* later; (*lugar*) further. **~mente** *adv* later, subsequently
últimamente *adv* (*recientemente*) recently; (*al final*) finally; (*en último caso*) as a last resort
ultim ar *vt* complete. **~átum** *m* ultimatum
último *a* last; (*más reciente*) latest; (*más lejano*) furthest; (*más alto*) top; (*más bajo*) bottom; (*fig*, *extremo*) extreme. **estar en las últimas** be on one's last legs; (*sin dinero*) be down to one's last penny. **por ~** finally. **ser lo ~** (*muy bueno*) be marvellous; (*muy malo*) be awful. **vestido a la última** dressed in the latest fashion
ultra *a* ultra, extreme
ultraj ante *a* outrageous. **~e** *m* outrage
ultramar *m* overseas countries. **de ~, en ~** overseas
ultramarino *a* overseas. **~s** *mpl* groceries. **tienda de ~s** grocer's (shop) (*Brit*), grocery store (*Amer*)
ultranza a ~ (*con decisión*) decisively; (*extremo*) extreme
ultra|sónico *a* ultrasonic. **~vi-oleta** *a* invar ultraviolet
ulular *vi* howl; (*búho*) hoot

umbilical *a* umbilical
umbral *m* threshold
umbrío, umbroso *a* shady
un *art indef m* (*pl* **unos**) a. **—a** one. **~os** *a pl* some
una *art indef f* a. **la ~** one o'clock
un ánime *a* unanimous. **~animidad** *f* unanimity
undécimo *a* eleventh
ung ir [14] *vt* anoint. **~üento** *m* ointment
únic amente *adv* only. **~o** *a* only; (*fig*, *incomparable*) unique
unicornio *m* unicorn
unid ad *f* unit; (*cualidad*) unity. **~o** *a* united
unifica ción *f* unification. **~r** [7] *vt* unite, unify
uniform ar *vt* standardize; (*poner uniforme a*) put into uniform. **~e** *a* & *m* uniform. **~idad** *f* uniformity
uni génito *a* only. **~lateral** *a* unilateral
uni ón *f* union; (*cualidad*) unity; (*tec*) joint. **~r** *vt* join; mix (*líquidos*). **~rse** *vpr* join together
unísono *m* unison. **al ~** in unison
unitario *a* unitary
universal *a* universal
universi dad *f* university. **U~dad a Distancia** Open University. **~tario** *a* university
universo *m* universe
uno *a* one; (*en plural*) some. **—pron** one; (*alguien*) someone, somebody. **—m** one. **~ a otro** each other. **~ y otro** both. (**los**) **~s... (los) otros** some... others
untar *vt* grease; (*med*) rub; (*fig*, *sobornar*, *fam*) bribe
uña *f* nail; (*de animal*) claw; (*casco*) hoof
upa *int* up!
uranio *m* uranium
Urano *m* Uranus
urban idad *f* politeness. **~ismo** *m* town planning. **~ístico** *a*

urban. ~**ización** f development.
~**izar** [10] vt civilize; develop
(terreno). ~**o** a urban
urbe f big city
urdimbre f warp
urdir vt (fig) plot
urgencia f urgency; (emergencia) emergency; (necesidad)
urgent need. ~**ente** a urgent.
~**ir** [14] vi be urgent. **carta** f
~**ente** express letter
urinario m urinal
urna f urn; (pol) ballot box
urraca f magpie
URSS abrev (historia) (Unión de
Repúblicas Socialistas Soviéticas) USSR, Union of Soviet
Socialist Republics
Uruguay m. **el** ~ Uruguay
uruguayo a & m Uruguayan
us|ado a used; (ropa etc) worn.
~**anza** f usage, custom. ~**ar** vt
use; (llevar) wear. ~**o** m use;
(costumbre) usage, custom. **al**
~**o** (de moda) in fashion; (a la
manera de) in the style of. **de** ~**o**
externo for external use
usted pron you
usual a usual
usuario a user
usur|a f usury. ~**ero** m usurer
usurpar vt usurp
usuta f (Arg) sandal
utensilio m tool; (de cocina)
utensil. ~**s** mpl equipment
útero m womb
útil a useful. ~**es** mpl
implements
utili|dad f usefulness. ~**tario** a
utilitarian; (coche) utility. ~**zación** f use, utilization. ~**zar** [10]
vt use, utilize
uva f grape. ~ **pasa** raisin. **mala**
~ bad mood

V

vaca f cow; (carne) beef
vacaciones fpl holiday(s). **estar**
de ~ be on holiday. **ir de** ~ go
on holiday
vaca|nte a vacant. —f vacancy.
~**r** [7] vi fall vacant
vaci|ar [20] vt empty; (ahuecar)
hollow out; (en molde) cast; (afilar) sharpen. ~**edad** f emptiness; (tontería) silly thing,
frivolity
vacila|ción f hesitation. ~**nte** a
unsteady; (fig) hesitant. ~**r** vi
sway; (dudar) hesitate; (fam)
tease
vacío a empty; (vanidoso)
vain. —m empty space; (estado)
emptiness; (en física) vacuum;
(fig) void
vacuidad f emptiness; (tontería)
silly thing, frivolity
vacuna f vaccine. ~**ción** f vaccination. ~**r** vt vaccinate
vacuno a bovine
vacuo a empty
vade m bland
vade|ar vt ford. ~**o** m ford
vaga|bundear vi wander.
~**bundo** a vagrant; (perro)
stray. —m tramp. ~**r** [12] vi wander (about)
vagina f vagina
vago a vague; (holgazán) idle;
(foto) blurred. —m idler
vagón m carriage; (de mercancías) truck, wagon. ~**ón**
restaurante dining-car. ~**oneta**
f truck
vahído m dizzy spell
vaho m breath; (vapor) steam.
~**s** mpl inhalation
vaina f sheath; (bot) pod
vainilla f vanilla
vaivén m swaying; (de tráfico)
coming and going; (fig, de suerte)

change. **vaivenes** *mpl* (*fig*) ups and downs

vajilla *f* dishes, crockery. **lavar la ~** wash up

vale *m* voucher; (*pagaré*) IOU. **~dero** *a* valid

valenciano *a* from Valencia

valent|ía *f* courage; (*acción*) brave deed. **~ón** *m* braggart

valer [42] *vt* be worth; (*costar*) cost; (*fig, significar*) mean. —*vi* be worth; (*costar*) cost; (*servir*) be of use; (*ser valedero*) be valid; (*estar permitido*) be allowed. —*m* worth. **~ la pena** be worthwhile, be worth it. **¿cuánto vale?** how much is it?. **no ~ para nada** be useless. **¡vale!** all right!, OK! (*fam*). **¿vale?** all right?, OK? (*fam*)

valeroso *a* courageous

valgo *vb véase* **valer**

valía *f* worth

validez *f* validity. **dar ~ a** validate

válido *a* valid

valiente *a* brave; (*valentón*) boastful; (*en sentido irónico*) fine. —*m* brave person; (*valentón*) braggart

valija *f* case; (*de correos*) mailbag. **~ diplomática** diplomatic bag

val|ioso *a* valuable. **~or** *m* value, worth; (*descaro, fam*) nerve. **~ores** *mpl* securities. **~oración** *f* valuation. **~orar** *vt* value. **conceder ~or a** attach importance to. **objetos** *mpl* **de ~or** valuables. **sin ~or** worthless

vals *m invar* waltz

válvula *f* valve

valla *f* fence; (*fig*) barrier

valle *m* valley

vampiro *m* vampire

vanagloriarse [20 *o regular*] *vpr* boast

vanamente *adv* uselessly, in vain

vandalismo *m* vandalism

vándalo *m* vandal

vanguardia *f* vanguard. **de ~** (*en arte, música etc*) avant-garde

vanid|ad *f* vanity. **~oso** *a* vain

vano *a* vain; (*inútil*) useless. **en ~** in vain

vapor *m* steam; (*gas*) vapour; (*naut*) steamer. **~izador** *m* spray. **~izar** [10] vaporize. **al ~** (*culin*) steamed

vaquer|ía *f* dairy. **~o** *m* cowherd, cowboy. **~os** *mpl* jeans

vara *f* stick; (*de autoridad*) staff; (*medida*) yard

varar *vi* run aground

varia|ble *a & f* variable. **~ción** *f* variation. **~nte** *f* version. **~ntes** *fpl* hors d'oeuvres. **~r** [20] *vt* change; (*dar variedad a*) vary. —*vi* vary; (*cambiar*) change

varice *f* varicose vein

varicela *f* chickenpox

varicoso *a* having varicose veins

variedad *f* variety

varilla *f* stick; (*de metal*) rod

vario *a* varied; (*en plural*) several

varita *f* wand

variz *f* varicose vein

var|ón *a* male. —*m* man; (*niño*) boy. **~onil** *a* manly

vasco *a & m* Basque. **~ongado** *a* Basque. **~uence** *a & m* Basque. **las V~ongadas** the Basque provinces

vasectomía *f* vasectomy

vaselina *f* Vaseline (P), petroleum jelly

vasija *f* pot, container

vaso *m* glass; (*anat*) vessel

vástago *m* shoot; (*descendiente*) descendant; (*varilla*) rod

vasto *a* vast

Vaticano *m* Vatican

vaticin|ar vt prophesy. **~io** m prophesy

vatio m watt

vaya vb véase **ir**

Vd abrev (Usted) you

vecin|dad f neighbourhood, vicinity; (vecinos) neighbours. **~dario** m inhabitants, neighbourhood. **~o** a neighbouring; (de al lado) next-door. —m neighbour

veda|do m preserve. **~do de caza** game preserve. **~r** vt prohibit

vega f fertile plain

vegeta|ción f vegetation. **~l** a vegetable. —m plant, vegetable. **~r** vi grow; (persona) vegetate. **~riano** a & m vegetarian

vehemente a vehement

vehículo m vehicle

veinte a & m twenty. **~na** f score

veinti|cinco a & m twenty-five. **~cuatro** a & m twenty-four. **~dós** a & m twenty-two. **~nueve** a & m twenty-nine. **~ocho** a & m twenty-eight. **~séis** a & m twenty-six. **~siete** a & m twenty-seven. **~trés** a & m twenty-three. **~ún** a twenty-one. **~uno** a & m (delante de nombre masculino **veintún**) twenty-one

vejar vt humiliate; (molestar) vex

vejez f old age

vejiga f bladder; (med) blister

vela f (naut) sail; (de cera) candle; (falta de sueño) sleeplessness; (vigilia) vigil. **pasar la noche en ~** have a sleepless night

velada f evening party

vela|do a veiled; (foto) blurred. **~r** vt watch over; (encubrir) veil; (foto) blur. —vi stay awake, not sleep. **~r por** look after. **~rse** vpr (foto) blur

velero m sailing-ship

veleta f weather vane

velo m veil

veloc|idad f speed; (auto etc) gear. **~ímetro** m speedometer. **~ista** m & f sprinter. **a toda ~idad** at full speed

velódromo m cycle-track

veloz a fast, quick

vell|o m down. **~ón** m fleece. **~udo** a hairy

vena f vein; (en madera) grain. **estar de/en ~** be in the mood

venado m deer; (culin) venison

vencedor a winning. —m winner

vencejo m (pájaro) swift

venc|er [9] vt beat; (superar) overcome. —vi win; (plazo) expire. **~erse** vpr collapse; (persona) control o.s. **~ido** a beaten; (com, atrasado) in arrears. **darse por ~ido** give up. los **~idos** mpl (en deportes etc) the losers

venda f bandage. **~je** m dressing. **~r** vt bandage

vendaval m gale

vende|dor a selling. —m seller, salesman. **~dor ambulante** pedlar. **~r** vt sell. **~rse** vpr sell. **~rse caro** play hard to get. **se ~** for sale

vendimia f grape harvest; (de vino) vintage, year

Venecia f Venice

veneciano a Venetian

veneno m poison; (fig, malevolencia) spite. **~so** a poisonous

venera f scallop shell

venera|ble a venerable. **~ción** f reverence. **~r** vt revere

venéreo a venereal

venero m (yacimiento) seam; (de agua) spring; (fig) source

venezolano a & m Venezuelan

Venezuela f Venezuela

venga|nza f revenge. **~r** [12] vt avenge. **~rse** vpr take revenge (de, por for) (de, en on). **~tivo** a vindictive

vengo vb véase **venir**

venia f (*permiso*) permission

venial a venial

veni|da f arrival; (*vuelta*) return. **~dero** a coming. **~r** [53] vi come; (*estar, ser*) be. **~r a para** come to. **~r bien** suit. **la semana que viene** next week. **¡venga!** come on!

venta f sale; (*posada*) inn. **en ~** for sale

ventaj|a f advantage. **~oso** a advantageous

ventan|a f window; (*de la nariz*) nostril. **~illa** f window

ventarrón m (*fam*) strong wind

ventear vt (*olfatear*) sniff

ventero m innkeeper

ventila|ción f ventilation. **~dor** m fan. **~r** vt air

vent|isca f blizzard. **~olera** f gust of wind. **~osa** f sucker. **~osidad** f wind, flatulence. **~oso** a windy

ventrílocuo m ventriloquist

ventrudo a pot-bellied

ventur|a f happiness; (*suerte*) luck. **~oso** a happy, lucky. **a la ~a** at random. **echar la buena ~a a** uno tell s.o.'s fortune. **por ~a** by chance; (*afortunadamente*) fortunately

Venus f Venus

ver [43] vt see; watch (*televisión*). **~vi** see. **~se** vpr see o.s.; (*encontrarse*) find o.s.; (*dos personas*) meet. **a mi (modo de) ~** in my view. **a ~** let's see. **de buen ~** good-looking. **dejarse ~** show. **¡hábrase visto!** did you ever! **no poder ~** not be able to stand. **no tener nada que ~ con** have nothing to do with. **¡para que veas!** so there! **vamos a ~** let's see. **ya lo veo** that's obvious. **ya ~ás** you'll see. **ya ~emos** we'll see

vera f edge; (*de río*) bank

veracruzano a from Veracruz

veran|eante m & f tourist, holiday-maker. **~ear** vi spend one's holiday. **~eo** m (*summer*) holiday. **~iego** a summer. **~o** m summer. **casa** f **de ~eo** summer-holiday home. **ir de ~eo** go on holiday. **lugar** m **de ~eo** holiday resort

veras fpl. **de ~** really

veraz a truthful

verbal a verbal

verbena f (*bot*) verbena; (*fiesta*) fair; (*baile*) dance

verbo m verb. **~so** a verbose

verdad f truth. **¿~?** isn't it?, aren't they?, won't it? etc. **~eramente** adv really. **~ero** a true; (*fig*) real. **a decir ~** to tell the truth. **de ~** really. **la pura ~** the plain truth. **si bien es ~ que** although

verd|e a green; (*fruta etc*) unripe; (*chiste etc*) dirty, blue. — m green; (*hierba*) grass. **~or** m greenness

verdugo m executioner; (*fig*) tyrant

verdu|lería f greengrocer's (shop). **~lero** m greengrocer. **~ra** f (*green*) vegetable(s)

vereda f path; (*LAm, acera*) pavement (*Brit*), sidewalk (*Amer*)

veredicto m verdict

vergel m large garden; (*huerto*) orchard

verg|onzoso a shameful; (*tímido*) shy. **~üenza** f shame; (*timidez*) shyness. **¡es una ~üenza!** it's a disgrace! **me da ~üenza** I'm ashamed; (*tímido*) I'm shy about. **tener ~üenza** be ashamed; (*tímido*) be shy

verídico a true

verifica|ción f verification. **~r** [7] vt check. **~rse** vpr take place; (*resultar verdad*) come true

verja f grating; (*cerca*) railings; (*puerta*) iron gate

vermú m, **vermut** m vermouth

vernáculo *a* vernacular

verosímil *a* likely; ⟨*relato etc*⟩ credible

verraco *m* boar

verruga *f* wart

versado *a* versed

versar *vi* turn. **~ sobre** be about

versátil *a* versatile; (*fig*) fickle

versión *f* version; (*traducción*) translation

verso *m* verse; (*línea*) line

vértebra *f* vertebra

verte|**dero** *m* rubbish tip; (*desaguadero*) drain. **~dor** *m* drain. **~r** [1] *vt* pour; (*derramar*) spill. —*vi* flow

vertical *a* & *f* vertical

vértice *f* vertex

vertiente *f* slope

vertiginoso *a* dizzy

vértigo *m* dizziness; (*med*) vertigo. **de ~** (*fam*) amazing

vesania *f* rage; (*med*) insanity

vesícula *f* blister. **~ biliar** gall-bladder

vespertino *a* evening

vestíbulo *m* hall; (*de hotel, teatro etc*) foyer

vestido *m* (*de mujer*) dress; (*ropa*) clothes

vestigio *m* trace. **~s** *mpl* remains

vest|**imenta** *f* clothing. **~ir** [5] *vt* (*ponerse*) put on; (*llevar*) wear; dress ⟨*niño etc*⟩. —*vi* dress; (*llevar*) wear. **~se** *vpr* get dressed; (*llevar*) wear. **~uario** *m* wardrobe; (*cuarto*) dressing-room

Vesuvio *m* Vesuvius

vetar *vt* veto

veterano *a* veteran

veterinari|**a** *f* veterinary science. **~o** *a* veterinary. —*m* vet (*fam*), veterinary surgeon (*Brit*), veterinarian (*Amer*)

veto *m* veto. **poner el ~ a** veto

vetusto *a* ancient

vez *f* time; (*turno*) turn. **a la ~** at the same time; (*de una vez*) in one go. **alguna que otra ~** from time to time. **alguna ~** sometimes; (*en preguntas*) ever. **algunas veces** sometimes. **a su ~** in (his) turn. **a veces** sometimes. **cada ~ más** more and more. **de una ~** in one go. **de una ~ para siempre** once and for all. **de ~ en cuando** from time to time. **dos veces** twice. **2 veces 4** 2 times 4. **en ~ de** instead of. **érase una ~, había una ~** once upon a time. **muchas veces** often. **otra ~** again. **pocas veces, rara ~** rarely. **repetidas veces** again and again. **tal ~** perhaps. **una ~ (que)** once

vía *f* road; (*rail*) line; (*anat*) tract; (*fig*) way. —*prep* via. **~ aérea** by air. **~ de comunicación** *f* means of communication. **~ férrea** railway (*Brit*), railroad (*Amer*). **~ rápida** fast lane. **estar en ~s de** be in the process of

viab|**ilidad** *f* viability. **~le** *a* viable

viaducto *m* viaduct

viaj|**ante** *m* & *f* commercial traveller. **~ar** *vi* travel. **~e** *m* journey; (*corto*) trip. **~e de novios** honeymoon. **~ero** *m* traveller; (*pasajero*) passenger. **¡buen ~e!** have a good journey!

víbora *f* viper

vibra|**ción** *f* vibration. **~nte** *a* vibrant. **~r** *vt/i* vibrate

vicario *m* vicar

vice... *pref* vice-...

viceversa *adv* vice versa

vici|**ado** *a* corrupt; (*aire*) stale. **~ar** *vt* corrupt; (*estropear*) spoil. **~o** *m* vice; (*mala costumbre*) bad habit. **~oso** *a* dissolute; ⟨*círculo*⟩ vicious

vicisitud *f* vicissitude

víctima f victim; (*de un accidente*) casualty

victori|a f victory. **~oso** a victorious

vid f vine

vida f life; (*duración*) lifetime. **¡~ mía!** my darling! **de por ~** for life. **en mi ~** never (in my life). **en ~ de** during the lifetime of. **estar en ~** be alive

vídeo m video recorder

video|cinta f videotape. **~juego** m video game

vidriar vt glaze

vidri|era f stained glass window; (*puerta*) glass door; (*LAm, escaparate*) shop window. **~ería** f glass works. **~ero** m glazier. **~o** m glass. **~oso** a glassy

vieira f scallop

viejo a old. **—m** old person

Viena f Vienna

viene vb véase **venir**

viento m wind. **hacer ~** be windy

vientre m belly; (*matriz*) womb; (*intestino*) bowels. **llevar un niño en el ~** be pregnant

viernes m Friday. **V~ Santo** Good Friday

viga f beam; (*de metal*) girder

vigen|cia f validity. **~te** a valid; (*ley*) in force. **entrar en ~cia** come into force

vigésimo a twentieth

vigía f (*torre*) watch-tower; (*persona*) lookout

vigil|ancia f vigilance. **~ante** a vigilant. **~m** watchman, supervisor. **~ar** vt keep an eye on. **—vi** be vigilant; (*vigía etc*) keep watch. **~ia** f vigil; (*relig*) fasting

vigor m vigour; (*vigencia*) force. **~oso** a vigorous. **entrar en ~** come into force

vil a vile. **~eza** f vileness; (*acción*) vile deed

vilipendiar vt abuse

vilo. en ~ in the air

villa f town; (*casa*) villa. **la V~** Madrid

villancico m (Christmas) carol

villano a rustic; (*grosero*) coarse

vinagre m vinegar. **~ra** f vinegar bottle. **~ras** fpl cruet. **~ta** f vinaigrette (sauce)

vincular vt bind

vínculo m bond

vindicar [7] vt avenge; (*justificar*) vindicate

vine vb véase **venir**

vinicult|or m wine-grower. **~ura** f wine growing

vino m wine. **~ de Jerez** sherry. **~ de la casa** house wine. **~ de mesa** table wine

viña f, **viñedo** m vineyard

viola f viola; (*músico*) viola player

violación f violation; (*de una mujer*) rape

violado a & m violet

violar vt violate; break (*ley*); rape (*mujer*)

violen|cia f violence; (*fuerza*) force; (*embarazo*) embarrassment. **~tar** vt force; break into (*casa etc*). **~tarse** upr force o.s. **~to** a violent; (*fig*) awkward. **hacer ~cia** a force

violeta a invar & f violet

violín m violin; (*músico*) violinist. **~inista** m & f violinist. **~ón** m double bass; (*músico*) double-bass player. **~onc(h)elista** m & f cellist. **~onc(h)elo** m cello

viraje m turn. **~r** vt turn. **—vi** turn; (*fig*) change direction

virgen a & f virgin. **~inal** a virginal. **~inidad** f virginity

Virgo m Virgo

viril a virile. **~idad** f virility

virtual a virtual

virtud f virtue; (*capacidad*) ability. **en ~ de** by virtue of

virtuoso a virtuous. **—m** virtuoso

viruela f smallpox. **picado de ~s** pock-marked

virulé. a la ~ (fam) crooked; (estropeado) damaged

virulento a virulent

virus m invar virus

visa|**do** m visa. **~r** vt endorse

visceras fpl entrails

viscos|**a** f viscose. **~o** a viscous

visera f visor; (de gorra) peak

visib|**ilidad** f visibility. **~le** a visible

visig|**odo** a Visigothic. —m Visigoth. **~ótico** a Visigothic

visillo m (cortina) net curtain

visi|**ón** f vision; (vista) sight. **~onario** a & m visionary

visita f visit; (persona) visitor. **~ de cumplido** courtesy call. **~nte** m & f visitor. **~r** vt visit. **tener ~** have visitors

vislumbr|**ar** vt glimpse. **~e** f glimpse; (resplandor, fig) glimmer

viso m sheen; (aspecto) appearance

visón m mink

visor m viewfinder

víspera f day before, eve

vista f sight, vision; (aspecto, mirada) look; (panorama) view. **apartar la ~** look away; (fig) turn a blind eye. **a primera ~, a simple ~** at first sight. **clavar la ~ en** stare at. **con ~s a** with a view to. **en ~ de** in view of, considering. **estar a la ~** be obvious. **hacer la ~ gorda** turn a blind eye. **perder de ~** lose sight of. **tener a la ~** have in front of one. **volver la ~ atrás** look back

vistazo m glance. **dar/echar un ~** a glance at

visto a seen; (corriente) common; (considerado) considered. —vb véase **vestir. ~ bueno** passed. **~ que** since. **bien ~** acceptable. **está ~ que** it's obvious that. **lo**

nunca ~ an unheard-of thing. **mal ~** unacceptable. **por lo ~** apparently

vistoso a colourful, bright

visual a visual. —f glance. **echar una ~ a** have a look at

vital a vital. **~icio** a life. —m (life) annuity. **~idad** f vitality

vitamina f vitamin

viticult|**or** m wine-grower. **~ura** f wine growing

vitorear vt cheer

vítreo a vitreous

vitrina f showcase

vituper|**ar** vt censure. **~io** m censure. **~ios** mpl abuse

viud|**a** f widow. **~ez** f widowhood. **~o** a widowed. —m widower

viva m cheer

vivacidad f liveliness

vivamente adv vividly; (sinceramente) sincerely

vivaz a (bot) perennial; (vivo) lively

víveres mpl supplies

vivero m nursery; (fig) hotbed

viveza f vividness; (de inteligencia) sharpness; (de carácter) liveliness

vívido a true

vívido a vivid

vivienda f housing; (casa) house; (piso) flat

viviente a living

vivificar [7] vt (animar) enliven

vivir vt live through. —vi live. —m life. **~ de** live on. **de mal ~** dissolute. **¡viva!** hurray! **¡viva el rey!** long live the king!

vivisección f vivisection

vivo a alive; (viviente) living; (color) bright; (listo) clever; (fig) lively. **a lo ~, al ~** vividly

Vizcaya f Biscay

vizconde m viscount. **~sa** f viscountess

vocab|**lo** m word. **~ulario** m vocabulary

vocación *f* vocation

vocal *a* vocal. —*f* vowel. —*m & f* member. ~**ista** *m & f* vocalist

voce|ar *vt* call *(mercancías)*; *(fig)* proclaim. —*vi* shout. ~**río** *m* shouting

vociferar *vi* shout

vodka *m & f* vodka

vola|da *f* flying. ~**dor** *a* flying. —*m* rocket. ~**ndas. en ~ndas** in the air; *(fig, rápidamente)* very quickly. ~**nte** *a* flying. —*m* *(auto)* steering-wheel; *(nota)* note; *(rehilete)* shuttlecock; *(tec)* flywheel. ~**r** [2] *vt* blow up. —*vi* fly; *(desaparecer, fam)* disappear

volátil *a* volatile

volcán *m* volcano. ~**ico** *a* volcanic

volc|ar [2 & 7] *vt* knock over; *(adrede)* empty out. —*vi* overturn. ~**carse** *vpr* fall over; *(vehículo)* overturn; *(fig)* do one's utmost. ~**carse en** throw o.s. into

vol(e)ibol *m* volleyball

volquete *m* tipper, dump truck

voltaje *m* voltage

volte|ar *vt* turn over; *(en el aire)* toss; ring *(campanas)*. ~**reta** *f* somersault

voltio *m* volt

voluble *a* *(fig)* fickle

volum|en *m* volume; *(importancia)* importance. ~**inoso** *a* voluminous

voluntad *f* will; *(fuerza de voluntad)* will-power; *(deseo)* wish; *(intención)* intention. **buena ~** goodwill. **mala ~** ill will

voluntario *a* voluntary. —*m* volunteer. ~**so** *a* willing; *(obstinado)* wilful

voluptuoso *a* voluptuous

volver [2, *pp* vuelto] *vt* turn; *(de arriba a abajo)* turn over; *(devolver)* restore. —*vi* return; *(fig)* revert. ~**se** *vpr* turn round; *(regresar)* turn; *(hacerse)*

become. ~ **a hacer algo** do sth again. ~ **en sí** come round

vomitar *vt* bring up. —*vi* be sick, vomit. ~**ivo** *m* emetic. —*a* disgusting

vómito *m* vomit; *(acción)* vomiting

vorágine *f* maelstrom

voraz *a* voracious

vos *pron* *(LAm)* you

vosotros *pron* you; *(reflexivo)* yourselves. **el libro de ~** your book

vot|ación *f* voting; *(voto)* vote. ~**ante** *m & f* voter. ~**ar** *vt* vote for. —*vi* vote. ~**o** *m* vote; *(relig)* vow; *(maldición)* curse. **hacer ~os** pray for hope for

voy *vb véase* **ir**

voz *f* voice; *(grito)* shout; *(rumor)* rumour; *(palabra)* word. ~ **pública** public opinion. **aclarar la ~** clear one's throat. **a media ~** softly. **a una ~** unanimously. **dar voces** shout. **en ~ alta** loudly

vuelco *m* upset. **el corazón me dio un ~** my heart missed a beat

vuelo *m* flight; *(acción)* flying; *(de ropa)* flare. **al ~** in flight; *(fig)* in passing

vuelta *f* turn; *(curva)* bend; *(paseo)* walk; *(revolución)* revolution; *(regreso)* return; *(dinero)* change. **a la ~** on one's return; *(de página)* over the page. **a la ~ de la esquina** round the corner. **dar la ~ al mundo** go round the world. **dar una ~** go for a walk. **estar de ~** be back. **¡hasta la ~!** see you soon!

vuelvo *vb véase* **volver**

vuestro *a* your. —*pron* yours. **un amigo ~** a friend of yours

vulg|ar *a* vulgar; *(persona)* common. ~**aridad** *f* ordinariness; *(trivialidad)* triviality; *(grosería)* vulgarity. ~**arizar** [10] *vt* popularize. **~o** *m* common people

vulnerab|ilidad *f* vulnerability. **~le** *a* vulnerable

W

wáter *m* toilet

whisky /'wiski/ *m* whisky

X

xenofobia *f* xenophobia

xilófono *m* xylophone

Y

y *conj* and

ya *adv* already; (*ahora*) now; (*luego*) later; (*en seguida*) immediately; (*pronto*) soon. —*int* of course! **~ no** no longer. **~ que** since. |**~**, **~!** oh yes!, all right!

yacaré *m* (*LAm*) alligator

yac|er [44] *vi* lie. **~imiento** *m* deposit; (*de petróleo*) oilfield

yanqui *m* & *f* American, Yank(ee)

yate *m* yacht

yegua *f* mare

yeísmo *m* pronunciation of the Spanish *ll* like the Spanish *y*

yelmo *m* helmet

yema *f* (*bot*) bud; (*de huevo*) yolk; (*golosina*) sweet. **~ del dedo** fingertip

yergo *vb véase* **erguir**

yermo *a* uninhabited; (*no cultivable*) barren. —*m* wasteland

yerno *m* son-in-law

yerro *m* mistake. —*vb véase* **errar**

yerto *a* stiff

yeso *m* gypsum; (*arquit*) plaster. **~ mate** plaster of Paris

yo *pron* I. —*m* ego. **~ mismo** I myself. **soy ~** it's me

yodo *m* iodine

yoga *m* yoga

yogur *m* yog(h)urt

York. **de ~** (*jamón*) cooked

yuca *f* yucca

Yucatán *m* Yucatán

yugo *m* yoke

Yugoslavia *f* Yugoslavia

yugoslavo *a* & *m* Yugoslav

yunque *m* anvil

yunta *f* yoke

yuxtaponer [34] *vt* juxtapose

yuyo *m* (*Arg*) weed

Z

zafarse *vpr* escape; get out of (*obligación etc*)

zafarrancho *m* (*confusión*) mess; (*riña*) quarrel

zafio *a* coarse

zafiro *m* sapphire

zaga *f* rear. **no ir en ~** not be inferior

zaguán *m* hall

zaherir [4] *vt* hurt one's feelings

zahorí *m* clairvoyant; (*de agua*) water diviner

zaino *a* (*caballo*) chestnut; (*vaca*) black

zalamer|ía *f* flattery. **~o** *a* flattering. —*m* flatterer

zamarra *f* (*piel*) sheepskin; (*prenda*) sheepskin jacket

zamarrear *vt* shake

zamba *f* (*esp LAm*) South American dance; (*samba*) samba

zambulli|da *f* dive. **~r** [22] *vt* plunge. **~rse** *vpr* dive

zamparse *vpr* fall; (*comer*) gobble up

zanahoria *f* carrot

zancad|a f stride. ~illa f trip. echar la ~illa a uno, poner la ~illa a uno trip s.o. up

zanc|o m stilt. ~udo a long-legged. —m (LAm) mosquito

zanganear vi idle

zángano m drone; (persona) idler

zangolotear vt fiddle with. —vi rattle; (persona) fidget

zanja f ditch. ~r vt (fig) settle

zapapico m pickaxe

zapat|ear vt/i tap with one's feet. ~ería f shoe shop; (arte) shoe-making. ~ero m shoemaker; (el que remienda zapatos) cobbler. ~illa f slipper. ~illas deportivas trainers. ~o m shoe

zaragata f turmoil

Zaragoza f Saragossa

zarand|a f sieve. ~ear vt sieve; (sacudir) shake

zarcillo m earring

zarpa f claw, paw

zarpar vi weigh anchor

zarza f bramble. ~mora f blackberry

zarzuela f musical, operetta

zascandil m scatterbrain

zenit m zenith

zigzag m zigzag. ~uear vi zigzag

zinc m zinc

zipizape m (fam) row

zócalo m skirting-board; (pedestal) plinth

zodiaco m, zodíaco m zodiac

zona f zone; (área) area

zoo m zoo. ~logía f zoology. ~lógico a zoological

zoólogo m zoologist

zopenco a stupid. —m idiot

zoquete m (de madera) block; (persona) blockhead

zorr|a f fox; (hembra) vixen. ~o m fox

zozobra f (fig) anxiety. ~r vi be shipwrecked; (fig) be ruined

zueco m clog

zulú a & m Zulu

zumb|ar vt (fam) give (golpe etc). —vi buzz. ~ido m buzzing

zumo m juice

zurci|do m darning. ~r [9] vt darn

zurdo a left-handed; (mano) left

zurrar vt (fig, dar golpes, fam) beat up

zurriago m whip

zutano m so-and-so

ENGLISH-SPANISH
INGLÉS-ESPAÑOL

A

a /ə, eɪ/ *indef art* (*before vowel* **an**) un *m*; una *f*

aback /ə'bæk/ *adv.* **be taken ~** quedar desconcertado

abacus /'æbəkəs/ *n* ábaco *m*

abandon /ə'bændən/ *vt* abandonar. *—n* abandono *m*, desenfado *m*. **~ed** *a* abandonado; (*behaviour*) perdido. **~ment** *n* abandono *m*

abase /ə'beɪs/ *vt* degradar. **~ment** *n* degradación *f*

abashed /ə'bæʃt/ *a* confuso

abate /ə'beɪt/ *vt* disminuir. *—vi* disminuir; (*storm etc*) calmarse. **~ment** *n* disminución *f*

abattoir /'æbətwɑː(r)/ *n* matadero *m*

abbess /'æbis/ *n* abadesa *f*

abbey /'æbi/ *n* abadía *f*

abbot /'æbət/ *n* abad *m*

abbreviat|**e** /ə'briːvieɪt/ *vt* abreviar. **~ion** /-'eɪʃn/ *n* abreviatura *f*; (*act*) abreviación *f*

ABC /'eɪbiː'siː/ *n* abecé *m*, abecedario *m*

abdicat|**e** /'æbdikeɪt/ *vt/i* abdicar. **~ion** /-'eɪʃn/ *n* abdicación *f*

abdom|**en** /'æbdəmən/ *n* abdomen *m*. **~inal** /-'dɒmɪnl/ *a* abdominal

abduct /æb'dʌkt/ *vt* secuestrar. **~ion** /-ʃn/ *n* secuestro *m*. **~or** *n* secuestrador *m*

aberration /æbə'reɪʃn/ *n* aberración *f*

abet /ə'bet/ *vt* (*pt* **abetted**) (*jurid*) ser cómplice de

abeyance /ə'beɪəns/ *n.* **in ~** en suspenso

abhor /əb'hɔː(r)/ *vt* (*pt* **abhorred**) aborrecer. **~rence** /-'hɒrəns/ *n* aborrecimiento *m*; (*thing*) abominación *f*. **~rent** /-'hɒrənt/ *a* aborrecible

abide /ə'baɪd/ *vt* (*pt* **abided**) soportar. *—vi* (*old use*, *pt* **abode**) morar. **~ by** atenerse a; cumplir (*promise*)

abiding /ə'baɪdɪŋ/ *a* duradero, permanente

ability /ə'bɪləti/ *n* capacidad *f*; (*cleverness*) habilidad *f*

abject /'æbdʒekt/ *a* (*wretched*) miserable; (*vile*) abyecto

ablaze /ə'bleɪz/ *a* en llamas

able /'eɪbl/ *a* (**-er**, **-est**) capaz. **be ~** poder; (*know how to*) saber

ablutions /ə'bluːʃnz/ *npl* ablución *f*

ably /'eɪblɪ/ *adv* hábilmente

abnormal /æb'nɔːml/ *a* anormal. **~ity** /-'mæləti/ *n* anormalidad *f*

aboard /ə'bɔːd/ *adv* a bordo. *—prep* a bordo de

abode /ə'bəʊd/ *see* **abide**. *—n* (*old use*) domicilio *m*

abolish /ə'bɒlɪʃ/ *vt* suprimir, abolir

abolition /æbə'lɪʃn/ n supresión f, abolición f

abominable /ə'bɒmɪnəbl/ a abominable

abominat|e /ə'bɒmɪneɪt/ vt abominar. ~**ion** /-'neɪʃn/ n abominación f

aborigin|al /æbə'rɪdʒənl/ a & n aborigen (m & f), indígena (m & f). ~**es** /-i:z/ npl aborígenes mpl

abort /ə'bɔːt/ vt hacer abortar. —vi abortar. ~**ion** /-ʃn/ n aborto m provocado; (fig) aborto m. ~**ionist** n abortista m & f. ~**ive** a abortivo; (fig) fracasado

abound /ə'baʊnd/ vi abundar (**in** de, en)

about /ə'baʊt/ adv (approximately) alrededor de; (here and there) por todas partes; (in existence) por aquí. ~ **here** por aquí. **be** ~ **to** estar a punto de. **be up and** ~ estar levantado. —prep sobre; (around) alrededor de; (somewhere in) en. **talk** ~ hablar de. ~**face** n (fig) cambio m rotundo. ~**turn** n (fig) cambio m rotundo

above /ə'bʌv/ adv arriba. —prep encima de; (more than) más de. ~ **all** sobre todo. ~**board** a honrado. —adv abiertamente. ~**mentioned** a susodicho

abrasi|on /ə'breɪʒn/ n abrasión f. ~**ve** /ə'breɪsɪv/ a & n abrasivo (m); (fig) agresivo, brusco

abreast /ə'brest/ adv de frente. **keep** ~ **of** mantenerse al corriente de

abridge /ə'brɪdʒ/ vt abreviar. ~**ment** n abreviación f; (abstract) resumen m

abroad /ə'brɔːd/ adv (be) en el extranjero; (go) al extranjero; (far and wide) por todas partes

abrupt /ə'brʌpt/ a brusco. ~**ly** adv (suddenly) repentinamente; (curtly) bruscamente. ~**ness** n brusquedad f

abscess /'æbsɪs/ n absceso m

abscond /əb'skɒnd/ vi fugarse

absen|ce /'æbsəns/ n ausencia f; (lack) falta f. ~**t** /'æbsənt/ a ausente. /æb'sent/ vr. ~ **o.s.** ausentarse. ~**tly** adv distraídamente. ~**t-minded** a distraído. ~**t-mindedness** n distracción f, despiste m

absentee /æbsən'ti:/ n ausente m & f. ~**ism** n absentismo m

absinthe /'æbsɪnθ/ n ajenjo m

absolute /'æbsəluːt/ a absoluto. ~**ly** adv absolutamente

absolution /æbsə'luːʃn/ n absolución f

absolve /əb'zɒlv/ vt (from sin) absolver; (from obligation) liberar

absor|b /əb'zɔːb/ vt absorber. ~**bent** a absorbente. ~**ption** n absorción f

abstain /əb'steɪn/ vi abstenerse (**from** de)

abstemious /əb'stiːmɪəs/ a abstemio

abstention /əb'stenʃn/ n abstención f

abstinen|ce /'æbstɪnəns/ n abstinencia f. ~**t** a abstinente

abstract /'æbstrækt/ a abstracto. —n (quality) abstracto m; (summary) resumen m. /əb'strækt/ vt extraer; (summarize) resumir. ~**ion** /-ʃn/ n abstracción f

abstruse /əb'struːs/ a abstruso

absurd /əb'sɜːd/ a absurdo. ~**ity** n absurdo m, disparate m

abundan|ce /ə'bʌndəns/ n abundancia f. ~**t** a abundante

abuse /ə'bjuːz/ vt (misuse) abusar de; (ill-treat) maltratar; (insult) insultar. /ə'bjuːs/ n abuso m; (insults) insultos mpl

abusive /ə'bjuːsɪv/ a injurioso

abut /ə'bʌt/ vi (pt abutted) confinar (**on** con)

abysmal /ə'bɪzməl/ a abismal;
(*bad, fam*) pésimo; (*fig*) profundo

abyss /ə'bɪs/ n abismo m

acacia /ə'keɪʃə/ n acacia f

academic /ækə'demɪk/ a académico; (*pej*) teórico. —n universitario m, catedrático m. ~ian /-də'mɪʃn/ n académico m

academy /ə'kædəmɪ/ n academia f. ~ of music conservatorio m

accede /ək'si:d/ vi. ~ to acceder a (*request*); tomar posesión de (*office*). ~ to the throne subir al trono

accelerat|e /ək'seləreɪt/ vt acelerar. ~ion /-'reɪʃn/ n aceleración f. ~or n acelerador m

accent /'æksent/ n acento m. /æk'sent/ vt acentuar

accentuate /ək'sentʃʊeɪt/ vt acentuar

accept /ək'sept/ vt aceptar. ~able a aceptable. ~ance n aceptación f; (*approval*) aprobación f

access /'ækses/ n accceso m. ~ibility /-ɪ'bɪlətɪ/ n accesibilidad f. ~ible /ək'sesəbl/ a accesible; (*person*) tratable

accession /æk'seʃn/ n (*to power, throne etc*) ascenso m; (*thing added*) adquisición f

accessory /ək'sesərɪ/ a accesorio. —n accesorio m, complemento m; (*jurid*) cómplice m & f

accident /'æksɪdənt/ n accidente m; (*chance*) casualidad f. by ~ por accidente, por descuido, sin querer; (*by chance*) por casualidad. ~al /-'dentl/ a accidental, fortuito. ~ally /-'dentlɪ/ adv por accidente, por descuido, sin querer; (*by chance*) por casualidad

acclaim /ə'kleɪm/ vt aclamar. —n aclamación f

acclimatiz|ation /əklaɪmət-aɪ'zeɪʃn/ n aclimatación f. ~e /ə'klaɪmətaɪz/ vt aclimatar. —vi aclimatarse

accolade /'ækəleɪd/ n (*of knight*) acolada f; (*praise*) encomio m

accommodat|e /ə'kɒmədeɪt/ vt (*give hospitality to*) alojar; (*adapt*) acomodar; (*supply*) proveer; (*oblige*) complacer. ~ing a complaciente. ~ion /-'deɪʃn/ n alojamiento m; (*rooms*) habitaciones fpl

accompan|iment /ə'kʌmpənɪmənt/ n acompañamiento m. ~ist n acompañante m & f. ~y /ə'kʌmpənɪ/ vt acompañar

accomplice /ə'kʌmplɪs/ n cómplice m & f

accomplish /ə'kʌmplɪʃ/ vt (*complete*) acabar; (*achieve*) realizar; (*carry out*) llevar a cabo. ~ed a consumado. ~ment n realización f; (*ability*) talento m; (*thing achieved*) triunfo m, logro m

accord /ə'kɔ:d/ vi concordar. —vt conceder. —n acuerdo m; (*harmony*) armonía f. of one's own ~ espontáneamente. ~ance n. in ~ance with de acuerdo con

according /ə'kɔ:dɪŋ/ adv. ~ to según. ~ly adv en conformidad; (*therefore*) por consiguiente

accordion /ə'kɔ:dɪən/ n acordeón m

accost /ə'kɒst/ vt abordar

account /ə'kaʊnt/ n cuenta f; (*description*) relato m; (*importance*) importancia f. on ~ of a causa de. on no ~ de ninguna manera. on this ~ por eso. take into ~ tener en cuenta. —vt considerar. ~ for dar cuenta de, explicar

accountab|ility /əkaʊntə'bɪlətɪ/ n responsabilidad f. ~le a responsable (for de)

accountan|cy /əˈkaʊntənsɪ/ n contabilidad f. **~t** n contable m & f

accoutrements /əˈkuːtrəmənts/ npl equipo m

accredited /əˈkredɪtɪd/ a acreditado; (*authorized*) autorizado

accrue /əˈkruː/ vi acumularse

accumulat|e /əˈkjuːmjʊleɪt/ vt acumular. —vi acumularse. **~ion** /-ˈleɪʃn/ n acumulación f. **~or** n (*elec*) acumulador m

accura|cy /ˈækjərəsɪ/ n exactitud f, precisión f. **~te** a exacto, preciso

accusation /ækjuːˈzeɪʃn/ n acusación f. **~e** vt acusar

accustom /əˈkʌstəm/ vt acostumbrar. **~ed** a acostumbrado. **get ~ed (to)** acostumbrarse (a)

ace /eɪs/ n as m

acetate /ˈæsɪteɪt/ n acetato m

ache /eɪk/ n dolor m. —vi doler. **my leg ~s** me duele la pierna

achieve /əˈtʃiːv/ vt realizar; lograr (*success*). **~ment** n realización f; (*feat*) éxito m; (*thing achieved*) proeza f, logro m

acid /ˈæsɪd/ a & n ácido (m). **~ity** /əˈsɪdətɪ/ n acidez f

acknowledge /əkˈnɒlɪdʒ/ vt reconocer. **~ receipt of** acusar recibo de. **~ment** n reconocimiento m; (*com*) acuse m de recibo

acme /ˈækmɪ/ n cima f

acne /ˈæknɪ/ n acné m

acorn /ˈeɪkɔːn/ n bellota f

acoustic /əˈkuːstɪk/ a acústico. **~s** npl acústica f

acquaint /əˈkweɪnt/ vt. **~ s.o. with** poner a uno al corriente de. **be ~ed with** conocer (*person*); saber (*fact*). **~ance** n conocimiento m; (*person*) conocido m

acquiesce /ækwɪˈes/ vi consentir (**in** en). **~nce** n aquiescencia f, consentimiento m

acquire /əˈkwaɪə(r)/ vt adquirir; aprender (*language*). **~re a taste for** tomar gusto a. **~sition** /ækwɪˈzɪʃn/ n adquisición f. **~sitive** /-ˈkwɪzətɪv/ a codicioso

acquit /əˈkwɪt/ vt (pt **acquitted**) absolver; **~ o.s. well** defenderse bien, tener éxito. **~tal** n absolución f

acre /ˈeɪkə(r)/ n acre m. **~age** n superficie f (en acres)

acrid /ˈækrɪd/ a acre

acrimon|ious /ækrɪˈməʊnɪəs/ a cáustico, mordaz. **~y** /ˈækrɪmənɪ/ n acrimonia f, acritud f

acrobat /ˈækrəbæt/ n acróbata m & f. **~ic** /-ˈbætɪk/ a acrobático. **~ics** /-ˈbætɪks/ npl acrobacia f

acronym /ˈækrənɪm/ n acrónimo m, siglas fpl

across /əˈkrɒs/ adv & prep (*side to side*) de un lado al otro; (*on other side*) del otro lado de; (*crosswise*) a través de. **go** or **walk ~** atravesar

act /ækt/ n acto m; (*action*) acción f; (*in variety show*) número m; (*decree*) decreto m. —vt hacer (*part, role*). —vi actuar; (*pretend*) fingir; (*function*) funcionar. **~ as** actuar de. **~ for** representar. **~ing** a interino. —n (*of play*) representación f; (*by actor*) interpretación f; (*profession*) profesión f de actor

action /ˈækʃn/ n acción f; (*jurid*) demanda f; (*plot*) argumento m. **out of ~** (*on sign*) no funciona. **put out of ~** inutilizar. **take ~** tomar medidas

activate /ˈæktɪveɪt/ vt activar

activ|e /ˈæktɪv/ a activo; (*energetic*) enérgico; (*volcano*) en actividad. **~ity** /-ˈtɪvətɪ/ n actividad f

act|or /ˈæktə(r)/ n actor m. **~ress** n actriz f

actual /'æktʃʊəl/ *a* verdadero.
~ity /-'ælətɪ/ *n* realidad *f.* **~ly**
adv en realidad, efectivamente;
(*even*) incluso

actuary /'æktʃʊərɪ/ *n* actuario *m*

actuate /'æktjʊeɪt/ *vt* accionar,
impulsar

acumen /'ækjʊmen/ *n* perspi-
cacia *f*

acupuncture /'ækjʊpʌŋktʃə(r)/
n acupuntura *f.* **~ist** *n* acu-
punturista *m & f*

acute /ə'kjuːt/ *a* agudo. **~ly** *adv*
agudamente. **~ness** *n* agudeza *f*

ad /æd/ *n* (*fam*) anuncio *m*

AD /eɪ'diː/ *abbr* (*Anno Domini*)
d.J.C.

adamant /'ædəmənt/ *a* inflexible

Adam's apple /'ædəmz'æpl/ *n*
nuez *f* (de Adán)

adapt /ə'dæpt/ *vt* adaptar. —*vi*
adaptarse

adaptability /ədæptə'bɪlətɪ/ *n*
adaptabilidad *f.* **~le** /ə'dæptəbl/
a adaptable

adaptation /ædæp'teɪʃn/ *n* adaptación *f*; (*of book etc*) versión *f*

adaptor /ə'dæptə(r)/ *n* (*elec*)
adaptador *m*

add /æd/ *vt* añadir. —*vi* sumar. **~
up** sumar; (*fig*) tener sentido. **~
up to** equivaler a

adder /'ædə(r)/ *n* víbora *f*

addict /'ædɪkt/ *n* adicto *m*; (*fig*)
entusiasta *m & f.* **~ed** /ə'dɪktɪd/
a. **~ed to** adicto a; (*fig*) fanático
de. **~ion** /-ʃn/ *n* (*med*) dependencia *f*; (*fig*) afición *f.* **~ive** *a*
que crea dependencia

adding machine /'ædɪŋməʃiːn/ *n*
máquina *f* de sumar, sumadora *f*

addition /ə'dɪʃn/ *n* suma *f.* **in ~**
además. **~al** /-ʃnl/ *a* suplementario

additive /'ædɪtɪv/ *a & n* aditivo
(*m*)

address /ə'dres/ *n* señas *fpl*,
dirección *f*; (*speech*) discurso
m. —*vt* poner la dirección;

(*speak to*) dirigirse a. **~ee**
/ædre'siː/ *n* destinatario *m*

adenoids /'ædɪnɔɪdz/ *npl* veg-
etaciones *fpl* adenoideas

adept /'ædept/ *a* y experto (*m*)

adequacy /'ædɪkwəsɪ/ *n* suficiencia *f.* **~te** *a* suficiente, adecuado. **~tely** *adv* suficientemente, adecuadamente

adhere /əd'hɪə(r)/ *vi* adherirse
(**to** a); observar (*rule*). **~nce**
/-rəns/ *n* adhesión *f*; (*to rules*)
observancia *f*

adhesion /əd'hiːʒn/ *n* adherencia
f

adhesive /əd'hiːsɪv/ *a & n* ad-
hesivo (*m*)

ad infinitum /ædɪnfɪ'naɪtəm/ *adv*
hasta el infinito

adjacent /ə'dʒeɪsnt/ *a* contiguo

adjective /'ædʒɪktɪv/ *n* adjetivo
m

adjoin /ə'dʒɔɪn/ *vt* lindar con.
~ing *a* contiguo

adjourn /ə'dʒɜːn/ *vt* aplazar; suspender (*meeting etc*). —*vi* sus-
penderse. **~ to** trasladarse a

adjudicate /ə'dʒuːdɪkeɪt/ *vt*
juzgar. —*vi* actuar como juez

adjust /ə'dʒʌst/ *vt* ajustar (*machine*); (*arrange*) arreglar. —*vi.*
~ (to) adaptarse (a). **~able** *a*
ajustable. **~ment** *n* adaptación
f; (*tec*) ajuste *m*

ad lib /æd'lɪb/ *a* improvisado. —
vi (*pt* -**libbed**) (*fam*) improvisar

administer /əd'mɪnɪstə(r)/ *vt*
administrar, dar, proporcionar

administration /ədmɪnɪ-
'streɪʃn/ *n* administra-
ción *f.* **~or** *n* administrador *m*

admirable /'ædmərəbl/ *a* admirable

admiral /'ædmərəl/ *n* almirante
m

admiration /ædmə'reɪʃn/ *n*
admiración *f*

admire /əd'maɪə(r)/ vt admirar. **~r** /-'maɪərə(r)/ n admirador m; (suitor) enamorado m

admissible /əd'mɪsəbl/ a admisible

admission /əd'mɪʃn/ n admisión f; (entry) entrada f

admit /əd'mɪt/ vt (pt admitted) dejar entrar; (acknowledge) admitir, reconocer. **~** to confesar. **be ~ted** (to hospital etc) ingresar. **~tance** n entrada f. **~tedly** adv es verdad que

admoni|sh /əd'mɒnɪʃ/ vt reprender; (advise) aconsejar. **~tion** /-'nɪʃn/ n represión f

ado /ə'duː/ n alboroto m; (trouble) dificultad f. **without more ~** en seguida, sin más

adolescen|ce /ædə'lesns/ n adolescencia f. **~t** a & n adolescente (m & f)

adopt /ə'dɒpt/ vt adoptar. **~ed** a (child) adoptivo. **~ion** /-ʃn/ n adopción f. **~ive** a adoptivo

ador|able /ə'dɔːrəbl/ a adorable. **~ation** /ædə'reɪʃn/ n adoración f. **~e** /ə'dɔː(r)/ vt adorar

adorn /ə'dɔːn/ vt adornar. **~ment** n adorno m

adrenalin /ə'drenəlɪn/ n adrenalina f

adrift /ə'drɪft/ a & adv a la deriva

adroit /ə'drɔɪt/ a diestro

adulation /ædjʊ'leɪʃn/ n adulación f

adult /'ædʌlt/ a & n adulto (m)

adulterat|ion /ədʌltə'reɪʃn/ n adulteración f. **~e** /ə'dʌltəreɪt/ vt adulterar

adulter|er /ə'dʌltərə(r)/ n adúltero m. **~ess** n adúltera f. **~ous** a adúltero. **~y** n adulterio m

advance /əd'vɑːns/ vt adelantar. —vi adelantarse. —n adelanto m. **in ~** con anticipación, por adelantado. **~d** a avanzado; (studies) superior. **~ment** n adelanto m; (in job) promoción f

advantage /əd'vɑːntɪdʒ/ n ventaja f. **take ~ of** aprovecharse de; abusar de (person). **~ous** /ædvən'teɪdʒəs/ a ventajoso

advent /'ædvənt/ n venida f. **A~** n adviento m

adventur|e /əd'ventʃə(r)/ n aventura f. **~er** n aventurero m. **~ous** a (person) aventurero; (cosa) arriesgado; (fig, bold) llamativo

adverb /'ædvɜːb/ n adverbio m

adversary /'ædvəsərɪ/ n adversario m

advers|e /'ædvɜːs/ a adverso, contrario, desfavorable. **~ity** /əd'vɜːsətɪ/ n infortunio m

advert /'ædvɜːt/ n (fam) anuncio m. **~ise** /'ædvətaɪz/ vt anunciar. —vi hacer publicidad; (seek, sell) poner un anuncio. **~isement** /əd'vɜːtɪsmənt/ n anuncio m. **~iser** /-ə(r)/ n anunciante m & f

advice /əd'vaɪs/ n consejo m; (report) informe m

advis|able /əd'vaɪzəbl/ a aconsejable. **~e** vt aconsejar; (inform) avisar. **~e against** aconsejar en contra de. **~er** n consejero m; (consultant) asesor m. **~ory** a consultivo

advocate /'ædvəkət/ n defensor m; (jurid) abogado m. /'ædvəkeɪt/ vt recomendar

aegis /'iːdʒɪs/ n égida f. **under the ~ of** bajo la tutela de, patrocinado por

aeon /'iːən/ n eternidad f

aerial /'eərɪəl/ a aéreo. —n antena f

aerobatics /eərə'bætɪks/ npl acrobacia f aérea

aerobics /eə'rɒbɪks/ npl aeróbica f

aerodrome /'eərədrəʊm/ n aeródromo m

aerodynamic /eərəʊdaɪ'næmɪk/ a aerodinámico

aeroplane /ˈeərəpleɪn/ n avión m

aerosol /ˈeərəsɒl/ n aerosol m

aesthetic /iːsˈθetɪk/ a estético

afar /əˈfɑː(r)/ adv lejos

affable /ˈæfəbl/ a afable

affair /əˈfeə(r)/ n asunto m. (love) ~ aventura f, amorío m. ~s npl (business) negocios mpl

affect /əˈfekt/ vt afectar; (pretend) fingir

affect|ation /æfekˈteɪʃn/ n afectación f. ~ed a afectado, amanerado

affection /əˈfekʃn/ n cariño m; (disease) afección f. ~ate /-ʃənət/ a cariñoso

affiliate /əˈfɪlɪeɪt/ vt afiliar. ~ion /-ˈeɪʃn/ n afiliación f

affinity /əˈfɪnəti/ n afinidad f

affirm /əˈfɜːm/ vt afirmar. ~ation /æfəˈmeɪʃn/ n afirmación f

affirmative /əˈfɜːmətɪv/ a afirmativo. —n respuesta f afirmativa

affix /əˈfɪks/ vt sujetar; añadir (signature); pegar (stamp)

afflict /əˈflɪkt/ vt afligir. ~ion /-ʃn/ n aflicción f, pena f

affluen|ce /ˈæfluəns/ n riqueza f. ~t a rico. —n (geog) afluente m

afford /əˈfɔːd/ vt permitirse; (provide) dar

affray /əˈfreɪ/ n reyerta f

affront /əˈfrʌnt/ n afrenta f, ofensa f. —vt afrentar, ofender

afield /əˈfiːld/ adv. far ~ muy lejos

aflame /əˈfleɪm/ adv & a en llamas

afloat /əˈfləʊt/ adv a flote

afoot /əˈfʊt/ adv. sth is ~ se está tramando algo

aforesaid /əˈfɔːsed/ a susodicho

afraid /əˈfreɪd/ a. be ~ tener miedo (of a); (be sorry) sentir, lamentar

afresh /əˈfreʃ/ adv de nuevo

Africa /ˈæfrɪkə/ n África f. ~n a & n africano (m)

after /ˈɑːftə(r)/ adv después; (behind) detrás. —prep después de; (behind) detrás de. be ~ (seek) buscar, andar en busca de. —conj después de que. —a posterior

afterbirth /ˈɑːftəbɜːθ/ n placenta f

after-effect /ˈɑːftərɪfekt/ n consecuencia f, efecto m secundario

aftermath /ˈɑːftəmæθ/ n secuelas fpl

afternoon /ɑːftəˈnuːn/ n tarde f

aftershave /ˈɑːftəʃeɪv/ n loción f para después del afeitado

afterthought /ˈɑːftəθɔːt/ n ocurrencia f tardía

afterwards /ˈɑːftəwədz/ adv después

again /əˈgen/ adv otra vez; (besides) además. ~ and ~ una y otra vez

against /əˈgenst/ prep contra, en contra de

age /eɪdʒ/ n edad f. of ~ mayor de edad. under ~ menor de edad. —vt/i (pres p ageing) envejecer. ~d /ˈeɪdʒd/ a de ... años. ~d 10 de 10 años, que tiene 10 años. ~d /ˈeɪdʒɪd/ a viejo, anciano. ~less a siempre joven; (eternal) eterno, inmemorial. ~s (fam) siglos mpl

agency /ˈeɪdʒənsi/ n agencia f, organismo m, oficina f; (means) mediación f

agenda /əˈdʒendə/ npl orden m del día

agent /ˈeɪdʒənt/ n agente m & f; (representative) representante m & f

agglomeration /əglɒməˈreɪʃn/ n aglomeración f

aggravate /ˈægrəveɪt/ vt agravar; (irritate, fam) irritar. ~ion /-ˈveɪʃn/ n agravación f, (irritation, fam) irritación f

aggregate /ˈægrɪgət/ a total. —n conjunto m. /ˈægrɪgeɪt/ vt agregar. —vi ascender a

aggress|ion /əˈgreʃn/ n agresión f. ~**ive** a agresivo. ~**iveness** n agresividad f. ~**or** n agresor m

aggrieved /əˈgriːvd/ a apenado, ofendido

aghast /əˈgɑːst/ a horrorizado

agile /ˈædʒaɪl/ a ágil. ~**ity** /əˈdʒɪlətɪ/ n agilidad f

agitat|e /ˈædʒɪteɪt/ vt agitar. ~**ion** /-ˈteɪʃn/ n agitación f, excitación f. ~**or** n agitador m

agnostic /ægˈnɒstɪk/ a & n agnóstico (m). ~**ism** /-sɪzəm/ n agnosticismo m

ago /əˈgəʊ/ adv hace. **a long time** ~ hace mucho tiempo. **3 days** ~ hace 3 días

agog /əˈgɒg/ a ansioso

agon|ize /ˈægənaɪz/ vi atormentarse. ~**izing** a atroz, angustioso, doloroso. ~**y** n dolor m (agudo); (mental) angustia f

agree /əˈgriː/ vt acordar. —vi estar de acuerdo; (of figures) concordar; (get on) entenderse. ~ **with** (of food etc) sentar bien a. ~**able** /əˈgriːəbl/ a agradable. **be** ~**able** (willing) estar de acuerdo. ~**d** a (time, place) convenido. ~**ment** /əˈgriːmənt/ n acuerdo m. **in** ~**ment** de acuerdo

agricultur|al /ægrɪˈkʌltʃərəl/ a agrícola. ~**e** /ˈægrɪkʌltʃə(r)/ n agricultura f

aground /əˈgraʊnd/ adv. **run** ~ (of ship) varar, encallar

ahead /əˈhed/ adv delante; (of time) antes de. **be** ~ ir delante

aid /eɪd/ vt ayudar. —n ayuda f. **in** ~ **of** a beneficio de

aide /eɪd/ n (Amer) ayudante m & f

AIDS /eɪdz/ n (med) SIDA m

ail /eɪl/ vt afligir. ~**ing** a enfermo. ~**ment** n enfermedad f

aim /eɪm/ vt apuntar; (fig) dirigir. —vi apuntar; (fig) pretender. —n puntería f; (fig) propósito m. ~**less** a, ~**lessly** adv sin objeto, sin rumbo

air /eə(r)/ n aire m. **be on the** ~ estar en el aire. **put on** ~**s** darse aires. —vt airear. —a (base etc) aéreo. ~**borne** a en el aire; (mil) aerotransportado. ~**conditioned** a climatizado, con aire acondicionado. ~**craft** /ˈeəkrɑːft/ n (pl invar) avión m. ~**field** /ˈeəfiːld/ n aeródromo m. **A~ Force** fuerzas fpl aéreas. ~**gun** /ˈeəgʌn/ n escopeta f de aire comprimido. ~**lift** /ˈeəlɪft/ n puente m aéreo. ~**line** /ˈeəlaɪn/ n línea f aérea. ~**lock** /ˈeəlɒk/ n (in pipe) burbuja f de aire; (chamber) esclusa f de aire. ~**mail** n correo m aéreo. ~**man** /ˈeəmən/ n (pl -men) n aviador m. ~**port** /ˈeəpɔːt/ n aeropuerto m. ~**tight** /ˈeətaɪt/ a hermético. ~**worthy** /ˈeəwɜːðɪ/ a en condiciones de vuelo. ~**y** /ˈeərɪ/ a (-ier, -iest) aireado; (manner) ligero

aisle /aɪl/ n nave f lateral; (gangway) pasillo m

ajar /əˈdʒɑː(r)/ adv & a entreabierto

akin /əˈkɪn/ a semejante (**a** to)

alabaster /ˈæləbɑːstə(r)/ n alabastro m

alacrity /əˈlækrətɪ/ n prontitud f

alarm /əˈlɑːm/ n alarma f; (clock) despertador m. —vt asustar. ~**ist** n alarmista m & f

alas /əˈlæs/ int ¡ay!, ¡ay de mí!

albatross /ˈælbətrɒs/ n albatros m

albino /ælˈbiːnəʊ/ a & n albino (m)

album /ˈælbəm/ n álbum m

alchem|ist /ˈælkəmɪst/ *n* alquimista *m & f.* **~y** *n* alquimia *f*

alcohol /ˈælkəhɒl/ *n* alcohol *m.* **~ic** /-ˈhɒlɪk/ *a & n* alcohólico (*m*). **~ism** *n* alcoholismo *m*

alcove /ˈælkəʊv/ *n* nicho *m*

ale /eɪl/ *n* cerveza *f*

alert /əˈlɜːt/ *a* vivo; (*watchful*) vigilante. **—** *n* alerta *f.* **on the ~** alerta. **—vt** avisar. **~ness** *n* vigilancia *f*

algebra /ˈældʒɪbrə/ *n* álgebra *f*

Algeria /ælˈdʒɪərɪə/ *n* Argelia *f.* **~n** *a & n* argelino (*m*)

alias /ˈeɪlɪəs/ *n* (*pl* **-ases**) alias *m invar.* **—adv** alias

alibi /ˈælɪbaɪ/ *n* (*pl* **-is**) coartada *f*

alien /ˈeɪlɪən/ *n* extranjero *m.* **—** *a* ajeno

alienat|e /ˈeɪlɪəneɪt/ *vt* enajenar. **~ion** /-ˈneɪʃn/ *n* enajenación *f*

alight[1] /əˈlaɪt/ *vi* bajar; ⟨*bird*⟩ posarse

alight[2] /əˈlaɪt/ *a* ardiendo; ⟨*light*⟩ encendido

align /əˈlaɪn/ *vt* alinear. **~ment** *n* alineación *f*

alike /əˈlaɪk/ *a* parecido, semejante. **look** *or* **be ~** parecerse. **—** *adv* de la misma manera

alimony /ˈælɪmənɪ/ *n* pensión *f* alimenticia

alive /əˈlaɪv/ *a* vivo. **~ to** sensible a. **~ with** lleno de

alkali /ˈælkəlaɪ/ *n* (*pl* **-is**) álcali *m.* **~ne** *a* alcalino

all /ɔːl/ *a & pron* todo. **~ but one** todos excepto uno. **~ of it** todo. **—adv** completamente. **~ but** casi. **~ in** (*fam*) rendido. **~ of a sudden** de pronto. **~ over** (*finished*) acabado; (*everywhere*) por todas partes. **~ right!** ¡vale! **be ~ for** estar a favor de. **not at ~** de ninguna manera; (*after thanks*) ¡no hay de qué!

allay /əˈleɪ/ *vt* aliviar ⟨*pain*⟩; aquietar ⟨*fears etc*⟩

all-clear /ɔːlˈklɪə(r)/ *n* fin *m* de (la) alarma

allegation /ælɪˈɡeɪʃn/ *n* alegato *m*

allege /əˈledʒ/ *vt* alegar. **~dly** /-ɪdlɪ/ *adv* según se dice, supuestamente

allegiance /əˈliːdʒəns/ *n* lealtad *f*

allegor|ical /ælɪˈɡɒrɪkl/ *a* alegórico. **~y** /ˈælɪɡərɪ/ *n* alegoría *f*

allerg|ic /əˈlɜːdʒɪk/ *a* alérgico. **~y** /ˈælədʒɪ/ *n* alergia *f*

alleviat|e /əˈliːvɪeɪt/ *vt* aliviar. **~ion** /-ˈeɪʃn/ *n* alivio *m*

alley /ˈælɪ/ *n* (*pl* **-eys**) *n* callejuela *f*; (*for bowling*) bolera *f*

alliance /əˈlaɪəns/ *n* alianza *f*

allied /ˈælaɪd/ *a* aliado

alligator /ˈælɪɡeɪtə(r)/ *n* caimán *m*

allocat|e /ˈæləkeɪt/ *vt* asignar; (*share out*) repartir. **~ion** /-ˈkeɪʃn/ *n* asignación *f*; (*share*) ración *f*; (*distribution*) reparto *m*

allot /əˈlɒt/ *vt* (*pt* **allotted**) asignar. **~ment** *n* asignación *f*; (*share*) ración *f*; (*land*) parcela *f*

all-out /ˈɔːlˈaʊt/ *a* máximo

allow /əˈlaʊ/ *vt* permitir; (*grant*) conceder; (*reckon on*) prever; (*agree*) admitir. **~ for** tener en cuenta. **~ance** /əˈlaʊəns/ *n* concesión *f*; (*pension*) pensión *f*; (*com*) rebaja *f.* **make ~ances for** ser indulgente con; (*take into account*) tener en cuenta

alloy /ˈælɒɪ/ *n* aleación *f.* /əˈlɔɪ/ *vt* alear

all-round /ɔːlˈraʊnd/ *a* completo

allude /əˈluːd/ *vi* aludir

allure /əˈlʊə(r)/ *vt* atraer. **—** *n* atractivo *m*

allusion /əˈluːʒn/ *n* alusión *f*

ally /ˈælaɪ/ *n* aliado *m.* /əˈlaɪ/ *vt* aliarse

almanac /ˈɔːlmənæk/ *n* almanaque *m*

almighty /ɔːlˈmaɪtɪ/ *a* todopoderoso; (*big, fam*) enorme. **—** *n.* **the A~** el Todopoderoso *m*

almond /ˈɑːmənd/ n almendra f; (tree) almendro (m)

almost /ˈɔːlməʊst/ adv casi

alms /ɑːmz/ n limosna f

alone /əˈləʊn/ a solo. —adv sólo, solamente

along /əˈlɒŋ/ prep por, a lo largo de. —adv. ~ with junto con. all ~ todo el tiempo. come ~ venga

alongside /əlɒŋˈsaɪd/ adv (naut) al costado. —prep al lado de

aloof /əˈluːf/ adv apartado. —a reservado. ~ness n reserva f

aloud /əˈlaʊd/ adv en voz alta

alphabet /ˈælfəbet/ n alfabeto m. ~ical /-ˈbetɪkl/ a alfabético

alpine /ˈælpaɪn/ a alpino

Alps /ælps/ npl. the ~ los Alpes mpl

already /ɔːlˈredɪ/ adv ya

Alsatian /ælˈseɪʃn/ n (geog) alsaciano m; (dog) pastor m alemán

also /ˈɔːlsəʊ/ adv también; (moreover) además

altar /ˈɔːltə(r)/ n altar m

alter /ˈɔːltə(r)/ vt cambiar. —vi cambiarse. ~ation /-ˈreɪʃn/ n modificación f; (to garment) arreglo m

alternate /ɔːlˈtɜːnət/ a alterno. /ˈɔːltəneɪt/ vt/i alternar. ~ly adv alternativamente

alternative /ɔːlˈtɜːnətɪv/ a alternativo. —n alternativa f. ~ly adv en cambio, por otra parte

although /ɔːlˈðəʊ/ conj aunque

altitude /ˈæltɪtjuːd/ n altitud f

altogether /ɔːltəˈgeðə(r)/ adv completamente; (on the whole) en total

altruis|m /ˈæltruːɪzəm/ n altruismo m. ~t /ˈæltruːɪst/ n altruista m & f. ~tic /-ˈɪstɪk/ a altruista

aluminium /æljʊˈmɪnɪəm/ n aluminio m

always /ˈɔːlweɪz/ adv siempre

am /æm/ see be

a.m. /ˈeɪem/ abbr (ante meridiem) de la mañana

amalgamate /əˈmælgəmeɪt/ vt amalgamar. —vi amalgamarse

amass /əˈmæs/ vt amontonar

amateur /ˈæmətə(r)/ n aficionado m. —a no profesional; (in sports) amateur. ~ish a (pej) torpe, chapucero

amaze /əˈmeɪz/ vt asombrar. ~ed a asombrado, estupefacto. be ~ed at quedarse asombrado de, asombrarse de. ~ement n asombro m. ~ingly adv extraordinariamente

ambassador /æmˈbæsədə(r)/ n embajador m

amber /ˈæmbə(r)/ n ámbar m; (auto) luz f amarilla

ambidextrous /æmbɪˈdekstrəs/ a ambidextro

ambience /ˈæmbɪəns/ n ambiente m

ambigu|ity /æmbɪˈgjuːəti/ n ambigüedad f. ~ous /æmˈbɪgjʊəs/ a ambiguo

ambit /ˈæmbɪt/ n ámbito m

ambition /æmˈbɪʃn/ n ambición f. ~ous a ambicioso

ambivalen|ce /æmˈbɪvələns/ n ambivalencia f. ~t a ambivalente

amble /ˈæmbl/ vi andar despacio, andar sin prisa

ambulance /ˈæmbjʊləns/ n ambulancia f

ambush /ˈæmbʊʃ/ n emboscada f. —vt tender una emboscada a

amen /ɑːˈmen/ int amén

amenable /əˈmiːnəbl/ a. ~ to (responsive) sensible a, flexible a

amend /əˈmend/ vt enmendar. ~ment n enmienda f. ~s npl. make ~s reparar

amenities /əˈmiːnətiz/ npl atractivos mpl, comodidades fpl, instalaciones fpl

America /əˈmerɪkə/ n América; (North America) Estados mpl

Unidos. **~n** a & a americano
(m); (North American) estadounidense (m & f). **~nize** v
americanizar

amethyst /'æmɪθɪst/ n amatista f.
amiable /'eɪmɪəbl/ a simpático
amicable /'æmɪkəbl/ a amistoso.
~y adv amistosamente
amid(st) /ə'mɪd(st)/ prep entre,
en medio de
amiss /ə'mɪs/ a malo. —adv mal.
sth ~ algo que no va bien. take
sth ~ llevar algo a mal
ammonia /ə'məʊnɪə/ n amoníaco
m, amoniaco m
ammunition /æmjʊ'nɪʃn/ n
municiones fpl
amnesia /æm'niːzɪə/ n amnesia f
amnesty /'æmnəstɪ/ n amnistía f
amok /ə'mɒk/ adv. run ~ volverse loco
among(st) /ə'mʌŋ(st)/ prep entre
amoral /eɪ'mɒrəl/ a amoral
amorous /'æmərəs/ a amoroso
amorphous /ə'mɔːfəs/ a amorfo
amount /ə'maʊnt/ n cantidad f;
(total) total m, suma f. —vi. ~ to
sumar; (fig) equivaler a,
significar
amp(ere) /'æmp(eə(r))/ n
amperio m
amphibi|an /æm'fɪbɪən/ n anfi-
bio m. **~ous** a anfibio
amphitheatre /'æmfɪθɪətə(r)/ n
anfiteatro m
ample /'æmpl/ a (-er, -est)
amplio; (enough) suficiente;
(plentiful) abundante. **~y** adv
ampliamente, bastante
amplif|ier /'æmplɪfaɪə(r)/ n am-
plificador m. **~y** vt ampli-
ficar
amputat|e /'æmpjʊteɪt/ vt ampu-
tar. **~ion** /-'teɪʃn/ n amputación
f
amus|e /ə'mjuːz/ vt divertir.
~ement n diversión f. **~ing** a
divertido

an /ən, æn/ see a
anachronism /ə'nækrənɪzəm/ n
anacronismo m
anaemi|a /ə'niːmɪə/ n anemia f.
~c a anémico
anaesthe|sia /ænɪs'θiːzɪə/ n anes-
tesia f. **~tic** /ænɪs'θetɪk/ n anestésico m. **~tist** /ə'niːsθɪtɪst/ n
anestesista m f
anagram /'ænəgræm/ n anagrama m
analogy /ə'nælədʒɪ/ n analogía f
analys|e /'ænəlaɪz/ vt analizar.
~is /ə'næləsɪs/ n (pl -yses /-siːz/)
n análisis m. **~t** /'ænəlɪst/ n analista m & f
analytic(al) /ænə'lɪtɪk(əl)/ a ana-
lítico
anarch|ist /'ænəkɪst/ n anar-
quista m & f. **~y** n anarquía f
anathema /ə'næθəmə/ n anatema
m
anatom|ical /ænə'tɒmɪkl/ a ana-
tómico. **~y** /ə'nætəmɪ/ n ana-
tomía f
ancest|or /'ænsestə(r)/ n ante-
pasado m. **~ral** /-'sestrəl/ a
ancestral. **~ry** /'ænsestrɪ/ n
ascendencia f
anchor /'æŋkə(r)/ n ancla f. —vt
anclar; (fig) sujetar. —vi anclar
anchovy /'æntʃəvɪ/ n (fresh)
boquerón m; (tinned) anchoa f
ancient /'eɪnʃənt/ a antiguo,
viejo
ancillary /æn'sɪlərɪ/ a auxiliar
and /ənd, ænd/ conj y; (before i-
and hi-) e. go ~ see him vete a
verle. more ~ more siempre
más, cada vez más. try ~ come
ven si puedes, trata de venir
Andalusia /ændə'luːzjə/ f Andalucía f
anecdote /'ænɪkdəʊt/ n anécdota
f
anew /ə'njuː/ adv de nuevo
angel /'eɪndʒl/ n ángel m. **~ic**
/æn'dʒelɪk/ a angélico

anger /'æŋgə(r)/ n ira f. —vt enojar

angle[1] /'æŋgl/ n ángulo m; (fig) punto m de vista

angle[2] /'æŋgl/ vi pescar con caña. ~ **for** (fig) buscar. ~**r** /-ə(r)/ n pescador m

Anglican /'æŋglɪkən/ a & n anglicano (m)

Anglo-... /'æŋgləʊ/ pref anglo.

Anglo-Saxon /'æŋgləʊ'sæksn/ a & n anglosajón (m)

angr|ily /'æŋgrɪli/ adv con enojo. ~**y** /'æŋgrɪ/ a (-ier, -iest) enojado. **get** ~**y** enfadarse

anguish /'æŋgwɪʃ/ n angustia f

angular /'æŋgjʊlə(r)/ a angular; (face) anguloso

animal /'ænɪməl/ a & n animal (m)

animat|e /'ænɪmət/ a vivo. /'ænɪmeɪt/ vt animar. ~**ion** /-'meɪʃn/ n animación f

animosity /ænɪ'mɒsəti/ n animosidad f

aniseed /'ænɪsi:d/ n anís m

ankle /'æŋkl/ n tobillo m. ~ **sock** escarpín m, calcetín m

annals /'ænlz/ npl anales mpl

annex /ə'neks/ vt anexionar. ~**ation** /ænek'seɪʃn/ n anexión f

annexe /'æneks/ n anexo m, dependencia f

annihilat|e /ə'naɪəleɪt/ vt aniquilar. ~**ion** /-'leɪʃn/ n aniquilación f

anniversary /ænɪ'vɜ:sərɪ/ n aniversario m

annotat|e /'ænəteɪt/ vt anotar. ~**ion** /-'teɪʃn/ n anotación f

announce /ə'naʊns/ vt anunciar, comunicar. ~**ment** n anuncio m, aviso m, declaración f. ~**r** /-ə(r)/ n (radio, TV) locutor m

annoy /ə'nɔɪ/ vt molestar. ~**ance** n disgusto m. ~**ed** a enfadado. ~**ing** a molesto

annual /'ænjʊəl/ a anual. —n anuario m. ~**ly** adv cada año

annuity /ə'nju:əti/ n anualidad f. **life** ~ renta f vitalicia

annul /ə'nʌl/ vt (pt **annulled**) anular. ~**ment** n anulación f

anoint /ə'nɔɪnt/ vt ungir

anomal|ous /ə'nɒmələs/ a anómalo. ~**y** n anomalía f

anon /ə'nɒn/ adv (old use) dentro de poco

anonymous /ə'nɒnɪməs/ a anónimo

anorak /'ænəræk/ n anorac m

another /ə'nʌðə(r)/ a & pron otro (m). ~ **10 minutes** 10 minutos más. **in** ~ **way** de otra manera. **one** ~ unos a otros

answer /'ɑ:nsə(r)/ n respuesta f; (solution) solución f. —vt contestar a; escuchar, oír (prayer). —vi contestar. ~ **back** replicar. ~ **for** ser responsable de. ~**able** a responsable. ~**ing-machine** n contestador m automático

ant /ænt/ n hormiga f

antagoni|sm /æn'tægənɪzəm/ n antagonismo m. ~**stic** /-'nɪstɪk/ a antagónico, opuesto. ~**ze** /æn'tægənaɪz/ vt provocar la enemistad de

Antarctic /æn'tɑ:ktɪk/ a antártico. —n Antártico m

ante-... /æntɪ/ pref ante...

antecedent /æntɪ'si:dnt/ n antecedente m

antelope /'æntɪləʊp/ n antílope m

antenatal /'æntɪneɪtl/ a prenatal

antenna /æn'tenə/ n antena f

anthem /'ænθəm/ n himno m

anthill /'ænthɪl/ n hormiguero m

anthology /æn'θɒlədʒɪ/ n antología f

anthropolog|ist /ænθrə'pɒlədʒɪst/ n antropólogo m. ~**y** n antropología f

anti-... /æntɪ/ pref anti... ~**aircraft** a antiaéreo

antibiotic /æntɪbaɪ'ɒtɪk/ a & n antibiótico (m)

antibody /'æntɪbɒdɪ/ n anti-cuerpo m

antic /'æntɪk/ n payasada f, travesura f

anticipat|e /æn'tɪsɪpeɪt/ vt anticiparse a; (foresee) prever; (forestall) prevenir. ∼ion /-'peɪʃn/ n anticipación f; (expectation) esperanza f

anticlimax /æntɪ'klaɪmæks/ n decepción f

anticlockwise /æntɪ'klɒkwaɪz/ adv & a en sentido contrario al de las agujas del reloj, hacia la izquierda

anticyclone /æntɪ'saɪkləʊn/ n anticiclón m

antidote /'æntɪdəʊt/ m antídoto m

antifreeze /'æntɪfriːz/ n anticongelante m

antipathy /æn'tɪpəθɪ/ n antipatía f

antiquarian /æntɪ'kweərɪən/ a & n anticuario (m)

antiquated /'æntɪkweɪtɪd/ a anticuado

antique /æn'tiːk/ a antiguo. —n antigüedad f. ∼ dealer anticuario m. ∼ shop tienda f de antigüedades

antiquity /æn'tɪkwətɪ/ n antigüedad f

anti-Semitic /æntɪsɪ'mɪtɪk/ a antisemítico

antiseptic /æntɪ'septɪk/ a & n antiséptico (m)

antisocial /æntɪ'səʊʃl/ a antisocial

antithesis /æn'tɪθəsɪs/ n (pl -eses /-siːz/) antítesis f

antler /'æntlər/ n cornamenta f

anus /'eɪnəs/ n ano m

anvil /'ænvɪl/ n yunque m

anxiety /æŋ'zaɪətɪ/ n ansiedad f; (worry) inquietud f; (eagerness) anhelo m

anxious /'æŋkʃəs/ a inquieto; (eager) deseoso. ∼ly adv con

inquietud; (eagerly) con impaciencia

any /'enɪ/ a algún m; (negative) ningún m; (whatever) cualquier; (every) todo. a ∼ moment en cualquier momento. have you ∼ wine? ¿tienes vino? —pron alguno; (negative) ninguno. have we ∼? ¿tenemos algunos? not ∼ ninguno. —adv (a little) un poco, algo. is it ∼ better? ¿está algo mejor? it isn't ∼ good no sirve para nada

anybody /'enɪbɒdɪ/ pron alguien; (after negative) nadie. ∼ can do it cualquiera sabe hacerlo, cualquiera puede hacerlo

anyhow /'enɪhaʊ/ adv de todas formas; (in spite of all) a pesar de todo; (badly) de cualquier modo

anyone /'enɪwʌn/ pron alguien; (after negative) nadie

anything /'enɪθɪŋ/ pron algo; (whatever) cualquier cosa; (after negative) nada. ∼ but todo menos

anyway /'enɪweɪ/ adv de todas formas

anywhere /'enɪweə(r)/ adv en cualquier parte; (after negative) en ningún sitio; (everywhere) en todas partes. ∼ else en cualquier otro lugar. ∼ you go dondequiera que vayas

apace /ə'peɪs/ adv rápidamente

apart /ə'pɑːt/ adv aparte; (separated) apartado, separado. ∼ from aparte de. come ∼ romperse. take ∼ desmontar

apartheid /ə'pɑːtheɪt/ n segregación f racial, apartheid m

apartment /ə'pɑːtmənt/ n (Amer) apartamento m

apath|etic /æpə'θetɪk/ a apático, indiferente. ∼y /'æpəθɪ/ n apatía f

ape /eɪp/ n mono m. —vt imitar

aperient /ə'pɪərɪənt/ a & n laxante (m)

aperitif /ə'perətif/ n aperitivo m

aperture /'æpətjʊə(r)/ n abertura f

apex /'eɪpeks/ n ápice m

aphorism /'æfərɪzəm/ n aforismo m

aphrodisiac /æfrə'dɪzɪæk/ a & n afrodisíaco (m), afrodisiaco (m)

apiece /ə'piːs/ adv cada uno

aplomb /ə'plɒm/ n aplomo m

apolog|etic /əplɒ'dʒetɪk/ a lleno de disculpas. be ~etic disculparse. ~ize /ə'pɒlədʒaɪz/ vi disculparse (for de). ~y /ə'pɒlədʒɪ/ n disculpa f; (poor specimen) birria f

apostle /ə'pɒsl/ n apóstol m

apostrophe /ə'pɒstrəfɪ/ n (punctuation mark) apóstrofo m

appal /ə'pɔːl/ vt (pt appalled) horrorizar. ~ling a espantoso

apparatus /æpə'reɪtəs/ n aparato m

apparel /ə'pærəl/ n ropa f, indumentaria f

apparent /ə'pærənt/ a aparente; (clear) evidente. ~ly adv por lo visto

apparition /æpə'rɪʃn/ n aparición f

appeal /ə'piːl/ vi apelar; (attract) atraer. —n llamamiento m; (attraction) atractivo m; (jurid) apelación f. ~ing a atrayente

appear /ə'pɪə(r)/ vi aparecer; (arrive) llegar; (seem) parecer; (on stage) actuar. ~ance n aparición f; (aspect) aspecto m

appease /ə'piːz/ vt aplacar; (pacify) apaciguar

append /ə'pend/ vt adjuntar. ~age /ə'pendɪdʒ/ n añadidura f

appendicitis /əpendɪ'saɪtɪs/ n apendicitis f

appendix /ə'pendɪks/ n (pl -ices -ɪsiːz/) (of book) apéndice m. (pl -ixes) (anat) apéndice m

appertain /æpə'teɪn/ vi relacionarse (to con)

appetite /'æpɪtaɪt/ n apetito m

appetiz|er /'æpɪtaɪzə(r)/ n aperitivo m. ~ing a apetitoso

applaud /ə'plɔːd/ vt/i aplaudir. ~se n aplausos mpl

apple /'æpl/ n manzana f. ~-tree n manzano m

appliance /ə'plaɪəns/ n aparato m. electrical ~ electrodoméstico m

applicable /'æplɪkəbl/ a aplicable; (relevant) pertinente

applicant /'æplɪkənt/ n candidato m, solicitante m & f

application /æplɪ'keɪʃn/ n aplicación f; (request) solicitud f. ~ form formulario m (de solicitud)

appl|ied /ə'plaɪd/ a aplicado. ~y /ə'plaɪ/ vt aplicar. —vi aplicarse; (ask) dirigirse. ~y for solicitar (job etc)

appoint /ə'pɔɪnt/ vt nombrar; (fix) señalar. ~ment n cita f; (job) empleo m

apportion /ə'pɔːʃn/ vt repartir

apposite /'æpəzɪt/ a apropiado

apprais|al /ə'preɪzl/ n evaluación f. ~e vt evaluar

appreciable /ə'priːʃəbl/ a sensible; (considerable) considerable

appreciat|e /ə'priːʃɪeɪt/ vt apreciar; (understand) comprender; (be grateful for) agradecer. —vi (increase value) aumentar en valor. ~ion /-'eɪʃn/ n aprecio m; (gratitude) agradecimiento m. ~ive /ə'priːʃɪətɪv/ a (grateful) agradecido

apprehend /æprɪ'hend/ vt detener; (understand) comprender. ~sion /-ʃn/ n detención f; (fear) recelo m

apprehensive /æprɪ'hensɪv/ a aprensivo

apprentice /ə'prentɪs/ n aprendiz m. —vt poner de aprendiz. ~ship n aprendizaje m

approach /ə'prəʊtʃ/ vt acercarse
a. —vi acercarse. —n acer-
camiento m; (to problem)
enfoque m; (access) acceso m.
make ~es to dirigirse a. ~able
a accesible

approbation /æprə'beɪʃn/ n
aprobación f

appropriate /ə'prəʊprɪət/ a apropiado. /ə'prəʊprɪeɪt/ vt apropi-
arse de. ~ly adv apropiadamente

approval /ə'pruːvl/ n aprobación
f. on ~ a prueba

approv|**e** /ə'pruːv/ vt/i aprobar.
~ingly adv con aprobación

approximat|**e** /ə'prɒksɪmət/ a
aproximado. /ə'prɒksɪmeɪt/ vt
aproximarse a. ~ely adv aproximadamente. ~ion /-'meɪʃn/ n
aproximación f

apricot /'eɪprɪkɒt/ n albaricoque
m, chabacano m (Mex). ~-tree
n albaricoquero m, chabacano m
(Mex)

April /'eɪprəl/ n abril m. ~ fool!
¡inocentón!

apron /'eɪprən/ n delantal m

apropos /æprə'pəʊ/ adv a
propósito

apse /æps/ n ábside m

apt /æpt/ a apropiado; (pupil)
listo. be ~ to tener tendencia a

aptitude /'æptɪtjuːd/ n aptitud f

aptly /'æptlɪ/ adv acertadamente

aqualung /'ækwəlʌŋ/ n pulmón
m acuático

aquarium /ə'kweərɪəm/ n (pl
-ums) acuario m

Aquarius /ə'kweərɪəs/ n Acuario m

aquatic /ə'kwætɪk/ a acuático

aqueduct /'ækwɪdʌkt/ n acueducto m

aquiline /'ækwɪlaɪn/ a aquilino

Arab /'ærəb/ a & n árabe m. ~ian
/ə'reɪbɪən/ a árabe m. ~ic /'ærəbɪk/
a & n árabe (m). ~ic numerals
números mpl arábigos

arable /'ærəbl/ a cultivable

arbiter /'ɑːbɪtə(r)/ n árbitro m

arbitrary /'ɑːbɪtrərɪ/ a arbitrario

arbitrat|**e** /'ɑːbɪtreɪt/ vi arbitrar.
~ion /-'treɪʃn/ n arbitraje m.
~or n árbitro m

arc /ɑːk/ n arco m

arcade /ɑː'keɪd/ n arcada f;
(around square) soportales mpl;
(shops) galería f. amusement ~
galería f de atracciones

arcane /ɑː'keɪn/ a misterioso

arch[1] /ɑːtʃ/ n arco m. —vt
arquear. —vi arquearse

arch[2] /ɑːtʃ/ a malicioso

archaeolog|**ical** /ɑːkɪə'lɒdʒɪkl/ a
arqueológico. ~ist /ɑːkɪ'ɒlədʒɪst/
n arqueólogo m. ~y /ɑːkɪ'ɒlədʒɪ/
n arqueología f

archaic /ɑː'keɪɪk/ a arcaico

archbishop /ɑːtʃ'bɪʃəp/ n arzobispo m

arch-enemy /ɑːtʃ'enəmɪ/ n enemigo m jurado

archer /'ɑːtʃə(r)/ n arquero m. ~y
n tiro m al arco

archetype /'ɑːkɪtaɪp/ n arquetipo
m

archipelago /ɑːkɪ'peləgəʊ/ n (pl
-os) archipiélago m

architect /'ɑːkɪtekt/ n arquitecto
m. ~ure /'ɑːkɪtektʃə(r)/ n arqui-
tectura f. ~ural /-'tektʃərəl/ a
arquitectónico

archiv|**es** /'ɑːkaɪvz/ npl archivo
m. ~ist /-ɪvɪst/ n archivero m

archway /'ɑːtʃweɪ/ n arco m

Arctic /'ɑːktɪk/ a ártico. —n
Ártico m

arctic /'ɑːktɪk/ a glacial

ardent /'ɑːdənt/ a ardiente, fer-
voroso, apasionado. ~ly adv
ardientemente

ardour /'ɑːdə(r)/ n ardor m, fervor
m, pasión f

arduous /'ɑːdjʊəs/ a arduo

are /ɑː(r)/ see be

area /'eərɪə/ n (surface) superficie f; (region) zona f; (fig)
campo m

arena /əˈriːnə/ n arena f; (in circus) pista f; (in bullring) ruedo m

aren't /ɑːnt/ = are not

Argentina /ɑːdʒənˈtiːnə/ n Argentina f. **~ian** /-ˈtɪnɪən/ a & n argentino (m)

arguable /ˈɑːɡjʊəbl/ a discutible

argue /ˈɑːɡjuː/ vi discutir; (reason) razonar

argument /ˈɑːɡjʊmənt/ n disputa f; (reasoning) argumento m. **~ative** /-ˈmentətɪv/ a discutidor

arid /ˈærɪd/ a árido

Aries /ˈeərɪːz/ n Aries m

arise /əˈraɪz/ vi (pt arose, pp arisen) levantarse; (fig) surgir. **~ from** resultar de

aristocracy /ærɪˈstɒkrəsɪ/ n aristocracia f. **~t** /ˈærɪstəkræt/ n aristócrata m & f. **~tic** /-ˈkrætɪk/ a aristocrático

arithmetic /əˈrɪθmətɪk/ n aritmética f

ark /ɑːk/ n (relig) arca f

arm[1] /ɑːm/ n brazo m. **~ in ~** cogidos del brazo

arm[2] /ɑːm/ n. **~s** npl armas fpl. **—vt** armar

armada /ɑːˈmɑːdə/ n armada f

armament /ˈɑːməmənt/ n armamento m

armchair /ˈɑːmtʃeə(r)/ n sillón m

armed robbery /ɑːmdˈrɒbərɪ/ n robo m a mano armada

armful /ˈɑːmfʊl/ n brazada f

armistice /ˈɑːmɪstɪs/ n armisticio m

armlet /ˈɑːmlɪt/ n brazalete m

armour /ˈɑːmə(r)/ n armadura f. **~ed** a blindado

armoury /ˈɑːmərɪ/ n arsenal m

armpit /ˈɑːmpɪt/ n sobaco m, axila f

army /ˈɑːmɪ/ n ejército m

aroma /əˈrəʊmə/ n aroma m. **~tic** /ærəˈmætɪk/ a aromático

arose /əˈrəʊz/ see **arise**

around /əˈraʊnd/ adv alrededor; (near) cerca. **all ~** por todas partes. **—prep** alrededor de; (with time) a eso de

arouse /əˈraʊz/ vt despertar

arpeggio /ɑːˈpedʒɪəʊ/ n arpegio m

arrange /əˈreɪndʒ/ vt arreglar; (fix) fijar. **~ment** n arreglo m; (agreement) acuerdo m; (pl, plans) preparativos mpl

array /əˈreɪ/ vt (dress) ataviar; (mil) formar. **—n** atavío m; (mil) orden m; (fig) colección f, conjunto m

arrears /əˈrɪəz/ npl atrasos mpl. **in ~** atrasado en pagos

arrest /əˈrest/ vt detener; llamar (attention). **—n** detención f. **under ~** detenido

arrival /əˈraɪvl/ n llegada f. **new ~al** recien llegado m. **~e** /əˈraɪv/ vi llegar

arrogance /ˈærəɡəns/ n arrogancia f. **~t** a arrogante. **~tly** adv con arrogancia

arrow /ˈærəʊ/ n flecha f

arsenal /ˈɑːsənl/ n arsenal m

arsenic /ˈɑːsnɪk/ n arsénico m

arson /ˈɑːsn/ n incendio m provocado. **~ist** n incendiario m

art[1] /ɑːt/ n arte m. **A~s** npl (Univ) Filosofía y Letras fpl. **fine ~s** bellas artes fpl

art[2] /ɑːt/ (old use, with thou) = are

artefact /ˈɑːtɪfækt/ n artefacto m

arterial /ɑːˈtɪərɪəl/ a arterial. **~ road** n carretera f nacional

artery /ˈɑːtərɪ/ n arteria f

artesian /ɑːˈtiːzjən/ a. **~ well** pozo m artesiano

artful /ˈɑːtfʊl/ a astuto. **~ness** n astucia f

art gallery /ˈɑːtɡælərɪ/ n museo m de pinturas, pinacoteca f, galería f de arte

arthritic /ɑːˈθrɪtɪk/ a artrítico. **~s** /ɑːˈθraɪtɪs/ n artritis f

artichoke /ˈɑːtɪtʃəʊk/ n alcachofa f. **Jerusalem ~** pataca f

article /ˈɑːtɪkl/ n artículo m. ~ **of clothing** prenda f de vestir. **leading** ~ artículo de fondo

articulate /ɑːˈtɪkjʊlət/ a articulado; ⟨person⟩ elocuente. ~ /ɑːˈtɪkjʊleɪt/ vt/i articular. ~**ed lorry** n camión m con remolque. ~**ion** /-ˈleɪʃn/ n articulación f

artifice /ˈɑːtɪfɪs/ n artificio m

artificial /ɑːtɪˈfɪʃl/ a artificial; ⟨hair etc⟩ postizo

artillery /ɑːˈtɪlərɪ/ n artillería f

artisan /ɑːtɪˈzæn/ n artesano m

artist /ˈɑːtɪst/ n artista m & f

artiste /ɑːˈtiːst/ n ⟨in theatre⟩ artista m & f

artist|**ic** /ɑːˈtɪstɪk/ a artístico. ~**ry** n arte m, habilidad f

artless /ˈɑːtlɪs/ a ingenuo

arty /ˈɑːtɪ/ a ⟨fam⟩ que se las da de artista

as /æz, əz/ adv & conj como; ⟨since⟩ ya que; ⟨while⟩ mientras. ~ **big** ~ tan grande como. ~ **far** ~ ⟨distance⟩ hasta; ⟨qualitative⟩ en cuanto a. ~ **far** ~ **I know** que yo sepa. ~ **if** como si. ~ **long** ~ mientras. ~ **much** ~ tanto como. ~ **soon** ~ tan pronto como. ~ **well** también

asbestos /æzˈbestos/ n amianto m, asbesto m

ascend /əˈsend/ vt/i subir. ~**t** /əˈsent/ n subida f

ascertain /æsəˈteɪn/ vt averiguar

ascetic /əˈsetɪk/ a ascético. ~n asceta m & f

ascribe /əˈskraɪb/ vt atribuir

ash[1] /æʃ/ n ceniza f

ash[2] /æʃ/ n. ~(**-tree**) fresno m

ashamed /əˈʃeɪmd/ a avergonzado. **be** ~ avergonzarse

ashen /ˈæʃn/ a ceniciento

ashore /əˈʃɔː(r)/ adv a tierra. **go** ~ desembarcar

ash: ~**tray** /ˈæʃtreɪ/ n cenicero m. **A~ Wednesday** n Miércoles m de Ceniza

Asia /ˈeɪʃə/ n Asia f. ~n a & n asiático (m). ~**tic** /-ɪˈætɪk/ a asiático

aside /əˈsaɪd/ adv a un lado. —n ⟨in theatre⟩ aparte m

asinine /ˈæsɪnaɪn/ a estúpido

ask /ɑːsk/ vt pedir; preguntar ⟨question⟩; ⟨invite⟩ invitar. ~ **about** enterarse de. ~ **after** pedir noticias de. ~ **for help** pedir ayuda. ~ **for trouble** buscarse problemas. ~ **s.o. in** invitar a uno a pasar

askance /əˈskæns/ adv. **look** ~ **at** mirar de soslayo

askew /əˈskjuː/ adv & a ladeado

asleep /əˈsliːp/ adv & a dormido. **fall** ~ dormirse, quedar dormido

asparagus /əˈspærəgəs/ n espárrago m

aspect /ˈæspekt/ n aspecto m; ⟨of house etc⟩ orientación f

aspersions /əˈspɜːʃnz/ npl. **cast** ~ **on** difamar

asphalt /ˈæsfælt/ n asfalto m. —vt asfaltar

asphyxia /æsˈfɪksɪə/ n asfixia f. ~**te** /əsˈfɪksɪeɪt/ vt asfixiar. ~**tion** /-ˈeɪʃn/ n asfixia f

aspic /ˈæspɪk/ n gelatina f

aspir|**ation** /æspəˈreɪʃn/ n aspiración f. ~**e** /əˈspaɪə(r)/ vi aspirar

aspirin /ˈæspriːn/ n aspirina f

ass /æs/ n asno m; ⟨fig, fam⟩ imbécil m

assail /əˈseɪl/ vt asaltar. ~**ant** n asaltador m

assassin /əˈsæsɪn/ n asesino m. ~**ate** /əˈsæsɪneɪt/ vt asesinar. ~**ation** /-ˈeɪʃn/ n asesinato m

assault /əˈsɔːlt/ n ⟨mil⟩ ataque m; ⟨jurid⟩ atentado m. —vt asaltar

assemblage /əˈsemblɪdʒ/ n ⟨of things⟩ colección f; ⟨of people⟩ reunión f; ⟨mec⟩ montaje m

assemble /əˈsembl/ vt reunir; ⟨mec⟩ montar. —vi reunirse

assembly /ə'sembli/ *n* reunión *f*; (*pol etc*) asamblea *f*. ∼ **line** *n* línea *f* de montaje

assent /ə'sent/ *n* asentimiento *m*. —*vi* asentir

assert /ə'sɜːt/ *vt* afirmar; hacer valer (*one's rights*). ∼**ion** /-ʃn/ *n* afirmación *f*. ∼**ive** *a* positivo, firme

assess /ə'ses/ *vt* valorar; (*determine*) determinar; fijar (*tax etc*). ∼**ment** *n* valoración *f*

asset /'æset/ *n* (*advantage*) ventaja *f*; (*pl, com*) bienes *mpl*

assiduous /ə'sɪdjʊəs/ *a* asiduo

assign /ə'saɪn/ *vt* asignar; (*appoint*) nombrar

assignation /æsɪɡ'neɪʃn/ *n* asignación *f*; (*meeting*) cita *f*

assignment /ə'saɪnmənt/ *n* asignación *f*, misión *f*; (*task*) tarea *f*

assimilate /ə'sɪmɪleɪt/ *vt* asimilar. —*vi* asimilarse. ∼**ion** /-'eɪʃn/ *n* asimilación *f*

assist /ə'sɪst/ *vt*/*i* ayudar. ∼**ance** *n* ayuda *f*. ∼**ant** /ə'sɪstənt/ *n* ayudante *m* & *f*; (*shop*) dependienta *f*, dependiente *m*. —*a* auxiliar, adjunto

associat|e /ə'səʊʃɪeɪt/ *vt* asociar. —*vi* asociarse. /ə'səʊ-ʃɪət/ *a* asociado. —*n* colega *m* & *f*; (*com*) socio *m*. ∼**ion** /-'eɪʃn/ *n* asociación *f*. A∼**ion** football *n* fútbol *m*

assort|ed /ə'sɔːtɪd/ *a* surtido. ∼**ment** *n* surtido *m*

assume /ə'sjuːm/ *vt* suponer; tomar (*power, attitude*); asumir (*role, burden*)

assumption /ə'sʌmpʃn/ *n* suposición *f*. the A∼ la Asunción *f*

assur|ance /ə'ʃʊərəns/ *n* seguridad *f*; (*insurance*) seguro *m*. ∼**e** /ə'ʃʊə(r)/ *vt* asegurar. ∼**ed** *a* seguro. ∼**edly** /-rɪdlɪ/ *adv* seguramente

asterisk /'æstərɪsk/ *n* asterisco *m*

astern /ə'stɜːn/ *adv* a popa

asthma /'æsmə/ *n* asma *f*. ∼**tic** /-'mætɪk/ *a* & *n* asmático (*m*)

astonish /ə'stɒnɪʃ/ *vt* asombrar. ∼**ing** *a* asombroso. ∼**ment** *n* asombro *m*

astound /ə'staʊnd/ *vt* asombrar

astray /ə'streɪ/ *adv* & *a*. **go** ∼ extraviarse. **lead** ∼ llevar por mal camino

astride /ə'straɪd/ *adv* a horcajadas. —*prep* a horcajadas sobre

astringent /ə'strɪndʒənt/ *a* astringente; (*fig*) austero. —*n* astringente *m*

astrolog|er /ə'strɒlədʒə(r)/ *n* astrólogo *m*. ∼**y** *n* astrología *f*

astronaut /'æstrənɔːt/ *n* astronauta *m* & *f*

astronom|er /ə'strɒnəmə(r)/ *n* astrónomo *m*. ∼**ical** /æstrə-'nɒmɪkl/ *a* astronómico. ∼**y** /ə'strɒnəmɪ/ *n* astronomía *f*

astute /ə'stjuːt/ *a* astuto. ∼**ness** *n* astucia *f*

asunder /ə'sʌndə(r)/ *adv* en pedazos; (*in two*) en dos

asylum /ə'saɪləm/ *n* asilo *m*. **lunatic** ∼ manicomio *m*

at /ət, æt/ *prep* a. ∼ **home** en casa. ∼ **night** por la noche. ∼ **Robert's** en casa de Roberto. ∼ **once** en seguida; (*simultaneously*) a la vez. ∼ **sea** en el mar. ∼ **the station** en la estación. ∼ **times** a veces. **not** ∼ **all** nada; (*after thanks*) ¡de nada!

ate /et/ *see* eat

atheis|m /'eɪθɪəzm/ *n* ateísmo *m*. ∼**t** /-st/ *n* ateo *m*

athlet|e /'æθliːt/ *n* atleta *m* & *f*. ∼**ic** /-'letɪk/ *a* atlético. ∼**ics** /-'letɪks/ *npl* atletismo *m*

Atlantic /ət'læntɪk/ *a* & *n* atlántico (*m*). —*n*. ∼ (**Ocean**) Océano (*m*) Atlántico *m*

atlas /'ætləs/ *n* atlas *m*

atmospher|e /'ætməsfɪə(r)/ *n* atmósfera *f*; (*fig*) ambiente *m*.

~**ic** /-'ferɪk/ *a* atmosférico. ~**ics** /-'ferɪks/ *npl* parásitos *mpl*

atom /'ætəm/ *n* átomo *m*. ~**ic** /ə'tɒmɪk/ *a* atómico

atomize /'ætəmaɪz/ *vt* atomizar. ~**r** /'ætəmaɪzə(r)/ *n* atomizador *m*

atone /ə'təʊn/ *vi*. ~ **for** expiar. ~**ment** *n* expiación *f*

atrocious /ə'trəʊʃəs/ *a* atroz. ~**ty** /-'trɒsətɪ/ *n* atrocidad *f*

atrophy /'ætrəfɪ/ *n* atrofia *f*

attach /ə'tætʃ/ *vt* sujetar; adjuntar (*document etc*). **be** ~**ed to** (*be fond of*) tener cariño a

attaché /ə'tæʃeɪ/ *n* agregado *m*. ~ **case** maletín *m*

attachment /ə'tætʃmənt/ *n* (*affection*) cariño *m*; (*tool*) accesorio *m*

attack /ə'tæk/ *n* ataque *m*. —*vt/i* atacar. ~**er** *n* agresor *m*

attain /ə'teɪn/ *vt* conseguir. ~**able** *a* alcanzable. ~**ment** *n* logro *m*. ~**ments** *npl* conocimientos *mpl*, talento *m*

attempt /ə'tempt/ *vt* intentar. —*n* tentativa *f*, (*attack*) atentado *m*

attend /ə'tend/ *vt* asistir a; (*escort*) acompañar. —*vi* prestar atención. ~ **to** (*look after*) ocuparse de. ~**ance** *n* asistencia *f*; (*people present*) concurrencia *f*. ~**ant** /ə'tendənt/ *a* concomitante. —*n* encargado *m*; (*servant*) sirviente *m*

attention /ə'tenʃn/ *n* atención *f*. ~**!** (*mil*) ¡firmes! **pay** ~ prestar atención

attentive /ə'tentɪv/ *a* atento. ~**ness** *n* atención *f*

attenuate /ə'tenjʊeɪt/ *vt* atenuar

attest /ə'test/ *vt* atestiguar. —*vi* dar testimonio. ~**ation** /æte'steɪʃn/ *n* testimonio *m*

attic /'ætɪk/ *n* desván *m*

attire /ə'taɪə(r)/ *n* atavío *m*. —*vt* vestir

attitude /'ætɪtjuːd/ *n* postura *f*

attorney /ə'tɜːnɪ/ *n* (*pl* -**eys**) apoderado *m*; (*Amer*) abogado *m*

attract /ə'trækt/ *vt* atraer. ~**ion** /-ʃn/ *n* atracción *f*; (*charm*) atractivo *m*

attractive /ə'træktɪv/ *a* atractivo; (*interesting*) atrayente. ~**ness** *n* atractivo *m*

attribute /ə'trɪbjuːt/ *vt* atribuir. /'ætrɪbjuːt/ *n* atributo *m*

attrition /ə'trɪʃn/ *n* desgaste *m*.

aubergine /'əʊbəʒiːn/ *n* berenjena *f*

auburn /'ɔːbən/ *a* castaño

auction /'ɔːkʃn/ *n* subasta *f*. —*vt* subastar. ~**eer** /-ʃə'nɪə(r)/ *n* subastador *m*

audacious /ɔː'deɪʃəs/ *a* audaz. ~**ty** /-'æsətɪ/ *n* audacia *f*

audible /'ɔːdəbl/ *a* audible

audience /'ɔːdɪəns/ *n* (*interview*) audiencia *f*; (*teatro, radio*) público *m*

audio-visual /ɔːdɪəʊ'vɪʒʊəl/ *a* audiovisual

audit /'ɔːdɪt/ *n* revisión *f* de cuentas. —*vt* revisar

audition /ɔː'dɪʃn/ *n* audición *f*. —*vt* dar audición a

auditor /'ɔːdɪtə(r)/ *n* interventor *m* de cuentas

auditorium /ɔːdɪ'tɔːrɪəm/ *n* sala *f*, auditorio *m*

augment /ɔːg'ment/ *vt* aumentar

augur /'ɔːgə(r)/ *vt* augurar. **it** ~**s well** es de buen agüero

august /ɔː'gʌst/ *a* augusto

August /'ɔːgəst/ *n* agosto *m*

aunt /ɑːnt/ *n* tía *f*

au pair /əʊ'peə(r)/ *n* chica *f* au pair

aura /'ɔːrə/ *n* atmósfera *f*, halo *m*

auspices /'ɔːspɪsɪz/ *npl* auspicios *mpl*

auspicious /ɔː'spɪʃəs/ *a* propicio

austere /ɔː'stɪə(r)/ *a* austero. ~**ity** /-'erətɪ/ *n* austeridad *f*

Australia /ɒ'streɪlɪə/ *n* Australia *f*. ~**n** *a* & *n* australiano *m*

Austria /ˈɒstrɪə/ n Austria f. ∼n a & n austríaco (m)

authentic /ɔːˈθentɪk/ a auténtico. ∼ate /ɔːˈθentɪkeɪt/ vt autenticar. ∼ity /-ənˈtɪsɪtɪ/ n autenticidad f

author /ˈɔːθə(r)/ n autor m. ∼ess n autora f

authoritarian /ɔːθɒrɪˈteərɪən/ a autoritario

authoritative /ɔːˈθɒrɪtətɪv/ a autorizado; (manner) autoritario

authority /ɔːˈθɒrətɪ/ n autoridad f, (permission) autorización f

authorization /ɔːθəraɪˈzeɪʃn/ n autorización f. ∼e /ˈɔːθəraɪz/ vt autorizar

authorship /ˈɔːθəʃɪp/ n profesión f de autor; (origin) paternidad f literaria

autistic /ɔːˈtɪstɪk/ a autista

autobiography /ɔːtəʊbaɪˈɒgrəfɪ/ n autobiografía f

autocracy /ɔːˈtɒkrəsɪ/ n autocracia f. ∼t /ˈɔːtəkræt/ n autócrata m & f. ∼tic /-ˈkrætɪk/ a autocrático

autograph /ˈɔːtəgrɑːf/ n autógrafo m. ∼vt firmar

automate /ˈɔːtəmeɪt/ vt automatizar. ∼ic /ɔːtəˈmætɪk/ a automático. ∼ion /ɔːtəˈmeɪʃn/ n automatización f. ∼on /ɔːˈtɒmətən/ n autómata m

automobile /ˈɔːtəmɒbiːl/ n (Amer) coche m, automóvil m

autonomous /ɔːˈtɒnəməs/ a autónomo. ∼y n autonomía f

autopsy /ˈɔːtɒpsɪ/ n autopsia f

autumn /ˈɔːtəm/ n otoño m. ∼al /-ˈtʌmnəl/ a de otoño, otoñal

auxiliary /ɔːgˈzɪlɪərɪ/ a auxiliar. ∼n asistente m; (verb) verbo m auxiliar; (pl, troops) tropas fpl auxiliares

avail /əˈveɪl/ vt/i servir. ∼ o.s. of aprovecharse de. ∼n ventaja f. **to no** ∼ inútil

availability /əveɪləˈbɪlətɪ/ n disponibilidad f. ∼le /əˈveɪləbl/ a disponible

avalanche /ˈævəlɑːnʃ/ n avalancha f

avarice /ˈævərɪs/ n avaricia f. ∼ious /-ˈrɪʃəs/ a avaro

avenge /əˈvendʒ/ vt vengar

avenue /ˈævənjuː/ n avenida f, (fig) vía f

average /ˈævərɪdʒ/ n promedio m. **on** ∼ por término medio. –a medio. –vt calcular el promedio de. –vi alcanzar un promedio de

averse /əˈvɜːs/ a enemigo (to de). **be** ∼**e** to sentir repugnancia por, no gustarle. ∼ion /-ʃn/ n repugnancia f

avert /əˈvɜːt/ vt (turn away) apartar; (ward off) desviar

aviary /ˈeɪvɪərɪ/ n pajarera f

aviation /eɪvɪˈeɪʃn/ n aviación f

aviator /ˈeɪvɪeɪtə(r)/ n (old use) aviador m

avid /ˈævɪd/ a ávido. ∼ity /-ˈvɪdətɪ/ n avidez f

avocado /ævəˈkɑːdəʊ/ n (pl -os) aguacate m

avoid /əˈvɔɪd/ vt evitar. ∼able a evitable. ∼ance n el evitar m

avuncular /əˈvʌŋkjʊlə(r)/ a de tío

await /əˈweɪt/ vt esperar

awake /əˈweɪk/ vt/i (pt awoke, pp awoken) despertar. –a despierto. **wide** ∼ completamente despierto; (fig) despabilado. ∼n /əˈweɪkən/ vt/i despertar. ∼ning n el despertar m

award /əˈwɔːd/ vt otorgar; (jurid) adjudicar. ∼n premio m; (jurid) adjudicación f; (scholarship) beca f

aware /əˈweə(r)/ a consciente. **are you** ∼ that? ¿te das cuenta de que? ∼ness n conciencia f

awash /əˈwɒʃ/ a inundado

away /əˈweɪ/ adv (absent) fuera; (far) lejos; (persistently) sin parar. —*a & n.* ~ **(match)** partido *m* fuera de casa

awe /ɔ:/ *n* temor *m.* ~**some** *a* imponente. ~**struck** *a* atemorizado

awful /'ɔ:fʊl/ *a* terrible, malísimo. ~**ly** *adv* terriblemente

awhile /ə'waɪl/ *adv* un rato

awkward /'ɔ:kwəd/ *a* difícil; (*inconvenient*) inoportuno; (*clumsy*) desmañado; (*embarrassed*) incómodo. ~**ly** *adv* con dificultad; (*clumsily*) de manera torpe. ~**ness** *n* dificultad *f;* (*discomfort*) molestia *f;* (*clumsiness*) torpeza *f*

awning /'ɔ:nɪŋ/ *n* toldo *m*

awoke, awoken /ə'wəʊk, ə'wəʊkən/ *see* **awake**

awry /ə'raɪ/ *adv a* ladeado. **go** ~ salir mal

axe /æks/ *n* hacha *f.* —*vt* (*pres p* **axing**) cortar con hacha; (*fig*) recortar

axiom /'æksɪəm/ *n* axioma *m*

axis /'æksɪs/ *n* (*pl* **axes** /-i:z/) eje *m*

axle /'æksl/ *n* eje *m*

ay(e) /aɪ/ *adv & n* sí (*m*)

B

BA *abbr see* **bachelor**

babble /'bæbl/ *vi* balbucir; (*chatter*) parlotear; (*of stream*) murmullar. —*n* balbuceo *m;* (*chatter*) parloteo *m;* (*of stream*) murmullo *m*

baboon /bə'bu:n/ *n* mandril *m*

baby /'beɪbɪ/ *n* niño *m,* bebé *m;* (*Amer, sl*) chica *f.* ~**ish** /'beɪbɪʃ/ *a* infantil. ~**-sit** *vi* cuidar a los niños, hacer de canguro. ~**sitter** *n* persona *f* que cuida a los niños, canguro *m*

bachelor /'bætʃələ(r)/ *n* soltero *m.* **B**~ **of Arts** (**BA**) licenciado

m en filosofía y letras. **B**~ **of Science** (**BSc**) licenciado *m* en ciencias

back /bæk/ *n* espalda *f;* (*of car*) parte *f* trasera; (*of chair*) respaldo *m;* (*of cloth*) revés *m;* (*of house*) parte *f* de atrás; (*of animal, book*) lomo *m;* (*of hand, document*) dorso *m;* (*football*) defensa *m & f.* ~ **of beyond** en el quinto pino. —*a* trasero; (*taxes*) atrasado. —*adv* atrás; (*returned*) de vuelta. —*vt* apoyar; (*betting*) apostar a; dar marcha atrás a ⟨*car*⟩. —*vi* retroceder; ⟨*car*⟩ dar marcha atrás. ~ **down** *vi* volverse atrás. ~ **out** *vi* retirarse. ~ **up** *vt* (*auto*) retroceder. ~**ache** /'bækeɪk/ *n* dolor *m* de espalda. ~**bencher** *n* (*pol*) diputado *m* sin poder ministerial. ~**biting** /'bækbaɪtɪŋ/ *n* maledicencia *f.* ~**bone** /'bækbəʊn/ *n* columna *f* vertebral; (*fig*) pilar *m.* ~**chat** /'bæktʃæt/ *n* impertinencias *fpl.* ~**date** /bæk'deɪt/ *vt* antedatar. ~**er** /bækə(r)/ *n* partidario *m;* (*com*) financiador *m.* ~**fire** /bæk'faɪə(r)/ *vi* (*auto*) petardear; (*fig*) fallar, salir el tiro por la culata. ~**gammon** /bæk'gæmən/ *n* backgammon *m.* ~**ground** /'bækgraʊnd/ *n* fondo *m;* (*environment*) antecedentes *mpl.* ~**hand** /'bækhænd/ *n* (*sport*) revés *m.* ~**handed** *a* dado con el dorso de la mano; (*fig*) equívoco, ambiguo. ~**hander** *n* (*sport*) revés *m;* (*fig*) ataque *m* indirecto; (*bribe, sl*) soborno *m.* ~**ing** /'bækɪŋ/ *n* apoyo *m.* ~**lash** /'bæklæʃ/ *n* reacción *f.* ~**log** /'bæklɒg/ *n* atrasos *mpl.* ~**side** /bæk'saɪd/ *n* (*fam*) trasero *m.* ~**stage** /bæk'steɪdʒ/ *a* de bastidores. —*adv* entre bastidores. ~**stroke** /'bækstrəʊk/ *n* (*tennis etc*) revés *m;* (*swimming*) braza

f de espaldas. **~-up** n apoyo m.
~ward /'bækwəd/ a *(step etc)*
hacia atrás; *(retarded)* atrasado.
~wards /'bækwədz/ adv hacia
atrás; *(fall)* de espaldas; *(back to
front)* al revés. **go ~wards and
forwards** ir de acá para allá.
~water /'bækwɔːtə(r)/ n agua f
estancada; *(fig)* lugar m
apartado

bacon /'beɪkən/ n tocino m

bacteria /bæk'tɪərɪə/ npl bac-
terias fpl. **~l** a bacteriano

bad /bæd/ a (**worse**, **worst**)
malo; *(serious)* grave; *(harmful)*
nocivo; *(language)* indecente.
feel ~ sentirse mal

bade /beɪd/ see **bid**

badge /bædʒ/ n distintivo m,
chapa f

badger /'bædʒə(r)/ n tejón m. —vt
acosar

bad: **~ly** adv mal. **want ~ly**
desear muchísimo. **~ly off** mal
de dinero. **~-mannered** a mal
educado

badminton /'bædmɪntən/ n bád-
minton m

bad-tempered /bæd'tempəd/ a
(always) de mal genio; *(tem-
porarily)* de mal humor

baffle /'bæfl/ vt desconcertar

bag /bæg/ n bolsa f; *(handbag)*
bolso m. —vt (pt **bagged**) ensa-
car; *(take)* coger (not LAm), agarrar (LAm). **~s** npl *(luggage)*
equipaje m. **~s of** *(fam)* montones de

baggage /'bægɪdʒ/ n equipaje m

baggy /'bægɪ/ a *(clothes)* holgado

bagpipes /'bægpaɪps/ npl gaita f

Bahamas /bə'hɑːməz/ npl. **the ~**
las Bahamas fpl

bail[1] /beɪl/ n caución, fianza f. —
vt poner en libertad bajo fianza.
~ s.o. out obtener la libertad de
uno bajo fianza

bail[2] /beɪl/ n *(cricket)* travesaño
m

bail[3] /beɪl/ vt *(naut)* achicar

bailiff /'beɪlɪf/ n alguacil m;
(estate) administrador m

bait /beɪt/ n cebo m. —vt cebar;
(torment) atormentar

bak|e /beɪk/ vt cocer al horno. —
vi cocerse. **~er** n panadero m.
~ery /'beɪkərɪ/ n panadería f.
~ing n cocción f; *(batch)* hornada f. **~ing-powder** n levadura f en polvo

balance /'bæləns/ n equilibrio m;
(com) balance m; *(sum)* saldo m;
(scales) balanza f; *(remainder)*
resto m. —vt equilibrar; *(com)*
saldar; nivelar *(budget)*. —vi
equilibrarse; *(com)* saldarse. **~d**
a equilibrado

balcony /'bælkənɪ/ n balcón m

bald /bɔːld/ a (-**er**, -**est**) calvo;
(tyre) desgastado

balderdash /'bɔːldədæʃ/ n tonterías fpl

bald: **~ly** adv escuetamente.
~ness n calvicie f

bale /beɪl/ n bala f, fardo m. —vi.
~ out lanzarse en paracaídas

Balearic /bælɪ'ærɪk/ a. **~
Islands** Islas fpl Baleares

baleful /'beɪlfʊl/ a funesto

balk /bɔːk/ vt frustrar. —vi. **~
(at)** resistirse (a)

ball[1] /bɔːl/ n bola f; *(tennis etc)*
pelota f; *(football etc)* balón m; *(of
yarn)* ovillo m

ball[2] /bɔːl/ *(dance)* baile m

ballad /'bæləd/ n balada f

ballast /'bæləst/ n lastre m

ball: **~-bearing** n cojinete m de
bolas. **~-cock** n llave f de bola

ballerina /bælə'riːnə/ f bailarina
f

ballet /'bæleɪ/ n ballet m

ballistic /bə'lɪstɪk/ a balístico.
~s n balística f

balloon /bə'luːn/ n globo m

balloonist /bə'luːnɪst/ n aero-
nauta m & f

ballot /'bælət/ n votación f. ~
(-paper) n papeleta f. ~box n
urna f
ball-point /'bɔːlpɔɪnt/ n. ~ (pen)
bolígrafo m
ballroom /'bɔːlruːm/ n salón m
de baile
ballyhoo /bælɪ'huː/ n (publicity)
publicidad f sensacionalista;
(uproar) jaleo m
balm /bɑːm/ n bálsamo m. ~y a
(mild) suave; (sl) chiflado
baloney /bə'ləʊnɪ/ n (sl) tonterías fpl
balsam /'bɔːlsəm/ n bálsamo m
balustrade /bælə'streɪd/ n barandilla f
bamboo /bæm'buː/ n bambú m
bamboozle /bæm'buːzl/ vt engañar
ban /bæn/ vt (pt banned) prohibir. ~ from excluir de. —n prohibición f
banal /bə'nɑːl/ a banal. ~ity
/-ælətɪ/ n banalidad f
banana /bə'nɑːnə/ n plátano m,
banana f (LAm). ~-tree plátano
m, banano m
band[1] /bænd/ n banda f
band[2] /bænd/ n (mus) orquesta f;
(military, brass) banda f. —vi. ~
together juntarse
bandage /'bændɪdʒ/ n venda f. —
vt vendar
b & b abbr (bed and breakfast)
cama f y desayuno
bandit /'bændɪt/ n bandido m
bandstand /'bændstænd/ n
quiosco m de música
bandwagon /'bændwægən/ n.
jump on the ~ (fig) subirse al
carro
bandy[1] /'bændɪ/ a (-ier, -iest)
patizambo
bandy[2] /'bændɪ/ vt. ~ about
repetir. be bandied about estar
en boca de todos
bandy-legged /'bændɪlegd/ a
patizambo

bane /beɪn/ n (fig) perdición f.
~ful a funesto
bang /bæŋ/ n (noise) ruido m;
(blow) golpe m; (of gun) estampido m; (of door) golpe m. —vt/i
golpear. —adv exactamente. —
int ¡pum!
banger /'bæŋə(r)/ n petardo m;
(culin, sl) salchicha f
bangle /'bæŋgl/ n brazalete m
banish /'bænɪʃ/ vt desterrar
banisters /'bænɪstəz/ npl barandilla f
banjo /'bændʒəʊ/ n (pl -os) banjo
m
bank[1] /bæŋk/ n (of river) orilla
f. —vt cubrir (fire). —vi (aviat)
ladearse
bank[2] /bæŋk/ n banco m. —vt
depositar. —vi contar con. ~
with tener una cuenta con. ~er
n banquero m. ~ holiday n día
m festivo, fiesta f. ~ing n (com)
banca f. ~note f ~ /bæŋknəʊt/ n
billete m de banco
bankrupt /'bæŋkrʌpt/ a & n que-
brado (m). —vt hacer quebrar.
~cy n bancarrota f, quiebra f
banner /'bænə(r)/ n bandera f; (in
demonstration) pancarta f
banns /bænz/ npl amone-
staciones fpl
banquet /'bæŋkwɪt/ n banquete
m
bantamweight /'bæntəmweɪt/ n
peso m gallo
banter /'bæntə(r)/ n chanza f. —
vi chancearse
bap /bæp/ n panecillo m blando
baptism /'bæptɪzəm/ n bautismo
m; (act) bautizo m
Baptist /'bæptɪst/ n bautista m &
f
baptize /bæp'taɪz/ vt bautizar
bar /bɑː(r)/ n barra f; (on window)
reja f; (of chocolate) tableta f; (of
soap) pastilla f; (pub) bar m;
(mus) compás m; (jurid) abogacía f; (fig) obstáculo m. —vt (pt

barred) atrancar ⟨door⟩; (exclude) excluir; (prohibit) prohibir. —prep excepto

barbar|ian /ba:'beərɪən/ a & n bárbaro (m). ~ic /ba:'bærɪk/ a bárbaro. ~ity /-ətɪ/ n barbaridad f. ~ous /'ba:bərəs/ a bárbaro

barbecue /'ba:bɪkju:/ n barbacoa f. —vt asar a la parilla

barbed /ba:bd/ a. ~ **wire** alambre m de espinas

barber /'ba:bə(r)/ n peluquero m, barbero m

barbiturate /ba:'bɪtjʊrət/ n barbitúrico m

bare /beə(r)/ a (-er, est) desnudo; ⟨room⟩ con pocos muebles; (mere) simple; (empty) vacío. — vt desnudar; (uncover) descubrir. ~ **one's teeth** mostrar los dientes. ~**back** /'beəbæk/ adv a pelo. ~**faced** /'beəfeɪst/ a descarado. ~**foot** a descalzo. ~**headed** /'beəhedɪd/ a descubierto. ~**ly** adv apenas. ~**ness** n desnudez f

bargain /'ba:gɪn/ n (agreement) pacto m; (good buy) ganga f. — vi negociar; (haggle) regatear. ~ **for** esperar, contar con

barge /ba:dʒ/ n barcaza f. —vi. ~ **in** irrumpir

baritone /'bærɪtəʊn/ n barítono m

barium /'beərɪəm/ n bario m

bark¹ /ba:k/ n (of dog) ladrido m. —vi ladrar

bark² /ba:k/ (of tree) corteza f

barley /'ba:lɪ/ n cebada f. ~ **water** n hordiate m

bar: ~**maid** /'ba:meɪd/ n camarera f. ~**man** /'ba:mən/ n (pl -men) camarero m

barmy /'ba:mɪ/ a (sl) chiflado

barn /ba:n/ n granero m

barometer /bə'rɒmɪtə(r)/ n barómetro m

baron /'bærən/ n barón m. ~**ess** n baronesa f

baroque /bə'rɒk/ a & n barroco (m)

barracks /'bærəks/ npl cuartel m

barrage /'bæra:ʒ/ n (mil) barrera f; (dam) presa f; (of questions) bombardeo m

barrel /'bærəl/ n tonel m; (of gun) cañón m. ~**organ** n organillo m

barren /'bærən/ a estéril. ~**ness** n esterilidad f, aridez f

barricade /bærɪ'keɪd/ n barricada f. —vt cerrar con barricadas

barrier /'bærɪə(r)/ n barrera f

barring /'ba:rɪŋ/ prep salvo

barrister /'bærɪstə(r)/ n abogado m

barrow /'bærəʊ/ n carro m; (wheelbarrow) carretilla f

barter /'ba:tə(r)/ n trueque m. —vt trocar

base /beɪs/ n base f. —vt basar. — a vil

baseball /'beɪsbɔ:l/ n béisbol m

baseless /'beɪslɪs/ a infundado

basement /'beɪsmənt/ n sótano m

bash /bæʃ/ vt golpear. —n golpe m. **have a** ~ (sl) probar

bashful /'bæʃfl/ a tímido

basic /'beɪsɪk/ a básico, fundamental. ~**ally** adv fundamentalmente

basil /'bæzl/ n albahaca f

basilica /bə'zɪlɪkə/ n basílica f

basin /'beɪsn/ n (for washing) palangana f; (for food) cuenco m; (geog) cuenca f

basis /'beɪsɪs/ n (pl bases /-si:z/) base f

bask /ba:sk/ vi asolearse; (fig) gozar (in de)

basket /'ba:skɪt/ n cesta f; (big) cesto m. ~**ball** /'ba:skɪtbɔ:l/ n baloncesto m

Basque /ba:sk/ a & n vasco (m). ~ **Country** n País m Vasco. ~ **Provinces** npl Vascongadas fpl

bass[1] /beɪs/ a bajo. —n (mus) bajo m

bass[2] /bæs/ n (marine fish) róbalo m; (freshwater fish) perca f

bassoon /bə'su:n/ n fagot m

bastard /'bɑ:stəd/ a & n bastardo (m). **you ~!** (fam) ¡cabrón!

baste /beɪst/ vt (sew) hilvanar; (culin) lard(e)ar

bastion /'bæstɪən/ n baluarte m

bat[1] /bæt/ n bate m; (for table tennis) raqueta f. **off one's own ~** por sí solo. —vt (pt batted) golpear. —vi batear

bat[2] /bæt/ n (mammal) murciélago m

bat[3] /bæt/ vt. **without ~ting an eyelid** sin pestañear

batch /bætʃ/ n (of people) grupo m; (of papers) lío m; (of goods) remesa f; (of bread) hornada f

bated /'beɪtɪd/ a. **with ~ breath** con aliento entrecortado

bath /bɑːθ/ n (pl -s /bɑːðz/) baño m; (tub) bañera f; (pl, swimming pool) piscina f. —vt bañar. —vi bañarse

bathe /beɪð/ vt bañar. —vi bañarse. —n baño m. **~r** /-ə(r)/ n bañista m & f

bathing /'beɪðɪŋ/ n baños mpl. **~-costume** n traje m de baño

bathroom /'bɑːθrʊm/ n cuarto m de baño

batman /'bætmən/ n (pl -men) (mil) ordenanza f

baton /'bætən/ n (mil) bastón m; (mus) batuta f

batsman /'bætsmən/ n (pl -men) bateador m

battalion /bə'tælɪən/ n batallón m

batter[1] /'bætə(r)/ vt apalear

batter[2] /'bætə(r)/ n batido m para rebozar, albardilla f

batter: **~ed** a (car etc) estropeado; (wife etc) golpeado. **~ing** n (fam) bombardeo m

battery /'bætərɪ/ n (mil, auto) batería f; (of torch, radio) pila f

battle /'bætl/ n batalla f; (fig) lucha f. —vi luchar. **~axe** /'bætlæks/ n (woman, fam) arpía f. **~field** /'bætlfiːld/ n campo m de batalla. **~ments** /'bætlmənts/ npl almenas fpl. **~ship** /'bætlʃɪp/ n acorazado m

batty /'bætɪ/ a (sl) chiflado

baulk /bɔːlk/ vt frustrar. —vi. **~ (at)** resistirse (a)

bawd|iness /'bɔːdɪnəs/ n obscenidad f. **~y** /'bɔːdɪ/ a (-ier, -iest) obsceno, verde

bawl /bɔːl/ vt/i gritar

bay[1] /beɪ/ n (geog) bahía f

bay[2] /beɪ/ n (bot) laurel m

bay[3] /beɪ/ n (of dog) ladrido m. **keep at ~** mantener a raya. —vi ladrar

bayonet /'beɪənet/ n bayoneta f

bay window /beɪ'wɪndəʊ/ n ventana f salediza

bazaar /bə'zɑː(r)/ n bazar m

BC /biː'siː/ abbr (before Christ) a. de C., antes de Cristo

be /biː/ vi (pres am, are, is; pt was, were; pp been) (position or temporary) estar; (permanent) ser. **~ cold/hot, etc** tener frío/calor, etc. **~ reading/singing, etc** (aux) leer/cantar, etc. **~ at** may sea como fuere. **he is 30** (age) tiene 30 años. **he is to come** (must) tiene que venir. **how are you?** ¿cómo estás? **how much is it?** ¿cuánto vale?, ¿cuánto es? **have been to** haber estado en. **it is cold/hot, etc** (weather) hace frío/calor, etc

beach /biːtʃ/ n playa f

beachcomber /'biːtʃkəʊmə(r)/ n raquero m

beacon /'biːkən/ n faro m

bead /biːd/ n cuenta f; (of glass) abalorio m

beak /biːk/ n pico m

beaker /'biːkə(r)/ n jarra f, vaso m

beam /biːm/ n viga f; (of light) rayo m; (naut) bao m. —vt emitir. —vi irradiar; (smile) sonreír. **~ends** npl. be on one's **~ends** no tener más dinero. **~ing** a radiante

bean /biːn/ n judía; (broad bean) haba f, (of coffee) grano m

beano /'biːnəʊ/ n (pl -os) (fam) juerga f

bear[1] /beə(r)/ vt (pt bore, pp borne) llevar; parir «niño»; (endure) soportar. **~ right** torcer a la derecha. **~ in mind** tener en cuenta. **~ with** tener paciencia con

bear[2] /beə(r)/ n oso m

bearable /'beərəbl/ a soportable

beard /bɪəd/ n barba f. **~ed** a barbudo

bearer /'beərə(r)/ n portador m; (of passport) poseedor m

bearing /'beərɪŋ/ n comportamiento m; (relevance) relación f; (mec) cojinete m. **get one's ~s** orientarse

beast /biːst/ n bestia f; (person) bruto m. **~ly** /'biːstlɪ/ a (-ier, -iest) bestial; (fam) horrible

beat /biːt/ vt (pt beat, pp beaten) golpear; (culin) batir; (defeat) derrotar; (better) sobrepasar; (baffle) dejar perplejo. **~ a retreat** (mil) batirse en retirada. **~ it** (sl) largarse. —vi (heart) latir. —n latido m; (mus) ritmo m; (of policeman) ronda f. **~ up** dar una paliza a; (culin) batir. **~er** n batidor m. **~ing** n paliza f

beautician /bjuː'tɪʃn/ n esteticista m & f

beautiful /'bjuːtɪfl/ a hermoso. **~ly** adv maravillosamente

beautify /'bjuːtɪfaɪ/ vt embellecer

beauty /'bjuːtɪ/ n belleza f. **~ parlour** n salón m de belleza. **~ spot** (on face) lunar m; (site) lugar m pintoresco

beaver /'biːvə(r)/ n castor m

became /bɪ'keɪm/ see become

because /bɪ'kɒz/ conj porque. —adv. **~ of** a causa de

beck /bek/ n. be at the **~ and call of** estar a disposición de

beckon /'bekən/ vt/i. **~ (to)** hacer señas a

become /bɪ'kʌm/ vt (pt became, pp become) sentar bien. —vi hacerse, llegar a ser, volverse, convertirse en. **what has ~ of her?** ¿qué es de ella?

becoming /bɪ'kʌmɪŋ/ a (clothes) favorecedor

bed /bed/ n cama f; (layer) estrato m; (of sea, river) fondo m; (of flowers) macizo m. —vi (pt bedded). **~ down** acostarse. **~ and breakfast (b & b)** cama y desayuno. **~bug** /'bedbʌg/ n chinche f. **~clothes** /'bedkləʊðz/ npl, **~ding** n ropa f de cama

bedevil /bɪ'devl/ vt (pt bedevilled) (torment) atormentar

bedlam /'bedləm/ n confusión f, manicomio m

bed: ~pan /'bedpæn/ n orinal m de cama. **~post** /'bedpəʊst/ n columna f de la cama

bedraggled /bɪ'dræɡld/ a sucio

bed: ~ridden /'bedrɪdn/ a encamado. **~room** /'bedrʊm/ n dormitorio m, habitación f. **~side** /'bedsaɪd/ n cabecera f. **~-sitting-room** /bed'sɪtɪŋruːm/ n salón m con cama, estudio m. **~spread** /'bedspred/ n colcha f. **~time** /'bedtaɪm/ n hora f de acostarse

bee /biː/ n abeja f. **make a ~-line for** ir en línea recta hacia

beech /biːtʃ/ n haya f

beef /biːf/ n carne f de vaca, carne f de res (LAm). —vi (sl) quejarse. ~**burger** /'biːfbɜːgə(r)/ n hamburguesa f

beefeater /'biːfiːtə(r)/ n alabardero m de la torre de Londres

beefsteak /biːf'steɪk/ n filete m, bistec m, bife m (Arg)

beefy /'biːfɪ/ a (-ier, -iest) musculoso

beehive /'biːhaɪv/ n colmena f

been /biːn/ see **be**

beer /bɪə(r)/ n cerveza f

beet /biːt/ n remolacha f

beetle /'biːtl/ n escarabajo m

beetroot /'biːtruːt/ n invar remolacha f

befall /bɪ'fɔːl/ vt (pt **befell**, pp **befallen**) acontecer a. —vi acontecer

befit /bɪ'fɪt/ vt (pt **befitted**) convenir a

before /bɪ'fɔː(r)/ prep (time) antes de; (place) delante de. ~ **leaving** antes de marcharse. —adv (place) delante; (time) antes. a week ~ una semana antes. the week ~ la semana anterior. —conj (time) antes de que. ~ **he leaves** antes de que se vaya. ~**hand** /bɪ'fɔːhænd/ adv de antemano

befriend /bɪ'frend/ vt ofrecer amistad a

beg /beg/ vt/i (pt **begged**) mendigar; (entreat) suplicar; (ask) pedir. ~ **s.o.'s pardon** pedir perdón a uno. **I** ~ **your pardon!** ¡perdone Vd! **I** ~ **your pardon?** ¿cómo? **it's going** ~**ging** no lo quiere nadie

began /bɪ'gæn/ see **begin**

beget /bɪ'get/ vt (pt **begot**, pp **begotten**, pres p **begetting**) engendrar

beggar /'begə(r)/ n mendigo m; (sl) individuo m, tío m (fam)

begin /bɪ'gɪn/ vt/i (pt **began**, pp **begun**, pres p **beginning**) comenzar, empezar. ~**ner** /n principiante m & f. ~**ning** /n principio m

begot, begotten /bɪ'got, bɪ'gotn/ see **beget**

begrudge /bɪ'grʌdʒ/ vt envidiar; (give) dar de mala gana

beguile /bɪ'gaɪl/ vt engañar, seducir; (entertain) entretener

begun /bɪ'gʌn/ see **begin**

behalf /bɪ'hɑːf/ n. **on** ~ **of** de parte de, en nombre de

behav|e /bɪ'heɪv/ vi comportarse, portarse. ~ (**o.s.**) portarse bien. ~**iour** /bɪ'heɪvjə(r)/ n comportamiento m

behead /bɪ'hed/ vt decapitar

beheld /bɪ'held/ see **behold**

behind /bɪ'haɪnd/ prep detrás de. —adv detrás; (late) atrasado. —n (fam) trasero m

behold /bɪ'həʊld/ vt (pt **beheld**) (old use) mirar, contemplar

beholden /bɪ'həʊldən/ a agradecido

being /'biːɪŋ/ n ser m. **come into** ~ nacer

belated /bɪ'leɪtɪd/ a tardío

belch /beltʃ/ vi eructar. —vt. ~ **out** arrojar (smoke)

belfry /'belfrɪ/ n campanario m

Belgi|an /'beldʒən/ a & n belga (m & f). ~**um** /'beldʒəm/ n Bélgica f

belie /bɪ'laɪ/ vt desmentir

belief /bɪ'liːf/ n (trust) fe f; (opinion) creencia f. ~**ve** /bɪ'liːv/ vt/i creer. **make** ~**ve** fingir. ~**ver** /-ə(r)/ n creyente m & f; (supporter) partidario m

belittle /bɪ'lɪtl/ vt empequeñecer; (fig) despreciar

bell /bel/ n campana f; (on door) timbre m

belligerent /bɪ'lɪdʒərənt/ a & n beligerante (m & f)

bellow /'beləʊ/ vt gritar. —vi bramar

bellows /'beləʊz/ npl fuelle m

belly /'belɪ/ n vientre m. ~ful /'belɪfʊl/ n panzada f. **have a ~ful of** (sl) estar harto de

belong /bɪ'lɒŋ/ vi pertenecer; (club) ser socio (**to** de)

belongings /bɪ'lɒŋɪŋz/ npl pertenencias fpl. **personal ~** efectos mpl personales

beloved /bɪ'lʌvɪd/ a & n querido (m)

below /bɪ'ləʊ/ prep debajo de; (fig) inferior a. —adv abajo

belt /belt/ n cinturón m; (area) zona f. —vt (fig) rodear; (sl) pegar

bemused /bɪ'mju:zd/ a perplejo

bench /bentʃ/ n banco m. **the B~** (jurid) la magistratura f

bend /bend/ vt (pt & pp **bent**) doblar; torcer (arm, leg). —vi doblarse; (road) torcerse. —n curva f. **~ down/over** inclinarse

beneath /bɪ'ni:θ/ prep debajo de; (fig) inferior a. —adv abajo

benediction /benɪ'dɪkʃn/ n bendición f

benefactor /'benɪfæktə(r)/ n bienhechor m, benefactor m

beneficial /benɪ'fɪʃl/ a provechoso

beneficiary /benɪ'fɪʃərɪ/ a & n beneficiario m

benefit /'benɪfɪt/ n provecho m, ventaja f; (allowance) subsidio m; (financial gain) beneficio m. —vt (pt **benefited**, pres p **benefiting**) aprovechar. —vi aprovecharse

benevolence /bɪ'nevələns/ n benevolencia f. **~t** a bénévolo

benign /bɪ'naɪn/ a benigno

bent /bent/ see **bend**. —n inclinación f. —a encorvado; (sl) corrompido

bequeath /bɪ'kwi:ð/ vt legar

bequest /bɪ'kwest/ n legado m

bereave|d /bɪ'ri:vd/ n. **the ~d** la familia f del difunto. **~ment** n pérdida f; (mourning) luto m

bereft /bɪ'reft/ a. **~ of** privado de

beret /'bereɪ/ n boina f

Bermuda /bə'mju:də/ n Islas fpl Bermudas

berry /'berɪ/ n baya f

berserk /bə'sɜ:k/ a. **go ~** volverse loco, perder los estribos

berth /bɜ:θ/ n litera f; (anchorage) amarradero m. **give a wide ~ to** evitar. —vi atracar

beseech /bɪ'si:tʃ/ vt (pt **besought**) suplicar

beset /bɪ'set/ vt (pt **beset**, pres p **besetting**) acosar

beside /bɪ'saɪd/ prep al lado de. **be ~ o.s.** estar fuera de sí

besides /bɪ'saɪdz/ prep además de; (except) excepto. —adv además

besiege /bɪ'si:dʒ/ vt asediar; (fig) acosar

besought /bɪ'sɔ:t/ see **beseech**

bespoke /bɪ'spəʊk/ a (tailor) que confecciona a la medida

best /best/ a (el) mejor. **the ~ thing is to...** lo mejor es... —adv (lo) mejor. **like ~** preferir. —n lo mejor. **at ~** a lo más. **do one's ~** hacer todo lo posible. **make the ~ of** contentarse con. **~ man** n padrino m (de boda)

bestow /bɪ'stəʊ/ vt conceder

bestseller /best'selə(r)/ n éxito m de librería, bestseller m

bet /bet/ n apuesta f. —vt/i (pt **bet** or **betted**) apostar

betray /bɪ'treɪ/ vt traicionar. **~al** n traición f

betroth|al /bɪ'trəʊðəl/ n esponsales mpl. **~ed** a prometido

better /'betə(r)/ a & adv mejor. **~ off** en mejores condiciones; (richer) más rico. **get ~** mejorar. **all the ~** tanto mejor. **I'd ~** más vale que. **the ~ part of** la mayor parte de. **the sooner the ~** cuanto antes mejor. —*vt* mejorar; (*beat*) sobrepasar. —*n* superior *m*. **get the ~ of** vencer a. **one's ~s** sus superiores *mpl*

between /bɪ'twiːn/ *prep* entre.— *adv* en medio

beverage /'bevərɪdʒ/ *n* bebida *f*

bevy /'bevɪ/ *n* grupo *m*

beware /bɪ'weə(r)/ *vi* tener cuidado. —*int* ¡cuidado!

bewilder /bɪ'wɪldə(r)/ *vt* desconcertar. **~ment** *n* aturdimiento *m*

bewitch /bɪ'wɪtʃ/ *vt* hechizar

beyond /bɪ'jɒnd/ *prep* más allá de; (*fig*) fuera de. **~ doubt** sin lugar a duda. **~ reason** irrazonable. —*adv* más allá

bias /'baɪəs/ *n* predisposición *f*; (*prejudice*) prejuicio *m*; (*sewing*) sesgo *m*. —*vt* (*pt* biased) influir en. **~ed** *a* parcial

bib /bɪb/ *n* babero *m*

Bible /'baɪbl/ *n* Biblia *f*

biblical /'bɪblɪkl/ *a* bíblico

bibliography /bɪblɪ'ɒgrəfɪ/ *n* bibliografía *f*

biceps /'baɪseps/ *n* bíceps *m*

bicker /'bɪkə(r)/ *vi* altercar

bicycle /'baɪsɪkl/ *n* bicicleta *f*. — *vi* ir en bicicleta

bid /bɪd/ *n* (*offer*) oferta *f*; (*attempt*) tentativa *f*. —*vi* hacer una oferta. —*vt* (*pt* bid, pres *p* **bidding**) ofrecer; (*pt* bid, *pp* bidden, pres *p* bidding) mandar; dar (*welcome, good-day etc*). **~der** *n* postor *m*. **~ding** *n* (*at auction*) ofertas *fpl*; (*order*) mandato *m*

bide /baɪd/ *vt*. **~ one's time** esperar el momento oportuno

biennial /baɪ'enɪəl/ *a* bienal. — *n* (*event*) bienal *f*; (*bot*) planta *f* bienal

bifocals /baɪ'fəʊklz/ *npl* gafas *fpl* bifocales, anteojos *mpl* bifocales (*LAm*)

big /bɪg/ *a* (**bigger, biggest**) grande; (*generous, sl*) generoso. —*adv*. **talk ~** farronear

bigamist /'bɪgəmɪst/ *n* bígamo *m*. **~ous** *a* bígamo. **~y** *n* bigamía *f*

big-headed /bɪg'hedɪd/ *a* engreído

bigot /'bɪgət/ *n* fanático *m*. **~ed** *a* fanático. **~ry** *n* fanatismo *m*

bigwig /'bɪgwɪg/ *n* (*fam*) pez *m* gordo

bike /baɪk/ *n* (*fam*) bicicleta *f*, bici *f* (*fam*)

bikini /bɪ'kiːnɪ/ *n* (*pl* -is) biquini *m*, bikini *m*

bilberry /'bɪlbərɪ/ *n* arándano *m*

bile /baɪl/ *n* bilis *f*

bilingual /baɪ'lɪŋgwəl/ *a* bilingüe

bilious /'bɪlɪəs/ *a* (*med*) bilioso

bill[1] /bɪl/ *n* cuenta *f*; (*invoice*) factura *f*; (*notice*) cartel *m*; (*Amer, banknote*) billete *m*; (*pol*) proyecto *m* de ley. —*vt* pasar la factura; (*in theatre*) anunciar

bill[2] /bɪl/ *n* (*of bird*) pico *m*

billet /'bɪlɪt/ *n* (*mil*) alojamiento *m*. —*vt* alojar

billiards /'bɪlɪədz/ *n* billar *m*

billion /'bɪlɪən/ *n* billón *m*; (*Amer*) mil millones *mpl*

billy-goat /'bɪlɪgəʊt/ *n* macho *m* cabrío

bin /bɪn/ *n* recipiente *m*; (*for rubbish*) cubo *m*; (*for waste paper*) papelera *f*

bind /baɪnd/ *vt* (*pt* **bound**) atar; encuadernar (*book*); (*jurid*) obligar. —*n* (*sl*) lata *f*. **~ing** /'baɪndɪŋ/ *n* (*of books*) encuadernación *f*; (*braid*) ribete *m*

binge /bɪndʒ/ *n* (*sl*) (*of food*) comilona *f*; (*of drink*) borrachera *f*. **go on a ~** ir de juerga

bingo /'bɪŋgəʊ/ *n* bingo *m*

binoculars /bɪ'nɒkjʊləz/ *npl* prismáticos *mpl*

biochemistry /baɪəʊ'kemɪstrɪ/ n bioquímica f

biograph|er /baɪ'ɒgrəfə(r)/ n biógrafo m. **~y** n biografía f

biolog|ical /baɪə'lɒdʒɪkl/ a biológico. **~ist** n biólogo m. **~y** /baɪ'ɒlədʒɪ/ n biología f

biped /'baɪped/ n bípedo m

birch /bɜːtʃ/ n (tree) abedul m; (whip) férula f

bird /bɜːd/ n ave f; (small) pájaro m; (fam) tipo m; (girl, sl) chica f

Biro /'baɪərəʊ/ n (pl -os) (P) bolígrafo m, biromen m (Arg)

birth /bɜːθ/ n nacimiento m. **~ certificate** n partida f de nacimiento. **~control** n control m de la natalidad. **~day** /'bɜːθdeɪ/ n cumpleaños m invar. **~mark** /'bɜːθmɑːk/ n marca f de nacimiento. **~rate** n natalidad f. **~right** /'bɜːθraɪt/ n derechos mpl de nacimiento

biscuit /'bɪskɪt/ n galleta f

bisect /baɪ'sekt/ vt bisecar

bishop /'bɪʃəp/ n obispo m

bit¹ /bɪt/ n trozo m; (quantity) poco m

bit² /bɪt/ see **bite**

bit³ /bɪt/ n (of horse) bocado m; (mec) broca f

bitch /bɪtʃ/ n perra f; (woman, fam) mujer f maligna, bruja f (fam). **~vi** (fam) quejarse (about de). **~y** a malintencionado

bit|e /baɪt/ vt/i (pt bit, pp bitten) morder. **~e one's nails** morderse las uñas. **—n** mordisco m; (mouthful) bocado m; (of insect etc) picadura f. **~ing** /'baɪtɪŋ/ a mordaz

bitter /'bɪtə(r)/ a amargo; (of weather) glacial. **to the ~ end** hasta el final. **—n** cerveza f amarga. **~ly** adv amargamente. **it's ~ly cold** hace un frío glacial. **~ness** n amargor m; (resentment) amargura f

bizarre /bɪ'zɑː(r)/ a extraño

blab /blæb/ vi (pt **blabbed**) chismear

black /blæk/ a (-er, -est) negro. **~ and blue** amoratado. **—n** negro m. **—vt** ennegrecer; limpiar (shoes). **~ out** desmayarse; (make dark) apagar las luces de

blackball /'blækbɔːl/ vt votar en contra de

blackberry /'blækbərɪ/ n zarzamora f

blackbird /'blækbɜːd/ n mirlo m

blackboard /'blækbɔːd/ n pizarra f

blackcurrant /blæk'kʌrənt/ n casis f

blacken /'blækən/ vt ennegrecer. **—vi** ennegrecerse

blackguard /'blægɑːd/ n canalla m

blackleg /'blækleg/ n esquirol m

blacklist /'blæklɪst/ vt poner en la lista negra

blackmail /'blækmeɪl/ n chantaje m. **—vt** chantajear. **~er** n chantajista m & f

black-out /'blækaʊt/ n apagón m; (med) desmayo m; (of news) censura f

blacksmith /'blæksmɪθ/ n herrero m

bladder /'blædə(r)/ n vejiga f

blade /bleɪd/ n hoja f; (razorblade) cuchilla f. **~ of grass** brizna f de hierba

blame /bleɪm/ vt echar la culpa a. **be to ~** tener la culpa. **—n** culpa f. **~less** a inocente

bland /blænd/ a (-er, -est) suave

blandishments /'blændɪʃmənts/ npl halagos mpl

blank /blæŋk/ a en blanco; (cartridge) sin bala; (fig) vacío. **—verse** n verso m suelto. **—n** blanco m

blanket /'blæŋkɪt/ n manta f; (fig) capa f. **—vt** (pt **blanketed**) (fig) cubrir (in, with de)

blare /bleə(r)/ *vi* sonar muy
fuerte. —*n* estrépito *m*

blarney /ˈblɑːnɪ/ *n* coba *f*. —*vt* dar
coba

blasé /ˈblɑːzeɪ/ *a* hastiado

blasphem|e /blæsˈfiːm/ *vt/i* blas-
femar. ~**er** *n* blasfemador *m*.
~**ous** /ˈblæsfəməs/ *a* blasfemo.
~**y** /ˈblæsfəmɪ/ *n* blasfemia *f*

blast /blɑːst/ *n* explosión *f*; (*gust*)
ráfaga *f*; (*sound*) toque *m*. —*vt*
volar. ~**ed** *a* maldito. ~**
furnace** *n* alto horno *m*. ~**off** *n*
(*of missile*) despegue *m*

blatant /ˈbleɪtnt/ *a* patente;
(*shameless*) descarado

blaze /bleɪz/ *n* llamarada *f*; (*of
light*) resplandor *m*; (*fig*) arranque *m*. —*vi* arder en llamas; (*fig*)
brillar. ~ **a trail** abrir un
camino

blazer /ˈbleɪzə(r)/ *n* chaqueta *f*

bleach /bliːtʃ/ *n* lejía *f*; (*for hair*)
decolorante *m*. —*vt* blanquear;
decolorar ⟨*hair*⟩. —*vi*
blanquearse

bleak /bliːk/ *a* (**-er, -est**) deso-
lado; (*fig*) sombrío

bleary /ˈblɪərɪ/ *a* ⟨*eyes*⟩ nublado;
(*indistinct*) indistinto

bleat /bliːt/ *n* balido *m*. —*vi* balar

bleed /bliːd/ *vt/i* (*pt* **bled**)
sangrar

bleep /bliːp/ *n* pitido *m*. ~**er** *n*
busca *m*, buscapersonas *m*

blemish /ˈblemɪʃ/ *n* tacha *f*

blend /blend/ *n* mezcla *f*. —*vt*
mezclar. —*vi* combinarse

bless /bles/ *vt* bendecir. ~ **you!**
(*on sneezing*) ¡Jesús! ~**ed** *a*
bendito. **be** ~**ed with** estar dotado de. ~**ing** *n* bendición *f*;
(*advantage*) ventaja *f*

blew /bluː/ *see* **blow**

blight /blaɪt/ *n* añublo *m*, tizón
m; (*fig*) plaga *f*. —*vt* añublar, ati-
zonar; (*fig*) destrozar

blighter /ˈblaɪtə(r)/ *n* (*sl*) tío *m*
(*fam*), sinvergüenza *m*

blind /blaɪnd/ *a* ciego. ~ **alley** *n*
callejón *m* sin salida. —*n* persiana *f*; (*fig*) pretexto *m*. —*vt*
cegar. ~**fold** /ˈblaɪndfəʊld/ *a* &
adv con los ojos vendados. —*n*
venda *f*. —*vt* vendar los ojos.
~**ly** *adv* a ciegas. ~**ness** *n* ceg-
uera *f*

blink /blɪŋk/ *vi* parpadear; (*of
light*) centellear

blinkers /ˈblɪŋkəz/ *npl* anteojeras *fpl*; (*auto*) intermitente *m*

bliss /blɪs/ *n* felicidad *f*. ~**ful** *a*
feliz. ~**fully** *adv* felizmente;
(*completely*) completamente

blister /ˈblɪstə(r)/ *n* ampolla *f*. —
vi formarse ampollas

blithe /blaɪð/ *a* alegre

blitz /blɪts/ *n* bombardeo *m*
aéreo. —*vt* bombardear

blizzard /ˈblɪzəd/ *n* ventisca *f*

bloated /ˈbləʊtɪd/ *a* hinchado
(**with de**)

bloater /ˈbləʊtə(r)/ *n* arenque *m*
ahumado

blob /blɒb/ *n* gota *f*; (*stain*) mancha *f*

bloc /blɒk/ *n* (*pol*) bloque *m*

block /blɒk/ *n* bloque *m*; (*of
wood*) zoquete *m*; (*of buildings*)
manzana *f*, cuadra *f* (*LAm*); (*in
pipe*) obstrucción *f*. **in** ~ **letters**
en letra de imprenta. **traffic** ~
embotellamiento *m*. —*vt*
obstruir. ~**ade** /blɒˈkeɪd/ *n* blo-
queo *m*. —*vt* bloquear. ~**age** *n*
obstrucción *f*

blockhead /ˈblɒkhed/ *n* (*fam*)
zopenco *m*

bloke /bləʊk/ *n* (*fam*) tío *m* (*fam*),
tipo *m*

blond /blɒnd/ *a* & *n* rubio (*m*).
~**e** *a* & *n* rubia (*f*)

blood /blʌd/ *n* sangre *f*. ~ **count**
n recuento *m* sanguíneo. ~**
curdling** *a* horripilante

bloodhound /ˈblʌdhaʊnd/ *n* sabueso *m*

blood: ~ **pressure** n tensión f arterial. **high ~ pressure** hipertensión f. ~**shed** /'blʌdʃed/ n efusión f de sangre, derramamiento m de sangre, matanza f. ~**shot** /'blʌdʃɒt/ a sanguinolento; ⟨eye⟩ inyectado de sangre. ~**stream** /'blʌdstri:m/ n sangre f

bloodthirsty /'blʌdθɜːstɪ/ a sanguinario

bloody /'blʌdɪ/ a (-ier, -iest) sangriento; ⟨stained⟩ ensangrentado; (sl) maldito. ~**y-minded** a (fam) terco

bloom /blu:m/ n flor f. —vi florecer

bloomer /'blu:mə(r)/ n (sl) metedura f de pata

blooming a floreciente; (fam) maldito

blossom /'blɒsəm/ n flor f. —vi florecer. ~ **out (into)** ⟨fig⟩ llegar a ser

blot /blɒt/ n borrón m. —vt (pt blotted) manchar; ⟨dry⟩ secar. ~ **out** oscurecer

blotch /blɒtʃ/ n mancha f. ~**y** a lleno de manchas

blotter /'blɒtə(r)/ n, **blotting-paper** /'blɒtɪŋpeɪpə(r)/ n papel m secante

blouse /blaʊz/ n blusa f

blow[1] /bləʊ/ vt (pt blew, pp blown) soplar; fundir ⟨fuse⟩; tocar ⟨trumpet⟩. —vi soplar; ⟨fuse⟩ fundirse; ⟨sound⟩ sonar. —n ⟨puff⟩ soplo m. ~ **down** vt derribar. ~ **out** apagar ⟨candle⟩. ~ **over** pasar. ~ **up** vt inflar; ⟨explode⟩ volar; ⟨photo⟩ ampliar. —vi ⟨explode⟩ estallar; ⟨burst⟩ reventar

blow[2] /bləʊ/ n (incl fig) golpe m

blow-dry /'bləʊdraɪ/ vt secar con secador

blowlamp /'bləʊlæmp/ n soplete m

blow: ~**out** n (of tyre) reventón m. ~**up** n (photo) ampliación f

blowzy /'blaʊzɪ/ a desaliñado

blubber /'blʌbə(r)/ n grasa f de ballena

bludgeon /'blʌdʒən/ n cachiporra f. —vt aporrear

blue /blu:/ a (-er, -est) azul; ⟨joke⟩ verde. —n azul m. **out of the** ~ totalmente inesperado. ~**s** npl. **have the** ~**s** tener tristeza

bluebell /'blu:bel/ n campanilla f

bluebottle /'blu:bɒtl/ n moscarda f

blueprint /'blu:prɪnt/ n ferroprusiato m; ⟨fig, plan⟩ anteproyecto m

bluff /blʌf/ a ⟨person⟩ brusco. —n ⟨poker⟩ farol m. —vt engañar. —vi ⟨poker⟩ tirarse un farol

blunder /'blʌndə(r)/ vi cometer un error. —n metedura f de pata

blunt /blʌnt/ a desafilado; ⟨person⟩ directo, abrupto. —vt desafilar. ~**ly** adv francamente. ~**ness** n embotadura f; ⟨fig⟩ franqueza f, brusquedad f

blur /blɜː(r)/ n impresión f indistinta. —vt (pt blurred) hacer borroso

blurb /blɜːb/ n resumen m publicitario

blurt /blɜːt/ vt. ~ **out** dejar escapar

blush /blʌʃ/ vi ruborizarse. —n sonrojo m

bluster /'blʌstə(r)/ vi ⟨weather⟩ bramar; ⟨person⟩ fanfarronear. ~**y** a tempestuoso

boar /bɔː(r)/ n verraco m

board /bɔːd/ n tabla f, tablero m; (for recreation) tablón m; (food) pensión f; ⟨admin⟩ junta f. ~ **and lodging** casa y comida. **above** ~ correcto. **full** ~ pensión f completa. **go by the** ~ ser abandonado. —vt alojar; ⟨naut⟩

embarcar en. —*vi* alojarse ⟨with en casa de⟩; ⟨at school⟩ ser interno. ~**er** *n* huésped *m*; ⟨schol⟩ interno *m*. ~**ing-house** *n* casa *f* de huéspedes, pensión *f*. ~**ing-school** *n* internado *m*

boast /bəʊst/ *vt* enorgullecerse de. —*vi* jactarse. —*n* jactancia *f*. ~**er** *n* jactancioso *m*. ~**ful** *a* jactancioso

boat /bəʊt/ *n* barco *m*; ⟨large⟩ navío *m*; ⟨small⟩ barca *f*

boater /ˈbəʊtə(r)/ *n* ⟨hat⟩ canotié *m*

boatswain /ˈbəʊsn/ *n* contramaestre *m*

bob[1] /bɒb/ *vi* ⟨pt bobbed⟩ menearse, subir y bajar. ~ **up** presentarse súbitamente

bob[2] /bɒb/ *n invar* ⟨sl⟩ chelín *m*

bobbin /ˈbɒbɪn/ *n* carrete *m*; ⟨in sewing machine⟩ canilla *f*

bobby /ˈbɒbɪ/ *n* ⟨fam⟩ policía *m*, poli *m* ⟨fam⟩

bobsleigh /ˈbɒbsleɪ/ *n* bob (-sleigh) *m*

bode /bəʊd/ *vi* presagiar. ~ **well/ill** ser de buen/mal agüero

bodice /ˈbɒdɪs/ *n* corpiño *m*

bodily /ˈbɒdɪlɪ/ *a* físico, corporal. —*adv* físicamente; ⟨in person⟩ en persona

body /ˈbɒdɪ/ *n* cuerpo *m*. ~**guard** /ˈbɒdɪgɑːd/ *n* guardaespaldas *m invar*. ~**work** *n* carrocería *f*

boffin /ˈbɒfɪn/ *n* ⟨sl⟩ científico *m*

bog /bɒg/ *n* ciénaga *f*. —*vt* ⟨pt bogged⟩. **get** ~**ged down** empantanarse

bogey /ˈbəʊgɪ/ *n* duende *m*; ⟨nuisance⟩ pesadilla *f*

boggle /ˈbɒgl/ *vi* sobresaltarse. **the mind** ~**s** ¡no es posible!

bogus /ˈbəʊgəs/ *a* falso

bogy /ˈbəʊgɪ/ *n* duende *m*; ⟨nuisance⟩ pesadilla *f*

boil[1] /bɔɪl/ *vt/i* hervir. **be** ~**ing hot** estar ardiendo; ⟨weather⟩

hacer mucho calor. ~ **away** evaporarse. ~ **down to** reducirse a. ~ **over** rebosar

boil[2] /bɔɪl/ *n* furúnculo *m*

boiled /bɔɪld/ *a* hervido; ⟨egg⟩ pasado por agua

boiler /ˈbɔɪlə(r)/ *n* caldera *f*. ~ **suit** *n* mono *m*

boisterous /ˈbɔɪstərəs/ *a* ruidoso, bullicioso

bold /bəʊld/ *a* (-er, -est) audaz. ~**ness** *n* audacia *f*

Bolivia /bəˈlɪvɪə/ *n* Bolivia *f*. ~**n** *a & n* boliviano (*m*)

bollard /ˈbɒləd/ *n* ⟨naut⟩ noray *m*; ⟨Brit, auto⟩ poste *m*

bolster /ˈbəʊlstə(r)/ *n* cabezal *m*. —*vt*. ~ **up** sostener

bolt /bəʊlt/ *n* cerrojo *m*; ⟨for nut⟩ perno *m*; ⟨lightning⟩ rayo *m*; ⟨leap⟩ fuga *f*. —*vt* echar el cerrojo a ⟨door⟩; engullir ⟨food⟩. —*vi* fugarse. —*adv*. ~ **upright** rígido

bomb /bɒm/ *n* bomba *f*. —*vt* bombardear. ~**ard** /bɒmˈbɑːd/ *vt* bombardear

bombastic /bɒmˈbæstɪk/ *a* ampuloso

bomb: ~**er** /ˈbɒmə(r)/ *n* bombardero *m*. ~**ing** *n* bombardeo *m*. ~**shell** *n* bomba *f*

bonanza /bəˈnænzə/ *n* bonanza *f*

bond /bɒnd/ *n* ⟨agreement⟩ obligación *f*; ⟨link⟩ lazo *m*; ⟨com⟩ bono *m*

bondage /ˈbɒndɪdʒ/ *n* esclavitud *f*

bone /bəʊn/ *n* hueso *m*; ⟨of fish⟩ espina *f*. —*vt* deshuesar. ~**-dry** *a* completamente seco. ~ **idle** *a* holgazán

bonfire /ˈbɒnfaɪə(r)/ *n* hoguera *f*

bonnet /ˈbɒnɪt/ *n* gorra *f*; ⟨auto⟩ capó *m*, tapa *f* del motor ⟨Mex⟩

bonny /ˈbɒnɪ/ *a* (-ier, -iest) bonito

bonus /ˈbəʊnəs/ *n* prima *f*; ⟨fig⟩ plus *m*

bony /'bəʊnɪ/ a (-ier, -iest) huesudo; ⟨fish⟩ lleno de espinas

boo /buː/ int ¡bu! —vt/i abuchear

boob /buːb/ n (mistake, sl) metedura f de pata. —vi (sl) meter la pata

booby /'buːbɪ/ n bobo m. ~ trap trampa f; (mil) trampa f explosiva

book /bʊk/ n libro m; (of cheques etc) talonario m; (notebook) libreta f; (exercise book) cuaderno m; (pl, com) cuentas fpl. —vt (enter) registrar; (reserve) reservar. —vi reservar. ~able a que se puede reservar. ~case /'bʊkkeɪs/ n estantería f, librería f. ~ing-office (in theatre) taquilla f; (rail) despacho m de billetes. ~let /'bʊklɪt/ n folleto m

bookkeeping /'bʊkkiːpɪŋ/ n contabilidad f

bookmaker /'bʊkmeɪkə(r)/ n corredor m de apuestas

book: ~mark /'bʊkmɑː(r)k/ n señal f. ~seller /'bʊkselə(r)/ n librero m. ~shop /'bʊkʃɒp/ n librería f. ~stall /'bʊkstɔːl/ n quiosco m de libros. ~worm /'bʊkwɜːm/ n (fig) ratón m de biblioteca

boom /buːm/ vi retumbar; (fig) prosperar. —n estampido m; (com) auge m

boon /buːn/ n beneficio m

boor /bʊə(r)/ n patán m. ~ish a grosero

boost /buːst/ vt estimular; reforzar ⟨morale⟩; aumentar ⟨price⟩; (publicize) hacer publicidad por. —n empuje m. ~er n (med) revacunación f

boot /buːt/ n bota f; (auto) maletero m, baúl m (LAm). **get the ~** (sl) ser despedido

booth /buːð/ n cabina f; (at fair) puesto m

booty /'buːtɪ/ n botín m

booze /buːz/ vi (fam) beber mucho. —n (fam) alcohol m; (spree) borrachera f

border /'bɔːdə(r)/ n borde m; (frontier) frontera f; (in garden) arriate m. —vi. ~ on lindar con

borderline /'bɔːdəlaɪn/ n línea f divisoria. ~ case n caso m dudoso

bore[1] /bɔː(r)/ vt (tec) taladrar. —vi taladrar

bore[2] /bɔː(r)/ vt (annoy) aburrir. —n (person) pelmazo m; (thing) lata f

bore[3] /bɔː(r)/ see bear[1]

boredom /'bɔːdəm/ n aburrimiento m

boring /'bɔːrɪŋ/ a aburrido, pesado

born /bɔːn/ a nato. **be ~** nacer

borne /bɔːn/ see bear[1]

borough /'bʌrə/ n municipio m

borrow /'bɒrəʊ/ vt pedir prestado

Borstal /'bɔːstl/ n reformatorio m

bosh /bɒʃ/ int & n (sl) tonterías (fpl)

bosom /'bʊzəm/ n seno m. ~ friend n amigo m íntimo

boss /bɒs/ n (fam) jefe m. —vt (about) (fam) dar órdenes a. ~y /'bɒsɪ/ a mandón

botan|ical /bə'tænɪkl/ a botánico. ~ist /'bɒtənɪst/ n botánico m. ~y /'bɒtənɪ/ n botánica f

botch /bɒtʃ/ vt chapucear. —n chapuza f

both /bəʊθ/ a & pron ambos (mpl), los dos (mpl). —adv al mismo tiempo, a la vez

bother /'bɒðə(r)/ vt molestar; (worry) preocupar. ~ it! int ¡caramba! ~ vi molestarse. ~ about preocuparse de. ~ doing tenerse la molestia de hacer. —n molestia f

bottle /'bɒtl/ n botella f; (for baby) biberón m. —vt embotellar.

up (fig) reprimir. **~neck** /'bɒtlnek/ n (traffic jam) embotellamiento m. **~opener** n destapador m, abrebotellas m invar; (corkscrew) sacacorchos m invar

bottom /'bɒtəm/ n fondo m; (of hill) pie m; (buttocks) trasero m. **—a** último, inferior. **~less** a sin fondo

bough /bau/ n rama f

bought /bɔːt/ see buy

boulder /'bəʊldə(r)/ n canto m

boulevard /'buːləvɑːd/ n bulevar m

bounce /bauns/ vt hacer rebotar. —vi rebotar; ⟨person⟩ saltar; ⟨cheque, sl⟩ ser rechazado. —n rebote m. **~ing** /'baunsɪŋ/ a robusto

bound¹ /baund/ vi saltar. —n salto m

bound² /baund/ n. out of **~s** zona f prohibida

bound³ /baund/ a. be **~** for dirigirse a

bound⁴ /baund/ see bind. **~ to** obligado a; (certain) seguro de

boundary /'baundərɪ/ n límite m

boundless /'baundlɪs/ a ilimitado

bountiful /'bauntɪfl/ a abundante

bouquet /bu'keɪ/ n ramo m; (perfume) aroma m; (of wine) buqué m, nariz f

bout /baut/ n período m; (med) ataque m; (sport) encuentro m

bow¹ /bəʊ/ n (weapon, mus) arco m; (knot) lazo m

bow² /bau/ n reverencia f. —vi inclinarse. —vt inclinar

bow³ /bau/ n (naut) proa f

bowels /'bauəlz/ npl intestinos mpl; (fig) entrañas fpl

bowl¹ /bəʊl/ n cuenco m; (for washing) palangana f; (of pipe) cazoleta f

bowl² /bəʊl/ n (ball) bola f. —vt (cricket) arrojar. —vi (cricket) arrojar la pelota. **~ over** derribar

bow-legged /bəʊ'legɪd/ a estevado

bowler¹ /'bəʊlə(r)/ n (cricket) lanzador m

bowler² /'bəʊlə(r)/ n. **~** (hat) hongo m, bombín m

bowling /'bəʊlɪŋ/ n bolos mpl

bow-tie /bəʊ'taɪ/ n corbata f de lazo, pajarita f

box¹ /bɒks/ n caja f; (for jewels etc) estuche m; (in theatre) palco m

box² /bɒks/ vt boxear contra. **~ s.o.'s ears** dar una manotada a uno. —vi boxear. **~er** n boxeador m. **~ing** n boxeo m

box: B~ing Day n el 26 de diciembre. **~office** n taquilla f. **~room** n trastero m

boy /bɔɪ/ n chico m, muchacho m; (young) niño m

boycott /'bɔɪkɒt/ vt boicotear. —n boicoteo m

boy: ~friend n novio m. **~hood** n niñez f. **~ish** a de muchacho; (childish) infantil

bra /braː/ n sostén m, sujetador m

brace /breɪs/ n abrazadera f; (dental) aparato m. —vt asegurar. **~ o.s.** prepararse. **~s** npl tirantes mpl

bracelet /'breɪslɪt/ n pulsera f

bracing /'breɪsɪŋ/ a vigorizante

bracken /'brækən/ n helecho m

bracket /'brækɪt/ n soporte m; (group) categoría f; (typ) paréntesis m invar. **square ~s** corchetes mpl. —vt poner entre paréntesis; (join together) agrupar

brag /bræg/ vi (pt bragged) jactarse (about de)

braid /breɪd/ n galón m; (of hair) trenza f

brain /brein/ n cerebro m. —vt romper la cabeza

brain-child /'breintʃaild/ n invento m

brain: ~ **drain** (fam) fuga f de cerebros. ~**less** a estúpido. ~**s** npl (fig) inteligencia f

brainstorm /'breinstɔːm/ n ataque m de locura; (Amer, brainwave) idea f genial

brainwash /'breinwɒʃ/ vt lavar el cerebro

brainwave /'breinweiv/ n idea f genial

brainy /'breini/ a (-ier, -iest) inteligente

braise /breiz/ vt cocer a fuego lento

brake /breik/ n freno m. **disc** ~ freno de disco. **hand** ~ freno de mano. —vt/i frenar. ~ **fluid** n líquido m de freno. ~ **lining** n forro m del freno. ~ **shoe** n zapata f del freno

bramble /'bræmbl/ n zarza f

bran /bræn/ n salvado m

branch /brɑːntʃ/ n rama f, (of road) bifurcación f; (com) sucursal m; (fig) ramo m. —vi. ~ **off** bifurcarse. ~ **out** ramificarse

brand /brænd/ n marca f; (iron) hierro m. —vt marcar; (reputation) tildar de

brandish /'brændiʃ/ vt blandir

brand-new /brænd'njuː/ a flamante

brandy /'brændi/ n coñac m

brash /bræʃ/ a descarado

brass /brɑːs/ n latón m. **get down to** ~ **tacks** (fig) ir al grano. **top** ~ (sl) peces mpl gordos. ~**y** a (-ier, -iest) descarado

brassière /'bræsjeə(r)/ n sostén m, sujetador m

brat /bræt/ n (pej) mocoso m

bravado /brə'vɑːdəʊ/ n bravata f

brave /breiv/ a (-er, -est) valiente. —n (Red Indian) guerrero m indio. —vt afrontar. ~**ry** /-əri/ n valentía f, valor m

brawl /brɔːl/ n alboroto m. —vi pelearse

brawn /brɔːn/ n músculo m; (strength) fuerza f muscular. ~**y** a musculoso

bray /brei/ n rebuzno m. —vi rebuznar

brazen /'breizn/ a descarado

brazier /'breiziə(r)/ n brasero m

Brazil /brə'zil/ n el Brasil m. ~**ian** a & n brasileño (m)

breach /briːtʃ/ n violación f; (of contract) incumplimiento m; (gap) brecha f. —vt abrir una brecha en

bread /bred/ n pan m. **loaf of** ~ pan. ~**crumbs** /'bredkrʌmz/ npl migajas fpl; (culin) pan rallado. ~**line** n. **on the** ~**line** en la miseria

breadth /bredθ/ n anchura f

bread-winner /'bredwinə(r)/ n sostén m de la familia, cabeza f de familia

break /breik/ vt (pt broke, pp broken) romper; quebrantar (law); batir (record); comunicar (news); interrumpir (journey). —vi romperse; (news) divulgarse. —n ruptura f; (interval) intervalo m; (chance, fam) oportunidad f; (in weather) cambio m. ~ **away** escapar. ~ **down** vt derribar; analizar (figures). —vi estropearse; (auto) averiarse; (med) sufrir un colapso; (cry) deshacerse en lágrimas. ~ **into** forzar (house etc); (start doing) ponerse a. ~ **off** interrumpirse. ~ **out** (war, disease) estallar; (run away) escaparse. ~ **up** romperse; (schools) terminar. ~**able** a frágil. ~**age** n rotura f

breakdown /'breikdaʊn/ n (tec) falla f; (med) colapso m, crisis f nerviosa; (of figures) análisis f

breaker /ˈbreɪkə(r)/ n (*wave*) cachón m

breakfast /ˈbrekfəst/ n desayuno m

breakthrough /ˈbreɪkθruː/ n adelanto m

breakwater /ˈbreɪkwɔːtə(r)/ n rompeolas m invar

breast /brest/ n pecho m; (*of chicken etc*) pechuga f. **~stroke** n braza f de pecho

breath /breθ/ n aliento m, respiración f. **out of ~** sin aliento. **under one's ~** a media voz. **~alyser** /ˈbreθəlaɪzə(r)/ n alcoholímetro m

breathe /briːð/ vt/i respirar. **~er** /ˈbriːðə(r)/ n descanso m, pausa f. **~ing** n respiración f

breathtaking /ˈbreθteɪkɪŋ/ a impresionante

bred /bred/ see **breed**

breeches /ˈbrɪtʃɪz/ npl calzones mpl

breed /briːd/ vt/i (pt **bred**) reproducirse; (*fig*) engendrar. —n raza f. **~er** n criador m. **~ing** n cría f; (*manners*) educación f

breeze /briːz/ n brisa f. **~y** a de mucho viento; (*person*) despreocupado. **it is ~y** hace viento

Breton /ˈbretən/ a & n bretón (m)

brew /bruː/ vt hacer. —vi fermentar; (*tea*) reposar; (*fig*) prepararse. —n infusión f. **~er** n cervecero m. **~ery** n fábrica f de cerveza, cervecería f

bribe /braɪb/ n soborno m. —vt sobornar. **~ry** /-ərɪ/ n soborno m

brick /brɪk/ n ladrillo m. —vt. **~ up** tapar con ladrillos. **~layer** /ˈbrɪkleɪə(r)/ n albañil m

bridal /ˈbraɪdl/ n nupcial

bride /braɪd/ m novia f. **~groom** /ˈbraɪdɡrʊm/ n novio m. **~smaid** /ˈbraɪdzmeɪd/ n dama f de honor

bridge[1] /brɪdʒ/ n puente m; (*of nose*) caballete m. —vt tender un puente sobre. **~ a gap** llenar un vacío

bridge[2] /brɪdʒ/ n (*cards*) bridge m

bridle /ˈbraɪdl/ n brida f. —vt embridar. **~path** n camino m de herradura

brief /briːf/ a (-er, -est) breve. —n (*jurid*) escrito m. —vt dar instrucciones a. **~case** /ˈbriːfkeɪs/ n maletín m. **~ly** adv brevemente. **~s** npl (*man's*) calzoncillos mpl; (*woman's*) bragas fpl

brigade /brɪˈɡeɪd/ n brigada f. **~ier** /-əˈdɪə(r)/ n general m de brigada

bright /braɪt/ a (-er, -est) brillante, claro; (*clever*) listo; (*cheerful*) alegre. **~en** /ˈbraɪtn/ vt aclarar; hacer más alegre (*house etc*). —vi (*weather*) aclararse; (*face*) animarse. **~ly** adv brillantemente. **~ness** n claridad f

brilliance /ˈbrɪljəns/ n brillantez f, brillo m. **~t** a brillante

brim /brɪm/ n borde m; (*of hat*) ala f. —vi (pt **brimmed**). **~ over** desbordarse

brine /braɪn/ n salmuera f

bring /brɪŋ/ vt (pt **brought**) traer (*thing*); conducir (*person*, *vehicle*). **~ about** causar. **~ back** devolver. **~ down** derribar; rebajar (*price*). **~ off** lograr. **~ on** causar. **~ out** sacar; lanzar (*product*); publicar (*book*). **~ round/to** hacer volver en sí (*unconscious person*). **~ up** (*med*) vomitar; educar (*children*); plantear (*question*)

brink /brɪŋk/ n borde m

brisk /brɪsk/ a (-er, -est) enérgico, vivo. **~ness** n energía f

bristle /ˈbrɪsl/ n cerda f. —vi erizarse. **~ing with** erizado de

Brit|ain /'brɪtən/ n Gran Bretaña f. **~ish** /'brɪtɪʃ/ a británico. **the ~ish** los británicos. **~on** /'brɪtən/ n británico m

Brittany /'brɪtənɪ/ n Bretaña f

brittle /'brɪtl/ a frágil, quebradizo

broach /brəʊtʃ/ vt abordar ⟨subject⟩; espitar ⟨cask⟩

broad /brɔːd/ a (-er, -est) ancho. **in ~ daylight** en pleno día. **~bean** n haba f

broadcast /'brɔːdkɑːst/ n emisión f. —vt (pt broadcast) emitir. —vi hablar por la radio. **~ing** n radiodifusión. —n radiodifusión f

broad: **~en** /'brɔːdn/ vt ensanchar. —vi ensancharse. **~ly** adv en general. **~minded** a de miras amplias, tolerante, liberal

brocade /brə'keɪd/ n brocado m

broccoli /'brɒkəlɪ/ n invar brécol m

brochure /'brəʊʃə(r)/ n folleto m

brogue /brəʊg/ n abarca f; ⟨accent⟩ acento m regional

broke /brəʊk/ see **break**. —a (sl) sin blanca

broken /'brəʊkən/ see **break**. —a. **~ English** inglés m chapurreado. **~hearted** a con el corazón destrozado

broker /'brəʊkə(r)/ n corredor m

brolly /'brɒlɪ/ n (fam) paraguas m invar

bronchitis /brɒŋ'kaɪtɪs/ n bronquitis f

bronze /brɒnz/ n bronce m. —vt broncear. —vi broncearse

brooch /brəʊtʃ/ n broche m

brood /bruːd/ n cría f; (joc) prole m. —vi empollar; (fig) meditar. **~y** a contemplativo

brook[1] /brʊk/ n arroyo m

brook[2] /brʊk/ vt soportar

broom /bruːm/ n hiniesta f; (brush) escoba f. **~stick** /'bruːmstɪk/ n palo m de escoba

broth /brɒθ/ n caldo m

brothel /'brɒθl/ n burdel m

brother /'brʌðə(r)/ n hermano m. **~hood** n fraternidad f, (relig) hermandad f. **~in-law** n cuñado m. **~ly** a fraternal

brought /brɔːt/ see **bring**

brow /braʊ/ n frente f; (of hill) cima f

browbeat /'braʊbiːt/ vt (pt -beat, pp -beaten) intimidar

brown /braʊn/ a (-er, -est) marrón; ⟨skin⟩ moreno; ⟨hair⟩ castaño. —n marrón m. —vt poner moreno; (culin) dorar. —vi ponerse moreno; (culin) dorarse. **be ~ed off** (sl) estar hasta la coronilla

Brownie /'braʊnɪ/ n niña f exploradora

browse /braʊz/ vi (in a shop) curiosear; ⟨animal⟩ pacer

bruise /bruːz/ n magulladura f. —vt magullar; machucar ⟨fruit⟩. —vi magullarse; ⟨fruit⟩ machacarse

brunch /brʌntʃ/ n (fam) desayuno m tardío

brunette /bruː'net/ n morena f

brunt /brʌnt/ n. **the ~ of** lo más fuerte de

brush /brʌʃ/ n cepillo m; (large) escoba; (for decorating) brocha f; (artist's) pincel; (skirmish) escaramuza f. —vt cepillar. **~against** rozar. **~ aside** rechazar. **~ off** (rebuff) desairar. **~ up (on)** refrescar

brusque /bruːsk/ a brusco. **~ly** adv bruscamente

Brussels /'brʌslz/ n Bruselas f. **~sprout** col m de Bruselas

brutal /'bruːtl/ a brutal. **~ity** /-'tælɪt/ n brutalidad f

brute /bruːt/ n bestia f. **~ force** fuerza f bruta

BSc abbr see **bachelor**

bubble /'bʌbl/ n burbuja f. —vi burbujear. **~ over** desbordarse

bubbly /'bʌblɪ/ a burbujeante. —
n (fam) champaña m, champán
m (fam)

buck¹ /bʌk/ a macho. —n (deer)
ciervo m. —vi (of horse) corco-
vear. ~ **up** (hurry, sl) darse
prisa; (cheer up, sl) animarse

buck² /bʌk/ (Amer, sl) dólar m

buck³ /bʌk/ n. **pass the** ~ **to s.o.**
echarle a uno el muerto

bucket /'bʌkɪt/ n cubo m

buckle /'bʌkl/ n hebilla f. —vt
abrochar. —vi torcerse. ~ **down
to** dedicarse con empeño a

bud /bʌd/ n brote m. —vi (pt bud-
ded) brotar.

Buddhism /'bʊdɪzəm/ n budis-
mo m. ~**t** /'bʊdɪst/ a & n bud-
ista (m & f)

budding /'bʌdɪŋ/ a (fig) en
ciernes

buddy /'bʌdɪ/ n (fam) compañero
m, amigote m (fam)

budge /bʌdʒ/ vt mover. —vi
moverse

budgerigar /'bʌdʒərɪgɑ:(r)/ n periquito m

budget /'bʌdʒɪt/ n presupuesto
m. —vi (pt budgeted)
presupuestar

buff /bʌf/ n (colour) color m de
ante; (fam) aficionado m. —vt
pulir

buffalo /'bʌfələʊ/ n (pl -oes or -o)
búfalo m

buffer /'bʌfə(r)/ n parachoques m
invar. ~ **state** n estado m tapón

buffet /'bʊfeɪ/ n (meal, counter)
bufé m. /'bʌfɪt/ n golpe m; (slap)
bofetada f. —vt (pt buffeted)
golpear

buffoon /bə'fu:n/ n payaso m,
bufón m

bug /bʌg/ n bicho m; (germ, sl)
microbio m; (device, sl) micrófono m oculto. —vt (pt
bugged) ocultar un micrófono
en; intervenir (telephone);
(Amer, sl) molestar

bugbear /'bʌgbeə(r)/ n pesadilla
f

buggy /'bʌgɪ/ n. **baby** ~ (esp
Amer) cochecito m de niño

bugle /'bju:gl/ n corneta f

build /bɪld/ vt/i (pt built) construir. ~ **up** vt urbanizar;
(increase) aumentar. —n (of person) figura f, tipo m. ~**er** n con-
structor m. ~**up** n aumento m;
(of gas etc) acumulación f; (fig)
propaganda f

built /bɪlt/ see build. ~**in** a
empotrado. ~**up area** n zona f
urbanizada

bulb /bʌlb/ n bulbo m; (elec) bombilla f. ~**ous** a bulboso

Bulgaria /bʌl'geərɪə/ n Bulgaria
f. ~**n** a & n búlgaro (m)

bulge /bʌldʒ/ n protuberancia
f. —vi pandearse; (jut out) sobresalir. ~**ing** a abultado; (eyes)
saltón

bulk /bʌlk/ n bulto m, volumen
m. **in** ~ a granel; (loose) suelto.
the ~ **of** la mayor parte de. ~**y** a
voluminoso

bull /bʊl/ n toro m

bulldog /'bʊldɒg/ n buldog m

bulldozer /'bʊldəʊzə(r)/ n oruga
f aplanadora, buldózer m

bullet /'bʊlɪt/ n bala f

bulletin /'bʊlətɪn/ n anuncio m;
(journal) boletín m

bullet-proof /'bʊlɪtpru:f/ a a
prueba de balas

bullfight /'bʊlfaɪt/ n corrida f (de
toros). ~**er** n torero m

bullion /'bʊljən/ n (gold) oro m
en barras; (silver) plata f en
barras

bull-: ~**ring** /'bʊlrɪŋ/ n plaza f de
toros. ~**'s-eye** n centro m del
blanco, diana f

bully /'bʊlɪ/ n matón m. —vt
intimidar. ~**ing** n intimidación
f

bum¹ /bʌm/ n (bottom, sl) trasero
m

bum[2] /bʌm/ n (Amer, sl) holgazán m

bumble-bee /'bʌmblbi:/ n abejorro m

bump /bʌmp/ vt chocar contra. —vi dar sacudidas. —n choque m; (swelling) chichón m. ~ **into** chocar contra; (meet) encontrar

bumper /'bʌmpə(r)/ n parachoques m invar. —a abundante. ~ **edition** n edición f especial

bumpkin /'bʌmpkɪn/ n patán m, paleto m (fam)

bumptious /'bʌmpʃəs/ a presuntuoso

bun /bʌn/ n bollo m; (hair) moño m

bunch /bʌntʃ/ n manojo m; (of people) grupo m; (of bananas, grapes) racimo m, (of flowers) ramo m

bundle /'bʌndl/ n bulto m; (of papers) legajo m; (of nerves) manojo m. —vt. ~ **up** atar

bung /bʌŋ/ n tapón m. —vt tapar; (sl) tirar

bungalow /'bʌŋgələʊ/ n casa f de un solo piso, chalé m, bungalow m

bungle /'bʌŋgl/ vt chapucear

bunion /'bʌnjən/ n juanete m

bunk /bʌŋk/ n litera f

bunker /'bʌŋkə(r)/ n carbonera f; (golf) obstáculo m; (mil) refugio m, búnker m

bunkum /'bʌŋkəm/ n tonterías fpl

bunny /'bʌnɪ/ n conejito m

buoy /bɔɪ/ n boya f. —vt. ~ **up** hacer flotar; (fig) animar

buoyan|cy /'bɔɪənsɪ/ n flotabilidad f; (fig) optimismo m. ~**t** /'bɔɪənt/ a boyante; (fig) alegre

burden /'bɜːdn/ n carga f. —vt cargar (**with** de). ~**some** a pesado

bureau /'bjʊərəʊ/ n (pl -**eaux** /-əʊz/) escritorio m; (office) oficina f

bureaucra|cy /bjʊə'rɒkrəsɪ/ n burocracia f. ~**t** /'bjʊərəkræt/ n burócrata m & f. ~**tic** /-'krætɪk/ a burocrático

burgeon /'bɜːdʒən/ vi brotar; (fig) crecer

burgl|ar /'bɜːglə(r)/ n ladrón m. ~**ary** n robo m con allanamiento de morada. ~**e** /'bɜːgl/ vt robar con allanamiento

Burgundy /'bɜːgəndɪ/ n Borgoña f; (wine) vino m de Borgoña

burial /'berɪəl/ n entierro m

burlesque /bɜː'lesk/ n burlesco m

burly /'bɜːlɪ/ a (-**ier**, -**iest**) corpulento

Burma /'bɜːmə/ Birmania f. ~**ese** /-'miːz/ a & n birmano (m)

burn /bɜːn/ vt (pt **burned** or **burnt**) quemar. —vi quemarse. ~ **down** vt destruir con fuego. —n quemadura f. ~**er** n quemador m. ~**ing** a ardiente; (food) que quema; (question) candente

burnish /'bɜːnɪʃ/ vt lustrar, pulir

burnt /bɜːnt/ see **burn**

burp /bɜːp/ n (fam) eructo m. —vi (fam) eructar

burr /bɜː(r)/ n (bot) erizo m

burrow /'bʌrəʊ/ n madriguera f. —vt excavar

bursar /'bɜːsə(r)/ n tesorero m. ~**y** /'bɜːsərɪ/ n beca f

burst /bɜːst/ vt (pt **burst**) reventar. —vi reventarse; (tyre) pincharse. —n reventón m; (mil) ráfaga f; (fig) explosión f. ~ **of laughter** carcajada f

bury /'berɪ/ vt enterrar; (hide) ocultar

bus /bʌs/ n (pl **buses**) autobús m, camión m (Mex). —vi (pt **bussed**) ir en autobús

bush /bʊʃ/ n arbusto m; (land) monte m. ~y a espeso

busily /'bɪzɪlɪ/ adv afanosamente

business /'bɪznɪs/ n negocio m; (com) negocios mpl; (profession) ocupación f; (fig) asunto m. **mind one's own** ~ ocuparse de sus propios asuntos. ~**-like** a práctico, serio. ~**man** n hombre m de negocios

busker /'bʌskə(r)/ n músico m ambulante

bus-stop /'bʌsstɒp/ n parada f de autobús

bust[1] /bʌst/ n busto m; (chest) pecho m

bust[2] /bʌst/ vt (pt busted or **bust**) (sl) romper. —vi romperse. —a roto. **go** ~ (sl) quebrar

bustle /'bʌsl/ vi apresurarse. —n bullicio m

bust-up /'bʌstʌp/ n (sl) riña f

busy /'bɪzɪ/ a (-ier, -iest) ocupado; (street) concurrido. —vt. ~ **o.s. with** ocuparse de

busybody /'bɪzɪbɒdɪ/ n entrometido m

but /bʌt/ conj pero; (after negative) sino. —prep menos. ~ **for** si no fuera por. **last** ~ **one** penúltimo. —adv solamente

butane /'bjuːteɪn/ n butano m

butcher /'bʊtʃə(r)/ n carnicero m. —vt matar; (fig) hacer una carnicería con. ~**y** n carnicería f, matanza f

butler /'bʌtlə(r)/ n mayordomo m

butt /bʌt/ n (of gun) culata f; (of cigarette) colilla f; (target) blanco m. —vi topar. ~ **in** interrumpir

butter /'bʌtə(r)/ n mantequilla f. —vt untar con mantequilla. ~ **up** vt (fam) lisonjear, dar jabón a. ~**-bean** n judía f

buttercup /'bʌtəkʌp/ n ranúnculo m

butter-fingers /'bʌtəfɪŋgəz/ n manazas m invar, torpe m

butterfly /'bʌtəflaɪ/ n mariposa f

buttock /'bʌtək/ n nalga f

button /'bʌtn/ n botón m. —vt abotonar. —vi abotonarse. ~**hole** n ojal m. —vt (fig) detener

buttress /'bʌtrɪs/ n contrafuerte m. —vt apoyar

buxom /'bʌksəm/ a (woman) rollizo

buy /baɪ/ vt (pt bought) comprar. —n compra f. ~**er** n comprador m

buzz /bʌz/ n zumbido m; (phone call, fam) llamada f. —vi zumbar. ~ **off** (sl) largarse. ~**er** n timbre m

by /baɪ/ prep por; (near) cerca de; (before) antes de; (according to) según. ~ **and large** en conjunto, en general. ~ **car** en coche. ~**oneself** por sí solo

bye-bye /'baɪbaɪ/ int (fam) ¡adiós!

by-election /'baɪɪlekʃn/ n elección f parcial

bygone /'baɪgɒn/ a pasado

by-law /'baɪlɔː/ n reglamento m (local)

bypass /'baɪpɑːs/ n carretera f de circunvalación. —vt evitar

by-product /'baɪprɒdʌkt/ n subproducto m

bystander /'baɪstændə(r)/ n espectador m

byword /'baɪwɜːd/ n sinónimo m. **be a** ~ **for** ser conocido por

C

cab /kæb/ n taxi m; (of lorry, train) cabina f

cabaret /'kæbəreɪ/ n espectáculo m

cabbage /'kæbɪdʒ/ n col m, repollo m

cabin /'kæbɪn/ n cabaña f; (in ship) camarote m; (in plane) cabina f

cabinet /'kæbɪnɪt/ n (cupboard) armario m; (for display) vitrina f. C~ (pol) gabinete m. ~-maker n ebanista m & f

cable /'keɪbl/ n cable m. —vt cablegrafiar. ~ railway n funicular m

cache /kæʃ/ n (place) escondrijo m; (things) reservas fpl escondidas. —vt ocultar

cackle /'kækl/ n (of hen) cacareo m; (laugh) risotada f. —vi cacarear; (laugh) reírse a carcajadas

cacophon|ous /kə'kɒfənəs/ a cacofónico. ~y n cacofonía f

cactus /'kæktəs/ n (pl -ti /-taɪ/) cacto m

cad /kæd/ n sinvergüenza m. ~dish a desvergonzado

caddie /'kædɪ/ n (golf) portador m de palos

caddy /'kædɪ/ n cajita f

cadence /'keɪdəns/ n cadencia f

cadet /kə'det/ n cadete m

cadge /kædʒ/ vt/i gorronear. ~r /-ə(r)/ n gorrón m

Caesarean /sɪ'zeərɪən/ a cesáreo. ~ section n cesárea f

café /'kæfeɪ/ n cafetería f

cafeteria /kæfɪ'tɪərɪə/ n autoservicio m

caffeine /'kæfiːn/ n cafeína f

cage /keɪdʒ/ n jaula f. —vt enjaular

cagey /'keɪdʒɪ/ a (fam) evasivo

Cairo /'kaɪərəʊ/ n el Cairo m

cajole /kə'dʒəʊl/ vt engatusar. ~ry n engatusamiento m

cake /keɪk/ n pastel m, tarta f; (sponge) bizcocho m. ~ of soap pastilla f de jabón. ~d a incrustado

calamit|ous /kə'læmɪtəs/ a desastroso. ~y /kə'læmətɪ/ n calamidad f

calcium /'kælsɪəm/ n calcio m

calculat|e /'kælkjʊleɪt/ vt/i calcular; (Amer) suponer. ~ing a calculador. ~ion /-'leɪʃn/ n cálculo m. ~or n calculadora f

calculus /'kælkjʊləs/ n (pl -li) cálculo m

calendar /'kælɪndə(r)/ n calendario m

calf /kɑːf/ n (pl calves) ternero m

calf /kɑːf/ n (pl calves) (of leg) pantorrilla f

calibre /'kælɪbə(r)/ n calibre m

calico /'kælɪkəʊ/ n calicó m

call /kɔːl/ vt/i llamar. —n llamada f; (shout) grito m; (visit) visita f. be on ~ estar de guardia. long distance ~ conferencia f. ~ back vt hacer volver; (on phone) volver a llamar. —vi volver; (on phone) volver a llamar. ~ for pedir; (fetch) ir a buscar. ~ off cancelar. ~ on visitar. ~ out dar voces. ~ together convocar. ~ up (mil) llamar al servicio militar; (phone) llamar. ~-box n cabina f telefónica. ~er n visita f; (phone) el que llama m. ~ing n vocación f

callous /'kæləs/ a insensible, cruel. ~ness n crueldad f

callow /'kæləʊ/ a (-er, -est) inexperto

calm /kɑːm/ a (-er, -est) tranquilo; (weather) calmoso. —n tranquilidad f, calma f. —vt calmar. —vi calmarse. ~ness n tranquilidad f, calma f

calorie /'kælərɪ/ n caloría f

camber /'kæmbə(r)/ n curvatura f

came /keɪm/ see come

camel /'kæml/ n camello m

camellia /kə'miːljə/ n camelia f

cameo /'kæmɪəʊ/ n (pl -os) cameo m

camera /'kæmərə/ n máquina f (fotográfica); (TV) cámara f

∼man *n* (*pl* -men) operador *m*, cámara *m*

camouflage /'kæməflɑːʒ/ *n* camuflaje *m*. —*vt* encubrir; (*mil*) camuflar

camp[1] /kæmp/ *n* campamento *m*. —*vi* acamparse

camp[2] /kæmp/ *a* (*affected*) amanerado

campaign /kæm'peɪn/ *n* campaña *f*. —*vi* hacer campaña

camp: ∼**bed** *n* catre *m* de tijera. ∼**er** *n* campista *m* & *f*; (*vehicle*) caravana *f*. ∼**ing** *n* camping *m*. **go** ∼**ing** hacer camping. ∼**site** /'kæmpsaɪt/ *n* camping *m*

campus /'kæmpəs/ *n* (*pl* -puses) ciudad *f* universitaria

can[1] /kæn/ *v aux* (*pt* could) (*be able to*) poder; (*know how to*) saber. ∼**not** (*neg*), ∼'**t** (*neg*, *fam*). **I** ∼**not**/∼'**t go** no puedo ir

can[2] /kæn/ *n* lata *f*. —*vt* (*pt* canned) enlatar. ∼**ned music** música *f* grabada

Canad|**a** /'kænədə/ *n* el Canadá *m*. ∼**ian** /kə'neɪdɪən/ *a* & *n* canadiense (*m* & *f*)

canal /kə'næl/ *n* canal *m*

canary /kə'neəri/ *n* canario *m*

cancel /'kænsl/ *vt/i* (*pt* cancelled) anular; cancelar (*contract etc*); suspender (*appointment etc*); (*delete*) tachar. ∼**lation** /-'leɪʃn/ *n* cancelación *f*

cancer /'kænsə(r)/ *n* cáncer *m*. **C**∼ *n* (*Astr*) Cáncer *m*. ∼**ous** *a* canceroso

candid /'kændɪd/ *a* franco

candida|**cy** /'kændɪdəsɪ/ *n* candidatura *f*. ∼**te** /'kændɪdeɪt/ *n* candidato *m*

candle /'kændl/ *n* vela *f*. ∼**stick** /'kændlstɪk/ *n* candelero *m*

candour /'kændə(r)/ *n* franqueza *f*

candy /'kændɪ/ *n* (*Amer*) caramelo *m*. ∼**floss** *n* algodón *m* de azúcar

cane /keɪn/ *n* caña *f*; (*for baskets*) mimbre *m*; (*stick*) bastón *m*. —*vt* (*strike*) castigar con palmeta

canine /'keɪnaɪn/ *a* canino

canister /'kænɪstə(r)/ *n* bote *m*

cannabis /'kænəbɪs/ *n* cáñamo *m* índico, hachís *m*, mariguana *f*

cannibal /'kænɪbl/ *n* caníbal *m*. ∼**ism** *n* canibalismo *m*

cannon /'kænən/ *n invar* cañón *m*. ∼ **shot** cañonazo *m*

cannot /'kænət/ *see* can[1]

canny /'kænɪ/ *a* astuto

canoe /kə'nuː/ *n* canoa *f*, piragua *f*. —*vi* ir en canoa. ∼**ist** *n* piragüista *m f*

canon /'kænən/ *n* canon *m*; (*person*) canónigo *m*. ∼**ize** /'kænənaɪz/ *vt* canonizar

can-opener /'kænəʊpnə(r)/ *n* abrelatas *m invar*

canopy /'kænəpɪ/ *n* dosel *m*; (*of parachute*) casquete *m*

cant /kænt/ *n* jerga *f*

can't /kɑːnt/ *see* can[1]

cantankerous /kæn'tæŋkərəs/ *a* malhumorado

canteen /kæn'tiːn/ *n* cantina *f*; (*of cutlery*) juego *m*; (*flask*) cantimplora *f*

canter /'kæntə(r)/ *n* medio galope *m*. —*vi* ir a medio galope

canvas /'kænvəs/ *n* lona *f*; (*artist's*) lienzo *m*

canvass /'kænvəs/ *vi* hacer campaña, solicitar votos. ∼**ing** *n* solicitación *f* (de votos)

canyon /'kænjən/ *n* cañón *m*

cap /kæp/ *n* gorra *f*; (*lid*) tapa *f*; (*of cartridge*) cápsula *f*; (*academic*) birrete *m*; (*of pen*) capuchón *m*; (*mec*) casquete *m*. —*vt* (*pt* capped) tapar, poner cápsula a; (*outdo*) superar

capab|**ility** /keɪpə'bɪlətɪ/ *n* capacidad *f*. ∼**le** /'keɪpəbl/ *a* capaz. ∼**ly** *adv* competentemente

capacity /kə'pæsətɪ/ *n* capacidad *f*; (*function*) calidad *f* cape[1] /keɪp/ n (cloak) capa f

cape[2] /keɪp/ n (geog) cabo m

caper[1] /'keɪpə(r)/ vi brincar. −n salto m; (fig) travesura f

caper[2] /'keɪpə(r)/ n (culin) alcaparra f

capital /'kæpɪtl/ a capital. ∼ letter n mayúscula f. −n (town) capital f; (money) capital m

capitalis|m /'kæpɪtəlɪzəm/ n capitalismo m. ∼t a & n capitalista (m & f)

capitalize /'kæpɪtəlaɪz/ vt capitalizar; (typ) escribir con mayúsculas. ∼ on aprovechar

capitulat|e /kə'pɪtʃʊleɪt/ vi capitular. ∼ion /-'leɪʃn/ n capitulación f

capon /'keɪpən/ n capón m

capricious /kə'prɪʃəs/ a caprichoso

Capricorn /'kæprɪkɔ:n/ n Capricornio m

capsicum /'kæpsɪkəm/ n pimiento m

capsize /kæp'saɪz/ vt hacer zozobrar. −vi zozobrar

capsule /'kæpsju:l/ n cápsula f

captain /'kæptɪn/ n capitán m. − vt capitanear

caption /'kæpʃn/ n (heading) título m; (of cartoon etc) leyenda f

captivate /'kæptɪveɪt/ vt encantar

captiv|e /'kæptɪv/ a & n cautivo (m). ∼ity /-'tɪvətɪ/ n cautiverio m, cautividad f

capture /'kæptʃə(r)/ vt prender; llamar (attention); (mil) tomar. −n apresamiento m; (mil) toma f

car /ka:(r)/ n coche m, carro m (LAm)

carafe /kə'ræf/ n jarro m, garrafa f

caramel /'kærəməl/ n azúcar m quemado; (sweet) caramelo m

carat /'kærət/ n quilate m

caravan /'kærəvæn/ n caravana f

carbohydrate /ka:bəʊ'haɪdreɪt/ n hidrato m de carbono

carbon /'ka:bən/ n carbono m; (paper) carbón m. ∼ copy copia f al carbón

carburettor /ka:bjʊ'retə(r)/ n carburador m

carcass /'ka:kəs/ n cadáver m, esqueleto m

card /ka:d/ n tarjeta f; (for games) carta f; (membership) carnet m; (records) ficha f

cardboard /'ka:dbɔ:d/ n cartón m

cardiac /'ka:dɪæk/ a cardíaco

cardigan /'ka:dɪgən/ n chaqueta f de punto, rebeca f

cardinal /'ka:dɪnl/ a cardinal. − n cardenal m

card-index /'ka:dɪndeks/ n fichero m

care /keə(r)/ n cuidado m; (worry) preocupación f; (protection) cargo m. ∼ of a cuidado de, en casa de. take ∼ of cuidar de (person); ocuparse de (matter). −vi interesarse. I don't ∼ me es igual. ∼ about interesarse por. ∼ for cuidar de; (like) querer

career /kə'rɪə(r)/ n carrera f. −vi correr a toda velocidad

carefree /'keəfri:/ a despreocupado

careful /'keəfʊl/ a cuidadoso; (cautious) prudente. ∼ly adv con cuidado

careless /'keəlɪs/ a negligente; (not worried) indiferente. ∼ly adv descuidadamente. ∼ness n descuido m

caress /kə'res/ n caricia f. −vt acariciar

caretaker /'keəteɪkə(r)/ n vigilante m; (of flats etc) portero m

car-ferry /'ka:feri/ n transbordador m de coches

cargo /'ka:gəʊ/ n (pl -oes) carga f

Caribbean /kærɪ'bi:ən/ a caribe. ∼ Sea n mar m Caribe

caricature /ˈkærɪkətʃʊə(r)/ n caricatura f. —vt caricaturizar

carnage /ˈkɑːnɪdʒ/ n carnicería f, matanza f

carnal /ˈkɑːnl/ a carnal

carnation /kɑːˈneɪʃn/ n clavel m

carnival /ˈkɑːnɪvl/ n carnaval m

carol /ˈkærəl/ n villancico m

carouse /kəˈraʊz/ vi correrse una juerga

carousel /kærəˈsel/ n tiovivo m

carp[1] /kɑːp/ n invar carpa f

carp[2] /kɑːp/ vi. ~ **at** quejarse de

car park /ˈkɑːpɑːk/ n aparcamiento m

carpent|er /ˈkɑːpɪntə(r)/ n carpintero m. **~ry** n carpintería f

carpet /ˈkɑːpɪt/ n alfombra f. **be on the ~** (fam) recibir un rapapolvo; (under consideration) estar sobre el tapete. —vt alfombrar. **~-sweeper** n escoba f mecánica

carriage /ˈkærɪdʒ/ n coche m; (mec) carro m; (transport) transporte m; (cost, bearing) porte m

carriageway /ˈkærɪdʒweɪ/ n calzada f, carretera f

carrier /ˈkærɪə(r)/ n transportista m & f; (company) empresa f de transportes; (med) portador m. **~-bag** bolsa f

carrot /ˈkærət/ n zanahoria f

carry /ˈkærɪ/ vt llevar; transportar (goods); (involve) llevar consigo, implicar. —vi (sounds) llegar, oírse. **~ off** llevarse. **~ on** continuar; (complain, fam) quejarse. **~ out** realizar; cumplir (promise, threat). **~-cot** n capazo m

cart /kɑːt/ n carro m. —vt acarrear; (carry, fam) llevar

cartilage /ˈkɑːtɪlɪdʒ/ n cartílago m

carton /ˈkɑːtən/ n caja f (de cartón)

cartoon /kɑːˈtuːn/ n caricatura f, chiste m; (strip) historieta f; (film) dibujos mpl animados. **~ist** n caricaturista m & f

cartridge /ˈkɑːtrɪdʒ/ n cartucho m

carve /kɑːv/ vt tallar; trinchar (meat)

cascade /kæsˈkeɪd/ n cascada f. —vi caer en cascadas

case /keɪs/ n caso m; (jurid) proceso m; (crate) cajón m; (box) caja f; (suitcase) maleta f. **in any ~** en todo caso. **in ~ he comes** por si viene. **in ~ of** en caso de. **lower ~** caja f baja, minúscula f. **upper ~** caja f alta, mayúscula f

cash /kæʃ/ n dinero m efectivo. **pay (in) ~** pagar al contado. —vt cobrar. **~ in (on)** aprovecharse de. **~ desk** n caja f

cashew /ˈkæʃuː/ n anacardo m

cashier /kæˈʃɪə(r)/ n cajero m

cashmere /kæʃˈmɪə(r)/ n casimir m, cachemir m

casino /kəˈsiːnəʊ/ n (pl **-os**) casino m

cask /kɑːsk/ n barril m

casket /ˈkɑːskɪt/ n cajita f

casserole /ˈkæsərəʊl/ n cacerola f; (stew) cazuela f

cassette /kəˈset/ n casete m

cast /kɑːst/ vt (pt cast) arrojar; fundir (metal); dar (vote); (in theatre) repartir. —n lanzamiento m; (in play) reparto m; (mould) molde m

castanets /kæstəˈnets/ npl castañuelas fpl

castaway /ˈkɑːstəweɪ/ n náufrago m

caste /kɑːst/ n casta f

cast: **~ iron** n hierro m fundido. **~-iron** a de hierro fundido; (fig) sólido

castle /ˈkɑːsl/ n castillo m; (chess) torre f

cast-offs /ˈkɑːstɒfs/ npl desechos mpl

castor /ˈkɑːstə(r)/ n ruedecilla f

castor oil /ˈkɑːstərɔɪl/ n aceite m de ricino

castor sugar /ˈkɑːstəʃʊgə(r)/ n azúcar m extrafino

castrat|e /'kæstreɪt/ vt castrar.
~ion /-ʃn/ n castración f

casual /'kæʒʊəl/ a casual; ‹meeting› fortuito; ‹work› ocasional;
‹attitude›   despreocupado;
‹clothes› informal, de sport. ~ly
adv de paso

casualt|y /'kæʒʊəltɪ/ n accidente
m; ‹injured› víctima f, herido m;
‹dead› víctima f, muerto m. ~ies
npl ‹mil› bajas fpl

cat /kæt/ n gato m

cataclysm /'kætəklɪzəm/ n cataclismo m

catacomb /'kætəkuːm/ n cata-
cumba f

catalogue /'kætəlɒg/ n catálogo
m. —vt catalogar

catalyst /'kætəlɪst/ n catalizador
m

catamaran /kætəmə'ræn/ n catamarán m

catapult /'kætəpʌlt/ n catapulta f;
‹child's› tirador m, tirachinos m
invar

cataract /'kætərækt/ n catarata f

catarrh /kə'tɑː(r)/ n catarro m

catastroph|e /kə'tæstrəfɪ/ n cat-
ástrofe m. ~ic /kætə'strɒfɪk/ a
catastrófico

catch /kætʃ/ vt (pt caught) coger
(not LAm), agarrar; ‹grab› asir;
tomar ‹train, bus›; ‹unawares›
sorprender; ‹understand› comprender; contraer ‹disease›. ~ a
cold resfriarse. ~ sight of avistar. —vi ‹get stuck› engancharse; ‹fire› prenderse. —n
cogida f; ‹of fish› pesca f; ‹on
door› pestillo m; ‹on window›
cerradura f. ~ on ‹fam› hacerse
popular. ~ up poner al día. ~ up
with alcanzar; ponerse al corriente de ‹news etc›

catching /'kætʃɪŋ/ a contagioso

catchment /'kætʃmənt/ n. ~
area n zona f de captación

catch-phrase /'kætʃfreɪz/ n eslogan m

catchword /'kætʃwɜːd/ n eslogan
m, consigna f

catchy /'kætʃɪ/ a pegadizo

catechism /'kætɪkɪzəm/ n catecismo m

categorical /kætɪ'gɒrɪkl/   a
categórico

category /'kætɪgərɪ/ n categoría f

cater /'keɪtə(r)/ vi proveer comida a. ~ for proveer a ‹needs›.
~er n proveedor m

caterpillar /'kætəpɪlə(r)/ n oruga
f

cathedral /kə'θiːdrəl/ n catedral
f

catholic /'kæθəlɪk/ a universal.
C~ a & n católico (m). C~ism
/kə'θɒlɪsɪzm/ n catolicismo m

catnap /'kætnæp/ n sueñecito m

cat's eyes /'kætsaɪz/ npl cat-
afotos mpl

cattle /'kætl/ npl ganado m
(vacuno)

catt|y /'kætɪ/ a malicioso. ~walk
/'kætwɔːk/ n pasarela f

caucus /'kɔːkəs/ n comité m
electoral

caught /kɔːt/ see catch

cauldron /'kɔːldrən/ n caldera f

cauliflower /'kɒlɪflaʊə(r)/ n coliflor f

cause /kɔːz/ n causa f, motivo
m. —vt causar

causeway /'kɔːzweɪ/ n calzada f
elevada, carretera f elevada

caustic /'kɔːstɪk/ a & n cáustico
(m)

cauterize /'kɔːtəraɪz/ vt cauterizar

caution /'kɔːʃn/ n cautela f;
‹warning› advertencia f. —vt
advertir; ‹jurid› amonestar

cautious /'kɔːʃəs/ a cauteloso,
prudente. ~ly adv con precaución, cautelosamente

cavalcade /kævəl'keɪd/ n cabalgata f

cavalier /kævə'lɪə(r)/   a
arrogante

cavalry /'kævəlrɪ/ n caballería f

cave /keɪv/ n cueva f. —vi. ~ **in** hundirse. ~**man** n (pl -men) troglodita m

cavern /'kævən/ n caverna f, cueva f

caviare /'kævɪɑ:(r)/ n caviar m

caving /'keɪvɪŋ/ n espeleología f

cavity /'kævətɪ/ n cavidad f, (in tooth) caries f

cavort /kə'vɔ:t/ vi brincar

cease /si:s/ vt/i cesar. —n. **without** ~ sin cesar. ~**fire** n tregua f, alto m el fuego. ~**less** a incesante

cedar /'si:də(r)/ n cedro m

cede /si:d/ vt ceder

cedilla /sɪ'dɪlə/ n cedilla f

ceiling /'si:lɪŋ/ n techo m

celebrat|e /'selɪbreɪt/ vt celebrar. —vi divertirse. ~**ed** /'selɪbreɪtɪd/ a célebre. ~**ion** /-'breɪʃn/ n celebración f; (party) fiesta f

celebrity /sɪ'lebrɪtɪ/ n celebridad f

celery /'selərɪ/ n apio m

celestial /sɪ'lestjəl/ a celestial

celiba|cy /'selɪbəsɪ/ n celibato m. ~**te** /'selɪbət/ a & n célibe (m & f)

cell /sel/ n celda f; (biol) célula f; (elec) pila f

cellar /'selə(r)/ n sótano m; (for wine) bodega f

cell|ist /'tʃelɪst/ n violonc(h)elo m & f, violonc(h)elista m & f. ~**o** /'tʃeləʊ/ n (pl -os) violonc(h)elo m

Cellophane /'seləfeɪn/ n (P) celofán m (P)

cellular /'seljʊlə(r)/ a celular

celluloid /'seljʊlɔɪd/ n celuloide m

cellulose /'seljʊləʊs/ n celulosa f

Celt /kelt/ n celta m & f. ~**ic** a céltico

cement /sɪ'ment/ n cemento m. —vt cementar; (fig) consolidar

cemetery /'semətrɪ/ n cementerio m

cenotaph /'senətɑ:f/ n cenotafio m

censor /'sensə(r)/ n censor m. —vt censurar. ~**ship** n censura f

censure /'senʃə(r)/ n censura f. —vt censurar

census /'sensəs/ n censo m

cent /sent/ n centavo m

centenary /sen'ti:nərɪ/ n centenario m

centigrade /'sentɪgreɪd/ a centígrado

centilitre /'sentɪli:tə(r)/ n centilitro m

centimetre /'sentɪmi:tə(r)/ n centímetro m

centipede /'sentɪpi:d/ n ciempiés m invar

central /'sentrəl/ a central; (of town) céntrico. ~ **heating** n calefacción f central. ~**ize** vt centralizar. ~**ly** adv (situated) en el centro

centre /'sentə(r)/ n centro m. —vt (pt centred) vi concentrarse

centrifugal /sen'trɪfjʊgəl/ a centrífugo

century /'sentʃərɪ/ n siglo m

ceramic /sɪ'ræmɪk/ a cerámico. ~**s** npl cerámica f

cereal /'sɪərɪəl/ n cereal m

cerebral /'serɪbrəl/ a cerebral

ceremon|ial /serɪ'məʊnɪəl/ a & n ceremonial (m). ~**ious** /-'məʊnɪəs/ a ceremonioso. ~**y** /'serɪmənɪ/ n ceremonia f

certain /'sɜ:tn/ a cierto. **for** ~ seguro. **make** ~ **of** asegurarse de. ~**ly** adv desde luego. ~**ty** n certeza f

certificate /sə'tɪfɪkət/ n certificado m; (of birth, death etc) partida f

certify /'sɜ:tɪfaɪ/ vt certificar

cessation /se'seɪʃn/ n cesación f

cesspit /'sespɪt/ n, **cesspool** /'sespu:l/ n pozo m negro; (fam) sentina f

chafe /tʃeɪf/ vt rozar. —vi rozarse; (fig) irritarse

chaff /tʃæf/ vt zumbarse de

chaffinch /'tʃæfɪntʃ/ n pinzón m

chagrin /'ʃægrɪn/ n disgusto m

chain /tʃeɪn/ n cadena f. —vt encadenar. ~ **reaction** n reacción f en cadena. **~-smoker** n fumador m que siempre tiene un cigarrillo encendido. ~ **store** n sucursal m

chair /tʃeə(r)/ n silla f; (univ) cátedra f. —vt presidir. **~-lift** n telesilla m

chairman /'tʃeəmən/ n (pl -men) presidente m

chalet /'ʃæleɪ/ n chalé m

chalice /'tʃælɪs/ n cáliz m

chalk /tʃɔːk/ n creta f; (stick) tiza f. **~y** a cretáceo

challeng|e /'tʃælɪndʒ/ n desafío m; (fig) reto m. —vt desafiar; (question) poner en duda. **~ing** a estimulante

chamber /'tʃeɪmbə(r)/ n (old use) cámara f. **~maid** /'tʃeɪmbəmeɪd/ n camarera f. **~-pot** n orinal m. **~s** npl despacho m, bufete m

chameleon /kə'miːljən/ n camaleón m

chamois /'ʃæmɪ/ n gamuza f

champagne /ʃæm'peɪn/ n champaña m, champán m (fam)

champion /'tʃæmpɪən/ n campeón m. —vt defender. **~ship** n campeonato m

chance /tʃɑːns/ n casualidad f; (likelihood) probabilidad f; (opportunity) oportunidad f; (risk) riesgo m. **by** ~ por casualidad. —a fortuito. —vt arriesgar. —vi suceder. **~ upon** tropezar con

chancellor /'tʃɑːnsələ(r)/ n canciller m; (univ) rector m. **C~ of the Exchequer** Ministro m de Hacienda

chancy /'tʃɑːnsɪ/ a arriesgado; (uncertain) incierto

chandelier /ʃændə'lɪə(r)/ n araña f (de luces)

change /tʃeɪndʒ/ vt cambiar; (substitute) reemplazar. ~ **one's mind** cambiar de idea. —vi cambiarse. —n cambio m; (small coins) suelto m. ~ **of life** menopausia f. **~able** a cambiable; (weather) variable. **~-over** n cambio m

channel /'tʃænl/ n canal m; (fig) medio m. **the C~ Islands** npl las islas fpl Anglonormandas. **the (English) C~** el canal de la Mancha. —vt (pt **channelled**) acanalar; (fig) encauzar

chant /tʃɑːnt/ n canto m. —vt/i cantar; (fig) salmodiar

chao|s /'keɪɒs/ n caos m, desorden m. **~tic** /-'ɒtɪk/ a caótico, desordenado

chap¹ /tʃæp/ n (crack) grieta f. —vt (pt **chapped**) agrietar. —vi agrietarse

chap² /tʃæp/ n (fam) hombre m, tío m (fam)

chapel /'tʃæpl/ n capilla f

chaperon /'ʃæpərəʊn/ n acompañanta f. —vt acompañar

chaplain /'tʃæplɪn/ n capellán m

chapter /'tʃæptə(r)/ n capítulo m

char¹ /tʃɑː(r)/ vt (pt **charred**) carbonizar

char² /tʃɑː(r)/ n asistenta f

character /'kærəktə(r)/ n carácter m; (in play) personaje m. **in ~** característico

characteristic /kærəktə'rɪstɪk/ a característico. **~ally** adv típicamente

characterize /'kærəktəraɪz/ vt caracterizar

charade /ʃə'rɑːd/ n charada f, farsa f

charcoal /'tʃɑːkəʊl/ n carbón m vegetal; (for drawing) carboncillo m

charge /tʃɑːdʒ/ n precio m; (elec, mil) carga f; (jurid) acusación f; (task, custody) encargo m; (responsibility) responsabilidad f. **in ~ of** responsable de, encargado de. **take ~ of** encargarse de. —vt pedir; (elec, mil) cargar; (jurid) acusar; (entrust) encargar. —vi cargar; (money) cobrar. **~able** a a cargo (de)

chariot /ˈtʃærɪət/ n carro m

charisma /kəˈrɪzmə/ n carisma m. **~tic** /-ˈmætɪk/ a carismático

charitable /ˈtʃærɪtəbl/ a caritativo

charity /ˈtʃærɪtɪ/ n caridad f; (society) institución f benéfica

charlatan /ˈʃɑːlətən/ n charlatán m

charm /tʃɑːm/ n encanto m; (spell) hechizo m; (on bracelet) dije m, amuleto m. —vt encantar. **~ing** a encantador

chart /tʃɑːt/ n (naut) carta f de marear; (table) tabla f. —vt poner en una carta de marear

charter /ˈtʃɑːtə(r)/ n carta f. —vt conceder carta a, estatuir; alquilar (bus, train); fletar (plane, ship). **~ed accountant** n contador m titulado. **~ flight** n vuelo m charter

charwoman /ˈtʃɑːwʊmən/ n (pl -women) asistenta f

chary /ˈtʃeərɪ/ a cauteloso

chase /tʃeɪs/ vt perseguir. —vi correr. —n persecución f. **~ away, ~ off** ahuyentar

chasm /ˈkæzəm/ n abismo m

chassis /ˈʃæsɪ/ n chasis m

chaste /tʃeɪst/ a casto

chastise /tʃæsˈtaɪz/ vt castigar

chastity /ˈtʃæstɪtɪ/ n castidad f

chat /tʃæt/ n charla f. **have a ~** charlar. —vi (pt chatted) charlar

chattels /ˈtʃætlz/ n bienes mpl muebles

chatter /ˈtʃætə(r)/ n charla f. —vi charlar. **his teeth are ~ing** le castañetean los dientes. **~box** /ˈtʃætəbɒks/ n parlanchín m

chatty a hablador; (style) familiar

chauffeur /ˈʃəʊfə(r)/ n chófer m

chauvinis|m /ˈʃəʊvɪnɪzəm/ n patriotería f; (male) machismo m. **~t** /ˈʃəʊvɪnɪst/ n patriotero m; (male) machista m & f

cheap /tʃiːp/ a (-er, -est) barato; (poor quality) de baja calidad; (rate) económico. **~en** /ˈtʃiːpən/ vt abaratar. **~(ly)** adv barato, a bajo precio. **~ness** n baratura f

cheat /tʃiːt/ vt defraudar; (deceive) engañar. —vi (at cards) hacer trampas. —n trampa f; (person) tramposo m

check[1] /tʃek/ vt comprobar; (examine) inspeccionar; (curb) detener; (chess) dar jaque a. —vi comprobar. —n comprobación f; (of tickets) control m; (curb) freno m; (chess) jaque m; (bill, Amer) cuenta f. **~ in** registrarse; (at airport) facturar el equipaje. **~ out** pagar la cuenta y marcharse. **~ up** comprobar. **~ up on** investigar

check[2] /tʃek/ n (pattern) cuadro m. **~ed** a a cuadros

checkmate /ˈtʃekmeɪt/ n jaque m mate. —vt dar mate a

check-up /ˈtʃekʌp/ n examen m

cheek /tʃiːk/ n mejilla f; (fig) descaro m. **~bone** n pómulo m. **~y** a descarado

cheep /tʃiːp/ vi piar

cheer /tʃɪə(r)/ n alegría f; (applause) viva m. —vt alegrar; (applaud) aplaudir. —vi alegrarse; (applaud) aplaudir. **~ up!** ¡anímate! ¡ánimo! **~ful** a alegre. **~fulness** n alegría f

cheerio /tʃɪərɪˈəʊ/ int (fam) ¡adiós!, ¡hasta luego!

cheer: ∼less /'tʃɪəlɪs/ a triste.
∼s! ¡salud!

cheese /tʃiːz/ n queso m

cheetah /'tʃiːtə/ n guepardo m

chef /ʃef/ n cocinero m

chemical /'kemɪkl/ a químico. —
n producto m químico

chemist /'kemɪst/ n far-
macéutico m; (scientist) químico
m. ∼ry n química f. ∼'s (shop)
n farmacia f

cheque /tʃek/ n cheque m, talón
m. ∼-book n talonario m

chequered /'tʃekəd/ a a cuadros;
(fig) con altibajos

cherish /'tʃerɪʃ/ vt cuidar; (love)
querer; abrigar (hope)

cherry /'tʃerɪ/ n cereza f. ∼-tree
n cerezo m

cherub /'tʃerəb/ n (pl -im) (angel)
querubín m

chess /tʃes/ n ajedrez m.
∼-board n tablero m de ajedrez

chest /tʃest/ n pecho m; (box)
cofre m, cajón m. ∼ of drawers
n cómoda f

chestnut /'tʃesnʌt/ n castaña f.
∼-tree n castaño m

chew /tʃuː/ vt masticar; (fig)
rumiar. ∼ing-gum n chicle m

chic /ʃiːk/ a elegante. —n elegancia f

chick /tʃɪk/ n polluelo m. ∼en
/'tʃɪkɪn/ n pollo m. —a (sl)
cobarde. —vt out (sl) retirarse. ∼en-pox n varicela f

chicory /'tʃɪkərɪ/ n (in coffee)
achicoria f; (in salad) escarola f

chide /tʃaɪd/ vt (pt chided)
reprender

chief /tʃiːf/ n jefe m. —a
principal. ∼ly adv prin-
cipalmente

chilblain /'tʃɪlbleɪn/ n sabañón
m

child /tʃaɪld/ n (pl children
/'tʃɪldrən/) niño m; (offspring)
hijo m. ∼birth /'tʃaɪldbɜːθ/ n
parto m. ∼hood n niñez f. ∼ish

a infantil. ∼less a sin hijos.
∼like a inocente, infantil

Chile /'tʃɪlɪ/ n Chile m. ∼an a &
n chileno (m)

chill /tʃɪl/ n frío m; (illness)
resfriado m. —a frío. —vt
enfriar; refrigerar (food)

chilli /'tʃɪlɪ/ n (pl -ies) chile m

chilly /'tʃɪlɪ/ a frío

chime /tʃaɪm/ n carillón m. —vt
tocar (bells); dar (hours). —vi
repicar

chimney /'tʃɪmnɪ/ n (pl -eys)
chimenea f. ∼-pot n cañón m de
chimenea. ∼-sweep n des-
hollinador m

chimpanzee /tʃɪmpæn'ziː/ n
chimpancé m

chin /tʃɪn/ n barbilla f

china /'tʃaɪnə/ n porcelana f

China /'tʃaɪnə/ n China f. ∼ese
/-'niːz/ a & n chino (m)

chink¹ /tʃɪŋk/ n (crack) grieta f

chink² /tʃɪŋk/ n (sound) tintín
m. —vt hacer tintinear. —vi
tintinear

chip /tʃɪp/ n pedacito m; (splinter) astilla f; (culin) patata f frita;
(gambling) ficha f. have a ∼ on
one's shoulder guardar
rencor. —vt (pt chipped)
desportillar. —vi desportillarse.
∼ in (fam) interrumpir; (with
money) contribuir

chiropodist /kɪ'rɒpədɪst/ n cal-
lista m & f

chirp /tʃɜːp/ n pío m. —vi piar

chirpy /'tʃɜːpɪ/ a alegre

chisel /'tʃɪzl/ n formón m. —vt (pt
chiselled) cincelar

chit /tʃɪt/ n vale m, nota f

chit-chat /'tʃɪttʃæt/ n cháchara f

chivalr|ous /'ʃɪvəlrəs/ a caba-
lleroso. ∼y /'ʃɪvlrɪ/ n caba-
llerosidad f

chive /tʃaɪv/ n cebollino m

chlorine /'klɔːriːn/ n cloro f

chock /tʃɒk/ n calzo m. ∼-a-
block a, ∼-full a atestado

chocolate /'tʃɒklɪt/ n chocolate m; (individual sweet) bombón m
choice /tʃɔɪs/ n elección f; (preference) preferencia f. —a escogido
choir /'kwaɪə(r)/ n coro m. ~boy /'kwaɪəbɔɪ/ n niño m de coro
choke /tʃəʊk/ vt sofocar. —vi sofocarse. —n (auto) estrangulador m, estárter m
cholera /'kɒlərə/ n cólera m
cholesterol /kə'lestərɒl/ n colesterol m
choose /tʃuːz/ vt/i (pt chose, pp chosen) elegir. ~y /'tʃuːzɪ/ a (fam) exigente
chop /tʃɒp/ vt (pt chopped) cortar. —n (culin) chuleta f. ~ down talar. ~ off cortar. ~per n hacha f; (butcher's) cuchilla f, (sl) helicóptero m
choppy /'tʃɒpɪ/ a picado
chopstick /'tʃɒpstɪk/ n palillo m (chino)
choral /'kɔːrəl/ a coral
chord /kɔːd/ n cuerda f; (mus) acorde m
chore /tʃɔː(r)/ n tarea f, faena f. **household** ~s npl faenas fpl domésticas
choreographer /kɒrɪ'ɒgrəfə(r)/ n coreógrafo m
chorister /'kɒrɪstə(r)/ n (singer) corista m & f
chortle /'tʃɔːtl/ n risita f alegre. —vi reírse alegremente
chorus /'kɔːrəs/ n coro m; (of song) estribillo m
chose, chosen /tʃəʊz, 'tʃəʊzn/ see **choose**
Christ /kraɪst/ n Cristo m
christen /'krɪsn/ vt bautizar. ~ing n bautizo m
Christian /'krɪstʃən/ a & n cristiano (m). ~ name n nombre m de pila
Christmas /'krɪsməs/ n Navidad f; (period) Navidades fpl. —a de Navidad, navideño. ~box n

aguinaldo m. ~ day n día m de Navidad. ~ Eve n Nochebuena f. **Father** ~ n Papá m Noel. **Happy** ~! ¡Felices Pascuas!
chrom|e /krəʊm/ n cromo m. ~ium /'krəʊmɪəm/ n cromo m. ~ium plating n cromado m
chromosome /'krəʊməsəʊm/ n cromosoma m
chronic /'krɒnɪk/ a crónico; (bad, fam) terrible
chronicle /'krɒnɪkl/ n crónica f. —vt historiar
chronolog|ical /krɒnə'lɒdʒɪkl/ a cronológico. ~y /krə'nɒlədʒɪ/ n cronología f
chrysanthemum /krɪ'sænθəməm/ n crisantemo m
chubby /'tʃʌbɪ/ a (-ier, -iest) regordete; (face) mofletudo
chuck /tʃʌk/ vt (fam) arrojar. ~ out tirar
chuckle /'tʃʌkl/ n risa f ahogada. —vi reírse entre dientes
chuffed /tʃʌft/ a (sl) contento
chug /tʃʌg/ vi (pt chugged) (of motor) traquetear
chum /tʃʌm/ n amigo m, compinche m. ~my a. be ~my (2 people) ser muy amigos. be ~my with ser muy amigo de
chump /tʃʌmp/ n (sl) tonto m. ~ chop n chuleta f
chunk /tʃʌŋk/ n trozo m grueso. ~y /tʃʌŋkɪ/ a macizo
church /tʃɜːtʃ/ n iglesia f. ~yard /'tʃɜːtʃjɑːd/ n cementerio m
churlish /'tʃɜːlɪʃ/ a grosero
churn /tʃɜːn/ n (for milk) lechera f, cántara f; (for butter) mantequera f. —vt agitar. ~ out producir en profusión
chute /ʃuːt/ n tobogán m
chutney /'tʃʌtnɪ/ n (pl -eys) condimento m agridulce
cider /'saɪdə(r)/ n sidra f
cigar /sɪ'gɑː(r)/ n puro m

cigarette /sɪgə'ret/ n cigarillo m. ~**-holder** n boquilla f

cine-camera /'sɪnɪkæmərə/ n cámara f, tomavistas m invar

cinema /'sɪnəmə/ n cine m

cinnamon /'sɪnəmən/ n canela f

cipher /'saɪfə(r)/ n (math, fig) cero m; (secret system) cifra f

circle /'sɜːkl/ n círculo m; (in theatre) anfiteatro m. —vt girar alrededor de. —vi dar vueltas

circuit /'sɜːkɪt/ n circuito m; (chain) cadena f

circuitous /sɜː'kjuːɪtəs/ a indirecto

circular /'sɜːkjʊlə(r)/ a & n circular (f)

circularize /'sɜːkjʊləraɪz/ vt enviar circulares a

circulat|**e** /'sɜːkjʊleɪt/ vt hacer circular. —vi circular. ~**ion** /-'leɪʃn/ n circulación f; (of journals) tirada f

circumcis|**e** /'sɜːkəmsaɪz/ vt circuncidar. ~**ion** /-'sɪʒn/ n circuncisión f

circumference /sə'kʌmfərəns/ n circunferencia f

circumflex /'sɜːkəmfleks/ a & n circunflejo (m)

circumspect /'sɜːkəmspekt/ a circunspecto

circumstance /'sɜːkəmstəns/ n circunstancia f. ~**s** (means) npl situación f económica

circus /'sɜːkəs/ n circo m

cistern /'sɪstən/ n depósito m; (of WC) cisterna f

citadel /'sɪtədl/ n ciudadela f

citation /saɪ'teɪʃn/ n citación f

cite /saɪt/ vt citar

citizen /'sɪtɪzn/ n ciudadano m; (inhabitant) habitante m & f. ~**ship** n ciudadanía f

citrus /'sɪtrəs/ n. ~ **fruits** cítricos mpl

city /'sɪtɪ/ n ciudad f; **the C**~ el centro m financiero de Londres

civic /'sɪvɪk/ a cívico. ~**s** npl cívica f

civil /'sɪvl/ a civil, cortés

civilian /sɪ'vɪlɪən/ a & n civil (m & f). ~ **clothes** npl traje m de paisano

civility /sɪ'vɪlətɪ/ n cortesía f

civiliz|**ation** /sɪvɪlaɪ'zeɪʃn/ n civilización f. ~**e** /'sɪvəlaɪz/ vt civilizar.

civil: ~ **servant** n funcionario m. ~ **service** n administración f pública

civvies /'sɪvɪz/ npl. **in** ~ (sl) en traje m de paisano

clad /klæd/ see CLOTHE

claim /kleɪm/ vt reclamar; (assert) pretender. —n reclamación f; (right) derecho m; (jurid) demanda f. ~**ant** n demandante m & f; (to throne) pretendiente m

clairvoyant /kleə'vɔɪənt/ n clarividente m & f

clam /klæm/ n almeja f

clamber /'klæmbə(r)/ vi trepar a gatas

clammy /'klæmɪ/ a (-ier, -iest) húmedo

clamour /'klæmə(r)/ n clamor m. —vi. ~ **for** pedir a voces

clamp /klæmp/ n abrazadera f. (auto) cepo m. —vt sujetar con abrazadera. ~ **down on** reprimir

clan /klæn/ n clan m

clandestine /klæn'destɪn/ a clandestino

clang /klæŋ/ n sonido m metálico

clanger /'klæŋə(r)/ n (sl) metedura f de pata

clap /klæp/ vt (pt clapped) aplaudir; batir ⟨hands⟩. —vi aplaudir. —n palmada f; (of thunder) trueno m

claptrap /'klæptræp/ n charlatanería f, tonterías fpl

claret /'klærət/ n clarete m

clarif·ication /klærɪfɪ'keɪʃn/ n aclaración f. **~y** /'klærɪfaɪ/ vt aclarar. —vi aclararse

clarinet /klærɪ'net/ n clarinete m

clarity /'klærɪtɪ/ n claridad f

clash /klæʃ/ n choque m; (noise) estruendo m; (contrast) contraste m; (fig) conflicto m. —vt golpear. —vi encontrarse; (dates) coincidir; (opinions) estar en desacuerdo; (colours) desentonar

clasp /klɑːsp/ n cierre m. —vt agarrar; apretar (hand); (fasten) abrochar

class /klɑːs/ n clase f. **evening ~** n clase nocturna. —vt clasificar

classic /'klæsɪk/ a & n clásico (m). **~al** a clásico. **~s** npl estudios mpl clásicos

classif·ication /klæsɪfɪ'keɪʃn/ n clasificación f. **~y** /'klæsɪfaɪ/ vt clasificar

classroom /'klɑːsruːm/ n aula f

classy /'klɑːsɪ/ a (sl) elegante

clatter /'klætə(r)/ n estrépito m. —vi hacer ruido

clause /klɔːz/ n cláusula f; (gram) oración f

claustrophobia /klɔːstrə'fəʊbɪə/ n claustrofobia f

claw /klɔː/ n garra f; (of cat) uña f; (of crab) pinza f; (device) garfio m. —vt arañar

clay /kleɪ/ n arcilla f

clean /kliːn/ a (-er, -est) limpio; (stroke) neto. —adv completamente. —vt limpiar. —vi hacer la limpieza. **~ up** hacer la limpieza. **~-cut** a bien definido. **~er** n mujer f de la limpieza. **~liness** /'klenlɪnɪs/ n limpieza f

cleans·e /klenz/ vt limpiar; (fig) purificar. **~ing cream** n crema f desmaquilladora

clear /klɪə(r)/ a (-er, -est) claro; (transparent) transparente; (without obstacles) libre; (profit) neto; (sky) despejado. **keep ~ of** evitar. —adv claramente. —vt despejar; liquidar (goods); (jurid) absolver; (jump over) saltar por encima de; quitar (table). —vi (weather) despejarse; (fog) disolverse. **~ off** vi (sl), **~ out** vi (sl) largarse. **~ up** vt (tidy) poner en orden; aclarar (mystery); —vi (weather) despejarse

clearance /'klɪərəns/ n espacio m libre; (removal of obstructions) despeje m; (authorization) permiso m; (by customs) despacho m; (by security) acreditación f. **~ sale** n liquidación f

clearing /'klɪərɪŋ/ n claro m

clearly /'klɪəlɪ/ adv evidentemente

clearway /'klɪəweɪ/ n carretera f en la que no se permite parar

cleavage /'kliːvɪdʒ/ n escote m; (fig) división f

cleav·e /kliːv/ vt (pt cleaved, clove or cleft; pp cloven or cleft) hender. —vi henderse

clef /klef/ n (mus) clave f

cleft /kleft/ see **cleave**

clemen·cy /'klemənsɪ/ n clemencia f. **~t** a clemente

clench /klentʃ/ vt apretar

clergy /'klɜːdʒɪ/ n clero m. **~man** n (pl -men) clérigo m

cleric /'klerɪk/ n clérigo m. **~al** a clerical; (of clerks) de oficina

clerk /klɑːk/ n empleado m; (jurid) escribano m

clever /'klevə(r)/ a (-er, -est) listo; (skilful) hábil. **~ly** adv inteligentemente; (with skill) hábilmente. **~ness** n inteligencia f

cliché /'kliːʃeɪ/ n tópico m, frase f hecha

click /klɪk/ n golpecito m. —vi chascar; (sl) llevarse bien

client /'klaɪənt/ n cliente m & f

clientele /kliːɑːn'tel/ n clientela f

cliff /klɪf/ n acantilado m

climat|e /'klaɪmɪt/ n clima m. **~ic** /-'mætɪk/ a climático

climax /'klaɪmæks/ n punto m culminante

climb /klaɪm/ vt subir ⟨stairs⟩; trepar ⟨tree⟩; escalar ⟨mountain⟩. —vi subir. —n subida f. **~ down** bajar; ⟨fig⟩ volverse atrás, rajarse. **~er** n ⟨sport⟩ alpinista m & f; ⟨plant⟩ trepadora f

clinch /klɪntʃ/ vt cerrar ⟨deal⟩

cling /klɪŋ/ vi ⟨pt clung⟩ agarrarse; ⟨stick⟩ pegarse

clinic /'klɪnɪk/ n clínica f. **~al** /'klɪnɪkl/ a clínico

clink /klɪŋk/ n sonido m metálico. —vt hacer tintinear. —vi tintinear

clinker /'klɪŋkə(r)/ n escoria f

clip¹ /klɪp/ n ⟨for paper⟩ sujetapapeles m invar; ⟨for hair⟩ horquilla f. —vt ⟨pt clipped⟩ ⟨join⟩ sujetar

clip² /klɪp/ n ⟨with scissors⟩ tijeretada f; ⟨blow, fam⟩ golpe m. —vt ⟨pt clipped⟩ ⟨cut⟩ cortar; ⟨fam⟩ golpear. **~pers** /'klɪpəz/ npl ⟨for hair⟩ maquinilla f para cortar el pelo; ⟨for nails⟩ cortauñas m invar. **~ping** n recorte m

clique /kliːk/ n pandilla f

cloak /kləʊk/ n capa f. **~room** /'kləʊkruːm/ n guardarropa m; ⟨toilet⟩ servicios mpl

clobber /'klɒbə(r)/ n ⟨sl⟩ trastos mpl. —vt ⟨sl⟩ dar una paliza a

clock /klɒk/ n reloj m. **grandfather** ~ reloj de caja. —vi. **~ in** fichar, registrar la llegada. **~wise** /'klɒkwaɪz/ a adv en el sentido de las agujas del reloj, a la derecha. **~work** /'klɒkwɜːk/ n mecanismo m de relojería. **like ~work** con precisión

clod /klɒd/ n terrón m

clog /klɒg/ n zueco m. —vt ⟨pt clogged⟩ atascar. —vi atascarse

cloister /'klɔɪstə(r)/ n claustro m

close¹ /kləʊs/ a ⟨-er, -est⟩ cercano; ⟨together⟩ apretado; ⟨friend⟩ íntimo; ⟨weather⟩ bochornoso; ⟨link etc⟩ estrecho; ⟨game, battle⟩ reñido. **have a ~ shave** ⟨fig⟩ escaparse de milagro. —adv cerca. —n recinto m

close² /kləʊz/ vt cerrar. —vi cerrarse; ⟨end⟩ terminar. —n fin m. **~d shop** n empresa f que emplea solamente a miembros del sindicato

close: **~ly** adv de cerca; ⟨with attention⟩ atentamente; ⟨exactly⟩ exactamente. **~ness** n proximidad f; ⟨togetherness⟩ intimidad f

closet /'klɒzɪt/ n ⟨Amer⟩ armario m

close-up /'kləʊsʌp/ n ⟨cinema etc⟩ primer plano m

closure /'kləʊʒə(r)/ n cierre m

clot /klɒt/ n ⟨culin⟩ grumo m; ⟨med⟩ coágulo m; ⟨sl⟩ tonto m. —vi ⟨pt clotted⟩ cuajarse

cloth /klɒθ/ n tela f; ⟨duster⟩ trapo m; ⟨table-cloth⟩ mantel m

cloth|e /kləʊð/ vt ⟨pt clothed or clad⟩ vestir. **~es** /kləʊðz/ npl, **~ing** n ropa f

cloud /klaʊd/ n nube f. —vi nublarse. **~burst** /'klaʊdbɜːst/ n chaparrón m. **~y** a ⟨-ier, -iest⟩ nublado; ⟨liquid⟩ turbio

clout /klaʊt/ n bofetada f. —vt abofetear

clove /kləʊv/ n clavo m

clove² /kləʊv/ n. **~ of garlic** n diente m de ajo

clove³ /kləʊv/ see **cleave**

clover /'kləʊvə(r)/ n trébol m

clown /klaʊn/ n payaso m. —vi hacer el payaso

cloy /klɔɪ/ vt empalagar

club /klʌb/ n club m; ⟨weapon⟩ porra f; ⟨at cards⟩ trébol m. —vt ⟨pt clubbed⟩ aporrear. —vi. **~**

together reunirse, pagar a escote

cluck /klʌk/ vi cloquear

clue /kluː/ n pista f; (in crosswords) indicación f. **not to have a ~** no tener la menor idea

clump /klʌmp/ n grupo m. —vt agrupar. —vi pisar fuertemente

clums|iness /ˈklʌmzɪnɪs/ n torpeza f. **~y** /ˈklʌmzɪ/ a (-ier, -iest) torpe

clung /klʌŋ/ see **cling**

cluster /ˈklʌstə(r)/ n grupo m. —vi agruparse

clutch /klʌtʃ/ vt agarrar. —n (auto) embrague m

clutter /ˈklʌtə(r)/ n desorden m. —vt llenar desordenadamente

coach /kəʊtʃ/ n autocar m; (of train) vagón m; (horse-drawn) coche m; (sport) entrenador m. —vt dar clases particulares; (sport) entrenar

coagulate /kəʊˈægjʊleɪt/ vt coagular. —vi coagularse

coal /kəʊl/ n carbón m. **~field** /ˈkəʊlfiːld/ n yacimiento m de carbón

coalition /kəʊəˈlɪʃn/ n coalición f

coarse /kɔːs/ a (-er, -est) grosero; (material) basto. **~ness** n grosería f; (texture) basteza f

coast /kəʊst/ n costa f. —vi (with cycle) deslizarse cuesta abajo; (with car) ir en punto muerto. **~al** a costero. **~er** /ˈkəʊstə(r)/ n (ship) barco m de cabotaje; (for glass) posavasos m invar. **~guard** /ˈkəʊstɡɑːd/ n guardacostas m invar. **~line** /ˈkəʊstlaɪn/ n litoral m

coat /kəʊt/ n abrigo m; (jacket) chaqueta f; (of animal) pelo m; (of paint) mano f. —vt cubrir, revestir. **~ing** n capa f. **~ of arms** n escudo m de armas

coax /kəʊks/ vt engatusar

cob /kɒb/ n (of corn) mazorca f

cobble¹ /ˈkɒbl/ n guijarro m, adoquín m. —vt empedrar con guijarros, adoquinar

cobble² /ˈkɒbl/ vt (mend) remendar. **~r** /ˈkɒblə(r)/ n (old use) remendón m

cobweb /ˈkɒbweb/ n telaraña f

cocaine /kəˈkeɪn/ n cocaína f

cock /kɒk/ n gallo m; (mec) grifo m; (of gun) martillo m. —vt amartillar (gun); aguzar (ears). **~-and-bull story** n patraña f. **~erel** /ˈkɒkərəl/ n gallo m. **~-eyed** a (sl) torcido

cockle /ˈkɒkl/ n berberecho m

cockney /ˈkɒknɪ/ a & n (pl -eys) londinense (m & f) (del este de Londres)

cockpit /ˈkɒkpɪt/ n (in aircraft) cabina f del piloto

cockroach /ˈkɒkrəʊtʃ/ n cucaracha f

cocksure /kɒkˈʃʊə(r)/ a presuntuoso

cocktail /ˈkɒkteɪl/ n cóctel m. **fruit ~** macedonia f de frutas

cock-up /ˈkɒkʌp/ n (sl) lío m

cocky /ˈkɒkɪ/ a (-ier, -iest) engreído

cocoa /ˈkəʊkəʊ/ n cacao m; (drink) chocolate m

coconut /ˈkəʊkənʌt/ n coco m

cocoon /kəˈkuːn/ n capullo m

cod /kɒd/ n (pl cod) bacalao m, abadejo m

coddle /ˈkɒdl/ vt mimar; (culin) cocer a fuego lento

code /kəʊd/ n código m; (secret) cifra f

codify /ˈkəʊdɪfaɪ/ vt codificar

cod-liver oil /ˈkɒdlɪvə(r)ɔɪl/ n aceite m de hígado de bacalao

coeducational /kəʊedʒʊˈkeɪʃənl/ a mixto

coerce /kəʊˈɜːs/ vt obligar. **~ion** /-ʃn/ n coacción f

coexist /kəʊɪɡˈzɪst/ vi coexistir. **~ence** n coexistencia f

coffee /'kɒfɪ/ n café m. **~-mill** n molinillo m de café. **~-pot** n cafetera f

coffer /'kɒfə(r)/ n cofre m

coffin /'kɒfɪn/ n ataúd m

cog /kɒg/ n diente m, (fig) pieza f

cogent /'kəʊdʒənt/ a convincente

cohabit /kəʊˈhæbɪt/ vi cohabitar

coherent /kəʊˈhɪərənt/ a coherente

coil /kɔɪl/ vt enrollar. —n rollo m; (one ring) vuelta f

coin /kɔɪn/ n moneda f. —vt acuñar. **~age** n sistema m monetario

coincide /kəʊɪnˈsaɪd/ vi coincidir

coinciden|ce /kəʊˈɪnsɪdəns/ n casualidad f. **~tal** /-ˈdentl/ a casual; (coinciding) coincidente

coke /kəʊk/ n (coal) coque m

colander /'kʌləndə(r)/ n colador m

cold /kəʊld/ a (-er, -est) frío. be ~ tener frío. it is ~ hace frío. —n frío m; (med) resfriado m. have a ~ estar constipado. **~-blooded** a insensible. ~ **cream** n crema f. ~ **feet** (fig) miedtis f. **~-ness** n frialdad f. **~-shoulder** vt tratar con frialdad. ~ **sore** n herpes m labial. ~ **storage** n conservación f en frigorífico

coleslaw /'kəʊlslɔː/ n ensalada f de col

colic /'kɒlɪk/ n cólico m

collaborat|e /kəˈlæbəreɪt/ vi colaborar. **~ion** /-ˈreɪʃn/ n colaboración f. **~or** n colaborador m

collage /'kɒlɑːʒ/ n collage m

collaps|e /kəˈlæps/ vi derrumbarse; (med) sufrir un colapso. —n derrumbamiento m; (med) colapso m. **~ible** /kəˈlæpsəbl/ a plegable

collar /'kɒlə(r)/ n cuello m; (for animals) collar m. —vt (fam) hurtar. **~-bone** n clavícula f

colleague /'kɒliːg/ n colega m & f

collect /kəˈlekt/ vt reunir; (hobby) coleccionar; (pick up) recoger; recaudar (rent). —vi (people) reunirse; (things) acumularse. **~ed** /kəˈlektɪd/ a convincente /kəˈlektɪd/ a reunido; (person) tranquilo. **~ion** /-ʃn/ n colección f; (in church) colecta f; (of post) recogida f. **~ive** /kəˈlektɪv/ a colectivo. **~or** n coleccionista m & f; (of taxes) recaudador m

college /'kɒlɪdʒ/ n colegio m; (of art, music etc) escuela f; (univ) colegio m mayor

collide /kəˈlaɪd/ vi chocar

colliery /'kɒlɪərɪ/ n mina f de carbón

collision /kəˈlɪʒn/ n choque m

colloquial /kəˈləʊkwɪəl/ a familiar. **~ism** n expresión f familiar.

collusion /kəˈluːʒn/ n connivencia f

colon /'kəʊlən/ n (gram) dos puntos mpl; (med) colon m

colonel /'kɜːnl/ n coronel m

colon|ial /kəˈləʊnɪəl/ a colonial. **~ize** /'kɒlənaɪz/ vt colonizar. **~y** /'kɒlənɪ/ n colonia f

colossal /kəˈlɒsl/ a colosal

colour /'kʌlə(r)/ n color m. off ~ (fig) indispuesto. —a de color(es), en color(es). —vt colorar; (dye) teñir. —vi (blush) sonrojarse. **~ bar** n barrera f racial. **~-blind** a daltoniano. **~ed** /'kʌləd/ a de color. **~ful** a lleno de color; (fig) pintoresco. **~less** a incoloro. **~s** npl (flag) bandera f

colt /kəʊlt/ n potro m

column /'kɒləm/ n columna f. **~ist** /'kɒləmnɪst/ n columnista m & f

coma /'kəʊmə/ n coma m

comb /kəʊm/ n peine m. —vt peinar; (search) registrar

combat /'kɒmbæt/ n combate m. —vt (pt combated) combatir.

~ant /-ətənt/ *n* combatiente *m* & *f*

combination /kɒmbɪ'neɪʃn/ *n* combinación *f*

combine /kəm'baɪn/ *vt* combinar. —*vi* combinarse. /'kɒmbaɪn/ *n* asociación *f*. ~ **harvester** *n* cosechadora *f*

combustion /kəm'bʌstʃən/ *n* combustión *f*

come /kʌm/ *vi* (*pt* **came**, *pp* **come**) venir; (*occur*) pasar. ~ **about** ocurrir. ~ **across** encontrarse con (*person*); encontrar (*object*). ~ **apart** deshacerse. ~ **away** marcharse. ~ **back** volver. ~ **by** obtener; (*pass*) pasar. ~ **down** bajar. ~ **in** entrar. ~ **in for** recibir. ~ **into** heredar (*money*). ~ **off** desprenderse; (*succeed*) tener éxito. ~ **off it!** (*fam*) ¡no me vengas con eso! ~ **out** salir; (*result*) resultar. ~ **round** (*after fainting*) volver en sí; (*be converted*) cambiar de idea. ~ **to** llegar a (*decision etc*). ~ **up** subir; (*fig*) salir. ~ **up with** proponer (*idea*)

comeback /'kʌmbæk/ *n* retorno *m*; (*retort*) réplica *f*

comedian /kə'miːdɪən/ *n* cómico *m*

comedown /'kʌmdaʊn/ *n* revés *m*

comedy /'kɒmədɪ/ *n* comedia *f*

comely /'kʌmlɪ/ *a* (-**ier**, -**iest**) (*old use*) bonito

comet /'kɒmɪt/ *n* cometa *m*

comeuppance /kʌm'ʌpəns/ *n* (*Amer*) merecido *m*

comfort /'kʌmfət/ *n* bienestar *m*; (*consolation*) consuelo *m*. —*vt* consolar. ~**ortable** *a* cómodo; (*wealthy*) holgado. ~**y** /'kʌmfɪ/ *a* (*fam*) cómodo

comic /'kɒmɪk/ *a* cómico. —*n* cómico *m*; (*periodical*) tebeo *m*. ~**al** *a* cómico. ~ **strip** *n* historieta *f*

coming /'kʌmɪŋ/ *n* llegada *f*. —*a* próximo; (*week*, *month etc*) que viene. ~ **and going** ir y venir

comma /'kɒmə/ *n* coma *f*

command /kə'mɑːnd/ *n* orden *f*; (*mastery*) dominio *m*. —*vt* mandar; (*deserve*) merecer

commandeer /kɒmən'dɪə(r)/ *vt* requisar

commander /kə'mɑːndə(r)/ *n* comandante *m*

commanding /kə'mɑːndɪŋ/ *a* imponente

commandment /kə'mɑːndmənt/ *n* mandamiento *m*

commando /kə'mɑːndəʊ/ *n* (*pl* -**os**) comando *m*

commemorat|**e** /kə'meməreɪt/ *vt* conmemorar. ~**ion** /-'reɪʃn/ *n* conmemoración *f*. ~**ive** /-ətɪv/ *a* conmemorativo

commence /kə'mens/ *vt/i* empezar. ~**ment** *n* principio *m*

commend /kə'mend/ *vt* alabar; (*entrust*) encomendar. ~**able** *a* loable. ~**ation** /kɒmen'deɪʃn/ *n* elogio *m*

commensurate /kə'menʃərət/ *a* proporcionado

comment /'kɒment/ *n* observación *f*. —*vi* hacer observaciones

commentary /'kɒməntrɪ/ *n* comentario *m*; (*radio*, *TV*) reportaje *m*

commentat|**e** /'kɒmənteɪt/ *vi* narrar. ~**or** *n* (*radio*, *TV*) locutor *m*

commerc|**e** /'kɒmɜːs/ *n* comercio *m*. ~**ial** /-ʃl/ *a* comercial. —*n* anuncio *m*. ~**ialize** *vt* comercializar

commiserat|**e** /kə'mɪzəreɪt/ *vt* compadecer. —*vi* compadecerse (**with de**). ~**ion** /-'reɪʃn/ *n* conmiseración *f*

commission /kə'mɪʃn/ *n* comisión *f*. **out of** ~ fuera de servicio. —*vt* encargar; (*mil*) nombrar

commissionaire /kəmɪʃə'neə(r)/ n portero m

commissioner /kə'mɪʃənə(r)/ n comisario m; (of police) jefe m

commit /kə'mɪt/ vt (pt committed) cometer; (entrust) confiar. ~ o.s. comprometerse. ~ to memory aprender de memoria. ~ment n compromiso m

committee /kə'mɪtɪ/ n comité m

commodity /kə'mɒdətɪ/ n producto m, artículo m

common /'kɒmən/ a (-er, -est) común; (usual) corriente; (vulgar) ordinario. —n ejido m

commoner /'kɒmənə(r)/ n plebeyo m

common: ~ **law** n derecho m consuetudinario. ~**ly** adv comúnmente. C~ **Market** n Mercado m Común

commonplace /'kɒmənpleɪs/ a banal. —n banalidad f

common: ~**room** n sala f común, salón m común. ~ **sense** n sentido m común

Commonwealth /'kɒmənwelθ/ n. **the** ~ la Mancomunidad f Británica

commotion /kə'məʊʃn/ n confusión f

communal /'kɒmjʊnl/ a comunal

commune¹ /'kɒmju:n/ n comuna f

commune² /kə'mju:n/ vi comunicarse

communicat|e /kə'mju:nɪkeɪt/ vt comunicar. —vi comunicarse. ~**ion** /-'keɪʃn/ n comunicación f. ~**ive** /-ətɪv/ a comunicativo

communion /kə'mju:nɪən/ n comunión f

communiqué /kə'mju:nɪkeɪ/ n comunicado m

communis|m /'kɒmjʊnɪzəm/ n comunismo m. ~**t** /'kɒmjʊnɪst/ n comunista m & f

community /kə'mju:nətɪ/ n comunidad f. ~ **centre** n centro m social

commute /kə'mju:t/ vi viajar diariamente. —vt (jurid) conmutar. ~**r** /-ə(r)/ n viajero m diario

compact /kəm'pækt/ a compacto. /'kɒmpækt/ n (for powder) polvera f. ~ **disc** /'kɒm-/ n disco m compacto

companion /kəm'pænɪən/ n compañero m. ~**ship** n compañerismo m

company /'kʌmpənɪ/ n compañía f; (guests, fam) visita f; (com) sociedad f

compar|able /'kɒmpərəbl/ a comparable. ~**ative** /kəm'pærətɪv/ a comparativo; (fig) relativo. —n (gram) comparativo m. ~**e** /kəm'peə(r)/ vt comparar. —vi poderse comparar. ~**ison** /kəm'pærɪsn/ n comparación f

compartment /kəm'pɑ:tmənt/ n compartimiento m; (on train) departamento m

compass /'kʌmpəs/ n brújula f. ~**es** npl compás m

compassion /kəm'pæʃn/ n compasión f. ~**ate** a compasivo

compatibility /kəmpætə'bɪlətɪ/ n compatibilidad f. ~**le** /kəm'pætəbl/ a compatible

compatriot /kəm'pætrɪət/ n compatriota m & f

compel /kəm'pel/ vt (pt compelled) obligar. ~**ling** a irresistible

compendium /kəm'pendɪəm/ n compendio m

compensat|e /'kɒmpənseɪt/ vt compensar; (for loss) indemnizar. —vi compensar. ~**ion** /-'seɪʃn/ n compensación f; (financial) indemnización f

compère /'kɒmpeə(r)/ n presentador m. —vt presentar

compete /kəm'piːt/ vi competir
competen|ce /'kɒmpətəns/ n
competencia f, aptitud f. ~t
/'kɒmpətənt/ a competente,
capaz
competit|ion /kɒmpə'tɪʃn/ n
(contest) concurso m; (com)
petencia f. ~ive /kəm'petətɪv/ a
competidor; (price) competitivo.
~or /kəm'petɪtə(r)/ n competidor m; (in contest) concursante m & f
compile /kəm'paɪl/ vt compilar.
~r /-ə(r)/ n recopilador m, com-
pilador m
complacen|cy /kəm'pleɪsənsɪ/ n
satisfacción f de sí mismo. ~t
/kəm'pleɪsnt/ a satisfecho de sí
mismo
complain /kəm'pleɪn/ vi. ~
(about) quejarse (de). ~ of
(med) sufrir de. ~t /kəm'pleɪnt/
n queja f; (med) enfermedad f
complement /'kɒmplɪmənt/ n
complemento m. ~t vt com-
plementar. ~ary /-'mentrɪ/ a
complementario
complet|e /kəm'pliːt/ a completo;
(finished) acabado; (downright)
total. —vt acabar; llenar (a
form). ~ely adv comple-
tamente. ~ion /-ʃn/ n conclusión f
complex /'kɒmpleks/ a complejo. —n complejo m
complexion /kəm'plekʃn/ n tez f;
(fig) aspecto m
complexity /kəm'pleksətɪ/ n
complejidad f
complian|ce /kəm'plaɪəns/ n
sumisión f. in ~ce with de
acuerdo con. ~t a sumiso
complicat|e /'kɒmplɪkeɪt/ vt
complicar. ~ed a complicado.
~ion /-'keɪʃn/ n complicación f
complicity /kəm'plɪsətɪ/ n com-
plicidad f
compliment /'kɒmplɪmənt/ n
cumplido m; (amorous) piropo

m. —vt felicitar. ~ary /-'mentrɪ/
a halagador; (given free) de
favor; ~s npl saludos mpl
comply /kəm'plaɪ/ vi. ~ with
conformarse con
component /kəm'pəʊnənt/ a & n
componente (m)
compose /kəm'pəʊz/ vt componer. ~ o.s. tranquilizarse. ~d a
sereno
compos|er /kəm'pəʊzə(r)/ n com-
positor m. ~ition /kɒmpə'zɪʃn/
n composición f
compost /'kɒmpɒst/ n abono m
composure /kəm'pəʊʒə(r)/ n serenidad f
compound[1] /'kɒmpaʊnd/ n compuesto m. ~ a compuesto; (fracture) complicado. /kəm'paʊnd/
vt componer; agravar (problem
etc). —vi (settle) arreglarse
compound[2] /'kɒmpaʊnd/ n
(enclosure) recinto m
comprehen|d /kɒmprɪ'hend/ vt
comprender. ~sion /kɒmprɪ-
'henʃn/ n comprensión f
comprehensive /kɒmprɪ-
'hensɪv/ a extenso; (insurance) a
todo riesgo. ~ school n instituto
m
compress /'kɒmpres/ n (med)
compresa f. /kəm'pres/ vt com-
primir; (fig) condensar. ~ion
/-ʃn/ n compresión f
comprise /kəm'praɪz/ vt comprender
compromise /'kɒmprəmaɪz/ n
acuerdo m, acomodo m, arreglo
m. —vt comprometer. —vi llegar
a un acuerdo
compuls|ion /kəm'pʌlʃn/ n obli-
gación f, impulso m. ~ive
/kəm'pʌlsɪv/ a compulsivo.
~ory /kəm'pʌlsərɪ/ a
obligatorio
compunction /kəm'pʌŋkʃn/ n
remordimiento m

computer /kəm'pju:tə(r)/ n ordenador m. ~**ize** vt instalar ordenadores en. **be** ~**ized** tener ordenador

comrade /'kɒmreid/ n camarada m & f. ~**ship** n camaradería f

con[1] /kɒn/ vt (pt **conned**) (fam) estafar. —n (fam) estafa f

con[2] /kɒn/ see **pro and con**

concave /'kɒŋkeɪv/ a cóncavo

conceal /kən'si:l/ vt ocultar. ~**ment** n encubrimiento m

concede /kən'si:d/ vt conceder

conceit /kən'si:t/ n vanidad f. ~**ed** a engreído

conceiv|able /kən'si:vəbl/ a concebible. ~**ably** adv. **may** ~**ably** es concebible que. ~**e** /kən'si:v/ vt/i concebir

concentrat|e /'kɒnsəntreɪt/ vt concentrar. —vi concentrarse. ~**ion** /-'treɪʃn/ n concentración f. ~**ion camp** n campo m de concentración

concept /'kɒnsept/ n concepto m

conception /kən'sepʃn/ n concepción f

conceptual /kən'septʃʊəl/ a conceptual

concern /kən'sɜ:n/ n asunto m; (worry) preocupación f; (com) empresa f. —vt tener que ver con; (deal with) tratar de. **as far as I'm** ~**ed** en cuanto a mí. be ~**ed about** preocuparse por. ~**ing** prep acerca de

concert /'kɒnsət/ n concierto m. **in** ~ de común acuerdo. ~**ed** /kən'sɜ:tɪd/ a concertado

concertina /kɒnsə'ti:nə/ n concertina f

concerto /kən'tʃɜ:təʊ/ n (pl -os) concierto m

concession /kən'seʃn/ n concesión f

conciliat|e /kən'sɪlieɪt/ vt conciliar. ~**ion** /-'eɪʃn/ n conciliación f

concise /kən'saɪs/ a conciso. ~**ly** adv concisamente. ~**ness** n concisión f

conclu|de /kən'klu:d/ vt concluir. —vi concluirse. ~**ding** a final. ~**sion** n conclusión f

conclusive /kən'klu:sɪv/ a decisivo. ~**ly** adv concluyentemente

concoct /kən'kɒkt/ vt confeccionar; (fig) inventar. ~**ion** /-ʃn/ n mezcla f; (drink) brebaje m

concourse /'kɒŋkɔ:s/ n (rail) vestíbulo m

concrete /'kɒŋkri:t/ n hormigón m. —a concreto. —vt cubrir con hormigón

concur /kən'kɜ:(r)/ vi (pt concurred) estar de acuerdo

concussion /kən'kʌʃn/ n conmoción f cerebral

condemn /kən'dem/ vt condenar. ~**ation** /kɒndem'neɪʃn/ n condenación f, condena f; (censure) censura f

condens|ation /kɒnden'seɪʃn/ n condensación f. ~**e** /kən'dens/ vt condensar. —vi condensarse

condescend /kɒndɪ'send/ vi dignarse (**to** a). ~**ing** a superior

condiment /'kɒndɪmənt/ n condimento m

condition /kən'dɪʃn/ n condición f. **on** ~ **that** a condición de que. —vt condicionar. ~**al** a condicional. ~**er** n acondicionador m; (for hair) suavizante m

condolences /kən'dəʊlənsɪz/ npl pésame m

condom /'kɒndɒm/ n condón m

condone /kən'dəʊn/ vt condonar

conducive /kən'dju:sɪv/ a. **be** ~ **to** ser favorable a

conduct /kən'dʌkt/ vt conducir; dirigir (orchestra). /'kɒndʌkt/ n conducta f. ~**or** /kən'dʌktə(r)/ n director m; (of bus) cobrador m. ~**ress** n cobradora f

cone /kəʊn/ n cono m; (for ice-cream) cucurucho m

confectioner /kən'fekʃənə(r)/ n pastelero m. **~y** n dulces mpl; golosinas fpl

confederation /kənfedə'reɪʃn/ n confederación f

confer /kən'fɜ:(r)/ vt (pt conferred) conferir. —vi consultar

conference /'kɒnfərəns/ n congreso m

confess /kən'fes/ vt confesar. —vi confesarse. **~ion** /-ʃn/ n confesión f. **~ional** n confes(i)onario m. **~or** n confesor m

confetti /kən'feti/ n confeti m, confetis mpl

confide /kən'faɪd/ vt/i confiar

confiden|ce /'kɒnfɪdəns/ n confianza f; (secret) confidencia f. **~ce trick** n estafa f, timo m. **~t** /'kɒnfɪdənt/ a seguro

confidential /kɒnfɪ'denʃl/ a confidencial

confine /kən'faɪn/ vt confinar; (limit) limitar. **~ment** n (imprisonment) prisión f; (med) parto m

confines /'kɒnfaɪnz/ npl confines mpl

confirm /kən'fɜ:m/ vt confirmar. **~ation** /kɒnfə'meɪʃn/ n confirmación f. **~ed** a (fam) maldito

confiscat|e /'kɒnfɪskeɪt/ vt confiscar. **~ion** /-'keɪʃn/ n confiscación f

conflagration /kɒnflə'greɪʃn/ n conflagración f

conflict /'kɒnflɪkt/ n conflicto m. /kən'flɪkt/ vi chocar. **~ing** /kən-/ a contradictorio

conform /kən'fɔ:m/ vt conformar. —vi conformarse. **~ist** n conformista m & f

confound /kən'faʊnd/ vt confundir. **~ed** a (fam) maldito

confront /kən'frʌnt/ vt hacer frente a; (face) enfrentarse con.

~ation /kɒnfrʌn'teɪʃn/ n confrontación f

confus|e /kən'fju:z/ vt confundir. **~ing** a desconcertante. **~ion** /-ʒn/ n confusión f

congeal /kən'dʒi:l/ vt coagular. —vi coagularse

congenial /kən'dʒi:nɪəl/ a simpático

congenital /kən'dʒenɪtl/ a congénito

congest|ed /kən'dʒestɪd/ a congestionado. **~ion** /-tʃən/ n congestión f

congratulat|e /kən'grætjʊleɪt/ vt felicitar. **~ions** /-'leɪʃnz/ npl felicitaciones fpl

congregat|e /'kɒŋgrɪgeɪt/ vi congregarse. **~ion** /-'geɪʃn/ n asamblea f; (relig) fieles mpl, feligreses mpl

congress /'kɒŋgres/ n congreso m. **C~** (Amer) el Congreso

conic(al) /'kɒnɪk(l)/ a cónico

conifer /'kɒnɪfə(r)/ n conífera f

conjecture /kən'dʒektʃə(r)/ n conjetura f. —vt conjeturar. —vi hacer conjeturas

conjugal /'kɒndʒʊgl/ a conyugal

conjugat|e /'kɒndʒʊgeɪt/ vt conjugar. **~ion** /-'geɪʃn/ n conjugación f

conjunction /kən'dʒʌŋkʃn/ n conjunción f

conjur|e /'kʌndʒə(r)/ vi hacer juegos de manos. —vt. **~e up** evocar. **~or** n prestidigitador m

conk /kɒŋk/ vi. **~ out** (sl) fallar; (person) desmayarse

conker /'kɒŋkə(r)/ n (fam) castaña f de Indias

conman /'kɒnmæn/ n (fam) estafador m, timador m

connect /kə'nekt/ vt conectar; (elec) conectar. —vi unirse; (elec) conectarse. **~ with** (train) enlazar con. **~ed** a unido; (related) relacionado. **be ~ed with** tener que ver con, estar emparentado con

connection /kəˈnekʃn/ n unión f; (rail) enlace m; (elec, mec) conexión f; (fig) relación f. **in ~ with** a propósito de, con respecto a. **~s** npl relaciones fpl

conniv|ance /kəˈnaɪvəns/ n connivencia f. **~e** /kəˈnaɪv/ vi. **~e at** hacer la vista gorda a

connoisseur /kɒnəˈsɜː(r)/ n experto m

connot|ation /kɒnəˈteɪʃn/ n connotación f. **~e** /kəˈnəʊt/ vt connotar; (imply) implicar

conquer /ˈkɒŋkə(r)/ vt conquistar; (fig) vencer. **~or** n conquistador m

conquest /ˈkɒŋkwest/ n conquista f

conscience /ˈkɒnʃəns/ n conciencia f

conscientious /kɒnʃɪˈenʃəs/ a concienzudo

conscious /ˈkɒnʃəs/ a consciente; (deliberate) intencional. **~ly** adv a sabiendas. **~ness** n consciencia f; (med) conocimiento m

conscript /ˈkɒnskrɪpt/ n recluta m. /kənˈskrɪpt/ vt reclutar. **~ion** /kənˈskrɪpʃn/ n reclutamiento m

consecrate /ˈkɒnsɪkreɪt/ vt consagrar. **~ion** /-ˈkreɪʃn/ n consagración f

consecutive /kənˈsekjʊtɪv/ a sucesivo

consensus /kənˈsensəs/ n consenso m

consent /kənˈsent/ vi consentir. **~** n consentimiento m

consequen|ce /ˈkɒnsɪkwəns/ n consecuencia f. **~t** /ˈkɒnsɪkwənt/ a consiguiente. **~tly** adv por consiguiente

conservation /kɒnsəˈveɪʃn/ n conservación f, preservación f. **~ist** /kɒnsəˈveɪʃənɪst/ n conservacionista m & f

conservative /kənˈsɜːvətɪv/ a conservador; (modest) prudente,

moderado. **C~** a & n conservador (m)

conservatory /kənˈsɜːvətrɪ/ n (greenhouse) invernadero m

conserve /kənˈsɜːv/ vt conservar

consider /kənˈsɪdə(r)/ vt considerar; (take into account) tomar en cuenta. **~able** /kənˈsɪdərəbl/ a considerable. **~ably** adv considerablemente

considerat|e /kənˈsɪdərət/ a considerado. **~ion** /-ˈreɪʃn/ n consideración f

considering /kənˈsɪdərɪŋ/ prep en vista de

consign /kənˈsaɪn/ vt consignar; (send) enviar. **~ment** n envío m

consist /kənˈsɪst/ vi. **~ of** consistir en

consistency /kənˈsɪstənsɪ/ n consistencia f; (fig) coherencia f

consistent /kənˈsɪstənt/ a coherente; (unchanging) constante. **~ with** compatible con. **~ly** adv constantemente

consolation /kɒnsəˈleɪʃn/ n consuelo m

console /kənˈsəʊl/ vt consolar

consolidat|e /kənˈsɒlɪdeɪt/ vt consolidar. **—vi** consolidarse. **~ion** /-ˈdeɪʃn/ n consolidación f

consonant /ˈkɒnsənənt/ n consonante f

consort /ˈkɒnsɔːt/ n consorte m & f. /kənˈsɔːt/ vi. **~ with** asociarse con

consortium /kənˈsɔːtɪəm/ n (pl -tia) consorcio m

conspicuous /kənˈspɪkjʊəs/ a (easily seen) visible; (showy) llamativo; (noteworthy) notable

conspir|acy /kənˈspɪrəsɪ/ n complot m, conspiración f. **~e** /kənˈspaɪə(r)/ vi conspirar

constable /ˈkʌnstəbl/ n policía m, guardia m. **~ulary** /kənˈstæbjʊlərɪ/ n policía f

constant /ˈkɒnstənt/ a constante. **~ly** adv constantemente

constellation /kɒnstə'leɪʃn/ n constelación f

consternation /kɒnstə'neɪʃn/ n consternación f

constipat|ed /'kɒnstɪpeɪtɪd/ a estreñido. ~**ion** /-'peɪʃn/ n estreñimiento m

constituen|cy /kən'stɪtjʊənsɪ/ n distrito m electoral. ~**t** /kən'stɪtjʊənt/ n componente m. (pol) elector m

constitut|e /'kɒnstɪtjuːt/ vt constituir. ~**ion** /-'tjuːʃn/ n constitución f. ~**ional** /-'tjuːʃənl/ a constitucional. —n paseo m

constrain /kən'streɪn/ vt forzar, obligar, constreñir. ~**t** /kən'streɪnt/ n fuerza f

constrict /kən'strɪkt/ vt apretar. ~**ion** /-ʃn/ n constricción f

construct /kən'strʌkt/ vt construir. ~**ion** /-ʃn/ n construcción f. ~**ive** /kən'strʌktɪv/ a constructivo

construe /kən'struː/ vt interpretar; (gram) construir

consul /'kɒnsl/ n cónsul m. ~**ar** /-jʊlə(r)/ a consular. ~**ate** /-ət/ n consulado m

consult /kən'sʌlt/ vt/i consultar. ~**ant** /kən'sʌltənt/ n asesor m; (med) especialista m & f; (tec) consejero m técnico. ~**ation** /kɒnsəl'teɪʃn/ n consulta f

consume /kən'sjuːm/ vt consumir; (eat) comer; (drink) beber. ~**r** /-ə(r)/ n consumidor m. —a de consumo. ~**rism** /kən'sjuːmərɪzəm/ n protección f del consumidor, consumismo m

consummat|e /'kɒnsəmeɪt/ vt consumar. ~**ion** /-'meɪʃn/ n consumación f

consumption /kən'sʌmpʃn/ n consumo m; (med) tisis f

contact /'kɒntækt/ n contacto m. —vt ponerse en contacto con

contagious /kən'teɪdʒəs/ a contagioso

contain /kən'teɪn/ vt contener. ~**er** n recipiente m; (com) contenedor m

contaminat|e /kən'tæmɪneɪt/ vt contaminar. ~**ion** /-'neɪʃn/ n contaminación f

contemplate /'kɒntəmpleɪt/ vt contemplar; (consider) considerar. ~**ion** /-'pleɪʃn/ n contemplación f

contemporary /kən'tempərərɪ/ a & n contemporáneo (m)

contempt /kən'tempt/ n desprecio m. ~**ible** a despreciable. ~**uous** /-tjʊəs/ a desdeñoso

contend /kən'tend/ vt sostener. —vi contender. ~**er** n contendiente m & f

content[1] /'kɒntent/ a satisfecho. —n vt contentar

content[2] /'kɒntent/ n contenido m

contented /kən'tentɪd/ a satisfecho

contention /kən'tenʃn/ n contienda f; (opinion) opinión f, argumento m

contentment /kən'tentmənt/ n contento m

contest /'kɒntest/ n (competition) concurso m; (fight) contienda f. /kən'test/ vt disputar. ~**ant** n contendiente m & f, concursante m & f

context /'kɒntekst/ n contexto m

continent /'kɒntɪnənt/ n continente m. the C~ Europa f. ~**al** /-'nentl/ a continental

contingency /kən'tɪndʒənsɪ/ n contingencia f

contingent /kən'tɪndʒənt/ a & n contingente (m)

continu|al /kən'tɪnjʊəl/ a continuo. ~**ance** /kən'tɪnjʊəns/ n continuación f. ~**ation** /-ʊ'eɪʃn/ n continuación f. ~**e** /kən'tɪnjuː/ vt/i continuar; (resume) seguir. ~**ed** a continuo. ~**ity** /kɒntɪ'njuːətɪ/ n continuidad *f.* **∼ity girl** (*cinema*, *TV*) secretaria *f* de rodaje. **∼ous** *adv* continuamente

contort /kən'tɔ:t/ *vt* retorcer. **∼ion** /-ʃn/ *n* contorsión *f.* **∼ionist** /-ʃənɪst/ *n* contorsionista *m* & *f*

contour /'kɒntʊə(r)/ *n* contorno *m.* **∼ line** *n* curva *f* de nivel

contraband /'kɒntrəbænd/ *n* contrabando *m*

contraception /kɒntrə'sepʃn/ *n* contracepción *f.* **∼ve** /kɒntrə'septɪv/ *a & n* anticonceptivo (*m*)

contract /'kɒntrækt/ *n* contrato *m.* /kən'trækt/ *vt* contraer. —*vi* contraerse. **∼ion** /kən'trækʃn/ *n* contracción *f.* **∼or** /kən'træktə(r)/ *n* contratista *m* & *f*

contradict /kɒntrə'dɪkt/ *vt* contradecir. **∼ion** /-ʃn/ *n* contradicción *f.* **∼ory** *a* contradictorio

contraption /kən'træpʃn/ *n* (*fam*) artilugio *m*

contrary /'kɒntrərɪ/ *a & n* contrario (*m*). **on the ∼** al contrario. —*adv.* **∼ to** contrariamente a. /kən'treərɪ/ *a* terco

contrast /'kɒntrɑːst/ *n* contraste *m.* /kən'trɑːst/ *vt* poner en contraste. —*vi* contrastar. **∼ing** *a* contrastante

contraven|e /kɒntrə'viːn/ *vt* contravenir. **∼tion** /-'venʃn/ *n* contravención *f*

contribut|e /kən'trɪbjuːt/ *vt/i* contribuir. **∼e to** escribir para ⟨*newspaper*⟩. **∼ion** /kɒntrɪ'bjuːʃn/ *n* contribución *f*; (*from salary*) cotización *f.* **∼or** *n* contribuyente *m* & *f*, (*to newspaper*) colaborador *m*

contrite /'kɒntraɪt/ *a* arrepentido, pesaroso

contriv|ance /kən'traɪvəns/ *n* invención *f.* **∼e** /kən'traɪv/ *vt* idear. **∼e to** conseguir

control /kən'trəʊl/ *vt* (*pt* **controlled**) controlar. —*n* control *m.* **∼s** *npl* (*mec*) mandos *mpl*

controvers|ial /kɒntrə'vɜ:ʃl/ *a* polémico, discutible. **∼y** /'kɒntrəvɜːsɪ/ *n* controversia *f*

conundrum /kə'nʌndrəm/ *n* adivinanza *f*; (*problem*) enigma *m*

conurbation /kɒnɜː'beɪʃn/ *n* conurbación *f*

convalesce /kɒnvə'les/ *vi* convalecer. **∼nce** *n* convalecencia *f.* **∼nt** *a & n* convaleciente (*m & f*). **∼nt home** *n* casa *f* de convalecencia

convector /kən'vektə(r)/ *n* estufa *f* de convección

convene /kən'viːn/ *vt* convocar. —*vi* reunirse

convenien|ce /kən'viːnɪəns/ *n* conveniencia *f*, comodidad *f.* **all modern ∼ces** todas las comodidades. **at your ∼ce** según le convenga. **∼ces** *npl* servicios *mpl.* **∼t** /kən'viːnɪənt/ *a* cómodo; (*place*) bien situado; (*time*) oportuno. **be ∼t** convenir. **∼tly** *adv* convenientemente

convent /'kɒnvənt/ *n* convento *m*

convention /kən'venʃn/ *n* convención *f*; (*meeting*) congreso *m.* **∼al** *a* convencional

converge /kən'vɜːdʒ/ *vi* convergir

conversant /kən'vɜːsənt/ *a.* **∼ with** versado en

conversation /kɒnvə'seɪʃn/ *n* conversación *f.* **∼al** *a* de la conversación. **∼alist** *n* hábil conversador *m*

converse¹ /kən'vɜːs/ *vi* conversar

converse² /'kɒnvɜːs/ *a* inverso. —*n* lo contrario. **∼ly** *adv* a la inversa

conver|sion /kən'vɜːʃn/ *n* conversión *f.* **∼t** /kən'vɜːt/ *vt* convertir. /'kɒnvɜːt/ *n* converso *m.*

~**tible** /kən'vɜːtɪbl/ a convertible. —n (auto) descapotable m

convex /kɒn'veks/ a convexo

convey /kən'veɪ/ vt llevar; transportar (goods); comunicar (idea, feeling). ~**ance** n transporte m. ~**or belt** n cinta f transportadora

convict /kən'vɪkt/ vt condenar. /'kɒnvɪkt/ n presidiario m. ~**ion** /kən'vɪkʃn/ n condena f; (belief) creencia f

convinc|e /kən'vɪns/ vt convencer. ~**ing** a convincente

convivial /kən'vɪvɪəl/ a alegre

convoke /kən'vəʊk/ vt convocar

convoluted /'kɒnvəluːtɪd/ a enrollado; (argument) complicado

convoy /'kɒnvɔɪ/ n convoy m

convuls|e /kən'vʌls/ vt convulsionar. **be ~ed with laughter** desternillarse de risa. ~**ion** /-ʃn/ n convulsión f

coo /kuː/ vi arrullar

cook /kʊk/ vt cocinar; (alter, fam) falsificar. ~ **up** (fam) inventar. —n cocinero m

cooker /'kʊkə(r)/ n cocina f

cookery /'kʊkərɪ/ n cocina f

cookie /'kʊkɪ/ n (Amer) galleta f

cool /kuːl/ a (-er, -est) fresco; (calm) tranquilo; (unfriendly) frío. —n fresco m; (sl) calma f. —vt enfriar. —vi enfriarse. ~**down** (person) calmarse. ~**ly** adv tranquilamente. ~**ness** n frescura f

coop /kuːp/ n gallinero m. —vt. ~ **up** encerrar

co-operat|e /kəʊ'ɒpəreɪt/ vi cooperar. ~**ion** /-'reɪʃn/ n cooperación f

cooperative /kəʊ'ɒpərətɪv/ a cooperativo. —n cooperativa f

co-opt /kəʊ'ɒpt/ vt cooptar

co-ordinat|e /kəʊ'ɔːdɪneɪt/ vt coordinar. ~**ion** /-'neɪʃn/ n coordinación f

cop /kɒp/ vt (pt copped) (sl) prender. —n (sl) policía f

cope /kəʊp/ vi (fam) arreglárselas. ~ **with** enfrentarse con

copious /'kəʊpɪəs/ a abundante

copper[1] /'kɒpə(r)/ n cobre m; (coin) perra f. —a de cobre

copper[2] /'kɒpə(r)/ n (sl) policía m

coppice /'kɒpɪs/ n, **copse** /kɒps/ n bosquecillo m

Coptic /'kɒptɪk/ a copto

copulat|e /'kɒpjʊleɪt/ vi copular. ~**ion** /-'leɪʃn/ n cópula f

copy /'kɒpɪ/ n copia f; (typ) material m. —vt copiar

copyright /'kɒpɪraɪt/ n derechos mpl de autor

copy-writer /'kɒpɪraɪtə(r)/ n redactor m de textos publicitarios

coral /'kɒrəl/ n coral m

cord /kɔːd/ n cuerda f; (fabric) pana f. ~**s** npl pantalones mpl de pana

cordial /'kɔːdɪəl/ a & n cordial (m)

cordon /'kɔːdn/ n cordón m. —vt. ~ **off** acordonar

corduroy /'kɔːdərɔɪ/ n pana f

core /kɔː(r)/ n (of apple) corazón m; (fig) meollo m

cork /kɔːk/ n corcho m. —vt taponar. ~**screw** /'kɔːkskruː/ n sacacorchos m invar

corn[1] /kɔːn/ n (wheat) trigo m; (Amer) maíz m; (seed) grano m

corn[2] /kɔːn/ n (hard skin) callo m

corned /kɔːnd/ a. ~ **beef** n carne f de vaca en lata

corner /'kɔːnə(r)/ n ángulo m; (inside) rincón m; (outside) esquina f; (football) saque m de esquina. —vt arrinconar; (com) acaparar. ~**stone** n piedra f angular

cornet /'kɔːnɪt/ n (mus) corneta f; (for ice-cream) cucurucho m

cornflakes /'kɔːnfleɪks/ npl copos mpl de maíz

cornflour /'kɔːnflaʊə(r)/ n harina f de maíz

cornice /'kɔːnɪs/ n cornisa f

cornucopia /kɔːnjʊ'kəʊpɪə/ n cuerno m de la abundancia

Cornish /'kɔːnɪʃ/ a de Cornualles. ～**wall** /'kɔːnwəl/ n Cornualles m

corny /'kɔːnɪ/ a (a (trite, fam) gastado; (mawkish) sentimental, sensiblero

corollary /kə'rɒlərɪ/ n corolario m

coronary /'kɒrənərɪ/ n trombosis f coronaria

coronation /kɒrə'neɪʃn/ n coronación f

coroner /'kɒrənə(r)/ n juez m de primera instancia

corporal[1] /'kɔːpərəl/ n cabo m

corporal[2] /'kɔːpərəl/ a corporal

corporate /'kɔːpərət/ a corporativo

corporation /kɔːpə'reɪʃn/ n corporación f; (of town) ayuntamiento m

corps /kɔː(r)/ n (pl corps /kɔːz/) cuerpo m

corpse /kɔːps/ n cadáver m

corpulent /'kɔːpjʊlənt/ a gordo, corpulento

corpuscle /'kɔːpʌsl/ n glóbulo m

corral /kə'rɑːl/ n (Amer) corral m

correct /kə'rekt/ a correcto; (time) exacto. —vt corregir. ～**ion** /-ʃn/ n corrección f

correlat|e /'kɒrəleɪt/ vt poner en correlación. ～**ion** /-'leɪʃn/ n correlación f

correspond /kɒrɪ'spɒnd/ vi corresponder; (write) escribirse. ～**ence** n correspondencia f. ～**ent** n corresponsal m & f

corridor /'kɒrɪdɔː(r)/ n pasillo m

corroborate /kə'rɒbəreɪt/ vt corroborar

corro|de /kə'rəʊd/ vt corroer. —vi corroerse. ～**sion** n corrosión f

corrugated /'kɒrəgeɪtɪd/ a ondulado. ～ **iron** n hierro m ondulado

corrupt /kə'rʌpt/ a corrompido. —vt corromper. ～**ion** /-ʃn/ n corrupción f

corset /'kɔːsɪt/ n corsé m

Corsica /'kɔːsɪkə/ n Córcega f. ～**n** a & n corso (m)

cortège /'kɔːteɪʒ/ n cortejo m

cos /kɒs/ n lechuga f romana

cosh /kɒʃ/ n cachiporra f. —vt aporrear

cosiness /'kəʊzɪnɪs/ n comodidad f

cosmetic /kɒz'metɪk/ a & n cosmético (m)

cosmic /'kɒzmɪk/ a cósmico

cosmonaut /'kɒzmənɔːt/ n cosmonauta m & f

cosmopolitan /kɒzmə'pɒlɪtən/ a & n cosmopolita (m & f)

cosmos /'kɒzmɒs/ n cosmos m

Cossack /'kɒsæk/ a & n cosaco (m)

cosset /'kɒsɪt/ vt (pt cosseted) mimar

cost /kɒst/ vi (pt cost) costar, valer. —vt (pt costed) calcular el coste de. —n precio m. at all ～s cueste lo que cueste. to one's ～ a sus expensas. ～s npl (jurid) costas fpl

Costa Rica /kɒstə'riːkə/ n Costa f Rica. ～**n** a & n costarricense (m & f), costarriqueño (m)

costly /'kɒstlɪ/ a (-ier, -iest) caro, costoso

costume /'kɒstjuːm/ n traje m

cosy /'kəʊzɪ/ a (-ier, -iest) cómodo; (place) acogedor. —n cubierta f (de tetera)

cot /kɒt/ n cuna f

cottage /'kɒtɪdʒ/ n casita f de campo. ～ **cheese** n requesón m. ～ **industry** n industria f casera.

~ **pie** n carne f picada con puré de patatas

cotton /'kɒtn/ n algodón m. —vi. ~ **on** (sl) comprender. ~ **wool** n algodón hidrófilo

couch /kaʊtʃ/ n sofá m. —vt expresar

couchette /ku:'ʃet/ n litera f

cough /kɒf/ vi toser. —n tos f. ~ **up** (sl) pagar. ~ **mixture** n jarabe m para la tos

could /kʊd, kəd/ pt of **can**

couldn't /'kʊdnt/ = **could not**

council /'kaʊnsl/ n consejo m; (of town) ayuntamiento m. ~ **house** n vivienda f protegida. ~**lor** /'kaʊnsələ(r)/ n concejal m

counsel /'kaʊnsl/ n consejo m; (pl invar) (jurid) abogado m. ~**lor** n consejero m

count[1] /kaʊnt/ n recuento m. —vt/i contar

count[2] /kaʊnt/ n (nobleman) conde m

countdown /'kaʊntdaʊn/ n cuenta f atrás

countenance /'kaʊntɪnəns/ n semblante m. —vt aprobar

counter /'kaʊntə(r)/ n (in shop etc) mostrador m; (token) ficha f. —adv. ~ **to** en contra de. —a opuesto. —vt oponerse a; parar ⟨blow⟩. —vi contraatacar

counter... /'kaʊntə(r)/ pref contra...

counteract /kaʊntər'ækt/ vt contrarrestar

counter-attack /'kaʊntərətæk/ n contraataque m. —vt/i contraatacar

counterbalance /'kaʊntəbæləns/ n contrapeso m. —vt/i contrapesar

counterfeit /'kaʊntəfɪt/ a falsificado. —n falsificación f. —vt falsificar

counterfoil /'kaʊntəfɔɪl/ n talón m

counterpart /'kaʊntəpɑ:t/ n equivalente m; (person) homólogo m

counter-productive /'kaʊntəprə'dʌktɪv/ a contraproducente

countersign /'kaʊntəsaɪn/ vt refrendar

countess /'kaʊntɪs/ n condesa f

countless /'kaʊntlɪs/ a innumerable

countrified /'kʌntrɪfaɪd/ a rústico

country /'kʌntrɪ/ n (native land) país m; (countryside) campo m. ~ **folk** n gente f del campo. **go to the** ~ ir al campo; (pol) convocar elecciones generales

countryman /'kʌntrɪmən/ n (pl -men) campesino m; (of one's own country) compatriota m

countryside /'kʌntrɪsaɪd/ n campo m

county /'kaʊntɪ/ n condado m, provincia f

coup /ku:/ n golpe m

coupé /'ku:peɪ/ n cupé m

couple /'kʌpl/ n (of things) par m; (of people) pareja f; (married) matrimonio m. **a** ~ **of** un par de. —vt unir; (tec) acoplar. —vi copularse

coupon /'ku:pɒn/ n cupón m

courage /'kʌrɪdʒ/ n valor m. ~**ous** /kə'reɪdʒəs/ a valiente. ~**ously** adv valientemente

courgette /kʊə'ʒet/ n calabacín m

courier /'kʊrɪə(r)/ n mensajero m; (for tourists) guía m & f

course /kɔ:s/ n curso m; (behaviour) conducta f; (aviat, naut) rumbo m; (culin) plato m; (for golf) campo m. **in due** ~ a su debido tiempo. **in the** ~ **of** en el transcurso de, durante. **of** ~ desde luego, por supuesto

court /kɔ:t/ n corte f; (tennis) pista f; (jurid) tribunal m. —vt cortejar; buscar ⟨danger⟩

courteous /'kɜ:tɪəs/ a cortés

courtesan /ˌkɔːtɪˈzæn/ n (old use) cortesana f

courtesy /ˈkɜːtəsɪ/ n cortesía f

court: ~**ier** /ˈkɔːtɪə(r)/ n (old use) cortesano m. ~ **martial** n (pl **courts martial**) consejo m de guerra. ~-**martial** vt (pt ~-**martialled**) juzgar en consejo de guerra. ~**ship** /ˈkɔːtʃɪp/ n cortejo m

courtyard /ˈkɔːtjɑːd/ n patio m

cousin /ˈkʌzn/ n primo m. **first** ~ primo carnal. **second** ~ primo segundo

cove /kəʊv/ n cala f

covenant /ˈkʌvənənt/ n acuerdo m

Coventry /ˈkɒvntrɪ/ n. **send to** ~ hacer el vacío

cover /ˈkʌvə(r)/ vt cubrir; (journalism) hacer un reportaje sobre. ~ **up** cubrir; (fig) ocultar. —n cubierta f; (shelter) abrigo m; (lid) tapa f; (for furniture) funda f; (pretext) pretexto m; (of magazine) portada f. ~**age** /ˈkʌvərɪdʒ/ n reportaje m. ~ **charge** n precio m del cubierto. ~**ing** n cubierta f. ~**ing letter** n carta f explicatoria, carta f adjunta

covet /ˈkʌvɪt/ vt codiciar

cow /kaʊ/ n vaca f

coward /ˈkaʊəd/ n cobarde m. ~**ly** a cobarde. ~**ice** /ˈkaʊədɪs/ n cobardía f

cowboy /ˈkaʊbɔɪ/ n vaquero m

cower /ˈkaʊə(r)/ vi encogerse, acobardarse

cowl /kaʊl/ n capucha f; (of chimney) sombrerete m

cowshed /ˈkaʊʃed/ n establo m

coxswain /ˈkɒksn/ n timonel m

coy /kɔɪ/ a (-**er**, -**est**) (falsamente) tímido, remilgado

crab[1] /kræb/ n cangrejo m

crab[2] /kræb/ vi (pt **crabbed**) quejarse

crab-apple /ˈkræbæpl/ n manzana f silvestre

crack /kræk/ n grieta f; (noise) crujido m; (of whip) chasquido m; (joke, sl) chiste m. —a (fam) de primera. —vt agrietar; chasquear (whip, fingers); cascar (nut); gastar (joke); resolver (problem). —vi agrietarse. **get** ~**ing** (fam) darse prisa. ~ **down on** (fam) tomar medidas enérgicas contra. ~ **up** vi fallar; (person) volverse loco. ~**ed** /krækt/ a (sl) chiflado

cracker /ˈkrækə(r)/ n petardo m; (culin) galleta f; (culin, Amer) galleta f

crackers /ˈkrækəz/ a (sl) chiflado

crackl|e /ˈkrækl/ vi crepitar. —n crepitación f, crujido m. ~**ing** /ˈkræklɪŋ/ n crepitación f, crujido m; (of pork) chicharrón m

crackpot /ˈkrækpɒt/ n (sl) chiflado m

cradle /ˈkreɪdl/ n cuna f. —vt acunar

craft /krɑːft/ n destreza f; (technique) arte f; (cunning) astucia f. —n invar (boat) barco m

craftsman /ˈkrɑːftsmən/ n (pl -**men**) artesano m. ~**ship** n artesanía f

crafty /ˈkrɑːftɪ/ a (-**ier**, -**iest**) astuto

crag /kræg/ n despeñadero m. ~**gy** a peñascoso

cram /kræm/ vt (pt **crammed**) rellenar. ~ **with** llenar de. —vi (for exams) empollar. ~-**full** a atestado

cramp /kræmp/ n calambre m

cramped /kræmpt/ a apretado

cranberry /ˈkrænbərɪ/ n arándano m

crane /kreɪn/ n grúa f; (bird) grulla f. —vt estirar (neck)

crank[1] /kræŋk/ n manivela f

crank[2] /kræŋk/ n (person) excéntrico m. ~**y** a excéntrico

cranny /ˈkrænɪ/ n grieta f

crash /kræʃ/ *n* accidente *m*; *(noise)* estruendo *m*; *(collision)* choque *m*; *(com)* quiebra *f*. —*vt* estrellar. —*vi* quebrar con estrépito; *(have accident)* tener un accidente; *(car etc)* chocar; *(fail)* fracasar. ~ **course** *n* curso *m* intensivo. ~**helmet** *n* casco *m* protector. ~**land** *vi* hacer un aterrizaje de emergencia, hacer un aterrizaje forzoso

crass /kræs/ *a* craso, burdo

crate /kreɪt/ *n* cajón *m*. —*vt* embalar

crater /'kreɪtə(r)/ *n* cráter *m*

cravat /krə'væt/ *n* corbata *f*, fular *m*

crav|e /kreɪv/ *vi.* ~**e for** anhelar. ~**ing** *n* ansia *f*

crawl /krɔːl/ *vi* andar a gatas; *(move slowly)* avanzar lentamente; *(drag o.s.)* arrastrarse. —*n (swimming)* crol *m*. **at a** ~ a paso lento. ~ **to** humillarse ante. ~ **with** hervir de

crayon /'kreɪən/ *n* lápiz *m* de color

craze /kreɪz/ *n* manía *f*

craz|iness /'kreɪzɪnɪs/ *n* locura *f*. ~**y** /'kreɪzɪ/ *a* (-**ier**, -**iest**) loco. **be** ~**y about** andar loco por. ~**y paving** *n* enlosado *m* irregular

creak /kriːk/ *n* crujido *m*; *(of hinge)* chirrido *m*. —*vi* crujir; *(hinge)* chirriar

cream /kriːm/ *n* crema *f*; *(fresh)* nata *f*. —*a (colour)* color de crema. —*vt (remove)* desnatar; *(beat)* batir. ~ **cheese** *n* queso *m* de nata. ~**y** *a* cremoso

crease /kriːs/ *n* pliegue *m*; *(crumple)* arruga *f*. —*vt* plegar; *(wrinkle)* arrugar. —*vi* arrugarse

creat|e /kriː'eɪt/ *vt* crear. ~**ion** /-ʃn/ *n* creación *f*. ~**ive** *a* creativo. ~**or** *n* creador *m*

creature /'kriːtʃə(r)/ *n* criatura *f*, bicho *m*, animal *m*

crèche /kreɪʃ/ *n* guardería *f* infantil

credence /'kriːdns/ *n* creencia *f*, fe *f*

credentials /krɪ'denʃlz/ *npl* credenciales *mpl*

credib|ility /kredə'bɪlɪtɪ/ *n* credibilidad *f*. ~**le** /'kredəbl/ *a* creíble

credit /'kredɪt/ *n* crédito *m*; *(honour)* honor *m*. **take the** ~ **for** atribuirse el mérito de. —*vt (pt credited)* acreditar; *(believe)* creer. ~ **s.o. with** atribuir a uno. ~**able** *a* loable. ~ **card** *n* tarjeta *f* de crédito. ~**or** *n* acreedor *m*

credulous /'kredjʊləs/ *a* crédulo

creed /kriːd/ *n* credo *m*

creek /kriːk/ *n* ensenada *f*. **up the** ~ *(sl)* en apuros

creep /kriːp/ *vi (pt crept)* arrastrarse; *(plant)* trepar. —*n (sl)* persona *f* desagradable. ~**er** *n* enredadera *f*. ~**s** /kriːps/ *npl*. **give s.o. the** ~**s** dar repugnancia a uno

cremat|e /krɪ'meɪt/ *vt* incinerar. ~**ion** /-ʃn/ *n* cremación *f*. ~**orium** /kremə'tɔːrɪəm/ *n (pl* -**ia**) crematorio *m*

Creole /'kriːəʊl/ *a & n* criollo (*m*)

crêpe /kreɪp/ *n* crespón *m*

crept /krept/ *see* **creep**

crescendo /krɪ'ʃendəʊ/ *n (pl* -**os**) crescendo *m*

crescent /'kresnt/ *n* media luna *f*; *(street)* calle *f* en forma de media luna

cress /kres/ *n* berro *m*

crest /krest/ *n* cresta *f*; *(coat of arms)* blasón *m*

Crete /kriːt/ *n* Creta *f*

cretin /'kretɪn/ *n* cretino *m*

crevasse /krɪ'væs/ *n* grieta *f*

crevice /'krevɪs/ *n* grieta *f*

crew[1] /kruː/ *n* tripulación *f*; *(gang)* pandilla *f*

crew[2] /kruː/ *see* **crow**[2]

crew: ~ **cut** *n* corte *m* al rape. ~ **neck** *n* cuello *m* redondo

crib /krɪb/ *n* cuna *f*; (*relig*) belén *m*; (*plagiarism*) plagio *m*. —*vt/i* (*pt* **cribbed**) plagiar

crick /krɪk/ *n* calambre *m*; (*in neck*) torticolis *f*

cricket[1] /'krɪkɪt/ *n* criquet *m*

cricket[2] /'krɪkɪt/ *n* (*insect*) grillo *m*

cricketer /'krɪkɪtə(r)/ *n* jugador *m* de criquet

crim|**e** /kraɪm/ *n* crimen *m*; (*acts*) criminalidad *f*. ~**inal** /'krɪmɪnl/ *a* & *n* criminal (*m*)

crimp /krɪmp/ *vt* rizar

crimson /'krɪmzn/ *a* & *n* carmesí (*m*)

cringe /krɪndʒ/ *vi* encogerse; (*fig*) humillarse

crinkle /'krɪŋkl/ *vt* arrugar. —*vi* arrugarse. —*n* arruga *f*

crinoline /'krɪnəlɪn/ *n* miriñaque *m*

cripple /'krɪpl/ *n* lisiado *m*, mutilado *m*. —*vt* lisiar; (*fig*) paralizar

crisis /'kraɪsɪs/ *n* (*pl* **crises** /'kraɪsiːz/) crisis *f*

crisp /krɪsp/ *a* (-**er**, -**est**) (*culin*) crujiente; (*air*) vigorizador. ~**s** *npl* patatas *fpl* fritas a la inglesa

criss-cross /'krɪskrɒs/ *a* entrecruzado. —*vt* entrecruzar. —*vi* entrecruzarse

criterion /kraɪ'tɪərɪən/ *n* (*pl* -**ia**) criterio *m*

critic /'krɪtɪk/ *n* crítico *m*

critical /'krɪtɪkl/ *a* crítico. ~**ly** *adv* críticamente; (*ill*) gravemente

critici|**sm** /'krɪtɪsɪzəm/ *n* crítica *f*. ~**ze** /'krɪtɪsaɪz/ *vt/i* criticar

croak /krəʊk/ *n* (*of person*) gruñido *m*; (*of frog*) canto *m*. —*vi* gruñir; (*frog*) croar

crochet /'krəʊʃeɪ/ *n* croché *m*, ganchillo *m*. —*vt* hacer ganchillo

crock[1] /krɒk/ *n* (*person*, *fam*) vejancón *m*; (*old car*) cacharro *m*

crock[2] /krɒk/ *n* vasija *f* de loza

crockery /'krɒkərɪ/ *n* loza *f*

crocodile /'krɒkədaɪl/ *n* cocodrilo *m*. ~ **tears** *npl* lágrimas *fpl* de cocodrilo

crocus /'krəʊkəs/ *n* (*pl* -**es**) azafrán *m*

crony /'krəʊnɪ/ *n* amigote *m*

crook /krʊk/ *n* (*fam*) maleante *m* & *f*, estafador *m*, criminal *m*; (*stick*) cayado *m*; (*of arm*) pliegue *m*

crooked /'krʊkɪd/ *a* torcido; (*winding*) tortuoso; (*dishonest*) poco honrado

croon /kruːn/ *vt/i* canturrear

crop /krɒp/ *n* cosecha *f*; (*fig*) montón *m*. —*vt* (*pt* **cropped**) *vi* cortar. ~ **up** surgir

cropper /'krɒpə(r)/ *n*. **come a** ~ (*fall*, *fam*) caer; (*fail*, *fam*) fracasar

croquet /'krəʊkeɪ/ *n* croquet *m*

croquette /krə'ket/ *n* croqueta *f*

cross /krɒs/ *n* cruz *f*; (*of animals*) cruce *m*. —*vt/i* cruzar; (*oppose*) contrariar. ~ **off** tachar. ~ **o.s.** santiguarse. ~ **out** tachar. ~ **s.o.'s mind** ocurrírsele a uno. — *a* enfadado. **talk at** ~ **purposes** hablar sin entenderse

crossbar /'krɒsbɑː(r)/ *n* travesaño *m*

cross-examine /krɒsɪg'zæmɪn/ *vt* interrogar

cross-eyed /'krɒsaɪd/ *a* bizco

crossfire /'krɒsfaɪə(r)/ *n* fuego *m* cruzado

crossing /'krɒsɪŋ/ *n* (*by boat*) travesía *f*; (*on road*) paso *m* para peatones

crossly /'krɒslɪ/ *adv* con enfado

cross-reference /krɒs'refrəns/ *n* referencia *f*

crossroads /'krɒsrəʊdz/ *n* cruce *m* (de carreteras)

cross-section /krɒs'sekʃn/ n sección f transversal; (fig) muestra f representativa

crosswise /'krɒswaɪz/ adv al través

crossword /'krɒswɜːd/ n crucigrama m

crotch /krɒtʃ/ n entrepiernas fpl

crotchety /'krɒtʃɪtɪ/ a de mal genio

crouch /kraʊtʃ/ vi agacharse

crow[1] /krəʊ/ n cuervo m. **as the ~ flies** en línea recta

crow[2] /krəʊ/ vi (pt **crew**) cacarear

crowbar /'krəʊbɑː(r)/ n palanca f

crowd /kraʊd/ n muchedumbre f. —vi amontonar; (fill) llenar. —vi amontonarse; (gather) reunirse. **~ed** a atestado

crown /kraʊn/ n corona f; (of hill) cumbre f; (of head) coronilla f. —vt coronar; poner una corona a (tooth). **C~ Court** n tribunal m regional. **C~ prince** n príncipe m heredero

crucial /'kruːʃl/ a crucial

crucifix /'kruːsɪfɪks/ n crucifijo m. **~ion** /-'fɪkʃn/ n crucifixión f

crucify /'kruːsɪfaɪ/ vt crucificar

crude /kruːd/ a (-er, -est) (raw) crudo; (rough) tosco; (vulgar) ordinario

cruel /krʊəl/ a (**crueller, cruellest**) cruel. **~ty** n crueldad f

cruet /'kruːɪt/ n vinagreras fpl

cruise /kruːz/ n crucero m. —vi hacer un crucero; (of car) circular lentamente. **~r** n crucero m

crumb /krʌm/ n migaja f

crumble /'krʌmbl/ vt desmenuzar. —vi desmenuzarse; (collapse) derrumbarse

crummy /'krʌmɪ/ a (-ier, -iest) (sl) miserable

crumpet /'krʌmpɪt/ n bollo m blando

crumple /'krʌmpl/ vt arrugar; estrujar (paper). —vi arrugarse

crunch /krʌntʃ/ vt hacer crujir; (bite) ronzar, morder, masticar. —n crujido m; (fig) momento m decisivo

crusade /kruː'seɪd/ n cruzada f. **~r** /-ə(r)/ n cruzado m

crush /krʌʃ/ vt aplastar; arrugar (clothes); estrujar (paper). —n (crowd) aglomeración f. **have a ~ on** (sl) estar perdido por. **orange ~** n naranjada f

crust /krʌst/ n corteza f. **~y** a (bread) de corteza dura; (person) malhumorado

crutch /krʌtʃ/ n muleta f; (anat) entrepiernas fpl

crux /krʌks/ n (pl **cruxes**) punto m más importante, quid m, busilis m

cry /kraɪ/ n grito m. **be a far ~ from** (fig) distar mucho de. —vi llorar; (call out) gritar. **~ off** rajarse. **~-baby** n llorón m

crypt /krɪpt/ n cripta f

cryptic /'krɪptɪk/ a enigmático

crystal /'krɪstl/ n cristal m. **~lize** vt cristalizar. —vi cristalizarse

cub /kʌb/ n cachorro m. **C~ (Scout)** n niño m explorador

Cuba /'kjuːbə/ n Cuba f. **~n** a & n cubano (m)

cubby-hole /'kʌbɪhəʊl/ n casilla f; (room) chiribitil m, cuchitril m

cube /kjuːb/ n cubo m. **~ic** a cúbico

cubicle /'kjuːbɪkl/ n cubículo m; (changing room) caseta f

cubism /'kjuːbɪzm/ n cubismo m. **~t** a & n cubista (m & f)

cuckold /'kʌkəʊld/ n cornudo m

cuckoo /'kʊkuː/ n cuco m, cuclillo m

cucumber /'kjuːkʌmbə(r)/ n pepino m

cuddle /'kʌdl/ vt abrazar. —vi abrazarse. —n abrazo m. **~y** a mimoso

cudgel /'kʌdʒl/ n porra f. —vt (pt cudgelled) aporrear

cue[1] /kju:/ n indicación f; (in theatre) pie m

cue[2] /kju:/ n (in billiards) taco m

cuff /kʌf/ n puño m; (blow) bofetada f. speak off the ~ hablar de improviso. —vt abofetear. ~-link n gemelo m

cul-de-sac /'kʌldəsæk/ n callejón m sin salida

culinary /'kʌlɪnərɪ/ a culinario

cull /kʌl/ vt coger (flowers); entresacar (animals)

culminate /'kʌlmɪneɪt/ vi culminar. ~ion /-'neɪʃn/ n culminación f

culottes /ku'lɒts/ npl falda f pantalón

culprit /'kʌlprɪt/ n culpable m

cult /kʌlt/ n culto m

cultivate /'kʌltɪveɪt/ vt cultivar. ~ion /-'veɪʃn/ n cultivo m; (fig) cultura f

cultural /'kʌltʃərəl/ a cultural. ~e /'kʌltʃə(r)/ n cultura f; (bot etc) cultivo m. ~ed a cultivado; (person) culto

cumbersome /'kʌmbəsəm/ a incómodo; (heavy) pesado

cumulative /'kju:mjʊlətɪv/ a cumulativo

cunning /'kʌnɪŋ/ a astuto. —n astucia f

cup /kʌp/ n taza f; (prize) copa f

cupboard /'kʌbəd/ n armario m

Cup Final /kʌp'faɪnl/ n final f del campeonato

cupful /'kʌpfʊl/ n taza f

cupidity /kju:'pɪdɪtɪ/ n codicia f

curable /'kjʊərəbl/ a curable

curate /'kjʊərət/ n coadjutor m

curator /kjʊə'reɪtə(r)/ n (of museum) conservador m

curb /kɜ:b/ n freno m. —vt refrenar

curdle /'kɜ:dl/ vt cuajar. —vi cuajarse; (milk) cortarse

curds /kɜ:dz/ npl cuajada f, requesón m

cure /kjʊə(r)/ vt curar. —n cura f

curfew /'kɜ:fju:/ n queda f; (signal) toque m de queda

curio /'kjʊərɪəʊ/ n (pl -os) curiosidad f

curious /'kjʊərɪəs/ a curioso. ~sity /-'ɒsɪtɪ/ n curiosidad f

curl /kɜ:l/ vt rizar (hair). ~ o.s. up acurrucarse. —vi (hair) rizarse; (paper) arrollarse. —n rizo m. ~er n bigudí m, rulo m. ~y /-lɪ/ a (-ier, -iest) rizado

currant /'kʌrənt/ n pasa f de Corinto

currency /'kʌrənsɪ/ n moneda f; (acceptance) uso m (corriente)

current /'kʌrənt/ a & n corriente (f). ~ events asuntos mpl de actualidad. ~ly adv actualmente

curriculum /kə'rɪkjʊləm/ n (pl -la) programa m de estudios. ~ vitae n curriculum m vitae

curry[1] /'kʌrɪ/ n curry m

curry[2] /'kʌrɪ/ vt. ~ favour with congraciarse con

curse /kɜ:s/ n maldición f; (oath) palabrota f. —vt maldecir. —vi decir palabrotas

cursory /'kɜ:sərɪ/ a superficial

curt /kɜ:t/ a brusco

curtail /kɜ:'teɪl/ vt abreviar; reducir (expenses)

curtain /'kɜ:tn/ n cortina f; (in theatre) telón m

curtsy /'kɜ:tsɪ/ n reverencia f. —vi hacer una reverencia

curve /kɜ:v/ n curva f. —vt encurvar. —vi encorvarse; (road) torcerse

cushion /'kʊʃn/ n cojín m. —vt amortiguar (a blow); (fig) proteger

cushy /'kʊʃɪ/ a (-ier, -iest) (fam) fácil

custard /'kʌstəd/ n natillas fpl

custodian /kʌˈstəʊdɪən/ n custodio m

custody /ˈkʌstədɪ/ n custodia f. **be in ~** (jurid) estar detenido

custom /ˈkʌstəm/ n costumbre f; (com) clientela f

customary /ˈkʌstəmərɪ/ a acostumbrado

customer /ˈkʌstəmə(r)/ n cliente m

customs /ˈkʌstəmz/ npl aduana f. **~ officer** n aduanero m

cut /kʌt/ vt/i (pt cut, pres p cutting) cortar; reducir (prices). — n corte m; (reduction) reducción f. **~ across** atravesar. **~ back**, **~ down** reducir. **~ in** interrumpir. **~ off** cortar; (phone) desconectar; (fig) aislar. **~ out** recortar; (omit) suprimir. **~ through** atravesar. **~ up** cortar en pedazos. **be ~ up about** (fig) afligirse por

cute /kjuːt/ a (-er, -est) (fam) listo; (Amer) mono

cuticle /ˈkjuːtɪkl/ n cutícula f

cutlery /ˈkʌtlərɪ/ n cubiertos mpl

cutlet /ˈkʌtlɪt/ n chuleta f

cut-price /ˈkʌtpraɪs/ a a precio reducido

cut-throat /ˈkʌtθrəʊt/ a despiadado

cutting /ˈkʌtɪŋ/ a cortante; (remark) mordaz. — n (from newspaper) recorte m; (of plant) esqueje m

cyanide /ˈsaɪənaɪd/ n cianuro m

cybernetics /saɪbəˈnetɪks/ n cibernética f

cyclamen /ˈsɪkləmən/ n ciclamen m

cycle /ˈsaɪkl/ n ciclo m; (bicycle) bicicleta f. —vi ir en bicicleta

cyclic(al) /ˈsaɪklɪk(l)/ a cíclico

cycling /ˈsaɪklɪŋ/ n ciclismo m. **~st** n ciclista m & f

cyclone /ˈsaɪkləʊn/ n ciclón m

cylinder /ˈsɪlɪndə(r)/ n cilindro m. **~ head** (auto) n culata f. **~rical** /-ˈlɪndrɪkl/ a cilíndrico

cymbal /ˈsɪmbl/ n címbalo m

cynic /ˈsɪnɪk/ n cínico m. **~al** a cínico. **~ism** /-sɪzəm/ n cinismo m

cypress /ˈsaɪprəs/ n ciprés m

Cypriot /ˈsɪprɪət/ a & n chipriota (m & f). **~us** /ˈsaɪprəs/ n Chipre f

cyst /sɪst/ n quiste m

czar /zɑː(r)/ n zar m

Czech /tʃek/ a & n checo (m). **the ~ Republic** n la república f Checa

Czechoslovak /tʃekəʊˈsləʊvæk/ a & n (history) checoslovaco (m). **~ia** /-əˈvækɪə/ n (history) Checoslovaquia f

D

dab /dæb/ vt (pt dabbed) tocar ligeramente. —n toque m suave. **a ~ of** un poquito de

dabble /ˈdæbl/ vi. **~ in** meterse (superficialmente) en. **~r** /ə(r)/ n aficionado m

dad /dæd/ n (fam) papá m. **~dy** n (children's use) papá m. **~dy-long-legs** n típula f

daffodil /ˈdæfədɪl/ n narciso m

daft /dɑːft/ a (-er, -est) tonto

dagger /ˈdæɡə(r)/ n puñal m

dahlia /ˈdeɪlɪə/ n dalia f

daily /ˈdeɪlɪ/ a diario. —adv diariamente, cada día. —n diario m; (cleaner, fam) asistenta f

dainty /ˈdeɪntɪ/ a (-ier, -iest) delicado

dairy /ˈdeərɪ/ n vaquería f; (shop) lechería f. —a lechero

dais /ˈdeɪɪs/ n estrado m

daisy /ˈdeɪzɪ/ n margarita f

dale /deɪl/ n valle m

dally /ˈdælɪ/ vi tardar; (waste time) perder el tiempo

dam /dæm/ n presa f. —vt (pt dammed) embalsar

damag|e /'dæmɪdʒ/ n daño m; (pl, jurid) daños mpl y perjuicios mpl. —vt (fig) dañar, estropear. **~ing** a perjudicial

damask /'dæmask/ n damasco m

dame /deɪm/ n (old use) dama f; (Amer, sl) chica f

damn /dæm/ vt condenar; (curse) maldecir. —int ¡córcholis! —a maldito. —n. **I don't care a ~** (no) me importa un comino. **~ation** /-'neɪʃn/ n condenación f, perdición f

damp /dæmp/ n humedad f. —a (-er, -est) húmedo. —vt mojar; (fig) ahogar. **~er** /'dæmpə(r)/ n apagador m, sordina f; (fig) aguafiestas m invar. **~ness** n humedad f

damsel /'dæmzl/ n (old use) doncella f

dance /dɑːns/ vt/i bailar. —n baile m. **~hall** n salón m de baile. **~r** /-ə(r)/ n bailador m; (professional) bailarín m

dandelion /'dændɪlaɪən/ n diente m de león

dandruff /'dændrʌf/ n caspa f

dandy /'dændɪ/ n petimetre m

Dane /deɪn/ n danés m

danger /'deɪndʒə(r)/ n peligro m; (risk) riesgo m. **~ous** a peligroso

dangle /'dæŋgl/ vt balancear. —vi suspender, colgar

Danish /'deɪnɪʃ/ a danés. —m (lang) danés m

dank /dæŋk/ a (-er, -est) húmedo, malsano

dare /deə(r)/ vt desafiar. —vi atreverse a. **I ~ say** probablemente. —n desafío m

daredevil /'deədevl/ n atrevido m

daring /'deərɪŋ/ a atrevido

dark /dɑːk/ a (-er, -est) oscuro; (gloomy) sombrío; (skin, hair) moreno. —n oscuridad f; (nightfall) atardecer. **in the ~** a oscuras. **~en** /'dɑːkən/ vt oscurecer. —

vi oscurecerse. **~ horse** n persona f de talentos desconocidos. **~ness** n oscuridad f. **~room** n cámara f oscura

darling /'dɑːlɪŋ/ a querido. —n querido m

darn /dɑːn/ vt zurcir

dart /dɑːt/ n dardo m. —vi lanzarse; (run) precipitarse. **~board** /'dɑːtbɔːd/ n blanco m. **~s** npl los dardos mpl

dash /dæʃ/ vi precipitarse. **~ off** marcharse apresuradamente. **~ out** salir corriendo. —vt lanzar; (break) romper; defraudar (hopes). —n carrera f; (small amount) poquito m; (stroke) raya f. **cut a ~** causar sensación

dashboard /'dæʃbɔːd/ n tablero m de mandos

dashing /'dæʃɪŋ/ a vivo; (showy) vistoso

data /'deɪtə/ npl datos mpl. **~ processing** n proceso m de datos

date[1] /deɪt/ n fecha f; (fam) cita f. **to ~** hasta la fecha. —vt fechar; (go out with, fam) salir con. —vi datar; (be old-fashioned) quedar anticuado

date[2] /deɪt/ n (fruit) dátil m

dated /'deɪtɪd/ a pasado de moda

daub /dɔːb/ vt embadurnar

daughter /'dɔːtə(r)/ n hija f. **~-in-law** n nuera f

daunt /dɔːnt/ vt intimidar

dauntless /'dɔːntlɪs/ a intrépido

dawdle /'dɔːdl/ vi andar despacio; (waste time) perder el tiempo. **~r** /-ə(r)/ n rezagado m

dawn /dɔːn/ n amanecer m. —vi amanecer; (fig) nacer. **it ~ed on me that** caí en la cuenta de que, comprendí que

day /deɪ/ n día m; (whole day) jornada f; (period) época f. **~break** n amanecer m. **~dream** n ensueño m. —vi soñar despierto

~**light** /'deɪlaɪt/ n luz f del día.
~**time** /'deɪtaɪm/ n día m

daze /deɪz/ vt aturdir. —n aturdimiento m. **in a** ~ aturdido

dazzle /'dæzl/ vt deslumbrar

deacon /'di:kən/ n diácono m

dead /ded/ a muerto; (numb) entumecido. ~ **centre** justo en medio. —adv completamente. ~**beat** rendido. ~ **on time** justo a tiempo. ~ **slow** muy lento. **stop** ~ parar en seco. —n muertos mpl. **in the** ~ **of night** en plena noche. **the** ~ los muertos mpl. ~**en** /'dedn/ vt amortiguar ⟨sound, blow⟩; calmar ⟨pain⟩. ~**end** n callejón m sin salida. ~ **heat** n empate m

deadline /'dedlaɪn/ n fecha f tope, fin m de plazo

deadlock /'dedlɒk/ n punto m muerto

deadly /'dedlɪ/ a (-ier, -iest) mortal; (harmful) nocivo; (dreary) aburrido

deadpan /'dedpæn/ a impasible

deaf /def/ a (-er, -est) sordo. ~-**aid** n audífono m. ~**en** /'defn/ vt ensordecer. ~**ening** a ensordecedor. ~ **mute** n sordomudo m. ~**ness** n sordera f

deal /di:l/ n (transaction) negocio m; (agreement) pacto m; (of cards) reparto m; (treatment) trato m; (amount) cantidad f. **a great** ~ muchísimo. —vt (pt dealt) distribuir; dar ⟨a blow, cards⟩. —vi. ~ **in** comerciar en. ~ **with** tratar con ⟨person⟩; tratar de ⟨subject etc⟩; ocuparse de ⟨problem etc⟩. ~**er** n comerciante m. ~**ings** /'di:lɪŋz/ npl trato m

dean /di:n/ n deán m; (univ) decano m

dear /dɪə(r)/ a (-er, -est) querido; (expensive) caro. —n querido m; (child) pequeño m. —adv caro. —int ¡Dios mío! ~ **me!** ¡Dios mío!

~**ly** adv tiernamente; (pay) caro; (very much) muchísimo

dearth /dɜ:θ/ n escasez f

death /deθ/ n muerte f. ~ **duty** n derechos mpl reales. ~**ly** a mortal; (silence) profundo. —adv como la muerte. ~**'s head** n calavera f. ~**trap** n lugar m peligroso.

débâcle /deɪ'bɑ:kl/ n fracaso m, desastre m

debar /dɪ'bɑ:(r)/ vt (pt **debarred**) excluir

debase /dɪ'beɪs/ vt degradar

debat|able /dɪ'beɪtəbl/ a discutible. ~**e** /dɪ'beɪt/ n debate m. —vt debatir, discutir. —vi discutir; (consider) considerar

debauch /dɪ'bɔ:tʃ/ vt corromper. ~**ery** n libertinaje m

debilit|ate /dɪ'bɪlɪteɪt/ vt debilitar. ~**y** /dɪ'bɪlɪtɪ/ n debilidad f

debit /'debɪt/ n debe m. —vt. ~ **s.o.'s account** cargar en cuenta a uno

debonair /debə'neə(r)/ a alegre

debris /'debri:/ n escombros mpl

debt /det/ n deuda f. **be in** ~ tener deudas. ~**or** n deudor m

debutante /'debju:tɑ:nt/ n (old use) debutante f

decade /dekeɪd/ n década f

decaden|ce /'dekədəns/ n decadencia f. ~**t** /'dekədənt/ a decadente

decant /dɪ'kænt/ vt decantar. ~**er** /ə(r)/ n garrafa f

decapitate /dɪ'kæpɪteɪt/ vt decapitar

decay /dɪ'keɪ/ vi decaer; ⟨tooth⟩ cariarse. —n decadencia f; ⟨of tooth⟩ caries f

deceased /dɪ'si:st/ a difunto

deceit /dɪ'si:t/ n engaño m. ~**ful** a falso. ~**fully** adv falsamente

deceive /dɪ'si:v/ vt engañar

December /dɪ'sembə(r)/ n diciembre m

decen|cy /'di:sənsı/ n decencia f. ~t /'di:snt/ a decente; (good, fam) bueno; (kind, fam) amable. ~tly adv decentemente

decentralize /di:'sentrəlaız/ vt descentralizar

decept|ion /dɪ'sepʃn/ n engaño m. ~ve /dɪ'septɪv/ a engañoso

decibel /'desɪbel/ n decibel(io) m

decide /dɪ'saɪd/ vt/i decidir. ~d /-ɪd/ a resuelto; (unquestionable) indudable. ~dly /-ɪdlɪ/ adv decididamente; (unquestionably) indudablemente

decimal /'desɪml/ a & n decimal (f). ~ point n coma f (decimal)

decimate /'desɪmeɪt/ vt diezmar

decipher /dɪ'saɪfə(r)/ vt descifrar

decision /dɪ'sɪʒn/ n decisión f

decisive /dɪ'saɪsɪv/ a decisivo; (manner) decidido. ~ly adv de manera decisiva

deck /dek/ n cubierta f; (of cards, Amer) baraja f. top ~ (of bus) imperial m. ~ (of) adornar. ~ chair n tumbona f

declaim /dɪ'kleɪm/ vt declamar

declar|ation /deklə'reɪʃn/ n declaración f. ~e /dɪ'kleə(r)/ vt declarar

decline /dɪ'klaɪn/ vt rehusar; (gram) declinar. ~vi disminuir; (deteriorate) deteriorarse; (fall) bajar. ~n decadencia f; (decrease) disminución f; (fall) baja f

decode /di:'kəʊd/ vt descifrar

decompos|e /di:kəm'pəʊz/ vt descomponer. ~vi descomponerse. ~ition /-ɒmpə'zɪʃn/ n descomposición f

décor /'deɪkɔ:(r)/ n decoración f

decorat|e /'dekəreɪt/ vt decorar; empapelar y pintar (room). ~ion /-'reɪʃn/ n (act) decoración f; (ornament) adorno m. ~ive /-ətɪv/ a decorativo. ~or /'dekəreɪtə(r)/ n pintor m decorador. interior ~or decorador m de interiores

decorum /dɪ'kɔ:rəm/ n decoro m

decoy /'di:kɔɪ/ n señuelo m. /dɪ'kɔɪ/ vt atraer con señuelo

decrease /dɪ'kri:s/ vt disminuir. ~vi disminuirse. /'di:kri:s/ n disminución f

decree /dɪ'kri:/ n decreto m; (jurid) sentencia f. ~vt (pt decreed) decretar

decrepit /dɪ'krepɪt/ a decrépito

decry /dɪ'kraɪ/ vt denigrar

dedicat|e /'dedɪkeɪt/ vt dedicar. ~ion /-'keɪʃn/ n dedicación f; (in book) dedicatoria f

deduce /dɪ'dju:s/ vt deducir

deduct /dɪ'dʌkt/ vt deducir. ~ion /-ʃn/ n deducción f

deed /di:d/ n hecho m; (jurid) escritura f

deem /di:m/ vt juzgar, considerar

deep /di:p/ a (-er, est) adv profundo. get into ~ waters meterse en honduras. go off the ~ end enfadarse. ~adv profundamente. be ~ in thought estar absorto en sus pensamientos. ~en /'di:pən/ vt profundizar. ~vi hacerse más profundo. ~freeze n congelador m. ~ly adv profundamente

deer /dɪə(r)/ n invar ciervo m

deface /dɪ'feɪs/ vt desfigurar

defamation /defə'meɪʃn/ n difamación f

default /dɪ'fɔ:lt/ vi faltar. ~n. by ~ en rebeldía. in ~ of en ausencia de

defeat /dɪ'fi:t/ vt vencer; (frustrate) frustrar. ~n derrota f; (of plan etc) fracaso m. ~ism /dɪ'fi:tɪzm/ n derrotismo m. ~ist /dɪ'fi:tɪst/ n derrotista m & f

defect /'di:fekt/ n defecto m. /dɪ'fekt/ vi desertar. ~ to pasar a. ~ion /dɪ'fekʃn/ n deserción f. ~ive /dɪ'fektɪv/ a defectuoso

defence /dɪˈfens/ n defensa f. **∼less** a indefenso

defend /dɪˈfend/ vt defender. **∼ant** n (jurid) acusado m

defensive /dɪˈfensɪv/ a defensivo. —n defensiva f

defer /dɪˈfɜː(r)/ vt (pt **deferred**) aplazar

deferen|ce /ˈdefərəns/ n deferencia f. **∼tial** /-ˈrenʃl/ a deferente

defian|ce /dɪˈfaɪəns/ n desafío m. **in ∼ce of** a despecho de. a desafiante. **∼tly** adv con tono retador

deficien|cy /dɪˈfɪʃənsɪ/ n falta f. **∼t** /dɪˈfɪʃnt/ a deficiente. **be ∼t in** carecer de

deficit /ˈdefɪsɪt/ n déficit m

defile /dɪˈfaɪl/ vt ensuciar; (fig) deshonrar

define /dɪˈfaɪn/ vt definir

definite /ˈdefɪnɪt/ a determinado; (clear) claro; (firm) categórico. **∼ly** adv claramente; (certainly) seguramente

definition /defɪˈnɪʃn/ n definición f

definitive /dɪˈfɪnɪtɪv/ a definitivo

deflat|e /dɪˈfleɪt/ vt desinflar. —vi desinflarse. **∼ion** /-ʃn/ n (com) deflación f

deflect /dɪˈflekt/ vt desviar. —vi desviarse

deform /dɪˈfɔːm/ vt deformar. **∼ed** a deforme. **∼ity** n deformidad f

defraud /dɪˈfrɔːd/ vt defraudar

defray /dɪˈfreɪ/ vt pagar

defrost /diːˈfrɒst/ vt descongelar

deft /deft/ a (**-er, -est**) hábil. **∼ness** n destreza f

defunct /dɪˈfʌŋkt/ a difunto

defuse /diːˈfjuːz/ vt desactivar ‹bomb›; (fig) calmar

defy /dɪˈfaɪ/ vt desafiar; (resist) resistir

degenerate /dɪˈdʒenəreɪt/ vi degenerar. /dɪˈdʒenərət/ a & n degenerado (m)

degrad|ation /degrəˈdeɪʃn/ n degradación f. **∼e** /dɪˈgreɪd/ vt degradar

degree /dɪˈgriː/ n grado m; (univ) licenciatura f; (rank) rango m. **to a certain ∼** hasta cierto punto. **to a ∼** (fam) sumamente

dehydrate /diːˈhaɪdreɪt/ vt deshidratar

de-ice /diːˈaɪs/ vt descongelar

deign /deɪn/ vi. **∼ to** dignarse

deity /ˈdiːɪtɪ/ n deidad f

deject|ed /dɪˈdʒektɪd/ a desanimado. **∼ion** /-ʃn/ n abatimiento m

delay /dɪˈleɪ/ vt retardar; (postpone) aplazar. —vi demorarse. —n demora f

delectable /dɪˈlektəbl/ a deleitable

delegat|e /ˈdelɪgeɪt/ vt delegar. /ˈdelɪgət/ n delegado m. **∼ion** /-ˈgeɪʃn/ n delegación f

delet|e /dɪˈliːt/ vt tachar. **∼ion** /-ʃn/ n tachadura f

deliberat|e /dɪˈlɪbəreɪt/ vt/i deliberar. /dɪˈlɪbərət/ a intencionado; (steps etc) pausado. **∼ely** adv a propósito. **∼ion** /-ˈreɪʃn/ n deliberación f

delica|cy /ˈdelɪkəsɪ/ n delicadeza f; (food) manjar m; (sweet food) golosina f. **∼te** /ˈdelɪkət/ a delicado

delicatessen /delɪkəˈtesn/ n charcutería f fina

delicious /dɪˈlɪʃəs/ a delicioso

delight /dɪˈlaɪt/ n placer m. —vt encantar. —vi deleitarse. **∼ed** a encantado. **∼ful** a delicioso

delineat|e /dɪˈlɪnɪeɪt/ vt delinear. **∼ion** /-ˈeɪʃn/ n delineación f

delinquen|cy /dɪˈlɪŋkwənsɪ/ n delincuencia f. **∼t** /dɪˈlɪŋkwənt/ a & n delincuente (m & f)

deliri|ous /dɪˈlɪrɪəs/ a delirante.
~**um** n delirio m

deliver /dɪˈlɪvə(r)/ vt entregar;
(utter) pronunciar; (aim) lanzar;
(set free) librar; (med) asistir al
parto de. ~**ance** n liberación f.
~**y** n entrega f. (of post) reparto
m; (med) parto m

delta /ˈdeltə/ n (geog) delta m

delude /dɪˈluːd/ vt engañar. ~
o.s. engañarse

deluge /ˈdeljuːdʒ/ n diluvio m

delusion /dɪˈluːʒn/ n ilusión f

de luxe /dɪˈlʌks/ a de lujo

delve /delv/ vi cavar. ~ **into**
(investigate) investigar

demagogue /ˈdeməgɒg/ n demagogo m

demand /dɪˈmɑːnd/ vt exigir. —n
petición f. (claim) reclamación f.
(com) demanda f. **in** ~ muy popular, muy solicitado. **on** ~ a solicitud. ~**ing** a exigente. ~**s** npl
exigencias fpl

demarcation /diːmɑːˈkeɪʃn/ n
demarcación f

demean /dɪˈmiːn/ vt. ~ o.s.
degradarse. ~**our** /dɪˈmiːnə(r)/
n conducta f

demented /dɪˈmentɪd/ a demente

demerara /deməˈreərə/ n. ~
(sugar) n azúcar m moreno

demise /dɪˈmaɪz/ n fallecimiento
m

demo /ˈdeməʊ/ n (pl -os) (fam)
manifestación f

demobilize /diːˈməʊbɪlaɪz/ vt
desmovilizar

democra|cy /dɪˈmɒkrəsɪ/ n demo-
cracia f. ~**t** /ˈdeməkræt/ n demó-
crata m & f. ~**tic** /-ˈkrætɪk/ a
democrático

demoli|sh /dɪˈmɒlɪʃ/ vt derribar.
~**tion** /deməˈlɪʃn/ n demolición
f

demon /ˈdiːmən/ n demonio m

demonstrat|e /ˈdemənstreɪt/ vt
demostrar. —vi manifestarse,
hacer una manifestación. ~**ion**

/-ˈstreɪʃn/ n demostración f. (pol
etc) manifestación f

demonstrative /dɪˈmɒnstrətɪv/
a demostrativo

demonstrator /ˈdemənstreɪtə(r)/
n demostrador m: (pol etc) manifestante m & f

demoralize /dɪˈmɒrəlaɪz/ vt
desmoralizar

demote /dɪˈməʊt/ vt degradar

demure /dɪˈmjʊə(r)/ a recatado

den /den/ n (of animal) guarida f,
madriguera f

denial /dɪˈnaɪəl/ n denegación f.
(statement) desmentimiento m

denigrate /ˈdenɪgreɪt/ vt denigrar

denim /ˈdenɪm/ n dril m (de algodón azul grueso). ~**s** npl pantalón m vaquero

Denmark /ˈdenmɑːk/ n Dinamarca f

denomination /dɪnɒmɪˈneɪʃn/ n
denominación f; (relig) secta f

denote /dɪˈnəʊt/ vt denotar

denounce /dɪˈnaʊns/ vt denunciar

dens|e /dens/ a (-er, -est) espeso,
(person) torpe. ~**ely** adv densamente. ~**ity** n densidad f

dent /dent/ n abolladura f. —vt
abollar

dental /ˈdentl/ a dental. ~ **surgeon** n dentista m & f

dentist /ˈdentɪst/ n dentista m &
f. ~**ry** n odontología f

denture /ˈdentʃə(r)/ n dentadura
f postiza

denude /dɪˈnjuːd/ vt desnudar;
(fig) despojar

denunciation /dɪnʌnsɪˈeɪʃn/ n
denuncia f

deny /dɪˈnaɪ/ vt negar; desmentir
(rumour); (disown) renegar

deodorant /diːˈəʊdərənt/ a & n
desodorante (m)

depart /dɪˈpɑːt/ vi marcharse;
(train etc) salir. ~ **from** apartarse de

department /dɪˈpɑːtmənt/ n departamento m; (com) sección f. ~ **store** n grandes almacenes mpl

departure /dɪˈpɑːtʃə(r)/ n partida f; (of train etc) salida f. ~ **from** (fig) desviación f

depend /dɪˈpend/ vi depender. ~ **on** depender de; (rely) contar con. ~**able** a seguro. ~**ant** /dɪˈpendənt/ n familiar m & f dependiente. ~**ence** n dependencia f. ~**ent** a dependiente. be ~**ent on** depender de

depict /dɪˈpɪkt/ vt pintar; (in words) describir

deplete /dɪˈpliːt/ vt agotar

deplor|able /dɪˈplɔːrəbl/ a lamentable. ~**e** /dɪˈplɔː(r)/ vt lamentar

deploy /dɪˈplɔɪ/ vt desplegar. —vi desplegarse

depopulate /diːˈpɒpjʊleɪt/ vt despoblar

deport /dɪˈpɔːt/ vt deportar. ~**ation** /diːpɔːˈteɪʃn/ n deportación f

depose /dɪˈpəʊz/ vt deponer

deposit /dɪˈpɒzɪt/ vt (pt deposited) depositar. —n depósito m. ~**or** n depositante m & f

depot /ˈdepəʊ/ n depósito m; (Amer) estación f

deprav|e /dɪˈpreɪv/ vt depravar. ~**ity** /-ˈprævətɪ/ n depravación f

deprecate /ˈdeprɪkeɪt/ vt desaprobar

depreciat|e /dɪˈpriːʃɪeɪt/ vt depreciar. —vi depreciarse. ~**ion** /-ˈeɪʃn/ n depreciación f

depress /dɪˈpres/ vt deprimir; (press down) apretar. ~**ion** /-ʃn/ n depresión f

depriv|ation /deprɪˈveɪʃn/ n privación f. ~**e** /dɪˈpraɪv/ vt. ~ **of** privar de

depth /depθ/ n profundidad f. be out of one's ~ perder pie; (fig)

meterse en honduras. **in the ~s of** en lo más hondo de

deputation /depjʊˈteɪʃn/ n diputación f

deputize /ˈdepjʊtaɪz/ vi. ~ **for** sustituir a

deputy /ˈdepjʊtɪ/ n sustituto m. ~ **chairman** n vicepresidente m

derail /dɪˈreɪl/ vt hacer descarrilar. ~**ment** n descarrilamiento m

deranged /dɪˈreɪndʒd/ a ⟨mind⟩ trastornado

derelict /ˈderəlɪkt/ a abandonado

deri|de /dɪˈraɪd/ vt mofarse de. ~**sion** /-ˈrɪʒn/ n mofa f. ~**sive** a burlón. ~**sory** /dɪˈraɪsərɪ/ a mofador; (offer etc) irrisorio

deriv|ation /derɪˈveɪʃn/ n derivación f. ~**ative** /dɪˈrɪvətɪv/ a & n derivado (m). ~**e** /dɪˈraɪv/ vt/i derivar

derogatory /dɪˈrɒgətrɪ/ a despectivo

derv /dɜːv/ n gasóleo m

descen|d /dɪˈsend/ vt/i descender, bajar. ~**dant** n descendiente m & f. ~**t** /dɪˈsent/ n descenso m; (lineage) descendencia f

descri|be /dɪˈskraɪb/ vt describir. ~**ption** /-ˈkrɪpʃn/ n descripción f. ~**ptive** /-ˈkrɪptɪv/ a descriptivo

desecrat|e /ˈdesɪkreɪt/ vt profanar. ~**ion** /-ˈkreɪʃn/ n profanación f

desert[1] /dɪˈzɜːt/ vt abandonar. —vi (mil) desertar

desert[2] /ˈdezət/ a & n desierto (m)

deserter /dɪˈzɜːtə(r)/ n desertor m

deserts /dɪˈzɜːts/ npl lo merecido. **get one's ~** llevarse su merecido

deserv|e /dɪˈzɜːv/ vt merecer. ~**edly** adv merecidamente.

~ing *a* (*person*) digno de; (*action*) meritorio

design /dɪˈzaɪn/ *n* diseño *m*; (*plan*) proyecto *m*; (*pattern*) modelo *m*; (*aim*) propósito *m*. **have ~s on** poner la mira en. — *vt* diseñar; (*plan*) proyectar

designate /ˈdezɪgneɪt/ *vt* designar; (*appoint*) nombrar. ~**ion** /-ˈneɪʃn/ *n* denominación *f*; (*appointment*) nombramiento *m*

designer /dɪˈzaɪnə(r)/ *n* diseñador *m*; (*of clothing*) modisto *m*; (*in theatre*) escenógrafo *m*

desirab|ility /dɪzaɪərəˈbɪlətɪ/ *n* conveniencia *f*. ~**le** /dɪˈzaɪrəbl/ *a* deseable

desire /dɪˈzaɪə(r)/ *n* deseo *m*. —*vt* desear

desist /dɪˈzɪst/ *vi* desistir

desk /desk/ *n* escritorio *m*; (*at school*) pupitre *m*; (*in hotel*) recepción *f*; (*com*) caja *f*

desolat|e /ˈdesələt/ *a* desolado; (*uninhabited*) deshabitado. ~**ion** /-ˈleɪʃn/ *n* desolación *f*

despair /dɪˈspeə(r)/ *n* desesperación *f*. —*vi*. ~ **of** desesperarse de

desperat|e /ˈdespərət/ *a* desesperado; (*dangerous*) peligroso. ~**ely** *adv* desesperadamente. ~**ion** /-ˈreɪʃn/ *n* desesperación *f*

despicable /dɪˈspɪkəbl/ *a* despreciable

despise /dɪˈspaɪz/ *vt* despreciar

despite /dɪˈspaɪt/ *prep* a pesar de

despondenc|y /dɪˈspɒndənsɪ/ *n* abatimiento *m*. ~**t** /dɪˈspɒndənt/ *a* desanimado

despot /ˈdespɒt/ *n* déspota *m*

dessert /dɪˈzɜːt/ *n* postre *m*. ~**spoon** *n* cuchara *f* de postre

destination /destɪˈneɪʃn/ *n* destino *m*

destine /ˈdestɪn/ *vt* destinar

destiny /ˈdestɪnɪ/ *n* destino *m*

destitute /ˈdestɪtjuːt/ *a* indigente. ~ **of** desprovisto de

destroy /dɪˈstrɔɪ/ *vt* destruir

destroyer /dɪˈstrɔɪə(r)/ *n* (*naut*) destructor *m*

destruct|ion /dɪˈstrʌkʃn/ *n* destrucción *f*. ~**ve** *a* destructivo

desultory /ˈdesəltrɪ/ *a* irregular

detach /dɪˈtætʃ/ *vt* separar. ~**able** *a* separable. ~**ed** *a* separado. ~**ed house** *n* chalet *m*. ~**ment** /dɪˈtætʃmənt/ *n* separación *f*; (*mil*) destacamento *m*; (*fig*) indiferencia *f*

detail /ˈdiːteɪl/ *n* detalle *m*. —*vt* detallar; (*mil*) destacar. ~**ed** *a* detallado

detain /dɪˈteɪn/ *vt* detener; (*delay*) retener. ~**ee** /diːteɪˈniː/ *n* detenido *m*

detect /dɪˈtekt/ *vt* percibir; (*discover*) descubrir. ~**ion** /-ʃn/ *n* descubrimiento *m*, detección *f*. ~**or** *n* detector *m*

detective /dɪˈtektɪv/ *n* detective *m*. ~ **story** *n* novela *f* policíaca

detention /dɪˈtenʃn/ *n* detención *f*

deter /dɪˈtɜː(r)/ *vt* (*pt* **deterred**) disuadir; (*prevent*) impedir

detergent /dɪˈtɜːdʒənt/ *a & n* detergente (*m*)

deteriorat|e /dɪˈtɪərɪəreɪt/ *vi* deteriorarse. ~**ion** /-ˈreɪʃn/ *n* deterioro *m*

determination /dɪtɜːmɪˈneɪʃn/ *n* determinación *f*

determine /dɪˈtɜːmɪn/ *vt* determinar; (*decide*) decidir. ~**d** *a* determinado; (*resolute*) resuelto

deterrent /dɪˈterənt/ *n* fuerza *f* de disuasión

detest /dɪˈtest/ *vt* aborrecer. ~**able** *a* odioso

detonat|e /ˈdetəneɪt/ *vt* hacer detonar. —*vi* detonar. ~**ion** /-ˈneɪʃn/ *n* detonación *f*. ~**or** *n* detonador *m*

detour /ˈdiːtʊə(r)/ *n* desviación *f*

detract /dɪˈtrækt/ *vi*. ~ **from** (*lessen*) disminuir

detriment /'detrɪmənt/ n perjuicio m. ~al /-'mentl/ a perjudicial

devaluation /diː'væljuː'eɪʃn/ n desvalorización f. ~e /diː'vælju:/ vt desvalorizar

devastate /'devəsteɪt/ vt devastar. ~ing a devastador; (fig) arrollador

develop /dɪ'veləp/ vt desarrollar; contraer (illness); urbanizar (land). ~ vi desarrollarse; (show) aparecerse. ~er n (foto) revelador m. ~ing country n país m en vías de desarrollo. ~ment n desarrollo m. (new) ~ment novedad f

deviant /'diːvɪənt/ a desviado

deviate /'diːvɪeɪt/ vi desviarse. ~ion /-'eɪʃn/ n desviación f

device /dɪ'vaɪs/ n dispositivo m; (scheme) estratagema f

devil /'devl/ n diablo m. ~ish a diabólico

devious /'diːvɪəs/ a tortuoso

devise /dɪ'vaɪz/ vt idear

devoid /dɪ'vɔɪd/ a. ~ of desprovisto de

devolution /diːvə'luːʃn/ n descentralización f; (of power) delegación f

devote /dɪ'vəʊt/ vt dedicar. ~ed a leal. ~edly adv con devoción f. ~ee /devə'tiː/ n partidario m. ~ion /-ʃn/ n dedicación f. ~ions npl (relig) oraciones fpl

devour /dɪ'vaʊə(r)/ vt devorar

devout /dɪ'vaʊt/ a devoto

dew /djuː/ n rocío m

dexterity /dek'sterətɪ/ n destreza f. ~(e)rous /'dekstrəs/ a diestro

diabetes /daɪə'biːtiːz/ n diabetes f. ~ic /-'betɪk/ a & n diabético (m)

diabolical /daɪə'bɒlɪkl/ a diabólico

diadem /'daɪədəm/ n diadema f

diagnose /'daɪəgnəʊz/ vt diagnosticar. ~is /daɪəg'nəʊsɪs/ n (pl -oses /-siːz/) diagnóstico m

diagonal /daɪ'ægənl/ a & n diagonal (f)

diagram /'daɪəgræm/ n diagrama m

dial /daɪəl/ n cuadrante m; (on phone) disco m. ~ vt (pt dialled) marcar

dialect /'daɪəlekt/ n dialecto m

dial: ~ling code n prefijo m. ~ling tone n señal f para marcar

dialogue /'daɪəlɒg/ n diálogo m

diameter /daɪ'æmɪtə(r)/ n diámetro m

diamond /'daɪəmənd/ n diamante m; (shape) rombo m. ~s npl (cards) diamantes mpl

diaper /'daɪəpə(r)/ n (Amer) pañal m

diaphanous /daɪ'æfənəs/ a diáfano

diaphragm /'daɪəfræm/ n diafragma m

diarrhoea /daɪə'rɪə/ n diarrea f

diary /'daɪərɪ/ n diario m; (book) agenda f

diatribe /'daɪətraɪb/ n diatriba f

dice /daɪs/ n invar dado m. ~ vt (culin) cortar en cubitos

dicey /'daɪsɪ/ a (sl) arriesgado

dictate /dɪk'teɪt/ vt/i dictar. ~es /'dɪkteɪts/ npl dictados mpl. ~ion /dɪk'teɪʃn/ n dictado m

dictator /dɪk'teɪtə(r)/ n dictador m. ~ship n dictadura f

diction /'dɪkʃn/ n dicción f

dictionary /'dɪkʃənərɪ/ n diccionario m

did /dɪd/ see do

didactic /daɪ'dæktɪk/ a didáctico

diddle /dɪdl/ vt (sl) estafar

didn't /'dɪdnt/ = did not

die[1] /daɪ/ vi (pres p dying) morir. **be dying to** morirse por. ~ **down** disminuir. ~ **out** extinguirse

die² /daɪ/ n (tec) cuño m

die-hard /ˈdaɪhɑːd/ n intransigente m & f

diesel /ˈdiːzl/ n (fuel) gasóleo m. **~ engine** n motor m diesel

diet /ˈdaɪət/ n alimentación f; (restricted) régimen m. —vi estar a régimen. **~etic** /daɪəˈtetɪk/ a dietético. **~itian** n dietético m

differ /ˈdɪfə(r)/ vi ser distinto; (disagree) no estar de acuerdo. **~ence** /ˈdɪfrəns/ n diferencia f; (disagreement) desacuerdo m. **~ent** /ˈdɪfrənt/ a distinto, diferente

differential /dɪfəˈrenʃl/ a & n diferencial (f). **~te** /dɪfəˈrenʃɪeɪt/ vt diferenciar. —vi diferenciarse

differently /ˈdɪfrəntlɪ/ adv de otra manera

difficult /ˈdɪfɪkəlt/ a difícil. **~y** n dificultad f

diffiden|ce /ˈdɪfɪdəns/ n falta f de confianza. **~t** /ˈdɪfɪdənt/ a que falta confianza

diffus|e /dɪˈfjuːs/ a difuso. /dɪˈfjuːz/ vt difundir. —vi difundirse. **~ion** /-ʒn/ n difusión f

dig /dɪg/ n (poke) empujón m; (poke with elbow) codazo m; (remark) indirecta f; (archaeol) excavación f. —vt (pt dug, pres p digging) cavar; (thrust) empujar. —vi cavar. **~ out** extraer. **~ up** desenterrar. **~s** npl (fam) alojamiento m

digest /ˈdaɪdʒest/ n resumen m. —vt digerir. **~ible** a digerible. **~ion** /-ʃn/ n digestión f. **~ive** a digestivo

digger /ˈdɪgə(r)/ n (mec) excavadora f

digit /ˈdɪdʒɪt/ n cifra f; (finger) dedo m. **~al** /ˈdɪdʒɪtl/ a digital

dignified /ˈdɪgnɪfaɪd/ a solemne. **~y** /ˈdɪgnɪfaɪ/ vt dignificar

dignitary /ˈdɪgnɪtərɪ/ n dignatario m

dignity /ˈdɪgnətɪ/ n dignidad f

digress /daɪˈgres/ vi divagar. **~ from** apartarse de. **~ion** /-ʃn/ n digresión f

dike /daɪk/ n dique m

dilapidated /dɪˈlæpɪdeɪtɪd/ a ruinoso

dilat|e /daɪˈleɪt/ vt dilatar. —vi dilatarse. **~ion** /-ʃn/ n dilatación f

dilatory /ˈdɪlətərɪ/ a dilatorio, lento

dilemma /daɪˈlemə/ n dilema m

diligen|ce /ˈdɪlɪdʒəns/ n diligencia f. **~t** /ˈdɪlɪdʒənt/ a diligente

dilly-dally /ˈdɪlɪdælɪ/ vi (fam) perder el tiempo

dilute /daɪˈljuːt/ vt diluir

dim /dɪm/ a (dimmer, dimmest) (weak) débil; (dark) oscuro; (stupid, fam) torpe. —vt (pt dimmed) amortiguar. —vi apagarse. **~ the headlines** bajar los faros

dime /daɪm/ n (Amer) moneda f de diez centavos

dimension /daɪˈmenʃn/ n dimensión f

diminish /dɪˈmɪnɪʃ/ vt/i disminuir

diminutive /dɪˈmɪnjʊtɪv/ a diminuto. —n diminutivo m

dimness /ˈdɪmnɪs/ n debilidad f; (of room etc) oscuridad f

dimple /ˈdɪmpl/ n hoyuelo m

din /dɪn/ n jaleo m

dine /daɪn/ vi cenar. **~r** /-ə(r)/ n comensal m & f; (rail) coche m restaurante

dinghy /ˈdɪŋgɪ/ n (inflatable) bote m neumático

ding|iness /ˈdɪndʒɪnɪs/ n suciedad f. **~y** /ˈdɪndʒɪ/ a (-ier, -iest) miserable, sucio

dining-room /ˈdaɪnɪŋruːm/ n comedor m

dinner /ˈdɪnə(r)/ n cena f. **~-jacket** n esmoquin m. **~ party** n cena f

dinosaur /'daɪnɔːsɔ:(r)/ n dinosaurio m

dint /dɪnt/ n. **by ∼ of** a fuerza de

diocese /'daɪəsɪs/ n diócesis f

dip /dɪp/ vt (pt **dipped**) sumergir. —vi bajar. **∼ into** hojear ‹book›. —n ‹slope› inclinación f; (in sea) baño m

diphtheria /dɪf'θɪərɪə/ n difteria f

diphthong /'dɪfθɒŋ/ n diptongo m

diploma /dɪ'pləʊmə/ n diploma m

diplomacy /dɪ'pləʊməsɪ/ n diplomacia f

diplomat /'dɪpləmæt/ n diplomático m. **∼ic** /-'mætɪk/ a diplomático

dipstick /'dɪpstɪk/ n (auto) varilla f del nivel de aceite

dire /daɪə(r)/ a (-er, -est) terrible; ‹need, poverty› extremo

direct /dɪ'rekt/ a directo. —adv directamente. —vt dirigir; (show the way) indicar

direction /dɪ'rekʃn/ n dirección f. **∼s** npl instrucciones fpl

directly /dɪ'rektlɪ/ adv directamente; (at once) en seguida. —conj (fam) en cuanto

director /dɪ'rektə(r)/ n director m

directory /dɪ'rektərɪ/ n guía f

dirge /dɜːdʒ/ n canto m fúnebre

dirt /dɜːt/ n suciedad f. **∼track** n (sport) pista f de ceniza. **∼y** /dɜːtɪ/ a (-ier, -iest) sucio. **∼y trick** n mala jugada f. **∼y word** n palabrota f. —vt ensuciar

disability /dɪsə'bɪlətɪ/ n invalidez f

disable /dɪs'eɪbl/ vt incapacitar. **∼d** a minusválido

disabuse /dɪsə'bju:z/ vt desengañar

disadvantage /dɪsəd'vɑːntɪdʒ/ n desventaja f. **∼d** a desventajado

disagree /dɪsə'gri:/ vi no estar de acuerdo; ‹food, climate› sentar mal a. **∼able** /dɪsə'gri:əbl/ a desagradable. **∼ment** n desacuerdo m; (quarrel) riña f

disappear /dɪsə'pɪə(r)/ vi desaparecer. **∼ance** n desaparición f

disappoint /dɪsə'pɔɪnt/ vt desilusionar, decepcionar. **∼ment** n desilusión f, decepción f

disapproval /dɪsə'pru:vl/ n desaprobación f. **∼e** /dɪsə'pru:v/ vi. **∼ of** desaprobar

disarm /dɪs'ɑːm/ vt/i desarmar. **∼ament** n desarme m

disarray /dɪsə'reɪ/ n desorden m

disaster /dɪ'zɑːstə(r)/ n desastre m. **∼rous** a catastrófico

disband /dɪs'bænd/ vt disolver. —vi disolverse

disbelief /dɪsbɪ'li:f/ n incredulidad f

disc /dɪsk/ n disco m

discard /dɪs'kɑːd/ vt descartar; abandonar ‹beliefs etc›

discern /dɪ'sɜːn/ vt percibir. **∼ible** a perceptible. **∼ing** a perspicaz

discharge /dɪs'tʃɑːdʒ/ vt descargar; cumplir ‹duty›; ‹dismiss› despedir; poner en libertad ‹prisoner›; (mil) licenciar. /'dɪstʃɑːdʒ/ n descarga f; (med) secreción f; (mil) licenciamiento m; (dismissal) despedida f

disciple /dɪ'saɪpl/ n discípulo m

disciplinarian /dɪsɪplɪ'neərɪən/ n ordenancista m & f. **∼ary** a disciplinario. **∼e** /'dɪsɪplɪn/ n disciplina f. —vt disciplinar; (punish) castigar

disc jockey /'dɪskdʒɒkɪ/ n (on radio) pinchadiscos m & f invar

disclaim /dɪs'kleɪm/ vt desconocer. **∼er** n renuncia f

disclose /dɪs'kləʊz/ vt revelar. **∼ure** /-ʒə(r)/ n revelación f

disco /'dɪskəʊ/ n (pl -os) (fam) discoteca f

discolo|ur /dɪsˈkʌlə(r)/ vt decolorar. —vi decolorarse. ~ration /-ˈreɪʃn/ n decoloración f

discomfort /dɪsˈkʌmfət/ n malestar m; (lack of comfort) incomodidad f

disconcert /dɪskənˈsɜːt/ vt desconcertar

disconnect /dɪskəˈnekt/ vt separar; (elec) desconectar

disconsolate /dɪsˈkɒnsələt/ a desconsolado

discontent /dɪskənˈtent/ n descontento m. ~ed a descontento

discontinue /dɪskənˈtɪnjuː/ vt interrumpir

discord /ˈdɪskɔːd/ n discordia f; (mus) disonancia f. ~ant /-ˈskɔːdənt/ a discorde; (mus) disonante

discothèque /ˈdɪskətek/ n discoteca f

discount /ˈdɪskaʊnt/ n descuento m. /dɪsˈkaʊnt/ vt hacer caso omiso de; (com) descontar

discourage /dɪsˈkʌrɪdʒ/ vt desanimar; (dissuade) disuadir

discourse /ˈdɪskɔːs/ n discurso m

discourteous /dɪsˈkɜːtɪəs/ a descortés

discover /dɪsˈkʌvə(r)/ vt descubrir. ~y n descubrimiento m

discredit /dɪsˈkredɪt/ vt (pt discredited) desacreditar. —n descrédito m

discreet /dɪsˈkriːt/ a discreto. ~ly adv discretamente

discrepancy /dɪˈskrepənsɪ/ n discrepancia f

discretion /dɪsˈkreʃn/ n discreción f

discriminat|e /dɪsˈkrɪmɪneɪt/ vt/i discriminar. ~e between distinguir entre. ~ing a perspicaz. ~ion /-ˈneɪʃn/ n discernimiento m; (bias) discriminación f

discus /ˈdɪskəs/ n disco m

discuss /dɪˈskʌs/ vt discutir. ~ion /-ʃn/ n discusión f

disdain /dɪsˈdeɪn/ n desdén m. —vt desdeñar. ~ful a desdeñoso

disease /dɪˈziːz/ n enfermedad f. ~d a enfermo

disembark /dɪsɪmˈbɑːk/ vt/i desembarcar

disembodied /dɪsɪmˈbɒdɪd/ a incorpóreo

disenchant /dɪsɪnˈtʃɑːnt/ vt desencantar. ~ment n desencanto m

disengage /dɪsɪnˈɡeɪdʒ/ vt soltar. ~ the clutch desembragar. ~ment n soltura f

disentangle /dɪsɪnˈtæŋɡl/ vt desenredar

disfavour /dɪsˈfeɪvə(r)/ n desaprobación f. fall into ~ (person) caer en desgracia; (custom, word) caer en desuso

disfigure /dɪsˈfɪɡə(r)/ vt desfigurar

disgorge /dɪsˈɡɔːdʒ/ vt arrojar; (river) descargar; (fig) restituir

disgrace /dɪsˈɡreɪs/ n deshonra f. (disfavour) desgracia f. —vt deshonrar. ~ful a vergonzoso

disgruntled /dɪsˈɡrʌntld/ a descontento

disguise /dɪsˈɡaɪz/ vt disfrazar. —n disfraz m. in ~ disfrazado

disgust /dɪsˈɡʌst/ n repugnancia f, asco m. —vt repugnar, dar asco. ~ing a repugnante, asqueroso

dish /dɪʃ/ n plato m. —vt. ~ out (fam) distribuir. ~ up servir. ~cloth /ˈdɪʃklɒθ/ n bayeta f

dishearten /dɪsˈhɑːtn/ vt desanimar

dishevelled /dɪˈʃevld/ a desaliñado; (hair) despeinado

dishonest /dɪsˈɒnɪst/ a (person) poco honrado; (means) fraudulento. ~y n falta f de honradez

dishonour /dɪs'ɒnə(r)/ n deshonra f. —vt deshonrar. ∼able a deshonroso. ∼ably adv deshonrosamente

dishwasher /'dɪʃwɒʃə(r)/ n lavaplatos m & f

disillusion /dɪsɪ'luːʒn/ vt desilusionar. ∼ment n desilusión f

disincentive /dɪsɪn'sentɪv/ n freno m

disinclined /dɪsɪn'klaɪnd/ a poco dispuesto

disinfect /dɪsɪn'fekt/ vt desinfectar. ∼ant n desinfectante m

disinherit /dɪsɪn'herɪt/ vt desheredar

disintegrate /dɪs'ɪntɪgreɪt/ vt desintegrar. —vi desintegrarse

disinterested /dɪs'ɪntrəstɪd/ a desinteresado

disjointed /dɪs'dʒɔɪntɪd/ a inconexo

disk /dɪsk/ n disco m

dislike /dɪs'laɪk/ n aversión f. —vt tener aversión a

dislocat|**e** /'dɪsləkeɪt/ vt dislocar(se) ⟨limb⟩. ∼ion /-'keɪʃn/ n dislocación f

dislodge /dɪs'lɒdʒ/ vt sacar; ⟨oust⟩ desalojar

disloyal /dɪs'lɔɪəl/ a desleal. ∼ty n deslealtad f

dismal /'dɪzməl/ a triste; ⟨bad⟩ fatal

dismantle /dɪs'mæntl/ vt desarmar

dismay /dɪs'meɪ/ n consternación f. —vt consternar

dismiss /dɪs'mɪs/ vt despedir; ⟨reject⟩ rechazar. ∼al n despedida f; ⟨of idea⟩ abandono m

dismount /dɪs'maʊnt/ vi apearse

disobedien|**ce** /dɪsə'biːdɪəns/ n desobediencia f. ∼t /dɪsə'biːdɪənt/ a desobediente

disobey /dɪsə'beɪ/ vt/i desobedecer

disorder /dɪs'ɔːdə(r)/ n desorden m; ⟨ailment⟩ trastorno m. ∼ly a desordenado

disorganize /dɪs'ɔːgənaɪz/ vt desorganizar

disorientate /dɪs'ɔːrɪənteɪt/ vt desorientar

disown /dɪs'əʊn/ vt repudiar

disparaging /dɪs'pærɪdʒɪŋ/ a despreciativo. ∼ly adv con desprecio

disparity /dɪs'pærətɪ/ n disparidad f

dispassionate /dɪs'pæʃənət/ a desapasionado

dispatch /dɪs'pætʃ/ vt enviar. —n envío m; ⟨report⟩ despacho m. ∼-rider n correo m

dispel /dɪs'pel/ vt (pt **dispelled**) disipar

dispensable /dɪs'pensəbl/ a prescindible

dispensary /dɪs'pensərɪ/ n farmacia f

dispensation /dɪspen'seɪʃn/ n distribución f; ⟨relig⟩ dispensa f

dispense /dɪs'pens/ vt distribuir; ⟨med⟩ preparar; ⟨relig⟩ dispensar; administrar ⟨justice⟩. ∼ with prescindir de. ∼r /-ə(r)/ n ⟨mec⟩ distribuidor m automático; ⟨med⟩ farmacéutico m

dispers|**al** /dɪs'pɜːsl/ n dispersión f. ∼e /dɪs'pɜːs/ vt dispersar. —vi dispersarse

dispirited /dɪs'pɪrɪtɪd/ a desanimado

displace /dɪs'pleɪs/ vt desplazar

display /dɪs'pleɪ/ vt mostrar; exhibir ⟨goods⟩; manifestar ⟨feelings⟩. —n exposición f; ⟨of feelings⟩ manifestación f; ⟨pej⟩ ostentación f

displeas|**e** /dɪs'pliːz/ vt desagradar. be ∼ed with estar disgustado con. ∼ure /-'pleʒə(r)/ n desagrado m

dispos|**able** /dɪs'pəʊzəbl/ a desechable. ∼al n ⟨of waste⟩ eliminación f. at s.o.'s ∼al a la disposición de uno. ∼e /dɪs'pəʊz/ vt disponer. be well

~ed towards estar bien dispuesto hacia. —vi. ~e of deshacerse de

disposition /dɪspə'zɪʃn/ n disposición f

disproportionate /dɪsprə'pɔ:ʃənət/ a desproporcionado

disprove /dɪs'pru:v/ vt refutar

dispute /dɪs'pju:t/ vt disputar. —n disputa f. **in** ~ disputado

disqualif|ication /dɪskwɒlɪfɪ'keɪʃn/ n descalificación f. ~y /dɪs'kwɒlɪfaɪ/ vt incapacitar; (sport) descalificar

disquiet /dɪs'kwaɪət/ n inquietud f

disregard /dɪsrɪ'gɑ:d/ vt no hacer caso de. —n indiferencia f (for a)

disrepair /dɪsrɪ'peə(r)/ n mal estado m

disreputable /dɪs'repjʊtəbl/ a de mala fama

disrepute /dɪsrɪ'pju:t/ n descrédito m

disrespect /dɪsrɪs'pekt/ n falta f de respeto

disrobe /dɪs'rəʊb/ vt desvestir. —vi desvestirse

disrupt /dɪs'rʌpt/ vt interrumpir; trastornar (plans). ~ion /-ʃn/ n interrupción f; (disorder) desorganización f. ~ive a desbaratador

dissatisfaction /dɪsætɪs'fækʃn/ n descontento m

dissatisfied /dɪs'sætɪsfaɪd/ a descontento

dissect /dɪ'sekt/ vt disecar. ~ion /-ʃn/ n disección f

disseminate /dɪ'semɪneɪt/ vt diseminar. ~ion /-'neɪʃn/ n diseminación f

dissent /dɪ'sent/ vi disentir. —n disentimiento m

dissertation /dɪsə'teɪʃn/ n disertación f; (univ) tesis f

disservice /dɪs'sɜ:vɪs/ n mal servicio m

dissident /'dɪsɪdənt/ a & n disidente (m & f)

dissimilar /dɪ'sɪmɪlə(r)/ a distinto

dissipate /'dɪsɪpeɪt/ vt disipar; (fig) desvanecer. ~d a disoluto

dissociate /dɪ'səʊʃɪeɪt/ vt disociar

dissolute /'dɪsəlu:t/ a disoluto. ~ion /dɪsə'lu:ʃn/ n disolución f

dissolve /dɪ'zɒlv/ vt disolver. —vi disolverse

dissuade /dɪ'sweɪd/ vt disuadir

distan|ce /'dɪstəns/ n distancia f. **from a** ~**ce** desde lejos. **in the** ~**ce** a lo lejos. ~**t** /'dɪstənt/ a lejano; (aloof) frío

distaste /dɪs'teɪst/ n aversión f. ~**ful** a desagradable

distemper[1] /dɪs'tempə(r)/ n (paint) temple m. —vt pintar al temple

distemper[2] /dɪs'tempə(r)/ n (of dogs) moquillo m

distend /dɪs'tend/ vt dilatar. —vi dilatarse

distil /dɪs'tɪl/ vt (pt distilled) destilar. ~**lation** /-'leɪʃn/ n destilación f. ~**lery** /dɪs'tɪlərɪ/ n destilería f

distinct /dɪs'tɪŋkt/ a distinto; (clear) claro; (marked) marcado. ~**ion** /-ʃn/ n distinción f; (in exam) sobresaliente m. ~**ive** a distintivo. ~**ly** adv claramente

distinguish /dɪs'tɪŋgwɪʃ/ vt/i distinguir. ~**ed** a distinguido

distort /dɪs'tɔ:t/ vt torcer. ~**ion** /-ʃn/ n deformación f

distract /dɪs'trækt/ vt distraer. ~**ed** a aturdido. ~**ing** a molesto. ~**ion** /-ʃn/ n distracción f; (confusion) aturdimiento m

distraught /dɪs'trɔ:t/ a aturdido

distress /dɪs'tres/ n angustia f; (poverty) miseria f; (danger) peligro m. —vt afligir. ~**ing** a penoso

distribut|e /dɪsˈtrɪbjuːt/ vt distribuir. **∼ion** /-ˈbjuːʃn/ n distribución f. **∼or** n distribuidor m; (auto) distribuidor m de encendido

district /ˈdɪstrɪkt/ n distrito m; (of town) barrio m

distrust /dɪsˈtrʌst/ n desconfianza f. — vt desconfiar de

disturb /dɪsˈtɜːb/ vt molestar; (perturb) inquietar; (move) desordenar; (interrupt) interrumpir. **∼ance** n disturbio m; (tumult) alboroto m. **∼ed** a trastornado. **∼ing** a inquietante

disused /dɪsˈjuːzd/ a fuera de uso

ditch /dɪtʃ/ n zanja f; (for irrigation) acequia f. — vt (sl) abandonar

dither /ˈdɪðə(r)/ vi vacilar

ditto /ˈdɪtəʊ/ adv ídem

divan /dɪˈvæn/ n diván m

dive /daɪv/ vi tirarse de cabeza; (rush) meterse (precipitadamente); (underwater) bucear. — n salto m; (of plane) picado m; (place, fam) taberna f. **∼r** n saltador m; (underwater) buzo m

diverge /daɪˈvɜːdʒ/ vi divergir. **∼nt** /daɪˈvɜːdʒənt/ a divergente

divers|e /daɪˈvɜːs/ a diverso. **∼ify** /daɪˈvɜːsɪfaɪ/ vt diversificar. **∼ity** /daɪˈvɜːsətɪ/ n diversidad f

diver|sion /daɪˈvɜːʃn/ n desvío m; (distraction) diversión f. **∼t** /daɪˈvɜːt/ vt desviar; (entertain) divertir

divest /daɪˈvest/ vt. **∼ of** despojar de

divide /dɪˈvaɪd/ vt dividir. — vi dividirse

dividend /ˈdɪvɪdend/ n dividendo m

divine /dɪˈvaɪn/ a divino

diving-board /ˈdaɪvɪŋbɔːd/ n trampolín m

diving-suit /ˈdaɪvɪŋsuːt/ n escafandra f

divinity /dɪˈvɪnɪtɪ/ n divinidad f

division /dɪˈvɪʒn/ n división f

divorce /dɪˈvɔːs/ n divorcio m. — vt divorciarse de; (judge) divorciar. — vi divorciarse. **∼e** /dɪvɔːˈsiː/ n divorciado m

divulge /daɪˈvʌldʒ/ vt divulgar

DIY abbr see **do-it-yourself**

dizz|iness /ˈdɪzɪnɪs/ n vértigo m. **∼y** /ˈdɪzɪ/ a (-ier, -iest) mareado; (speed) vertiginoso. **be or feel ∼y** marearse

do /duː/ vt (3 sing pres **does**, pt **did**, pp **done**) hacer; (swindle, sl) engañar. — vi hacer; (fare) ir; (be suitable) convenir; (be enough) bastar. — n (pl **dos** or **do's**) (fam) fiesta f. — v aux. **∼ you speak Spanish? Yes I ∼** ¿habla Vd español? Sí. **doesn't he?, don't you?** ¿verdad? **∼ come in!** (emphatic) ¡pase Vd! **∼ away with** abolir. **∼ in** (exhaust, fam) agotar; (kill, sl) matar. **∼ out** (clean) limpiar. **∼ up** abotonar ⟨coat etc⟩; renovar ⟨house⟩. **∼ with** tener que ver con; (need) necesitar. **∼ without** prescindir de. **∼ne for** (fam) arruinado. **∼ne in** (fam) agotado. **well ∼ne** (culin) bien hecho. **well ∼ne!** ¡muy bien!

docile /ˈdəʊsaɪl/ a dócil

dock[1] /dɒk/ n dique m. — vt poner en dique. — vi atracar al muelle

dock[2] /dɒk/ n (jurid) banquillo m de los acusados

dock: ∼er n estibador m. **∼yard** /ˈdɒkjɑːd/ n astillero m

doctor /ˈdɒktə(r)/ n médico m, doctor m; (univ) doctor m. — vt castrar ⟨cat⟩; (fig) adulterar

doctorate /ˈdɒktərət/ n doctorado m

doctrine /ˈdɒktrɪn/ n doctrina f

document /ˈdɒkjʊmənt/ n documento m. **∼ary** /-ˈmentrɪ/ a & n documental (m)

doddering /ˈdɒdərɪŋ/ a chocho

dodge /dɒdʒ/ vt esquivar. —vi esquivarse. —n regate m; (fam) truco m

dodgems /'dɒdʒəmz/ npl autos mpl de choque

dodgy /'dɒdʒɪ/ a (-ier, -iest) ⟨awkward⟩ difícil

does /dʌz/ see do

doesn't /'dʌznt/ = does not

dog /dɒg/ n perro m. —vt (pt dogged) perseguir. **~-collar** n (relig, fam) alzacuello m. **~-eared** a ⟨book⟩ sobado

dogged /'dɒgɪd/ a obstinado

doghouse /'dɒghaʊs/ n (Amer) perrera f. **in the ~** (sl) en desgracia

dogma /'dɒgmə/ n dogma m. **~tic** /-'mætɪk/ a dogmático

dogsbody /'dɒgzbɒdɪ/ n (fam) burro m de carga

doh /dəʊ/ n (mus, first note of any musical scale) do m

doily /'dɔɪlɪ/ n tapete m

doings /'duːɪŋz/ npl (fam) actividades fpl

do-it-yourself /duːɪtjɔːˈself/ (abbr **DIY**) n bricolaje m. **~ enthusiast** n manitas m

doldrums /'dɒldrəmz/ npl. **be in the ~** estar abatido

dole /dəʊl/ vt. **~ out** distribuir. —n (fam) subsidio m de paro. **on the ~** (fam) parado

doleful /'dəʊlfl/ a triste

doll /dɒl/ n muñeca f. —vt. **~ up** (fam) emperejilar

dollar /'dɒlə(r)/ n dólar m

dollop /'dɒləp/ n (fam) masa f

dolphin /'dɒlfɪn/ n delfín m

domain /dəʊˈmeɪn/ n dominio m; (fig) campo m

dome /dəʊm/ n cúpula f. **~d** a abovedado

domestic /dəˈmestɪk/ a doméstico; ⟨trade, flights, etc⟩ nacional

domesticated a ⟨animal⟩ domesticado

domesticity /dɒmeˈstɪsɪtɪ/ n domesticidad f

domestic: **~ science** n economía f doméstica. **~ servant** n doméstico m

dominant /'dɒmɪnənt/ a dominante

dominat|e /'dɒmɪneɪt/ vt/i dominar. **~ion** /-'neɪʃn/ n dominación f

domineer /dɒmɪˈnɪə(r)/ vi tiranizar

Dominican Republic /dəmɪnɪkən rɪˈpʌblɪk/ n República f Dominicana

dominion /dəˈmɪnjən/ n dominio m

domino /'dɒmɪnəʊ/ n (pl **~es**) ficha f de dominó. **~es** npl (game) dominó m

don¹ /dɒn/ n profesor m

don² /dɒn/ vt (pt **donned**) ponerse

donate /dəʊˈneɪt/ vt donar. **~ion** /-ʃn/ n donativo m

done /dʌn/ see do

donkey /'dɒŋkɪ/ n burro m. **~-work** n trabajo m penoso

donor /'dəʊnə(r)/ n donante m & f

don't /dəʊnt/ = do not

doodle /'duːdl/ vi garrapatear

doom /duːm/ n destino m; (death) muerte f. —vt. **be ~ed to** ser condenado a

doomsday /'duːmzdeɪ/ n día m del juicio final

door /dɔː(r)/ n puerta f. **~man** /'dɔːmæn/ n (pl **-men**) portero m. **~mat** /'dɔːmæt/ n felpudo m. **~step** /'dɔːstep/ n peldaño m. **~way** /'dɔːweɪ/ n entrada f

dope /dəʊp/ n (fam) droga f; (idiot, sl) imbécil m. —vt (fam) drogar. **~y** a (sl) tonto

dormant /'dɔːmənt/ a inactivo

dormer /'dɔːmə(r)/ n. **~ (window)** buhardilla f

dormitory /'dɔːmɪtrɪ/ n dormitorio m

dormouse /'dɔːmaʊs/ n (pl -mice) lirón m

dos|age /'dəʊsɪdʒ/ n dosis f. ~e /dəʊs/ n dosis f

doss /dɒs/ vi (sl) dormir. ~house n refugio m

dot /dɒt/ n punto m. on the ~ in punto. —vt (pt dotted) salpicar. **be ~ted with** estar salpicado de

dote /dəʊt/ vi. ~ on adorar

dotted line /dɒtɪd'laɪn/ n línea f de puntos

dotty /'dɒtɪ/ a (-ier, -iest) (fam) chiflado

double /'dʌbl/ a doble. —adv doble, dos veces. —n (person) doble m & f. **at the ~** corriendo. —vt doblar; (efforts etc). —vi doblarse. ~**-bass** n contrabajo m. ~ **bed** n cama f de matrimonio. ~**-breasted** a cruzado. ~**-chin** n papada f. ~**-cross** vt traicionar. ~**-dealing** n doblez m & f. ~**-decker** n autobús m de dos pisos. ~ **Dutch** n galimatías m. ~**-jointed** a con articulaciones dobles. ~**s** npl (tennis) doble m

doubt /daʊt/ n duda f. —vt dudar; (distrust) dudar de, desconfiar de. ~**ful** a dudoso. ~**less** adv sin duda

doubly /'dʌblɪ/ adv doblemente

dough /dəʊ/ n masa f; (money, sl) dinero m, pasta f (sl)

doughnut /'dəʊnʌt/ n buñuelo m

douse /daʊs/ vt mojar; apagar (fire)

dove /dʌv/ n paloma f

dowager /'daʊədʒə(r)/ n viuda f (con bienes o título del marido)

dowdy /'daʊdɪ/ a (-ier, -iest) poco atractivo

down[1] /daʊn/ adv abajo. ~ **with** abajo. **come** ~ bajar. **go** ~ bajar; (sun) ponerse. —prep

abajo. —a (sad) triste. —vt derribar; (drink, fam) beber

down[2] /daʊn/ n (feathers) plumón m

down-and-out /'daʊnənd'aʊt/ n vagabundo m

downcast /'daʊnkɑːst/ a abatido

downfall /'daʊnfɔːl/ n caída f; (fig) perdición f

downgrade /daʊn'greɪd/ vt degradar

down-hearted /daʊn'hɑːtɪd/ a abatido

downhill /daʊn'hɪl/ adv cuesta abajo

down payment /'daʊnpeɪmənt/ n depósito m

downpour /'daʊnpɔː(r)/ n aguacero m

downright /'daʊnraɪt/ a completo; (honest) franco. —adv completamente

downs /daʊnz/ npl colinas fpl

downstairs /daʊn'steəz/ adv abajo. /'daʊnsteəz/ a de abajo

downstream /'daʊnstriːm/ adv río abajo

down-to-earth /daʊntʊ'ɜːθ/ a práctico

downtrodden /'daʊntrɒdn/ a oprimido

down: ~ **under** en las antípodas; (in Australia) en Australia. ~**ward** /'daʊnwəd/ a & adv, ~**wards** adv hacia abajo

dowry /'daʊrɪ/ n dote f

doze /dəʊz/ vi dormitar. ~ **off** dormitar, dar una cabezada. —n sueño m ligero

dozen /'dʌzn/ n docena f. ~**s** of (fam) miles de, muchos

Dr abbr (Doctor) Dr, Doctor m. ~ **Broadley** (el) Doctor Broadley

drab /dræb/ a poco atractivo

draft /drɑːft/ n borrador m; (outline) bosquejo m; (com) letra f de cambio; (Amer, mil) reclutamiento m; (Amer, of air) corriente f de aire. —vt bosquejar;

drag /dræg/ *vt* (*pt* dragged) arrastrar; rastrear ‹*river*›. —*vi* arrastrarse por el suelo. —*n* (*fam*) lata *f*. **in** ~ (*man, sl*) vestido de mujer

dragon /'drægən/ *n* dragón *m*

dragon-fly /'drægənflaɪ/ *n* libélula *f*

drain /dreɪn/ *vt* desaguar; apurar ‹*tank, glass*›; (*fig*) agotar. —*vi* escurrirse. —*n* desaguadero *m*. **be a** ~ **on** agotar. ~**ing-board** *n* escurridero *m*

drama /'drɑːmə/ *n* drama *m*; (*art*) arte *m* teatral. ~**tic** /drə'mætɪk/ *a* dramático. ~**tist** /'dræmətɪst/ *n* dramaturgo *m*. ~**tize** /'dræmətaɪz/ *vt* adaptar al teatro; (*fig*) dramatizar

drank /dræŋk/ *see* **drink**

drape /dreɪp/ *vt* cubrir; (*hang*) colgar. ~**s** *npl* (*Amer*) cortinas *fpl*

drastic /'dræstɪk/ *a* drástico

draught /drɑːft/ *n* corriente *f* de aire. ~ **beer** *n* cerveza *f* de barril. ~**s** *n pl* (*game*) juego *m* de damas

draughtsman /'drɑːftsmən/ *n* (*pl* -men) diseñador *m*

draughty /'drɑːftɪ/ *a* lleno de corrientes de aire

draw /drɔː/ *vt* (*pt* drew, *pp* drawn) tirar; (*attract*) atraer; dibujar ‹*picture*›; trazar ‹*line*›; retirar ‹*money*›. ~ **the line** at trazar el límite. —*vi* (*sport*) empatar; dibujar ‹*pictures*›; (*in lottery*) sortear. —*n* (*sport*) empate *m*; (*in lottery*) sorteo *m*. ~ **in** ‹*days*› acortarse. ~ **out** sacar ‹*money*›. ~ **up** pararse; redactar ‹*document*›; acercar ‹*chair*›

drawback /'drɔːbæk/ *n* desventaja *f*

drawbridge /'drɔːbrɪdʒ/ *n* puente *m* levadizo

drawer /drɔː(r)/ *n* cajón *m*. ~**s** /drɔːz/ *npl* calzoncillos *mpl*; (*women's*) bragas *fpl*

drawing /'drɔːɪŋ/ *n* dibujo *m*. ~**pin** *n* chinche *m*, chincheta *f*

drawing-room /'drɔːɪŋruːm/ *n* salón *m*

drawl /drɔːl/ *n* habla *f* lenta

drawn /drɔːn/ *see* **draw**. —*a* ‹*face*› ojeroso

dread /dred/ *n* terror *m*. —*vt* temer. ~**ful** /dredfl/ *a* terrible. ~**fully** *adv* terriblemente

dream /driːm/ *n* sueño *m*. —*vt/i* (*pt* **dreamed** *or* **dreamt**) soñar. —*a* ideal. ~ **up** idear. ~**er** *n* soñador *m*. ~**y** *a* soñador

drear|iness /'drɪərɪnɪs/ *n* tristeza *f*; (*monotony*) monotonía *f*. ~**y** /'drɪərɪ/ *a* (-ier, -iest) triste; (*boring*) monótono

dredge[1] /dredʒ/ *n* draga *f*. —*vt* dragar

dredge[2] /dredʒ/ *n* (*culin*) espolvorear

dredger[1] /'dredʒə(r)/ *n* draga *f*

dredger[2] /'dredʒə(r)/ *n* (*for sugar*) espolvoreador *m*

dregs /dregz/ *npl* heces *fpl*; (*fig*) hez *f*

drench /drentʃ/ *vt* empapar

dress /dres/ *n* vestido *m*; (*clothing*) ropa *f*. —*vt* vestir; (*decorate*) adornar; (*med*) vendar; (*culin*) aderezar, aliñar. —*vi* vestirse. ~ **circle** *n* primer palco *m*

dresser[1] /'dresə(r)/ *n* (*furniture*) aparador *m*

dresser[2] /'dresə(r)/ *n* (*in theatre*) camarero *m*

dressing /'dresɪŋ/ *n* (*sauce*) aliño *m*; (*bandage*) vendaje *m*. ~**case** *n* neceser *m*. ~**down** *n* rapapolvo *m*, reprensión *f*. ~**gown** *n* bata *f*. ~**room** *n* tocador *m*; (*in theatre*) camarín *m*. ~**table** *n* tocador *m*

dressmak|er /ˈdresmeɪkə(r)/ n modista m & f. **~ing** n costura f

dress rehearsal /ˈdresrɪhɜːsl/ n ensayo m general

dressy /ˈdresɪ/ a (-ier, -iest) elegante

drew /druː/ see draw

dribble /ˈdrɪbl/ vi gotear; ⟨baby⟩ babear; ⟨in football⟩ regatear

dribs and drabs /drɪbznˈdræbz/ npl. in ~ poco a poco, en cantidades pequeñas

drie|d /draɪd/ a ⟨food⟩ seco; ⟨fruit⟩ paso. **~r** /ˈdraɪə(r)/ n secador m

drift /drɪft/ vi ir a la deriva; ⟨snow⟩ amontonarse. —n ⟨movement⟩ dirección f; ⟨of snow⟩ montón m; ⟨meaning⟩ significado m. **~er** n persona f sin rumbo. **~wood** /ˈdrɪftwʊd/ n madera f flotante

drill /drɪl/ n ⟨tool⟩ taladro m; ⟨training⟩ ejercicio m; ⟨fig⟩ lo normal. —vt taladrar, perforar; ⟨train⟩ entrenar. —vi entrenarse

drily /ˈdraɪlɪ/ adv secamente

drink /drɪŋk/ vt/i ⟨pt drank, pp drunk⟩ beber. —n bebida f. **~able** a bebible; ⟨water⟩ potable. **~er** n bebedor m. **~ing-water** n agua f potable

drip /drɪp/ vi ⟨pt dripped⟩ gotear. —n gota f; ⟨med⟩ goteo m intravenoso; ⟨person, sl⟩ mentecato m. **~-dry** a que no necesita plancharse

dripping /ˈdrɪpɪŋ/ n ⟨culin⟩ pringue m

drive /draɪv/ vt ⟨pt drove, pp driven⟩ empujar; conducir, manejar ⟨LAm⟩ ⟨car etc⟩. **~ in** clavar ⟨nail⟩. **~ s.o. mad** volver loco a uno. —vi conducir. **~ in** ⟨in car⟩ entrar en coche. —n paseo m; ⟨road⟩ calle f; ⟨private road⟩ camino m de entrada; ⟨fig⟩ energía f; ⟨pol⟩ campaña f. **~ at**

querer decir. **~r** /ˈdraɪvə(r)/ n conductor m, chófer m ⟨LAm⟩

drivel /ˈdrɪvl/ n tonterías fpl

driving /ˈdraɪvɪŋ/ n conducción f. **~-licence** n carné m de conducir. **~ school** n autoescuela f

drizzl|e /ˈdrɪzl/ n llovizna f. —vi lloviznar. **~y** a lloviznoso

dromedary /ˈdromədərɪ/ n dromedario m

drone /drəʊn/ n ⟨noise⟩ zumbido m; ⟨bee⟩ zángano m. —vi zumbar; ⟨fig⟩ hablar en voz monótona; ⟨idle, fam⟩ holgazanear

drool /druːl/ vi babear

droop /druːp/ vt inclinar. —vi inclinarse; ⟨flowers⟩ marchitarse

drop /drop/ n gota f; ⟨fall⟩ caída f; ⟨decrease⟩ baja f; ⟨of cliff⟩ precipicio m. —vt ⟨pt dropped⟩ dejar caer; ⟨lower⟩ bajar. —vi caer. **~ in on** pasar por casa de. **~ off** ⟨sleep⟩ dormirse. **~ out** retirarse; ⟨student⟩ abandonar los estudios. **~-out** n marginado m

droppings /ˈdropɪŋz/ npl excremento m

dross /dros/ n escoria f

drought /draʊt/ n sequía f

drove¹ /drəʊv/ see drive

drove² /drəʊv/ n manada f

drown /draʊn/ vt ahogar. —vi ahogarse

drowsy /ˈdraʊzɪ/ a soñoliento

drudge /drʌdʒ/ n esclavo m del trabajo. **~ry** /-ərɪ/ n trabajo m pesado

drug /drʌg/ n droga f; ⟨med⟩ medicamento m. —vt ⟨pt drugged⟩ drogar. **~ addict** n toxicómano m

drugstore /ˈdrʌgstɔː(r)/ n ⟨Amer⟩ farmacia f ⟨que vende otros artículos también⟩

drum /drʌm/ n tambor m; ⟨for oil⟩ bidón m. —vi ⟨pt drummed⟩ tocar el tambor. —vt. **~ into s.o.**

inculcar en la mente de uno.
~**mer** n tambor m; (in group)
batería f. ~**s** npl batería f.
~**stick** /'drʌmstik/ n baqueta f,
(culin) pierna f (de pollo)
drunk /drʌŋk/ see **drink**. —a
borracho. **get** ~ emborracharse. ~**ard** n borracho m.
~**en** a borracho. ~**enness** n
embriaguez f
dry /drai/ a (**drier, driest**)
seco. —vt secar. —vi secarse. ~
up (fam) secar los platos.
~-**clean** vt limpiar en seco.
~-**cleaner** n tintorero m. ~
cleaner's (shop) tintorería f.
~**ness** n sequedad f
dual /'dju:əl/ a doble. ~ **carriageway** n autovía f, carretera
f de doble calzada. ~**purpose** a
de doble uso
dub /dʌb/ vt (pt **dubbed**) doblar
(film); (nickname) apodar
dubious /'dju:biəs/ a dudoso;
(person) sospechoso
duchess /'dʌtʃis/ n duquesa f
duck[1] /dʌk/ n pato m
duck[2] /dʌk/ vt sumergir; bajar
(head etc). —vi agacharse
duckling /'dʌkliŋ/ n patito m
duct /dʌkt/ n conducto m
dud /dʌd/ a inútil; (cheque) sin
fondos; (coin) falso
due /dju:/ a debido; (expected)
esperado. ~ **to** debido a. —adv.
~ **north** npl derechos mpl al
norte. ~**s** npl derechos mpl
duel /'dju:əl/ n duelo m
duet /dju:'et/ n dúo m
duffle /'dʌfl/ a. ~ **bag** n bolsa f de
lona. ~-**coat** n trenca f
dug /dʌg/ see **dig**
duke /dju:k/ n duque m
dull /dʌl/ a (**-er, -est**) (weather)
gris; (colour) apagado; (person,
play, etc) pesado; (sound) sordo;
(stupid) torpe. —vt aliviar
(pain); entorpecer (mind)
duly /'dju:li/ adv debidamente

dumb /dʌm/ a (**-er, -est**) mudo;
(fam) estúpido
dumbfound /dʌm'faʊnd/ vt
pasmar
dummy /'dʌmi/ n muñeco m; (of
tailor) maniquí m; (of baby) chupete m. —a falso. ~ **run** n
prueba f
dump /dʌmp/ vt descargar; (fam)
deshacerse de. —n vertedero m;
(mil) depósito m; (fam) lugar m
desagradable. **be down in the**
~**s** estar deprimido
dumpling /'dʌmpliŋ/ n bola f de
masa hervida
dumpy /'dʌmpi/ a (**-ier, -iest**)
regordete
dunce /dʌns/ n burro m
dung /dʌŋ/ n excremento m;
(manure) estiércol m
dungarees /dʌŋgə'ri:z/ npl mono
m peto m
dungeon /'dʌndʒən/ n calabozo
m
dunk /dʌŋk/ vt remojar
duo /'dju:əʊ/ n dúo m
dupe /dju:p/ vt engañar. —n
inocentón m
duplicat|e /'dju:plikət/ a & n
duplicado (m). /'dju:plikeit/ vt
duplicar; (on machine) reproducir. ~**or** n multicopista f
duplicity /dju:'plisəti/ n doblez f
durable /'djʊərəbl/ a resistente;
(enduring) duradero
duration /djʊ'reiʃn/ n duración f
duress /djʊ'res/ n coacción f
during /'djʊəriŋ/ prep durante
dusk /dʌsk/ n crepúsculo m
dusky /'dʌski/ a (**-ier, -iest**)
oscuro
dust /dʌst/ n polvo m. —vt quitar
el polvo a; (sprinkle) espolvorear
dustbin /'dʌstbin/ n cubo m de la
basura
dust-cover /'dʌstkʌvə(r)/ n
sobrecubierta f
duster /'dʌstə(r)/ n trapo m

dust-jacket /'dʌstdʒækɪt/ n sobrecubierta f

dustman /'dʌstmən/ n (pl -men) basurero m

dustpan /'dʌstpæn/ n recogedor m

dusty /'dʌstɪ/ a (-ier, -iest) polvoriento

Dutch /dʌtʃ/ a & n holandés (m). go ~ pagar a escote. ~man n holandés m. ~woman n holandesa f

dutiful /'dju:tɪfl/ a obediente

duty /'dju:tɪ/ n deber m; (tax) derechos mpl de aduana. on ~ de servicio. ~-free a libre de impuestos

duvet /dju:veɪ/ n edredón m

dwarf /dwɔ:f/ n (pl -s) enano m. —vt empequeñecer

dwell /dwel/ vi (pt dwelt) morar. ~ on dilatarse. ~er n habitante m & f. ~ing n morada f

dwindle /'dwɪndl/ vi disminuir

dye /daɪ/ vt (pres p dyeing) teñir. —n tinte m

dying /'daɪɪŋ/ see die

dynamic /daɪ'næmɪk/ a dinámico. ~s npl dinámica f

dynamite /'daɪnəmaɪt/ n dinamita f. —vt dinamitar

dynamo /'daɪnəməʊ/ n dinamo f, dínamo f

dynasty /'dɪnəstɪ/ n dinastía f

dysentery /'dɪsəntrɪ/ n disentería f

dyslexia /dɪs'leksɪə/ n dislexia f

E

each /i:tʃ/ a cada. —pron cada uno. ~ one cada uno. ~ other uno a otro, el uno al otro. they love ~ other se aman

eager /'i:gə(r)/ a impaciente; (enthusiastic) ávido. ~ly adv

con impaciencia. ~ness n impaciencia f, ansia f

eagle /'i:gl/ n águila f

ear[1] /ɪə(r)/ n oído m; (outer) oreja f

ear[2] /ɪə(r)/ n (of corn) espiga f

ear: ~ache /'ɪəreɪk/ n dolor m de oído. ~drum n tímpano m

earl /ɜ:l/ n conde m

early /'ɜ:lɪ/ a (-ier, -iest) temprano; (before expected time) prematuro. in the ~ spring a principios de la primavera. —adv temprano; (ahead of time) con anticipación

earmark /'ɪəmɑ:k/ vt. ~ for destinar a

earn /ɜ:n/ vt ganar; (deserve) merecer

earnest /'ɜ:nɪst/ a serio. in ~ en serio

earnings /'ɜ:nɪŋz/ npl ingresos m; (com) ganacias fpl

ear: ~phones /'ɪəfəʊnz/ npl auricular m. ~ring n pendiente m

earshot /'ɪəʃɒt/ n. within ~ al alcance del oído

earth /ɜ:θ/ n tierra f. —vt (elec) conectar a tierra. ~ly a terrenal

earthenware /'ɜ:θnweə(r)/ n loza f de barro

earthquake /'ɜ:θkweɪk/ n terremoto m

earthy /'ɜ:θɪ/ a terroso; (coarse) grosero

earwig /'ɪəwɪg/ n tijereta f

ease /i:z/ n facilidad f; (comfort) tranquilidad f. at ~ a gusto; (mil) en posición de descanso. ill at ~ molesto. with ~ fácilmente. —vt calmar; aliviar (pain); tranquilizar (mind); (loosen) aflojar. —vi calmarse; (lessen) disminuir

easel /'i:zl/ n caballete m

east /i:st/ n este m, oriente m. —a del este, oriental. —adv hacia el este.

Easter /'i:stə(r)/ n Semana f Santa; (relig) Pascua f de Resurrección. − **egg** n huevo m de Pascua

east: ~**erly** a este; (wind) del este. ~**ern** a del este, oriental. ~**ward** adv, ~**wards** adv hacia el este

easy /'i:zi/ a (-ier, -iest) fácil; (relaxed) tranquilo. **go** ~ **on** (fam) tener cuidado con. **take it** ~ no preocuparse. −int ¡despacio! ~ **chair** n sillón m. ~**going** a acomodadizo

eat /i:t/ vt/i (pt ate, pp eaten) comer. ~ **into** corroer. ~**able** a comestible. ~**er** n comedor m

eau-de-Cologne /ɔʊdəkə'ləʊn/ n agua f de colonia

eaves /i:vz/ npl alero m

eavesdrop /'i:vzdrɒp/ vi (pt -dropped) escuchar a escondidas

ebb /eb/ n reflujo m. −vi bajar; (fig) decaer

ebony /'ebənɪ/ n ébano m

ebullient /ɪ'bʌlɪənt/ a exuberante

EC /i:'si:/ abbr (European Community) CE (Comunidad f Europea)

eccentric /ɪk'sentrɪk/ a & n excéntrico (m). ~**ity** /eksen'trɪsətɪ/ n excentricidad f

ecclesiastical /ɪkli:zɪ'æstɪkl/ a eclesiástico

echelon /'eʃəlɒn/ n escalón m

echo /'ekəʊ/ n (pl -oes) eco m. −vt (pt echoed, pres p echoing) repetir; (imitate) imitar. −vi hacer eco

eclectic /ɪk'lektɪk/ a & n ecléctico (m)

eclipse /ɪ'klɪps/ n eclipse m. −vt eclipsar

ecology /ɪ'kɒlədʒɪ/ n ecología f

economic /i:kə'nɒmɪk/ a económico. ~**ical** a económico. ~**ics** n economía f. ~**ist**

/ɪ'kɒnəmɪst/ n economista m & f. ~**ize** /ɪ'kɒnəmaɪz/ vi economizar. ~**y** /ɪ'kɒnəmɪ/ n economía f

ecstasy /'ekstəsɪ/ n éxtasis f. ~**tic** /ɪk'stætɪk/ a extático. ~**tically** adv con éxtasis

Ecuador /'ekwədɔ:(r)/ n el Ecuador m

ecumenical /i:kju:'menɪkl/ a ecuménico

eddy /'edɪ/ n remolino m

edge /edʒ/ n borde m, margen m; (of knife) filo m; (of town) afueras fpl. **have the** ~ **on** (fam) llevar la ventaja a. **on** ~ nervioso. −vt ribetear; (move) mover poco a poco. −vi avanzar cautelosamente. ~**ways** adv de lado

edging /'edʒɪŋ/ n borde m; (sewing) ribete m

edgy /'edʒɪ/ a nervioso

edible /'edɪbl/ a comestible

edict /'i:dɪkt/ n edicto m

edifice /'edɪfɪs/ n edificio m

edify /'edɪfaɪ/ vt edificar

edit /'edɪt/ vt dirigir (newspaper); preparar una edición de (text); (write) redactar; montar (film). ~**ed by** a cargo de. ~**ion** /ɪ'dɪʃn/ n edición f. ~**or** /'edɪtə(r)/ n (of newspaper) director m; (of text) redactor m. ~**orial** /edɪ'tɔ:rɪəl/ a editorial. −n artículo m de fondo. ~**or in chief** n jefe m de redacción

educat|e /'edʒʊkeɪt/ vt instruir, educar. ~**ed** a culto. ~**ion** /-'keɪʃn/ n enseñanza f; (culture) cultura f; (upbringing) educación f. ~**ional** /-'keɪʃənl/ a instructivo

EEC /i:'i:si:/ abbr (European Economic Community) CEE (Comunidad f Económica Europea)

eel /i:l/ n anguila f

eerie /'ɪərɪ/ a (-ier, -iest) misterioso

efface /ɪ'feɪs/ vt borrar
effect /ɪ'fekt/ n efecto m. **in ~** efectivamente. **take ~** entrar en vigor. —vt efectuar
effective /ɪ'fektɪv/ a eficaz; (striking) impresionante; (mil) efectivo. **~ly** adv eficazmente. **~ness** n eficacia f
effeminate /ɪ'femɪnət/ a afeminado
effervescent /efə'vesnt/ a efervescente
effete /ɪ'fiːt/ a agotado
efficien|cy /ɪ'fɪʃənsɪ/ n eficiencia f; (mec) rendimiento m. **~t** /ɪ'fɪʃnt/ a eficiente. **~tly** adv eficientemente
effigy /'efɪdʒɪ/ n efigie f
effort /'efət/ n esfuerzo m. **~less** a fácil
effrontery /ɪ'frʌntərɪ/ n descaro m
effusive /ɪ'fjuːsɪv/ a efusivo
e.g. /ɪː'dʒiː/ abbr (exempli gratia) p.ej., por ejemplo
egalitarian /ɪgælɪ'teərɪən/ a & n igualitario (m)
egg[1] /eg/ n huevo m
egg[2] /eg/ vt. **~ on** (fam) incitar
egg-cup /'egkʌp/ n huevera f
egg-plant /'egplɑːnt/ n berenjena f
eggshell /'egʃel/ n cáscara f de huevo
ego /'iːgəʊ/ n (pl -os) yo m. **~ism** n egoísmo m. **~ist** n egoísta m & f. **~centric** /iːgəʊ'sentrɪk/ a egocéntrico. **~tism** n egotismo m. **~tist** n egotista m & f
Egypt /'iːdʒɪpt/ n Egipto m. **~ian** /ɪ'dʒɪpʃn/ a & n egipcio (m)
eh /eɪ/ int (fam) ¡eh!
eiderdown /'aɪdədaʊn/ n edredón m
eight /eɪt/ a & n ocho (m)
eighteen /eɪ'tiːn/ a & n dieciocho (m). **~th** a & n decimoctavo (m)
eighth /eɪtθ/ a & n octavo (m)
eight|ieth /'eɪtɪəθ/ a & n ochenta (m), octogésimo (m). **~y** /'eɪtɪ/ a & n ochenta (m)

either /'aɪðə(r)/ a cualquiera de los dos; (negative) ninguno de los dos; (each) cada. —pron uno u otro; (with negative) ni uno ni otro. —adv (negative) tampoco. —conj o. **~ he or** o él o; (with negative) ni él ni
ejaculate /ɪ'dʒækjʊleɪt/ vt/i (exclaim) exclamar
eject /ɪ'dʒekt/ vt expulsar, echar
eke /iːk/ vt. **~ out** hacer bastar; (increase) complementar
elaborate /ɪ'læbərət/ a complicado. /ɪ'læbəreɪt/ vt elaborar. —vi explicarse
elapse /ɪ'læps/ vi (of time) transcurrir
elastic /ɪ'læstɪk/ a & n elástico (m). **~ band** n goma f (elástica)
elasticity /ɪlæ'stɪsətɪ/ n elasticidad f
elat|ed /ɪ'leɪtɪd/ a regocijado. **~ion** /-ʃn/ n regocijo m
elbow /'elbəʊ/ n codo m
elder[1] /'eldə(r)/ a & n mayor (m)
elder[2] /'eldə(r)/ n (tree) saúco m
elderly /'eldəlɪ/ a mayor, anciano
eldest /'eldɪst/ a & n el mayor (m)
elect /ɪ'lekt/ vt elegir. **~ to do** decidir hacer. —a electo. **~ion** /-ʃn/ n elección f
elector /ɪ'lektə(r)/ n elector m. **~al** a electoral. **~ate** n electorado m
electric /ɪ'lektrɪk/ a eléctrico. **~al** a eléctrico. **~ blanket** n manta f eléctrica. **~ian** /ɪlek'trɪʃn/ n electricista m & f. **~ity** /ɪlek'trɪsətɪ/ n electricidad f
electrify /ɪ'lektrɪfaɪ/ vt electrificar; (fig) electrizar
electrocute /ɪ'lektrəkjuːt/ vt electrocutar
electrolysis /ɪlek'trɒlɪsɪs/ n electrólisis f
electron /ɪ'lektrɒn/ n electrón m

electronic /ɪlek'trɒnɪk/ a electrónico. **~s** n electrónica f

elegan|ce /'eligəns/ n elegancia f. **~t** /'eligənt/ a elegante. **~tly** adv elegantemente

element /'elimənt/ n elemento m. **~ary** /-'mentrɪ/ a elemental

elephant /'elifənt/ n elefante m

elevat|e /'eliveɪt/ vt elevar. **~ion** /-'veɪʃn/ n elevación f. **~or** /'eliveɪtə(r)/ n (Amer) ascensor m

eleven /ɪ'levn/ a & n once (m). **~th** a & n undécimo (m)

elf /elf/ n (pl elves) duende m

elicit /ɪ'lɪsɪt/ vt sacar

eligible /'elɪdʒəbl/ a elegible. be **~ for** tener derecho a

eliminat|e /ɪ'lɪmɪneɪt/ vt eliminar. **~ion** /-'neɪʃn/ n eliminación f

élite /eɪ'li:t/ n elite f, élite m

elixir /ɪ'lɪksɪə(r)/ n elixir m

ellip|se /ɪ'lɪps/ n elipse f. **~tical** a elíptico

elm /elm/ n olmo m

elocution /elə'kju:ʃn/ n elocución f

elongate /'i:lɒŋgeɪt/ vt alargar

elope /ɪ'ləʊp/ vi fugarse con el amante. **~ment** n fuga f

eloquen|ce /'eləkwəns/ n elocuencia f. **~t** /'eləkwənt/ a elocuente. **~tly** adv con elocuencia

El Salvador /el'sælvədɔ:(r)/ n El Salvador m

else /els/ adv más. everybody **~** todos los demás. nobody **~** ningún otro, nadie más. nothing **~** nada más. or **~** o bien. some-where **~** en otra parte

elsewhere /els'weə(r)/ adv en otra parte

elucidate /ɪ'lu:sɪdeɪt/ vt aclarar

elude /ɪ'lu:d/ vt eludir

elusive /ɪ'lu:sɪv/ a esquivo

emaciated /ɪ'meɪʃɪeɪtɪd/ a esquelético

emanate /'eməneɪt/ vi emanar

emancipat|e /ɪ'mænsɪpeɪt/ vt emancipar. **~ion** /-'peɪʃn/ n emancipación f

embalm /ɪm'ba:m/ vt embalsamar

embankment /ɪm'bæŋkmənt/ n terraplén m; (of river) dique m

embargo /ɪm'ba:gəʊ/ n (pl -oes) prohibición f

embark /ɪm'ba:k/ vt embarcar. **—vi** embarcarse. **~ on** (fig) emprender. **~ation** /emba:'keɪʃn/ n (of people) embarco m; (of goods) embarque m

embarrass /ɪm'bærəs/ vt desconcertar; (shame) dar vergüenza. **~ment** n desconcierto m; (shame) vergüenza f

embassy /'embəsɪ/ n embajada f

embed /ɪm'bed/ vt (pt embedded) embutir; (fig) fijar

embellish /ɪm'belɪʃ/ vt embellecer. **~ment** n embellecimiento m

embers /'embəz/ npl ascua f

embezzle /ɪm'bezl/ vt desfalcar. **~ment** n desfalco m

embitter /ɪm'bɪtə(r)/ vt amargar

emblem /'embləm/ n emblema m

embodi|ment /ɪm'bɒdɪmənt/ n encarnación f. **~y** /ɪm'bɒdɪ/ vt encarnar; (include) incluir

emboss /ɪm'bɒs/ vt grabar en relieve, repujar. **~ed** a en relieve, repujado

embrace /ɪm'breɪs/ vt abrazar; (fig) abarcar. **—vi** abrazarse. **—n** abrazo m

embroider /ɪm'brɔɪdə(r)/ vt bordar. **~y** n bordado m

embroil /ɪm'brɔɪl/ vt enredar

embryo /'embrɪəʊ/ n (pl -os) embrión m. **~nic** /-'ɒnɪk/ a embrionario

emend /ɪ'mend/ vt enmendar

emerald /'emərəld/ n esmeralda f

emerge /ɪ'mɜ:dʒ/ vi salir. **~nce** /-əns/ n aparición f

emergency /ı'mɜːdʒənsı/ n emergencia f. **in an ~** en caso de emergencia. **~ exit** n salida f de emergencia

emery /'eməri/ n esmeril m. **~board** n lima f de uñas

emigrant /'emɪɡrənt/ n emigrante m & f

emigrat|e /'emɪɡreɪt/ vi emigrar. **~ion** /-'ɡreɪʃn/ n emigración f

eminen|ce /'emɪnəns/ n eminencia f. **~t** /'emɪnənt/ a eminente. **~tly** adv eminentemente

emissary /'emɪsərı/ n emisario m

emission /ı'mɪʃn/ n emisión f

emit /ı'mɪt/ vt (pt **emitted**) emitir

emollient /ı'mɒlɪənt/ a & n emoliente (m)

emoti|on /ı'məʊʃn/ n emoción f. **~onal** a emocional; (person) emotivo; (moving) conmovedor. **~ve** /ı'məʊtɪv/ a emotivo

empathy /'empəθı/ n empatía f

emperor /'empərə(r)/ n emperador m

emphas|is /'emfəsɪs/ n (pl **~ses** /-siːz/) énfasis m. **~ze** /'emfəsaɪz/ vt subrayar; (single out) destacar

emphatic /ım'fætɪk/ a categórico; (resolute) decidido

empire /'empaɪə(r)/ n imperio m

empirical /ım'pɪrɪkl/ a empírico

employ /ım'plɔɪ/ vt emplear. **~ee** /emplɔɪ'iː/ n empleado m. **~er** n patrón m. **~ment** n empleo m. **~ment agency** n agencia f de colocaciones

empower /ım'paʊə(r)/ vt autorizar (**to do** a hacer)

empress /'emprıs/ n emperatriz f

empt|ies /'emptız/ npl envases mpl. **~iness** n vacío m. **~y** /'emptı/ a vacío; (promise) vano. **on an ~y stomach** con el estómago vacío. —vt vaciar. —vi vaciarse

emulate /'emjʊleɪt/ vt emular

emulsion /ı'mʌlʃn/ n emulsión f

enable /ı'neɪbl/ vt. **~ s.o.** to permitir a uno

enact /ı'nækt/ vt (jurid) decretar; (in theatre) representar

enamel /ı'næml/ n esmalte m. —vt (pt **enamelled**) esmaltar

enamoured /ı'næməd/ a. **be ~ of** estar enamorado de

encampment /ın'kæmpmənt/ n campamento m

encase /ın'keıs/ vt encerrar

enchant /ın'tʃɑːnt/ vt encantar. **~ing** a encantador. **~ment** n encanto m

encircle /ın'sɜːkl/ vt rodear

enclave /'enkleıv/ n enclave m

enclos|e /ın'kləʊz/ vt cercar (land); (with letter) adjuntar; (in receptacle) encerrar. **~ed** a (space) encerrado; (com) adjunto. **~ure** /ın'kləʊʒə(r)/ n cercamiento m; (area) recinto m; (com) documento m adjunto

encompass /ın'kʌmpəs/ vt cercar; (include) incluir, abarcar

encore /'ɒŋkɔː(r)/ int ¡bis! —n bis m, repetición f

encounter /ın'kaʊntə(r)/ vt encontrar. —n encuentro m

encourage /ın'kʌrıdʒ/ vt animar; (stimulate) estimular. **~ment** n estímulo m

encroach /ın'krəʊtʃ/ vi. **~ on** invadir (land); quitar (time). **~ment** n usurpación f

encumb|er /ın'kʌmbə(r)/ vt (hamper) estorbar; (burden) cargar. **be ~ered with** estar cargado de. **~rance** n estorbo m; (burden) carga f

encyclical /ın'sıklıkl/ n encíclica f

encyclopaedi|a /ınsaıklə'piːdıə/ n enciclopedia f. **~c** a enciclopédico

end /end/ n fin m; (furthest point) extremo m. **in the ~** por fin.

make ~s **meet** poder llegar a fin de mes. **no** ~ (fam) muy. **no** ~ **of** muchísimos. **on** ~ de pie; (consecutive) seguido. —vt/i terminar, acabar

endanger /ɪnˈdeɪndʒə(r)/ vt arriesgar

endearing /ɪnˈdɪərɪŋ/ a simpático. ~**ment** n palabra f cariñosa

endeavour /ɪnˈdevə(r)/ n tentativa f. —vi. ~ **to** esforzarse por

ending /ˈendɪŋ/ n fin m

endive /ˈendɪv/ n escarola f, endibia f

endless /ˈendlɪs/ a interminable; (patience) infinito

endorse /ɪnˈdɔːs/ vt endosar; (fig) aprobar. ~**ment** n endoso m; (fig) aprobación f; (auto) nota f de inhabilitación

endow /ɪnˈdaʊ/ vt dotar

endurable /ɪnˈdjʊərəbl/ a aguantable. ~**ance** n resistencia f. ~**e** /ɪnˈdjʊə(r)/ vt aguantar. —vi durar. ~**ing** a perdurable

enemy /ˈenəmɪ/ n & a enemigo (m)

energetic /enəˈdʒetɪk/ a enérgico. ~**y** /ˈenədʒɪ/ n energía f

enervate /ˈenəveɪt/ vt debilitar. ~**ing** a debilitante

enfold /ɪnˈfəʊld/ vt envolver; (in arms) abrazar

enforce /ɪnˈfɔːs/ vt aplicar; (impose) imponer; hacer cumplir (law). ~**d** a forzado

engage /ɪnˈgeɪdʒ/ vt emplear (staff); (reserve) reservar; ocupar (attention); (mec) hacer engranar. —vi (mec) engranar. ~**d** a prometido; (busy) ocupado. **get** ~**d** prometerse. ~**ment** n compromiso m; (undertaking) obligación f

engaging /ɪnˈgeɪdʒɪŋ/ a atractivo

engender /ɪnˈdʒendə(r)/ vt engendrar

engine /ˈendʒɪn/ n motor m; (of train) locomotora f. ~**driver** n maquinista m

engineer /endʒɪˈnɪə(r)/ n ingeniero m; (mechanic) mecánico m. —vt (contrive, fam) lograr. ~**ing** n ingeniería f

England /ˈɪŋglənd/ n Inglaterra f

English /ˈɪŋglɪʃ/ a inglés. —n (lang) inglés m; (people) ingleses mpl. ~**man** n inglés m. ~**woman** n inglesa f. **the** ~ **Channel** n el canal m de la Mancha

engrave /ɪnˈgreɪv/ vt grabar. ~**ing** n grabado m

engrossed /ɪnˈgrəʊst/ a absorto

engulf /ɪnˈgʌlf/ vt tragar(se)

enhance /ɪnˈhɑːns/ vt aumentar

enigma /ɪˈnɪgmə/ n enigma m. ~**tic** /enɪgˈmætɪk/ a enigmático

enjoy /ɪnˈdʒɔɪ/ vt gozar de. ~ **o.s.** divertirse. **I** ~ **reading** me gusta la lectura. ~**able** a agradable. ~**ment** n placer m

enlarge /ɪnˈlɑːdʒ/ vt agrandar; (foto) ampliar. —vi agrandarse. ~ **upon** extenderse sobre. ~**ment** n (foto) ampliación f

enlighten /ɪnˈlaɪtn/ vt aclarar; (inform) informar. ~**ment** n aclaración f. **the E~ment** el siglo m de la luces

enlist /ɪnˈlɪst/ vt alistar; (fig) conseguir. —vi alistarse

enliven /ɪnˈlaɪvn/ vt animar

enmity /ˈenmɪtɪ/ n enemistad f

ennoble /ɪˈnəʊbl/ vt ennoblecer

enormity /ɪˈnɔːmətɪ/ n enormidad f. ~**ous** /ɪˈnɔːməs/ a enorme

enough /ɪˈnʌf/ a & adv bastante. —n bastante m, suficiente m. —int ¡basta!

enquire /ɪnˈkwaɪə(r)/ vt/i preguntar. ~**e about** informarse de. ~**y** n pregunta f; (investigation) investigación f

enrage /ɪnˈreɪdʒ/ vt enfurecer

enrapture /ɪn'ræptʃə(r)/ *vt* extasiar

enrich /ɪn'rɪtʃ/ *vt* enriquecer

enrol /ɪn'rəʊl/ *vt* (*pt* **enrolled**) inscribir; matricular ⟨*student*⟩. —*vi* inscribirse; ⟨*student*⟩ matricularse. **∼ment** *n* inscripción *f*; (*of student*) matrícula *f*

ensconce /ɪn'skɒns/ *vt*. ∼ **o.s.** arrellanarse

ensemble /ɒn'sɒmbl/ *n* conjunto *m*

enshrine /ɪn'ʃraɪn/ *vt* encerrar

ensign /'ensaɪn/ *n* enseña *f*

enslave /ɪn'sleɪv/ *vt* esclavizar

ensue /ɪn'sju:/ *vi* resultar, seguirse

ensure /ɪn'ʃʊə(r)/ *vt* asegurar

entail /ɪn'teɪl/ *vt* suponer; acarrear ⟨*trouble etc*⟩

entangle /ɪn'tæŋgl/ *vt* enredar. **∼ment** *n* enredo *m*; (*mil*) alambrada *f*

enter /'entə(r)/ *vt* entrar en; (*write*) escribir; matricular ⟨*school etc*⟩; hacerse socio de ⟨*club*⟩. —*vi* entrar

enterprise /'entəpraɪz/ *n* empresa *f*; (*fig*) iniciativa *f*

enterprising /'entəpraɪzɪŋ/ *a* emprendedor

entertain /entə'teɪn/ *vt* divertir; recibir ⟨*guests*⟩; abrigar ⟨*ideas, hopes*⟩; (*consider*) considerar. **∼ment** *n* diversión *f*; (*performance*) espectáculo *m*; (*reception*) recepción *f*

enthral /ɪn'θrɔːl/ *vt* (*pt* **enthralled**) cautivar

enthuse /ɪn'θjuːz/ *vi*. ∼ **over** entusiasmarse por

enthusiasm /ɪn'θjuːzɪæzəm/ *n* entusiasmo *m*. **∼tic** /-'æstɪk/ *a* entusiasta; ⟨*thing*⟩ entusiástico. **∼tically** /-'æstɪklɪ/ *adv* con entusiasmo. **∼t** /ɪn'θjuːzɪæst/ *n* entusiasta *m & f*

entice /ɪn'taɪs/ *vt* atraer. **∼ment** *n* atracción *f*

entire /ɪn'taɪə(r)/ *a* entero. **∼ly** *adv* completamente. **∼ty** /ɪn'taɪərətɪ/ *n*. **in its ∼ty** en su totalidad

entitle /ɪn'taɪtl/ *vt* titular; (*give a right*) dar derecho a. **be ∼d to** tener derecho a. **∼ment** *n* derecho *m*

entity /'entətɪ/ *n* entidad *f*

entomb /ɪn'tuːm/ *vt* sepultar

entrails /'entreɪlz/ *npl* entrañas *fpl*

entrance[1] /'entrəns/ *n* entrada *f*; (*right to enter*) admisión *f*

entrance[2] /ɪn'trɑːns/ *vt* encantar

entrant /'entrənt/ *n* participante *m & f*; (*in exam*) candidato *m*

entreat /ɪn'triːt/ *vt* suplicar. **∼y** *n* súplica *f*

entrench /ɪn'trentʃ/ *vt* atrincherar

entrust /ɪn'trʌst/ *vt* confiar

entry /'entrɪ/ *n* entrada *f*; (*of street*) bocacalle *f*; (*note*) apunte *m*

entwine /ɪn'twaɪn/ *vt* entrelazar

enumerate /ɪ'njuːməreɪt/ *vt* enumerar

enunciate /ɪ'nʌnsɪeɪt/ *vt* pronunciar; (*state*) enunciar

envelop /ɪn'veləp/ *vt* (*pt* **enveloped**) envolver

envelope /'envələʊp/ *n* sobre *m*

enviable /'envɪəbl/ *a* envidiable

envious /'envɪəs/ *a* envidioso. **∼ly** *adv* con envidia

environment /ɪn'vaɪərənmənt/ *n* medio *m* ambiente. **∼al** /-'mentl/ *a* ambiental

envisage /ɪn'vɪzɪdʒ/ *vt* prever; (*imagine*) imaginar

envoy /'envɔɪ/ *n* enviado *m*

envy /'envɪ/ *n* envidia *f*. —*vt* envidiar

enzyme /'enzaɪm/ *n* enzima *f*

epaulette /'epəʊlet/ *n* charretera *f*

ephemeral /ı'femərəl/ *a* efímero

epic /'epık/ *n* épica *f.* —*a* épico

epicentre /'episentə(r)/ *n* epicentro *m*

epicure /'epıkjuə(r)/ *n* sibarita *m & f,* (*gourmet*) gastrónomo *m*

epidemic /epı'demık/ *n* epidemia *f.* —*a* epidémico

epilep|sy /'epılepsı/ *n* epilepsia *f.* ~**tic** /-'leptık/ *a & n* epiléptico (*m*)

epilogue /'epılɒg/ *n* epílogo *m*

episode /'epısəud/ *n* episodio *m*

epistle /ı'pısl/ *n* epístola *f*

epitaph /'epıta:f/ *n* epitafio *m*

epithet /'epıθet/ *n* epíteto *m*

epitom|e /ı'pıtəmı/ *n* epítome *m,* personificación *f.* ~**ize** *vt* epitomar, personificar, ser la personificación de

epoch /'i:pɒk/ *n* época *f.* ~**making** *a* que hace época

equal /'i:kwəl/ *a* n igual (*m & f*). ~ **to** (*a task*) a la altura de. —*vt* (*pt* **equalled**) ser igual a; (*math*) ser. ~**ity** /ı'kwɒlətı/ *n* igualdad *f.* ~**ize** /'i:kwəlaız/ *vt/i* igualar. ~**izer** /-ə(r)/ *n* (*sport*) tanto *m* de empate. ~**ly** *adv* igualmente

equanimity /ekwə'nımıtı/ *n* ecuanimidad *f*

equate /ı'kweıt/ *vt* igualar

equation /ı'kweıʒn/ *n* ecuación *f*

equator /ı'kweıtə(r)/ *n* ecuador *m.* ~**ial** /ekwə'tɔ:rıəl/ *a* ecuatorial

equestrian /ı'kwestrıən/ *a* ecuestre

equilateral /i:kwı'lætərəl/ *a* equilátero

equilibrium /i:kwı'lıbrıəm/ *n* equilibrio *m*

equinox /'i:kwınɒks/ *n* equinoccio *m*

equip /ı'kwıp/ *vt* (*pt* **equipped**) equipar. ~**ment** *n* equipo *m*

equitable /'ekwıtəbl/ *a* equitativo

equity /'ekwətı/ *n* equidad *f;* (*pl, com*) acciones *fpl* ordinarias

equivalen|ce /ı'kwıvələns/ *n* equivalencia *f.* ~**t** /ı'kwıvələnt/ *a & n* equivalente (*m*)

equivocal /ı'kwıvəkl/ *a* equívoco

era /'ıərə/ *n* era *f*

eradicate /ı'rædıkeıt/ *vt* extirpar

erase /ı'reız/ *vt* borrar. ~**r** /-ə(r)/ *n* borrador *m*

erect /ı'rekt/ *a* erguido. —*vt* levantar. ~**ion** /-ʃn/ *n* erección *f,* montaje *m*

ermine /'ɜ:mın/ *n* armiño *m*

ero|de /ı'rəud/ *vt* desgastar. ~**sion** /-ʒn/ *n* desgaste *m*

erotic /ı'rɒtık/ *a* erótico. ~**ism** /-sızəm/ *n* erotismo *m*

err /ɜ:(r)/ *vi* errar; (*sin*) pecar

errand /'erənd/ *n* recado *m*

erratic /ı'rætık/ *a* irregular; (*person*) voluble

erroneous /ı'rəunıəs/ *a* erróneo

error /'erə(r)/ *n* error *m*

erudit|e /'eru:daıt/ *a* erudito. ~**ion** /-'dıʃn/ *n* erudición *f*

erupt /ı'rʌpt/ *vi* estar en erupción; (*fig*) estallar. ~**ion** /-ʃn/ *n* erupción *f*

escalat|e /'eskəleıt/ *vt* intensificar. —*vi* intensificarse. ~**ion** /-'leıʃn/ *n* intensificación *f*

escalator /'eskəleıtə(r)/ *n* escalera *f* mecánica

escapade /eskə'peıd/ *n* aventura *f*

escape /ı'skeıp/ *vi* escaparse. —*vt* evitar. —*n* fuga *f;* (*avoidance*) evasión *f.* **have a narrow** ~**e** escapar por un pelo. ~**ism** /ı'skeıpızəm/ *n* escapismo *m*

escarpment /ıs'ka:pmənt/ *n* escarpa *f*

escort /'eskɔ:t/ *n* acompañante *m;* (*mil*) escolta *f.* /ıs'kɔ:t/ *vt* acompañar; (*mil*) escoltar

Eskimo /'eskıməu/ *n* (*pl* **-os, -o**) esquimal (*m & f*)

especial /ɪˈspeʃl/ *a* especial. ~**ly** *adv* especialmente

espionage /ˈespɪɒnɑːʒ/ *n* espionaje *m*

esplanade /ˌespləˈneɪd/ *n* paseo *m* marítimo

Esq. /ɪˈskwaɪə(r)/ *abbr* (*Esquire*) (*in address*). **E. Ashton** ~ Sr. D. E. Ashton

essay /ˈeseɪ/ *n* ensayo *m*; (*at school*) composición *f*

essence /ˈesns/ *n* esencia *f*. **in** ~ esencialmente

essential /ɪˈsenʃl/ *a* esencial. ~*n* lo esencial. ~**ly** *adv* esencialmente

establish /ɪˈstæblɪʃ/ *vt* establecer; (*prove*) probar. ~**ment** *n* establecimiento *m*. **the E**~**ment** los que mandan, el sistema *m*

estate /ɪˈsteɪt/ *n* finca *f*; (*possessions*) bienes *mpl*. ~ **agent** *n* agente *m* inmobiliario. ~ **car** *n* furgoneta *f*

esteem /ɪˈstiːm/ *vt* estimar. ~*n* estimación *f*, estima *f*

estimate /ˈestɪmət/ *n* cálculo *m*; (*com*) presupuesto *m*. /ˈestɪmeɪt/ *vt* calcular. ~**ion** /-ˈmeɪʃn/ *n* estima *f*, estimación *f*; (*opinion*) opinión *f*

estranged /ɪsˈtreɪndʒd/ *a* alejado

estuary /ˈestjʊərɪ/ *n* estuario *m*

etc. /etˈsetrə/ *abbr* (*et cetera*) etc., etcétera

etching /ˈetʃɪŋ/ *n* aguafuerte *m*

eternal /ɪˈtɜːnl/ *a* eterno

eternity /ɪˈtɜːnətɪ/ *n* eternidad *f*

ether /ˈiːθə(r)/ *n* éter *m*

ethereal /ɪˈθɪərɪəl/ *a* etéreo

ethic /ˈeθɪk/ *n* ética *f*. ~**s** *npl* ética *f*. ~**al** *a* ético

ethnic /ˈeθnɪk/ *a* étnico

ethos /ˈiːθɒs/ *n* carácter *m* distintivo

etiquette /ˈetɪket/ *n* etiqueta *f*

etymology /etɪˈmɒlədʒɪ/ *n* etimología *f*

eucalyptus /juːkəˈlɪptəs/ *n* (*pl* -tuses) eucalipto *m*

eulogy /ˈjuːlədʒɪ/ *n* encomio *m*

euphemism /ˈjuːfəmɪzəm/ *n* eufemismo *m*

euphoria /juːˈfɔːrɪə/ *n* euforia *f*

Europe /ˈjʊərəp/ *n* Europa *f*. ~**an** /-ˈpɪən/ *a & n* europeo (*m*)

euthanasia /juːθəˈneɪzɪə/ *n* eutanasia *f*

evacuate /ɪˈvækjʊeɪt/ *vt* evacuar; desocupar (*building*). ~**ion** /-ˈeɪʃn/ *n* evacuación *f*

evade /ɪˈveɪd/ *vt* evadir

evaluate /ɪˈvæljʊeɪt/ *vt* evaluar

evangelical /iːvænˈdʒelɪkl/ *a* evangélico. ~**st** /ɪˈvændʒəlɪst/ *n* evangelista *m f*

evaporate /ɪˈvæpəreɪt/ *vi* evaporarse. ~**ion** /-ˈreɪʃn/ *n* evaporación *f*

evasion /ɪˈveɪʒn/ *n* evasión *f*

evasive /ɪˈveɪsɪv/ *a* evasivo

eve /iːv/ *n* víspera *f*

even /ˈiːvn/ *a* regular; (*flat*) llano; (*surface*) liso; (*amount*) igual; (*number*) par. **get** ~ **with** desquitarse con. ~*vt* nivelar. ~ **up** igualar. ~*adv* aun, hasta, incluso. ~ **if** aunque. ~ **so** aun así. **not** ~ ni siquiera

evening /ˈiːvnɪŋ/ *n* tarde *f*; (*after dark*) noche *f*. ~ **class** *n* clase *f* nocturna. ~ **dress** *n* (*man's*) traje *m* de etiqueta; (*woman's*) traje *m* de noche

evensong /ˈiːvnsɒŋ/ *n* vísperas *fpl*

event /ɪˈvent/ *n* acontecimiento *m*; (*sport*) prueba *f*. **in the** ~ **of** en caso de. ~**ful** *a* lleno de acontecimientos

eventual /ɪˈventʃʊəl/ *a* final, definitivo. ~**ity** /-ˈælətɪ/ *n* eventualidad *f*. ~**ly** *adv* finalmente

ever /ˈevə(r)/ *adv* jamás, nunca; (*at all times*) siempre. ~ **after** desde entonces. ~ **since** desde entonces. ~*conj* después de que.

~ **so** (*fam*) muy. **for** ~ para siempre. **hardly** ~ casi nunca

evergreen /'evəgri:n/ *a* de hoja perenne. —*n* árbol *m* de hoja perenne

everlasting /'evəlɑːstɪŋ/ *a* eterno

every /'evrɪ/ *a* cada, todo. ~ **child** todos los niños. ~ **one** cada uno. ~ **other day** cada dos días

everybody /'evrɪbɒdɪ/ *pron* todo el mundo

everyday /'evrɪdeɪ/ *a* todos los días

everyone /'evrɪwʌn/ *pron* todo el mundo. ~ **else** todos los demás

everything /'evrɪθɪŋ/ *pron* todo

everywhere /'evrɪweə(r)/ *adv* en todas partes

evict /ɪ'vɪkt/ *vt* desahuciar. ~**ion** /-ʃn/ *n* desahucio *m*

eviden|ce /'evɪdəns/ *n* evidencia *f*; (*proof*) pruebas *fpl*; (*jurid*) testimonio *m*. ~**ce of** señales de. **in** ~**ce** visible. ~**t** /'evɪdənt/ *a* evidente. ~**tly** *adv* evidentemente

evil /'iːvl/ *a* malo. —*n* mal *m*, maldad *f*

evocative /ɪ'vɒkətɪv/ *a* evocador

evoke /ɪ'vəʊk/ *vt* evocar

evolution /iːvə'luːʃn/ *n* evolución *f*

evolve /ɪ'vɒlv/ *vt* desarrollar. —*vi* desarrollarse, evolucionar

ewe /juː/ *n* oveja *f*

ex... /eks/ *pref* ex...

exacerbate /ɪg'zæsəbeɪt/ *vt* exacerbar

exact /ɪg'zækt/ *a* exacto. —*vt* exigir (**from** a). ~**ing** *a* exigente. ~**itude** *n* exactitud *f*. ~**ly** *adv* exactamente

exaggerat|e /ɪg'zædʒəreɪt/ *vt* exagerar. ~**ion** /-'reɪʃn/ *n* exageración *f*

exalt /ɪg'zɔːlt/ *vt* exaltar

exam /ɪg'zæm/ *n* (*fam*) examen *m*. ~**ination** /ɪgzæmɪ'neɪʃn/ *n* examen *m*. ~**ine** /ɪg'zæmɪn/ *vt*

examinar; interrogar (*witness*). ~**iner** /-ə(r)/ *n* examinador *m*

example /ɪg'zɑːmpl/ *n* ejemplo *m*. **make an** ~ **of** infligir castigo ejemplar a

exasperat|e /ɪg'zæspəreɪt/ *vt* exasperar. ~**ion** /-'reɪʃn/ *n* exasperación *f*

excavat|e /'ekskəveɪt/ *vt* excavar. ~**ion** /-'veɪʃn/ *n* excavación *f*

exceed /ɪk'siːd/ *vt* exceder. ~**ingly** *adv* extremadamente

excel /ɪk'sel/ *vi* (*pt* **excelled**) sobresalir. —*vt* superar

excellen|ce /'eksələns/ *n* excelencia *f*. ~**t** /'eksələnt/ *a* excelente. ~**tly** *adv* excelentemente

except /ɪk'sept/ *prep* excepto, con excepción de. ~ **for** con excepción de. —*vt* exceptuar. ~**ing** *prep* con excepción de.

exception /ɪk'sepʃən/ *n* excepción *f*. **take** ~ **to** ofenderse por. ~**al** /ɪk'sepʃənl/ *a* excepcional. ~**ally** *adv* excepcionalmente

excerpt /'eksɜːpt/ *n* extracto *m*

excess /ɪk'ses/ *n* exceso *m*. /'ekses/ *a* excedente. ~ **fare** *n* suplemento *m*. ~ **luggage** *n* exceso *m* de equipaje

excessive /ɪk'sesɪv/ *a* excesivo. ~**ly** *adv* excesivamente

exchange /ɪks'tʃeɪndʒ/ *vt* cambiar. —*n* cambio *m*. (**telephone**) ~ central *f* telefónica

exchequer /ɪks'tʃekə(r)/ *n* (*pol*) erario *m*, hacienda *f*

excise[1] /'eksaɪz/ *n* impuestos *mpl* indirectos

excise[2] /ek'saɪz/ *vt* quitar

excit|able /ɪk'saɪtəbl/ *a* excitable. ~**e** /ɪk'saɪt/ *vt* emocionar; (*stimulate*) excitar. ~**ed** *a* entusiasmado. ~**ement** *n* emoción *f*; (*enthusiasm*) entusiasmo *m*. ~**ing** *a* emocionante

exclaim /ɪk'skleɪm/ *vi* exclamar. ~**mation** /eksklə'meɪʃn/

exclamación f. **~mation mark**
n signo m de admiración f, punto
m de exclamación

exclu|de /ɪk'skluːd/ vt excluir.
~sion /-ʒən/ n exclusión f

exclusive /ɪk'skluːsɪv/ a exclusivo; ⟨club⟩ selecto. **o of** exclu-
yendo. **~ly** adv exclusivamente

excomunicate /ekskə'mjuːnɪ-
keɪt/ vt excomulgar

excrement /'ekskrɪmənt/ n excremento m

excruciating /ɪk'skruːʃɪeɪtɪŋ/ a
atroz, insoportable

excursion /ɪk'skɜːʃn/ n excursión f

excus|able a /ɪk'skjuːzəbl/ a per-
donable. **~e** /ɪk'skjuːz/ vt perdonar. **~e from** dispensar de.
~e me! ¡perdón! /ɪk'skjuːs/ n
excusa f

ex-directory /eksdɪ'rektərɪ/ a
que no está en la guía telefónica

execrable /'eksɪkrəbl/ a execrable

execut|e /'eksɪkjuːt/ vt ejecutar.
~ion /eksɪ'kjuːʃn/ n ejecución f.
~ioner n verdugo m

executive /ɪg'zekjʊtɪv/ a & n
ejecutivo (m)

executor /ɪg'zekjʊtə(r)/ n ⟨jurid⟩
testamentario m

exemplary /ɪg'zemplərɪ/ a ejemplar

exemplify /ɪg'zemplɪfaɪ/ vt ilustrar

exempt /ɪg'zempt/ a exento. —vt
dispensar. **~ion** /-ʃn/ n exen-
ción f

exercise /'eksəsaɪz/ n ejercicio
m. —vt ejercer. —vi hacer ejercicios. **~ book** n cuaderno m

exert /ɪg'zɜːt/ vt ejercer. **~ o.s.**
esforzarse. **~ion** /-ʃn/ n
esfuerzo m

exhal|ation /ekshə'leɪʃn/ n
exhalación f. **~e** /eks'heɪl/ vt/i
exhalar

exhaust /ɪg'zɔːst/ vt agotar. —n
⟨auto⟩ tubo m de escape. **~ed** a
agotado. **~ion** /-stʃən/ n ago-
tamiento m. **~ive** /ɪg'zɔːstɪv/ a
exhaustivo

exhibit /ɪg'zɪbɪt/ vt exponer;
⟨jurid⟩ exhibir; ⟨fig⟩ mostrar. —
n objeto m expuesto; ⟨jurid⟩ documento m

exhibition /eksɪ'bɪʃn/ n exposición f; ⟨act of showing⟩ demostración f; ⟨univ⟩ beca f. **~ist** n
exhibicionista m & f

exhibitor /ɪg'zɪbɪtə(r)/ n expos-
itor m

exhilarat|e /ɪg'zɪləreɪt/ vt ale-
grar. **~ion** /-'reɪʃn/ n regocijo m

exhort /ɪg'zɔːt/ vt exhortar

exile /'eksaɪl/ n exilio m; ⟨person⟩
exiliado m. —vt desterrar

exist /ɪg'zɪst/ vi existir. **~ence** n
existencia f. **in ~ence** existente

existentialism /egzɪs'tenʃəl-
ɪzəm/ n existencialismo
m

exit /'eksɪt/ n salida f

exodus /'eksədəs/ n éxodo m

exonerate /ɪg'zɒnəreɪt/ vt disculpar

exorbitant /ɪg'zɔːbɪtənt/ a exorbitante

exorcis|e /'eksɔːsaɪz/ vt exorci-
zar. **~m** /-sɪzəm/ n exorcismo m

exotic /ɪg'zɒtɪk/ a exótico

expand /ɪk'spænd/ vt extender;
dilatar ⟨metal⟩; ⟨develop⟩ desarrollar. —vi extenderse;
⟨develop⟩ desarrollarse; ⟨metal⟩
dilatarse

expanse /ɪk'spæns/ n extensión f

expansion /ɪk'spænʃn/ n extensión f; ⟨of metal⟩ dilatación f

expansive /ɪk'spænsɪv/ a ex-
pansivo

expatriate /eks'pætrɪət/ a & n
expatriado (m)

expect /ɪk'spekt/ vt esperar;
⟨suppose⟩ suponer; ⟨demand⟩

contar con. **I** ~ **so** supongo que sí

expectan|cy /ɪk'spektənsɪ/ n esperanza f. **life ~cy** esperanza f de vida. **~t** /ɪk'spektənt/ a expectante. **~t mother** n futura madre f

expectation /ekspek'teɪʃn/ n esperanza f

expedien|cy /ɪk'spiːdɪənsɪ/ n conveniencia f. **~t** /ɪk'spiːdɪənt/ a conveniente

expedite /'ekspɪdaɪt/ vt acelerar

expedition /ekspɪ'dɪʃn/ n expedición f. **~ary** a expedicionario

expel /ɪk'spel/ vt (pt expelled) expulsar

expend /ɪk'spend/ vt gastar. **~able** a prescindible

expenditure /ɪk'spendɪtʃə(r)/ n gastos mpl

expens|e /ɪk'spens/ n gasto m; (fig) costa f. **at s.o.'s ~e** a costa de uno. **~ive** /ɪk'spensɪv/ a caro. **~ively** adv costosamente

experience /ɪk'spɪərɪəns/ n experiencia f. —vt experimentar. **~d** a experto

experiment /ɪk'sperɪmənt/ n experimento m. —vi experimentar. **~al** /-'mentl/ a experimental

expert /'ekspɜːt/ a & n experto (m). **~ise** /eksfɜː'tiːz/ n pericia f. **~ly** adv hábilmente

expir|e /ɪk'spaɪə(r)/ vi expirar. **~y** n expiración f

expla|in /ɪk'spleɪn/ vt explicar. **~nation** /eksplə'neɪʃn/ n explicación f. **~natory** /ɪks'plænətərɪ/ a explicativo

expletive /ɪk'spliːtɪv/ n palabrota f

explicit /ɪk'splɪsɪt/ a explícito

explode /ɪk'spləʊd/ vt hacer explotar; (tec) explosionar. —vi estallar

exploit /'eksplɔɪt/ n hazaña f. /ɪk'splɔɪt/ vt explotar. **~ation** /eksplɔɪ'teɪʃn/ n explotación f

explor|ation /eksplə'reɪʃn/ n exploración f. **~atory** /ɪk'splɒrətrɪ/ a exploratorio. **~e** /ɪk'splɔː(r)/ vt explorar. **~er** n explorador m

explosion /ɪk'spləʊʒn/ n explosión f. **~ve** a & n explosivo (m)

exponent /ɪk'spəʊnənt/ n exponente m

export /ɪk'spɔːt/ vt exportar. /'ekspɔːt/ n exportación f. **~er** /ɪks'pɔːtə(r)/ n exportador m

expos|e /ɪk'spəʊz/ vt exponer; (reveal) descubrir. **~ure** /-ʒə(r)/ n exposición f. **die of ~ure** morir de frío

expound /ɪk'spaʊnd/ vt exponer

express[1] /ɪk'spres/ vt expresar

express[2] /ɪk'spres/ a expreso; (letter) urgente. —adv (by express post) por correo urgente. —n (train) rápido m, expreso m

expression /ɪk'spreʃn/ n expresión f

expressive /ɪk'spresɪv/ a expresivo

expressly /ɪk'spreslɪ/ adv expresamente

expulsion /ɪk'spʌlʃn/ n expulsión f

expurgate /'ekspəgeɪt/ vt expurgar

exquisite /'ekskwɪzɪt/ a exquisito. **~ly** adv primorosamente

ex-serviceman /eks'sɜːvɪsmən/ n (pl -men) excombatiente m

extant /ek'stænt/ a existente

extempore /ek'stempərɪ/ a improvisado. —adv de improviso

exten|d /ɪk'stend/ vt extender; (prolong) prolongar; ensanchar (house). —vi extenderse. **~sion** n extensión f; (of road, time) prolongación f; (building) anejo m; (com) prórroga f

extensive /ɪk'stensɪv/ a extenso. **~ly** adv extensamente

extent /ɪk'stent/ n extensión f; (fig) alcance. **to a certain ~** hasta cierto punto

extenuate /ɪk'stenjoeɪt/ vt atenuar

exterior /ɪk'stɪərɪə(r)/ a & n exterior (m)

exterminat|e /ɪk'stɜ:mɪneɪt/ vt exterminar. **~ion** /-'neɪʃn/ n exterminio m

external /ɪk'stɜ:nl/ a externo. **~ly** adv externamente

extinct /ɪk'stɪŋkt/ a extinto. **~ion** /-ʃn/ n extinción f

extinguish /ɪk'stɪŋgwɪʃ/ vt extinguir. **~er** n extintor m

extol /ɪk'stəʊl/ vt (pt extolled) alabar

extort /ɪk'stɔ:t/ vt sacar por la fuerza. **~ion** /-ʃn/ n exacción f. **~ionate** /ɪk'stɔ:ʃənət/ a exorbitante

extra /'ekstrə/ a suplementario. —adv extraordinariamente. —n suplemento m; (cinema) extra m & f

extract /'ekstrækt/ n extracto m. /ɪk'strækt/ vt extraer; (fig) arrancar. **~ion** /-ʃn/ n extracción f; (lineage) origen m

extradit|e /'ekstrədaɪt/ vt extraditar. **~ion** /-'dɪʃn/ n extradición f

extramarital /ekstrə'mærɪtl/ a fuera del matrimonio

extramural /ekstrə'mjʊərəl/ a fuera del recinto universitario; (for external students) para estudiantes externos

extraordinary /ɪk'strɔ:dnrɪ/ a extraordinario

extra-sensory /ekstrə'sensərɪ/ a extrasensorial

extravagan|ce /ɪk'strævəgəns/ n prodigalidad f, extravagancia f. **~t** /ɪk'strævəgənt/ a pródigo, extravagante

extrem|e /ɪk'stri:m/ a & n extremo (m). **~ely** adv extremadamente. **~ist** n extremista

m & f. **~ity** /ɪk'stremətɪ/ n extremidad f

extricate /'ekstrɪkeɪt/ vt desenredar, librar

extrovert /'ekstrəvɜ:t/ n extrovertido m

exuberan|ce /ɪg'zju:bərəns/ n exuberancia f. **~t** /ɪg'zju:bərənt/ a exuberante

exude /ɪg'zju:d/ vt rezumar

exult /ɪg'zʌlt/ vi exultar

eye /aɪ/ n ojo m. **keep an ~ on** no perder de vista. **see ~ to ~** estar de acuerdo con. —vt (pt eyed, pres p eyeing) mirar. **~ball** /'aɪbɔ:l/ n globo m del ojo. **~brow** /'aɪbraʊ/ n ceja f. **~ful** /'aɪfʊl/ n (fam) espectáculo m sorprendente. **~lash** /'aɪlæʃ/ n pestaña f. **~let** /'aɪlɪt/ n ojete m. **~lid** /'aɪlɪd/ n párpado m. **~opener** n (fam) revelación f. **~shadow** /n sombra f de ojos, sombreador m. **~sight** /'aɪsaɪt/ n vista f. **~sore** /'aɪsɔ:(r)/ n (fig, fam) monstruosidad f, horror m. **~witness** /'aɪwɪtnɪs/ n testigo m ocular

F

fable /'feɪbl/ n fábula f

fabric /'fæbrɪk/ n tejido m, tela f

fabrication /fæbrɪ'keɪʃn/ n invención f

fabulous /'fæbjʊləs/ a fabuloso

façade /fə'sɑ:d/ n fachada f

face /feɪs/ n cara f, rostro m; (of watch) esfera f; (aspect) aspecto m. **~ down(wards)** boca abajo. **~ up(wards)** boca arriba. **in the ~ of** frente a. **lose ~** quedar mal. **pull ~s** hacer muecas. —vt mirar hacia; (house) dar a; (confront) enfrentarse con. —vi volverse. **~ up to** enfrentarse con.

~ flannel n paño m (para lavarse la cara). **~less** a anónimo. **~lift** n cirugía f estética en la cara

facet /ˈfæsɪt/ n faceta f

facetious /fəˈsiːʃəs/ a chistoso, gracioso

facial /ˈfeɪʃl/ a facial. —n masaje m facial

facile /ˈfæsaɪl/ a fácil

facilitate /fəˈsɪlɪteɪt/ vt facilitar

facility /fəˈsɪlɪtɪ/ n facilidad f

facing /ˈfeɪsɪŋ/ n revestimiento m. **~s** npl (on clothes) vueltas fpl

facsimile /fækˈsɪmɪlɪ/ n facsímile m

fact /fækt/ n hecho m. **as a matter of ~**, **in ~** en realidad, a decir verdad

faction /ˈfækʃn/ n facción f

factor /ˈfæktə(r)/ n factor m

factory /ˈfæktərɪ/ n fábrica f

factual /ˈfæktʃʊəl/ a basado en hechos, factual

faculty /ˈfækəltɪ/ n facultad f

fad /fæd/ n manía f, capricho m

fade /feɪd/ vi (colour) descolorarse; (flowers) marchitarse; (light) apagarse; (memory, sound) desvanecerse

faeces /ˈfiːsiːz/ npl excrementos mpl

fag¹ /fæg/ n (chore, fam) faena f; (cigarette, sl) cigarillo m, pitillo m

fag² /fæg/ n (homosexual, Amer, sl) marica m

fagged /fægd/ a. **~ (out)** rendido

fah /fɑː/ n (mus, fourth note of any musical scale) fa m

fail /feɪl/ vi fallar; (run short) acabarse. he **~ed to arrive** no llegó. —vt no aprobar (exam); suspender (candidate); (disappoint) fallar. ~ **s.o.** (words etc) faltarle a uno. —n. **without ~** sin falta

failing /ˈfeɪlɪŋ/ n defecto m. —prep a falta de

failure /ˈfeɪljə(r)/ n fracaso m; (person) fracasado m; (med) ataque m; (mec) fallo m. ~ **to do** dejar m de hacer

faint /feɪnt/ a (-er, -est) (weak) débil; (indistinct) indistinto. —vi ~ estar mareado. **the ~est idea** la más remota idea. —vi desmayarse. —n desmayo m. **~-hearted** a pusilánime, cobarde. **~ly** adv (weakly) débilmente; (indistinctly) indistintamente. **~ness** n debilidad f

fair¹ /feə(r)/ a (-er, -est) (just) justo; (weather) bueno; (amount) razonable; (hair) rubio; (skin) blanco. ~ **play** n juego m limpio. —adv limpio

fair² /feə(r)/ n feria f

fair: **~ly** adv (justly) justamente; (rather) bastante. **~ness** n justicia f

fairy /ˈfeərɪ/ n hada f. **~land** n país m de las hadas. ~ **story,** **~-tale** cuento m de hadas

fait accompli /feɪtəˈkɒmpliː/ n hecho m consumado

faith /feɪθ/ n (trust) confianza f; (relig) fe f. **~ful** a fiel. **~fully** adv fielmente. **~fulness** n fidelidad f. **~healing** n curación f por la fe

fake /feɪk/ n falsificación f; (person) impostor m. —a falso. —vt falsificar; (pretend) fingir

fakir /ˈfeɪkɪə(r)/ n faquir m

falcon /ˈfɔːlkən/ n halcón m

Falkland /ˈfɔːlklənd/ n. **the ~ Islands** npl las islas fpl Malvinas

fall /fɔːl/ vi (pt fell, pp fallen) caer. —n caída f; (autumn, Amer) otoño m; (in price) baja f. ~ **back on** recurrir a. ~ **down** (fall) caer; (be unsuccessful) fracasar. ~ **for** (fam) enamorarse de (person); (fam) dejarse engañar por (trick). ~ **in** (mil) formar filas. ~ **off** (diminish) disminuir. ~ **out**

(*quarrel*) reñir (**with** con); (*drop out*) caer. ~ **over** caer(se). ~ **over sth** tropezar con algo. ~ **short** caer insuficiente. ~ **through** fracasar

fallacy /'fæləsɪ/ n error m

fallible /'fælɪbl/ a falible

fallout /'fɔːlaʊt/ n lluvia f radiactiva

fallow /'fæləʊ/ a en barbecho

false /fɔːls/ a falso. ~**hood** n mentira f. ~**ly** adv falsamente. ~**ness** n falsedad f

falsetto /fɔːl'setəʊ/ n (pl -os) falsete m

falsify /'fɔːlsɪfaɪ/ vt falsificar

falter /'fɔːltə(r)/ vi vacilar

fame /feɪm/ n fama f. ~**d** a famoso

familiar /fə'mɪlɪə(r)/ a familiar. **be** ~ **with** conocer. ~**ity** /-'ærətɪ/ n familiaridad f. ~**ize** vt familiarizar

family /'fæmɪlɪ/ n familia f. ~ a de (la) familia, familiar

famine /'fæmɪn/ n hambre f, hambruna f (Amer)

famished /'fæmɪʃt/ a hambriento

famous /'feɪməs/ a famoso. ~**ly** adv (fam) a las mil maravillas

fan[1] /fæn/ n abanico m; (mec) ventilador m. —vt (pt **fanned**) abanicar; soplar (*fire*). —vi. ~ **out** desparramarse en forma de abanico

fan[2] /fæn/ n (of person) admirador m; (enthusiast) aficionado m, entusiasta m & f

fanatic /fə'nætɪk/ n fanático m. ~**al** a fanático. ~**ism** /-sɪzəm/ n fanatismo m

fan belt /'fænbelt/ n correa f de ventilador

fancier /'fænsɪə(r)/ n aficionado m

fanciful /'fænsɪfl/ a (*imaginative*) imaginativo; (*unreal*) imaginario

fancy /'fænsɪ/ n fantasía f; (*liking*) gusto m. **take a** ~ **to** tomar cariño a (*person*); aficionarse a (*thing*). —a de lujo; (*extravagant*) excesivo. —vt (*imagine*) imaginar; (*believe*) creer; (*want, fam*) apetecer a. ~ **dress** n disfraz m

fanfare /'fænfeə(r)/ n fanfarria f

fang /fæŋ/ n (of animal) colmillo m; (of snake) diente m

fanlight /'fænlaɪt/ n montante m

fantasize /'fæntəsaɪz/ vi fantasear

fantastic /fæn'tæstɪk/ a fantástico

fantasy /'fæntəsɪ/ n fantasía f

far /fɑː(r)/ adv lejos; (*much*) mucho. **as** ~ **as** hasta. **as** ~ **as I know** que yo sepa. **by** ~ mucho. —a (*further, furthest o farther, farthest*) lejano

far-away /'fɑːrəweɪ/ a lejano

farce /fɑːs/ n farsa f. ~**ical** a ridículo

fare /feə(r)/ n (*for transport*) tarifa f; (*food*) comida f. —vi irle. **how did you** ~? ¿qué tal te fue?

Far East /fɑː(r)'iːst/ n Extremo/Lejano Oriente m

farewell /feə'wel/ int a n adiós (m)

far-fetched /fɑː'fetʃt/ a improbable

farm /fɑːm/ n granja f. —vt cultivar. ~ **out** arrendar. —vi ser agricultor. ~**er** n agricultor m. ~**house** n granja f. ~**ing** n agricultura f. ~**yard** n corral m

far: ~**-off** a lejano. ~**-reaching** a trascendental. ~**-seeing** a clarividente. ~**-sighted** a hipermétrope; (fig) clarividente

farther, farthest /'fɑːðə(r), 'fɑːðəst/ see **far**

fascinate /'fæsɪneɪt/ vt fascinar. ~**ion** /-'neɪʃn/ n fascinación f

fascis|m /'fæʃɪzəm/ n fascismo m. ~**t** /'fæʃɪst/ a & n fascista (m & f)

fashion /'fæʃn/ n (manner) manera f; (vogue) moda f. ~able a de moda

fast[1] /fɑːst/ a (-er, -est) rápido; (clock) adelantado; (secure) fijo; (colours) sólido. —adv rápidamente; (securely) firmemente. ~ **asleep** profundamente dormido

fast[2] /fɑːst/ vi ayunar. —n ayuno m

fasten /'fɑːsn/ vt/i sujetar; cerrar (windows, doors); abrochar (belt etc). ~**er**, ~**ing** n (on box, window) cierre m; (on door) cerrojo m

fastidious /fə'stɪdɪəs/ a exigente, minucioso

fat /fæt/ n grasa f. —a (fatter, fattest) gordo; (meat) que tiene mucha grasa; (thick) grueso. **a ~ lot of** (sl) muy poco

fatal /'feɪtl/ a mortal; (fateful) fatídico

fatalism /'feɪtəlɪzəm/ n fatalismo m. ~**t** n fatalista m & f

fatality /fə'tælətɪ/ n calamidad f; (death) muerte f

fatally /'feɪtəlɪ/ adv mortalmente; (by fate) fatalmente

fate /feɪt/ n destino m; (one's lot) suerte f. ~**d** a predestinado. ~**ful** a fatídico

fat-head /'fæthed/ n imbécil m

father /'fɑːðə(r)/ n padre m. ~**hood** n paternidad f. ~**in-law** m (pl **fathers-in-law**) suegro m. ~**ly** a paternal

fathom /'fæðəm/ n braza f. —vt. ~ (**out**) comprender

fatigue /fə'tiːg/ n fatiga f. —vt fatigar

fat: ~**ness** n gordura f. ~**ten** vt/i engordar; (animal) ~**tening** a que engorda. ~**ty** a graso. —n (fam) gordinflón m

fatuous /'fætjʊəs/ a fatuo

faucet /'fɔːsɪt/ n (Amer) grifo m

fault /fɔːlt/ n defecto m; (blame) culpa f; (tennis) falta f; (geol)

falla f. **at** ~ culpable. —vt criticar. ~**less** a impecable. ~**y** a defectuoso

fauna /'fɔːnə/ n fauna f

faux pas /fəʊ'pɑː/ n (pl **faux pas** /fəʊ'pɑː/) n metedura f de pata, paso m en falso

favour /'feɪvə(r)/ n favor m. —vt favorecer; (support) estar a favor de; (prefer) preferir. ~**able** a favorable. ~**ably** adv favorablemente

favourite /'feɪvərɪt/ a & n preferido (m). ~**ism** n favoritismo m

fawn[1] /fɔːn/ n cervato m. —a color de cervato, beige, beis

fawn[2] /fɔːn/ vi. ~ **on** adular

fax /fæks/ n telefacsímil m, fax m

fear /fɪə(r)/ n miedo m. —vt temer. ~**ful** a (frightening) espantoso; (frightened) temeroso. ~**less** a intrépido. ~**lessness** n intrepidez f. ~**some** a espantoso

feasibility /fiːzə'bɪlətɪ/ n viabilidad f. ~**le** /'fiːzəbl/ a factible; (likely) posible

feast /fiːst/ n (relig) fiesta f; (meal) banquete m, comilona f. —vt banquetear, festejar. ~ **on** regalarse con

feat /fiːt/ n hazaña f

feather /'feðə(r)/ n pluma f. —vt. ~ **one's nest** hacer su agosto. ~**brained** a tonto. ~**weight** n peso m pluma

feature /'fiːtʃə(r)/ n (on face) facción f; (characteristic) característica f; (in newspaper) artículo m; ~ (**film**) película f principal, largometraje m. —vt presentar; (give prominence to) destacar. —vi figurar

February /'febrʊərɪ/ n febrero m

feckless /'feklɪs/ a inepto; (irresponsible) irreflexivo

fed /fed/ see **feed**. —a. ~ **up** (sl) harto (**with** de)

federal /ˈfedərəl/ a federal

federation /fedəˈreɪʃn/ n federación f

fee /fiː/ n (professional) honorarios mpl; (enrolment) derechos mpl; (club) cuota f

feeble /ˈfiːbl/ a (-er, -est) débil. **~-minded** a imbécil

feed /fiːd/ vt (pt fed) dar de comer a; (supply) alimentar. —vi comer. —n (for animals) pienso m; (for babies) comida f. **~back** n reacciones fpl, comentarios mpl

feel /fiːl/ vt (pt felt) sentir; (touch) tocar; (think) parecerle. **do you ~ it's a good idea?** te parece buena idea? **I ~ it is necessary** me parece necesario. **~ as if** tener la impresión de que. **~ hot/hungry** tener calor/hambre. **~ like** (want, fam) tener ganas de. **~ up to** sentirse capaz de

feeler /ˈfiːlə(r)/ n (of insects) antena f. **put out a ~** (fig) hacer un sondeo

feeling /ˈfiːlɪŋ/ n sentimiento m; (physical) sensación f

feet /fiːt/ see **foot**

feign /feɪn/ vt fingir

feint /feɪnt/ n finta f

felicitous /fəˈlɪsɪtəs/ a feliz, oportuno

feline /ˈfiːlaɪn/ a felino

fell[1] /fel/ see **fall**

fell[2] /fel/ vt derribar

fellow /ˈfeləʊ/ n (fam) tipo m; (comrade) compañero m; (society) socio m. **~ countryman** n compatriota m & f. **~ passenger/traveller** n compañero m de viaje. **~ship** n compañerismo m; (group) asociación f

felony /ˈfeləni/ n crimen m

felt[1] /felt/ n fieltro m

felt[2] /felt/ see **feel**

female /ˈfiːmeɪl/ a hembra; (voice, sex etc) femenino. —n mujer f; (animal) hembra f

feminine /ˈfemənɪn/ a & n femenino (m). **~nity** /-ˈnɪnɪti/ n feminidad f. **~st** n feminista m & f

fenc|e /fens/ n cerca f; (person, sl) perista m & f (fam). —vt. **~e (in)** encerrar, cercar. —vi (sport) practicar la esgrima. **~er** n esgrimidor m. **~ing** n (sport) esgrima f

fend /fend/ vi. **~ for o.s.** valerse por sí mismo. —vt. **~ off** defenderse de

fender /ˈfendə(r)/ n guardafuego m; (mudguard, Amer) guardabarros m invar; (naut) defensa f

fennel /ˈfenl/ n hinojo m

ferment /ˈfɜːment/ n fermento m; (fig) agitación f. /fəˈment/ vt/i fermentar. **~ation** /-ˈteɪʃn/ n fermentación f

fern /fɜːn/ n helecho m

feroci|ous /fəˈrəʊʃəs/ a feroz. **~ty** /-ˈrɒsɪti/ n ferocidad f

ferret /ˈferɪt/ n hurón m. —vi (pt ferreted) huronear. —vt. **~ out** descubrir

ferry /ˈferi/ n ferry m. —vt transportar

fertil|e /ˈfɜːtaɪl/ a fértil; (biol) fecundo. **~ity** /-ˈtɪlɪti/ n fertilidad f; (biol) fecundidad f

fertilize /ˈfɜːtɪlaɪz/ vt abonar; (biol) fecundar. **~r** n abono m

fervent /ˈfɜːvənt/ a ferviente

fervour /ˈfɜːvə(r)/ n fervor m

fester /ˈfestə(r)/ vi enconarse

festival /ˈfestɪvl/ n fiesta f; (of arts) festival m

festive /ˈfestɪv/ a festivo. **~ season** n temporada f de fiestas

festivity /feˈstɪvɪti/ n festividad f

festoon /feˈstuːn/ vi. **~ with** adornar de

fetch /fetʃ/ vt (go for) ir a buscar; (bring) traer; (be sold for) venderse por

fetching /ˈfetʃɪŋ/ a atractivo

fête /feɪt/ n fiesta f. —vt festejar

fetid /ˈfetɪd/ a fétido

fetish /ˈfetɪʃ/ n fetiche m; (psychy) obsesión f

fetter /ˈfetə(r)/ vt encadenar. —s npl grilletes mpl

fettle /ˈfetl/ n condición f

feud /fjuːd/ n enemistad f (inveterada)

feudal /ˈfjuːdl/ a feudal. —ism n feudalismo m

fever /ˈfiːvə(r)/ n fiebre f. —ish a febril

few /fjuː/ a pocos. —n pocos mpl. **a** ~ unos (pocos). **a good** ~, **quite a** ~ (fam) muchos. —**er** a & n menos. —**est** a & n el menor número m

fiancé /frˈɒnseɪ/ n novio m. —**e** /frˈɒnseɪ/ n novia f

fiasco /frˈæskəʊ/ n (pl -os) fiasco m

fib /fɪb/ n mentirijilla f. —**ber** n mentiroso m

fibre /ˈfaɪbə(r)/ n fibra f. —**glass** n fibra f de vidrio

fickle /ˈfɪkl/ a inconstante

fiction /ˈfɪkʃn/ n ficción f. **(works of)** ~ novelas fpl. —**al** a novelesco

fictitious /fɪkˈtɪʃəs/ a ficticio

fiddle /ˈfɪdl/ n (fam) violín m; (swindle, sl) trampa f. —vt (sl) falsificar. ~ **with** juguetear con, toquetear, manosear. —**r** n (fam) violinista m & f; (cheat, sl) tramposo m

fidelity /fɪˈdelətɪ/ n fidelidad f

fidget /ˈfɪdʒɪt/ vi (pt fidgeted) moverse, ponerse nervioso. ~ **with** juguetear con. —n azogado m. —**y** a azogado

field /fiːld/ n campo m. ~ **day** n gran ocasión f. ~ **glasses** npl gemelos mpl. **F**~ **Marshal** n mariscal de campo, capitán m general. —**work** n investigaciones fpl en el terreno

fiend /fiːnd/ n demonio m. —**ish** a diabólico

fierce /fɪəs/ a (-er, -est) feroz; (attack) violento. —**ness** n ferocidad f, violencia f

fiery /ˈfaɪərɪ/ a (-ier, -iest) ardiente

fifteen /fɪfˈtiːn/ a & n quince (m). —**th** a & n quince (m), decimoquinto (m). —n (fraction) quinzavo m

fifth /fɪfθ/ a & n quinto (m). ~ **column** n quinta columna f

fiftieth /ˈfɪftɪəθ/ a & n cincuenta (m). —**y** a & n cincuenta (m). —**y-**~**y** mitad y mitad, a medias. **a** ~**y-**~**y chance** una posibilidad f de cada dos

fig /fɪg/ n higo m

fight /faɪt/ vi/t (pt fought) luchar; (quarrel) disputar. ~ **shy of** evitar. —n lucha f; (quarrel) disputa f; (mil) combate m. ~ **back** defenderse. ~ **off** rechazar (attack); luchar contra (illness). —**er** n luchador m; (mil) combatiente m & f; (aircraft) avión m de caza. —**ing** n luchas fpl

figment /ˈfɪgmənt/ n invención f

figurative /ˈfɪgjʊrətɪv/ a figurado

figure /ˈfɪgə(r)/ n (number) cifra f; (diagram) figura f; (shape) forma f; (of woman) tipo m. —vt imaginar. —vi figurar. **that** ~**s** (Amer, fam) es lógico. ~ **out** explicarse. —**head** n testaferro m, mascarón m de proa. ~ **of speech** n tropo m, figura f. ~**s** npl (arithmetic) aritmética f

filament /ˈfɪləmənt/ n filamento m

filch /fɪltʃ/ vt hurtar

file[1] /faɪl/ n carpeta f; (set of papers) expediente m. —vt archivar (papers)

file[2] /faɪl/ n (row) fila f. —vi. **in** entrar en fila. ~ **past** desfilar ante

file[3] /fail/ n (tool) lima f. —vt limar

filings /'failɪnz/ npl limaduras fpl

fill /fil/ vt llenar. —vi llenarse. ~ **in** rellenar (form). ~ **out** (get fatter) engordar. ~ **up** (auto) llenar, repostar. —n. **eat one's** ~ hartarse de comer. **have had one's** ~ **of** estar harto de

fillet /'filit/ n filete m. —vt (pt **filleted**) cortar en filetes

filling /'filɪŋ/ n (in tooth) empaste m. ~ **station** n estación f de servicio

film /film/ n película f. —vt filmar. ~ **star** n estrella f de cine. ~**strip** n tira f de película

filter /'filtə(r)/ n filtro m. —vt filtrar. —vi filtrarse. ~**tipped** a con filtro

filth /filθ/ n inmundicia f. ~**iness** n inmundicia f. ~**y** a inmundo

fin /fin/ n aleta f

final /'faɪnl/ a último; (conclusive) decisivo. —n (sport) final f. ~**s** npl (schol) exámenes mpl de fin de curso

finale /fi'nɑːlɪ/ n final m

final: ~**ist** n finalista m & f. ~**ize** vt concluir. ~**ly** adv (lastly) finalmente, por fin; (once and for all) definitivamente

financ|**e** /'faɪnæns/ n finanzas fpl. —vt financiar. ~**ial** /faɪ'nænʃl/ a financiero. ~**ially** adv económicamente. ~**ier** /faɪ'nænsɪə(r)/ n financiero m

finch /fintʃ/ n pinzón m

find /faɪnd/ vt (pt **found**) encontrar. ~ **out** enterarse de. ~**er** n el m que encuentra, descubridor m. ~**ings** npl resultados mpl

fine[1] /faɪn/ a (-er, -est) fino; (excellent) excelente. —adv muy bien; (small) en trozos pequeños

fine[2] /faɪn/ n multa f. —vt multar

fine: ~ **arts** npl bellas artes fpl. ~**ly** adv (admirably) espléndidamente; (cut) en trozos pequeños. ~**ry** /'faɪnərɪ/ n galas fpl

finesse /fi'nes/ n tino m

finger /'fɪŋgə(r)/ n dedo m. —vt tocar. ~**nail** n uña f. ~**print** n huella f dactilar. ~**stall** n dedil m. ~**tip** n punta f del dedo

finicking /'fɪnɪkɪŋ/ a, **finicky** /'fɪnɪkɪ/ a melindroso

finish /'fɪnɪʃ/ vt/i terminar. ~ **doing** terminar de hacer. ~ **up doing** terminar por hacer. —n fin m; (of race) llegada f, meta f; (appearance) acabado m

finite /'faɪnaɪt/ a finito

Finland /'fɪnlənd/ n Finlandia f. ~**n** n finlandés m. ~**nish** a & n finlandés (m)

fiord /fjɔːd/ n fiordo m

fir /fɜː(r)/ n abeto m

fire /faɪə(r)/ n fuego m; (conflagration) incendio m. —vt disparar (bullet etc); (dismiss) despedir; (fig) excitar, enardecer, inflamar. —vi tirar. ~**arm** n arma f de fuego. ~ **brigade** n cuerpo m de bomberos. ~**cracker** n (Amer) petardo m. ~ **department** n (Amer) cuerpo m de bomberos. ~**engine** n coche m de bomberos. ~**escape** n escalera f de incendios. ~**light** n lumbre f. ~**man** n bombero m. ~**place** n chimenea f. ~**side** n hogar m. ~ **station** n parque m de bomberos. ~**wood** n leña f. ~**work** n fuego m artificial

firing-squad /'faɪərɪŋskwɒd/ n pelotón m de ejecución

firm[1] /fɜːm/ n empresa f

firm[2] /fɜːm/ a (-er, -est) firme. ~**ly** adv firmemente. ~**ness** n firmeza f

first /fɜːst/ a primero. **at** ~ **hand** directamente. **at** ~ **sight** a primera vista. —n primero m. —adv primero; (first time) por primera vez. ~ **of all** ante todo. ~ **aid** n primeros auxilios mpl. ~**-born** a primogénito. ~**-class** a de primera clase. ~ **floor** n primer piso m; (Amer) planta f baja. **F~ Lady** n (Amer) Primera Dama f. ~**ly** adv en primer lugar. ~ **name** n nombre m de pila. ~**-rate** a excelente

fiscal /ˈfɪskl/ a fiscal

fish /fɪʃ/ n (usually invar) (alive in water) pez m; (food) pescado m. —vi pescar. ~ **for** pescar. ~ **out** (take out, fam) sacar. ~**ing** ir de pesca. ~**erman** /ˈfɪʃəmən/ n pescador m. ~**ing** n pesca f. ~**ing-rod** n caña f de pesca. ~**monger** n pescadero m. ~**shop** n pescadería f. ~**y** a ⟨smell⟩ a pescado; (questionable, fam) sospechoso

fission /ˈfɪʃn/ n fisión f

fist /fɪst/ n puño m

fit[1] /fɪt/ a (**fitter, fittest**) conveniente; (healthy) sano; (good enough) adecuado; (able) capaz. —n (of clothes) corte m. —vt (pt **fitted**) (adapt) adaptar; (be the right size for) sentar bien a; (install) colocar. —vi encajar; (in certain space) caber; ⟨clothes⟩ sentar. ~ **out** equipar. ~ **up** equipar

fit[2] /fɪt/ n ataque m

fitful /ˈfɪtfl/ a irregular

fitment /ˈfɪtmənt/ n mueble m

fitness /ˈfɪtnɪs/ n (buena) salud f; (of remark) conveniencia f

fitting /ˈfɪtɪŋ/ a apropiado. —n (of clothes) prueba f. ~**s** /ˈfɪtɪŋz/ npl (in house) accesorios mpl

five /faɪv/ a & n cinco (m). ~**r** /ˈfaɪvə(r)/ n (fam) billete m de cinco libras

fix /fɪks/ vt (make firm, attach, decide) fijar; (mend, deal with) arreglar. —n. **in a** ~ en un aprieto. ~**ation** /-eɪʃn/ n fijación f. ~**ed** a fijo

fixture /ˈfɪkstʃə(r)/ n (sport) partido m. ~**s** (in house) accesorios mpl

fizz /fɪz/ vi burbujear. —n efervescencia f. ~**le out** fracasar. ~**y** a efervescente; ⟨water⟩ con gas

flab /flæb/ n (fam) flaccidez f

flabbergast /ˈflæbəgɑːst/ vt pasmar

flabby /ˈflæbɪ/ a flojo

flag /flæg/ n bandera f. —vt (pt **flagged**). ~ **down** hacer señales de parada a. —vi (pt **flagged**) (weaken) flaquear; ⟨interest⟩ decaer; ⟨conversation⟩ languidecer

flagon /ˈflægən/ n botella f grande, jarro m

flag-pole /ˈflægpəʊl/ n asta f de bandera

flagrant /ˈfleɪgrənt/ a (glaring) flagrante; (scandalous) escandaloso

flagstone /ˈflægstəʊn/ n losa f

flair /fleə(r)/ n don m (**for** de)

flak|**e** /fleɪk/ n copo m; (of paint, metal) escama f. —vi desconcharse. ~**e out** (fam) caer rendido. ~**y** a escamoso

flamboyant /flæmˈbɔɪənt/ a ⟨clothes⟩ vistoso; ⟨manner⟩ extravagante

flame /fleɪm/ n llama f. —vi llamear

flamingo /fləˈmɪŋgəʊ/ n (pl -o(e)s) flamenco m

flammable /ˈflæməbl/ a inflamable

flan /flæn/ n tartaleta f, tarteleta f

flank /flæŋk/ n (of animal) ijada f, flanco m; (of person) costado m; (of mountain) falda f; (mil) flanco m

flannel /ˈflænl/ n franela f (de lana); (for face) paño m (para lavarse la cara). ~**ette** n franela f (de algodón), muletón m

flap /flæp/ vi (pt **flapped**) ondear; ⟨wings⟩ aletear; ⟨become agitated, fam⟩ ponerse nervioso. —vt sacudir; batir ⟨wings⟩. —n ⟨of pocket⟩ cartera f; ⟨of table⟩ ala f. **get into a ~** ponerse nervioso

flare /fleə(r)/ —n llamarada f; ⟨mil⟩ bengala f; ⟨in skirt⟩ vuelo m. —vi. **~ up** llamear; ⟨fighting⟩ estallar; ⟨person⟩ encolerizarse. **~d** a ⟨skirt⟩ acampanada

flash /flæʃ/ —vi brillar; ⟨on and off⟩ destellar. —vt despedir; ⟨aim torch⟩ dirigir; ⟨flaunt⟩ hacer ostentación de. **~ past** pasar como un rayo. —n relámpago m; ⟨of news, camera⟩ flash m. **~back** n escena f retrospectiva. **~light** n ⟨torch⟩ linterna f

flashy /'flæʃɪ/ a ostentoso

flask /flɑːsk/ n frasco m; ⟨vacuum flask⟩ termo m

flat[1] /flæt/ a ⟨flatter, flattest⟩ llano; ⟨tyre⟩ desinflado; ⟨refusal⟩ categórico; ⟨fare, rate⟩ fijo; ⟨mus⟩ desafinado. —adv. **~ out** ⟨at top speed⟩ a toda velocidad

flat[2] /flæt/ n ⟨rooms⟩ piso m, apartamento m; ⟨tyre⟩ ⟨fam⟩ pinchazo m; ⟨mus⟩ bemol m

flat: **~ly** adv categóricamente. **~ness** n llanura f. **~ten** /'flætn/ vt allanar, aplanar. —vi allanarse, aplanarse

flatter /flætə(r)/ vt adular. **~er** n adulador m. **~ing** a ⟨clothes⟩ favorecedor. **~y** n adulación f

flatulence /'flætjʊləns/ n flatulencia f

flaunt /flɔːnt/ vt hacer ostentación de

flautist /'flɔːtɪst/ n flautista m & f

flavour /'fleɪvə(r)/ n sabor m. —vt condimentar. **~ing** n condimento m

flaw /flɔː/ n defecto m. **~less** a perfecto

flax /flæks/ n lino m. **~en** a de lino; ⟨hair⟩ rubio

flea /fliː/ n pulga f

fleck /flek/ n mancha f, pinta f

fled /fled/ see **flee**

fledged /fledʒd/ a. **fully ~** ⟨doctor etc⟩ hecho y derecho; ⟨member⟩ de pleno derecho

fledg(e)ling /'fledʒlɪŋ/ n pájaro m volantón

flee /fliː/ vi (pt **fled**) huir. —vt huir de

fleece /fliːs/ n vellón m. —vt ⟨rob⟩ desplumar

fleet /fliːt/ n ⟨naut, aviat⟩ flota f; ⟨of cars⟩ parque m

fleeting /'fliːtɪŋ/ a fugaz

Flemish /'flemɪʃ/ a & n flamenco (m)

flesh /fleʃ/ n carne f. **in the ~** en persona. **one's own ~ and blood** los de su sangre. **~y** a ⟨fruit⟩ carnoso

flew /fluː/ see **fly**[1]

flex /fleks/ vt doblar; flexionar ⟨muscle⟩. —n ⟨elec⟩ cable m, flexible m

flexibility /fleksə'bɪlətɪ/ n flexibilidad f. **~le** /'fleksəbl/ a flexible

flexitime /'fleksɪ'taɪm/ n horario m flexible

flick /flik/ n golpecito m. —vt dar un golpecito a. **~ through** hojear

flicker /'flikə(r)/ vi temblar; ⟨light⟩ parpadear. —n temblor m; ⟨of hope⟩ resquicio m; ⟨of light⟩ parpadeo m

flick: **~-knife** n navaja f de muelle. **~s** npl cine m

flier /'flaɪə(r)/ n aviador m; ⟨circular, Amer⟩ prospecto m, folleto m

flies /flaɪz/ npl ⟨on trousers, fam⟩ bragueta f

flight /flaɪt/ n vuelo m; ⟨fleeing⟩ huida f, fuga f. **~ of stairs** tramo m de escalera f. **put to** poner en fuga. **take (to)** ~ darse a la fuga. **~-deck** n cubierta f de vuelo

flighty /flaɪtɪ/ a (-ier, -iest) frívolo

flimsy /flɪmzɪ/ a (-ier, -iest) flojo, débil, poco substancioso

flinch /flɪntʃ/ vi (draw back) retroceder (from ante). **without** ~ing (without wincing) sin pestañear

fling /flɪŋ/ vt (pt **flung**) arrojar. —n. **have a** ~ echar una cana al aire

flint /flɪnt/ n pedernal m; (for lighter) piedra f

flip /flɪp/ vt (pt **flipped**) dar un golpecito a. ~ **through** hojear. —n golpecito m. ~ **side** n otra cara f

flippant /flɪpənt/ a poco serio; (disrespectful) irrespetuoso

flipper /flɪpə(r)/ n aleta f

flirt /flɜːt/ vi coquetear. —n (woman) coqueta f; (man) mariposón m, coqueto m. ~**ation** /-ˈteɪʃn/ n coqueteo m

flit /flɪt/ vi (pt **flitted**) revolotear

float /fləʊt/ vi flotar. —vt hacer flotar. —n flotador m; (on fishing line) corcho m; (cart) carroza f

flock /flɒk/ n (of birds) bandada f; (of sheep) rebaño m; (of people) muchedumbre f, multitud f. —vi congregarse

flog /flɒg/ vt (pt **flogged**) (beat) azotar; (sell, sl) vender

flood /flʌd/ n inundación f; (fig) torrente m. —vt inundar. —vi (building etc) inundarse; (river) desbordar

floodlight /flʌdlaɪt/ n foco m. —vt (pt **floodlit**) iluminar (con focos)

floor /flɔː(r)/ n suelo m; (storey) piso m; (for dancing) pista f. —vt (knock down) derribar; (baffle) confundir

flop /flɒp/ vi (pt **flopped**) dejarse caer pesadamente; (fail, sl) fracasar. —n (sl) fracaso m. ~**py** a flojo

flora /flɔːrə/ n flora f

floral /flɔːrəl/ a floral

florid /flɒrɪd/ a florido

florist /flɒrɪst/ n florista m & f

flounce /flaʊns/ n volante m

flounder[1] /flaʊndə(r)/ vi avanzar con dificultad, no saber qué hacer

flounder[2] /flaʊndə(r)/ n (fish) platija f

flour /flaʊə(r)/ n harina f

flourish /flʌrɪʃ/ vi prosperar. —vt blandir. —n ademán m elegante; (in handwriting) rasgo m. ~**ing** a próspero

floury /flaʊərɪ/ a harinoso

flout /flaʊt/ vt burlarse de

flow /fləʊ/ vi correr; (hang loosely) caer. ~ **into** (river) desembocar en. —n flujo m; (jet) chorro m; (stream) corriente f; (of words, tears) torrente m. ~ **chart** n organigrama m

flower /flaʊə(r)/ n flor f. ~**-bed** n macizo m de flores. ~**ed** a floreado, de flores. ~**y** a florido

flown /fləʊn/ see **fly**[1]

flu /fluː/ n (fam) gripe f

fluctuate /flʌktjʊeɪt/ vi fluctuar. ~**ion** /-eɪʃn/ n fluctuación f

flue /fluː/ n humero m

fluency /fluːənsɪ/ n facilidad f. ~**t** a (style) fluido; (speaker) elocuente. **be** ~**t (in a language)** hablar (un idioma) con soltura. ~**tly** adv con fluidez; (lang) con soltura

fluff /flʌf/ n pelusa f. ~**y** a (-ier, -iest) velloso

fluid /fluːɪd/ a & n fluido (m)

fluke /fluːk/ n (stroke of luck) chiripa f

flung /flʌŋ/ see **fling**

flunk /flʌŋk/ vt (Amer, fam) ser suspendido en ⟨exam⟩; suspender ⟨person⟩. —vi (fam) ser suspendido

fluorescent /fluə'resnt/ a fluorescente

fluoride /'fluəraid/ n fluoruro m

flurry /'flʌri/ n (squall) ráfaga f; (fig) agitación f

flush¹ /flʌʃ/ vi ruborizarse. —vt limpiar con agua. ~ the toilet tirar de la cadena. —n (blush) rubor m; (fig) emoción f

flush² /flʌʃ/ a. ~ (with) a nivel (con)

flush³ /flʌʃ/ vt/i. ~ out (drive out) echar fuera

fluster /'flʌstə(r)/ vt poner nervioso

flute /flu:t/ n flauta f

flutter /'flʌtə(r)/ vi ondear; ⟨bird⟩ revolotear. —n (of wings) revoloteo m; (fig) agitación f

flux /flʌks/ n flujo m. **be in a state of** ~ estar siempre cambiando

fly¹ /flai/ vi (pt flew, pp flown) volar; ⟨passenger⟩ ir en avión; ⟨flag⟩ flotar; ⟨rush⟩ correr. —vt pilotar ⟨aircraft⟩; transportar en avión ⟨passengers, goods⟩; izar ⟨flag⟩. —n (of trousers) bragueta f

fly² /flai/ n mosca f

flyer /'flaiə(r)/ n aviador m; (circular, Amer) prospecto m, folleto m

flying /'flaiiŋ/ a volante; ⟨hasty⟩ relámpago invar. —n (activity) aviación f. ~ **visit** n visita f relámpago

fly: ~**leaf** n guarda f. ~**over** n paso m elevado. ~**weight** n peso m mosca

foal /fəul/ n potro m

foam /fəum/ n espuma f. ~ **(rubber)** n goma f espuma. —vi espumar

fob /fɒb/ vt (pt fobbed). ~ **off on** s.o. (palm off) encajar a uno

focal /'fəukl/ a focal

focus /'fəukəs/ n (pl -cuses or -ci /-sai/) foco m; (fig) centro m. **in** ~ enfocado. **out of** ~ desenfocado. —vt/i (pt **focused**) enfocar(se); (fig) concentrar

fodder /'fɒdə(r)/ n forraje m

foe /fəu/ n enemigo m

foetus /'fi:təs/ n (pl -tuses) feto m

fog /fɒg/ n niebla f. —vt (pt **fogged**) envolver en niebla; ⟨photo⟩ velar. —vi. ~ **(up)** empañarse; ⟨photo⟩ velarse

fog(e)y /'fəugi/ n. **be an old** ~ estar chapado a la antigua

foggy /'fɒgi/ a (-ier, -iest) nebuloso. **it is** ~ hay niebla

foghorn /'fɒghɔːn/ n sirena f de niebla

foible /'fɔibl/ n punto m débil

foil¹ /fɔil/ vt (thwart) frustrar

foil² /fɔil/ n papel m de plata; (fig) contraste m

foist /fɔist/ vt encajar (on a)

fold¹ /fəuld/ vt doblar; cruzar ⟨arms⟩. —vi doblarse; ⟨fail⟩ fracasar. —n pliegue m

fold² /fəuld/ n (for sheep) redil m

folder /'fəuldə(r)/ n (file) carpeta f; (leaflet) folleto m

folding /'fəuldiŋ/ a plegable

foliage /'fəuliidʒ/ n follaje m

folk /fəuk/ n gente f. —a popular. ~**lore** n folklore m. ~**s** npl ⟨one's relatives⟩ familia f

follow /'fɒləu/ vt/i seguir. ~ **up** seguir; (investigate further) investigar. ~**er** n seguidor m. ~**ing** n partidarios mpl. —a siguiente. —prep después de

folly /'fɒli/ n locura f

foment /fə'ment/ vt fomentar

fond /fɒnd/ a (-er, -est) (loving) cariñoso; ⟨hope⟩ vivo. **be** ~ **of s.o.** tener(l) cariño a uno. **be** ~ **of sth** ser aficionado a algo

fondle /'fɒndl/ vt acariciar

fondness /ˈfɒndnɪs/ n cariño m;
(for things) afición f

font /fɒnt/ n pila f bautismal

food /fuːd/ n alimento m, comida
f. ~ **processor** n robot m de
cocina, batidora f

fool /fuːl/ n tonto m. —vt
engañar. —vi hacer el tonto

foolhardy /ˈfuːlhɑːdɪ/ a temerario

foolish /ˈfuːlɪʃ/ a tonto. ~**ly** adv
tontamente. ~**ness** n tontería f

foolproof /ˈfuːlpruːf/ a infalible,
a toda prueba, a prueba de
tontos

foot /fʊt/ n (pl **feet**) pie m; (measure) pie m (=30,48 cm); (of
animal, furniture) pata f. **get
under s.o.'s feet** estorbar a
uno. **on** ~ a pie. **on/to one's
feet** de pie. **put one's** ~ **in it**
meter la pata. —vt pagar (bill).
~ **it** ir andando

footage /ˈfʊtɪdʒ/ n (of film) secuencia f

football /ˈfʊtbɔːl/ n (ball) balón
m; (game) fútbol m. ~**er** n futbolista m & f

footbridge /ˈfʊtbrɪdʒ/ n puente
m para peatones

foothills /ˈfʊthɪlz/ npl estri-
baciones fpl

foothold /ˈfʊthəʊld/ n punto m
de apoyo m

footing /ˈfʊtɪŋ/ n pie m

footlights /ˈfʊtlaɪts/ npl can-
dilejas fpl

footloose /ˈfʊtluːs/ a libre

footman /ˈfʊtmən/ n lacayo m

footnote /ˈfʊtnəʊt/ n nota f (al pie
de la página)

foot: ~**path** n (in country) senda
f; (in town) acera f, vereda f
(Arg), banqueta f (Mex). ~**print**
n huella f. ~**sore** a. **be** ~**sore**
tener los pies doloridos. ~**step**
n paso m. ~**stool** n escabel m.
~**wear** n calzado m

for /fɔː(r)/, unstressed /fə(r)/ prep
(expressing purpose) para; (on

behalf of) por; (in spite of) a pesar
de; (during) durante; (in favour
of) a favor de. **he has been in
Madrid** ~ **two months** hace
dos meses que está en Madrid. —
conj ya que

forage /ˈfɒrɪdʒ/ vi forrajear. —n
forraje m

foray /ˈfɒreɪ/ n incursión f

forbade /fəˈbæd/ see **forbid**

forbear /fɔːˈbeər/ vt/i (pt
forbore, pp **forborne**) contenerse. ~**ance** n paciencia f

forbid /fəˈbɪd/ vt (pt **forbade**, pp
forbidden) prohibir (s.o. to do
a uno hacer). ~ **s.o. sth** prohibir
algo a uno

forbidding /fəˈbɪdɪŋ/ a imponente

force /fɔːs/ n fuerza f. **come into**
~ entrar en vigor. **the** ~**s** las
fuerzas fpl armadas. —vt forzar.
~ **on** imponer a. ~**d** a forzado.
~**feed** vt alimentar a la fuerza.
~**ful** /ˈfɔːsfʊl/ a enérgico

forceps /ˈfɔːseps/ n invar tenazas
fpl; (for obstetric use) fórceps m
invar; (for dental use) gatillo m

forcible /ˈfɔːsəbl/ a a la fuerza.
~**y** adv a la fuerza

ford /fɔːd/ n vado m, botadero m
(Mex). —vt vadear

fore /fɔː(r)/ a anterior. —n. **come
to the** ~ hacerse evidente

forearm /ˈfɔːrɑːm/ n antebrazo m

foreboding /fɔːˈbəʊdɪŋ/ n presentimiento m

forecast /ˈfɔːkɑːst/ vt (pt **forecast**)
pronosticar. —n pronóstico m

forecourt /ˈfɔːkɔːt/ n patio m

forefathers /ˈfɔːfɑːðəz/ npl ante-
pasados mpl

forefinger /ˈfɔːfɪŋɡə(r)/ n (dedo
m) índice m

forefront /ˈfɔːfrʌnt/ n vanguardia f. **in the** ~ a/en vanguardia, en primer plano

foregone /ˈfɔːɡɒn/ a. ~ **con-
clusion** resultado m previsto

foreground /ˈfɔːɡraʊnd/ n primer plano m

forehead /ˈfɒrɪd/ n frente f

foreign /ˈfɒrən/ a extranjero; (trade) exterior; (travel) al extranjero, en el extranjero. ~er n extranjero m. F~ Secretary n ministro m de Asuntos Exteriores

foreman /ˈfɔːmən/ n capataz m, caporal m

foremost /ˈfɔːməʊst/ a primero. —adv. **first and** ~ ante todo

forensic /fəˈrensɪk/ a forense

forerunner /ˈfɔːrʌnə(r)/ n precursor m

foresee /fɔːˈsiː/ vt (pt -saw, pp -seen) prever. ~able a previsible

foreshadow /fɔːˈʃædəʊ/ vt presagiar

foresight /ˈfɔːsaɪt/ n previsión f

forest /ˈfɒrɪst/ n bosque m

forestall /fɔːˈstɔːl/ vt anticiparse a

forestry /ˈfɒrɪstrɪ/ n silvicultura f

foretaste /ˈfɔːteɪst/ n anticipación f

foretell /fɔːˈtel/ vt (pt foretold) predecir

forever /fəˈrevə(r)/ adv para siempre

forewarn /fɔːˈwɔːn/ vt prevenir

foreword /ˈfɔːwɜːd/ n prefacio m

forfeit /ˈfɔːfɪt/ n (penalty) pena f; (in game) prenda f; (fine) multa f. —vt perder

forgave /fəˈɡeɪv/ see **forgive**

forge[1] /fɔːdʒ/ n fragua f. —vt fraguar; (copy) falsificar

forge[2] /fɔːdʒ/ vi avanzar. ~ **ahead** adelantarse rápidamente

forge: ~r /ˈfɔːdʒə(r)/ n falsificador m. ~ry n falsificación f

forget /fəˈɡet/ vt (pt forgot, pp forgotten) olvidar. ~ **o.s.** propasarse, extralimitarse. —vi

olvidar(se). **I forgot** se me olvidó. ~ful a olvidadizo. ~ful of olvidando. ~me-not n nomeolvides f invar

forgive /fəˈɡɪv/ vt (pt forgave, pp forgiven) perdonar. ~ness n perdón m

forgo /fɔːˈɡəʊ/ vt (pt forwent, pp forgone) renunciar a

fork /fɔːk/ n tenedor m; (for digging) horca f; (in road) bifurcación f. —vi (road) bifurcarse. ~ **out** (sl) aflojar la bolsa (fam), pagar. ~ed a ahorquillado; (road) bifurcado. ~lift **truck** n carretilla f elevadora

forlorn /fəˈlɔːn/ a (hopeless) desesperado; (abandoned) abandonado. ~ **hope** n empresa f desesperada

form /fɔːm/ n forma f; (document) impreso m, formulario m; (schol) clase f. —vt formar; (vi formarse

formal /ˈfɔːml/ a formal; (person) formalista; (dress) de etiqueta. ~ity /-ˈmælətɪ/ n formalidad f. ~ly adv oficialmente

format /ˈfɔːmæt/ n formato m

formation /fɔːˈmeɪʃn/ n formación f

formative /ˈfɔːmətɪv/ a formativo

former /ˈfɔːmə(r)/ a anterior; (first of two) primero. ~ly adv antes

formidable /ˈfɔːmɪdəbl/ a formidable

formless /ˈfɔːmlɪs/ a informe

formula /ˈfɔːmjʊlə/ n (pl -ae /-iː/ or -as) fórmula f

formulate /ˈfɔːmjʊleɪt/ vt formular

fornicate /ˈfɔːnɪkeɪt/ vi fornicar. ~ion /-ˈkeɪʃn/ n fornicación f

forsake /fəˈseɪk/ vt (pt forsook, pp forsaken) abandonar

fort /fɔːt/ n (mil) fuerte m

forte /ˈfɔːteɪ/ n (talent) fuerte m

forth /fɔːθ/ adv en adelante. **and so** ~ y así sucesivamente. **go back and** ~ ir y venir

forthcoming /fɔːθˈkʌmɪŋ/ a próximo, venidero; (sociable, fam) comunicativo

forthright /ˈfɔːθraɪt/ a directo

forthwith /fɔːθˈwɪθ/ adv inmediatamente

fortieth /ˈfɔːtɪɪθ/ a cuarenta, cuadragésimo. —n cuadragésima parte f

fortification /fɔːtɪfɪˈkeɪʃn/ n fortificación f. ~y /ˈfɔːtɪfaɪ/ vt fortificar

fortitude /ˈfɔːtɪtjuːd/ n valor m

fortnight /ˈfɔːtnaɪt/ n quince días mpl, quincena f. ~ly a bimensual. —adv cada quince días

fortress /ˈfɔːtrɪs/ n fortaleza f

fortuitous /fɔːˈtjuːɪtəs/ a fortuito

fortunate /ˈfɔːtʃənət/ a afortunado. **be** ~ tener suerte. ~ly adv afortunadamente

fortune /ˈfɔːtʃuːn/ n fortuna f. **have the good** ~ to tener la suerte de. ~-teller n adivino m

forty /ˈfɔːtɪ/ a & n cuarenta (m). ~ **winks** un sueñecito m

forum /ˈfɔːrəm/ n foro m

forward /ˈfɔːwəd/ a delantero; (advanced) precoz; (pert) impertinente. —n (sport) delantero m. —adv adelante. **come** ~ presentarse. **go** ~ avanzar. —vt hacer seguir (letter); enviar (goods); (fig) favorecer. ~ness n precocidad f

forwards /ˈfɔːwədz/ adv adelante

fossil /ˈfɒsl/ a & n fósil m

foster /ˈfɒstə(r)/ vt (promote) fomentar; criar (child). ~-**child** n hijo m adoptivo. ~-**mother** n madre f adoptiva

fought /fɔːt/ see **fight**

foul /faul/ a (-er, -est) (smell, weather) asqueroso; (dirty) sucio; (language) obsceno; (air) viciado. ~ **play** n jugada f sucia;

(crime) delito m. —n (sport) falta f. —vt ensuciar; manchar (reputation). ~-**mouthed** a obsceno

found[1] /faund/ see **find**

found[2] /faund/ vt fundar

found[3] /faund/ vt (tec) fundir

foundation /faunˈdeɪʃn/ n fundación f; (basis) fundamento. ~s npl (archit) cimientos mpl

founder[1] /ˈfaundə(r)/ n fundador m

founder[2] /ˈfaundə(r)/ vi (ship) hundirse

foundry /ˈfaundrɪ/ n fundición f

fountain /ˈfauntɪn/ n fuente f. ~-**pen** n estilográfica f

four /fɔː(r)/ a & n cuatro (m). ~**fold** a cuádruple. —adv cuatro veces. ~-**poster** n cama f con cuatro columnas

foursome /ˈfɔːsəm/ n grupo m de cuatro personas

fourteen /fɔːˈtiːn/ a & n catorce (m). ~**th** a & n catorce (m), decimocuarto (m). —n (fraction) catorceavo m

fourth /fɔːθ/ a & n cuarto (m)

fowl /faul/ n ave f

fox /fɒks/ n zorro m, zorra f. —vt (baffle) dejar perplejo; (deceive) engañar

foyer /ˈfɔɪeɪ/ n (hall) vestíbulo m

fraction /ˈfrækʃn/ n fracción f

fractious /ˈfrækʃəs/ a díscolo

fracture /ˈfræktʃə(r)/ n fractura f. —vt fracturar. —vi fracturarse

fragile /ˈfrædʒaɪl/ a frágil

fragment /ˈfrægmənt/ n fragmento m. ~**ary** a fragmentario

fragrance /ˈfreɪgrəns/ n fragancia f. ~**t** a fragante

frail /freɪl/ a (-er, -est) frágil

frame /freɪm/ n, (of picture, door, window) marco m; (of spectacles) montura f; (fig, structure) estructura f; (temporary state) estado m. ~ **of mind** estado m de ánimo. —vt enmarcar; (fig) formular; (*jurid, sl*) incriminar falsamente. ~**up** *n* (*sl*) complot *m*

framework /'freɪmwɜːk/ *n* estructura *f*; (*context*) marco *m*

France /frɑːns/ *n* Francia *f*

franchise /'fræntʃaɪz/ *n* (*pol*) derecho *m* a votar; (*com*) concesión *f*

Franco... /'fræŋkəʊ/ *pref* franco...

frank /fræŋk/ *a* sincero. ~*vt* franquear. ~**ly** *adv* sinceramente. ~**ness** *n* sinceridad *f*

frantic /'fræntɪk/ *a* frenético. ~ **with** loco de

fraternal /frə'tɜːnl/ *a* fraternal

fraternity /frə'tɜːnɪtɪ/ *n* fraternidad *f*; (*club*) asociación *f*

fraternize /'frætənaɪz/ *vi* fraternizar

fraud /frɔːd/ *n* (*deception*) fraude *m*; (*person*) impostor *m*. ~**ulent** *a* fraudulento

fraught /frɔːt/ *a* (*tense*) tenso. ~ **with** cargado de

fray[1] /freɪ/ *vt* desgastar. ~*vi* deshilacharse

fray[2] /freɪ/ *n* riña *f*

freak /friːk/ *n* (*caprice*) capricho *m*; (*monster*) monstruo *m*; (*person*) chalado *m*. ~*a* anormal. ~**ish** *a* anormal

freckle /'frekl/ *n* peca *f*. ~**d** *a* pecoso

free /friː/ *a* (*freer* /'friːə(r)/, *freest* /'friːɪst/) libre; (*gratis*) gratis; (*lavish*) generoso. ~ **kick** *n* golpe *m* franco. ~ **of charge** gratis. ~ **speech** *n* libertad *f* de expresión. **give a** ~ **hand** carta blanca. ~*vt* (*pt* **freed**) (*set at liberty*) poner en libertad; (*relieve from*) liberar (**from/of** de); (*untangle*) desenredar; (*loosen*) soltar

freedom /'friːdəm/ *n* libertad *f*

freehold /'friːhəʊld/ *n* propiedad *f* absoluta

freelance /'friːlɑːns/ *a* independiente

freely /'friːlɪ/ *adv* libremente

Freemason /'friːmeɪsn/ *n* masón *m*. ~**ry** *n* masonería *f*

free-range /friːreɪndʒ/ *a* (*eggs*) de granja

freesia /'friːzjə/ *n* fresia *f*

freeway /'friːweɪ/ *n* (*Amer*) autopista *f*

freeze /friːz/ *vt* (*pt* **froze**, *pp* **frozen**) helar; congelar (*food, wages*). ~*vi* helarse, congelarse; (*become motionless*) quedarse inmóvil. ~*n* helada *f*; (*of wages, prices*) congelación *f*. ~**er** *n* congelador *m*. ~**ing** *a* glacial. ~*n* congelación *f*. **below** ~**ing** bajo cero

freight /freɪt/ *n* (*goods*) mercancías *fpl*; (*hire of ship etc*) flete *m*. ~**er** *n* (*ship*) buque *m* de carga

French /frentʃ/ *a* francés. ~*n* (*lang*) francés *m*. ~**man** *n* francés *m*. ~**-speaking** *a* francófono. ~ **window** *n* puertaventana *f*. ~**woman** *n* francesa *f*

frenzied /'frenzɪd/ *a* frenético. ~**y** *n* frenesí *m*

frequency /'friːkwənsɪ/ *n* frecuencia *f*

frequent /frɪ'kwent/ *vt* frecuentar. /'friːkwənt/ *a* frecuente. ~**ly** *adv* frecuentemente

fresco /'freskəʊ/ *n* (*pl* -**o(e)s**) fresco *m*

fresh /freʃ/ *a* (-**er**, -**est**) fresco; (*different, additional*) nuevo; (*cheeky*) fresco, descarado; (*water*) dulce. ~**en** *vi* refrescar. ~**en up** (*person*) refrescarse. ~**ly** *adv* recientemente. ~**man** *n* estudiante *m* de primer año. ~**ness** *n* frescura *f*

fret /fret/ *vi* (*pt* **fretted**) inquietarse. ~**ful** *a* (*discontented*) quejoso; (*irritable*) irritable

Freudian /'frɔɪdjən/ a freudiano

friar /'fraɪə(r)/ n fraile m

friction /'frɪkʃn/ n fricción f

Friday /'fraɪdeɪ/ n viernes m. Good ~ Viernes Santo

fridge /frɪdʒ/ n (fam) nevera f, refrigerador m, refrigeradora f

fried /fraɪd/ see **fry**. —a frito

friend /frend/ n amigo m. ~liness /'frendlɪnɪs/ n simpatía f. ~ly a (-ier, -iest) simpático. F~ly Society n mutualidad f. ~ship /'frendʃɪp/ n amistad f

frieze /friːz/ n friso m

frigate /'frɪgət/ n fragata f

fright /fraɪt/ n susto m; (person) espantajo m; (thing) horror m

frighten /'fraɪtn/ vt asustar. ~ off ahuyentar. ~ed a asustado. be ~ed tener miedo (of de)

frightful /'fraɪtfl/ a espantoso, horrible. ~ly adv terriblemente

frigid /'frɪdʒɪd/ a frío; (psych) frígido. ~ity /-'dʒɪdɪtɪ/ n frigidez f

frill /frɪl/ n volante m. ~s npl (fig) adornos mpl. with no ~s sencillo

fringe /frɪndʒ/ n (sewing) fleco m; (ornamental border) franja f; (of hair) flequillo m; (of area) periferia f; (of society) margen m. ~ benefits npl beneficios mpl suplementarios. ~ theatre n teatro m de vanguardia

frisk /frɪsk/ vt (search) cachear

frisky /'frɪskɪ/ a (-ier, -iest) retozón; (horse) fogoso

fritter[1] /'frɪtə(r)/ n buñuelo m

fritter[2] /'frɪtə(r)/ vt. ~ away desperdiciar

frivol|ity /frɪ'vɒlɪtɪ/ n frivolidad f. ~ous /'frɪvələs/ a frívolo

frizzy /'frɪzɪ/ a crespo

fro /frəʊ/ see **to and fro**

frock /frɒk/ n vestido m; (of monk) hábito m

frog /frɒg/ n rana f. have a ~ in one's throat tener carraspera

frogman /'frɒgmən/ n hombre m rana

frolic /'frɒlɪk/ vi (pt frolicked) retozar. —n broma f

from /frɒm/, unstressed /frəm/ prep de; (with time, prices, etc) a partir de; (habit, conviction) por; (according to) según. take ~ (away from) quitar a

front /frʌnt/ n parte f delantera; (of building) fachada f; (of clothes) delantera f; (mil, pol) frente f; (of book) principio m; (fig, appearance) apariencia f; (sea front) paseo m marítimo. in ~ of delante de. put a bold ~ on hacer de tripas corazón, mostrar firmeza. —a delantero; (first) primero. ~age n fachada f. ~al a frontal; (attack) de frente. ~ door n puerta f principal. ~ page n (of newspaper) primera plana f

frontier /'frʌntɪə(r)/ n frontera f

frost /frɒst/ n (freezing) helada f; (frozen dew) escarcha f. ~bite n congelación f. ~bitten a congelado. ~ed a (glass) esmerilado. ~ed a (glass) esmerilado

frosting /'frɒstɪŋ/ n (icing, Amer) azúcar m glaseado

frosty a (weather) de helada; (window) escarchado; (fig) glacial

froth /frɒθ/ n espuma f. —vi espumar. ~y a espumoso

frown /fraʊn/ vi fruncir el entrecejo. ~ on desaprobar. —n ceño m

froze /frəʊz/, **frozen** /'frəʊzn/ see **freeze**

frugal /'fruːgl/ a frugal. ~ly adv frugalmente

fruit /fruːt/ n (bot, on tree, fig) fruto m; (as food) fruta f. ~erer n frutero m. ~ful /'fruːtfl/ a fértil; (fig) fructífero. ~less a infructuoso. ~ machine n (máquina f) tragaperras m. ~ salad n macedonia f de frutas.

~y /ˈfruːtɪ/ a ⟨taste⟩ que sabe a fruta

fruition /fruːˈɪʃn/ n. **come to** ~ realizarse

frump /frʌmp/ n espantajo m

frustrat e /frʌˈstreɪt/ vt frustrar. ~ion /-ʃn/ n frustración f; ⟨disappointment⟩ decepción f

fry[1] /fraɪ/ vt (pt **fried**) freír. ~ freírse

fry[2] /fraɪ/ n (pl **fry**). **small** ~ gente f de poca monta

frying-pan /ˈfraɪɪŋpæn/ n sartén f

fuchsia /ˈfjuːʃə/ n fucsia f

fuddy-duddy /ˈfʌdɪdʌdɪ/ n. **be a** ~ (sl) chapado a la antigua

fudge /fʌdʒ/ n dulce m de azúcar

fuel /ˈfjuːəl/ n combustible m; ⟨for car engine⟩ carburante m; (fig) pábulo m. ~ vt (pt **fuelled**) alimentar de combustible

fugitive /ˈfjuːdʒɪtɪv/ a & n fugitivo (m)

fugue /fjuːg/ n (mus) fuga f

fulfil /fʊlˈfɪl/ vt (pt **fulfilled**) cumplir (con) ⟨promise, obligation⟩; satisfacer ⟨condition⟩; realizar ⟨hopes, plans⟩; llevar a cabo ⟨task⟩. ~ment n ⟨of promise, obligation⟩ cumplimiento m; ⟨of hopes, plans⟩ satisfacción f; ⟨of task⟩ ejecución f

full /fʊl/ a (-er, -est) lleno, ⟨bus, hotel⟩ completo; ⟨skirt⟩ amplio; ⟨account⟩ detallado. **at** ~ **speed** a máxima velocidad. **be** ~ **(up)** ⟨with food⟩ no poder más. **in** ~ **swing** en plena marcha. —n. **in** ~ sin quitar nada. **to the** ~ completamente. **write in** ~ escribir con todas las letras. ~ **back** n (sport) defensa m & f. ~-**blooded** a vigoroso. ~ **moon** n plenilunio m. ~-**scale** a ⟨drawing⟩ de tamaño natural; (fig) amplio. ~ **stop** n punto m; ⟨at

end of paragraph, fig⟩ punto m final. ~ **time** a de jornada completa. ~y adv completamente

fulsome /ˈfʊlsəm/ a excesivo

fumble /ˈfʌmbl/ vi buscar (torpemente)

fume /fjuːm/ vi humear; (fig, be furious) estar furioso. ~s npl humo m

fumigate /ˈfjuːmɪgeɪt/ vt fumigar

fun /fʌn/ n ⟨amusement⟩ diversión f; ⟨merriment⟩ alegría f. **for** ~ en broma. **have** ~ divertirse. **make** ~ **of** burlarse de

function /ˈfʌŋkʃn/ n ⟨purpose, duty⟩ función f; ⟨reception⟩ recepción f. ~i vi funcionar. ~al a funcional

fund /fʌnd/ n fondo m. ~ vt proveer fondos para

fundamental /fʌndəˈmentl/ a fundamental

funeral /ˈfjuːnərəl/ n funeral m, funerales mpl. ~a fúnebre

fun-fair /ˈfʌnfeə(r)/ n parque m de atracciones

fungus /ˈfʌŋgəs/ n (pl -**gi** /-gaɪ/) hongo m

funicular /fjuːˈnɪkjʊlə(r)/ n funicular m

funk /fʌŋk/ m ⟨fear, sl⟩ miedo m; ⟨state of depression, Amer, sl⟩ depresión f. **be in a (blue)** ~ tener (mucho) miedo; (Amer) estar (muy) deprimido. —vi rajarse

funnel /ˈfʌnl/ n ⟨for pouring⟩ embudo m; ⟨of ship⟩ chimenea f

funn ily /ˈfʌnɪlɪ/ adv graciosamente; ⟨oddly⟩ curiosamente. ~y a (-ier, -iest) divertido, gracioso; ⟨odd⟩ curioso, raro. ~y-**bone** n cóndilo m del húmero. ~y **business** n engaño m

fur /fɜː(r)/ n pelo m; ⟨pelt⟩ piel f; ⟨in kettle⟩ sarro m

furbish /ˈfɜːbɪʃ/ vt pulir; ⟨renovate⟩ renovar

furious /'fjʊərɪəs/ a furioso. ~**ly** adv furiosamente

furnace /'fɜːnɪs/ n horno m

furnish /'fɜːnɪʃ/ vt (with furniture) amueblar; (supply) proveer. ~**ings** npl muebles mpl, mobiliario m

furniture /'fɜːnɪtʃə(r)/ n muebles mpl, mobiliario m

furrier /'fʌrɪə(r)/ n peletero m

furrow /'fʌrəʊ/ n surco m

furry /'fɜːrɪ/ a peludo

further /'fɜːðə(r)/ a más lejano; (additional) nuevo. —adv más lejos; (more) además. —vt fomentar. ~**rmore** adv además. ~**rmost** a más lejano. ~**st** a más lejano. —adv más lejos

furtive /'fɜːtɪv/ a furtivo

fury /'fjʊərɪ/ n furia f

fuse[1] /fjuːz/ vt (melt) fundir; (fig, unite) fusionar. ~ **the lights** fundir los plomos. —vi fundirse; (fig) fusionarse. —n fusible m, plomo m

fuse[2] /fjuːz/ n (of bomb) mecha f

fuse-box /'fjuːzbɒks/ n caja f de fusibles

fuselage /'fjuːzəlɑːʒ/ n fuselaje m

fusion /'fjuːʒn/ n fusión f

fuss /fʌs/ n (commotion) jaleo m. **kick up a** ~ armar un lío, armar una bronca, protestar. **make a** ~ of tratar con mucha atención. ~**y** a (-ier, -iest) (finicky) remilgado; (demanding) exigente; (ornate) recargado

fusty /'fʌstɪ/ a (-ier, -iest) que huele a cerrado

futile /'fjuːtaɪl/ a inútil, vano

future /'fjuːtʃə(r)/ a futuro. —n futuro m, porvenir m; (gram) futuro m. **in** ~ en lo sucesivo, de ahora en adelante

futuristic /fjuːtʃə'rɪstɪk/ a futurista

fuzz /fʌz/ n (fluff) pelusa f; (police, sl) policía f, poli f (fam)

fuzzy /'fʌzɪ/ a (hair) crespo; (photograph) borroso

G

gab /gæb/ n charla f. **have the gift of the** ~ tener un pico de oro

gabardine /gæbə'diːn/ n gabardina f

gabble /'gæbl/ vt decir atropelladamente. —vi hablar atropelladamente. —n torrente m de palabras

gable /'geɪbl/ n aguilón m

gad /gæd/ vi (pt gadded). ~ **about** callejear

gadget /'gædʒɪt/ n chisme m

Gaelic /'geɪlɪk/ a & n gaélico (m)

gaffe /gæf/ n plancha f, metedura f de pata

gag /gæg/ n mordaza f; (joke) chiste m. —vt (pt gagged) amordazar

gaga /'gɑːgɑː/ a (sl) chocho

gaiety /'geɪətɪ/ n alegría f

gaily /'geɪlɪ/ adv alegremente

gain /geɪn/ vt ganar; (acquire) adquirir; (obtain) conseguir. —vi (clock) adelantar. —n ganancia f; (increase) aumento m. ~**ful** a lucrativo

gainsay /geɪn'seɪ/ vt (pt gainsaid) (formal) negar

gait /geɪt/ n modo m de andar

gala /'gɑːlə/ n fiesta f; (sport) competición f

galaxy /'gæləksɪ/ n galaxia f

gale /geɪl/ n vendaval m; (storm) tempestad f

gall /gɔːl/ n bilis f; (fig) hiel f; (impudence) descaro m

gallant /'gælənt/ a (brave) valiente; (chivalrous) galante. ~**ry** n valor m

gall-bladder /'gɔːlblædə(r)/ n vesícula f biliar

galleon /'gælɪən/ n galeón m

gallery /'gælərɪ/ n galería f

galley /'gælɪ/ n (ship) galera f; (ship's kitchen) cocina f. ~ (proof) (typ) galerada f

Gallic /'gælɪk/ a gálico. ~ism /n galicismo m

gallivant /'gælɪvænt/ vi (fam) callejear

gallon /'gælən/ n galón m (imperial = 4,546l; Amer = 3,785l)

gallop /'gæləp/ n galope m. —vi (pt galloped) galopar

gallows /'gæləʊz/ n horca f

galore /gə'lɔː(r)/ adv en abundancia

galosh /gə'lɒʃ/ n chanclo m

galvanize /'gælvənaɪz/ vt galvanizar

gambit /'gæmbɪt/ n (in chess) gambito m; (fig) táctica f

gamble /'gæmbl/ vt/i jugar. ~e on contar con. —n (venture) empresa f arriesgada; (bet) jugada f; (risk) riesgo m. ~er n jugador m. ~ing n juego m

game[1] /geɪm/ n juego m; (match) partido m; (animals, birds) caza f. ~a valiente. ~ for listo para

game[2] /geɪm/ a (lame) cojo

gamekeeper /'geɪmkiːpə(r)/ n guardabosque m

gammon /'gæmən/ n jamón m ahumado

gamut /'gæmət/ n gama f

gamy /'geɪmɪ/ a manido

gander /'gændə(r)/ n ganso m

gang /gæŋ/ n pandilla f; (of workmen) equipo m. —vi. ~ up unirse (on contra)

gangling /'gæŋglɪŋ/ a larguirucho

gangrene /'gæŋgriːn/ n gangrena f

gangster /'gæŋstə(r)/ n bandido m, gángster m

gangway /'gæŋweɪ/ n pasillo m; (of ship) pasarela f

gaol /dʒeɪl/ n cárcel f. ~bird n criminal m empedernido. ~er n carcelero m

gap /gæp/ n vacío m; (breach) brecha f; (in time) intervalo m; (deficiency) laguna f; (difference) diferencia f

gape /geɪp/ vi quedarse boquiabierto; (be wide open) estar muy abierto. ~ing a abierto; (person) boquiabierto

garage /'gærɑːʒ/ n garaje m; (petrol station) gasolinera f; (for repairs) taller m. —vt dejar en (el) garaje

garb /gɑːb/ n vestido m

garbage /'gɑːbɪdʒ/ n basura f

garble /'gɑːbl/ vt mutilar

garden /'gɑːdn/ n (of flowers) jardín m; (of vegetables/fruit) huerto m. —vi trabajar en el jardín/huerto. ~er n jardinero/hortelano m. ~ing n jardinería/horticultura f

gargantuan /gɑː'gæntjʊən/ a gigantesco

gargle /'gɑːgl/ vi hacer gárgaras. n gargarismo m

gargoyle /'gɑːgɔɪl/ n gárgola f

garish /'geərɪʃ/ a chillón

garland /'gɑːlənd/ n guirnalda f

garlic /'gɑːlɪk/ n ajo m

garment /'gɑːmənt/ n prenda f (de vestir)

garnet /'gɑːnɪt/ n granate m

garnish /'gɑːnɪʃ/ vt aderezar. —n aderezo m

garret /'gærət/ n guardilla f, buhardilla f

garrison /'gærɪsn/ n guarnición f

garrulous /'gærələs/ a hablador

garter /'gɑːtə(r)/ n liga f

gas /gæs/ n (pl gases) gas m; (med) anestésico m; (petrol, Amer, fam) gasolina f. —vt (pt gassed) asfixiar con gas. —vi (fam) charlar. ~ fire n estufa f de gas

gash /gæʃ/ n cuchillada f. —vt acuchillar

gasket /'gæskɪt/ n junta f

gas: ~ **mask** n careta f antigás a invar. ~ **meter** n contador m de gas

gasoline /'gæsəliːn/ n (petrol, Amer) gasolina f

gasometer /gæ'sɒmɪtə(r)/ n gasómetro m

gasp /gɑːsp/ vi jadear; (with surprise) quedarse boquiabierto. — n jadeo m

gas: ~ **ring** n hornillo m de gas. ~ **station** n (Amer) gasolinera f

gastric /'gæstrɪk/ a gástrico

gastronomy /gæ'strɒnəmɪ/ n gastronomía f

gate /geɪt/ n puerta f; (of metal) verja f; (barrier) barrera f

gateau /'gætəʊ/ n (pl **gateaux**) tarta f

gate: ~**crasher** n intruso m (que ha entrado sin ser invitado o sin pagar). ~**way** n puerta f

gather /'gæðə(r)/ vt reunir (people, things); (accumulate) acumular; (pick up) recoger; recoger (flowers); (fig, infer) deducir; (sewing) fruncir. ~ **speed** acelerar. —vi (people) reunirse; (things) acumularse. ~**ing** n reunión f

gauche /gəʊʃ/ a torpe

gaudy /'gɔːdɪ/ a (-ier, -iest) chillón

gauge /geɪdʒ/ n (measurement) medida f; (rail) entrevía f; (instrument) indicador m. —vt medir; (fig) estimar

gaunt /gɔːnt/ a macilento; (grim) lúgubre

gauntlet /'gɔːntlɪt/ n. **run the ~ of** estar sometido a

gauze /gɔːz/ n gasa f

gave /geɪv/ see **give**

gawk /gɔːk/ vi. ~ **at** mirar como un tonto

gawky /'gɔːkɪ/ a (-ier, -iest) torpe

gawp /gɔːp/ vi. ~ **at** mirar como un tonto

gay /geɪ/ a (-er, -est) (joyful) alegre; (homosexual, fam) homosexual, gay (fam)

gaze /geɪz/ vi. ~ **(at)** mirar (fijamente). —n mirada f (fija)

gazelle /gə'zel/ n gacela f

gazette /gə'zet/ n boletín m oficial, gaceta f

gazump /gə'zʌmp/ vt aceptar un precio más elevado de otro comprador

GB abbr see **Great Britain**

gear /gɪə(r)/ n equipo m; (tec) engranaje m; (auto) marcha f. **in ~** engranado. **out of ~** desengranado. —vt adaptar. ~**box** n (auto) caja f de cambios

geese /giːs/ see **goose**

geezer /'giːzə(r)/ n (sl) tipo m

gelatine /'dʒelətiːn/ n gelatina f

gelignite /'dʒelɪgnaɪt/ n gelignita f

gem /dʒem/ n piedra f preciosa

Gemini /'dʒemɪnaɪ/ n (astr) Gemelos mpl, Géminis mpl

gen /dʒen/ n (sl) información f

gender /'dʒendə(r)/ n género m

gene /dʒiːn/ n gene m

genealogy /dʒiːnɪ'ælədʒɪ/ n genealogía f

general /'dʒenərəl/ a general. — n general m. **in ~** generalmente. ~ **election** n elecciones fpl generales

generaliz|ation /dʒenərəlaɪ'zeɪʃn/ n generalización f. ~**e** vt/i generalizar

generally /'dʒenərəlɪ/ adv generalmente

general practitioner /'dʒenərəl præk'tɪʃənə(r)/ n médico m de cabecera

generate /'dʒenəreɪt/ vt producir; (elec) generar

generation /dʒenəˈreɪʃn/ n generación f

generator /ˈdʒenəreɪtə(r)/ n (elec) generador m

genero|sity /dʒenəˈrɒsəti/ n generosidad f. ~**us** /ˈdʒenərəs/ a (plentiful) abundante

genetic /dʒɪˈnetɪk/ a genético. ~**s** n genética f

Geneva /dʒɪˈniːvə/ n Ginebra f

genial /ˈdʒiːnɪəl/ a simpático, afable; (climate) suave, templado

genital /ˈdʒenɪtl/ a genital. ~**s** npl genitales mpl

genitive /ˈdʒenɪtɪv/ a & n genitivo (m)

genius /ˈdʒiːnɪəs/ n (pl -uses) genio m

genocide /ˈdʒenəsaɪd/ n genocidio m

genre /ʒɑːŋr/ n género m

gent /dʒent/ n (sl) señor m. ~**s** n aseo m de caballeros

genteel /dʒenˈtiːl/ a distinguido; (excessively refined) cursi

gentle /ˈdʒentl/ a (-er, -est) (mild, kind) amable, dulce; (slight) ligero; (hint) discreto

gentlefolk /ˈdʒentlfəʊk/ npl gente f de buena familia

gentleman /ˈdʒentlmən/ n señor m; (well-bred) caballero m

gentleness /ˈdʒentlnɪs/ n amabilidad f

gentlewoman /ˈdʒentlwʊmən/ n señora f (de buena familia)

gently /ˈdʒentlɪ/ adv amablemente; (slowly) despacio

gentry /ˈdʒentrɪ/ npl pequeña aristocracia f

genuflect /ˈdʒenjuːflekt/ vi doblar la rodilla

genuine /ˈdʒenjʊɪn/ a verdadero; (person) sincero

geographer /dʒɪˈɒɡrəfə(r)/ n geógrafo m. ~**ical** /dʒɪəˈɡræfɪkl/ a geográfico. ~**y** /dʒɪˈɒɡrəfɪ/ n geografía f

geolog|ical /dʒɪəˈlɒdʒɪkl/ a geológico. ~**ist** n geólogo m. ~**y** /dʒɪˈɒlədʒɪ/ n geología f

geometr|ic(al) /dʒɪəˈmetrɪk(l)/ a geométrico. ~**y** /dʒɪˈɒmətrɪ/ n geometría f

geranium /dʒəˈreɪnɪəm/ n geranio m

geriatrics /dʒerɪˈætrɪks/ n geriatría f

germ /dʒɜːm/ n (rudiment, seed) germen m; (med) microbio m

German /ˈdʒɜːmən/ a & n alemán (m). ~**ic** /dʒəˈmænɪk/ a germánico. ~ **measles** n rubéola f. ~ **shepherd (dog)** n (perro m) pastor m alemán. ~**y** n Alemania f

germicide /ˈdʒɜːmɪsaɪd/ n germicida m

germinate /ˈdʒɜːmɪneɪt/ vi germinar. ~tr hacer germinar

gerrymander /ˈdʒerɪmændə(r)/ n falsificación f electoral

gestation /dʒeˈsteɪʃn/ n gestación f

gesticulate /dʒeˈstɪkjʊleɪt/ vi hacer ademanes, gesticular

gesture /ˈdʒestʃə(r)/ n ademán m; (fig) gesto m

get /get/ vt (pt & pp **got**, pp Amer **gotten**, pres p **getting**) obtener, tener; (catch) coger (not LAm), agarrar (esp LAm); (buy) comprar; (find) encontrar; (fetch) buscar, traer; (understand, sl) comprender, caer (fam). ~ **s.o. to do sth** conseguir que uno haga algo. —vi (go) ir; (become) hacerse; (start to) empezar a; (manage) conseguir. ~ **married** casarse. ~ **ready** prepararse. ~ **about** (person) salir mucho; (after illness) levantarse. ~ **along** (manage) ir tirando; (progress) hacer progresos. ~ **along with** llevarse bien con. ~ **at** (reach) llegar a; (imply) querer decir. ~ **away** salir; (escape)

escaparse. ~ **back** vi volver. —
vt (recover) recobrar. ~ **by**
(manage) ir tirando; (pass)
pasar. ~ **down** bajar; (depress)
deprimir. ~ **in** entrar; subir
⟨vehicle⟩; (arrive) llegar. ~ **off**
bajar de ⟨train, car etc⟩; (leave)
irse; (jurid) salir absuelto. ~ **on**
(progress) hacer progresos; (succeed) tener éxito. ~ **on with** (be
on good terms with) llevarse bien
con; (continue) seguir. ~ **out**
⟨person⟩ salir; (take out) sacar. ~
out of (fig) librarse de. ~ **over**
reponerse de ⟨illness⟩. ~ **round**
soslayar ⟨difficulty etc⟩; engatusar ⟨person⟩. ~ **through**
(pass) pasar; (finish) terminar;
(on phone) comunicar con. ~ **up**
levantarse; (climb) subir;
(organize) preparar. ~**away** ~n
huida f. ~**up** n traje m

geyser /ˈgiːzə(r)/ n calentador m
de agua; (geog) géiser m

Ghana /ˈɡɑːnə/ n Ghana f

ghastly /ˈɡɑːstlɪ/ a (-ier, -iest)
horrible; (pale) pálido

gherkin /ˈɡɜːkɪn/ n pepinillo m

ghetto /ˈɡetəʊ/ n (pl -os) (Jewish
quarter) judería f; (ethnic set-
tlement) barrio m pobre habit-
ado por un grupo étnico

ghost /ɡəʊst/ n fantasma m. ~**ly**
a espectral

ghoulish /ˈɡuːlɪʃ/ a macabro

giant /ˈdʒaɪənt/ n gigante m. —a
gigantesco

gibberish /ˈdʒɪbərɪʃ/ n jerigonza
f

gibe /dʒaɪb/ n mofa f

giblets /ˈdʒɪblɪts/ npl menudillos
mpl

Gibraltar /dʒɪˈbrɔːltə(r)/ n Gibraltar m

giddiness /ˈɡɪdɪnɪs/ n vértigo m.
~**y** a (-ier, -iest) mareado;
⟨speed⟩ vertiginoso. be/feel ~**y**
estar/sentirse mareado

gift /ɡɪft/ n regalo m; (ability) don
m. ~**ed** a dotado de talento.
~**-wrap** vt envolver para regalo

gig /ɡɪɡ/ n (fam) concierto m

gigantic /dʒaɪˈɡæntɪk/ a gigantesco

giggle /ˈɡɪɡl/ vi reírse tontamente. —n risita f. **the** ~**s** la risa
f tonta

gild /ɡɪld/ vt dorar

gills /ɡɪlz/ npl agallas fpl

gilt /ɡɪlt/ a dorado. ~**-edged** a
(com) de máxima garantía

gimmick /ˈɡɪmɪk/ n truco m

gin /dʒɪn/ n ginebra f

ginger /ˈdʒɪndʒə(r)/ n jengibre
m. —a rojizo. —vt. ~ **up** animar.
~ **ale** n, ~ **beer** n cerveza f de
jengibre. ~**bread** n pan m de
jengibre

gingerly /ˈdʒɪndʒəlɪ/ adv cautelosamente

gingham /ˈɡɪŋəm/ n guinga f

gipsy /ˈdʒɪpsɪ/ n gitano m

giraffe /dʒɪˈrɑːf/ n jirafa f

girder /ˈɡɜːdə(r)/ n viga f

girdle /ˈɡɜːdl/ n (belt) cinturón m;
(corset) corsé m

girl /ɡɜːl/ n chica f, muchacha f;
(child) niña f. ~**friend** n amiga
f, (of boy) novia f. ~**hood** n (up
to adolescence) niñez f; (adolescence) juventud f. ~**ish** a de
niña; (boy) afeminado

giro /ˈdʒaɪrəʊ/ n (pl -os) giro m
(bancario)

girth /ɡɜːθ/ n circunferencia f

gist /dʒɪst/ n lo esencial invar

give /ɡɪv/ vt (pt **gave**, pp **given**)
dar; (deliver) entregar; regalar
⟨present⟩; prestar ⟨aid, atten-
tion⟩; (grant) conceder; (yield)
ceder; (devote) dedicar. ~ **o.s. to**
darse a. —vi dar; (yield) ceder;
(stretch) estirarse. —n elasticidad f. ~ **away** regalar; descubrir ⟨secret⟩. ~ **back** devolver. ~
in (yield) rendirse. ~ **off** emitir.
~ **o.s. up** entregarse (a). ~ **out**

distribuir; (announce) anunciar; (become used up) agotarse. —over (devote) dedicar; (stop, fam) dejar de (be). ~ up (renounce) renunciar a; (yield) ceder

given /'gɪvn/ see give. —a dado. ~ name n nombre m de pila

glacier /'glæsɪə(r)/ n glaciar m

glad /glæd/ a contento. ~den vt alegrar

glade /gleɪd/ n claro m

gladiator /'glædɪeɪtə(r)/ n gladiador m

gladiolus /glædɪ'əʊləs/ n (pl -li /-laɪ/) estoque m, gladiolo m, gladíolo m

gladly /'glædlɪ/ adv alegremente; (willingly) con mucho gusto

glamorize /'glæməraɪz/ vt embellecer. ~rous /-rəs/ a atractivo. ~ur n encanto m

glance /glɑːns/ n ojeada f. —vi. ~ at dar un vistazo a

gland /glænd/ n glándula f

glare /gleə(r)/ vi deslumbrar; (stare angrily) mirar airadamente. —n deslumbramiento m; (stare, fig) mirada f airada. ~ing a deslumbrador; (obvious) manifiesto

glass /glɑːs/ n (material) vidrio m; (without stem or for wine) vaso m; (with stem) copa f; (for beer) caña f; (mirror) espejo m. ~es npl (spectacles) gafas fpl, anteojos (LAm) mpl. ~y a vítreo

glaze /gleɪz/ vt poner cristales a (windows, doors); vidriar (pottery). —n barniz m; (for pottery) esmalte m. ~d a (object) vidriado; (eye) vidrioso

gleam /gliːm/ n destello m. —vi destellar

glean /gliːn/ vt espigar

glee /gliː/ n regocijo m. ~ club n orfeón m. ~ful a regocijado

glen /glen/ n cañada f

glib /glɪb/ a de mucha labia; (reply) fácil. ~ly adv con poca sinceridad

glide /glaɪd/ vi deslizarse; (plane) planear. ~er n planeador m. ~ing n planeo m

glimmer /'glɪmə(r)/ n destello m. —vi destellar

glimpse /glɪmps/ n vislumbre f. catch a ~ of vislumbrar. —vt vislumbrar

glint /glɪnt/ n destello m. —vi destellar

glisten /'glɪsn/ vi brillar

glitter /'glɪtə(r)/ vi brillar. —n brillo m

gloat /gləʊt/ vi. ~ on/over regodearse

global /'gləʊbl/ a (world-wide) mundial; (all-embracing) global

globe /gləʊb/ n globo m

globule /'glɒbjuːl/ n glóbulo m

gloom /gluːm/ n oscuridad f; (sadness, fig) tristeza f. ~y a (-ier, -iest) triste; (pessimistic) pesimista

glorify /'glɔːrɪfaɪ/ vt glorificar

glorious /'glɔːrɪəs/ a espléndido; (deed, hero etc) glorioso

glory /'glɔːrɪ/ n gloria f; (beauty) esplendor m. —vi. ~ in enorgullecerse de. ~-hole n (untidy room) leonera f

gloss /glɒs/ n lustre m. —a brillante. —vi. ~ over (make light of) minimizar; (cover up) encubrir

glossary /'glɒsərɪ/ n glosario m

glossy /'glɒsɪ/ a brillante

glove /glʌv/ n guante m. ~ compartment n (auto) guantera f, gaveta f. ~d a enguantado

glow /gləʊ/ vi brillar; (with health) rebosar de; (with passion) enardecerse. —n incandescencia f; (of cheeks) rubor m

glower /'glaʊə(r)/ vi. ~ (at) mirar airadamente

glowing /'gləʊɪŋ/ a incandescente; (account) entusiasta; (complexion) rojo; (with health) rebosante de

glucose /'gluːkəʊs/ n glucosa f

glue /gluː/ n cola f. —vt (pres p **gluing**) pegar

glum /glʌm/ a (**glummer, glummest**) triste

glut /glʌt/ n superabundancia f

glutton /ˈglʌtn/ n glotón m. **~ous** a glotón. **~y** n glotonería f

glycerine /ˈglɪsəriːn/ n glicerina f

gnarled /nɑːld/ a nudoso

gnash /næʃ/ vt. **~ one's teeth** rechinar los dientes

gnat /næt/ n mosquito m

gnaw /nɔː/ vt/i roer

gnome /nəʊm/ n gnomo m

go /ɡəʊ/ vi (pt **went**, pp **gone**) ir; (leave) irse; (work) funcionar; (become) hacerse; (be sold) venderse; (vanish) desaparecer. **~ ahead!** ¡adelante! **it's your ~** te toca a ti. **make a ~ of** tener éxito en. **~ across** cruzar. **~ away** irse. **~ back** volver. **~ back on** faltar a (promise etc). **~ by** pasar. **~ down** bajar; (sun) ponerse. **~ for** buscar, traer; (like) gustar; (attack, sl) atacar. **~ in** entrar. **~ in for** presentarse para (exam). **~ off** (leave) irse; (go bad) pasarse; (explode) estallar. **~ on** seguir; (happen) pasar. **~ out** salir; (light, fire) apagarse. **~ over** (check) examinar. **~ round** (be enough) ser bastante. **~ through** (suffer) sufrir; (check) examinar. **~ under** hundirse. **~ up** subir. **~ without** pasarse sin

goad /ɡəʊd/ vt aguijonear

go-ahead /ˈɡəʊəhed/ n luz f verde. —a dinámico

goal /ɡəʊl/ n fin m, objeto m; (sport) gol m. **~ie** n (fam) portero m. **~keeper** n portero m.

~post n poste m (de la portería)

goat /ɡəʊt/ n cabra f

goatee /ɡəʊˈtiː/ n perilla f, barbas fpl de chivo

gobble /ˈgɒbl/ vt engullir

go-between /ˈgəʊbɪtwiːn/ n intermediario m

goblet /ˈgɒblɪt/ n copa f

goblin /ˈgɒblɪn/ n duende m

God /gɒd/ n Dios m. **~-forsaken** a olvidado de Dios

god /gɒd/ n dios m. **~child** n ahijado m. **~daughter** n ahijada f. **~dess** /ˈgɒdɪs/ n diosa f. **~father** n padrino m. **~ly** a devoto. **~mother** n madrina f. **~send** n beneficio m inesperado. **~son** n ahijado m

go-getter /ɡəʊˈɡetə(r)/ n persona f ambiciosa

goggle /ˈgɒgl/ vi. **~ (at)** mirar con los ojos desmesuradamente abiertos

goggles /ˈgɒglz/ npl gafas fpl protectoras

going /ˈgəʊɪŋ/ n camino m; (racing) (estado m del) terreno m. **it is slow/hard ~** es lento/difícil. —a (price) actual; (concern) en funcionamiento. **~s-on** npl actividades fpl anormales, tejemaneje m

gold /ɡəʊld/ n oro m. —a de oro. **~en** /ˈgəʊldən/ a (de oro); (in colour) dorado; (opportunity) único. **~en wedding** n bodas fpl de oro. **~fish** n invar pez m de colores, carpa f dorada. **~mine** n mina f de oro; (fig) fuente f de gran riqueza. **~-plated** a chapado en oro. **~smith** n orfebre m

golf /gɒlf/ n golf m. **~-course** n campo m de golf. **~er** n jugador m de golf

golly /ˈgɒlɪ/ int ¡caramba!

golosh /gəˈlɒʃ/ n chanclo m

gondola /ˈgɒndələ/ n góndola f. **~ier** /gɒndəˈlɪə(r)/ n gondolero m

gone /gɒn/ *see* go. —*a* pasado. ~ **six o'clock** después de las seis

gong /gɒŋ/ *n* (*gong*) *m*

good /gʊd/ *a* (**better**, **best**) bueno, (*before masculine singular noun*) buen. ~ **after-noon!** ¡buenas tardes! ~ **evening!** (*before dark*) ¡buenas tardes!; (*after dark*) ¡buenas noches! G~ **Friday** *n* Viernes *m* Santo. ~ **morning!** ¡buenos días! ~ **name** *n* (buena) reputación *f*. ~ **night!** ¡buenas noches! **a** ~ **deal** bastante. **as** ~ **as** (*almost*) casi. **be** ~ **with** entender. **do** ~ hacer bien. **feel** ~ sentirse bien. **have a** ~ **time** divertirse. **it is** ~ **for you** te sentará bien. —*n* bien *m*. **for** ~ para siempre. **it is no** ~ **shouting/ etc** es inútil gritar/etc.

goodbye /gʊd'baɪ/ *int* ¡adiós! —*n* adiós *m*. **say** ~ **to** despedirse de

good: ~**-for-nothing** *a* & *n* inútil (*m*). ~**-looking** *a* guapo

goodness /'gʊdnɪs/ *n* bondad *f*. ~**!**, ~ **gracious!**, ~ **me!**, **my** ~**!** ¡Dios mío!

goods /gʊdz/ *npl* (*merchandise*) mercancías *fpl*

goodwill /gʊd'wɪl/ *n* buena voluntad *f*

goody /'gʊdɪ/ *n* (*culin*, *fam*) golosina *f*; (*in film*) bueno *m*. ~**-goody** *n* mojigato *m*

gooey /'gu:ɪ/ *a* (**gooier**, **gooiest**) (*sl*) pegajoso; (*fig*) sentimental

goof /gu:f/ *vi* (*Amer*, *blunder*) cometer una pifia. ~**y** *a* (*sl*) necio

goose /gu:s/ *n* (*pl* **geese**) oca *f*

gooseberry /'gʊzbərɪ/ *n* uva *f* espina, grosella *f*

goose-flesh /'gu:sfleʃ/ *n*, **goose-pimples** /'gu:spɪmplz/ *n* carne *f* de gallina

gore /gɔ:(r)/ *n* sangre *f*. —*vt* cornear

gorge /gɔ:dʒ/ *n* (*geog*) garganta *f*. —*vt*. ~ **o.s.** hartarse (**on** de)

gorgeous /'gɔ:dʒəs/ *a* magnífico

gorilla /gə'rɪlə/ *n* gorila *m*

gormless /'gɔ:mlɪs/ *a* (*sl*) idiota

gorse /gɔ:s/ *n* aulaga *f*

gory /'gɔ:rɪ/ *a* (**-ier**, **-iest**) (*covered in blood*) ensangrentado; (*horrific*, *fig*) horrible

gosh /gɒʃ/ *int* ¡caramba!

go-slow /gəʊ'sləʊ/ *n* huelga *f* de celo

gospel /'gɒspl/ *n* evangelio *m*

gossip /'gɒsɪp/ *n* (*idle chatter*) charla *f*; (*tittle-tattle*) comadreo *m*; (*person*) chismoso *m*. —*vi* (*pt* **gossiped**) (*chatter*) charlar; (*repeat scandal*) comadrear. ~**y** *a* chismoso

got /gɒt/ *see* get. **have** ~ tener. **have** ~ **to** do tener que hacer

Gothic /'gɒθɪk/ *a* (*archit*) gótico; (*people*) godo

gouge /gaʊdʒ/ *vt*. ~ **out** arrancar

gourmet /'gʊəmeɪ/ *n* gastrónomo *m*

gout /gaʊt/ *n* (*med*) gota *f*

govern /'gʌvn/ *vt*/*i* gobernar

governess /'gʌvənɪs/ *n* institutriz *f*

government /'gʌvənmənt/ *n* gobierno *m*. ~**al** /gʌvən'mentl/ *a* gubernamental

governor /'gʌvənə(r)/ *n* gobernador *m*

gown /gaʊn/ *n* vestido *m*; (*of judge*, *teacher*) toga *f*

GP *abbr* *see* **general practitioner**

grab /græb/ *vt* (*pt* **grabbed**) agarrar

grace /greɪs/ *n* gracia *f*. ~**ful** *a* elegante

gracious /'greɪʃəs/ *a* (*kind*) amable; (*elegant*) elegante

gradation /grə'deɪʃn/ *n* gradación *f*

grade /greɪd/ *n* clase *f*, categoría *f*; (*of goods*) clase *f*, calidad *f*; (*on* *scale*) grado *m*; (*school mark*) nota *f*; (*class, Amer*) curso *m*. ~ **school** *n* (*Amer*) escuela *f* primaria. —*vt* clasificar; (*schol*) calificar

gradient /ˈgreɪdɪənt/ *n* (*slope*) pendiente *f*

gradual /ˈgrædʒʊəl/ *a* gradual. ~**ly** *adv* gradualmente

graduat|e /ˈgrædjʊət/ *n* (*univ*) licenciado. —*vi* /ˈgrædjʊeɪt/ licenciarse. —*vt* graduar. ~**ion** /-ˈeɪʃn/ *n* entrega *f* de títulos

graffiti /grəˈfiːtiː/ *npl* pintada *f*

graft[1] /grɑːft/ *n* (*med, bot*) injerto *m*. —*vt* injertar

graft[2] /grɑːft/ *n* (*bribery, fam*) corrupción *f*

grain /greɪn/ *n* grano *m*

gram /græm/ *n* gramo *m*

grammar /ˈgræmə(r)/ *n* gramática *f*. ~**tical** /grəˈmætɪkl/ *a* gramatical

gramophone /ˈgræməfəʊn/ *n* tocadiscos *m invar*

grand /grænd/ *a* (**-er, -est**) magnífico; (*excellent, fam*) estupendo. ~**child** *n* nieto *m*. ~**daughter** *n* nieta *f*

grandeur /ˈgrændʒə(r)/ *n* grandiosidad *f*

grandfather /ˈgrændfɑːðə(r)/ *n* abuelo *m*

grandiose /ˈgrændɪəʊs/ *a* grandioso

grand: ~**mother** *n* abuela *f*. ~**parents** *npl* abuelos *mpl*. ~ **piano** *n* piano *m* de cola. ~**son** *n* nieto *m*

grandstand /ˈgrænstænd/ *n* tribuna *f*

granite /ˈgrænɪt/ *n* granito *m*

granny /ˈgrænɪ/ *n* (*fam*) abuela *f*, nana *f* (*fam*)

grant /grɑːnt/ *vt* conceder; (*give*) donar; (*admit*) admitir (that que). **take for ~ed** dar por sentado. —*n* concesión *f*; (*univ*) beca *f*

granulated /ˈgrænjʊleɪtɪd/ *a*. ~ **sugar** *n* azúcar *m* granulado

granule /ˈgrænuːl/ *n* gránulo *m*

grape /greɪp/ *n* uva *f*

grapefruit /ˈgreɪpfruːt/ *n invar* toronja *f*, pomelo *m*

graph /grɑːf/ *n* gráfica *f*

graphic /ˈgræfɪk/ *a* gráfico

grapple /ˈgræpl/ *vi*. ~ **with** intentar vencer

grasp /grɑːsp/ *vt* agarrar. —*n* (*hold*) agarro *m*; (*strength of hand*) apretón *m*; (*reach*) alcance *m*; (*fig*) comprensión *f*

grasping /ˈgrɑːspɪŋ/ *a* avaro

grass /grɑːs/ *n* hierba *f*. ~**hopper** *n* saltamontes *m invar*. ~**land** *n* pradera *f*. ~ **roots** *npl* base *f* popular. —*a* popular. ~**y** *a* cubierto de hierba

grate /greɪt/ *n* (*fireplace*) parrilla *f*. —*vt* rallar. ~ **one's teeth** hacer rechinar los dientes. —*vi* rechinar

grateful /ˈgreɪtfl/ *a* agradecido. ~**ly** *adv* con gratitud

grater /ˈgreɪtə(r)/ *n* rallador *m*

gratif|ied /ˈgrætɪfaɪd/ *a* contento. ~**y** *vt* satisfacer; (*please*) agradar a. ~**ying** *a* agradable

grating /ˈgreɪtɪŋ/ *n* reja *f*

gratis /ˈgrɑːtɪs/ *a & adv* gratis (*a invar*)

gratitude /ˈgrætɪtjuːd/ *n* gratitud *f*

gratuitous /grəˈtjuːɪtəs/ *a* gratuito

gratuity /grəˈtjuːətɪ/ *n* (*tip*) propina *f*; (*gift of money*) gratificación *f*

grave[1] /greɪv/ *n* sepultura *f*

grave[2] /greɪv/ *a* (**-er, -est**) (*serious*) serio. /grɑːv/ *a*. ~ **accent** *n* acento *m* grave

grave-digger /ˈgreɪvdɪgə(r)/ *n* sepulturero *m*

gravel /ˈgrævl/ *n* grava *f*

gravely /ˈgreɪvlɪ/ *a* (*seriously*) seriamente

grave: ~stone n lápida f. ~yard n cementerio m

gravitate /ˈgræviteit/ vi gravitar. ~ion /-ˈteiʃn/ n gravitación f

gravity /ˈgrævəti/ n gravedad f

gravy /ˈgreivi/ n salsa f

graze¹ /greiz/ vt/i (eat) pacer

graze² /greiz/ (touch) rozar; (scrape) raspar. ~n rozadura f

grease /griːs/ n grasa f. ~vt engrasar. ~e-paint n maquillaje m. ~e-proof paper n papel m a prueba de grasa, apergaminado m. ~y a grasiento

great /greit/ a (-er, -est) grande, (before singular noun) gran; (very good, fam) estupendo. G~ Britain n Gran Bretaña f. ~grandfather n bisabuelo m. ~grandmother n bisabuela f. ~ly /ˈgreitli/ adv (very) muy; (much) mucho. ~ness n grandeza f

Greece /griːs/ n Grecia f

greed /griːd/ n avaricia f; (for food) glotonería f. ~y a avaro; (for food) glotón

Greek /griːk/ a & n griego (m)

green /griːn/ a (-er, -est) verde; (fig) crédulo. ~n verde m; (grass) césped m. ~ belt n zona f verde. ~ery n verdor m. ~fingers npl habilidad f con las plantas

greengage /ˈgriːngeidʒ/ n (plum) claudia f

greengrocer /ˈgriːnɡrəʊsə(r)/ n verdulero m

greenhouse /ˈgriːnhaʊs/ n invernadero m

green: ~ light n luz f verde. ~s npl verduras fpl

Greenwich Mean Time /ˈgrenɪtʃˈmiːntaim/ n hora f media de Greenwich

greet /griːt/ vt saludar; (receive) recibir. ~ing n saludo m. ~ings npl (in letter) recuerdos mpl

gregarious /griˈgeəriəs/ a gregario

grenade /griˈneid/ n granada f

grew /gruː/ see grow

grey /grei/ a (-er, -est) gris (m). —vi (hair) encanecer

greyhound /ˈgreihaʊnd/ n galgo m

grid /grid/ n reja f. (network, elec) red f; (culin) parrilla f; (on map) cuadrícula f

grief /griːf/ n dolor m. come to ~ (person) sufrir un accidente; (fail) fracasar

grievance /ˈɡriːvns/ n queja f

grieve /griːv/ vt afligir. —vi afligirse. ~ for llorar

grievous /ˈgriːvəs/ a doloroso; (serious) grave

grill /gril/ n (cooking device) parrilla f; (food) parrillada f, asado m, asada f. —vt asar a la parrilla; (interrogate) interrogar

grille /gril/ n rejilla f

grim /grim/ a (grimmer, grimmest) severo

grimace /ˈgriməs/ n mueca f. —vi hacer muecas

grim|e /graim/ n mugre f. ~y a mugriento

grin /grin/ vt (pt grinned) sonreír. —n sonrisa f (abierta)

grind /graind/ vt (pt ground) moler (coffee, corn etc); (pulverize) pulverizar; (sharpen) afilar. ~ one's teeth hacer rechinar los dientes. —n faena f

grip /grip/ vt (pt gripped) agarrar; (interest) captar la atención de. —n (hold) agarro m; (strength of hand) apretón m. come to ~s encararse (with a/con)

gripe /graip/ n. ~s npl (med) cólico m

grisly /ˈgrizli/ a (-ier, -iest) horrible

gristle /ˈgrisl/ n cartílago m

grit /grɪt/ *n* arena *f*; (*fig*) valor *m*, aguante *m*. —*vt* (*pt* gritted) echar arena en (*road*). ~ one's teeth (*fig*) acorazarse

grizzle /'grɪzl/ *vi* lloriquear

groan /grəʊn/ *vi* gemir. —*n* gemido *m*

grocer /'grəʊsə(r)/ *n* tendero *m*. ~ies *npl* comestibles *mpl*. ~y *n* tienda *f* de comestibles

grog /grɒg/ *n* grog *m*

groggy /'grɒgɪ/ *a* (*weak*) débil; (*unsteady*) inseguro; (*ill*) malucho

groin /grɔɪn/ *n* ingle *f*

groom /gruːm/ *n* mozo *m* de caballos; (*bridegroom*) novio *m*. —*vt* almohazar (*horses*); (*fig*) preparar. well-~ed *a* bien arreglado

groove /gruːv/ *n* ranura *f*; (*in record*) surco *m*

grope /grəʊp/ *vi* (*find one's way*) moverse a tientas. ~ for buscar a tientas

gross /grəʊs/ *a* (-er, -est) (*coarse*) grosero; (*fat*) bruto; (*fat*) grueso; (*flagrant*) grave. —*n invar* gruesa *f*. ~ly *adv* groseramente; (*very*) enormemente

grotesque /grəʊ'tesk/ *a* grotesco

grotto /'grɒtəʊ/ *n* (*pl* -oes) gruta *f*

grotty /'grɒtɪ/ *a* (*sl*) desagradable; (*dirty*) sucio

grouch /graʊtʃ/ *vi* (*grumble, fam*) rezongar

ground¹ /graʊnd/ *n* suelo *m*; (*area*) terreno *m*; (*reason*) razón *f*; (*elec, Amer*) toma *f* de tierra. —*vt* varar (*ship*); prohibir despegar (*aircraft*). ~s *npl* jardines *mpl*; (*sediment*) poso *m*

ground² /graʊnd/ *see* grind

ground: ~ floor *n* planta *f* baja. ~ rent *n* alquiler *m* del terreno

grounding /'graʊndɪŋ/ *n* base *f*, conocimientos *mpl* (in de)

groundless /'graʊndlɪs/ *a* infundado

ground: ~sheet *n* tela *f* impermeable. ~swell *n* mar *m* de fondo. ~work *n* trabajo *m* preparatorio

group /gruːp/ *n* grupo *m*. —*vt* agrupar. —*vi* agruparse

grouse¹ /graʊs/ *n*, *pl invar* (*bird*) urogallo *m*. red ~ lagópodo *m* escocés

grouse² /graʊs/ *vi* (*grumble, fam*) rezongar

grove /grəʊv/ *n* arboleda *f*. lemon ~ *n* limonar *m*. olive ~ *n* olivar *m*. orange ~ *n* naranjal *m*. pine ~ *n* pinar *m*

grovel /'grɒvl/ *vi* (*pt* grovelled) arrastrarse, humillarse. ~ling *a* servil

grow /grəʊ/ *vi* (*pt* grew, *pp* grown) crecer; (*cultivated plant*) cultivarse; (*become*) volverse, ponerse. —*vt* cultivar. ~ up hacerse mayor. ~er *n* cultivador *m*

growl /graʊl/ *vi* gruñir. —*n* gruñido *m*

grown /grəʊn/ *see* grow. —*a* adulto. ~up *a* & *n* adulto (*m*)

growth /grəʊθ/ *n* crecimiento *m*; (*increase*) aumento *m*; (*development*) desarrollo *m*; (*med*) tumor *m*

grub /grʌb/ *n* (*larva*) larva *f*; (*food, sl*) comida *f*

grubby /'grʌbɪ/ *a* (-ier, -iest) mugriento

grudge /grʌdʒ/ *vt* dar de mala gana; (*envy*) envidiar. ~e doing molestarle hacer. he ~ed paying le molestó pagar. —*n* rencor *m*. bear/have a ~ guardar rencor a alguien. ~ingly *adv* de mala gana

gruelling /'gruːəlɪŋ/ *a* agotador

gruesome /'gruːsəm/ *a* horrible

gruff /grʌf/ *a* (-er, -est) (*manners*) brusco; (*voice*) ronco

grumble /ˈgrʌmbl/ vi rezongar

grumpy /ˈgrʌmpɪ/ a (-ier, -iest) malhumorado

grunt /grʌnt/ vi gruñir. —n gruñido m

guarant|ee /gærənˈtiː/ n garantía f. —vt garantizar. —or n garante m & f

guard /gɑːd/ vt proteger; (watch) vigilar. —vi. ~ **against** guardar de. —n (vigilance, mil group) guardia f; (person) guardia m; (on train) jefe m de tren

guarded /ˈgɑːdɪd/ a cauteloso

guardian /ˈgɑːdɪən/ n guardián m; (of orphan) tutor m

guer(r)illa /gəˈrɪlə/ n guerrillero m. ~ **warfare** n guerra f de guerrillas

guess /ges/ vt/i adivinar; (suppose, Amer) creer. —n conjetura f. ~**work** n conjetura f(pl)

guest /gest/ n invitado m; (in hotel) huésped m. ~**house** n casa f de huéspedes

guffaw /gʌˈfɔː/ n carcajada f. —vi reírse a carcajadas

guidance /ˈgaɪdəns/ n (advice) consejos mpl; (information) información f

guide /gaɪd/ n (person) guía m & f; (book) guía f. **Girl G~** exploradora f, guía f (fam). —vt guiar. ~**book** n guía f. ~**d missile** n proyectil m teledirigido. ~**lines** npl pauta f

guild /gɪld/ n gremio m

guile /gaɪl/ n astucia f

guillotine /ˈgɪlətiːn/ n guillotina f

guilt /gɪlt/ n culpabilidad f. ~**y** a culpable

guinea-pig /ˈgɪnɪpɪg/ n (including fig) cobaya f

guise /gaɪz/ n (external appearance) apariencia f; (style) manera f

guitar /gɪˈtɑː(r)/ n guitarra f. ~**ist** n guitarrista m & f

gulf /gʌlf/ n (part of sea) golfo m; (hollow) abismo m

gull /gʌl/ n gaviota f

gullet /ˈgʌlɪt/ n esófago m

gullible /ˈgʌləbl/ a crédulo

gully /ˈgʌlɪ/ n (ravine) barranco m

gulp /gʌlp/ vt. ~ **down** tragarse de prisa. —vi tragar; (from fear etc) sentir dificultad para tragar. —n trago m

gum[1] /gʌm/ n goma f; (for chewing) chicle m. —vt (pt gummed) engomar

gum[2] /gʌm/ n (anat) encía f. ~**boil** /ˈgʌmbɔɪl/ n flemón m

gumboot /ˈgʌmbuːt/ n bota f de agua

gumption /ˈgʌmpʃn/ n (fam) iniciativa f; (common sense) sentido m común

gun /gʌn/ n (pistol) pistola f; (rifle) fusil m; (large) cañón m. —vt (pt gunned). ~ **down** abatir a tiros. ~**fire** n tiros mpl

gunge /gʌndʒ/ n (sl) materia f sucia (y pegajosa)

gun: ~**man** /ˈgʌnmən/ n pistolero m. ~**ner** /ˈgʌnə(r)/ n artillero m. ~**powder** n pólvora f. ~**shot** n disparo m

gurgle /ˈgɜːgl/ n (of liquid) gorgoteo m; (of baby) gorjeo m. —vi (liquid) gorgotear; (baby) gorjear

guru /ˈguruː/ n (pl -us) mentor m

gush /gʌʃ/ vi. ~ (**out**) salir a borbotones. —n (of liquid) chorro m; (fig) torrente m. ~**ing** a efusivo

gusset /ˈgʌsɪt/ n escudete m

gust /gʌst/ n ráfaga f; (of smoke) bocanada f

gusto /ˈgʌstəʊ/ n entusiasmo m

gusty /ˈgʌstɪ/ a borrascoso

gut /gʌt/ n tripa f, intestino m. —vt (pt gutted) destripar; (fire) destruir. ~**s** npl tripas fpl; (courage, fam) valor m

gutter /'gʌtə(r)/ n (on roof) canalón m; (in street) cuneta f, (slum, fig) arroyo m. **~snipe** n golfillo m

guttural /'gʌtərəl/ a gutural

guy /gaɪ/ n (man, fam) hombre m, tío m (fam)

guzzle /'gʌzl/ vt/i soplarse, tragarse

gym /dʒɪm/ n (gymnasium, fam) gimnasio m; (gymnastics, fam) gimnasia f

gymkhana /dʒɪmkɑːnə/ n gincana f, gymkhana f

gymnasium /dʒɪm'neɪzɪəm/ n gimnasio m

gymnast /'dʒɪmnæst/ n gimnasta m & f. **~ics** npl gimnasia f

gym-slip /'dʒɪmslɪp/ n túnica f (de gimnasia)

gynaecolog|ist /gaɪnɪˈkɒlədʒɪst/ n ginecólogo m. **~y** n ginecología f

gypsy /'dʒɪpsɪ/ n gitano m

gyrate /dʒaɪəˈreɪt/ vi girar

gyroscope /'dʒaɪərəskəʊp/ n giroscopio m

H

haberdashery /hæbə'dæʃərɪ/ n mercería f

habit /'hæbɪt/ n costumbre f; (costume, relig) hábito m. **be in the ~ of** (+ infinitive), soler (+ infinitive). **get into the ~ of** (+ gerund) acostumbrarse a (+ infinitive)

habitable /'hæbɪtəbl/ a habitable

habitat /'hæbɪtæt/ n hábitat m

habitation /hæbɪ'teɪʃn/ n habitación f

habitual /hə'bɪtjʊəl/ a habitual; (smoker, liar) inveterado. **~ly** adv de costumbre

hack /hæk/ n (old horse) jamelgo m; (writer) escritorzuelo m. —vt cortar. **~ to pieces** cortar en pedazos

hackney /'hæknɪ/ a. **~ carriage** n coche m de alquiler, taxi m

hackneyed /'hæknɪd/ a manido

had /hæd/ see **have**

haddock /'hædək/ n invar eglefino m. **smoked ~** n eglefino m ahumado

haemorrhage /'hemərɪdʒ/ n hemorragia f

haemorrhoids /'hemərɔɪdz/ npl hemorroides fpl, almorranas fpl

hag /hæg/ n bruja f

haggard /'hægəd/ a ojeroso

haggle /'hægl/ vi regatear

Hague /heɪg/ n. **The ~** La Haya f

hail¹ /heɪl/ n granizo m. —vi granizar

hail² /heɪl/ vt (greet) saludar; llamar (taxi). —vi. **~ from** venir de

hailstone /'heɪlstəʊn/ n grano m de granizo

hair /heə(r)/ n pelo m. **~brush** n cepillo m para el pelo. **~cut** n corte m de pelo. **have a ~cut** cortarse el pelo. **~do** n (fam) peinado m. **~dresser** n peluquero m. **~dresser's (shop)** n peluquería f. **~dryer** n secador m. **~pin** n horquilla f. **~pin bend** n curva f cerrada. **~raising** a espeluznante. **~style** n peinado m

hairy /'heərɪ/ a (-ier, -iest) peludo; (terrifying, sl) espeluznante

hake /heɪk/ n invar merluza f

halcyon /'hælsɪən/ a sereno. **~ days** npl época f feliz

hale /heɪl/ a robusto

half /hɑːf/ n (pl halves) mitad f. —a medio. **~ a dozen** media docena f. **~ an hour** media hora f. —adv medio, a medias. **~back** n (sport) medio m. **~caste** a & n mestizo (m). **~hearted** a poco entusiasta

~**-term** n vacaciones fpl de medio trimestre. ~**-time** n (sport) descanso m. ~**way** a medio. —adv a medio camino. ~**-wit** n imbécil m & f. at ~**mast** a media asta

halibut /'hælɪbət/ n invar hipogloso m, halibut m

hall /hɔːl/ n (room) sala f; (mansion) casa f solariega; (entrance) vestíbulo m. ~ **of residence** n colegio m mayor

hallelujah /hælɪ'luːjə/ int & n aleluya (f)

hallmark /'hɔːlmɑːk/ n (on gold etc) contraste m; (fig) sello m (distintivo)

hallo /hə'ləʊ/ int = **hello**

hallow /'hæləʊ/ vt santificar. **H~e'en** n víspera f de Todos los Santos

hallucination /həluːsɪ'neɪʃn/ n alucinación f

halo /'heɪləʊ/ n (pl **-oes**) aureola f

halt /hɔːlt/ n alto m. —vt parar. —vi pararse

halve /hɑːv/ vt dividir por mitad

ham /hæm/ n jamón m; (theatre, sl) racionista m & f

hamburger /'hæmbɜːgə(r)/ n hamburguesa f

hamlet /'hæmlɪt/ n aldea f, caserío m

hammer /'hæmə(r)/ n martillo m. —vt martill(e)ar; (defeat, fam) machacar

hammock /'hæmək/ n hamaca f

hamper[1] /'hæmpə(r)/ n cesta f

hamper[2] /'hæmpə(r)/ n estorbar, poner trabas

hamster /'hæmstə(r)/ n hámster m

hand /hænd/ n (including cards) mano f; (of clock) manecilla f; (writing) escritura f, letra f; (worker) obrero m. **at** ~ a mano. **by** ~ a mano. **lend a** ~ echar una mano. **on** ~ a mano. **on**

one's ~**s** (fig) en (las) manos de uno. **on the one** ~... **on the other** ~ por un lado... por otro. **out of** ~ fuera de control. **to** ~ a mano. ~ **dar.** ~ **down** pasar. ~ **in** entregar. ~ **over** entregar. ~ **out** distribuir. ~**bag** n bolso m, cartera f (LAm). ~**book** n (manual) manual m; (guidebook) guía f. ~**cuffs** npl esposas fpl. ~**ful** /'hændfʊl/ n puñado m; (person, fam) persona f difícil. ~**luggage** n equipaje m de mano. ~**out** n folleto m; (money) limosna f

handicap /'hændɪkæp/ n desventaja f; (sport) handicap m. —vt (pt **handicapped**) imponer impedimentos a

handicraft /'hændɪkrɑːft/ n artesanía f

handiwork /'hændɪwɜːk/ n obra f, trabajo m manual

handkerchief /'hæŋkətʃɪf/ n (pl **-fs**) pañuelo m

handle /'hændl/ n (of door etc) tirador m; (of implement) mango m; (of cup, bag, basket etc) asa f. —vt manejar; (touch) tocar; (control) controlar

handlebar /'hændlbɑː(r)/ n (on bicycle) manillar m

handshake /'hændʃeɪk/ n apretón m de manos

handsome /'hænsəm/ a (goodlooking) guapo; (generous) generoso; (large) considerable

handwriting /'hændraɪtɪŋ/ n escritura f, letra f

handy /'hændɪ/ a (**-ier**, **-iest**) (useful) cómodo; (person) diestro; (near) a mano. ~**man** n hombre m habilidoso

hang /hæŋ/ vt (pt hung) colgar; (pt **hanged**) (capital punishment) ahorcar. —vi colgar; (hair) caer. —n. **get the** ~ **of sth** coger el truco de algo. ~ **about** holgazanear. ~ **on** (hold out)

resistir; (wait, sl) esperar. ~ **out**
vi tender; (live, sl) vivir. ~ **up**
(telephone) colgar

hangar /'hæŋə(r)/ n hangar m

hanger /'hæŋə(r)/ n (for clothes)
percha f. ~**on** n parásito m, peg-
ote m

hang-gliding /'hæŋɡlaɪdɪŋ/ n
vuelo m libre

hangman /'hæŋmən/ n verdugo
m

hangover /'hæŋəʊvə(r)/ n (after
drinking) resaca f

hang-up /'hæŋʌp/ n (sl) complejo
m

hanker /'hæŋkə(r)/ vi. ~ **after**
anhelar. ~**ing** n anhelo m

hanky-panky /'hæŋkɪpæŋkɪ/ n
(trickery, sl) trucos mpl

haphazard /hæp'hæzəd/ a fortuito. ~**ly** adv al azar

hapless /'hæplɪs/ a des-
afortunado

happen /'hæpən/ vi pasar,
suceder, ocurrir. **if he ~s to
come** si acaso viene. ~**ing** n
acontecimiento m

happily /'hæpɪlɪ/ adv felizmente; (fortunately) afortunadamente. ~**iness** n
felicidad f. ~**y** a (-ier, -iest) feliz.
~**y-go-lucky** a despreocupado.
~**y medium** n término m medio

harangue /hə'ræŋ/ n arenga f. —
vt arengar

harass /'hærəs/ vt acosar.
~**ment** n tormento m

harbour /'hɑːbə(r)/ n puerto m. —
vt encubrir (criminal); abrigar
(feelings)

hard /hɑːd/ a (-er, -est) duro;
(difficult) difícil. ~ **of hearing**
duro de oído. —adv mucho;
(pull) fuerte. ~ **by** (muy) cerca.
~ **done by** tratado injustamente. ~ **up** (fam) sin un
cuarto. ~**board** n chapa f de
madera, tabla f. ~**boiled egg** n
huevo m duro. ~**en** /'hɑːdn/ vt

endurecer. —vi endurecerse.
~**headed** a realista

hardly /'hɑːdlɪ/ adv apenas. ~
ever casi nunca

hardness /'hɑːdnɪs/ n dureza f

hardship /'hɑːdʃɪp/ n apuro m

hard: ~ **shoulder** n arcén m. ~
ware n ferretería f; (computer)
hardware m. ~**working** a
trabajador

hardy /'hɑːdɪ/ a (-ier, -iest) (bold)
audaz; (robust) robusto; (bot)
resistente

hare /heə(r)/ n liebre f. ~
brained a aturdido

harem /'hɑːriːm/ n harén m

haricot /'hærɪkəʊ/ n. ~ **bean**
alubia f, judía f

hark /hɑːk/ vi escuchar. ~ **back**
to volver a

harlot /'hɑːlət/ n prostituta f

harm /hɑːm/ n daño m. **there is
no ~ in** (+ gerund) no hay ningún mal en (+ infinitive). —vt
hacer daño a (person); dañar
(thing); perjudicar (interests).
~**ful** a perjudicial. ~**less** a
inofensivo

harmonica /hɑː'mɒnɪkə/ n armónica f

harmonious /hɑː'məʊnɪəs/ a
armonioso. ~**ize** vt/i armonizar. ~**y** n armonía f

harness /'hɑːnɪs/ n (for horses)
guarniciones fpl; (for children)
andadores mpl. —vt poner guarniciones a (horse); (fig)
aprovechar

harp /hɑːp/ n arpa f. —vi. ~ **on**
(about) machacar. ~**ist** /'hɑː-
pɪst/ n arpista m & f

harpoon /hɑː'puːn/ n arpón m

harpsichord /'hɑːpsɪkɔːd/ n clavicémbalo m, clave m

harrowing /'hærəʊɪŋ/ a desgarrador

harsh /hɑːʃ/ a (-er, -est) duro,
severo; (taste, sound) áspero.

~ly *adv* severamente. ~ness *n*
severidad *f*

harvest /'hɑːvɪst/ *n* cosecha *f*. —*vt*
cosechar. ~er *n* (person) segador; (machine) cosechadora *f*

has /hæz/ *see* have

hash /hæʃ/ *n* picadillo *m*. make a
~ of sth hacer algo con los pies,
estropear algo

hashish /'hæʃiːʃ/ *n* hachís *m*

hassle /'hæsl/ *n* (quarrel) pelea *f*;
(difficulty) problema *m*, dificultad *f*; (bother, fam) pena *f*, follón *m*, lío *m*. —*vt* (harass)
acosar, dar la lata

haste /heɪst/ *n* prisa *f*. in ~ de
prisa. make ~ darse prisa

hasten /'heɪsn/ *vt* apresurar. —*vi*
apresurarse, darse prisa

hast|ily /'heɪstɪlɪ/ *adv* de prisa.
~y *a* (-ier, -iest) precipitado;
(rash) irreflexivo

hat /hæt/ *n* sombrero *m*. a ~
trick *n* tres victorias *fpl*
consecutivas

hatch¹ /hætʃ/ *n* (for food) ventanilla *f*; (naut) escotilla *f*

hatch² /hætʃ/ *vt* empollar (eggs);
tramar (plot). —*vi* salir del
cascarón

hatchback /'hætʃbæk/ *n* (coche
m) cincopuertas *m invar*, coche
m con puerta trasera

hatchet /'hætʃɪt/ *n* hacha *f*

hate /heɪt/ *n* odio *m*. —*vt* odiar.
~ful *a* odioso

hatred /'heɪtrɪd/ *n* odio *m*

haughty /'hɔːtɪ/ *a* (-ier, -iest)
altivo

haul /hɔːl/ *vt* arrastrar; transportar (goods). —*n* (catch)
redada *f*; (stolen goods) botín *m*;
(journey) recorrido *m*. ~age *n*
transporte *m*. ~ier *n* transportista *m & f*

haunch /hɔːntʃ/ *n* anca *f*

haunt /hɔːnt/ *vt* frecuentar. —*n*
sitio *m* preferido. ~ed house *n*

casa *f* frecuentada por fantasmas

Havana /hə'vænə/ *n* La Habana *f*

have /hæv/ *vt* (3 sing pres tense
has, *pt* had) tener; (eat, drink)
tomar. ~ it out with resolver el
asunto. ~ sth done hacer hacer
algo. ~ to do tener que hacer. —
v aux haber. ~ just done acabar
de hacer. —*n*. the ~s and
~nots los ricos *mpl* y los pobres
mpl

haven /'heɪvn/ *n* puerto *m*; (refuge) refugio *m*

haversack /'hævəsæk/ *n* mochila
f

havoc /'hævək/ *n* estragos *mpl*

haw /hɔː/ *see* hum

hawk¹ /hɔːk/ *n* halcón *m*

hawk² /hɔːk/ *vt* vender por las
calles. ~er *n* vendedor *m*
ambulante

hawthorn /'hɔːθɔːn/ *n* espino *m*
(blanco)

hay /heɪ/ *n* heno *m*. ~ fever *n*
fiebre *f* del heno. ~stack *n*
almiar *m*

haywire /'heɪwaɪə(r)/ *a*. go ~
(plans) desorganizarse; (machine) estropearse

hazard /'hæzəd/ *n* riesgo *m*. —*vt*
arriesgar; aventurar (guess).
~ous *a* arriesgado

haze /heɪz/ *n* neblina *f*

hazel /'heɪzl/ *n* avellano *m*.
~nut *n* avellana *f*

hazy /'heɪzɪ/ *a* (-ier, -iest)
nebuloso

he /hiː/ *pron* él. —*n* (animal)
macho *m*; (man) varón *m*

head /hed/ *n* cabeza *f*; (leader)
jefe *m*; (of beer) espuma *f*. ~s or
tails cara o cruz. ~ a principal.
~ waiter *n* jefe *m* de
comedor. —*vt* encabezar. ~ the
ball dar un cabezazo. ~ for dirigirse a. ~ache *n* dolor *m* de cabeza. ~dress *n* tocado *m*. ~er *n*
(football) cabezazo *m*. ~ first

adv de cabeza. **~gear** *n* tocado *m*

heading /'hedɪŋ/ *n* título *m*, encabezamiento *m*

headlamp /'hedlæmp/ *n* faro *m*

headland /'hedlənd/ *n* promontorio *m*

headlight /'hedlaɪt/ *n* faro *m*

headline /'hedlaɪn/ *n* titular *m*

headlong /'hedlɒŋ/ *adv* de cabeza; (*precipitately*) precipitadamente

head: **~master** *n* director *m*. **~mistress** *n* directora *f*. **~on** *a* & *adv* de frente. **~phone** *n* auricular *m*, audífono *m* (*LAm*)

headquarters /hed'kwɔːtəz/ *n* (*of organization*) sede *f*; (*of business*) oficina *f* central; (*mil*) cuartel *m* general

headstrong /'hedstrɒŋ/ *a* testarudo

headway /'hedweɪ/ *n* progreso *m*. **make ~** hacer progresos

heady /'hedɪ/ *a* (**-ier, -iest**) (*impetuous*) impetuoso; (*intoxicating*) embriagador

heal /hiːl/ *vt* curar. —*vi* (*wound*) cicatrizarse; (*fig*) curarse

health /helθ/ *n* salud *f*. **~y** *a* sano

heap /hiːp/ *n* montón *m*. —*vt* amontonar. **~s of** (*fam*) montones de, muchísimos

hear /hɪə(r)/ *vt/i* (*pt* **heard** /hɜːd/) oír. **~, ~!** ¡bravo! **no ~ of** (*refuse to allow*) no querer oír. **~ about** oír hablar de. **~ from** recibir noticias de. **~ of** oír hablar de

hearing /'hɪərɪŋ/ *n* oído *m*; (*of witness*) audición *f*. **~aid** *n* audífono *m*

hearsay /'hɪəseɪ/ *n* rumores *mpl*. **from ~** según los rumores

hearse /hɜːs/ *n* coche *m* fúnebre

heart /hɑːt/ *n* corazón *m*. **at ~** en el fondo. **by ~** de memoria. **lose ~** descorazonarse. **~ache** *n* pena *f*. **~ attack** *n* ataque *m* al

corazón. **~break** *n* pena *f*. **~breaking** *a* desgarrador. **~broken** *a*. **be ~broken** partírsele el corazón

heartburn /'hɑːtbɜːn/ *n* acedía *f*

hearten /'hɑːtn/ *vt* animar

heartfelt /'hɑːtfelt/ *a* sincero

hearth /hɑːθ/ *n* hogar *m*

heartily /'hɑːtɪlɪ/ *adv* de buena gana; (*sincerely*) sinceramente

heart: **~less** *a* cruel. **~searching** *n* examen *m* de conciencia. **~to~** *a* abierto

hearty /'hɑːtɪ/ *a* (*sincere*) sincero; (*meal*) abundante

heat /hiːt/ *n* calor *m*; (*contest*) eliminatoria *f*. —*vt* calentar. —*vi* calentarse. **~ed** *a* (*fig*) acalorado. **~er** /'hiːtə(r)/ *n* calentador *m*

heath /hiːθ/ *n* brezal *m*, descampado *m*, terreno *m* baldío

heathen /'hiːðn/ *n* & *a* pagano (*m*)

heather /'heðə(r)/ *n* brezo *m*

heat: **~ing** *n* calefacción *f*. **~stroke** *n* insolación *f*. **~wave** *n* ola *f* de calor

heave /hiːv/ *vt* (*lift*) levantar; exhalar (*sigh*); (*throw, fam*) lanzar. —*vi* (*retch*) sentir náuseas

heaven /'hevn/ *n* cielo *m*. **~ly** *a* celestial; (*astronomy*) celeste; (*excellent, fam*) divino

heavily /'hevɪlɪ/ *adv* pesadamente; (*smoke, drink*) mucho. **~y** *a* (**-ier, -iest**) pesado; (*sea*) grueso; (*traffic*) denso; (*work*) duro. **~yweight** *n* peso *m* pesado

Hebrew /'hiːbruː/ *a* & *n* hebreo (*m*)

heckle /'hekl/ *vt* interrumpir (*speaker*)

hectic /'hektɪk/ *a* febril

hedge /hedʒ/ *n* seto *m* vivo. —*vt* rodear con seto vivo. —*vi* escaparse por la tangente

hedgehog /'hedʒhɒg/ *n* erizo *m*

heed /hiːd/ vt hacer caso de. —n atención f. **pay ~ to** hacer caso de. **~less** a desatento

heel /hiːl/ n talón m; (of shoe) tacón m. **down at ~, down at the ~s** (Amer) desharrapado

hefty /'heftɪ/ a (-ier, -iest) (sturdy) fuerte; (heavy) pesado

heifer /'hefə(r)/ n novilla f

height /haɪt/ n altura f; (of person) estatura f; (of fame, glory) cumbre f; (of joy, folly, pain) colmo m

heighten /'haɪtn/ vt (raise) elevar; (fig) aumentar

heinous /'heɪnəs/ a atroz

heir /eə(r)/ n heredero m. **~ess** n heredera f; (of fame) **~loom** /'eəluːm/ n reliquia f heredada

held /held/ see **hold**[1]

helicopter /'helɪkɒptə(r)/ n helicóptero m

heliport /'helɪpɔːt/ n helipuerto m

hell /hel/ n infierno m. **~-bent** a resuelto. **~ish** a infernal

hello /hə'ləʊ/ int ¡hola!; (telephone, caller) ¡oiga!, ¡bueno! (Mex), ¡hola! (Arg); (telephone, person answering) ¡diga!, ¡bueno! (Mex), ¡hola! (Arg); (surprise) ¡vaya! **say ~ to** saludar

helm /helm/ n (of ship) timón m

helmet /'helmɪt/ n casco m

help /help/ vt/i ayudar. **he cannot ~ laughing** no puede menos de reír. **~ o.s. to** servirse. **it cannot be ~ed** no hay más remedio. —n ayuda f; (charwoman) asistenta f. **~er** n ayudante m. **~ful** a útil; (person) amable

helping /'helpɪŋ/ n porción f

helpless /'helplɪs/ a (unable to manage) incapaz; (powerless) impotente

helter-skelter /heltə'skeltə(r)/ n tobogán m. —adv atropelladamente

hem /hem/ n dobladillo m. —vt (pt **hemmed**) hacer un dobladillo. **~ in** encerrar

hemisphere /'hemɪsfɪə(r)/ n hemisferio m

hemp /hemp/ n (plant) cáñamo m; (hashish) hachís m

hen /hen/ n gallina f

hence /hens/ adv de aquí. **~forth** adv de ahora en adelante

henchman /'hentʃmən/ n secuaz m

henna /'henə/ n alheña f

hen-party /'henpɑːtɪ/ n (fam) reunión f de mujeres

henpecked /'henpekt/ a dominado por su mujer

her /hɜː(r)/ pron (accusative) la; (dative) le; (after prep) ella. **I know ~** la conozco. —a su, sus pl

herald /'herəld/ vt anunciar

heraldry /'herəldrɪ/ n heráldica f

herb /hɜːb/ n hierba f. **~s** npl hierbas fpl finas

herbaceous /hɜː'beɪʃəs/ a herbáceo

herbalist /'hɜːbəlɪst/ n herbolario m

herculean /hɜːkjʊ'liːən/ a hercúleo

herd /hɜːd/ n rebaño m. —vt. **~ together** reunir

here /hɪə(r)/ adv aquí. **~!** (take this) ¡tenga! **~abouts** adv por aquí. **~after** adv en el futuro. **~by** adv por este medio; (in letter) por la presente

hereditary /hɪ'redɪtərɪ/ a hereditario. **~y** /hɪ'redɪtɪ/ n herencia f

heresy /'herəsɪ/ n herejía f. **~tic** n hereje m & f

herewith /hɪə'wɪð/ adv adjunto

heritage /'herɪtɪdʒ/ n herencia f; (fig) patrimonio m

hermetic /hɜːˈmetɪk/ a hermético

hermit /ˈhɜːmɪt/ n ermitaño m

hernia /ˈhɜːnɪə/ n hernia f

hero /ˈhɪərəʊ/ n (pl -oes) héroe m. ~ic a heroico

heroin /ˈherəʊɪn/ n heroína f

hero: ~ine /ˈherəʊɪn/ n heroína f. ~ism /ˈherəʊɪzm/ n heroísmo m

heron /ˈherən/ n garza f real

herring /ˈherɪŋ/ n arenque m

hers /hɜːz/ poss pron suyo m, suya f, suyos mpl, suyas fpl, de ella

herself /hɜːˈself/ pron ella misma; (reflexive) se; (after prep) sí

hesitant /ˈhezɪtənt/ a vacilante

hesitate /ˈhezɪteɪt/ vi vacilar. ~ion /-ˈteɪʃn/ n vacilación f

hessian /ˈhesɪən/ n arpillera f

het /het/ a. ~ up (sl) nervioso

heterogeneous /hetərəʊˈdʒiːnɪəs/ a heterogéneo

heterosexual /hetərəʊˈseksjʊəl/ a heterosexual

hew /hjuː/ vt (pp hewn) cortar; (cut into shape) tallar

hexagon /ˈheksəgən/ n hexágono m. ~al /-ˈægənl/ a hexagonal

hey /heɪ/ int ¡eh!

heyday /ˈheɪdeɪ/ n apogeo m

hi /haɪ/ int (fam) ¡hola!

hiatus /haɪˈeɪtəs/ n (pl -tuses) hiato m

hibernate /ˈhaɪbəneɪt/ vi hibernar. ~ion n hibernación f

hibiscus /haɪˈbɪskəs/ n hibisco m

hiccup /ˈhɪkʌp/ n hipo m. have (the) ~s tener hipo. —vi tener hipo

hide[1] /haɪd/ vt (pt hid, pp hidden) esconder. —vi esconderse

hide[2] /haɪd/ n piel f, cuero m

hideous /ˈhɪdɪəs/ a (dreadful) horrible; (ugly) feo

hide-out /ˈhaɪdaʊt/ n escondrijo m

hiding[1] /ˈhaɪdɪŋ/ n (thrashing) paliza f

hiding[2] /ˈhaɪdɪŋ/ n. go into ~ esconderse

hierarchy /ˈhaɪərɑːkɪ/ n jerarquía f

hieroglyph /ˈhaɪərəglɪf/ n jeroglífico m

hi-fi /ˈhaɪfaɪ/ a de alta fidelidad. —n (equipo m de) alta fidelidad (f)

higgledy-piggledy /hɪgldɪˈpɪgldɪ/ adv en desorden

high /haɪ/ a (-er, -est) alto; (price) elevado; (number, speed) grande; (wind) fuerte; (intoxicated, fam) ebrio; (voice) agudo; (meat) manido. in the ~ season en plena temporada. —n alto nivel m. a (new) ~ un récord m. —adv alto

highbrow /ˈhaɪbraʊ/ a & n intelectual (m & f)

higher education /haɪər edʒʊˈkeɪʃn/ n enseñanza f superior

high-falutin /haɪfəˈluːtɪn/ a pomposo

high-handed /haɪˈhændɪd/ a despótico

high jump /ˈhaɪdʒʌmp/ n salto m de altura

highlight /ˈhaɪlaɪt/ n punto m culminante. —vt destacar

highly /ˈhaɪlɪ/ adv muy; (paid) muy bien. ~ strung a nervioso

highness /ˈhaɪnɪs/ n (title) alteza f

high: ~rise building n rascacielos m. ~ school n instituto m. ~speed a de gran velocidad. ~ spot n (fam) punto m culminante. ~ street n calle f mayor. ~strung a (Amer) nervioso. ~ tea n merienda f substanciosa

highway /ˈhaɪweɪ/ n carretera f. ~man n salteador m de caminos

hijack /'haɪdʒæk/ vt secuestrar. —n secuestro m. ~**er** n secuestrador

hike /haɪk/ n caminata f. —vi darse la caminata. ~**r** n excursionista m & f

hilarious /hɪ'leərɪəs/ a (funny) muy divertido

hill /hɪl/ n colina f; (slope) cuesta f. ~**billy** n rústico m. ~**side** n ladera f. ~**y** a montuoso

hilt /hɪlt/ n (of sword) puño m. **to the** ~ totalmente

him /hɪm/ pron le, lo; (after prep) él. **I know** ~ le/lo conozco

himself /hɪm'self/ pron él mismo; (reflexive) se

hind /haɪnd/ a trasero

hinder /'hɪndə(r)/ vt estorbar; (prevent) impedir

hindrance /'hɪndrəns/ n obstáculo m

hindsight /'haɪnsaɪt/ n. **with** ~ retrospectivamente

Hindu /hɪn'duː/ n & a hindú (m & f). ~**ism** n hinduismo m

hinge /hɪndʒ/ n bisagra f. —vi. ~ **on** (depend on) depender de

hint /hɪnt/ n indirecta f; (advice) consejo m. —vt dar a entender. —vi soltar una indirecta. ~ **at** hacer alusión a

hinterland /'hɪntəlænd/ n interior m

hip /hɪp/ n cadera f

hippie /'hɪpɪ/ n hippie m & f

hippopotamus /hɪpə'pɒtəməs/ n (pl -muses or -mi) hipopótamo m

hire /haɪə(r)/ vt alquilar (thing); contratar (person). —n alquiler m. ~**purchase** n compra f a plazos

hirsute /'hɜːsjuːt/ a hirsuto

his /hɪz/ a su, sus pl. —poss pron el suyo m, la suya f, los suyos mpl, las suyas fpl

Hispanic /hɪ'spænɪk/ a hispánico. ~**ist** /'hɪspənɪst/ n hispanista m & f. ~**o...** pref hispano...

hiss /hɪs/ n silbido. —vt/i silbar

histor ian /hɪ'stɔːrɪən/ n historiador m. ~**ic(al)** /hɪ'stɒrɪkl/ a histórico. ~**y** /'hɪstərɪ/ n historia f. **make** ~**y** pasar a la historia

histrionic /hɪstrɪ'ɒnɪk/ a histriónico

hit /hɪt/ vt (pt hit, pres p hitting) golpear; (collide with) chocar con; (affect) dar con; (affect) afectar. ~ **it off** with hacer buenas migas con. —n (blow) golpe m; (fig) éxito m. ~ **on** vi encontrar, dar con

hitch /hɪtʃ/ vt (fasten) atar. —n (snag) problema m. ~ **a lift**, ~**hike** vi hacer autostop, hacer dedo (Arg), pedir aventón (Mex). ~**hiker** n autostopista m & f

hither /'hɪðə(r)/ adv acá. ~ **and thither** acá y allá

hitherto /'hɪðətuː/ adv hasta ahora

hit-or-miss /'hɪtɔː'mɪs/ a (fam) a la buena de Dios, a ojo

hive /haɪv/ n colmena f. —vt. ~ **off** separar; (industry) desnacionalizar

hoard /hɔːd/ vt acumular. —n provisión f; (of money) tesoro m

hoarding /'hɔːdɪŋ/ n cartelera f, valla f publicitaria

hoar-frost /'hɔːfrɒst/ n escarcha f

hoarse /hɔːs/ a (-er, -est) ronco. ~**ness** n (of voice) ronquera f; (of sound) ronquedad f

hoax /həʊks/ n engaño m. —vt engañar

hob /hɒb/ n repisa f; (of cooker) fogón m

hobble /'hɒbl/ vi cojear

hobby /'hɒbɪ/ n pasatiempo m

hobby-horse /'hɒbɪhɔːs/ n (toy) caballito m (de niño); (fixation) caballo m de batalla

hobnail /'hɒbneɪl/ n clavo m

hob-nob /'hɒbnɒb/ *vi* (*pt* hob-
nobbed). ~ **with** codearse con

hock[1] /hɒk/ *n* vino *m* del Rin

hock[2] /hɒk/ *vt* (*pawn, sl*)
empeñar

hockey /'hɒkɪ/ *n* hockey *m*

hodgepodge /'hɒdʒpɒdʒ/ *n* mezcolanza *f*

hoe /həʊ/ *n* azada *f*. —*vt* (*pres p*
hoeing) azadonar

hog /hɒg/ *n* cerdo *m*. —*vt* (*pt*
hogged) (*fam*) acaparar

hoist /hɔɪst/ *vt* levantar; izar
(*flag*). —*n* montacargas *m invar*

hold[1] /həʊld/ *vt* (*pt* held) tener;
(*grasp*) coger (*not* LAm), agarrar; (*contain*) contener; mantener (*interest*); (*believe*) creer;
contener (*breath*). ~ **one's
tongue** callarse. —*vi* mantenerse. —*n* asidero *m*; (*influence*) influencia *f*. **get** ~ **of**
agarrar; (*fig, acquire*) adquirir.
~ **back** (*contain*) contener; (*conceal*) ocultar. ~ **on** (*stand firm*)
resistir; (*wait*) esperar. ~ **on to**
(*keep*) guardar; (*cling to*) agarrarse a. ~ **out** *vt* (*offer*)
ofrecer. —*vi* (*resist*) resistir. ~
over aplazar. ~ **up** (*support*)
sostener; (*delay*) retrasar; (*rob*)
atracar. ~ **with** aprobar

hold[2] /həʊld/ *n* (*of ship*) bodega *f*

holdall /'həʊldɔːl/ *n* bolsa *f* (de
viaje)

holder /'həʊldə(r)/ *n* tenedor *m*;
(*of post*) titular *m*; (*for object*)
soporte *m*

holding /'həʊldɪŋ/ *n* (*land*) propiedad *f*

hold-up /'həʊldʌp/ *n* atraco *m*

hole /həʊl/ *n* agujero *m*; (*in
ground*) hoyo *m*; (*in road*) bache
m. —*vt* agujerear

holiday /'hɒlɪdeɪ/ *n* vacaciones
fpl; (*public*) fiesta *f*. —*vi* pasar
las vacaciones. ~**maker** *n* ver-
aneante *m*

holiness /'həʊlɪnɪs/ *n* santidad *f*

Holland /'hɒlənd/ *n* Holanda *f*

hollow /'hɒləʊ/ *a & n* hueco
(*m*). —*vt* ahuecar

holly /'hɒlɪ/ *n* acebo *m*. ~**hock** *n*
malva *f* real

holocaust /'hɒləkɔːst/ *n* holocausto *m*

holster /'həʊlstə(r)/ *n* pistolera *f*

holy /'həʊlɪ/ *a* (-ier, -iest) santo,
sagrado. **H~ Ghost** *n*, **H~
Spirit** *n* Espíritu *m* Santo. ~
water *n* agua *f* bendita

homage /'hɒmɪdʒ/ *n* homenaje *m*

home /həʊm/ *n* casa *f*; (*insti-
tution*) asilo *m*; (*for soldiers*)
hogar *m*; (*native land*) patria *f*.
feel at ~ with sentirse como en
su casa. —*a* casera, de casa; (*of
family*) de familia; (*pol*) interior;
(*match*) de casa. —*adv*. (**at**) en
casa. **H~ Counties** *npl* región *f*
alrededor de Londres. ~**land** *n*
patria *f*. ~**less** *a* sin hogar. ~**ly**
/'həʊmlɪ/ *a* (-ier, -iest) casero;
(*ugly*) feo. **H~ Office** *n* Ministerio *m* del Interior. **H~ Secretary** *n* Ministro *m* del
Interior. ~**sick** *a*. **be** ~**sick**
tener morriña. ~ **town** *n* ciudad
f natal. ~ **truths** *npl* las verdades *fpl* del barquero, las cuatro verdades *fpl*. ~**ward**
/'həʊmwəd/ *a* (*journey*) de
vuelta. —*adv* hacia casa.
~**work** *n* deberes *mpl*

homicide /'hɒmɪsaɪd/ *n* homicidio *m*

homoeopath|**ic** /ˌhəʊmɪəʊ-
'pæθɪk/ *a* homeopático. ~**y**
/-'ɒpəθɪ/ *n* homeopatía *f*

homogeneous /ˌhəʊməʊ'dʒiː-
nɪəs/ *a* homogéneo

homosexual /ˌhəʊməʊ'seksjʊəl/
a & n homosexual (*m*)

hone /həʊn/ *vt* afilar

honest /'ɒnɪst/ *a* honrado;
(*frank*) sincero. ~**ly** *adv* hon-
radamente. ~**y** *n* honradez *f*

honey /'hʌnɪ/ n miel f; (person, fam) cielo m, cariño m. ∼**comb** /'hʌnɪkəʊm/ n panal m

honeymoon /'hʌnɪmuːn/ n luna f de miel

honeysuckle /'hʌnɪsʌkl/ n madreselva f

honk /hɒŋk/ vi tocar la bocina

honorary /'ɒnərərɪ/ a honorario

honour /'ɒnə(r)/ n honor m. ∼vt honrar. ∼**able** a honorable

hood /hʊd/ n capucha f; (car roof) capota f; (car bonnet) capó m

hoodlum /'huːdləm/ n gamberro m, matón m

hoodwink /'hʊdwɪŋk/ vt engañar

hoof /huːf/ n (pl hoofs or hooves) casco m

hook /hʊk/ n gancho m; (on garment) corchete m; (for fishing) anzuelo m. **by** ∼ **or by crook** por fas o por nefas, por las buenas o por las malas. **get s.o. off the** ∼ sacar a uno de un apuro. **off the** ∼ ⟨telephone⟩ descolgado. —vt enganchar. —vi engancharse

hooked /hʊkt/ a ganchudo. ∼ **on** (sl) adicto a

hooker /'hʊkə(r)/ n (rugby) talonador m; (Amer, sl) prostituta f

hookey /'hʊkɪ/ n. **play** ∼ (Amer, sl) hacer novillos

hooligan /'huːlɪɡən/ n gamberro m

hoop /huːp/ n aro m

hooray /hʊ'reɪ/ int & n ¡viva! (m)

hoot /huːt/ n (of horn) bocinazo m; (of owl) ululato m. —vi tocar la bocina; ⟨owl⟩ ulular

hooter /'huːtə(r)/ n (of car) bocina f; (of factory) sirena f

Hoover /'huːvə(r)/ n (P) aspiradora f. —vt pasar la aspiradora

hop¹ /hɒp/ vi (pt hopped) saltar a la pata coja. ∼ **in** (fam) subir. ∼ **it** (sl) largarse. ∼ **out** (fam) bajar. —n salto m; (flight) etapa f

hop² /hɒp/ n. ∼**(s)** lúpulo m

hope /həʊp/ n esperanza f. —vt/i esperar. ∼ **for** esperar. ∼**ful** a esperanzador. ∼**fully** adv con optimismo; (it is hoped) se espera. ∼**less** a desesperado. ∼**lessly** adv sin esperanza

hopscotch /'hɒpskɒtʃ/ n tejo m

horde /hɔːd/ n horda f

horizon /hə'raɪzn/ n horizonte m

horizontal /hɒrɪ'zɒntl/ a horizontal. ∼**ly** adv horizontalmente

hormone /'hɔːməʊn/ n hormona f

horn /hɔːn/ n cuerno m; (of car) bocina f; (mus) trompa f. —vt. ∼ **in** (sl) entrometerse. ∼**ed** a con cuernos

hornet /'hɔːnɪt/ n avispón m

horny /'hɔːnɪ/ a ⟨hands⟩ calloso

horoscope /'hɒrəskəʊp/ n horóscopo m

horri|ble /'hɒrəbl/ a horrible. ∼**d** /'hɒrɪd/ a horrible

horrif|ic /hə'rɪfɪk/ a horroroso. ∼**y** /'hɒrɪfaɪ/ vt horrorizar

horror /'hɒrə(r)/ n horror m. ∼ **film** n película f de miedo

hors-d'oevre /ɔː'dɜːvr/ n entremés m

horse /hɔːs/ n caballo m. ∼**back** n. **on** ∼**back** a caballo

horse chestnut /hɔːs'tʃesnʌt/ n castaña f de Indias

horse: ∼**man** n jinete m. ∼**play** n payasadas fpl. ∼**power** (unit) caballo m (de fuerza). ∼**racing** n carreras fpl de caballos

horseradish /'hɔːsrædɪʃ/ n rábano m picante

horse: ∼**sense** n (fam) sentido m común. ∼**shoe** /'hɔːsʃuː/ n herradura f

horsy /ˈhɔːsɪ/ *a (face etc)* caballuno

horticultur|al /hɔːtɪˈkʌltʃərəl/ *a* hortícola. **~e** /ˈhɔːtɪkʌltʃə(r)/ *n* horticultura *f*

hose /həʊz/ *n (tube)* manga *f.* *—vt (water)* regar con una manga; *(clean)* limpiar con una manga. **~-pipe** *n* manga *f*

hosiery /ˈhəʊzɪərɪ/ *n* calcetería *f*

hospice /ˈhɒspɪs/ *n* hospicio *m*

hospitabl|e /hɒˈspɪtəbl/ *a* hospitalario. **~y** *adv* con hospitalidad

hospital /ˈhɒspɪtl/ *n* hospital *m*

hospitality /hɒspɪˈtælɪtɪ/ *n* hospitalidad *f*

host[1] /həʊst/ *n.* **a ~ of** un montón de

host[2] /həʊst/ *n (master of house)* huésped *m*, anfitrión *m*

host[3] /həʊst/ *n (relig)* hostia *f*

hostage /ˈhɒstɪdʒ/ *n* rehén *m*

hostel /ˈhɒstl/ *n (for students)* residencia *f.* **youth ~** albergue *m* juvenil

hostess /ˈhəʊstɪs/ *n* huéspeda *f*, anfitriona *f*

hostil|e /ˈhɒstaɪl/ *a* hostil. **~ity** *n* hostilidad *f*

hot /hɒt/ *a (hotter, hottest)* caliente; *(culin)* picante; *(news)* de última hora. **be/feel ~** tener calor. **in ~ water** *(fam)* en un apuro. **it is ~** hace calor. *—vt/i.* **~ up** *(fam)* calentarse

hotbed /ˈhɒtbed/ *n (fig)* semillero *m*

hotchpotch /ˈhɒtʃpɒtʃ/ *n* mezcolanza *f*

hot dog /hɒtˈdɒg/ *n* perrito *m* caliente

hotel /həʊˈtel/ *n* hotel *m.* **~ier** *n* hotelero *m*

hot: ~-head *n* impetuoso *m.* **~-headed** *a* impetuoso. **~-house** *n* invernadero *m.* **~-line** *n* teléfono *m* rojo. **~-plate**

calentador *m.* **~-water bottle** *n* bolsa *f* de agua caliente

hound /haʊnd/ *n* perro *m* de caza. *—vt* perseguir

hour /aʊə(r)/ *n* hora *f.* **~ly** *a* & *adv* cada hora. **~ly pay** *n* sueldo *m* por hora. **paid ~ly** pagado por hora

house /haʊs/ *n (pl* **-s** /ˈhaʊzɪz/) casa *f*; *(theatre building)* sala *f*; *(theatre audience)* público *m*; *(pol)* cámara *f.* /haʊz/ *vt* alojar; *(keep)* guardar. **~boat** *n* casa *f* flotante. **~breaking** *n* robo *m* de casa. **~hold** /ˈhaʊshəʊld/ *n* casa *f*, familia *f.* **~holder** *n* dueño *m* de una casa; *(head of household)* cabeza *f* de familia. **~keeper** *n* ama *f* de llaves. **~keeping** *n* gobierno *m* de la casa. **~maid** *n* criada *f*, mucama *f (LAm).* **H~ of Commons** *n* Cámara *f* de los Comunes. **~proud** *a* meticuloso. **~warming** *n* inauguración *f* de una casa. **~wife** /ˈhaʊswaɪf/ *n* ama *f* de casa. **~work** *n* quehaceres *mpl* domésticos

housing /ˈhaʊzɪŋ/ *n* alojamiento *m.* **~ estate** *n* urbanización *f*

hovel /ˈhɒvl/ *n* casucha *f*

hover /ˈhɒvə(r)/ *vi (bird, threat etc)* cernerse; *(loiter)* rondar. **~craft** *n* aerodeslizador *m*

how /haʊ/ *adv* cómo. **~ about a walk?** ¿qué le parece si damos un paseo? **~ are you?** ¿cómo está Vd? **~ do you do?** *(in introduction)* mucho gusto. **~ long?** ¿cuánto tiempo? **~ many?** ¿cuántos? **~ much?** ¿cuánto? **~ often?** ¿cuántas veces? **and ~!** ¡y cómo!

however /haʊˈevə(r)/ *adv (with verb)* de cualquier manera de (+ *subjunctive*); *(with adjective or adverb)* por... que (+ *subjunctive*); *(nevertheless)* no

obstante, sin embargo. ~ **much
it rains** por mucho que llueva

howl /haʊl/ n aullido. —vi aullar

howler /'haʊlə(r)/ n (fam) plancha f

HP abbr see **hire-purchase**

hp abbr see **horsepower**

hub /hʌb/ n (of wheel) cubo m;
(fig) centro m

hubbub /'hʌbʌb/ n barahúnda f

hub-cap /'hʌbkæp/ n tapacubos
m invar

huddle /'hʌdl/ vi apiñarse

hue[1] /hjuː/ n (colour) color m

hue[2] /hjuː/ n. ~ **and cry** clamor
m

huff /hʌf/ n. **in a** ~ enojado

hug /hʌg/ vt (pt **hugged**) abrazar; (keep close to) no apartarse
de. —n abrazo m

huge /hjuːdʒ/ a enorme. ~**ly** adv
enormemente

hulk /hʌlk/ n (of ship) barco m
viejo; (person) armatoste m

hull /hʌl/ n (of ship) casco m

hullabaloo /hʌləbə'luː/ n tumulto m

hullo /hə'ləʊ/ int = **hello**

hum /hʌm/ vt/i (pt **hummed**)
(person) canturrear; (insect,
engine) zumbar. —n zumbido m.
~ (**or hem**) **and haw** (**or ha**)
vacilar

human /'hjuːmən/ a & n humano
(m). ~ **being** n ser m humano

humane /hjuː'meɪn/ a humano

humanism /'hjuːmənɪzəm/ n
humanismo m

humanitarian /hjuːmænɪ
'teərɪən/ a humanitario

humanity /hjuː'mænətɪ/ n humanidad f

humble /'hʌmbl/ a (-er, -est)
humilde. —vt humillar. ~**y** adv
humildemente

humbug /'hʌmbʌg/ n (false talk)
charlatanería f; (person) charlatán m; (sweet) caramelo m de
menta

humdrum /'hʌmdrʌm/ a monótono

humid /'hjuːmɪd/ a húmedo.
~**ifier** n humedecedor m. ~**ity**
/hjuː'mɪdətɪ/ n humedad f

humiliat|**e** /hjuː'mɪlɪeɪt/ vt hum-
illar. ~**ion** /-'eɪʃn/ n hum-
illación f

humility /hjuː'mɪlətɪ/ n humil-
dad f

humorist /'hjuːmərɪst/ n humor-
ista m & f

humo|**rous** /'hjuːmərəs/ a diverti-
do. ~**rously** adv con gracia.
~**ur** n humorismo m; (mood)
humor m. **sense of** ~**ur** n sentido m del humor

hump /hʌmp/ n montecillo m; (of
the spine) joroba f. **the** ~ (sl)
malhumor m. —vt encorvarse;
(hoist up) llevar al hombro

hunch /hʌntʃ/ vt encorvar. ~**ed
up** encorvado. —n presentimiento m; (lump) joroba f.
~**back** /'hʌntʃbæk/ n jorobado
m

hundred /'hʌndrəd/ a ciento,
(before noun) cien. —n ciento m.
~**fold** a céntuplo. —adv cien
veces. ~**s of** centenares de. ~**th**
a centésimo. —n centésimo m,
centésima parte f

hundredweight /'hʌndrədweɪt/
n 50,8kg; (Amer) 45,36kg

hung /hʌŋ/ see **hang**

Hungar|**ian** /hʌŋ'geərɪən/ a & n
húngaro (m). ~**y** /'hʌŋgərɪ/ n
Hungría f

hunger /'hʌŋgə(r)/ n hambre f. —
vi. ~ **for** tener hambre de.
~**-strike** n huelga f de hambre

hungr|**ily** /'hʌŋgrəlɪ/ adv ávi-
damente. ~**y** a (-ier, -iest) hambriento. **be** ~**y** tener hambre

hunk /hʌŋk/ n (buen) pedazo m

hunt /hʌnt/ vt/i cazar. ~ **for**
buscar. —n caza f. ~**er** n cazador
m. ~**ing** n caza f

hurdle /'hɜːdl/ n (sport) valla f; (fig) obstáculo m

hurdy-gurdy /'hɜːdɪgɜːdɪ/ n organillo m

hurl /hɜːl/ vt lanzar

hurly-burly /'hɜːlɪbɜːlɪ/ n tumulto m

hurrah /hʊ'rɑː/, **hurray** /hʊ'reɪ/ int & n ¡viva! (m)

hurricane /'hʌrɪkən/ n huracán m

hurried /'hʌrɪd/ a apresurado. **~ly** adv apresuradamente

hurry /'hʌrɪ/ vi apresurarse, darse prisa. —vt apresurar, dar prisa a. —n prisa f. **be in a ~** tener prisa

hurt /hɜːt/ vt/i (pt hurt) herir. —n (injury) herida f; (harm) daño m. **~ful** a hiriente; (harmful) dañoso

hurtle /'hɜːtl/ vt lanzar. —vi. **~ along** mover rápidamente

husband /'hʌzbənd/ n marido m

hush /hʌʃ/ vt acallar. —n silencio m. **~ up** ocultar (affair). **~ ~** a (fam) muy secreto

husk /hʌsk/ n cáscara f

husky /'hʌskɪ/ a (-ier, -iest) (hoarse) ronco; (burly) fornido

hussy /'hʌsɪ/ n desvergonzada f

hustle /'hʌsl/ vt (jostle) empujar. —vi (hurry) darse prisa. —n empuje m. **~ and bustle** n bullicio m

hut /hʌt/ n cabaña f

hutch /hʌtʃ/ n conejera f

hyacinth /'haɪəsɪnθ/ n jacinto m

hybrid /'haɪbrɪd/ a & n híbrido (m)

hydrangea /haɪ'dreɪndʒə/ n hortensia f

hydrant /'haɪdrənt/ n. **(fire) ~** n boca f de riego

hydraulic /haɪ'drɔːlɪk/ a hidráulico

hydroelectric /haɪdrəʊɪ'lektrɪk/ a hidroeléctrico

hydrofoil /'haɪdrəfɔɪl/ n aerodeslizador m

hydrogen /'haɪdrədʒən/ n hidrógeno m. **~ bomb** n bomba f de hidrógeno. **~ peroxide** n peróxido m de hidrógeno

hyena /haɪ'iːnə/ n hiena f

hygien|e /'haɪdʒiːn/ n higiene f. **~ic** a higiénico

hymn /hɪm/ n himno m

hyper... /'haɪpə(r)/ pref hiper...

hypermarket /'haɪpəmɑːkɪt/ n hipermercado m

hyphen /'haɪfn/ n guión m. **~ate** vt escribir con guión

hypno|sis /hɪp'nəʊsɪs/ n hipnosis f. **~tic** /-'nɒtɪk/ a hipnótico. **~tism** /hɪpnə'tɪzəm/ n hipnotismo m. **~tist** n hipnotista m & f. **~tize** vt hipnotizar

hypochondriac /haɪpə'kɒn drɪæk/ n hipocondríaco m

hypocrisy /hɪ'pɒkrəsɪ/ n hipocresía f

hypocrit|e /'hɪpəkrɪt/ n hipócrita m & f. **~ical** a hipócrita

hypodermic /haɪpə'dɜːmɪk/ a hipodérmico. —n jeringa f hipodérmica

hypothe|sis /haɪ'pɒθəsɪs/ n (pl -theses /-siːz/) hipótesis f. **~tical** /-ə'θetɪkl/ a hipotético

hysteri|a /hɪ'stɪərɪə/ n histerismo m. **~cal** /-'terɪkl/ a histérico. **~cs** /hɪ'sterɪks/ npl histerismo m. **have ~cs** ponerse histérico; (laugh) morir de risa

I

I /aɪ/ pron yo

ice /aɪs/ n hielo m. —vt helar; glasear (cake). —vi. **~ (up)** helarse. **~berg** n iceberg m, témpano m. **~-cream** n helado m. **~-cube**

cubito *m* de hielo. ~ **hockey** *n* hockey *m* sobre hielo

Iceland /'aisland/ *n* Islandia *f.* ~**er** *n* islandés *m.* ~**ic** /-'lændik/ *a* islandés

ice lolly /ais'loli/ polo *m*, paleta *f* (*LAm*)

icicle /'aisikl/ *n* carámbano *m*

icing /'aisiŋ/ *n* (*sugar*) azúcar *m* glaseado

icon /'aikɒn/ *n* icono *m*

icy /'aisi/ *a* (-**ier**, -**iest**) glacial

idea /ai'dia/ *n* idea *f*

ideal /ai'dial/ *a* ideal. ─*n* ideal *m.* ~**ism** *n* idealismo *m.* ~**ist** *n* idealista *m & f.* ~**istic** /-'listik/ *a* idealista. ~**ize** *vt* idealizar. ~**ly** *adv* idealmente

identical /ai'dentikl/ *a* idéntico

identif ication /aidentifi'keiʃn/ *n* identificación *f.* ~**y** /ai'dentifai/ *vt* identificar. ─*vi.* ~**y with** identificarse con

identikit /ai'dentikit/ *n* retrato-robot *m*

identity /ai'dentiti/ *n* identidad *f*

ideolog ical /aidia'lɒdʒikl/ *a* ideológico. ~**y** /aidi'ɒlədʒi/ *n* ideología *f*

idiocy /'idiəsi/ *n* idiotez *f*

idiom /'idiəm/ *n* locución *f.* ~**atic** /-'mætik/ *a* idiomático

idiosyncrasy /idiə'siŋkrəsi/ *n* idiosincrasia *f*

idiot /'idiət/ *n* idiota *m & f.* ~**ic** /-'ɒtik/ *a* idiota

idle /'aidl/ *a* (-**er**, -**est**) ocioso; (*lazy*) holgazán; (*out of work*) desocupado; (*machine*) parado. ─*vi* (*engine*) marchar en vacío. ─*vt.* ~ **away** perder. ~**ness** *n* ociosidad *f.* ~**r** /-ə(r)/ *n* ocioso *m*

idol /'aidl/ *n* ídolo *m.* ~**ize** *vt* idolatrar

idyllic /i'dilik/ *a* idílico

i.e. /ai'i:/ *abbr* (*id est*) es decir

if /if/ *conj* si

igloo /'iglu:/ *n* iglú *m*

ignite /ig'nait/ *vt* encender. ─*vi* encenderse

ignition /ig'niʃn/ *n* ignición *f;* (*auto*) encendido *m.* ~ (**switch**) *n* contacto *m*

ignoramus /ignə'reiməs/ *n* (*pl* -**muses**) ignorante

ignoran ce /'ignərəns/ *n* ignorancia *f.* ~**t** *a* ignorante. ~**tly** *adv* por ignorancia

ignore /ig'nɔ:(r)/ *vt* no hacer caso de

ilk /ilk/ *n* ralea *f*

ill /il/ *a* enfermo; (*bad*) malo. ~ **will** *n* mala voluntad *f.* ─*adv* mal. ~ **at ease** inquieto. ─*n* mal *m.* ~-**advised** *a* imprudente. ~-**bred** *a* mal educado

illegal /i'li:gl/ *a* ilegal

illegible /i'ledʒəbl/ *a* ilegible

illegitima cy /ili'dʒitiməsi/ *n* ilegitimidad *f.* ~**te** *a* ilegítimo

ill: ~-fated *a* malogrado. ~-**gotten** *a* mal adquirido

illitera cy /i'litərəsi/ *n* analfabetismo *m.* ~**te** *a & n* analfabeto (*m*)

ill: ~-natured *a* poco afable. ~**ness** *n* enfermedad *f*

illogical /i'lɒdʒikl/ *a* ilógico

ill: ~-starred *a* malogrado. ~-**treat** *vt* maltratar

illuminat e /i'lu:mineit/ *vt* iluminar. ~**ion** /-'neiʃn/ *n* iluminación *f*

illus ion /i'lu:ʒn/ *n* ilusión *f.* ~**sory** *a* ilusorio

illustrat e /'iləstreit/ *vt* ilustrar. ~**ion** *n* (*example*) ejemplo *m;* (*picture in book*) grabado *m*, lámina *f.* ~**ive** *a* ilustrativo

illustrious /i'lʌstriəs/ *a* ilustre

image /'imidʒ/ *n* imagen *f.* ~**ry** *n* imágenes *fpl*

imagin able /i'mædʒinəbl/ *a* imaginable. ~**ary** *a* imaginario. ~**ation** /-'neiʃn/ *n* imaginación *f.* ~**ative** *a* imaginativo. ~**e** *vt* imaginar(se)

imbalance /ɪmˈbæləns/ n desequilibrio m

imbecil|e /ˈɪmbəsiːl/ a & n imbécil (m & f). **~ity** /-ˈsɪlətɪ/ n imbecilidad f

imbibe /ɪmˈbaɪb/ vt embeber; (drink) beber

imbue /ɪmˈbjuː/ vt empapar (**with** de)

imitat|e /ˈɪmɪteɪt/ vt imitar. **~ion** /-ˈteɪʃn/ n imitación f. **~or** n imitador m

immaculate /ɪˈmækjʊlət/ a inmaculado

immaterial /ɪməˈtɪərɪəl/ a inmaterial; (unimportant) insignificante

immature /ɪməˈtjʊə(r)/ a inmaduro

immediate /ɪˈmiːdɪət/ a inmediato. **~ly** adv inmediatamente. **~ly you hear me en** cuanto me oigas. —conj en cuanto (+ subj)

immense /ɪˈmens/ a inmenso. **~ely** adv inmensamente; (very much, fam) muchísimo. **~ity** n inmensidad f

immers|e /ɪˈmɜːs/ vt sumergir. **~ion** /ɪˈmɜːʃn/ n inmersión f. **~ion heater** n calentador m de inmersión

immigra|nt /ˈɪmɪgrənt/ a & n inmigrante (m & f). **~te** vi inmigrar. **~tion** /-ˈgreɪʃn/ n inmigración f

imminen|ce /ˈɪmɪnəns/ n inminencia f. **~t** a inminente

immobil|e /ɪˈməʊbaɪl/ a inmóvil. **~ize** /-bɪlaɪz/ vt inmovilizar

immoderate /ɪˈmɒdərət/ a inmoderado

immodest /ɪˈmɒdɪst/ a inmodesto

immoral /ɪˈmɒrəl/ a inmoral. **~ity** /ɪməˈrælətɪ/ n inmoralidad f

immortal /ɪˈmɔːtl/ a inmortal. **~ity** /-ˈtælətɪ/ n inmortalidad f. **~ize** vt inmortalizar

immun|e /ɪˈmjuːn/ a inmune (**from, to** a, contra). **~ity** n inmunidad f. **~ization** /ɪmjʊnaɪˈzeɪʃn/ n inmunización f. **~ize** vt inmunizar

imp /ɪmp/ n diablillo m

impact /ˈɪmpækt/ n impacto m

impair /ɪmˈpeə(r)/ vt perjudicar

impale /ɪmˈpeɪl/ vt empalar

impart /ɪmˈpɑːt/ vt comunicar

impartial /ɪmˈpɑːʃl/ a imparcial. **~ity** /-ɪˈælɪtɪ/ n imparcialidad f

impassable /ɪmˈpɑːsəbl/ a (barrier etc) infranqueable; (road) impracticable

impasse /æmˈpɑːs/ n callejón m sin salida

impassioned /ɪmˈpæʃnd/ a apasionado

impassive /ɪmˈpæsɪv/ a impasible

impatien|ce /ɪmˈpeɪʃəns/ n impaciencia f. **~t** a impaciente. **~tly** adv con impaciencia

impeach /ɪmˈpiːtʃ/ vt acusar

impeccable /ɪmˈpekəbl/ a impecable

impede /ɪmˈpiːd/ vt estorbar

impediment /ɪmˈpedɪmənt/ n obstáculo m. (speech) **~** n defecto m del habla

impel /ɪmˈpel/ vt (pt impelled) impeler

impending /ɪmˈpendɪŋ/ a inminente

impenetrable /ɪmˈpenɪtrəbl/ a impenetrable

imperative /ɪmˈperətɪv/ a imprescindible. —n (gram) imperativo m

imperceptible /ɪmpəˈseptəbl/ a imperceptible

imperfect /ɪmˈpɜːfɪkt/ a imperfecto. **~ion** /ə-ˈfekʃn/ n imperfección f

imperial /ɪmˈpɪərɪəl/ a imperial. **~ism** n imperialismo m

imperil /ɪmˈperəl/ vt (pt imperilled) poner en peligro

imperious /ɪmˈpɪərɪəs/ *a* imperioso

impersonal /ɪmˈpɜːsənl/ *a* impersonal

impersonate /ɪmˈpɜːsəneɪt/ *vt* hacerse pasar por; (*mimic*) imitar. ~**ion** /-ˈneɪʃn/ *n* imitación *f*. ~**or** *n* imitador *m*

impertinence /ɪmˈpɜːtɪnəns/ *n* impertinencia *f*. ~**t** *a* impertinente. ~**tly** *adv* impertinentemente

impervious /ɪmˈpɜːvɪəs/ *a*. ~ **to** impermeable a; (*fig*) insensible a

impetuous /ɪmˈpetjʊəs/ *a* impetuoso

impetus /ˈɪmpɪtəs/ *n* ímpetu *m*

impinge /ɪmˈpɪndʒ/ *vi*. ~ **on** afectar a

impish /ˈɪmpɪʃ/ *a* travieso

implacable /ɪmˈplækəbl/ *a* implacable

implant /ɪmˈplɑːnt/ *vt* implantar

implement /ˈɪmplɪmənt/ *n* herramienta *f*. /ˈɪmplɪment/ *vt* realizar

implicate /ˈɪmplɪkeɪt/ *vt* implicar. ~**ion** /-ˈkeɪʃn/ *n* implicación *f*

implicit /ɪmˈplɪsɪt/ *a* (*implied*) implícito; (*unquestioning*) absoluto

implied /ɪmˈplaɪd/ *a* implícito

implore /ɪmˈplɔː(r)/ *vt* implorar

imply /ɪmˈplaɪ/ *vt* implicar; (*mean*) querer decir; (*insinuate*) dar a entender

impolite /ɪmpəˈlaɪt/ *a* mal educado

imponderable /ɪmˈpɒndərəbl/ *a* & *n* imponderable (*m*)

import /ɪmˈpɔːt/ *vt* importar. /ˈɪmpɔːt/ *n* (*article*) importación *f*; (*meaning*) significación *f*

importance /ɪmˈpɔːtəns/ *n* importancia *f*. ~**t** *a* importante

importation /ɪmpɔːˈteɪʃn/ *n* importación *f*

importer /ɪmˈpɔːtə(r)/ *n* importador *m*

impose /ɪmˈpəʊz/ *vt* imponer. — *vi*. ~ **on** abusar de la amabilidad de

imposing /ɪmˈpəʊzɪŋ/ *a* imponente

imposition /ɪmpəˈzɪʃn/ *n* imposición *f*; (*fig*) molestia *f*

impossibility /ɪmpɒsəˈbɪlətɪ/ *n* imposibilidad *f*. ~**le** *a* imposible

impostor /ɪmˈpɒstə(r)/ *n* impostor *m*

impotence /ˈɪmpətəns/ *n* impotencia *f*. ~**t** *a* impotente

impound /ɪmˈpaʊnd/ *vt* confiscar

impoverish /ɪmˈpɒvərɪʃ/ *vt* empobrecer

impracticable /ɪmˈpræktɪkəbl/ *a* impracticable

impractical /ɪmˈpræktɪkl/ *a* poco práctico

imprecise /ɪmprɪˈsaɪs/ *a* impreciso

impregnable /ɪmˈpregnəbl/ *a* inexpugnable

impregnate /ˈɪmpregneɪt/ *vt* impregnar (**with** de)

impresario /ɪmprɪˈsɑːrɪəʊ/ *n* (*pl* -os) empresario *m*

impress /ɪmˈpres/ *vt* impresionar; (*imprint*) imprimir. ~ **on s.o.** hacer entender a uno

impression /ɪmˈpreʃn/ *n* impresión *f*. ~**able** *a* impresionable

impressive /ɪmˈpresɪv/ *a* impresionante

imprint /ˈɪmprɪnt/ *n* impresión *f*. /ɪmˈprɪnt/ *vt* imprimir

imprison /ɪmˈprɪzn/ *vt* encarcelar. ~**ment** *n* encarcelamiento *m*

improbability /ɪmprɒbəˈbɪlətɪ/ *n* improbabilidad *f*. ~**le** *a* improbable

impromptu /ɪmˈprɒmptjuː/ *a* improvisado. —*adv* de improviso

improper /ɪmˈprɒpə(r)/ *a* impropio; (*incorrect*) incorrecto

impropriety /ɪmprə'praɪətɪ/ n inconveniencia f

improve /ɪm'pruːv/ vt mejorar. —vi mejorar(se). ~ment n mejora f

improvisation /ɪmprəvaɪ'zeɪʃn/ n improvisación f. ~e vt/i improvisar

imprudent /ɪm'pruːdənt/ a imprudente

impudence /'ɪmpjudəns/ n insolencia f. ~t a insolente

impulse /'ɪmpʌls/ n impulso m. on ~ sin reflexionar

impulsive /ɪm'pʌlsɪv/ a irreflexivo. ~ly adv sin reflexionar

impunity /ɪm'pjuːnətɪ/ n impunidad f. with ~ impunemente

impure /ɪm'pjʊə(r)/ a impuro. ~ity n impureza f

impute /ɪm'pjuːt/ vt imputar

in /ɪn/ prep en, dentro de. ~ a firm manner de una manera terminante. ~ an hour('s time) dentro de una hora. ~ doing al hacer. ~ so far as en cuanto que. ~ the evening por la tarde. ~ the main por la mayor parte. ~ the rain bajo la lluvia. ~ the sun al sol. one ~ ten uno de cada diez. the best ~ el mejor de. —adv (inside) dentro; (at home) en casa; (in fashion) de moda. —n. the ~s and outs of los detalles mpl de

inability /ɪnə'bɪlətɪ/ n incapacidad f

inaccessible /ɪnæk'sesəbl/ a inaccesible

inaccuracy /ɪn'ækjʊrəsɪ/ n inexactitud f. ~te a inexacto

inaction /ɪn'ækʃn/ n inacción f

inactive /ɪn'æktɪv/ a inactivo. ~ity /-'tɪvətɪ/ n inactividad f

inadequacy /ɪn'ædɪkwəsɪ/ a insuficiencia f. ~te a insuficiente

inadmissible /ɪnəd'mɪsəbl/ a inadmisible

inadvertently /ɪnəd'vɜːtəntlɪ/ adv por descuido

inadvisable /ɪnəd'vaɪzəbl/ a no aconsejable

inane /ɪ'neɪn/ a estúpido

inanimate /ɪn'ænɪmət/ a inanimado

inappropriate /ɪnə'prəʊprɪət/ a inoportuno

inarticulate /ɪnɑː'tɪkjʊlət/ a incapaz de expresarse claramente

inasmuch as /ɪnəz'mʌtʃəz/ adv ya que

inattentive /ɪnə'tentɪv/ a desatento

inaudible /ɪn'ɔːdəbl/ a inaudible

inaugural /ɪ'nɔːgjʊrəl/ a inaugural

inaugurate /ɪ'nɔːgjʊreɪt/ vt inaugurar. ~ion /-'reɪʃn/ n inauguración f

inauspicious /ɪnɔː'spɪʃəs/ a poco propicio

inborn /'ɪnbɔːn/ a innato

inbred /ɪn'bred/ a (inborn) innato

incalculable /ɪn'kælkjʊləbl/ a incalculable

incapability /ɪnkeɪpə'bɪlətɪ/ n incapacidad f. ~le a incapaz

incapacitate /ɪnkə'pæsɪteɪt/ vt incapacitar. ~y n incapacidad f

incarcerate /ɪn'kɑːsəreɪt/ vt encarcelar. ~ion /-'reɪʃn/ n encarcelamiento m

incarnate /ɪn'kɑːnət/ a encarnado. ~ion /-'neɪʃn/ n encarnación f

incautious /ɪn'kɔːʃəs/ a incauto. ~ly adv incautamente

incendiary /ɪn'sendɪərɪ/ a incendiario. —n (person) incendiario m; (bomb) bomba f incendiaria

incense¹ /'ɪnsens/ n incienso m

incense² /ɪn'sens/ vt enfurecer

incentive /ɪn'sentɪv/ n incentivo m; (payment) prima f de incentivo

inception /ɪnˈsepʃn/ n principio m

incertitude /ɪnˈsɜːtɪtjuːd/ n incertidumbre f

incessant /ɪnˈsesnt/ a incesante. **~ly** adv sin cesar

incest /ˈɪnsest/ n incesto m. **~uous** /-ˈsestjʊəs/ a incestuoso

inch /ɪntʃ/ n pulgada f (= 2,54cm). —vi avanzar palmo a palmo

incidence /ˈɪnsɪdəns/ n frecuencia f

incident /ˈɪnsɪdənt/ n incidente m

incidental /ɪnsɪˈdentl/ a fortuito. **~ly** adv incidentemente; (by the way) a propósito

incinerat|e /ɪnˈsɪnəreɪt/ vt incinerar. **~or** n incinerador m

incipient /ɪnˈsɪpɪənt/ a incipiente

incision /ɪnˈsɪʒn/ n incisión f

incisive /ɪnˈsaɪsɪv/ a incisivo

incite /ɪnˈsaɪt/ vt incitar. **~ment** n incitación f

inclement /ɪnˈklemənt/ a inclemente

inclination /ɪnklɪˈneɪʃn/ n inclinación f

incline[1] /ɪnˈklaɪn/ vt inclinar. —vi inclinarse. **be ~d to** tener tendencia a

incline[2] /ˈɪnklaɪn/ n cuesta f

includ|e /ɪnˈkluːd/ vt incluir. **~ding** prep incluso. **~sion** /-ʒn/ n inclusión f

inclusive /ɪnˈkluːsɪv/ a inclusivo. **be ~ of** incluir. —adv inclusive

incognito /ɪnkɒɡˈniːtəʊ/ adv de incógnito

incoherent /ɪnkəʊˈhɪərənt/ a incoherente

income /ˈɪnkʌm/ n ingresos mpl. **~ tax** n impuesto m sobre la renta

incoming /ˈɪnkʌmɪŋ/ a ⟨tide⟩ ascendente; ⟨tenant etc⟩ nuevo

incomparable /ɪnˈkɒmpərəbl/ a incomparable

incompatible /ɪnkəmˈpætəbl/ a incompatible

incompeten|ce /ɪnˈkɒmpɪtəns/ n incompetencia f. **~t** a incompetente

incomplete /ɪnkəmˈpliːt/ a incompleto

incomprehensible /ɪnkɒmprɪˈhensəbl/ a incomprensible

inconceivable /ɪnkənˈsiːvəbl/ a inconcebible

inconclusive /ɪnkənˈkluːsɪv/ a poco concluyente

incongruous /ɪnˈkɒŋɡrʊəs/ a incongruente

inconsequential /ɪnkɒnsɪˈkwenʃl/ a sin importancia

inconsiderate /ɪnkənˈsɪdərət/ a desconsiderado

inconsisten|cy /ɪnkənˈsɪstənsɪ/ n inconsecuencia f. **~t** a inconsecuente. **be ~t with** no concordar con

inconspicuous /ɪnkənˈspɪkjʊəs/ a que no llama la atención. **~ly** adv sin llamar la atención

incontinen|ce /ɪnˈkɒntɪnəns/ n incontinencia f. **~t** a incontinente

inconvenien|ce /ɪnkənˈviːnɪəns/ a incomodidad f; ⟨drawback⟩ inconveniente m. **~t** a incómodo; ⟨time⟩ inoportuno

incorporat|e /ɪnˈkɔːpəreɪt/ vt incorporar; (include) incluir. **~ion** /-ˈreɪʃn/ n incorporación f

incorrect /ɪnkəˈrekt/ a incorrecto

incorrigible /ɪnˈkɒrɪdʒəbl/ a incorregible

incorruptible /ɪnkəˈrʌptəbl/ a incorruptible

increase /ˈɪnkriːs/ n aumento m (in, of de). /ɪnˈkriːs/ vt/i aumentar

increasing /ɪnˈkriːsɪŋ/ a creciente. **~ly** adv cada vez más

incredible /ɪn'kredəbl/ a increíble

incredulous /ɪn'kredjʊləs/ a incrédulo

increment /'ɪnkrɪmənt/ n aumento m

incriminat|e /ɪn'krɪmɪneɪt/ vt acriminar. ~ing a acriminador

incubat|e /'ɪŋkjʊbeɪt/ vt incubar. ~ion /-'beɪʃn/ n incubación f. ~or n incubadora f

inculcate /'ɪnkʌlkeɪt/ vt inculcar

incumbent /ɪn'kʌmbənt/ n titular. —a. **be ~ on** incumbir a

incur /ɪn'kɜː(r)/ vt (pt incurred) incurrir en; contraer (debts)

incurable /ɪn'kjʊərəbl/ a incurable

incursion /ɪn'kɜːʃn/ n incursión f

indebted /ɪn'detɪd/ a. **~ to s.o.** estar en deuda con uno

indecen|cy /ɪn'diːsnsɪ/ n indecencia f. ~t a indecente

indecisi|on /ɪndɪ'sɪʒn/ n indecisión f. ~ve /ɪndɪ'saɪsɪv/ a indeciso

indeed /ɪn'diːd/ adv en efecto; (really?) ¿de veras?

indefatigable /ɪndɪ'fætɪɡəbl/ a incansable

indefinable /ɪndɪ'faɪnəbl/ a indefinible

indefinite /ɪn'defɪnət/ a indefinido. ~ly adv indefinidamente

indelible /ɪn'delɪbl/ a indeleble

indemni|fy /ɪn'demnɪfaɪ/ vt indemnizar. ~ty /-ətɪ/ n indemnización f

indent /ɪn'dent/ vt endentar (text). ~ation /-'teɪʃn/ n mella f

independen|ce /ɪndɪ'pendəns/ n independencia f. ~t a independiente. ~tly adv independientemente. ~tly of independientemente de

indescribable /ɪndɪ'skraɪbəbl/ a indescriptible

indestructible /ɪndɪ'strʌktəbl/ a indestructible

indeterminate /ɪndɪ'tɜːmɪnət/ a indeterminado

index /'ɪndeks/ n (pl indexes) índice m. —vt poner índice a; (enter in the/an index) poner en el/un índice. **~ finger** n (dedo m) índice m. **~-linked** a indexado

India /'ɪndɪə/ n la India f. **~n** a & n indio (m). **~n summer** n veranillo m de San Martín

indicat|e /'ɪndɪkeɪt/ vt indicar. ~ion /-'keɪʃn/ n indicación f. ~ive /ɪn'dɪkətɪv/ a & n indicativo (m). ~or /'ɪndɪkeɪtə(r)/ n indicador m

indict /ɪn'daɪt/ vt acusar. ~ment n acusación f

indifferen|ce /ɪn'dɪfrəns/ n indiferencia f. ~t a indiferente; (not good) mediocre

indigenous /ɪn'dɪdʒɪnəs/ a indígena

indigesti|ble /ɪndɪ'dʒestəbl/ a indigesto. ~on /-tʃən/ n indigestión f

indigna|nt /ɪn'dɪɡnənt/ a indignado. ~tion /-'neɪʃn/ n indignación f

indignity /ɪn'dɪɡnətɪ/ n indignidad f

indigo /'ɪndɪɡəʊ/ n añil (m)

indirect /ɪndɪ'rekt/ a indirecto. ~ly adv indirectamente

indiscre|et /ɪndɪ'skriːt/ a indiscreto. ~tion /-'kreʃn/ n indiscreción f

indiscriminate /ɪndɪ'skrɪmɪnət/ a indistinto. ~ly adv indistintamente

indispensable /ɪndɪ'spensəbl/ a imprescindible

indispos|ed /ɪndɪ'spəʊzd/ a indispuesto. ~ition /-ə'zɪʃn/ n indisposición f

indisputable /ɪndɪ'spjuːtəbl/ a indiscutible

indissoluble /ɪndɪˈsɒljʊbl/ a indisoluble

indistinct /ɪndɪˈstɪŋkt/ a indistinto

indistinguishable /ɪndɪˈstɪŋgwɪʃ əbl/ a indistinguible

individual /ɪndɪˈvɪdjʊəl/ a individual. —n individuo m. ~ist n individualista m & f. ~ity n individualidad f. ~ly adv individualmente

indivisible /ɪndɪˈvɪzəbl/ a indivisible

Indo-China /ɪndəʊˈtʃaɪnə/ n Indochina f

indoctrinate /ɪnˈdɒktrɪneɪt/ vt adoctrinar. ~ion /-ˈneɪʃn/ n adoctrinamiento m

indolen|ce /ˈɪndələns/ n indolencia f. ~t a indolente

indomitable /ɪnˈdɒmɪtəbl/ a indomable

Indonesia /ɪndəʊˈniːzɪə/ n Indonesia f. ~n a & n indonesio (m)

indoor /ˈɪndɔː(r)/ a interior; ⟨clothes etc⟩ de casa; ⟨covered⟩ cubierto. ~s adv dentro; ⟨at home⟩ en casa

induce /ɪnˈdjuːs/ vt inducir; ⟨cause⟩ provocar. ~ment n incentivo m

induct /ɪnˈdʌkt/ vt instalar; ⟨mil, Amer⟩ incorporar

indulge /ɪnˈdʌldʒ/ vt satisfacer ⟨desires⟩; complacer ⟨person⟩. — vi. ~ in entregarse a. ~nce /ɪnˈdʌldʒəns/ n ⟨of desires⟩ satisfacción f; ⟨relig⟩ indulgencia f. ~nt a indulgente

industrial /ɪnˈdʌstrɪəl/ a industrial; ⟨unrest⟩ laboral. ~ist n industrial m & f. ~ized a industrializado

industrious /ɪnˈdʌstrɪəs/ a trabajador

industry /ˈɪndəstrɪ/ n industria f; ⟨zeal⟩ aplicación f

inebriated /ɪˈniːbrɪeɪtɪd/ a borracho

inedible /ɪnˈedɪbl/ a incomible

ineffable /ɪnˈefəbl/ a inefable

ineffective /ɪnɪˈfektɪv/ a ineficaz; ⟨person⟩ incapaz

ineffectual /ɪnɪˈfektjʊəl/ a eficaz

inefficien|cy /ɪnɪˈfɪʃnsɪ/ n ineficacia f; ⟨of person⟩ incompetencia f. ~t a ineficaz; ⟨person⟩ incompetente

ineligible /ɪnˈelɪdʒəbl/ a inelegible. be ~ for no tener derecho a

inept /ɪˈnept/ a inepto

inequality /ɪnɪˈkwɒlətɪ/ n desigualdad f

inert /ɪˈnɜːt/ a inerte

inertia /ɪˈnɜːʃə/ n inercia f

inescapable /ɪnɪˈskeɪpəbl/ a ineludible

inestimable /ɪnˈestɪməbl/ a inestimable

inevitab|le /ɪnˈevɪtəbl/ a inevitable. ~ly adv inevitablemente

inexact /ɪnɪgˈzækt/ a inexacto

inexcusable /ɪnɪkˈskjuːsəbl/ a imperdonable

inexhaustible /ɪnɪgˈzɔːstəbl/ a inagotable

inexorable /ɪnˈeksərəbl/ a inexorable

inexpensive /ɪnɪkˈspensɪv/ a económico, barato

inexperience /ɪnɪkˈspɪərɪəns/ n falta f de experiencia. ~d a inexperto

inexplicable /ɪnɪkˈsplɪkəbl/ a inexplicable

inextricable /ɪnɪkˈstrɪkəbl/ a inextricable

infallibility /ɪnˈfæləbɪlətɪ/ n infalibilidad f. ~le a infalible

infam|ous /ˈɪnfəməs/ a infame. ~y n infamia f

infan|cy /ˈɪnfənsɪ/ n infancia f. ~t n niño m. ~tile /ˈɪnfəntaɪl/ a infantil

infantry /ˈɪnfəntrɪ/ n infantería f

infatuated /ɪnˈfætjʊeɪtɪd/ a. be ~ed with encapricharse por

~ion /-'eɪʃn/ n encaprichamiento m

infect /ɪn'fekt/ vt infectar; (fig) contagiar. ~ **s.o. with** contagiar a uno. ~**ion** /-'fekʃn/ n infección f; (fig) contagio m. ~**ious** /ɪn'fekʃəs/ a contagioso

infer /ɪn'fɜː(r)/ vt (pt **inferred**) deducir. ~**ence** /'ɪnfərəns/ n deducción f

inferior /ɪn'fɪərɪə(r)/ a inferior. —n inferior m & f. ~**ity** /-'ɒrətɪ/ n inferioridad f

infernal /ɪn'fɜːnl/ a infernal. ~**ly** adv (fam) atrozmente

inferno /ɪn'fɜːnəʊ/ n (pl -os) infierno m

infertil|e /ɪn'fɜːtaɪl/ a estéril. ~**ity** /-'tɪlətɪ/ n esterilidad f

infest /ɪn'fest/ vt infestar. ~**ation** /-'steɪʃn/ n infestación f

infidelity /ɪnfɪ'delətɪ/ n infidelidad f

infighting /'ɪnfaɪtɪŋ/ n lucha f cuerpo a cuerpo; (fig) riñas fpl (internas)

infiltrat|e /ɪnfɪl'treɪt/ vt infiltrar. —vi infiltrarse. ~**ion** /-'treɪʃn/ n infiltración f

infinite /'ɪnfɪnət/ a infinito. ~**ly** adv infinitamente

infinitesimal /ɪnfɪnɪ'tesɪml/ a infinitesimal

infinitive /ɪn'fɪnətɪv/ n infinitivo m

infinity /ɪn'fɪnətɪ/ n (infinite distance) infinito m; (infinite quantity) infinidad f

infirm /ɪn'fɜːm/ a enfermizo

infirmary /ɪn'fɜːmərɪ/ n hospital m; (sick bay) enfermería f

infirmity /ɪn'fɜːmətɪ/ n enfermedad f; (weakness) debilidad f

inflam|e /ɪn'fleɪm/ vt inflamar. ~**mable** /ɪn'flæməbl/ a inflamable. ~**mation** /-ə'meɪʃn/ n inflamación f. ~**matory** /ɪn'flæmətərɪ/ a inflamatorio

inflate /ɪn'fleɪt/ vt inflar

inflation /ɪn'fleɪʃn/ n inflación f. ~**ary** a inflacionario

inflection /ɪn'flekʃn/ n inflexión f

inflexible /ɪn'fleksəbl/ a inflexible

inflict /ɪn'flɪkt/ vt infligir (**on** a)

inflow /'ɪnfləʊ/ n afluencia f

influence /'ɪnfloəns/ n influencia f. **under the ~** (drunk, fam) borracho. —vt influir, influenciar (esp LAm)

influential /ɪnfloʊ'enʃl/ a influyente

influenza /ɪnfloʊ'enzə/ n gripe f

influx /'ɪnflʌks/ n afluencia f

inform /ɪn'fɔːm/ vt informar. **keep ~ed** tener al corriente

informal /ɪn'fɔːml/ a (simple) sencillo, sin ceremonia; (unofficial) oficioso. ~**ity** n falta f de ceremonia. ~**ly** adv sin ceremonia

inform|ant /ɪn'fɔːmənt/ n informador m. ~**ation** /ɪnfə'meɪʃn/ n información f. ~**ative** /ɪn'fɔːmətɪv/ a informativo. ~**er** /ɪn'fɔːmə(r)/ n denunciante m

infra-red /ɪnfrə'red/ a infrarrojo

infrequent /ɪn'friːkwənt/ a poco frecuente. ~**ly** adv raramente

infringe /ɪn'frɪndʒ/ vt infringir. ~ **on** usurpar. ~**ment** n infracción f

infuriate /ɪn'fjʊərɪeɪt/ vt enfurecer

infus|e /ɪn'fjuːz/ vt infundir. ~**ion** /-ʒn/ n infusión f

ingen|ious /ɪn'dʒiːnɪəs/ a ingenioso. ~**uity** /ɪndʒɪ'njuːətɪ/ n ingeniosidad f

ingenuous /ɪn'dʒenjʊəs/ a ingenuo

ingest /ɪn'dʒest/ vt ingerir

ingot /'ɪŋgət/ n lingote m

ingrained /ɪn'greɪnd/ a arraigado

ingratiate /ɪn'greɪʃɪeɪt/ vt. ~ **o.s. with** congraciarse con

ingratitude /ɪn'grætɪtjuːd/ n ingratitud f

ingredient /ɪn'griːdɪənt/ n ingrediente m

ingrowing /'ɪngrəʊɪŋ/ a. ~ **nail** n uñero m, uña f encarnada

inhabit /ɪn'hæbɪt/ vt habitar. ~**able** a habitable. ~**ant** n habitante m

inhale /ɪn'heɪl/ vt aspirar. —vi (tobacco) aspirar el humo

inherent /ɪn'hɪərənt/ a inherente. ~**ly** adv intrínsecamente

inherit /ɪn'herɪt/ vt heredar. ~**ance** n herencia f

inhibit /ɪn'hɪbɪt/ vt inhibir. **be** ~**ed** tener inhibiciones. ~**ion** /-'bɪʃn/ n inhibición f

inhospitable /ɪnhə'spɪtəbl/ a (place) inhóspito; (person) inhospitalario

inhuman /ɪn'hjuːmən/ a inhumano. ~**e** /ɪnhjuː'meɪn/ a inhumano. ~**ity** /ɪnhjuː'mænətɪ/ n inhumanidad f

inimical /ɪ'nɪmɪkl/ a hostil

inimitable /ɪ'nɪmɪtəbl/ a inimitable

iniquit|ous /ɪ'nɪkwɪtəs/ a inicuo. ~**y** /-ətɪ/ n iniquidad f

initial /ɪ'nɪʃl/ n inicial f. —vt (pt **initialled**) firmar con iniciales. **he** ~**led the document** firmó el documento con sus iniciales. —a inicial. ~**ly** adv al principio

initiat|e /ɪ'nɪʃɪeɪt/ vt iniciar; promover (scheme etc). ~**ion** /-'eɪʃn/ n iniciación f

initiative /ɪ'nɪʃɪtɪv/ n iniciativa f

inject /ɪn'dʒekt/ vt inyectar; (fig) injertar (new element). ~**ion** /-ʃn/ n inyección f

injunction /ɪn'dʒʌŋkʃn/ n (court order) entredicho m

injur|e /'ɪndʒə(r)/ vt (wound) herir; (fig, damage) perjudicar. ~**y** /'ɪndʒərɪ/ n herida f; (damage) perjuicio m

injustice /ɪn'dʒʌstɪs/ n injusticia f

ink /ɪŋk/ n tinta f

inkling /'ɪŋklɪŋ/ n atisbo m

ink: ~**well** n tintero m. ~**y** a manchado de tinta

inland /'ɪnlənd/ a interior. —adv tierra adentro. **I**~ **Revenue** n Hacienda f

in-laws /'ɪnlɔːz/ npl parientes mpl políticos

inlay /ɪn'leɪ/ vt (pt **inlaid**) taracear, incrustar. /'ɪnleɪ/ n taracea f, incrustación f

inlet /'ɪnlet/ n ensenada f; (tec) entrada f

inmate /'ɪnmeɪt/ n (of asylum) internado m; (of prison) preso m

inn /ɪn/ n posada f

innards /'ɪnədz/ npl tripas fpl

innate /ɪ'neɪt/ a innato

inner /'ɪnə(r)/ a interior; (fig) íntimo. ~**most** a más íntimo. ~**tube** n cámara f de aire, llanta f (LAm)

innings /'ɪnɪŋz/ n invar turno m

innkeeper /'ɪnkiːpə(r)/ n posadero m

innocen|ce /'ɪnəsns/ n inocencia f. ~**t** a & n inocente (m & f)

innocuous /ɪ'nɒkjʊəs/ a inocuo

innovat|e /'ɪnəveɪt/ vi innovar. ~**ion** /-'veɪʃn/ n innovación f. ~**or** n innovador m

innuendo /ɪnjuː'endəʊ/ n (pl -oes) insinuación f

innumerable /ɪ'njuːmərəbl/ a innumerable

inoculat|e /ɪ'nɒkjʊleɪt/ vt inocular. ~**ion** /-'leɪʃn/ n inoculación f

inoffensive /ɪnə'fensɪv/ a inofensivo

inoperative /ɪn'ɒpərətɪv/ a inoperante

inopportune /ɪn'ɒpətjuːn/ a inoportuno

inordinate /ɪ'nɔːdɪnət/ a excesivo. ~**ly** adv excesivamente

in-patient /'ɪnpeɪʃnt/ *n* paciente *m* interno

input /'ɪnput/ *n* (*data*) datos *mpl*; (*comput process*) entrada *f*, input *m*; (*elec*) energía *f*

inquest /'ɪnkwest/ *n* investigación *f* judicial

inquir|e /ɪn'kwaɪə(r)/ *vi* preguntar. **~y** *n* (*question*) pregunta *f*; (*investigation*) investigación *f*

inquisition /ɪnkwɪ'zɪʃn/ *n* inquisición *f*

inquisitive /ɪn'kwɪzətɪv/ *a* inquisitivo

inroad /'ɪnrəʊd/ *n* incursión *f*

inrush /'ɪnrʌʃ/ *n* irrupción *f*

insan|e /ɪn'seɪn/ *a* loco. **~ity** /-'sænətɪ/ *n* locura *f*

insanitary /ɪn'sænɪtərɪ/ *a* insalubre

insatiable /ɪn'seɪʃəbl/ *a* insaciable

inscri|be /ɪn'skraɪb/ *vt* inscribir; dedicar ⟨*book*⟩. **~ption** /-ɪpʃn/ *n* inscripción *f*; (*in book*) dedicatoria *f*

inscrutable /ɪn'skruːtəbl/ *a* inescrutable

insect /'ɪnsekt/ *n* insecto *m*. **~icide** /ɪn'sektɪsaɪd/ *n* insecticida *f*

insecur|e /ɪnsɪ'kjʊə(r)/ *a* inseguro. **~ity** *n* inseguridad *f*

insemination /ɪnsemɪ'neɪʃn/ *n* inseminación *f*

insensible /ɪn'sensəbl/ *a* insensible; (*unconscious*) sin conocimiento

insensitive /ɪn'sensətɪv/ *a* insensible

inseparable /ɪn'sepərəbl/ *a* inseparable

insert /'ɪnsɜːt/ *n* materia *f* insertada. /ɪn'sɜːt/ *vt* insertar. **~ion** /-ʃn/ *n* inserción *f*

inshore /ɪn'ʃɔː(r)/ *a* costero

inside /ɪn'saɪd/ *n* interior *m*. **~ out** al revés; (*thoroughly*) a fondo. —*a* interior. —*adv*

dentro. —*prep* dentro de. **~s** *npl* tripas *fpl*

insidious /ɪn'sɪdɪəs/ *a* insidioso

insight /'ɪnsaɪt/ *n* (*perception*) penetración *f*, revelación *f*

insignia /ɪn'sɪɡnɪə/ *npl* insignias *fpl*

insignificant /ɪnsɪɡ'nɪfɪkənt/ *a* insignificante

insincer|e /ɪnsɪn'sɪə(r)/ *a* poco sincero. **~ity** /-'serətɪ/ *n* falta *f* de sinceridad *f*

insinuat|e /ɪn'sɪnjʊeɪt/ *vt* insinuar. **~ion** /-'eɪʃn/ *n* insinuación *f*

insipid /ɪn'sɪpɪd/ *a* insípido

insist /ɪn'sɪst/ *vt/i* insistir. **~ on** insistir en; (*demand*) exigir

insisten|ce /ɪn'sɪstəns/ *n* insistencia *f*. **~t** *a* insistente. **~tly** *adv* con insistencia

insolen|ce /'ɪnsələns/ *n* insolencia *f*. **~t** *a* insolente

insoluble /ɪn'sɒljʊbl/ *a* insoluble

insolvent /ɪn'sɒlvənt/ *a* insolvente

insomnia /ɪn'sɒmnɪə/ *n* insomnio *m*. **~c** /-iæk/ *n* insomne *m & f*

inspect /ɪn'spekt/ *vt* inspeccionar; revisar ⟨*ticket*⟩. **~ion** /-ʃn/ *n* inspección *f*. **~or** *n* inspector *m*; (*on train, bus*) revisor *m*

inspir|ation /ɪnspə'reɪʃn/ *n* inspiración *f*. **~e** /ɪn'spaɪə(r)/ *vt* inspirar

instability /ɪnstə'bɪlətɪ/ *n* inestabilidad *f*

install /ɪn'stɔːl/ *vt* instalar. **~ation** /-ə'leɪʃn/ *n* instalación *f*

instalment /ɪn'stɔːlmənt/ *n* (*payment*) plazo *m*; (*of serial*) entrega *f*

instance /'ɪnstəns/ *n* ejemplo *m*; (*case*) caso *m*. **for ~** por ejemplo. **in the first ~** en primer lugar

instant /'ɪnstənt/ *a* inmediato; ⟨*food*⟩ instantáneo. —*n* instante

m. ~aneous /ɪnstənˈteɪnɪəs/ *a*
instantáneo. ~ly /ˈɪnstəntlɪ/ *adv*
inmediatamente

instead /ɪnˈsted/ *adv* en cambio.
~ **of doing** en vez de hacer. ~ **of
s.o.** en lugar de uno

instep /ˈɪnstep/ *n* empeine *m*

instigat|**e** /ˈɪnstɪgeɪt/ *vt* instigar.
~**ion** /-ˈgeɪʃn/ *n* instigación *f*.
~**or** *n* instigador *m*

instil /ɪnˈstɪl/ *vt* (*pt* **instilled**)
infundir

instinct /ˈɪnstɪŋkt/ *n* instinto *m*.
~**ive** /ɪnˈstɪŋktɪv/ *a* instintivo

institut|**e** /ˈɪnstɪtjuːt/ *n* instituto
m. —*vt* instituir; iniciar (*enquiry
etc*). ~**ion** /-ˈtjuːʃn/ *n* institución
f

instruct /ɪnˈstrʌkt/ *vt* instruir;
(*order*) mandar. ~ **s.o. in sth**
enseñar algo a uno. ~**ion** /-ʃn/
n instrucción *f*. ~**ions** /-ʃnz/ *npl*
(*for use*) modo *m* de empleo.
~**ive** *a* instructivo

instrument /ˈɪnstrəmənt/ *n* instrumento *m*. ~**al** /ɪnstrə
ˈmentl/ *a* instrumental. **be** ~**al in**
contribuir a. ~**alist** *n* instru-
mentalista *m* & *f*

insubordinat|**e** /ɪnsəˈbɔːdɪnət/ *a*
insubordinado. ~**ion** /-ˈneɪʃn/ *n*
insubordinación *f*

insufferable /ɪnˈsʌfərəbl/ *a* insufrible, insoportable

insufficient /ɪnsəˈfɪʃnt/ *a* insuficiente. ~**ly** *adv* insuficientemente

insular /ˈɪnsjʊlə(r)/ *a* insular;
(*narrow-minded*) de miras
estrechas

insulat|**e** /ˈɪnsjʊleɪt/ *vt* aislar.
~**ing tape** *n* cinta *f* aisladora/
aislante. ~**ion** /-ˈleɪʃn/ *n* aislamiento *m*

insulin /ˈɪnsjʊlɪn/ *n* insulina *f*

insult /ɪnˈsʌlt/ *vt* insultar.
/ˈɪnsʌlt/ *n* insulto *m*

insuperable /ɪnˈsjuːpərəbl/ *a*
insuperable

insur|**ance** /ɪnˈʃʊərəns/ *n* seguro
m. ~**e** *vt* asegurar. ~**e that** asegurarse de que

insurgent /ɪnˈsɜːdʒənt/ *a* & *n*
insurrecto (*m*)

insurmountable /ɪnsəˈmaʊnt-
əbl/ *a* insuperable

insurrection /ɪnsəˈrekʃn/ *n* in-
surrección *f*

intact /ɪnˈtækt/ *a* intacto

intake /ˈɪnteɪk/ *n* (*quantity*)
número *m*; (*mec*) admisión *f*; (*of
food*) consumo *m*

intangible /ɪnˈtændʒəbl/ *a* intangible

integral /ˈɪntɪgrəl/ *a* íntegro. **be
an** ~ **part of** ser parte inte-
grante de

integrat|**e** /ˈɪntɪgreɪt/ *vt*
integrar. —*vi* integrarse. ~**ion**
/-ˈgreɪʃn/ *n* integración *f*

integrity /ɪnˈtegrətɪ/ *n* integridad *f*

intellect /ˈɪntəlekt/ *n* intelecto *m*.
~**ual** *a* & *n* intelectual (*m*)

intelligen|**ce** /ɪnˈtelɪdʒəns/ *n*
inteligencia *f*; (*information*)
información *f*. ~**t** *a* inteligente.
~**tly** *adv* inteligentemente.
~**tsia** /ɪntelɪˈdʒentsɪə/ *n* intel-
ectualidad *f*

intelligible /ɪnˈtelɪdʒəbl/ *a* inteligible

intemperance /ɪnˈtempərəns/ *n*
inmoderación *f*

intend /ɪnˈtend/ *vt* destinar. ~ **to
do** tener la intención de hacer.
~**ed** *a* intencionado. —*n* (*future
spouse*) novio *m*

intense /ɪnˈtens/ *a* intenso; (*person*) apasionado. ~**ly** *adv* intensamente; (*very*) sumamente

intensif|**ication** /ɪntensɪfɪˈkeɪʃn/
n intensificación *f*. ~**y** /-faɪ/
vt intensificar

intensity /ɪnˈtensətɪ/ *n* intensidad *f*

intensive /ɪnˈtensɪv/ *a* intensivo.
~ **care** *n* asistencia *f* intensiva,
cuidados *mpl* intensivos

intent /ɪn'tent/ n propósito m. — a atento. ~ on absorto en. ~ on doing resuelto a hacer

intention /ɪn'tenʃn/ n intención f. ~al a intencional

intently /ɪn'tentlɪ/ adv atentamente

inter /ɪn'tɜː(r)/ vt (pt interred) enterrar

inter... /'ɪntə(r)/ pref inter..., entre...

interact /ɪntər'ækt/ vi obrar recíprocamente. ~ion /-ʃn/ n interacción f

intercede /ɪntə'siːd/ vi interceder

intercept /ɪntə'sept/ vt interceptar. ~ion /-ʃn/ n interceptación f; (in geometry) intersección f

interchange /ɪntət'ʃeɪndʒ/ n (road junction) cruce m. ~able /-'tʃeɪndʒəbl/ a intercambiable

intercom /'ɪntəkom/ n intercomunicador m

interconnected /ɪntəkə'nektɪd/ a relacionado

intercourse /'ɪntəkɔːs/ n trato m; (sexual) trato m sexual

interest /'ɪntrɪst/ n interés m; (advantage) ventaja f. —vt interesar. ~ed a interesado. be ~ed in interesarse por. ~ing a interesante

interfere /ɪntə'fɪə(r)/ vi entrometerse. ~ in entrometerse en. ~ with entrometerse en, interferir en; interferir (radio). ~nce n interferencia f

interim /'ɪntərɪm/ a provisional. —n. in the ~ entre tanto

interior /ɪn'tɪərɪə(r)/ a & n interior (m)

interjection /ɪntə'dʒekʃn/ n interjección f

interlock /ɪntə'lɒk/ vt/i (tec) engranar

interloper /'ɪntələʊpə(r)/ n intruso m

interlude /'ɪntəluːd/ n intervalo m; (theatre, music) interludio m

intermarriage /ɪntə'mærɪdʒ/ n matrimonio m entre personas de distintas razas. ~y vi casarse (con personas de distintas razas)

intermediary /ɪntə'miːdɪərɪ/ a & n intermediario (m)

intermediate /ɪntə'miːdɪət/ a intermedio

interminable /ɪn'tɜːmɪnəbl/ a interminable

intermission /ɪntə'mɪʃn/ n pausa f; (theatre) descanso m

intermittent /ɪntə'mɪtnt/ a intermitente. ~ly adv con discontinuidad

intern /ɪn'tɜːn/ vt internar. /'ɪntɜːn/ n (doctor, Amer) interno m

internal /ɪn'tɜːnl/ a interior. ~ly adv interiormente

international /ɪntə'næʃənl/ a & n internacional (m)

internee /ˌɪntɜː'niː/ n internado m

internment /ɪn'tɜːnmənt/ n internamiento m

interplay /'ɪntəpleɪ/ n interacción f

interpolate /ɪn'tɜːpəleɪt/ vt interpolar

interpret /ɪn'tɜːprɪt/ vt/i interpretar. ~ation /-'teɪʃn/ n interpretación f. ~er n intérprete m & f

interrelated /ɪntərɪ'leɪtɪd/ a interrelacionado

interrogate /ɪn'terəgeɪt/ vt interrogar. ~ion /-'geɪʃn/ n interrogación f; (session of questions) interrogatorio m

interrogative /ɪntə'rɒgətɪv/ a & n interrogativo (m)

interrupt /ɪntə'rʌpt/ vt interrumpir. ~ion /-ʃn/ n interrupción f

intersect /ɪntə'sekt/ vt cruzar. —vi (roads) cruzarse; (geometry) intersecarse. ~ion /-ʃn/ n (*roads*) cruce *m*; (*geometry*) intersección *f*

interspersed /ɪntə'spɜːst/ *a* disperso. ~ **with** salpicado de

intertwine /ɪntə'twaɪn/ *vt* entrelazar. —*vi* entrelazarse

interval /'ɪntəvl/ *n* intervalo *m*; (*theatre*) descanso *m*. **at ~s** a intervalos

intervene /ɪntə'viːn/ *vi* intervenir. **~tion** /-'venʃn/ *n* intervención *f*

interview /'ɪntəvjuː/ *n* entrevista *f*. —*vt* entrevistarse con. **~er** *n* entrevistador *m*

intestin|al /ɪn'testaɪnl/ *a* intestinal. **~e** /ɪn'testɪn/ *n* intestino *m*

intimacy /'ɪntɪməsɪ/ *n* intimidad *f*

intimate[1] /'ɪntɪmət/ *a* íntimo

intimate[2] /'ɪntɪmeɪt/ *vt* (*state*) anunciar; (*imply*) dar a entender

intimately /'ɪntɪmətlɪ/ *adv* íntimamente

intimidat|e /ɪn'tɪmɪdeɪt/ *vt* intimidar. **~ion** /-'deɪʃn/ *n* intimidación *f*

into /'ɪntuː/, *unstressed* /'ɪntə/ *prep* en; (*translate*) a

intolerable /ɪn'tɒlərəbl/ *a* intolerable

intoleran|ce /ɪn'tɒlərəns/ *n* intolerancia *f*. **~t** *a* intolerante

intonation /ɪntə'neɪʃn/ *n* entonación *f*

intoxicat|e /ɪn'tɒksɪkeɪt/ *vt* embriagar; (*med*) intoxicar. **~ed** *a* ebrio. **~ion** /-'keɪʃn/ *n* embriaguez *f*; (*med*) intoxicación *f*

intra... /'ɪntrə/ *pref* intra...

intractable /ɪn'træktəbl/ *a* (*person*) intratable; (*thing*) muy difícil

intransigent /ɪn'trænsɪdʒənt/ *a* intransigente

intransitive /ɪn'trænsɪtɪv/ *a* intransitivo

intravenous /ɪntrə'viːnəs/ *a* intravenoso

intrepid /ɪn'trepɪd/ *a* intrépido

intrica|cy /'ɪntrɪkəsɪ/ *n* complejidad *f*. **~te** *a* complejo

intrigu|e /ɪn'triːg/ *vt/i* , intrigar. —*n* intriga *f*. **~ing** *a* intrigante

intrinsic /ɪn'trɪnsɪk/ *a* intrínseco. **~ally** *adv* intrínsecamente

introduc|e /ɪntrə'djuːs/ *vt* introducir; presentar (*person*). **~tion** /ɪntrə'dʌkʃn/ *n* introducción *f*; (*to person*) presentación *f*. **~tory** /-tərɪ/ *a* preliminar

introspective /ɪntrə'spektɪv/ *a* introspectivo

introvert /'ɪntrəvɜːt/ *n* introvertido *m*

intru|de /ɪn'truːd/ *vi* entrometerse; (*disturb*) molestar. **~der** *n* intruso *m*. **~sion** *n* intrusión *f*

intuiti|on /ɪntjuː'ɪʃn/ *n* intuición *f*. **~ve** /ɪn'tjuːɪtɪv/ *a* intuitivo

inundat|e /'ɪnʌndeɪt/ *vt* inundar. **~ion** /-'deɪʃn/ *n* inundación *f*

invade /ɪn'veɪd/ *vt* invadir. **~r** /-ə(r)/ *n* invasor *m*

invalid[1] /'ɪnvəlɪd/ *n* enfermo *m*, inválido *m*

invalid[2] /ɪn'vælɪd/ *a* nulo. **~ate** *vt* invalidar

invaluable /ɪn'væljʊəbl/ *a* inestimable

invariab|le /ɪn'veərɪəbl/ *a* invariable. **~y** *adv* invariablemente

invasion /ɪn'veɪʒn/ *n* invasión *f*

invective /ɪn'vektɪv/ *n* invectiva *f*

inveigh /ɪn'veɪ/ *vi* dirigir invectivas (**against** contra)

inveigle /ɪn'veɪgl/ *vt* engatusar, persuadir

invent /ɪn'vent/ *vt* inventar. **~ion** /-'venʃn/ *n* invención *f*. **~ive** *a* inventivo. **~or** *n* inventor *m*

inventory /'ɪnvəntərɪ/ n inventario m

invers|e /ɪn'vɜːs/ a & n inverso (m). **~ely** adv inversamente. **~ion** /ɪn'vɜːʃn/ n inversión f

invert /ɪn'vɜːt/ vt invertir. **~ed commas** npl comillas fpl

invest /ɪn'vest/ vt invertir. **—**vi. **~ in** hacer una inversión f

investigat|e /ɪn'vestɪgeɪt/ vt investigar. **~ion** /-'geɪʃn/ n investigación f. **under ~ion** sometido a examen. **~or** n investigador m

inveterate /ɪn'vetərət/ a inveterado

invidious /ɪn'vɪdɪəs/ a (hateful) odioso; (unfair) injusto

invigilat|e /ɪn'vɪdʒɪleɪt/ vi vigilar. **~or** n celador m

invigorate /ɪn'vɪgəreɪt/ vt vigorizar; (stimulate) estimular

invincible /ɪn'vɪnsɪbl/ a invencible

invisible /ɪn'vɪzəbl/ a invisible

invit|ation /ɪnvɪ'teɪʃn/ n invitación f. **~e** /ɪn'vaɪt/ vt invitar; (ask for) pedir. **~ing** a atrayente

invoice /'ɪnvɔɪs/ n factura f. **—**vt facturar

invoke /ɪn'vəʊk/ vt invocar

involuntary /ɪn'vɒləntərɪ/ a involuntario

involve /ɪn'vɒlv/ vt enredar. **~d** a (complex) complicado. **~d in** embrollado en. **~ment** n enredo m

invulnerable /ɪn'vʌlnərəbl/ a invulnerable

inward /'ɪnwəd/ a interior. **—**adv interiormente. **~s** adv hacia/para dentro

iodine /'aɪədiːn/ n yodo m

iota /aɪ'əʊtə/ n (amount) pizca f

IOU /aɪəʊ'juː/ abbr (I owe you) pagaré m

IQ /aɪ'kjuː/ abbr (intelligence quotient) cociente m intelectual

Iran /ɪ'rɑːn/ n Irán m. **~ian** /ɪ'reɪnɪən/ a & n iraní (m)

Iraq /ɪ'rɑːk/ n Irak m. **~i** a & n iraquí (m)

irascible /ɪ'ræsəbl/ a irascible

irate /aɪ'reɪt/ a colérico

ire /aɪə(r)/ n ira f

Ireland /'aɪələnd/ n Irlanda f

iris /'aɪərɪs/ n (anat) iris m; (bot) lirio m

Irish /'aɪərɪʃ/ a irlandés. **—**n (lang) irlandés m. **~man** n irlandés m. **~woman** n irlandesa f

irk /ɜːk/ vt fastidiar. **~some** a fastidioso

iron /'aɪən/ n hierro m; (appliance) plancha f. **—**a de hierro. **—**vt planchar. **~ out** allanar. **I~ Curtain** n telón m de acero

ironic(al) /aɪ'rɒnɪk(l)/ a irónico

ironing-board /'aɪənɪŋbɔːd/ n tabla f de planchar

ironmonger /'aɪənmʌŋgə(r)/ n ferretero m. **~y** n ferretería f

ironwork /'aɪənwɜːk/ n herraje m

irony /'aɪərənɪ/ n ironía f

irrational /ɪ'ræʃənl/ a irracional

irreconcilable /ɪrekən'saɪləbl/ a irreconciliable

irrefutable /ɪrɪ'fjuːtəbl/ a irrefutable

irregular /ɪ'regjʊlə(r)/ a irregular. **~ity** /-'lærətɪ/ n irregularidad f

irrelevan|ce /ɪ'reləvəns/ n inoportunidad f, impertinencia f. **~t** a no pertinente

irreparable /ɪ'repərəbl/ a irreparable

irreplaceable /ɪrɪ'pleɪsəbl/ a irreemplazable

irrepressible /ɪrɪ'presəbl/ a irreprimible

irresistible /ɪrɪ'zɪstəbl/ a irresistible

irresolute /ɪˈrezəluːt/ *a* irresoluto, indeciso

irrespective /ɪrɪˈspektɪv/ *a*. **∼ of** sin tomar en cuenta

irresponsible /ɪrɪˈspɒnsəbl/ *a* irresponsable

irretrievable /ɪrɪˈtriːvəbl/ *a* irrecuperable

irreverent /ɪˈrevərənt/ *a* irreverente

irreversible /ɪrɪˈvɜːsəbl/ *a* irreversible; (*decision*) irrevocable

irrevocable /ɪˈrevəkəbl/ *a* irrevocable

irrigat|**e** /ˈɪrɪgeɪt/ *vt* regar; (*med*) irrigar. **∼ion** /-ˈgeɪʃn/ *n* riego *m*; (*med*) irrigación *f*

irritable /ˈɪrɪtəbl/ *a* irritable

irritat|**e** /ˈɪrɪteɪt/ *vt* irritar. **∼ion** /-ˈteɪʃn/ *n* irritación *f*

is /ɪz/ *see* **be**

Islam /ˈɪzlɑːm/ *n* Islam *m*. **∼ic** /ɪzˈlæmɪk/ *a* islámico

island /ˈaɪlənd/ *n* isla *f*. **traffic ∼** *n* refugio *m* (en la calle). **∼er** *n* isleño *m*

isle /aɪl/ *n* isla *f*

isolat|**e** /ˈaɪsəleɪt/ *vt* aislar. **∼ion** /-ˈleɪʃn/ *n* aislamiento *m*

isotope /ˈaɪsətəʊp/ *n* isotopo *m*

Israel /ˈɪzreɪl/ *n* Israel *m*. **∼i** /ɪzˈreɪlɪ/ *a & n* israelí (*m*)

issue /ˈɪʃuː/ *n* asunto *m*; (*outcome*) resultado *m*; (*of magazine etc*) número *m*; (*of stamps*) emisión *f*; (*offspring*) descendencia *f*. **at ∼** en cuestión. **take ∼ with** oponerse a. **—***vt* distribuir; emitir (*stamps etc*); publicar (*book*). **—***vi*. **∼ from** salir de

isthmus /ˈɪsməs/ *n* istmo *m*

it /ɪt/ *pron* (*subject*) él, ella, ello; (*direct object*) lo, la; (*indirect object*) le; (*after preposition*) él, ella, ello. **∼ is hot** hace calor. **∼ is me** soy yo. **far from ∼** ni mucho menos. **that's ∼** eso es. **who is ∼?** ¿quién es?

italic /ɪˈtælɪk/ *a* bastardilla *m*. **∼s** *npl* (letra *f*) bastardilla *f*

ital|**ian** /ɪˈtæljən/ *a & n* italiano (*m*). **I∼y** /ˈɪtəli/ *n* Italia *f*

itch /ɪtʃ/ *n* picazón *f*. **—***vi* picar. **I'm ∼ing to** rabio por. **my arm ∼es** me pica el brazo. **∼y** *a* que pica

item /ˈaɪtəm/ *n* artículo *m*; (*on agenda*) asunto *m*. **news ∼** *n* noticia *f*. **∼ize** *vt* detallar

itinerant /aɪˈtɪnərənt/ *a* ambulante

itinerary /aɪˈtɪnərəri/ *n* itinerario *m*

its /ɪts/ *a* su, sus (*pl*). **—***pron* (el) suyo *m*, (la) suya *f*, (los) suyos *mpl*, (las) suyas *fpl*

it's /ɪts/ = **it is**, **it has**

itself /ɪtˈself/ *pron* él mismo, ella misma, ello mismo; (*reflexive*) se; (*after prep*) sí mismo, sí misma

ivory /ˈaɪvərɪ/ *n* marfil *m*. **∼ tower** *n* torre *f* de marfil

ivy /ˈaɪvɪ/ *n* hiedra *f*

J

jab /dʒæb/ *vt* (*pt* **jabbed**) pinchar; (*thrust*) hurgonear. **—***n* pinchazo *m*

jabber /ˈdʒæbə(r)/ *vi* barbullar. **—***n* farfulla *f*

jack /dʒæk/ *n* (*mec*) gato *m*; (*cards*) sota *f*. **—***vt*. **∼ up** alzar con gato

jackal /ˈdʒækl/ *n* chacal *m*

jackass /ˈdʒækæs/ *n* burro *m*

jackdaw /ˈdʒækdɔː/ *n* grajilla *f*

jacket /ˈdʒækɪt/ *n* chaqueta *f*, saco *m* (*LAm*); (*of book*) sobrecubierta *f*, camisa *f*

jack-knife /ˈdʒæknaɪf/ *n* navaja *f*

jackpot /ˈdʒækpɒt/ *n* premio *m* gordo. **hit the ∼** sacar el premio gordo

jade /dʒeɪd/ n (stone) jade m

jaded /ˈdʒeɪdɪd/ a cansado

jagged /ˈdʒægɪd/ a dentado

jaguar /ˈdʒægjʊə(r)/ n jaguar m

jail /dʒeɪl/ n cárcel m. criminal m emperdernido. ~er n carcelero m

jalopy /dʒəˈlɒpɪ/ n cacharro m

jam[1] /dʒæm/ vt (pt jammed) interferir con (radio); (traffic) embotellar; (people) agolparse en. —vi obstruirse; (mechanism etc) atascarse. —n (of people) agolpamiento m; (of traffic) embotellamiento m; (situation, fam) apuro m

jam[2] /dʒæm/ n mermelada f

Jamaica /dʒəˈmeɪkə/ n Jamaica f

jamboree /dʒæmbəˈriː/ n reunión f

jam-packed /ˈdʒæmˈpækt/ a atestado

jangle /ˈdʒæŋgl/ n sonido m metálico (y áspero). —vt/i sonar discordemente

janitor /ˈdʒænɪtə(r)/ n portero m

January /ˈdʒænjʊərɪ/ n enero m

Japan /dʒəˈpæn/ n el Japón m. ~ese /dʒæpəˈniːz/ a & n japonés (m)

jar[1] /dʒɑː(r)/ n tarro m, frasco m

jar[2] /dʒɑː(r)/ vi (pt jarred) (sound) sonar mal; (colours) chillar. —vt sacudir

jar[3] /dʒɑː(r)/ n. on the ~ (ajar) entreabierto

jargon /ˈdʒɑːgən/ n jerga f

jarring /ˈdʒɑːrɪŋ/ a discorde

jasmine /ˈdʒæsmɪn/ n jazmín m

jaundice /ˈdʒɔːndɪs/ n icteria f. ~d a (envious) envidioso; (bitter) amargado

jaunt /dʒɔːnt/ n excursión f

jaunty /ˈdʒɔːntɪ/ a (-ier, -iest) garboso

javelin /ˈdʒævəlɪn/ n jabalina f

jaw /dʒɔː/ n mandíbula f. —vi (talk lengthily, sl) hablar por los codos

jay /dʒeɪ/ n arrendajo m. ~-walk vi cruzar la calle descuidadamente

jazz /dʒæz/ n jazz m. —vt. ~ up animar. ~y a chillón

jealous /ˈdʒeləs/ a celoso. ~y n celos mpl

jeans /dʒiːnz/ npl (pantalones mpl) vaqueros mpl

jeep /dʒiːp/ n jeep m

jeer /dʒɪə(r)/ vt/i. ~ at mofarse de, befar; (boo) abuchear. —n mofa f; (boo) abucheo m

jell /dʒel/ vi cuajar. ~ied a en gelatina

jelly /ˈdʒelɪ/ n jalea f. ~fish n medusa f

jeopardize /ˈdʒepədaɪz/ vt arriesgar. ~y n peligro m

jerk /dʒɜːk/ n sacudida f; (fool, sl) idiota m & f. —vt sacudir. ~ily adv a sacudidas. ~y a espasmódico

jersey /ˈdʒɜːzɪ/ n (pl -eys) jersey m

jest /dʒest/ n broma f. —vi bromear. ~er n bufón m

Jesus /ˈdʒiːzəs/ n Jesús m

jet[1] /dʒet/ n (stream) chorro m; (plane) yet n, avión m de propulsión por reacción

jet[2] /dʒet/ n (mineral) azabache m. ~-black a de azabache, como el azabache

jet: ~ lag n cansancio m retardado después de un vuelo largo. have ~ lag estar desfasado. ~-propelled a (de propulsión) a reacción

jettison /ˈdʒetɪsn/ vt echar al mar; (fig, discard) deshacerse de

jetty /ˈdʒetɪ/ n muelle m

Jew /dʒuː/ n judío m

jewel /ˈdʒuːəl/ n joya f. ~led a enjoyado. ~ler n joyero m. ~lery n joyas fpl

Jew: ~ess n judía f. ~ish a judío. ~ry /ˈdʒʊərɪ/ n los judíos mpl

jib[1] /dʒɪb/ n (sail) foque m

jib² /dʒɪb/ *vi* (pt **jibbed**) rehusar.
~ at oponerse a.

jiffy /'dʒɪfɪ/ *n* momentito *m*. **do sth in a ~** hacer algo en un santiamén

jig /dʒɪg/ *n* (*dance*) giga *f*

jiggle /'dʒɪgl/ *vt* zangolotear

jigsaw /'dʒɪgsɔ:/ *n* rompecabezas *m invar*

jilt /dʒɪlt/ *vt* plantar, dejar plantado

jingle /'dʒɪŋgl/ *vt* hacer sonar. —*vi* tintinear. —*n* tintineo *m*; (*advert*) anuncio *m* cantado

jinx /dʒɪŋks/ *n* (*person*) gafe *m*; (*spell*) maleficio *m*

jitter|s /'dʒɪtəz/ *npl*. **have the ~s** estar nervioso. **~y** /-ərɪ/ *a* nervioso. **be ~y** estar nervioso

job /dʒɒb/ *n* trabajo *m*; (*post*) empleo *m*, puesto *m*. **have a ~ doing** costar trabajo hacer. **it is a good ~ that** menos mal que. **~centre** *n* bolsa *f* de trabajo. **~less** *a* sin trabajo.

jockey /'dʒɒkɪ/ *n* jockey *m*. —*vi* (*manoeuvre*) maniobrar (**for** para)

jocular /'dʒɒkjʊlə(r)/ *a* jocoso

jog /dʒɒg/ *vt* (pt **jogged**) empujar; refrescar (*memory*). —*vi* hacer footing. **~ging** *n* jogging *m*

join /dʒɔɪn/ *vt* unir, juntar; hacerse socio de (*club*); hacerse miembro de (*political group*); alistarse en (*army*); reunirse con (*another person*). —*vi* (*roads etc*) empalmar; (*rivers*) confluir. **~ in** participar (en). **~ up** (*mil*) alistarse. —*n* juntura

joiner /'dʒɔɪnə(r)/ *n* carpintero *m*

joint /dʒɔɪnt/ *a* común. **~ author** *n* coautor *m*. —*n* juntura *f*; (*anat*) articulación *f*; (*culin*) asado *m*; (*place*, sl) garito *m*; (*marijuana*, sl) cigarillo *m* de marijuana. **out of ~** descoyuntado. **~ly** *adv* conjuntamente

joist /dʒɔɪst/ *n* viga *f*

jok|e /dʒəʊk/ *n* broma *f*; (*funny story*) chiste *m*. —*vi* bromear. **~er** *n* bromista *m & f*; (*cards*) comodín *m*. **~ingly** *adv* en broma

joll|ification /dʒɒlɪfɪ'keɪʃn/ *n* jolgorio *m*. **~ity** *n* jolgorio *m*. **~y** *a* (**-ier, -iest**) alegre. —*adv* (*fam*) muy

jolt /dʒɒlt/ *vt* sacudir. —*vi* (*vehicle*) traquetear. —*n* sacudida *f*

Jordan /'dʒɔ:dən/ *n* Jordania *f*. **~ian** *a & n* /-'deɪnɪən/ jordano *m*

jostle /'dʒɒsl/ *vt/i* empujar(se)

jot /dʒɒt/ *n* pizca *f*. —*vt* (pt **jotted**) apuntar. **~ter** *n* bloc *m*

journal /'dʒɜ:nl/ *n* (*diary*) diario *m*; (*newspaper*) periódico *m*; (*magazine*) revista *f*. **~ese** /dʒɜ:nə'li:z/ *n* jerga *f* periodística. **~ism** *n* periodismo *m*. **~ist** *n* periodista *m & f*

journey /'dʒɜ:nɪ/ *n* viaje *m*. —*vi* viajar

jovial /'dʒəʊvɪəl/ *a* jovial

jowl /dʒaʊl/ *n* (*jaw*) quijada *f*; (*cheek*) mejilla *f*. **cheek by ~** muy cerca

joy /dʒɔɪ/ *n* alegría *f*. **~ful** *a* alegre. **~ride** *n* paseo *m* en coche sin permiso del dueño. **~ous** *a* alegre

jubila|nt /'dʒu:bɪlənt/ *a* jubiloso. **~tion** /-'leɪʃn/ *n* júbilo *m*

jubilee /'dʒu:bɪli:/ *n* aniversario *m* especial

Judaism /'dʒu:deɪɪzəm/ *n* judaísmo *m*

judder /'dʒʌdə(r)/ *vi* vibrar. —*n* vibración *f*

judge /dʒʌdʒ/ *n* juez *m*. —*vt* juzgar. **~ment** *n* juicio *m*

judicia|l /dʒu:'dɪʃl/ *a* judicial. **~ry** *n* magistratura *f*

judicious /dʒu:'dɪʃəs/ *a* juicioso

judo /'dʒu:dəʊ/ *n* judo *m*

jug /dʒʌg/ n jarra f

juggernaut /'dʒʌgənɔːt/ n (lorry) camión m grande

juggle /'dʒʌgl/ vt/i hacer juegos malabares (con). **~r** n malabarista m & f

juice /dʒuːs/ n jugo m, zumo m. **~y** a jugoso, zumoso; ⟨story etc⟩ (fam) picante

juke-box /'dʒuːkbɒks/ n tocadiscos m invar tragaperras

July /dʒuːˈlaɪ/ n julio m

jumble /'dʒʌmbl/ vt mezclar. —n (muddle) revoltijo m. **~ sale** n venta f de objetos usados, mercadillo m

jumbo /'dʒʌmbəʊ/ a. **~ jet** n jumbo m

jump /dʒʌmp/ vt/i saltar. **~ the gun** obrar prematuramente. **~ the queue** colarse. —vi saltar; ⟨start⟩ asustarse; ⟨prices⟩ alzarse. **~ at** apresurarse a aprovechar. —n salto m; ⟨start⟩ susto m; ⟨increase⟩ aumento m

jumper /'dʒʌmpə(r)/ n jersey m; ⟨dress, Amer⟩ mandil m, falda f con peto

jumpy /'dʒʌmpɪ/ a nervioso

junction /'dʒʌŋkʃn/ n juntura f; ⟨of roads⟩ cruce m, entronque m (LAm); ⟨rail⟩ empalme m, entronque m (LAm)

juncture /'dʒʌŋktʃə(r)/ n momento m; ⟨state of affairs⟩ coyuntura f

June /dʒuːn/ n junio m

jungle /'dʒʌŋgl/ n selva f

junior /'dʒuːnɪə(r)/ a ⟨in age⟩ más joven (to que); ⟨in rank⟩ subalterno. —n menor m. **~ school** n escuela f

junk /dʒʌŋk/ n trastos mpl viejos. —vt (fam) tirar

junkie /'dʒʌŋkɪ/ n (sl) drogadicto m

junk shop /'dʒʌŋkʃɒp/ n tienda f de trastos viejos

junta /'dʒʌntə/ n junta f

jurisdiction /dʒʊərɪs'dɪkʃn/ n jurisdicción f

jurisprudence /dʒʊərɪs'pruːdəns/ n jurisprudencia f

juror /'dʒʊərə(r)/ n jurado m

jury /'dʒʊərɪ/ n jurado m

just /dʒʌst/ a (fair) justo. —adv exactamente; (slightly) apenas; (only) sólo, solamente. **~ as tall** tan alto como. **~ listen!** ¡escucha! **he has ~ left** acaba de marcharse

justice /'dʒʌstɪs/ n justicia f. **J~ of the Peace** juez m de paz

justifiable /dʒʌstɪ'faɪəbl/ a justificable. **~iably** adv con razón. **~ication** /dʒʌstɪfɪ'keɪʃn/ n justificación f. **~y** /'dʒʌstɪfaɪ/ vt justificar

justly /'dʒʌstlɪ/ adv con justicia

jut /dʒʌt/ vi (pt jutted). **~ out** sobresalir

juvenile /'dʒuːvənaɪl/ a juvenil; (childish) infantil. —n joven m & f. **~ court** n tribunal m de menores

juxtapose /dʒʌkstə'pəʊz/ vt yuxtaponer

K

kaleidoscope /kə'laɪdəskəʊp/ n calidoscopio m

kangaroo /kæŋgə'ruː/ n canguro m

kapok /'keɪpɒk/ n miraguano m

karate /kə'rɑːtɪ/ n karate m

kebab /kɪ'bæb/ n broqueta f

keel /kiːl/ n ⟨of ship⟩ quilla f. —vi. **~ over** volcarse

keen /kiːn/ a (-er, -est) ⟨interest, feeling⟩ vivo; ⟨wind, mind, analysis⟩ penetrante; ⟨edge⟩ afilado; ⟨appetite⟩ bueno; ⟨eyesight⟩ agudo; ⟨eager⟩ entusiasta. **be ~ on** gustarle a uno. **he's ~ on**

Shostakovich le gusta Shostakovich. **~ly** *adv* vivamente; ⟨*enthusiastically*⟩ con entusiasmo. **~ness** *n* intensidad *f*; ⟨*enthusiasm*⟩ entusiasmo *m*.

keep /kiːp/ *vt* (*pt* **kept**) guardar; cumplir ⟨*promise*⟩; tener ⟨*shop, animals*⟩; mantener ⟨*family*⟩; observar ⟨*rule*⟩; celebrate⟩ celebrar; ⟨*delay*⟩ detener; ⟨*prevent*⟩ impedir. —*vi* ⟨*food*⟩ conservarse; ⟨*remain*⟩ quedarse. —*n* subsistencia *f*; ⟨*of castle*⟩ torreón *m.* **for ~s** (*fam*) para siempre. **~ back** *vt* retener. —*vi* no acercarse. **~ in** no dejar salir. **~ in with** mantenerse en buenas relaciones con. **~ out** no dejar entrar. **~ up** mantener. **~ up (with)** estar al día (en). **~er** *n* guarda *m*

keeping /ˈkiːpɪŋ/ *n* cuidado *m.* **in ~ with** de acuerdo con

keepsake /ˈkiːpseɪk/ *n* recuerdo *m*

keg /keg/ *n* barrilete *m*

kennel /ˈkenl/ *n* perrera *f*

Kenya /ˈkenjə/ *n* Kenia *f*

kept /kept/ *see* **keep**

kerb /kɜːb/ *n* bordillo *m*

kerfuffle /kəˈfʌfl/ *n* ⟨*fuss, fam*⟩ lío *m*

kernel /ˈkɜːnl/ *n* almendra *f*; ⟨*fig*⟩ meollo *m*

kerosene /ˈkerəsiːn/ *n* queroseno *m*

ketchup /ˈketʃʌp/ *n* salsa *f* de tomate

kettle /ˈketl/ *n* hervidor *m*

key /kiː/ *n* llave *f*; ⟨*of typewriter, piano etc*⟩ tecla *f.* —*a* clave. —*vt.* **~ up** excitar. **~board** *n* teclado *m.* **~hole** *n* ojo *m* de la cerradura. **~note** *n* ⟨*mus*⟩ tónica *f*; ⟨*speech*⟩ idea *f* fundamental. **~ring** *n* llavero *m.* **~stone** *n* piedra *f* clave

khaki /ˈkɑːkɪ/ *a* caqui

kibbutz /kɪˈbʊts/ *n* (*pl* **-im** /-iːm/ *or* **-es**) kibbutz *m*

kick /kɪk/ *vt* dar una patada a; ⟨*animals*⟩ tirar una coz a. —*vi* dar patadas; ⟨*firearm*⟩ dar culatazo. —*n* patada *f*; ⟨*of animal*⟩ coz *f*; ⟨*of firearm*⟩ culatazo *m*; ⟨*thrill, fam*⟩ placer *m.* **~ out** (*fam*) echar a patadas. **~ back** *n* culatazo *m*; ⟨*payment*⟩ soborno *m.* **~off** *n* ⟨*sport*⟩ saque *m* inicial

kid /kɪd/ *n* ⟨*young goat*⟩ cabrito *m*; ⟨*leather*⟩ cabritilla *f*; ⟨*child, sl*⟩ chaval *m.* —*vt* (*pt* **kidded**) tomar el pelo a. —*vi* bromear

kidnap /ˈkɪdnæp/ *vt* (*pt* **kidnapped**) secuestrar. **~ping** *n* secuestro *m*

kidney /ˈkɪdnɪ/ *n* riñón *m.* —*a* renal

kill /kɪl/ *vt* matar; ⟨*fig*⟩ acabar con. —*n* matanza *f*; ⟨*in hunt*⟩ pieza *f* ⟨*fpl*⟩. **~er** *n* matador *m*; ⟨*murderer*⟩ asesino *m.* **~ing** *n* matanza *f*; ⟨*murder*⟩ asesinato *m.* —*a* ⟨*funny, fam*⟩ para morirse de risa; ⟨*tiring, fam*⟩ agotador. **~joy** *n* aguafiestas *m & f invar*

kiln /kɪln/ *n* horno *m*

kilo /ˈkiːləʊ/ *n* (*pl* **-os**) kilo *m*

kilogram(me) /ˈkɪləgræm/ *n* kilogramo *m*

kilohertz /ˈkɪləhɜːts/ *n* kilohercio *m*

kilometre /ˈkɪləmiːtə(r)/ *n* kilómetro *m*

kilowatt /ˈkɪləwɒt/ *n* kilovatio *m*

kilt /kɪlt/ *n* falda *f* escocesa

kin /kɪn/ *n* parientes *mpl.* **next of ~** pariente *m* más próximo, parientes *mpl* más próximos

kind[1] /kaɪnd/ *n* clase *f.* **~ of** ⟨*somewhat, fam*⟩ un tanto. **in ~** en especie. **be two of a ~** ser tal para cual

kind[2] /kaɪnd/ *a* amable

kindergarten /ˈkɪndəgɑːtn/ *n* escuela *f* de párvulos

kind-hearted /kaɪnd'hɑːtɪd/ a bondadoso

kindle /'kɪndl/ vt/i encender(se)

kind: ~**liness** n bondad f. ~**ly** a (-ier, -iest) bondadoso. —adv bondadosamente; (please) haga el favor de. ~**ness** n bondad f

kindred /'kɪndrɪd/ a emparentado. ~ **spirits** npl almas fpl afines

kinetic /kɪ'netɪk/ a cinético

king /kɪŋ/ n rey m

kingdom /'kɪŋdəm/ n reino m

kingpin /'kɪŋpɪn/ n (person) persona f clave; (thing) piedra f angular

king-size(d) /'kɪŋsaɪz(d)/ a extraordinariamente grande

kink /kɪŋk/ n (in rope) retorcimiento m; (fig) manía f. ~**y** a (fam) pervertido

kiosk /'kiːɒsk/ n quiosco m. **telephone** ~ cabina f telefónica

kip /kɪp/ n (sl) sueño m. —vi (pt kipped) dormir

kipper /'kɪpə(r)/ n arenque m ahumado

kiss /kɪs/ n beso m. —vt/i besar(se)

kit /kɪt/ n avíos mpl; (tools) herramientos mpl. —vt (pt kitted). ~ **out** equipar de. ~**bag** n mochila f

kitchen /'kɪtʃɪn/ n cocina f. ~**ette** /kɪtʃɪ'net/ n cocina f pequeña. ~ **garden** n huerto m

kite /kaɪt/ n (toy) cometa f

kith /kɪθ/ n. ~ **and kin** amigos mpl y parientes mpl

kitten /'kɪtn/ n gatito m

kitty /'kɪtɪ/ n (fund) fondo m común

kleptomaniac /kleptəʊ'meɪnɪæk/ n cleptómano m

knack /næk/ n truco m

knapsack /'næpsæk/ n mochila f

knave /neɪv/ n (cards) sota f

knead /niːd/ vt amasar

knee /niː/ n rodilla f. ~**cap** n rótula f

kneel /niːl/ vi (pt knelt). ~ (**down**) arrodillarse

knees-up /'niːzʌp/ n (fam) baile m

knell /nel/ n toque m de difuntos

knelt /nelt/ see **kneel**

knew /njuː/ see **know**

knickerbockers /'nɪkəbɒkəz/ npl pantalón m bombacho

knickers /'nɪkəz/ npl bragas fpl

knick-knack /'nɪknæk/ n chuchería f

knife /naɪf/ n (pl knives) cuchillo m. —vt acuchillar

knight /naɪt/ n caballero m; (chess) caballo m. —vt conceder el título de Sir a. ~**hood** n título m de Sir

knit /nɪt/ vt (pt knitted or knit) tejer. —vi hacer punto. ~ **one's brow** fruncir el ceño. ~**ting** n labor f de punto. ~**wear** n artículos mpl de punto

knob /nɒb/ n botón m; (of door, drawer etc) tirador m. ~**bly** a nudoso

knock /nɒk/ vt golpear; (criticize) criticar. —vi golpear; (at door) llamar. —n golpe m. ~ **about** vt maltratar. —vi rodar. ~ **down** derribar; atropellar (person); rebajar (prices). ~ **off** vt hacer caer; (complete quickly, fam) despachar; (steal, sl) birlar. —vi (finish work, fam) terminar, salir del trabajo. ~ **out** (by blow) dejar sin conocimiento; (eliminate) eliminar; (tire) agotar. ~ **over** tirar; atropellar (person). ~ **up** preparar de prisa (meal etc). ~**down** a (price) de saldo. ~**er** n aldaba f. ~**-kneed** a patizambo. ~**out** n (boxing) knock-out m

knot /nɒt/ n nudo m. —vt (pt knotted) anudar. ~**ty** /'nɒtɪ/ a nudoso

know /nəʊ/ vt (pt **knew**) saber; (be acquainted with) conocer. — vi saber. —n. be in the ~ estar al tanto. ~ **about** entender (cars etc.). ~ of saber de. ~**all** n, ~-**it-all** (Amer) n sabelotodo & f. ~-**how** n habilidad f. ~**ingly** adv deliberadamente

knowledge /'nɒlɪdʒ/ n conocimiento m; (learning) conocimientos mpl. ~**able** a informado

known /nəʊn/ see **know**. —a conocido

knuckle /'nʌkl/ n nudillo m. —vi. ~ **under** someterse

Koran /kə'rɑːn/ n Corán m, Alcorán m

Korea /kə'rɪə/ n Corea f

kosher /'kəʊʃə(r)/ a preparado según la ley judía

kowtow /kaʊ'taʊ/ vi humillarse (to ante)

kudos /'kjuːdɒs/ n prestigio m

L

lab /læb/ n (fam) laboratorio m

label /'leɪbl/ n etiqueta f. —vt (pt **labelled**) poner etiqueta a; (fig, describe as) describir como

laboratory /lə'bɒrətərɪ/ n laboratorio m

laborious /lə'bɔːrɪəs/ a penoso

labour /'leɪbə(r)/ n trabajo m; (workers) mano f de obra. in ~ de parto. —vi trabajar. —vt insistir en

Labour /'leɪbə(r)/ n el partido m laborista. —a laborista

laboured /'leɪbəd/ a penoso

labourer /'leɪbərə(r)/ n obrero, a m; (on farm) labriego m

labyrinth /'læbərɪnθ/ n laberinto m

lace /leɪs/ n encaje m; (of shoe) cordón m, agujeta f (Mex). —vt

(fasten) atar. ~ **with** echar a (a drink)

lacerate /'læsəreɪt/ vt lacerar

lack /læk/ n falta f. ~ **for** of por falta de. —vt faltarle a uno. be ~**ing** money carece de dinero. be ~**ing** faltar

lackadaisical /,lækə'deɪzɪkl/ a indolente, apático

lackey /'lækɪ/ n lacayo m

laconic /lə'kɒnɪk/ a lacónico

lacquer /'lækə(r)/ n laca f

lad /læd/ n muchacho m

ladder /'lædə(r)/ n escalera f (de mano); (in stocking) carrera f. —vt hacer una carrera en. —vi hacerse una carrera

laden /'leɪdn/ a cargado (with de)

ladle /'leɪdl/ n cucharón m

lady /'leɪdɪ/ n señora f. young ~ señorita f. ~-**bird** n, ~-**bug** n (Amer) mariquita f. ~ **friend** n amiga f. ~-**in-waiting** n dama f de honor. ~-**like** a distinguido. ~**ship** n Señora f

lag¹ /læg/ vi (pt **lagged**). ~ (**behind**) retrasarse. —n (interval) intervalo m

lag² /læg/ vt (pt **lagged**) revestir (pipes)

lager /'lɑːgə(r)/ n cerveza f dorada

laggard /'lægəd/ n holgazán m

lagging /'lægɪŋ/ n revestimiento m calorífugo

lagoon /lə'guːn/ n laguna f

lah /lɑː/ n (mus, sixth note of any musical scale) la m

laid /leɪd/ see **lay**¹

lain /leɪn/ see **lie**¹

lair /leə(r)/ n guarida f

laity /'leɪətɪ/ n laicado m

lake /leɪk/ n lago m

lamb /læm/ n cordero m. ~**swool** n lana f de cordero

lame /leɪm/ a (-er, -est) cojo; (excuse) poco convincente. ~**ly** adv (argue) con poca convicción f

lament /lə'mènt/ n lamento m. — vt/i lamentarse (de). ~able /'læməntəbl/ a lamentable

laminated /'læmɪneɪtɪd/ a laminado

lamp /læmp/ n lámpara f. ~post n farol m. ~shade n pantalla f

lance /lɑːns/ n lanza f. —vt (med) abrir con lanceta. ~corporal n cabo m interino

lancet /'lɑːnsɪt/ n lanceta f

land /lænd/ n tierra f; (country) país m; (plot) terreno m. —a terrestre; (breeze) de tierra; (policy, reform) agrario. —vt desembarcar; (obtain) conseguir; dar (blow); (put) meter. —vi (from ship) desembarcar; (aircraft) aterrizar; (fall) caer. ~ up ir a parar

landed /'lændɪd/ a hacendado

landing /'lændɪŋ/ n desembarque m; (aviat) aterrizaje m; (top of stairs) descanso m. ~stage n desembarcadero m

landlady /'lændleɪdɪ/ n propietaria f; (of inn) patrona f

land-locked /'lændlɒkt/ a rodeado de tierra

landlord /'lændlɔːd/ n propietario m; (of inn) patrón m

land: ~mark n punto m destacado. ~scape /'lændskeɪp/ n paisaje m. —vt ajardinar. ~slide n desprendimiento m de tierras; (pol) victoria f arrolladora

lane /leɪn/ n (path, road) camino m; (strip of road) carril m; (aviat) ruta f

language /'læŋgwɪdʒ/ n idioma m; (speech, style) lenguaje m

languid /'læŋgwɪd/ a lánguido. ~ish /'læŋgwɪʃ/ vi languidecer. ~or /'læŋgə(r)/ n languidez f

lank /læŋk/ a larguirucho; (hair) lacio. ~y /'læŋkɪ/ a (-ier, -iest) larguirucho

lantern /'læntən/ n linterna f

lap¹ /læp/ n regazo m

lap² /læp/ n (sport) vuelta f. —vt/i (pt lapped) ~ over traslapar(se)

lap³ /læp/ vt (pt lapped). ~ up beber a lengüetazos; (fig) aceptar con entusiasmo. —vi (waves) chapotear

lapel /lə'pel/ n solapa f

lapse /læps/ vi (decline) degradarse; (expire) caducar; (time) transcurrir. ~ into recaer en. —n error m; (of time) intervalo m

larceny /'lɑːsənɪ/ n robo m

lard /lɑːd/ n manteca f de cerdo

larder /'lɑːdə(r)/ n despensa f

large /lɑːdʒ/ a (-er, -est) grande, (before singular noun) gran. —n. at ~ en libertad. ~ly adv en gran parte. ~ness n (gran) tamaño m

largesse /lɑː'ʒes/ n generosidad f

lark¹ /lɑːk/ n alondra f

lark² /lɑːk/ n broma f; (bit of fun) travesura f. —vi andar de juerga

larva /'lɑːvə/ n (pl -vae /-viː/) larva f

laryn|gitis /lærɪn'dʒaɪtɪs/ n laringitis f. ~x /'lærɪŋks/ n laringe f

lascivious /lə'sɪvɪəs/ a lascivo

laser /'leɪzə(r)/ n láser m

lash /læʃ/ vt azotar. ~ out (spend) gastar. ~ out against atacar. —n latigazo m; (eyelash) pestaña f

lashings /'læʃɪŋz/ npl. ~ of (cream etc, sl) montones de

lass /læs/ n muchacha f

lassitude /'læsɪtjuːd/ n lasitud f

lasso /læ'suː/ n (pl -os) lazo m

last¹ /lɑːst/ a último; (week etc) pasado. ~ Monday n el lunes pasado. have the ~ word decir la última palabra. the ~ straw n el colmo m. —adv por último; (most recently) la última vez. he came ~ llegó el último. —n último m; (remainder) lo que queda. ~ but one penúltimo. at (long) ~ en fin.

last[2] /lɑːst/ *vi* durar. ~ **out** sobrevivir

last[3] /lɑːst/ *n* horma *f*

lasting /ˈlɑːstɪŋ/ *a* duradero

last: ~**ly** *adv* por último. ~ **night** *n* anoche *m*

latch /lætʃ/ *n* picaporte *m*

late /leɪt/ *a* (-er, -est) (*not on time*) tarde; (*recent*) reciente; (*former*) antiguo, ex; (*fruit*) tardío; (*hour*) avanzado; (*deceased*) difunto. **in** ~ **July** a fines de julio. **the** ~ **Dr Phillips** el difunto Dr. Phillips. —*adv* tarde. **of** ~ últimamente. ~**ly** *adv* últimamente. ~**ness** *n* (*delay*) retraso *m*; (*of hour*) lo avanzado

latent /ˈleɪtnt/ *a* latente

lateral /ˈlætərəl/ *a* lateral

latest /ˈleɪtɪst/ *a* último. **at the** ~ a más tardar

lathe /leɪð/ *n* torno *m*

lather /ˈlɑːðə(r)/ *n* espuma *f.* —*vt* enjabonar. —*vi* hacer espuma

Latin /ˈlætɪn/ *n* (*lang*) latín *m.* — *a* latino

latitude /ˈlætɪtjuːd/ *n* latitud *f*

latrine /ləˈtriːn/ *n* letrina *f*

latter /ˈlætə(r)/ *a* último; (*of two*) segundo. —*n.* **the** ~ éste *m*, ésta *f*, éstos *mpl*, éstas *fpl.* ~**day** *a* moderno. ~**ly** *adv* últimamente

lattice /ˈlætɪs/ *n* enrejado *m*

laudable /ˈlɔːdəbl/ *a* laudable

laugh /lɑːf/ *vi* reír(se) (**at** de). —*n* risa *f.* ~**able** *a* ridículo. ~**ing- stock** *n* hazmerreír *m invar.* ~**ter** /ˈlɑːftə(r)/ *n* (*act*) risa *f*; (*sound of laughs*) risas *fpl*

launch[1] /lɔːntʃ/ *vt* lanzar. —*n* lanzamiento *m.* ~ (**out**) **into** lanzarse a

launch[2] /lɔːntʃ/ *n* (*boat*) lancha *f*

launching pad /ˈlɔːntʃɪŋpæd/ *n* plataforma *f* de lanzamiento

launder /ˈlɔːndə(r)/ *vt* lavar (y planchar). ~**erette** *n* lavandería *f* automática. ~**ress** *n* lavandera

f. ~**ry** /ˈlɔːndrɪ/ *n* (*place*) lavandería *f*; (*dirty clothes*) ropa *f* sucia; (*clean clothes*) colada *f*

laurel /ˈlɒrəl/ *n* laurel *m*

lava /ˈlɑːvə/ *n* lava *f*

lavatory /ˈlævətərɪ/ *n* retrete *m.* **public** ~ servicios *mpl*

lavender /ˈlævəndə(r)/ *n* lavanda *f*

lavish /ˈlævɪʃ/ *a* (*person*) pródigo; (*plentiful*) abundante; (*lush*) suntuoso. —*vt* prodigar. ~**ly** *adv* profusamente

law /lɔː/ *n* ley *f*; (*profession, subject of study*) derecho *m.* ~-**abiding** *a* observante de la ley. ~ **and order** *n* orden *m* público. ~ **court** *n* tribunal *m.* ~**ful** *a* (*permitted by law*) lícito; (*recognized by law*) legítimo. ~**fully** *adv* legalmente. ~**less** *a* sin leyes

lawn /lɔːn/ *n* césped *m.* ~-**mower** *n* cortacésped *f.* ~ **tennis** *n* tenis *m* (sobre hierba)

lawsuit /ˈlɔːsuːt/ *n* pleito *m*

lawyer /ˈlɔːjə(r)/ *n* abogado *m*

lax /læks/ *a* descuidado; (*morals etc*) laxo

laxative /ˈlæksətɪv/ *n* laxante *m*

laxity /ˈlæksətɪ/ *n* descuido *m*

lay[1] /leɪ/ *vt* (*pt* **laid**) poner (*incl table, eggs*); tender (*trap*); formar (*plan*). ~ **hands on** echar mano a. ~ **hold of** agarrar. ~ **waste** asolar. ~ **aside** dejar a un lado. ~ **down** dejar a un lado; imponer (*condition*). ~ **into** (*sl*) dar una paliza a. ~ **off** *vt* despedir (*worker*). —*vi* (*fam*) terminar. ~ **on** (*provide*) proveer. ~ **out** (*design*) disponer; (*display*) exponer; desembolsar (*money*). ~ **up** (*store*) guardar; obligar a guardar cama (*person*)

lay[2] /leɪ/ *a* (*non-clerical*) laico; (*opinion etc*) profano

lay[3] /leɪ/ *see* **lie**

layabout /ˈleɪəbaʊt/ n holgazán m

lay-by /ˈleɪbaɪ/ n apartadero m

layer /ˈleɪə(r)/ n capa f

layette /leɪˈet/ n canastilla f

layman /ˈleɪmən/ n lego m

lay-off /ˈleɪɒf/ n paro m forzoso

layout /ˈleɪaʊt/ n disposición f

laze /leɪz/ vi holgazanear; (relax) descansar

laz|iness /ˈleɪzɪnɪs/ n pereza f. ~y a perezoso. ~y-bones n holgazán m

lb. abbr (pound) libra f

lead[1] /liːd/ vt (pt led) conducir; dirigir (team); llevar (life); (induce) inducir a. —vi (go first) ir delante; (road) ir, conducir; (in cards) salir. —n mando m; (clue) pista f; (leash) correa f; (in theatre) primer papel m; (wire) cable m; (example) ejemplo m. in the ~ en cabeza. ~ away llevar. ~ up to preparar el terreno para

lead[2] /led/ n plomo m; (of pencil) mina f. ~en /ˈledn/ a de plomo

leader /ˈliːdə(r)/ n jefe m; (leading article) editorial m. ~ship n dirección f

leading /ˈliːdɪŋ/ a principal; (in front) delantero. ~ article n editorial m

leaf /liːf/ n (pl leaves) hoja f. —vi. ~ through hojear

leaflet /ˈliːflɪt/ n folleto m

leafy /ˈliːfɪ/ a frondoso

league /liːg/ n liga f. be in ~ with concharbarse con

leak /liːk/ n (hole) agujero m; (of gas, liquid) escape m; (of information) filtración f; (in roof) gotera f; (in boat) vía f de agua. —vi (receptacle, gas, liquid) salirse; (information) filtrarse; (drip) gotear; (boat) hacer agua. —vt dejar escapar; filtrar (information). ~age n = leak. ~y a (receptacle) agujereado;

(roof) que tiene goteras; (boat) que hace agua

lean[1] /liːn/ vt (pt leaned or leant /lent/) apoyar. —vi inclinarse. ~ against apoyarse en. ~ on apoyarse en. ~out asomarse (of a). ~ over inclinarse

lean[2] /liːn/ a (-er, -est) magro. —n carne f magra

leaning /ˈliːnɪŋ/ a inclinado. —n inclinación f

leanness /ˈliːnnɪs/ n (of meat) magrez f; (of person) flaqueza f

lean-to /ˈliːntuː/ n colgadizo m

leap /liːp/ vi (pt leaped or leapt /lept/) saltar. —n salto m. ~frog n salto m, saltacabrilla f. —vi (pt -frogged) jugar a saltacabrilla. ~ year n año m bisiesto

learn /lɜːn/ vt/i (pt learned or learnt) aprender (to do a hacer). ~ed /ˈlɜːnɪd/ a culto. ~er /ˈlɜːnə(r)/ n principiante m; (apprentice) aprendiz m; (student) estudiante m & f. ~ing n saber m

lease /liːs/ n arriendo m. —vt arrendar

leash /liːʃ/ n correa f

least /liːst/ a. the ~ (smallest amount of) mínimo; (slightest) menor; (smallest) más pequeño. —n lo menos. at ~ por lo menos. not in the ~ en absoluto. —adv menos

leather /ˈleðə(r)/ n piel f, cuero m

leave /liːv/ vt (pt left) dejar; (depart from) marcharse de. ~ alone dejar de tocar (thing); dejar en paz (person). be left (over) quedar. —vi marcharse; (train) salir. —n permiso m. on ~ (mil) de permiso. take one's ~ of despedirse de. ~ out omitir

leavings /ˈliːvɪŋz/ npl restos mpl

Leban|on /ˈlebənən/ n el Líbano m. ~ese /-'niːz/ a & n libanés (m)

lecher /ˈletʃə(r)/ n libertino m.
~**ous** a lascivo. ~**y** n lascivia f

lectern /ˈlektɜːn/ n atril m; (in church) facistol m

lecture /ˈlektʃə(r)/ n conferencia f; (univ) clase f; (rebuke) sermón m. —vt/i dar una conferencia (a); (univ) dar clases (a); (rebuke) sermonear. ~**r** n conferenciante m; (univ) profesor m

led /led/ see **lead**[1]

ledge /ledʒ/ n repisa f; (of window) antepecho m

ledger /ˈledʒə(r)/ n libro m mayor

lee /liː/ n sotavento m; (fig) abrigo m

leech /liːtʃ/ n sanguijuela f

leek /liːk/ n puerro m

leer /lɪə(r)/ vi. ~ (**at**) mirar impúdicamente. —n mirada f impúdica

leeway /ˈliːweɪ/ n deriva f; (fig, freedom of action) libertad f de acción. **make up** ~ recuperar los atrasos

left[1] /left/ a izquierdo. —adv a la izquierda. —n izquierda f

left[2] /left/ see **leave**

left: ~**-hand** a izquierdo.
~**-handed** a zurdo. ~**ist** n izquierdista m & f. ~ **luggage** n consigna f. ~**overs** npl restos mpl

left-wing /ˈleftwɪŋ/ a izquierdista

leg /leg/ n pierna f; (of animal, furniture) pata f; (of pork) pernil m; (of lamb) pierna f; (of journey) etapa f. **on its last** ~**s** en las últimas

legacy /ˈlegəsɪ/ n herencia f

legal /ˈliːgl/ a (permitted by law) lícito; (recognized by law) legítimo; (affairs etc) jurídico. ~ **aid** n abogacía f de pobres. ~**ity** /-ˈgælətɪ/ n legalidad f. ~**ize** vt legalizar. ~**ly** adv legalmente

legation /lɪˈgeɪʃn/ n legación f

legend /ˈledʒənd/ n leyenda f.
~**ary** a legendario

leggings /ˈlegɪŋz/ npl polainas fpl

legib|**ility** /ˈledʒəbɪlətɪ/ n legibilidad f. ~**le** a legible. ~**ly** adv legiblemente

legion /ˈliːdʒən/ n legión f

legislat|**e** /ˈledʒɪsleɪt/ vi legislar.
~**ion** /-ˈleɪʃn/ n legislación f.
~**ive** a legislativo. ~**ure** /-eɪtʃə(r)/ n cuerpo m legislativo

legitima|**cy** /lɪˈdʒɪtɪməsɪ/ f legitimidad f. ~**te** a legítimo

leisure /ˈleʒə(r)/ n ocio m. **at one's** ~ cuando tenga tiempo.
~**ly** adv sin prisa

lemon /ˈlemən/ n limón m. ~**ade** /leməˈneɪd/ n (fizzy) gaseosa f (de limón); (still) limonada f

lend /lend/ vt (pt lent) prestar. ~ **itself to** prestarse a. ~**er** n prestador m; (moneylender) prestamista m & f. ~**ing** n préstamo m. ~**ing library** n biblioteca f de préstamo

length /leŋθ/ n largo m; (in time) duración f; (of cloth) largo m; (of road) tramo m. **at** ~ (at last) por fin. **at (great)** ~ detalladamente. ~**en** /ˈleŋθən/ vt alargar. —vi alargarse. ~**ways** adv a lo largo. ~**y** a largo

lenien|**cy** /ˈliːnɪənsɪ/ n indulgencia f. ~**t** a indulgente. ~**tly** adv con indulgencia

lens /lenz/ n lente f. **contact** ~**es** npl lentillas fpl

lent /lent/ see **lend**

Lent /lent/ n cuaresma f

lentil /ˈlentl/ n (bean) lenteja f

Leo /ˈliːəʊ/ n (astr) Leo m

leopard /ˈlepəd/ n leopardo m

leotard /ˈliːətɑːd/ n leotardo m

lep|**er** /ˈlepə(r)/ n leproso m.
~**rosy** /ˈleprəsɪ/ n lepra f

lesbian /ˈlezbɪən/ n lesbiana f. —a lesbiano

lesion /ˈliːʒn/ n lesión f

less /les/ a (in quantity) menos; (in size) menor. —adv & prep menos. ∼ **than** menos que; (with numbers) menos de. —n menor m. ∼ **and** ∼ cada vez menos. **none** the ∼ sin embargo. ∼**en** /'lesn/ vt/i disminuir. ∼**er** /'lesə(r)/ a menor

lesson /'lesn/ n clase f

lest /lest/ conj por miedo de que

let /let/ vt (pt **let**, pres p **letting**) dejar; (lease) alquilar. ∼ **me do it** déjame hacerlo. —v aux. ∼'s **go!** ¡vamos!, ¡vámonos! ∼'s **see** (vamos) a ver. ∼'s **talk/drink** hablemos/bebamos. —n alquiler m. ∼ **down** bajar; (deflate) desinflar; (fig) defraudar. ∼ **go** soltar. ∼ **in** dejar entrar. ∼ **off** disparar (gun); (cause to explode) hacer explotar; (firework); (excuse) perdonar. ∼ **off steam** (fig) desfogarse. ∼ **on** (sl) revelar. ∼ **out** dejar salir. ∼ **through** dejar pasar. ∼ **up** disminuir. ∼**down** n desilusión f

lethal /'li:θl/ a (dose, wound) mortal; (weapon) mortífero

letharg|**ic** /lɪ'tɑ:dʒɪk/ a letárgico. ∼**y** /'leθədʒɪ/ n letargo m

letter /'letə(r)/ n (of alphabet) letra f; (written message) carta f. ∼**bomb** n carta f explosiva. ∼**box** n buzón m. ∼**head** n membrete m. ∼**ing** n letras fpl

lettuce /'letɪs/ n lechuga f

let-up /'letʌp/ n (fam) descanso m

leukaemia /lu:'ki:mɪə/ n leucemia f

level /'levl/ a (flat) llano; (on surface) horizontal; (in height) a nivel; (in score) igual; (spoonful) raso. —n nivel m. **be on the** ∼ (fam) ser honrado. —vt (pt **levelled**) nivelar; (aim) apuntar. ∼ **crossing** n paso m a nivel. ∼**headed** a juicioso

lever /'li:və(r)/ n palanca f. —vt apalancar. ∼**age** /'li:vərɪdʒ/ n apalancamiento m

levity /'levətɪ/ n ligereza f

levy /'levɪ/ vt exigir (tax). —n impuesto m

lewd /lu:d/ a (-er, -est) lascivo

lexicography /leksɪ'kɒgrəfɪ/ n lexicografía f

lexicon /'leksɪkən/ n léxico m

liable /'laɪəbl/ a. **be** ∼ **to do** tener tendencia a hacer. ∼ **for** responsable de. ∼ **to** susceptible de; expuesto a (fine)

liability /laɪə'bɪlətɪ/ n responsabilidad f; (disadvantage, fam) inconveniente m. **liabilities** npl (debts) deudas fpl

liais|**e** /lɪ'eɪz/ vi hacer un enlace, enlazar. ∼**on** /lɪ'eɪzɒn/ n enlace m; (love affair) lío m

liar /'laɪə(r)/ n mentiroso m

libel /'laɪbl/ n libelo m. —vt (pt **libelled**) difamar (por escrito)

Liberal /'lɪbərəl/ a & n liberal (m & f)

liberal /'lɪbərəl/ a liberal; (generous) generoso; (tolerant) tolerante. ∼**ly** adv liberalmente; (generously) generosamente; (tolerantly) tolerantemente

liberat|**e** /'lɪbəreɪt/ vt liberar. ∼**ion** /-'reɪʃn/ n liberación f

libertine /'lɪbəti:n/ n libertino m

liberty /'lɪbətɪ/ n libertad f. **be at** ∼ **to** estar autorizado para. **take liberties** tomarse libertades. **take the** ∼ **of** tomarse la libertad de

libido /lɪ'bi:dəʊ/ n (pl -os) libido m

Libra /'li:brə/ n (astr) Libra f

librar|**ian** /laɪ'breərɪən/ n bibliotecario m. ∼**y** /'laɪbrərɪ/ n biblioteca f

libretto /lɪ'bretəʊ/ n (pl -os) libreto m

Libya /'lɪbɪə/ n Libia f. ∼**n** a & n libio (m)

lice /laɪs/ see **louse**

licence /'laɪsns/ n licencia f, permiso m; (fig, liberty) libertad f. ∼

plate *n* (placa *f* de) matrícula *f*. **driving** ~ carné *m* de conducir

license /'laɪsns/ *vt* autorizar

licentious /laɪ'senʃəs/ *a* licencioso

lichen /'laɪkən/ *n* liquen *m*

lick /lɪk/ *vt* lamer; (*defeat*, *sl*) dar una paliza a. ~ **one's chops** relamerse. —*n* lametón *m*

licorice /'lɪkərɪs/ *n* (*Amer*) regaliz *m*

lid /lɪd/ *n* tapa *f*; (*of pan*) cobertera *f*

lido /'liːdəʊ/ *n* (*pl* **-os**) piscina *f*

lie[1] /laɪ/ *vi* (*pt* **lay**, *pp* **lain**, *pres p* **lying**) echarse; (*state*) estar echado; (*remain*) quedarse; (*be*) estar, encontrarse; (*in grave*) yacer. **be lying** estar echado. ~ **down** acostarse. ~ **low** quedarse escondido

lie[2] /laɪ/ *n* mentira *f*. —*vi* (*pt* **lied**, *pres p* **lying**) mentir. **give the** ~ **to** desmentir

lie-in /laɪ'ɪn/ *n*. **have a** ~**in** quedarse en la cama

lieu /ljuː/ *n*. **in** ~ **of** en lugar de

lieutenant /lefˈtenənt/ *n* (*mil*) teniente *m*

life /laɪf/ *n* (*pl* **lives**) vida *f*. ~**belt** *n* cinturón *m* salvavidas. ~**boat** *n* lancha *f* de salvamento; (*on ship*) bote *m* salvavidas. ~**buoy** *n* boya *f* salvavidas. ~ **cycle** *n* ciclo *m* vital. ~**guard** *n* bañero *m*. ~**jacket** *n* chaleco *m* salvavidas. ~**less** *a* sin vida. ~**like** *a* natural. ~**line** *n* cuerda *f* salvavidas; (*fig*) cordón *m* umbilical. ~**long** *a* de toda la vida. ~**size(d)** *a* de tamaño natural. ~**time** *n* vida *f*

lift /lɪft/ *vt* levantar; (*steal*, *fam*) robar. —*vi* (*fog*) disiparse. —*n* ascensor *m*, elevador *m* (*LAm*). **give a** ~ **to s.o.** llevar a uno en su coche, dar aventón a uno (*LAm*). ~**off** *n* (*aviat*) despegue *m*

ligament /'lɪgəmənt/ *n* ligamento *m*

light[1] /laɪt/ *n* luz *f*; (*lamp*) lámpara *f*, luz *f*; (*flame*) fuego *m*; (*headlight*) faro *m*. **bring to** ~ sacar a luz. **come to** ~ salir a luz. **have you got a** ~? ¿tienes fuego? **the** ~**s** *npl* (*auto*, *traffic signals*) el semáforo *m*. —*a* claro. —*vt* (*pt* **lit** *or* **lighted**) encender; (*illuminate*) alumbrar. ~ **up** *vt/i* iluminar(se)

light[2] /laɪt/ *a* (**-er**, **-est**) (*not heavy*) ligero

lighten[1] /'laɪtn/ *vt* (*make less heavy*) aligerar

lighten[2] /'laɪtn/ *vt* (*give light to*) iluminar; (*make brighter*) aclarar

lighter /'laɪtə(r)/ *n* (*for cigarettes*) mechero *m*

light-fingered /laɪt'fɪŋgəd/ *a* largo de uñas

light-headed /laɪt'hedɪd/ *a* (*dizzy*) mareado; (*frivolous*) casquivano

light-hearted /laɪt'hɑːtɪd/ *a* alegre

lighthouse /'laɪthaʊs/ *n* faro *m*

lighting /'laɪtɪŋ/ *n* (*system*) alumbrado *m*; (*act*) iluminación *f*

light: ~**ly** *adv* ligeramente. ~**ness** *n* ligereza *f*

lightning /'laɪtnɪŋ/ *n* relámpago *m*. —*a* relámpago

lightweight /'laɪtweɪt/ *a* ligero. —*n* (*boxing*) peso *m* ligero

light-year /'laɪtjɪə(r)/ *n* año *m* luz

like[1] /laɪk/ *a* parecido. —*prep* como. —*conj* (*fam*) como. —*n* igual. **the** ~**s of you** la gente como tú

like[2] /laɪk/ *vt* gustarle (a uno). **I** ~ **chocolate** me gusta el chocolate. **I should** ~ quisiera. **they** ~ **swimming** (a ellos) les gusta

nadar. **would you** ~? ¿quieres?
~**able** *a* simpático. ~**s** *npl*
gustos *mpl*
likelihood /'laɪklɪhʊd/ *n* probabilidad *f*
likely *a* (-ier, -iest) probable. **he
is** ~ **to come** es probable que
venga. —*adv* probablemente.
not ~! ¡ni hablar!
like-minded /laɪk'maɪndɪd/ *a.*
be ~ tener las mismas opiniones
liken /'laɪkən/ *vt* comparar
likeness /'laɪknɪs/ *n* parecido *m.*
be a good ~ parecerse mucho
likewise /'laɪkwaɪz/ *adv* (*also*)
también; (*the same way*) lo
mismo
liking /'laɪkɪŋ/ *n* (*for thing*) afición *f*; (*for person*) simpatía *f*
lilac /'laɪlək/ *n* lila *f.* —*a* color de
lila
lilt /lɪlt/ *n* ritmo *m*
lily /'lɪlɪ/ *n* lirio *m.* ~ **of the valley** lirio *m* de los valles
limb /lɪm/ *n* miembro *m.* **out on
a** ~ aislado
limber /'lɪmbə(r)/ *vi.* ~ **up** hacer
ejercicios preliminares
limbo /'lɪmbəʊ/ *n* limbo *m.* **be in**
~ (*forgotten*) estar olvidado
lime[1] /laɪm/ *n* (*white substance*)
cal *f*
lime[2] /laɪm/ *n* (*fruit*) lima *f*
lime[3] /laɪm/ *n.* ~**-(-tree)** (*linden
tree*) tilo *m*
limelight /'laɪmlaɪt/ *n.* **be in the**
~ estar muy a la vista
limerick /'lɪmərɪk/ *n* quintilla *f*
humorística
limestone /'laɪmstəʊn/ *n* caliza *f*
limit /'lɪmɪt/ *n* límite *m.* —*vt*
limitar. ~**ation** /-'teɪʃn/ *n* limit-
ación *f.* ~**ed** *a* limitado. ~**ed
company** *n* sociedad *f* anónima
limousine /'lɪmǝziːn/ *n* limusina
f
limp[1] /lɪmp/ *vi* cojear. —*n* cojera
f. **have a** ~ cojear
limp[2] /lɪmp/ *a* (-er, -est) flojo

limpid /'lɪmpɪd/ *a* límpido
linctus /'lɪŋktəs/ *n* jarabe *m*
(para la tos)
line[1] /laɪn/ *n* línea *f*; (*track*) vía *f*;
(*wrinkle*) arruga *f*; (*row*) fila *f*; (*of
poem*) verso *m*; (*rope*) cuerda *f*;
(*of goods*) surtido *m*; (*queue,
Amer*) cola *f.* **in** ~ **with** de
acuerdo con. —*vt* (*on paper etc*)
rayar; bordear (*streets etc*). ~ **up**
alinearse; (*in queue*) hacer cola
line[2] /laɪn/ *vt* forrar; (*fill*) llenar
lineage /'lɪnɪɪdʒ/ *n* linaje *m*
linear /'lɪnɪə(r)/ *a* lineal
linen /'lɪnɪn/ *n* (*sheets etc*) ropa *f*
blanca; (*material*) lino *m*
liner /'laɪnə(r)/ *n* transatlántico
m
linesman /'laɪnzmən/ *n* (*football*)
juez *m* de línea
linger /'lɪŋgə(r)/ *vi* tardar en
marcharse; (*smells etc*) persistir.
~ **over** dilatarse en
lingerie /'lænʒərɪ/ *n* ropa *f* interior, lencería *f*
lingo /'lɪŋgəʊ/ *n* (*pl* -os) idioma
m; (*specialized vocabulary*) jerga
f
linguist /'lɪŋgwɪst/ *n* (*specialist
in languages*) políglota *m* & *f*;
(*specialist in linguistics*) lin-
güista *m* & *f.* ~**ic** /lɪŋ'gwɪstɪk/ *a*
lingüístico. ~**ics** *n* lingüística *f*
lining /'laɪnɪŋ/ *n* forro *m*; (*auto,
of brakes*) guarnición *f*
link /lɪŋk/ *n* (*of chain*) eslabón *m*;
(*fig*) lazo *m.* —*vt* eslabonar; (*fig*)
enlazar. ~ **up with** reunirse
con. ~**age** *n* enlace *m*
links /lɪŋks/ *n invar* campo *m* de
golf
lino /'laɪnəʊ/ *n* (*pl* -os) linóleo *m.*
~**leum** /lɪ'nəʊlɪəm/ *n* linóleo *m*
lint /lɪnt/ *n* (*med*) hilas *fpl*; (*fluff*)
pelusa *f*
lion /'laɪən/ *n* león *m.* **the** ~**'s
share** la parte *f* del león. ~**ess** *n*
leona *f*

lionize /'laɪənaɪz/ vt tratar como una celebridad

lip /lɪp/ n labio m; (edge) borde m. **pay ~ service to** aprobar de boquilla. **stiff upper ~** n imperturbabilidad f. **~-read** vt/i leer en los labios. **~salve** n crema f para los labios. **~stick** n lápiz m de labios.

liquefy /'lɪkwɪfaɪ/ vt/i licuar(se)

liqueur /lɪ'kjʊə(r)/ n licor m

liquid /'lɪkwɪd/ a & n líquido (m)

liquidate /'lɪkwɪdeɪt/ vt liquidar. **~ion** /-'deɪʃn/ n liquidación f

liquidize /'lɪkwɪdaɪz/ vt licuar. **~r** n licuadora f

liquor /'lɪkə(r)/ n bebida f alcohólica

liquorice /'lɪkərɪs/ n regaliz m

lira /'lɪərə/ n (pl **lire** /'lɪəreɪ/ or **liras**) lira f

lisle /laɪl/ n hilo m de Escocia

lisp /lɪsp/ n ceceo m. **speak with a ~** cecear. —vi cecear

lissom /'lɪsəm/ a flexible, ágil

list[1] /lɪst/ n lista f. —vt hacer una lista de; (enter in a list) inscribir

list[2] /lɪst/ vi (ship) escorar

listen /'lɪsn/ vi escuchar. **~ in (to)** escuchar. **~ to** escuchar. **~er** n oyente m & f

listless /'lɪstlɪs/ a apático

lit /lɪt/ see **light**[1]

litany /'lɪtənɪ/ n letanía f

literacy /'lɪtərəsɪ/ n capacidad f de leer y escribir

literal /'lɪtərəl/ a literal; (fig) prosaico. **~ly** adv al pie de la letra, literalmente

literary /'lɪtərərɪ/ a literario

literate /'lɪtərət/ a que sabe leer y escribir

literature /'lɪtərətʃə(r)/ n literatura f; (fig) impresos mpl

lithe /laɪð/ a ágil

lithograph /'lɪθəgrɑːf/ n litografía f

litigation /lɪtɪ'ɡeɪʃn/ n litigio m

litre /'liːtə(r)/ n litro m

litter /'lɪtə(r)/ n basura f; (of animals) camada f. —vt ensuciar; (scatter) esparcir. **~ed with** lleno de. **~bin** n papelera f

little /'lɪtl/ a pequeño; (not much) poco de. —n poco m. **a ~** un poco. **a ~ water** un poco de agua. —adv poco. **~ by ~** poco a poco. **~ finger** n meñique m

liturgy /'lɪtədʒɪ/ n liturgia f

live[1] /lɪv/ vt/i vivir. **~ down** lograr borrar. **~ it up** echar una cana al aire. **~ on** (feed o.s. on) vivir de; (continue) perdurar. **~ up to** vivir de acuerdo con; cumplir (a promise)

live[2] /laɪv/ a vivo; (wire) con corriente; (broadcast) en directo. **be a ~ wire** ser una persona enérgica

livelihood /'laɪvlɪhʊd/ n sustento m

liveliness /'laɪvlɪnɪs/ n vivacidad f. **~y** a (-ier, -iest) vivo

liven /'laɪvn/ vt/i. **~ up** animar(se); (cheer up) alegrar(se)

liver /'lɪvə(r)/ n hígado m

livery /'lɪvərɪ/ n librea f

livestock /'laɪvstɒk/ n ganado m

livid /'lɪvɪd/ a lívido; (angry, fam) furioso

living /'lɪvɪŋ/ a vivo. —n vida f. **~room** n cuarto m de estar, cuarto m de estancia (LAm)

lizard /'lɪzəd/ n lagartija f; (big) lagarto m

llama /'lɑːmə/ n llama f

load /ləʊd/ n (incl elec) carga f; (quantity) cantidad f; (weight, strain) peso m. —vt cargar. **~ed** a (incl dice) cargado; (wealthy, sl) muy rico. **~s of** (fam) montones de

loaf[1] /ləʊf/ n (pl **loaves**) pan m; (stick of bread) barra f

loaf[2] /ləʊf/ vi. **~ (about)** holgazanear. **~er** n holgazán m

loam /ləʊm/ n marga f

loan /ləʊn/ n préstamo m. **on ~** prestado. —vt prestar

loath /ləʊθ/ a poco dispuesto (**to** a)

loath|e /ləʊð/ vt odiar. **~ing** n odio m (**of** a). **~some** a odioso

lobby /ˈlɒbɪ/ n vestíbulo m; (pol) grupo m de presión. —vt hacer presión sobre

lobe /ləʊb/ n lóbulo m

lobster /ˈlɒbstə(r)/ n langosta f

local /ˈləʊkl/ a local. ~ (pub, fam) bar m. **the ~s** los vecinos mpl

locale /ləʊˈkɑːl/ n escenario m

local government /ˈləʊkl ˈɡʌvənmənt/ n gobierno m municipal

locality /ləʊˈkælətɪ/ n localidad f

localized /ˈləʊkəlaɪzd/ a localizado

locally /ˈləʊkəlɪ/ adv localmente; (nearby) en la localidad

locate /ləʊˈkeɪt/ vt (situate) situar; (find) encontrar

location /ləʊˈkeɪʃn/ n colocación f; (place) situación f. **on ~** fuera del estudio. **to film on ~ in Andalusia** rodar en Andalucía

lock[1] /lɒk/ n (of door etc) cerradura f; (on canal) esclusa f. —vt/i cerrar(se) con llave. ~ **in** encerrar. ~ **out** cerrar la puerta a. ~ **up** encerrar

lock[2] /lɒk/ n (of hair) mechón m. ~**s** npl pelo m

locker /ˈlɒkə(r)/ n armario m

locket /ˈlɒkɪt/ n medallón m

lock-out /ˈlɒkaʊt/ n lock-out m

locksmith /ˈlɒksmɪθ/ n cerrajero m

locomotion /ləʊkəˈməʊʃn/ n locomoción f

locomotive /ləʊkəˈməʊtɪv/ n locomotora f

locum /ˈləʊkəm/ n interino m

locust /ˈləʊkəst/ n langosta f

lodge /lɒdʒ/ n (in park) casa f del guarda; (of porter) portería f. —vt alojar; presentar ⟨complaint⟩; depositar ⟨money⟩. —vi alojarse. ~**r** /-ə(r)/ n huésped m

lodgings /ˈlɒdʒɪŋz/ n alojamiento m; (room) habitación f

loft /lɒft/ n desván m

lofty /ˈlɒftɪ/ a (-ier, -iest) elevado; (haughty) altanero

log /lɒɡ/ n (of wood) leño m; (naut) cuaderno m de bitácora. **sleep like a ~** dormir como un lirón. —vt (pt **logged**) apuntar; (travel) recorrer

logarithm /ˈlɒɡərɪðəm/ n logaritmo m

log-book /ˈlɒɡbʊk/ n cuaderno m de bitácora; (aviat) diario m de vuelo

loggerheads /ˈlɒɡəhedz/ npl. **be at ~ with** estar a matar con

logic /ˈlɒdʒɪk/ a lógica f. ~**al** a lógico. ~**ally** adv lógicamente

logistics /ləˈdʒɪstɪks/ n logística f

logo /ˈləʊɡəʊ/ n (pl -os) logotipo m

loin /lɔɪn/ n (culin) solomillo m. ~**s** npl ijadas fpl

loiter /ˈlɔɪtə(r)/ vi holgazanear

loll /lɒl/ vi repantigarse

lollipop /ˈlɒlɪpɒp/ n (boiled sweet) pirulí m. ~ **y** n (iced) polo m; (money, sl) dinero m

London /ˈlʌndn/ n Londres m. ~ a londinense. ~**er** n londinense m & f

lone /ləʊn/ a solitario. ~**ly** /ˈləʊnlɪ/ a (-ier, -iest) solitario. **feel ~ly** sentirse muy solo. ~**r** /ˈləʊnə(r)/ n solitario m. ~**some** a solitario

long[1] /lɒŋ/ a (-er, -est) largo. a ~ **time** mucho tiempo. **how ~ is it?** ¿cuánto tiempo de largo? **in the ~ run** a la larga. —adv largo/mucho tiempo. **as ~ as** (while) mientras; (provided that) con tal que (+ subjunctive).

before ~ dentro de poco. **so** ~!
¡hasta luego! **so** ~ **as** (*provided that*) con tal que (+ *subjunctive*)

long² /lɒŋ/ *vi.* ~ **for** anhelar

long-distance /lɒŋˈdɪstəns/ *a* de larga distancia. ~ **(tele)phone call** *n* conferencia *f*

longer /ˈlɒŋɡə(r)/ *adv.* **no** ~**er ya** no

longevity /lɒnˈdʒevətɪ/ *n* longevidad *f*

long: ~**face** *n* cara *f* triste. ~**hand** *n* escritura *f* a mano. ~**johns** *npl* (*fam*) calzoncillos largos. ~ **jump** *n* salto *m* de longitud

longing /ˈlɒŋɪŋ/ *n* anhelo *m*, ansia *f*

longitude /ˈlɒŋɡɪtjuːd/ *n* longitud *f*

long: ~**-playing record** *n* elepé *m.* ~**-range** *a* de gran alcance. ~**-sighted** *a* présbita. ~**standing** *a* de mucho tiempo. ~**-suffering** *a* sufrido. ~**-term** *a* a largo plazo. ~ **wave** *n* onda *f* larga. ~**-winded** *a* (*speaker etc*) prolijo

loo /luː/ *n* (*fam*) servicios *mpl*

look /lʊk/ *vt* mirar; (*seem*) parecer; representar (*age*). —*vi* mirar; (*seem*) parecer; (*search*) buscar. —*n* mirada *f*; (*appearance*) aspecto *m.* ~ **after** ocuparse de; cuidar (*person*). ~ **at** mirar. ~ **down** on despreciar. ~ **for** buscar. ~ **forward to** esperar con ansia. ~ **in on** pasar por casa de. ~ **into** investigar. ~ **like** (*resemble*) parecerse a. ~ **on to** ⟨*room, window*⟩ dar a. ~ **out** tener cuidado. ~ **out for** buscar; (*watch*) tener cuidado con. ~ **round** volver la cabeza. ~ **through** hojear. ~ **up** buscar ⟨*word*⟩; (*visit*) ir a ver. ~ **up to** respetar. ~**er-on** *n* espectador *m.* ~**ing-glass** *n* espejo *m.* ~**-out** *n* (*mil*) atalaya *f*; (*person*)

vigía *m.* ~**s** *npl* belleza *f.* **good** ~**s** *mpl* belleza *f*

loom¹ /luːm/ *n* telar *m*

loom² /luːm/ *vi* aparecerse

loony /ˈluːnɪ/ *a & n* (*sl*) chiflado (*m*) (*fam*), loco (*m*). ~ **bin** *n* (*sl*) manicomio *m*

loop /luːp/ *n* lazo *m.* —*vt* hacer presilla con

loophole /ˈluːphəʊl/ *n* (*in rule*) escapatoria *f*

loose /luːs/ *a* (-**er**, -**est**) (*untied*) suelto; (*not tight*) flojo; (*inexact*) vago; (*immoral*) inmoral; (*not packed*) suelto. **be at a** ~ **end**, **be at** ~ **ends** (*Amer*) no tener nada que hacer. ~**ly** *adv* sueltamente; (*roughly*) aproximadamente. ~**n** /ˈluːsn/ *vt* (*slacken*) aflojar; (*untie*) desatar

loot /luːt/ *n* botín *m.* —*vt* saquear. ~**er** *n* saqueador *m.* ~**ing** *n* saqueo *m*

lop /lɒp/ *vt* (*pt* **lopped**). ~ **off** cortar

lop-sided /lɒpˈsaɪdɪd/ *a* ladeado

loquacious /ləˈkweɪʃəs/ *a* locuaz

lord /lɔːd/ *n* señor *m*; (*British title*) lord *m.* **(good) L**~! ¡Dios mío! **the L**~ el Señor *m.* **the (House of) L**~**s** la Cámara *f* de los Lores. ~**ly** *a* señorial; (*haughty*) altivo. ~**ship** *n* señoría *f*

lore /lɔː(r)/ *n* tradiciones *fpl*

lorgnette /lɔːˈnjet/ *n* impertinentes *mpl*

lorry /ˈlɒrɪ/ *n* camión *m*

lose /luːz/ *vt/i* (*pt* **lost**) perder. ~**r** *n* perdedor *m*

loss /lɒs/ *n* pérdida *f.* **be at a** ~ estar perplejo. **be at a** ~ **for words** no encontrar palabras. **be at a** ~ **to** no saber cómo

lost /lɒst/ *see* **lose**. —*a* perdido. ~ **property** *n,* ~ **and found** (*Amer*) *n* oficina *f* de objetos perdidos. **get** ~ perderse

lot /lɒt/ *n* (*fate*) suerte *f*; (*at auction*) lote *m*; (*land*) solar *m*. **a ~ (of)** muchos. **quite a ~ of** (*fam*) bastante. **~s (of)** (*fam*) muchos. **the ~** todos *mpl*

lotion /ˈləʊʃn/ *n* loción *f*

lottery /ˈlɒtəri/ *n* lotería *f*

lotto /ˈlɒtəʊ/ *n* lotería *f*

lotus /ˈləʊtəs/ *n* (*pl* **-uses**) loto *m*

loud /laʊd/ *a* (**-er, -est**) fuerte; (*noisy*) ruidoso; (*gaudy*) chillón. **out ~** en voz alta. **~ hailer** *n* megáfono *m*. **~ly** *adv* (*speak etc*) en voz alta; (*noisily*) ruidosamente. **~speaker** *n* altavoz *m*

lounge /laʊndʒ/ *vi* repantigarse. **—** *n* salón *m*. **~ suit** *n* traje *m* de calle

louse /laʊs/ *n* (*pl* **lice**) piojo *m*

lousy /ˈlaʊzi/ *a* (**-ier, -iest**) piojoso; (*bad, sl*) malísimo

lout /laʊt/ *n* patán *m*

lovable /ˈlʌvəbl/ *a* adorable

love /lʌv/ *n* amor *m*; (*tennis*) cero *m*. **be in ~ with** estar enamorado de. **fall in ~ with** enamorarse de. **—** *vt* querer (*person*); gustarle mucho a uno, encantarle a uno (*things*). **I ~ milk** me encanta la leche. **~ affair** *n* amores *mpl*

lovely /ˈlʌvli/ *a* (**-ier, -iest**) hermoso; (*delightful, fam*) precioso. **have a ~ time** divertirse

lover /ˈlʌvə(r)/ *n* amante *m & f*

lovesick /ˈlʌvsɪk/ *a* atortolado

loving /ˈlʌvɪŋ/ *a* cariñoso

low[1] /ləʊ/ *a & adv* (**-er, -est**) bajo. **—** *n* (*low pressure*) área *f* de baja presión

low[2] /ləʊ/ *vi* mugir

lowbrow /ˈləʊbraʊ/ *a* poco culto

low-cut /ˈləʊkʌt/ *a* escotado

low-down /ˈləʊdaʊn/ *a* bajo. **—** *n* (*sl*) informes *mpl*

lower /ˈləʊə(r)/ *a & adv* *see* **low**[2]. **—** *vt* bajar. **~ o.s.** envilecerse

low-key /ləʊˈkiː/ *a* moderado

lowlands /ˈləʊləndz/ *npl* tierra *f* baja

lowly /ˈləʊli/ *a* (**-ier, -iest**) humilde

loyal /ˈlɔɪəl/ *a* leal. **~ly** *adv* lealmente. **~ty** *n* lealtad *f*

lozenge /ˈlɒzɪndʒ/ *n* (*shape*) rombo *m*; (*tablet*) pastilla *f*

LP /elˈpiː/ *abbr* (*long-playing record*) elepé *m*

Ltd /ˈlɪmɪtɪd/ *abbr* (*Limited*) S.A., Sociedad Anónima

lubricant /ˈluːbrɪkənt/ *n* lubricante *m*. **~te** /-ˈkeɪt/ *vt* lubricar. **~tion** /-ˈkeɪʃn/ *n* lubricación *f*

lucid /ˈluːsɪd/ *a* lúcido. **~ity** /-ˈsɪdətɪ/ *n* lucidez *f*

luck /lʌk/ *n* suerte *f*. **bad ~** *n* mala suerte *f*. **~ily** /ˈlʌkɪlɪ/ *adv* afortunadamente. **~y** *a* (**-ier, -iest**) afortunado

lucrative /ˈluːkrətɪv/ *a* lucrativo

lucre /ˈluːkə(r)/ *n* (*pej*) dinero *m*. **filthy ~** vil metal *m*

ludicrous /ˈluːdɪkrəs/ *a* ridículo

lug /lʌg/ *vt* (*pt* **lugged**) arrastrar

luggage /ˈlʌgɪdʒ/ *n* equipaje *m*. **~-rack** *n* rejilla *f*. **~-van** *n* furgón *m*

lugubrious /luːˈguːbrɪəs/ *a* lúgubre

lukewarm /ˈluːkwɔːm/ *a* tibio

lull /lʌl/ *vt* (*soothe, send to sleep*) adormecer; (*calm*) calmar. **—** *n* periodo *m* de calma

lullaby /ˈlʌləbaɪ/ *n* canción *f* de cuna

lumbago /lʌmˈbeɪgəʊ/ *n* lumbago *m*

lumber /ˈlʌmbə(r)/ *n* trastos *mpl* viejos; (*wood*) maderos *mpl*. **—** *vt*. **~ s.o.** with hacer que uno cargue con. **~jack** *n* leñador *m*

luminous /ˈluːmɪnəs/ *a* luminoso

lump[1] /lʌmp/ *n* protuberancia *f*; (*in liquid*) grumo *m*; (*of sugar*)

terrón m; (in throat) nudo m. —
vt. ~ together agrupar
lump² /lʌmp/ vt. ~ **it** (fam)
aguantarlo
lump: ~ **sum** n suma f global. ~y
a (sauce) grumoso; (bumpy) cubierto de protuberancias
lunacy /ˈluːnəsɪ/ n locura f
lunar /ˈluːnə(r)/ a lunar
lunatic /ˈluːnətɪk/ n loco m
lunch /lʌntʃ/ n comida f,
almuerzo m. —vi comer
luncheon /ˈlʌntʃən/ n comida f,
almuerzo m. ~ **meat** n carne f
en lata. ~ **voucher** n vale m de comida
lung /lʌŋ/ n pulmón m
lunge /lʌndʒ/ n arremetida f
lurch¹ /lɜːtʃ/ vi tambalearse
lurch² /lɜːtʃ/ n. **leave in the** ~
dejar en la estacada
lure /ljʊə(r)/ vt atraer. —n
(attraction) atractivo m
lurid /ˈljʊərɪd/ a chillón; (shocking) espeluznante
lurk /lɜːk/ vi esconderse; (in ambush) estar al acecho; (prowl)
rondar
luscious /ˈlʌʃəs/ a delicioso
lush /lʌʃ/ a exuberante. —n
(Amer, sl) borracho m
lust /lʌst/ n lujuria f; (fig) ansia
f. —vi. ~ **after** codiciar. ~**ful** a
lujurioso
lustre /ˈlʌstə(r)/ n lustre m
lusty /ˈlʌstɪ/ a (-ier, -iest) fuerte
lute /luːt/ n laúd m
Luxemburg /ˈlʌksəmbɜːg/ n Luxemburgo m
luxuriant /lʌɡˈzjʊərɪənt/ a exuberante
luxurious /lʌɡˈzjʊərɪəs/ a
lujoso. ~**y** /ˈlʌkʃərɪ/ n lujo m. —
a de lujo
lye /laɪ/ n lejía f
lying /ˈlaɪɪŋ/ see lie¹, lie². —n
mentiras fpl
lynch /lɪntʃ/ vt linchar
lynx /lɪŋks/ n lince m

lyre /ˈlaɪə(r)/ n lira f
lyric /ˈlɪrɪk/ a lírico. ~**al** a lírico.
~**ism** /-sɪzəm/ n lirismo m. ~**s**
npl letra f

M

MA abbr (Master of Arts) Master
m, grado m universitario entre
el de licenciado y doctor
mac /mæk/ n (fam) impermeable
m
macabre /məˈkɑːbrə/ a macabro
macaroni /mækəˈrəʊnɪ/ n macarrones mpl
macaroon /mækəˈruːn/ n mostachón m
mace¹ /meɪs/ n (staff) maza f
mace² /meɪs/ n (spice) macis f
Mach /mɑːk/ n. ~ (**number**) n
(número m de) Mach (m)
machiavellian /mækɪəˈvelɪən/ a
maquiavélico
machinations /mækɪˈneɪʃnz/ npl
maquinaciones fpl
machine /məˈʃiːn/ n máquina
f. —vt (sew) coser a máquina;
(tec) trabajar a máquina. ~**gun**
n ametralladora f. ~**ry** /məˈʃiː-
nərɪ/ n maquinaria f; (working
parts, fig) mecanismo m. ~ **tool**
n máquina f herramienta
machinist /məˈʃiːnɪst/ n maquinista m & f
machismo /mæˈtʃɪzməʊ/ n
machismo m. ~**o** a macho
mackerel /ˈmækrəl/ n invar
(fish) caballa f
mackintosh /ˈmækɪntɒʃ/ n
impermeable m
macrobiotic /mækrəʊbaɪˈɒtɪk/ a
macrobiótico

mad /mæd/ a (madder, maddest) loco; (foolish) insensato;
(dog) rabioso; (angry, fam)
furioso. **be** ~ **about** estar loco

por. **like** ~ como un loco; (a lot) muchísimo

Madagascar /mædə'gæskə(r)/ n Madagascar m

madam /'mædəm/ n señora f; (unmarried) señorita f

madcap /'mædkæp/ a atolondrado. —n locuelo m

madden /mædn/ vt (make mad) enloquecer; (make angry) enfurecer

made /meɪd/ see **make**. ~ **to measure** hecho a la medida

Madeira /mə'dɪərə/ n (wine) vino m de Madera

mad: ~**house** n manicomio m. ~**ly** adv (interested, in love etc) locamente; (frantically) como un loco. ~**man** n loco m. ~**ness** n locura f

madonna /mə'dɒnə/ n Virgen f María

madrigal /'mædrɪgl/ n madrigal m

maelstrom /'meɪlstrəm/ n remolino m

maestro /'maɪstrəʊ/ n (pl maestri /-stri:/ or os) maestro m

Mafia /'mæfɪə/ n mafia f

magazine /mægə'zi:n/ n revista f; (of gun) recámara f

magenta /mə'dʒentə/ a rojo purpúreo

maggot /'mægət/ n gusano m. ~**y** a agusanado

Magi /'meɪdʒaɪ/ npl. the ~ los Reyes mpl Magos

magic /'mædʒɪk/ n magia f. —a mágico. ~**al** a mágico. ~**ian** /mə'dʒɪʃn/ n mago m

magisterial /mædʒɪ'stɪərɪəl/ a magistral; (imperious) autoritario

magistrate /'mædʒɪstreɪt/ n magistrado m, juez m

magnanim|**ity** /mægnə'nɪmətɪ/ n magnanimidad f. ~**ous** /-'næn ɪməs/ a magnánimo

magnate /'mægneɪt/ n magnate m

magnesia /mæg'ni:ʒə/ n magnesia f

magnet /'mægnɪt/ n imán m. ~**ic** /-'netɪk/ a magnético. ~**ism** n magnetismo m. ~**ize** vt magnetizar

magnificen|**ce** /mæg'nɪfɪsns/ a magnificencia f. ~**t** a magnífico

magnif|**ication** /mægnɪfɪ'keɪʃn/ n aumento m. ~**ier** /-'faɪə(r)/ n lupa f, lente f de aumento. ~**y** /-'faɪ/ vt aumentar. ~**ying-glass** n lupa f, lente f de aumento

magnitude /'mægnɪtju:d/ n magnitud f

magnolia /mæg'nəʊlɪə/ n magnolia f

magnum /'mægnəm/ n botella f de litro y medio

magpie /'mægpaɪ/ n urraca f

mahogany /mə'hɒgənɪ/ n caoba f

maid /meɪd/ n (servant) criada f; (girl, old use) doncella f. **old** ~ solterona f

maiden /'meɪdn/ n doncella f. —a (aunt) soltera; (voyage) inaugural. ~**hood** n doncellez f, virginidad f, soltería f. ~**ly** adv virginal. ~ **name** n apellido m de soltera

mail[1] /meɪl/ n correo m; (letters) cartas fpl. —a postal, de correos. —vt (post) echar al correo; (send) enviar por correo

mail[2] /meɪl/ n (armour) (cota f de) malla f

mail: ~**ing list** n lista f de direcciones. ~**man** n (Amer) cartero m. ~ **order** n venta f por correo

maim /meɪm/ vt mutilar

main /meɪn/ n. (water/gas) ~ cañería f principal. **in the** ~ en su mayor parte. **the** ~**s** npl (elec) la red f eléctrica. —a principal. **a** ~ **road** n una carretera f. ~**land**

n continente *m*. ~**ly** *adv* principalmente. ~**spring** *n* muelle *m* real; (*fig, motive*) móvil *m* principal. ~**stay** *n* sostén *m*. ~**stream** *n* corriente *f* principal. ~ **street** *n* calle *f* principal

maintain /meɪnˈteɪn/ *vt* mantener

maintenance /ˈmeɪntənəns/ *n* mantenimiento *m*; (*allowance*) pensión *f* alimenticia

maisonette /meɪzəˈnet/ *n* (*small house*) casita *f*; (*part of house*) dúplex *m*

maize /meɪz/ *n* maíz *m*

majestic /məˈdʒestɪk/ *a* majestuoso

majesty /ˈmædʒəstɪ/ *n* majestad *f*

major /ˈmeɪdʒə(r)/ *a* mayor. **a ~ road** una calle *f* prioritaria. —*n* comandante *m*. —*vi*. ~ **in** (*univ, Amer*) especializarse en

Majorca /məˈdʒɔːkə/ *n* Mallorca *f*

majority /məˈdʒɒrɪtɪ/ *n* mayoría *f*. **the ~ of people** la mayoría *f* de la gente. ~ el mayoritario

make /meɪk/ *vt/i* (*pt* made) hacer; (*manufacture*) fabricar; ganar (*money*); tomar (*decision*); llegar a (*destination*). ~ **s.o. do sth** obligar a uno a hacer algo. **be made of** estar hecho de. **I cannot ~ anything of it** no me lo explico. **I ~ it two o'clock** yo tengo las dos. —*n* fabricación *f*; (*brand*) marca *f*. ~ **as if to** estar a punto de. ~ **believe** fingir. ~ **do** (*manage*) arreglarse. ~ **do with** (*content o.s.*) contentarse con. ~ **for** dirigirse a. ~ **good** *vi* tener éxito. —*vt* compensar; (*repair*) reparar. ~ **it** llegar; (*succeed*) tener éxito. ~ **it up** (*become reconciled*) hacer las paces. ~ **much of** dar mucha importancia a. ~ **off** escaparse (**with** con). ~ **out** *vt* distinguir; (*understand*) entender; (*draw*

up) extender; (*assert*) dar a entender. —*vi* arreglárselas. ~ **over** ceder (**to a**). ~ **up** formar; (*prepare*) preparar; inventar (*story*); (*apply cosmetics*) compensar. —*vi* hacer las paces. ~ **up** (*one's face*) maquillarse. ~ **up for** compensar; recuperar (*time*). ~ **up to** congraciarse con. ~**believe** *a* fingido, simulado. —*n* ficción *f*

maker /ˈmeɪkə(r)/ *n* fabricante *m* & *f*. **the M~** el Hacedor *m*, el Creador *m*

makeshift /ˈmeɪkʃɪft/ *n* expediente *m*. —*a* (*temporary*) provisional; (*improvised*) improvisado

make-up /ˈmeɪkʌp/ *n* maquillaje *m*

makeweight /ˈmeɪkweɪt/ *n* complemento *m*

making /ˈmeɪkɪŋ/ *n*. **be the ~ of** ser la causa del éxito de. **he has the ~s of** tiene madera de. **in the ~** en vías de formación

maladjust|ed /mæləˈdʒʌstɪd/ *a* inadaptado. ~**ment** *n* inadaptación *f*

maladministration /mæləd-mɪnɪˈstreɪʃn/ *n* mala administración *f*

malady /ˈmælədɪ/ *n* enfermedad *f*

malaise /mæˈleɪz/ *n* malestar *m*

malaria /məˈleərɪə/ *n* paludismo *m*

Malay /məˈleɪ/ *a & n* malayo (*m*). ~**sia** *n* Malasia *f*

male /meɪl/ *a* masculino; (*bot, tec*) macho. —*n* macho *m*; (*man*) varón *m*

malefactor /ˈmælɪfæktə(r)/ *n* malhechor *m*

malevolen|ce /məˈlevələns/ *n* malevolencia *f*. ~**t** *a* malévolo

malformation /mælfɔːˈmeɪʃn/ *n* malformación *f*. ~**ed** *a* deforme

malfunction /mælˈfʌŋkʃn/ *n* funcionamiento *m* defectuoso. —*vi* funcionar mal

malic|e /'mælɪs/ n rencor m.
bear s.o. ~e guardar rencor a
uno. **~ious** /mə'lɪʃəs/ a malévolo. **~iously** adv con
malevolencia

malign /mə'laɪn/ a maligno. —vt
calumniar

malignan|cy /mə'lɪgnənsɪ/ n
malignidad f. **~t** a maligno

malinger /mə'lɪŋgə(r)/ vi fingirse
enfermo. **~er** n enfermo m
fingido

malleable /'mælɪəbl/ a maleable

mallet /'mælɪt/ n mazo m

malnutrition /mælnjuː'trɪʃn/ n
desnutrición f

malpractice /mæl'præktɪs/ n
falta f profesional

malt /mɔːlt/ n malta f

Malt|a /'mɔːltə/ n Malta f. **~ese**
/-'tiːz/ a & n maltés (m)

maltreat /mæl'triːt/ vt maltratar.
~ment n maltrato m

malt whisky /mɔːlt'wɪskɪ/ n
güisqui m de malta

mammal /'mæml/ n mamífero m

mammoth /'mæməθ/ n mamut
m. —a gigantesco

man /mæn/ n (pl **men**) hombre
m; (in sports team) jugador m;
(chess) pieza f. **~ in the street**
hombre m de la calle. **to ~** de
hombre a hombre. —vt (pt
manned) guarnecer (de hombres); tripular ⟨ship⟩; servir
⟨guns⟩

manacle /'mænəkl/ n manilla
f. —vt poner esposas a

manage /'mænɪdʒ/ vt dirigir; llevar ⟨shop, affairs⟩; (handle)
manejar. —vi arreglárselas. **~
to do** lograr hacer. **~able** a
manejable. **~ment** n dirección f

manager /'mænɪdʒə(r)/ n director m; (of actor) empresario m.
~ess /-'res/ n directora f. **~ial**
/-'dʒɪərɪəl/ a directivo. **~ial
staff** n personal m dirigente

managing director /'mænɪdʒɪŋ
daɪ'rektə(r)/ n director m
gerente

mandarin /'mændərɪn/ n mandarín m; (orange) mandarina f

mandate /'mændeɪt/ n mandato
m

mandatory /'mændətərɪ/ a obligatorio

mane /meɪn/ n (of horse) crin f;
(of lion) melena f

manful /'mænfl/ a valiente

manganese /'mæŋgəniːz/ n man-
ganeso m

manger /'meɪndʒə(r)/ n pesebre
m

mangle¹ /'mæŋgl/ n (for wring-
ing) exprimidor m; (for smooth-
ing) máquina f de planchar

mangle² /'mæŋgl/ vt destrozar

mango /'mæŋgəʊ/ n (pl **-oes**)
mango m

mangy /'meɪndʒɪ/ a sarnoso

man: **~handle** vt maltratar.
~hole n registro m. **~hole
cover** n tapa f de registro.
~hood n edad f viril; (quality)
virilidad f. **~-hour** n hora-
hombre f. **~-hunt** n persecución
f

mania /'meɪnɪə/ n manía f. **~c**
/-ræk/ n maníaco m

manicur|e /'mænɪkjʊə(r)/ n
manicura f. —vt hacer la manicura a ⟨person⟩. **~ist** n manicuro
m

manifest /'mænɪfest/ a manifiesto. —vt mostrar. **~ation**
/-'steɪʃn/ n manifestación f

manifesto /mænɪ'festəʊ/ n (pl
-os) manifiesto m

manifold /'mænɪfəʊld/ a
múltiple

manipulat|e /mə'nɪpjʊleɪt/ vt
manipular. **~ion** /-'leɪʃn/ n mani-
pulación f

mankind /mæn'kaɪnd/ n la
humanidad f

man: ~**ly** *adv* viril. ~**made** *a* artificial

mannequin /ˈmænɪkɪn/ *n* maniquí *m*

manner /ˈmænə/ *n* manera *f*; (*behaviour*) comportamiento *m*; (*kind*) clase *f*. ~**ed** *a* amanerado. **bad-**~**ed** *a* mal educado. ~**s** *npl* (*social behaviour*) educación *f*. **have no** ~**s** no tener educación

mannerism /ˈmænərɪzəm/ *n* peculiaridad *f*

mannish /ˈmænɪʃ/ *a* (*woman*) hombruna

manoevre /məˈnuːvə(r)/ *n* maniobra *f*. —*vt/i* maniobrar

man-of-war /ˈmænəvˈwɔː(r)/ *n* buque *m* de guerra

manor /ˈmænə(r)/ *n* casa *f* solariega

manpower /ˈmænpaʊə(r)/ *n* mano *f* de obra

manservant /ˈmænsɜːvənt/ *n* criado *m*

mansion /ˈmænʃn/ *n* mansión *f*

man: ~**size(d)** *a* grande. ~**slaughter** *n* homicidio *m* impremeditado

mantelpiece /ˈmæntlpiːs/ *n* repisa *f* de chimenea

mantilla /mænˈtɪlə/ *n* mantilla *f*

mantle /ˈmæntl/ *n* manto *m*

manual /ˈmænjʊəl/ *a* manual. —*n* (*handbook*) manual *m*

manufacture /ˌmænjʊˈfæktʃə(r)/ *vt* fabricar. —*n* fabricación *f*. ~**r** /-ə(r)/ *n* fabricante *m*

manure /məˈnjʊə(r)/ *n* estiércol *m*

manuscript /ˈmænjʊskrɪpt/ *n* manuscrito *m*

many /ˈmenɪ/ *a* & *n* muchos (*mpl*). ~ **people** mucha gente *f*. ~ **a time** muchas veces. **a great/good** ~ muchísimos

map /mæp/ *n* mapa *m*; (*of streets etc*) plano *m*. —*vt* (*pt* **mapped**) levantar un mapa de. ~ **out** organizar

maple /ˈmeɪpl/ *n* arce *m*

mar /mɑː/ *vt* (*pt* **marred**) estropear; aguar ⟨*enjoyment*⟩

marathon /ˈmærəθən/ *n* maratón *m*

maraud|er /məˈrɔːdə(r)/ *n* merodeador *m*. ~**ing** *a* merodeador

marble /ˈmɑːbl/ *n* mármol *m*; (*for game*) canica *f*

March /mɑːtʃ/ *n* marzo *m*

march /mɑːtʃ/ *vi* (*mil*) marchar. ~ **off** irse. —*vt*. ~ **off** (*lead away*) llevarse. —*n* marcha *f*

marchioness /ˌmɑːʃəˈnes/ *n* marquesa *f*

march-past /ˈmɑːtʃpɑːst/ *n* desfile *m*

mare /meə(r)/ *n* yegua *f*

margarine /ˌmɑːdʒəˈriːn/ *n* margarina *f*

margin /ˈmɑːdʒɪn/ *n* margen *f*. ~**al** *a* marginal. ~**al seat** *n* (*pol*) escaño *m* inseguro. ~**ally** *adv* muy poco

marguerite /ˌmɑːɡəˈriːt/ *n* margarita *f*

marigold /ˈmærɪɡəʊld/ *n* caléndula *f*

marijuana /ˌmærɪˈhwɑːnə/ *n* marihuana *f*

marina /məˈriːnə/ *n* puerto *m* deportivo

marina|de /ˌmærɪˈneɪd/ *n* escabeche *m*. ~**te** /ˈmærɪneɪt/ *vt* escabechar

marine /məˈriːn/ *a* marino. —*n* (*sailor*) soldado *m* de infantería de marina; (*shipping*) marina *f*

marionette /ˌmærɪəˈnet/ *n* marioneta *f*

marital /ˈmærɪtl/ *a* marital, matrimonial. ~ **status** *n* estado *m* civil

maritime /ˈmærɪtaɪm/ *a* marítimo

marjoram /ˈmɑːdʒərəm/ *n* mejorana *f*

mark[1] /mɑːk/ *n* marca *f*; (*trace*) huella *f*; (*schol*) nota *f*; (*target*) blanco *m*. —*vt* marcar; poner nota a (*exam*). ~ **time** marcar el paso. ~ **out** trazar; escoger (*person*)

mark² /mɑːk/ *n* (*currency*) marco *m*

marked /mɑːkt/ *a* marcado. ~**ly** /-kɪdlɪ/ *adv* marcadamente

marker /'mɑːkə(r)/ *n* marcador *m*; (*for book*) registro *m*

market /'mɑːkɪt/ *n* mercado *m*. **on the** ~ en venta. —*vt* (*sell*) vender; (*launch*) comercializar. ~ **garden** *n* huerto *m*. ~**ing** *n* marketing *m*

marking /'mɑːkɪŋ/ *n* (*marks*) marcas *fpl*

marksman /'mɑːksmən/ *n* tirador *m*. ~**ship** *n* puntería *f*

marmalade /'mɑːməleɪd/ *n* mermelada *f* de naranja

marmot /'mɑːmət/ *n* marmota *f*

maroon /mə'ruːn/ *n* granate *m*. —*a* de color granate

marooned /mə'ruːnd/ *a* abandonado; (*snow-bound etc*) aislado

marquee /mɑː'kiː/ *n* tienda de campaña *f* grande; (*awning, Amer*) marquesina *f*

marquetry /'mɑːkɪtrɪ/ *n* marquetería *f*

marquis /'mɑːkwɪs/ *n* marqués *m*

marriage /'mærɪdʒ/ *n* matrimonio *m*; (*wedding*) boda *f*. ~**able** *a* casadero

married /'mærɪd/ *a* casado; (*life*) conjugal

marrow /'mærəʊ/ *n* (*of bone*) tuétano *m*; (*vegetable*) calabacín *m*

marry /'mærɪ/ *vt* casarse con; (*give or unite in marriage*) casar. —*vi* casarse. **get married** casarse

marsh /mɑːʃ/ *n* pantano *m*

marshal /'mɑːʃl/ *n* (*mil*) mariscal *m*; (*master of ceremonies*) maestro *m* de ceremonias; (*at sports*

events) oficial *m*. —*vt* (*pt marshalled*) ordenar; formar (*troops*)

marsh mallow /mɑːʃ'mæləʊ/ *n* (*plant*) malvavisco *m*

marshmallow /mɑːʃ'mæləʊ/ *n* (*sweet*) caramelo *m* blando

marshy /'mɑːʃɪ/ *a* pantanoso

martial /'mɑːʃl/ *a* marcial. ~ **law** *n* ley *f* marcial

Martian /'mɑːʃn/ *a* & *n* marciano (*m*)

martinet /mɑːtɪ'net/ *n* ordenancista *m* & *f*

martyr /'mɑːtə(r)/ *n* mártir *m* & *f*. —*vt* martirizar. ~**dom** *n* martirio *m*

marvel /'mɑːvl/ *n* maravilla *f*. —*vi* (*pt marvelled*) maravillarse (**at** con, de). ~**lous** /'mɑːvələs/ *a* maravilloso

Marxis|m /'mɑːksɪzəm/ *n* marxismo *m*. ~**t** *a* & *n* marxista (*m* & *f*)

marzipan /'mɑːzɪpæn/ *n* mazapán *m*

mascara /mæ'skɑːrə/ *n* rimel *m*

mascot /'mæskɒt/ *n* mascota *f*

masculin|e /'mæskjʊlɪn/ *a* & *n* masculino (*m*). ~**ity** /-'lɪnɪtɪ/ *n* masculinidad *f*

mash /mæʃ/ *n* mezcla *f*; (*potatoes, fam*) puré *m* de patatas. —*vt* (*crush*) machacar; (*mix*) mezclar. ~**ed potatoes** *n* puré *m* de patatas

mask /mɑːsk/ *n* máscara *f*. —*vt* enmascarar

masochis|m /'mæsəkɪzəm/ *n* masoquismo *m*. ~**t** *n* masoquista *m* & *f*

mason /'meɪsn/ *n* (*builder*) albañil *m*

Mason /'meɪsn/ *n*. ~ **masón** *m*. ~**ic** /mə'sɒnɪk/ *a* masónico

masonry /'meɪsnrɪ/ *n* albañilería *f*

masquerade /mɑːskə'reɪd/ n mascarada f. —vi. ~ **as** hacerse pasar por

mass[1] /mæs/ n masa f; (large quantity) montón m. **the ~es** npl las masas fpl. —vt/i agrupar(se)

mass[2] /mæs/ n (relig) misa f. **high ~** misa f mayor

massacre /'mæsəkə(r)/ n masacre f, matanza f. —vt masacrar

massage /'mæsɑːʒ/ n masaje m. —vt dar masaje a

masseu r /mæ'sɜː(r)/ n masajista m. ~**se** /mæ'sɜːz/ n masajista f

massive /'mæsɪv/ a massive; (heavy) macizo; (huge) enorme

mass: ~ **media** n medios mpl de comunicación. ~-**produce** vt fabricar en serie

mast /mɑːst/ n mástil m; (for radio, TV) torre f

master /'mɑːstə(r)/ n maestro m; (in secondary school) profesor m; (of ship) capitán m. —vt dominar. ~-**key** n llave f maestra. ~**ly** a magistral. ~**mind** n cerebro m. —vt dirigir. **M~ of Arts** master m, grado m universitario entre el de licenciado y el de doctor

masterpiece /'mɑːstəpiːs/ n obra f maestra

master-stroke /'mɑːstəstrəʊk/ n golpe m maestro

mastery /'mɑːstərɪ/ n dominio m; (skill) maestría f

masturbat e /'mæstəbeɪt/ vi masturbarse. ~**ion** /-'beɪʃn/ n masturbación f

mat /mæt/ n estera f; (at door) felpudo m

match[1] /mætʃ/ n (sport) partido m; (equal) igual m; (marriage) matrimonio m; (s.o. to marry) partido m. —vt emparejar; (equal) igualar; (clothes, colours) hacer juego con. —vi hacer juego

match[2] /mætʃ/ n (of wood) fósforo m; (of wax) cerilla f. ~**box** /'mætʃbɒks/ n (for wooden matches) caja f de fósforos; (for wax matches) caja f de cerillas

matching /'mætʃɪŋ/ a que hace juego

mate[1] /meɪt/ n compañero m; (of animals) macho m, hembra f; (assistant) ayudante m. —vt/i acoplar(se)

mate[2] /meɪt/ n (chess) mate m

material /mə'tɪərɪəl/ n material m; (cloth) tela f. —a material; (fig) importante. ~**istic** /-'lɪstɪk/ a materialista. ~**s** npl materiales mpl. **raw** ~**s** npl materias fpl primas

materialize /mə'tɪərɪəlaɪz/ vi materializarse

maternal /mə'tɜːnl/ a maternal; (relation) materno

maternity /mə'tɜːnɪtɪ/ n maternidad f. —a de maternidad. ~ **clothes** npl vestido m premamá. ~ **hospital** n maternidad f

matey /'meɪtɪ/ a (fam) simpático

mathematic ian /mæθəmə'tɪʃn/ n matemático m. ~**al** /-'mætɪkl/ a matemático. ~**s** /-'mætɪks/ n & npl matemáticas fpl

maths /mæθs/, **math** (Amer) n npl matemáticas fpl

matinée /'mætɪneɪ/ n función f de tarde

matriculat e /mə'trɪkjʊleɪt/ vt/i matricular(se). ~**ion** /-'leɪʃn/ n matriculación f

matrimon ial /mætrɪ'məʊnɪəl/ a matrimonial. ~**y** /'mætrɪmənɪ/ n matrimonio m

matrix /'meɪtrɪks/ n (pl matrices /-sɪːz/) matriz f

matron /'meɪtrən/ n (married, elderly) matrona f; (in school) ama f de llaves; (former use, in hospital) enfermera f jefe. ~**ly** a matronil

matt /mæt/ a mate

matted /'mætɪd/ a enmarañado

matter /'mætə(r)/ n (substance) materia f; (affair) asunto m; (pus) pus m. **as a ~ of fact** en realidad. **no ~** no importa. **what is the ~?** ¿qué pasa? —vi importar. **it does not ~** no importa. **~-of-fact** a realista

matting /'mætɪŋ/ n estera f

mattress /'mætrɪs/ n colchón m

mature /mə'tjʊə(r)/ a maduro. —vt/i madurar. **~ity** n madurez f

maul /mɔːl/ vt maltratar

Mauritius /mɔ'rɪʃəs/ n Mauricio m

mausoleum /mɔːsə'lɪəm/ n mausoleo m

mauve /məʊv/ a & n color (m) de malva

mawkish /'mɔːkɪʃ/ a empalagoso

maxim /'mæksɪm/ n máxima f

maxim|ize /'mæksɪmaɪz/ vt llevar al máximo. **~um** a & n (pl -ima) máximo (m)

may /meɪ/ v aux (pt might) poder. **~ I smoke?** ¿se permite fumar? **~ he be happy** ¡que sea feliz! **he ~/might come** puede que venga. **I ~/might as well stay** más vale quedarme. **it ~/might be true** puede ser verdad

May /meɪ/ n mayo m. **~ Day** n el primero m de mayo

maybe /'meɪbɪ/ adv quizá(s)

mayhem /'meɪhem/ n (havoc) alboroto m

mayonnaise /meɪə'neɪz/ n mayonesa f

mayor /meə(r)/ n alcalde m, alcaldesa f. **~ess** n alcaldesa f

maze /meɪz/ n laberinto m

me[1] /miː/ pron me; (after prep) mí. **he knows ~** me conoce. **it's ~** soy yo

me[2] /miː/ n (mus, third note of any musical scale) mi m

meadow /'medəʊ/ n prado m

meagre /'miːgə(r)/ a escaso

meal[1] /miːl/ n comida f

meal[2] /miːl/ n (grain) harina f

mealy-mouthed /miːlɪ'maʊðd/ a hipócrita

mean[1] /miːn/ vt (pt meant) (intend) tener la intención de, querer; (signify) querer decir, significar. **~ to do** tener la intención de hacer. **~ well** tener buenas intenciones. **be meant for** estar destinado a

mean[2] /miːn/ a (-er, -est) (miserly) tacaño; (unkind) malo; (poor) pobre

mean[3] /miːn/ a medio. —n medio m; (average) promedio m

meander /mɪ'ændə(r)/ vi (river) serpentear; (person) vagar

meaning /'miːnɪŋ/ n sentido m. **~ful** a significativo. **~less** a sin sentido

meanness /'miːnnɪs/ n (miserliness) tacañería f; (unkindness) maldad f

means /miːnz/ n medio m. **by all ~** por supuesto. **by no ~** de ninguna manera. —npl (wealth) recursos mpl. **~ test** n investigación f financial

meant /ment/ see **mean**[1]

meantime /'miːntaɪm/ adv entretanto. **in the ~** entretanto

meanwhile /'miːnwaɪl/ adv entretanto

measles /'miːzlz/ n sarampión m

measly /'miːzlɪ/ a (sl) miserable

measurable /'meʒərəbl/ a mensurable

measure /'meʒə(r)/ n medida f; (ruler) regla f. —vt/i medir. **~ up to** estar a la altura de. **~d** a (rhythmical) acompasado; (carefully considered) prudente. **~ment** n medida f

meat /miːt/ n carne f. **~y** a carnoso; (fig) sustancioso mechanic /mɪˈkænɪk/ n mecánico m. ~al /mɪˈkænɪkl/ a mecánico. ~s n mecánica f

mechanism /ˈmekənɪzəm/ n mecanismo m. ~ze vt mecanizar

medal /ˈmedl/ n medalla f

medallion /mɪˈdælɪən/ n medallón m

medallist /ˈmedəlɪst/ n ganador m de una medalla. be a gold ~ ganar una medalla de oro

meddle /ˈmedl/ vi entrometerse (in en); (tinker) tocar. ~ with (tinker) tocar. ~some a entrometido

media /ˈmiːdɪə/ see medium. —npl. the ~ npl los medios mpl de comunicación

mediate /ˈmiːdɪeɪt/ vi mediar. ~ion /-ˈeɪʃn/ n mediación f. ~or n mediador m

medical /ˈmedɪkl/ a médico; (student) de medicina. —n (fam) reconocimiento m médico

medicated /ˈmedɪkeɪtɪd/ a medicinal. ~ion /-ˈkeɪʃn/ n medicación f

medicine /ˈmedsɪn/ n medicina f. ~al /mɪˈdɪsɪnl/ a medicinal

medieval /medɪˈiːvl/ a medieval

mediocre /miːdɪˈəʊkə(r)/ a mediocre. ~ity /-ˈɒkrətɪ/ n mediocridad f

meditate /ˈmedɪteɪt/ vt/i meditar. ~ion /-ˈteɪʃn/ n meditación f

Mediterranean /medɪtəˈreɪnɪən/ a mediterráneo. —n. the ~ el Mediterráneo m

medium /ˈmiːdɪəm/ n (pl media) medio m; (pl mediums) (person) médium m. —a mediano

medley /ˈmedlɪ/ n popurrí m

meek /miːk/ a (-er, -est) manso

meet /miːt/ vt (pt met) encontrar; (bump into s.o.) encontrarse con; (see again) ver; (fetch) ir a buscar; (get to know, be introduced to) conocer. ~ the

bill pagar la cuenta. —vi encontrarse; (get to know) conocerse; (in session) reunirse. ~ with tropezar con (obstacles)

meeting /ˈmiːtɪŋ/ n reunión f; (accidental between two people) encuentro m; (arranged between two people) cita f

megalomania /megələʊˈmeɪnɪə/ n megalomanía f

megaphone /ˈmegəfəʊn/ n megáfono m

melancholic /melənˈkɒlɪk/ a melancólico. ~y /ˈmelənkɒlɪ/ n melancolía f. —a melancólico

mêlée /ˈmeleɪ/ n pelea f confusa

mellow /ˈmeləʊ/ a (-er, -est) (fruit, person) maduro; (sound, colour) dulce. —vt/i madurar(se)

melodic /mɪˈlɒdɪk/ a melódico. ~ous /mɪˈləʊdɪəs/ a melodioso

melodrama /ˈmelədrɑːmə/ n melodrama m. ~tic /-əˈmætɪk/ a melodramático

melody /ˈmelədɪ/ n melodía f

melon /ˈmelən/ n melón m

melt /melt/ vt (make liquid) derretir; fundir (metals). —vi (become liquid) derretirse; (metals) fundirse. ~ing-pot n crisol m

member /ˈmembə(r)/ n miembro m. M~ of Parliament n diputado m. ~ship n calidad f de miembro; (members) miembros mpl

membrane /ˈmembreɪn/ n membrana f

memento /mɪˈmentəʊ/ n (pl -oes) recuerdo m

memo /ˈmeməʊ/ n (pl -os) (fam) nota f

memoir /ˈmemwɑː(r)/ n memoria f

memorable /ˈmemərəbl/ a memorable

memorandum /meməˈrændəm/ n (pl -ums) nota f

memorial /mɪ'mɔːrɪəl/ n monumento m. —a conmemorativo

memorize /'meməraɪz/ vt aprender de memoria

memory /'meməri/ n (faculty) memoria f; (thing remembered) recuerdo m. **from ~ de** memoria. **in ~ of** en memoria de

men /men/ see **man**

menace /'menəs/ n amenaza f; (nuisance) pesado m. —vt amenazar. **~ingly** adv de manera amenazadora

menagerie /mɪ'nædʒəri/ n casa f de fieras

mend /mend/ vt reparar; (darn) zurcir. **~ one's ways** enmendarse. —n remiendo m. **be on the ~** ir mejorando

menfolk /'menfəʊk/ n hombres mpl

menial /'miːnɪəl/ a servil

meningitis /menɪn'dʒaɪtɪs/ n meningitis f

menopause /'menəpɔːz/ n menopausia f

menstruat|e /'menstrʊeɪt/ vi menstruar. **~ion** /-'eɪʃn/ n menstruación f

mental /'mentl/ a mental; (hospital) psiquiátrico

mentality /men'tæləti/ n mentalidad f

menthol /'menθɒl/ n mentol m. **~ated** a mentolado

mention /'menʃn/ vt mencionar. **don't ~ it!** ¡no hay de qué! —n mención f

mentor /'mentɔː(r)/ n mentor m

menu /'menjuː/ n (set meal) menú m; (a la carte) lista f (de platos)

mercantile /'mɜːkəntaɪl/ a mercantil

mercenary /'mɜːsɪnəri/ a & n mercenario (m)

merchandise /'mɜːtʃəndaɪz/ n mercancías fpl

merchant /'mɜːtʃənt/ n comerciante m. —a (ship, navy) mercante. **~ bank** n banco m mercantil

merci|ful /'mɜːsɪfl/ a misericordioso. **~fully** adv (fortunately, fam) gracias a Dios. **~less** /'mɜːsɪlɪs/ a despiadado

mercur|ial /mɜː'kjʊərɪəl/ a mercurial; (fig, active) vivo. **~y** /'mɜːkjʊrɪ/ n mercurio m

mercy /'mɜːsɪ/ n compasión f. **at the ~ of** a merced de

mere /mɪə(r)/ a simple. **~ly** adv simplemente

merest /'mɪərɪst/ a mínimo

merge /mɜːdʒ/ vt unir; fusionar (companies). —vi unirse; (companies) fusionarse. **~r** /-ə(r)/ n fusión f

meridian /mə'rɪdɪən/ n meridiano m

meringue /mə'ræŋ/ n merengue m

merit /'merɪt/ n mérito m. —vt (pt merited) merecer. **~orious** /-'tɔːrɪəs/ a meritorio

mermaid /'mɜːmeɪd/ n sirena f

merr|ily /'merɪlɪ/ adv alegremente. **~iment** /'merɪmənt/ n alegría f. **~y** /'meri/ a (-ier, -iest) alegre. **make ~** divertirse. **~y-go-round** n tiovivo m. **~y-making** n holgorio m

mesh /meʃ/ n malla f; (network) red f

mesmerize /'mezməraɪz/ vt hipnotizar

mess /mes/ n desorden m; (dirt) suciedad f; (mil) rancho m. **make a ~ of** chapucear, estropear. —vt. **~ up** desordenar; (dirty) ensuciar. —vi. **~ about** entretenerse. **~ with** (tinker with) manosear

message /'mesɪdʒ/ n recado m

messenger /'mesɪndʒə(r)/ n mensajero m

Messiah /mɪ'saɪə/ n Mesías m

Messrs /'mesəz/ *npl.* ~ Smith los señores *mpl* or Sres. Smith

messy /'mesɪ/ *a* (-ier, -iest) en desorden; (*dirty*) sucio

met /met/ *see* **meet**

metabolism /mɪ'tæbəlɪzəm/ *n* metabolismo *m*

metal /'metl/ *n* metal. —*a* de metal. ~**lic** /mɪ'tælɪk/ *a* metálico

metallurgy /mɪ'tælədʒɪ/ *n* metalurgia *f*

metamorphosis /metə'mɔːfəsɪs/ *n* (*pl* -**phoses** /-sɪːz/) metamorfosis *f*

metaphor /'metəfə(r)/ *n* metáfora *f*. ~**ical** /-'fɒrɪkl/ *a* metafórico

mete /miːt/ *vt.* ~ **out** repartir; dar (*punishment*)

meteor /'miːtɪə(r)/ *n* meteoro *m*

meteorite /'miːtɪəraɪt/ *n* meteorito *m*

meteorological /miːtɪərə'lɒdʒɪkl/ *a* meteorológico. ~**y** /-'rɒlədʒɪ/ *n* meteorología *f*

meter[1] /'miːtə(r)/ *n* contador *m*

meter[2] /'miːtə(r)/ *n* (*Amer*) = **metre**

method /'meθəd/ *n* método *m*

methodical /mɪ'θɒdɪkl/ *a* metódico

Methodist /'meθədɪst/ *a & n* metodista (*m & f*)

methylated /'meθɪleɪtɪd/ *a.* ~ **spirit** *n* alcohol *m* desnaturalizado

meticulous /mɪ'tɪkjʊləs/ *a* meticuloso

metre /'miːtə(r)/ *n* metro *m*

metric /'metrɪk/ *a* métrico. ~**ation** /-'keɪʃn/ *n* cambio *m* al sistema métrico

metropolis /mɪ'trɒpəlɪs/ *n* metrópoli *f*

metropolitan /metrə'pɒlɪtən/ *a* metropolitano

mettle /'metl/ *n* valor *m*

mew /mjuː/ *n* maullido *m*. —*vi* maullar

mews /mjuːz/ *npl* casas *fpl* pequeñas (que antes eran caballerizas)

Mexican /'meksɪkən/ *a & n* mejicano (*m*); (*in Mexico*) mexicano (*m*). ~**o** /-kəʊ/ *n* Méjico *m*; (*in Mexico*) México *m*

mezzanine /'metsəniːn/ *n* entresuelo *m*

mi /miː/ *n* (*mus, third note of any musical scale*) mi *m*

miaow /miː'aʊ/ *n & vi* = **mew**

mice /maɪs/ *see* **mouse**

mickey /'mɪkɪ/ *n.* **take the** ~ **out of** (*sl*) tomar el pelo a

micro... /'maɪkrəʊ/ *pref* micro...

microbe /'maɪkrəʊb/ *n* microbio *m*

microchip /'maɪkrəʊtʃɪp/ *n* pastilla *f*

microfilm /'maɪkrəʊfɪlm/ *n* microfilme *m*

microphone /'maɪkrəfəʊn/ *n* micrófono *m*

microprocessor /maɪkrəʊ'prəʊsesə(r)/ *n* microprocesador *m*

microscope /'maɪkrəskəʊp/ *n* microscopio *m.* ~**ic** /-'skɒpɪk/ *a* microscópico

microwave /'maɪkrəʊweɪv/ *n* microonda *f.* ~ **oven** *n* horno *m* de microondas

mid /mɪd/ *a.* **in** ~ **air** en pleno aire. **in** ~ **March** a mediados de marzo. **in** ~ **ocean** en medio del océano

midday /'mɪddeɪ/ *n* mediodía *m*

middle /'mɪdl/ *a* de en medio; (*quality*) mediano. —*n* medio *m.* **in the** ~ **of** en medio de. ~**-aged** *a* de mediana edad. **M**~ **Ages** *npl* Edad *f* Media. ~ **class** *n* clase *f* media. ~**class** *a* de la clase media. **M**~ **East** *n* Oriente *m* Medio. ~**man** *n* intermediario *m*

middling /'mɪdlɪŋ/ *a* regular

midge /mɪdʒ/ *n* mosquito *m*

midget /'mɪdʒɪt/ n enano m. —a minúsculo

Midlands /'mɪdləndz/ npl región f central de Inglaterra

midnight /'mɪdnaɪt/ n medianoche f

midriff /'mɪdrɪf/ n diafragma m; (fam) vientre m

midst /mɪdst/ n. in our ~ entre nosotros. in the ~ of en medio de

midsummer /mɪd'sʌmə(r)/ n pleno verano m; (solstice) solsticio m de verano

midway /mɪd'weɪ/ adv a medio camino

midwife /'mɪdwaɪf/ n comadrona f

midwinter /mɪd'wɪntə(r)/ n pleno invierno m

might[1] /maɪt/ see **may**

might[2] /maɪt/ n (strength) fuerza f; (power) poder m. ~y a (strong) fuerte; (powerful) poderoso; (very great, fam) enorme. —adv (fam) muy

migraine /'mi:greɪn/ n jaqueca f

migrant /'maɪgrənt/ a migratorio. —n (person) emigrante m & f

migrat|**e** /maɪ'greɪt/ vi emigrar. ~**ion** /-ʃn/ n migración f

mike /maɪk/ n (fam) micrófono m

mild /maɪld/ a (-er, -est) (person) apacible; (climate) templado; (slight) ligero; (taste) suave; (illness) benigno

mildew /'mɪldju:/ n moho m

mild: ~**ly** adv (slightly) ligeramente. ~**ness** n (of person) apacibilidad f; (of climate, illness) benignidad f; (of taste) suavidad f

mile /maɪl/ n milla f. ~**s better** (fam) mucho mejor. ~**s too big** (fam) demasiado grande. ~**age** n (loosely) kilometraje m

~**stone** n mojón m; (event, stage, fig) hito m

milieu /mɪ'ljɜ:/ n ambiente m

militant /'mɪlɪtənt/ a & n militante (m & f)

military /'mɪlɪtərɪ/ a militar

militate /'mɪlɪteɪt/ vi militar (**against** contra)

militia /mɪ'lɪʃə/ n milicia f

milk /mɪlk/ n leche f. —a (product) lácteo; (chocolate) con leche. —vt ordeñar (cow); (exploit) chupar. ~**man** n repartidor m de leche. ~ **shake** n batido m de leche. ~**y** a lechoso. **M~y Way** n Vía f Láctea

mill /mɪl/ n molino m; (for coffee, pepper) molinillo m; (factory) fábrica f. —vt moler. —vi. ~ **about/around** apiñarse, circular

millennium /mɪ'lenɪəm/ n (pl -ia or -iums) milenio m

miller /'mɪlə(r)/ n molinero m

millet /'mɪlɪt/ n mijo m

milli... /'mɪlɪ/ pref mili...

milligram(me) /'mɪlɪgræm/ n miligramo m

millimetre /'mɪlɪmi:tə(r)/ n milímetro m

milliner /'mɪlɪnə(r)/ n sombrerero m

million /'mɪlɪən/ n millón m. **a ~ pounds** un millón m de libras. ~**aire** n millonario m

millstone /'mɪlstəʊn/ n muela f (de molino); (fig, burden) losa f

mime /maɪm/ n pantomima f. —vt hacer en pantomima. —vi actuar de mimo

mimic /'mɪmɪk/ vt (pt **mimicked**) imitar. —n imitador m. ~**ry** n imitación f

mimosa /mɪ'məʊzə/ n mimosa f

minaret /mɪnə'ret/ n alminar m

mince /mɪns/ vt desmenuzar; picar (meat). **not to ~ matters/words** no tener pelos en la lengua. —n carne f picada.

∼**meat** n conserva f de fruta picada. **make** ∼**meat of s.o.** hacer trizas a uno. ∼ **pie** n pastel m con frutas picadas. ∼**r** n máquina f de picar carne

mind /maɪnd/ n mente f; (sanity) juicio m; (opinion) parecer m; (intention) intención f. **be on one's** ∼ preocuparle a uno. —vt (look after) cuidar; (heed) hacer caso de. **I don't** ∼ me da igual. **I don't** ∼ **the noise** no me molesta el ruido. **never** ∼ no te preocupes, no se preocupe. ∼**er** n cuidador m. ∼**ful** a atento (of a). ∼**less** a estúpido

mine[1] /maɪn/ poss pron (el) mío m, (la) mía f, (los) míos mpl, (las) mías fpl. **it is** ∼ es mío

mine[2] /maɪn/ n mina f. —vt extraer. ∼**field** n campo m de minas. ∼**r** n minero m

mineral /ˈmɪnərəl/ a & n mineral (m). ∼ (**water**) n (fizzy soft drink) gaseosa f. ∼ **water** n (natural) agua f mineral

minesweeper /ˈmaɪnswiːpə(r)/ n (ship) dragaminas m invar

mingle /ˈmɪŋgl/ vt/i mezclar(se)

mingy /ˈmɪndʒɪ/ a tacaño

mini... /ˈmɪnɪ/ pref mini...

miniature /ˈmɪnɪtʃə(r)/ a & n miniatura (f)

mini: ∼**bus** n microbús m. ∼**cab** n taxi m

minim /ˈmɪnɪm/ n (mus) blanca f

minimal /ˈmɪnɪml/ a mínimo. ∼**ize** vt minimizar. ∼**um** a & n (pl -ima) mínimo (m)

mining /ˈmaɪnɪŋ/ n explotación f. —a minero

miniskirt /ˈmɪnɪskɜːt/ n minifalda f

minister /ˈmɪnɪstə(r)/ n ministro m; (relig) pastor m. ∼**erial** /-ˈstɪərɪəl/ a ministerial. ∼**ry** n ministerio m

mink /mɪŋk/ n visón m

minor /ˈmaɪnə(r)/ a (incl mus) menor; (of little importance) sin importancia. —n menor m & f de edad

minority /maɪˈnɒrɪtɪ/ n minoría f. —a minoritario

minster /ˈmɪnstə(r)/ n catedral f

minstrel /ˈmɪnstrəl/ n juglar m

mint[1] /mɪnt/ n (plant) menta f; (sweet) caramelo m de menta

mint[2] /mɪnt/ n. **the M**∼ n casa f de la moneda. **a** ∼ un dineral m. —vt acuñar. **in** ∼ **condition** como nuevo

minuet /mɪnjuˈet/ n minué m

minus /ˈmaɪnəs/ prep menos; (without, fam) sin. —n (sign) menos m. ∼ **sign** n menos m

minuscule /ˈmɪnəskjuːl/ a minúsculo

minute[1] /ˈmɪnɪt/ n minuto m. ∼**s** npl (of meeting) actas fpl

minute[2] /maɪˈnjuːt/ a minúsculo; (detailed) minucioso

minx /mɪŋks/ n chica f descarada

miracle /ˈmɪrəkl/ n milagro m. ∼**ulous** /mɪˈrækjələs/ a milagroso

mirage /ˈmɪrɑːʒ/ n espejismo m

mire /maɪə(r)/ n fango m

mirror /ˈmɪrə(r)/ n espejo m. —vt reflejar

mirth /mɜːθ/ n (merriment) alegría f; (laughter) risas fpl

misadventure /ˌmɪsədˈventʃə(r)/ n desgracia f

misanthropist /mɪˈzænθrəpɪst/ n misántropo m

misapprehension /ˌmɪsæprɪˈhenʃn/ n malentendido m

misbehave /ˌmɪsbɪˈheɪv/ vi portarse mal. ∼**iour** n mala conducta f

miscalculate /ˌmɪsˈkælkjʊleɪt/ vt/i calcular mal. ∼**ion** /-ˈleɪʃn/ n desacierto m

miscarr|**iage** /ˈmɪskærɪdʒ/ n aborto m. ∼**iage of justice** n error m judicial. ∼**y** vi abortar

miscellaneous /misə'leiniəs/ a vario

mischief /'mistʃif/ n (foolish conduct) travesura f; (harm) daño m. get into ~ cometer travesuras. make ~ armar un lío

mischievous /'mistʃivəs/ a travieso; (malicious) perjudicial

misconception /miskən'sepʃn/ n equivocación f

misconduct /mis'kɒndʌkt/ n mala conducta f

misconstrue /miskən'stru:/ vt interpretar mal

misdeed /mis'di:d/ n fechoría f

misdemeanour /misdi'mi:nə(r)/ n fechoría f

misdirect /misdi'rekt/ vt dirigir mal (person)

miser /'maizə(r)/ n avaro m

miserable /'mizərəbl/ a (sad) triste; (wretched) miserable; (weather) malo

miserly /'maizəli/ a avariento

misery /'mizəri/ n (unhappiness) tristeza f; (pain) sufrimiento m; (poverty) pobreza f; (person, fam) aguafiestas m & f

misfire /mis'faiə(r)/ vi fallar

misfit /'misfit/ n (person) inadaptado m; (thing) cosa f mal ajustada

misfortune /mis'fɔ:tʃu:n/ n desgracia f

misgiving /mis'givin/ n (doubt) duda f; (apprehension) presentimiento m

misguided /mis'gaidid/ a equivocado. be ~ equivocarse

mishap /'mishæp/ n desgracia f

misinform /misin'fɔ:m/ vt informar mal

misinterpret /misin'tɜ:prit/ vt interpretar mal

misjudge /mis'dʒʌdʒ/ vt juzgar mal

mislay /mis'lei/ vt (pt mislaid) extraviar

mislead /mis'li:d/ vt (pt misled) engañar. ~ing a engañoso

mismanage /mis'mænidʒ/ vt administrar mal. ~ment n mala administración f

misnomer /mis'nəumə(r)/ n nombre m equivocado

misplace /mis'pleis/ vt colocar mal; (lose) extraviar

misprint /'misprint/ n errata f

misquote /mis'kwəut/ vt citar mal

misrepresent /misrepri'zent/ vt describir engañosamente

miss¹ /mis/ vt (fail to hit) errar; (notice absence of) echar de menos; perder (train). ~ the point no comprender. −n fallo m. ~ out omitir

miss² /mis/ n (pl misses) señorita f

misshapen /mis'ʃeipən/ a deforme

missile /'misail/ n proyectil m

missing /'misin/ a (person) (absent) ausente; (person) (after disaster) desaparecido; (lost) perdido. be ~ faltar

mission /'miʃn/ n misión f. ~ary /'miʃənəri/ n misionero m

missive /'misiv/ n misiva f

misspell /mis'spel/ vt (pt misspelt or misspelled) escribir mal

mist /mist/ n neblina f; (at sea) bruma f. −vt/i empañar(se)

mistake /mi'steik/ n error m. −vt (pt mistook, pp mistaken) equivocarse de; (misunderstand) entender mal. ~ for tomar por. ~n /ˈən/ a equivocado. be ~n equivocarse. ~nly adv equivocadamente

mistletoe /'misltəu/ n muérdago m

mistreat /mis'tri:t/ vt maltratar

mistress /'mistris/ n (of house) señora f; (primary school teacher) maestra f; (secondary *school teacher*) profesora *f*; (*lover*) amante *f*

mistrust /mɪs'trʌst/ *a* (*school etc*) desconfiar de. —*n* desconfianza *f*

misty /'mɪstɪ/ *a* (-**ier**, -**iest**) nebuloso; (*day*) de niebla; (*glass*) empañado. **it is ~** hay neblina

misunderstand /mɪsʌndə'stænd/ *vt* (*pt* -**stood**) entender mal. **~ing** *n* malentendido *m*

misuse /mɪs'juːz/ *vt* emplear mal; abusar de (*power etc*). /mɪs'juːs/ *n* mal uso *m*; (*unfair use*) abuso *m*

mite /maɪt/ *n* (*insect*) ácaro *m*, garrapata *f*; (*child*) niño *m* pequeño

mitigate /'mɪtɪgeɪt/ *vt* mitigar

mitre /'maɪtə(r)/ *n* (*head-dress*) mitra *f*

mitten /'mɪtn/ *n* manopla *f*; (*leaving fingers exposed*) mitón *m*

mix /mɪks/ *vt/i* mezclar(se). **~ up** mezclar; (*confuse*) confundir. **~ with** frecuentar (*people*). —*n* mezcla *f*

mixed /mɪkst/ *a* (*school etc*) mixto; (*assorted*) variado. **be ~ up** estar confuso

mixer /'mɪksə(r)/ *n* (*culin*) batidora *f*. **be a good ~** tener don de gentes

mixture /'mɪkstʃə(r)/ *n* mezcla *f*

mix-up /'mɪksʌp/ *n* lío *m*

moan /məʊn/ *n* gemido *m*. —*vi* gemir; (*complain*) quejarse (*about* de). **~er** *n* refunfuñador *m*

moat /məʊt/ *n* foso *m*

mob /mɒb/ *n* (*crowd*) muchedumbre *f*; (*gang*) pandilla *f*; (*masses*) populacho *m*. —*vt* (*pt* **mobbed**) acosar

mobile /'məʊbaɪl/ *a* móvil. **~ home** *n* caravana *f*, *n* móvil *m*. **~ity** /məʊ'bɪlɪtɪ/ *n* movilidad *f*

mobiliz|ation /məʊbɪlaɪ'zeɪʃn/ *n* movilización *f*. **~e** /'məʊbɪlaɪz/ *vt/i* movilizar

moccasin /'mɒkəsɪn/ *n* mocasín *m*

mocha /'mɒkə/ *n* moca *m*

mock /mɒk/ *vt* burlarse de. —*vi* burlarse. —*a* fingido

mockery /'mɒkərɪ/ *n* burla *f*. **a ~ of** una parodia *f* de

mock-up /'mɒkʌp/ *n* maqueta *f*

mode /məʊd/ *n* (*way, method*) modo *m*; (*fashion*) moda *f*

model /'mɒdl/ *n* modelo *m*; (*mock-up*) maqueta *f*; (*for fashion*) maniquí *m*. —*a* (*exemplary*) ejemplar; (*car etc*) en miniatura. —*vt* (*pt* **modelled**) modelar; presentar (*clothes*). —*vi* ser maniquí; (*pose*) posar. **~ling** *n* profesión *f* de maniquí

moderate /'mɒdərət/ *a* & *n* moderado (*m*). /'mɒdəreɪt/ *vt/i* moderar(se). **~ly** /'mɒdərətlɪ/ *adv* (*in moderation*) moderadamente; (*fairly*) medianamente

moderation /mɒdə'reɪʃn/ *n* moderación *f*. **in ~** con moderación

modern /'mɒdn/ *a* moderno. **~ize** *vt* modernizar

modest /'mɒdɪst/ *a* modesto. **~y** *n* modestia *f*

modicum /'mɒdɪkəm/ *n*. **a ~ of** un poquito *m* de

modification /mɒdɪfɪ'keɪʃn/ *n* modificación *f*. **~y** /-faɪ/ *vt/i* modificar(se)

modulat|e /'mɒdjʊleɪt/ *vt/i* modular. **~ion** /-'leɪʃn/ *n* modulación *f*

module /'mɒdjuːl/ *n* módulo *m*

mogul /'məʊgəl/ *n* (*fam*) magnate *m*

mohair /'məʊheə(r)/ *n* mohair *m*

moist /mɔɪst/ *a* (-**er**, -**est**) húmedo. **~en** /'mɔɪsn/ *vt* humedecer

moisture /'mɔɪstʃə(r)/ *n* humedad *f*. **~ize** /'mɔɪstʃəraɪz/ *vt* humedecer. **~izer** *n* crema *f* hidratante

molar /'məʊlə(r)/ n muela f

molasses /mə'læsɪz/ n melaza f

mold /məʊld/ (Amer) = **mould**

mole[1] /məʊl/ n (animal) topo m

mole[2] /məʊl/ n (on skin) lunar m

mole[3] /məʊl/ n (breakwater) malecón m

molecule /'mɒlɪkjuːl/ n molécula f

molehill /'məʊlhɪl/ n topera f

molest /mə'lest/ vt importunar

mollify /'mɒlɪfaɪ/ vt apaciguar

mollusc /'mɒləsk/ n molusco m

mollycoddle /'mɒlɪkɒdl/ vt mimar

molten /'məʊltən/ a fundido

mom /mɒm/ n (Amer) mamá f

moment /'məʊmənt/ n momento m. **~arily** /'məʊməntərɪlɪ/ adv momentáneamente. **~ary** a momentáneo

momentous /mə'mentəs/ a importante

momentum /mə'mentəm/ n momento m; (speed) velocidad f; (fig) ímpetu m

Monaco /'mɒnəkəʊ/ n Mónaco m

monarch /'mɒnək/ n monarca m. **~ist** n monárquico m. **~y** n monarquía f

monastery /'mɒnəstərɪ/ n monasterio m. **~ic** /mə'næstɪk/ a monástico

Monday /'mʌndeɪ/ n lunes m

monetarist /'mʌnɪtərɪst/ n monetarista m & f. **~y** a monetario

money /'mʌnɪ/ n dinero m. **~box** n hucha f. **~ed** a adinerado. **~lender** n prestamista m & f. **~ order** n giro m postal. **~s** npl cantidades fpl de dinero. **~spinner** n mina f de dinero

mongol /'mɒŋgl/ n & a (med) mongólico (m)

mongrel /'mʌŋgrəl/ n perro m mestizo

monitor /'mɒnɪtə(r)/ n (pupil) monitor m & f; (tec) monitor

m. **~vt** controlar; escuchar (a broadcast)

monk /mʌŋk/ n monje m

monkey /'mʌŋkɪ/ n mono m. **~nut** n cacahuete m, maní m (LAm). **~wrench** n llave f inglesa

mono /'mɒnəʊ/ a monofónico

monocle /'mɒnəkl/ n monóculo m

monogram /'mɒnəgræm/ n monograma m

monologue /'mɒnəlɒg/ n monólogo m

monopolize /mə'nɒpəlaɪz/ vt monopolizar. **~y** n monopolio m

monosyllabic /mɒnəsɪ'læbɪk/ a monosilábico. **~le** /-'sɪləbl/ n monosílabo m

monotone /'mɒnətəʊn/ n monotonía f. **speak in a ~** hablar con una voz monótona

monotonous /mə'nɒtənəs/ a monótono. **~y** n monotonía f

monsoon /mɒn'suːn/ n monzón m

monster /'mɒnstə(r)/ n monstruo m

monstrosity /mɒn'strɒsɪtɪ/ n monstruosidad f

monstrous /'mɒnstrəs/ a monstruoso

montage /mɒn'tɑːʒ/ n montaje m

month /mʌnθ/ n mes m. **~ly** /'mʌnθlɪ/ a mensual. **—adv** mensualmente. **—n** (periodical) revista f mensual

monument /'mɒnjʊmənt/ n monumento m. **~al** /-'mentl/ a monumental

moo /muː/ n mugido m. **—vi** mugir

mooch /muːtʃ/ vi (sl) haraganear. **—vt** (Amer, sl) birlar

mood /muːd/ n humor m. **be in the ~ for** tener ganas de. **in a good/bad ~** de buen/mal humor. **~y** a (-ier, -iest) de humor cambiadizo; (*bad-tempered*) malhumorado

moon /muːn/ *n* luna *f*. **~light** *n* luz *f* de la luna. **~lighting** *n* (*fam*) pluriempleo *m*. **~lit** *a* iluminado por la luna; (*night*) de luna

moor[1] /mʊə(r)/ *n* (*open land*) páramo *m*

moor[2] /mʊə(r)/ *vt* amarrar. **~ings** *npl* (*ropes*) amarras *fpl*; (*place*) amarradero *m*

Moor /mʊə(r)/ *n* moro *m*

moose /muːs/ *n invar* alce *m*

moot /muːt/ *a* discutible. —*vt* proponer (*question*)

mop /mɒp/ *n* fregona *f*. **~ of hair** pelambrera *f*. —*vt* (*pt* mopped) fregar. **~ (up)** limpiar

mope /məʊp/ *vi* estar abatido.

moped /ˈməʊped/ *n* ciclomotor *m*

moral /ˈmɒrəl/ *a* moral. —*n* moraleja *f*. **~s** *npl* moralidad *f*

morale /məˈrɑːl/ *n* moral *f*

moral|ist /ˈmɒrəlɪst/ *n* moralista *m* & *f*. **~ity** /məˈrælətɪ/ *n* moralidad *f*. **~ize** *vi* moralizar. **~ly** *adv* moralmente

morass /məˈræs/ *n* (*marsh*) pantano *m*; (*fig, entanglement*) embrollo *m*

morbid /ˈmɔːbɪd/ *a* morboso

more /mɔː(r)/ *a* & *n* & *adv* más. **~ and ~** cada vez más. **~ or less** más o menos. **once ~** una vez más. **some ~** más

moreover /mɔːˈrəʊvə(r)/ *adv* además

morgue /mɔːg/ *n* depósito *m* de cadáveres

moribund /ˈmɒrɪbʌnd/ *a* moribundo

morning /ˈmɔːnɪŋ/ *n* mañana *f*; (*early hours*) madrugada *f*. **at 11 o'clock in the ~** a las once de la mañana. **in the ~** por la mañana

Morocc|an /məˈrɒkən/ *a* & *n* marroquí (*m* & *f*). **~o** /-kəʊ/ *n* Marruecos *mpl*

moron /ˈmɔːrɒn/ *n* imbécil *m* & *f*

morose /məˈrəʊs/ *a* malhumorado

morphine /ˈmɔːfiːn/ *n* morfina *f*

Morse /mɔːs/ *n* Morse *m*. **~ (code)** *n* alfabeto *m* Morse

morsel /ˈmɔːsl/ *n* pedazo *m*; (*mouthful*) bocado *m*

mortal /ˈmɔːtl/ *a* & *n* mortal (*m*). **~ity** /-ˈtælɪt/ *n* mortalidad *f*

mortar /ˈmɔːtə(r)/ *n* (*all senses*) mortero *m*

mortgage /ˈmɔːgɪdʒ/ *n* hipoteca *f*. —*vt* hipotecar

mortify /ˈmɔːtɪfaɪ/ *vt* mortificar

mortuary /ˈmɔːtjʊərɪ/ *n* depósito *m* de cadáveres

mosaic /məʊˈzeɪk/ *n* mosaico *m*

Moscow /ˈmɒskəʊ/ *n* Moscú *m*

Moses /ˈməʊzɪz/ *a*. **~ basket** *n* moisés *m*

mosque /mɒsk/ *n* mezquita *f*

mosquito /mɒsˈkiːtəʊ/ *n* (*pl* -oes) mosquito *m*

moss /mɒs/ *n* musgo *m*. **~y** *a* musgoso

most /məʊst/ *a* más. **for the ~ part** en su mayor parte. —*n* la mayoría *f*. **~ of** la mayor parte de. **at ~** a lo más. **make the ~ of** aprovechar al máximo. —*adv* más; (*very*) muy. **~ly** *adv* principalmente

MOT *abbr* (*Ministry of Transport*). **~ (test)** ITV, inspección *f* técnica de vehículos

motel /məʊˈtel/ *n* motel *m*

moth /mɒθ/ *n* mariposa *f* (nocturna); (*in clothes*) polilla *f*. **~-ball** *n* bola *f* de naftalina. **~-eaten** *a* apolillado

mother /ˈmʌðə(r)/ *n* madre *f*. —*vt* cuidar como a un hijo. **~hood** *n* maternidad *f*. **~-in-law** *n* (*pl* **~s-in-law**) suegra *f*. **~land** *n* patria *f*. **~ly** *adv* maternalmente. **~-of-pearl** *n* nácar *m*. **M~'s Day** *n* el día *m* de la

Madre. ~-to-be n futura madre f. ~ tongue n lengua f materna

motif /məʊ'tiːf/ n motivo m

motion /'məʊʃn/ n movimiento m; (proposal) moción f. —vt/i. ~ (to) s.o. to hacer señas a uno para que. ~less a inmóvil

motivat|e /'məʊtɪveɪt/ vt motivar. ~ion /-'veɪʃn/ n motivación f

motive /'məʊtɪv/ n motivo m

motley /'mɒtlɪ/ a abigarrado

motor /'məʊtə(r)/ n motor m; (car) coche m. —a motor; (fem) motora, motriz. —vi ir en coche. ~ bike n (fam) motocicleta f, moto f (fam). ~ boat n lancha f motora. ~cade /'məʊtəkeɪd/ n (Amer) desfile m de automóviles. ~ car n coche m, automóvil m. ~ cycle n motocicleta f. ~cyclist n motociclista m & f. ~ing n automovilismo m. ~ist n automovilista m & f. ~ize vt motorizar. ~way n autopista f

mottled /'mɒtld/ a abigarrado

motto /'mɒtəʊ/ n (pl -oes) lema m

mould¹ /məʊld/ n molde m. —vt moldear

mould² /məʊld/ n (fungus, rot) moho m

moulding /'məʊldɪŋ/ n (on wall etc) moldura f

mouldy /'məʊldɪ/ a mohoso

moult /məʊlt/ vi mudar

mound /maʊnd/ n montículo m; (pile, fig) montón m

mount¹ /maʊnt/ vt/i subir. —n montura f. ~ up aumentar

mount² /maʊnt/ n (hill) monte m

mountain /'maʊntɪn/ n montaña f. ~eer /maʊntɪ'nɪə(r)/ n alpinista m & f. ~eering n alpinismo m. ~ous /'maʊntɪnəs/ a montañoso

mourn /mɔːn/ vt llorar. —vi lamentarse. ~ for llorar la muerte de. ~er n persona f que

acompaña el cortejo fúnebre. ~ful a triste. ~ing n luto m

mouse /maʊs/ n (pl mice) ratón m. ~trap n ratonera f

mousse /muːs/ n (dish) crema f batida

moustache /mə'staːʃ/ n bigote m

mousy /'maʊsɪ/ a (hair) pardusco; (fig) tímido

mouth /maʊð/ vt formar con los labios. /maʊθ/ n boca f. ~ful n bocado m. ~organ n armónica f. ~piece n (mus) boquilla f; (fig, person) portavoz f, vocero m (LAm). ~wash n enjuague m

movable /'muːvəbl/ a móvil, movible

move /muːv/ vt/i mover; mudarse de (house); (with emotion) conmover; (propose) proponer. —vi moverse; (be in motion) estar en movimiento; (progress) hacer progresos; (take action) tomar medidas; (depart) irse. ~ (out) irse. —n movimiento m; (in game) jugada f; (player's turn) turno m; (removal) mudanza f. on the ~ en movimiento. ~ along (hacer) circular. ~ away alejarse. ~ back (hacer) retroceder. ~ forward (hacer) avanzar. ~ in instalarse. ~ on (hacer) circular. ~ over apartarse. ~ment n /'muːvmənt/ n movimiento m

movie /'muːvɪ/ n (Amer) película f. the ~s npl el cine m

moving /'muːvɪŋ/ a en movimiento; (touching) conmovedor

mow /məʊ/ vt (pt mowed or mown) segar. ~ down derribar. ~er n (for lawn) cortacésped m inv

MP abbr see **Member of Parliament**

Mr /'mɪstə(r)/ abbr (pl Messrs) (Mister) señor m. ~ Coldbeck (el) Sr. Coldbeck

Mrs /'mɪsɪz/ abbr (pl **Mrs**) (Missis) señora f. ~ **Andrews** (la) Sra. Andrews. the ~ **Andrews** (las) Sras. Andrews

Ms /mɪz/ abbr (title of married or unmarried woman) señora f, señorita f. **Ms Lawton** (la) Sra. Lawton

much /mʌtʃ/ a & n mucho (m). —adv mucho; (before pp) muy. ~ **as** por mucho que. ~ **the same** más o menos lo mismo. **so** ~ tanto. **too** ~ demasiado

muck /mʌk/ n estiércol m; (dirt, fam) suciedad f. —vi. ~ **about** (sl) perder el tiempo. ~ **about with** (sl) juguetear con. —vt. ~ **up** (sl) echar a perder. ~ **in** (sl) participar. ~**y** a sucio

mucus /'mjuːkəs/ n moco m

mud /mʌd/ n lodo m, barro m

muddle /'mʌdl/ vt embrollar. —vi. ~ **through** salir del paso. —n desorden m; (mix-up) lío m

muddy /'mʌdɪ/ a lodoso; ⟨hands etc⟩ cubierto de lodo

mudguard /'mʌdɡɑːd/ n guardabarros m invar

muff /mʌf/ n manguito m

muffin /'mʌfɪn/ n mollete m

muffle /'mʌfl/ vt tapar; amortiguar ⟨a sound⟩. ~**r** n (scarf) bufanda f

mug /mʌɡ/ n tazón m; (for beer) jarra f; (face, sl) cara f, jeta f (sl); (fool, sl) primo m. —vt (pt **mugged**) asaltar. ~**ger** n asaltador m. ~**ging** n asalto m

muggy /'mʌɡɪ/ a bochornoso

Muhammadan /mə'hæmɪdən/ a & n mahometano (m)

mule[1] /mjuːl/ n mula f, mulo m

mule[2] /mjuːl/ n (slipper) babucha f

mull[1] /mʌl/ vt. ~ **over** reflexionar sobre

mull[2] /mʌl/ vt calentar con especias ⟨wine⟩

multi... /'mʌltɪ/ pref multi...

multicoloured /mʌltɪ'kʌləd/ a multicolor

multifarious /mʌltɪ'feərɪəs/ a múltiple

multinational /mʌltɪ'næʃənl/ a & n multinacional (f)

multiple /'mʌltɪpl/ a & n múltiplo (m). ~**ication** /mʌltɪplɪ'keɪʃn/ n multiplicación f. ~**y** /'mʌltɪplaɪ/ vt/i multiplicar(se)

multitude /'mʌltɪtjuːd/ n multitud f

mum[1] /mʌm/ n (fam) mamá f (fam)

mum[2] /mʌm/ a. **keep** ~ (fam) guardar silencio

mumble /'mʌmbl/ vt decir entre dientes. —vi hablar entre dientes

mummify /'mʌmɪfaɪ/ vt/i momificar(se)

mummy[1] /'mʌmɪ/ n (mother, fam) mamá f (fam)

mummy[2] /'mʌmɪ/ n momia f

mumps /mʌmps/ n paperas fpl

munch /mʌntʃ/ vt/i mascar

mundane /mʌn'deɪn/ a mundano m

municipal /mjuː'nɪsɪpl/ a municipal. ~**ity** /-'pælətɪ/ n municipio m

munificent /mjuː'nɪfɪsənt/ a munífico

munitions /mjuː'nɪʃnz/ npl municiones fpl

mural /'mjʊərəl/ a & n mural (f)

murder /'mɜːdə(r)/ n asesinato m. —vt asesinar. ~**er** n asesino m. ~**ess** n asesina f. ~**ous** a homicida

murky /'mɜːkɪ/ a (-ier, -iest) oscuro

murmur /'mɜːmə(r)/ n murmullo m. —vt/i murmurar

muscle /'mʌsl/ n músculo m. —vi. ~ **in** (Amer, sl) meterse por fuerza en

muscular /'mʌskjʊlə(r)/ *a* muscular; (*having well-developed muscles*) musculoso

muse /mjuːz/ *vi* meditar

museum /mjuːˈzɪəm/ *n* museo *m*

mush /mʌʃ/ *n* pulpa *f*

mushrom /'mʌʃrʊm/ *n* champiñón *m*; (*bot*) seta *f*. —*vi* (*appear in large numbers*) crecer como hongos

mushy /'mʌʃɪ/ *a* pulposo

music /'mjuːzɪk/ *n* música *f*. ~al *a* musical; (*instrument*) de música; (*talented*) que tiene don de música. —*n* comedia *f* musical. ~ hall *n* teatro *m* de variedades. ~ian /mjuːˈzɪʃn/ *n* músico *m*

musk /mʌsk/ *n* almizcle *m*

Muslim /'mʊzlɪm/ *a* & *n* musulmán (*m*)

muslin /'mʌzlɪn/ *n* muselina *f*

musquash /'mʌskwɒʃ/ *n* ratón *m* almizclero

mussel /'mʌsl/ *n* mejillón *m*

must /mʌst/ *v aux* deber, tener que. **he ~ be old** debe ser viejo. **I ~ have done it** debo haberlo hecho. **you ~ go** debes marcharte. —*n*. **be a ~** ser imprescindible

mustard /'mʌstəd/ *n* mostaza *f*

muster /'mʌstə(r)/ *vt/i* reunir(se)

musty /'mʌstɪ/ *a* (**-ier, -iest**) que huele a cerrado

mutation /mjuːˈteɪʃn/ *n* mutación *f*

mute /mjuːt/ *a* & *n* mudo (*m*). ~d *a* (*sound*) sordo; (*criticism*) callado

mutilat|**e** /'mjuːtɪleɪt/ *vt* mutilar. ~ion /-'leɪʃn/ *n* mutilación *f*

mutin|**ous** /'mjuːtɪnəs/ *a* (*sailor etc*) amotinado; (*fig*) rebelde. ~y *n* motín *m*. —*vi* amotinarse

mutter /'mʌtə(r)/ *vt/i* murmurar

mutton /'mʌtn/ *n* cordero *m*

mutual /'mjuːtʃʊəl/ *a* mutuo; (*common, fam*) común. ~ly *adv* mutuamente

muzzle /'mʌzl/ *n* (*snout*) hocico *m*; (*device*) bozal *m*; (*of gun*) boca *f*. —*vt* poner el bozal a

my /maɪ/ *a* mi, mis *pl*

myopic /maɪˈɒpɪk/ *a* miope

myriad /'mɪrɪəd/ *n* miríada *f*

myself /maɪˈself/ *pron* yo mismo *m*, yo misma *f*; (*reflexive*) me; (*after prep*) mí (mismo) *m*, mí (misma) *f*

myster|**ious** /mɪˈstɪərɪəs/ *a* misterioso. ~y /'mɪstərɪ/ *n* misterio *m*

mystic /'mɪstɪk/ *a* & *n* místico (*m*). ~al *a* místico. ~ism /-sɪzm/ *n* misticismo *m*

mystif|**ication** /mɪstɪfɪˈkeɪʃn/ *n* confusión *f*. ~y /-faɪ/ *vt* dejar perplejo

mystique /mɪˈstiːk/ *n* mística *f*

myth /mɪθ/ *n* mito *m*. ~ical *a* mítico. ~ology /mɪˈθɒlədʒɪ/ *n* mitología *f*

N

N *abbr* (*north*) norte *m*

nab /næb/ *vt* (*pt* **nabbed**) (*arrest, sl*) coger (*not LAm*), agarrar (*esp LAm*)

nag /næg/ *vt* (*pt* **nagged**) fastidiar; (*scold*) regañar. —*vi* criticar

nagging /'nægɪŋ/ *a* persistente, regañón

nail /neɪl/ *n* clavo *m*; (*of finger, toe*) uña *f*. **pay on the ~** pagar a tocateja. —*vt* clavar. ~ **polish** *n* esmalte *m* para las uñas

naïve /naɪˈiːv/ *a* ingenuo

naked /'neɪkɪd/ *a* desnudo. **to the ~ eye** a simple vista. ~ly *adv* desnudamente. ~ness *n* desnudez *f*

namby-pamby /næmbɪˈpæmbɪ/ *a* & *n* ñoño (*m*)

name /neɪm/ n nombre m; (fig) fama f. —vt nombrar; (fix) fijar. **be ~d after** llevar el nombre de. **~less** a anónimo. **~ly** /neɪmlɪ/ adv a saber. **~sake** /neɪmseɪk/ n (person) tocayo m

nanny /nænɪ/ n niñera f. **~goat** n cabra f

nap[1] /næp/ n (sleep) sueñecito m; (after lunch) siesta f. —vi (pt **napped**) echarse un sueño. **catch s.o. ~ping** coger a uno desprevenido

nap[2] /næp/ n (fibres) lanilla f

nape /neɪp/ n nuca f

napkin /næpkɪn/ n (at meals) servilleta f; (for baby) pañal m

nappy /næpɪ/ n pañal m

narcotic /nɑːˈkɒtɪk/ a & n narcótico m

narrat|e /nəˈreɪt/ vt contar. **~ion** /-ʃn/ n narración f. **~ive** /nærətɪv/ n relato m. —or /nəˈreɪtə(r)/ n narrador m

narrow /nærəʊ/ a (-er, -est) estrecho. **have a ~ escape** escaparse por los pelos. —vt estrechar; (limit) limitar. —vi estrecharse. **~ly** adv estrechamente; (just) por poco. **~-minded** a de miras estrechas. **~ness** n estrechez f

nasal /neɪzl/ a nasal

nast|ily /nɑːstɪlɪ/ adv desagradablemente; (maliciously) con malevolencia. **~iness** n (malice) malevolencia f. **~y** a (-ier, -iest) desagradable; (malicious) malévolo; (weather) malo; (taste, smell) asqueroso; (wound) grave; (person) antipático

natal /neɪtl/ a natal

nation /neɪʃn/ n nación f

national /næʃənl/ a nacional. —n súbdito m. **~ anthem** n himno m nacional. **~ism** n nacionalismo m. **~ity** /næʃəˈnælɪtɪ/ n

nacionalidad f. **~ize** vt nacionalizar. **~ly** adv a nivel nacional

nationwide /neɪʃnwaɪd/ a nacional

native /neɪtɪv/ n natural m & f. **be a ~ of** ser natural de. —a nativo; (country, town) natal; (inborn) innato. **~ speaker of Spanish** hispanohablante m & f. **~ language** n lengua f materna

Nativity /nəˈtɪvɪtɪ/ n. **the ~** la Natividad f

NATO /neɪtəʊ/ abbr (North Atlantic Treaty Organization) OTAN f, Organización f del Tratado del Atlántico Norte

natter /nætə(r)/ vi (fam) charlar. —n (fam) charla f

natural /nætʃərəl/ a natural. **~ history** n historia f natural. **~ist** n naturalista m & f

naturaliz|ation /nætʃərəlaɪˈzeɪʃn/ n. naturalización f. **~e** vt naturalizar

naturally /nætʃərəlɪ/ adv (of course) naturalmente; (by nature) por naturaleza

nature /neɪtʃə(r)/ n naturaleza f; (kind) género m; (of person) carácter m

naught /nɔːt/ n (old use) nada f; (maths) cero m

naught|ily /nɔːtɪlɪ/ adv mal. **~y** a (-ier, -iest) malo; (child) travieso; (joke) verde

nause|a /nɔːzɪə/ n náusea f. **~ate** vt dar náuseas a. **~ous** a nauseabundo

nautical /nɔːtɪkl/ a náutico. **~ mile** n milla f marina

naval /neɪvl/ a naval; (officer) de marina

Navarre /nəˈvɔː(r)/ n Navarra f. **~se** a navarro

nave /neɪv/ n (of church) nave f

navel /neɪvl/ n ombligo m

navigable /nævɪɡəbl/ a navegable

navigat e /'nævɪgeɪt/ *vt* navegar por ⟨*sea etc*⟩; gobernar ⟨*ship*⟩. — *vi* navegar. **~ion** *n* navegación *f*. **~or** *n* navegante *m*

navvy /'nævɪ/ *n* peón *m* caminero

navy /'neɪvɪ/ *n* marina *f*. **~ (blue)** azul *m* marino

NE *abbr* (*north-east*) noreste *m*

near /nɪə(r)/ *adv* cerca. **~ at hand** muy cerca. **~ by** *adv* cerca. **draw ~** acercarse. — *prep.* **~ (to)** cerca de. — *a* cercano. — *vt* acercarse a. **~by** *a* cercano. **N~ East** *n* Oriente *m* Próximo. **~ly** /nɪəlɪ/ *adv* casi. **not ~ly** as pretty as no es ni con mucho tan guapa como. **~ness** /nɪənɪs/ *n* proximidad *f*

neat /niːt/ *a* (*-er, -est*) pulcro; ⟨*room etc*⟩ bien arreglado; ⟨*clever*⟩ diestro; ⟨*ingenious*⟩ hábil; ⟨*whisky, brandy etc*⟩ solo. **~ly** *adv* pulcramente. **~ness** *n* pulcritud *f*

nebulous /'nebjʊləs/ *a* nebuloso

necessar ies /'nesəsərɪz/ *npl* lo indispensable. **~ily** /nesə'serɪlɪ/ *adv* necesariamente. **~y** *a* necesario, imprescindible

necessit ate /nə'sesɪteɪt/ *vt* necesitar. **~y** /nɪ'sesətɪ/ *n* necesidad *f*; ⟨*thing*⟩ cosa *f* indispensable

neck /nek/ *n* (*of person, bottle, dress*) cuello *m*; (*of animal*) pescuezo *m*. **~ and ~** parejos. **~lace** /'nekləs/ *n* collar *m*. **~line** *n* escote *m*. **~tie** *n* corbata *f*

nectar /'nektə(r)/ *n* néctar *m*

nectarine /'nektə'riːn/ *n* nectarina *f*

née /neɪ/ *a* de soltera

need /niːd/ *n* necesidad *f*. — *vt* necesitar; ⟨*demand*⟩ exigir. **you ~ not speak** no tienes que hablar

needle /'niːdl/ *n* aguja *f*. — *vt* ⟨*annoy, fam*⟩ pinchar

needless /'niːdlɪs/ *a* innecesario. **~ly** *adv* innecesariamente

needlework /'niːdlwɜːk/ *n* costura *f*; (*embroidery*) bordado *m*

needy /'niːdɪ/ *a* (*-ier, -iest*) necesitado

negation /nɪ'geɪʃn/ *n* negación *f*

negative /'negətɪv/ *a* negativo. — *n* (*of photograph*) negativo *m*; (*word, gram*) negativa *f*. **~ly** *adv* negativamente

neglect /nɪ'glekt/ *vt* descuidar; no cumplir con ⟨*duty*⟩. **~ to do** dejar de hacer. — *n* descuido *m*, negligencia *f*. (**state of**) **~** abandono *m*. **~ful** *a* descuidado

négligé /'neglɪʒeɪ/ *n* bata *f*, salto *m* de cama

negligen ce /'neglɪdʒəns/ *n* negligencia *f*, descuido *m*. **~t** *a* descuidado

negligible /'neglɪdʒəbl/ *a* insignificante

negotiable /nɪ'gəʊʃəbl/ *a* negociable

negotiat e /nɪ'gəʊʃɪeɪt/ *vt/i* negociar. **~ion** /-'eɪʃn/ *n* negociación *f*. **~or** *n* negociador *m*

Negr ess /'niːgrɪs/ *n* negra *f*. **~o** *n* (*pl* -oes) negro *m*. — *a* negro

neigh /neɪ/ *n* relincho *m*. — *vi* relinchar

neighbour /'neɪbə(r)/ *n* vecino *m*. **~hood** *n* vecindad *f*, barrio *m*. **in the ~hood of** alrededor de. **~ing** *a* vecino. **~ly** /'neɪbəlɪ/ *a* amable

neither /'naɪðə(r)/ *a & pron* ninguno *m* de los dos, ni el uno *m* ni el otro *m*. — *adv* ni. **~ big nor small** ni grande ni pequeño. **~ shall I come** no voy yo tampoco. — *conj* tampoco

neon /'niːɒn/ *n* neón *m*. — *a* ⟨*lamp etc*⟩ de neón

nephew /'nevjuː/ *n* sobrino *m*

nepotism /'nepətɪzəm/ *m* nepotismo *m*

nerve /nɜːv/ n nervio m; (*courage*) valor m; (*calm*) sangre f fría; (*impudence, fam*) descaro m. **~-racking** a exasperante. **~s** npl (*before exams etc*) nervios mpl

nervous /ˈnɜːvəs/ a nervioso. **be/feel ~** (*afraid*) tener miedo (**of** a). **~ly** adv (*tensely*) nerviosamente; (*timidly*) tímidamente. **~ness** n nerviosidad f; (*fear*) miedo m

nervy /ˈnɜːvɪ/ a see **nervous**; (*Amer, fam*) descarado

nest /nest/ n nido m. **-ví** anidar. **~-egg** n (*money*) ahorros mpl

nestle /ˈnesl/ vi acomodarse. **~ up to** arrimarse a

net /net/ n red f. **-vt** (*pt netted*) coger (*not LAm*), agarrar (*esp LAm*). **-a** (*material etc*) neto

netball /ˈnetbɔːl/ n baloncesto m

Netherlands /ˈneðələndz/ npl. **the ~** los Países mpl Bajos

netting /ˈnetɪŋ/ n (*nets*) redes fpl; (*wire*) malla f; (*fabric*) tul m

nettle /ˈnetl/ n ortiga f

network /ˈnetwɜːk/ n red f

neuralgia /njʊəˈrældʒɪə/ n neuralgia f

neuro|**sis** /njʊəˈrəʊsɪs/ n (*pl -oses* /-siːz/) neurosis f. **~tic** a & n neurótico (m)

neuter /ˈnjuːtə(r)/ a & n neutro (m). **-vt** castrar (*animals*)

neutral /ˈnjuːtrəl/ a neutral; (*colour*) neutro; (*elec*) neutro. **~** (*gear*) (*auto*) punto m muerto. **~ity** /-ˈtrælɪtɪ/ n neutralidad f

neutron /ˈnjuːtrɒn/ n neutrón m. **~ bomb** n bomba f de neutrones

never /ˈnevə(r)/ adv nunca, jamás; (*not, fam*) no. **~ again** nunca más. **~ mind** (*don't worry*) no te preocupes, no se preocupe; (*it doesn't matter*) no importa. **he ~ smiles** no sonríe nunca. **I ~ saw him** (*fam*) no le vi. **~-ending** a interminable

nevertheless /nevəðəˈles/ adv sin embargo, no obstante

new /njuː/ a (*-er, -est*) (*new to owner*) nuevo (*placed before noun*); (*brand new*) nuevo (*placed after noun*). **~-born** a recién nacido. **~comer** n recién llegado m. **~-fangled** a (*pej*) moderno. **~-laid egg** n huevo m fresco. **~ly** adv nuevamente; (*recently*) recién. **~ly-weds** npl recién casados mpl. **~ moon** n luna f nueva. **~ness** n novedad f

news /njuːz/ n noticias fpl; (*broadcasting, press*) informaciones fpl; (*on TV*) telediario m; (*on radio*) diario m hablado. **~agent** n vendedor m de periódicos. **~caster** n locutor m. **~letter** n boletín m. **~paper** n periódico m. **~reader** n locutor m. **~reel** n noticiario m, nodo m (*in Spain*)

newt /njuːt/ n tritón m

new year /njuːˈjɪə(r)/ n año m nuevo. **N~'s Day** n día m de Año Nuevo. **N~'s Eve** n noche f vieja

New Zealand /njuːˈziːlənd/ n Nueva Zelanda f. **~er** n neozelandés m

next /nekst/ a próximo; (*week, month etc*) que viene, próximo; (*adjoining*) vecino; (*following*) siguiente. **—adv** la próxima vez; (*afterwards*) después. **—n** siguiente m. **~ to** junto a. **~ to nothing** casi nada. **~ door** al lado (**to** de). **~-door** de al lado. **~-best** mejor alternativa f. **~ of kin** n pariente m más próximo, parientes mpl más próximos

nib /nɪb/ n (*of pen*) plumilla f

nibble /ˈnɪbl/ vt|i mordisquear. **—n** mordisco m

nice /naɪs/ a (*-er, -est*) agradable; (*likeable*) simpático; (*kind*) amable; (*pretty*) bonito; (*weather*) bueno; (*subtle*) sutil. **~ly** adv agradablemente;

(*kindly*) amablemente; (*well*) bien

nicety /'naɪsətɪ/ n (*precision*) precisión f; (*detail*) detalle. **to a ~** exactamente

niche /nɪtʃ, niːʃ/ n (*recess*) nicho m; (*fig*) buena posición f

nick /nɪk/ n corte m pequeño; (*prison, sl*) cárcel f. **in the ~ of time** justo a tiempo. —vt (*steal, arrest, sl*) birlar

nickel /'nɪkl/ n níquel m; (*Amer*) moneda f de cinco centavos

nickname /'nɪkneɪm/ n apodo m; (*short form*) diminutivo m. —vt apodar

nicotine /'nɪkətiːn/ n nicotina f

niece /niːs/ n sobrina f

nifty /'nɪftɪ/ a (*sl*) (*smart*) elegante

Nigeria /naɪ'dʒɪərɪə/ n Nigeria f. **~n** a & n nigeriano (m)

niggardly /'nɪgədlɪ/ a (*person*) tacaño; (*thing*) miserable

niggling /'nɪglɪŋ/ a molesto

night /naɪt/ n noche f; (*evening*) tarde f. —a nocturno, de noche. **~cap** n (*hat*) gorro m de dormir; (*drink*) bebida f (tomada antes de acostarse). **~club** n sala f de fiestas, boîte f. **~dress** n camisón m. **~fall** n anochecer m. **~gown** n camisón m

nightingale /'naɪtɪŋgeɪl/ n ruiseñor m

night: **~life** n vida f nocturna. **~ly** adv todas las noches. **~mare** n pesadilla f. **~school** n escuela f nocturna. **~time** n noche f. **~watchman** n sereno m

nil /nɪl/ n nada f; (*sport*) cero m

nimble /'nɪmbl/ a (**-er, -est**) ágil

nine /naɪn/ a & n nueve (m)

nineteen /naɪn'tiːn/ a & n diecinueve (m). **~th** a & n diecinueve (m), decimonoveno (m)

ninet|ieth /'naɪntɪəθ/ a & n noventa, nonagésimo. **~y** a & n noventa (m)

ninth /naɪnθ/ a & n noveno (m)

nip[1] /nɪp/ vt (*pt* **nipped**) (*pinch*) pellizcar; (*bite*) mordisquear. —vi (*rush, sl*) correr. —n (*pinch*) pellizco m; (*cold*) frío m

nip[2] /nɪp/ n (*of drink*) trago m

nipper /'nɪpə(r)/ n (*sl*) chaval m

nipple /'nɪpl/ n pezón m; (*of baby's bottle*) tetilla f

nippy /'nɪpɪ/ a (**-ier, -iest**) (*nimble, fam*) ágil; (*quick, fam*) rápido; (*chilly, fam*) fresquito

nitrogen /'naɪtrədʒən/ n nitrógeno m

nitwit /'nɪtwɪt/ n (*fam*) imbécil m & f

no /nəʊ/ a ninguno. **~ entry** prohibido el paso. **~ man's land** n tierra f de nadie. **~ smoking** se prohíbe fumar. **~ way!** (*Amer, fam*) ¡ni hablar! —adv no. —n (*pl* **noes**) no m

nobility /nəʊ'bɪlətɪ/ n nobleza f

noble /'nəʊbl/ a (**-er, -est**) noble. **~man** n noble m

nobody /'nəʊbədɪ/ pron nadie m. —n nadie m. **~ is there** no hay nadie. **he knows ~** no conoce a nadie

nocturnal /nɒk'tɜːnl/ a nocturno

nod /nɒd/ vt (*pt* **nodded**). **~ one's head** asentir con la cabeza. —vi (*in agreement*) asentir con la cabeza; (*in greeting*) saludar; (*be drowsy*) dar cabezadas. —n inclinación f de cabeza

nodule /'nɒdjuːl/ n nódulo m

nois|e /nɔɪz/ n ruido m. **~eless** a silencioso. **~ily** /'nɔɪzɪlɪ/ adv ruidosamente. **~y** a (**-ier, -iest**) ruidoso

nomad /'nəʊmæd/ n nómada m & f. **~ic** /-'mædɪk/ a nómada

nominal /'nɒmɪnl/ a nominal

nominat|e /'nɒmɪneɪt/ vt nombrar; (*put forward*) proponer. **~ion** /-'neɪʃn/ n nombramiento m

non-... /nɒn/ pref no ...

nonagenarian /nəʊnədʒɪ-ˈneərɪən/ a & n nonagenario (m), noventón (m)

nonchalant /ˈnɒnʃələnt/ a imperturbable

non-commissioned /nɒnkə-ˈmɪʃnd/ a. ~ officer n suboficial m

non-committal /nɒnkəˈmɪtl/ a evasivo

nondescript /ˈnɒndɪskrɪpt/ a inclasificable, anodino

none /nʌn/ pron (person) nadie, ninguno; (thing) ninguno, nada. ~ of nada de. ~ of us ninguno de nosotros. I have ~ no tengo nada. —adv no, de ninguna manera. he is ~ the happier no está más contento

nonentity /nɒˈnentətɪ/ n nulidad f

non-existent /nɒnɪgˈzɪstənt/ a inexistente

nonplussed /nɒnˈplʌst/ a perplejo

nonsens|e /ˈnɒnsns/ n tonterías fpl, disparates mpl. ~ical /-ˈsensɪkl/ a absurdo

non-smoker /nɒnˈsməʊkə(r)/ n persona f que no fuma; (rail) departamento m de no fumadores

non-starter /nɒnˈstɑːtə(r)/ n (fam) proyecto m imposible

non-stop /nɒnˈstɒp/ a (train) directo; (flight) sin escalas. —adv sin parar; (by train) directamente; (by air) sin escalas

noodles /ˈnuːdlz/ npl fideos mpl

nook /nʊk/ n rincón m

noon /nuːn/ n mediodía m

no-one /ˈnəʊwʌn/ pron nadie. see **nobody**

noose /nuːs/ n nudo m corredizo

nor /nɔː(r)/ conj ni, tampoco. neither blue ~ red ni azul ni rojo. he doesn't play the piano, ~

do I no sabe tocar el piano, ni yo tampoco

Nordic /ˈnɔːdɪk/ a nórdico

norm /nɔːm/ n norma f; (normal) lo normal

normal /ˈnɔːml/ a normal. ~cy n (Amer) normalidad f. ~ity /-ˈmælətɪ/ n normalidad f. ~ly adv normalmente

Norman /ˈnɔːmən/ a & n normando (m)

Normandy /ˈnɔːməndɪ/ n Normandía f

north /nɔːθ/ n norte m. —a del norte, norteño. —adv hacia el norte. **N~ America** América f del Norte, Norteamérica f. **N~ American** a & n norteamericano (m). ~**east** n nordeste m. ~**erly** /nɔːˈðəlɪ/ a del norte. ~**ern** /ˈnɔːðən/ a del norte. ~**erner** n norteño m. **N~ Sea** n mar m del Norte. ~**ward** a hacia el norte. ~**wards** adv hacia el norte. ~**west** n noroeste m

Norway /ˈnɔːweɪ/ n Noruega f. ~**egian** a & n noruego (m)

nose /nəʊz/ n nariz f. —vi. ~ **about** curiosear. ~**bleed** n hemorragia f nasal. ~**dive** n picado m

nostalgia /nɒˈstældʒə/ n nostalgia f. ~**c** a nostálgico

nostril /ˈnɒstrɪl/ n nariz f; (of horse) ollar m

nosy /ˈnəʊzɪ/ a (-ier, -iest) (fam) entrometido

not /nɒt/ adv no. ~ **at all** no... nada; (after thank you) de nada. ~ **yet** aún no. **I do** ~ **know** no sé. **I suppose** ~ supongo que no

notable /ˈnəʊtəbl/ a notable. —n (person) notabilidad f. ~**y** /ˈnəʊtəblɪ/ adv notablemente

notary /ˈnəʊtərɪ/ n notario m

notation /nəʊˈteɪʃn/ n notación f

notch /nɒtʃ/ n muesca f. —vt. ~ **up** apuntar (score etc)

note /nəʊt/ n nota f; (banknote) billete m. **take ~s** tomar apuntes. —vt notar. **~book** n libreta f. **~d** a célebre. **~paper** n papel m de escribir. **~worthy** a notable

nothing /'nʌθɪŋ/ pron nada. **he eats ~** no come nada. **for ~** (free) gratis; (in vain) inútilmente. —n nada f; (person) nulidad f; (thing of no importance) fruslería f; (zero) cero m. —adv de ninguna manera. **~ big** nada grande. **~ else** nada más. **~ much** poca cosa

notice /'nəʊtɪs/ n (attention) atención f; (advert) anuncio m; (sign) letrero m; (poster) cartel m; (termination of employment) despido m; (warning) aviso m. **(advance) ~** previo aviso m. **(of dismissal)** despido m. **take ~ of** prestar atención a, hacer caso a (person); hacer caso de (thing). —vt notar. **~able** a evidente. **~ably** adv visiblemente. **~board** n tablón m de anuncios

notification /nəʊtɪfɪ'keɪʃn/ n aviso m, notificación f. **~y** vt avisar

notion /'nəʊʃn/ n (concept) concepto m; (idea) idea f. **~s** npl (sewing goods etc, Amer) artículos mpl de mercería

notoriety /nəʊtə'raɪətɪ/ n notoriedad f; (pej) mala fama f. **~ous** /nəʊ'tɔːrɪəs/ a notorio. **~ously** adv notoriamente

notwithstanding /nɒtwɪθ'stændɪŋ/ prep a pesar de. —adv sin embargo

nougat /'nuːgɑː/ n turrón m

nought /nɔːt/ n cero m

noun /naʊn/ n sustantivo m, nombre m

nourish /'nʌrɪʃ/ vt alimentar; (incl fig) nutrir. **~ment** n alimento m

novel /'nɒvl/ n novela f. —a nuevo. **~ist** n novelista m & f. **~ty** n novedad f

November /nəʊ'vembə(r)/ n noviembre m

novice /'nɒvɪs/ n principiante m & f

now /naʊ/ adv ahora. **~ and again**, **~ and then** de vez en cuando. **just ~** ahora mismo; (a moment ago) hace poco. —conj ahora que

nowadays /'naʊədeɪz/ adv hoy (en) día

nowhere /'nəʊweə(r)/ adv en/por ninguna parte; (after motion towards) a ninguna parte

noxious /'nɒkʃəs/ a nocivo

nozzle /'nɒzl/ n boquilla f; (tec) tobera f

nuance /'njuːɑːns/ n matiz m

nuclear /'njuːklɪə(r)/ a nuclear

nucleus /'njuːklɪəs/ n (pl **-lei** /-lɪaɪ/) núcleo m

nude /njuːd/ a & n desnudo (m). **in the ~** desnudo

nudge /nʌdʒ/ vt dar un codazo a. —n codazo m

nudism /'njuːdɪzəm/ n desnudismo m. **~st** n nudista m & f. **~ty** /'njuːdətɪ/ n desnudez f

nuisance /'njuːsns/ n (thing, event) fastidio m; (person) pesado m. **be a ~** dar la lata

null /nʌl/ a nulo. **~ify** vt anular

numb /nʌm/ a entumecido. —vt entumecer

number /'nʌmbə(r)/ n número m. —vt numerar; (count, include) contar. **~-plate** n matrícula f

numeracy /'njuːmərəsɪ/ n conocimientos mpl de matemáticas

numeral /'njuːmərəl/ n número m

numerate /'njuːmərət/ a que tiene buenos conocimientos de matemáticas

numerical /njuː'merɪkl/ a numérico

numerous /ˈnjuːmərəs/ a numeroso

nun /nʌn/ n monja f

nurse /nɜːs/ n enfermera f, enfermero m; (nanny) niñera f. **wet ~** n nodriza f. —vt cuidar; abrigar ⟨hope etc⟩. **~maid** n niñera f

nursery /ˈnɜːsəri/ n cuarto m de los niños; (for plants) vivero m. **(day) ~** n guardería f infantil. **~ rhyme** n canción f infantil. **~ school** n escuela f de párvulos

nursing home /ˈnɜːsɪŋhəʊm/ n (for old people) asilo m de ancianos

nurture /ˈnɜːtʃə(r)/ vt alimentar

nut /nʌt/ n (walnut, Brazil nut etc) nuez f; (hazlenut) avellana f; (peanut) cacahuete m; (tec) tuerca f; (crazy person, sl) chiflado m. **~crackers** npl cascanueces m invar

nutmeg /ˈnʌtmeg/ n nuez f moscada

nutrient /ˈnjuːtrɪənt/ n alimento m

nutrit|ion /njuːˈtrɪʃn/ n nutrición f. **~ious** a nutritivo

nuts /nʌts/ a (crazy, sl) chiflado

nutshell /ˈnʌtʃel/ n cáscara f de nuez. **in a ~** en pocas palabras

nuzzle /ˈnʌzl/ vt acariciar con el hocico

NW abbr (north-west) noroeste m

nylon /ˈnaɪlɒn/ n nailon m. **~s** npl medias fpl de nailon

nymph /nɪmf/ n ninfa f

O

oaf /əʊf/ n (pl oafs) zoquete m

oak /əʊk/ n roble m

OAP /əʊeɪˈpiː/ abbr (old-age pensioner) n pensionista m & f

oar /ɔː(r)/ n remo m. **~sman** /ˈɔːzmən/ n (pl -men) remero m

oasis /əʊˈeɪsɪs/ n (pl oases /-siːz/) oasis m invar

oath /əʊθ/ n juramento m; (swear-word) palabrota f

oat|meal /ˈəʊtmiːl/ n harina f de avena. **~s** /əʊts/ npl avena f

obedien|ce /əˈbiːdɪəns/ n obediencia f. **~t** /əˈbiːdɪənt/ a obediente. **~tly** adv obedientemente

obelisk /ˈɒbəlɪsk/ n obelisco m

obes|e /əʊˈbiːs/ a obeso. **~ity** n obesidad f

obey /əʊˈbeɪ/ vt obedecer; cumplir ⟨instructions etc⟩

obituary /əˈbɪtʃʊərɪ/ n necrología f

object /ˈɒbdʒɪkt/ n objeto m. /əbˈdʒekt/ vi oponerse

objection /əbˈdʒekʃn/ n objeción f. **~able** /əbˈdʒekʃnəbl/ a censurable; (unpleasant) desagradable

objective /əbˈdʒektɪv/ a & n objetivo (m). **~ively** adv objetivamente

objector /əbˈdʒektə(r)/ n objetante m & f

obligat|ion /ɒblɪˈgeɪʃn/ n obligación f. **be under an ~ation** to tener obligación de. **~atory** /əˈblɪgətrɪ/ a obligatorio. **~e** /əˈblaɪdʒ/ vt obligar; (do a small service) hacer un favor a. **~ed** a agradecido. **much ~ed!** ¡muchas gracias! **~ing** a atento

oblique /əˈbliːk/ a oblicuo

obliterat|e /əˈblɪtəreɪt/ vt borrar. **~ion** /-ˈreɪʃn/ n borradura f

oblivi|on /əˈblɪvɪən/ n olvido m. **~ous** /əˈblɪvɪəs/ a (unaware) inconsciente (to, of de)

oblong /ˈɒblɒŋ/ a & n oblongo (m)

obnoxious /əbˈnɒkʃəs/ a odioso

oboe /ˈəʊbəʊ/ n oboe m

obscen|e /əbˈsiːn/ a obsceno. **~ity** /-enətɪ/ n obscenidad f

obscure /əbˈskjʊə(r)/ a oscuro. —vt oscurecer; (conceal) esconder; (*confuse*) confundir. **~ity** *n* oscuridad *f*

obsequious /əbˈsiːkwɪəs/ *a* obsequioso

observan|ce /əbˈzɜːvəns/ *n* observancia *f*. **~t** /əbˈzɜːvənt/ *a* observador

observation /ɒbzəˈveɪʃn/ *n* observación *f*

observatory /əbˈzɜːvətrɪ/ *n* observatorio *m*

observe /əbˈzɜːv/ *vt* observar. **~r** *n* observador *m*

obsess /əbˈses/ *vt* obsesionar. **~ion** /-ʃn/ *n* obsesión *f*. **~ive** *a* obsesivo

obsolete /ˈɒbsəliːt/ *a* desusado

obstacle /ˈɒbstəkl/ *n* obstáculo *m*

obstetrics /əbˈstetrɪks/ *n* obstetricia *f*

obstina|cy /ˈɒbstɪnəsɪ/ *n* obstinación *f*. **~te** /ˈɒbstɪnət/ *a* obstinado. **~tely** *adv* obstinadamente

obstreperous /əbˈstrepərəs/ *a* turbulento, ruidoso, protestón

obstruct /əbˈstrʌkt/ *vt* obstruir. **~ion** /-ʃn/ *n* obstrucción *f*

obtain /əbˈteɪn/ *vt* obtener. **—***vi* prevalecer. **—able** *a* asequible

obtrusive /əbˈtruːsɪv/ *a* importuno

obtuse /əbˈtjuːs/ *a* obtuso

obviate /ˈɒbvɪeɪt/ *vt* evitar

obvious /ˈɒbvɪəs/ *a* obvio. **~ly** *adv* obviamente

occasion /əˈkeɪʒn/ *n* ocasión *f*, oportunidad *f*. **on** **~** de vez en cuando. **—***vt* ocasionar. **~al** /əˈkeɪʒənl/ *a* poco frecuente. **~ally** *adv* de vez en cuando

occult /ɒˈkʌlt/ *a* oculto

occupant /ˈɒkjʊpənt/ *n* ocupante *m & f*. **~ation** /ɒkjʊˈpeɪʃn/ *n* ocupación *f*; (*job*) trabajo *m*, profesión *f*. **~ational** *a* profesional. **~ier** *n* ocupante *m & f*. **~y** /ˈɒkjʊpaɪ/ *vt* ocupar

occur /əˈkɜː(r)/ *vi* (*pt* occurred) ocurrir, suceder; (*exist*) encontrarse. **it ~red to me that** se me ocurrió que. **~rence** /əˈkʌrəns/ *n* suceso *m*, acontecimiento *m*

ocean /ˈəʊʃn/ *n* océano *m*

o'clock /əˈklɒk/ *adv*. **it is 7 ~** son las siete

octagon /ˈɒktəgən/ *n* octágono *m*

octane /ˈɒkteɪn/ *n* octano *m*

octave /ˈɒktɪv/ *n* octava *f*

October /ɒkˈtəʊbə(r)/ *n* octubre *m*

octopus /ˈɒktəpəs/ *n* (*pl* **-puses**) pulpo *m*

oculist /ˈɒkjʊlɪst/ *n* oculista *m & f*

odd /ɒd/ *a* (**-er**, **-est**) extraño, raro; (*number*) impar; (*one of pair*) sin pareja; (*occasional*) poco frecuente; (*left over*) sobrante. **fifty-~** unos cincuenta, cincuenta y pico. **the ~ one out** la excepción *f*. **~ity** *n* (*thing*) curiosidad *f*; (*person*) excéntrico *m*. **~ly** *adv* extrañamente. **~ly enough** por extraño que parezca. **~ment** /ˈɒdmənt/ *n* retazo *m*. **~s** /ɒdz/ *npl* probabilidades *fpl*; (*in betting*) apuesta *f*. **~s and ends** retazos *mpl*. **at ~s** de punta, de malas

ode /əʊd/ *n* oda *f*

odious /ˈəʊdɪəs/ *a* odioso

odour /ˈəʊdə(r)/ *n* olor *m*. **~less** *a* inodoro

of /ɒv, əv/ *prep* de. **a friend ~ mine** un amigo mío. **how kind ~ you** es Vd muy amable

off /ɒf/ *adv* lejos; (*light etc*) apagado; (*tap*) cerrado; (*food*) pasado. **—***prep* de, desde; (*away from*) fuera de; (*distant from*) lejos de. **be better ~** estar mejor. **be ~** marcharse. **day ~** *n* día *m* de asueto, día *m* libre

offal /ˈɒfl/ *n* menudos *mpl*, asaduras *fpl*

off: ~**beat** a insólito. ~ **chance** n posibilidad f remota. ~ **colour** a indispuesto

offen|ce /əˈfens/ n ofensa f; (illegal act) delito m. **take** ~**ce** ofenderse. ~**d** /əˈfend/ vt ofender. ~**der** n delincuente m & f. ~**sive** /əˈfensɪv/ a ofensivo; (disgusting) repugnante. —n ofensiva f

offer /ˈɒfə(r)/ vt ofrecer. —n oferta f. **on** ~ en oferta

offhand /ɒfˈhænd/ a (casual) desenvuelto; (brusque) descortés. —adv de improviso

office /ˈɒfɪs/ n oficina f; (post) cargo m

officer /ˈɒfɪsə(r)/ n oficial m; (policeman) policía f, guardia m; (of organization) director m

official /əˈfɪʃl/ a & n oficial (m). ~**ly** adv oficialmente

officiate /əˈfɪʃɪeɪt/ vi oficiar. ~ **as** desempeñar las funciones de

officious /əˈfɪʃəs/ a oficioso

offing /ˈɒfɪŋ/ n. **in the** ~ en perspectiva

off: ~**licence** n tienda f de bebidas alcohólicas. ~**load** vt descargar. ~**putting** a (disconcerting, fam) desconcertante; (repellent) repugnante. ~**set** /ˈɒfset/ vt (pt ~**set**, pres p ~**setting**) contrapesar. ~**shoot** /ˈɒfʃuːt/ n retoño m; (fig) ramificación f. ~**side** /ɒfˈsaɪd/ a (sport) fuera de juego. ~**spring** /ˈɒfsprɪŋ/ n invar progenie f. ~**stage** a entre bastidores. ~**white** a blancuzco, color hueso

often /ˈɒfn/ adv muchas veces, con frecuencia, a menudo. **how** ~? ¿cuántas veces?

ogle /ˈəʊgl/ vt comerse con los ojos

ogre /ˈəʊgə(r)/ n ogro m

oh /əʊ/ int ¡oh!, ¡ay!

oil /ɔɪl/ n aceite m; (petroleum) petróleo m. —vt lubricar. ~**field** /ˈɔɪlfiːld/ n yacimiento m petrolífero. ~**painting** n pintura f al óleo. ~**rig** /ˈɔɪlrɪg/ n plataforma f de perforación. ~**skins** /ˈɔɪlskɪnz/ npl chubasquero m. ~**y** a aceitoso; (food) grasiento

ointment /ˈɔɪntmənt/ n ungüento m

OK /əʊˈkeɪ/ int ¡vale!, ¡de acuerdo! —a bien; (satisfactory) satisfactorio. —adv muy bien

old /əʊld/ a (-er, -est) viejo; (not modern) anticuado; (former) antiguo. **how** ~ **is she?** ¿cuántos años tiene? **she is ten years** ~ tiene diez años. **of** ~ de antaño. ~ **age** n vejez f. ~**fashioned** a anticuado. ~ **maid** n solterona f. ~**world** a antiguo

oleander /əʊlɪˈændə(r)/ n adelfa f

olive /ˈɒlɪv/ n (fruit) aceituna f; (tree) olivo m. —a de oliva; (colour) aceitunado

Olympic /əˈlɪmpɪk/ a olímpico. ~**s** npl, ~ **Games** npl Juegos mpl Olímpicos

omelette /ˈɒmlɪt/ n tortilla f, tortilla f de huevos (Mex)

om|en /ˈəʊmen/ n agüero m. ~**inous** /ˈɒmɪnəs/ a siniestro

omi|ssion /əˈmɪʃn/ n omisión f. ~**t** /əˈmɪt/ vt (pt omitted) omitir

omnipotent /ɒmˈnɪpətənt/ a omnipotente

on /ɒn/ prep en, sobre. ~ **foot** a pie. ~ **Monday** el lunes. ~ **Mondays** los lunes. ~ **seeing** al ver. ~ **the way** de camino. —adv (light etc) encendido; (put on) puesto, poco natural; (machine) en marcha; (tap) abierto. ~ **and off** de vez en cuando. ~ **and** ~ sin cesar. **and so** ~ y así sucesivamente. **be** ~ **at** (fam) criticar. **go** ~ continuar. **later** ~ más tarde

once /wʌns/ *adv* una vez; (*formerly*) antes. —*conj* una vez que. **at ~** en seguida. **~over** *n* (*fam*) ojeada *f*

oncoming /'ɒnkʌmɪŋ/ *a* que se acerca; (*traffic*) que viene en sentido contrario, de frente

one /wʌn/ *a & n* uno (*m*). —*pron* uno. **~ another** el uno al otro. **~ by** ~ uno a uno. **~ never knows** nunca se sabe. **the blue** ~ el azul. **this** ~ éste. **~off** *a* (*fam*) único

onerous /'ɒnərəs/ *a* oneroso

one: **~self** /wʌn'self/ *pron* (*subject*) uno mismo; (*object*) se; (*after prep*) sí (mismo). **by ~self** solo. **~sided** *a* unilateral. **~way** *a* (*street*) de dirección única; (*ticket*) de ida

onion /'ʌnɪən/ *n* cebolla *f*

onlooker /'ɒnlʊkə(r)/ *n* espectador *m*

only /'əʊnlɪ/ *a* único. **~ son** *n* hijo *m* único. —*adv* sólo, solamente. ~ **just** apenas. ~ **too** *de* veras. —*conj* pero, sólo que

onset /'ɒnset/ *n* principio *m*; (*attack*) ataque *m*

onslaught /'ɒnslɔːt/ *n* ataque *m* violento

onus /'əʊnəs/ *n* responsabilidad *f*

onward(s) /'ɒnwəd(z)/ *a & adv* hacia adelante

onyx /'ɒnɪks/ *n* ónice *f*

ooze /uːz/ *vt/i* rezumar

opal /'əʊpl/ *n* ópalo *m*

opaque /əʊ'peɪk/ *a* opaco

open /'əʊpən/ *a* abierto; (*free to all*) público; (*undisguised*) manifiesto; (*question*) discutible; (*view*) despejado. ~ **sea** *n* alta mar *f*. ~ **secret** *n* secreto *m* a voces. **O~ University** *n* Universidad *f* a Distancia. **half-~** *a* medio abierto. **in the ~** *n* al aire libre. —*vt/i* abrir. **~ended** *a* abierto. **~er** /'əʊpənə(r)/ *n* (*for tins*) abrelatas *m* invar; (*for*

bottles with caps) abrebotellas *m* invar; (*corkscrew*) sacacorchos *m* invar. **eye~er** *n* (*fam*) revelación *f*. **~ing** /'əʊpənɪŋ/ *n* abertura *f*; (*beginning*) principio *m*; (*job*) vacante *m*. **~ly** /'əʊpənlɪ/ *adv* abiertamente. **~minded** *a* imparcial

opera /'ɒprə/ *n* ópera *f*. **~ glasses** *npl* gemelos *mpl* de teatro

operate /'ɒpəreɪt/ *vt* hacer funcionar. —*vi* funcionar; (*medicine etc*) operar. ~ **on** (*med*) operar a

operatic /ɒpə'rætɪk/ *a* operístico

operation /ɒpə'reɪʃn/ *n* operación *f*; (*mec*) funcionamiento *m*. **in** ~ en vigor. **~al** /ɒpə'reɪʃnl/ *a* operacional

operative /'ɒpərətɪv/ *a* operativo; (*law etc*) en vigor

operator *n* operario *m*; (*telephonist*) telefonista *m & f*

operetta /ɒpə'retə/ *n* opereta *f*

opinion /ə'pɪnɪən/ *n* opinión *f*. **in my** ~ a mi parecer. **~ated** *a* dogmático

opium /'əʊpɪəm/ *n* opio *m*

opponent /ə'pəʊnənt/ *n* adversario *m*

opportune /'ɒpətjuːn/ *a* oportuno. **~ist** /ɒp'tjuːnɪst/ *n* oportunista *m & f*. **~ity** /ɒpə'tjuːnətɪ/ *n* oportunidad *f*

oppos|**e** /ə'pəʊz/ *vt* oponerse a. **~ed to** en contra de. **be ~ed to** oponerse a. **~ing** *a* opuesto

opposite /'ɒpəzɪt/ *a* opuesto; (*facing*) de enfrente. —*n* contrario *m*. —*adv* enfrente. —*prep* enfrente de. ~ **number** *n* homólogo *m*

opposition /ɒpə'zɪʃn/ *n* oposición *f*; (*resistence*) resistencia *f*

oppress /ə'pres/ *vt* oprimir. **~ion** /-ʃn/ *n* opresión *f*. **~ive** *a* (*cruel*) opresivo; (*heat*) sofocante. **~or** *n* opresor *m* opt /ɒpt/ vi. ~ for elegir. ~ out negarse a participar

optic|al /'ɒptɪkl/ a óptico. ~ian /ɒp'tɪʃn/ n óptico m

optimis|m /'ɒptɪmɪzəm/ n optimismo m. ~t /'ɒptɪmɪst/ n optimista m & f. ~tic /-'mɪstɪk/ a optimista

optimum /'ɒptɪməm/ n lo óptimo, lo mejor

option /'ɒpʃn/ n opción f. ~al /'ɒpʃənl/ a facultativo

opulen|ce /'ɒpjʊləns/ n opulencia f. ~t /'ɒpjʊlənt/ a opulento

or /ɔː(r)/ conj o; (before Spanish o- and ho-) u; (after negative) ni. ~ else si no, o bien

oracle /'ɒrəkl/ n oráculo m

oral /'ɔːrəl/ a oral. —n (fam) examen m oral

orange /'ɒrɪndʒ/ n naranja f; (tree) naranjo m; (colour) color m naranja. —a de color naranja. ~ade n naranjada f

orator /'ɒrətə(r)/ n orador m

oratorio /ɒrə'tɔːrɪəʊ/ n (pl -os) oratorio m

oratory /'ɒrətrɪ/ n oratoria f

orb /ɔːb/ n orbe m

orbit /'ɔːbɪt/ n órbita f. —vt orbitar

orchard /'ɔːtʃəd/ n huerto m

orchestra /'ɔːkɪstrə/ n orquesta f. ~l /-'kestrəl/ a orquestal. ~te /'ɔːkɪstreɪt/ vt orquestar

orchid /'ɔːkɪd/ n orquídea f

ordain /ɔː'deɪn/ vt ordenar

ordeal /ɔː'diːl/ n prueba f dura

order /'ɔːdə(r)/ n orden m; (com) pedido m. in ~ that para, in ~ to para. —vt (command) mandar; (com) pedir

orderly /'ɔːdəlɪ/ a ordenado. —n asistente m & f

ordinary /'ɔːdɪnrɪ/ a corriente; (average) medio; (mediocre) ordinario

ordination /ɔːdɪ'neɪʃn/ n ordenación f

ore /ɔː(r)/ n mineral m

organ /'ɔːgən/ n órgano m

organic /ɔː'gænɪk/ a orgánico

organism /'ɔːgənɪzəm/ n organismo m

organist /'ɔːgənɪst/ n organista m & f

organiz|ation /ɔːgənaɪ'zeɪʃn/ n organización f. ~e /'ɔːgənaɪz/ vt organizar. ~er n organizador m

orgasm /'ɔːgæzəm/ n orgasmo m

orgy /'ɔːdʒɪ/ n orgía f

Orient /'ɔːrɪənt/ n Oriente m. ~al /-'entl/ a & n oriental (m & f)

orientat|e /'ɔːrɪəntet/ vt orientar. ~ion /-'teɪʃn/ n orientación f

orifice /'ɒrɪfɪs/ n orificio m

origin /'ɒrɪdʒɪn/ n origen m. ~al /ə'rɪdʒənl/ a original. ~ality /-'nælɪt/ n originalidad f. ~ally adv originalmente. ~ate /ə'rɪdʒəneɪt/ vi. ~ate from provenir de. ~ator n autor m

ormolu /'ɔːməluː/ n similor m

ornament /'ɔːnəmənt/ n adorno m. ~al /-'mentl/ a de adorno. ~ation /-en'teɪʃn/ n ornamentación f

ornate /ɔː'neɪt/ a adornado; (style) florido

ornithology /ɔːnɪ'θɒlədʒɪ/ n ornitología f

orphan /'ɔːfn/ n huérfano m. —vt dejar huérfano. ~age n orfanato m

orthodox /'ɔːθədɒks/ a ortodoxo. ~y n ortodoxia f

orthopaedic /ɔːθə'piːdɪk/ a ortopédico. ~s n ortopedia f

oscillate /'ɒsɪleɪt/ vi oscilar

ossify /'ɒsɪfaɪ/ vt osificar. —vi osificarse

ostensible /ɒs'tensɪbl/ a aparente. ~y adv aparentemente

ostentat|ion /ɒsten'teɪʃn/ n ostentación f. ~ious a ostentoso

osteopath /ˈɒstɪəpæθ/ n osteópata m & f. **~y** /-ˈɒpəθɪ/ n osteopatía f

ostracize /ˈɒstrəsaɪz/ vt excluir

ostrich /ˈɒstrɪtʃ/ n avestruz m

other /ˈʌðə(r)/ a & n & pron otro (m). **~ than** de otra manera que. **the ~ one** el otro. **~wise** /ˈʌðəwaɪz/ adv de otra manera; (or) si no

otter /ˈɒtə(r)/ n nutria f

ouch /aʊtʃ/ int ¡ay!

ought /ɔːt/ v aux deber. **I ~ to see it** debería verlo. **he ~ to have done it** debería haberlo hecho

ounce /aʊns/ n onza f (= 28.35 gr.)

our /ˈaʊə(r)/ a nuestro. **~s** /ˈaʊəz/ poss pron el nuestro, la nuestra, los nuestros, las nuestras. **~selves** /aʊəˈselvz/ pron (subject) nosotros mismos, nosotras mismas; (reflexive) nos; (after prep) nosotros (mismos), nosotras (mismas)

oust /aʊst/ vt expulsar, desalojar

out /aʊt/ adv fuera; (light) apagado; (in blossom) en flor; (in error) equivocado. **~and-~** cien por cien. **~ of date** anticuado; (not valid) caducado. **~ of doors** fuera. **~ of order** estropeado; (sign) no funciona. **~ of place** fuera de lugar; (fig) inoportuno. **~ of print** agotado. **~ of sorts** indispuesto. **~ of stock** agotado. **~ of tune** desafinado. **~ of work** parado, desempleado. **be ~** equivocarse. **be ~ of** quedarse sin. **be ~ to** estar resuelto a. **a five ~ of six** cinco de cada seis. **made ~ of** hecho de

outbid /aʊtˈbɪd/ vt (pt **-bid**, pres p **-bidding**) ofrecer más que

outboard /ˈaʊtbɔːd/ a fuera borda

outbreak /ˈaʊtbreɪk/ n (of anger) arranque m; (of war) comienzo m; (of disease) epidemia f

outbuilding /ˈaʊtbɪldɪŋ/ n dependencia f

outburst /ˈaʊtbɜːst/ n explosión f

outcast /ˈaʊtkɑːst/ n paria m & f

outcome /ˈaʊtkʌm/ n resultado m

outcry /ˈaʊtkraɪ/ n protesta f

outdated /aʊtˈdeɪtɪd/ a anticuado

outdo /aʊtˈduː/ vt (pt **-did**, pp **-done**) superar

outdoor /ˈaʊtdɔː(r)/ a al aire libre. **~s** /-ˈdɔːz/ adv al aire libre

outer /ˈaʊtə(r)/ a exterior

outfit /ˈaʊtfɪt/ n equipo m; (clothes) traje m. **~ter** n camisero m

outgoing /ˈaʊtɡəʊɪŋ/ a (minister etc) saliente; (sociable) abierto. **~s** npl gastos mpl

outgrow /æʊtˈɡrəʊ/ vt (pt **-grew**, pp **-grown**) crecer más que (person); hacerse demasiado grande para (clothes). **he's ~n his trousers** le quedan pequeños los pantalones

outhouse /ˈaʊthaʊs/ n dependencia f

outing /ˈaʊtɪŋ/ n excursión f

outlandish /aʊtˈlændɪʃ/ a extravagante

outlaw /ˈaʊtlɔː/ n proscrito m. — vt proscribir

outlay /ˈaʊtleɪ/ n gastos mpl

outlet /ˈaʊtlet/ n salida f

outline /ˈaʊtlaɪn/ n contorno m; (summary) resumen m. —vt trazar; (describe) dar un resumen de

outlive /aʊtˈlɪv/ vt sobrevivir a

outlook /ˈaʊtlʊk/ n perspectiva f

outlying /ˈaʊtlaɪɪŋ/ a remoto

outmoded /aʊtˈməʊdɪd/ a anticuado

outnumber /aʊtˈnʌmbə(r)/ vt sobrepasar en número

outpatient /'aʊtpeɪʃnt/ n paciente m externo

outpost /'aʊtpəʊst/ n avanzada f

output /'aʊtpʊt/ n producción f

outrage /'aʊtreɪdʒ/ n ultraje m. —vt ultrajar. **~ous** /aʊt'reɪdʒəs/ a escandaloso, atroz

outright /'aʊtraɪt/ adv completamente; (at once) inmediatamente; (frankly) francamente. —a completo; (refusal) rotundo

outset /'aʊtset/ n principio m

outside /'aʊtsaɪd/ a & n exterior (m). /aʊt'saɪd/ adv fuera. —prep fuera de. **~r** /aʊt'saɪdə(r)/ n forastero m; (in race) caballo m no favorito

outsize /'aʊtsaɪz/ a de tamaño extraordinario

outskirts /'aʊtskɜːts/ npl afueras fpl

outspoken /aʊt'spəʊkn/ a franco. **be ~** no tener pelos en la lengua

outstanding /aʊt'stændɪŋ/ a excepcional; (not settled) pendiente; (conspicuous) sobresaliente

outstretched /aʊt'stretʃt/ a extendido

outstrip /aʊt'strɪp/ vt (pt -stripped) superar

outward /'aʊtwəd/ a externo; (journey) de ida. **~ly** adv por fuera, exteriormente. **~(s)** adv hacia fuera

outweigh /aʊt'weɪ/ vt pesar más que; (fig) valer más que

outwit /aʊt'wɪt/ vt (pt -witted) ser más listo que

oval /'əʊvl/ a oval(ado). —n óvalo m

ovary /'əʊvərɪ/ n ovario m

ovation /əʊ'veɪʃn/ n ovación f

oven /'ʌvn/ n horno m

over /'əʊvə(r)/ prep por encima de; (across) al otro lado de; (during) durante; (more than) más

de. **~ and above** por encima de. —adv por encima; (ended) terminado; (more) más; (in excess) de sobra. **~ again** otra vez. **~ and ~** una y otra vez. **~ here** por aquí. **~ there** por allí. **all ~** por todas partes

over /'əʊvə(r)/ pref sobre..., super...

overall /əʊvər'ɔːl/ a global; (length, cost) total. —adv en conjunto. /'əʊvərɔːl/ n, **~s** npl mono m

overawe /əʊvər'ɔː/ vt intimidar

overbalance /əʊvə'bæləns/ vt hacer perder el equilibrio. —vi perder el equilibrio

overbearing /əʊvə'beərɪŋ/ a dominante

overboard /əʊvə'bɔːd/ adv al agua

overbook /əʊvə'bʊk/ vt aceptar demasiadas reservaciones para

overcast /əʊvə'kɑːst/ a nublado

overcharge /əʊvə'tʃɑːdʒ/ vt (fill too much) sobrecargar; (charge too much) cobrar demasiado

overcoat /'əʊvəkəʊt/ n abrigo m

overcome /əʊvə'kʌm/ vt (pt -came, pp -come) superar, vencer. **be ~ by** estar abrumado de

overcrowded /əʊvə'kraʊdɪd/ a atestado (de gente)

overdo /əʊvə'duː/ vt (pt -did, pp -done) exagerar; (culin) cocer demasiado

overdose /'əʊvədəʊs/ n sobredosis f

overdraft /'əʊvədrɑːft/ n giro m en descubierto

overdraw /əʊvə'drɔː/ vt (pt -drew, pp -drawn) girar en descubierto. **be ~n** tener un saldo deudor

overdue /əʊvə'djuː/ a retrasado; (belated) tardío; (bill) vencido y no pagado

overestimate /əʊvər'estɪmeɪt/ vt sobrestimar

overflow /əʊvə'fləʊ/ vi desbordarse. /'əʊvəfləʊ/ n (excess) exceso m; (outlet) rebosadero m

overgrown /əʊvə'grəʊn/ a demasiado grande; (garden) cubierto de hierbas

overhang /əʊvə'hæŋ/ vt (pt -hung) sobresalir por encima de; (fig) amenazar. —vi sobresalir. /'əʊvəhæŋ/ n saliente f

overhaul /əʊvə'hɔːl/ vt revisar. /'əʊvəhɔːl/ n revisión f

overhead /əʊvə'hed/ adv por encima. /'əʊvəhed/ a de arriba. **~s** npl gastos mpl generales

overhear /əʊvə'hɪə(r)/ vt (pt -heard) oír por casualidad

overjoyed /əʊvə'dʒɔɪd/ a muy contento. **he was ~** rebosaba de alegría

overland /'əʊvəlænd/ a terrestre. —adv por tierra

overlap /əʊvə'læp/ vt (pt -lapped) traslapar. —vi traslaparse

overleaf /əʊvə'liːf/ adv a la vuelta. **see ~** véase al dorso

overload /əʊvə'ləʊd/ vt sobrecargar

overlook /əʊvə'lʊk/ vt dominar; (building) dar a; (forget) olvidar; (oversee) inspeccionar; (forgive) perdonar

overnight /əʊvə'naɪt/ adv por la noche, durante la noche; (fig, instantly) de la noche a la mañana. **stay ~** pasar la noche. —a de noche

overpass /'əʊvəpɑːs/ n paso m a desnivel, paso m elevado

overpay /əʊvə'peɪ/ vt (pt -paid) pagar demasiado

overpower /əʊvə'paʊə(r)/ vt subyugar; dominar (opponent); (fig) abrumar. **~ing** a abrumador

overpriced /əʊvə'praɪst/ a demasiado caro

overrate /əʊvə'reɪt/ vt supervalorar

overreach /əʊvə'riːtʃ/ vr. **~ o.s.** extralimitarse

overreact /əʊvərɪ'ækt/ vi reaccionar excesivamente

override /əʊvə'raɪd/ vt (pt -rode, pp -ridden) pasar por encima de. **~ing** a dominante

overripe /'əʊvəraɪp/ a pasado, demasiado maduro

overrule /əʊvə'ruːl/ vt anular; denegar (claim)

overrun /əʊvə'rʌn/ vt (pt -ran, pp -run, pres p -running) invadir; exceder (limit)

overseas /əʊvə'siːz/ a de ultramar. —adv al extranjero, en ultramar

oversee /əʊvə'siː/ vt (pt -saw, pp -seen) vigilar. **~r** /'əʊvəsɪə(r)/ n supervisor m

overshadow /əʊvə'ʃædəʊ/ vt (darken) sombrear; (fig) eclipsar

overshoot /əʊvə'ʃuːt/ vt (pt -shot) excederse. **~ the mark** pasarse de la raya

oversight /'əʊvəsaɪt/ n descuido m

oversleep /əʊvə'sliːp/ vi (pt -slept) despertarse tarde. **I overslept** se me pegaron las sábanas

overstep /əʊvə'step/ vt (pt -stepped) pasar de. **~ the mark** pasarse de la raya

overt /'əʊvɜːt/ a manifiesto

overtak|e /əʊvə'teɪk/ vt/i (pt -took, pp -taken) sobrepasar; (auto) adelantar. **~ing** n adelantamiento m

overtax /əʊvə'tæks/ vt exigir demasiado

overthrow /əʊvə'θrəʊ/ vt (pt -threw, pp -thrown) derrocar. /'əʊvəθrəʊ/ n derrocamiento m

overtime /'əʊvətaɪm/ n horas fpl extra

overtone /'əʊvətəʊn/ n (fig) matiz m

overture /'əʊvətjʊə(r)/ n obertura f. ~s npl (fig) propuestas fpl

overturn /əʊvə'tɜːn/ vt/i volcar

overweight /'əʊvəweit/ a demasiado pesado. **be ~** pesar demasiado, ser gordo

overwhelm /əʊvə'welm/ vt aplastar; (with emotion) abrumar. ~ing a aplastante; (fig) abrumador

overwork /əʊvə'wɜːk/ vt hacer trabajar demasiado. —vi trabajar demasiado. —n trabajo m excesivo

ovulation /ɒvjʊ'leiʃn/ n ovulación f

owe /əʊ/ vt deber. ~ing a debido. ~ing to a causa de

owl /aʊl/ n lechuza f, búho m

own /əʊn/ a propio. **get one's ~ back** (fam) vengarse. **hold one's ~** mantenerse firme, saber defenderse. **on one's ~** por su cuenta. —vt poseer, tener. —vi. **~ up (to)** confesar. **~er** n propietario m, dueño m. **~ership** n posesión f; (right) propiedad f

ox /ɒks/ n (pl oxen) buey m

oxide /'ɒksaid/ n óxido m

oxygen /'ɒksidʒən/ n oxígeno m

oyster /'ɔistə(r)/ n ostra f

P

p /piː/ abbr (pence, penny) penique(s) (m/pl)

pace /peis/ n paso m. —vi. **~ up and down** pasearse de aquí para allá. **~-maker** n (runner) el que marca el paso; (med) marcapasos m invar. **keep ~ with** andar al mismo paso que

Pacific /pə'sifik/ a pacífico. —n. **~ (Ocean)** (Océano m) Pacífico m

pacif|ist /'pæsifist/ n pacifista m & f. **~y** /'pæsifai/ vt apaciguar

pack /pæk/ n fardo m; (of cards) baraja f; (of hounds) jauría f; (of wolves) manada f; (large amount) montón m. —vt empaquetar; hacer (suitcase); (press down) apretar. —vi hacer la maleta. **~age** /'pækidʒ/ n paquete m. —vt empaquetar. **~age deal** n acuerdo m global. **~age tour** n viaje m organizado. **~ed lunch** almuerzo m frío. **~ed out** (fam) de bote en bote. **~et** /'pækit/ n paquete m. **send ~ing** echar a paseo

pact /pækt/ n pacto m, acuerdo m

pad /pæd/ n almohadilla f; (for writing) bloc m; (for ink) tampón m; (flat, fam) piso m. —vt (pt padded) rellenar. **~ding** n relleno m. —vi andar a pasos quedos. **launching ~** plataforma f de lanzamiento

paddle[1] /'pædl/ n canalete m

paddle[2] /'pædl/ vi mojarse los pies

paddle-steamer /'pædlstiːmə(r)/ n vapor m de ruedas

paddock /'pædək/ n recinto m; (field) prado m

paddy /'pædi/ n arroz m con cáscara. **~-field** n arrozal m

padlock /'pædlɒk/ n candado m. —vt cerrar con candado

paediatrician /piːdiə'triʃn/ n pediatra m & f

pagan /'peigən/ a & n pagano (m)

page[1] /peidʒ/ n página f. —vt paginar

page[2] /peidʒ/ n (in hotel) botones m invar. —vt llamar

pageant /'pædʒənt/ n espectáculo m (histórico). **~ry** n boato m

pagoda /pə'gəʊdə/ n pagoda f

paid /peɪd/ *see* pay. —*a.* **put ~ to**
(*fam*) acabar con

pail /peɪl/ *n* cubo *m*

pain /peɪn/ *n* dolor *m*. **~ in the
neck** (*fam*) (*persona*) pesado *m*;
⟨*thing*⟩ lata *f*. **be in ~** tener
dolores. **~s** *npl* (*effort*) esfuerzos
mpl. **be at ~s** esmerarse. —*vt*
doler. **~ful** /'peɪnfl/ *a* doloroso;
(*laborious*) penoso. **~killer** *n*
calmante *m*. **~less** *a* indoloro.
~staking /'peɪnzteɪkɪŋ/ *a*
esmerado

paint /peɪnt/ *n* pintura *f*. —*vt/i*
pintar. **~er** *n* pintor *m*. **~ing** *n*
pintura *f*

pair /peə(r)/ *n* par *m*; (*of people*)
pareja *f*. **~ of trousers** pantalón
m, pantalones *mpl*. —*vi* emparejarse. **~ off** emparejarse

pajamas /pə'dʒɑ:məz/ *npl* pijama
m

Pakistan /pɑ:kɪ'stɑ:n/ *n* el Pakistán
m. **~i** *a & n* paquistaní (*m & f*)

pal /pæl/ *n* (*fam*) amigo *m*

palace /'pælɪs/ *n* palacio *m*

palat|able /'pælətəbl/ *a* sabroso;
(*fig*) aceptable. **~e** /'pælət/ *n* paladar *m*

palatial /pə'leɪʃl/ *a* suntuoso

palaver /pə'lɑ:və(r)/ *n* (*fam*) lío *m*

pale[1] /peɪl/ *a* (**-er, -est**) pálido;
⟨*colour*⟩ claro. —*vi* palidecer

pale[2] /peɪl/ *n* estaca *n*

paleness /'peɪlnɪs/ *n* palidez *f*

Palestin|e /'pælɪstaɪn/ *n* Palest-
ina *f*. **~ian** /-'stɪnɪən/ *a & n* el
palestino (*m*)

palette /'pælɪt/ *n* paleta *f*.
~knife *n* espátula *f*

pall[1] /pɔːl/ *n* paño *m* mortuorio;
(*fig*) capa *f*

pall[2] /pɔːl/ *vi.* **~ (on)** perder su
sabor (para)

pallid /'pælɪd/ *a* pálido

palm /pɑːm/ *n* palma *f*. —*vt.* **~ off**
encajar (**on** a). **~ist** /'pɑːmɪst/ *n*
quiromántico *m*. **P~ Sunday** *n*
Domingo *m* de Ramos

palpable /'pælpəbl/ *a* palpable

palpitat|e /'pælpɪteɪt/ *vi* palpitar.
~ion /-'teɪʃn/ *n* palpitación *f*

paltry /'pɔːltrɪ/ *a* (**-ier, -iest**)
insignificante

pamper /'pæmpə(r)/ *vt* mimar

pamphlet /'pæmflɪt/ *n* folleto *m*

pan /pæn/ *n* cacerola *f*; (*for fry-
ing*) sartén *f*; (*of scales*) platillo
m; (*of lavatory*) taza *f*

panacea /pænə'sɪə/ *n* panacea *f*

panache /pæ'næʃ/ *n* brío *m*

pancake /'pænkeɪk/ *n* hojuela *f*,
crêpe *f*

panda /'pændə/ *n* panda *m*. **~ car**
n coche *m* de la policía

pandemonium /pændɪ'məʊnɪəm/
n pandemonio *m*

pander /'pændə(r)/ *vi.* **~ to**
complacer

pane /peɪn/ *n* (*of glass*) vidrio *m*

panel /'pænl/ *n* panel *m*; (*group
of people*) jurado *m*. **~ling** *n*
paneles *mpl*

pang /pæŋ/ *n* punzada *f*

panic /'pænɪk/ *n* pánico *m*. —*vi*
(*pt* **panicked**) ser preso de
pánico. **~stricken** *a* preso de
pánico

panoram|a /pænə'rɑːmə/ *n* pan-
orama *m*. **~ic** /-'ræmɪk/ *a*
panorámico

pansy /'pænzɪ/ *n* pensamiento *m*;
(*effeminate man, fam*) maricón
m

pant /pænt/ *vi* jadear

pantechnicon /pæn'teknɪkən/ *n*
camión *m* de mudanzas

panther /'pænθə(r)/ *n* pantera *f*

panties /'pæntɪz/ *npl* bragas *fpl*

pantomime /'pæntəmaɪm/ *n*
pantomima *f*

pantry /'pæntrɪ/ *n* despensa *f*

pants /pænts/ *npl* (*man's underwear, fam*) calzoncillos *mpl*;
(*woman's underwear, fam*)
bragas *fpl*; (*trousers, fam*) pantalones *mpl*

papa|cy /'peɪpəsɪ/ n papado m. ~la papal

paper /'peɪpə(r)/ n papel m; (newspaper) periódico m; (exam) examen m; (document) documento m. on ~ en teoría. –vt empapelar, tapizar (LAm). ~back /'peɪpəbæk/ a en rústica. – n libro m en rústica. ~clip n sujetapapeles m invar, clip m. ~weight /'peɪpəweɪt/ n pisapapeles m invar. ~work n papeleo m, trabajo m de oficina

papier mâché /'pæpɪeɪ'mæʃeɪ/ n cartón m piedra

par /pɑː(r)/ n par f; (golf) par m. feel below ~ no estar en forma. on a ~ with a la par con

parable /'pærəbl/ n parábola f

parachut|e /'pærəʃuːt/ n paracaídas m invar. –vi lanzarse en paracaídas. ~ist n paracaidista m & f

parade /pə'reɪd/ n desfile m; (street) paseo m; (display) alarde m. –vi desfilar. –vt hacer alarde de

paradise /'pærədaɪs/ n paraíso m

paradox /'pærədɒks/ n paradoja f. ~ical /-'dɒksɪkl/ a paradójico

paraffin /'pærəfɪn/ n queroseno m

paragon /'pærəgən/ n dechado m

paragraph /'pærəgrɑːf/ n párrafo m

parallel /'pærəlel/ a paralelo. –n paralelo m; (line) paralela f. –vt ser paralelo a

paraly|se /'pærəlaɪz/ vt paralizar. ~sis /-sɪs/ n (pl -ses /-siːz/) parálisis f. ~tic /pærə'lɪtɪk/ a & n paralítico m

parameter /pə'ræmɪtə(r)/ n parámetro m

paramount /'pærəmaʊnt/ a supremo

paranoia /pærə'nɔɪə/ n paranoia f

parapet /'pærəpɪt/ n parapeto m

paraphernalia /pærəfə'neɪlɪə/ n trastos mpl

paraphrase /'pærəfreɪz/ n paráfrasis f. –vt parafrasear

paraplegic /pærə'pliːdʒɪk/ n parapléjico m

parasite /'pærəsaɪt/ n parásito m

parasol /'pærəsɒl/ n sombrilla f

paratrooper /'pærətruːpə(r)/ n paracaidista m

parcel /'pɑːsl/ n paquete m

parch /pɑːtʃ/ vt resecar. be ~ed tener mucha sed

parchment /'pɑːtʃmənt/ n pergamino m

pardon /'pɑːdn/ n perdón m; (jurid) indulto m. I beg your ~! ¡perdone Vd! I beg your ~? ¿cómo?, ¿mande? (Mex). –vt perdonar

pare /peə(r)/ vt cortar (nails); (peel) pelar, mondar

parent /'peərənt/ n (father) padre m; (mother) madre f; (source) origen m. ~s npl padres mpl. ~al /pə'rentl/ a de los padres

parenthesis /pə'renθəsɪs/ n (pl -theses /-siːz/) paréntesis m invar

parenthood /'peərənthʊd/ n paternidad f, maternidad f

Paris /'pærɪs/ n París m

parish /'pærɪʃ/ n parroquia f; (municipal) municipio m. ~ioner /pə'rɪʃənə(r)/ n feligrés m

Parisian /pə'rɪzɪən/ a & n parisino (m)

parity /'pærətɪ/ n igualdad f

park /pɑːk/ n parque m. –vt/i aparcar. ~ oneself vr (fam) instalarse

parka /'pɑːkə/ n anorak m

parking-meter /'pɑːkɪŋmiːtə(r)/ n parquímetro m

parliament /'pɑːləmənt/ n parlamento m. ~ary /-'mentrɪ/ a parlamentario

parlour /'pɑːlə(r)/ n salón m

parochial /pəˈrəʊkɪəl/ a parroquial; (*fig*) pueblerino

parody /ˈpærədɪ/ n parodia f. —vt parodiar

parole /pəˈrəʊl/ n libertad f bajo palabra, libertad f provisional. **on ~** libre bajo palabra. —vt liberar bajo palabra

paroxysm /ˈpærəksɪzəm/ n paroxismo m

parquet /ˈpɑːkeɪ/ n. **~ floor** parqué m

parrot /ˈpærət/ n papagayo m

parry /ˈpærɪ/ vt parar; (*avoid*) esquivar. —n parada f

parsimonious /pɑːsɪˈməʊnɪəs/ a parsimonioso

parsley /ˈpɑːslɪ/ n perejil m

parsnip /ˈpɑːsnɪp/ n pastinaca f

parson /ˈpɑːsn/ n cura m, párroco m

part /pɑːt/ n parte f; (*of machine*) pieza f; (*of serial*) entrega f; (*in play*) papel m; (*side in dispute*) partido m. **on the ~ of** por parte de. —adv en parte. —vt separar. **~ with** vt separarse de. —vi separarse

partake /pɑːˈteɪk/ vt (*pt* -**took**, *pp* -**taken**) participar. **~ of** compartir

partial /ˈpɑːʃl/ a parcial. **be ~ to** ser aficionado a. **~ity** /-ɪˈælɪtɪ/ n parcialidad f. **~ly** adv parcialmente

participa|nt /pɑːˈtɪsɪpənt/ n participante m & f. **~te** /pɑːˈtɪsɪpeɪt/ vi participar. **~tion** /-ˈpeɪʃn/ n participación f

participle /ˈpɑːtɪsɪpl/ n participio m

particle /ˈpɑːtɪkl/ n partícula f

particular /pəˈtɪkjʊlə(r)/ a particular; (*precise*) meticuloso; (*fastidious*) quisquilloso. —n. **in ~** especialmente. **~ly** adv especialmente. **~s** npl detalles mpl

parting /ˈpɑːtɪŋ/ n separación f; (*in hair*) raya f. —a de despedida

partisan /pɑːtɪˈzæn/ n partidario m

partition /pɑːˈtɪʃn/ n partición f; (*wall*) tabique m. —vt dividir en parte

partly /ˈpɑːtlɪ/ adv en parte

partner /ˈpɑːtnə(r)/ n socio m; (*sport*) pareja f. **~ship** n asociación f; (*com*) sociedad f

partridge /ˈpɑːtrɪdʒ/ n perdiz f

part-time /ˈpɑːtˈtaɪm/ a & adv a tiempo parcial

party /ˈpɑːtɪ/ n reunión f, fiesta f; (*group*) grupo m; (*pol*) partido m; (*jurid*) parte f. **~ line** n (*telephone*) línea f colectiva

pass /pɑːs/ vt pasar; (*in front of*) pasar por delante de; (*overtake*) adelantar; (*approve*) aprobar (*exam, bill, law*); hacer (*remark*); pronunciar (*judgement*). **~ down** transmitir. **~ over** pasar por alto de. **~ round** distribuir. **~ through** pasar por; (*cross*) atravesar. **~ up** (*fam*) dejar pasar. —vi pasar; (*in exam*) aprobar. **~ away** morir. **~ out** (*fam*) desmayarse. —n (*permit*) permiso m; (*in mountains*) puerto m, desfiladero m; (*sport*) pase m; (*in exam*) aprobado m. **make a ~ at** (*fam*) hacer proposiciones amorosas a. **~able** /ˈpɑːsəbl/ a pasable; (*road*) transitable

passage /ˈpæsɪdʒ/ n paso m; (*voyage*) travesía f; (*corridor*) pasillo m; (*in book*) pasaje m

passenger /ˈpæsɪndʒə(r)/ n pasajero m

passer-by /pɑːsəˈbaɪ/ n (*pl* **passers-by**) transeúnte m & f

passion /ˈpæʃn/ n pasión f. **~ate** a apasionado. **~ately** adv apasionadamente

passive /ˈpæsɪv/ a pasivo. **~ness** n pasividad f

passmark /ˈpɑːsmɑːk/ n aprobado m

Passover /ˈpɑːsəʊvə(r)/ n Pascua f de los hebreos

passport /ˈpɑːspɔːt/ n pasaporte m

password /ˈpɑːswɜːd/ n contraseña f

past /pɑːst/ a & n pasado (m). in times ~ en tiempos pasados. the ~ week n la semana f pasada. —prep por delante de; (beyond) más allá de. —adv por delante. drive ~ pasar en coche. go ~ pasar

paste /peɪst/ n pasta f; (adhesive) engrudo m. —vt (fasten) pegar; (cover) engrudar. ~board /ˈpeɪstbɔːd/ n cartón m. ~ jewellery n joyas fpl de imitación

pastel /ˈpæstl/ a & n pastel (m)

pasteurize /ˈpæstʃəraɪz/ vt pasteurizar

pastiche /pæˈstiːʃ/ n pastiche m

pastille /ˈpæstl/ n pastilla f

pastime /ˈpɑːstaɪm/ n pasatiempo m

pastoral /ˈpɑːstərəl/ a pastoral

pastr|ies npl pasteles mpl, pastas fpl. ~y /ˈpeɪstrɪ/ n pasta f

pasture /ˈpɑːstʃə(r)/ n pasto m

pasty[1] /ˈpæstɪ/ n empanada f

pasty[2] /ˈpeɪstɪ/ a pastoso; (pale) pálido

pat[1] /pæt/ vt (pt patted) dar palmaditas en; acariciar ‹dog etc›. —n palmadita f; (of butter) porción f

pat[2] /pæt/ adv en el momento oportuno

patch /pætʃ/ n pedazo m; (period) período m; (repair) remiendo m; (piece of ground) terreno m. not a ~ on (fam) muy inferior a. —vt remendar. ~ up arreglar. ~work n labor m de retazos; (fig) mosaico m. ~y a desigual

pâté /ˈpæteɪ/ n pasta f, pasté m

patent /ˈpeɪtnt/ a patente. —n patente f. —vt patentar. ~ leather n charol m. ~ly adv evidentemente

patern|al /pəˈtɜːnl/ a paterno. ~ity /pəˈtɜːnətɪ/ n paternidad f

path /pɑːθ/ n (pl -s /pɑːðz/) sendero m; (sport) pista f; (of rocket) trayectoria f; (fig) camino m

pathetic /pəˈθetɪk/ a patético, lastimoso

pathology /pəˈθɒlədʒɪ/ n patología f

pathos /ˈpeɪθɒs/ n patetismo f

patien|ce /ˈpeɪʃns/ n paciencia f. ~t /ˈpeɪʃnt/ a & n paciente (m & f). ~tly adv con paciencia

patio /ˈpætɪəʊ/ n (pl -os) patio m

patriarch /ˈpeɪtrɪɑːk/ n patriarca m

patrician /pəˈtrɪʃn/ a & n patricio (m)

patriot /ˈpætrɪət/ n patriota m & f. ~ic /-ˈɒtɪk/ a patriótico. ~ism n patriotismo m

patrol /pəˈtrəʊl/ n patrulla f. —vt/i patrullar

patron /ˈpeɪtrən/ n (of the arts etc) mecenas m & f; (customer) cliente m & f; (of charity) patrocinador m. ~age /ˈpætrənɪdʒ/ n patrocinio m; (of shop etc) clientela f. ~ize vt ser cliente de; (fig) tratar con condescendencia

patter[1] /ˈpætə(r)/ n (of steps) golpeteo m; (of rain) tamborileo m. —vi correr con pasos ligeros; (rain) tamborilear

patter[2] /ˈpætə(r)/ n (speech) jerga f; (chatter) parloteo m

pattern /ˈpætn/ n diseño m; (model) modelo m; (sample) muestra f; (manner) modo m; (in dressmaking) patrón m

paunch /pɔːntʃ/ n panza f

pauper /ˈpɔːpə(r)/ n indigente m & f, pobre m & f

pause /pɔːz/ n pausa f. —vi hacer una pausa

pave /peɪv/ vt pavimentar. ~ the way for preparar el terreno para

pavement /ˈpeɪvmənt/ n pavimento m; (at side of road) acera f

pavilion /pəˈvɪlɪən/ n pabellón m

paving-stone /ˈpeɪvɪŋstəʊn/ n losa f

paw /pɔː/ n pata f; (of cat) garra f. —vi tocar con la pata; (person) manosear

pawn[1] /pɔːn/ n (chess) peón m; (fig) instrumento m

pawn[2] /pɔːn/ vt empeñar. —n. in ~ en prenda. **~broker** /pɔːn ˈbrəʊkə(r)/ n prestamista m & f. **~shop** n monte m de piedad

pawpaw /ˈpɔːpɔː/ n papaya f

pay /peɪ/ vt (pt **paid**) pagar; prestar (attention); hacer (compliment, visit). ~ **back** devolver. ~ **cash** pagar al contado. ~ **in** ingresar. ~ **off** pagar. ~ **out** pagar. —vi pagar; (be profitable) rendir. —n paga f. **in the** ~ **of** al servicio de. **~able** /ˈpeɪəbl/ a pagadero. **~ment** /ˈpeɪmənt/ n pago m. **~off** n (sl) liquidación f; (fig) ajuste m de cuentas. **~roll** /ˈpeɪrəʊl/ n nómina f. ~ **up** pagar

pea /piː/ n guisante m

peace /piːs/ n paz f. ~ **of mind** tranquilidad f. **~able** a pacífico. **~ful** /ˈpiːsfl/ a tranquilo. **~maker** /ˈpiːsmeɪkə(r)/ n pacificador m

peach /piːtʃ/ n melocotón m, durazno m (LAm); (tree) melocotonero m, duraznero m (LAm)

peacock /ˈpiːkɒk/ n pavo m real

peak /piːk/ n cumbre f; (maximum) máximo m. ~ **hours** npl horas fpl punta. **~ed cap** n gorra f de visera

peaky /ˈpiːkɪ/ a pálido

peal /piːl/ n repique m. **~s of laughter** risotadas fpl

peanut /ˈpiːnʌt/ n cacahuete m, maní m (Mex). **~s** (sl) una bagatela f

pear /peə(r)/ n pera f; (tree) peral m

pearl /pɜːl/ n perla f. **~y** a nacarado

peasant /ˈpeznt/ n campesino m

peat /piːt/ n turba f

pebble /ˈpebl/ n guijarro m

peck /pek/ vt picotear; (kiss, fam) dar un besito a. —n picotazo m; (kiss) besito m. **~ish** /ˈpekɪʃ/ a. **be ~ish** (fam) tener hambre, tener gazuza (fam)

peculiar /prˈkjuːlɪə(r)/ a raro; (special) especial. **~ity** /-ˈærɪtɪ/ n rareza f; (feature) particularidad f

pedal /ˈpedl/ n pedal m. —vi pedalear

pedantic /prˈdæntɪk/ a pedante

peddle /ˈpedl/ vt vender por las calles

pedestal /ˈpedɪstl/ n pedestal m

pedestrian /prˈdestrɪən/ n peatón m. —a de peatones; (dull) prosaico. ~ **crossing** n paso m de peatones

pedigree /ˈpedɪgriː/ n linaje m; (of animal) pedigrí m. —a (animal) de raza

pedlar /ˈpedlə(r)/ n buhonero m, vendedor m ambulante

peek /piːk/ vi mirar a hurtadillas

peel /piːl/ n cáscara f. —vt pelar (fruit, vegetables). —vi pelarse. **~ings** npl peladuras fpl, monda f

peep[1] /piːp/ vi mirar a hurtadillas. —n mirada f furtiva

peep[2] /piːp/ (bird) piar. —n pío m

peep-hole /ˈpiːphəʊl/ n mirilla f

peer[1] /pɪə(r)/ vi mirar. ~ **at** escudriñar

peer[2] /pɪə(r)/ n par m, compañero m. **~age** n pares mpl

peeved /piːvd/ a (sl) irritado. **~ish** /ˈpiːvɪʃ/ a picajoso

peg /peg/ n clavija f; (for washing) pinza f; (hook) gancho m; (for tent) estaca f. **off the** ~ **de**

percha. —*vt* (*pt* **pegged**) fijar ⟨*precios*⟩. ~ **away at** afanarse por

pejorative /prɪˈdʒɒrətɪv/ *a* peyorativo, despectivo

pelican /ˈpelɪkən/ *n* pelícano *m*. ~ **crossing** *n* paso *m* de peatones (con semáforo)

pellet /ˈpelɪt/ *n* pelotilla *f*; (*for gun*) perdigón *m*

pelt[1] /pelt/ *n* pellejo *m*

pelt[2] /pelt/ *vt* tirar. —*vi* llover a cántaros

pelvis /ˈpelvɪs/ *n* pelvis *f*

pen[1] /pen/ *n* (*enclosure*) recinto *m*

pen[2] /pen/ *n* (*for writing*) pluma *f*, estilográfica *f*; (*ball-point*) bolígrafo *m*

penal /ˈpiːnl/ *a* penal. ~**ize** *vt* castigar. ~**ty** /ˈpenltɪ/ *n* castigo *m*; (*fine*) multa *f*. ~**ty kick** *n* (*football*) penalty *m*

penance /ˈpenəns/ *n* penitencia *f*

pence /pens/ *see* penny

pencil /ˈpensl/ *n* lápiz *m*. —*vt* (*pt* **pencilled**) escribir con lápiz. ~**sharpener** *n* sacapuntas *m invar*

pendant /ˈpendənt/ *n* dije *m*, medallón *m*

pending /ˈpendɪŋ/ *a* pendiente. —*prep* hasta

pendulum /ˈpendjʊləm/ *n* péndulo *m*

penetra|**te** /ˈpenɪtreɪt/ *vt/i* penetrar. ~**ing** *a* penetrante. ~**ion** /-ˈtreɪʃn/ *n* penetración *f*

penguin /ˈpengwɪn/ *n* pingüino *m*

penicillin /penɪˈsɪlɪn/ *n* penicilina *f*

peninsula /pəˈnɪnsjʊlə/ *n* península *f*

penis /ˈpiːnɪs/ *n* pene *m*

peniten|**ce** /ˈpenɪtəns/ *n* penitencia *f*. ~**t** /ˈpenɪtənt/ *a & n* penitente (*m & f*). ~**tiary** /penɪˈtenʃərɪ/ *n* (*Amer*) cárcel *f*

pen: ~**knife** /ˈpennaɪf/ *n* (*pl* **penknives**) navaja *f*; (*small*) cortaplumas *m invar*. ~**name** *n* seudónimo *m*

pennant /ˈpenənt/ *n* banderín *m*

penn|**iless** /ˈpenɪlɪs/ *a* sin un céntimo. ~**y** /ˈpenɪ/ *n* (*pl* **pennies** *or* **pence**) penique *m*

pension /ˈpenʃn/ *n* pensión *f* (*for retirement*) jubilación *f*. —*vt* pensionar. ~**able** *a* con derecho a pensión; (*age*) de la jubilación. ~**er** *n* jubilado *m*. ~ **off** jubilar

pensive /ˈpensɪv/ *a* pensativo

pent-up /ˈpentʌp/ *a* reprimido; (*confined*) encerrado

pentagon /ˈpentəgən/ *n* pentágono *m*

Pentecost /ˈpentɪkɒst/ *n* Pentecostés *m*

penthouse /ˈpenthaʊs/ *n* ático *m*

penultimate /penˈʌltɪmət/ *a* penúltimo

penury /ˈpenjʊrɪ/ *n* penuria *f*

peony /ˈpiːənɪ/ *n* peonía *f*

people /ˈpiːpl/ *npl* gente *f*; (*citizens*) pueblo *m*. ~ **say** se dice. **English** ~ los ingleses *mpl*. **my** ~ (*fam*) mi familia *f*. —*vt* poblar

pep /pep/ *n* vigor *m*. —*vt*. ~ **up** animar

pepper /ˈpepə(r)/ *n* pimienta *f*; (*vegetable*) pimiento *m*. —*vt* sazonar con pimienta. ~**y** *a* picante. ~**corn** /ˈpepəkɔːn/ *n* grano *m* de pimienta. ~**corn rent** *n* alquiler *m* nominal

peppermint /ˈpepəmɪnt/ *n* menta *f*; (*sweet*) pastilla *f* de menta

pep talk /ˈpeptɔːk/ *n* palabras *fpl* animadoras

per /pɜː(r)/ *prep* por. ~ **annum** al año. ~ **cent** por ciento. ~ **head** por cabeza, por persona. **ten miles** ~ **hour** diez millas por hora

perceive /pəˈsiːv/ *vt* percibir; (*notice*) darse cuenta de

percentage /pə'sentɪdʒ/ n porcentaje m

perceptible /pə'septəbl/ a perceptible. ~on /pə'sepʃn/ n percepción f. ~ve a perspicaz

perch[1] /pɜːtʃ/ n (of bird) percha f. —vi posarse

perch[2] /pɜːtʃ/ (fish) perca f

percolat|e /'pɜːkəleɪt/ vt filtrar. —vi filtrarse. ~or n cafetera f

percussion /pə'kʌʃn/ n percusión f

peremptory /pə'remptərɪ/ a perentorio

perennial /pə'renɪəl/ a & n perenne (m)

perfect /'pɜːfɪkt/ a perfecto. /pə'fekt/ vt perfeccionar. ~ion /pə'fekʃn/ n perfección f. to ~ion a la perfección. ~ionist n perfeccionista m & f. ~ly /'pɜːfɪktlɪ/ adv perfectamente

perforat|e /'pɜːfəreɪt/ vt perforar. ~ion /-'reɪʃn/ n perforación f

perform /pə'fɔːm/ vt hacer, realizar; representar (play); desempeñar (role); (mus) interpretar. ~ an operation (med) operar. ~ance n ejecución f; (of play) representación f; (of car) rendimiento m; (fuss, fam) jaleo m. ~er n artista m & f

perfume /'pɜːfjuːm/ n perfume m

perfunctory /pə'fʌŋktərɪ/ a superficial

perhaps /pə'hæps/ adv quizá(s), tal vez

peril /'perəl/ n peligro m. ~ous a arriesgado, peligroso

perimeter /pə'rɪmɪtə(r)/ n perímetro m

period /'pɪərɪəd/ n periodo m; (lesson) clase f; (gram) punto m. —a de (la) época. ~ic /-'ɒdɪk/ a periódico. ~ical /pɪərɪ'ɒdɪkl/ n revista f. ~ically /-'ɒdɪklɪ/ adv periódico

peripher|al /pə'rɪfərəl/ a periférico. ~y /pə'rɪfərɪ/ n periferia f

periscope /'perɪskəʊp/ n periscopio m

perish /'perɪʃ/ vi perecer; (rot) estropearse. ~able a perecedero. ~ing a (fam) glacial

perjur|e /'pɜːdʒə(r)/ vr. ~e o.s. perjurarse. ~y n perjurio m

perk[1] /pɜːk/ n gaje m

perk[2] /pɜːk/ vt/i. ~ up vt reanimar. —vi reanimarse. ~y a alegre

perm /pɜːm/ n permanente f. —vt hacer una permanente a

permanen|ce /'pɜːmənəns/ n permanencia f. ~t /'pɜːmənənt/ a permanente. ~tly adv permanentemente

permea|ble /'pɜːmɪəbl/ a permeable. ~te /'pɜːmɪeɪt/ vt penetrar; (soak) empapar

permissible /pə'mɪsəbl/ a permisible

permission /pə'mɪʃn/ n permiso m

permissive /pə'mɪsɪv/ a indulgente. ~ness n tolerancia f. ~ society n sociedad f permisiva

permit /pə'mɪt/ vt (pt permitted) permitir. /'pɜːmɪt/ n permiso m

permutation /pɜːmjuː'teɪʃn/ n permutación f

pernicious /pə'nɪʃəs/ a pernicioso

peroxide /pə'rɒksaɪd/ n peróxido m

perpendicular /pɜːpən'dɪkjʊlə(r)/ a & n perpendicular (f)

perpetrat|e /'pɜːpɪtreɪt/ vt cometer. ~or n autor m

perpetual /pə'petʃʊəl/ a perpetuo. ~te /pə'petʃʊeɪt/ vt perpetuar. ~tion /-'eɪʃn/ n perpetuación f

perplex /pə'pleks/ vt dejar perplejo. ~ed a perplejo. ~ing a

desconcertante. ~ity n per-
plejidad f
persecute /'pɜːsɪkjuːt/ vt perseguir. ~ion /-'kjuːʃn/ n persecución f
persever|ance /pɜːsɪ'vɪərəns/ n
perseverancia f. ~e /pɜːsɪ'vɪə(r)/
vi perseverar, persistir
Persian /'pɜːʃn/ a persa. the ~
Gulf n el golfo m Pérsico. —n
persa (m & f); (lang) persa m
persist /pə'sɪst/ vi persistir.
~ence n persistencia f. ~ent a
persistente; (continual) continuo. ~ently adv persis-
tentemente
person /'pɜːsn/ n persona f
personal /'pɜːsənl/ a personal
personality /pɜːsə'nælətɪ/ n per-
sonalidad f; (on TV) personaje m
personally /'pɜːsənlɪ/ adv per-
sonalmente; (in person) en
persona
personify /pə'sɒnɪfaɪ/ vt per-
sonificar
personnel /pɜːsə'nel/ n personal
m
perspective /pə'spektɪv/ n perspectiva f
perspicacious /pɜːspɪ'keɪʃəs/ a
perspicaz
perspir|ation /pɜːspə'reɪʃn/ n
sudor m. ~e /pəs'paɪə(r)/ vi
sudar
persua|de /pə'sweɪd/ vt per-
suadir. ~sion n persuasión f.
~sive a persu-
asivo. ~sively adv de manera
persuasiva
pert /pɜːt/ a (saucy) impertinente; (lively) animado
pertain /pə'teɪn/ vi. ~ to relacionarse con
pertinent /'pɜːtɪnənt/ a pertinente. ~ly adv pertinentemente
pertly /'pɜːtlɪ/ adv impertinentemente
perturb /pə'tɜːb/ vt perturbar
Peru /pə'ruː/ n el Perú m

perus|al /pə'ruːzl/ n lectura f cui-
dadosa. ~e /pə'ruːz/ vt leer
cuidadosamente
Peruvian /pə'ruːvɪən/ a & n peruano (m)
pervade /pə'veɪd/ vt difundirse
por. ~sive a penetrante
pervers|e /pə'vɜːs/ a (stubborn)
terco; (wicked) perverso. ~sity
n terquedad f; (wickedness) per-
versidad f. ~sion n perversión
f. ~t /pə'vɜːt/ vt pervertir. /'pɜː
vɜːt/ n pervertido m
pessimis|m /'pesɪmɪzəm/ n pes-
imismo m. ~t /'pesɪmɪst/ n pesimista m & f. ~tic /-'mɪstɪk/ a
pesimista
pest /pest/ n insecto m nocivo,
plaga f; (person) pelma m; (thing)
lata f
pester /'pestə(r)/ vt importunar
pesticide /'pestɪsaɪd/ n pesticida f
pet /pet/ n animal m doméstico;
(favourite) favorito m. —a preferido. —vt (pt petted) acariciar
petal /'petl/ n pétalo m
peter /'piːtə(r)/ vi. ~ out (supplies) agotarse; (disappear)
desaparecer
petite /pə'tiːt/ a (of woman)
chiquita
petition /pɪ'tɪʃn/ n petición f. —
vt dirigir una petición a
pet name /'petneɪm/ n apodo m
cariñoso
petrify /'petrɪfaɪ/ vt petrificar. —
vi petrificarse
petrol /'petrl/ n gasolina f.
~eum /pɪ'trəʊlɪəm/ n petróleo
m. ~ gauge n indicador m de
nivel de gasolina. ~ pump n (in
car) bomba f de gasolina; (at garage) surtidor m de gasolina. ~
station n gasolinera f. ~ tank n
depósito m de gasolina
petticoat /'petɪkəʊt/ n enaguas
fpl
pett|iness /'petɪnɪs/ n mez-
quindad f. ~y /'petɪ/ a (-ier,

-iest) insignificante; (*mean*) mezquino. **~y cash** *n* dinero *m* para gastos menores. **~y officer** *n* suboficial *m* de marina

petulan|ce /'petjuləns/ *n* irritabilidad *f*. **~t** /'petjulənt/ *a* irritable

pew /pju:/ *n* banco *m* (de iglesia)

pewter /'pju:tə(r)/ *n* peltre *m*

phallic /'fælɪk/ *a* fálico

phantom /'fæntəm/ *n* fantasma *m*

pharmaceutical /fɑ:mə'sju:tɪkl/ *a* farmacéutico

pharmac|ist /'fɑ:məsɪst/ *n* farmacéutico *m*. **~y** /'fɑ:məsɪ/ *n* farmacia *f*

pharyngitis /færɪn'dʒaɪtɪs/ *n* faringitis *f*

phase /feɪz/ *n* etapa *f*. —*vt*. **~ in** introducir progresivamente. **~ out** retirar progresivamente

PhD *abbr* (*Doctor of Philosophy*) *n* Doctor *m* en Filosofía

pheasant /'feznt/ *n* faisán *m*

phenomenal /fɪ'nɒmɪnl/ *a* fenomenal

phenomenon /fɪ'nɒmɪnən/ *n* (*pl* **-ena**) fenómeno *m*

phew /fju:/ *int* ¡uy!

phial /'faɪəl/ *n* frasco *m*

philanderer /fɪ'lændərə(r)/ *n* mariposón *m*

philanthrop|ic /fɪlən'θrɒpɪk/ *a* filantrópico. **~ist** /fɪ'lænθrəpɪst/ *n* filántropo *m*

philatel|ist /fɪ'lætəlɪst/ *n* filatelista *m* & *f*. **~y** /fɪ'lætəlɪ/ *n* filatelia *f*

philharmonic /fɪlhɑ:'mɒnɪk/ *a* filarmónico

Philippines /'fɪlɪpi:nz/ *npl* Filipinas *fpl*

philistine /'fɪlɪstaɪn/ *a* & *n* filisteo (*m*)

philosoph|er /fɪ'lɒsəfə(r)/ *n* filósofo *m*. **~ical** /-ə'sɒfɪkl/ *a* filosófico. **~y** /fɪ'lɒsəfɪ/ *n* filosofía *f*

phlegm /flem/ *n* flema *f*. **~atic** /fleg'mætɪk/ *a* flemático

phobia /'fəʊbɪə/ *n* fobia *f*

phone /fəʊn/ *n* (*fam*) teléfono *m*. —*vt/i* llamar por teléfono. **~ back** (*caller*) volver a llamar; (*person called*) llamar. **~ box** *n* cabina *f* telefónica

phonetic /fə'netɪk/ *a* fonético. **~s** *n* fonética *f*

phoney /'fəʊnɪ/ *a* (**-ier, -iest**) (*sl*) falso. —*n* (*sl*) farsante *m* & *f*

phosphate /'fɒsfeɪt/ *n* fosfato *m*

phosphorus /'fɒsfərəs/ *n* fósforo *m*

photo /'fəʊtəʊ/ *n* (*pl* **-os**) (*fam*) fotografía *f*, foto *f* (*fam*)

photocopy /'fəʊtəʊkɒpɪ/ *n* fotocopia *f*. —*vt* fotocopiar

photogenic /fəʊtəʊ'dʒenɪk/ *a* fotogénico

photograph /'fəʊtəgrɑ:f/ *n* fotografía *f*. —*vt* hacer una fotografía de, sacar fotos de. **~er** /fə'tɒgrəfə(r)/ *n* fotógrafo *m*. **~ic** /-'græfɪk/ *a* fotográfico. **~y** /fə'tɒgrəfɪ/ *n* fotografía *f*

phrase /freɪz/ *n* frase *f*, locución *f*, expresión *f*. —*vt* expresar. **~-book** *n* libro *m* de frases

physical /'fɪzɪkl/ *a* físico

physician /fɪ'zɪʃn/ *n* médico *m*

physic|ist /'fɪzɪsɪst/ *n* físico *m*. **~s** /'fɪzɪks/ *n* física *f*

physiology /fɪzɪ'ɒlədʒɪ/ *n* fisiología *f*

physiotherap|ist /fɪzɪəʊ-'θerəpɪst/ *n* fisioterapeuta *m* & *f*. **~y** /fɪzɪəʊ'θerəpɪ/ *n* fisioterapia *f*

physique /fɪ'zi:k/ *n* constitución *f*; (*appearance*) físico *m*

pian|ist /'pɪənɪst/ *n* pianista *m* & *f*. **~o** /pɪ'ænəʊ/ *n* (*pl* **-os**) piano *m*

piccolo /'pɪkələʊ/ *n* flautín *m*, píccolo *m*

pick[1] /pɪk/ (*tool*) pico *m*

pick[2] /pɪk/ *vt* escoger; recoger (*flowers etc*); forzar (*a lock*); (*dig*)

picar. ～ **a quarrel** buscar
camorra. ～ **holes in** criticar.
—*n* (*choice*) selección *f*; (*the best*)
lo mejor. ～ **on** *vt* (*nag*) meterse
con. ～ **out** *vt* escoger; (*identify*)
identificar; destacar (*colour*). ～
up *vt* recoger; (*lift*) levantar;
(*learn*) aprender; adquirir
〈*habit, etc*〉; obtener 〈*information*〉; contagiarse de 〈*illness*〉.
—*vi* mejorar; (*med*) reponerse

pickaxe /'pikæks/ *n* pico *m*

picket /'pɪkɪt/ *n* (*striker*) huelguista *m* & *f*; (*group of strikers*)
piquete *m*; (*stake*) estaca *f*. ～
line *n* piquete *m*. —*vt* vigilar por
piquetes. —*vi* estar de guardia

pickle /'pɪkl/ *n* (*in vinegar*)
encurtido *m*; (*in brine*) salmuera
f. **in a** ～ (*fam*) en un apuro. —*vt*
encurtir. ～**s** *npl* encurtido *m*

pick: ～**pocket** /'pɪkpɒkɪt/ *n* ratero *m*. ～**up** *n* (*sl*) ligue *m*;
(*truck*) camioneta *f*; (*stylus-
holder*) fonocaptor *m*, brazo *m*

picnic /'pɪknɪk/ *n* comida *f* cam-
pestre. —*vi* (*pt* **picnicked**) merendar en el campo

pictorial /pɪk'tɔːrɪəl/ *a* ilustrado

picture /'pɪktʃə(r)/ *n* (*painting*)
cuadro *m*; (*photo*) fotografía *f*;
(*drawing*) dibujo *m*; (*beautiful
thing*) preciosidad *f*; (*film*) película *f*; (*fig*) descripción *f*. **the** ～**s**
npl el cine *m*. —*vt* imaginarse;
(*describe*) describir

picturesque /pɪktʃə'resk/ *a*
pintoresco

piddling /'pɪdlɪŋ/ *a* (*fam*)
insignificante

pidgin /'pɪdʒɪn/ *a*. ～ **English** *n*
inglés *m* corrompido

pie /paɪ/ *n* empanada *f*; (*sweet*)
pastel *m*, tarta *f*

piebald /'paɪbɔːld/ *a* pío

piece /piːs/ *n* pedazo *m*; (*coin*)
moneda *f*; (*in game*) pieza *f*. **a** ～
of advice un consejo *m*. **a** ～ **of
news** una noticia *f*. **take to** ～**s**

desmontar. —*vt*. ～ **together**
juntar. ～**meal** /'piːsmiːl/ *a* gradual; (*unsystematic*) poco sistemático. —*adv* poco a poco.
～**work** *n* trabajo *m* a destajo

pier /pɪə(r)/ *n* muelle *m*

pierce /pɪəs/ *vt* perforar. ～**ing** *a*
penetrante

piety /'paɪətɪ/ *n* piedad *f*

piffle /'pɪfl/ *n* (*sl*) tonterías *fpl*.
～**ing** *a* (*sl*) insignificante

pig /pɪg/ *n* cerdo *m*

pigeon /'pɪdʒɪn/ *n* paloma *f*;
(*culin*) pichón *m*. ～**-hole** *n* casilla *f*

pig: ～**gy** /'pɪgɪ/ *a* (*greedy, fam*)
glotón. ～**gy-back** *adv* a cuestas.
～**gy bank** *n* hucha *f*. ～**headed**
a terco

pigment /'pɪgmənt/ *n* pigmento
m. ～**ation** /-'teɪʃn/ *n* pig-
mentación *f*

pig: ～**skin** /'pɪgskɪn/ *n* piel *m* de
cerdo. ～**sty** /'pɪgstaɪ/ *n* pocilga *f*

pigtail /'pɪgteɪl/ *n* (*plait*) trenza *f*

pike /paɪk/ *n* *invar* (*fish*) lucio *m*

pilchard /'pɪltʃəd/ *n* sardina *f*

pile[1] /paɪl/ *n* (*heap*) montón *m*. —
vt amontonar. ～ **it on**
exagerar. —*vi* amontonarse. ～
up *vt* amontonar. —*vi* amontonarse. ～**s** /paɪlz/ *npl* (*med*)
almorranas *fpl*

pile[2] /paɪl/ *n* (*of fabric*) pelo *m*

pile-up /'paɪlʌp/ *n* accidente *m*
múltiple

pilfer /'pɪlfə(r)/ *vt/i* hurtar.
～**age** *n*, ～**ing** *n* hurto *m*

pilgrim /'pɪlgrɪm/ *n* peregrino.
～**age** *n* peregrinación *f*

pill /pɪl/ *n* píldora *f*

pillage /'pɪlɪdʒ/ *n* saqueo *m*. —*vt*
saquear

pillar /'pɪlə(r)/ *n* columna *f*.
～**-box** *n* buzón *m*

pillion /'pɪlɪən/ *n* asiento *m* trasero. **ride** ～ ir en el asiento
trasero

pillory /'pɪlərɪ/ *n* picota *f*

pillow /'pɪləʊ/ n almohada f.
~case /'pɪləʊkeɪs/ n funda f de
almohada

pilot /'paɪlət/ n piloto m. —vt
pilotar. **~light** n fuego m piloto

pimp /pɪmp/ n alcahuete m

pimple /'pɪmpl/ n grano m

pin /pɪn/ n alfiler m; (mec) perno
m. **~s and needles** hormigueo
m. —vt (pt **pinned**) prender con
alfileres; (hold down) enclavijar;
(fix) sujetar. **~ s.o. down** obligar a uno a que se decida. **~ up**
fijar

pinafore /'pɪnəfɔː(r)/ n delantal
m. **~ dress** n mandil m

pincers /'pɪnsəz/ npl tenazas fpl

pinch /pɪntʃ/ vt pellizcar; (steal,
sl) hurtar. —vi (shoe) apretar. —
n pellizco m; (small amount)
pizca f. **at a ~** en caso de
necesidad

pincushion /'pɪnkʊʃn/ n acerico
m

pine¹ /paɪn/ n pino m

pine² /paɪn/ vi. **~ away** consumirse. **~ for** suspirar por

pineapple /'paɪnæpl/ n piña f,
ananás m

ping /pɪŋ/ n sonido m agudo.
~pong /'pɪŋpɒŋ/ n pimpón m,
ping-pong m

pinion /'pɪnjən/ vt maniatar

pink /pɪŋk/ a & n color (m) de
rosa

pinnacle /'pɪnəkl/ n pináculo m

pin: ~point vt determinar con
precisión f. **~stripe** /'pɪnstraɪp/
n raya f fina

pint /paɪnt/ n pinta f (= 0.57 litre)

pin-up /'pɪnʌp/ n (fam) fotografía
f de mujer

pioneer /paɪə'nɪə(r)/ n pionero
m. —vt ser el primer promotor
de, promover

pious /'paɪəs/ a piadoso

pip¹ /pɪp/ n (seed) pepita f

pip² /pɪp/ (time signal) señal f

pip³ /pɪp/ (on uniform) estrella f

pipe /paɪp/ n tubo m; (mus) car-
amillo m; (for smoking) pipa f. —
vt conducir por tuberías.
~down (fam) bajar la voz, callarse. **~cleaner** n limpiapipas m
invar. **~dream** n ilusión f.
~line /'paɪplaɪn/ n tubería f; (for
oil) oleoducto m. **in the ~line**
en preparación f. **~r** n flautista
m & f

piping /'paɪpɪŋ/ n tubería f. **~
hot** muy caliente, hirviendo

piquant /'piːkənt/ a picante

pique /piːk/ n resentimiento m

pira|**cy** /'paɪərəsɪ/ n piratería f.
~te /'paɪərət/ n pirata m

pirouette /pɪrʊ'et/ n pirueta f. —
vi piruetear

Pisces /'paɪsiːz/ n (astr) Piscis m

pistol /'pɪstl/ n pistola f

piston /'pɪstən/ n pistón m

pit /pɪt/ n foso m; (mine) mina f;
(of stomach) boca f. —vt (pt
pitted) marcar con hoyos;
(fig) oponer. **~ o.s. against**
medirse con

pitch¹ /pɪtʃ/ n brea f

pitch² /pɪtʃ/ (degree) grado m;
(mus) tono m; (sport) campo
m. —vt lanzar; armar (tent).
~into (fam) atacar. —vi caerse;
(ship) cabecear. **~ in** (fam) contribuir. **~ed battle** n batalla f
campal

pitch-black /pɪtʃ'blæk/ a oscuro
como boca de lobo

pitcher /'pɪtʃə(r)/ n jarro m

pitchfork /'pɪtʃfɔːk/ n horca f

piteous /'pɪtɪəs/ a lastimoso

pitfall /'pɪtfɔːl/ n trampa f

pith /pɪθ/ n (of orange, lemon)
médula f; (fig) meollo m

pithy /'pɪθɪ/ a (**-ier**, **-iest**)
conciso

piti|**ful** /'pɪtɪfl/ a lastimoso.
~less a despiadado

pittance /'pɪtns/ n sueldo m
irrisorio

pity /'pɪtɪ/ n piedad f; (regret) lástima f. —vt compadecerse de

pivot /'pɪvət/ n pivote m. —vt montonar sobre un pivote. —vi girar sobre un pivote; (fig) depender (on de)

pixie /'pɪksɪ/ n duende m

placard /'plækɑːd/ n pancarta f; (poster) cartel m

placate /plə'keɪt/ vt apaciguar

place /pleɪs/ n lugar m; (seat) asiento m; (post) puesto m; (house, fam) casa f. **take** ~ tener lugar. —vt poner, colocar; (remember) recordar; (identify) identificar. **be** ~**d** (in race) colocarse. ~**mat** n salvamanteles m invar. ~**ment** /'pleɪsmənt/ n colocación f

placid /'plæsɪd/ a plácido

plagiari|sm /'pleɪdʒərɪzm/ n plagio m. ~**ze** /'pleɪdʒəraɪz/ vt plagiar

plague /pleɪg/ n peste f; (fig) plaga f. —vt atormentar

plaice /pleɪs/ n invar platija f

plaid /plæd/ n tartán m

plain /pleɪn/ a (-er, -est) claro; (simple) sencillo; (candid) franco; (ugly) feo. **in** ~ **clothes** en traje de paisano. —adv claramente. —n llanura f. ~**ly** adv claramente; (frankly) francamente; (simply) sencillamente. ~**ness** n claridad f; (simplicity) sencillez f

plaintiff /'pleɪntɪf/ n demandante m & f

plait /plæt/ vt trenzar. —n trenza f

plan /plæn/ n proyecto m; (map) plano m. —vt (pt **planned**) planear, proyectar; (intend) proponerse

plane[1] /pleɪn/ n (tree) plátano m

plane[2] /pleɪn/ n (level) nivel m; (aviat) avión m. —a plano

plane[3] /pleɪn/ n (tool) cepillo m. —vt cepillar

planet /'plænɪt/ n planeta m. ~**ary** a planetario

plank /plæŋk/ n tabla f

planning /'plænɪŋ/ n planificación f. **family** ~ planificación familiar. **town** ~ n urbanismo m

plant /plɑːnt/ n planta f; (mec) maquinaria f; (factory) fábrica f. —vt plantar; (place in position) colocar. ~**ation** /plæn'teɪʃn/ n plantación f

plaque /plæk/ n placa f

plasma /'plæzmə/ n plasma m

plaster /'plɑːstə(r)/ n yeso m; (adhesive) esparadrapo m; (for setting bones) escayola f. ~ **of Paris** n yeso m mate. —vt enyesar; (med) escayolar (broken bone); (cover) cubrir (with de). ~**ed** a (fam) borracho

plastic /'plæstɪk/ a & n plástico (m)

Plasticine /'plæstɪsiːn/ n (P) pasta f de modelar, plastilina f (P)

plastic surgery /'plæstɪk'sɜːdʒərɪ/ n cirugía f estética

plate /pleɪt/ n plato m; (of metal) chapa f; (silverware) vajilla f de plata; (in book) lámina f. —vt (cover with metal) chapear

plateau /'plætəʊ/ n (pl **plateaux**) n meseta f

plateful /'pleɪtfl/ n (pl -**fuls**) plato m

platform /'plætfɔːm/ n plataforma f; (rail) andén m

platinum /'plætɪnəm/ n platino m

platitude /'plætɪtjuːd/ n tópico m, perogrullada f, lugar m común

platonic /plə'tɒnɪk/ a platónico

platoon /plə'tuːn/ n pelotón m

platter /'plætə(r)/ n fuente f, plato m grande

plausible /'plɔːzəbl/ a plausible; (person) convincente

play /pleɪ/ vt jugar; (act role) desempeñar el papel de; tocar ⟨instrument⟩. ~ **safe** no arriesgarse. ~ **up to** halagar. —vi jugar. ~**ed out** agotado. ~ **boy** n juego m; (drama) obra f de teatro. ~ **on words** n juego m de palabras. ~ **down** vt minimizar. ~ **on** vi aprovecharse de. ~ **boy** /ˈpleɪbɔɪ/ n calavera m. ~**er** n jugador m; (mus) músico m. ~**ful** /ˈpleɪfl/ a juguetón. ~**fully** adv jugando; (jokingly) en broma. ~**ground** /ˈpleɪgraʊnd/ n parque m de juegos infantiles; (in school) campo m de recreo. ~**group** n jardín m de la infancia. ~**ing** /ˈpleɪɪŋ/ n juego m. ~**ing-card** n naipe m. ~**ing-field** n campo m de deportes. ~**mate** /ˈpleɪmeɪt/ n compañero m (de juego). ~**pen** n corralito m. ~**thing** n juguete m. ~**wright** /ˈpleɪraɪt/ n dramaturgo m

plc /piːelˈsiː/ abbr (public limited company) S.A., sociedad f anónima

plea /pliː/ n súplica f; (excuse) excusa f; (jurid) defensa f

plead /pliːd/ vt (jurid) alegar; (as excuse) pretextar. —vi suplicar; (jurid) abogar. ~ **with** suplicar

pleasant /ˈpleznt/ a agradable

pleas|e /pliːz/ int por favor. —vt agradar, dar gusto a. —vi agradar; (wish) querer. ~ **o.s.** hacer lo que quiera. **do as you ~** haz lo que quieras. ~**ed** a contento. ~**ed with** satisfecho de. ~**ing** a agradable

pleasur|e /ˈpleʒə(r)/ n placer m. ~**able** a agradable

pleat /pliːt/ n pliegue m. —vt hacer pliegues en

plebiscite /ˈplebɪsɪt/ n plebiscito m

plectrum /ˈplektrəm/ n plectro m

pledge /pledʒ/ n prenda f; (promise) promesa f. —vt empeñar; (promise) prometer

plent|iful /ˈplentɪfl/ a abundante. ~**y** /ˈplentɪ/ n abundancia f. ~**y (of)** muchos (de)

pleurisy /ˈplʊərəsɪ/ n pleuresía f

pliable /ˈplaɪəbl/ a flexible

pliers /ˈplaɪəz/ npl alicates mpl

plight /plaɪt/ n situación f (difícil)

plimsolls /ˈplɪmsɒlz/ npl zapatillas fpl de lona

plinth /plɪnθ/ n plinto m

plod /plɒd/ vi (pt plodded) caminar con paso pesado; (work hard) trabajar laboriosamente. ~**der** n empollón m

plonk /plɒŋk/ n (sl) vino m peleón

plop /plɒp/ n paf m. —vi (pt plopped) caerse con un paf

plot /plɒt/ n complot m; (of novel etc) argumento m; (piece of land) parcela f. —vt (pt plotted) tramar; (mark out) trazar. —vi conspirar

plough /plaʊ/ n arado m. —vt/i arar. ~ **through** avanzar laboriosamente por

ploy /plɔɪ/ n (fam) estratagema f, truco m

pluck /plʌk/ vt arrancar; depilarse ⟨eyebrows⟩; desplumar ⟨bird⟩; recoger ⟨flowers⟩. ~ **up courage** hacer de tripas corazón. —n valor m. ~**y** a (-ier, -iest) valiente

plug /plʌg/ n tapón m; (elec) enchufe m; (auto) bujía f. —vt (pt plugged) tapar; (advertise, fam) dar publicidad a. ~ **in** (elec) enchufar

plum /plʌm/ n ciruela f; (tree) ciruelo m

plumage /ˈpluːmɪdʒ/ n plumaje m

plumb /plʌm/ a vertical. —n plomada f. —adv verticalmente; (exactly) exactamente. —vt sondar

plumb|er /'plʌmə(r)/ n fontanero m. ~ing n instalación f sanitaria, instalación f de cañerías

plume /pluːm/ n pluma f

plum job /plʌm'dʒɒb/ n (fam) puesto m estupendo

plummet /'plʌmɪt/ n plomada f. —vi caer a plomo, caer en picado

plump /plʌmp/ a (-er, -est) rechoncho. —vt. ~ for elegir. ~ness n gordura f

plum pudding /plʌm'pʊdɪŋ/ n budín m de pasas

plunder /'plʌndə(r)/ n (act) saqueo m; (goods) botín m. —vt saquear

plunge /plʌndʒ/ vt hundir; (in water) sumergir. —vi zambullirse; (fall) caer. —n salto m. ~r (for sink) desatascador m; (mec) émbolo m. ~ing a (neckline) bajo, escotado

plural /'plʊərəl/ a & n plural (m)

plus /plʌs/ prep más. —a positivo. —n signo m más; (fig) ventaja f. **five ~** más de cinco

plush /plʌʃ/ n felpa f. —a de felpa, afelpado; (fig) lujoso. ~y a lujoso

plutocrat /'pluːtəkræt/ n plutócrata m & f

plutonium /pluː'təʊnjəm/ n plutonio m

ply /plaɪ/ vt manejar (tool); ejercer (trade). ~ s.o. with drink dar continuamente de beber a uno. ~wood n contrachapado m

p.m. /piː'em/ abbr (post meridiem) de la tarde

pneumatic /njuː'mætɪk/ a neumático

pneumonia /njuː'məʊnjə/ n pulmonía f

PO /piː'əʊ/ abbr (Post Office) oficina f de correos

poach /pəʊtʃ/ vt escalfar (egg); cocer (fish etc); (steal) cazar en vedado. ~er n cazador m furtivo

pocket /'pɒkɪt/ n bolsillo m; (of air, resistance) bolsa f. **be in ~** salir ganado. **be out of ~** salir perdiendo. —vt poner en el bolsillo. ~-book (notebook) libro m de bolsillo; (purse, Amer) cartera f; (handbag, Amer) bolso m. ~-money n dinero m para los gastos personales

pock-marked /'pɒkmɑːkt/ a (face) picado de viruelas

pod /pɒd/ n vaina f

podgy /'pɒdʒɪ/ a (-ier, -iest) rechoncho

poem /'pəʊɪm/ n poesía f

poet /'pəʊɪt/ n poeta m. ~ess n poetisa f. ~ic /-'etɪk/ a, ~ical /-'etɪkl/ a poético. **P~ Laureate** poeta laureado. ~ry /'pəʊɪtrɪ/ n poesía f

poignant /'pɔɪnjənt/ a conmovedor

point /pɔɪnt/ n punto m; (sharp end) punta f; (significance) lo importante; (elec) toma f de corriente. **good ~s** cualidades fpl. **to the ~** pertinente. **up to a ~** hasta cierto punto. **what is the ~?** ¿para qué?, ¿a qué fin? —vt (aim) apuntar; (show) indicar. ~ **out** señalar. —vi señalar. ~-**blank** a & adv a boca de jarro, a quemarropa. ~**ed** /'pɔɪntɪd/ a puntiagudo; (fig) mordaz. ~**er** /'pɔɪntə(r)/ n indicador m; (dog) perro m de muestra; (clue, fam) indicación f. ~**less** /'pɔɪntlɪs/ a inútil

poise /pɔɪz/ n equilibrio m; (elegance) elegancia f; (fig) aplomo m. ~**d** a en equilibrio. ~**d for** listo para

poison /'pɔɪzn/ n veneno m. —vt envenenar. ~**ous** a venenoso; (chemical etc) tóxico

poke /pəʊk/ vt empujar; atizar ⟨fire⟩. ~ **fun at** burlarse de. ~ **out** asomar ⟨head⟩. —vi hurgar; ⟨pry⟩ meterse. ~ **about** fisgonear. —n empuje m

poker[1] /ˈpəʊkə(r)/ n atizador m

poker[2] /ˈpəʊkə(r)/ ⟨cards⟩ póquer m. ~**-face** n cara f inmutable

poky /ˈpəʊki/ a (-ier, -iest) estrecho

Poland /ˈpəʊlənd/ n Polonia f

polar /ˈpəʊlə(r)/ a polar. ~ **bear** n oso m blanco

polarize /ˈpəʊləraɪz/ vt polarizar

Pole /pəʊl/ polaco n

pole[1] /pəʊl/ n palo m; ⟨for flag⟩ asta f

pole[2] /pəʊl/ ⟨geog⟩ polo m. ~**-star** n estrella f polar

polemic /pəˈlemɪk/ a polémico. —n polémica f

police /pəˈliːs/ n policía f. —vt vigilar. ~**man** /pəˈliːsmən/ n (pl **-men**) policía m, guardia m. ~ **record** n antecedentes mpl penales. ~ **state** n estado m policíaco. ~ **station** n comisaría f. ~**woman** /-wʊmən/ n (pl **-women**) mujer m policía

policy[1] /ˈpɒlɪsɪ/ n política f

policy[2] /ˈpɒlɪsɪ/ ⟨insurance⟩ póliza f (de seguros)

polio(myelitis) /ˈpəʊlɪəʊ(maɪəˈlaɪtɪs)/ n polio(mielitis) f

polish /ˈpɒlɪʃ/ n ⟨for shoes⟩ betún m; ⟨for floor⟩ cera f; ⟨for nails⟩ esmalte m de uñas; ⟨shine⟩ brillo m; ⟨fig⟩ finura f. **nail** ~ esmalte m de uñas. —vt pulir; limpiar ⟨shoes⟩; encerar ⟨floor⟩. ~ **off** despachar. ~**ed** a pulido; ⟨manner⟩ refinado. ~**er** n pulidor m; ⟨machine⟩ pulidora f

Polish /ˈpəʊlɪʃ/ a & n polaco (m)

polite /pəˈlaɪt/ a cortés. ~**ly** adv cortésmente. ~**ness** n cortesía f

political /pəˈlɪtɪkl/ a político. ~**ian** /pɒlɪˈtɪʃn/ n político m. ~**s** /ˈpɒlətɪks/ n política f

polka /ˈpɒlkə/ n polca f. ~ **dots** npl diseño m de puntos

poll /pəʊl/ n elección f; ⟨survey⟩ encuesta f. —vt obtener ⟨votes⟩

pollen /ˈpɒlən/ n polen m

polling-booth /ˈpəʊlɪŋbuːð/ n cabina f de votar

pollut|e /pəˈluːt/ vt contaminar. ~**ion** /-ʃn/ n contaminación f

polo /ˈpəʊləʊ/ n polo m. ~**-neck** n cuello m vuelto

poltergeist /ˈpɒltəgaɪst/ n duende m

polyester /pɒlɪˈestə(r)/ n poliéster m

polygam|ist /pəˈlɪgəmɪst/ n polígamo m. ~**ous** a polígamo. ~**y** /pəˈlɪgəmɪ/ n poligamia f

polyglot /ˈpɒlɪglɒt/ a & n poliglota (m & f)

polygon /ˈpɒlɪgən/ n polígono m

polyp /ˈpɒlɪp/ n pólipo m

polystyrene /pɒlɪˈstaɪriːn/ n poliestireno m

polytechnic /pɒlɪˈteknɪk/ n escuela f politécnica

polythene /ˈpɒlɪθiːn/ n polietileno m. ~ **bag** n bolsa f de plástico

pomegranate /ˈpɒmɪgrænɪt/ n ⟨fruit⟩ granada f

pommel /ˈpʌml/ n pomo m

pomp /pɒmp/ n pompa f

pompon /ˈpɒmpɒn/ n pompón m

pompo|sity /pɒmˈpɒsɪtɪ/ n pomposidad f. ~**us** /ˈpɒmpəs/ a pomposo

poncho /ˈpɒntʃəʊ/ n (pl **-os**) poncho m

pond /pɒnd/ n charca f; ⟨artificial⟩ estanque m

ponder /ˈpɒndə(r)/ vt considerar.—vi reflexionar. ~**ous** /ˈpɒndərəs/ a pesado

pong /pɒŋ/ n ⟨sl⟩ hedor m. —vi ⟨sl⟩ apestar

pontiff /ˈpɒntɪf/ n pontífice m. ~**ical** /-ˈtɪfɪkl/ a pontifical; ⟨fig⟩

dogmático. ~icate /pon'tıfıkeıt/ vi pontificar

pontoon /pon'tu:n/ n pontón m. ~ **bridge** n puente m de pontones

pony /'pəʊnı/ n poni m. ~tail n cola f de caballo. ~trekking n excursionismo m en poni

poodle /'pu:dl/ n perro m de lanas, caniche m

pool¹ /pu:l/ n charca f; (artificial) estanque m. (swimming-)~ n piscina f

pool² /pu:l/ (common fund) fondos mpl comunes; (snooker) billar m americano. —vt aunar. ~s npl quinielas fpl

poor /pʊə(r)/ a (-er, -est) pobre; (not good) malo. **be in** ~ **health** estar mal de salud. ~ly a (fam) indispuesto. —adv pobremente; (badly) mal

pop¹ /pɒp/ n ruido m seco; (of bottle) taponazo m. —vt (pt popped) hacer reventar; (put) poner. ~ **in** vi entrar; (visit) pasar por. ~ **out** vi saltar; (person) salir un rato. ~ **up** vi surgir, aparecer

pop² /pɒp/ a (popular) pop invar. —n (fam) música f pop. ~ **art** n arte m pop

popcorn /'pɒpkɔ:n/ n palomitas fpl

pope /pəʊp/ n papa m

popgun /'pɒpgʌn/ n pistola f de aire comprimido

poplar /'pɒplə(r)/ n chopo m

poplin /'pɒplın/ n popelina f

poppy /'pɒpı/ n amapola f

popular /'pɒpjʊlə(r)/ a popular. ~ity /-'lærətı/ n popularidad f. ~ize vt popularizar

populate /'pɒpjʊleıt/ vt poblar. ~ion /-'leıʃn/ n población f; (number of inhabitants) habitantes mpl

porcelain /'pɔ:səlın/ n porcelana f

porch /pɔ:tʃ/ n porche m

porcupine /'pɔ:kjʊpaın/ n puerco m espín

pore¹ /pɔ:(r)/ n poro m

pore² /pɔ:(r)/ vi. ~ **over** estudiar detenidamente

pork /pɔ:k/ n cerdo m

porn /pɔ:n/ n (fam) pornografía f. ~ographic /-ə'græfık/ a pornográfico. ~ography /pɔ:'nɒgrəfı/ n pornografía f

porous /'pɔ:rəs/ a poroso

porpoise /'pɔ:pəs/ n marsopa f

porridge /'pɒrıdʒ/ n gachas fpl de avena

port¹ /pɔ:t/ n puerto m; (porthole) portilla f. ~ **of call** puerto de escala

port² /pɔ:t/ (naut, left) babor m. —a de babor

port³ /pɔ:t/ (wine) oporto m

portable /'pɔ:təbl/ a portátil

portent /'pɔ:tent/ n presagio m

porter /'pɔ:tə(r)/ n portero m; (for luggage) mozo m. ~**age** n porte m

portfolio /pɔ:t'fəʊljəʊ/ n (pl -os) cartera f

porthole /'pɔ:thəʊl/ n portilla f

portico /'pɔ:tıkəʊ/ n (pl -oes) pórtico m

portion /'pɔ:ʃn/ n porción f. —vt repartir

portly /'pɔ:tlı/ a (-ier, -iest) corpulento

portrait /'pɔ:trıt/ n retrato m

portray /pɔ:'treı/ vt retratar; (represent) representar. ~al n retrato m

Portugal /'pɔ:tjʊgl/ n Portugal m. ~**uese** /-'gi:z/ a & n portugués (m)

pose /pəʊz/ n postura f. —vt colocar; hacer ‹question›; plantear ‹problem›. —vi posar. ~ **as** hacerse pasar por. ~**r** /'pəʊzə(r)/ n pregunta f difícil

posh /pɒʃ/ a (sl) elegante

position /pə'zɪʃn/ n posición f;
(job) puesto m; (status) rango
m. —vt colocar

positive /'pozətɪv/ a positivo;
(real) verdadero; (certain)
seguro. —n (foto) positiva f. —ly
adv positivamente

possess /pə'zes/ vt poseer. ∼ion
/pə'zeʃn/ n posesión f. take
∼ion of tomar posesión de.
∼ions npl posesiones fpl; (jurid)
bienes mpl. ∼ive /pə'zesɪv/ a
posesivo. ∼or n poseedor m

possib|ility /posə'bɪlətɪ/ n pos-
ibilidad f. ∼le /'posəbl/ a
posible. ∼ly adv posiblemente

post[1] /pəʊst/ n (pole) poste m. —
vt fijar (notice)

post[2] /pəʊst/ (place) puesto m

post[3] /pəʊst/ (mail) correo m. —
vt echar (letter). **keep s.o.**
∼ed tener a uno al corriente

post... /pəʊst/ pref post

post: ∼age /'pəʊstɪdʒ/ n fran-
queo m. ∼al /'pəʊstl/ a postal.
∼al order n giro m postal.
∼box n buzón m. ∼card
/'pəʊstkɑːd/ n (tarjeta f) postal f.
∼code n código m postal

post-date /pəʊst'deɪt/ vt poner
fecha posterior a

poster /'pəʊstə(r)/ n cartel m

poste restante /pəʊst'restɑːnt/ n
lista f de correos

posteri|or /po'stɪərɪə(r)/ a pos-
terior. —n trasero m. ∼ty
/po'sterətɪ/ n posteridad f

posthumous /'postjʊməs/ a
póstumo. ∼ly adv después de la
muerte

post: ∼man /'pəʊstmən/ n (pl
-men) cartero m. ∼mark
/'pəʊstmɑːk/ n matasellos m
invar. ∼master /pəʊstmɑːstə(r)/ n
administrador m de correos. ∼mis-
tress /'pəʊstmɪstrɪs/ n admin-
istradora f de correos

post-mortem /pəʊst'mɔːtəm/ n
autopsia f

Post Office /'pəʊstɒfɪs/ n oficina
f de correos, correos mpl

postpone /pəʊst'pəʊn/ vt
aplazar. ∼ment n aplazamiento
m

postscript /'pəʊstskrɪpt/ n posdata f

postulant /'postjʊlənt/ n postu-
lante m & f

postulate /'postjʊleɪt/ vt
postular

posture /'postʃə(r)/ n postura
f. —vi adoptar una postura

posy /'pəʊzɪ/ n ramillete m

pot /pot/ n (for cooking) olla f; (for
flowers) tiesto m; (marijuana, sl)
mariguana f. **go to** ∼ (sl) echarse a perder. —vt (pt **potted**)
poner en tiesto

potassium /pə'tæsjəm/ n potasio
m

potato /pə'teɪtəʊ/ n (pl -oes) patata f, papa f (LAm)

pot: ∼-belly n barriga f.
∼-boiler n obra f literaria
escrita sólo para ganar dinero

poten|cy /'pəʊtənsɪ/ n potencia f.
∼t /'pəʊtnt/ a potente; (drink)
fuerte

potentate /'pəʊtənteɪt/ n poten-
tado m

potential /pəʊ'tenʃl/ a & n pot-
encial (m). ∼ity /-ʃɪ'ælətɪ/ n pot-
encialidad f. ∼ly adv
potencialmente

pot-hole /'pothəʊl/ n caverna f;
(in road) bache m. ∼r n espeleólogo m

potion /'pəʊʃn/ n poción f

pot: ∼ **luck** n lo que haya.
∼-**shot** n tiro m al azar. ∼ted
/'potɪd/ see **pot**. —a (food) en
conserva

potter[1] /'potə(r)/ n alfarero m

potter[2] /'potə(r)/ vi hacer pequeños trabajos agradables, no
hacer nada de particular

pottery /'potərɪ/ n cerámica f

potty /'potɪ/ a (-ier, -iest) (sl) chiflado. −n orinal m

pouch /pautʃ/ n bolsa f; pequeña

pouffe /puːf/ n (stool) taburete m

poulterer /'pəultərə(r)/ n pollero m

poultice /'pəultɪs/ n cataplasma f

poultry /'pəultrɪ/ n aves fpl de corral

pounce /pauns/ vi saltar, atacar de repente. −n salto m, ataque m repentino

pound[1] /paund/ n (weight) libra f (= 454g); (money) libra f (esterlina)

pound[2] /paund/ n (for cars) depósito m

pound[3] /paund/ vt (crush) machacar; (bombard) bombardear. −vi golpear; (heart) palpitar; (walk) ir con pasos pesados

pour /pɔː(r)/ vt verter. ∼ out servir (drink). −vi fluir; (rain) llover a cántaros. ∼ in (people) entrar en tropel. ∼ing rain n lluvia f torrencial. ∼ out (people) salir en tropel

pout /paut/ vi hacer pucheros. −n puchero m, mala cara f

poverty /'povətɪ/ n pobreza f

powder /'paudə(r)/ n polvo m; (cosmetic) polvos mpl. −vt polvorear; (pulverize) pulverizar. ∼ one's face ponerse polvos en la cara. ∼ed a en polvo. ∼y a polvoriento

power /'pauə(r)/ n poder m; (elec) corriente f; (energy) energía f; (nation) potencia f. ∼ cut n apagón m. ∼ed a con motor. ∼ed by impulsado por. ∼ful a poderoso. ∼less a impotente. ∼station n central f eléctrica

practicable /'præktɪkəbl/ a practicable

practical /'præktɪkl/ a práctico. ∼ joke n broma f pesada. ∼ly adv prácticamente

practice /'præktɪs/ n práctica f; (custom) costumbre f; (exercise) ejercicio m; (sport) entrenamiento m; (clients) clientela f. be in ∼ce (doctor, lawyer) ejercer. be out of ∼ce no estar en forma. in ∼ce (in fact) en la práctica; (on form) en forma. ∼se /'præktɪs/ vt hacer ejercicios en; (put into practice) poner en práctica; (sport) entrenarse en; ejercer (profession). −vi ejercitarse; (professional) ejercer. −∼sed a experto

practitioner /præk'tɪʃənə(r)/ n profesional m & f. general ∼ médico m de cabecera. medical ∼ médico m

pragmatic /præg'mætɪk/ a pragmático

prairie /'preərɪ/ n pradera f

praise /preɪz/ vt alabar. −n alabanza f. ∼worthy a loable

pram /præm/ n cochecito m de niño

prance /prɑːns/ vi (horse) hacer cabriolas; (person) pavonearse

prank /præŋk/ n travesura f

prattle /'prætl/ vi parlotear. −n parloteo m

prawn /prɔːn/ n gamba f

pray /preɪ/ vi rezar. ∼er /preə(r)/ n oración f. ∼ for rogar pre.. /priː/ pref pre...

preach /priːtʃ/ vt/i predicar. ∼er n predicador m

preamble /priː'æmbl/ n preámbulo m

pre-arrange /priːə'reɪndʒ/ vt arreglar de antemano. ∼ment n arreglo m previo

precarious /prɪ'keərɪəs/ a precario. ∼ly adv precariamente

precaution /prɪ'kɔːʃn/ n precaución f. ∼ary a de precaución; (preventive) preventivo

precede /prɪ'siːd/ vt preceder

precedence /'presɪdəns/ n precedencia f. ∼t /'presɪdənt/ n precedente m preceding /prɪˈsiːdɪŋ/ a precedente

precept /ˈpriːsept/ n precepto m

precinct /ˈpriːsɪŋkt/ n recinto m; ~ zona f peatonal. ~s npl contornos mpl

pedestrian ~ zona f peatonal.

precious /ˈpreʃəs/ a precioso. — adv (fam) muy

precipice /ˈpresɪpɪs/ n precipicio m

precipitat|e /prɪˈsɪpɪteɪt/ vt precipitar. /prɪˈsɪpɪtət/ n precipitado m. —a precipitado. ~ion /-ˈteɪʃn/ n precipitación f

precipitous /prɪˈsɪpɪtəs/ a escarpado

précis /ˈpreɪsiː/ n (pl précis /-siːz/) resumen m

precis|e /prɪˈsaɪs/ a preciso; (careful) meticuloso. ~ely adv precisamente. ~ion /-ˈsɪʒn/ n precisión f

preclude /prɪˈkluːd/ vt (prevent) impedir; (exclude) excluir

precocious /prɪˈkəʊʃəs/ a precoz. ~ly adv precozmente

preconce|ived /priːkənˈsiːvd/ a preconcebido. ~ption /-ˈsepʃn/ n preconcepción f

precursor /priːˈkɜːsə(r)/ n precursor m

predator /ˈpredətə(r)/ n animal m de rapiña. ~y a de rapiña

predecessor /ˈpriːdɪsesə(r)/ n predecesor m, antecesor m

predestin|ation /priːdestɪˈneɪʃn/ n predestinación f. ~e /priːˈdestɪn/ vt predestinar

predicament /prɪˈdɪkəmənt/ n apuro m

predicat|e /ˈpredɪkət/ n predicado m. ~ive /prɪˈdɪkətɪv/ a predicativo

predict /prɪˈdɪkt/ vt predecir. ~ion /-ʃn/ n predicción f

predilection /priːdɪˈlekʃn/ n predilección f

predispose /priːdɪˈspəʊz/ vt predisponer

predomina|nt /prɪˈdɒmɪnənt/ a predominante. ~te /prɪˈdɒmɪneɪt/ vi predominar

pre-eminent /priːˈemɪnənt/ a preeminente

pre-empt /priːˈempt/ vt adquirir por adelantado, adelantarse a

preen /priːn/ vt limpiar, arreglar. ~ o.s atildarse

prefab /ˈpriːfæb/ n (fam) casa f prefabricada. ~ricated /-ˈfæbrɪkeɪtɪd/ a prefabricado

preface /ˈprefəs/ n prólogo m

prefect /ˈpriːfekt/ n monitor m; (official) prefecto m

prefer /prɪˈfɜː(r)/ vt (pt preferred) preferir. ~able /ˈprefrəbl/ a preferible. ~ence /ˈprefrəns/ n preferencia f. ~ential /-əˈrenʃl/ a preferente

prefix /ˈpriːfɪks/ n (pl -ixes) prefijo m

pregnan|cy /ˈpregnənsɪ/ n embarazo m. ~t /ˈpregnənt/ a embarazada

prehistoric /priːhɪˈstɒrɪk/ a prehistórico

prejudge /priːˈdʒʌdʒ/ vt prejuzgar

prejudice /ˈpredʒʊdɪs/ n prejuicio m; (harm) perjuicio m. — vt predisponer; (harm) perjudicar. ~d a parcial

prelate /ˈprelət/ n prelado m

prelimina|ries /prɪˈlɪmɪnərɪz/ npl preliminares mpl. ~y /prɪˈlɪmɪnərɪ/ a preliminar

prelude /ˈpreljuːd/ n preludio m

pre-marital /priːˈmærɪtl/ a prematrimonial

premature /ˈpremətjʊə(r)/ a prematuro

premeditated /priːˈmedɪteɪtɪd/ a premeditado

premier /ˈpremɪə(r)/ a primero. —n (pol) primer ministro

première /ˈpremɪə(r)/ n estreno m

premises /'premɪsɪz/ *npl* local *m*.
on the ~ en el local

premiss /'premɪs/ *n* premisa *f*

premium /'priːmɪəm/ *n* premio
m. **at a ~** muy solicitado

premonition /priːmə'nɪʃn/ *n*
presentimiento *m*

preoccup|ation /priːɒkju'peɪʃn/
n preocupación *f*. **~ied**
/-'ɒkjupaɪd/ *a* preocupado

prep /prep/ *n* deberes *mpl*.

preparation /prepə'reɪʃn/ *n* preparación *f*. **~s** *npl* preparativos
mpl

preparatory /prɪ'pærətrɪ/ *a* preparatorio. **~ school** *n* escuela *f*
primaria privada

prepare /prɪ'peə(r)/ *vt* preparar. —*vi* prepararse. **~d to**
dispuesto a

prepay /priː'peɪ/ *vt* (*pt* **-paid**)
pagar por adelantado

preponderance /prɪ'pɒndərəns/
n preponderancia *f*

preposition /prepə'zɪʃn/ *n* preposición *f*

prepossessing /priːpə'zesɪŋ/ *a*
atractivo

preposterous /prɪ'pɒstərəs/ *a*
absurdo

prep school /'prepskuːl/ *n*
escuela *f* primaria privada

prerequisite /priː'rekwɪzɪt/ *n*
requisito *m* previo

prerogative /prɪ'rɒgətɪv/ *n* prerrogativa *f*

Presbyterian /prezbɪ'tɪərɪən/ *a*
& *n* presbiteriano (*m*)

prescri|be /prɪ'skraɪb/ *vt* pres-
cribir; (*med*) recetar. **~ption**
/-'ɪpʃn/ *n* prescripción *f*; (*med*)
receta *f*

presence /'prezns/ *n* presencia *f*;
(*attendance*) asistencia *f*. **~ of
mind** presencia *f* de ánimo

present[1] /'preznt/ *a* & *n* presente
(*m* & *f*). **at ~** actualmente. **for
the ~** por ahora

present[2] /'preznt/ *n* (*gift*) regalo
m

present[3] /prɪ'zent/ *vt* presentar;
(*give*) obsequiar. **~ s.o. with**
obsequiar a uno con. **~able** *a*
presentable. **~ation** /prezn-
'teɪʃn/ *n* presentación *f*; (*ceremony*) ceremonia *f* de entrega

presently /'prezntlɪ/ *adv* dentro
de poco

preserv|ation /prezə'veɪʃn/ *n*
conservación *f*. **~ative** /prɪ'zɜː-
vətɪv/ *n* preservativo *m*. **~e**
/prɪ'zɜːv/ *vt* conservar; (*maintain*) mantener; (*culin*) poner en
conserva. —*n* coto *m*; (*jam*) con-
fitura *f*

preside /prɪ'zaɪd/ *vi* presidir. **~
over** presidir

presiden|cy /'prezɪdənsɪ/ *n*
presidencia *f*. **~t** /'prezɪdənt/
n presidente *m*. **~tial**
/-'denʃl/ *a* presidencial

press /pres/ *vt* apretar; exprimir
(*fruit etc*); (*insist on*) insistir en;
(*iron*) planchar. **be ~ed for**
tener poco. —*vi* apretar; (*time*)
apremiar; (*fig*) urgir. **~ on** seguir adelante. —*n* presión *f*;
(*mec*, *newspapers*) prensa *f*;
(*printing*) imprenta *f*. **~ conference** *n* rueda *f* de prensa. **~
cutting** *n* recorte *m* de periódico. **~ing** /-ɪŋ/ *a* urgente.
~stud *n* automático *m*. **~up** *n*
plancha *f*

pressure /'preʃə(r)/ *n* presión
f. —*vt* hacer presión sobre. **~
cooker** *n* olla *f* a presión. **~
group** *n* grupo *m* de presión

pressurize /'preʃəraɪz/ *vt* hacer
presión sobre

prestig|e /pre'stiːʒ/ *n* prestigio *m*.
~ious /pre'stɪdʒəs/ *a* prestigioso

presum|ably /prɪ'zjuːməblɪ/ *adv*
presumiblemente, prob-
ablemente. **~e** /prɪ'zjuːm/ *vt* presumir. **~e (up)on** *vi* abusar de.

~ption /-'zʌmpʃn/ n presunción f. **~ptuous** /prɪ'zʌmptʃʊəs/ a presuntuoso

presuppose /pri:sə'pəʊz/ vt presuponer

preten|ce /prɪ'tens/ n fingimiento m; (claim) pretensión f; (pretext) pretexto m. **~d** /prɪ'tend/ vt i fingir. **~d to** (lay claim) pretender

pretentious /prɪ'tenʃəs/ a pretencioso

pretext /'pri:tekst/ n pretexto m

pretty /'prɪtɪ/ a (-ier, -iest) adv bonito, lindo (esp LAm); (person) guapo

prevail /prɪ'veɪl/ vi predominar; (win) prevalecer. **~ on** persuadir

prevalen|ce /'prevələns/ n costumbre f. **~t** /'prevələnt/ a extendido

prevaricate /prɪ'værɪkeɪt/ vi despistar

prevent /prɪ'vent/ vt impedir. **~able** a evitable. **~ion** /-ʃn/ n prevención f. **~ive** a preventivo

preview /'pri:vju:/ n preestreno m, avance m

previous /'pri:vɪəs/ a anterior. **~ to** antes de. **~ly** adv anteriormente, antes

pre-war /pri:'wɔ:(r)/ a de antes de la guerra

prey /preɪ/ n presa f; (fig) víctima f. **bird of ~** n ave f de rapiña. —vi. **~ on** alimentarse de; (worry) atormentar

price /praɪs/ n precio m. —vt fijar el precio de. **~less** a inapreciable; (amusing, fam) muy divertido. **~y** a (fam) caro

prick /prɪk/ vt i pinchar. **~ up one's ears** aguzar las orejas. —n pinchazo m

prickl|e /'prɪkl/ n (bot) espina f; (of animal) púa f; (sensation) picor m. **~y** a espinoso; (animal) lleno de púas; (person) quisquilloso

pride /praɪd/ n orgullo m. **~ of place** n puesto m de honor. —vr. **~ o.s. on** enorgullecerse de

priest /pri:st/ n sacerdote m. **~hood** n sacerdocio m. **~ly** a sacerdotal

prig /prɪg/ n mojigato m. **~gish** a mojigato

prim /prɪm/ a (primmer, primmest) estirado; (prudish) gazmoño

primarily /'praɪmərɪlɪ/ adv en primer lugar

primary /'praɪmərɪ/ a primario; (chief) principal. **~ school** n escuela f primaria

prime[1] /praɪm/ vt cebar (gun); (prepare) preparar; aprestar (surface)

prime[2] /praɪm/ a principal; (first rate) excelente. **~ minister** n primer ministro m. —n. **be in one's ~** estar en la flor de la vida

primer[1] /'praɪmə(r)/ n (of paint) primera mano f

primer[2] /'praɪmə(r)/ (book) silabario m

primeval /praɪ'mi:vl/ a primitivo

primitive /'prɪmɪtɪv/ a primitivo

primrose /'prɪmrəʊz/ n primavera f

prince /prɪns/ n príncipe m. **~ly** a principesco. **~ss** /prɪn'ses/ n princesa f

principal /'prɪnsəpl/ a principal. —n (of school etc) director m

principality /prɪnsɪ'pælətɪ/ n principado m

principally /'prɪnsɪpəlɪ/ adv principalmente

principle /'prɪnsəpl/ n principio m. **in ~** en principio. **on ~** por principio

print /prɪnt/ vt imprimir; (write in capitals) escribir con letras de molde. —n (of finger, foot) huella f; (letters) caracteres mpl; (of *design)* estampado *m*; *(picture)* grabado *m*; *(photo)* copia *f*. **in** ~ ⟨*book*⟩ disponible. **out of** ~ agotado. ~**ed matter** *n* impresos *mpl*. ~**er** /'prɪntə(r)/ *n* impresor *m*; *(machine)* impresora *f*. ~**ing** *n* tipografía *f*. ~**out** *n* listado *m*

prior /'praɪə(r)/ *n* prior *m*. —*a* anterior. ~ **to** antes de

priority /praɪ'ɒrətɪ/ *n* prioridad *f*

priory /'praɪərɪ/ *n* priorato *m*

prise /praɪz/ *vt* apalancar. ~ **open** abrir por fuerza

prism /'prɪzəm/ *n* prisma *m*

prison /'prɪzn/ *n* cárcel *m*. ~**er** *n* prisionero *m*; *(in prison)* preso *m*; *(under arrest)* detenido *m*. ~ **officer** *n* carcelero *m*

pristine /'prɪstiːn/ *a* prístino

privacy /'prɪvəsɪ/ *n* intimidad *f*; *(private life)* vida *f* privada. **in** ~ en la intimidad

private /'praɪvət/ *a* privado; *(confidential)* personal; ⟨*lessons, house*⟩ particular; *(ceremony)* en la intimidad. —*n* soldado *m* raso. **in** ~ en privado; *(secretly)* en secreto. ~ **eye** *n (fam)* detective *m* privado. ~**ly** *adv* en privado; *(inwardly)* interiormente

privation /praɪ'veɪʃn/ *n* privación *f*

privet /'prɪvɪt/ *n* alheña *f*

privilege /'prɪvɪlɪdʒ/ *n* privilegio *m*. ~**d** *a* privilegiado

privy /'prɪvɪ/ *a*. ~ **to** al corriente de

prize /praɪz/ *n* premio *m*. —*a* ⟨*idiot etc*⟩ de remate. —*vt* estimar. ~**fighter** *n* boxeador *m* profesional. ~**giving** *n* reparto *m* de premios. ~**winner** *n* premiado *m*

pro /prəʊ/ *n*. ~**s and cons** el pro *m* y el contra *m*

probab|ility /prɒbə'bɪlətɪ/ *n* probabilidad *f*. ~**le** /'prɒbəbl/ *a* probable. ~**ly** *adv* probablemente

probation /prə'beɪʃn/ *n* prueba *f*; *(jurid)* libertad *f* condicional. ~**ary** *a* de prueba

probe /prəʊb/ *n* sonda *f*; *(fig)* encuesta *f*. —*vt* sondar. —*vi*. ~ **into** investigar

problem /'prɒbləm/ *n* problema *m*. —*a* difícil. ~**atic** /-'mætɪk/ *a* problemático

procedure /prə'siːdʒə(r)/ *n* procedimiento *m*

proceed /prə'siːd/ *vi* proceder. ~**ing** *n* procedimiento *m*. ~**ings** /prə'siːdɪŋz/ *npl (report)* actas *fpl*; *(jurid)* proceso *m*

proceeds /'prəʊsiːdz/ *npl* ganancias *fpl*

process /'prəʊses/ *n* proceso *m*. **in** ~ **of** en vías de. **in the** ~ **of time** con el tiempo. —*vt* tratar; revelar ⟨*photo*⟩. ~**ion** /prə'seʃn/ *n* desfile *m*

proclaim /prə'kleɪm/ *vt* proclamar. ~**mation** /prɒklə'meɪʃn/ *n* proclamación *f*

procrastinate /prəʊ'kræstɪneɪt/ *vi* aplazar, demorar, diferir

procreation /prəʊkrɪ'eɪʃn/ *n* procreación *f*

procure /prə'kjʊə(r)/ *vt* obtener

prod /prɒd/ *vt (pt prodded)* empujar; *(with elbow)* dar un codazo a. —*vi* dar con el dedo. —*n* empuje *m*; *(with elbow)* codazo *m*

prodigal /'prɒdɪgl/ *a* pródigo

prodigious /prə'dɪdʒəs/ *a* prodigioso

prodigy /'prɒdɪdʒɪ/ *n* prodigio *m*

produce /prə'djuːs/ *vt (show)* presentar; *(bring out)* sacar; poner en escena ⟨*play*⟩; *(cause)* causar; *(manufacture)* producir. /'prɒdjuːs/ *n* productos *mpl*. ~**r** /prə'djuːsə(r)/ *n* productor *m*; *(in theatre)* director *m*

product /'prɒdʌkt/ *n* producto *m*. ~**ion** /prə'dʌkʃn/ *n* producción *f*; *(of play)* representación *f*

productive /prəˈdʌktɪv/ a productivo. **~ity** /prɒdʌkˈtɪvətɪ/ n productividad f

profane /prəˈfeɪn/ a profano; (blasphemous) blasfemo. **~ity** /-ˈfænɪtɪ/ n profanidad f

profess /prəˈfes/ vt profesar; (pretend) pretender

profession /prəˈfeʃn/ n profesión f. **~al** a & n profesional (m & f)

professor /prəˈfesə(r)/ n catedrático m; (Amer) profesor m

proffer /ˈprɒfə(r)/ vt ofrecer

proficien|cy /prəˈfɪʃənsɪ/ n competencia f. **~t** /prəˈfɪʃnt/ a competente

profile /ˈprəʊfaɪl/ n perfil m

profit /ˈprɒfɪt/ n (com) ganancia f; (fig) provecho m. **—vi. ~ from** sacar provecho de. **~able** a provechoso

profound /prəˈfaʊnd/ a profundo. **~ly** adv profundamente

profuse /prəˈfjuːs/ a profuso. **~ely** adv profusamente. **~ion** /-ʒn/ n profusión f

progeny /ˈprɒdʒənɪ/ n progenie f

prognosis /prɒgˈnəʊsɪs/ n (pl -oses) pronóstico m

program(me) /ˈprəʊgræm/ n programa m. **—vt** (pt programmed) programar. **~mer** n programador m

progress /ˈprəʊgres/ n progreso m, progresos mpl; (development) desarrollo m. **in ~** en curso. /prəˈgres/ vi hacer progresos; (develop) desarrollarse. **~ion** /prəˈgreʃn/ n progresión f

progressive /prəˈgresɪv/ a progresivo; (reforming) progresista. **~ly** adv progresivamente

prohibit /prəˈhɪbɪt/ vt prohibir. **~ive** /-bətɪv/ a prohibitivo

project /prəˈdʒekt/ vt proyectar. **—vi** (stick out) sobresalir. /ˈprɒdʒekt/ n proyecto m

projectile /prəˈdʒektaɪl/ n proyectil m

projector /prəˈdʒektə(r)/ n proyector m

proletari|an /prəʊlɪˈteərɪən/ a & n proletario (m). **~at** /prəʊlɪˈteərɪət/ n proletariado m

prolif|erate /prəˈlɪfəreɪt/ vi proliferar. **~eration** /-ˈreɪʃn/ n proliferación f. **~ic** /prəˈlɪfɪk/ a prolífico

prologue /ˈprəʊlɒg/ n prólogo m

prolong /prəˈlɒŋ/ vt prolongar

promenade /prɒməˈnɑːd/ n paseo m; (along beach) paseo m marítimo. **—vi** pasear. **—vi** pasearse. **~ concert** n concierto m (que forma parte de un festival de música clásica en Londres, en que no todo el público tiene asientos)

prominen|ce /ˈprɒmɪnəns/ n prominencia f; (fig) importancia f. **~t** /ˈprɒmɪnənt/ a prominente; (important) importante; (conspicuous) conspicuo

promiscu|ity /prɒmɪˈskjuːətɪ/ n libertinaje m. **~ous** /prəˈmɪskjʊəs/ a libertino

promise /ˈprɒmɪs/ n promesa f. **—vt/i** prometer. **~ing** a prometedor; (person) que promete

promontory /ˈprɒməntrɪ/ n promontorio m

promote /prəˈməʊt/ vt promover. **~ion** /-ˈməʊʃn/ n promoción f

prompt /prɒmpt/ a pronto; (punctual) puntual. **—adv** en punto. **—vt** incitar; apuntar (actor). **~er** n apuntador m. **~ly** adv puntualmente. **~ness** n prontitud f

promulgate /ˈprɒmʌlgeɪt/ vt promulgar

prone /prəʊn/ a echado boca abajo. **~ to** propenso a

prong /prɒŋ/ n (of fork) diente m

pronoun /ˈprəʊnaʊn/ n pronombre m

pronounce /prəˈnaʊns/ vt pronunciar; (declare) declarar. ~ement n declaración f. ~ed /prəˈnaʊnst/ a pronunciado; (noticeable) marcado

pronunciation /prənʌnsɪˈeɪʃn/ n pronunciación f

proof /pruːf/ n prueba f, (of alcohol) graduación f normal. —a. ~ against a prueba de. ~reading n corrección f de pruebas

prop[1] /prɒp/ n puntal m; (fig) apoyo m. —vt (pt propped) apoyar. ~ against (lean) apoyar en

prop[2] /prɒp/ (in theatre, fam) accesorio m

propaganda /prɒpəˈgændə/ n propaganda f

propagat|e /ˈprɒpəgeɪt/ vt propagar. —vi propagarse. ~ion /-ˈgeɪʃn/ n propagación f

propel /prəˈpel/ vt (pt propelled) propulsar. ~ler /prəˈpelə(r)/ n hélice f

propensity /prəˈpensɪtɪ/ n propensión f

proper /ˈprɒpə(r)/ a correcto; (suitable) apropiado; (gram) propio; (real, fam) verdadero. ~ly adv correctamente

property /ˈprɒpətɪ/ n propiedad f; (things owned) bienes mpl. —a inmobiliario

prophe|cy /ˈprɒfəsɪ/ n profecía f. ~sy /ˈprɒfɪsaɪ/ vt/i profetizar. ~t /ˈprɒfɪt/ n profeta m. ~tic /prəˈfetɪk/ a profético

propitious /prəˈpɪʃəs/ a propicio

proportion /prəˈpɔːʃn/ n porción f. ~al a, ~ate a proporcional

propos|al /prəˈpəʊzl/ n propuesta f. ~al of marriage oferta f de matrimonio. ~e /prəˈpəʊz/ vt proponer. —vi hacer una oferta de matrimonio

proposition /prɒpəˈzɪʃn/ n proposición f; (project, fam) asunto m

propound /prəˈpaʊnd/ vt proponer

proprietor /prəˈpraɪətə(r)/ n propietario m

propriety /prəˈpraɪətɪ/ n decoro m

propulsion /prəˈpʌlʃn/ n propulsión f

prosaic /prəˈzeɪk/ a prosaico

proscribe /prəˈskraɪb/ vt proscribir

prose /prəʊz/ n prosa f

prosecut|e /ˈprɒsɪkjuːt/ vt procesar; (carry on) proseguir. ~ion /-ˈkjuːʃn/ n proceso m. ~or n acusador m. **Public P~or** fiscal m

prospect /ˈprɒspekt/ n vista f; (expectation) perspectiva f. /prəˈspekt/ vi prospectar

prospective /prəˈspektɪv/ a probable; (future) futuro

prospector /prəˈspektə(r)/ n prospector m, explorador m

prospectus /prəˈspektəs/ n prospecto m

prosper /ˈprɒspə(r)/ vi prosperar. ~ity /-ˈsperətɪ/ n prosperidad f. ~ous /ˈprɒspərəs/ a próspero

prostitut|e /ˈprɒstɪtjuːt/ n prostituta f. ~ion /-ˈtjuːʃn/ n prostitución f

prostrate /ˈprɒstreɪt/ a echado boca abajo; (fig) postrado

protagonist /prəˈtægənɪst/ n protagonista m & f

protect /prəˈtekt/ vt proteger. ~ion /-ʃn/ n protección f. ~ive /prəˈtektɪv/ a protector. ~or n protector m

protégé /ˈprɒtɪʒeɪ/ n protegido m. ~e n protegida f

protein /ˈprəʊtiːn/ n proteína f

protest /ˈprəʊtest/ n protesta f. **under** ~ bajo protesta.

/prə'test/ *vt/i* protestar. ~er *n* (*demonstrator*) manifestante *m* & *f*

Protestant /'prɒtɪstənt/ *a* & *n* protestante (*m* & *f*)

protocol /'prəʊtəkɒl/ *n* protocolo *m*

prototype /'prəʊtətaɪp/ *n* prototipo *m*

protract /prə'trækt/ *vt* prolongar

protractor /prə'træktə(r)/ *n* transportador *m*

protrude /prə'truːd/ *vi* sobresalir

protuberance /prə'tjuːbərəns/ *n* protuberancia *f*

proud /praʊd/ *a* orgulloso. ~**ly** *adv* orgullosamente

prove /pruːv/ *vt* probar. —*vi* resultar. ~**n** *a* probado

provenance /'prɒvənəns/ *n* procedencia *f*

proverb /'prɒvɜːb/ *n* proverbio *m*. ~**ial** /prə'vɜːbɪəl/ *a* proverbial

provide /prə'vaɪd/ *vt* proveer. —*vi*. ~ **against** precaverse de. ~ **for** (*allow for*) prever; mantener (*person*). ~**d** /prə'vaɪdɪd/ *conj*. ~ (**that**) con tal que

providen|**ce** /'prɒvɪdəns/ *n* providencia *f*. ~**t** *a* providente. ~**tial** /prɒvɪ'denʃl/ *a* providencial

providing /prə'vaɪdɪŋ/ *conj*. ~ **that** con tal que

provin|**ce** /'prɒvɪns/ *n* provincia *f*; (*fig*) competencia *f*. ~**ial** /prə'vɪnʃl/ *a* provincial

provision /prə'vɪʒn/ *n* provisión *f*; (*supply*) suministro *m*; (*stipulation*) condición *f*. ~**s** *npl* comestibles *mpl*

provisional /prə'vɪʒənl/ *a* provisional. ~**ly** *adv* provisionalmente

proviso /prə'vaɪzəʊ/ *n* (*pl* **-os**) condición *f*

provo|**cation** /prɒvə'keɪʃn/ *n* provocación *f*. ~**cative** /-'vɒkətɪv/ *a* provocador. ~**ke** /prə'vəʊk/ *vt* provocar

prow /praʊ/ *n* proa *f*

prowess /'praʊɪs/ *n* habilidad *f*; (*valour*) valor *m*

prowl /praʊl/ *vi* merodear. —*n* ronda *f*. **be on the** ~ merodear. ~**er** *n* merodeador *m*

proximity /prɒk'sɪmətɪ/ *n* proximidad *f*

proxy /'prɒksɪ/ *n* poder *m*. **by** ~ por poder

prude /pruːd/ *n* mojigato *m*

pruden|**ce** /'pruːdəns/ *n* prudencia *f*. ~**t** /'pruːdənt/ *a* prudente. ~**tly** *adv* prudentemente

prudish /'pruːdɪʃ/ *a* mojigato

prune[1] /pruːn/ *n* ciruela *f* pasa

prune[2] /pruːn/ *vt* podar

pry /praɪ/ *vi* entrometerse

psalm /sɑːm/ *n* salmo *m*

pseudo.. /'sjuːdəʊ/ *pref* seudo...

pseudonym /'sjuːdənɪm/ *n* seudónimo *m*

psychiatr|**ic** /saɪkɪ'ætrɪk/ *a* psiquiátrico. ~**ist** /saɪ'kaɪətrɪst/ *n* psiquiatra *m* & *f*. ~**y** /saɪ'kaɪətrɪ/ *n* psiquiatría *f*

physic /'saɪkɪk/ *a* psíquico

psycho-analys|**e** /saɪkəʊ'ænəlaɪz/ *vt* psicoanalizar. ~**is** /saɪkəʊ'næləsɪs/ *n* psicoanálisis *m*. ~**t** /-ɪst/ *n* psicoanalista *m* & *f*

psycholog|**ical** /saɪkə'lɒdʒɪkl/ *a* psicológico. ~**ist** /saɪ'kɒlədʒɪst/ *n* psicólogo *m*. ~**y** /saɪ'kɒlədʒɪ/ *n* psicología *f*

psychopath /'saɪkəpæθ/ *n* psicópata *m* & *f*

pub /pʌb/ *n* bar *m*

puberty /'pjuːbətɪ/ *n* pubertad *f*

pubic /'pjuːbɪk/ *a* pubiano, púbico

public /'pʌblɪk/ *a* público

publican /'pʌblɪkən/ *n* tabernero *m*

publication /pʌblɪ'keɪʃn/ n publicación f

public house /pʌblɪk'haʊs/ n bar m

publicity /pʌb'lɪsəti/ n publicidad f

publicize /'pʌblɪsaɪz/ vt publicar, anunciar

publicly /'pʌblɪkli/ adv públicamente

public school /pʌblɪk'sku:l/ n colegio m privado; (Amer) instituto m

public-spirited /pʌblɪk'spɪrɪtɪd/ a cívico

publish /'pʌblɪʃ/ vt publicar. ~er n editor m. ~ing n publicación f

puck /pʌk/ n (ice hockey) disco m

pucker /'pʌkə(r)/ vt arrugar. —vi arrugarse

pudding /'pʊdɪŋ/ n postre m; (steamed) budín m

puddle /'pʌdl/ n charco m

pudgy /'pʌdʒi/ a (-ier, -iest) rechoncho

puerile /'pjʊəraɪl/ a pueril

puff /pʌf/ n soplo m; (for powder) borla f. —vt/i soplar. ~ at chupar (pipe). ~ out apagar (candle); (swell up) hinchar. ~ed a (out of breath) sin aliento. ~ pastry n hojaldre m. ~y /'pʌfi/ a hinchado

pugnacious /pʌg'neɪʃəs/ a belicoso

pug-nosed /'pʌgnəʊzd/ a chato

pull /pʊl/ vt tirar de; sacar ⟨tooth⟩; torcer ⟨muscle⟩. ~ a face hacer una mueca. ~ a fast one hacer una mala jugada. ~ down derribar ⟨building⟩. ~ off quitarse; (fig) lograr. ~ one's weight poner de su parte. ~ out sacar. ~ s.o.'s leg tomar el pelo a uno. ~ up ⟨uproot⟩ desarraigar; ⟨reprimand⟩ reprender. —vi tirar (at de). ~ away

(auto) alejarse. ~ back retirarse. ~ in (enter) entrar; (auto) parar. ~ o.s. together tranquilizarse. ~ out (auto) salirse. ~ through recobrar la salud. ~ up (auto) parar. —n tirón m; (fig) atracción f; (influence) influencia f. give a ~ tirar

pulley /'pʊli/ n polea f

pullover /'pʊləʊvə(r)/ n jersey m

pulp /pʌlp/ n pulpa f; (for paper) pasta f

pulpit /'pʊlpɪt/ n púlpito m

pulsate /'pʌlseɪt/ vi pulsar

pulse /pʌls/ n (med) pulso m

pulverize /'pʌlvəraɪz/ vt pulverizar

pumice /'pʌmɪs/ n piedra f pómez

pummel /'pʌml/ vt (pt pummelled) aporrear

pump[1] /pʌmp/ n bomba f; —vt sacar con una bomba; (fig) sonsacar. ~ up inflar

pump[2] /pʌmp/ (plimsoll) zapatilla f de lona; (dancing shoe) escarpín m

pumpkin /'pʌmpkɪn/ n calabaza f

pun /pʌn/ n juego m de palabras

punch[1] /pʌntʃ/ vt dar un puñetazo a; (perforate) perforar; hacer ⟨hole⟩. —n puñetazo m; (vigour, sl) empuje m; (device) punzón m

punch[2] /pʌntʃ/ (drink) ponche m

punch: ~-drunk a aturdido a golpes. ~ line n gracia f. ~-up n riña f

punctilious /pʌŋk'tɪlɪəs/ a meticuloso

punctual /'pʌŋktʃʊəl/ a puntual. ~ity /-'ælətɪ/ n puntualidad f. ~ly adv puntualmente

punctuate /'pʌŋktʃʊeɪt/ vt puntuar. ~ion /-'eɪʃn/ n puntuación f

puncture /'pʌŋktʃə(r)/ n (in tyre) pinchazo m. —vt pinchar. —vi pincharse

pundit /ˈpʌndɪt/ n experto m

pungency /ˈpʌndʒənsɪ/ n acritud f; (fig) mordacidad f. ~t /ˈpʌndʒənt/ a acre; (remark) mordaz

punish /ˈpʌnɪʃ/ vt castigar. ~able a castigable. ~ment n castigo m

punitive /ˈpjuːnɪtɪv/ a punitivo

punk /pʌŋk/ a (music, person) punk

punnet /ˈpʌnɪt/ n canastilla f

punt¹ /pʌnt/ n (boat) batea f

punt² /pʌnt/ vi apostar. ~er n apostante m & f

puny /ˈpjuːnɪ/ a (-ier, -iest) diminuto; (weak) débil; (petty) insignificante

pup /pʌp/ n cachorro m

pupil¹ /ˈpjuːpl/ n alumno m

pupil² /ˈpjuːpl/ (of eye) pupila f

puppet /ˈpʌpɪt/ n títere m

puppy /ˈpʌpɪ/ n cachorro m

purchase /ˈpɜːtʃəs/ vt comprar. —n compra f. ~r n comprador m

pure /ˈpjʊə(r)/ a (-er, -est) puro. ~ly adv puramente. ~ity n pureza f

purée /ˈpjʊəreɪ/ n puré m

purgatory /ˈpɜːgətrɪ/ n purgatorio m

purge /pɜːdʒ/ vt purgar. —n purga f

purification /pjʊərɪfɪˈkeɪʃn/ n purificación f. ~y /ˈpjʊərɪfaɪ/ vt purificar

purist /ˈpjʊərɪst/ n purista m & f

puritan /ˈpjʊərɪtən/ n puritano m. ~ical /-ˈtænɪkl/ a puritano

purl /pɜːl/ n (knitting) punto m del revés

purple /ˈpɜːpl/ a purpúreo, morado. —n púrpura f

purport /pəˈpɔːt/ vt. ~ to be pretender ser

purpose /ˈpɜːpəs/ n propósito m; (determination) resolución f. on ~ a propósito. to no ~ en vano.

~-built a construido especialmente. ~ful a (resolute) resuelto. ~ly adv a propósito

purr /pɜː(r)/ vi ronronear

purse /pɜːs/ n monedero m; (Amer) bolso m, cartera f (LAm). —vt fruncir

pursue /pəˈsjuː/ vt perseguir, seguir. ~r n perseguidor m. ~it /pəˈsjuːt/ n persecución f; (fig) ocupación f

purveyor /pəˈveɪə(r)/ n proveedor m

pus /pʌs/ n pus m

push /pʊʃ/ vt empujar; apretar (button). —vi empujar. —n empuje m; (effort) esfuerzo m; (drive) dinamismo m. at a ~ en caso de necesidad. get the ~ (sl) ser despedido. ~ aside vt apartar. ~ back vt hacer retroceder. ~ off vi (sl) marcharse. ~ on vi seguir adelante. ~ up vt levantar. ~-button telephone n teléfono m de teclas. ~-chair n sillita f con ruedas. ~ing /ˈpʊʃɪŋ/ a ambicioso. ~-over n (fam) cosa f muy fácil, pan comido. ~y a (pej) ambicioso

puss /pʊs/ n minino m

put /pʊt/ vt (pt put, pres p putting) poner; (express) expresar; (say) decir; (estimate) estimar; hacer (question). ~ across comunicar; (deceive) engañar. ~ aside poner aparte. ~ away guardar. ~ back devolver; retrasar (clock). ~ by guardar; ahorrar (money). ~ down depositar; (suppress) suprimir; (write) apuntar; (kill) sacrificar. ~ forward avanzar. ~ in introducir; (submit) presentar. ~ in for pedir. ~ off aplazar; (disconcert) desconcertar. ~ on (wear) ponerse; cobrar (speed); encender (light). ~ one's foot down mantenerse firme. ~ out (*extinguish*) apagar; (*inconvenience*) incomodar; extender ⟨*hand*⟩; (*disconcert*) desconcertar. ~ **to sea** hacerse a la mar. ~ **through** (*phone*) poner. ~ **up** levantar; subir ⟨*price*⟩; alojar ⟨*guest*⟩. ~ **up** (*fam*) no moverse

putrefy /'pjuːtrɪfaɪ/ *vi* pudrirse

putt /pʌt/ *n* (*golf*) golpe *m* suave

putty /'pʌtɪ/ *n* masilla *f*

put-up /'pʊtʌp/ *a.* ~ **job** *n* confabulación *f*

puzzle /'pʌzl/ *n* enigma *m*; (*game*) rompecabezas *m invar.* —*vt* dejar perplejo. —*vi* calentarse los sesos. ~**ing** *a* incomprensible; (*odd*) curioso

pygmy /'pɪgmɪ/ *n* pigmeo *m*

pyjamas /pə'dʒɑːməz/ *npl* pijama *m*

pylon /'paɪlən/ *n* pilón *m*

pyramid /'pɪrəmɪd/ *n* pirámide *f*

python /'paɪθn/ *n* pitón *m*

Q

quack[1] /kwæk/ *n* (*of duck*) graznido *m*

quack[2] /kwæk/ (*person*) charlatán *m*. ~ **doctor** *n* curandero *m*

quadrangle /'kwɒdræŋgl/ *n* cuadrilátero *m*; (*court*) patio *m*

quadruped /'kwɒdruped/ *n* cuadrúpedo *m*

quadruple /'kwɒdrʊpl/ *a & n* cuádruplo (*m*). —*vt* cuadruplicar. —*t* /-plət/ *n* cuatrillizo *m*

quagmire /'kwæɡmaɪə(r)/ *n* ciénaga *f*; (*fig*) atolladero *m*

quail /kweɪl/ *n* codorniz *f*

quaint /kweɪnt/ *a* (-**er**, -**est**) pintoresco; (*odd*) curioso

quake /kweɪk/ *vi* temblar. —*n* (*fam*) terremoto *m*

Quaker /'kweɪkə(r)/ *n* cuáquero (*m*)

qualification /ˌkwɒlɪfɪ'keɪʃn/ *n* título *m*; (*requirement*) requisito *m*; (*ability*) capacidad *f*; (*fig*) reserva *f*

qualified /'kwɒlɪfaɪd/ *a* cualificado; (*limited*) limitado; (*with degree, diploma*) titulado. ~**y** /'kwɒlɪfaɪ/ *vt* calificar; (*limit*) limitar. —*vi* sacar el título; (*sport*) clasificarse; (*fig*) llenar los requisitos

qualitative /'kwɒlɪtətɪv/ *a* cualitativo

quality /'kwɒlɪtɪ/ *n* calidad *f*; (*attribute*) cualidad *f*

qualm /kwɑːm/ *n* escrúpulo *m*

quandary /'kwɒndrɪ/ *n*. **in a** ~ en un dilema

quantitative /'kwɒntɪtətɪv/ *a* cuantitativo

quantity /'kwɒntɪtɪ/ *n* cantidad *f*

quarantine /'kwɒrəntiːn/ *n* cuarentena *f*

quarrel /'kwɒrəl/ *n* riña *f*. —*vi* (*pt* **quarrelled**) reñir. ~**some** *a* pendenciero

quarry[1] /'kwɒrɪ/ *n* (*excavation*) cantera *f*

quarry[2] /'kwɒrɪ/ *n* (*animal*) presa *f*

quart /kwɔːt/ *n* (poco más de un) litro *m*

quarter /'kwɔːtə(r)/ *n* cuarto *m*; (*of year*) trimestre *m*; (*district*) barrio *m*. **from all** ~**s** de todas partes. —*vt* dividir en cuartos; (*mil*) acuartelar. ~**s** *npl* alojamiento *m*

quartermaster /'kwɔːtəmɑːstə(r)/ *n* intendente *m*

quarter: ~**final** *n* cuarto *m* de final. ~**ly** *a* trimestral. —*adv* cada tres meses

quartet /kwɔː'tet/ *n* cuarteto *m*

quartz /kwɔːts/ *n* cuarzo *m*. —*a* ⟨*watch etc*⟩ de cuarzo

quash /kwɒʃ/ *vt* anular

quasi.. /'kweɪsaɪ/ *pref* cuasi...

quaver /'kweɪvə(r)/ *vi* temblar. —*n* (*mus*) corchea *f*

quay /kiː/ *n* muelle *m*

queasy /'kwiːzɪ/ *a* ⟨*stomach*⟩ delicado

queen /kwiːn/ *n* reina *f*. ∼ **mother** *n* reina *f* madre

queer /kwɪə(r)/ *a* (-er, -est) extraño; (*dubious*) sospechoso; (*ill*) indispuesto. —*n* (*sl*) homosexual *m*

quell /kwel/ *vt* reprimir

quench /kwentʃ/ *vt* apagar; sofocar ⟨*desire*⟩

querulous /'kwerʊləs/ *a* quejumbroso

query /'kwɪərɪ/ *n* pregunta *f*. —*vt* preguntar; (*doubt*) poner en duda

quest /kwest/ *n* busca *f*

question /'kwestʃən/ *n* pregunta *f*; (*for discussion*) cuestión *f*. **in** ∼ en cuestión. **out of the** ∼ imposible. **without** ∼ sin duda. —*vt* preguntar; ⟨*police etc*⟩ interrogar; (*doubt*) poner en duda. ∼**able** /'kwestʃənəbl/ *a* discutible. ∼ **mark** *n* signo *m* de interrogación. ∼**naire** /kwestʃə'neə(r)/ *n* cuestionario *m*

queue /kjuː/ *n* cola *f*. —*vi* (*pres p* **queuing**) hacer cola

quibble /'kwɪbl/ *vi* discutir; (*split hairs*) sutilizar

quick /kwɪk/ *a* (-er, -est) rápido. **be** ∼! ¡date prisa! —*adv* rápidamente. —*n* lo vivo. **to the** ∼ en lo vivo. ∼**en** /'kwɪkən/ *vt* acelerar. —*vi* acelerarse. ∼**ly** *adv* rápidamente. ∼**sand** /'kwɪksænd/ *n* arena *f* movediza. ∼**-tempered** *a* irascible

quid /kwɪd/ *n invar* (*sl*) libra *f* (esterlina)

quiet /'kwaɪət/ *a* (-er, -est) tranquilo; (*silent*) callado; (*discreet*) discreto. —*n* tranquilidad *f*. **on the** ∼ a escondidas. ∼**en**

/'kwaɪətn/ *vt* calmar. —*vi* calmarse. ∼**ly** *adv* tranquilamente; (*silently*) silenciosamente; (*discreetly*) discretamente. ∼**ness** *n* tranquilidad *f*

quill /kwɪl/ *n* pluma *f*

quilt /kwɪlt/ *n* edredón *m*. —*vt* acolchar

quince /kwɪns/ *n* membrillo *m*

quinine /kwɪ'niːn/ *n* quinina *f*

quintessence /kwɪn'tesns/ *n* quintaesencia *f*

quintet /kwɪn'tet/ *n* quinteto *m*

quintuplet /'kwɪntjuːplət/ *n* quintillizo *m*

quip /kwɪp/ *n* ocurrencia *f*

quirk /kwɜːk/ *n* peculiaridad *f*

quit /kwɪt/ *vt* (*pt* **quitted**) dejar. —*vi* abandonar; (*leave*) marcharse; (*resign*) dimitir. ∼ **doing** (*cease*, *Amer*) dejar de hacer

quite /kwaɪt/ *adv* bastante; (*completely*) totalmente; (*really*) verdaderamente. ∼ (**so**)! ¡claro! ∼ **a few** bastante

quits /kwɪts/ *a* a la par. **call it** ∼ darlo por terminado

quiver /'kwɪvə(r)/ *vi* temblar

quixotic /kwɪk'sɒtɪk/ *a* quijotesco

quiz /kwɪz/ *n* (*pl* **quizzes**) serie *f* de preguntas; (*game*) concurso *m*. —*vt* (*pt* **quizzed**) interrogar. ∼**zical** /'kwɪzɪkl/ *a* burlón

quorum /'kwɔːrəm/ *n* quórum *m*

quota /'kwəʊtə/ *n* cuota *f*

quot|**ation** /kwəʊ'teɪʃn/ *n* cita *f*; (*price*) presupuesto *m*. ∼**ation marks** *npl* comillas *fpl*. ∼**e** /kwəʊt/ *vt* citar; (*com*) cotizar. —*n* (*fam*) cita *f*; (*price*) presupuesto *m*. **in** ∼**es** *npl* entre comillas

quotient /'kwəʊʃnt/ *n* cociente *m*

R

rabbi /'ræbaɪ/ n rabino m

rabbit /'ræbɪt/ n conejo m

rabble /'ræbl/ n gentío m. **the ~** (pej) el populacho m

rabid /'ræbɪd/ a feroz; ⟨dog⟩ rabioso. **~es** /'reɪbi:z/ n rabia f

race[1] /reɪs/ n carrera f. —vt hacer correr ⟨horse⟩; acelerar ⟨engine⟩. —vi ⟨run⟩ correr, ir corriendo; ⟨rush⟩ ir de prisa

race[2] /reɪs/ ⟨group⟩ raza f

race: ~course /'reɪskɔ:s/ n hipódromo m. **~horse** /'reɪshɔ:s/ n caballo m de carreras. **~riots** /'reɪsraɪəts/ npl disturbios mpl raciales. **~track** /'reɪstræk/ n hipódromo m

racial /'reɪʃl/ a racial. **~ism** /-ɪzəm/ n racismo m

racing /'reɪsɪŋ/ n carreras fpl. **~ car** n coche m de carreras

racis|m /'reɪsɪzəm/ n racismo m. **~t** /'reɪsɪst/ a & n racista (m & f)

rack[1] /ræk/ n ⟨shelf⟩ estante m; ⟨for luggage⟩ rejilla f; ⟨for plates⟩ escurreplatos m invar. —vt. **~ one's brains** devanarse los sesos

rack[2] /ræk/ n. **go to ~ and ruin** quedarse en la ruina

racket[1] /'rækɪt/ n ⟨for sports⟩ raqueta f

racket[2] /'rækɪt/ ⟨din⟩ alboroto m; ⟨swindle⟩ estafa f. **~eer** /-ə'tɪə(r)/ n estafador m

raconteur /rækɒn'tɜ:/ n anecdotista m & f

racy /'reɪsɪ/ a (-ier, -iest) vivo

radar /'reɪdɑ:(r)/ n radar m

radian|ce /'reɪdɪəns/ n resplandor m. **~t** /'reɪdɪənt/ a radiante. **~tly** adv con resplandor

radiate /'reɪdɪeɪt/ vt irradiar. —vi divergir. **~ion** /-'eɪʃn/ n radiación f. **~or** /'reɪdɪeɪtə(r)/ n radiador m

radical /'rædɪkl/ a & n radical (m)

radio /'reɪdɪəʊ/ n (pl **-os**) radio f. —vt transmitir por radio

radioactiv|e /reɪdɪəʊ'æktɪv/ a radiactivo. **~ity** /-'tɪvəti/ n radiactividad f

radiograph|er /reɪdɪ'ɒgrəfə(r)/ n radiógrafo m. **~y** n radiografía f

radish /'rædɪʃ/ n rábano m

radius /'reɪdɪəs/ n (pl **-dii** /-dɪaɪ/) radio m

raffish /'ræfɪʃ/ a disoluto

raffle /'ræfl/ n rifa f

raft /rɑ:ft/ n balsa f

rafter /'rɑ:ftə(r)/ n cabrio m

rag[1] /ræg/ n andrajo m; ⟨for wiping⟩ trapo m; ⟨newspaper⟩ periodicucho m. **in ~s** ⟨person⟩ andrajoso; ⟨clothes⟩ hecho jirones

rag[2] /ræg/ n ⟨univ⟩ festival m estudiantil; ⟨prank, fam⟩ broma f pesada. —vt (pt ragged) ⟨sl⟩ tomar el pelo a

ragamuffin /'rægəmʌfɪn/ n granuja m, golfo m

rage /reɪdʒ/ n rabia f; ⟨fashion⟩ moda f. —vi estar furioso; ⟨storm⟩ bramar

ragged /'rægɪd/ a ⟨person⟩ andrajoso; ⟨clothes⟩ hecho jirones; ⟨edge⟩ mellado

raid /reɪd/ n ⟨mil⟩ incursión f; ⟨by police, etc⟩ redada f; ⟨by thieves⟩ asalto m. —vt ⟨mil⟩ atacar; ⟨police⟩ hacer una redada en; ⟨thieves⟩ asaltar. **~er** n invasor m; ⟨thief⟩ ladrón m

rail[1] /reɪl/ n barandilla f; ⟨for train⟩ riel m; ⟨rod⟩ barra f. **by ~** por ferrocarril

rail[2] /reɪl/ vi. **~ against**, **~ at** insultar

railing /'reɪlɪŋ/ n barandilla f; ⟨fence⟩ verja f

rail|road /'reɪlrəʊd/ n (Amer), **~way** /'reɪlweɪ/ n ferrocarril m

~**wayman** n (pl -men) ferroviario m. ~**way station** n estación f de ferrocarril

rain /reɪn/ n lluvia f. —vi llover. ~**bow** /'reɪnbəʊ/ n arco m iris. ~**coat** /'reɪnkəʊt/ n impermeable m. ~**fall** /'reɪnfɔ:l/ n precipitación f. ~**water** n agua f de lluvia. ~**y** /'reɪnɪ/ a (-ier, -iest) lluvioso

raise /reɪz/ vt levantar; (breed) criar; obtener (money etc); hacer (question); plantear (problem); subir (price). ~ **one's glass to** brindar por. ~ **one's hat** descubrirse. —n (Amer) aumento m

raisin /'reɪzn/ n (uva f) pasa f

rake[1] /reɪk/ n rastrillo m. —vt rastrillar; (search) buscar en. ~ **up** remover

rake[2] /reɪk/ n (man) calavera m

rake-off /'reɪkɒf/ n (fam) comisión f

rally /'rælɪ/ vt reunir; (revive) reanimar. —vi reunirse; (in sickness) recuperarse. —n reunión f; (recovery) recuperación f; (auto) rallye m

ram /ræm/ n carnero m. —vt (pt rammed) (thrust) meter por la fuerza; (crash into) chocar con

ramble /'ræmbl/ n excursión f a pie. —vi ir de paseo; (in speech) divagar. ~**e on** divagar. ~**er** n excursionista m & f. ~**ing** n (speech) divagador

ramification /ˌræmɪfɪ'keɪʃn/ n ramificación f

ramp /ræmp/ n rampa f

rampage /ræm'peɪdʒ/ vi alborotarse. /'ræmpeɪdʒ/ n. **go on the** ~ alborotarse

rampant /'ræmpənt/ a. **be** ~ (disease etc) estar extendido

rampart /'ræmpɑ:t/ n muralla f

ramshackle /'ræmʃækl/ a desvencijado

ran /ræn/ see **run**

ranch /rɑ:ntʃ/ n hacienda f

rancid /'rænsɪd/ a rancio

rancour /'ræŋkə(r)/ n rencor m

random /'rændəm/ a hecho al azar; (chance) fortuito. —n. **at** ~ al azar

randy /'rændɪ/ a (-ier, -iest) lujurioso, cachondo (fam)

rang /ræŋ/ see **ring**[2]

range /reɪndʒ/ n alcance m; (distance) distancia f; (series) serie f; (of mountains) cordillera f; (extent) extensión f; (com) surtido m; (open area) dehesa f; (stove) cocina f económica. —vi extenderse; (vary) variar

ranger /'reɪndʒə(r)/ n guardabosque m

rank[1] /ræŋk/ n posición f, categoría f; (row) fila f; (for taxis) parada f. **the** ~ **and file** la masa f. —vt clasificar. —vi clasificarse. ~**s** npl soldados mpl rasos

rank[2] /ræŋk/ a (-er, -est) exuberante; (smell) fétido; (fig) completo

rankle /'ræŋkl/ vi (fig) causar rencor

ransack /'rænsæk/ vt registrar; (pillage) saquear

ransom /'rænsəm/ n rescate m. **hold s.o. to** ~ exigir rescate por uno; (fig) hacer chantaje a uno. —vt rescatar; (redeem) redimir

rant /rænt/ vi vociferar

rap /ræp/ n golpe m seco. —vt/i (pt rapped) golpear

rapacious /rə'peɪʃs/ a rapaz

rape /reɪp/ n violar. —n violación f

rapid /'ræpɪd/ a rápido. ~**ity** /rə'pɪdətɪ/ n rapidez f. ~**s** /'ræpɪdz/ npl rápido m

rapist /'reɪpɪst/ n violador m

rapport /ræ'pɔ:(r)/ n armonía f, relación f

rapt /ræpt/ a (attention) profundo. ~ **in** absorto en

rapture /'ræptʃə(r)/ n éxtasis m. **~ous** a extático

rare[1] /reə(r)/ a (-er, -est) raro

rare[2] /reə(r)/ a (culin) poco hecho

rarefied /'reərifaid/ a enrarecido

rarely /'reəli/ adv raramente

rarity /'reərəti/ n rareza f

raring /'reəriŋ/ a (fam). **~ to** impaciente por

rascal /'rɑːskl/ n tunante m & f

rash[1] /ræʃ/ a (-er, -est) imprudente, precipitado

rash[2] /ræʃ/ n erupción f.

rasher /'ræʃə(r)/ n loncha f

rash|ly /'ræʃli/ adv imprudentemente, a la ligera. **~ness** n imprudencia f

rasp /rɑːsp/ n (file) escofina f

raspberry /'rɑːzbri/ n frambuesa f

rasping /'rɑːspiŋ/ a áspero

rat /ræt/ n rata f. **~** (pt ratted). **~ on** (desert) desertar; (inform on) denunciar, chivarse

rate /reit/ n (ratio) proporción f; (speed) velocidad f; (price) precio m; (of interest) tipo m. **at any ~** de todas formas. **at the ~ of** (on the basis of) a razón de. **at this ~** así. **—vt** valorar; (consider) considerar; (deserve, Amer) merecer. **—vi** ser considerado. **~able value** n valor m imponible. **~payer** /'reitpeiə(r)/ n contribuyente m & f. **~s** npl (taxes) impuestos mpl municipales

rather /'rɑːðə(r)/ adv mejor dicho; (fairly) bastante; (a little) un poco. **—int** claro. **I would ~ not** prefiero no

ratification /rætifi'keiʃn/ n ratificación f. **~y** /'rætifai/ vt ratificar

rating /'reitiŋ/ n clasificación f; (sailor) marinero m; (number, TV) índice m

ratio /'reiʃiəu/ n (pl -os) proporción f

ration /'ræʃn/ n ración f. **—vt** racionar

rational /'ræʃənəl/ a racional. **~ize** /'ræʃənəlaiz/ vt racionalizar

rat race /'rætreis/ n lucha f incesante para triunfar

rattle /'rætl/ vi traquetear. **—vt** (shake) agitar; (sl) desconcertar. **—n** traqueteo m; (toy) sonajero m. **~ off** (fig) decir de corrida

rattlesnake /'rætlsneik/ n serpiente f de cascabel

ratty /'ræti/ a (-ier, -iest) (sl) irritable

raucous /'rɔːkəs/ a estridente

ravage /'rævidʒ/ vt estragar. **~s** /'rævidʒiz/ npl estragos mpl

rave /reiv/ vi delirar; (in anger) enfurecerse. **~ about** entusiasmarse por

raven /'reivn/ n cuervo m. **—a** (hair) negro

ravenous /'rævənəs/ a voraz; (person) hambriento. **be ~** morirse de hambre

ravine /rə'viːn/ n barranco m

raving /'reiviŋ/ a. **~ mad** loco de atar. **~s** npl divagaciones fpl

ravish /'ræviʃ/ vt (rape) violar. **~ing** a (enchanting) encantador

raw /rɔː/ a (-er, -est) crudo; (not processed) bruto; (wound) en carne viva; (inexperienced) inexperto; (weather) crudo. **~ deal** n tratamiento m injusto, injusticia f. **~ materials** npl materias fpl primas

ray /rei/ n rayo m

raze /reiz/ vt arrasar

razor /'reizə(r)/ n navaja f de afeitar; (electric) maquinilla f de afeitar

Rd abbr (Road) C/, Calle f

re[1] /riː/ prep con referencia a. **—pref** re...

re[2] /rei/ n (mus, second note of any musical scale) re m reach / riːtʃ/ vt alcanzar; (extend) extender; (arrive at) llegar a; (achieve) lograr; (hand over) pasar, dar. —vi extenderse. —n alcance m. **within ~ of** al alcance de; (close to) a corta distancia de

react /rɪˈækt/ vi reaccionar. **~ion** /rɪˈækʃn/ n reacción f. **~ionary** a & n reaccionario (m)

reactor /rɪˈæktə(r)/ n reactor m

read /riːd/ vt (pt read /red/) leer; (study) estudiar; (interpret) interpretar. —vi leer; (instrument) indicar. —n (fam) lectura f. **~ out** vt leer en voz alta. **~able** a interesante, agradable; (clear) legible. **~er** /ˈriːdə(r)/ n lector m. **~ership** n lectores m

readi|ly /ˈredɪlɪ/ adv (willingly) de buena gana; (easily) fácilmente. **~ness** /ˈredɪnɪs/ n prontitud f. **in ~ness** preparado, listo

reading /ˈriːdɪŋ/ n lectura f

readjust /riːəˈdʒʌst/ vt reajustar. —vi readaptarse (**to** a)

ready /ˈredɪ/ a (-ier, -iest) listo, preparado; (quick) pronto. **~-made** a confeccionado. **~ money** n dinero m contante. **~ reckoner** n baremo m. **get ~** prepararse

real /rɪəl/ a verdadero. —adv (Amer, fam) verdaderamente. **~ estate** n bienes mpl raíces

realis|m /ˈrɪəlɪzəm/ n realismo m. **~t** /ˈrɪəlɪst/ n realista m & f. **~tic** /-ˈlɪstɪk/ a realista. **~tically** /-ˈlɪstɪklɪ/ adv de manera realista

reality /rɪˈælətɪ/ n realidad f

realiz|ation /rɪəlaɪˈzeɪʃn/ n comprensión f; (com) realización f. **~e** /ˈrɪəlaɪz/ vt darse cuenta de; (fulfil, com) realizar

really /ˈrɪəlɪ/ adv verdaderamente

realm /relm/ n reino m

ream /riːm/ n resma f

reap /riːp/ vt segar; (fig) cosechar

re: **~appear** /riːəˈpɪə(r)/ vi reaparecer. **~appraisal** /riːəˈpreɪzl/ n revaluación f

rear¹ /rɪə(r)/ n parte f de atrás. —a posterior, trasero

rear² /rɪə(r)/ vt (bring up, breed) criar. **~ one's head** levantar la cabeza. —vi (horse) encabritarse. **~ up** (horse) encabritarse

rear: **~-admiral** n contraalmirante m. **~guard** /ˈrɪəgɑːd/ n retaguardia f

re: **~arm** /riːˈɑːm/ vt rearmar. —vi rearmarse. **~arrange** /riːəˈreɪndʒ/ vt arreglar de otra manera

reason /ˈriːzn/ n razón f, motivo m. **within ~** dentro de lo razonable. —vi razonar

reasonable /ˈriːzənəbl/ a razonable

reasoning /ˈriːznɪŋ/ n razonamiento m

reassur|ance /riːəˈʃʊərəns/ n promesa f tranquilizadora; (guarantee) garantía f. **~e** /riːəˈʃʊə(r)/ vt tranquilizar

rebate /ˈriːbeɪt/ n reembolso m; (discount) rebaja f

rebel /ˈrebl/ n rebelde m & f. /rɪˈbel/ vi (pt rebelled) rebelarse. **~lion** rebelión f. **~lious** a rebelde

rebound /rɪˈbaʊnd/ vi rebotar; (fig) recaer. —/ˈriːbaʊnd/ n rebote m. **on the ~** (fig) por reacción

rebuff /rɪˈbʌf/ vt rechazar. —n desaire m

rebuild /riːˈbɪld/ vt (pt rebuilt) reconstruir

rebuke /rɪˈbjuːk/ vt reprender. —n reprensión f

rebuttal /rɪˈbʌtl/ n refutación f

recall /rɪˈkɔːl/ vt (call s.o. back) llamar; (remember) recordar. —n llamada f recant /rɪˈkænt/ vi retractarse

recap /ˈriːkæp/ vt/i (pt recapped) (fam) resumir. —n (fam) resumen m

recapitulate /ˌriːkəˈpɪtʃʊleɪt/ vt/i resumir. ~ion /-ˈleɪʃn/ n resumen m

recapture /riːˈkæptʃə(r)/ vt recobrar; (recall) hacer revivir

recede /rɪˈsiːd/ vi retroceder. ~ing a (forehead) huidizo

receipt /rɪˈsiːt/ n recibo m. ~s npl (com) ingresos mpl

receive /rɪˈsiːv/ vt recibir. ~r /-ə(r)/ n (of stolen goods) perista m & f, (of phone) auricular m

recent /ˈriːsnt/ a reciente. ~ly adv recientemente

receptacle /rɪˈseptəkl/ n recipiente m

reception /rɪˈsepʃn/ n recepción f; (welcome) acogida f. ~ist n recepcionista m & f

receptive /rɪˈseptɪv/ a receptivo

recess /rɪˈses/ n hueco m; (holiday) vacaciones fpl. (fig) parte f recóndita

recession /rɪˈseʃn/ n recesión f

recharge /riːˈtʃɑːdʒ/ vt cargar de nuevo, recargar

recipe /ˈresɪpɪ/ n receta f

recipient /rɪˈsɪpɪənt/ n recipiente m & f, (of letter) destinatario m

reciprocal /rɪˈsɪprəkl/ a recíproco

reciprocate /rɪˈsɪprəkeɪt/ vt corresponder a

recital /rɪˈsaɪtl/ n (mus) recital m

recite /rɪˈsaɪt/ vt recitar; (list) enumerar

reckless /ˈrekləs/ a imprudente. ~ly adv imprudentemente. ~ness n imprudencia f

reckon /ˈrekən/ vt/i calcular; (consider) considerar; (think) pensar. ~ on (rely) contar con. ~ing n cálculo m

reclaim /rɪˈkleɪm/ vt reclamar; recuperar (land)

recline /rɪˈklaɪn/ vi recostarse. ~ing a acostado; (seat) reclinable

recluse /rɪˈkluːs/ n solitario m

recognition /ˌrekəgˈnɪʃn/ n reconocimiento m. beyond ~tion irreconocible. ~ze /ˈrekəgnaɪz/ vt reconocer

recoil /rɪˈkɔɪl/ vi retroceder. —n (of gun) culatazo m

recollect /ˌrekəˈlekt/ vt recordar. ~ion /-ʃn/ n recuerdo m

recommend /ˌrekəˈmend/ vt recomendar. ~ation /-ˈdeɪʃn/ n recomendación f

recompense /ˈrekəmpens/ vt recompensar. —n recompensa f

reconcile /ˈrekənsaɪl/ vt reconciliar (people); conciliar (facts). ~e o.s. resignarse (to a). ~iation /-sɪlɪˈeɪʃn/ n reconciliación f

recondition /ˌriːkənˈdɪʃn/ vt reacondicionar, arreglar

reconnaissance /rɪˈkɒnɪsns/ n reconocimiento m

reconnoitre /ˌrekəˈnɔɪtə(r)/ vt (pres p -tring) (mil) reconocer. —vi hacer un reconocimiento

re:~consider /ˌriːkənˈsɪdə(r)/ vt volver a considerar. ~construct /ˌriːkənˈstrʌkt/ vt reconstruir. ~construction /-ʃn/ n reconstrucción f

record /rɪˈkɔːd/ vt (in register) registrar; (in diary) apuntar; (mus) grabar. /ˈrekɔːd/ n (file) documentación f, expediente m; (mus) disco m; (sport) récord m. off the ~ en confianza. ~er /rɪˈkɔːdə(r)/ n registrador m; (mus) flauta f dulce. ~ing n grabación f. ~player n tocadiscos m invar

recount /rɪˈkaʊnt/ vt contar, relatar, referir

re-count /riːˈkaʊnt/ vt recontar. /ˈriːkaʊnt/ n (pol) recuento m

recoup /rɪˈkuːp/ vt recuperar

recourse /rɪˈkɔːs/ n recurso m. **have ~ to** recurrir a

recover /rɪˈkʌvə(r)/ vt recuperar. —vi reponerse. **~y** n recuperación f

recreation /rekrɪˈeɪʃn/ n recreo m. **~al** a de recreo

recrimination /rɪkrɪmɪˈneɪʃn/ n recriminación f

recruit /rɪˈkruːt/ n recluta m. —vt reclutar. **~ment** n reclutamiento m

rectangle /ˈrektæŋgl/ n rectángulo m. **~ular** /-ˈtæŋgjʊlə(r)/ a rectangular

rectification /rektɪfɪˈkeɪʃn/ n rectificación f. **~y** /ˈrektɪfaɪ/ vt rectificar

rector /ˈrektə(r)/ n párroco m; (of college) rector m. **~y** n rectoría f

recumbent /rɪˈkʌmbənt/ a recostado

recuperate /rɪˈkuːpəreɪt/ vt recuperar. —vi reponerse. **~ion** /-ˈreɪʃn/ n recuperación f

recur /rɪˈkɜː(r)/ vi (pt recurred) repetirse. **~rence** /rɪˈkʌrns/ n repetición f. **~rent** /rɪˈkʌrənt/ a repetido

recycle /riːˈsaɪkl/ vt reciclar

red /red/ a (redder, reddest) rojo. —n rojo m. **in the ~** (account) en descubierto. **~breast** /ˈredbrest/ n petirrojo m. **~brick** /ˈredbrɪk/ a (univ) de reciente fundación. **~den** /ˈredn/ vt enrojecer. —vi enrojecerse. **~dish** a rojizo

redecorate /riːˈdekəreɪt/ vt pintar de nuevo

redeem /rɪˈdiːm/ vt redimir. **~eming quality** n cualidad f compensadora. **~mption** /-ˈdempʃn/ n redención f

redeploy /riːdɪˈplɔɪ/ vt disponer de otra manera; (mil) cambiar de frente

red: ~-handed a en flagrante. **~ herring** (fig) pista f falsa. **~-hot** a al rojo; (news) de última hora

Red Indian /red'ɪndjən/ n piel m & f roja

redirect /riːdaɪˈrekt/ vt reexpedir

red: ~-letter day n día m señalado, día m memorable. **~ light** n luz f roja. **~ness** n rojez f

redo /riːˈduː/ vt (pt redid, pp redone) rehacer

redouble /rɪˈdʌbl/ vt redoblar

redress /rɪˈdres/ vt reparar. —n reparación f

red tape /red'teɪp/ n (fig) papeleo m

reduce /rɪˈdjuːs/ vt reducir. —vi reducirse; (slim) adelgazar. **~tion** /ˈdʌkʃn/ n reducción f

redundan|cy /rɪˈdʌndənsɪ/ n superfluidad f; (unemployment) desempleo m. **~t** /rɪˈdʌndənt/ a superfluo. **be made ~t** perder su empleo

reed /riːd/ n caña f; (mus) lengüeta f

reef /riːf/ n arrecife m

reek /riːk/ n mal olor m. —vi. **~ (of)** apestar

reel /riːl/ n carrete m. —vi dar vueltas; (stagger) tambalearse. —vt. **~ off** (fig) enumerar

refectory /rɪˈfektərɪ/ n refectorio m

refer /rɪˈfɜː(r)/ vt (pt referred) remitir. —vi referirse. **~ to** referirse a; (consult) consultar

referee /refəˈriː/ n árbitro m; (for job) referencia f. —vi (pt refereed) arbitrar

reference /ˈrefrəns/ n referencia f. **~ book** n libro m de consulta. **in ~ to, with ~ to** en cuanto a; (com) respecto a

referendum /refəˈrendəm/ n (pl -ums) referéndum m

refill /riːˈfil/ vt rellenar. /ˈriːfil/ n recambio m

refine /rɪˈfaɪn/ vt refinar. ∼d a refinado. ∼ment n refinamiento m; (tec) refinación f. ∼ry /-ərɪ/ n refinería f

reflect /rɪˈflekt/ vt reflejar. —vi reflejar; (think) reflexionar. ∼ upon perjudicar. ∼ion /-ʃn/ n reflexión f; (image) reflejo m. ∼ive /rɪˈflektɪv/ a reflector; (thoughtful) pensativo. ∼or n reflector m

reflex /ˈriːfleks/ a & n reflejo (m)

reflexive /rɪˈfleksɪv/ a (gram) reflexivo

reform /rɪˈfɔːm/ vt reformar. —vi reformarse. —n reforma f. ∼er n reformador m

refract /rɪˈfrækt/ vt refractar

refrain[1] /rɪˈfreɪn/ n estribillo m

refrain[2] /rɪˈfreɪn/ vi abstenerse (from de)

refresh /rɪˈfreʃ/ vt refrescar. ∼er /rɪˈfreʃə(r)/ a (course) de repaso. ∼ing a refrescante. ∼ments npl (food and drink) refrigerio m

refrigerate /rɪˈfrɪdʒəreɪt/ vt refrigerar. ∼or n nevera f, refrigeradora f (LAm)

refuel /riːˈfjuːəl/ vt/i (pt refuelled) repostar

refuge /ˈrefjuːdʒ/ n refugio m. take ∼e refugiarse. ∼e /refjʊˈdʒiː/ n refugiado m

refund /rɪˈfʌnd/ vt reembolsar. /ˈriːfʌnd/ n reembolso m

refurbish /riːˈfɜːbɪʃ/ vt renovar

refusal /rɪˈfjuːzl/ n negativa f

refuse[1] /rɪˈfjuːz/ vt rehusar. —vi negarse

refuse[2] /refjuːs/ n basura f

refute /rɪˈfjuːt/ vt refutar

regain /rɪˈgeɪn/ vt recobrar

regal /ˈriːgl/ a real

regale /rɪˈgeɪl/ vt festejar

regalia /rɪˈgeɪlɪə/ npl insignias fpl

regard /rɪˈgaːd/ vt mirar; (consider) considerar. as ∼s en cuanto a. —n mirada f; (care) atención f; (esteem) respeto m. ∼ing prep en cuanto a. ∼less /rɪˈgaːdlɪs/ adv a pesar de todo. ∼less of sin tener en cuenta. ∼s npl saludos mpl. kind ∼s npl recuerdos mpl

regatta /rɪˈgætə/ n regata f

regency /ˈriːdʒənsɪ/ n regencia f

regenerate /rɪˈdʒenəreɪt/ vt regenerar

regent /ˈriːdʒənt/ n regente m & f

regime /reɪˈʒiːm/ n régimen m

regiment /ˈredʒɪmənt/ n regimiento m. ∼al /-ˈmentl/ a del regimiento. ∼ation /-enˈteɪʃn/ n reglamentación f rígida

region /ˈriːdʒən/ n región f. in the ∼ of alrededor de. ∼al a regional

register /ˈredʒɪstə(r)/ n registro m. —vt registrar; matricular (vehicle); declarar (birth); certificar (letter); facturar (luggage); (indicate) indicar; (express) expresar. —vi (enrol) inscribirse; (fig) producir impresión. ∼ office n registro m civil

registrar /redʒɪˈstraː(r)/ n secretario m del registro civil; (univ) secretario m general

registration /redʒɪˈstreɪʃn/ n registración f; (in register) inscripción f; (of vehicle) matrícula f

registry /ˈredʒɪstrɪ/ n. ∼ office n registro m civil

regression /rɪˈgreʃn/ n regresión f

regret /rɪˈgret/ n pesar m. —vt (pt regretted) lamentar. I ∼ that siento (que). ∼fully adv con pesar. ∼table a lamentable. ∼tably adv lamentablemente

regular /'regjʊlə(r)/ *a* regular; (*usual*) habitual. **—n** (*fam*) cliente *m* habitual. **~ity** /-'lærətɪ/ *n* regularidad *f*. **~ly** *adv* regularmente

regulat|e /'regjʊleɪt/ *vt* regular. **~ion** /-'leɪʃn/ *n* arreglo *m*; (*rule*) regla *f*

rehabilitat|e /ri:hə'bɪlɪteɪt/ *vt* rehabilitar. **~ion** /-'teɪʃn/ *n* rehabilitación *f*

rehash /ri:'hæʃ/ *vt* volver a presentar. /'ri:hæʃ/ *n* refrito *m*

rehears|al /rɪ'hɜ:sl/ *n* ensayo *m*. **~e** /rɪ'hɜ:s/ *vt* ensayar

reign /reɪn/ *n* reinado *m*. **—vi** reinar

reimburse /ri:ɪm'bɜ:s/ *vt* reembolsar

reins /reɪnz/ *npl* riendas *fpl*

reindeer /'reɪndɪə(r)/ *n invar* reno *m*

reinforce /ri:ɪn'fɔ:s/ *vt* reforzar. **~ment** *n* refuerzo *m*

reinstate /ri:ɪn'steɪt/ *vt* reintegrar

reiterate /ri:'ɪtəreɪt/ *vt* reiterar

reject /rɪ'dʒekt/ *vt* rechazar. /'ri:dʒekt/ *n* producto *m* defectuoso. **~ion** /'dʒekʃn/ *n* rechazamiento *m*, rechazo *m*

rejoic|e /rɪ'dʒɔɪs/ *vi* regocijarse. **~ing** *n* regocijo *m*

rejoin /rɪ'dʒɔɪn/ *vt* reunirse con; (*answer*) replicar. **~der** /rɪ'dʒɔɪndə(r)/ *n* réplica *f*

rejuvenate /rɪ'dʒu:vəneɪt/ *vt* rejuvenecer

rekindle /ri:'kɪndl/ *vt* reavivar

relapse /rɪ'læps/ *n* recaída *f*. —*vi* recaer; (*into crime*) reincidir

relat|e /rɪ'leɪt/ *vt* contar; (*connect*) relacionar. —*vi* relacionarse (**to** con). **~d** *a* emparentado; (*ideas etc*) relacionado

relation /rɪ'leɪʃn/ *n* relación *f*; (*person*) pariente *m & f*. **~ship** *n* relación *f*; (*blood tie*) parentesco *m*; (*affair*) relaciones *fpl*

relative /'relətɪv/ *n* pariente *m & f*. **—a** relativo. **~ly** *adv* relativamente

relax /rɪ'læks/ *vt* relajar. —*vi* relajarse. **~ation** /ri:læk'seɪʃn/ *n* relajación *f*; (*rest*) descanso *m*; (*recreation*) recreo *m*. **~ing** *a* relajante

relay /'ri:leɪ/ *n* relevo *m*. **~** (*race*) *n* carrera *f* de relevos. /rɪ'leɪ/ *vt* retransmitir

release /rɪ'li:s/ *vt* soltar; poner en libertad (*prisoner*); lanzar (*bomb*); estrenar (*film*); (*mec*) desenganchar; publicar (*news*); emitir (*smoke*). **—n** liberación *f*; (*of film*) estreno *m*; (*record*) disco *m* nuevo

relegate /'relɪgeɪt/ *vt* relegar

relent /rɪ'lent/ *vi* ceder. **~less** *a* implacable; (*continuous*) incesante

relevan|ce /'reləvəns/ *n* pertinencia *f*. **~t** /'reləvənt/ *a* pertinente

reliab|ility /rɪlaɪə'bɪlətɪ/ *n* fiabilidad *f*. **~le** /rɪ'laɪəbl/ *a* seguro; (*person*) de fiar; (*com*) serio

relian|ce /rɪ'laɪəns/ *n* dependencia *f*; (*trust*) confianza *f*. **~t** *a* confiado

relic /'relɪk/ *n* reliquia *f*. **~s** *npl* restos *mpl*

relief /rɪ'li:f/ *n* alivio *m*; (*assistance*) socorro *m*; (*outline*) relieve *m*. **~ve** /rɪ'li:v/ *vt* aliviar; (*take over from*) relevar

religio|n /rɪ'lɪdʒən/ *n* religión *f*. **~us** /rɪ'lɪdʒəs/ *a* religioso

relinquish /rɪ'lɪnkwɪʃ/ *vt* abandonar, renunciar

relish /'relɪʃ/ *n* gusto *m*; (*culin*) salsa *f*. —*vt* saborear. **I don't ~ the idea** no me gusta la idea

relocate /ri:ləʊ'keɪt/ *vt* colocar de nuevo

reluctan|ce /rɪ'lʌktəns/ *n* desgana *f*. **~t** /rɪ'lʌktənt/ *a* mal dispuesto. **be ~t to** no tener ganas de. **~tly** *adv* de mala gana rely /rɪˈlaɪ/ vi. ~ on contar con; (trust) fiarse de; (depend) depender

remain /rɪˈmeɪn/ vi quedar. ~der /rɪˈmeɪndə(r)/ n resto m. ~s npl restos mpl; (left-overs) sobras fpl

remand /rɪˈmɑːnd/ vt. ~ in custody mantener bajo custodia. — n. on ~ bajo custodia

remark /rɪˈmɑːk/ n observación f. —vt observar. ~able a notable

remarry /riːˈmæri/ vi volver a casarse

remedial /rɪˈmiːdɪəl/ a remediador

remedy /ˈremədɪ/ n remedio m. —vt remediar

remember /rɪˈmembə(r)/ vt acordarse de. —vi acordarse. ~rance n recuerdo m

remind /rɪˈmaɪnd/ vt recordar. ~er n recordatorio m; (letter) notificación f

reminisce /remɪˈnɪs/ vi recordar el pasado. ~nces npl recuerdos mpl. ~nt /remɪˈnɪsnt/ a. be ~nt of recordar

remiss /rɪˈmɪs/ a negligente

remission /rɪˈmɪʃn/ n remisión f; (of sentence) reducción f de condena

remit /rɪˈmɪt/ vt (pt remitted) perdonar; enviar (money). —vi moderarse. ~tance n remesa f

remnant /ˈremnənt/ n resto m; (of cloth) retazo m; (trace) vestigio m

remonstrate /ˈremənstreɪt/ vi protestar

remorse /rɪˈmɔːs/ n remordimiento m. ~ful a lleno de remordimiento. ~less a implacable

remote /rɪˈməʊt/ a remoto; (slight) leve; (person) distante. ~ control n mando m a distancia. ~ly adv remotamente.

~ness n lejanía f; (isolation) aislamiento m, alejamiento m; (fig) improbabilidad f

removable /rɪˈmuːvəbl/ a movible; (detachable) de quita y pon, separable. ~al n eliminación f; (from house) mudanza f. ~e /rɪˈmuːv/ vt quitar; (dismiss) despedir; (get rid of) eliminar; (do away with) suprimir

remunerate /rɪˈmjuːnəreɪt/ vt remunerar. ~ion /-ˈreɪʃn/ n remuneración f. ~ive a remunerador

Renaissance /rəˈneɪsəns/ n Renacimiento m

rend /rend/ vt (pt rent) rasgar

render /ˈrendə(r)/ vt rendir; (com) presentar; (mus) interpretar; prestar (help etc). ~ing n (mus) interpretación f

rendezvous /ˈrɒndɪvuː/ n (pl -vous /-vuːz/) cita f

renegade /ˈrenɪgeɪd/ n renegado m

renew /rɪˈnjuː/ vt renovar; (resume) reanudar. ~able a renovable. ~al n renovación f

renounce /rɪˈnaʊns/ vt renunciar a; (disown) repudiar

renovate /ˈrenəveɪt/ vt renovar. ~ion /-ˈveɪʃn/ n renovación f

renown /rɪˈnaʊn/ n fama f. ~ed a célebre

rent¹ /rent/ n alquiler m. —vt alquilar

rent² /rent/ see rend

rental /ˈrentl/ n alquiler m

renunciation /rɪnʌnsɪˈeɪʃn/ n renuncia f

reopen /riːˈəʊpən/ vt reabrir. — vi reabrirse. ~ing n reapertura f

reorganize /riːˈɔːgənaɪz/ vt reorganizar

rep¹ /rep/ n (com, fam) representante m & f

rep² /rep/ (theatre, fam) teatro m de repertorio

repair /rɪˈpeə(r)/ vt reparar; remendar (clothes, shoes). —n reparación f; (patch) remiendo m. **in good ~** en buen estado

repartee /repɑːˈtiː/ n ocurrencias fpl

repatriat|e /riːˈpætrieit/ vt repatriar. **~ion** /-ˈeiʃn/ n repatriación f

repay /riːˈpei/ vt (pt **repaid**) reembolsar; pagar (debt); (reward) recompensar. **~ment** n reembolso m, pago m

repeal /rɪˈpiːl/ vt abrogar. —n abrogación f

repeat /rɪˈpiːt/ vt repetir. —vi repetir(se). —n repetición f. **~edly** /rɪˈpiːtɪdli/ adv repetidas veces

repel /rɪˈpel/ vt (pt **repelled**) repeler. **~lent** a repelente

repent /rɪˈpent/ vi arrepentirse. **~ance** n arrepentimiento m. **~ant** a arrepentido

repercussion /riːpəˈkʌʃn/ n repercusión f

reperto|ire /ˈrepətwɑː(r)/ n repertorio m. **~ry** /ˈrepətri/ n repertorio m. **~ry (theatre)** n teatro m de repertorio

repetit|ion /repɪˈtiʃn/ n repetición f. **~ious** /-ˈtiʃəs/ a, **~ive** /rɪˈpetətiv/ a que se repite; (dull) monótono

replace /rɪˈpleis/ vt reponer; (take the place of) sustituir. **~ment** n sustitución f; (person) sustituto m. **~ment part** n recambio m

replay /ˈriːplei/ n (sport) repetición f del partido; (recording) repetición f inmediata

replenish /rɪˈpleniʃ/ vt reponer; (refill) rellenar

replete /rɪˈpliːt/ a repleto

replica /ˈreplikə/ n copia f

reply /rɪˈplai/ vt/i contestar. —n respuesta f

report /rɪˈpɔːt/ vt anunciar; (denounce) denunciar. —vi presentar un informe; (present o.s.) presentarse. —n informe m; (schol) boletín m; (rumour) rumor m; (newspaper) reportaje m; (sound) estallido m. **~age** /repɔːˈtɑːʒ/ n reportaje m. **~edly** adv según se dice. **~er** /rɪˈpɔːtə(r)/ n reportero m, informador m

repose /rɪˈpəʊz/ n reposo m

repository /rɪˈpɒzitri/ n depósito m

repossess /riːpəˈzes/ vt recuperar

reprehen|d /repriˈhend/ vt reprender. **~sible** /-səbl/ a reprensible

represent /repriˈzent/ vt representar. **~ation** /-ˈteiʃn/ n representación f. **~ative** /repriˈzentətiv/ a representativo. —n representante m & f

repress /rɪˈpres/ vt reprimir. **~ion** /-ʃn/ n represión f. **~ive** a represivo

reprieve /rɪˈpriːv/ n indulto m; (fig) respiro m. —vt indultar; (fig) aliviar

reprimand /ˈreprimɑːnd/ vt reprender. —n reprensión f

reprint /ˈriːprint/ n reimpresión f; (offprint) tirada f aparte. /riːˈprint/ vt reimprimir

reprisal /rɪˈpraizl/ n represalia f

reproach /rɪˈprəʊtʃ/ vt reprochar. —n reproche m. **~ful** a de reproche, reprobador. **~fully** adv con reproche

reprobate /ˈreprəbeit/ n malvado m; (relig) réprobo m

reproduc|e /riːprəˈdjuːs/ vt reproducir. —vi reproducirse. **~tion** /-ˈdʌkʃn/ n reproducción f. **~tive** /-ˈdʌktiv/ a reproductor

reprove /rɪˈpruːv/ vt reprender

reptile /ˈreptail/ n reptil m

republic /rɪ'pʌblɪk/ n república f. ~**an** a & n republicano (m)

repudiate /rɪ'pju:dɪeɪt/ vt repudiar; (refuse to recognize) negarse a reconocer

repugnan|ce /rɪ'pʌgnəns/ n repugnancia f. ~**t** /rɪ'pʌgnənt/ a repugnante

repuls|e /rɪ'pʌls/ vt rechazar, repulsar. ~**ion** /-ʃn/ n repulsión f. ~**ive** a repulsivo

reputable /'repjʊtəbl/ a acreditado, de confianza, honroso

reputation /repjʊ'teɪʃn/ n reputación f

repute /rɪ'pju:t/ n reputación f. ~**d** /-ɪd/ a supuesto. ~**dly** adv según se dice

request /rɪ'kwest/ n petición f. — vt pedir. ~ **stop** n parada f discrecional

require /rɪ'kwaɪə(r)/ vt requerir; (need) necesitar; (demand) exigir. ~**d** a necesario. ~**ment** n requisito m

requisite /'rekwɪzɪt/ a necesario. —n requisito m

requisition /rekwɪ'zɪʃn/ n requisición f. —vt requisar

resale /'ri:seɪl/ n reventa f

rescind /rɪ'sɪnd/ vt rescindir

rescue /'reskju:/ vt salvar. —n salvamento m. ~**r** /-ə(r)/ n salvador m

research /rɪ'sɜ:tʃ/ n investigación f. —vt investigar. ~**er** n investigador m

resembl|ance /rɪ'zembləns/ n parecido m. ~**e** /rɪ'zembl/ vt parecerse a

resent /rɪ'zent/ vt resentirse por. ~**ful** a resentido. ~**ment** n resentimiento m

reservation /rezə'veɪʃn/ n reserva f; (booking) reservación f

reserve /rɪ'zɜ:v/ vt reservar. —n reserva f; (in sports) suplente m & f. ~**d** a reservado

reservist /rɪ'zɜ:vɪst/ n reservista m & f

reservoir /'rezəvwɑ:(r)/ n embalse m; (tank) depósito m

reshape /ri:'ʃeɪp/ vt formar de nuevo, reorganizar

reshuffle /ri:'ʃʌfl/ vt (pol) reorganizar. —n (pol) reorganización f

reside /rɪ'zaɪd/ vi residir

residen|ce /'rezɪdəns/ n residencia f. ~**ce permit** n permiso m de residencia. **be in ~ce** (doctor etc) interno. ~**t** /'rezɪdənt/ a & n residente (m & f). ~**tial** /rezɪ'denʃl/ a residencial

residue /'rezɪdju:/ n residuo m

resign /rɪ'zaɪn/ vt/i dimitir. ~ **o.s. to** resignarse a. ~**ation** /rezɪg'neɪʃn/ n resignación f; (from job) dimisión f. ~**ed** a resignado

resilien|ce /rɪ'zɪlɪəns/ n elasticidad f; (of person) resistencia f. ~**t** /rɪ'zɪlɪənt/ a elástico; (person) resistente

resin /'rezɪn/ n resina f

resist /rɪ'zɪst/ vt resistir. —vi resistirse. ~**ance** n resistencia f. ~**ant** a resistente

resolute /'rezəlu:t/ a resuelto. ~**ion** /-'lu:ʃn/ n resolución f

resolve /rɪ'zɒlv/ vt resolver. ~ **to do** resolverse a hacer. —n resolución f. ~**d** a resuelto

resonan|ce /'rezənəns/ n resonancia f. ~**t** /'rezənənt/ a resonante

resort /rɪ'zɔ:t/ vi. ~ **to** recurrir a. —n recurso m; (place) lugar m turístico. **in the last ~** como último recurso

resound /rɪ'zaʊnd/ vi resonar. ~**ing** a resonante

resource /rɪ'sɔ:s/ n recurso m. ~**ful** a ingenioso. ~**fulness** n ingeniosidad f

respect /rɪ'spekt/ n (esteem) respeto m; (aspect) respecto m.

with ~ to con respecto a. —vt respetar

respectab|ility /rɪspektə'bɪlətɪ/ n respetabilidad f. **~le** /rɪ'spektəbl/ a respetable. **~ly** adv respetablemente

respectful /rɪ'spektfl/ a respetuoso

respective /rɪ'spektɪv/ a respectivo. **~ly** adv respectivamente

respiration /respə'reɪʃn/ n respiración f

respite /'respaɪt/ n respiro m, tregua f

resplendent /rɪ'splendənt/ a resplandeciente

respond /rɪ'spɒnd/ vi responder. **~se** /rɪ'spɒns/ n respuesta f; (reaction) reacción f

responsib|ility /rɪspɒnsə'bɪlətɪ/ n responsabilidad f. **~le** /rɪ'spɒnsəbl/ a responsable; (job) de responsabilidad. **~ly** adv con formalidad

responsive /rɪ'spɒnsɪv/ a que reacciona bien. **~ to** sensible a

rest¹ /rest/ vt descansar; (lean) apoyar; (place) poner, colocar. — vi descansar; (lean) apoyarse. — n descanso m; (mus) pausa f

rest² /rest/ n (remainder) resto m, lo demás; (people) los demás, los otros mpl. —vi (remain) quedar

restaurant /'restərɒnt/ n restaurante m

restful /'restfl/ a sosegado

restitution /restɪ'tjuːʃn/ n restitución f

restive /'restɪv/ a inquieto

restless /'restlɪs/ a inquieto. **~ly** adv inquietamente. **~ness** n inquietud f

restor|ation /restə'reɪʃn/ n restauración f. **~e** /rɪ'stɔː(r)/ vt restablecer; restaurar (building); (put back in position) reponer; (return) devolver

restrain /rɪ'streɪn/ vt contener. **~ o.s.** contenerse. **~ed** a (moderate) moderado; (in control of self) comedido. **~t** n restricción f; (moderation) moderación f

restrict /rɪ'strɪkt/ vt restringir. **~ion** /-ʃn/ n restricción f. **~ive** /rɪ'strɪktɪv/ a restrictivo

result /rɪ'zʌlt/ n resultado m. — vi. **~ from** resultar de. **~ in** dar como resultado

resume /rɪ'zjuːm/ vt reanudar. — vi continuar

résumé /'rezjʊmeɪ/ n resumen m

resumption /rɪ'zʌmpʃn/ n continuación f

resurgence /rɪ'sɜːdʒəns/ n resurgimiento m

resurrect /rezə'rekt/ vt resucitar. **~ion** /-ʃn/ n resurrección f

resuscitat|e /rɪ'sʌsɪteɪt/ vt resucitar. **~ion** /-'teɪʃn/ n resucitación f

retail /'riːteɪl/ n venta f al por menor. —a & adv al por menor. —vt vender al por menor. —vi venderse al por menor. **~er** n minorista m & f

retain /rɪ'teɪn/ vt retener; (keep) conservar

retainer /rɪ'teɪnə(r)/ n (fee) anticipo m

retaliat|e /rɪ'tælɪeɪt/ vi desquitarse. **~ion** /-'eɪʃn/ n represalias fpl

retarded /rɪ'tɑːdɪd/ a retrasado

retentive /rɪ'tentɪv/ a (memory) bueno

rethink /riː'θɪŋk/ vt (pt rethought) considerar de nuevo

reticen|ce /'retɪsns/ n reserva f. **~t** /'retɪsnt/ a reservado, callado

retina /'retɪnə/ n retina f

retinue /'retɪnjuː/ n séquito m

retire /rɪ'taɪə(r)/ vi (from work) jubilarse; (withdraw) retirarse; (go to bed) acostarse. —vt jubilar. **~ed** _a_ jubilado. **~ement** _n_ jubilación _f._ **~ing** /rɪ'taɪərɪŋ/ _a_ reservado

retort /rɪ'tɔːt/ _vt/i_ replicar. —_n_ réplica _f_

retrace /riː'treɪs/ _vt_ repasar. **~ one's steps** volver sobre sus pasos

retract /rɪ'trækt/ _vt_ retirar. —_vi_ retractarse

retrain /riː'treɪn/ _vt_ reciclar, reeducar

retreat /rɪ'triːt/ _vi_ retirarse. —_n_ retirada _f,_ ⟨place⟩ refugio _m_

retrial /riː'traɪəl/ _n_ nuevo proceso _m_

retribution /retrɪ'bjuːʃn/ _n_ justo _m_ castigo

retriev|al /rɪ'triːvl/ _n_ recuperación _f._ **~e** /rɪ'triːv/ _vt_ ⟨recover⟩ recuperar; ⟨save⟩ salvar; ⟨put right⟩ reparar. **~er** _n_ ⟨dog⟩ perro _m_ cobrador

retrograde /'retrəgreɪd/ _a_ retrógrado

retrospect /'retrəspekt/ _n_ retrospección _f._ **in ~** retrospectivamente. **~ive** /-'spektɪv/ _a_ retrospectivo

return /rɪ'tɜːn/ _vi_ volver; ⟨reappear⟩ reaparecer. —_vt_ devolver; ⟨com⟩ declarar; ⟨pol⟩ elegir. —_n_ vuelta _f;_ ⟨com⟩ ganancia _f;_ ⟨restitution⟩ devolución _f._ **~ of income** _n_ declaración _f_ de ingresos. **in ~ for** a cambio de. **many happy ~s!** ¡feliz cumpleaños! **~ing** /rɪ'tɜːnɪŋ/ _a._ **~ing officer** _n_ escrutador _m._ **~ match** _n_ partido _m_ de desquite. **~ ticket** _n_ billete _m_ de ida y vuelta. **~s** _npl_ ⟨com⟩ ingresos _mpl_

reunion /riː'juːnɪən/ _n_ reunión _f_

reunite /riːjuː'naɪt/ _vt_ reunir

rev /rev/ _n_ ⟨auto, fam⟩ revolución _f._ —_vt/i._ **~ (up)** ⟨pt revved⟩ ⟨auto, fam⟩ acelerar(se)

revamp /riː'væmp/ _vt_ renovar

reveal /rɪ'viːl/ _vt_ revelar. **~ing** _a_ revelador

revel /revl/ _vi_ ⟨pt revelled⟩ jaranear. **~ in** deleitarse en. **~ry** _n_ juerga _f_

revelation /revə'leɪʃn/ _n_ revelación _f_

revenge /rɪ'vendʒ/ _n_ venganza _f;_ ⟨sport⟩ desquite _m._ **take ~** vengarse. —_vt_ vengar. **~ful** _a_ vindicativo, vengativo

revenue /'revənjuː/ _n_ ingresos _mpl_

reverberate /rɪ'vɜːbəreɪt/ _vi_ ⟨light⟩ reverberar; ⟨sound⟩ resonar

revere /rɪ'vɪə(r)/ _vt_ venerar. **reverence** /'revərəns/ _n_ reverencia _f_

reverend /'revərənd/ _a_ reverendo

reverent /'revərənt/ _a_ reverente

reverie /'revərɪ/ _n_ ensueño _m_

revers /rɪ'vɪə/ _n_ ⟨pl **revers** /rɪ'vɪəz/⟩ _n_ solapa _f_

revers|al /rɪ'vɜːsl/ _n_ inversión _f._ **~e** /rɪ'vɜːs/ _a_ inverso. —_n_ contrario _m;_ ⟨back⟩ revés _m;_ ⟨auto⟩ marcha _f_ atrás. —_vt_ invertir; anular ⟨decision⟩; ⟨auto⟩ dar marcha atrás a. —_vi_ ⟨auto⟩ dar marcha atrás

revert /rɪ'vɜːt/ _vi._ **~ to** volver a

review /rɪ'vjuː/ _n_ repaso _m;_ ⟨mil⟩ revista _f;_ ⟨of book, play, etc⟩ crítica _f._ —_vt_ analizar ⟨situation⟩; reseñar ⟨book, play, etc⟩. **~er** _n_ crítico _m_

revile /rɪ'vaɪl/ _vt_ injuriar

revis|e /rɪ'vaɪz/ _vt_ revisar; ⟨schol⟩ repasar. **~ion** /-ɪʒn/ _n_ revisión _f;_ ⟨schol⟩ repaso _m_

reviv|al /rɪ'vaɪvl/ _n_ restablecimiento _m;_ ⟨of faith⟩ despertar _m;_ ⟨of play⟩ reestreno _m._ **~e** /rɪ'vaɪv/ _vt_ restablecer; resucitar ⟨person⟩. —_vi_ restablecerse; ⟨person⟩ volver en sí

revoke /rɪ'vəʊk/ _vt_ revocar

revolt /rɪ'vəʊlt/ vi sublevarse. —
vt dar asco a. —n sublevación f

revolting /rɪ'vəʊltɪŋ/ a
asqueroso

revolution /revə'luːʃn/ n revolución f. ~**ary** a & n revo-
lucionario (m). ~**ize** vt
revolucionar

revolve /rɪ'vɒlv/ vi girar

revolver /rɪ'vɒlvə(r)/ n revólver
m

revolving /rɪ'vɒlvɪŋ/ a giratorio

revue /rɪ'vjuː/ n revista f

revulsion /rɪ'vʌlʃn/ n asco m

reward /rɪ'wɔːd/ n recompensa
f. —vt recompensar. ~**ing** a
remunerador; (worthwhile) que
vale la pena

rewrite /riː'raɪt/ vt (pt rewrote,
pp rewritten) escribir de
nuevo; (change) redactar de
nuevo

rhapsody /'ræpsədɪ/ n rapsodia f

rhetoric /'retərɪk/ n retórica f.
~**al** /rɪ'tɒrɪkl/ a retórico

rheumatic /ruː'mætɪk/ a reumá-
tico. ~**sm** /'ruːmətɪzəm/ n
reumatismo m

rhinoceros /raɪ'nɒsərəs/ n (pl
-oses) rinoceronte m

rhubarb /'ruːbɑːb/ n ruibarbo m

rhyme /raɪm/ n rima f; (poem)
poesía f. —vt/i rimar

rhythm /'rɪðəm/ n ritmo m.
~**ic(al)** /'rɪðmɪk(l)/ a rítmico

rib /rɪb/ n costilla f. —vt (pt
ribbed) (fam) tomar el pelo a

ribald /'rɪbld/ a obsceno, verde

ribbon /'rɪbən/ n cinta f

rice /raɪs/ n arroz m. ~ **pudding**
n arroz con leche

rich /rɪtʃ/ a (-er, -est) rico. —n
ricos mpl. ~**es** npl riquezas fpl.
~**ly** adv ricamente. ~**ness** n
riqueza f

rickety /'rɪkətɪ/ a (shaky) cojo,
desvencijado

ricochet /'rɪkəʃeɪ/ n rebote m. —
vi rebotar

rid /rɪd/ vt (pt rid, pres p rid-
ding) librar (of de). get ~ of
deshacerse de. ~**dance** /'rɪdns/
n. good ~**dance**! ¡qué alivio!

ridden /'rɪdn/ see ride. —a (in-
fested) infestado. ~ **by** (oppressed) agobiado de

riddle[1] /'rɪdl/ n acertijo m

riddle[2] /'rɪdl/ vt acribillar. be ~d
with estar lleno de

ride /raɪd/ vi (pt rode, pp ridden) (on horseback) montar; (go)
ir (en bicicleta, a caballo etc).
take s.o. for a ~ (fam) enga-
ñarle a uno. —vt montar a (horse);
ir en (bicycle); recorrer (distance). —n (on horse) cabalgata
f; (in car) paseo m en coche. ~**r**
/-ə(r)/ n jinete m; (cyc-
list) ciclista m & f; (in document)
cláusula f adicional

ridge /rɪdʒ/ n línea f, arruga f;
(mountain) cresta f; (of roof)
caballete m

ridicule /'rɪdɪkjuːl/ n irrisión
f. —vt ridiculizar. ~**ous** /rɪ
'dɪkjʊləs/ a ridículo

riding /'raɪdɪŋ/ n equitación f

rife /raɪf/ a difundido. ~ **with**
lleno de

riff-raff /'rɪfræf/ n gentuza f

rifle[1] /'raɪfl/ n fusil m

rifle[2] /'raɪfl/ vt saquear

rifle-range /'raɪflreɪndʒ/ n
campo m de tiro

rift /rɪft/ n grieta f; (fig) ruptura f

rig[1] /rɪg/ vt (pt rigged)
aparejar. —n (at sea) plataforma
f de perforación. ~ **up** vt
improvisar

rig[2] /rɪg/ vt (pej) amañar

right /raɪt/ a (correct, fair)
exacto, justo; (morally) bueno;
(not left) derecho; (suitable)
adecuado. —n (entitlement)
derecho m; (not left) derecha f.
(not evil) bien m. ~ **of way** n
(auto) prioridad f. be in the ~

tener razón. **on the ~** a la derecha. **put ~** rectificar. —*vt* enderezar; (*fig*) corregir. —*adv* a la derecha; (*directly*) derecho; (*completely*) completamente; (*well*) bien. **~ away** *adv* inmediatamente. **~ angle** *n* ángulo *m* recto

righteous /'raɪtʃəs/ *a* recto; (*cause*) justo

right: **~ful** /'raɪtfʊl/ *a* legítimo. **~fully** *adv* legítimamente. **~hand man** *n* brazo *m* derecho. **~ly** *adv* justamente. **~wing** *a* (*pol*) *n* derechista

rigid /'rɪdʒɪd/ *a* rígido. **~ity** /-'dʒɪdətɪ/ *n* rigidez *f*

rigmarole /'rɪgmərəʊl/ *n* galimatías *m invar*

rig|orous /'rɪgərəs/ *a* riguroso. **~our** /'rɪgə(r)/ *n* rigor *m*

rig-out /'rɪgaʊt/ *n* (*fam*) atavío *m*

rile /raɪl/ *vt* (*fam*) irritar

rim /rɪm/ *n* borde *m*; (*of wheel*) llanta *f*; (*of glasses*) montura *f*. **~med** *a* bordeado

rind /raɪnd/ *n* corteza *f*; (*of fruit*) cáscara *f*

ring /rɪŋ/ *n* (*circle*) círculo *m*; (*circle of metal etc*) aro *m*; (*on finger*) anillo *m*; (*on finger with stone*) sortija *f*; (*boxing*) cuadrilátero *m*; (*bullring*) ruedo *m*, redondel *m*, plaza *f*; (*for circus*) pista *f*; —*vt* rodear

ring² /rɪŋ/ *n* (*of bell*) toque *m*; (*tinkle*) tintineo *m*; (*telephone call*) llamada *f*. —*vt* (*pt* **rang**, *pp* **rung**) hacer sonar; (*telephone*) llamar por teléfono. **~ the bell** tocar el timbre. —*vi* sonar. **~ back** *vt/i* volver a llamar. **~ off** *vi* colgar. **~ up** *vt* llamar por teléfono

ring: **~leader** /'rɪŋliːdə(r)/ *n* cabecilla *f*. **~ road** *n* carretera *f* de circunvalación

rink /rɪŋk/ *n* pista *f*

rinse /rɪns/ *vt* enjuagar. —*n* aclarado *m*; (*of dishes*) enjuague *m*; (*for hair*) reflejo *m*

riot /'raɪət/ *n* disturbio *m*; (*of colours*) profusión *f*. **run ~** desenfrenarse. —*vi* amotinarse. **~er** *n* amotinador *m*. **~ous** *a* tumultuoso

rip /rɪp/ *vt* (*pt* **ripped**) rasgar. —*vi* rasgarse. **let ~** (*fig*) soltar. —*n* rasgadura *f*. **~ off** *vt* (*sl*) robar. **~cord** *n* (*of parachute*) cuerda *f* de abertura

ripe /raɪp/ *a* (**-er, -est**) maduro. **~n** /'raɪpən/ *vt/i* madurar. **~ness** *n* madurez *f*

rip-off /'rɪpɒf/ *n* (*sl*) timo *m*

ripple /'rɪpl/ *n* rizo *m*; (*sound*) murmullo *m*. —*vt* rizar. —*vi* rizarse

rise /raɪz/ *vi* (*pt* **rose**, *pp* **risen**) levantarse; (*rebel*) sublevarse; (*river*) crecer; (*prices*) subir. —*n* subida *f*; (*land*) altura *f*; (*increase*) aumento *m*; (*to power*) ascenso *m*. **give ~ to** ocasionar. **~r** /-ə(r)/ *n* **early ~r** *n* madrugador *m*

rising /'raɪzɪŋ/ *n* (*revolt*) sublevación *f*. —*a* (*sun*) naciente. **~ generation** *n* nueva generación

risk /rɪsk/ *n* riesgo *m*. —*vt* arriesgar. **~y** *a* (**-ier, -iest**) arriesgado

risqué /'rɪːskeɪ/ *a* subido de color

rissole /'rɪsəʊl/ *n* croqueta *f*

rite /raɪt/ *n* rito *m*

ritual /'rɪtʃʊəl/ *a & n* ritual (*m*)

rival /'raɪvl/ *a & n* rival (*m*). —*vt* (*pt* **rivalled**) rivalizar con. **~ry** *n* rivalidad *f*

river /'rɪvə(r)/ *n* río *m*

rivet /'rɪvɪt/ *n* remache *m*. —*vt* remachar. **~ing** *a* fascinante

Riviera /rɪvɪ'eərə/ *n*. **the (French) ~** la Costa *f* Azul. **the (Italian) ~** la Riviera *f* (Italiana)

rivulet /'rɪvjʊlɪt/ *n* riachuelo *m*

road /rəʊd/ n (*in town*) calle f; (*between towns*) carretera f; (*way*) camino m. **on the ~** en camino. **~hog** n conductor m descortés. **~house** n albergue m. **~map** n mapa m de carreteras. **~side** /ˈrəʊdsaɪd/ n borde m de la carretera. **~ sign** n señal f de tráfico. **~way** /ˈrəʊdweɪ/ n calzada f. **~works** npl obras fpl. **~worthy** /ˈrəʊdwɜːðɪ/ a (*vehicle*) seguro

roam /rəʊm/ vi vagar

roar /rɔː(r)/ n rugido m; (*laughter*) carcajada f. —vt/i rugir. **~ past** (*vehicles*) pasar con estruendo. **~ with laughter** reírse a carcajadas. **~ing** /ˈrɔːrɪŋ/ a (*trade etc*) activo

roast /rəʊst/ vt asar; tostar (*coffee*). —vi asarse; (*person, coffee*) tostarse. —a & n asado (m). **~ beef** n rosbif m

rob /rɒb/ vt (pt **robbed**) robar; asaltar (*bank*). **~ of** privar de. **~ber** n ladrón m; (*of bank*) atracador m. **~bery** n robo m

robe /rəʊb/ n manto m; (*univ etc*) toga f. **bath-~** n albornoz m

robin /ˈrɒbɪn/ n petirrojo m

robot /ˈrəʊbɒt/ n robot m, autómata m

robust /rəʊˈbʌst/ a robusto

rock[1] /rɒk/ n roca f; (*boulder*) peñasco m; (*sweet*) caramelo m en forma de barra; (*of Gibraltar*) peñón m. **on the ~s** (*drink*) con hielo; (*fig*) arruinado. **be on the ~s** (*marriage etc*) andar mal

rock[2] /rɒk/ vt mecer; (*shake*) sacudir. —vi mecerse; (*shake*) sacudirse. —n (*mus*) música f rock

rock: ~bottom a (*fam*) bajísimo. **~ery** /ˈrɒkərɪ/ n cuadro m alpino, rocalla f

rocket /ˈrɒkɪt/ n cohete m

rock: ~ing-chair n mecedora f. **~ing-horse** n caballo m de balancín. **~y** /ˈrɒkɪ/ a (-**ier**, -**iest**)

rocoso; (*fig, shaky*) bamboleante

rod /rɒd/ n vara f; (*for fishing*) caña f; (*metal*) barra f

rode /rəʊd/ *see* **ride**

rodent /ˈrəʊdnt/ n roedor m

rodeo /rəˈdeɪəʊ/ n (pl -**os**) rodeo m

roe[1] /rəʊ/ n (*fish eggs*) hueva f

roe[2] /rəʊ/ n (pl **roe**, or **roes**) (*deer*) corzo m

rogue /rəʊg/ n pícaro m. **~ish** a picaresco

role /rəʊl/ n papel m

roll /rəʊl/ vt hacer rodar; (*roll up*) enrollar; (*flatten lawn*) allanar; aplanar (*pastry*). —vi rodar; (*ship*) balancearse; (*on floor*) revolcarse. **be ~ing** (*in money*) (*fam*) nadar (en dinero). —n rollo m; (*of ship*) balanceo m; (*of drum*) redoble m; (*thunder*) retumbo m; (*bread*) panecillo m; (*list*) lista f. **~ over** vi (*turn over*) dar una vuelta. **~ up** vt enrollar; arremangar (*sleeve*). —vi (*fam*) llegar. **~call** n lista f

roller /ˈrəʊlə(r)/ n rodillo m; (*wheel*) rueda f; (*for hair*) rulo m, bigudí m. **~-coaster** n montaña f rusa. **~-skate** n patín m de ruedas

rollicking /ˈrɒlɪkɪŋ/ a alegre

rolling /ˈrəʊlɪŋ/ a ondulado. **~-pin** n rodillo m

Roman /ˈrəʊmən/ a & n romano (m). **~ Catholic** a & n católico (m) (romano)

romance /rəʊˈmæns/ n novela f romántica; (*love*) amor m; (*affair*) aventura f

Romania /rəʊˈmeɪnɪə/ n Rumania f. **~n** a & n rumano (m)

romantic /rəʊˈmæntɪk/ a romántico. **~ism** n romanticismo m

Rome /rəʊm/ n Roma f

romp /rɒmp/ vi retozar. —n retozo m

rompers /'rɒmpəz/ *npl* pelele *m*

roof /ru:f/ *n* techo *m*, tejado *m*; (*of mouth*) paladar *m*. —*vt* techar. ~**-garden** *n* jardín *m* en la azotea. ~**-rack** *n* baca *f*. ~**-top** *n* tejado *m*

rook[1] /rʊk/ *n* grajo *m*

rook[2] /rʊk/ (*in chess*) torre *f*

room /ru:m/ *n* cuarto *m*, habitación *f*; (*bedroom*) dormitorio *m*; (*space*) sitio *m*; (*large hall*) sala *f*. ~**y** *a* espacioso; (*clothes*) holgado

roost /ru:st/ *n* percha *f*. —*vi* descansar. ~**er** *n* gallo *m*

root[1] /ru:t/ *n* raíz *f*. **take** ~ echar raíces. —*vt* hacer arraigar. —*vi* echar raíces, arraigarse

root[2] /ru:t/ *vt/i*. ~ **about** *vi* hurgar. ~ **for** *vi* (*Amer, sl*) alentar. ~ **out** *vt* extirpar

rootless /'ru:tlɪs/ *a* desarraigado

rope /rəʊp/ *n* cuerda *f*. **know the** ~**s** estar al corriente. —*vt* atar. ~ **in** *vt* agarrar

rosary /'rəʊzərɪ/ *n* (*relig*) rosario *m*

rose[1] /rəʊz/ *n* rosa *f*; (*nozzle*) roseta *f*

rose[2] /rəʊz/ *see* **rise**

rosé /'rəʊzeɪ/ *n* (*vino m*) rosado *m*

rosette /rəʊ'zet/ *n* escarapela *f*

roster /'rɒstə(r)/ *n* lista *f*

rostrum /'rɒstrəm/ *n* tribuna *f*

rosy /'rəʊzɪ/ *a* (**-ier, -iest**) rosado; (*skin*) sonrosado

rot /rɒt/ *vt* (*pt* **rotted**) pudrir. —*vi* pudrirse. —*n* putrefacción *f*; (*sl*) tonterías *fpl*

rota /'rəʊtə/ *n* lista *f*

rotary /'rəʊtərɪ/ *a* giratorio, rotativo

rotat|**e** /rəʊ'teɪt/ *vt* girar; (*change round*) alternar. —*vi* girar; (*change round*) alternarse. ~**ion** /-ʃn/ *n* rotación *f*

rote /rəʊt/ *n*. **by** ~ maquinalmente, de memoria

rotten /'rɒtn/ *a* podrido; (*fam*) desagradable

rotund /rəʊ'tʌnd/ *a* redondo; (*person*) regordete

rouge /ru:ʒ/ *n* colorete *m*

rough /rʌf/ *a* (**-er, -est**) áspero; (*person*) tosco; (*bad*) malo; (*ground*) accidentado; (*violent*) brutal; (*approximate*) aproximado; (*diamond*) bruto. —*adv* duro. ~ **copy** *n*, ~ **draft** *n* borrador *m*. —*n* (*ruffian*) matón *m*. —*vt*. ~ **it** vivir sin comodidades. ~ **out** *vt* esbozar

roughage /'rʌfɪdʒ/ *n* alimento *m* indigesto, afrecho *m*; (*for animals*) forraje *m*

rough: ~**-and-ready** *a* improvisado. ~**-and-tumble** *n* riña *f*. ~**ly** *adv* toscamente; (*more or less*) más o menos. ~**ness** *n* aspereza *f*; (*lack of manners*) incultura *f*; (*crudeness*) tosquedad *f*

roulette /ru:'let/ *n* ruleta *f*

round /raʊnd/ *a* (**-er, -est**) redondo. —*n* círculo *m*; (*slice*) tajada *f*; (*of visits, drinks*) ronda *f*; (*of competition*) vuelta *f*; (*boxing*) asalto *m*. —*prep* alrededor de. —*adv* alrededor. ~ **about** (*approximately*) aproximadamente. **come** ~ **to**, **go** ~ **to** (*a friend etc*) pasar por casa de. —*vt* redondear; doblar (*corner*). ~ **off** *vt* terminar. ~ **up** *vt* reunir; redondear (*price*)

roundabout /'raʊndəbaʊt/ *n* tiovivo *m*; (*for traffic*) glorieta *f*. —*a* indirecto

rounders /'raʊndəz/ *n* juego *m* parecido al béisbol

round: ~**ly** *adv* (*bluntly*) francamente. ~ **trip** *n* viaje *m* de ida y vuelta. ~**up** *n* reunión *f*; (*of suspects*) redada *f*

rous|**e** /raʊz/ *vt* despertar. ~**ing** *a* excitante

rout /raʊt/ n derrota f. —vt derrotar

route /ruːt/ n ruta f; (naut, aviat) rumbo m; (of bus) línea f

routine /ruːˈtiːn/ n rutina f. —a rutinario

rov|e /rəʊv/ vt/i vagar (por). ~ing a errante

row[1] /rəʊ/ n fila f

row[2] /rəʊ/ n (in boat) paseo m en bote (de remos). —vi remar

row[3] /raʊ/ n (noise, fam) ruido m; (quarrel) pelea f. —vi (fam) pelearse

rowdy /ˈraʊdɪ/ a (-ier, -iest) n ruidoso

rowing /ˈrəʊɪŋ/ n remo m. ~-boat n bote m de remos

royal /ˈrɔɪəl/ a real. ~ist a & n monárquico (m). ~ly adv magníficamente. ~ty /ˈrɔɪəltɪ/ n familia f real; (payment) derechos mpl de autor

rub /rʌb/ vt (pt rubbed) frotar. ~ it in insistir en algo. —n frotamiento m. ~ off on s.o. vi pegársele a uno. ~ out vt borrar

rubber /ˈrʌbə(r)/ n goma f. ~ band n goma f (elástica). ~ stamp n sello m de goma. ~-stamp vt (fig) aprobar maquinalmente. ~y a parecido al caucho

rubbish /ˈrʌbɪʃ/ n basura f; (junk) trastos mpl; (fig) tonterías fpl. ~y a sin valor

rubble /ˈrʌbl/ n escombros; (small) cascajo m

ruby /ˈruːbɪ/ n rubí m

rucksack /ˈrʌksæk/ n mochila f

rudder /ˈrʌdə(r)/ n timón m

ruddy /ˈrʌdɪ/ a (-ier, -iest) rubicundo; (sl) maldito

rude /ruːd/ a (-er, -est) descortés, mal educado; (improper) indecente; (brusque) brusco. ~ly adv con descortesía. ~ness n descortesía f

rudiment /ˈruːdɪmənt/ n rudimento m. ~ary /-ˈmentrɪ/ a rudimentario

rueful /ˈruːfl/ a triste

ruffian /ˈrʌfɪən/ n rufián m

ruffle /ˈrʌfl/ vt despeinar ⟨hair⟩; arrugar ⟨clothes⟩. —n (frill) volante m, fruncido m

rug /rʌg/ n tapete m; (blanket) manta f

Rugby /ˈrʌgbɪ/ n. ~ (football) n rugby m

rugged /ˈrʌgɪd/ a desigual; (landscape) accidentado; (fig) duro

ruin /ˈruːɪn/ n ruina f. —vt arruinar. ~ous a ruinoso

rule /ruːl/ n regla f; (custom) costumbre f; (pol) dominio m. as a ~ por regla general. —vt gobernar; (master) dominar; (jurid) decretar; (decide) decidir. ~ out vt descartar. ~d paper n papel m rayado

ruler /ˈruːlə(r)/ n (sovereign) soberano m; (leader) gobernante m & f; (measure) regla f

ruling /ˈruːlɪŋ/ a (class) dirigente. —n decisión f

rum /rʌm/ n ron m

rumble /ˈrʌmbl/ vi retumbar; ⟨stomach⟩ hacer ruidos. —n retumbo m; (of stomach) ruido m

ruminant /ˈruːmɪnənt/ a & n rumiante (m)

rummage /ˈrʌmɪdʒ/ vi hurgar

rumour /ˈruːmə(r)/ n rumor m. —vt. it is ~ed that se dice que

rump /rʌmp/ n (of horse) grupa f; (of fowl) rabadilla f. ~ steak n filete m

rumpus /ˈrʌmpəs/ n (fam) jaleo m

run /rʌn/ vi (pt ran, pp run, pres p running) correr; (flow) fluir; (pass) pasar; (function) funcionar; (melt) derretirse; ⟨bus etc⟩ circular; (play) representarse (continuamente)

⟨colours⟩ correrse; ⟨in election⟩ presentarse. —vt tener ⟨house⟩; ⟨control⟩ dirigir; correr ⟨risk⟩; ⟨drive⟩ conducir; ⟨pass⟩ pasar; ⟨present⟩ presentar; forzar ⟨blockade⟩. ~ **a temperature** tener fiebre. —n corrida f, carrera f; ⟨journey⟩ viaje m; ⟨outing⟩ paseo m, excursión f; ⟨distance travelled⟩ recorrido m; ⟨ladder⟩ carrera f; ⟨ski⟩ pista f; ⟨series⟩ serie f. **at a** ~ corriendo. **have the** ~ **of** tener a su disposición. **in the long** ~ a la larga. **on the** ~ de fuga. ~ **across** vi toparse con ⟨friend⟩. ~ **away** vi escaparse. ~ **down** vi bajar corriendo; ⟨clock⟩ quedarse sin cuerda. —vt ⟨auto⟩ atropellar; ⟨belittle⟩ denigrar. ~ **in** vt rodar ⟨vehicle⟩. —vi entrar corriendo. ~ **into** vt toparse con ⟨friend⟩; ⟨hit⟩ chocar con. ~ **off** vt tirar ⟨copies etc⟩. ~ **out** vi salir corriendo; ⟨liquid⟩ salirse; ⟨fig⟩ agotarse. ~ **out of** quedar sin. ~ **over** vt ⟨auto⟩ atropellar. ~ **through** vt traspasar; ⟨revise⟩ repasar. ~ **up** vt hacerse ⟨bill⟩. —vi subir corriendo. ~ **up against** tropezar con ⟨difficulties⟩. ~**away** /'rʌnəwei/ a fugitivo; ⟨success⟩ decisivo; ⟨inflation⟩ galopante. —n fugitivo m. ~ **down** ⟨person⟩ agotado. ~**down** n informe m detallado

rung¹ /rʌŋ/ n ⟨of ladder⟩ peldaño m

rung² /rʌŋ/ see **ring**

run: ~**ner** /'rʌnə(r)/ n corredor m; ⟨on sledge⟩ patín m. ~**ner bean** n judía f escarlata. ~**ner-up** n sub-campeón m, segundo m. ~**ning** /'rʌnɪŋ/ n ⟨race⟩ carrera f. **be in the** ~**ning** tener posibilidades de ganar. —a en marcha; ⟨water⟩ corriente; ⟨commentary⟩ en directo. **four times** ~**ning** cuatro veces seguidas.

~**ny** /rʌnɪ/ a líquido; ⟨nose⟩ que moquea. ~**-of-the-mill** a ordinario. ~**up** n período m que precede. ~**way** /'rʌnwei/ n pista f

rupture /'rʌptʃə(r)/ n ruptura f; ⟨med⟩ hernia f. —vt/i quebrarse

rural /'rʊərəl/ a rural

ruse /ru:z/ n ardid m

rush¹ /rʌʃ/ n ⟨haste⟩ prisa f; ⟨crush⟩ bullicio m. —vi precipitarse. —vt apresurar; ⟨mil⟩ asaltar

rush² /rʌʃ/ n ⟨plant⟩ junco m

rush-hour /'rʌʃaʊə(r)/ n hora f punta

rusk /rʌsk/ n galleta f, tostada f

russet /'rʌsɪt/ a rojizo. —n ⟨apple⟩ manzana f rojiza

Russia /'rʌʃə/ n Rusia f. ~**n** a & n ruso (m)

rust /rʌst/ n orín m. —vt oxidar. —vi oxidarse

rustic /'rʌstɪk/ a rústico

rustle /'rʌsl/ vt hacer susurrar; ⟨Amer⟩ robar. ~ **up** ⟨fam⟩ preparar. —vi susurrar

rust: ~**-proof** a inoxidable. ~**y** a ⟨-ier, -iest⟩ oxidado

rut /rʌt/ n surco m. **in a** ~ en la rutina de siempre

ruthless /'ru:θlɪs/ a despiadado. ~**ness** n crueldad f

rye /raɪ/ n centeno m

S

S abbr ⟨south⟩ sur m

sabbath /'sæbəθ/ n día m de descanso; ⟨Christian⟩ domingo m; ⟨Jewish⟩ sábado m

sabbatical /sə'bætɪkl/ a sabático

sabot|**age** /'sæbətɑ:ʒ/ n sabotaje m. —vt sabotear. ~**eur** /-'tɜ:(r)/ n saboteador n

saccharin /'sækərɪn/ n sacarina f

sachet /'sæʃeɪ/ n bolsita f

sack¹ /sæk/ n saco m. **get the ~** (fam) ser despedido. —vt (fam) despedir. **~ing** n arpillera f, (fam) despido m

sack² /sæk/ vt (plunder) saquear

sacrament /'sækrəmənt/ n sacramento m

sacred /'seɪkrɪd/ a sagrado

sacrifice /'sækrɪfaɪs/ n sacrificio m. —vt sacrificar

sacrilege /'sækrɪlɪdʒ/ n sacrilegio m. **~ious** /-'lɪdʒəs/ a sacrílego

sacrosanct /'sækrəʊsæŋkt/ a sacrosanto

sad /sæd/ a (sadder, saddest) triste. **~den** /'sædn/ vt entristecer

saddle /'sædl/ n silla f. **be in the ~** (fig) tener las riendas. —vt ensillar (horse). **~ s.o. with** (fig) cargar a uno con. **~bag** n alforja f

sad: **~ly** adv tristemente; (fig) desgraciadamente. **~ness** n tristeza f

sadis|m /'seɪdɪzəm/ n sadismo m. **~t** /'seɪdɪst/ n sádico m. **~tic** /sə'dɪstɪk/ a sádico

safari /sə'fɑːrɪ/ n safari m

safe /seɪf/ a (-er, -est) seguro; (out of danger) salvo; (cautious) prudente. **~ and sound** sano y salvo. —n caja f fuerte. **~ deposit** n caja f de seguridad. **~guard** /'seɪfgɑːd/ n salvaguardia f. —vt salvaguardar. **~ly** adv sin peligro; (in safe place) en lugar seguro. **~ty** /'seɪftɪ/ n seguridad f. **~ty belt** n cinturón m de seguridad. **~ty-pin** n imperdible m. **~ty-valve** n válvula f de seguridad

saffron /'sæfrən/ n azafrán m

sag /sæg/ vi (pt sagged) hundirse; (give) aflojarse

saga /'sɑːgə/ n saga f

sage¹ /seɪdʒ/ n (wise person) sabio m. —a sabio

sage² /seɪdʒ/ n (herb) salvia f

sagging /'sægɪŋ/ a hundido; (fig) decaído

Sagittarius /sædʒɪ'teərɪəs/ n (astr) Sagitario m

sago /'seɪgəʊ/ n sagú m

said /sed/ see **say**

sail /seɪl/ n vela f; (trip) paseo m (en barco). —vi navegar; (leave) partir; (sport) practicar la vela; (fig) deslizarse. —vt manejar (boat). **~ing** n (sport) vela f. **~ing-boat** n, **~ing-ship** n barco m de vela. **~or** /'seɪlə(r)/ n marinero m

saint /seɪnt, before name sənt/ n santo m. **~ly** a santo

sake /seɪk/ n. **for the ~ of** por, por el amor de

salacious /sə'leɪʃəs/ a salaz

salad /'sæləd/ n ensalada f. **~ bowl** n ensaladera f. **~ cream** n mayonesa f. **~-dressing** n aliño m

salar|ied /'sælərɪd/ a asalariado. **~y** /'sælərɪ/ n sueldo m

sale /seɪl/ n venta f; (at reduced prices) liquidación f. **for ~** (sign) se vende. **on ~** en venta. **~able** /'seɪləbl/ a vendible. **~sman** /'seɪlzmən/ n (pl -men) vendedor m; (in shop) dependiente m; (traveller) viajante m. **~swoman** n (pl -women) vendedora f; (in shop) dependienta f

salient /'seɪlɪənt/ a saliente, destacado

saliva /sə'laɪvə/ n saliva f

sallow /'sæləʊ/ a (-er, -est) amarillento

salmon /'sæmən/ n invar salmón m. **~ trout** n trucha f salmonada

salon /'sælɒn/ n salón m

saloon /sə'luːn/ n (on ship) salón m; (Amer, bar) bar m; (auto) turismo m

salt /sɔːlt/ n sal f. —a salado. —vt salar. **~cellar** n salero m. **~y** a salado

salutary /'sæljotri/ a saludable

salute /sə'luːt/ n saludo m. —vt saludar. —vi hacer un saludo

salvage /'sælvidʒ/ n salvamento m; (goods) objetos mpl salvados. —vt salvar

salvation /sæl'veiʃn/ n salvación f

salve /sælv/ n ungüento m

salver /'sælvə(r)/ n bandeja f

salvo /'sælvəʊ/ n (pl -os) salva f

same /seim/ a igual (as que); (before noun) mismo (as que). at the ~ time al mismo tiempo. —pron. the ~ el mismo, la misma, los mismos, las mismas. do the ~ as hacer como. —adv. the ~ de la misma manera. all the ~ de todas formas

sample /'saːmpl/ n muestra f. —vt probar (food)

sanatorium /sænə'tɔːriəm/ n (pl -ums) sanatorio m

sanctify /'sæŋktifai/ vt santificar

sanctimonious /sæŋkti- 'məʊniəs/ a beato

sanction /'sæŋkʃn/ n sanción f. —vt sancionar

sanctity /'sæŋktəti/ n santidad f

sanctuary /'sæŋktʃʊəri/ n (relig) santuario m; (for wildlife) reserva f; (refuge) asilo m

sand /sænd/ n arena f. —vt enarenar. ~s npl (beach) playa f

sandal /'sændl/ n sandalia f

sand: ~castle n castillo m de arena. **~paper** /'sændpeipə(r)/ n papel m de lija. —vt lijar. **~storm** /'sændstɔːm/ n tempestad f de arena

sandwich /'sænwidʒ/ n bocadillo m, sandwich m. —vt. ~ed between intercalado

sandy /'sændi/ a arenoso

sane /sein/ a (-er, -est) (person) cuerdo; (judgement, policy) razonable. ~ly adv sensatamente

sang /sæŋ/ see **sing**

sanitary /'sænitri/ a higiénico; (system etc) sanitario. ~ **towel** n, ~ **napkin** n (Amer) compresa f (higiénica)

sanitation /sæni'teiʃn/ n higiene f; (drainage) sistema m sanitario

sanity /'sæniti/ n cordura f; (fig) sensatez f

sank /sæŋk/ see **sink**

Santa Claus /'sæntəklɔːz/ n Papá m Noel

sap /sæp/ n (in plants) savia f. —vt (pt sapped) agotar

sapling /'sæpliŋ/ n árbol m joven

sapphire /'sæfaiə(r)/ n zafiro m

sarcasm /'saːkæzəm/ n sarcasmo m. ~**tic** /-'kæstik/ a sarcástico

sardine /saː'diːn/ n sardina f

Sardinia /saː'diniə/ n Cerdeña f. ~n a & n sardo (m)

sardonic /saː'dɒnik/ a sardónico

sash /sæʃ/ n (over shoulder) banda f; (round waist) fajín m. ~**window** n ventana f de guillotina

sat /sæt/ see **sit**

satanic /sə'tænik/ a satánico

satchel /'sætʃl/ n cartera f

satellite /'sætəlait/ n & a satélite (m)

satiate /'seiʃieit/ vt saciar

satin /'sætin/ n raso m. —a de raso; (like satin) satinado

satire /'sætaiə(r)/ n sátira f. ~**ical** /sə'tirikl/ a satírico. ~**ist** /'sætərist/ n satírico m. ~**ize** /'sætəraiz/ vt satirizar

satisfaction /sætis'fækʃn/ n satisfacción f

satisfactor ily /sætis'fæktərili/ adv satisfactoriamente. ~**y** /sætis'fæktəri/ a satisfactorio

satisfy /'sætisfai/ vt satisfacer; (convince) convencer. ~**ing** a satisfactorio

satsuma /sæt'suːmə/ n mandarina f

saturat e /'sætʃəreit/ vt saturar, empapar. ~**ed** a saturado.

empapado. ~**ion** /-'reɪʃn/ n saturación f

Saturday /'sætədeɪ/ n sábado m

sauce /sɔːs/ n salsa f; (cheek) descaro m. ~**pan** /'sɔːspən/ n cazo m

saucer /'sɔːsə(r)/ n platillo m

saucy /'sɔːsɪ/ a (-ier, -iest) descarado

Saudi Arabia /saʊdɪə'reɪbɪə/ n Arabia f Saudí

sauna /'sɔːnə/ n sauna f

saunter /'sɔːntə(r)/ vi deambular, pasearse

sausage /'sɒsɪdʒ/ n salchicha f

savage /'sævɪdʒ/ a salvaje; (fierce) feroz; (furious, fam) rabioso. —n salvaje m & f. —vt atacar. ~**ry** n ferocidad f

sav|e /seɪv/ vt salvar; ahorrar (money, time); (prevent) evitar. —n (football) parada f. —prep salvo, con excepción de. ~**er** n ahorrador m. ~**ing** n ahorro m. ~**ings** npl ahorros mpl

saviour /'seɪvɪə(r)/ n salvador m

savour /'seɪvə(r)/ n sabor m. —vt saborear. ~**y** a (appetizing) sabroso; (not sweet) no dulce. —n aperitivo m (no dulce)

saw[1] /sɔː/ see **see**[1]

saw[2] /sɔː/ n sierra f. —vt (pt sawed, pp sawn) serrar. ~**dust** /'sɔːdʌst/ n serrín m. ~**n** /sɔːn/ see **saw**

saxophone /'sæksəfəʊn/ n saxófono m

say /seɪ/ vt/i (pt said /sed/) decir; rezar (prayer). **I** ~**!** int me digas! —n have a opinión; (in decision) voz en capítulo. **have no** ~ no tener ni voz ni voto. ~**ing** /'seɪɪŋ/ n refrán m

scab /skæb/ n costra f; (blackleg, fam) esquirol m

scaffold /'skæfəʊld/ n (gallows) cadalso m, patíbulo m. ~**ing**

/'skæfəldɪŋ/ n (for workmen) andamio m

scald /skɔːld/ vt escaldar; calentar (milk etc). —n escaldadura f

scale[1] /skeɪl/ n escala f

scale[2] /skeɪl/ n (of fish) escama f

scale[3] /skeɪl/ vt (climb) escalar. ~ **down** vt reducir (proporcionalmente)

scales /skeɪlz/ npl (for weighing) balanza f, peso m

scallop /'skɒləp/ n venera f; (on dress) festón m

scalp /skælp/ n cuero m cabelludo. —vt quitar el cuero cabelludo a

scalpel /'skælpəl/ n escalpelo m

scamp /skæmp/ n bribón m

scamper /'skæmpə(r)/ vi. ~ **away** marcharse corriendo

scampi /'skæmpɪ/ npl gambas fpl grandes

scan /skæn/ vt (pt **scanned**) escudriñar; (quickly) echar un vistazo a; (radar) explorar. —vi (poetry) estar bien medido

scandal /'skændl/ n escándalo m; (gossip) chismorreo m. ~**ize** /'skændəlaɪz/ vt escandalizar. ~**ous** a escandaloso

Scandinavia /skændɪ'neɪvɪə/ n Escandinavia f. ~**n** a & n escandinavo (m)

scant /skænt/ a escaso. ~**ily** adv insuficientemente. ~**y** /'skæntɪ/ a (-ier, -iest) escaso

scapegoat /'skeɪpɡəʊt/ n cabeza f de turco

scar /skɑː(r)/ n cicatriz f. —vt (pt **scarred**) dejar una cicatriz en. —vi cicatrizarse

scarc|e /skeəs/ a (-er, -est) escaso. **make o.s.** ~**e** (fam) mantenerse lejos. ~**ely** /'skeəslɪ/ adv apenas. ~**ity** n escasez f

scare /skeə(r)/ vt asustar. **be** ~**d** tener miedo. —n susto m.

~crow /'skeɒkrəʊ/ *n* espantapájaros *m invar*. **~monger** /'skeɒmʌŋgə(r)/ *n* alarmista *m* & *f*

scarf /skɑːf/ *n* (*pl* **scarves**) bufanda *f*; (*over head*) pañuelo *m*

scarlet /'skɑːlət/ *a* escarlata *f*. **~ fever** *n* escarlatina *f*

scary /'skeərɪ/ *a* (**-ier, -iest**) que da miedo

scathing /'skeɪðɪŋ/ *a* mordaz

scatter /'skætə(r)/ *vt* (*throw*) esparcir; (*disperse*) dispersar. — *vi* dispersarse. **~brained** *a* atolondrado. **~ed** *a* disperso; (*occasional*) esporádico

scatty /'skætɪ/ *a* (**-ier, -iest**) (*sl*) atolondrado

scavenge /'skævɪndʒ/ *vi* buscar (en la basura). **~r** /-ə(r)/ *n* (*vagrant*) persona *f* que busca objetos en la basura

scenario /sɪ'nɑːrɪəʊ/ *n* (*pl* **-os**) argumento *m*; (*of film*) guión *m*

scen|e /siːn/ *n* escena *f*; (*sight*) vista *f*; (*fuss*) lío *m*. **behind the ~es** entre bastidores. **~ery** /'siːnərɪ/ *n* paisaje *m*; (*in theatre*) decorado *m*. **~ic** /'siːnɪk/ *a* pintoresco

scent /sent/ *n* olor *m*; (*perfume*) perfume *m*; (*trail*) pista *f*. —*vt* presentir; (*make fragrant*) perfumar

sceptic /'skeptɪk/ *n* escéptico *m*. **~al** *a* escéptico. **~ism** /-sɪzəm/ *n* escepticismo *m*

sceptre /'septə(r)/ *n* cetro *m*

schedule /'ʃedjuːl, 'skedʒuːl/ *n* programa *f*; (*timetable*) horario *m*. **behind ~** con retraso. **on ~** sin retraso. —*vt* proyectar. **~d flight** *n* vuelo *m* regular

scheme /skiːm/ *n* proyecto *m*; (*plot*) intriga *f*. —*vi* hacer proyectos; (*pej*) intrigar. **~r** *n* intrigante *m* & *f*

schism /'sɪzəm/ *n* cisma *f*

schizophrenic /skɪtsə'frenɪk/ *a* & *n* esquizofrénico (*m*)

scholar /'skɒlə(r)/ *n* erudito *m*. **~ly** *a* erudito. **~ship** *n* erudición *f*; (*grant*) beca *f*

scholastic /skə'læstɪk/ *a* escolar

school /skuːl/ *n* escuela *f*; (*of univ*) facultad *f*. —*a* (*age, holidays, year*) escolar. —*vt* enseñar; (*discipline*) disciplinar. **~boy** /'skuːlbɔɪ/ *n* colegial *m*. **~girl** /-gɜːl/ *n* colegiala *f*. **~ing** *n* instrucción *f*. **~master** /'skuːlmɑːstə(r)/ *n* (*primary*) maestro *m*; (*secondary*) profesor *m*. **~mistress** *n* (*primary*) maestra *f*; (*secondary*) profesora *f*. **~teacher** *n* (*primary*) maestro *m*; (*secondary*) profesor *m*

schooner /'skuːnə(r)/ *n* goleta *f*; (*glass*) vaso *m* grande

sciatica /saɪ'ætɪkə/ *n* ciática *f*

scien|ce /'saɪəns/ *n* ciencia *f*. **~ce fiction** *n* ciencia *f* ficción. **~tific** /-'tɪfɪk/ *a* científico. **~tist** /'saɪəntɪst/ *n* científico *m*

scintillate /'sɪntɪleɪt/ *vi* centellear

scissors /'sɪsəz/ *npl* tijeras *fpl*

sclerosis /sklə'rəʊsɪs/ *n* esclerosis *f*

scoff /skɒf/ *vt* (*sl*) zamparse. —*vi*. **~ at** mofarse de

scold /skəʊld/ *vt* regañar. **~ing** *n* regaño *m*

scone /skɒn/ *n* (tipo *m* de) bollo *m*

scoop /skuːp/ *n* paleta *f*; (*news*) noticia *f* exclusiva. —*vt*. **~ out** excavar. **~ up** recoger

scoot /skuːt/ *vi* (*fam*) largarse corriendo. **~er** /'skuːtə(r)/ *n* escúter *m*; (*for child*) patinete *m*

scope /skəʊp/ *n* alcance *m*; (*opportunity*) oportunidad *f*

scorch /skɔːtʃ/ *vt* chamuscar. **~er** *n* (*fam*) día *m* de mucho calor. **~ing** *a* (*fam*) de mucho calor

score /skɔː(r)/ *n* tanteo *m*; *(mus)* partitura *f*; *(twenty)* veintena *f*; *(reason)* motivo *m*. **on that ~** en cuanto a eso. —*vt* marcar; *(slash)* rayar; *(mus)* instrumentar; conseguir *(success)*. —*vi* marcar un tanto; *(keep score)* tantear. **~ over s.o.** aventajar a. **~r** /-ə(r)/ *n* tanteador *m*

scorn /skɔːn/ *n* desdén m. —*vt* desdeñar. **~ful** *a* desdeñoso. **~fully** *adv* desdeñosamente

Scorpio /ˈskɔːpɪəʊ/ *n* *(astr)* Escorpión *m*

scorpion /ˈskɔːpɪən/ *n* escorpión *m*

Scot /skɒt/ *n* escocés *m*. **~ch** /skɒtʃ/ *a* escocés. —*n* güisqui *m*

scotch /skɒtʃ/ *vt* frustrar; *(suppress)* suprimir

scot-free /skɒtˈfriː/ *a* impune; *(gratis)* sin pagar

Scot: **~land** /ˈskɒtlənd/ *n* Escocia *f*. **~s** *a* escocés. **~sman** *n* escocés *m*. **~swoman** *n* escocesa *f*. **~tish** *a* escocés *f*

scoundrel /ˈskaʊndrəl/ *n* canalla *f*

scour /ˈskaʊə(r)/ *vt* estregar; *(search)* registrar. **~er** *n* estropajo *m*

scourge /skɜːdʒ/ *n* azote *m*

scout /skaʊt/ *n* explorador *m*. **Boy S~** explorador *m*. —*vi*. **~ (for)** buscar

scowl /skaʊl/ *n* ceño *m*. —*vi* fruncir el entrecejo

scraggy /ˈskrægɪ/ *a* (-ier, -iest) descarnado

scram /skræm/ *vi* *(sl)* largarse

scramble /ˈskræmbl/ *vi* *(clamber)* gatear. **~ for** pelearse para obtener. —*vt* revolver *(eggs)*. —*n* *(difficult climb)* subida *f* difícil; *(struggle)* lucha *f*

scrap /skræp/ *n* pedacito *m*; *(fight, fam)* pelea *f*. —*vt* *(pt* **scrapped)** desechar. **~-book** *n*

álbum *m* de recortes. **~s** *npl* sobras *fpl*

scrape /skreɪp/ *n* raspadura *f*; *(fig)* apuro *m*. —*vt* raspar; *(graze)* arañar; *(rub)* frotar. —*vi*. **~ through** lograr pasar; aprobar por los pelos *(exam)*. **~ together** reunir. **~r** /-ə(r)/ *n* raspador *m*

scrap: **~ heap** *n* montón *m* de deshechos. **~-iron** *n* chatarra *f*

scrappy /ˈskræpɪ/ *a* fragmentario, pobre, de mala calidad

scratch /skrætʃ/ *vt* rayar; *(with nail etc)* arañar; rascar *(itch)*. —*vi* arañar. —*n* raya *f*; *(from nail etc)* arañazo *m*. **start from ~** empezar sin nada, empezar desde el principio. **up to ~** al nivel requerido

scrawl /skrɔːl/ *n* garrapato *m*. —*vt/i* garrapatear

scrawny /ˈskrɔːnɪ/ *a* (-ier, -iest) descarnado

scream /skriːm/ *vt/i* gritar. —*n* grito *m*

screech /skriːtʃ/ *vi* gritar; *(brakes etc)* chirriar. —*n* grito *m*; *(of brakes etc)* chirrido *m*

screen /skriːn/ *n* pantalla *f*; *(folding)* biombo *m*. —*vt* *(hide)* ocultar; *(protect)* proteger; proyectar *(film)*; seleccionar *(candidates)*

screw /skruː/ *n* tornillo *m*. —*vt* atornillar. **~driver** /ˈskruːdraɪvə(r)/ *n* destornillador *m*. **~ up** atornillar; entornar *(eyes)*; torcer *(face)*; *(ruin, sl)* arruinar. **~y** /ˈskruːɪ/ *a* (-ier, -iest) *(sl)* chiflado

scribble /ˈskrɪbl/ *vt/i* garrapatear. —*n* garrapato *m*

scribe /skraɪb/ *n* copista *m & f*

script /skrɪpt/ *n* escritura *f*; *(of film etc)* guión *m*

Scriptures /ˈskrɪptʃəz/ *npl* Sagradas Escrituras *fpl*

script-writer /ˈskrɪptraɪtə(r)/ *n* guionista *m & f*

scroll /skrəʊl/ n rollo m (de pergamino)

scrounge /skraʊndʒ/ vt/i obtener de gorra; (steal) birlar. **~r** /-ə(r)/ n gorrón m

scrub /skrʌb/ n (land) maleza f; (clean) fregado m. —vt/i (pt scrubbed) fregar

scruff /skrʌf/ n. the ~ of the neck el cogote m

scruffy /'skrʌfɪ/ a (-ier, -iest) desaliñado

scrum /skrʌm/ n, **scrummage** /'skrʌmɪdʒ/ n (Rugby) melée f

scrup|le /'skruːpl/ n escrúpulo m. **~ulous** /'skruːpjʊləs/ a escrupuloso. **~ulously** adv escrupulosamente

scrutin|ize /'skruːtɪnaɪz/ vt escudriñar. **~y** /'skruːtɪnɪ/ n examen m minucioso

scuff /skʌf/ vt arañar (shoes)

scuffle /'skʌfl/ n pelea f

scullery /'skʌlərɪ/ n trascocina f

sculpt /skʌlpt/ vt/i esculpir. **~or** n escultor m. **~ure** /-tʃə(r)/ n escultura f. —vt/i esculpir

scum /skʌm/ n espuma f; (people, pej) escoria f

scurf /skɜːf/ n caspa f

scurrilous /'skʌrɪləs/ a grosero

scurry /'skʌrɪ/ vi correr

scurvy /'skɜːvɪ/ n escorbuto m

scuttle[1] /'skʌtl/ n cubo m del carbón

scuttle[2] /'skʌtl/ vt barrenar (ship)

scuttle[3] /'skʌtl/ vi. ~ away correr, irse de prisa

scythe /saɪð/ n guadaña f

SE abbr (south-east) sudeste m

sea /siː/ n mar m. at ~ en el mar; (fig) confuso. by ~ por mar. **~board** /'siːbɔːd/ n litoral m. **~farer** /'siːfeərə(r)/ n marinero m. **~food** /'siːfuːd/ n mariscos mpl. **~gull** /'siːgʌl/ n gaviota f. **~horse** n caballito m de mar, hipocampo m

seal[1] /siːl/ n sello m. —vt sellar. ~ off acordonar (area)

seal[2] /siːl/ n (animal) foca f

sea level /'siːlevl/ n nivel m del mar

sealing-wax /'siːlɪŋwæks/ n lacre m

sea lion /'siːlaɪən/ n león m marino

seam /siːm/ n costura f; (of coal) veta f

seaman /'siːmən/ n (pl -men) marinero m

seamy /'siːmɪ/ a. the ~ side n el lado m sórdido, el revés m

seance /'seɪɑːns/ n sesión f de espiritismo

sea: **~plane** /'siːpleɪn/ n hidroavión f. **~port** /'siːpɔːt/ n puerto m de mar

search /sɜːtʃ/ vt registrar; (examine) examinar. —vi buscar. —n (for sth) búsqueda f; (of sth) registro m. **in ~ of** en busca de. ~ for buscar. **~ing** a penetrante. **~party** n equipo m de salvamento. **~light** /'sɜːtʃlaɪt/ n reflector m

sea: **~scape** /'siːskeɪp/ n marina f. **~shore** n orilla f del mar. **~sick** /'siːsɪk/ a mareado. **be ~sick** marearse. **~side** /'siːsaɪd/ n playa f

season /'siːzn/ n estación f; (period) temporada f. —vt (culin) sazonar; secar (wood). **~able** a propio de la estación. **~al** a estacional. **~ed** /'siːznd/ a (fig) experto. **~ing** n condimento m. **~ticket** n billete m de abono

seat /siːt/ n asiento m; (place) lugar m; (of trousers) fondillos mpl; (bottom) trasero m. **take a ~** sentarse. —vt sentar; (have seats for) tener asientos para. **~belt** n cinturón m de seguridad

sea: ~**urchin** n erizo m de mar. ~**weed** /'si:wi:d/ n alga f. ~**worthy** /'si:wɜ:ðɪ/ a en estado de navegar

secateurs /'sekətɜːz/ npl tijeras fpl de podar

sece|de /sɪ'si:d/ vi separarse. ~**ssion** /-eʃn/ n secesión f

seclu|de /sɪ'klu:d/ vt aislar. ~**ded** a aislado. ~**sion** /-ʒn/ n aislamiento m

second¹ /'sekənd/ a & n segundo (m). **on** ~ **thoughts** pensándolo bien. —adv (in race etc) en segundo lugar. —vt apoyar. ~**s** npl (goods) artículos m de segunda calidad; (more food, fam) otra porción f

second² /sɪ'kɒnd/ vt (transfer) trasladar temporalmente

secondary /'sekəndrɪ/ a secundario. ~ **school** n instituto m

second: ~**best** a segundo. ~**class** a de segunda clase. ~**hand** a de segunda mano. ~**ly** adv en segundo lugar. ~**rate** a mediocre

secre|cy /'si:krəsɪ/ n secreto m. ~**t** /'si:krɪt/ a & n secreto (m). **in** ~**t** en secreto

secretar|ial /sekrə'teərɪəl/ a de secretario. ~**iat** /sekrə'teərɪət/ n secretaría f. ~**y** /'sekrətrɪ/ n secretario m. **S**~ **of State** ministro m; (Amer) Ministro m de Asuntos Exteriores

secrete /sɪ'kri:t/ vt (med) secretar. ~**ion** /-ʃn/ n secreción f

secretive /'si:krɪtɪv/ a reservado

secretly /'si:krɪtlɪ/ adv en secreto

sect /sekt/ n secta f. ~**arian** /-'teərɪən/ a sectario

section /'sekʃn/ n sección f; (part) parte f

sector /'sektə(r)/ n sector m

secular /'sekjʊlə(r)/ a seglar

secur|e /sɪ'kjʊə(r)/ a seguro; (fixed) fijo. —vt asegurar; (obtain) obtener. ~**ely** adv seguramente. ~**ity** /sɪ'kjʊərətɪ/ n seguridad f; (for loan) garantía f, fianza f

sedate /sɪ'deɪt/ a sosegado

sedat|ion /sɪ'deɪʃn/ n sedación f. ~**ive** /'sedətɪv/ a & n sedante (m)

sedentary /'sedəntrɪ/ a sedentario

sediment /'sedɪmənt/ n sedimento m

seduc|e /sɪ'dju:s/ vt seducir. ~**er** /-ə(r)/ n seductor m. ~**tion** /sɪ'dʌkʃn/ n seducción f. ~**tive** /-tɪv/ a seductor

see¹ /si:/ —vt (pt **saw**, pp **seen**) ver; (understand) comprender; (notice) notar; (escort) acompañar. ~**ing that** visto que. ~ **you later!** ¡hasta luego! —vi ver; (understand) comprender. ~ **about** ocuparse de. ~ **off** despedirse de. ~ **through** llevar a cabo; descubrir el juego de ‹person›. ~ **to** ocuparse de

see² /si:/ n diócesis f

seed /si:d/ n semilla f; (fig) germen m; (tennis) preseleccionado m. ~**ling** n plantón m. **go to** ~ granar; (fig) echarse a perder. ~**y** /'si:dɪ/ a (-ier, -iest) sórdido

seek /si:k/ vt (pt **sought**) buscar. ~ **out** buscar

seem /si:m/ vi parecer. ~**ingly** adv aparentemente

seemly /'si:mlɪ/ a (-ier, -iest) correcto

seen /si:n/ see **see**¹

seep /si:p/ vi filtrarse. ~**age** n filtración f

see-saw /'si:sɔ:/ n balancín m

seethe /si:ð/ vi (fig) hervir. **be seething with anger** estar furioso

see-through /'si:θru:/ a transparente

segment /ˈsegmənt/ n segmento m; (of orange) gajo m

segregat|e /ˈsegrɪgeɪt/ vt segregar. **~ion** /-ˈgeɪʃn/ n segregación f

seiz|e /siːz/ vt agarrar; (jurid) incautarse de. **~e on** vi valerse de. **~e up** vi (tec) agarrotarse. **~ure** /ˈsiːʒə(r)/ n incautación f; (med) ataque m

seldom /ˈseldəm/ adv raramente

select /sɪˈlekt/ vt escoger; (sport) seleccionar. —a selecto; (exclusive) exclusivo. **~ion** /-ʃn/ n selección f. **~ive** a selectivo

self /self/ n (pl selves) sí mismo. **~-addressed** a con su propia dirección. **~-assurance** n confianza f en sí mismo. **~-assured** a seguro de sí mismo. **~-catering** a con facilidades para cocinar. **~-centred** a egocéntrico. **~-confidence** n confianza f en sí mismo. **~-confident** a seguro de sí mismo. **~-conscious** a cohibido. **~-contained** a independiente. **~-control** n dominio m de sí mismo. **~-defence** n defensa f propia. **~-denial** n abnegación f. **~-employed** a que trabaja por cuenta propia. **~-esteem** n amor m propio. **~-evident** a evidente. **~-government** n autonomía f. **~-important** a presumido. **~-indulgent** a inmoderado. **~-interest** n interés m propio. **~ish** /ˈselfɪʃ/ a egoísta. **~ishness** n egoísmo m. **~less** /ˈselflɪs/ a desinteresado. **~-made** a rico por su propio esfuerzo. **~-opinionated** a intransigente; (arrogant) engreído. **~-pity** n compasión f de sí mismo. **~-portrait** n autorretrato m. **~-possessed** a dueño de sí mismo. **~-reliant** a independiente. **~-respect** n amor m propio. **~-righteous** a

santurrón. **~-sacrifice** n abnegación f. **~-satisfied** a satisfecho de sí mismo. **~-seeking** a egoísta. **~-service** n & a autoservicio (m). **~-styled** a sedicente, llamado. **~-sufficient** a independiente. **~-willed** a terco

sell /sel/ vt (pt sold) vender. **be sold on** (fam) entusiasmarse por. **be sold out** estar agotado. —vi venderse. **~-by date** n fecha f de caducidad. **~ off** vt liquidar. **~ up** vt vender todo. **~er** n vendedor m

Sellotape /ˈseləteɪp/ n (P) (papel m) celo m, cinta f adhesiva

sell-out /ˈselaʊt/ n (betrayal, fam) traición f

semantic /sɪˈmæntɪk/ a semántico. **~s** n semántica f

semaphore /ˈseməfɔː(r)/ n semáforo m

semblance /ˈsembləns/ n apariencia f

semen /ˈsiːmən/ n semen m

semester /sɪˈmestə(r)/ n (Amer) semestre m

semi... /ˈsemɪ/ pref semi...

semi|breve /ˈsemɪbriːv/ n semibreve f, redonda f. **~circle** /ˈsemɪskɜːl/ n semicírculo m. **~circular** /-ˈsɜːkjʊlə(r)/ a semicircular. **~colon** /semɪˈkəʊlən/ n punto m y coma. **~detached** /semɪdɪˈtætʃt/ a (house) adosado. **~final** /semɪˈfaɪnl/ n semifinal f

seminar /ˈsemɪnɑː(r)/ n seminario m

seminary /ˈsemɪnərɪ/ n (college) seminario m

semiquaver /ˈsemɪkweɪvə(r)/ n (mus) semicorchea f

Semit|e /ˈsiːmaɪt/ n semita m & f. **~ic** /sɪˈmɪtɪk/ a semítico

semolina /seməˈliːnə/ n sémola f

senat|e /ˈsenɪt/ n senado m. **~or** /-ətə(r)/ n senador m

send /send/ vt/i (pt sent) enviar. **~ away** despedir. **~ away for**

senile /'si:naɪl/ a senil. **~ity** /sɪ'nɪlətɪ/ n senilidad f

senior /'si:nɪə(r)/ a mayor; (in rank) superior; (partner etc) principal. —n mayor m & f. ~ **citizen** n jubilado m. **~ity** /-'ɒrətɪ/ n antigüedad f

sensation /sen'seɪʃn/ n sensación f. **~al** a sensacional

sense /sens/ n sentido m; (common sense) sensación f. make ~ vt tener sentido. **make ~ of** comprender. **~less** a insensato; (med) sin sentido

sensibilities /sensɪ'bɪlətɪz/ npl susceptibilidad f. **~ibility** /sensɪ'bɪlətɪ/ n sensibilidad f

sensible /'sensəbl/ a sensato; (clothing) práctico

sensitive /'sensɪtɪv/ a sensible; (touchy) susceptible. **~ity** /-'tɪvətɪ/ n sensibilidad f

sensory /'sensərɪ/ a sensorio

sensual /'senʃʊəl/ a sensual. **~ity** /-'ælətɪ/ n sensualidad f

sensuous /'sensʊəs/ a sensual

sent /sent/ see send

sentence /'sentəns/ n frase f; (jurid) sentencia f; (punishment) condena f. —vt. **~ to** condenar a

sentiment /'sentɪmənt/ n sentimiento m; (opinion) opinión f. **~al** /-'mentl/ a sentimental. **~ality** /-'tæləti/ n sentimentalismo m

sentry /'sentrɪ/ n centinela f

separable /'sepərəbl/ a separable

separate¹ /'separət/ a separado; (independent) independiente. **~ly** adv por separado. **~s** npl coordinados mpl

separate² /'separeɪt/ vt separar. —vi separarse. **~ion** /-'reɪʃn/ n separación f. **~ist** /'separatɪst/ n separatista m & f

September /sep'tembə(r)/ n se(p)-tiembre m

septic /'septɪk/ a séptico. **~ tank** n fosa f séptica

sequel /'si:kwəl/ n continuación f; (consequence) consecuencia f

sequence /'si:kwəns/ n sucesión f; (of film) secuencia f

sequin /'si:kwɪn/ n lentejuela f

serenade /serə'neɪd/ n serenata f. —vt dar serenata a

serene /sɪ'ri:n/ a sereno. **~ity** /-enətɪ/ n serenidad f

sergeant /'sɑ:dʒənt/ n sargento m

serial /'sɪərɪəl/ n serial m. —a de serie. **~ize** vt publicar por entregas

series /'sɪəri:z/ n serie f

serious /'sɪərɪəs/ a serio. **~ly** adv seriamente; (ill) gravemente. **take ~ly** tomar en serio. **~ness** n seriedad f

sermon /'sɜ:mən/ n sermón m

serpent /'sɜ:pənt/ n serpiente f

serrated /sɪ'reɪtɪd/ a serrado

serum /'sɪərəm/ n pl (-a) suero m

servant /'sɜ:vənt/ n criado m; (fig) servidor m

serve /sɜ:v/ vt servir; (in the army etc) prestar servicio; cumplir (sentence). **~ as** servir de. **~ its purpose** servir para el caso. **it ~s you right** ¡bien te lo mereces! ¡te está bien merecido! —vi servir. —n (in tennis) saque m

service /'sɜ:vɪs/ n servicio m; (maintenance) revisión f. **of ~ to** útil a. —vt revisar (car etc). **~able** /'sɜ:vɪsəbl/ a práctico; (durable) duradero. **~ charge** n servicio m. **~man** /'sɜ:vɪsmən/ n (pl -men) militar m. **~s** npl (mil) fuerzas fpl armadas. **~ station** n estación f de servicio

serviette /sɜ:vɪ'et/ n servilleta f

servile /'sɜːvaɪl/ a servil
session /'seʃn/ n sesión f; (univ) curso m
set /set/ vt (pt set, pres p setting) poner; poner en hora (clock etc); fijar (limit etc); (typ) componer. ~ **fire** to pegar fuego a. ~ **free** vt poner en libertad. —vi (sun) ponerse; (jelly) cuajarse. —n serie f; (of cutlery etc) juego m; (tennis) set m; (TV, radio) aparato m; (of hair) marcado m; (in theatre) decorado m; (of people) círculo m. —a fijo. **be** ~ **on** estar resuelto a. ~ **about** vi empezar a. ~ **back** vt (delay) retardar; (cost, sl) costar. ~ **off** vi salir. — vt (make start) poner en marcha; hacer estallar (bomb). ~ **out** vt (expound) exponer —vi (leave) salir. ~ **sail** salir. ~ **the table** poner la mesa. ~ **up** vt establecer. ~**back** n revés m. ~ **square** n escuadra f de dibujar
settee /se'tiː/ n sofá m
setting /'setɪŋ/ n (of sun) puesta f; (of jewel) engaste m; (in theatre) escenario m; (typ) composición f. ~**lotion** n fijador m
settle /'setl/ vt (arrange) arreglar; (pay) pagar; fijar (date); calmar (nerves). —vi (come to rest) posarse; (live) instalarse. ~ **down** calmarse; (become orderly) sentar la cabeza. ~ **for** aceptar. ~ **up** ajustar cuentas. ~**ment** /'setlmənt/ n establecimiento m; (agreement) acuerdo m; (place) colonia f. ~**r** /-ə(r)/ n colonizador m
set: ~-**to** n pelea f. ~-**up** n (fam) sistema m
seven /'sevn/ a & n siete (m). ~**teen** /sevn'tiːn/ a & n diecisiete (m). ~**teenth** a & n decimoséptimo (m). ~**th** a & n séptimo (m). ~**tieth** a & n setenta (m), septuagésimo (m). ~**ty** /'sevntɪ/ a & n setenta (m)

sever /'sevə(r)/ vt cortar; (fig) romper
several /'sevrəl/ a & pron varios
severance /'sevrəns/ n (breaking off) ruptura f
sever|**e** /sɪ'vɪə(r)/ a (-er, -est) severo; (violent) violento; (serious) grave; (weather) riguroso. ~**ely** adv severamente; (seriously) gravemente. ~**ity** /-'verətɪ/ n severidad f; (violence) violencia f; (seriousness) gravedad f
sew /səʊ/ vt/i (pt sewed, pp sewn, or sewed) coser
sew age /'suːɪdʒ/ n aguas fpl residuales. ~**er** /'suːə(r)/ n cloaca f
sewing /'səʊɪŋ/ n costura f. ~ **machine** n máquina f de coser
sewn /səʊn/ see **sew**
sex /seks/ n sexo m. **have** ~ tener relaciones sexuales. —a sexual. ~**ist** /'seksɪst/ a & n sexista (m & f)
sextet /seks'tet/ n sexteto m
sexual /'sekʃʊəl/ a sexual. ~ **intercourse** n relaciones fpl sexuales. ~**ity** /-'ælətɪ/ n sexualidad f
sexy /'seksɪ/ a (-ier, -iest) excitante, sexy, provocativo
shabb|**ily** /'ʃæbɪlɪ/ adv pobremente; (act) mezquinamente. ~**iness** n pobreza f; (meanness) mezquindad f. ~**y** /'ʃæbɪ/ a (-ier, -iest) (clothes) gastado; (person) pobremente vestido; (mean) mezquino
shack /ʃæk/ n choza f
shackles /'ʃæklz/ npl grillos mpl, grilletes mpl
shade /ʃeɪd/ n sombra f; (of colour) matiz m; (for lamp) pantalla f. a ~ **better** un poquito mejor. —vt dar sombra a
shadow /'ʃædəʊ/ n sombra f. **S~ Cabinet** n gobierno m en la

sombra. —vt (follow) seguir. ~y a (fig) vago

shady /'ʃeɪdɪ/ a (-ier, -iest) sombreado; (fig) dudoso

shaft /ʃɑːft/ n (of arrow) astil m; (mec) eje m; (of light) rayo m; (of lift, mine) pozo m

shaggy /'ʃægɪ/ a (-ier, -iest) peludo

shak|**e** /ʃeɪk/ vt (pt **shook**, pp **shaken**) sacudir; agitar (bottle); (shock) desconcertar. ~e **hands with** estrechar la mano a. —vi temblar. ~e **off** vi deshacerse de. —n sacudida f. ~e-up n reorganización f. ~y /'ʃeɪkɪ/ a (-ier, -iest) tembloroso; (table etc) inestable; (unreliable) incierto

shall /ʃæl/ v, aux (first person in future tense). **I ~ go** iré. **we ~ see** veremos

shallot /ʃə'lɒt/ n chalote m

shallow /'ʃæləʊ/ a (-er, -est) poco profundo; (fig) superficial

sham /ʃæm/ n farsa f; (person) impostor m. —a falso; (affected) fingido. —vt (pt **shammed**) fingir

shambles /'ʃæmblz/ npl (mess, fam) desorden m total

shame /ʃeɪm/ n vergüenza f. **what a ~!** ¡qué lástima! —vt avergonzar. ~**faced** /'ʃeɪmfeɪst/ a avergonzado. ~**ful** a vergonzoso. ~**fully** adv vergonzosamente. ~**less** a desvergonzado

shampoo /ʃæm'puː/ n champú m. —vt lavar

shamrock /'ʃæmrɒk/ n trébol m

shandy /'ʃændɪ/ n cerveza f con gaseosa, clara f

shan't /ʃɑːnt/ = **shall not**

shanty /'ʃæntɪ/ n chabola f. ~ **town** n chabolas fpl

shape /ʃeɪp/ n forma f. —vt formar; determinar (future). —vi formarse. ~ **up** prometer.

~less a informe. ~**ly** /'ʃeɪplɪ/ a (-ier, -iest) bien proporcionado

share /ʃeə(r)/ n porción f; (com) acción f. **go ~s** compartir. —vt compartir; (divide) dividir. —vi participar. ~ **in** participar en. ~**holder** /'ʃeəhəʊldə(r)/ n accionista m & f. ~**out** n reparto m

shark /ʃɑːk/ n tiburón m; (fig) estafador m

sharp /ʃɑːp/ a (-er, -est) (knife etc) afilado; (pin etc) puntiagudo; (pain, sound) agudo; (taste) acre; (sudden, harsh) brusco; (well defined) marcado; (dishonest) poco escrupuloso; (clever) listo. —adv en punto. **at seven o'clock ~** a las siete en punto. —n (mus) sostenido m. ~**en** /'ʃɑːpn/ vt afilar; sacar punta a (pencil). ~**ener** n (mec) afilador m; (for pencils) sacapuntas m invar. ~**ly** adv bruscamente

shatter /'ʃætə(r)/ vt hacer añicos. —vi hacerse añicos. ~**ed** a (exhausted) agotado

shav|**e** /ʃeɪv/ vt afeitar. —vi afeitarse. —n afeitado m. **have a ~e** afeitarse. ~**en** a (face) afeitado; (head) rapado. ~**er** n maquinilla f (de afeitar). ~**ing-brush** n brocha f de afeitar. ~**ing-cream** n crema f de afeitar

shawl /ʃɔːl/ n chal m

she /ʃiː/ pron ella. —n hembra f

sheaf /ʃiːf/ n (pl **sheaves**) gavilla f

shear /ʃɪə(r)/ vt (pp **shorn**, or **sheared**) esquilar. ~**s** /ʃɪəz/ npl tijeras fpl grandes

sheath /ʃiːθ/ n (pl -s /ʃiːðz/) vaina f; (contraceptive) condón m. ~**e** /ʃiːð/ vt envainar

shed¹ /ʃed/ n cobertizo m

shed² /ʃed/ vt (pt **shed**, pres p **shedding**) perder; derramar (tears); despojarse de (clothes). ~ **light on** aclarar

sheen /ʃiːn/ n lustre m

sheep /ʃiːp/ n invar oveja f.
~dog n perro m pastor. **~ish**
/ˈʃiːpiʃ/ a vergonzoso. **~ishly**
adv tímidamente. **~skin** /ˈʃiːp
skɪn/ n piel f de carnero, zamarra f

sheer /ʃɪə(r)/ a puro; (steep) perpendicular; (fabric) muy fino. —
adv a pico

sheet /ʃiːt/ n sábana f; (of paper)
hoja f; (of glass) lámina f; (of ice)
capa f

sheikh /ʃeɪk/ n jeque m

shelf /ʃelf/ n (pl **shelves**) estante
m. **be on the ~** quedarse para
vestir santos

shell /ʃel/ n concha f; (of egg) cáscara f; (of building) casco m;
(explosive) proyectil m. —vt
desgranar (peas etc); (mil) bombardear. **~fish** /ˈʃelfɪʃ/ n invar
(crustacean) crustáceo m; (mollusc) marisco m

shelter /ˈʃeltə(r)/ n refugio m,
abrigo m. —vt abrigar; (protect)
proteger; (give lodging to) dar
asilo a. —vi abrigarse. **~ed** a
(spot) abrigado; (life etc)
protegido

shelv|e /ʃelv/ vt (fig) dar car-
petazo a. **~ing** /ˈʃelvɪŋ/ n estantería f

shepherd /ˈʃepəd/ n pastor m. —
vt guiar. **~ess** /-ˈdes/ n pastora f.
~'s pie n carne f picada con
puré de patatas

sherbet /ˈʃɜːbət/ n (Amer, water-
ice) sorbete m

sheriff /ˈʃerɪf/ n alguacil m, sheriff m

sherry /ˈʃerɪ/ n (vino m de) jerez
m

shield /ʃiːld/ n escudo m. —vt
proteger

shift /ʃɪft/ vt cambiar; cambiar
de sitio (furniture etc); echar
(blame etc). —n cambio m;
(work) turno m; (workers) tanda

f. **make ~** arreglárselas. **~less**
/ˈʃɪftlɪs/ a holgazán

shifty /ˈʃɪftɪ/ a (-ier, -iest)
taimado

shilling /ˈʃɪlɪŋ/ n chelín m

shilly-shally /ˈʃɪlɪʃælɪ/ vi ti-
tubear

shimmer /ˈʃɪmə(r)/ vi rielar,
relucir. —n luz f trémula

shin /ʃɪn/ n espinilla f

shine /ʃaɪn/ vi (pt **shone**)
brillar. —vt sacar brillo a. **~ on**
dirigir (torch). —n brillo m

shingle /ˈʃɪŋl/ n (pebbles) guijarros mpl

shingles /ˈʃɪŋlz/ npl (med) herpes mpl & fpl

shiny /ˈʃaɪnɪ/ a (-ier, -iest)
brillante

ship /ʃɪp/ n buque m, barco m. —
vt (pt **shipped**) transportar;
(send) enviar; (load) embarcar.
~building /ˈʃɪpbɪldɪŋ/ n construcción f naval. **~ment** n
envío m. **~per** n expedidor m.
~ping n envío m; (ships) barcos
mpl. **~shape** /ˈʃɪpʃeɪp/ adv & a
en buen orden, en regla.
~wreck /ˈʃɪprek/ n naufragio
m. **~wrecked** a naufragado. be
~wrecked naufragar. **~yard**
/ˈʃɪpjɑːd/ n astillero m

shirk /ʃɜːk/ vt esquivar. **~er** n
gandul m

shirt /ʃɜːt/ n camisa f. **in ~
sleeves** en mangas de camisa.
~y /ˈʃɜːtɪ/ a (sl) enfadado

shiver /ˈʃɪvə(r)/ vi temblar. —n
escalofrío m

shoal /ʃəʊl/ n banco m

shock /ʃɒk/ n sacudida f; (fig)
susto m; (elec) descarga f; (med)
choque m. —vt escandalizar.
~ing a escandaloso; (fam)
espantoso. **~ingly** adv terriblemente

shod /ʃɒd/ see **shoe**

shodd|ily /ˈʃɒdɪlɪ/ adv mal. **~y**
/ˈʃɒdɪ/ a (-ier, -iest) mal hecho,
de pacotilla

shoe /ʃuː/ n zapato m; (of horse) herradura f. —vt (pt **shod**, pres p **shoeing**) herrar ‹horse›. **be well shod** estar bien calzado. ~**horn** /ˈʃuːhɔːn/ n calzador m. ~**lace** n cordón m de zapato. ~**maker** /ˈʃuːmeɪkə(r)/ n zapatero m. ~**polish** n betún m. ~**string** n. **on a** ~**string** con poco dinero. ~**tree** n horma f

shone /ʃɒn/ see **shine**

shoo /ʃuː/ vt ahuyentar

shook /ʃʊk/ see **shake**

shoot /ʃuːt/ vt (pt **shot**) disparar; rodar ‹film›. —vi ‹hunt› cazar. —n (bot) retoño m; (hunt) cacería f. ~ **down** vt derribar. ~ **out** vi (rush) salir disparado. ~ **up** ‹prices› subir de repente; ‹grow› crecer. ~**ing-range** n campo m de tiro

shop /ʃɒp/ n tienda f; (work-shop) taller m. **talk** ~ hablar de su trabajo. —vi (pt **shopping**) hacer compras. ~ **around** buscar el mejor precio. **go** ~**ping** ir de compras. ~ **assistant** n dependiente m. ~**keeper** /ˈʃɒpkiːpə(r)/ n tendero m. ~**lifter** n ratero m (de tiendas). ~**lifting** n ratería f (de tiendas). ~**per** n comprador m. ~**ping** /ˈʃɒpɪŋ/ n compras fpl. ~**ping bag** n bolsa f de la compra. ~**ping centre** n centro m comercial. ~ **steward** n enlace m sindical. ~**window** n escaparate m

shore /ʃɔː(r)/ n orilla f

shorn /ʃɔːn/ see **shear**

short /ʃɔːt/ a (-er, -est) corto; (not lasting) breve; (person) bajo; (curt) brusco. **a** ~ **time ago** hace poco. **be** ~ **of** necesitar. **Mick is** ~ **for Michael** Mick es el diminutivo de Michael. —adv (stop) en seco. ~ **of doing** a menos que no hagamos. —n. **in** ~ en resumen.

~**age** /ˈʃɔːtɪdʒ/ n escasez f. ~**bread** /ˈʃɔːtbred/ n galleta f de mantequilla. ~**change** vt estafar, engañar. ~ **circuit** n cortocircuito m. ~**coming** /ʃɔːtkʌmɪŋ/ n deficiencia f. ~ **cut** n atajo m. ~**en** /ˈʃɔːtn/ vt acortar. ~**hand** /ˈʃɔːthænd/ n taquigrafía f. ~**hand typist** n taquimecanógrafo m, taquimeca f (fam). ~**lived** a efímero. ~**ly** /ˈʃɔːtlɪ/ adv dentro de poco. ~**s** npl pantalón m corto. ~**sighted** a miope. ~**tempered** a de mal genio

shot /ʃɒt/ see **shoot**. —n tiro m; (person) tirador m; (photo) foto f; (injection) inyección f. **like a** ~ como una bala; (willingly) de buena gana. ~**gun** n escopeta f

should /ʃʊd, ʃəd/ v, aux. **I** ~ **go** debería ir. **I** ~ **have seen him** debiera haberlo visto. **I** ~ **like** me gustaría. **if he** ~ **come** si viniese

shoulder /ˈʃəʊldə(r)/ n hombro m. —vt cargar con ‹responsibility›; llevar a hombros ‹burden›. ~**blade** n omóplato m. ~**strap** n correa f del hombro; (of bra etc) tirante m

shout /ʃaʊt/ n grito m. —vt/i gritar. ~ **at s.o.** gritarle a uno. ~ **down** vt hacer callar a gritos

shove /ʃʌv/ n empujón m. —vt empujar; (put, fam) poner. ~ **off** vi (fam) largarse

shovel /ˈʃʌvl/ n pala f. —vt (pt **shovelled**) mover con la pala

show /ʃəʊ/ vt (pt **showed**, pp **shown**) mostrar; (put on display) exponer; poner ‹film›. —vi (be visible) verse. —n demostración f; (exhibition) exposición f; (ostentation) pompa f; (in theatre) espectáculo m; (in cinema) sesión f. **on** ~ expuesto. ~ **off** vt lucir; (pej) ostentar. —vi presumir. ~ **up** vi destacar; (be

present) presentarse. —*vt*
(*unmask*) desenmascarar. ~
case *n* vitrina *f*. ~**down** *n* confrontación *f*

shower /ˈʃaʊə(r)/ *n* chaparrón *m*;
(*of blows etc*) lluvia *f*; (*for washing*) ducha *f*. **have a** ~
ducharse. —*vi* ducharse. —*vt*. ~
with colmar de. ~**proof**
/ˈʃaʊəpruːf/ *a* impermeable. ~**y**
a lluvioso

show: ~**jumping** *n* concurso *m*
hípico. ~**manship** /ˈʃəʊmənʃɪp/
n teatralidad *f*, arte *f* de presentar espectáculos

shown /ʃəʊn/ *see* **show**

show: ~**off** *n* fanfarrón *m*.
~**place** *n* lugar *m* de interés
turístico. ~**room** /ˈʃəʊruːm/ *n*
sala *f* de exposición *f*

showy /ˈʃəʊɪ/ *a* (-**ier**, -**iest**)
llamativo; (*person*) ostentoso

shrank /ʃræŋk/ *see* **shrink**

shrapnel /ˈʃræpnəl/ *n* metralla *f*

shred /ʃred/ *n* pedazo *m*; (*fig*)
pizca *f*. —*vt* (*pt* **shredded**) hacer
tiras; (*culin*) cortar en tiras.
~**der** *n* desfibradora *f*, trituradora *f*

shrew /ʃruː/ *n* musaraña *f*.
(*woman*) arpía *f*

shrewd /ʃruːd/ *a* (-**er**, -**est**)
astuto. ~**ness** *n* astucia *f*

shriek /ʃriːk/ *n* chillido *m*. —*vt/i*
chillar

shrift /ʃrɪft/ *n*. **give s.o. short** ~
despachar a uno con
brusquedad

shrill /ʃrɪl/ *a* agudo

shrimp /ʃrɪmp/ *n* camarón *m*

shrine /ʃraɪn/ *n* (*place*) lugar *m*
santo; (*tomb*) sepulcro *m*

shrink /ʃrɪŋk/ *vt* (*pt* **shrank**, *pp*
shrunk) encoger. —*vi* encogerse; (*draw back*) retirarse;
(*lessen*) disminuir. ~**age** *n* encogimiento *m*

shrivel /ˈʃrɪvl/ *vi* (*pt* **shrivelled**)
(*dry up*) secarse; (*become
wrinkled*) arrugarse

shroud /ʃraʊd/ *n* sudario *m*; (*fig*)
velo *m*. —*vt* (*veil*) velar

Shrove /ʃrəʊv/ *n*. ~ **Tuesday** *n*
martes *m* de carnaval

shrub /ʃrʌb/ *n* arbusto *m*

shrug /ʃrʌg/ *vt* (*pt* **shrugged**)
encogerse de hombros. —*n* encogimiento *m* de hombros

shrunk /ʃrʌŋk/ *see* **shrink**

shrunken /ˈʃrʌŋkən/ *a* encogido

shudder /ˈʃʌdə(r)/ *vi* estremecerse. —*n* estremecimiento *m*

shuffle /ˈʃʌfl/ *vi* arrastrar los
pies. —*vt* barajar (*cards*). —*n*
arrastramiento *m* de los pies; (*of
cards*) barajadura *f*

shun /ʃʌn/ *vt* (*pt* **shunned**)
evitar

shunt /ʃʌnt/ *vt* apartar, desviar

shush /ʃʊʃ/ *int* ¡chitón!

shut /ʃʌt/ *vt* (*pt* **shut**, *pres p*
shutting) cerrar. —*vi* cerrarse.
~ **down** cerrar. ~ **up** *vt* cerrar;
(*fam*) hacer callar. —*vi* callarse.
~**down** *n* cierre *m*. ~**ter**
/ˈʃʌtə(r)/ *n* contraventana *f*;
(*photo*) obturador *m*

shuttle /ˈʃʌtl/ *n* lanzadera *f*;
(*train*) tren *m* de enlace. —*vt*
transportar. —*vi* ir y venir.
~**cock** /ˈʃʌtlkɒk/ *n* volante *m*. ~
service *n* servicio *m* de enlace

shy /ʃaɪ/ *a* (-**er**, -**est**) tímido.
—*vi* (*pt* **shied**) asustarse. ~ **away
from** huir. ~**ness** *n* timidez *f*

Siamese /saɪəˈmiːz/ *a* siamés

sibling /ˈsɪblɪŋ/ *n* hermano *m*,
hermana *f*

Sicil|ian /sɪˈsɪljən/ *a* & *n* siciliano (*m*). ~**y** /ˈsɪsɪlɪ/ *n* Sicilia *f*

sick /sɪk/ *a* enfermo; (*humour*)
negro; (*fed up, fam*) harto. **be** ~
(*vomit*) vomitar. **be** ~ **of** (*fig*)
estar harto de. **feel** ~ sentir
náuseas. —*n* /ˈsɪkən/ *vt* dar
asco. —*vi* caer enfermo. **be**
~**ening for** incubar

sickle /ˈsɪkl/ *n* hoz *f*

sick: **∼ly** /'sɪklɪ/ a (-ier, -iest) enfermizo; ⟨taste, smell etc⟩ nauseabundo. **∼ness** /'sɪknɪs/ n enfermedad f. **∼-room** n cuarto m del enfermo

side /saɪd/ n lado m; (of river) orilla f; (of hill) ladera f; (team) equipo m; (fig) parte f. **∼ by ∼** uno al lado del otro. **on the ∼** (sideline) como actividad secundaria; (secretly) a escondidas. **—a** lateral. **—vi. ∼ with** tomar el partido de. **∼board** /'saɪdbɔːd/ n aparador m. **∼boards** npl, **∼burns** npl (sl) patillas fpl. **∼-car** n sidecar m. **∼-effect** n efecto m secundario. **∼light** /'saɪdlaɪt/ n luz f de posición. **∼line** /'saɪdlaɪn/ n actividad f secundaria. **∼-road** n calle f secundaria. **∼-saddle** n silla f de mujer. **ride ∼-saddle** adv a mujeriegas. **∼-show** n atracción f secundaria. **∼-step** vt evitar. **∼-track** vt desviar del asunto. **∼-walk** /'saɪdwɔːk/ n (Amer) acera f, vereda f (LAm). **∼ways** /'saɪdweɪz/ a & adv de lado. **∼-whiskers** npl patillas fpl

siding /'saɪdɪŋ/ n apartadero m

sidle /'saɪdl/ vi avanzar furtivamente. **∼ up to** acercarse furtivamente

siege /siːdʒ/ n sitio m, cerco m

siesta /sɪ'estə/ n siesta f

sieve /sɪv/ n cernedor m. —vt cerner

sift /sɪft/ vt cerner. —vi. **∼ through** examinar

sigh /saɪ/ n suspiro. —vi suspirar

sight /saɪt/ n vista f; (spectacle) espectáculo m; (on gun) mira f. **at (first)** **∼** a primera vista. **catch ∼ of** vislumbrar. **lose ∼ of** perder de vista. **on ∼** a primera vista. **within ∼ of** (near)

cerca de. —vt ver, divisar. **∼-seeing** /'saɪtsiːɪŋ/ n visita f turística. **∼seer** /-ə(r)/ n turista m & f

sign /saɪn/ n señal f. —vt firmar. **∼ on**, **∼ up** vt inscribir. —vi inscribirse

signal /'sɪgnəl/ n señal f. —vt (pt **signalled**) comunicar; hacer señas a ⟨person⟩. **∼-box** n casilla f del guardavía. **∼man** /'sɪgnəlmən/ n (pl -men) guardavía f

signatory /'sɪgnətərɪ/ n firmante m & f

signature /'sɪgnətʃə(r)/ n firma f. **∼ tune** n sintonía f

signet-ring /'sɪgnɪtrɪŋ/ n anillo m de sello

significance /sɪg'nɪfɪkəns/ n significado m. **∼t** /sɪg'nɪfɪkənt/ a significativo; (important) importante. **∼tly** adv significativamente

signify /'sɪgnɪfaɪ/ vt significar. —vi (matter) importar, tener importancia

signpost /'saɪnpəʊst/ n poste m indicador

silence /'saɪləns/ n silencio m. —vt hacer callar. **∼cer** /-ə(r)/ n silenciador m. **∼t** /'saɪlənt/ a silencioso; (film) mudo. **∼tly** adv silenciosamente

silhouette /sɪluː'et/ n silueta f. —vt. **be ∼d** perfilarse, destacarse (against contra)

silicon /'sɪlɪkən/ n silicio m. **∼ chip** n pastilla f de silicio

silk /sɪlk/ n seda f. **∼en** a, **∼y** a (of silk) de seda; (like silk) sedoso. **∼worm** n gusano m de seda

sill /sɪl/ n antepecho m; (of window) alféizar m; (of door) umbral m

silly /'sɪlɪ/ a (-ier, -iest) tonto. —n. **∼billy** (fam) tonto m

silo /'saɪləʊ/ n (pl -os) silo m

silt /sɪlt/ n sedimento m

silver /'sɪlvə(r)/ n plata f. ~ plated a bañado en plata, plateado. ~side /'sɪlvəsaɪd/ n (culin) contra f. ~smith /'sɪlvəsmɪθ/ n platero m. ~ware /'sɪlvəweə(r)/ n plata f. ~ wedding n bodas fpl de plata. ~y a plateado; (sound) argentino

similar /'sɪmɪlə(r)/ a parecido. ~arity /-ɪ'lærətɪ/ n parecido m. ~arly adv de igual manera

simile /'sɪmɪlɪ/ n símil m

simmer /'sɪmə(r)/ vt/i hervir a fuego lento; (fig) hervir. ~ down calmarse

simple /'sɪmpl/ a (-er, -est) sencillo; (person) ingenuo. ~e-minded a ingenuo. ~eton /'sɪmpltən/ n simplón m. ~icity /-'plɪsətɪ/ n sencillez f. ~ification /-ɪ'keɪʃn/ n simplificación f. ~ify /'sɪmplɪfaɪ/ vt simplificar. ~y adv sencillamente; (absolutely) absolutamente

simulat|e /'sɪmjʊleɪt/ vt simular. ~ion /-'leɪʃn/ n simulación f

simultaneous /sɪml'teɪnɪəs/ a simultáneo. ~ly adv simultáneamente

sin /sɪn/ n pecado m. —vi (pt sinned) pecar

since /sɪns/ prep desde. —adv desde entonces. —conj desde que; (because) ya que

sincer|e /sɪn'sɪə(r)/ a sincero. ~ely adv sinceramente. ~ity /-'serətɪ/ n sinceridad f

sinew /'sɪnjuː/ n tendón m. ~s npl músculos mpl

sinful /'sɪnfl/ a pecaminoso; (shocking) escandaloso

sing /sɪŋ/ vt/i (pt sang, pp sung) cantar

singe /sɪndʒ/ vt (pres p singeing) chamuscar

singer /'sɪŋə(r)/ n cantante m & f

single /'sɪŋgl/ a único; (not double) sencillo; (unmarried) soltero; (bed, room) individual. —n (tennis) juego de individual; (ticket) billete m sencillo. —vt. ~e out escoger; (distinguish) distinguir. ~e-handed a & adv sin ayuda. ~e-minded a resuelto

singlet /'sɪŋglɪt/ n camiseta f

singly /'sɪŋglɪ/ adv uno a uno

singsong /'sɪŋsɒŋ/ a monótono. —n. have a ~ cantar juntos

singular /'sɪŋgjʊlə(r)/ n singular f. —a singular; (uncommon) raro; (noun) en singular. ~ly adv singularmente

sinister /'sɪnɪstə(r)/ a siniestro

sink /sɪŋk/ vt (pt sank, pp sunk) hundir; perforar (well); invertir (money). —vi hundirse; (patient) debilitarse. —n fregadero m. ~ in vi penetrar

sinner /'sɪnə(r)/ n pecador m

sinuous /'sɪnjʊəs/ a sinuoso

sinus /'saɪnəs/ n (pl -uses) seno m

sip /sɪp/ n sorbo m. —vt (pt sipped) sorber

siphon /'saɪfən/ n sifón m. vt. ~ out sacar con sifón

sir /sɜː(r)/ n señor m. S~ n (title) sir m

siren /'saɪərən/ n sirena f

sirloin /'sɜːlɔɪn/ n solomillo m, lomo m bajo

sirocco /sɪ'rɒkəʊ/ n siroco m

sissy /'sɪsɪ/ n hombre m afeminado, marica m, mariquita m; (coward) gallina m & f

sister /'sɪstə(r)/ n hermana f; (nurse) enfermera f jefe. S~ Mary Sor María. ~-in-law n (pl ~s-in-law) cuñada f. ~ly a de hermana; (like sister) como hermana

sit /sɪt/ vt (pt sat, pres p sitting) sentar. —vi sentarse; (committee etc) reunirse. be ~ting estar sentado. ~ back vi (fig)

relajarse. ~ **down** *vi* sentarse.
~ **for** *vi* presentarse a ⟨*exam*⟩;
posar para ⟨*portrait*⟩. ~ **up** *vi*
enderezarse; ⟨*stay awake*⟩ velar.
~**in** *n* ocupación *f*

site /saɪt/ *n* sitio *m*. **building** ~
n solar *m*. —*vt* situar

sit: ~**ting** *n* sesión *f*; ⟨*in restaurant*⟩ turno *m*. ~**ting-room**
n cuarto *m* de estar

situat|**e** /ˈsɪtjʊeɪt/ *vt* situar. ~**ed**
a situado. ~**ion** /ˈeɪʃn/ *n* situación *f*; ⟨*job*⟩ puesto *m*

six /sɪks/ *a* & *n* seis (*m*). ~**teen**
/sɪkˈstiːn/ *a* & *n* dieciséis (*m*).
~**teenth** *a* & *n* decimosexto (*m*).
~**th** *a* & *n* sexto (*m*). ~**tieth** *a*
& *n* sesenta (*m*), sexagésimo (*m*).
~**ty** /ˈsɪkstɪ/ *a* & *n* sesenta (*m*)

size /saɪz/ *n* tamaño *m*; ⟨*of
clothes*⟩ talla *f*; ⟨*of shoes*⟩ número
m; ⟨*extent*⟩ magnitud *f*. —*vt*. ~
up ⟨*fam*⟩ juzgar. ~**able** *a* bastante grande

sizzle /ˈsɪzl/ *vi* crepitar

skate[1] /skeɪt/ *n* patín *m*. —*vi* patinar. ~**board** /ˈskeɪtbɔːd/ *n*
monopatín *m*. ~**r** *n* patinador *m*

skate[2] /skeɪt/ *n invar* ⟨*fish*⟩ raya *f*

skating /ˈskeɪtɪŋ/ *n* patinaje *m*.
~**rink** *n* pista *f* de patinaje

skein /skeɪn/ *n* madeja *f*

skelet|**al** /ˈskelɪtl/ *a* esquelético.
~**on** /ˈskelɪtn/ *n* esqueleto *m*.
~**on staff** *n* personal *m* reducido

sketch /sketʃ/ *n* esbozo *m*; ⟨*drawing*⟩ dibujo *m*; ⟨*in theatre*⟩ pieza *f*
corta y divertida. —*vt* es-
bozar. —*vi* dibujar. ~**y** /ˈsketʃɪ/ *a*
(**-ier, -iest**) incompleto

skew /skjuː/ *n*. **on the** ~ sesgado

skewer /ˈskjuːə(r)/ *n* broqueta *f*

ski /skiː/ *n* (*pl* **skis**) esquí *m*. —*vi*
(*pt* **skied,** *pres p* **skiing**)
esquiar. **go** ~**ing** ir a esquiar

skid /skɪd/ *vi* (*pt* **skidded**)
patinar. —*n* patinazo *m*

ski: ~**er** *n* esquiador *m*. ~**ing** *n*
esquí *m*

skilful /ˈskɪlfl/ *a* diestro

ski-lift /ˈskiːlɪft/ *n* telesquí *m*

skill /skɪl/ *n* destreza *f*, habilidad
f. ~**ed** *a* hábil; ⟨*worker*⟩
cualificado

skim /skɪm/ *vt* (*pt* **skimmed**)
espumar; desnatar ⟨*milk*⟩; ⟨*glide
over*⟩ rozar. ~ **over** *vt* rasar. ~
through *vi* hojear

skimp /skɪmp/ *vt* escatimar. ~**y**
/ˈskɪmpɪ/ *a* (**-ier, -iest**) insuficiente; ⟨*skirt, dress*⟩ corto

skin /skɪn/ *n* piel *f*. —*vt* (*pt*
skinned) despellejar; pelar
⟨*fruit*⟩. ~**-deep** *a* superficial.
~**-diving** *n* natación *f* submarina. ~**flint** /ˈskɪnflɪnt/ *n* tacaño
m. ~**ny** /ˈskɪnɪ/ *a* (**-ier, -iest**)
flaco

skint /skɪnt/ *a* (*sl*) sin una perra

skip[1] /skɪp/ *vi* (*pt* **skipped**) *vi*
saltar; ⟨*with rope*⟩ saltar a la
comba. —*vt* saltar. —*n* salto *m*

skip[2] /skɪp/ *n* ⟨*container*⟩ cuba *f*

skipper /ˈskɪpə(r)/ *n* capitán *m*

skipping-rope /ˈskɪpɪŋrəʊp/ *n*
comba *f*

skirmish /ˈskɜːmɪʃ/ *n* escaramuza *f*

skirt /skɜːt/ *n* falda *f*. —*vt* rodear;
⟨*go round*⟩ ladear

skirting-board /ˈskɜːtɪŋbɔːd/ *n*
rodapié *m*, zócalo *m*

skit /skɪt/ *n* pieza *f* satírica

skittish /ˈskɪtɪʃ/ *a* juguetón;
⟨*horse*⟩ nervioso

skittle /ˈskɪtl/ *n* bolo *m*

skive /skaɪv/ *vi* (*sl*) gandulear

skivvy /ˈskɪvɪ/ *n* (*fam*) criada *f*

skulk /skʌlk/ *vi* avanzar furtivamente; ⟨*hide*⟩ esconderse

skull /skʌl/ *n* cráneo *m*;
⟨*remains*⟩ calavera *f*. ~**-cap** *n*
casquete *m*

skunk /skʌŋk/ *n* mofeta *f*; ⟨*person*⟩ canalla *f*

sky /skaɪ/ n cielo m. ∼-blue a & n azul (m) celeste. ∼jack /ˈskaɪdʒæk/ vt secuestrar. ∼jacker n secuestrador m. ∼light /ˈskaɪlaɪt/ n tragaluz m. ∼scraper /ˈskaɪskreɪpə(r)/ n rascacielos m invar

slab /slæb/ n bloque m; (of stone) losa f; (of chocolate) tableta f

slack /slæk/ a (-er, -est) flojo; (person) negligente; (period) de poca actividad. —n (of rope) parte f floja. —vt aflojar. —vi aflojarse; (person) descansar. ∼en /ˈslækən/ vt aflojar. —vi aflojarse; (person) descansar. ∼en (off) vt aflojar. ∼ off (fam) aflojar

slacks /slæks/ npl pantalones mpl

slag /slæg/ n escoria f

slain /sleɪn/ see slay

slake /sleɪk/ vt apagar

slam /slæm/ vt (pt slammed) golpear; (throw) arrojar; (criticize, sl) criticar. ∼ the door dar un portazo. —vi cerrarse de golpe. —n golpe m; (of door) portazo m

slander /ˈslɑːndə(r)/ n calumnia f. —vt difamar. ∼ous a calumnioso

slang /slæŋ/ n jerga f, argot m. ∼y a vulgar

slant /slɑːnt/ vt inclinar; presentar con parcialidad (news). —n inclinación f; (point of view) punto m de vista

slap /slæp/ vt (pt slapped) abofetear; (on the back) dar una palmada; (put) arrojar. —n bofetada f; (on back) palmada f. —adv de lleno. ∼dash /ˈslæpdæʃ/ a descuidado. ∼happy a (fam) despreocupado; (dazed, fam) aturdido. ∼stick /ˈslæpstɪk/ n payasada f. ∼up a (sl) de primera categoría

slash /slæʃ/ vt acuchillar; (fig) reducir radicalmente. —n cuchillada f

slat /slæt/ n tablilla f

slate /sleɪt/ n pizarra f. —vt (fam) criticar

slaughter /ˈslɔːtə(r)/ vt masacrar; matar (animal). —n carnicería f; (of animals) matanza f. ∼house /ˈslɔːtəhaʊs/ n matadero m

Slav /slɑːv/ a & n eslavo (m)

slav|**e** /sleɪv/ n esclavo m. —vi trabajar como un negro. ∼**e-driver** n negrero m. ∼**ery** /-ərɪ/ n esclavitud f. ∼**ish** /ˈsleɪvɪʃ/ a servil

Slavonic /sləˈvɒnɪk/ a eslavo

slay /sleɪ/ vt (pt slew, pp slain) matar

sleazy /ˈsliːzɪ/ a (-ier, -iest) (fam) sórdido

sledge /sledʒ/ n trineo m. ∼**hammer** n almádena f

sleek /sliːk/ a (-er, -est) liso, brillante; (elegant) elegante

sleep /sliːp/ n sueño m. go to ∼ dormirse. —vi (pt slept) dormir. —vt poder alojar. ∼er n durmiente m & f; (on track) traviesa f; (berth) coche-cama m. ∼**ily** adv soñolientamente. ∼**ing-bag** n saco m de dormir. ∼**ing-pill** n somnífero m. ∼**less** a insomne. ∼**lessness** n insomnio m. ∼**walker** n sonámbulo m. ∼y /ˈsliːpɪ/ a (-ier, -iest) soñoliento. be ∼y tener sueño

sleet /sliːt/ n aguanieve f. —vi caer aguanieve

sleeve /sliːv/ n manga f; (for record) funda f. up one's ∼ en reserva. ∼**less** a sin mangas

sleigh /sleɪ/ n trineo m

sleight /slaɪt/ n. ∼ of hand prestidigitación f

slender /ˈslendə(r)/ a delgado; (fig) escaso

slept /slept/ see sleep

sleuth /slu:θ/ n investigador m

slew[1] /slu:/ see **slay**

slew[2] /slu:/ vi (turn) girar

slice /slaɪs/ n lonja f; (of bread) rebanada f; (of sth round) rodaja f; (implement) paleta f. —vt cortar; rebanar (bread)

slick /slɪk/ a liso; (cunning) astuto. —n. (oil)-~ capa f de aceite

slid|e /slaɪd/ vt (pt **slid**) deslizar. —vi resbalar. ~e over pasar por alto de. —n resbalón m; (in playground) tobogán m; (for hair) pasador m; (photo) diapositiva f; (fig, fall) baja f. ~e-rule n regla f de cálculo. ~ing a corredizo. ~ing scale n escala f móvil

slight /slaɪt/ a (-er, -est) ligero; (slender) delgado. —vt ofender. —n desaire m. ~est a mínimo. not in the ~est en absoluto. ~ly adv un poco

slim /slɪm/ a (slimmer, slimmest) delgado. —vi (pt slimmed) adelgazar

slime /slaɪm/ n légamo m, lodo m, fango m

slimness /'slɪmnɪs/ n delgadez f

slimy /'slaɪmɪ/ a legamoso, fangoso, viscoso; (fig) rastrero

sling /slɪŋ/ n honda f; (toy) tirador; (med) cabestrillo m. —vt (pt slung) lanzar

slip /slɪp/ vt (pt **slipped**) deslizar. ~ s.o.'s mind olvidársele a uno. —vi deslizarse. —n resbalón m; (mistake) error m; (petticoat) combinación f; (paper) trozo m. ~ of the tongue n lapsus m linguae. give the ~ to zafarse de, dar esquinazo a. ~ away vi escabullirse. ~ into vi ponerse (clothes). ~ up vi (fam) equivocarse

slipper /'slɪpə(r)/ n zapatilla f

slippery /'slɪpərɪ/ a resbaladizo

slip-**road** n rampa f de acceso. ~**shod** /'slɪpʃɒd/ a descuidado. ~**up** n (fam) error m

slit /slɪt/ n raja f; (cut) corte m. —vt (pt **slit**, pres p **slitting**) rajar; (cut) cortar

slither /'slɪðə(r)/ vi deslizarse

sliver /'slɪvə(r)/ n trocito m; (splinter) astilla f

slobber /'slɒbə(r)/ vi babear

slog /slɒg/ vt (pt **slogged**) golpear. —vi trabajar como un negro. —n golpetazo m; (hard work) trabajo m penoso

slogan /'sləʊgən/ n eslogan m

slop /slɒp/ vt (pt **slopped**) derramar. —vi derramarse. ~s npl (fam) agua f sucia

slop|e /sləʊp/ vi inclinarse. —vt inclinar. —n declive m, pendiente m. ~ing a inclinado

sloppy /'slɒpɪ/ a (-ier, -iest) (wet) mojado; (food) líquido; (work) descuidado; (person) desaliñado; (fig) sentimental

slosh /slɒʃ/ vi (fam) chapotear. —vt (hit, sl) pegar

slot /slɒt/ n ranura f. —vt (pt **slotted**) encajar

sloth /sləʊθ/ n pereza f

slot-**machine** /'slɒtməʃi:n/ n distribuidor m automático; (for gambling) máquina f tragaperras

slouch /slaʊtʃ/ vi andar cargado de espaldas; (in chair) repanchigarse

Slovak /'sləʊvæk/ a & n eslovaco (m). ~**ia** /sləʊ'vækɪə/ n Eslovaquia f

slovenl|iness /'slʌvnlɪnɪs/ n despreocupación f. ~**y** /'slʌvnlɪ/ a descuidado

slow /sləʊ/ a (-er, -est) lento. be ~ (clock) estar atrasado. in ~ motion a cámara lenta. —adv despacio. —vt retardar. —vi ir más despacio. ~ down, ~ up vt retardar. —vi ir más despacio.

~**coach** /'sləʊkəʊtʃ/ n tardón m. ~**ly** adv despacio. ~**ness** n lentitud f

sludge /slʌdʒ/ n fango m; (sediment) sedimento m

slug /slʌg/ n babosa f; (bullet) posta f. ~**gish** /'slʌgɪʃ/ a lento

sluice /sluːs/ n (gate) compuerta f; (channel) canal m

slum /slʌm/ n tugurio m

slumber /'slʌmbə(r)/ n sueño m. —vi dormir

slump /slʌmp/ n baja f repentina; (in business) depresión f. —vi bajar repentinamente; (flop down) dejarse caer pesadamente; (collapse) desplomarse

slung /slʌŋ/ see **sling**

slur /slɜː(r)/ vt/i (pt slurred) articular mal. —n dicción f defectuosa; (discredit) calumnia f

slush /slʌʃ/ n nieve f medio derretida; (fig) sentimentalismo m. ~ **fund** n fondos mpl secretos para fines deshonestos. ~**y** a (road) cubierto de nieve medio derretida

slut /slʌt/ n mujer f desaseada

sly /slaɪ/ a (slyer, slyest) (crafty) astuto; (secretive) furtivo. **on the** ~ **a** escondidas. ~**ly** adv astutamente

smack[1] /smæk/ n golpe m; (on face) bofetada f. —adv (fam) de lleno. —vt pegar

smack[2] /smæk/ vi. ~ **of** saber a; (fig) oler a

small /smɔːl/ a (-er, -est) pequeño. —n. **the** ~ **of the** back la región f lumbar. ~ **ads** npl anuncios mpl por palabras. ~ **change** n cambio m. ~**holding** /'smɔːlhəʊldɪŋ/ n parcela f. ~**pox** /'smɔːlpɒks/ n viruela f. ~ **talk** n charla f. ~**time** a (fam) de poca monta

smarmy /'smɑːmɪ/ a (-ier, -iest) (fam) zalamero

smart /smɑːt/ a (-er, -est) elegante; (clever) inteligente; (brisk) rápido. —vi escocer. ~**en** /'smɑːtn/ vt arreglar. —vi arreglarse. ~**en up** vi arreglarse. ~**ly** adv elegantemente; (quickly) rápidamente. ~**ness** n elegancia f

smash /smæʃ/ vt romper; (into little pieces) hacer pedazos; batir (record). —vi romperse; (collide) chocar (into con). —n (noise) estruendo m; (collision) choque m; (com) quiebra f. ~**ing** /'smæʃɪŋ/ a (fam) estupendo

smattering /'smætərɪŋ/ n conocimientos mpl superficiales

smear /smɪə(r)/ vt untar (with de); (stain) manchar (with de); (fig) difamar. —n mancha f; (med) frotis m

smell /smel/ n olor m; (sense) olfato m. —vt/i (pt smelt) oler. ~**y** a maloliente

smelt[1] /smelt/ see **smell**

smelt[2] /smelt/ vt fundir

smile /smaɪl/ n sonrisa f. —vi sonreír(se)

smirk /smɜːk/ n sonrisa f afectada

smite /smaɪt/ vt (pt smote, pp smitten) golpear

smith /smɪθ/ n herrero m

smithereens /smɪðə'riːnz/ npl añicos mpl. **smash to** ~ hacer añicos

smitten /'smɪtn/ see **smite**. —a encaprichado (with por)

smock /smɒk/ n blusa f, bata f

smog /smɒg/ n niebla f con humo

smok|**e** /sməʊk/ n humo m. —vt/i fumar. ~**eless** a sin humo. ~**er** /-ə(r)/ n fumador m. ~**e-screen** n cortina f de humo. ~**y** a (room) lleno de humo

smooth /smuːð/ a (-er, -est) liso; (sound, movement) suave; (sea) tranquilo; (manners) zalamero. —vt alisar; (fig) allanar. ~**ly** adv suavemente

smote /sməʊt/ *see* smite

smother /'smʌðə(r)/ *vt* sofocar; (*cover*) cubrir

smoulder /'sməʊldə(r)/ *vi* arder sin llama; (*fig*) arder

smudge /smʌdʒ/ *n* borrón *m*, mancha *f*. —*vt* tiznar. —*vi* tiznarse

smug /smʌg/ *a* (**smugger**, **smuggest**) satisfecho de sí mismo

smuggl|e /'smʌgl/ *vt* pasar de contrabando. ~**er** *n* contrabandista *m & f*. ~**ing** *n* contrabando *m*

smug: ~**ly** *adv* con suficiencia. ~**ness** *n* suficiencia *f*

smut /smʌt/ *n* tizne *m*; (*mark*) tiznajo *m*. ~**ty** *a* (-**ier**, -**iest**) tiznado; (*fig*) obsceno

snack /snæk/ *n* tentempié *m*. ~**bar** *n* cafetería *f*

snag /snæg/ *n* problema *m*; (*in cloth*) rasgón *m*

snail /sneɪl/ *n* caracol *m*. ~**'s pace** *n* paso *m* de tortuga

snake /sneɪk/ *n* serpiente *f*

snap /snæp/ *vt* (*pt* **snapped**) (*break*) romper; castañetear (*fingers*). —*vi* romperse; (*say*) contestar bruscamente; (*whip*) chasquear. ~ **at** (*dog*) intentar morder; (*say*) contestar bruscamente. —*n* chasquido *m*; (*photo*) foto *f*. —*a* instantáneo. ~ **up** *vt* agarrar. ~**py** /'snæpɪ/ *a* (-**ier**, -**iest**) (*fam*) rápido. **make it** ~**py!** (*fam*) ¡date prisa! ~**shot** /'snæpʃɒt/ *n* foto *f*

snare /sneə(r)/ *n* trampa *f*

snarl /snɑːl/ *vi* gruñir. —*n* gruñido *m*

snatch /snætʃ/ *vt* agarrar; (*steal*) robar. —*n* arrebatamiento *m*; (*short part*) trocito *m*; (*theft*) robo *m*

sneak /sniːk/ —*n* soplón *m*. —*vi*. ~ **in** entrar furtivamente. ~ **out** salir furtivamente

sneakers /'sniːkəz/ *npl* zapatillas *fpl* de lona

sneak|ing /'sniːkɪŋ/ *a* furtivo. ~**y** *a* furtivo

sneer /snɪə(r)/ *n* sonrisa *f* de desprecio. —*vi* sonreír con desprecio. ~ **at** hablar con desprecio a

sneeze /sniːz/ *n* estornudo *m*. —*vi* estornudar

snide /snaɪd/ *a* (*fam*) despreciativo

sniff /snɪf/ *vt* oler. —*vi* aspirar por la nariz. —*n* aspiración *f*

snigger /'snɪgə(r)/ *n* risa *f* disimulada. —*vi* reír disimuladamente

snip /snɪp/ *vt* (*pt* **snipped**) tijeretear. —*n* tijeretada *f*; (*bargain*, *sl*) ganga *f*

snipe /snaɪp/ *vi* disparar desde un escondite. ~**r** /ə(r)/ *n* tirador *m* emboscado, francotirador *m*

snippet /'snɪpɪt/ *n* retazo *m*

snivel /'snɪvl/ *vi* (*pt* **snivelled**) lloriquear. ~**ling** *a* llorón

snob /snɒb/ *n* esnob *m*. ~**bery** *n* esnobismo *m*. ~**bish** *a* esnob

snooker /'snuːkə(r)/ *n* billar *m*

snoop /snuːp/ *vi* (*fam*) curiosear

snooty /'snuːtɪ/ *a* (*fam*) desdeñoso

snooze /snuːz/ *n* sueñecito *m*. —*vi* echarse un sueñecito

snore /snɔː(r)/ *n* ronquido *m*. —*vi* roncar

snorkel /'snɔːkl/ *n* tubo *m* respiratorio

snort /snɔːt/ *n* bufido *m*. —*vi* bufar

snout /snaʊt/ *n* hocico *m*

snow /snəʊ/ *n* nieve *f*. —*vi* nevar. **be** ~**ed under with** estar inundado por. ~**ball** /'snəʊbɔːl/ *n* bola *f* de nieve. ~**drift** *n* nieve amontonada. ~**drop** /'snəʊdrɒp/ *n* campanilla *f* de invierno. ~**fall** /'snəʊfɔːl/ *n* nevada *f*. ~**flake** /'snəʊfleɪk/ *n* copo *m* de nieve. **∼man** /'snəʊmæn/ *n* (*pl* -men) muñeco *m* de nieve. **∼plough** /*n* quitanieves *m invar*. **∼storm** /'snəʊstɔːm/ *n* nevasca *f*. **∼y** *a* (*place*) de nieves abundantes; (*weather*) con nevadas seguidas

snub /snʌb/ *vt* (*pt* **snubbed**) desairar. —*n* desaire *m*. **∼-nosed** /'snʌbnəʊzd/ *a* chato

snuff /snʌf/ *n* rapé *m*. —*vt* despabilar (*candle*). **∼ out** apagar (*candle*)

snuffle /'snʌfl/ *vi* respirar ruidosamente

snug /snʌg/ *a* (**snugger**, **snuggest**) cómodo; (*tight*) ajustado

snuggle /'snʌgl/ *vi* acomodarse

so /səʊ/ *adv* (*before a or adv*) tan; (*thus*) así. —*conj* así que. **∼ am I** yo tambien. **∼ as to** para. **∼ far** *adv* (*time*) hasta ahora; (*place*) hasta aquí. **∼ far as I know** que yo sepa. **∼ long!** (*fam*) hasta luego! **∼ much** tanto. **∼ that** *conj* para que. **and ∼ forth, and ∼ on** y así sucesivamente. **if ∼** si es así. **I think ∼** creo que sí. **or ∼** más o menos

soak /səʊk/ *vt* remojar. —*vi* remojarse. **∼ in** penetrar. **∼ up** absorber. **∼ing** *a* empapado. —*n* remojón *m*

so-and-so /'səʊənsəʊ/ *n* fulano *m*

soap /səʊp/ *n* jabón *m*. —*vt* enjabonar. **∼ powder** *n* jabón en polvo. **∼y** *a* jabonoso

soar /sɔː(r)/ *vi* elevarse; (*price etc*) ponerse por las nubes

sob /sɒb/ *n* sollozo *m*. —*vi* (*pt* **sobbed**) sollozar

sober /'səʊbə(r)/ *a* sobrio; (*colour*) discreto

so-called /'səʊkɔːld/ *a* llamado, supuesto

soccer /'sɒkə(r)/ *n* (*fam*) fútbol *m*

sociable /'səʊʃəbl/ *a* sociable

social /'səʊʃl/ *a* social; (*sociable*) sociable. —*n* reunión *f*. **∼ism**

/-zəm/ *n* socialismo *m*. **∼ist** /'səʊʃəlɪst/ *a & n* socialista *m & f*. **∼ize** /'səʊʃəlaɪz/ *vt* socializar. **∼ly** *adv* socialmente. **∼ security** *n* seguridad *f* social. **∼ worker** *n* asistente *m* social. **∼ society** /sə'saɪətɪ/ *n* sociedad *f*

sociological /səʊsɪə'lɒdʒɪkl/ *a* sociológico. **∼ist** *n* sociólogo *m*. **∼y** /səʊsɪ'ɒlədʒɪ/ *n* sociología *f*

sock[1] /sɒk/ *n* calcetín *m*

sock[2] /sɒk/ *vt* (*sl*) pegar

socket /'sɒkɪt/ *n* hueco *m*; (*of eye*) cuenca *f*; (*wall plug*) enchufe *m*; (*for bulb*) portalámparas *m invar*, casquillo *m*

soda /'səʊdə/ *n* sosa *f*; (*water*) soda *f*. **∼-water** *n* soda *f*

sodden /'sɒdn/ *a* empapado

sodium /'səʊdɪəm/ *n* sodio *m*

sofa /'səʊfə/ *n* sofá *m*

soft /sɒft/ *a* (**-er**, **-est**) blando; (*sound, colour*) suave; (*gentle*) dulce, tierno; (*silly*) estúpido. **∼ drink** *n* bebida *f* no alcohólica. **∼ spot** *n* debilidad *f*. **∼en** /'sɒfn/ *vt* ablandar; (*fig*) suavizar. —*vi* ablandarse; (*fig*) suavizarse. **∼ly** *adv* dulcemente. **∼ness** *n* blandura *f*; (*fig*) dulzura *f*. **∼ware** /'sɒftweə(r)/ *n* programación *f*, software *m*

soggy /'sɒgɪ/ *a* (**-ier**, **-iest**) empapado

soh /səʊ/ *n* (*mus, fifth note of any musical scale*) sol *m*

soil[1] /sɔɪl/ *n* suelo *m*

soil[2] /sɔɪl/ *vt* ensuciar. —*vi* ensuciarse

solace /'sɒləs/ *n* consuelo *m*

solar /'səʊlə(r)/ *a* solar. **∼ium** /sə'leərɪəm/ *n* (*pl* -**ia**) solario *m*

sold /səʊld/ *see* **sell**

solder /'səʊldə(r)/ *n* soldadura *f*. —*vt* soldar

soldier /'səʊldʒə(r)/ *n* soldado *m*. —*vi*. **∼ on** (*fam*) perseverar

sole[1] /səʊl/ *n* (*of foot*) planta *f*; (*of shoe*) suela *f*

sole[2] /səʊl/ (*fish*) lenguado *m*

sole[3] /səʊl/ *a* único, solo. **~ly** *adv* únicamente

solemn /ˈsɒləm/ *a* solemne. **~ity** /sə'lemnətɪ/ *n* solemnidad *f*. **~ly** *adv* solemnemente

solicit /sə'lɪsɪt/ *vt* solicitar. **—vi** importunar

solicitor /sə'lɪsɪtə(r)/ *n* abogado *m*; (*notary*) notario *m*

solicitous /sə'lɪsɪtəs/ *a* solícito

solid /'sɒlɪd/ *a* sólido; (*gold etc*) macizo; (*unanimous*) unánime; (*meal*) sustancioso. **—n** sólido *m*. **~arity** /sɒlɪ'dærətɪ/ *n* solidaridad *f*. **~ify** /sə'lɪdɪfaɪ/ *vt* solidificar. **—vi** solidificarse. **~ity** /sə'lɪdətɪ/ *n* solidez *f*. **~ly** *adv* sólidamente. **~s** *npl* alimentos *mpl* sólidos

soliloquy /sə'lɪləkwɪ/ *n* soliloquio *m*

solitaire /sɒlɪ'teə(r)/ *n* solitario *m*

solitary /'sɒlɪtrɪ/ *a* solitario

solitude /'sɒlɪtjuːd/ *n* soledad *f*

solo /'səʊləʊ/ *n* (*pl* **-os**) (*mus*) solo *m*. **~ist** *n* solista *m* & *f*

solstice /'sɒlstɪs/ *n* solsticio *m*

soluble /'sɒljʊbl/ *a* soluble

solution /sə'luːʃn/ *n* solución *f*

solvable /ˈsɒlvəbl/ *a* soluble

solve /sɒlv/ *vt* resolver

solvent /ˈsɒlvənt/ *a* & *n* solvente (*m*)

sombre /ˈsɒmbə(r)/ *a* sombrío

some /sʌm/ *a* alguno; (*a little*) un poco de. **~ day** algún día. **~ two hours** unas dos horas. **will you have ~ wine?** ¿quieres vino? **—** *pron* algunos; (*a little*) un poco. **~ of us** algunos de nosotros. **I want ~** quiero un poco. **—adv** (*approximately*) unos. **~body** /ˈsʌmbədɪ/ *pron* alguien. **—n** personaje *m*. **~how** /ˈsʌmhaʊ/ *adv* de algún modo. **~how or other** de una manera u otra. **~one**

/ˈsʌmwʌn/ *pron* alguien. **—n** personaje *m*

somersault /ˈsʌməsɔːlt/ *n* salto *m* mortal. **—vi** dar un salto mortal

some: **~thing** /ˈsʌmθɪŋ/ *pron* algo *m*. **~thing like** algo como; (*approximately*) cerca de. **~time** /ˈsʌmtaɪm/ *a* ex. **—adv** algún día; (*in past*) durante. **~time last summer** a (durante) el verano pasado. **~times** /ˈsʌmtaɪmz/ *adv* de vez en cuando, a veces. **~what** /ˈsʌmwɒt/ *adv* algo, un poco. **~where** /ˈsʌmweə(r)/ *adv* en alguna parte

son /sʌn/ *n* hijo *m*

sonata /sə'nɑːtə/ *n* sonata *f*

song /sɒŋ/ *n* canción *f*. **sell for a ~** vender muy barato. **~-book** *n* cancionero *m*

sonic /'sɒnɪk/ *a* sónico

son-in-law /ˈsʌnɪnlɔː/ *n* (*pl* **sons-in-law**) yerno *m*

sonnet /'sɒnɪt/ *n* soneto *m*

sonny /ˈsʌnɪ/ *n* (*fam*) hijo *m*

soon /suːn/ *adv* (**-er**, **-est**) pronto; (*in a short time*) dentro de poco; (*early*) temprano. **~ after** poco después. **~er or later** tarde o temprano. **as ~ as** en cuanto; **as ~ as possible** lo antes posible. **I would ~ not go** prefiero no ir

soot /sʊt/ *n* hollín *m*

sooth|e /suːð/ *vt* calmar. **~ing** *a* calmante

sooty /ˈsʊtɪ/ *a* cubierto de hollín

sophisticated /sə'fɪstɪkeɪtɪd/ *a* sofisticado; (*complex*) complejo

soporific /sɒpə'rɪfɪk/ *a* soporífero

sopping /'sɒpɪŋ/ *a*. **~ (wet)** empapado

soppy /'sɒpɪ/ *a* (**-ier**, **-iest**) (*fam*) sentimental; (*silly*, *fam*) tonto

soprano /sə'prɑːnəʊ/ *n* (*pl* **-os**) (*voice*) soprano *m*; (*singer*) soprano *f*

sorcerer /ˈsɔːsərə(r)/ n hechicero m

sordid /ˈsɔːdɪd/ a sórdido

sore /sɔː(r)/ a (-er, -est) que duele, dolorido; (distressed) penoso; (vexed) enojado. —n llaga f. ~**ly** /ˈsɔːlɪ/ adv gravemente. ~ **throat** n dolor m de garganta. **I've got a ~ throat** me duele la garganta

sorrow /ˈsɒrəʊ/ n pena f, tristeza f. ~**ful** a triste

sorry /ˈsɒrɪ/ a (-ier, -iest) arrepentido; (wretched) lamentable; (sad) triste. **be ~** sentirlo; (repent) arrepentirse. **be ~ for s.o.** (pity) compadecerse de uno. **~!** ¡perdón!, ¡perdone!

sort /sɔːt/ n clase f. (person, fam) tipo m. **be out of ~s** estar indispuesto; (irritable) estar de mal humor. —vt clasificar. ~ **out** (choose) escoger; (separate) separar; resolver (problem)

so-so /ˈsəʊsəʊ/ a & adv regular

soufflé /ˈsuːfleɪ/ n suflé m

sought /sɔːt/ see **seek**

soul /səʊl/ n alma f. ~**ful** /ˈsəʊlfl/ a sentimental

sound[1] /saʊnd/ n sonido m; ruido m. —vt sonar; (test) sondar. —vi sonar; (seem) parecer (**as if** que)

sound[2] /saʊnd/ a (-er, -est) sano; (argument etc) lógico; (secure) seguro. ~ **asleep** profundamente dormido

sound[3] /saʊnd/ n (strait) estrecho m

sound barrier /ˈsaʊndbærɪə(r)/ n barrera f del sonido

soundly /ˈsaʊndlɪ/ adv sólidamente; (asleep) profundamente

sound: ~**proof** a insonorizado. ~**track** n banda f sonora

soup /suːp/ n sopa f. **in the ~** (sl) en apuros

sour /saʊə(r)/ a (-er, -est) agrio; (cream, milk) cortado. —vt agriar. —vi agriarse

source /sɔːs/ n fuente f

south /saʊθ/ n sur m. —a del sur. —adv hacia el sur. **S~ Africa** n Africa f del Sur. **S~ America** n América f (del Sur), Sudamérica f. **S~ American** a & n sudamericano (m). ~**east** n sudeste m. ~**erly** /ˈsʌðəlɪ/ a sur; (wind) del sur. ~**ern** /ˈsʌðən/ a del sur, meridional. ~**erner** n meridional m. ~**ward** a sur; —adv hacia el sur. ~**wards** adv hacia el sur. ~**west** n sudoeste m

souvenir /suːvəˈnɪə(r)/ n recuerdo m

sovereign /ˈsɒvrɪn/ n & a soberano (m). ~**ty** n soberanía f

Soviet /ˈsəʊvɪət/ a (history) soviético. **the ~ Union** n la Unión f Soviética

sow[1] /səʊ/ vt (pt **sowed**, pp **sowed** or **sown**) sembrar

sow[2] /saʊ/ n cerda f

soya /ˈsɔɪə/ n. ~ **bean** n soja f

spa /spɑː/ n balneario m

space /speɪs/ n espacio m; (room) sitio m; (period) período m. —a (research etc) espacial. —vt espaciar. ~ **out** espaciar. ~**craft** /ˈspeɪskrɑːft/ n, ~**ship** n nave f espacial. ~**suit** n traje m espacial

spacious /ˈspeɪʃəs/ a espacioso

spade /speɪd/ n pala f. ~**s** npl (cards) picos mpl, picas fpl; (in Spanish pack) espadas fpl. ~**work** /ˈspeɪdwɜːk/ n trabajo m preparatorio

spaghetti /spəˈgetɪ/ n espaguetis mpl

Spain /speɪn/ n España f

span[1] /spæn/ n (of arch) luz f; (of time) espacio m; (of wings) envergadura f. —vt (pt **spanned**) extenderse sobre

span[2] /spæn/ see **spick**

Spaniard /ˈspænjəd/ n español m

spaniel /'spænjəl/ n perro m de aguas

Spanish /'spænɪʃ/ a & n español (m)

spank /spæŋk/ vt dar un azote a. ~**ing** n azote m

spanner /'spænə(r)/ n llave f

spar /spɑː(r)/ vi (pt **sparred**) entrenarse en el boxeo; (argue) disputar

spare /speə(r)/ vt salvar; (do without) prescindir de; (afford to give) dar; (use without restraint) escatimar. —a de reserva; (surplus) sobrante; (person) enjuto; (meal etc) frugal. ~ (**part**) n repuesto m. ~ **time** n tiempo m libre. ~ **tyre** n neumático m de repuesto

sparing /'speərɪŋ/ a frugal. ~**ly** adv frugalmente

spark /spɑːk/ n chispa f. —vt. ~ **off** (initiate) provocar. ~**ing-plug** n (auto) bujía f

sparkl|e /'spɑːkl/ vi centellear. —n centelleo m. ~**ing** a centelleante; (wine) espumoso

sparrow /'spærəʊ/ n gorrión m

sparse /spɑːs/ a escaso; (population) poco denso. ~**ly** adv escasamente

spartan /'spɑːtn/ a espartano

spasm /'spæzəm/ n espasmo m; (of cough) acceso m. ~**odic** /spæz'mɒdɪk/ a espasmódico

spastic /'spæstɪk/ n víctima f de parálisis cerebral

spat /spæt/ see **spit**

spate /speɪt/ n avalancha f

spatial /'speɪʃl/ a espacial

spatter /'spætə(r)/ vt salpicar (with de)

spatula /'spætjʊlə/ n espátula f

spawn /spɔːn/ n hueva f. —vi engendrar. —vi desovar

speak /spiːk/ vt/i (pt **spoke**, pp **spoken**) hablar. ~ **for** vi hablar en nombre de. ~ **up** vi hablar más fuerte. ~**er** /'spiːkə(r)/ n (in public) orador m; (loudspeaker) altavoz m. **be a Spanish** ~**er** hablar español

spear /spɪə(r)/ n lanza f. ~**head** /'spɪəhed/ n punta f de lanza. —vt (lead) encabezar. ~**mint** /'spɪəmɪnt/ n menta f verde

spec /spek/ n. **on** ~ (fam) por si acaso

special /'speʃl/ a especial. ~**ist** /'speʃəlɪst/ n especialista m & f. ~**ity** /-ɪ'ælətɪ/ n especialidad f. ~**ization** /-'zeɪʃn/ n especialización f. ~**ize** /'speʃəlaɪz/ vi especializarse. ~**ized** a especializado. ~**ty** n especialidad f. ~**ly** adv especialmente

species /'spiːʃiːz/ n especie f

specific /spə'sɪfɪk/ a específico. ~**ically** adv específicamente. ~**ication** /-ɪ'keɪʃn/ n especificación f; (details) descripción f. ~**y** /'spesɪfaɪ/ vt especificar

specimen /'spesɪmɪn/ n muestra f

speck /spek/ n manchita f; (particle) partícula f

speckled /'spekld/ a moteado

specs /speks/ npl (fam) gafas fpl, anteojos mpl (LAm)

spectac|le /'spektəkl/ n espectáculo m. ~**les** npl gafas fpl, anteojos mpl (LAm). ~**ular** /spek'tækjʊlə(r)/ a espectacular

spectator /spek'teɪtə(r)/ n espectador m

spectre /'spektə(r)/ n espectro m

spectrum /'spektrəm/ n (pl **-tra**) espectro m; (of ideas) gama f

speculat|e /'spekjʊleɪt/ vi especular. ~**ion** /-'leɪʃn/ n especulación f. ~**ive** /-lətɪv/ a especulativo. ~**or** n especulador m

sped /sped/ see **speed**

speech /spiːtʃ/ n (faculty) habla f; (address) discurso m. ~**less** a mudo

speed /spiːd/ n velocidad f; (*rapidity*) rapidez f; (*haste*) prisa f. —vi (pt **sped**) apresurarse. (pt **speeded**) (*drive too fast*) ir a una velocidad excesiva. ~ **up** vt acelerar. —vi acelerarse. ~**boat** /'spiːdbəʊt/ n lancha f motora. ~**ily** adv rápidamente. ~**ing** n exceso m de velocidad. ~**ometer** /spiː'dɒmɪtə(r)/ n velocímetro m. ~**way** /'spiːdweɪ/ n pista f; (*Amer*) autopista f. ~**y** /'spiːdɪ/ a (**-ier, -iest**) rápido

spell[1] /spel/ n (*magic*) hechizo m

spell[2] /spel/ vt/i (pt **spelled** or **spelt**) escribir; (*mean*) significar. ~ **out** vt deletrear; (*fig*) explicar. ~**ing** n ortografía f

spell[3] /spel/ (*period*) período m

spellbound /'spelbaʊnd/ a hechizado

spelt /spelt/ see **spell**[2]

spend /spend/ vt (pt **spent**) gastar; pasar ⟨*time etc*⟩; dedicar ⟨*care etc*⟩. —vi gastar dinero. ~**thrift** /'spendθrɪft/ n derrochador m

spent /spent/ see **spend**

sperm /spɜːm/ n (pl **sperms** or **sperm**) esperma f

spew /spjuː/ vt/i vomitar

spher|**e** /sfɪə(r)/ n esfera f. ~**ical** /'sferɪkl/ a esférico

sphinx /sfɪŋks/ n esfinge f

spice /spaɪs/ n especia f; (*fig*) sabor m

spick /spɪk/ a. ~ **and span** impecable

spicy /'spaɪsɪ/ a picante

spider /'spaɪdə(r)/ n araña f

spik|**e** /spaɪk/ n (*of metal etc*) punta f. ~**y** a puntiagudo; ⟨*person*⟩ quisquilloso

spill /spɪl/ vt (pt **spilled** or **spilt**) derramar. —vi derramarse. ~ **over** desbordarse

spin /spɪn/ vt (pt **spun**, pres p **spinning**) hacer girar; hilar ⟨*wool etc*⟩. —vi girar. —n vuelta f; (*short drive*) paseo m

spinach /'spɪnɪdʒ/ n espinacas fpl

spinal /'spaɪnl/ a espinal. ~ **cord** n médula f espinal

spindl|**e** /'spɪndl/ n (*for spinning*) huso m. ~**y** a larguirucho

spin-drier /spɪn'draɪə(r)/ n secador m centrífugo

spine /spaɪn/ n columna f vertebral; (*of book*) lomo m. ~**less** a (*fig*) sin carácter

spinning /'spɪnɪŋ/ n hilado m. ~**-top** n trompa f, peonza f. ~**-wheel** n rueca f

spin-off /'spɪnɒf/ n beneficio m incidental; (*by-product*) subproducto m

spinster /'spɪnstə(r)/ n soltera f; (*old maid, fam*) solterona f

spiral /'spaɪərəl/ a espiral, helicoidal. —n hélice f. —vi (pt **spiralled**) moverse en espiral. ~ **staircase** n escalera f de caracol

spire /'spaɪə(r)/ n (*archit*) aguja f

spirit /'spɪrɪt/ n espíritu m; (*boldness*) valor m. **in low** ~**s** abatido. —vt. ~ **away** hacer desaparecer. ~**ed** /'spɪrɪtɪd/ a animado, fogoso. ~**lamp** n lamparilla f de alcohol. ~**level** n nivel m de aire. ~**s** npl (*drinks*) bebidas fpl alcohólicas

spiritual /'spɪrɪtjʊəl/ a espiritual. —n canción f religiosa de los negros. ~**ualism** /-zəm/ n espiritismo m. ~**ualist** /'spɪrɪtjʊəlɪst/ n espiritista m & f

spit[1] /spɪt/ vt (pt **spat** or **spit**, pres p **spitting**) escupir. —vi escupir; (*rain*) lloviznar. —n esputo m; (*spittle*) saliva f

spit[2] /spɪt/ (*for roasting*) asador m

spite /spaɪt/ n rencor m. **in** ~ **of** a pesar de. —vt fastidiar. ~**ful** a rencoroso. ~**fully** adv con rencor

spitting image /spɪtɪŋˈɪmɪdʒ/ n vivo retrato m

spittle /spɪtl/ n saliva f

splash /splæʃ/ vt salpicar. —vi esparcirse; (person) chapotear. —n salpicadura f. (sound) chapoteo m; (of colour) mancha f; (drop, fam) gota f. ~ **about** vi chapotear. ~ **down** vi (spacecraft) amerizar

spleen /spli:n/ n bazo m; (fig) esplín m

splendid /splendɪd/ a espléndido

splendour /splendə(r)/ n esplendor m

splint /splɪnt/ n tablilla f

splinter /splɪntə(r)/ n astilla f. —vi astillarse. ~ **group** n grupo m disidente

split /splɪt/ vt (pt **split**, pres p **splitting**) hender, rajar; (tear) rajar; (divide) dividir; (share) repartir. ~ **one's sides** caerse de risa. —vi partirse; (divide) dividirse. ~ **on s.o.** (sl) traicionar. —n hendidura f. (tear) desgarrón m; (quarrel) ruptura f; (pol) escisión f. ~ **up** vi separarse. ~ **second** n fracción f de segundo

splurge /splɜ:dʒ/ vi (fam) derrochar

splutter /splʌtə(r)/ vi chisporrotear; (person) farfullar. —n chisporroteo m; (speech) farfulla f

spoil /spɔɪl/ vt (pt **spoilt** or **spoiled**) estropear, echar a perder; (ruin) arruinar; (indulge) mimar. —n botín m. ~**s** npl botín m. ~**sport** n aguafiestas m invar

spoke[1] /spəʊk/ see **speak**

spoke[2] /spəʊk/ n (of wheel) radio m

spoken /spəʊkən/ see **speak**

spokesman /spəʊksmən/ n (pl -men) portavoz m

sponge /spʌndʒ/ n esponja f. —vt limpiar con una esponja. —vi. ~**e on** vivir a costa de. ~**e-cake** n bizcocho m. ~**er** /-ə(r)/ n gorrón m. ~**y** a esponjoso

sponsor /spɒnsə(r)/ n patrocinador m; (surety) garante m. —vt patrocinar. ~**ship** n patrocinio m

spontane|ity /spɒntəˈneɪɪtɪ/ n espontaneidad f. ~**ous** /spɒnˈteɪnjəs/ a espontáneo. ~**ously** adv espontáneamente

spoof /spu:f/ n (sl) parodia f

spooky /spu:kɪ/ a (-ier, -iest) (fam) escalofriante

spool /spu:l/ n carrete m; (of sewing-machine) canilla f

spoon /spu:n/ n cuchara f. ~**fed** a (fig) mimado. ~**feed** vt (pt -fed) dar de comer con cuchara. ~**ful** n (pl -fuls) cucharada f

sporadic /spəˈrædɪk/ a esporádico

sport /spɔ:t/ n deporte m; (amusement) pasatiempo m; (person, fam) persona f alegre, buen chico m, buena chica f. **be a good** ~ ser buen perdedor. —vt lucir. ~**ing** a deportivo. ~**ing chance** n probabilidad f de éxito. ~**s car** n coche m deportivo. ~**s coat** n chaqueta f de sport. ~**sman** /spɔ:tsmən/ n, (pl -men), ~**swoman** /spɔ:ts wʊmən/ n (pl -women) deportista m & f

spot /spɒt/ n mancha f; (pimple) grano m; (place) lugar m; (in pattern) punto m; (drop) gota f; (a little, fam) poquito m. **in a** ~ (fam) en un apuro. **on the** ~ en el lugar; (without delay) en el acto. —vt (pt **spotted**) manchar; (notice, fam) observar, ver. ~ **check** n control m hecho al azar. ~**less** a inmaculado. ~**light** /spɒtlaɪt/ n reflector m. ~**ted** a moteado; (cloth) a puntos. ~**ty**

a (**-ier, -iest**) manchado; ‹*skin*› con granos

spouse /spaʊz/ *n* cónyuge *m* & *f*

spout /spaʊt/ *n* caño; (*jet*) chorro *m*. **up the ~** (*ruined, sl*) perdido. —*vi* chorrear

sprain /spreɪn/ *vt* torcer. —*n* torcedura *f*

sprang /spræŋ/ *see* **spring**

sprat /spræt/ *n* espadín *m*

sprawl /sprɔːl/ *vi* (*person*) repanchigarse; ‹*city etc*› extenderse

spray /spreɪ/ *n* (*of flowers*) ramo *m*; (*water*) rociada *f*; (*from sea*) espuma *f*; (*device*) pulverizador *m*. —*vt* rociar. **~-gun** *n* pistola *f* pulverizadora

spread /spred/ *vt* (*pt* **spread**) (*stretch, extend*) extender; untar ‹*jam etc*›; difundir ‹*idea, news*›. —*vi* extenderse; ‹*disease*› propagarse; ‹*idea, news*› difundirse. —*n* extensión *f*; (*paste*) pasta *f*; (*of disease*) propagación *f*; (*feast, fam*) comilona *f*. **~-eagled** *a* con los brazos y piernas extendidos

spree /spriː/ *n*. **go on a ~** (*have fun, fam*) ir de juerga

sprig /sprɪg/ *n* ramito *m*

sprightly /ˈspraɪtlɪ/ *a* (**-ier, -iest**) vivo

spring /sprɪŋ/ *n* (*season*) primavera *f*; (*device*) muelle *m*; (*elasticity*) elasticidad *f*; (*water*) manantial *m*. —*a* de primavera. —*vt* (*pt* **sprang**, *pp* **sprung**) hacer inesperadamente. —*vi* saltar; (*issue*) brotar. **~ from** *vi* provenir de. **~ up** *vi* surgir. **~board** *n* trampolín *m*. **~time** *n* primavera *f*. **~y** *a* (**-ier, -iest**) elástico

sprinkl|e /ˈsprɪŋkl/ *vt* salpicar; (*with liquid*) rociar. —*n* salpicadura *f*; (*of liquid*) rociada *f*. **~ed with** salpicado de. **~er** /-ə(r)/ *n* regadera *f*. **~ing**

/ˈsprɪŋklɪŋ/ *n* (*fig, amount*) poco *m*

sprint /sprɪnt/ *n* carrera *f*. —*vi* correr. **~er** *n* corredor *m*

sprite /spraɪt/ *n* duende *m*, hada *f*

sprout /spraʊt/ *vi* brotar. —*n* brote *m*. (**Brussels**) **~s** *npl* coles *fpl* de Bruselas

spruce /spruːs/ *a* elegante

sprung /sprʌŋ/ *see* **spring**. —*a* de muelles

spry /spraɪ/ *a* (**spryer, spryest**) vivo

spud /spʌd/ *n* (*sl*) patata *f*, papa *f* (*LAm*)

spun /spʌn/ *see* **spin**

spur /spɜː(r)/ *n* espuela *f*; (*stimulus*) estímulo *m*. **on the ~ of the moment** impulsivamente. —*vt* (*pt* **spurred**). **~ (on)** espolear; (*fig*) estimular

spurious /ˈspjʊərɪəs/ *a* falso. **~ly** *adv* falsamente

spurn /spɜːn/ *vt* despreciar; (*reject*) rechazar

spurt /spɜːt/ *vi* chorrear; (*make sudden effort*) hacer un esfuerzo repentino. —*n* chorro *m*; (*effort*) esfuerzo *m* repentino

spy /spaɪ/ *n* espía *m* & *f*. —*vt* divisar. —*vi* espiar. **~ out** *vt* reconocer. **~ing** *n* espionaje *m*

squabble /ˈskwɒbl/ *n* riña *f*. —*vi* reñir

squad /skwɒd/ *n* (*mil*) pelotón *m*; (*of police*) brigada *f*; (*sport*) equipo *m*

squadron /ˈskwɒdrən/ *n* (*mil*) escuadrón *m*; (*naut, aviat*) escuadrilla *f*

squalid /ˈskwɒlɪd/ *a* asqueroso; (*wretched*) miserable

squall /skwɔːl/ *n* turbión *m*. —*vi* chillar. **~y** *a* borrascoso

squalor /ˈskwɒlə(r)/ *n* miseria *f*

squander /ˈskwɒndə(r)/ *vt* derrochar

square /skweə(r)/ n cuadrado m; (open space in town) plaza f; (for drawing) escuadra f. —a cuadrado; (not owing) sin deudas, iguales; (honest) honrado; (meal) satisfactorio; (old-fashioned, sl) chapado a la antigua. **all ~** iguales. —vt (settle) arreglar; (math) cuadrar. —vi (agree) cuadrar. **~ up to** enfrentarse con. **~ly** adv directamente

squash /skwɒʃ/ vt aplastar; (suppress) suprimir. —n apiñamiento m; (drink) zumo m; (sport) squash m. **~y** a blando

squat /skwɒt/ vi (pt squatted) ponerse en cuclillas; (occupy illegally) ocupar sin derecho. —n casa f ocupada sin derecho. —a (dumpy) achaparrado. **~ter** /-ə(r)/ n ocupante m & f ilegal

squawk /skwɔːk/ n graznido m. —vi graznar

squeak /skwiːk/ n chillido m; (of door etc) chirrido m. —vi chillar; (door etc) chirriar. **~y** a chirriador

squeal /skwiːl/ n chillido m. —vi chillar. **~ on** (inform on, sl) denunciar

squeamish /ˈskwiːmɪʃ/ a delicado; (scrupulous) escrupuloso. **be ~ about snakes** tener horror a las serpientes

squeeze /skwiːz/ vt apretar; exprimir (lemon etc); (extort) extorsionar (**from** de). —vi (force one's way) abrirse paso. —n estrujón m; (of hand) apretón m. **credit ~** n restricción f de crédito

squelch /skweltʃ/ vi chapotear. —n chapoteo m

squib /skwɪb/ n (firework) buscapiés m invar

squid /skwɪd/ n calamar m

squiggle /ˈskwɪɡl/ n garabato m

squint /skwɪnt/ vi ser bizco; (look sideways) mirar de soslayo. —n estrabismo m

squire /ˈskwaɪə(r)/ n terrateniente m

squirm /skwɜːm/ vi retorcerse

squirrel /ˈskwɪrəl/ n ardilla f

squirt /skwɜːt/ vt arrojar a chorros. —vi salir a chorros. —n chorro m

St abbr (saint) S, San(to); (street) C/, Calle f

stab /stæb/ vt (pt stabbed) apuñalar. —n puñalada f; (pain) punzada f; (attempt, fam) tentativa f

stabil|ity /stəˈbɪlətɪ/ n estabilidad f. **~ze** /ˈsteɪbɪlaɪz/ vt estabilizar. **~zer** /-ə(r)/ n estabilizador m

stable[1] /ˈsteɪbl/ a (-er, -est) estable

stable[2] /ˈsteɪbl/ n cuadra f. —vt poner en una cuadra. **~boy** n mozo m de cuadra

stack /stæk/ n montón m. —vt amontonar

stadium /ˈsteɪdjəm/ n estadio m

staff /stɑːf/ n (stick) palo m; (employees) personal m; (mil) estado m mayor; (in school) profesorado m. —vt proveer de personal

stag /stæɡ/ n ciervo m. **~party** n reunión f de hombres, fiesta f de despedida de soltero

stage /steɪdʒ/ n (in theatre) escena f; (phase) etapa f; (platform) plataforma f. **go on the ~** hacerse actor. —vt representar; (arrange) organizar. **~coach** (hist) diligencia f. **~ fright** n miedo m al público. **~manager** n director m de escena. **~ whisper** n aparte m

stagger /ˈstæɡə(r)/ vi tambalearse. —vt asombrar; escalonar (holidays etc). —n tambaleo m. **~ing** a asombroso

stagna|nt /'stægnənt/ a estancado. **~te** /-stæg'neɪt/ vi estancarse. **~tion** /-ˈʃn/ n estancamiento m

staid /steɪd/ a serio, formal

stain /steɪn/ vt manchar; (colour) teñir. —n mancha f; (liquid) tinte m. **~ed glass window** n vidriera f de colores. **~less** /'steɪnlɪs/ a inmaculado. **~less steel** n acero m inoxidable. **~ remover** n quitamanchas m invar

stair /steə(r)/ n escalón m. **~s** npl escalera f. **flight of ~s** tramo m de escalera. **~case** /'steəkeɪs/ n, **~way** n escalera f

stake /steɪk/ n estaca f; (for execution) hoguera f; (wager) apuesta f; (com) intereses mpl. **at ~** en juego. —vt estacar; (wager) apostar. **~ a claim** reclamar

stalactite /'stæləktaɪt/ n estalactita f

stalagmite /'stæləgmaɪt/ n estalagmita f

stale /steɪl/ a (-er, -est) no fresco; (bread) duro; (smell) viciado; (news) viejo; (uninteresting) gastado. **~mate** /'steɪlmeɪt/ n (chess) ahogado m; (deadlock) punto m muerto

stalk[1] /stɔːk/ n tallo m

stalk[2] /stɔːk/ vi andar majestuosamente. —vt seguir; (animal) acechar

stall[1] /stɔːl/ n (stable) cuadra f; (in stable) casilla f; (in theatre) butaca f; (in market) puesto m; (kiosk) quiosco m

stall[2] /stɔːl/ vt parar (engine). —vi (engine) pararse; (fig) andar con rodeos

stallion /'stæljən/ n semental m

stalwart /'stɔːlwət/ n partidario m leal

stamina /'stæmɪnə/ n resistencia f

stammer /'stæmə(r)/ vi tartamudear. —n tartamudeo m

stamp /stæmp/ vt (with feet) patear; (press) estampar; poner un sello en (envelope); (with rubber stamp) sellar; (fig) señalar. —vi patear. —n sello m; (with foot) patada f; (mark) marca f, señal f. **~ out** (fig) acabar con

stampede /stæm'piːd/ n desbandada f; (fam) pánico m. —vi huir en desorden

stance /stɑːns/ n postura f

stand /stænd/ vi (pt stood) estar de pie; (rise) ponerse de pie; (be) encontrarse; (stay firm) permanecer; (pol) presentarse como candidato (for en). **~ to reason** ser lógico. —vt (endure) soportar; (place) poner; (offer) ofrecer. **~ a chance** tener una posibilidad. **~ one's ground** mantenerse firme. **I'll ~ you a drink** te invito a una copa. —n posición f, postura f; (stall) resistencia f; (for lamp etc) pie m, sostén m; (at market) puesto m; (booth) quiosco m; (sport) tribuna f. **~ around** no hacer nada. **~ back** retroceder. **~ by** vi estar preparado. —vt (support) apoyar. **~ down** vi retirarse. **~ for** vt representar. **~ in for** suplir a. **~ out** destacarse. **~ up** vi ponerse de pie. **~ up for** defender. **~ up to** vt resistir a

standard /'stændəd/ n norma f; (level) nivel m; (flag) estandarte m. —a normal, corriente. **~ize** vt uniformar. **~ lamp** n lámpara f de pie. **~s** npl valores mpl

stand: **~-by** n (person) reserva f; (at airport) lista f de espera. **~-in** n suplente m & f. **~ing** /'stændɪŋ/ a de pie; (upright) derecho. —n posición f; (duration) duración f. **~offish** a (fam) frío. **~point** /'stændpɔɪnt/

n punto *m* de vista. ~**still**
/ˈstændstɪl/ *n*. **at a** ~**still**
parado. **come to a** ~**still**
pararse

stank /stæŋk/ *see* **stink**

staple[1] /ˈsteɪpl/ *a* principal

staple[2] /ˈsteɪpl/ *n* grapa *f*. —*vt*
sujetar con una grapa. ~**r** /-ə(r)/
n grapadora *f*

star /stɑː/ *n* (*incl cinema, theatre*)
estrella *f*; (*asterisk*) asterisco
m. —*vi* (*pt* **starred**) ser el
protagonista

starboard /ˈstɑːbəd/ *n* estribor *m*

starch /stɑːtʃ/ *n* almidón *m*; (*in
food*) fécula *f*. —*vt* almidonar.
~**y** *a* almidonado; (*food*) fecu-
lento; (*fig*) formal

stardom /ˈstɑːdəm/ *n* estrellato *m*

stare /steə(r)/ *n* mirada *f* fija. —
vi. ~ **at** mirar fijamente

starfish /ˈstɑːfɪʃ/ *n* estrella *f* de
mar

stark /stɑːk/ *a* (-**er**, -**est**) rígido;
(*utter*) completo. —*adv* completamente

starlight /ˈstɑːlaɪt/ *n* luz *f* de las
estrellas

starling /ˈstɑːlɪŋ/ *n* estornino *m*

starry /ˈstɑːrɪ/ *a* estrellado. ~-
eyed *a* (*fam*) ingenuo, idealista

start /stɑːt/ *vt* empezar; poner en
marcha (*machine*); (*cause*)
provocar. —*vi* empezar; (*jump*)
sobresaltarse; (*leave*) partir;
(*car start*) arrancar. —*n* principio
m; (*leaving*) salida *f*; (*sport*) ventaja *f*; (*jump*) susto *m*. ~**er** *n*
(*sport*) participante *m* & *f*; (*auto*)
motor *m* de arranque; (*culin*)
primer plato *m*. ~**ing-point** *n*
punto *m* de partida

startle /ˈstɑːtl/ *vt* asustar

starv|ation /stɑːˈveɪʃn/ *n* hambre
f. ~**e** /stɑːv/ *vt* hacer morir de
hambre; (*deprive*) privar. —*vi*
morir de hambre

stash /stæʃ/ *vt* (*sl*) esconder

state /steɪt/ *n* estado *m*; (*grand
style*) pompa *f*. **S**~ *n* Estado *m*.
be in a ~ estar agitado. —*vt*
declarar; expresar (*views*); (*fix*)
fijar. —*a* del Estado; (*schol*) públi-
lico; (*with ceremony*) de gala.
~**less** *a* sin patria

stately /ˈsteɪtlɪ/ *a* (-**ier**, -**iest**)
majestuoso

statement /ˈsteɪtmənt/ *n* declara-
ración *f*; (*account*) informe *m*.
bank ~ *n* estado *m* de cuenta

stateroom /ˈsteɪtrʊm/ *n* (*on ship*)
camarote *m*

statesman /ˈsteɪtsmən/ *n* (*pl*
-**men**) estadista *m*

static /ˈstætɪk/ *a* inmóvil. ~**s** *n*
estática *f*; (*rad, TV*) parásitos
mpl atmosféricos, interfe-
rencias *fpl*

station /ˈsteɪʃn/ *n* estación *f*; (*status*) posición *f* social. —*vt* colocar; (*mil*) estacionar

stationary /ˈsteɪʃənərɪ/ *a* es-
tacionario

stationer /ˈsteɪʃənə(r)/ *n* pap-
elero *m*. ~'**s** (**shop**) *n* papelería
f. ~**y** *n* artículos *mpl* de
escritorio

station-wagon /ˈsteɪʃnwægən/ *n*
furgoneta *f*

statistic /stəˈtɪstɪk/ *n* estadística
f. ~**al** /stəˈtɪstɪkl/ *a* estadístico.
~**s** /stəˈtɪstɪks/ *n* (*science*) estadística *f*

statue /ˈstætʃuː/ *n* estatua *f*.
~**sque** /-ʊˈesk/ *a* escultural.
~**tte** /-ʊˈet/ *n* figurilla *f*

stature /ˈstætʃə(r)/ *n* talla *f*, estatura *f*

status /ˈsteɪtəs/ *n* posición *f*
social; (*prestige*) categoría *f*;
(*jurid*) estado *m*

statut|e /ˈstætʃuːt/ *n* estatuto *m*.
~**ory** /-ʊtrɪ/ *a* estatutario

staunch /stɔːntʃ/ *a* (-**er**, -**est**) leal.
~**ly** *adv* lealmente

stave /steɪv/ *n* (*mus*) pentagrama *m*. —*vt*. ~ **off** evitar

stay /steɪ/ n soporte m, sostén m; (of time) estancia f; (jurid) suspensión f. —vi quedar; (spend time) detenerse; (reside) alojarse. —vt matar ⟨hunger⟩. ~ **the course** terminar. ~ **in** quedar en casa. ~ **put** mantenerse firme. ~ **up** no acostarse. ~**ing-power** n resistencia f

stays /steɪz/ npl (old use) corsé m

stead /sted/ n. **in s.o.'s** ~ en lugar de uno. **stand s.o. in good** ~ ser útil a uno

steadfast /'stedfɑːst/ a firme

stead|ily /'stedɪlɪ/ adv firmemente; (regularly) regularmente. ~**y** /'stedɪ/ a (-ier, -iest) firme; (regular) regular; (dependable) serio

steak /steɪk/ n filete m

steal /stiːl/ vt (pt **stole**, pp **stolen**) robar. ~ **the show** llevarse los aplausos. ~ **in** vi entrar a hurtadillas. ~ **out** vi salir a hurtadillas

stealth /stelθ/ n. **by** ~ sigilosamente. ~**y** a sigiloso

steam /stiːm/ n vapor m; (energy) energía f. —vt (cook) cocer al vapor; empañar ⟨window⟩. —vi echar vapor. ~ **ahead** (fam) hacer progresos. ~ **up** vi ⟨glass⟩ empañar. ~**engine** n máquina f de vapor. ~**er** /'stiːmə(r)/ n (ship) barco m de vapor. ~**roller** /'stiːmrəʊlə(r)/ n apisonadora f. ~**y** a húmedo

steel /stiːl/ n acero m. —vt. ~ **o.s.** fortalecerse. ~ **industry** n industria f siderúrgica. ~ **wool** n estropajo m de acero. ~**y** a acerado; (fig) duro, inflexible

steep /stiːp/ a (-er, -est) escarpado; (price) (fam) exorbitante. —vt (soak) remojar. ~**ed in** (fig) empapado de

steeple /'stiːpl/ n aguja f, campanario m. ~**chase** /'stiːpltʃeɪs/ n carrera f de obstáculos

steep|ly adv de modo empinado. ~**ness** n lo escarpado

steer /stɪə(r)/ vt guiar; gobernar ⟨ship⟩. —vi (in ship) gobernar. ~ **clear of** evitar. ~**ing** n (auto) dirección f. ~**ing-wheel** n volante m

stem /stem/ n tallo m; (of glass) pie m; (of word) raíz f; (of ship) roda f. —vt (pt **stemmed**) detener. —vi. ~ **from** provenir de

stench /stentʃ/ n hedor m

stencil /'stensl/ n plantilla f; (for typing) cliché m. —vt (pt **stencilled**) estarcir

stenographer /ste'nɒɡrəfə(r)/ n (Amer) estenógrafo m

step /step/ vi (pt **stepped**) ir. ~ **down** retirarse. ~ **in** entrar; (fig) intervenir. ~ **up** vt aumentar. —n paso m; (surface) escalón m; (fig) medida f. **in** ~ (fig) de acuerdo con. **out of** ~ (fig) en desacuerdo con. ~**brother** /'stepbrʌðə(r)/ n hermanastro m. ~**daughter** n hijastra f. ~**father** n padrastro m. ~**ladder** n escalera f de tijeras. ~**mother** n madrastra f. ~**ping-stone** /'stepɪŋstəʊn/ n pasadera f; (fig) escalón m. ~**sister** n hermanastra f. ~**son** n hijastro m

stereo /'sterɪəʊ/ n (pl -os) cadena f estereofónica. —a estereofónico. ~**phonic** /sterɪəʊ'fɒnɪk/ a estereofónico. ~**type** /'sterɪəʊtaɪp/ n estereotipo m. ~**typed** a estereotipado

steril|e /'steraɪl/ a estéril. ~**ity** /stə'rɪlɪtɪ/ n esterilidad f. ~**ization** /-'zeɪʃn/ n esterilización f. ~**ize** /'sterɪlaɪz/ vt esterilizar

sterling /'stɜːlɪŋ/ n libras fpl esterlinas. —a (pound) esterlina; (fig) excelente. ~ **silver** n plata f de ley

stern[1] /stɜːn/ n (of boat) popa f

stern[2] /stɜ:n/ a (-er, -est) severo. ~**ly** adv severamente

stethoscope /'steθəskəʊp/ n estetoscopio m

stew /stju:/ vt/i guisar. —n guisado m. **in a ~** (fam) en un apuro

steward /stjʊəd/ n administrador m; (on ship, aircraft) camarero m. ~**ess** /-'des/ n camarera f; (on aircraft) azafata f

stick /stɪk/ n palo m; (for walking) bastón m; (of celery etc) tallo m. —vt (pt **stuck**) (glue) pegar; (put, fam) poner; (thrust) clavar; (endure, sl) soportar. —vi pegarse; (remain, fam) quedarse; (jam) bloquearse. **~ at** (fam) perseverar en. **~ out** sobresalir; (catch the eye, fam) resaltar. **~ to** aferrarse a; (promise) cumplir. **~ up for** (fam) defender. ~**er** /'stɪkə(r)/ n pegatina f. ~**ing-plaster** n esparadrapo m. **~-in-the-mud** n persona f chapada a la antigua

stickler /'stɪklə(r)/ n. **be a ~ for** insistir en

sticky /'stɪkɪ/ a (-ier, -iest) pegajoso; (label) engomado; (sl) difícil

stiff /stɪf/ a (-er, -est) rígido, (difficult) difícil; (manner) estirado; (drink) fuerte; (price) subido; (joint) tieso; (muscle) con agujetas. ~**en** /'stɪfn/ vt poner tieso. ~**ly** adv rígidamente. **~ neck** n tortícolis f. **~ness** n rigidez f

stifl|e /'staɪfl/ vt sofocar. **~ing** a sofocante

stigma /'stɪgmə/ n (pl **-as**) estigma m. (pl **stigmata** /'stɪgmətə/) (relig) estigma m. **~tize** vt estigmatizar

stile /staɪl/ n portillo m con escalones

stiletto /stɪ'letəʊ/ n (pl **-os**) estilete m. **~ heels** npl tacones mpl aguja

still[1] /stɪl/ a inmóvil; (peaceful) tranquilo; (drink) sin gas. —n silencio m. —adv todavía; (nevertheless) sin embargo

still[2] /stɪl/ n (apparatus) alambique m

still|born a nacido muerto. **~ life** n (pl **-s**) bodegón m. **~ness** n tranquilidad f

stilted /'stɪltɪd/ a artificial

stilts /stɪlts/ npl zancos mpl

stimul|ant /'stɪmjʊlənt/ n estimulante m. ~**ate** /'stɪmjʊleɪt/ vt estimular. **~ation** /-'leɪʃn/ n estímulo m. **~us** /'stɪmjʊləs/ n (pl **-li** /-laɪ/) estímulo m

sting /stɪŋ/ n picadura f; (organ) aguijón m. —vt/i (pt **stung**) picar

sting|iness /'stɪndʒɪnɪs/ n tacañería f. **~y** /'stɪndʒɪ/ a (-ier, -iest) tacaño

stink /stɪŋk/ n hedor m. —vi (pt **stank** or **stunk**, pp **stunk**) oler mal. —vt. **~ out** apestar (room); ahuyentar (person). ~**er** /-ə(r)/ n (sl) problema m difícil; (person) mal bicho m

stint /stɪnt/ n (work) trabajo m. —vi. **~ on** escatimar

stipple /'stɪpl/ vt puntear

stipulat|e /'stɪpjʊleɪt/ vt/i estipular. **~ion** /-'leɪʃn/ n estipulación f

stir /stɜ:(r)/ vt (pt **stirred**) remover, agitar; (mix) mezclar; (stimulate) estimular. —vi moverse. —n agitación f; (commotion) conmoción f

stirrup /'stɪrəp/ n estribo m

stitch /stɪtʃ/ n (in sewing) puntada f; (in knitting) punto m; (pain) dolor m de costado; (med) punto m de sutura. **be in ~es** (fam) desternillarse de risa. —vt coser

stoat /stəʊt/ n armiño m

stock /stɒk/ n (com, supplies) existencias fpl; (com, variety) surtido *m*; (*livestock*) ganado *m*; (*lineage*) linaje *m*; (*finance*) acciones *fpl*; (*culin*) caldo *m*; (*plant*) alhelí *m*. ~ **out of** ~ agotado. **take** ~ (*fig*) evaluar. —*vt* abastecer (**with de**). —*vi*. ~ **up** abastecerse (**with de**). ~**broker** /'stɒkbrəʊkə(r)/ *n* corredor *m* de bolsa. **S**~ **Exchange** *n* bolsa *f*. **well-~ed** *a* bien provisto

stocking /'stɒkɪŋ/ *n* media *f*

stock: ~**-in-trade** /'stɒkɪntreɪd/ *n* existencias *fpl*. ~**ist** /'stɒkɪst/ *n* distribuidor *m*. ~**pile** /'stɒkpaɪl/ *n* reservas *fpl*. —*vt* acumular. ~**still** *a* inmóvil. ~**taking** *n* (*com*) inventario *m*

stocky /'stɒkɪ/ *a* (**-ier, -iest**) achaparrado

stodge /stɒdʒ/ *n* (*fam*) comida *f* pesada. ~**y** *a* pesado

stoic /'stəʊɪk/ *n* estoico. ~**al** *a* estoico. ~**ally** *adv* estoicamente. ~**ism** /-sɪzəm/ *n* estoicismo *m*

stoke /stəʊk/ *vt* alimentar. ~**r** /'stəʊkə(r)/ *n* fogonero *m*

stole[1] /stəʊl/ *see* **steal**

stole[2] /stəʊl/ *n* estola *f*

stolen /'stəʊlən/ *see* **steal**

stolid /'stɒlɪd/ *a* impasible. ~**ly** *adv* impasiblemente

stomach /'stʌmək/ *n* estómago *m*. —*vt* soportar. ~**ache** *n* dolor *m* de estómago

ston|e /stəʊn/ *n* piedra *f*; (*med*) cálculo *m*; (*in fruit*) hueso *m*; (*weight, pl* **stone**) peso *m* de 14 libras (= *6,348 kg*). —*a* de piedra. —*vt* apedrear; deshuesar (*fruit*). ~**e-deaf** *a* sordo como una tapia. ~**emason** /'stəʊnweɪsn/ *n* albañil *m*. ~**ework** /'stəʊnwɜːk/ *n* cantería *f*. ~**y** *a* pedregoso; (*like stone*) pétreo

stood /stʊd/ *see* **stand**

stooge /stuːdʒ/ *n* (*in theatre*) compañero *m*; (*underling*) lacayo *m*

stool /stuːl/ *n* taburete *m*

stoop /stuːp/ *vi* inclinarse; (*fig*) rebajarse. —*n*. **have a** ~ ser cargado de espaldas

stop /stɒp/ *vt* (*pt* **stopped**) parar; (*cease*) terminar; tapar (*a leak etc*); (*prevent*) impedir; (*interrupt*) interrumpir. —*vi* pararse; (*stay, fam*) quedarse. —*n* (*bus etc*) parada *f*; (*gram*) punto *m*; (*mec*) tope *m*. ~ **dead** *vi* pararse en seco. ~**cock** /'stɒpkɒk/ *n* llave *f* de paso. ~**gap** /'stɒpgæp/ *n* remedio *m* provisional. ~**(-over)** *n* escala *f*. ~**page** /'stɒpɪdʒ/ *n* parada *f*; (*of work*) paro *m*; (*interruption*) interrupción *f*. ~**per** /'stɒpə(r)/ *n* tapón *m*. ~**press** *n* noticias *fpl* de última hora. ~**light** *n* luz *f* de freno. ~**watch** *n* cronómetro *m*

storage /'stɔːrɪdʒ/ *n* almacenamiento *m*. ~ **heater** *n* acumulador *m*. **in cold** ~ almacenaje *m* frigorífico

store /stɔː(r)/ *n* provisión *f*; (*shop, depot*) almacén *m*; (*fig*) reserva *f*. **in** ~ en reserva. **set** ~ **by** dar importancia a. —*vt* (*for future*) poner en reserva; (*in warehouse*) almacenar. ~ **up** *vt* acumular

storeroom /'stɔːruːm/ *n* despensa *f*

storey /'stɔːrɪ/ *n* (*pl* **-eys**) piso *m*

stork /stɔːk/ *n* cigüeña *f*

storm /stɔːm/ *n* tempestad *f*; (*mil*) asalto *m*. —*vi* rabiar. —*vt* (*mil*) asaltar. ~**y** *a* tempestuoso

story /'stɔːrɪ/ *n* historia *f*; (*in newspaper*) artículo *m*; (*fam*) mentira *f*, cuento *m*. ~**-teller** *n* cuentista *m & f*

stout /staʊt/ *a* (**-er, -est**) (*fat*) gordo; (*brave*) valiente. —*n* cerveza *f* negra. ~**ness** *n* corpulencia *f*

stove /stəʊv/ *n* estufa *f*

stow /stəʊ/ *vt* guardar; (*hide*) esconder. —*vi*. ~ **away** viajar de polizón. ~away /ˈstɔːsweɪ/ n polizón m

straddle /ˈstrædl/ vt estar a horcajadas

straggle /ˈstrægl/ vi rezagarse. ~y a desordenado

straight /streɪt/ a (-er, -est) derecho, recto; (tidy) en orden; (frank) franco; (drink) solo, puro; (hair) lacio. —adv derecho; (direct) directamente; (without delay) inmediatamente. ~ on todo recto. ~ out sin vacilar. go ~ enmendarse. —n recta f. ~ away inmediatamente. ~en /ˈstreɪtn/ vt enderezar. —vi enderezarse. ~ forward /streɪtˈfɔːwəd/ a franco; (easy) sencillo. ~forwardly adv francamente. ~ness n rectitud f

strain[1] /streɪn/ n (tension) tensión f; (injury) torcedura f. —vt estirar; (tire) cansar; (injure) torcer; (sieve) colar

strain[2] /streɪn/ n (lineage) linaje m; (streak) tendencia f

strained /streɪnd/ a forzado; (relations) tirante

strainer /ˈstreɪnə(r)/ n colador m

strains /streɪnz/ npl (mus) acordes mpl

strait /streɪt/ n estrecho m. ~jacket n camisa f de fuerza. ~laced a remilgado, gazmoño. ~s npl apuro m

strand /strænd/ n (thread) hebra f; (sand) playa f. —vi (ship) varar. be ~ed quedarse sin recursos

strange /streɪndʒ/ a (-er, -est) extraño, raro; (not known) desconocido; (unaccustomed) nuevo. ~ly adv extrañamente. ~ness n extrañeza f. ~r /ˈstreɪndʒə(r)/ n desconocido m

strangle /ˈstræŋgl/ vt estrangular; (fig) ahogar. ~lehold /ˈstræŋglhəʊld/ n (fig) dominio m

completo. ~ler /-ə(r)/ n estrangulador m. ~ulation /ˈstræŋgjʊˈleɪʃn/ n estrangulación f

strap /stræp/ n correa f; (of garment) tirante m. —vt (pt strapped) atar con correa; (flog) azotar

strapping /ˈstræpɪŋ/ a robusto

strata /ˈstrɑːtə/ see **stratum**

stratagem /ˈstrætədʒəm/ n estratagema f. ~egic /strəˈtiːdʒɪk/ a estratégico. ~egically adv estratégicamente. ~egist n estratega m & f. ~egy /ˈstrætədʒɪ/ n estrategia f

stratum /ˈstrɑːtəm/ n (pl strata) estrato m

straw /strɔː/ n paja f. the last ~ el colmo

strawberry /ˈstrɔːbərɪ/ n fresa f

stray /streɪ/ vi vagar; (deviate) desviarse (from de). —a (animal) extraviado, callejero; (isolated) aislado. —n animal m extraviado, animal m callejero

streak /striːk/ n raya f; (of madness) vena f. —vt rayar. —vi moverse como un rayo. ~y a (-ier, -iest) rayado; (bacon) entreverado

stream /striːm/ n arroyo m; (current) corriente f; (of people) desfile m; (schol) grupo m. —vi correr. ~ out vi (people) salir en tropel

streamer /ˈstriːmə(r)/ n (paper) serpentina f; (flag) gallardete m

streamline /ˈstriːmlaɪn/ vt dar línea aerodinámica a; (simplify) simplificar. ~d a aerodinámico

street /striːt/ n calle f. ~car /ˈstriːtkɑː/ n (Amer) tranvía m. ~ lamp n farol m. ~ map n, ~ plan n plano m

strength /streŋθ/ n fuerza f; (of wall etc) solidez f. on the ~ of a base de. ~en /ˈstreŋθn/ vt reforzar

strenuous /'strenjʊəs/ a enérgico; (*arduous*) arduo; (*tiring*) fatigoso. ~**ly** *adv* enérgicamente

stress /stres/ n énfasis f; (*gram*) acento m; (*mec, med, tension*) tensión f. —*vt* insistir en

stretch /stretʃ/ vt estirar; (*extend*) extender; (*exaggerate*) forzar. ~ **a point** hacer una excepción. —*vi* estirarse; (*extend*) extenderse. —n estirón m; (*period*) período m; (*of road*) tramo m. **at a** ~ seguido; (*in one go*) de un tirón. ~**er** /'stretʃə(r)/ n camilla f

strew /struː/ vt (*pt* strewed, *pp* **strewn** *or* strewed) esparcir; (*cover*) cubrir

stricken /'strɪkən/ a. ~ **with** afectado con

strict /strɪkt/ a (-er, -est) severo; (*precise*) estricto, preciso. ~**ly** *adv* estrictamente. ~**ly speaking** en rigor

stricture /'strɪktʃə(r)/ n crítica f; (*constriction*) constricción f

stride /straɪd/ vi (*pt* strode, *pp* **stridden**) andar a zancadas. —n zancada f. **take sth in one's** ~ hacer algo con facilidad, tomarse las cosas con calma

strident /'straɪdnt/ a estridente

strife /straɪf/ n conflicto m

strike /straɪk/ vt (*pt* struck) golpear; encender (*match*); encontrar (*gold etc*); (*clock*) dar. ~ (*go on strike*) declararse en huelga; (*be on strike*) estar en huelga; (*attack*) atacar; (*clock*) dar la hora. —n (*of workers*) huelga f; (*attack*) ataque m; (*find*) descubrimiento m. **on** ~ en huelga. ~ **off**, ~ **out** tachar. ~ **up a friendship** trabar amistad. ~**r** /'straɪkə(r)/ n huelguista m & f

striking /'straɪkɪŋ/ a impresionante

string /strɪŋ/ n cuerda f; (*of lies, pearls*) sarta f. **pull** ~s tocar todos los resortes. —*vt* (*pt* **strung**) (*thread*) ensartar. ~ **along** (*fam*) engañar. ~ **out** extender(se). ~**ed** a (*mus*) de cuerda

stringen|cy /'strɪndʒənsɪ/ n rigor m. ~**t** /'strɪndʒənt/ a riguroso

stringy /'strɪŋɪ/ a fibroso

strip /strɪp/ vt (*pt* **stripped**) desnudar; (*tear away, deprive*) quitar; desmontar (*machine*). —*vi* desnudarse. —n tira f. ~**cartoon** n historieta f

stripe /straɪp/ n raya f; (*mil*) galón m. ~**d** a a rayas, rayado

strip-: ~ **light** n tubo m fluorescente. ~**per** /-ə(r)/ n artista m & f de striptease. ~**tease** n número m del desnudo, striptease m

strive /straɪv/ vi (*pt* strove, *pp* striven). ~ **to** esforzarse por

strode /strəʊd/ *see* stride

stroke /strəʊk/ n golpe m; (*in swimming*) brazada f; (*med*) apoplejía f; (*of pen etc*) rasgo m; (*of clock*) campanada f; (*caress*) caricia f. —*vt* acariciar

stroll /strəʊl/ vi pasearse. —n paseo m

strong /strɒŋ/ a (-er, -est) fuerte. ~**box** n caja f fuerte. ~**hold** /'strɒŋhəʊld/ n fortaleza f; (*fig*) baluarte m. ~ **language** n palabras fpl fuertes, palabras fpl subidas de tono. ~**ly** *adv* (*greatly*) fuertemente; (*with energy*) enérgicamente; (*deeply*) profundamente. ~ **measures** npl medidas fpl enérgicas. ~**-minded** a resuelto. ~**-room** n cámara f acorazada

stroppy /'strɒpɪ/ a (sl) irascible

strove /strəʊv/ *see* strive

struck /strʌk/ *see* strike. ~ **on** (sl) entusiasta de

structur|al /'strʌktʃərəl/ a estructural. **~e** /'strʌktʃə(r)/ n estructura f

struggle /'strʌgl/ vi luchar. **~ to one's feet** levantarse con dificultad. —n lucha f

strum /strʌm/ vt/i (pt **strummed**) rasguear

strung /strʌŋ/ see **string**. —a. **~ up** (tense) nervioso

strut /strʌt/ n puntal m; (walk) pavoneo m. —vi (pt **strutted**) pavonearse

stub /stʌb/ n cabo m; (counterfoil) talón m; (of cigarette) colilla f; (of tree) tocón m. **~ out** (pt **stubbed**) apagar

stubble /'stʌbl/ n rastrojo m; (beard) barba f de varios días

stubborn /'stʌbən/ a terco. **~ly** adv tercamente. **~ness** n terquedad f

stubby /'stʌbɪ/ a (-ier, -iest) achaparrado

stucco /'stʌkəʊ/ n (pl -oes) estuco m

stuck /stʌk/ see **stick**. —a. (jammed) bloqueado; (in difficulties) en un apuro. **~ on** (sl) encantado con. **~-up** a (sl) presumido

stud[1] /stʌd/ n tachón m; (for collar) botón m. —vt (pt **studded**) tachonar. **~ded with** sembrado de

stud[2] /stʌd/ n (of horses) caballeriza f

student /'stju:dənt/ n estudiante m & f

studied /'stʌdɪd/ a deliberado

studio /'stju:dɪəʊ/ n (pl -os) estudio m. **~ couch** n sofá m cama. **~ flat** n estudio m de artista

studious /'stju:dɪəs/ a estudioso; (studied) deliberado. **~ly** adv estudiosamente; (carefully) cuidadosamente

study /'stʌdɪ/ n estudio m; (office) despacho m. —vt/i estudiar

stuff /stʌf/ n materia f, sustancia f; (sl) cosas fpl. —vt rellenar; disecar (animal); (cram) atiborrar; (block up) tapar; (put) meter de prisa. **~ing** n relleno m

stuffy /'stʌfɪ/ a (-ier, -iest) mal ventilado; (old-fashioned) chapado a la antigua

stumble /'stʌmbl/ vi tropezar. **~e across**, **~e on** tropezar con. —n tropezón m. **~ing-block** n tropiezo m, impedimento m

stump /stʌmp/ n cabo m; (of limb) muñón m; (of tree) tocón m. **~ed** /stʌmpt/ a (fam) perplejo. **~y** /'stʌmpɪ/ a (-ier, -iest) achaparrado

stun /stʌn/ vt (pt **stunned**) aturdir; (bewilder) pasmar. **~ning** a (fabulous, fam) estupendo

stung /stʌŋ/ see **sting**

stunk /stʌŋk/ see **stink**

stunt[1] /stʌnt/ n (fam) truco m publicitario

stunt[2] /stʌnt/ vt impedir el desarrollo de. **~ed** a enano

stupefy /'stju:pɪfaɪ/ vt dejar estupefacto

stupendous /stju:'pendəs/ a estupendo. **~ly** adv estupendamente

stupid /'stju:pɪd/ a estúpido. **~ity** /-'pɪdətɪ/ n estupidez f. **~ly** adv estúpidamente

stupor /'stju:pə(r)/ n estupor m

sturd|iness /'stɜːdɪnɪs/ n robustez f. **~y** /'stɜːdɪ/ a (-ier, -iest) robusto

sturgeon /'stɜːdʒən/ n (pl **sturgeon**) esturión m

stutter /'stʌtə(r)/ vi tartamudear. —n tartamudeo m

sty[1] /staɪ/ n (pl **sties**) pocilga f

sty[2] /staɪ/ n (pl **sties**) (med) orzuelo m

styl|e /staɪl/ n estilo m; (fashion) moda f. **in ~** con todo lujo. —vt diseñar. **~ish** /'staɪlɪʃ/ a elegante. **~ishly** *adv* elegantemente. **~ist** /'staɪlɪst/ *n* estilista *m & f*. **hair ~ist** *n* peluquero *m*. **~ized** /staɪlaɪzd/ *a* estilizado

stylus /'staɪləs/ *n* (*pl* -**uses**) aguja *f* (de tocadiscos)

suave /swɑːv/ *a* (*pej*) zalamero

sub... /sʌb/ *pref* sub...

subaquatic /sʌbə'kwætɪk/ *a* subacuático

subconscious /sʌb'kɒnʃəs/ *a & n* subconsciente (*m*). **~ly** *adv* de modo subconsciente

subcontinent /sʌb'kɒntɪnənt/ *n* subcontinente *m*

subcontract /sʌbkən'trækt/ *vt* subcontratar. **~or** /-ə(r)/ *n* subcontratista *m & f*

subdivide /sʌbdɪ'vaɪd/ *vt* subdividir

subdue /səb'djuː/ *vt* dominar (*feelings*); sojuzgar (*country*). **~d** *a* (*depressed*) abatido; (*light*) suave

subhuman /sʌb'hjuːmən/ *a* infrahumano

subject /'sʌbdʒɪkt/ *a* sometido. **~ to** sujeto a. **—** *n* súbdito *m*; (*theme*) asunto *m*; (*schol*) asignatura *f*, (*gram*) sujeto *m*; (*of painting, play, book etc*) tema *m*. /səb'dʒekt/ *vt* sojuzgar; (*submit*) someter. **~ion** /-ʃn/ *n* sometimiento *m*

subjective /səb'dʒektɪv/ *a* subjetivo. **~ly** *adv* subjetivamente

subjugate /'sʌbdʒʊgeɪt/ *vt* subyugar

subjunctive /səb'dʒʌŋktɪv/ *a & n* subjuntivo (*m*)

sublet /sʌb'let/ *vt* (*pt* sublet, *pres p* subletting) subarrendar

sublimate /'sʌblɪmeɪt/ *vt* sublimar. **~ion** /-'meɪʃn/ *n* sublimación *f*

sublime /sə'blaɪm/ *a* sublime. **~ly** *adv* sublimemente

submarine /sʌbmə'riːn/ *n* submarino *m*

submerge /səb'mɜːdʒ/ *vt* sumergir. **—vi** sumergirse

submission /səb'mɪʃn/ *n* sumisión *f*. **~ssive** /-sɪv/ *a* sumiso. **~t** /səb'mɪt/ *vt* (*pt* submitted) someter. **—vi** someterse

subordinate /sə'bɔːdɪnət/ *a & n* subordinado (*m*). /sə'bɔːdɪneɪt/ *vt* subordinar. **~ion** /-'neɪʃn/ *n* subordinación *f*

subscribe /səb'skraɪb/ *vi* suscribir. **~be to** suscribir (*fund*); (*agree*) estar de acuerdo con; abonarse a (*newspaper*). **~ber** /-ə(r)/ *n* abonado *m*. **~ption** /-rɪpʃn/ *n* suscripción *f*

subsequent /'sʌbsɪkwənt/ *a* subsiguiente. **~ly** *adv* posteriormente

subservient /səb'sɜːvjənt/ *a* servil

subside /səb'saɪd/ *vi* (*land*) hundirse; (*flood*) bajar; (*storm, wind*) amainar. **~nce** *n* hundimiento *m*

subsidiary /səb'sɪdɪərɪ/ *a* subsidiario. **—n** (*com*) sucursal *m*

subsidize /'sʌbsɪdaɪz/ *vt* subvencionar. **~y** /'sʌbsədɪ/ *n* subvención *f*

subsist /səb'sɪst/ *vi* subsistir. **~ence** *n* subsistencia *f*

subsoil /'sʌbsɔɪl/ *n* subsuelo *m*

subsonic /sʌb'sɒnɪk/ *a* subsónico

substance /'sʌbstəns/ *n* substancia *f*

substandard /sʌb'stændəd/ *a* inferior

substantial /səb'stænʃl/ *a* sólido; (*meal*) substancial; (*considerable*) considerable. **~ly** *adv* considerablemente

substantiate /səb'stænʃɪeɪt/ *vt* justificar

substitute /'sʌbstɪtjuːt/ *n* substituto *m*. **—vt/i** substituir. **~ion** /-'tjuːʃn/ *n* substitución *f*

subterfuge /'sʌbtəfjuːdʒ/ n subterfugio m

subterranean /sʌbtə'reɪnjən/ a subterráneo

subtitle /'sʌbtaɪtl/ n subtítulo m. ~ty n sutileza f

subtle /'sʌtl/ a (-er, -est) sutil. ~ty n sutileza f

subtract /səb'trækt/ vt restar. ~ion /-ʃn/ n resta f

suburb /'sʌbɜːb/ n barrio m. the ~s las afueras fpl. ~an /sə'bɜːbən/ a suburbano. ~ia /sə'bɜːbɪə/ n las afueras fpl

subvention /səb'venʃn/ n subvención f

subver|sion /səb'vɜːʃn/ n subversión f. ~sive /səb'vɜːsɪv/ a subversivo. ~t /səb'vɜːt/ vt subvertir

subway /'sʌbweɪ/ n paso m subterráneo; (Amer) metro m

succeed /sək'siːd/ vi tener éxito. —vt suceder a. ~ in doing lograr hacer. ~ing a sucesivo

success /sək'ses/ n éxito m. ~ful a que tiene éxito; (chosen) elegido

succession /sək'seʃn/ n sucesión f. in ~ sucesivamente, seguidos

successive /sək'sesɪv/ a sucesivo. ~ly adv sucesivamente

successor /sək'sesə(r)/ n sucesor m

succinct /sək'sɪŋkt/ a sucinto

succour /'sʌkə(r)/ vt socorrer. — n socorro m

succulent /'sʌkjʊlənt/ a suculento

succumb /sə'kʌm/ vi sucumbir

such /sʌtʃ/ a tal. —pron lo que, las que; (so much) tanto. and ~ y tal. —adv tan. ~ a big house una casa tan grande. ~ and tal o cual. ~ as it is tal como es. ~like a (fam) semejante, de ese tipo

suck /sʌk/ vt chupar; sorber ‹liquid›. ~ up absorber. ~ up to

(sl) dar coba a. ~er /'sʌkə(r)/ n (plant) chupón m; (person, fam) primo m

suckle /'sʌkl/ vt amamantar

suction /'sʌkʃn/ n succión f

sudden /'sʌdn/ a repentino. all of a ~ de repente. ~ly adv de repente. ~ness n lo repentino

suds /sʌdz/ npl espuma f (de jabón)

sue /suː/ vt (pres p suing) demandar (for por)

suede /sweɪd/ n ante m

suet /'suːɪt/ n sebo m

suffer /'sʌfə(r)/ vt sufrir; (tolerate) tolerar. —vi sufrir. ~ance /'sʌfərəns/ n. on ~ance por tolerancia. ~ing n sufrimiento m

suffic|e /sə'faɪs/ vi bastar. ~iency /sə'fɪʃənsɪ/ n suficiencia f. ~ient /sə'fɪʃnt/ a suficiente; (enough) bastante. ~iently adv suficientemente, bastante

suffix /'sʌfɪks/ n (pl -ixes) sufijo m

suffocat|e /'sʌfəkeɪt/ vt ahogar. —vi ahogarse. ~ion /-'keɪʃn/ n asfixia f

sugar /'ʃʊgə(r)/ n azúcar m & f. —vt azucarar. ~-bowl n azucarero m. ~ lump n terrón m de azúcar. ~y a azucarado

suggest /sə'dʒest/ vt sugerir. ~ible /sə'dʒestɪbl/ a sugestionable. ~ion /-tʃən/ n sugerencia f; (trace) traza f. ~ive /sə'dʒestɪv/ a sugestivo. be ~ive of evocar, recordar. ~ively adv sugestivamente

suicid|al /suːɪ'saɪdl/ a suicida. ~e /'suːɪsaɪd/ n suicidio m; (person) suicida m & f. commit ~e suicidarse

suit /suːt/ n traje m; (woman's) traje m de chaqueta; (cards) palo m; (jurid) pleito m. —vt convenir; ‹clothes› sentar bien a; (adapt) adaptar. be ~ed for ser apto para. **~ability** n conveniencia f. **~able** a adecuado. **~ably** adv convenientemente. **~case** /'suːtkeɪs/ n maleta f, valija f (LAm)

suite /swiːt/ n (of furniture) juego m; (of rooms) apartamento m; (retinue) séquito m

suitor /'suːtə(r)/ n pretendiente m

sulk /sʌlk/ vi enfurruñarse. **~s** npl enfurruñamiento m. **~y** a enfurruñado

sullen /'sʌlən/ a resentido. **~ly** adv con resentimiento

sully /'sʌlɪ/ vt manchar

sulphur /'sʌlfə(r)/ n azufre m. **~ic** /-'fjʊərɪk/ a sulfúrico. **~ic acid** n ácido m sulfúrico

sultan /'sʌltən/ n sultán m

sultana /sʌl'tɑːnə/ n pasa f gorrona

sultry /'sʌltrɪ/ a (-ier, -iest) (weather) bochornoso; (fig) sensual

sum /sʌm/ n suma f. —vt (pt summed). **~ up** resumir (situation); (assess) evaluar

summar|ily /'sʌmərɪlɪ/ adv sumariamente. **~ize** vt resumir. **~y** /'sʌmərɪ/ a sumario. —n resumen m

summer /'sʌmə(r)/ n verano m. **~house** n glorieta f, cenador m. **~time** n verano m. **~ time** hora f de verano. **~y** a veraniego

summit /'sʌmɪt/ n cumbre f. **~ conference** n conferencia f cumbre

summon /'sʌmən/ vt llamar; convocar (meeting, s.o. to meeting); (jurid) citar. **~ up** armarse de. **~s** /'sʌmənz/ n llamada f; (jurid) citación f. —vt citar

sump /sʌmp/ n (mec) cárter m

sumptuous /'sʌmptjʊəs/ a suntuoso. **~ly** adv suntuosamente

sun /sʌn/ n sol m. —vt (pt sunned). **~ o.s.** tomar el sol.

~bathe /'sʌnbeɪð/ vi tomar el sol. **~beam** /'sʌnbiːm/ n rayo m de sol. **~burn** /'sʌnbɜːn/ n quemadura f de sol. **~burnt** a quemado por el sol

sundae /'sʌndeɪ/ n helado m con frutas y nueces

Sunday /'sʌndeɪ/ n domingo m. **~ school** n catequesis f

sun: ~dial /'sʌndaɪl/ n reloj m de sol. **~down** /'sʌndaʊn/ n puesta f del sol

sundry /'sʌndrɪ/ a diversos. **all and ~** todo el mundo. **sundries** npl artículos mpl diversos

sunflower /'sʌnflaʊə(r)/ n girasol m

sung /sʌŋ/ see **sing**

sun-glasses /'sʌnglɑːsɪz/ npl gafas fpl de sol

sunk /sʌŋk/ see **sink**. **~en** /'sʌŋkən/ —a hundido

sunlight /'sʌnlaɪt/ n luz f del sol

sunny /'sʌnɪ/ a (-ier, -iest) (day) de sol; (place) soleado. **it is ~** hace sol

sun: ~rise /'sʌnraɪz/ n amanecer m, salida f del sol. **~roof** n techo m corredizo. **~set** /'sʌnset/ n puesta f del sol. **~shade** /'sʌnʃeɪd/ n quitasol m, sombrilla f; (awning) toldo m. **~shine** /'sʌnʃaɪn/ n sol m. **~spot** /'sʌnspɒt/ n mancha f solar. **~stroke** /'sʌnstrəʊk/ n insolación f. **~tan** n bronceado m. **~tanned** a bronceado. **~tan lotion** n bronceador m

sup /sʌp/ vt (pt supped) sorber

super /'suːpə(r)/ a (fam) estupendo

superannuation /suːpərænjʊ-'eɪʃn/ n jubilación f

superb /suː'pɜːb/ a espléndido. **~ly** adv espléndidamente

supercilious /suːpə'sɪlɪəs/ a desdeñoso

superficial /su:pə'fɪʃl/ a superficial. ~ity /-ɪ'ælətɪ/ n superficialidad f. ~ly adv superficialmente

superfluous /su:'pɜ:fluəs/ a superfluo

superhuman /su:pə'hju:mən/ a sobrehumano

superimpose /su:pərɪm'pəʊz/ vt sobreponer

superintend /su:pərɪn'tend/ vt vigilar. ~ence n dirección f. ~ent n director m; (of police) comisario m

superior /su:'pɪərɪə(r)/ a & n superior (m). ~ity /-'ɒrətɪ/ n superioridad f

superlative /su:'pɜ:lətɪv/ a & n superlativo (m)

superman /'su:pəmæn/ n (pl -men) superhombre m

supermarket /'su:pəma:kɪt/ n supermercado m

supernatural /su:pə'nætʃrəl/ a sobrenatural

superpower /'su:pəpaʊə(r)/ n superpotencia f

supersede /su:pə'si:d/ vt reemplazar, suplantar

supersonic /su:pə'sɒnɪk/ a supersónico

superstition /su:pə'stɪʃn/ n superstición f. ~us a supersticioso

superstructure /'su:pəstrʌktʃə(r)/ n superestructura f

supertanker /'su:pətæŋkə(r)/ n petrolero m gigante

supervene /su:pə'vi:n/ vi sobrevenir

supervis|e /'su:pəvaɪz/ vt supervisar. ~ion /-'vɪʒn/ n supervisión f. ~or /-zə(r)/ n supervisor m. ~ory a de supervisión

supper /'sʌpə(r)/ n cena f

supplant /sə'plɑ:nt/ vt suplantar

supple /sʌpl/ a flexible. ~ness n flexibilidad f

supplement /'sʌplɪmənt/ n suplemento m. —vt completar; (increase) aumentar. ~ary /-'mentərɪ/ a suplementario

supplier /sə'plaɪə(r)/ n suministrador m; (com) proveedor m. ~y /sə'plaɪ/ vt proveer; (feed) alimentar; satisfacer (a need). ~y with abastecer de. —n provisión f, suministro m. ~y and demand oferta f y demanda

support /sə'pɔ:t/ vt sostener; (endure) soportar, aguantar; (fig) apoyar. —n apoyo m; (tec) soporte m. ~er /-ə(r)/ n soporte m; (sport) seguidor m, hincha m & f. ~ive a alentador

suppose /sə'pəʊz/ vt suponer; (think) creer. be ~ed to deber. not be ~ed to (fam) no tener permiso para, no tener derecho a. ~edly adv según cabe suponer; (before adjective) presuntamente. ~ition /sʌpə'zɪʃn/ n suposición f

suppository /sə'pɒzɪtərɪ/ n supositorio m

suppress /sə'pres/ vt suprimir. ~ion n supresión f. ~or /-ə(r)/ n supresor m

suprem|acy /su:'preməsɪ/ n supremacía f. ~e /su:'pri:m/ a supremo

surcharge /'sɜ:tʃɑ:dʒ/ n sobreprecio m; (tax) recargo m

sure /ʃʊə(r)/ a (-er, -est) seguro, cierto. make ~ asegurarse. — adv (Amer, fam) ¡claro! ~ enough efectivamente. ~ footed a de pie firme. ~ly adv seguramente

surety /'ʃʊərətɪ/ n garantía f

surf /sɜ:f/ n oleaje m; (foam) espuma f

surface /'sɜ:fɪs/ n superficie f. — a superficial, de la superficie. — vt (smoothe) alisar; (cover) recubrir (with de). —vi salir a la

superficie; (*emerge*) emerger. ~
mail n por vía marítima

surfboard /'sɜːfbɔːd/ n tabla f de
surf

surfeit /'sɜːfɪt/ n exceso m

surfing /'sɜːfɪŋ/ n, **surf-riding**
/'sɜːfraɪdɪŋ/ n surf m

surge /sɜːdʒ/ vi (*crowd*) moverse
en tropel; (*waves*) encres-
parse. —n oleada f; (*elec*) sobre-
tensión f

surgeon /'sɜːdʒən/ n cirujano m

surgery /'sɜːdʒərɪ/ n cirugía f;
(*consulting room*) consultorio m;
(*consulting hours*) horas fpl de
consulta

surgical /'sɜːrdʒɪkl/ a quirúrgico

surliness /'sɜːlɪnɪs/ n aspereza f.
~y /'sɜːlɪ/ a (-ier, -iest) áspero

surmise /sə'maɪz/ vt conjeturar

surmount /sə'maunt/ vt superar

surname /'sɜːneɪm/ n apellido m

surpass /sə'pɑːs/ vt sobrepasar,
exceder

surplus /'sɜːpləs/ a & n excedente (m)

surprise /sə'praɪz/ n sorpresa
f. —vt sorprender. ~ing a sorprendente. ~ingly adv asom-
brosamente

surrealism /sə'rɪəlɪzəm/ n su-
rrealismo m. ~t n surrealista m
& f

surrender /sə'rendə(r)/ vt entregar. —vi entregarse. —n entrega
f; (*mil*) rendición f

surreptitious /sʌrəp'tɪʃəs/ a
clandestino

surrogate /'sʌrəgət/ n substituto
m

surround /sə'raund/ vt rodear;
(*mil*) cercar. —n borde m. ~ing
a circundante. ~ings npl al-
rededores mpl

surveillance /sɜː'veɪləns/ n
vigilancia f

survey /'sɜːveɪ/ n inspección f;
(*report*) informe m; (*general
view*) vista f de conjunto. /sə'veɪ/

vt examinar, inspeccionar;
(*inquire into*) hacer una
encuesta de. ~or n topógrafo m,
agrimensor m

survival /sə'vaɪvl/ n super-
vivencia f. ~e /sə'vaɪv/ vt/i sobrevivir. ~or /-ə(r)/ n superviviente
m & f

susceptibility /səseptə'bɪlətɪ/ n
susceptibilidad f. ~le /sə-
'septəbl/ a susceptible. ~le to
propenso a

suspect /sə'spekt/ vt sospechar.
/'sʌspekt/ a & n sospechoso (m)

suspend /sə'spend/ vt suspender.
~er /sə'spendə(r)/ n liga f. ~er
belt n liguero m. ~ers npl
(*Amer*) tirantes mpl

suspense /sə'spens/ n incertidumbre f; (*in film etc*) suspense
m

suspension /sə'spenʃn/ n suspensión f. ~ bridge n puente m
colgante

suspicion /sə'spɪʃn/ n sospecha f;
(*trace*) pizca f

suspicious /sə'spɪʃəs/ a descon-
fiado; (*causing suspicion*)
sospechoso

sustain /sə'steɪn/ vt sostener;
(*suffer*) sufrir

sustenance /'sʌstɪnəns/ n sustento m

svelte /svelt/ a esbelto

SW abbr (*south-west*) sudoeste m

swab /swɒb/ n (*med*) tapón m

swagger /'swægə(r)/ vi pavonearse

swallow[1] /'swɒləʊ/ vt/i tragar.
—n trago m. ~ up tragar; consumir (*savings etc*)

swallow[2] /'swɒləʊ/ n (*bird*)
golondrina f

swam /swæm/ see **swim**

swamp /swɒmp/ n pantano m. —
vt inundar; (*with work*) agobiar.
~y a pantanoso

swan /swɒn/ n cisne m

swank /swæŋk/ n (fam) ostentación f. —vi (fam) fanfarronear

swap /swɒp/ vt/i (pt **swapped**) (fam) (inter)cambiar. —n (fam) (inter)cambio m

swarm /swɔːm/ n enjambre m. —vi ⟨bees⟩ enjambrar; (fig) hormiguear

swarthy /ˈswɔːðɪ/ a (-ier, -iest) moreno

swastika /ˈswɒstɪkə/ n cruz f gamada

swat /swɒt/ vt (pt **swatted**) aplastar

sway /sweɪ/ vi balancearse. —vt ⟨influence⟩ influir en. —n balanceo m; ⟨rule⟩ imperio m

swear /sweə(r)/ vt/i (pt **swore**, pp **sworn**) jurar. **~ by** (fam) creer ciegamente en. **~word** n palabrota f

sweat /swet/ n sudor m. —vi sudar

sweat|er /ˈswetə(r)/ n jersey m. **~shirt** n sudadera f

swede /swiːd/ n naba f

Swede /swiːd/ n sueco m

Sweden /ˈswiːdn/ n Suecia f

Swedish /ˈswiːdɪʃ/ a & n sueco (m)

sweep /swiːp/ vt (pt **swept**) barrer; deshollinar ⟨chimney⟩. **~ the board** ganar todo. —vi barrer; ⟨road⟩ extenderse; ⟨go majestically⟩ moverse majestuosamente. —n barrido m; ⟨curve⟩ curva f; ⟨movement⟩ movimiento m; ⟨person⟩ deshollinador m. **~ away** vt barrer. **~ing** a amplio; ⟨changes etc⟩ radical; ⟨statement⟩ demasiado general. **~stake** n /ˈswiːpsteɪk/ n lotería f

sweet /swiːt/ a (-er, -est) dulce; ⟨fragrant⟩ fragante; ⟨pleasant⟩ agradable. **have a ~ tooth** ser dulcero. —n caramelo m; ⟨dish⟩ postre m. **~bread** n /ˈswiːtbred/ n lechecillas fpl. **~en** /ˈswiːtn/ vt

endulzar. **~ener** /-ə(r)/ n dulcificante m. **~heart** /ˈswiːthɑːt/ n amor m. **~ly** adv dulcemente. **~ness** n dulzura f. **~ pea** n guisante m de olor

swell /swel/ vt (pt **swelled**, pp **swollen** or **swelled**) hinchar; ⟨increase⟩ aumentar. —vi hincharse; ⟨increase⟩ aumentarse; ⟨river⟩ crecer. —a (fam) estupendo. —n ⟨of sea⟩ oleaje m. **~ing** n hinchazón m

swelter /ˈsweltə(r)/ vi sofocarse de calor

swept /swept/ see **sweep**

swerve /swɜːv/ vi desviarse

swift /swɪft/ a (-er, -est) rápido. —n ⟨bird⟩ vencejo m. **~ly** adv rápidamente. **~ness** n rapidez f

swig /swɪɡ/ vt (pt **swigged**) (fam) beber a grandes tragos. —n (fam) trago m

swill /swɪl/ vt enjuagar; ⟨drink⟩ beber a grandes tragos. —n ⟨food for pigs⟩ bazofia f

swim /swɪm/ vi (pt **swam**, pp **swum**) nadar; ⟨room, head⟩ dar vueltas. —n baño m. **~mer** n nadador m. **~ming-bath** n piscina f. **~mingly** /ˈswɪmɪŋlɪ/ adv a las mil maravillas. **~ming-pool** n piscina f. **~ming-trunks** npl bañador m. **~suit** n traje m de baño

swindle /ˈswɪndl/ vt estafar. —n estafa f. **~r** /-ə(r)/ n estafador m

swine /swaɪn/ npl cerdos mpl. —n ⟨pl **swine**⟩ ⟨person, fam⟩ canalla m

swing /swɪŋ/ vt (pt **swung**) balancear. —vi oscilar; ⟨person⟩ balancearse; ⟨turn round⟩ girar. —n balanceo m, vaivén m; ⟨seat⟩ columpio m; ⟨mus⟩ ritmo m. **in full ~** en plena actividad. **~ bridge** n puente m giratorio

swingeing /ˈswɪndʒɪŋ/ a enorme

swipe /swaip/ *vt* golpear; (*snatch, sl*) birlar. —*n* (*fam*) golpe *m*

swirl /swɜ:l/ *vi* arremolinarse. —*n* remolino *m*

swish /swiʃ/ *vt* silbar. —*a* (*fam*) elegante

Swiss /swis/ *a* & *n* suizo (*m*). ~ **roll** *n* bizcocho *m* enrollado

switch /switʃ/ *n* (*elec*) interruptor *m*; (*change*) cambio *m*. —*vt* cambiar; (*deviate*) desviar. ~ **off** (*elec*) desconectar; apagar (*light*). ~ **on** (*elec*) encender; arrancar (*engine*). ~**back** /'switʃbæk/ *n* montaña *f* rusa. ~**board** /'switʃbɔ:d/ *n* centralita *f*

Switzerland /'switsələnd/ *n* Suiza *f*

swivel /'swivl/ —*vi* (*pt* **swivelled**) girar

swollen /'swəʊlən/ *see* **swell**. —*a* hinchado

swoon /swu:n/ *vi* desmayarse

swoop /swu:p/ *vi* (*bird*) calarse; (*plane*) bajar en picado. —*n* calada *f*; (*by police*) redada *f*

sword /sɔ:d/ *n* espada *f*. ~**fish** /'sɔ:dfiʃ/ *n* pez *m* espada

swore /swɔ:(r)/ *see* **swear**

sworn /swɔ:n/ *see* **swear**. —*a* (*enemy*) jurado; (*friend*) leal

swot /swɒt/ *vt*/*i* (*pt* **swotted**) (*schol, sl*) empollar. —*n* (*schol, sl*) empollón *m*

swum /swʌm/ *see* **swim**

swung /swʌŋ/ *see* **swing**

sycamore /'sɪkəmɔ:(r)/ *n* plátano *m* falso

syllable /'sɪləbl/ *n* sílaba *f*

syllabus /'sɪləbəs/ *n* (*pl* **-buses**) programa *m* (de estudios)

symbol /'sɪmbl/ *n* símbolo *m*. ~**ic(al)** /-'bɒlɪk(l)/ *a* simbólico. ~**ism** *n* simbolismo *m*. ~**ize** *vt* simbolizar

symmetr|ical /sɪ'metrɪkl/ *a* simétrico. ~**y** /'sɪmɪtrɪ/ *n* simetría *f*

sympath|etic /sɪmpə'θetɪk/ *a* comprensivo; (*showing pity*) compasivo. ~**ize** /-aɪz/ *vi* comprender; (*pity*) compadecerse (**with de**). ~**izer** *n* (*pol*) simpatizante *m* & *f*. ~**y** /'sɪmpəθɪ/ *n* comprensión *f*; (*pity*) compasión *f*; (*condolences*) pésame *m*. **be in** ~**y with** estar de acuerdo con

symphon|ic /sɪm'fɒnɪk/ *a* sinfónico. ~**y** /'sɪmfənɪ/ *n* sinfonía *f*

symposium /sɪm'pəʊzɪəm/ *n* (*pl* **-ia**) simposio *m*

symptom /'sɪmptəm/ *n* síntoma *m*. ~**atic** /-'mætɪk/ *a* sintomático

synagogue /'sɪnəgɒg/ *n* sinagoga *f*

synchroniz|ation /sɪŋkrənaɪ'zeɪʃn/ *n* sincronización *f*. ~**e** /'sɪŋkrənaɪz/ *vt* sincronizar

syncopat|e /'sɪŋkəpeɪt/ *vt* sincopar. ~**ion** /-'peɪʃn/ *n* síncopa *f*

syndicate /'sɪndɪkət/ *n* sindicato *m*

syndrome /'sɪndrəʊm/ *n* síndrome *m*

synod /'sɪnəd/ *n* sínodo *m*

synonym /'sɪnənɪm/ *n* sinónimo *m*. ~**ous** /-'nɒnɪməs/ *a* sinónimo

synopsis /sɪ'nɒpsɪs/ *n* (*pl* **-opses** /-si:z/) sinopsis *f*, resumen *m*

syntax /'sɪntæks/ *n* sintaxis *f* invar

synthesis /'sɪnθəsɪs/ *n* (*pl* **-theses** /-si:z/) síntesis *f*. ~**ze** *vt* sintetizar

synthetic /sɪn'θetɪk/ *a* sintético

syphilis /'sɪfɪlɪs/ *n* sífilis *f*

Syria /'sɪrɪə/ *n* Siria *f*. ~**n** *a* & *n* sirio (*m*)

syringe /'sɪrɪndʒ/ *n* jeringa *f*. —*vt* jeringar

syrup /'sɪrəp/ *n* jarabe *m*, almíbar *m*; (*treacle*) melaza *f*. ~**y** *a* almibarado

system /'sɪstəm/ *n* sistema *m*; (*body*) organismo *m*; (*order*) método *m*. ~**atic** /-ə'mætɪk/ *a* sistemático. ~**atically**

tab 582 take

/-ə'mætɪklɪ/ adv sistemáticamente. **~s analyst** n analista m & f de sistemas

T

tab /tæb/ n (flap) lengüeta f; (label) etiqueta f. **keep ~s on** (fam) vigilar
tabby /'tæbɪ/ n gato m atigrado
tabernacle /'tæbənækl/ n tabernáculo m
table /'teɪbl/ n mesa f; (list) tabla f. **~ of contents** índice m. —vt presentar; (postpone) aplazar. **~cloth** n mantel m. **~mat** n salvamanteles m invar. **~spoon** /'teɪblspuːn/ n cucharón m, cuchara f sopera. **~spoonful** n (pl **-fuls**) cucharada f
tablet /'tæblɪt/ n (of stone) lápida f; (pill) tableta f; (of soap etc) pastilla f
table tennis /'teɪbltenɪs/ n tenis m de mesa, ping-pong m
tabloid /'tæblɔɪd/ n tabloide m
taboo /tə'buː/ a & n tabú (m)
tabulator /'tæbjʊleɪtə(r)/ n tabulador m
tacit /'tæsɪt/ a tácito
taciturn /'tæsɪtɜːn/ a taciturno
tack /tæk/ n tachuela f; (stitch) hilván m; (naut) virada f; (fig) línea f de conducta. —vt sujetar con tachuelas; (sew) hilvanar. **~ on** añadir. —vi virar
tackle /'tækl/ n (equipment) equipo m; (football) placaje m. —vt abordar (problem etc); (in rugby) hacer un placaje a
tacky /'tækɪ/ a pegajoso; (in poor taste) vulgar, de pacotilla
tact /tækt/ n tacto m. **~ful** a discreto. **~fully** adv discretamente
tactical /'tæktɪkl/ a táctico. **~s** /'tæktɪks/ npl táctica f
tactile /'tæktaɪl/ a táctil

tact: **~less** a indiscreto. **~lessly** adv indiscretamente
tadpole /'tædpəʊl/ n renacuajo m
tag /tæg/ n (on shoe-lace) herrete m; (label) etiqueta f. —vt (pt **tagged**) poner etiqueta a; (trail) seguir. —vi. **~ along** (fam) seguir
tail /teɪl/ n cola f. **~s** npl (tail-coat) frac m; (of coin) cruz f. —vt (sl) seguir. —vi. **~ off** disminuir. **~end** n extremo m final, cola f
tailor /'teɪlə(r)/ n sastre m. —vt confeccionar. **~-made** a hecho a la medida. **~-made for** (fig) hecho para
tailplane /'teɪlpleɪn/ n plano m de cola
taint /teɪnt/ n mancha f. —vt contaminar
take /teɪk/ vt (pt **took**, pp **taken**) tomar, coger (not LAm), agarrar (esp LAm); (contain) contener; (capture) capturar; (endure) aguantar; (require) requerir; tomar (bath); dar (walk); (carry) llevar; (accompany) acompañar; presentarse para (exam); sacar (photo); ganar (prize). **~ advantage of** aprovechar. **~ after** parecerse a. **~ away** quitar. **~ back** retirar (statement etc). **~ in** achicar (garment); (understand) comprender; (deceive) engañar. **~ off** quitarse (clothes); (mimic) imitar; (aviat) despegar. **~ o.s. off** marcharse. **~ on** (undertake) emprender; contratar (employee). **~ out** (remove) sacar. **~ over** tomar posesión de; (assume control) tomar el poder. **~ part** participar. **~ place** tener lugar. **~ sides** tomar partido. **~ to** dedicarse a; (like) tomar simpatía a (person); (like) aficionarse a (thing). **~ up** dedicarse a (hobby); (occupy) ocupar; (resume) rea-

nudar. ~ **up with** trabar amistad con. **be ~n ill** ponerse enfermo. —n presa f; ⟨photo, cinema, TV⟩ toma f

takings /'teɪkɪŋz/ npl ingresos mpl

take: ~**-off** n despegue m. ~**-over** n toma f de posesión.

talcum /'tælkəm/ n. ~ **powder** n ⟨polvos mpl de⟩ talco (m)

tale /teɪl/ n cuento m

talent /'tælənt/ n talento m. ~**ed** a talentoso

talisman /'tælɪzmən/ n talismán m

talk /tɔːk/ vt/i hablar. ~ **about** hablar de. ~ **over** discutir. —n conversación f; ⟨lecture⟩ conferencia f. **small** ~ charla f. ~**ative** a hablador. ~**er** n hablador m; ⟨chatterbox⟩ parlanchín m. ~**ing-to** n represión f

tall /tɔːl/ a (-er, -est) alto. ~ **story** n ⟨fam⟩ historia f inverosímil. **that's a ~ order** n ⟨fam⟩ eso es pedir mucho

tallboy /'tɔːlbɔɪ/ n cómoda f alta

tally /'tælɪ/ n tarja f; ⟨total⟩ total m. —vi corresponder (**with** a)

talon /'tælən/ n garra f

tambourine /tæmbə'riːn/ n pandereta f

tame /teɪm/ a (-er, -est) ⟨animal⟩ doméstico; ⟨person⟩ dócil; ⟨dull⟩ insípido. —vt domesticar; domar ⟨wild animal⟩. ~**ly** adv dócilmente. ~**r** /-ə(r)/ n domador m

tamper /'tæmpə(r)/ vi. ~ **with** manosear; ⟨alter⟩ alterar, falsificar

tampon /'tæmpən/ n tampón m

tan /tæn/ vt (pt **tanned**) curtir ⟨hide⟩; ⟨sun⟩ broncear. —vi ponerse moreno. —n bronceado m. —a ⟨colour⟩ de color canela

tandem /'tændəm/ n tándem m

tang /tæŋ/ n sabor m fuerte; ⟨smell⟩ olor m fuerte

tangent /'tændʒənt/ n tangente f

tangerine /tændʒə'riːn/ n mandarina f

tangible /'tændʒəbl/ a tangible. ~**y** adv perceptiblemente

tangle /'tæŋgl/ vt enredar. —vi enredarse. —n enredo m

tango /'tæŋgəʊ/ n (pl -os) tango m

tank /tæŋk/ n depósito m; ⟨mil⟩ tanque m

tankard /'tæŋkəd/ n jarra f, bock m

tanker /'tæŋkə(r)/ n petrolero m; ⟨truck⟩ camión m cisterna

tantaliz|e /'tæntəlaɪz/ vt atormentar. ~**ing** a atormentador; ⟨tempting⟩ tentador

tantamount /'tæntəmaʊnt/ a. ~ **to** equivalente a

tantrum /'tæntrəm/ n rabieta f

tap[1] /tæp/ n grifo m. **on** ~ disponible. —vt explotar ⟨resources⟩; interceptar ⟨phone⟩

tap[2] /tæp/ n ⟨knock⟩ golpe m ligero. —vt (pt **tapped**) golpear ligeramente. ~**-dance** n zapateado m

tape /teɪp/ n cinta f. —vt atar con cinta; ⟨record⟩ grabar. **have sth** ~**d** ⟨sl⟩ comprender perfectamente. ~**-measure** n cinta f métrica

taper /'teɪpə(r)/ n bujía f. —vt ahusar. —vi ahusarse. ~ **off** disminuir

tape: ~ **recorder** n magnetofón m, magnétofono m. ~ **recording** n grabación f

tapestry /'tæpɪstrɪ/ n tapicería f; ⟨product⟩ tapiz m

tapioca /tæpɪ'əʊkə/ n tapioca f

tar /tɑː(r)/ n alquitrán m. —vt (pt **tarred**) alquitranar

tard|ily /'tɑːdɪlɪ/ adv lentamente; ⟨late⟩ tardíamente. ~**y** /'tɑːdɪ/ a (-ier, -iest) ⟨slow⟩ lento; ⟨late⟩ tardío

target /'tɑːgɪt/ n blanco m; ⟨fig⟩ objetivo m

tariff /'tærɪf/ n tarifa f

tarmac /'tɑːmæk/ n pista f de aterrizaje. **T~** n (P) macádan m

tarnish /'tɑːnɪʃ/ vt deslustrar. —vi deslustrarse

tarpaulin /tɑː'pɔːlɪn/ n alquitranado m

tarragon /'tærəgən/ n estragón m

tart[1] /tɑːt/ n pastel m; (individual) pastelillo m

tart[2] /tɑːt/ n (sl, woman) prostituta f, fulana f (fam). —vt. **~ o.s. up** (fam) engalanarse

tart[3] /tɑːt/ a (-er, -est) ácido; (fig) áspero

tartan /'tɑːtn/ n tartán m, tela f escocesa

tartar /'tɑːtə(r)/ n tártaro m. **~ sauce** n salsa f tártara

task /tɑːsk/ n tarea f. **take to ~** reprender. **~ force** n destacamiento m especial

tassel /'tæsl/ n borla f

tast|e /teɪst/ n sabor m, gusto m; (small quantity) poquito m. —vt probar. —vi. **~e of** saber a. **~eful** a de buen gusto. **~eless** a soso; (fig) de mal gusto. **~y** a (-ier, -iest) sabroso

tat /tæt/ see **tit**[2]

tatter|ed /'tætəd/ a hecho jirones. **~s** /'tætəz/ npl andrajos mpl

tattle /'tætl/ vi charlar. —n charla f

tattoo[1] /tə'tuː/ n (mil) espectáculo m militar

tattoo[2] /tə'tuː/ vt tatuar. —n tatuaje m

tatty /'tætɪ/ a (-ier, -iest) gastado, en mal estado

taught /tɔːt/ see **teach**

taunt /tɔːnt/ vt mofarse de. **~ s.o. with sth** echar algo en cara a uno. —n mofa f

Taurus /'tɔːrəs/ n (astr) Tauro m

taut /tɔːt/ a tenso

tavern /'tævən/ n taberna f

tawdry /'tɔːdrɪ/ a (-ier, -iest) charro

tawny /'tɔːnɪ/ a bronceado

tax /tæks/ n impuesto m. —vt imponer contribuciones a ‹person›; gravar con un impuesto ‹thing›; (fig) poner a prueba. **~able** a imponible. **~ation** /-'seɪʃn/ n impuestos mpl. **~ collector** n recaudador m de contribuciones. **~-free** a libre de impuestos

taxi /'tæksɪ/ n (pl -is) taxi m. —vi (pt taxied, pres p taxiing) ‹aircraft› rodar por la pista. **~ rank** n parada f de taxis

taxpayer /'tækspeɪə(r)/ n contribuyente m & f

te /tiː/ n (mus, seventh note of any musical scale) si m

tea /tiː/ n té m. **~-bag** n bolsita f de té. **~-break** n descanso m para el té

teach /tiːtʃ/ vt/i (pt **taught**) enseñar. **~er** n profesor m; (primary) maestro m. **~-in** n seminario m. **~ing** n enseñanza f. —a docente. **~ing staff** n profesorado m

teacup /'tiːkʌp/ n taza f de té

teak /tiːk/ n teca f

tea-leaf /'tiːliːf/ n hoja f de té

team /tiːm/ n equipo m; (of horses) tiro m. —vi. **~ up** unirse. **~-work** n trabajo m en equipo

teapot /'tiːpɒt/ n tetera f

tear[1] /teə(r)/ vt (pt **tore**, pp **torn**) rasgar. —vi rasgarse; (run) precipitarse. —n rasgón m. **~ apart** desgarrar. **~ o.s. away** separarse

tear[2] /tɪə(r)/ n lágrima f. **in ~s** llorando

tearaway /'teərəweɪ/ n gamberro m

tear /tɪə(r)/: **~ful** a lloroso. **~-gas** n gas m lacrimógeno

tease /tiːz/ vt tomar el pelo a; cardar ‹cloth etc›. —n guasón m. —vr /-ɔ(r)/ n (fam) problema m difícil

tea: **~-set** n juego m de té. **~spoon** /'tiːspuːn/ n cucharilla *f.* ∼**spoonful** *n* (*pl* **-fuls**) (*amount*) cucharadita *f*

teat /tiːt/ *n* (*of animal*) teta *f*; (*for bottle*) tetilla *f*

tea-towel /ˈtiːtaʊəl/ *n* paño *m* de cocina

technical /ˈteknɪkl/ *a* técnico. ∼**ity** *n* /-ˈkæləti/ *n* detalle *m* técnico. ∼**ly** *adv* técnicamente

technician /tekˈnɪʃn/ *n* técnico *m*

technique /tekˈniːk/ *n* técnica *f*

technologist /tekˈnɒlədʒɪst/ *n* tecnólogo *m*. ∼**y** /tekˈnɒlədʒɪ/ *n* tecnología *f*

teddy bear /ˈtedɪbeə(r)/ *n* osito *m* de felpa, osito *m* de peluche

tedious /ˈtiːdɪəs/ *a* pesado. ∼**ly** *adv* pesadamente

tedium /ˈtiːdɪəm/ *n* aburrimiento *m*

tee /tiː/ *n* (*golf*) tee *m*

teem /tiːm/ *vi* abundar; (*rain*) llover a cántaros

teen|age /ˈtiːneɪdʒ/ *a* adolescente; (*for teenagers*) para jóvenes. ∼**ager** /-ə(r)/ *n* adolescente *m* & *f*, joven *m* & *f*. ∼**s** /tiːnz/ *npl.* **the** ∼**s** la adolescencia *f*

teeny /ˈtiːnɪ/ *a* (**-ier, -iest**) (*fam*) chiquito

teeter /ˈtiːtə(r)/ *vi* balancearse

teeth /tiːθ/ *see* **tooth**. ∼**e** /tiːð/ *vi* echar los dientes. ∼**ing troubles** *npl* (*fig*) dificultades *fpl* iniciales

teetotaller /tiːˈtəʊtələ(r)/ *n* abstemio *m*

telecommunications /telɪkəmjuːnɪˈkeɪʃnz/ *npl* telecomunicaciones *fpl*

telegram /ˈtelɪgræm/ *n* telegrama *m*

telegraph /ˈtelɪgrɑːf/ *n* telégrafo *m*. —*vt* telegrafiar. ∼**ic** /-ˈgræfɪk/ *a* telegráfico

telepath|ic /telɪˈpæθɪk/ *a* telepático. ∼**y** /tɪˈlepəθɪ/ *n* telepatía *f*

telephon|e /ˈtelɪfəʊn/ *n* teléfono *m*. —*vt* llamar por teléfono. ∼**e booth** *n* cabina *f* telefónica. ∼**e directory** *n* guía *f* telefónica. ∼**e exchange** *n* central *f* telefónica. ∼**ic** /-ˈfɒnɪk/ *a* telefónico. ∼**ist** /tɪˈlefənɪst/ *n* telefonista *m* & *f*

telephoto /telɪˈfəʊtəʊ/ *a.* ∼ **lens** *n* teleobjetivo *m*

teleprinter /ˈtelɪprɪntə(r)/ *n* teleimpresor *m*

telescop|e /ˈtelɪskəʊp/ *n* telescopio *m*. ∼**ic** /-ˈkɒpɪk/ *a* telescópico

televis|e /ˈtelɪvaɪz/ *vt* televisar. ∼**ion** /-ˈvɪʒn/ *n* televisión *f*. ∼**ion set** *n* televisor *m*

telex /ˈteleks/ *n* télex *m*. —*vt* enviar por télex

tell /tel/ *vt* (*pt* **told**) decir; contar (*story*); (*distinguish*) distinguir. —*vi* (*produce an effect*) tener efecto; (*know*) saber. ∼ **off** *vt* reprender. ∼**er** /ˈtelə(r)/ *n* (*in bank*) cajero *m*

telling /ˈtelɪŋ/ *a* eficaz

tell-tale /ˈtelteɪl/ *n* soplón *m*. —*a* revelador

telly /ˈtelɪ/ *n* (*fam*) televisión *f*, tele *f* (*fam*)

temerity /tɪˈmerətɪ/ *n* temeridad *f*

temp /temp/ *n* (*fam*) empleado *m* temporal

temper /ˈtempə(r)/ *n* (*disposition*) disposición *f*; (*mood*) humor *m*; (*fit of anger*) cólera *f*; (*of metal*) temple *m*. **be in a** ∼ estar de mal humor. **keep one's** ∼ contenerse. **lose one's** ∼ enfadarse, perder la paciencia. —*vt* templar ⟨*metal*⟩

temperament /ˈtemprəmənt/ *n* temperamento *m*. ∼**al** /-ˈmentl/ *a* caprichoso

temperance /ˈtempərəns/ *n* moderación *f*

temperate /ˈtempərət/ *a* moderado; ⟨*climate*⟩ templado

temperature /'temprɪtʃə(r)/ n temperatura f. **have a ~** tener fiebre

tempest /'tempɪst/ n tempestad f. **~uous** /-'pestjʊəs/ a tempestuoso

temple[1] /'templ/ n templo m

temple[2] /'templ/ (anat) sien f

tempo /'tempoʊ/ n (pl **-os** or **tempi**) ritmo m

temporar|ily /'tempərərəlɪ/ adv temporalmente. **~y** /'tempərərɪ/ a temporal, provisional

tempt /tempt/ vt tentar. **~ s.o. to** inducir a uno a. **~ation** /-'teɪʃn/ n tentación f. **~ing** a tentador

ten /ten/ a & n diez (m)

tenable /'tenəbl/ a sostenible

tenac|ious /tɪ'neɪʃəs/ a tenaz. **~ty** /-'æstɪ/ n tenacidad f

tenan|cy /'tenənsɪ/ n alquiler m. **~t** /'tenənt/ n inquilino m

tend[1] /tend/ vi. **~ to** tener tendencia a

tend[2] /tend/ vt cuidar

tendency /'tendənsɪ/ n tendencia f

tender[1] /'tendə(r)/ a tierno; (painful) dolorido

tender[2] /'tendə(r)/ n (com) oferta f. **legal ~** n curso m legal. **—vt** ofrecer, presentar

tender: ~ly adv tiernamente. **~ness** n ternura f

tendon /'tendən/ n tendón m

tenement /'tenəmənt/ n vivienda f

tenet /'tenɪt/ n principio m

tenfold /'tenfoʊld/ a diez veces mayor, décuplo. **—adv** diez veces

tenner /'tenə(r)/ n (fam) billete m de diez libras

tennis /'tenɪs/ n tenis m

tenor /'tenə(r)/ n tenor m

tens|e /tens/ a (**-er, -est**) tieso; (fig) tenso. **—n** (gram) tiempo m. **—vi. ~ up** tensarse. **~eness** n, **~ion** /'tenʃn/ n tensión f

tent /tent/ n tienda f, carpa f (LAm)

tentacle /'tentəkl/ n tentáculo m

tentative /'tentətɪv/ a provisional; (hesitant) indeciso. **~ly** adv provisionalmente; (timidly) tímidamente

tenterhooks /'tentəhʊks/ npl. **on ~** en ascuas

tenth /tenθ/ a & n décimo (m)

tenuous /'tenjʊəs/ a tenue

tenure /'tenjʊə(r)/ n posesión f

tepid /'tepɪd/ a tibio

term /tɜ:m/ n (of time) período m; (schol) trimestre m; (word etc) término m. **—vt** llamar. **~s** npl condiciones fpl; (com) precio m. **on bad ~s** en malas relaciones. **on good ~s** en buenas relaciones

terminal /'tɜ:mɪnl/ a terminal, final. **—n** (rail) estación f terminal; (elec) borne m. **(air) ~** n término m, terminal m

terminat|e /'tɜ:mɪneɪt/ vt terminar. **—vi** terminarse. **~ion** /-'neɪʃn/ n terminación f

terminology /tɜ:mɪ'nɒlədʒɪ/ n terminología f

terrace /'terəs/ n terraza f; (houses) hilera f de casas. **the ~s** npl (sport) las gradas fpl

terrain /tə'reɪn/ n terreno m

terrestrial /tɪ'restrɪəl/ a terrestre

terrib|le /'terəbl/ a terrible. **~y** adv terriblemente

terrier /'terɪə(r)/ n terrier m

terrific /tə'rɪfɪk/ a (excellent, fam) estupendo; (huge, fam) enorme. **~ally** adv (fam) terriblemente; (very well) muy bien

terrify /'terɪfaɪ/ vt aterrorizar. **~ing** a espantoso

territorial /terɪ'tɔ:rɪəl/ a territorial. **~y** /'terɪtrɪ/ n territorio m

terror /'terə(r)/ n terror m. ∼ism /-zəm/ n terrorismo m. ∼ist /'terərist/ n terrorista m & f. ∼ize /'terəraiz/ vt aterrorizar

terse /tɜ:s/ a conciso; (abrupt) brusco

test /test/ n prueba f; (exam) examen m. —vt probar; (examine) examinar

testament /'testəmənt/ n testamento m. **New T∼** Nuevo Testamento. **Old T∼** Antiguo Testamento

testicle /'testikl/ n testículo m

testify /'testifai/ vt atestiguar. —vi declarar

testimon|ial /testi'məʊniəl/ n certificado m; (of character) recomendación f. ∼y /'testiməni/ n testimonio m

test: ∼ **match** n partido m internacional. ∼**tube** n tubo m de ensayo, probeta f

testy /'testi/ a irritable

tetanus /'tetənəs/ n tétanos m invar

tetchy /'tetʃi/ a irritable

tether /'teðə(r)/ vt atar. —n. **be at the end of one's** ∼ no poder más

text /tekst/ n texto m. ∼**book** n libro m de texto

textile /'tekstail/ a & n textil (m)

texture /'tekstʃə(r)/ n textura f

Thai /tai/ a & n tailandés (m). ∼**land** n Tailandia f

Thames /temz/ n Támesis m

than /ðæn, ðən/ conj que; (with numbers) de

thank /θæŋk/ vt dar las gracias a, agradecer. ∼ **you** gracias. ∼**ful** /'θæŋkfl/ a agradecido. ∼**fully** adv con gratitud; (happily) afortunadamente. ∼**less** /'θæŋklis/ a ingrato. ∼**s** npl gracias fpl. ∼**s!** (fam) ¡gracias! ∼**s to** gracias a

that /ðæt, ðət/ a (pl those) ese, aquel, esa, aquella. —pron (pl those) ése, aquél, ésa, aquélla.

∼ **is** es decir. ∼**'s it!** ¡eso es! ∼ **is why** por eso. **is** ∼ **you?** ¿eres tú? **like** ∼ así. ∼**ly** tan. —rel pron que; (with prep) el que, la que, el cual, la cual. —conj que

thatch /θætʃ/ n techo m de paja. ∼**ed** a con techo de paja

thaw /θɔ:/ vt deshelar. —vi deshelarse; (snow) derretirse. —n deshielo m

the /ðə, ði:/ def art el, la, los, las. **at** ∼ a la, a la, a los, a las. **from** ∼ del, de la, de los, de las. **to** ∼ al, a la, a los, a las. —adv. **all** ∼ **bet-ter** tanto mejor

theatre /'θiətə(r)/ n teatro m. ∼**ical** /-'ætrikl/ a teatral

theft /θeft/ n hurto m

their /ðeə(r)/ a su, sus

theirs /ðeəz/ poss pron (el) suyo, (la) suya, (los) suyos, (las) suyas

them /ðem, ðəm/ pron (accusative) los, las; (dative) les; (after prep) ellos, ellas

theme /θi:m/ n tema m. ∼ **song** n motivo m principal

themselves /ðəm'selvz/ pron ellos mismos, ellas mismas; (reflexive) se; (after prep) sí mismos, sí mismas

then /ðen/ adv entonces; (next) luego, después. **by** ∼ para entonces. **now and** ∼ de vez en cuando. **since** ∼ desde entonces. —a de entonces

theolog|ian /θiə'ləʊdʒən/ n teólogo m. ∼**y** /θi'ɒlədʒi/ n teología f

theorem /'θiərəm/ n teorema m

theor|etical /θiə'retikl/ a teórico. ∼**y** /'θiəri/ n teoría f

therap|eutic /θerə'pju:tik/ a terapéutico. ∼**ist** n terapeuta m & f. ∼**y** /'θerəpi/ n terapia f

there /ðeə(r)/ adv ahí, allí. ∼ **are** hay. ∼ **he is** ahí está. ∼ **is** hay. **it is** ∼ ahí está. **down** ∼ ahí abajo. **up** ∼ ahí arriba. —int ¡vaya! ∼, ∼! ¡ya, ya! ∼**abouts**

adv por ahí. **~after** *adv*
después. **~by** *adv* por eso.
~fore /'ðeəfɔ:(r)/ *adv* por lo
tanto.

thermal /'θɜ:ml/ *a* termal

thermometer /θə'mɒmɪtə(r)/ *n*
termómetro *m*

thermonuclear /θɜ:məʊ'nju:-
klɪə(r)/ *a* termonuclear

Thermos /'θɜ:məs/ *n* (P) termo *m*

thermostat /'θɜ:məstæt/ *n* termostato *m*

thesaurus /θɪ'sɔ:rəs/ *n* (*pl* **-ri**
/-raɪ/) diccionario *m* de
sinónimos

these /ði:z/ *a* estos, estas. —*pron*
éstos, éstas

thesis /'θi:sɪs/ *n* (*pl* **theses** /-si:z/)
tesis *f*

they /ðeɪ/ *pron* ellos, ellas. **~ say
that** se dice que

thick /θɪk/ *a* (**-er, -est**) espeso;
(*dense*) denso; (*stupid, fam*)
torpe; (*close, fam*) íntimo. —*adv*
espesamente, densamente. —*n*.
in the ~ of en medio de. **~en**
/'θɪkən/ *vt* espesar. —*vi* espesarse

thicket /'θɪkɪt/ *n* matorral *m*

thick: **~ly** *adv* espesamente,
densamente. **~ness** *n* espesor *m*

thickset /θɪk'set/ *a* fornido

thick-skinned /θɪk'skɪnd/ *a*
insensible

thief /θi:f/ *n* (*pl* **thieves**) ladrón
m

thieve /θi:v/ *vt/i* robar. **~ing** *a*
ladrón

thigh /θaɪ/ *n* muslo *m*

thimble /'θɪmbl/ *n* dedal *m*

thin /θɪn/ *a* (**thinner, thinnest**)
delgado; (*person*) flaco; (*weak*)
débil; (*fine*) fino; (*sparse*)
escaso. —*adv* ligeramente. —*vt*
(*pt* **thinned**) adelgazar; (*dilute*)
diluir. **~ out** hacer menos
denso. —*vi* adelgazarse; (*diminish*) disminuir

thing /θɪŋ/ *n* cosa *f*. **for one ~** en
primer lugar. **just the ~** exactamente lo que se necesita. **poor
~!** ¡pobrecito! **~s** *npl* (*belongings*) efectos *mpl*; (*clothing*) ropa
f

think /θɪŋk/ *vt* (*pt* **thought**) pensar, creer. —*vi* pensar (**about,
of** en); (*carefully*) reflexionar;
(*imagine*) imaginarse. **~ better
of it** cambiar de idea. **I ~ so** creo
que sí. **~ over** *vt* pensar bien. **~
up** *vt* idear, inventar. **~er** *n* pensador *m*. **~-tank** *n* grupo *m* de
expertos

thin: **~ly** *adv* ligeramente.
~ness *n* delgadez *f*; (*of person*)
flaqueza *f*

third /θɜ:d/ *a* tercero. —*n* tercio
m, tercera parte *f*. **~-rate** *a* muy
inferior. **T~ World** *n* Tercer
Mundo *m*

thirst /θɜ:st/ *n* sed *f*. **~y** *a* sediento. **be ~y** tener sed

thirteen /θɜ:'ti:n/ *a* & *n* trece (*m*).
~th *a* & *n* decimotercero (*m*)

thirtieth /'θɜ:tɪəθ/ *a* & *n* trigésimo (*m*). **~y** /'θɜ:tɪ/ *a* & *n*
treinta (*m*)

this /ðɪs/ *a* (*pl* **these**) este, esta.
~ one éste, ésta. —*pron* (*pl*
these) éste, ésta, esto. **like ~** así

thistle /'θɪsl/ *n* cardo *m*

thong /θɒŋ/ *n* correa *f*

thorn /θɔ:n/ *n* espina *f*. **~y** *a*
espinoso

thorough /'θʌrə/ *a* completo;
(*deep*) profundo; (*cleaning etc*) a
fondo; (*person*) concienzudo

thoroughbred /'θʌrəbred/ *a* de
pura sangre

thoroughfare /'θʌrəfeə(r)/ *n*
calle *f*. **no ~** prohibido el paso

thoroughly /'θʌrəlɪ/ *adv*
completamente

those /ðəʊz/ *a* esos, aquellos,
esas, aquellas. —*pron* ésos,
aquéllos, ésas, aquéllas

though /ðəʊ/ conj aunque. —adv sin embargo. **as ~** como si

thought /θɔːt/ see **think**. —n pensamiento m; (idea) idea f. **~ful** /'θɔːtfl/ a pensativo; (considerate) atento. **~fully** adv pensativamente; (considerately) atentamente. **~less** /'θɔːtlɪs/ a irreflexivo; (inconsiderate) desconsiderado

thousand /'θaʊznd/ a & n mil (m). **~th** a & n milésimo m

thrash /θræʃ/ vt azotar; (defeat) derrotar. **~ out** discutir a fondo

thread /θred/ n hilo m; (of screw) rosca f. —vt ensartar. **~ one's way** abrirse paso. **~bare** /'θredbeər/ a raído

threat /θret/ n amenaza f. **~en** /'θretn/ vt/i amenazar. **~ening** a amenazador. **~eningly** adv de modo amenazador

three /θriː/ a & n tres (m). **~fold** a triple. —adv tres veces. **~some** /'θriːsəm/ n conjunto m de tres personas

thresh /θreʃ/ vt trillar

threshold /'θreʃhəʊld/ n umbral m

threw /θruː/ see **throw**

thrift /θrɪft/ n economía f, ahorro m. **~y** a frugal

thrill /θrɪl/ n emoción f. —vt emocionar. —vi emocionarse; (quiver) estremecerse. **be ~ed with** estar encantado de. **~er** /'θrɪlə(r)/ n (book) libro m de suspense; (film) película f de suspense. **~ing** a emocionante

thriv|e /θraɪv/ vi prosperar. **~ing** a próspero

throat /θrəʊt/ n garganta f. **have a sore ~** dolerle la garganta

throb /θrɒb/ vi (pt **throbbed**) palpitar; (with pain) dar punzadas; (fig) vibrar. —n palpitación f; (pain) punzada f; (fig) vibración f. **~bing** a (pain) punzante

throes /θrəʊz/ npl. **in the ~ of** en medio de

thrombosis /θrɒm'bəʊsɪs/ n trombosis f

throne /θrəʊn/ n trono m

throng /θrɒŋ/ n multitud f

throttle /'θrɒtl/ n (auto) acelerador m. —vt ahogar

through /θruː/ prep por, a través de; (during) durante; (by means of) por medio de; (thanks to) gracias a. —adv de parte a parte, de un lado a otro; (entirely) completamente; (to the end) hasta el final. **be ~** (finished) haber terminado. —a (train dec) directo

throughout /θruː'aʊt/ prep por todo; (time) en todo. —adv en todas partes; (all the time) todo el tiempo

throve /θrəʊv/ see **thrive**

throw /θrəʊ/ vt (pt **threw**, pp **thrown**) arrojar; (baffle etc) desconcertar. **~ a party** (fam) dar una fiesta. —n tiro m; (of dice) lance m. **~ away** vt tirar. **~ over** vt abandonar. **~ up** vi (vomit) vomitar. **~away** a desechable

thrush /θrʌʃ/ n tordo m

thrust /θrʌst/ vt (pt **thrust**) empujar; (push in) meter. —n empuje m. **~ (up)on** imponer a

thud /θʌd/ n ruido m sordo

thug /θʌg/ n bruto m

thumb /θʌm/ n pulgar m. **under the ~ of** dominado por. —vt hojear (book). **~ a lift** hacer autostop. **~index** n uñeros mpl

thump /θʌmp/ vt golpear. —vi (heart) latir fuertemente. —n porrazo m; (noise) ruido m sordo

thunder /'θʌndə(r)/ n trueno m. —vi tronar. **~ past** pasar con estruendo. **~bolt** /'θʌndəbəʊlt/ n rayo m. **~clap** /'θʌndəklæp/ n trueno m. **~storm** /'θʌndəstɔːm/ n tronada f. **~y** a con truenos

Thursday /'θɜːzdeɪ/ n jueves m

thus /ðʌs/ *adv* así

thwart /θwɔːt/ *vt* frustrar

thyme /taɪm/ *n* tomillo *m*

thyroid /ˈθaɪrɔɪd/ *n* tiroides *m* invar

tiara /tɪˈɑːrə/ *n* diadema *f*

tic /tɪk/ *n* tic *m*

tick[1] /tɪk/ *n* tictac *m*; (*mark*) señal *f*, marca *f*; (*instant, fam*) momentito *m*. —*vi* hacer tictac. —*vt*. ~ (**off**) marcar. ~ **off** *vt* (*sl*) reprender. ~ **over** *vi* (*of engine*) marchar en vacío

tick[2] /tɪk/ *n* (*insect*) garrapata *f*

tick[3] /tɪk/ *n*. **on** ~ (*fam*) a crédito

ticket /ˈtɪkɪt/ *n* billete *m*, boleto *m* (*LAm*); (*label*) etiqueta *f*; (*fine*) multa *f*. ~**-collector** *n* revisor *m*. ~**-office** *n* taquilla *f*

tickle /ˈtɪkl/ *vt* hacer cosquillas a; (*amuse*) divertir. —*n* cosquilleo *m*. ~**ish** /ˈtɪklɪʃ/ *a* cosquilloso; (*problem*) delicado. **be** ~**ish** tener cosquillas

tidal /ˈtaɪdl/ *a* de marea. ~ **wave** *n* maremoto *m*

tiddly-winks /ˈtɪdlɪwɪŋks/ *n* juego *m* de pulgas

tide /taɪd/ *n* marea *f*; (*of events*) curso *m*. —*vt*. ~ **over** ayudar a salir de un apuro

tidings /ˈtaɪdɪŋz/ *npl* noticias *fpl*

tid|**ily** /ˈtaɪdɪlɪ/ *adv* en orden; (*well*) bien. ~**iness** *n* orden *m*. ~**y** /ˈtaɪdɪ/ *a* (-**ier**, -**iest**) ordenado; (*amount, fam*) considerable. —*vt/i*. ~**y** (**up**) ordenar. ~**y o.s. up** arreglarse

tie /taɪ/ *vt* (*pres p* **tying**) atar; hacer ⟨a knot⟩; (*link*) vincular. —*vi* (*sport*) empatar. —*n* atadura *f*; (*necktie*) corbata *f*; (*link*) lazo *m*; (*sport*) empate *m*. ~ **in with** relacionar con. ~ **up** atar; (*com*) inmovilizar. **be** ~**d up** (*busy*) estar ocupado

tier /tɪə(r)/ *n* fila *f*; (*in stadium etc*) grada *f*; (*of cake*) piso *m*

tie-up /ˈtaɪʌp/ *n* enlace *m*

tiff /tɪf/ *n* riña *f*

tiger /ˈtaɪgə(r)/ *n* tigre *m*

tight /taɪt/ *a* (-**er**, -**est**) ⟨clothes⟩ ceñido; (*taut*) tieso; ⟨control etc⟩ riguroso; ⟨knot, nut⟩ apretado; (*drunk, fam*) borracho. —*adv* bien; (*shut*) herméticamente. ~ **corner** *n* (*fig*) apuro *m*. ~**en** /ˈtaɪtn/ *vt* apretar. —*vi* apretarse. ~**-fisted** *a* tacaño. ~**ly** *adv* bien; (*shut*) herméticamente. ~**ness** *n* estrechez *f*. ~**rope** /ˈtaɪtrəʊp/ *n* cuerda *f* floja. ~**s** /taɪts/ *npl* leotardos *mpl*

tile /taɪl/ *n* (*decorative*) azulejo *m*; (*on roof*) teja *f*; (*on floor*) baldosa *f*. —*vt* azulejar; tejar ⟨roof⟩; embaldosar ⟨floor⟩

till[1] /tɪl/ *prep* hasta. —*conj* hasta que

till[2] /tɪl/ *n* caja *f*

till[3] /tɪl/ *vt* cultivar

tilt /tɪlt/ *vt* inclinar. —*vi* inclinarse. —*n* inclinación *f*. **at full** ~ a toda velocidad

timber /ˈtɪmbə(r)/ *n* madera *f* (de construcción); (*trees*) árboles *mpl*

time /taɪm/ *n* tiempo *m*; (*moment*) momento *m*; (*occasion*) ocasión *f*; (*by clock*) hora *f*; (*epoch*) época *f*; (*rhythm*) compás *m*. ~ **off** tiempo libre. **at** ~**s** a veces. **behind the** ~**s** anticuado. **behind** ~ atrasado. **for the** ~ **being** por ahora. **from** ~ **to** ~ de vez en cuando. **have a good** ~ divertirse, pasarlo bien. **in a year's** ~ dentro de un año. **in no** ~ en un abrir y cerrar de ojos. **in** ~ a tiempo; (*eventually*) con el tiempo. **on** ~ a la hora, puntual. —*vt* elegir el momento; cronometrar ⟨race⟩. ~ **bomb** *n* bomba *f* de tiempo. ~**honoured** *a* consagrado. ~**lag** *n* intervalo *m*

timeless /ˈtaɪmlɪs/ *a* eterno

timely /ˈtaɪmlɪ/ *a* oportuno

timer /'taɪmə(r)/ n cronómetro m; (culin) avisador m; (with sand) reloj m de arena; (elec) interruptor m de reloj

timetable /'taɪmteɪbl/ n horario m

time zone /'taɪmzəʊn/ n huso m horario

timid /'tɪmɪd/ a tímido; (fearful) miedoso. **~ly** adv tímidamente

timing /'taɪmɪŋ/ n medida f del tiempo; (moment) momento m; (sport) cronometraje m

timorous /'tɪmərəs/ a tímido; (fearful) miedoso. **~ly** adv tímidamente

tin /tɪn/ n estaño m; (container) lata f. **~ foil** n papel m de estaño. **—**vt (pt tinned) conservar en lata, enlatar

tinge /tɪndʒ/ vt teñir (with de); (fig) matizar (with de). **—**n matiz m

tingle /'tɪŋgl/ vi sentir hormigueo; (with excitement) estremecerse

tinker /'tɪŋkə(r)/ n hojalatero m. **—**vi. **~ (with)** jugar con; (repair) arreglar

tinkle /'tɪŋkl/ n retintín m; (phone call, fam) llamada f

tin: **~ned** n en lata. **~ny** a metálico. **~opener** n abrelatas m invar. **~ plate** n hojalata f

tinpot /'tɪnpɒt/ a (pej) inferior

tinsel /'tɪnsl/ n oropel m

tint /tɪnt/ n matiz m

tiny /'taɪnɪ/ a (-ier, -iest) diminuto

tip[1] /tɪp/ n punta f

tip[2] /tɪp/ vt (pt tipped) (tilt) inclinar; (overturn) volcar; (pour) verter—vi inclinarse; (overturn) volcarse. **~ out** verter; (for rubbish) vertedero m. **~ out** verter

tip[3] /tɪp/ vt (reward) dar una propina a. **~ off** advertir. **—**n (reward) propina f; (advice) consejo m

tip-off /'tɪpɒf/ n advertencia f

tipped /'tɪpt/ a (cigarette) con filtro

tipple /'tɪpl/ vi beborrotear. **—**n bebida f alcohólica. **have a ~** tomar una copa

tipsy /'tɪpsɪ/ a achispado

tiptoe /'tɪptəʊ/ n. **on ~** de puntillas

tiptop /'tɪptɒp/ a (fam) de primera

tirade /taɪ'reɪd/ n diatriba f

tire /'taɪə(r)/ vt cansar. —vi cansarse. **~d** /'taɪəd/ a cansado. **~d of** harto de. **~d out** agotado. **~less** a incansable

tiresome /'taɪəsəm/ a (annoying) fastidioso; (boring) pesado

tiring /'taɪərɪŋ/ a cansado

tissue /'tɪʃuː/ n tisú m; (handkerchief) pañuelo m de papel. **~-paper** n papel m de seda

tit[1] /tɪt/ n (bird) paro m

tit[2] /tɪt/ n. **~ for tat** golpe por golpe

titbit /'tɪtbɪt/ n golosina f

titillate /'tɪtɪleɪt/ vt excitar

title /'taɪtl/ n título m. **~d** a con título nobiliario. **~-deed** n título m de propiedad. **~-role** n papel m principal

tittle-tattle /'tɪtltætl/ n cháchara f

titular /'tɪtjʊlə(r)/ a nominal

tizzy /'tɪzɪ/ n (sl). **get in a ~** ponerse nervioso

to /tuː, tə/ prep a; (towards) hacia; (in order to) para; (according to) según; (as far as) hasta; (with times) menos; (of) de. **give it ~ me** dámelo. **I don't want to** no quiero. **twenty ~ seven** (by clock) las siete menos veinte. **—**adv. **push ~, pull ~** cerrar. **~ and fro** adv de aquí para allá

toad /təʊd/ n sapo m

toadstool /'təʊdstuːl/ n seta f venenosa

toast /təʊst/ n pan m tostado, tostada f; (drink) brindis m. **drink a ~ to** brindar por. **~vt** brindar por. **~er** n tostador m de pan

tobacco /təˈbækəʊ/ n tabaco m. **~nist** n estanquero m. **~nist's shop** n estanco m

to-be /təˈbiː/ a futuro

toboggan /təˈbɒgən/ n tobogán m

today /təˈdeɪ/ n & adv hoy (m). **~ week** dentro de una semana

toddler /ˈtɒdlə(r)/ n niño m que empieza a andar

toddy /ˈtɒdɪ/ n ponche m

to-do /təˈduː/ n lío m

toe /təʊ/ n dedo m del pie; (of shoe) punta f. **big ~** dedo m gordo (del pie). **on one's ~s** (fig) alerta. **~vt. ~ the line** conformarse. **~hold** n punto m de apoyo

toff /tɒf/ n (sl) petimetre m

toffee /ˈtɒfɪ/ n caramelo m

together /təˈgeðə(r)/ adv junto, juntos; (at same time) a la vez. **~ with** junto con. **~ness** n compañerismo m

toil /tɔɪl/ vi afanarse. **—n** trabajo m

toilet /ˈtɔɪlɪt/ n servicio m, retrete m; (grooming) arreglo m, tocado m. **~paper** n papel m higiénico. **~ries** /ˈtɔɪlɪtrɪz/ npl artículos mpl de tocador. **~ water** n agua f de Colonia

token /ˈtəʊkən/ n señal f; (voucher) vale m; (coin) ficha f. **—a** simbólico

told /təʊld/ see **tell**. **—a. all ~** con todo

tolerab|le /ˈtɒlərəbl/ a tolerable; (not bad) regular. **~y** adv pasablemente

toleran|ce /ˈtɒlərəns/ n tolerancia f. **~t** /ˈtɒlərənt/ a tolerante. **~tly** adv con tolerancia

tolerate /ˈtɒləreɪt/ vt tolerar

toll¹ /təʊl/ n peaje m. **death ~** número m de muertos. **take a heavy ~** dejar muchas víctimas

toll² /təʊl/ vi doblar, tocar a muerto

tom /tɒm/ n gato m (macho)

tomato /təˈmɑːtəʊ/ n (pl ~oes) tomate m

tomb /tuːm/ n tumba f, sepulcro m

tomboy /ˈtɒmbɔɪ/ n marimacho m

tombstone /ˈtuːmstəʊn/ n lápida f sepulcral

tom-cat /ˈtɒmkæt/ n gato m (macho)

tome /təʊm/ n librote m

tomfoolery /tɒmˈfuːlərɪ/ n payasadas fpl, tonterías fpl

tomorrow /təˈmɒrəʊ/ n & adv mañana (f). **see you ~!** ¡hasta mañana!

ton /tʌn/ n tonelada f (= 1,016 kg). **~s of** (fam) montones de. **metric ~** tonelada f (métrica) (= 1,000 kg)

tone /təʊn/ n tono m. **—vt. ~ down** atenuar. **~ up** tonificar (muscles). **—vi.** n armonizar. **~deaf** a que no tiene buen oído

tongs /tɒŋz/ npl tenazas fpl; (for hair, sugar) tenacillas fpl

tongue /tʌŋ/ n lengua f. **~ in cheek** adv irónicamente. **~tied** a mudo. **get ~tied** trabársele la lengua. **~twister** n trabalenguas m invar

tonic /ˈtɒnɪk/ a tónico. **—n** (tonic water) tónica f; (med, fig) tónico m. **~ water** n tónica f

tonight /təˈnaɪt/ adv & n esta noche f; (evening) esta tarde (f)

tonne /tʌn/ n tonelada f (métrica)

tonsil /ˈtɒnsl/ n amígdala f. **~litis** /-ˈlaɪtɪs/ n amigdalitis f

too /tuː/ adv demasiado; (also) también. **~ many** a demasiados. **~ much** a & adv demasiado

took /tʊk/ see **take**

tool /tuːl/ n herramienta f.
~**bag** n bolsa f de herramientas

toot /tuːt/ n bocinazo m. —vt
tocar la bocina

tooth /tuːθ/ n (pl **teeth**) diente m;
(molar) muela f. ~**ache** /'tuːθ-
eɪk/ n dolor m de muelas.
~**brush** /'tuːθbrʌʃ/ n cepillo m
de dientes. ~**comb** /'tuːθkəʊm/ n
peine m de púa fina. ~**less** a
desdentado, sin dientes. ~**paste**
/'tuːθpeɪst/ n pasta f dentífrica.
~**pick** /'tuːθpɪk/ n palillo m de
dientes

top[1] /tɒp/ n cima f; (upper part)
parte f de arriba; (upper surface)
superficie f; (lid, of bottle) tapa f;
(of list) cabeza f. **from** ~ **to bottom** de arriba abajo. **on** ~ (**of**)
encima de; (besides) además. ~
más alto; (highest) superior,
principal; (maximum) máximo.
~ **floor** n último piso m. —vt (pt
topped) cubrir; (exceed)
exceder. ~ **up** vt llenar

top[2] /tɒp/ n (toy) trompa f, peonza f

top: ~ **hat** n chistera f. ~**heavy**
a más pesado arriba que abajo

topic /'tɒpɪk/ n tema m. ~**al**
/'tɒpɪkl/ a de actualidad

top: ~**less** /'tɒplɪs/ a (bather) con
los senos desnudos. ~**most**
/'tɒpməʊst/ a (el) más alto.
~**notch** a (fam) excelente

topography /tə'pɒɡrəfɪ/ n topografía f

topple /'tɒpl/ vi derribar; (overturn) volcar

top secret /tɒp'siːkrɪt/ a sumamente secreto

topsy-turvy /tɒpsɪ'tɜːvɪ/ adv & a
patas arriba

torch /tɔːtʃ/ n lámpara f de bolsillo; (flaming) antorcha f

tore /tɔː(r)/ see **tear**[1]

toreador /'tɒrɪədɔː(r)/ n torero m

torment /'tɔːment/ n tormento
m. /tɔː'ment/ vt atormentar

torn /tɔːn/ see **tear**[1]

tornado /tɔː'neɪdəʊ/ n (pl **-oes**)
tornado m

torpedo /tɔː'piːdəʊ/ n (pl **-oes**)
torpedo m. —vt torpedear

torpor /'tɔːpə(r)/ n apatía f

torrent /'tɒrənt/ n torrente m.
~**ial** /tə'renʃl/ a torrencial

torrid /'tɒrɪd/ a tórrido

torso /'tɔːsəʊ/ n (pl **-os**) torso m

tortoise /'tɔːtəs/ n tortuga f. ~**
shell** n carey m

tortuous /'tɔːtjʊəs/ a tortuoso

torture /'tɔːtʃə(r)/ n tortura f, tormento m. —vt atormentar. ~**r**
/-ə(r)/ n atormentador m, verdugo m

Tory /'tɔːrɪ/ a & n (fam) conservador (m)

toss /tɒs/ vt echar; (shake) sacudir. —vi agitarse. ~ **and turn**
(in bed) revolverse. ~ **up** echar
a cara o cruz

tot[1] /tɒt/ n nene m; (of liquor,
fam) trago m

tot[2] /tɒt/ vt (pt **totted**). ~ **up**
(fam) sumar

total /'təʊtl/ a & n total (m). —vt
(pt **totalled**) sumar

totalitarian /təʊtælɪ'teərɪən/ a
totalitario

total: ~**ity** /təʊ'tælətɪ/ n totalidad
f. ~**ly** adv totalmente

totter /'tɒtə(r)/ vi tambalearse.
~**y** a inseguro

touch /tʌtʃ/ vt tocar; (reach)
alcanzar; (move) conmover. —vi
tocarse. ~ n toque m; (sense)
tacto m; (contact) contacto m;
(trace) pizca f. **get in** ~ **with**
ponerse en contacto con. ~
down (aircraft) aterrizar. ~ **off**
disparar (gun); (fig) desencadenar. ~ **on** tratar levemente.
~ **up** retocar. ~**and-go** a incierto, dudoso

touching /'tʌtʃɪŋ/ a conmovedor

touchstone /'tʌtʃstəʊn/ n (fig)
piedra f de toque

touchy /'tʌtʃɪ/ a quisquilloso

tough /tʌf/ a (-er, -est) duro; (strong) fuerte, resistente. ∼en /ˈtʌfn/ vt endurecer. ∼ness n dureza f; (strength) resistencia f

toupee /ˈtuːpeɪ/ n postizo m, tupé m

tour /tʊə(r)/ n viaje m; (visit) visita f; (excursion) excursión f; (by team etc) gira f. —vt recorrer; (visit) visitar

touris|m /ˈtʊərɪzəm/ n turismo m. ∼t /ˈtʊərɪst/ n turista m & f. —a turístico. ∼t office n oficina f de turismo

tournament /ˈtɔːnəmənt/ n torneo m

tousle /ˈtaʊzl/ vt despeinar

tout /taʊt/ vi. ∼ (for) solicitar. —n solicitador m

tow /təʊ/ vt remolcar. —n remolque m. on ∼ a remolque. with his family in ∼ (fam) acompañado por su familia

toward(s) /təˈwɔːd(z)/ prep hacia

towel /ˈtaʊəl/ n toalla f. ∼ling n (fabric) toalla f

tower /ˈtaʊə(r)/ n torre f. —vi. ∼ above dominar. ∼ block n edificio m alto. ∼ing a altísimo; (rage) violento

town /taʊn/ n ciudad f, pueblo m. go to ∼ (fam) no escatimar dinero. ∼ hall n ayuntamiento m. ∼ planning n urbanismo m

tow-path /ˈtəʊpɑːθ/ n camino m de sirga

toxi|c /ˈtɒksɪk/ a tóxico. ∼n /ˈtɒksɪn/ n toxina f

toy /tɔɪ/ n juguete m. —vi. ∼ with jugar con (object); acariciar (idea). ∼shop n jugueteria f

trac|e /treɪs/ n huella f; (small amount) pizca f. —vt seguir la pista de; (draw) dibujar; (with tracing-paper) calcar; (track down) encontrar. ∼ing /ˈtreɪsɪŋ/ n calco m. ∼ing-paper n papel m de calcar

track /træk/ n huella f; (path) sendero m; (sport) pista f; (of rocket etc) trayectoria f; (rail) vía f. keep ∼ of vigilar. make ∼s (sl) marcharse. ∼ down vt localizar. ∼ suit n traje m de deporte, chandal m

tract¹ /trækt/ n (land) extensión f; (anat) aparato m

tract² /trækt/ n (pamphlet) opúsculo m

traction /ˈtrækʃn/ n tracción f

tractor /ˈtræktə(r)/ n tractor m

trade /treɪd/ n comercio m; (occupation) oficio m; (exchange) cambio m; (industry) industria f. —vi cambiar. ∼vi comerciar. ∼ in (give in part-exchange) dar como parte del pago. ∼ on aprovecharse de. ∼ mark n marca f registrada. ∼r /-ə(r)/ n comerciante m & f. ∼sman /ˈtreɪdzmən/ n (pl -men) (shopkeeper) tendero m. ∼ union n sindicato m. ∼ unionist n sindicalista m & f. ∼ wind n viento m alisio

trading /ˈtreɪdɪŋ/ n comercio m. ∼ estate n zona f industrial

tradition /trəˈdɪʃn/ n tradición f. ∼al a tradicional. ∼alist n tradicionalista m & f. ∼ally adv tradicionalmente

traffic /ˈtræfɪk/ n tráfico m. —vi (pt trafficked) comerciar (in en). ∼-lights npl semáforo m. ∼ warden n guardia m, controlador m de tráfico

trag|edy /ˈtrædʒɪdɪ/ n tragedia f. ∼ic /ˈtrædʒɪk/ a trágico. ∼ically adv trágicamente

trail /treɪl/ vi arrastrarse; (lag) rezagarse. —vt (track) seguir la pista de. —n estela f; (track) pista f. (path) sendero m. ∼er /ˈtreɪlə(r)/ n remolque m; (film) avance m

train /treɪn/ n tren m; (of dress) cola f; (series) sucesión f; (retinue) séquito m. —vt adiestrar; (sport) entrenar; educar (child); guiar (plant); domar (animal). —vi adiestrarse; (sport) entrenarse. **~ed** a (skilled) cualificado; (doctor) diplomado. **~ee** n aprendiz m. **~er** n (sport) entrenador m; (of animals) domador m. **~ers** mpl zapatillas fpl de deporte. **~ing** n instrucción f; (sport) entrenamiento m

traipse /treɪps/ vi (fam) vagar

trait /treɪ(t)/ n característica f, rasgo m

traitor /'treɪtə(r)/ n traidor m

tram /træm/ n tranvía m

tramp /træmp/ vt recorrer a pie. —vi andar con pasos pesados. —n (vagrant) vagabundo m; (sound) ruido m de pasos; (hike) paseo m largo

trample /'træmpl/ vt/i pisotear. **~ (on)** pisotear

trampoline /'træmpəliːn/ n trampolín m

trance /trɑːns/ n trance m

tranquil /'træŋkwɪl/ a tranquilo. **~lity** /-'kwɪlətɪ/ n tranquilidad f

tranquillize /'træŋkwɪlaɪz/ vt tranquilizar. **~r** /-ə(r)/ n tranquilizante m

transact /træn'zækt/ vt negociar. **~ion** /-ʃn/ n transacción f

transatlantic /trænzət'læntɪk/ a transatlántico

transcend /træn'send/ vt exceder. **~ent** a sobresaliente

transcendental /trænsen'dentl/ a trascendental

transcribe /træn'skraɪb/ vt transcribir; grabar (recorded sound)

transcript /'trænskrɪpt/ n copia f. **~ion** /-ɪpʃn/ n transcripción f

transfer /træns'fɜː(r)/ vt (pt transferred) trasladar; calcar (drawing). —vi trasladarse. **~ the charges** (on telephone)

llamar a cobro revertido. /'trænsfɜː(r)/ n traslado m; (paper) calcomanía f. **~able** a transferible

transfigur|ation /trænsfɪɡjʊ-'reɪʃn/ n transfiguración f. **~e** /træns'fɪɡə(r)/ vt transfigurar

transfix /træns'fɪks/ vt traspasar; (fig) paralizar

transform /træns'fɔːm/ vt transformar. **~ation** /-ə'meɪʃn/ n transformación f. **~er** /-ə(r)/ n transformador m

transfusion /træns'fjuːʒn/ n transfusión f

transgress /træns'ɡres/ vt traspasar, infringir. **~ion** /-ʃn/ n transgresión f; (sin) pecado m

transient /'trænzɪənt/ a pasajero

transistor /træn'zɪstə(r)/ n transistor m

transit /'trænsɪt/ n tránsito m

transition /træn'zɪʒn/ n transición f

transitive /'trænsɪtɪv/ a transitivo

transitory /'trænsɪtrɪ/ a transitorio

translat|e /trænz'leɪt/ vt traducir. **~ion** /-ʃn/ n traducción f. **~or** /-ə(r)/ n traductor m

translucen|ce /træns'luːsns/ n traslucidez f. **~t** /træns'luːsnt/ a traslúcido

transmission /træns'mɪʃn/ n transmisión f

transmit /trænz'mɪt/ vt (pt transmitted) transmitir. **~ter** /-ə(r)/ n transmisor m; (TV, radio) emisora f

transparen|cy /træns'pærənsɪ/ n transparencia f; (photo) diapositiva f. **~t** /træns'pærənt/ a transparente

transpire /træn'spaɪə(r)/ vi transpirar; (happen, fam) suceder, revelarse

transplant /træns'plɑːnt/ vt trasplantar. /'trænsplɑːnt/ n trasplante m

transport /træn'spɔ:t/ vt transportar. /'trænspɔ:t/ n transporte m. ~ation /-'teɪʃn/ n transporte m

transpos|e /træn'spəʊz/ vt transponer; (mus) transportar. ~ition /-pə'zɪʃn/ n transposición f. (mus) transporte m

transverse /'trænzvɜ:s/ a transverso

transvestite /trænz'vestaɪt/ n travestido m

trap /træp/ n trampa f. —vt (pt **trapped**) atrapar; (jam) atascar; (cut off) bloquear. **~door** /'træpdɔ:(r)/ n trampa f. (in theatre) escotillón m

trapeze /trə'pi:z/ n trapecio m

trappings /'træpɪŋz/ npl (fig) atavíos mpl

trash /træʃ/ n pacotilla f; (refuse) basura f; (nonsense) tonterías fpl. ~ can n (Amer) cubo m de la basura. ~y a de baja calidad

trauma /'trɔ:mə/ n trauma m. ~tic /-'mætɪk/ a traumático

travel /'trævl/ vi (pt **travelled**) viajar. —vt recorrer. —n viajar m. ~ler /-ə(r)/ n viajero m. ~ler's cheque n cheque m de viaje. ~ling n viaje m

traverse /træ'vɜ:s/ vt atravesar, recorrer

travesty /'trævɪstɪ/ n parodia f

trawler /'trɔ:lə(r)/ n pesquero m de arrastre

tray /treɪ/ n bandeja f

treacher|ous a traidor; (deceptive) engañoso. ~ously adv traidoramente. ~y /'tretʃərɪ/ n traición f

treacle /'tri:kl/ n melaza f

tread /tred/ vi (pt **trod**, pp **trodden**) andar. —on pisar. —vt pisar. —n (step) paso m; (of tyre) banda f de rodadura. ~mill /tredmɪl/ n pedal m. ~mill /'tredmɪl/ n rueda f de molino; (fig) rutina f

treason /'tri:zn/ n traición f

treasure /'treʒə(r)/ n tesoro m. —vt apreciar mucho; (store) guardar

treasur|er /'treʒərə(r)/ n tesorero m. ~y /'treʒərɪ/ n tesorería f. the T~y n el Ministerio m de Hacienda

treat /tri:t/ vt tratar; (consider) considerar. ~ s.o. invitar a uno. —n placer m; (present) regalo m

treatise /'tri:tɪz/ n tratado m

treatment /'tri:tmənt/ n tratamiento m

treaty /'tri:tɪ/ n tratado m

treble /'trebl/ a triple; (clef) de sol; (voice) de tiple. —vt triplicar. —vi triplicarse. —n tiple m & f

tree /tri:/ n árbol m

trek /trek/ n viaje m arduo, caminata f. —vi (pt **trekked**) hacer un viaje arduo

trellis /'trelɪs/ n enrejado m

tremble /'trembl/ vi temblar

tremendous /trɪ'mendəs/ a tremendo; (huge, fam) enorme. ~ly adv tremendamente

tremor /'tremə(r)/ n temblor m

tremulous /'tremjʊləs/ a tembloroso

trench /trentʃ/ n foso m, zanja f; (mil) trinchera f. ~ coat n trinchera f

trend /trend/ n tendencia f; (fashion) moda f. ~setter n persona f que lanza la moda. ~y a (-ier, -iest) (fam) a la última

trepidation /trepɪ'deɪʃn/ n inquietud f

trespass /'trespəs/ vi. ~ on entrar sin derecho; (fig) abusar de. ~er /-ə(r)/ n intruso m

tress /tres/ n trenza f

trestle /'tresl/ n caballete m. ~ table n mesa f de caballete

trews /tru:z/ npl pantalón m

trial /'traɪəl/ n prueba f; (jurid) proceso m; (ordeal) prueba f dura. ~ **and error** tanteo *m*. **be on** ~ estar a prueba; (*jurid*) ser procesado

triangle /'traɪæŋgl/ *n* triángulo *m*. ~**ular** /-'æŋgjʊlə(r)/ *a* triangular

tribal /'traɪbl/ *a* tribal. ~**e** /traɪb/ *n* tribu *f*

tribulation /trɪbjʊ'leɪʃn/ *n* tribulación *f*

tribunal /traɪ'bjuːnl/ *n* tribunal *m*

tributary /'trɪbjʊtrɪ/ *n* (*stream*) afluente *m*

tribute /'trɪbjuːt/ *n* tributo *m*. **pay** ~ **to** rendir homenaje a

trice /traɪs/ *n*. **in a** ~ en un abrir y cerrar de ojos

trick /trɪk/ *n* trampa *f*; engaño *m*; (*joke*) broma *f*; (*at cards*) baza *f*; (*habit*) manía *f*. **do the** ~ servir. **play a** ~ **on** gastar una broma a. —*vt* engañar. ~**ery** /'trɪkərɪ/ *n* engaño *m*

trickle /'trɪkl/ *vi* gotear. ~ **in** (*fig*) entrar poco a poco. ~ **out** (*fig*) salir poco a poco

trickster /'trɪkstə(r)/ *n* estafador *m*

tricky /'trɪkɪ/ *a* delicado, difícil

tricolour /'trɪkələ(r)/ *n* bandera *f* tricolor

tricycle /'traɪsɪkl/ *n* triciclo *m*

trident /'traɪdənt/ *n* tridente *m*

tried /traɪd/ *see* **try**

trifle /'traɪfl/ *n* bagatela *f*; (*culin*) bizcocho *m* con natillas, jalea, frutas y nata. —*vi*. ~**e with** jugar con. ~**ing** *a* insignificante

trigger /'trɪɡə(r)/ *n* (*of gun*) gatillo *m*. —*vt*. ~ (**off**) desencadenar

trigonometry /trɪɡə'nɒmɪtrɪ/ *n* trigonometría *f*

trilby /'trɪlbɪ/ *n* sombrero *m* de fieltro

trilogy /'trɪlədʒɪ/ *n* trilogía *f*

trim /trɪm/ *a* (**trimmer, trimmest**) arreglado. —*vt* (*pt*

trimmed) cortar; recortar ⟨*hair etc*⟩; (*adorn*) adornar. —*n* (*cut*) recorte *m*; (*decoration*) adorno *m*; (*state*) estado *m*. **in a** ~ **en buen estado;** (*fit*) en forma. ~**ming** *n* adorno *m*. ~**mings** *npl* recortes *mpl*; (*decorations*) adornos *mpl*; (*culin*) guarnición *f*

trinity /'trɪnɪtɪ/ *n* trinidad *f*. **the T**~ la Trinidad

trinket /'trɪŋkɪt/ *n* chuchería *f*

trio /'triːəʊ/ *n* (*pl* -**os**) trío *m*

trip /trɪp/ *vt* (*pt* **tripped**) hacer tropezar. —*vi* tropezar; (*go lightly*) andar con paso ligero. —*n* (*journey*) viaje *m*; (*outing*) excursión *f*; (*stumble*) traspié *m*. ~ **up** *vi* tropezar. —*vt* hacer tropezar

tripe /traɪp/ *n* callos *mpl*; (*nonsense, sl*) tonterías *fpl*

triple /'trɪpl/ *a* triple. —*vt* triplicar. —*vi* triplicarse. ~**ts** /'trɪplɪts/ *npl* trillizos *mpl*

triplicate /'trɪplɪkət/ *a* triplicado. **in** ~ por triplicado

tripod /'traɪpɒd/ *n* trípode *m*

tripper /'trɪpə(r)/ *n* (*on day trip etc*) excursionista *m & f*

triptych /'trɪptɪk/ *n* tríptico *m*

trite /traɪt/ *a* trillado

triumph /'traɪəmf/ *n* triunfo *m*. —*vi* triunfar (**over** sobre). ~**al** /-'ʌmfl/ *a* triunfal. ~**ant** /-'ʌmfnt/ *a* triunfante

trivial /'trɪvɪəl/ *a* insignificante. ~**ity** /-'ælɪtɪ/ *n* insignificancia *f*

trod, trodden /trɒd, trɒdn/ *see* **tread**

trolley /'trɒlɪ/ *n* (*pl* -**eys**) carretón *m*. **tea** ~ *n* mesita *f* de ruedas. ~**bus** *n* trolebús *m*

trombone /trɒm'bəʊn/ *n* trombón *m*

troop /truːp/ *n* grupo *m*. —*vi*. ~ **in** entrar en tropel. ~ **out** salir en tropel. —*vt*. ~**ing the colour** saludo *m* a la bandera. ~**er** *n* soldado *m* de caballería. ~**s** *npl* (*mil*) tropas *fpl*

trophy /'trəʊfɪ/ n trofeo m
tropic /'trɒpɪk/ n trópico m. **~al** a tropical. **~s** npl trópicos mpl
trot /trɒt/ n trote m. **on the ~** (fam) seguidos. —vi (pt **trotted**) trotar. **~ out** (produce, fam) producir
trotter /'trɒtə(r)/ n (culin) pie m de cerdo
trouble /'trʌbl/ n problema m; (awkward situation) apuro m; (inconvenience) molestia f; (conflict) conflicto m; (med) enfermedad f; (mec) avería f. **be in ~** estar en un apuro. **make ~** armar un lío. **take ~** tomarse la molestia. —vt (bother) molestar; (worry) preocupar. —vi molestarse; (worry) preocuparse. **be ~d about** preocuparse por. **~-maker** n alborotador m. **~some** a molesto
trough /trɒf/ n (for drinking) abrevadero m; (for feeding) pesebre m; (of wave) seno m; (atmospheric) mínimo m de presión
trounce /traʊns/ vt (defeat) derrotar; (thrash) pegar
troupe /truːp/ n compañía f
trousers /'traʊzəz/ npl pantalón m; pantalones mpl
trousseau /'truːsəʊ/ n (pl **-s** /-əʊz/) ajuar m
trout /traʊt/ n (pl **trout**) trucha f
trowel /'traʊəl/ n (garden) desplantador m; (for mortar) paleta f
truant /'truːənt/ n. **play ~** hacer novillos
truce /truːs/ n tregua f
truck[1] /trʌk/ n carro m; (rail) vagón m; (lorry) camión m
truck[2] /trʌk/ n (dealings) trato m
truculent /'trʌkjʊlənt/ a agresivo
trudge /trʌdʒ/ vi andar penosamente. —n caminata f penosa
true /truː/ a (-er, -est) verdadero; (loyal) leal; (genuine)

auténtico; (accurate) exacto. **come ~** realizarse
truffle /'trʌfl/ n trufa f; (chocolate) trufa f de chocolate
truism /'truːɪzəm/ n perogrullada f
truly /'truːlɪ/ adv verdaderamente; (sincerely) sinceramente; (faithfully) fielmente. **yours ~** (in letters) le saluda atentamente
trump /trʌmp/ n (cards) triunfo m. —vt fallar. **~ up** inventar
trumpet /'trʌmpɪt/ n trompeta f. **~er** /-ə(r)/ n trompetero m, trompeta m & f
truncated /trʌŋ'keɪtɪd/ a truncado
truncheon /'trʌntʃən/ n porra f
trundle /'trʌndl/ vt hacer rodar. —vi rodar
trunk /trʌŋk/ n tronco m; (box) baúl m; (of elephant) trompa f. **~-call** n conferencia f. **~-road** n carretera f (nacional). **~s** npl bañador m
truss /trʌs/ n (med) braguero m. **~ up** vi (culin) espetar
trust /trʌst/ n confianza f; (association) trust m. **on ~** a ojos cerrados; (com) al fiado. —vi confiar. **~ to** confiar en. —vt confiar en; (hope) esperar. **~ed** a leal
trustee /trʌs'tiː/ n administrador m
trust: **~ful** a confiado. **~fully** adv confiadamente. **~worthy** a, **~y** a digno de confianza
truth /truːθ/ n (pl **-s** /truːðz/) verdad f. **~ful** a veraz; (true) verídico. **~fully** adv sinceramente
try /traɪ/ vt (pt **tried**) probar; (be a strain on) poner a prueba; (jurid) procesar. **~ on** vt probarse (garment). **~ out** vt probar. —vi probar. **~ for** vi intentar conseguir. —n tentativa f, prueba f; (rugby) ensayo

m. ~**ing** *a* difícil; (*annoying*) molesto. ~**out** *n* prueba *f*

tryst /trɪst/ *n* cita *f*

T-shirt /'tiːʃɜːt/ *n* camiseta *f*

tub /tʌb/ *n* tina *f*; (*bath, fam*) baño *m*

tuba /'tjuːbə/ *n* tuba *f*

tubby /'tʌbɪ/ *a* (**-ier, -iest**) rechoncho

tube /tjuːb/ *n* tubo *m*; (*rail, fam*) metro *m*. **inner** ~ *n* cámara *f* de aire

tuber /'tjuːbə(r)/ *n* tubérculo *m*

tuberculosis /tjuːbɜːkjʊ'ləʊsɪs/ *n* tuberculosis *f*

tub|**ing** /'tjuːbɪŋ/ *n* tubería *f*, tubos *mpl.* ~**ular** *a* tubular

tuck /tʌk/ *n* pliegue *m.* —*vt* plegar; (*put*) meter; (*put away*) remeter; (*hide*) esconder. ~ **up** *vt* arropar (*child*). —*vi.* ~ **in(to)** (*eat, sl*) comer con buen apetito. ~**-shop** *n* confitería *f*

Tuesday /'tjuːzdeɪ/ *n* martes *m*

tuft /tʌft/ *n* (*of hair*) mechón *m*; (*of feathers*) penacho *m*; (*of grass*) manojo *m*

tug /tʌg/ *vt* (*pt* **tugged**) tirar de; (*tow*) remolcar. —*vi* tirar fuerte. —*n* tirón *m*; (*naut*) remolcador *m.* ~**-of-war** *n* lucha *f* de la cuerda; (*fig*) tira *m* y afloja

tuition /tjuːˈɪʃn/ *n* enseñanza *f*

tulip /'tjuːlɪp/ *n* tulipán *m*

tumble /'tʌmbl/ *vi* caerse. ~ **to** (*fam*) comprender. —*n* caída *f*

tumbledown /'tʌmbldaʊn/ *a* ruinoso

tumble-drier /tʌmbl'draɪə(r)/ *n* secadora *f* (eléctrica con aire de salida)

tumbler /'tʌmblə(r)/ *n* (*glass*) vaso *m*

tummy /'tʌmɪ/ *n* (*fam*) estómago *m*

tumour /'tjuːmə(r)/ *n* tumor *m*

tumult /'tjuːmʌlt/ *n* tumulto *m.* ~**uous** /-'mʌltjʊəs/ *a* tumultuoso

tuna /'tjuːnə/ *n* (*pl* **tuna**) atún *m*

tune /tjuːn/ *n* aire *m.* **be in** ~ estar afinado. **be out of** ~ estar desafinado. —*vt* afinar; (*in*tonizar ⟨radio, TV⟩; (*mec*) poner a punto. —*vi.* ~ **in (to)** ⟨radio, TV⟩ sintonizarse. ~ **up** afinar. ~**ful** *a* melodioso. ~**r** /-ə(r)/ *n* afinador *m*; ⟨radio, TV⟩ sintonizador *m*

tunic /'tjuːnɪk/ *n* túnica *f*

tuning-fork /'tjuːnɪŋfɔːk/ *n* diapasón *m*

Tunisia /tjuːˈnɪzɪə/ *n* Túnez *m.* ~**n** *a & n* tunecino (*m*)

tunnel /'tʌnl/ *n* túnel *m.* —*vi* (*pt* **tunnelled**) construir un túnel en

turban /'tɜːbən/ *n* turbante *m*

turbid /'tɜːbɪd/ *a* túrbido

turbine /'tɜːbaɪn/ *n* turbina *f*

turbo-jet /'tɜːbəʊdʒet/ *n* turborreactor *m*

turbot /'tɜːbət/ *n* rodaballo *m*

turbulen|**ce** /'tɜːbjʊləns/ *n* turbulencia *f.* ~**t** /'tɜːbjʊlənt/ *a* turbulento

tureen /təˈriːn/ *n* sopera *f*

turf /tɜːf/ *n* (*pl* **turfs** or **turves**) césped *m*; (*segment*) tepe *m.* **the** ~ *n* las carreras *fpl* de caballos. —*vt.* ~ **out** (*sl*) echar

turgid /'tɜːdʒɪd/ *a* ⟨language⟩ pomposo

Turk /tɜːk/ *n* turco *m*

turkey /'tɜːkɪ/ *n* (*pl* **-eys**) pavo *m*

Turk|**ey** /'tɜːkɪ/ *n* Turquía *f.* **T~ish** *a & n* turco (*m*)

turmoil /'tɜːmɔɪl/ *n* confusión *f*

turn /tɜːn/ *vt* hacer girar, dar vueltas a; volver ⟨direction, page, etc⟩; cumplir ⟨age⟩; dar ⟨hour⟩; doblar ⟨corner⟩; ⟨change⟩ cambiar; (*deflect*) desviar. ~ **the tables** volver las tornas. —*vi* girar, dar vueltas; (*become*) hacerse; (*change*) cambiar. —*n* vuelta *f*; (*in road*) curva *f*; (*change*) cambio *m*; (*sequence*) turno *m*; (*of mind*) disposición *f*; (*in theatre*) número *m*; (*fright*) susto *m*; (*of illness, fam*) ataque *m*. **bad** ~ mala jugada *f*. **good** ~ favor *m*. **in** ~ a su vez. **out of** ~ fuera de lugar. **to a** ~ (*culin*) en su punto. ~ **against** *vt* volverse en contra de. ~ **down** *vt* (*fold*) doblar; (*reduce*) bajar; (*reject*) rechazar. ~ **in** *vt* entregar. —*vi* (*go to bed, fam*) acostarse. ~ **off** *vt* cerrar (*tap*); apagar (*light, TV, etc*). —*vi* desviarse. ~ **on** *vt* abrir (*tap*); encender (*light etc*); (*attack*) atacar; (*attract, fam*) excitar. ~ **out** *vt* expulsar; apagar (*light etc*); (*produce*) producir; (*empty*) vaciar. —*vi* (*result*) resultar. ~ **round** *vi* dar la vuelta. ~ **up** *vi* aparecer. —*vt* (*find*) encontrar; levantar (*collar*); poner más fuerte (*gas*). ~**ed-up** *a* (*nose*) respingona. ~**ing** /'tɜːnɪŋ/ *n* vuelta *f*; (*road*) bocacalle *f*. ~**ing-point** *n* punto *m* decisivo.

turnip /'tɜːnɪp/ *n* nabo *m*

turn: ~**out** /-aʊt/ *n* (*of people*) concurrencia *f*; (*of goods*) producción *f*. ~**over** /'tɜːnəʊvə(r)/ *n* (*culin*) empanada *f*; (*com*) volumen *m* de negocios; (*of staff*) rotación *f*. ~**pike** /-paɪk/ *n* (*Amer*) autopista *f* de peaje. ~**stile** /'tɜːnstaɪl/ *n* torniquete *m*. ~**table** /'tɜːnteɪbl/ *n* plataforma *f* giratoria; (*on record-player*) plato *m* giratorio. ~**up** *n* (*of trousers*) vuelta *f*

turpentine /'tɜːpəntaɪn/ *n* trementina *f*

turquoise /'tɜːkwɔɪz/ *a & n* turquesa (*f*)

turret /'tʌrɪt/ *n* torrecilla *f*; (*mil*) torreta *f*

turtle /'tɜːtl/ *n* tortuga *f* de mar. ~**-neck** *n* cuello *m* alto

tusk /tʌsk/ *n* colmillo *m*

tussle /'tʌsl/ *vi* pelearse. —*n* pelea *f*

tussock /'tʌsək/ *n* montecillo *m* de hierbas

tutor /'tjuːtə(r)/ *n* preceptor *m*; (*univ*) director *m* de estudios, profesor *m*. ~**ial** /tjuːˈtɔːrɪəl/ *n* clase *f* particular

tuxedo /tʌkˈsiːdəʊ/ *n* (*pl* **-os**) (*Amer*) esmoquin *m*

TV /tiːˈviː/ *n* televisión *f*

twaddle /'twɒdl/ *n* tonterías *fpl*

twang /twæŋ/ *n* tañido *m*; (*in voice*) gangueo *m*. —*vt* hacer vibrar. —*vi* vibrar

tweed /twiːd/ *n* tela *f* gruesa de lana

tweet /twiːt/ *n* piada *f*. —*vi* piar

tweezers /'twiːzəz/ *npl* pinzas *fpl*

twel|fth /twelfθ/ *a & n* duodécimo (*m*). ~**ve** /twelv/ *a & n* doce (*m*)

twent|ieth /'twentɪəθ/ *a & n* vigésimo (*m*). ~**y** /'twentɪ/ *a & n* veinte (*m*)

twerp /twɜːp/ *n* (*sl*) imbécil *m*

twice /twaɪs/ *adv* dos veces

twiddle /'twɪdl/ *vt* hacer girar. ~ **one's thumbs** (*fig*) no tener nada que hacer. ~ **with** jugar con

twig[1] /twɪg/ *n* ramita *f*

twig[2] /twɪg/ *vt/i* (*pt* **twigged**) (*fam*) comprender

twilight /'twaɪlaɪt/ *n* crepúsculo *m*

twin /twɪn/ *a & n* gemelo *m*

twine /twaɪn/ *n* bramante *m*. —*vt* torcer. —*vi* enroscarse

twinge /twɪndʒ/ *n* punzada *f*; (*fig*) remordimiento *m* (de conciencia)

twinkle /'twɪŋkl/ *vi* centellear. —*n* centelleo *m*

twirl /twɜːl/ *vt* dar vueltas a. —*vi* dar vueltas. —*n* vuelta *f*

twist /twɪst/ *vt* torcer; (*roll*) enrollar; (*distort*) deformar. —*vi* torcerse; (*coil*) enroscarse.

twit ‹road› serpentear. —n torsión f; ‹curve› vuelta f; ‹of character› peculiaridad f

twit[1] /twɪt/ n (sl) imbécil m

twit[2] /twɪt/ vt (pt twitted) tomar el pelo a

twitch /twɪtʃ/ vt crispar. —vi crisparse. —n tic m; ‹jerk› tirón m

twitter /'twɪtə(r)/ vi gorjear. —n gorjeo m

two /tuː/ a & n dos (m). in ~ minds indeciso. ~-faced a falso, insincero. ~piece (suit) n traje m (de dos piezas). ~some /'tuːsəm/ n pareja f. ~-way a ‹traffic› de doble sentido

tycoon /taɪ'kuːn/ n magnate m

tying /'taɪɪŋ/ see tie

type /taɪp/ n tipo m. —vt/i escribir a máquina. ~cast a ‹actor› encasillado. ~script /'taɪp skrɪpt/ n texto m escrito a máquina. ~writer /'taɪpraɪtə(r)/ n máquina f de escribir. ~written /-ɪtn/ a escrito a máquina, mecanografiado

typhoid /'taɪfɔɪd/ n. ~ (fever) fiebre f tifoidea

typhoon /taɪ'fuːn/ n tifón m

typical /'tɪpɪkl/ a típico. ~ly adv típicamente

typify /'tɪpɪfaɪ/ vt tipificar

typing /'taɪpɪŋ/ n mecanografía f. ~st n mecanógrafo m

typography /taɪ'pɒgrəfɪ/ n tipografía f

tyrannical /tɪ'rænɪkl/ a tiránico. ~nize /'tɪrənaɪz/ vt tiranizar. ~ny /'tɪrənɪ/ n tiranía f. ~t /'taɪərənt/ n tirano m

tyre /'taɪə(r)/ n neumático m, llanta f (Amer)

U

ubiquitous /juː'bɪkwɪtəs/ a omnipresente, ubicuo

udder /'ʌdə(r)/ n ubre f

UFO /'juːfəʊ/ abbr (unidentified flying object) OVNI m, objeto m volante no identificado

ugliness /'ʌglɪnɪs/ n fealdad f. ~y /'ʌglɪ/ a (-ier, -iest) feo

UK /juː'keɪ/ abbr (United Kingdom) Reino m Unido

ulcer /'ʌlsə(r)/ n úlcera f. ~ous a ulceroso

ulterior /ʌl'tɪərɪə(r)/ a ulterior. ~ motive n segunda intención f

ultimate /'ʌltɪmət/ a último; ‹definitive› definitivo; ‹fundamental› fundamental. ~ly adv al final; (basically) en el fondo

ultimatum /ʌltɪ'meɪtəm/ n (pl -ums) ultimátum m invar

ultra... /'ʌltrə/ pref ultra...

ultramarine /ʌltrəmə'riːn/ n azul m marino

ultrasonic /ʌltrə'sɒnɪk/ a ultrasónico

ultraviolet /ʌltrə'vaɪələt/ a ultravioleta a invar

umbilical /ʌm'bɪlɪkl/ a umbilical. ~ cord n cordón m umbilical

umbrage /'ʌmbrɪdʒ/ n resentimiento m. take ~ ofenderse (at por)

umbrella /ʌm'brelə/ n paraguas m invar

umpire /'ʌmpaɪə(r)/ n árbitro m. —vt arbitrar

umpteen /ʌmp'tiːn/ a (sl) muchísimos. ~th a (sl) enésimo

UN /juː'en/ abbr (United Nations) ONU f, Organización f de las Naciones Unidas

un... /ʌn/ pref in..., des..., no, poco, sin

unabated /ʌnəˈbeɪtɪd/ *a* no disminuido

unable /ʌnˈeɪbl/ *a* incapaz (to de). be ~ to no poder

unabridged /ʌnəˈbrɪdʒd/ *a* íntegro

unacceptable /ʌnəkˈseptəbl/ *a* inaceptable

unaccountabl|e /ʌnəˈkaʊntəbl/ *a* inexplicable. ~y *adv* inexplicablemente

unaccustomed /ʌnəˈkʌstəmd/ *a* insólito. be ~ to a no estar acostumbrado a

unadopted /ʌnəˈdɒptɪd/ *a* (of road) privado

unadulterated /ʌnəˈdʌltəreɪtɪd/ *a* puro

unaffected /ʌnəˈfektɪd/ *a* sin afectación, natural

unaided /ʌnˈeɪdɪd/ *a* sin ayuda

unalloyed /ʌnəˈlɔɪd/ *a* puro

unanimous /juːˈnænɪməs/ *a* unánime. ~ly *adv* unánimemente

unannounced /ʌnəˈnaʊnst/ *a* sin previo aviso; (unexpected) inesperado

unarmed /ʌnˈɑːmd/ *a* desarmado

unassuming /ʌnəˈsjuːmɪŋ/ *a* modesto, sin pretensiones

unattached /ʌnəˈtætʃt/ *a* suelto; (unmarried) soltero

unattended /ʌnəˈtendɪd/ *a* sin vigilar

unattractive /ʌnəˈtræktɪv/ *a* poco atractivo

unavoidabl|e /ʌnəˈvɔɪdəbl/ *a* inevitable. ~y *adv* inevitablemente

unaware /ʌnəˈweə(r)/ *a* ignorante (of de). be ~ of ignorar. ~s /-eəz/ *adv* desprevenido

unbalanced /ʌnˈbælənst/ *a* desequilibrado

unbearabl|e /ʌnˈbeərəbl/ *a* inaguantable. ~y *adv* inaguantablemente

unbeat|able /ʌnˈbiːtəbl/ *a* insuperable. ~en *a* no vencido

unbeknown /ʌnbɪˈnəʊn/ *a* desconocido. ~ to me (fam) sin saberlo yo

unbelievable /ʌnbɪˈliːvəbl/ *a* increíble

unbend /ʌnˈbend/ *vt* (pt unbent) enderezar. —*vi* (relax) relajarse. ~ing *a* inflexible

unbiased /ʌnˈbaɪəst/ *a* imparcial

unbidden /ʌnˈbɪdn/ *a* espontáneo; (without invitation) sin ser invitado

unblock /ʌnˈblɒk/ *vt* desatascar

unbolt /ʌnˈbəʊlt/ *vt* desatrancar

unborn /ʌnˈbɔːn/ *a* no nacido todavía

unbounded /ʌnˈbaʊndɪd/ *a* ilimitado

unbreakable /ʌnˈbreɪkəbl/ *a* irrompible

unbridled /ʌnˈbraɪdld/ *a* desenfrenado

unbroken /ʌnˈbrəʊkən/ *a* (intact) intacto; (continuous) continuo

unburden /ʌnˈbɜːdn/ *vt*. ~ o.s. desahogarse

unbutton /ʌnˈbʌtn/ *vt* desabotonar, desabrochar

uncalled-for /ʌnˈkɔːldfɔː(r)/ *a* fuera de lugar; (unjustified) injustificado

uncanny /ʌnˈkænɪ/ *a* (-ier, -iest) misterioso

unceasing /ʌnˈsiːsɪŋ/ *a* incesante

unceremonious /ʌnserɪˈməʊnɪəs/ *a* informal; (abrupt) brusco

uncertain /ʌnˈsɜːtn/ *a* incierto; (changeable) variable. be ~ whether no saber exactamente si. ~ty *n* incertidumbre *f*

unchang|ed /ʌnˈtʃeɪndʒd/ *a* igual. ~ing *a* inmutable

uncharitable /ʌnˈtʃærɪtəbl/ *a* severo

uncivilized /ʌnˈsɪvɪlaɪzd/ *a* incivilizado

uncle /ˈʌŋkl/ n tío m

unclean /ʌnˈkliːn/ a sucio

unclear /ʌnˈklɪə(r)/ a poco claro

uncomfortable /ʌnˈkʌmfətəbl/ a incómodo; (*unpleasant*) desagradable. **feel** ∼ no estar a gusto

uncommon /ʌnˈkɒmən/ a raro. ∼**ly** adv extraordinariamente

uncompromising /ʌnˈkɒmprə-maɪzɪŋ/ a intransigente

unconcerned /ʌnkənˈsɜːnd/ a indiferente

unconditional /ʌnkənˈdɪʃənl/ a incondicional. ∼**ly** adv incondicionalmente

unconscious /ʌnˈkɒnʃəs/ a inconsciente; (*med*) sin sentido. ∼**ly** adv inconscientemente

unconventional /ʌnkənˈvenʃənl/ a poco convencional

uncooperative /ʌnkəʊˈɒpərətɪv/ a poco servicial

uncork /ʌnˈkɔːk/ vt descorchar, destapar

uncouth /ʌnˈkuːθ/ a grosero

uncover /ʌnˈkʌvə(r)/ vt descubrir

unctuous /ˈʌŋktjʊəs/ a untuoso; (*fig*) empalagoso

undecided /ʌndɪˈsaɪdɪd/ a indeciso

undeniabl|e /ʌndɪˈnaɪəbl/ a innegable. ∼**y** adv indiscutiblemente

under /ˈʌndə(r)/ prep debajo de; (*less than*) menos de; (*in the course of*) bajo, en. —adv debajo, abajo. ∼ **age** a menor de edad. ∼**way** adv en curso; (*on the way*) en marcha

under... pref sub...

undercarriage /ˈʌndəkærɪdʒ/ n (*aviat*) tren m de aterrizaje

underclothes /ˈʌndəkləʊðz/ npl ropa f interior

undercoat /ˈʌndəkəʊt/ n (*of paint*) primera mano f

undercover /ʌndəˈkʌvə(r)/ a secreto

undercurrent /ˈʌndəkʌrənt/ n corriente f submarina; (*fig*) tendencia f oculta

undercut /ˈʌndəkʌt/ vt (*pt* **undercut**) (*com*) vender más barato que

underdeveloped /ʌndədɪˈveləpt/ a subdesarrollado

underdog /ˈʌndədɒg/ n perdedor m. **the** ∼**s** npl los de abajo

underdone /ʌndəˈdʌn/ a (*meat*) poco hecho

underestimate /ʌndərˈestɪmeɪt/ vt subestimar

underfed /ʌndəˈfed/ a desnutrido

underfoot /ʌndəˈfʊt/ adv bajo los pies

undergo /ʌndəˈgəʊ/ vt (*pt* **-went**, *pp* **-gone**) sufrir

undergraduate /ʌndəˈgrædjʊət/ n estudiante m & f universitario (no licenciado)

underground /ʌndəˈgraʊnd/ adv bajo tierra; (*in secret*) clandestinamente. /ˈʌndəgraʊnd/ a subterráneo; (*secret*) clandestino. —n metro m

undergrowth /ˈʌndəgrəʊθ/ n maleza f

underhand /ʌndəˈhænd/ a (*secret*) clandestino; (*deceptive*) fraudulento

underlie /ʌndəˈlaɪ/ vt (*pt* **-lay**, *pp* **-lain**, *pres p* **-lying**) estar debajo de; (*fig*) estar a la base de

underline /ʌndəˈlaɪn/ vt subrayar

underling /ˈʌndəlɪŋ/ n subalterno m

underlying /ʌndəˈlaɪŋ/ a fundamental

undermine /ʌndəˈmaɪn/ vt socavar

underneath /ʌndəˈniːθ/ prep debajo de. —adv por debajo

underpaid /ʌndəˈpeɪd/ a mal pagado

underpants /ˈʌndəpænts/ npl calzoncillos mpl

underpass /ˈʌndəpɑːs/ n paso m subterráneo

underprivileged /ʌndəˈprɪvɪlɪdʒd/ a desvalido

underrate /ʌndəˈreɪt/ vt subestimar

undersell /ʌndəˈsel/ vt (pt -sold) vender más barato que

undersigned /ˈʌndəsaɪnd/ a abajo firmante

undersized /ʌndəˈsaɪzd/ a pequeño

understand /ʌndəˈstænd/ vt/i (pt -stood) entender, comprender. **~able** a comprensible. **~ing** /ʌndəˈstændɪŋ/ a comprensivo. —n comprensión f; (agreement) acuerdo m

understatement /ˈʌndəsteɪtmənt/ n subestimación f

understudy /ˈʌndəstʌdɪ/ n sobresaliente m & f (en el teatro)

undertake /ʌndəˈteɪk/ vt (pt -took, pp -taken) emprender; (assume responsibility) encargarse de

undertaker /ˈʌndəteɪkə(r)/ n empresario m de pompas fúnebres

undertaking /ʌndəˈteɪkɪŋ/ n empresa f; (promise) promesa f

undertone /ˈʌndətəʊn/ n. **in an ~** en voz baja

undertow /ˈʌndətəʊ/ n resaca f

undervalue /ʌndəˈvæljuː/ vt subvalorar

underwater /ʌndəˈwɔːtə(r)/ a submarino. —adv bajo el agua

underwear /ˈʌndəweə(r)/ n ropa f interior

underweight /ˈʌndəweɪt/ a de peso insuficiente. **be ~** estar flaco

underwent /ʌndəˈwent/ see **undergo**

underworld /ˈʌndəwɜːld/ n (criminals) hampa f

underwrite /ʌndəˈraɪt/ vt (pt -wrote, pp -written) (com) asegurar. **~r** /-ə(r)/ n asegurador m

undeserved /ʌndɪˈzɜːvd/ a inmerecido

undesirable /ʌndɪˈzaɪərəbl/ a indeseable

undeveloped /ʌndɪˈveləpt/ a sin desarrollar

undies /ˈʌndɪz/ npl (fam) ropa f interior

undignified /ʌnˈdɪgnɪfaɪd/ a indecoroso

undisputed /ʌndɪsˈpjuːtɪd/ a incontestable

undistinguished /ʌndɪsˈtɪŋwɪʃt/ a mediocre

undo /ʌnˈduː/ vt (pt -did, pp -done) deshacer; (ruin) arruinar; reparar (wrong). **leave ~ne** dejar sin hacer

undoubted /ʌnˈdaʊtɪd/ a indudable. **~ly** adv indudablemente

undress /ʌnˈdres/ vt desnudar. —vi desnudarse

undue /ʌnˈdjuː/ a excesivo

undulate /ˈʌndjʊleɪt/ vi ondular. **~ion** /-ˈleɪʃn/ n ondulación f

unduly /ʌnˈdjuːlɪ/ adv excesivamente

undying /ʌnˈdaɪɪŋ/ a eterno

unearth /ʌnˈɜːθ/ vt desenterrar

unearthly /ʌnˈɜːθlɪ/ a sobrenatural; (impossible, fam) absurdo. **~ hour** n hora intempestiva

uneasily /ʌnˈiːzɪlɪ/ adv inquietamente. **~y** /ʌnˈiːzɪ/ a incómodo; (worrying) inquieto

uneconomic /ʌniːkəˈnɒmɪk/ a poco rentable

uneducated /ʌnˈedjʊkeɪtɪd/ a inculto

unemploy|ed /ʌnɪm'plɔɪd/ a parado, desempleado; (*not in use*) inutilizado. **∼ment** n paro m, desempleo m

unending /ʌn'endɪŋ/ a interminable, sin fin

unequal /ʌn'iːkwəl/ a desigual

unequivocal /ʌnɪ'kwɪvəkl/ a inequívoco

unerring /ʌn'ɜːrɪŋ/ a infalible

unethical /ʌn'eθɪkl/ a sin ética, inmoral

uneven /ʌn'iːvn/ a desigual

unexceptional /ʌnɪk'sepʃənl/ a corriente

unexpected /ʌnɪk'spektɪd/ a inesperado

unfailing /ʌn'feɪlɪŋ/ a inagotable; (*constant*) constante; (*loyal*) leal

unfair /ʌn'feə(r)/ a injusto. **∼ly** adv injustamente. **∼ness** n injusticia f

unfaithful /ʌn'feɪθfl/ a infiel. **∼ness** n infidelidad f

unfamiliar /ʌnfə'mɪlɪə(r)/ a desconocido. **be ∼ with** desconocer

unfasten /ʌn'fɑːsn/ vt desabrochar (*clothes*); (*untie*) desatar

unfavourable /ʌn'feɪvərəbl/ a desfavorable

unfeeling /ʌn'fiːlɪŋ/ a insensible

unfit /ʌn'fɪt/ a inadecuado, no apto; (*unwell*) en mal estado físico; (*incapable*) incapaz

unflinching /ʌn'flɪntʃɪŋ/ a resuelto

unfold /ʌn'fəʊld/ vt desdoblar; (*fig*) revelar. *−vi* (*view etc*) extenderse

unforeseen /ʌnfɔː'siːn/ a imprevisto

unforgettable /ʌnfə'getəbl/ a inolvidable

unforgivable /ʌnfə'gɪvəbl/ a imperdonable

unfortunate /ʌn'fɔːtʃənət/ a desgraciado; (*regrettable*) lamentable. **∼ly** adv desgraciadamente

unfounded /ʌn'faʊndɪd/ a infundado

unfriendly /ʌn'frendlɪ/ a poco amistoso, frío

unfurl /ʌn'fɜːl/ vt desplegar

ungainly /ʌn'geɪnlɪ/ a desgarbado

ungodly /ʌn'gɒdlɪ/ a impío. **∼ hour** n (*fam*) hora f intempestiva

ungrateful /ʌn'greɪtfl/ a desagradecido

unguarded /ʌn'gɑːdɪd/ a indefenso; (*incautious*) imprudente, incauto

unhapp|ily /ʌn'hæpɪlɪ/ adv infelizmente; (*unfortunately*) desgraciadamente. **∼iness** n tristeza f. **∼y** /ʌn'hæpɪ/ a (-ier, -iest) infeliz, triste; (*unsuitable*) inoportuno. **∼y with** insatisfecho de (*plans etc*)

unharmed /ʌn'hɑːmd/ a ileso, sano y salvo

unhealthy /ʌn'helθɪ/ a (-ier, -iest) enfermizo; (*insanitary*) malsano

unhinge /ʌn'hɪndʒ/ vt desquiciar

unholy /ʌn'həʊlɪ/ a (-ier, -iest) impío; (*terrible, fam*) terrible

unhook /ʌn'hʊk/ vt desenganchar

unhoped /ʌn'həʊpt/ a. **∼ for** inesperado

unhurt /ʌn'hɜːt/ a ileso

unicorn /'juːnɪkɔːn/ n unicornio m

unification /juːnɪfɪ'keɪʃn/ n unificación f

uniform /'juːnɪfɔːm/ a & n uniforme (m). **∼ity** /-'fɔːmɪtɪ/ n uniformidad f. **∼ly** adv uniformemente

unify /'juːnɪfaɪ/ vt unificar

unilateral /juːnɪˈlætərəl/ a
unilateral

unimaginable /ʌnɪˈmædʒɪnəbl/
a inconcebible

unimpeachable /ʌnɪmˈpiːtʃəbl/
a irreprensible

unimportant /ʌnɪmˈpɔːtnt/ a
insignificante

uninhabited /ʌnɪnˈhæbɪtɪd/ a
inhabitado; (abandoned) des-
poblado

unintentional /ʌnɪnˈtenʃənl/ a
involuntario

union /ˈjuːnjən/ n unión f; (trade
union) sindicato m. ~ist n sindicalista m & f. U~ Jack n bandera f del Reino Unido

unique /juːˈniːk/ a único. ~ly
adv extraordinariamente

unisex /ˈjuːnɪseks/ a unisex(o)

unison /ˈjuːnɪsn/ n. in ~ al
unísono

unit /ˈjuːnɪt/ n unidad f; (of furniture etc) elemento m

unite /juːˈnaɪt/ vt unir. —vi
unirse. U~d Kingdom (UK) n
Reino m Unido. U~d Nations
(UN) n Organización f de las
Naciones Unidas (ONU). U~d
States (of America) (USA) n
Estados mpl Unidos (de Amér-
ica) (EE.UU.)

unity /ˈjuːnɪtɪ/ n unidad f; (fig)
acuerdo m

universal /juːnɪˈvɜːsl/ a universal. ~e /ˈjuːnɪvɜːs/ n universo m

university /juːnɪˈvɜːsətɪ/ n universidad f. —a universitario

unjust /ʌnˈdʒʌst/ a injusto

unkempt /ʌnˈkempt/ a desaseado

unkind /ʌnˈkaɪnd/ a poco
amable; (cruel) cruel. ~ly adv
poco amablemente. ~ness n
falta f de amabilidad; (cruelty)
crueldad f

unknown /ʌnˈnəʊn/ a desconocido

unlawful /ʌnˈlɔːfl/ a ilegal

unleash /ʌnˈliːʃ/ vt soltar; (fig)
desencadenar

unless /ʌnˈles, ənˈles/ conj a
menos que, a no ser que

unlike /ʌnˈlaɪk/ a diferente; (not
typical) impropio de. —prep a
diferencia de. ~lihood n improbabilidad f. ~ly /ʌnˈlaɪklɪ/ a
improbable

unlimited /ʌnˈlɪmɪtɪd/ a ilimitado

unload /ʌnˈləʊd/ vt descargar

unlock /ʌnˈlɒk/ vt abrir (con
llave)

unlucky /ʌnˈlʌkɪlɪ/ adv
desgraciadamente. ~y /ʌnˈlʌkɪ/
a (-ier, -iest) desgraciado; (number) de mala suerte

unmanly /ʌnˈmænlɪ/ a poco viril

unmanned /ʌnˈmænd/ a no
tripulado

unmarried /ʌnˈmærɪd/ a soltero.
~ mother n madre f soltera

unmask /ʌnˈmɑːsk/ vt desenmascarar. —vi quitarse la
máscara

unmentionable /ʌnˈmenʃənəbl/
a a que no se debe aludir

unmistakable /ʌnmɪˈsteɪkəbl/ a
inconfundible. ~y adv
claramente

unmitigated /ʌnˈmɪtɪgeɪtɪd/ a
(absolute) absoluto

unmoved /ʌnˈmuːvd/ a (fig) indiferente (by a), insensible (by a)

unnatural /ʌnˈnætʃərəl/ a no natural; (not normal) anormal

unnecessarily /ʌnˈnesəsərɪlɪ/
adv innecesariamente. ~y
/ʌnˈnesəsərɪ/ a innecesario

unnerve /ʌnˈnɜːv/ vt desconcertar

unnoticed /ʌnˈnəʊtɪst/ a inadvertido

unobtainable /ʌnəbˈteɪnəbl/ a
inasequible; (fig) inalcanzable

unobtrusive /ʌnəbˈtruːsɪv/ a
discreto

unofficial /ʌnəˈfɪʃl/ a no oficial.
~**ly** adv extraoficialmente

unpack /ʌnˈpæk/ vt desempaquetar ⟨parcel⟩; deshacer ⟨suitcase⟩. —vi deshacer la maleta

unpalatable /ʌnˈpælətəbl/ a desagradable

unparalleled /ʌnˈpærəleld/ a sin par

unpick /ʌnˈpɪk/ vt descoser

unpleasant /ʌnˈpleznt/ a desagradable. ~**ness** n lo desagradable

unplug /ʌnˈplʌg/ vt (elec) desenchufar

unpopular /ʌnˈpɒpjʊlə(r)/ a impopular

unprecedented /ʌnˈpresɪdentɪd/ a sin precedente

unpredictable /ʌnprɪˈdɪktəbl/ a imprevisible

unpremeditated /ʌnprɪˈmedɪteɪtɪd/ a impremeditado

unprepared /ʌnprɪˈpeəd/ a no preparado; (unready) desprevenido

unprepossessing /ʌnpriːpəˈzesɪŋ/ a poco atractivo

unpretentious /ʌnprɪˈtenʃəs/ a sin pretensiones, modesto

unprincipled /ʌnˈprɪnsɪpld/ a sin principios

unprofessional /ʌnprəˈfeʃənl/ a contrario a la ética profesional

unpublished /ʌnˈpʌblɪʃt/ a inédito

unqualified /ʌnˈkwɒlɪfaɪd/ a sin título; (fig) absoluto

unquestionabl|**e** /ʌnˈkwestʃənəbl/ a indiscutible. ~**y** adv indiscutiblemente

unquote /ʌnˈkwəʊt/ vi cerrar comillas

unravel /ʌnˈrævl/ vt (pt unravelled) desenredar; deshacer ⟨knitting etc⟩. —vi desenredarse

unreal /ʌnˈrɪəl/ a irreal. ~**istic** a poco realista

unreasonable /ʌnˈriːzənəbl/ a irrazonable

unrecognizable /ʌnrekəgˈnaɪzəbl/ a irreconocible

unrelated /ʌnrɪˈleɪtɪd/ a ⟨facts⟩ inconexo, sin relación; ⟨people⟩ no emparentado

unreliable /ʌnrɪˈlaɪəbl/ a ⟨person⟩ poco formal; ⟨machine⟩ poco fiable

unrelieved /ʌnrɪˈliːvd/ a no aliviado

unremitting /ʌnrɪˈmɪtɪŋ/ a incesante

unrepentant /ʌnrɪˈpentənt/ a impenitente

unrequited /ʌnrɪˈkwaɪtɪd/ a no correspondido

unreservedly /ʌnrɪˈzɜːvɪdlɪ/ adv sin reserva

unrest /ʌnˈrest/ n inquietud f; (pol) agitación f

unrivalled /ʌnˈraɪvld/ a sin par

unroll /ʌnˈrəʊl/ vt desenrollar. —vi desenrollarse

unruffled /ʌnˈrʌfld/ ⟨person⟩ imperturbable

unruly /ʌnˈruːlɪ/ a indisciplinado

unsafe /ʌnˈseɪf/ a peligroso; ⟨person⟩ en peligro

unsaid /ʌnˈsed/ a sin decir

unsatisfactory /ʌnsætɪsˈfæktərɪ/ a insatisfactorio

unsavoury /ʌnˈseɪvərɪ/ a desagradable

unscathed /ʌnˈskeɪðd/ a ileso

unscramble /ʌnˈskræmbl/ vt descifrar

unscrew /ʌnˈskruː/ vt destornillar

unscrupulous /ʌnˈskruːpjʊləs/ a sin escrúpulos

unseat /ʌnˈsiːt/ vt (pol) quitar el escaño a

unseemly /ʌnˈsiːmlɪ/ a indecoroso

unseen /ʌnˈsiːn/ a inadvertido. —n ⟨translation⟩ traducción f a primera vista

unselfish /ʌnˈselfiʃ/ *a* desinteresado

unsettle /ʌnˈsetl/ *vt* perturbar. **~d** *a* perturbado; (*weather*) variable; (*bill*) por pagar

unshakeable /ʌnˈʃeikəbl/ *a* firme

unshaven /ʌnˈʃeivn/ *a* sin afeitar

unsightly /ʌnˈsaitli/ *a* feo

unskilled /ʌnˈskild/ *a* inexperto. **~ worker** *n* obrero *m* no cualificado

unsociable /ʌnˈsəʊʃəbl/ *a* insociable

unsolicited /ʌnsəˈlisitid/ *a* no solicitado

unsophisticated /ʌnsəˈfisti keitid/ *a* sencillo

unsound /ʌnˈsaʊnd/ *a* defectuoso, erróneo. **of ~ mind** demente

unsparing /ʌnˈspeəriŋ/ *a* pródigo; (*cruel*) cruel

unspeakable /ʌnˈspi:kəbl/ *a* indecible

unspecified /ʌnˈspesifaid/ *a* no especificado

unstable /ʌnˈsteibl/ *a* inestable

unsteady /ʌnˈstedi/ *a* inestable; (*hand*) poco firme; (*step*) inseguro

unstinted /ʌnˈstintid/ *a* abundante

unstuck /ʌnˈstʌk/ *a* suelto. **come ~** despegarse; (*fail*, *fam*) fracasar

unstudied /ʌnˈstʌdid/ *a* natural

unsuccessful /ʌnsəkˈsesful/ *a* fracasado. **be ~** no tener éxito, fracasar

unsuitable /ʌnˈsu:təbl/ *a* inadecuado; (*inconvenient*) inconveniente

unsure /ʌnˈʃʊə(r)/ *a* inseguro

unsuspecting /ʌnsəˈspektiŋ/ *a* confiado

unthinkable /ʌnˈθiŋkəbl/ *a* inconcebible

untidily /ʌnˈtaidili/ *adv* desordenadamente. **~iness** *n* desorden *m*. **~y** /ʌnˈtaidi/ *a* (-ier, -iest) desordenado; (*person*) desaseado

untie /ʌnˈtai/ *vt* desatar

until /ənˈtil, ʌnˈtil/ *prep* hasta. **—conj** hasta que

untimely /ʌnˈtaimli/ *a* inoportuno; (*premature*) prematuro

untiring /ʌnˈtaiəriŋ/ *a* incansable

untold /ʌnˈtəʊld/ *a* incalculable

untoward /ʌntəˈwɔːd/ *a* (*inconvenient*) inconveniente

untried /ʌnˈtraid/ *a* no probado

untrue /ʌnˈtruː/ *a* falso

unused /ʌnˈjuːzd/ *a* nuevo. /ʌnˈjuːst/ *a*. **~ to** no acostumbrado a

unusual /ʌnˈjuːʒʊəl/ *a* insólito; (*exceptional*) excepcional. **~ly** *adv* excepcionalmente

unutterable /ʌnˈʌtərəbl/ *a* indecible

unveil /ʌnˈveil/ *vt* descubrir; (*disclose*) revelar

unwanted /ʌnˈwɒntid/ *a* superfluo; (*child*) no deseado

unwarranted /ʌnˈwɒrəntid/ *a* injustificado

unwelcome /ʌnˈwelkəm/ *a* desagradable; (*guest*) inoportuno

unwell /ʌnˈwel/ *a* indispuesto

unwieldy /ʌnˈwiːldi/ *a* difícil de manejar

unwilling /ʌnˈwiliŋ/ *a* no dispuesto. **be ~** no querer. **~ly** *adv* de mala gana

unwind /ʌnˈwaind/ *vt* (*pt* **unwound**) desenvolver. **—vi** desenvolverse; (*relax*, *fam*) relajarse

unwise /ʌnˈwaiz/ *a* imprudente

unwitting /ʌnˈwitiŋ/ *a* inconsciente; (*involuntary*) involuntario. **~ly** *adv* involuntariamente

unworthy /ʌnˈwɜːði/ *a* indigno

unwrap /ʌn'ræp/ *vt* (*pt* **unwrapped**) desenvolver, deshacer

unwritten /ʌn'rɪtn/ *a* no escrito; ⟨*agreement*⟩ tácito

up /ʌp/ *adv* arriba; (*upwards*) hacia arriba; (*higher*) más arriba; (*out of bed*) levantado; (*finished*) terminado. ~ **here** aquí arriba. ~ **in** (*fam*) versado en, fuerte en. ~ **there** allí arriba. ~ **to** hasta. **be one** ~ **on** llevar la ventaja a. **be** ~ **against** enfrentarse con. **be** ~ **to** tramar ⟨*plot*⟩; (*one's turn*) tocar a; a la altura de ⟨*task*⟩; (*reach*) llegar a. **come** ~ subir. **feel** ~ **to** it sentirse capaz. **go** ~ subir. **it's** ~ **to you** depende de ti. **what is** ~? ¿qué pasa? —*prep* arriba; (*on top of*) en lo alto de. —*vt* (*pt* **upped**) aumentar. —*n*. ~**s and downs** *npl* altibajos *mpl*

upbraid /ʌp'breɪd/ *vt* reprender

upbringing /'ʌpbrɪŋɪŋ/ *n* educación *f*

update /ʌp'deɪt/ *vt* poner al día

upgrade /ʌp'greɪd/ *vt* ascender ⟨*person*⟩; mejorar ⟨*equipment*⟩

upheaval /ʌp'hiːvl/ *n* trastorno *m*

uphill /'ʌphɪl/ *a* ascendente; (*fig*) arduo. —*adv* /ʌp'hɪl/ cuesta arriba. **go** ~ subir

uphold /ʌp'həʊld/ *vt* (*pt* **upheld**) sostener

upholster /ʌp'həʊlstə(r)/ *vt* tapizar. ~**er** /-rə(r)/ *n* tapicero *m*. ~**y** *n* tapicería *f*

upkeep /'ʌpkiːp/ *n* mantenimiento *m*

up-market /ʌp'mɑːkɪt/ *a* superior

upon /ə'pɒn/ *prep* en; (*on top of*) encima de. **once** ~ **a time** érase una vez

upper /'ʌpə(r)/ *a* superior. ~ **class** *n* clases *fpl* altas. ~ **hand** *n* dominio *m*, ventaja *f*. ~**most** *a* (el) más alto. —*n* (*of shoe*) pala *f*

uppish /'ʌpɪʃ/ *a* engreído

upright /'ʌpraɪt/ *a* derecho, (*piano*) vertical. —*n* montante *m*

uprising /'ʌpraɪzɪŋ/ *n* sublevación *f*

uproar /'ʌprɔː(r)/ *n* tumulto *m*. ~**ious** /-'rɔːrɪəs/ *a* tumultuoso

uproot /ʌp'ruːt/ *vt* desarraigar

upset /ʌp'set/ *vt* (*pt* **upset**, *presp* **upsetting**) trastornar; desbaratar ⟨*plan etc*⟩; (*distress*) alterar. —*n* /'ʌpset/ *n* trastorno *m*

upshot /'ʌpʃɒt/ *n* resultado *m*

upside-down /ʌpsaɪd'daʊn/ *adv* al revés; (*in disorder*) patas arriba. **turn** ~ volver

upstairs /ʌp'steəz/ *adv* arriba. /'ʌpsteəz/ *a* de arriba

upstart /'ʌpstɑːt/ *n* arribista *m* & *f*

upstream /ʌp'striːm/ *adv* río arriba; (*against the current*) contra la corriente

upsurge /'ʌpsɜːdʒ/ *n* aumento *m*; (*of anger etc*) arrebato *m*

uptake /'ʌpteɪk/ *n*. **quick on the** ~ muy listo

uptight /'ʌptaɪt/ *a* (*fam*) nervioso

up-to-date /ʌptə'deɪt/ *a* al día; ⟨*news*⟩ de última hora; (*modern*) moderno

upturn /'ʌptɜːn/ *n* aumento *m*; (*improvement*) mejora *f*

upward /'ʌpwəd/ *a* ascendente. —*adv* hacia arriba. ~**s** *adv* hacia arriba

uranium /jʊ'reɪnɪəm/ *n* uranio *m*

urban /'ɜːbən/ *a* urbano

urbane /ɜː'beɪn/ *a* cortés

urbanize /'ɜːbənaɪz/ *vt* urbanizar

urchin /'ɜːtʃɪn/ *n* pilluelo *m*

urge /ɜːdʒ/ *vt* incitar, animar. —*n* impulso *m*. ~ **on** animar

urgen|cy /'ɜːdʒənsɪ/ *n* urgencia *f*. ~**t** /'ɜːdʒənt/ *a* urgente. ~**tly** *adv* urgentemente

urin|ate /'juərɪneɪt/ *vi* orinar. **~e** /'juərɪn/ *n* orina *f*

urn /ɜːn/ *n* urna *f*

Uruguay /juərəgwaɪ/ *n* el Uruguay *m*. **~an** *a* & *n* uruguayo (*m*)

us /ʌs, əs/ *pron* nos; (*after prep*) nosotros, nosotras

US(A) /juːes'eɪ/ *abbr* (*United States (of America)*) EE.UU., Estados *mpl* Unidos

usage /'juːzɪdʒ/ *n* uso *m*

use /juːz/ *vt* emplear. /juːs/ *n* uso *m*, empleo *m*. **be of ~** servir. **it is no ~** es inútil, no sirve para nada. **make ~ of** servirse de. **~ up** agotar, consumir. **~d** /juːzd/ *a* ⟨*clothes*⟩ gastado. /juːst/ *pt*. **he ~d to say** decía, solía decir. — *a*. **~d to** acostumbrado a. **~ful** /'juːsfl/ *a* útil. **~fully** *adv* útilmente. **~less** *a* inútil; ⟨*person*⟩ incompetente. **~r** /-zə(r)/ *n* usuario *m*

usher /'ʌʃə(r)/ *n* ujier *m*; (*in theatre etc*) acomodador *m*. —*vt*. **~ in** hacer entrar. **~ette** *n* acomodadora *f*

USSR *abbr* (*history*) (*Union of Soviet Socialist Republics*) URSS

usual /'juːʒʊəl/ *a* usual, corriente; (*habitual*) acostumbrado, habitual. **as ~** como de costumbre, como siempre. **~ly** *adv* normalmente. **he ~ly wakes up early** suele despertarse temprano

usurer /'juːʒərə(r)/ *n* usurero *m*

usurp /joˈzɜːp/ *vt* usurpar. **~er** /-ə(r)/ *n* usurpador *m*

usury /'juːʒərɪ/ *n* usura *f*

utensil /juːˈtensl/ *n* utensilio *m*

uterus /'juːtərəs/ *n* útero *m*

utilitarian /juːtɪlɪˈteərɪən/ *a* utilitario

utility /juːˈtɪlətɪ/ *n* utilidad *f*. **public ~** *n* servicio *m* público. —*a* utilitario

utilize /'juːtɪlaɪz/ *vt* utilizar

utmost /'ʌtməʊst/ *a* extremo. — *n*. **one's ~** todo lo posible

utter[1] /'ʌtə(r)/ *a* completo

utter[2] /'ʌtə(r)/ *vt* (*speak*) pronunciar; dar ⟨*sigh*⟩; emitir ⟨*sound*⟩. **~ance** *n* expresión *f*

utterly /'ʌtəlɪ/ *adv* totalmente

U-turn /'juːtɜːn/ *n* vuelta *f*

V

vacan|cy /'veɪkənsɪ/ *n* (*job*) vacante *f*; (*room*) habitación *f* libre. **~t** *a* libre; (*empty*) vacío; ⟨*look*⟩ vago

vacate /vəˈkeɪt/ *vt* dejar

vacation /vəˈkeɪʃn/ *n* (*Amer*) vacaciones *fpl*

vaccin|ate /'væksɪneɪt/ *vt* vacunar. **~ation** /-ˈneɪʃn/ *n* vacunación *f*. **~e** /'væksiːn/ *n* vacuna *f*

vacuum /'vækjʊəm/ *n* (*pl* **-cuums** *or* **-cua**) vacío *m*. **~ cleaner** *n* aspiradora *f*. **~ flask** *n* termo *m*

vagabond /'vægəbɒnd/ *n* vagabundo *m*

vagary /'veɪgərɪ/ *n* capricho *m*

vagina /vəˈdʒaɪnə/ *n* vagina *f*

vagrant /'veɪgrənt/ *n* vagabundo *m*

vague /veɪg/ *a* (**-er, -est**) vago; ⟨*outline*⟩ indistinto. **be ~ about** no precisar. **~ly** *adv* vagamente

vain /veɪn/ *a* (**-er, -est**) vanidoso; (*useless*) vano, inútil. **in ~** en vano. **~ly** *adv* vanamente

valance /'væləns/ *n* cenefa *f*

vale /veɪl/ *n* valle *m*

valentine /'væləntaɪn/ *n* (*card*) tarjeta *f* del día de San Valentín

valet /'vælɪt, 'væleɪ/ *n* ayuda *m* de cámara

valiant /'vælɪənt/ *a* valeroso

valid /'vælɪd/ *a* válido; (*ticket*) valedero. **~ate** *vt* dar validez a;

(*confirm*) convalidar. **~ity**
/-'ɪdətɪ/ n validez f

valley /'vælɪ/ n (pl **-eys**) valle m

valour /'vælə(r)/ n valor m

valuable /'væljʊəbl/ a valioso.
~s npl objetos mpl de valor

valuation /væljʊ'eɪʃn/ n valoración f

value /'væljuː/ n valor m; (*usefulness*) utilidad f. **face ~** n valor
m nominal; (*fig*) significado m
literal. —vt valorar; (*cherish*)
apreciar. **~ added tax (VAT)** n
impuesto m sobre el valor añadido (IVA). **~d** a (*appreciated*)
apreciado, estimado. **~r** /-ə(r)/ n
tasador m

valve /vælv/ n válvula f

vampire /'væmpaɪə(r)/ n vampiro m

van /væn/ n furgoneta f; (*rail*)
furgón m

vandal /'vændl/ n vándalo m.
~ism /-əlɪzəm/ n vandalismo m.
~ize vt destruir

vane /veɪn/ n (*weathercock*)
veleta f; (*naut, aviat*) paleta f

vanguard /'vænɡɑːd/ n vanguardia f

vanilla /və'nɪlə/ n vainilla f

vanish /'vænɪʃ/ vi desaparecer

vanity /'vænɪtɪ/ n vanidad f. **~
case** n neceser m

vantage /'vɑːntɪdʒ/ n ventaja f.
~point n posición f ventajosa

vapour /'veɪpə(r)/ n vapor m

variable /'veərɪəbl/ a variable

varian|ce /'veərɪəns/ n. **at ~ce**
en desacuerdo. **~t** /'veərɪənt/ a
diferente. —n variante f

variation /veərɪ'eɪʃn/ n variación f

varicoloured /'veərɪkʌləd/ a
multicolor

varied /'veərɪd/ a variado

varicose /'værɪkəʊs/ a varicoso.
~ veins npl varices fpl

variety /və'raɪətɪ/ n variedad f.
~ show n espectáculo m de
variedades

various /'veərɪəs/ a diverso. **~ly**
adv diversamente

varnish /'vɑːnɪʃ/ n barniz m; (*for
nails*) esmalte m. —vt barnizar

vary /'veərɪ/ vt/i variar. **~ing** a
diverso

vase /vɑːz, Amer veɪs/ n jarrón m

vasectomy /və'sektəmɪ/ n vasectomía f

vast /vɑːst/ a vasto, enorme. **~ly**
adv enormemente. **~ness** n
inmensidad f

vat /væt/ n tina f

VAT /viːeɪ'tiː/ abbr (*value added
tax*) IVA m, impuesto m sobre el
valor añadido

vault /vɔːlt/ n (*roof*) bóveda f; (*in
bank*) cámara f acorazada;
(*tomb*) cripta f; (*cellar*) sótano m;
(*jump*) salto m. —vt/i saltar

vaunt /vɔːnt/ vt jactarse de

veal /viːl/ n ternera f

veer /vɪə(r)/ vi cambiar de dirección; (*naut*) virar

vegetable /'vedʒɪtəbl/ a vegetal. —n legumbre m; (*greens*)
verduras fpl

vegetarian /vedʒɪ'teərɪən/ a & n
vegetariano (m)

vegetate /'vedʒɪteɪt/ vi vegetar

vegetation /vedʒɪ'teɪʃn/ n vegetación f

vehemen|ce /'viːəməns/ n
vehemencia f. **~t** /'viːəmənt/ a
vehemente. **~tly** adv con
vehemencia

vehicle /'viːɪkl/ n vehículo m

veil /veɪl/ n velo m. **take the ~**
hacerse monja. —vt velar

vein /veɪn/ n vena f; (*mood*)
humor m. **~ed** a veteado

velocity /vɪ'lɒsɪtɪ/ n velocidad f

velvet /'velvɪt/ n terciopelo m.
~y a aterciopelado

venal /'viːnl/ a venal. **~ity**
/-'nælɪtɪ/ n venalidad f

vendetta /ven'detə/ n enemistad
f prolongada

vending-machine /'vendɪŋ məʃiːn/ *n* distribuidor *m* automático

vendor /'vendə(r)/ *n* vendedor *m*

veneer /və'nɪə(r)/ *n* chapa *f*; *(fig)* barniz *m*, apariencia *f*

venerable /'venərəbl/ *a* venerable

venereal /və'nɪərɪəl/ *a* venéreo

Venetian /və'niːʃn/ *a & n* veneciano (*m*). **v~ blind** *n* persiana *f* veneciana

vengeance /'vendʒəns/ *n* venganza *f*. **with a ~** *(fig)* con creces

venison /'venɪzn/ *n* carne *f* de venado

venom /'venəm/ *n* veneno *m*. **~ous** *a* venenoso

vent /vent/ *n* abertura *f*, *(for air)* respiradero *m*. **give ~ to** dar salida a. —*vt* hacer un agujero en; *(fig)* desahogar

ventilate /'ventɪleɪt/ *vt* ventilar. **~ion** /-'leɪʃn/ *n* ventilación *f*. **~or** /-ə(r)/ *n* ventilador *m*

ventriloquist /ven'trɪləkwɪst/ *n* ventrílocuo *m*

venture /'ventʃə(r)/ *n* empresa *f* (arriesgada). **at a ~** a la ventura. —*vt* arriesgar. —*vi* atreverse

venue /'venjuː/ *n* lugar *m* (de reunión)

veranda /və'rændə/ *n* terraza *f*

verb /vɜːb/ *n* verbo *m*

verbal /'vɜːbl/ *a* verbal. **~ly** *adv* verbalmente

verbatim /vɜː'beɪtɪm/ *adv* palabra por palabra, al pie de la letra

verbose /vɜː'bəʊs/ *a* prolijo

verdant /'vɜːdənt/ *a* verde

verdict /'vɜːdɪkt/ *n* veredicto *m*; *(opinion)* opinión *f*

verge /vɜːdʒ/ *n* borde *m*. **~ on** acercarse a

verger /'vɜːdʒə(r)/ *n* sacristán *m*

verification /verɪfɪ'keɪʃn/ *n* verificación *f*. **~y** /'verɪfaɪ/ *vt* verificar

veritable /'verɪtəbl/ *a* verdadero

vermicelli /vɜːmɪ'tʃelɪ/ *n* fideos *mpl*

vermin /'vɜːmɪn/ *n* sabandijas *fpl*

vermouth /'vɜːməθ/ *n* vermut *m*

vernacular /və'nækjʊlə(r)/ *n* lengua *f*; *(regional)* dialecto *m*

versatile /'vɜːsətaɪl/ *a* versátil. **~ity** /-'tɪlətɪ/ *n* versatilidad *f*

verse /vɜːs/ *n* estrofa *f*; *(poetry)* poesías *fpl*; *(of Bible)* versículo *m*

versed /vɜːst/ *a*. **~ in** versado en

version /'vɜːʃn/ *n* versión *f*

versus /'vɜːsəs/ *prep* contra

vertebra /'vɜːtɪbrə/ *n* (*pl* **-brae** /-briː/) vértebra *f*

vertical /'vɜːtɪkl/ *a & n* vertical (*f*). **~ly** *adv* verticalmente

vertigo /'vɜːtɪɡəʊ/ *n* vértigo *m*

verve /vɜːv/ *n* entusiasmo *m*, vigor *m*

very /'verɪ/ *adv* muy. **~ much** muchísimo. **~ well** muy bien. **the ~ first** el primero de todos. —*a* mismo. **the ~ thing** exactamente lo que hace falta

vespers /'vespəz/ *npl* vísperas *fpl*

vessel /'vesl/ *n* *(receptacle)* recipiente *m*; *(ship)* buque *m*; *(anat)* vaso *m*

vest /vest/ *n* camiseta *f*; *(Amer)* chaleco *m*. —*vt* conferir. **~ed interest** *n* interés *m* personal; *(jurid)* derecho *m* adquirido

vestige /'vestɪdʒ/ *n* vestigio *m*

vestment /'vestmənt/ *n* vestidura *f*

vestry /'vestrɪ/ *n* sacristía *f*

vet /vet/ *n* *(fam)* veterinario *m*. —*vt* (*pt* **vetted**) examinar

veteran /'vetərən/ *n* veterano *m*

veterinary /'vetərɪnərɪ/ *a* veterinario. **~ surgeon** *n* veterinario *m*

veto /'viːtəʊ/ *n* (*pl* **-oes**) veto *m*. —*vt* poner el veto a

vex /veks/ vt fastidiar. ~ation /-'seɪʃn/ n fastidio m. ~ed question n cuestión f controvertida. ~ing a fastidioso

via /'vaɪə/ prep por, por vía de

viab|ility /vaɪə'bɪlɪti/ n viabilidad f. ~le /'vaɪəbl/ a viable

viaduct /'vaɪədʌkt/ n viaducto m

vibrant /'vaɪbrənt/ a vibrante

vibrat|e /vaɪ'breɪt/ vt/i vibrar. ~ion /-ʃn/ n vibración f

vicar /'vɪkə(r)/ n párroco m. ~age /-rɪdʒ/ n casa f del párroco

vicarious /vɪ'keərɪəs/ a indirecto

vice¹ /vaɪs/ n vicio m

vice² /vaɪs/ n (tec) torno m de banco

vice... /'vaɪs/ pref vice...

vice versa /vaɪsɪ'vɜːsə/ adv viceversa

vicinity /vɪ'sɪnɪti/ n vecindad f. in the ~ of cerca de

vicious /'vɪʃəs/ a (spiteful) malicioso; (violent) atroz. ~ circle n círculo m vicioso. ~ly adv cruelmente

vicissitudes /vɪ'sɪsɪtjuːdz/ npl vicisitudes fpl

victim /'vɪktɪm/ n víctima f. ~ization /-aɪ'zeɪʃn/ n persecución f. ~ize vt victimizar

victor /'vɪktə(r)/ n vencedor m

Victorian /vɪk'tɔːrɪən/ a victoriano

victor|ious /vɪk'tɔːrɪəs/ a victorioso. ~y /'vɪktərɪ/ n victoria f

video /'vɪdɪəʊ/ a vídeo. ~n (fam) magnetoscopio m. ~ recorder n magnetoscopio m. ~tape n videocassette f

vie /vaɪ/ vi (pres p vying) rivalizar

view /vjuː/ n vista f; (mental survey) visión f de conjunto; (opinion) opinión f. in my ~ a mi juicio. in ~ of en vista de. on ~ expuesto. with a ~ to con miras

a. ~ vt ver; (visit) visitar; (consider) considerar. ~er /-ə(r)/ n espectador m; (TV) televidente m & f. ~finder /'vjuːfaɪndə(r)/ n visor m. ~point /'vjuːpɔɪnt/ n punto m de vista

vigil /'vɪdʒɪl/ n vigilia f. ~ance n vigilancia f. ~ant a vigilante. keep ~ velar

vigor|ous /'vɪɡərəs/ a vigoroso. ~ur /'vɪɡə(r)/ n vigor m

vile /vaɪl/ a (base) vil; (bad) horrible; (weather, temper) de perros

vilif|ication /vɪlɪfɪ'keɪʃn/ n difamación f. ~y /'vɪlɪfaɪ/ vt difamar

village /'vɪlɪdʒ/ n aldea f. ~r /-ə(r)/ n aldeano m

villain /'vɪlən/ n malvado m; (in story etc) malo m. ~ous a infame. ~y n infamia f

vim /vɪm/ n (fam) energía f

vinaigrette /vɪnɪ'ɡret/ n. ~ sauce n vinagreta f

vindicat|e /'vɪndɪkeɪt/ vt vindicar. ~ion /-'keɪʃn/ n vindicación f

vindictive /vɪn'dɪktɪv/ a vengativo. ~ness n carácter m vengativo

vine /vaɪn/ n vid f

vinegar /'vɪnɪɡə(r)/ n vinagre m. ~y a (person) avinagrado

vineyard /'vɪnjəd/ n viña f

vintage /'vɪntɪdʒ/ n (year) cosecha f. ~a (wine) añejo; (car) de época

vinyl /'vaɪnɪl/ n vinilo m

viola /vɪ'əʊlə/ n viola f

violat|e /'vaɪəleɪt/ vt violar. ~ion /-'leɪʃn/ n violación f

violen|ce /'vaɪələns/ n violencia f. ~t /'vaɪələnt/ a violento. ~tly adv violentamente

violet /'vaɪələt/ a & n violeta (f)

violin /vaɪə'lɪn/ n violín m. ~ist n violinista m & f

VIP /viːaɪ'piː/ abbr (very important person) personaje m viper /'vaɪpə(r)/ n víbora f

virgin /'vɜːdʒɪn/ a & n virgen (f). ~al a virginal. ~ity /və'dʒɪnətɪ/ n virginidad f

Virgo /'vɜːgəʊ/ n (astr) Virgo f

virile /'vɪraɪl/ a viril. ~ity /-'rɪlətɪ/ n virilidad f

virtual /'vɜːtʃʊəl/ a verdadero. a ~ failure prácticamente un fracaso. ~ly adv prácticamente

virtue /'vɜːtʃuː/ n virtud f. by ~ of, in ~ of en virtud de

virtuoso /vɜːtʃʊ'əʊzəʊ/ n (pl -si /-ziː/) virtuoso m

virtuous /'vɜːtʃʊəs/ a virtuoso

virulent /'vɪrʊlənt/ a virulento

virus /'vaɪərəs/ n (pl -uses) virus m

visa /'viːzə/ n visado m, visa f (LAm)

vis-a-vis /'viːzaːviː/ adv frente a frente. —prep respecto a; (opposite) en frente de

viscount /'vaɪkaʊnt/ n vizconde m. ~ess n vizcondesa f

viscous /'vɪskəs/ a viscoso

visibility /vɪzɪ'bɪlɪtɪ/ n visibilidad f. ~le /'vɪzɪbl/ a visible. ~ly adv visiblemente

vision /'vɪʒn/ n visión f; (sight) vista f. ~ary /'vɪʒənərɪ/ a & n visionario (m)

visit /'vɪzɪt/ vt visitar; hacer una visita a (person). —vi hacer visitas. —n visita f. ~or n visitante m & f; (guest) visita f; (in hotel) cliente m & f

visor /'vaɪzə(r)/ n visera f

vista /'vɪstə/ n perspectiva f

visual /'vɪʒʊəl/ a visual. ~ize /'vɪʒʊəlaɪz/ vt imaginar(se); (foresee) prever. ~ly adv visualmente

vital /'vaɪtl/ a vital; (essential) esencial

vitality /vaɪ'tælətɪ/ n vitalidad f

vital: ~ly /'vaɪtlɪ/ adv extremadamente. ~s npl órganos mpl

vitales. ~ statistics npl (fam) medidas fpl

vitamin /'vɪtəmɪn/ n vitamina f

vitiate /'vɪʃɪeɪt/ vt viciar

vitreous /'vɪtrɪəs/ a vítreo

vituperate /vɪ'tjuːpəreɪt/ vt vituperar. ~ion /-'reɪʃn/ n vituperación f

vivacious /vɪ'veɪʃəs/ a animado, vivo. ~ously adv animadamente. ~ty /-'væsətɪ/ n viveza f

vivid /'vɪvɪd/ a vivo. ~ly adv intensamente; (describe) gráficamente. ~ness n viveza f

vivisection /vɪvɪ'sekʃn/ n vivisección f

vixen /'vɪksn/ n zorra f

vocabulary /və'kæbjʊlərɪ/ n vocabulario m

vocal /'vəʊkl/ a vocal; (fig) franco. ~ist n cantante m & f

vocation /vəʊ'keɪʃn/ n vocación f. ~al a profesional

vociferate /və'sɪfəreɪt/ vt/i vociferar. ~ous a vociferador

vogue /vəʊg/ n boga f. in ~ de moda

voice /vɔɪs/ n voz f. —vt expresar

void /vɔɪd/ a vacío; (not valid) nulo. ~ of desprovisto de. —n vacío m. —vt anular

volatile /'vɒlətaɪl/ a volátil; (person) voluble

volcanic /vɒl'kænɪk/ a volcánico. ~o /vɒl'keɪnəʊ/ n (pl -oes) volcán m

volition /və'lɪʃn/ n. of one's own ~ de su propia voluntad

volley /'vɒlɪ/ n (pl -eys) (of blows) lluvia f; (of gunfire) descarga f cerrada

volt /vəʊlt/ n voltio m. ~age n voltaje m

voluble /'vɒljʊbl/ a locuaz

volume /'vɒljuːm/ n volumen m; (book) tomo m

voluminous /və'ljuːmɪnəs/ a voluminoso

voluntar|ily /'vɒləntərəlɪ/ *adv* voluntariamente. **~y** /'vɒləntərɪ/ *a* voluntario

volunteer /vɒlən'tɪə(r)/ *n* voluntario *m*. —*vt* ofrecer. —*vi* ofrecerse voluntariamente; (*mil*) alistarse como voluntario

voluptuous /və'lʌptjʊəs/ *a* voluptuoso

vomit /'vɒmɪt/ *vt/i* vomitar. —*n* vómito *m*

voracious /və'reɪʃəs/ *a* voraz

vot|e /vəʊt/ *n* voto *m*; (*right*) derecho *m* de votar. —*vi* votar. **~er** /-ə(r)/ *n* votante *m* & *f*. **~ing** *n* votación *f*

vouch /vaʊtʃ/ *vi.* **~ for** garantizar

voucher /'vaʊtʃə(r)/ *n* vale *m*

vow /vaʊ/ *n* voto *m*. —*vi* jurar

vowel /'vaʊəl/ *n* vocal *f*

voyage /'vɔɪɪdʒ/ *n* viaje *m* (en barco)

vulgar /'vʌlgə(r)/ *a* vulgar. **~ity** /-'gærətɪ/ *n* vulgaridad *f*. **~ize** *vt* vulgarizar

vulnerab|ility /vʌlnərə'bɪlɪtɪ/ *n* vulnerabilidad *f*. **~le** /'vʌlnərəbl/ *a* vulnerable

vulture /'vʌltʃə(r)/ *n* buitre *m*

vying /'vaɪɪŋ/ *see* **vie**

W

wad /wɒd/ *n* (*pad*) tapón *m*; (*bundle*) lío *m*; (*of notes*) fajo *m*; (*of cotton wool etc*) bolita *f*

wadding /'wɒdɪŋ/ *n* relleno *m*

waddle /'wɒdl/ *vi* contonearse

wade /weɪd/ *vi.* **~ through** abrirse paso entre; leer con dificultad (*book*)

wafer /'weɪfə(r)/ *n* barquillo *m*; (*relig*) hostia *f*

waffle[1] /'wɒfl/ *n* (*fam*) palabrería *f*. —*vi* (*fam*) divagar

waffle[2] /'wɒfl/ *n* (*culin*) gofre *m*

waft /wɒft/ *vt* llevar por el aire. —*vi* flotar

wag /wæg/ *vt* (*pt* **wagged**) menear. —*vi* menearse

wage /weɪdʒ/ *vt.* **~s** *npl* salario *m*. —*vt.* **~ war** hacer la guerra. **~r** /'weɪdʒə(r)/ *n* apuesta *f*. —*vt* apostar

waggle /'wægl/ *vt* menear. —*vi* menearse

wagon /'wægən/ *n* carro *m*; (*rail*) vagón *m*. **be on the ~** (*sl*) no beber

waif /weɪf/ *n* niño *m* abandonado

wail /weɪl/ *vi* lamentarse. —*n* lamento *m*

wainscot /'weɪnskət/ *n* revestimiento *m*, zócalo *m*

waist /weɪst/ *n* cintura *f*. **~band** *n* cinturón *m*

waistcoat /'weɪstkəʊt/ *n* chaleco *m*

waistline /'weɪstlaɪn/ *n* cintura *f*

wait /weɪt/ *vt/i* esperar; (*at table*) servir. **~ for** esperar. **~ on** servir. —*n* espera *f*. **lie in ~** acechar

waiter /'weɪtə(r)/ *n* camarero *m*

wait: **~ing-list** *n* lista *f* de espera. **~ing-room** *n* sala *f* de espera

waitress /'weɪtrɪs/ *n* camarera *f*

waive /weɪv/ *vt* renunciar a

wake[1] /weɪk/ *vt* (*pt* **woke**, *pp* **woken**) despertar. —*vi* despertarse. —*n* velatorio *m*. **~ up** *vt* despertar. —*vi* despertarse

wake[2] /weɪk/ *n* (*naut*) estela *f*. **in the ~ of** como resultado de, tras

waken /'weɪkən/ *vt* despertar. —*vi* despertarse

wakeful /'weɪkfl/ *a* insomne

Wales /weɪlz/ *n* País *m* de Gales

walk /wɔːk/ *vi* andar; (*not ride*) ir a pie; (*stroll*) pasearse. **~ out** salir; (*workers*) declararse en huelga. **~ out on** abandonar. —*vt* andar por (*streets*); llevar de paseo (*dog*). —*n* paseo *m*; (*gait*) modo *m* de andar; (*path*) sendero *m*. ~ **of life** clase *f* social. ~**about** /-ə'kəbaʊt/ *vt* (*of royalty*) encuentro *m* con el público. ~**er** /-ə(r)/ *n* paseante *m* & *f*

walkie-talkie /wɔːkɪ'tɔːkɪ/ *n* transmisor-receptor *m* portátil

walking /'wɔːkɪŋ/ *n* paseo *m*. ~**-stick** *n* bastón *m*

Walkman /'wɔːkmən/ *n* (P) estereo *m* personal, Walkman *m* (P), magnetófono *m* de bolsillo

walk: ~**out** *n* huelga *f*. ~**over** *n* victoria *f* fácil

wall /wɔːl/ *n* (*interior*) pared *f*; (*exterior*) muro *m*; (*in garden*) tapia *f*; (*of city*) muralla *f*. **go to the** ~ fracasar. **up the** ~ (*fam*) loco. —*vt* amurallar (*city*)

wallet /'wɒlɪt/ *n* cartera *f*, billetera *f* (*LAm*)

wallflower /'wɔːlflaʊə(r)/ *n* alhelí *m*

wallop /'wɒləp/ *vt* (*pt* **walloped**) (*sl*) golpear con fuerza. —*n* (*sl*) golpe *m* fuerte

wallow /'wɒləʊ/ *vi* revolcarse

wallpaper /'wɔːlpeɪpə(r)/ *n* papel *m* pintado

walnut /'wɔːlnʌt/ *n* nuez *f*; (*tree*) nogal *m*

walrus /'wɔːlrəs/ *n* morsa *f*

waltz /wɔːls/ *n* vals *m*. —*vi* valsar

wan /wɒn/ *a* pálido

wand /wɒnd/ *n* varita *f*

wander /'wɒndə(r)/ *vi* vagar; (*stroll*) pasearse; (*digress*) divagar; (*road, river*) serpentear. —*n* paseo *m*. ~**er** /-ə(r)/ *n* vagabundo *m*. ~**lust** /'wɒndəlʌst/ *n* pasión *f* por los viajes

wane /weɪn/ *vi* menguar. —*n*. **on the** ~ disminuyendo

wangle /'wæŋgl/ *vt* (*sl*) agenciarse

want /wɒnt/ *vt* querer; (*need*) necesitar; (*require*) exigir. —*vi*. ~ **for** carecer de. —*n* necesidad *f*; (*lack*) falta *f*; (*desire*) deseo *m*. ~**ed** *a* (*criminal*) buscado. ~**ing**

a (*lacking*) falto de. **be** ~**ing** carecer de

wanton /'wɒntən/ *a* (*licentious*) lascivo; (*motiveless*) sin motivo

war /wɔː(r)/ *n* guerra *f*. **at** ~ en guerra

warble /'wɔːbl/ *vt* cantar trinando. —*vi* gorjear. —*n* gorjeo *m*. ~**r** /-ə(r)/ *n* curruca *f*

ward /wɔːd/ *n* (*in hospital*) sala *f*; (*of town*) barrio *m*; (*child*) pupilo *m*. —*vt*. ~ **off** parar

warden /'wɔːdn/ *n* guarda *m*

warder /'wɔːdə(r)/ *n* carcelero *m*

wardrobe /'wɔːdrəʊb/ *n* armario *m*; (*clothes*) vestuario *m*

warehouse /'weəhaʊs/ *n* almacén *m*

wares /weəz/ *npl* mercancías *fpl*

war: ~**fare** /'wɔːfeə(r)/ *n* guerra *f*. ~**head** /'wɔːhed/ *n* cabeza *f* explosiva

warily /'weərɪlɪ/ *adv* cautelosamente

warlike /'wɔːlaɪk/ *a* belicoso

warm /wɔːm/ *a* (-**er**, -**est**) caliente; (*hearty*) caluroso. **be** ~ (*person*) tener calor. **it is** ~ hace calor. —*vt*. ~ (**up**) calentar; recalentar (*food*); (*fig*) animar. —*vi*. ~ (**up**) calentarse; (*fig*) animarse. ~ **to** tomar simpatía a (*person*); ir entusiasmándose por (*idea etc*). ~**-blooded** *a* de sangre caliente. ~**-hearted** *a* simpático. ~**ly** *adv* (*heartily*) calurosamente

warmonger /'wɔːmʌŋgə(r)/ *n* belicista *m* & *f*

warmth /wɔːmθ/ *n* calor *m*

warn /wɔːn/ *vt* avisar, advertir. ~**ing** *n* advertencia *f*; (*notice*) aviso *m*. ~ **off** (*advise against*) aconsejar en contra de; (*forbid*) impedir

warp /wɔːp/ *vt* deformar; (*fig*) pervertir. —*vi* deformarse

warpath /'wɔːpɑːθ/ *n*. **be on the** ~ buscar camorra

warrant /'wɒrənt/ n autorización f; (for arrest) orden f. — vt justificar. ~officer n suboficial m

warranty /'wɒrəntɪ/ n garantía f

warring /'wɔːrɪŋ/ a en guerra

warrior /'wɒrɪə(r)/ n guerrero m

warship /'wɔːʃɪp/ n buque m de guerra

wart /wɔːt/ n verruga f

wartime /'wɔːtaɪm/ n tiempo m de guerra

wary /'weərɪ/ a (-ier, -iest) cauteloso

was /wɒz, wɒz/ see **be**

wash /wɒʃ/ vt lavar; (flow over) bañar. —vi lavarse. —n lavado m; (dirty clothes) ropa f sucia; (wet clothes) colada f; (of ship) estela f. have a ~ lavarse. ~ out vt enjuagar; (fig) cancelar. ~ up vi fregar los platos. ~able a lavable. ~basin n lavabo m. ~ed-out a (pale) pálido; (tired) rendido. ~er /'wɒʃə(r)/ n arandela f; (washing-machine) lavadora f. ~ing /'wɒʃɪŋ/ n lavado m; (dirty clothes) ropa f sucia; (wet clothes) colada f. ~ing-machine n lavadora f. ~ing-powder n jabón m en polvo. ~ing-up n fregado m; (dirty plates etc) platos mpl para fregar. ~out n (sl) desastre m. ~room n (Amer) servicios mpl. ~stand n lavabo m. ~tub n tina f de lavar

wasp /wɒsp/ n avispa f

wastage /'weɪstɪdʒ/ n desperdicios mpl

waste /weɪst/ —a de desecho; (land) yermo. —n derroche m; (rubbish) desperdicio m; (of time) pérdida f. —vt derrochar; (not use) desperdiciar; (of time). —vi. ~ away consumirse. ~-disposal unit n trituradora f de basuras. ~ful a

dispendioso; (person) derrochador. ~-paper basket n papelera f. ~s npl tierras fpl baldías

watch /wɒtʃ/ vt mirar; (keep an eye on) vigilar; (take heed) tener cuidado con; ver ⟨TV.⟩. —vi mirar; (keep an eye on) vigilar. —n vigilancia f; (period of duty) guardia f; (timepiece) reloj m. on the ~ alerta. ~ out vi tener cuidado. ~-dog n perro m guardián; (fig) guardián m. ~ful a vigilante. ~maker /'wɒtʃmeɪkə(r)/ n relojero m. ~man /'wɒtʃmən/ n (pl -men) vigilante m. ~-tower n atalaya f. ~word /'wɒtʃwɜːd/ n santo m y seña

water /'wɔːtə(r)/ n agua f. by ~ (of travel) por mar. in hot ~ (fam) en un apuro. —vt regar (plants etc); (dilute) aguar, diluir. —vi ⟨eyes⟩ llorar. make s.o.'s mouth ~ hacérsele la boca agua. ~ down vt diluir; (fig) suavizar. ~-closet n wáter m. ~-colour n acuarela f. ~course /'wɔːtəkɔːs/ n arroyo m; (artificial) canal m. ~cress /'wɔːtəkres/ n berro m. ~fall /'wɔːtəfɔːl/ n cascada f. ~-ice n sorbete m. ~ing-can /'wɔːtərɪŋkæn/ n regadera f. ~-lily n nenúfar m. ~-line n línea f de flotación. ~logged /'wɔːtəlɒgd/ a saturado de agua, empapado. ~ main n cañería f principal. ~-melon n sandía f. ~-mill n molino m de agua. ~polo n polo m acuático. ~-power n energía f hidráulica. ~proof /'wɔːtəpruːf/ a impermeable m; ⟨watch⟩ sumergible. ~shed /'wɔːtəʃed/ n punto m decisivo. ~-skiing n esquí m acuático. ~-softener n ablandador m de agua. ~tight /'wɔːtətaɪt/ a hermético, estanco; (fig) irrecusable. ~way n canal m navegable. ~-wheel n rueda f hidráulica. ~wings npl flotadores mpl. ~works /'wɔ:tə-wɔ:ks/ n sistema m de abastecimiento de agua. ~y /'wɔ:-tərɪ/ a acuoso; (colour) pálido; (eyes) lloroso

watt /wɒt/ n vatio m

wave /weɪv/ n onda f; (of hand) señal f; (fig) oleada f. ~vt agitar; ondular (hair). ~vi (signal) hacer señales con la mano; (flag) flotar. ~band /'weɪvbænd/ n banda f de ondas. ~length /'weɪvleŋθ/ n longitud f de onda

waver /'weɪvə(r)/ vi vacilar

wavy /'weɪvɪ/ a (-ier, -iest) ondulado

wax¹ /wæks/ n cera f. ~vt encerar

wax² /wæks/ vi (moon) crecer

wax: ~en a céreo. ~work /'wækswɔːk/ n figura f de cera. ~y a céreo

way /weɪ/ n camino m; (distance) distancia f; (manner) manera f, modo m; (direction) dirección f; (means) medio m; (habit) costumbre f. be in the ~ estorbar. by the ~ a propósito. by ~ of a título de, por. either ~ de cualquier modo. in a ~ en cierta manera. in some ~s en ciertos modos. lead the ~ marcar el camino. make ~ dejar paso a. on the ~ en camino. out of the ~ remoto; (extraordinary) fuera de lo común. that ~ por allí. this ~ por aquí. under ~ en curso. ~bill n hoja f de ruta. ~farer /'weɪfeərə(r)/ n viajero m. ~in n entrada f

waylay /weɪ'leɪ/ vt (pt -laid) acechar; (detain) detener

way: ~out n salida f. ~out a ultramoderno, original. ~s npl costumbres fpl. ~side /'weɪsaɪd/ n borde m del camino

wayward /'weɪwəd/ a caprichoso

we /wiː/ pron nosotros, nosotras

weak /wiːk/ a (-er, -est) débil; (liquid) aguado, acuoso; (fig) flojo. ~en vt debilitar. ~kneed a irresoluto. ~ling /'wiːklɪŋ/ n persona f débil. ~ly adv débilmente. ~a enfermizo. ~ness n debilidad f

weal /wiːl/ n verdugón m

wealth /welθ/ n riqueza f. ~y a (-ier, -iest) rico

wean /wiːn/ vt destetar

weapon /'wepən/ n arma f

wear /weə(r)/ vt (pt wore, pp worn) llevar; (put on) ponerse; tener (expression etc); (damage) desgastar. ~vi desgastarse; (last) durar. ~n uso m; (damage) desgaste m; (clothing) ropa f. ~down vt desgastar; agotar (opposition etc). ~off vi desaparecer. ~on vi (time) pasar. ~out vt desgastar; (tire) agotar. ~able a que se puede llevar. ~and tear desgaste m

wearily /'wɪərɪlɪ/ adv cansadamente. ~iness n cansancio m. ~isome /'wɪərɪsəm/ a cansado. ~y /'wɪərɪ/ a (-ier, -iest) cansado. ~vt cansar. ~vi cansarse. ~y of cansarse de

weasel /'wiːzl/ n comadreja f

weather /'weðə(r)/ n tiempo m. under the ~ (fam) indispuesto. ~a meteorológico. ~vt curar (wood); (survive) superar. ~beaten a curtido. ~cock /'weðəkɒk/ n, ~vane n veleta f

weave /wiːv/ vt (pt wove, pp woven) tejer; entretejer (story etc); entrelazar (flowers etc). one's way abrirse paso. ~n tejido m. ~r /-ə(r)/ n tejedor m

web /web/ n tela f; (of spider) telaraña f; (on foot) membrana f. ~bing n cincha f

wed /wed/ vt (pt **wedded**) casarse con; ⟨priest etc⟩ casar. —vi casarse. **~ded to** (fig) unido a

wedding /'wedɪŋ/ n boda f. **~-cake** n pastel m de boda. **~-ring** n anillo m de boda

wedge /wedʒ/ n cuña f; ⟨space filler⟩ calce m. —vt acuñar; (push) apretar

wedlock /'wedlɒk/ n matrimonio m

Wednesday /'wenzdeɪ/ n miércoles m

wee /wi:/ a (fam) pequeñito

weed /wi:d/ n mala hierba f. —vt desherbar. **~-killer** n herbicida m. **~ out** eliminar. **~y** a ⟨person⟩ débil

week /wi:k/ n semana f. **~day** /'wi:kdeɪ/ n día m laborable. **~end** n fin m de semana. **~ly** /'wi:klɪ/ a semanal. —n semanario m. —adv semanalmente

weep /wi:p/ vi (pt **wept**) llorar. **~ing willow** n sauce m llorón

weevil /'wi:vɪl/ n gorgojo m

weigh /weɪ/ vt/i pesar. **~ anchor** levar anclas. **~ down** vt (fig) oprimir. **~ up** vt pesar; (fig) considerar

weight /weɪt/ n peso m. **~less** a ingrávido. **~lessness** n ingravidez f. **~-lifting** n halterofilia f, levantamiento m de pesos. **~y** a (-ier, -iest) pesado; (influential) influyente

weir /wɪə(r)/ n presa f

weird /wɪəd/ a (-er, -est) misterioso; (bizarre) extraño

welcome /'welkəm/ a bienvenido. **~ to do** libre de hacer. **you're ~e!** (after thank you) ¡de nada! —n bienvenida f; (reception) acogida f. —vt dar la bienvenida a; (appreciate) alegrarse de

welcoming /'welkəmɪŋ/ a acogedor

weld /weld/ vt soldar. —n soldadura f. **~er** n soldador m

welfare /'welfeə(r)/ n bienestar m; (aid) asistencia f social. **W~ State** n estado m benefactor. **~ work** n asistencia f social

well¹ /wel/ adv (**better, best**) bien. **~ done!** ¡bravo! **as ~** también. **as ~ as** tanto... como. **be ~** estar bien. **do ~** (succeed) tener éxito. **very ~** muy bien. —a bien. —int bueno; (surprise) ¡vaya! **I never!** ¡no me digas!

well² /wel/ n pozo m; (of staircase) caja f

well: **~-appointed** a bien equipado. **~-behaved** a bien educado. **~-being** n bienestar m. **~-bred** a bien educado. **~-disposed** a benévolo. **~-groomed** a bien aseado. **~-heeled** a (fam) rico

wellington /'welɪŋtən/ n bota f de agua

well: **~-knit** a robusto. **~-known** a conocido. **~-meaning** a, **~-meant** a bienintencionado. **~-off** a acomodado. **~-read** a culto. **~-spoken** a bienhablado. **~-to-do** a rico. **~-wisher** n bienqueriente m & f

Welsh /welʃ/ a & n galés (m). **~ rabbit** n pan m tostado con queso

welsh /welʃ/ vi. **~ on** no cumplir con

wench /wentʃ/ n (old use) muchacha f

wend /wend/ vt. **~ one's way** encaminarse

went /went/ see **go**

wept /wept/ see **weep**

were /wɜ:(r), wə(r)/ see **be**

west /west/ n oeste m. **the ~** el Occidente m. —a del oeste. —adv hacia el oeste, al oeste. **go ~** (sl) morir. **W~ Germany** n Alemania f Occidental. **~erly** a del

oeste. **~ern** a occidental. —n (film) película f del Oeste. **~erner** /-ənə(r)/ n occidental m & f. **W~ Indian** a & n antillano (m). **W~ Indies** npl Antillas fpl.
~ward a, **~ward(s)** adv hacia el oeste

wet /wet/ a (wetter, wettest) mojado; (rainy) lluvioso, de lluvia; (person, sl) soso. **~ paint** recién pintado. **get ~** mojarse. —vt (pt wetted) mojar, humedecer. **~ blanket** n aguafiestas m & f invar. **~ suit** n traje m de buzo

whack /wæk/ vt (fam) golpear. —n (fam) golpe m. **~ed** /wækt/ a (fam) agotado. **~ing** a (huge, sl) enorme. —n paliza f

whale /weɪl/ n ballena f. a **~ of a** (fam) maravilloso, enorme

wham /wæm/ int ¡zas!

wharf /wɔːf/ n (pl wharves or wharfs) muelle m

what /wɒt/ a el que, la que, lo que, lo, los que, las que; (in questions & exclamations) qué. —pron lo que; (interrogative) qué. **~ about going?** ¿si fuésemos? **~ about me?** ¿y yo? **~ for?** ¿para qué? **~ if?** ¿y si? **~ is it?** ¿qué es? **~ you need** lo que te haga falta. —int ¡cómo! **~ a fool!** ¡qué tonto!

whatever /wɒt'evə(r)/ a cualquiera. —pron (todo) lo que, cualquier cosa que

whatnot /'wɒtnɒt/ n chisme m

whatsoever /wɒtsəʊ'evə(r)/ a & pron = **whatever**

wheat /wiːt/ n trigo m. **~en** a de trigo

wheedle /'wiːdl/ vt engatusar

wheel /wiːl/ n rueda f. **at the ~** al volante. **steering-~** n volante m. —vt empujar (bicycle etc). —vi girar. **~ round** girar. **~barrow** /'wiːlbærəʊ/ n carretilla f. **~chair** /'wiːltʃeə(r)/ n silla f de ruedas

wheeze /wiːz/ vi resollar. —n resuello m

when /wen/ adv cuándo. —conj cuando

whence /wens/ adv de dónde

whenever /wen'evə(r)/ adv en cualquier momento; (every time that) cada vez que

where /weə(r)/ adv & conj donde; (interrogative) dónde. **~ are you going?** ¿adónde vas? **~ are you from?** ¿de dónde eres?

whereabouts /'weərəbaʊts/ adv dónde. —n paradero m

whereas /weər'æz/ conj por cuanto; (in contrast) mientras (que)

whereby /weə'baɪ/ adv por lo cual

whereupon /weərə'pɒn/ adv después de lo cual

wherever /weər'evə(r)/ adv (in whatever place) dónde (diablos). —conj dondequiera que

whet /wet/ vt (pt whetted) afilar; (fig) aguzar

whether /'weðə(r)/ conj si. **~ you like it or not** que te guste o no te guste. **I don't know ~ she will like it** no sé si le gustará

which /wɪtʃ/ a (in questions) qué. **~ one** cuál. **~ one of you** cuál de vosotros. —pron (in questions) cuál; (relative) que; (object) el cual, la cual, lo cual, los cuales, las cuales

whichever /wɪtʃ'evə(r)/ a cualquier. —pron cualquiera que, el que, la que

whiff /wɪf/ n soplo m; (of smoke) bocanada f; (smell) olorcillo m

while /waɪl/ n rato m. —conj mientras; (although) aunque. —vt. **~ away** pasar (time)

whilst /waɪlst/ conj = **while**

whim /wɪm/ n capricho m

whimper /'wɪmpə(r)/ vi lloriquear. —n lloriqueo m

whimsical /'wɪmzɪkl/ a caprichoso; (*odd*) extraño

whine /waɪn/ vi gimotear. —n gimoteo m

whip /wɪp/ n látigo m; (*pol*) oficial m disciplinario. —vt (*pt* **whipped**) azotar; (*culin*) batir; (*seize*) agarrar. ~**cord** n tralla f. ~**ped cream** n nata f batida. ~**ping-boy** /'wɪpɪŋbɔɪ/ n cabeza f de turco. ~**round** n colecta f. ~ **up** (*incite*) estimular

whirl /wɜːl/ vt hacer girar rápidamente. —vi girar rápidamente; (*swirl*) arremolinarse. —n giro m; (*swirl*) remolino m. ~**pool** /'wɜːlpuːl/ n remolino m. ~**wind** /'wɜːlwɪnd/ n torbellino m

whirr /wɜː(r)/ n zumbido m. —vi zumbar

whisk /wɪsk/ vt (*culin*) batir. —n (*culin*) batidor m. ~ **away** llevarse

whisker /'wɪskə(r)/ n pelo m. ~**s** npl (*of man*) patillas fpl; (*of cat etc*) bigotes mpl

whisky /'wɪskɪ/ n güisqui m

whisper /'wɪspə(r)/ vt decir en voz baja. —vi cuchichear; (*leaves etc*) susurrar. —n cuchicheo m; (*of leaves*) susurro m; (*rumour*) rumor m

whistle /'wɪsl/ n silbido m; (*instrument*) silbato m. —vi silbar. ~**stop** n (*pol*) breve parada f (en gira electoral)

white /waɪt/ a (-er, -est) blanco. ~ **go** ~ ponerse pálido. ~n blanco; (*of egg*) clara f. ~**bait** /'waɪtbeɪt/ n (pl ~**bait**) chanquetes mpl. ~**coffee** n café m con leche. ~**collar worker** n empleado m de oficina. ~ **elephant** n objeto m inútil y costoso

Whitehall /'waɪthɔːl/ n el gobierno m británico

white: ~ **horses** n cabrillas fpl. ~**hot** a (*metal*) candente. ~ **lie**

n mentirijilla f. ~**n** vt/i blanquear. ~**ness** n blancura f. **W~ Paper** n libro m blanco. ~**wash** /'waɪtwɒʃ/ n jalbegue m; (*fig*) encubrimiento m. —vt enjalbegar; (*fig*) encubrir

whiting /'waɪtɪŋ/ n (pl **whiting**) (*fish*) pescadilla f

whitlow /'wɪtləʊ/ n panadizo m

Whitsun /'wɪtsn/ n Pentecostés m

whittle /'wɪtl/ vt. ~ (**down**) tallar; (*fig*) reducir

whiz /wɪz/ vi (*pt* **whizzed**) silbar; (*rush*) ir a gran velocidad. ~ **past** pasar como un rayo. ~**kid** n (*fam*) joven m prometedor, promesa f

who /huː/ pron que, quien; (*interrogative*) quién; (*particular person*) el que, la que, los que, las que

whodunit /huː'dʌnɪt/ n (*fam*) novela f policíaca

whoever /huː'evə(r)/ pron quienquera que; (*interrogative*) quién (diablos)

whole /həʊl/ a entero; (*not broken*) intacto. —n todo m, conjunto m; (*total*) total m. **as a** ~ en conjunto. **on the** ~ por regla general. ~**hearted** a sincero. ~**meal** a integral

wholesale /'həʊlseɪl/ n venta f al por mayor. —a & adv al por mayor. ~**r** /-ə(r)/ n comerciante m & f al por mayor

wholesome /'həʊlsəm/ a saludable

wholly /'həʊlɪ/ adv completamente

whom /huːm/ pron que, a quien; (*interrogative*) a quién

whooping cough /'huːpɪŋkɒf/ n tos f ferina

whore /hɔː(r)/ n puta f

whose /huːz/ pron de quién. —a de quién; (*relative*) cuyo

why /waɪ/ *adv* por qué. —*int* ¡toma!

wick /wɪk/ *n* mecha *f*

wicked /'wɪkɪd/ *a* malo; (*mischievous*) travieso; (*very bad, fam*) malísimo. **~ness** *n* maldad *f*

wicker /'wɪkə(r)/ *n* mimbre *m* & *f*. —*a* de mimbre. **~work** *n* artículos *mpl* de mimbre

wicket /'wɪkɪt/ *n* (*cricket*) rastrillo *m*

wide /waɪd/ *a* (**-er, -est**) ancho; (*fully opened*) de par en par; (*far from target*) lejano; ⟨*knowledge etc*⟩ amplio. —*adv* lejos. **far and ~** por todas partes. **~ awake** *a* completamente despierto; (*fig*) despabilado. **~ly** *adv* extensamente, (*believed*) generalmente; (*different*) muy. **~n** *vt* ensanchar

widespread /'waɪdspred/ *a* extendido; (*fig*) difundido

widow /'wɪdəʊ/ *n* viuda *f*. **~ed** *a* viudo. **~er** *n* viudo *m*. **~hood** *n* viudez *f*

width /wɪdθ/ *n* anchura *f*. **in ~** de ancho

wield /wiːld/ *vt* manejar; ejercer ⟨*power*⟩

wife /waɪf/ *n* (*pl* **wives**) mujer *f*, esposa *f*

wig /wɪg/ *n* peluca *f*

wiggle /'wɪgl/ *vt* menear. —*vi* menearse

wild /waɪld/ *a* (**-er, -est**) salvaje; (*enraged*) furioso; ⟨*idea*⟩ extravagante; (*with joy*) loco; (*random*) al azar. —*adv* en estado salvaje. **run ~** crecer en estado salvaje. **~s** *npl* regiones *fpl* salvajes

wildcat /'waɪldkæt/ *a*. **~ strike** *n* huelga *f* salvaje

wilderness /'wɪldənɪs/ *n* desierto *m*

wild. **~fire** /'waɪldfaɪə(r)/ *n*. **spread like ~fire** correr como

un reguero de pólvora. **~goose chase** *n* empresa *f* inútil. **~life** /'waɪldlaɪf/ *n* fauna *f*. **~ly** *adv* violentamente; (*fig*) locamente

wilful /'wɪlfʊl/ *a* intencionado; (*self-willed*) terco. **~ly** *adv* intencionadamente; (*obstinately*) obstinadamente

will[1] /wɪl/ *v aux*. **~ you have some wine?** ¿quieres vino? **he ~ be** será. **you ~ be back soon, won't you?** volverás pronto, ¿no?

will[2] /wɪl/ *n* voluntad *f*; (*document*) testamento *m*

willing /'wɪlɪŋ/ *a* complaciente. **~ to** dispuesto a. **~ly** *adv* de buena gana. **~ness** *n* buena voluntad *f*

willow /'wɪləʊ/ *n* sauce *m*

will-power /'wɪlpaʊə(r)/ *n* fuerza *f* de voluntad

willy-nilly /wɪlɪ'nɪlɪ/ *adv* quieras que no

wilt /wɪlt/ *vi* marchitarse

wily /'waɪlɪ/ *a* (**-ier, -iest**) astuto

win /wɪn/ *vt* (*pt* **won**, *pres p* **winning**) ganar; (*achieve, obtain*) conseguir. —*vi* ganar. —*n* victoria *f*. **~ back** *vi* reconquistar. **~ over** *vt* convencer

wince /wɪns/ *vi* hacer una mueca de dolor. **without wincing** sin pestañear. —*n* mueca *f* de dolor

winch /wɪntʃ/ *n* cabrestante *m*. —*vt* levantar con el cabrestante

wind[1] /wɪnd/ *n* viento *m*; (*in stomach*) flatulencia *f*. **get the ~ up** (*sl*) asustarse. **get ~ of** enterarse de. **in the ~** en el aire. —*vt* dejar sin aliento.

wind[2] /waɪnd/ *vt* (*pt* **wound**) (*wrap around*) enrollar; dar cuerda a ⟨*clock etc*⟩. —*vi* ⟨*road etc*⟩ serpentear. **~ up** *vt* dar cuerda a ⟨*watch, clock*⟩; (*provoke*) agitar, poner nervioso; (*fig*) terminar, concluir

wind /wind/: ~bag n charlatán m. ~cheater n cazadora f

winder /'waɪndə(r)/ n devanador m; (of clock, watch) llave f

windfall /'wɪndfɔːl/ n fruta f caída; (fig) suerte f inesperada

winding /'waɪndɪŋ/ a tortuoso

wind instrument /'wɪnd-ɪnstrəmənt/ n instrumento m de viento

windmill /'wɪndmɪl/ n molino m (de viento)

window /'wɪndəʊ/ n ventana f; (in shop) escaparate m; (of vehicle, booking-office) ventanilla f. ~-box n jardinera f. ~-dresser n escaparatista m & f. ~-shop vi mirar los escaparates

windpipe /'wɪndpaɪp/ n tráquea f

windscreen /'wɪndskriːn/, windshield n (Amer) parabrisas m invar. ~-wiper n limpiaparabrisas m invar

wind /wɪnd/: ~-swept a barrido por el viento. ~y a (-ier, -iest) ventoso, de mucho viento. it is ~y hace viento

wine /waɪn/ n vino m. ~-cellar n bodega f. ~-glass n copa f. ~-grower n viticultor m. ~-growing n viticultura f. ~a vinícola. ~ list n lista f de vinos. ~-tasting n cata f de vinos

wing /wɪŋ/ n ala f, (auto) aleta f. under one's ~ bajo la protección de uno. ~ed a alado. ~er /-ə(r)/ n (sport) ala m & f. ~s npl (in theatre) bastidores mpl

wink /wɪŋk/ vi guiñar el ojo; (light etc) centellear. ~n. not to sleep a ~ no pegar ojo

winkle /'wɪŋkl/ n bígaro m

win: ~ner /-ə(r)/ n ganador m. ~ning-post n poste m de llegada. ~ning smile n sonrisa f encantadora. ~nings npl ganancias fpl

winsome /'wɪnsəm/ a atractivo

winter /'wɪntə(r)/ n invierno m. ~vi invernar. ~ry a invernal

wipe /waɪp/ vt limpiar; (dry) secar. ~n limpión m. give sth a ~ limpiar algo. ~ out (cancel) cancelar; (destroy) destruir; (obliterate) borrar. ~ up limpiar; (dry) secar

wire /waɪə(r)/ n alambre m; (elec) cable m; (telegram, fam) telegrama m

wireless /'waɪəlɪs/ n radio f

wire netting /waɪə'netɪŋ/ n alambrera f, tela f metálica

wiring n instalación f eléctrica

wiry /'waɪərɪ/ a (-ier, -iest) (person) delgado

wisdom /'wɪzdəm/ n sabiduría f. ~ tooth n muela f del juicio

wise /waɪz/ a (-er, -est) sabio; (sensible) prudente. ~-crack /'waɪzkræk/ n (fam) salida f. ~ly adv sabiamente; (sensibly) prudentemente

wish /wɪʃ/ n deseo m; (greeting) saludo m. with best ~es (in letters) un fuerte abrazo. ~vt desear. ~ on (fam) encajar a. ~ s.o. well desear buena suerte a uno. ~bone n espoleta f (de las aves). ~ful a deseoso. ~ful thinking n ilusiones fpl

wishy-washy /'wɪʃɪwɒʃɪ/ a soso; (person) sin convicciones, falto de entereza

wisp /wɪsp/ n manojito m; (of smoke) voluta f; (of hair) mechón m

wisteria /wɪs'tɪərɪə/ n glicina f

wistful /'wɪstfl/ a melancólico

wit /wɪt/ n gracia f; (person) persona f chistosa; (intelligence) ingenio m. be at one's ~s' end no saber qué hacer. live by one's ~s vivir de expedientes, vivir del cuento

witch /wɪtʃ/ n bruja f. ~craft n brujería f. ~-doctor n hechicero m

with /wɪð/ prep con; (cause, having) de. **be ~ it** (fam) estar al día, estar al tanto. **the man ~ the beard** el hombre de la barba

withdraw /wɪð'drɔː/ vt (pt **withdrew**, pp **withdrawn**) retirar. —vi apartarse. **~al** n retirada f. **~n** a (person) introvertido

wither /ˈwɪðə(r)/ vi marchitarse. —vt (fig) fulminar

withhold /wɪð'həʊld/ vt (pt **withheld**) retener; (conceal) ocultar (**from** a)

within /wɪ'ðɪn/ prep dentro de. —adv dentro. **~ sight** a la vista

without /wɪ'ðaʊt/ prep sin

withstand /wɪð'stænd/ vt (pt **~stood**) resistir a

witness /ˈwɪtnɪs/ n testigo m; (proof) testimonio m. —vt presenciar; firmar como testigo (document). **~-box** n tribuna f de los testigos

witticism /ˈwɪtɪsɪzəm/ n ocurrencia f

wittingly /ˈwɪtɪŋlɪ/ adv a sabiendas

witty /ˈwɪtɪ/ a (-ier, -iest) gracioso

wives /waɪvz/ see **wife**

wizard /ˈwɪzəd/ n hechicero m. **~ry** n hechicería f

wizened /ˈwɪznd/ a arrugado

wobbl|e /ˈwɒbl/ vi tambalearse; (voice, jelly, hand) temblar; (chair etc) balancearse. **~y** a (chair etc) cojo

woe /wəʊ/ n aflicción f. **~ful** a triste. **~begone** /ˈwəʊbɪgɒn/ a desconsolado

woke, woken /wəʊk, ˈwəʊkən/ see **wake**[1]

wolf /wʊlf/ n (pl **wolves**) lobo m. —vt (also **~ down**) zamparse. **~-whistle** n silbido m de admiración

woman /ˈwʊmən/ n (pl **women**) mujer f. **single ~** soltera f. **~ize** /ˈwʊmənaɪz/ vi ser mujeriego. **~ly** a femenino

womb /wuːm/ n matriz f

women /ˈwɪmɪn/ npl see **woman**. **~folk** /ˈwɪmɪnfəʊk/ npl mujeres fpl. **~'s lib** n movimiento m de liberación de la mujer

won /wʌn/ see **win**

wonder /ˈwʌndə(r)/ n maravilla f; (bewilderment) asombro m. **no ~** no es de extrañarse (**that** que). —vi admirarse. (reflect) preguntarse

wonderful /ˈwʌndəfl/ a maravilloso. **~ly** adv maravillosamente

won't /wəʊnt/ = **will not**

woo /wuː/ vt cortejar

wood /wʊd/ n madera f; (for burning) leña f; (area) bosque m; (in bowls) bola f. **out of the ~** (fig) fuera de peligro. **~cutter** n leñador m. **~ed** a poblado de árboles, boscoso. **~en** a de madera. **~land** n bosque m

woodlouse /ˈwʊdlaʊs/ n (pl **-lice**) cochinilla f

woodpecker /ˈwʊdpekə(r)/ n pájaro m carpintero

woodwind /ˈwʊdwɪnd/ n instrumentos mpl de viento de madera

woodwork /ˈwʊdwɜːk/ n carpintería f; (in room etc) maderaje m

woodworm /ˈwʊdwɜːm/ n carcoma f

woody /ˈwʊdɪ/ a leñoso

wool /wʊl/ n lana f. **pull the ~ over s.o.'s eyes** engañar a uno. **~len** a de lana. **~lens** npl ropa f de lana. **~ly** a (-ier, -iest) de lana; (fig) confuso. —n jersey m

word /wɜːd/ n palabra f; (news) noticia f. **by ~ of mouth** de palabra. **have ~s with** reñir con. **in one ~** en una palabra. **in other ~s** es decir. —vt expresar

~**ing** n expresión f. términos mpl. ~**perfect** a. **be** ~**perfect** saber de memoria. ~**processor** n procesador m de textos. ~**y** a prolijo

wore /wɔː(r)/ see **wear**

work /wɜːk/ n trabajo m; (arts) obra f. —vt hacer trabajar; manejar (machine). —vi trabajar; (machine) funcionar; (student) estudiar; (drug etc) tener efecto; (be successful) tener éxito. ~ **in** introducir(se). ~ **off** desahogar. ~ **out** vt resolver; (calculate) calcular; elaborar (plan). —vi (succeed) salir bien; (sport) entrenarse. ~ **up** vt desarrollar. —vi excitarse. ~**able** /wɜːkəbl/ a (project) factible. ~**aholic** /wɜːkəhɒlık/ n trabajador m obsesivo. ~**ed up** a agitado. ~**er** /wɜːkə(r)/ n trabajador m; (manual) obrero m

workhouse /wɜːkhaʊs/ n asilo m de pobres

work: ~**ing** /wɜːkıŋ/ a (day) laborable; (clothes etc) de trabajo. —n (mec) funcionamiento m. **in** ~**ing order** en estado de funcionamiento. ~**ing class** n clase f obrera. ~**ing-class** a de la clase obrera. ~**man** /wɜːkmən/ n (pl -men) obrero m. ~**manlike** /wɜːkmənlaɪk/ a concienzudo. ~**manship** n destreza f. ~**s** npl (building) fábrica f; (mec) mecanismo m. ~**shop** /wɜːkʃɒp/ n taller m. ~**to-rule** n huelga f de celo

world /wɜːld/ n mundo m. **a** ~ **of** enorme. **out of this** ~ maravilloso. —a mundial. ~**ly** a mundano. ~**wide** a universal

worm /wɜːm/ n lombriz f; (grub) gusano m. —vi. ~ **one's way** insinuarse. ~**eaten** a carcomido

worn /wɔːn/ see **wear**. —a gastado. ~**out** a gastado; (person) rendido

worr|**ied** /wʌrɪd/ a preocupado. ~**ier** /wʌrɪ/ a aprensivo m. ~**y** /wʌrɪ/ vt preocupar; (annoy) molestar. —vi preocuparse. —n preocupación f. ~**ying** a inquietante

worse /wɜːs/ a peor. —adv peor; (more) más. —n lo peor. ~**n** vt/i empeorar

worship /wɜːʃɪp/ n culto m; (title) señor, su señoría. —vt (pt **worshipped**) adorar

worst /wɜːst/ a (el) peor. —adv peor. —n lo peor. **get the** ~ **of it** llevar la peor parte

worsted /wʊstɪd/ n estambre m

worth /wɜːθ/ n valor m. —a. **be** ~ valer. **it is** ~ **trying** vale la pena probarlo. **it was** ~ **my while** (me) valió la pena. ~**less** a sin valor. ~**while** /wɜːθwaɪl/ a que vale la pena

worthy /wɜːðɪ/ a meritorio; (respectable) respetable; (laudable) loable

would /wʊd/ v aux. ~ **you come here please?** ¿quieres venir aquí? ~ **you go?** ¿irías tú? **he** ~ **come if he could** vendría si pudiese. **I** ~ **come every day** (used to) venía todos los días. **I** ~ **do it** lo haría yo. ~**be** a supuesto

wound[1] /wuːnd/ n herida f. —vt herir

wound[2] /waʊnd/ see **wind**[2]

wove, woven /wəʊv, wəʊvn/ see **weave**

wow /waʊ/ int ¡caramba!

wrangle /ræŋgl/ vi reñir. —n riña f

wrap /ræp/ vt (pt **wrapped**) envolver. **be** ~**ped up in** (fig) estar absorto en. —n bata f; (shawl) chal m. ~**per** /-ə(r)/ n, ~**ping** n envoltura f

wrath /rɒθ/ n ira f. **~ful** a iracundo

wreath /ri:θ/ n (pl -ths /-ðz/) guirnalda f; (for funeral) corona f

wreck /rek/ n ruina f; (sinking) naufragio m; (remains of ship) buque m naufragado. **be a nervous ~** tener los nervios destrozados. —vt hacer naufragar; (fig) arruinar. **~age** n restos mpl; (of building) escombros mpl

wren /ren/ n troglodito m

wrench /rentʃ/ vt arrancar; (twist) torcer. —n arranque m; (tool) llave f inglesa

wrest /rest/ vt arrancar (from a)

wrestl|e /ˈresl/ vi luchar. **~er** /-ə(r)/ n luchador m. **~ing** n lucha f

wretch /retʃ/ n desgraciado m; (rascal) tunante m & f. **~ed** a miserable; (weather) horrible, de perros; (dog etc) maldito

wriggle /ˈrɪgl/ vi culebrear. **~ out of** escaparse de. **~ through** deslizarse por. —n serpenteo m

wring /rɪŋ/ vt (pt wrung) retorcer. **~ out of** (obtain from) arrancar. **~ing wet** empapado

wrinkle /ˈrɪŋkl/ n arruga f. —vt arrugar. —vi arrugarse

wrist /rɪst/ n muñeca f. **~watch** n reloj m de pulsera

writ /rɪt/ n decreto m judicial

write /raɪt/ vt/i (pt wrote, pp written, pres p writing) escribir. **~ down** vt anotar. **~ off** vt cancelar; (fig) dar por perdido. **~ up** vt hacer un reportaje de; (keep up to date) poner al día. **~off** n pérdida f total. **~r** /-ə(r)/ n escritor m; (author) autor m. **~-up** n reportaje m; (review) crítica f

writhe /raɪð/ vi retorcerse

writing /ˈraɪtɪŋ/ n escribir m; (handwriting) letra f. **in ~** por

escrito. **~s** npl obras fpl. **~-paper** n papel m de escribir

written /ˈrɪtn/ see **write**

wrong /rɒŋ/ a incorrecto; (not just) injusto; (mistaken) equivocado. **be ~** no tener razón; (be mistaken) equivocarse. —adv mal. **go ~** equivocarse; (plan) salir mal; (car etc) estropearse. —n injusticia f; (evil) mal m. **in the ~** equivocado. —vt ser injusto con. **~ful** a injusto. **~ly** adv mal; (unfairly) injustamente

wrote /rəʊt/ see **write**

wrought /rɔ:t/ a. **~ iron** n hierro m forjado

wrung /rʌŋ/ see **wring**

wry /raɪ/ a (wryer, wryest) torcido; (smile) forzado. **~ face** n mueca f

X

xenophobia /zenəˈfəʊbɪə/ n xenofobia f

Xerox /ˈzɪərɒks/ n (P) fotocopiadora f. **xerox** n fotocopia f

Xmas /ˈkrɪsməs/ n abbr (Christmas) Navidad f, Navidades fpl

X-ray /ˈeksreɪ/ n radiografía f. **~s** npl rayos mpl X. —vt radiografiar

xylophone /ˈzaɪləfəʊn/ n xilófono m

Y

yacht /jɒt/ n yate m. **~ing** n navegación f a vela

yam /jæm/ n ñame m, batata f

yank /jæŋk/ vt (fam) arrancar violentamente

Yankee /'jæŋkɪ/ n (fam) yanqui m & f

yap /jæp/ vi (pt yapped) ⟨dog⟩ ladrar

yard[1] /jɑːd/ n (measurement) yarda f (= 0.9144 metre)

yard[2] /jɑːd/ n patio m; (Amer, garden) jardín m

yardage /'jɑːdɪdʒ/ n metraje m

yardstick /'jɑːdstɪk/ n (fig) criterio m

yarn /jɑːn/ n hilo m; (tale, fam) cuento m

yashmak /'jæʃmæk/ n velo m

yawn /jɔːn/ vi bostezar. —n bostezo m

year /jɪə(r)/ n año m. **be three ~s old** tener tres años. **~book** n anuario m. **~ling** /'jɜːlɪŋ/ n primal m. **~ly** a anual. —adv anualmente

yearn /jɜːn/ vi. **~ for** anhelar. **~ing** n ansia f

yeast /jiːst/ n levadura f

yell /jel/ vi gritar. —n grito m

yellow /'jeləʊ/ a & n amarillo (m). **~ish** a amarillento

yelp /jelp/ n gañido m. —vi gañir

yen /jen/ n muchas ganas fpl

yeoman /'jəʊmən/ n (pl -men). **Y~ of the Guard** alabardero m de la Casa Real

yes /jes/ adv & n sí (m)

yesterday /'jestədeɪ/ adv & n ayer (m). **the day before ~** anteayer m

yet /jet/ adv todavía, aún; (already) ya. **as ~** hasta ahora. —conj sin embargo

yew /juː/ n tejo m

Yiddish /'jɪdɪʃ/ n judeoalemán m

yield /jiːld/ vt producir. —vi ceder. —n producción f; (com) rendimiento m

yoga /'jəʊɡə/ n yoga m

yoghurt /'jɒɡət/ n yogur m

yoke /jəʊk/ n yugo m; (of garment) canesú m

yokel /'jəʊkl/ n patán m, palurdo m

yolk /jəʊk/ n yema f (de huevo)

yonder /'jɒndə(r)/ adv a lo lejos

you /juː/ pron (familiar form) tú, vos (Arg), (pl) vosotros, vosotras, ustedes (LAm); (polite form) usted, (pl) ustedes; (familiar, object) te, (pl) os, les (LAm); (polite, object) le, la, (pl) les; (familiar, after prep) ti, (pl) vosotros, vosotras, ustedes (LAm); (polite, after prep) usted, (pl) ustedes. **with ~** (familiar) contigo, (pl) con vosotros, con vosotras, con ustedes (LAm); (polite) con usted, (pl) con ustedes; (polite reflexive) consigo. **I know ~** te conozco, le conozco a usted. **you can't smoke here** aquí no se puede fumar

young /jʌŋ/ a (-er, -est) joven. **~ lady** n señorita f. **~ man** n joven m. **her ~ man** (boyfriend) su novio m. **the ~** npl los jóvenes mpl; (of animals) la cría f. **~ster** /'jʌŋstə(r)/ n joven m

your /jɔː(r)/ a (familiar) tu, (pl) vuestro; (polite) su

yours /jɔːz/ poss pron (el) tuyo, (pl) (el) vuestro, el de ustedes (LAm); (polite) el suyo. **a book of ~s** un libro tuyo, un libro suyo. **Y~s faithfully**, **Y~s sincerely** le saluda atentamente

yourself /jɔː'self/ pron (pl **yourselves**) (familiar, subject) tú mismo, tú misma, (pl) vosotros mismos, vosotras mismas, ustedes mismos (LAm), ustedes mismas (LAm); (polite, subject) usted mismo, usted misma, (pl) ustedes mismos, ustedes mismas; (familiar, object) te, (pl) os, se (LAm); (polite, object) se, (familiar, after prep) ti, (pl) vosotros, vosotras, ustedes (LAm); (polite, after prep) sí

youth /juːθ/ n (pl **youths** /juːðz/)
juventud f; (boy) joven m; (young
people) jóvenes mpl. ∼**ful** a
joven, juvenil. ∼**hostel** n albergue m para jóvenes

yowl /jaʊl/ vi aullar. —n aullido
m

Yugoslav /ˈjuːgəslɑːv/ a & n yugoslavo (m). ∼**ia** /ˈslɑːvɪə/ n Yugoslavia f

yule /juːl/ n, **yule-tide** /ˈjuːltaɪd/
n (old use) Navidades fpl

Z

zany /ˈzeɪnɪ/ a (-ier, -iest)
estrafalario

zeal /ziːl/ n celo m

zealot /ˈzelət/ n fanático m

zealous /ˈzeləs/ a entusiasta. ∼**ly**
/ˈzeləslɪ/ adv con entusiasmo

zebra /ˈzebrə/ n cebra f. ∼ **crossing** n paso m de cebra

zenith /ˈzenɪθ/ n cenit m

zero /ˈzɪərəʊ/ n (pl -os) cero m

zest /zest/ n gusto m; (peel) cáscara f

zigzag /ˈzɪgzæg/ n zigzag m. —vi
(pt **zigzagged**) zigzaguear

zinc /zɪŋk/ n cinc m

Zionis|m /ˈzaɪənɪzəm/ n sionismo
m. ∼**t** n sionista m & f

zip /zɪp/ n cremallera f. —vt. ∼
(**up**) cerrar (la cremallera)

Zip code /ˈzɪpkəʊd/ n (Amer)
código m postal

zip fastener /zɪpˈfɑːsnə(r)/ n cremallera f

zircon /ˈzɜːkən/ n circón m

zither /ˈzɪðə(r)/ n cítara f

zodiac /ˈzəʊdɪæk/ n zodiaco m

zombie /ˈzɒmbɪ/ n (fam) autómata m & f

zone /zəʊn/ n zona f

zoo /zuː/ n (fam) zoo m, jardín m
zoológico. ∼**logical** /zəʊə-
ˈlɒdʒɪkl/ a zoológico

zoolog|ist /zəʊˈɒlədʒɪst/ n
zoólogo m. ∼**y** /zəʊˈɒlədʒɪ/ n
zoología f

zoom /zuːm/ vi ir a gran velocidad. ∼ **in** (photo) acercarse
rápidamente. ∼ **past** pasar zum-
bando. ∼ **lens** n zoom m

Zulu /ˈzuːluː/ n zulú m & f

Numbers · Números

zero	0	cero
one (first)	1	uno (primero)
two (second)	2	dos (segundo)
three (third)	3	tres (tercero)
four (fourth)	4	cuatro (cuarto)
five (fifth)	5	cinco (quinto)
six (sixth)	6	seis (sexto)
seven (seventh)	7	siete (séptimo)
eight (eighth)	8	ocho (octavo)
nine (ninth)	9	nueve (noveno)
ten (tenth)	10	diez (décimo)
eleven (eleventh)	11	once (undécimo)
twelve (twelfth)	12	doce (duodécimo)
thirteen (thirteenth)	13	trece (decimotercero)
fourteen (fourteenth)	14	catorce (decimocuarto)
fifteen (fifteenth)	15	quince (decimoquinto)
sixteen (sixteenth)	16	dieciséis (decimosexto)
seventeen (seventeenth)	17	diecisiete (decimoséptimo)
eighteen (eighteenth)	18	dieciocho (decimoctavo)
nineteen (nineteenth)	19	diecinueve (decimonoveno)
twenty (twentieth)	20	veinte (vigésimo)
twenty-one (twenty-first)	21	veintiuno (vigésimo primero)
twenty-two (twenty-second)	22	veintidós (vigésimo segundo)
twenty-three (twenty-third)	23	veintitrés (vigésimo tercero)
twenty-four (twenty-fourth)	24	veinticuatro (vigésimo cuarto)
twenty-five (twenty-fifth)	25	veinticinco (vigésimo quinto)
twenty-six (twenty-sixth)	26	veintiséis (vigésimo sexto)

thirty (thirtieth)	30	treinta (trigésimo)
thirty-one (thirty-first)	31	treinta y uno (trigésimo primero)
forty (fortieth)	40	cuarenta (cuadragésimo)
fifty (fiftieth)	50	cincuenta (quincuagésimo)
sixty (sixtieth)	60	sesenta (sexagésimo)
seventy (seventieth)	70	setenta (septuagésimo)
eighty (eightieth)	80	ochenta (octogésimo)
ninety (ninetieth)	90	noventa (nonagésimo)
a/one hundred (hundredth)	100	cien (centésimo)
a/one hundred and one (hundred and first)	101	ciento uno (centésimo primero)
two hundred (two hundredth)	200	doscientos (ducentésimo)
three hundred (three hundredth)	300	trescientos (tricentésimo)
four hundred (four hundredth)	400	cuatrocientos (cuadringentésimo)
five hundred (five hundredth)	500	quinientos (quingentésimo)
six hundred (six hundredth)	600	seiscientos (sexcentésimo)
seven hundred (seven hundredth)	700	setecientos (septingentésimo)
eight hundred (eight hundredth)	800	ochocientos (octingentésimo)
nine hundred (nine hundredth)	900	novecientos (noningentésimo)
a/one thousand (thousandth)	1000	mil (milésimo)
two thousand (two thousandth)	2000	dos mil (dos milésimo)
a/one million (millionth)	1,000,000	un millón (millonésimo)

Spanish Verbs · Verbos españoles

Regular verbs:

in -ar (*e.g.* comprar)
Present: compr|o, ~as, ~a,
~amos, ~áis, ~an
Future: comprar|é, ~ás, ~á,
~emos, ~éis, ~án
Imperfect: compr|aba, ~abas,
~aba, ~ábamos, ~abais,
~aban
Preterite: compr|é, ~aste, ~ó,
~amos, ~asteis, ~aron
Present subjunctive: compr|e,
~es, ~e, ~emos, ~éis, ~en
Imperfect subjunctive: compr|ara,
~aras ~ara, ~áramos,
~arais, ~aran
compr|ase, ~ases, ~ase,
~ásemos, ~aseis, ~asen
Conditional: comprar|ía, ~ías,
~ía, ~íamos, ~íais, ~ían
Present participle: comprando
Past participle: comprado
Imperative: compra, comprad

in -er (*e.g.* beber)
Present: beb|o, ~es, ~e, ~emos,
~éis, ~en
Future: beber|é, ~ás, ~á,
~emos, ~éis, ~án
Imperfect: beb|ía, ~ías, ~ía,
~íamos, ~íais, ~ían
Preterite: beb|í, ~iste, ~ió,
~imos, ~isteis, ~ieron
Present subjunctive: beb|a, ~as,
~a, ~amos, ~áis, ~an
Imperfect subjunctive: beb|iera,
~ieras, ~iera, ~iéramos,
~ierais, ~ieran
beb|iese, ~ieses, ~iese,
~iésemos, ~ieseis, ~iesen
Conditional: beber|ía, ~ías, ~ía,
~íamos, ~íais, ~ían
Present participle: bebiendo
Past participle: bebido
Imperative: bebe, bebed

in -ir (*e.g.* vivir)
Present: viv|o, ~es, ~e, ~imos,
~ís, ~en
Future: vivir|é, ~ás, ~á,
~emos, ~éis, ~án
Imperfect: viv|ía, ~ías, ~ía,
~íamos, ~íais, ~ían
Preterite: viv|í, ~iste, ~ió,
~imos, ~isteis, ~ieron
Present subjunctive: viv|a, ~as,
~a, ~amos, ~áis, ~an
Imperfect subjunctive: viv|iera,
~ieras, ~iera, ~iéramos,
~ierais, ~ieran
viv|iese, ~ieses, ~iese,
~iésemos, ~ieseis, ~iesen
Conditional: vivir|ía, ~ías, ~ía,
~íamos, ~íais, ~ían
Present participle: viviendo
Past participle: vivido
Imperative: vive, vivid

Irregular verbs:
[1] **cerrar**
Present: cierro, cierras, cierra,
cerramos, cerráis, cierran
Present subjunctive: cierre,
cierres, cierre, cerremos,
cerréis, cierren
Imperative: cierra, cerrad

[2] **contar, mover**
Present: cuento, cuentas, cuenta,
contamos, contáis, cuentan
muevo, mueves, mueve,
movemos, movéis, mueven
Present subjunctive: cuente,
cuentes, cuente, contemos,
contéis, cuenten
mueva, muevas mueva,
movamos, mováis, muevan
Imperative: cuenta, contad
mueve, moved

[3] jugar
Present: juego, juegas, juega, jugamos, jugáis, juegan
Preterite: jugué, jugaste, jugó, jugamos, jugasteis, jugaron
Present subjunctive: juegue, juegues, juegue, juguemos, juguéis, jueguen

[4] sentir
Present: siento, sientes, siente, sentimos, sentís, sienten
Preterite: sentí, sentiste, sintió, sentimos, sentisteis, sintieron
Present subjunctive: sienta, sientas, sienta, sintamos, sintáis, sientan
Imperfect subjunctive: sint|iera, ~ieras, ~iera, ~iéramos, ~ierais, ~ieran
sint|iese, ~ieses, ~iese, ~iésemos, ~ieseis, ~iesen
Present participle: sintiendo
Imperative: siente, sentid

[5] pedir
Present: pido, pides, pide, pedimos, pedís, piden
Preterite: pedí, pediste, pidió, pedimos, pedisteis, pidieron
Present subjunctive: pid|a, ~as, ~a, ~amos, ~áis, ~an
Imperfect subjunctive: pid|iera, ~ieras, ~iera, ~iéramos, ~ierais, ~ieran
pid|iese, ~ieses, ~iese, ~iésemos, ~ieseis, ~iesen
Present participle: pidiendo
Imperative: pide, pedid

[6] dormir
Present: duermo, duermes, duerme, dormimos, dormís, duermen
Preterite: dormí, dormiste, durmió, dormimos, dormisteis, durmieron

Present subjunctive: duerma, duermas, duerma, durmamos, durmáis, duerman
Imperfect subjunctive: durm|iera, ~ieras, ~iera, ~iéramos, ~ierais, ~ieran
durm|iese, ~ieses, ~iese, ~iésemos, ~ieseis, ~iesen
Present participle: durmiendo
Imperative: duerme, dormid

[7] dedicar
Preterite: dediqué, dedicaste, dedicó, dedicamos, dedicasteis, dedicaron
Present subjunctive: dediqu|e, ~ues, ~e, ~emos, ~éis, ~en

[8] delinquir
Present: delinco, delinques, delinque, delinquimos, delinquís, delinquen
Present subjunctive: delinc|a, ~as, ~a, ~amos, ~áis, ~an

[9] vencer, esparcir
Present: venzo, vences, vence, vencemos, vencéis, vencen
esparzo, esparces, esparce, esparcimos, esparcís, esparcen
Present subjunctive: venz|a, ~as, ~a, ~amos, ~áis, ~an
esparz|a, ~as, ~a, ~amos, ~áis, ~an

[10] rechazar
Preterite: rechacé, rechazaste, rechazó, rechazamos, rechazasteis, rechazaron
Present subjunctive: rechac|e, ~es, ~e, ~emos, ~éis, ~en

[11] conocer, lucir
Present: conozco, conoces, conoce, conocemos, conocéis, conocen
luzco, luces, luce, lucimos, lucís, lucen

Present subjunctive: conozc|a,
~as, ~a, ~amos, ~áis, ~an
luzc|a, ~as, ~a, ~amos, ~áis,
~an

[12] pagar
Preterite: pagué, pagaste, pagó,
pagamos, pagasteis, pagaron
Present subjunctive: pagu|e, ~es,
~e, ~emos, ~éis, ~en

[13] distinguir
Present: distingo, distingues,
distingue, distinguimos,
distinguís, distinguen
Present subjunctive: disting|a,
~as, ~a, ~amos, ~áis, ~an

[14] acoger, afligir
Present: acojo, acoges, acoge,
acogemos, acogéis, acogen
aflijo, afliges, aflige, afligimos,
afligís, afligen
Present subjunctive: acoj|a, ~as,
~a, ~amos, ~áis, ~an
aflij|a, ~as, ~a, ~amos, ~áis,
~an

[15] averiguar
Preterite: averigüé, averiguaste,
averiguó, averiguamos,
averiguasteis, averiguaron
Present subjunctive: averigü|e,
~es, ~e, ~emos, ~éis, ~en

[16] agorar
Present: agüero, agüeras, agüera,
agoramos, agoráis, agüeran
Present subjunctive: agüere,
agüeres, agüere, agoremos,
agoréis, agüeren
Imperative: agüera, agorad

[17] huir
Present: huyo, huyes, huye,
huimos, huís, huyen
Preterite: huí, huiste, huyó,
huimos, huisteis, huyeron

Present subjunctive: huy|a, ~as,
~a, ~amos, ~áis, ~an
Imperfect subjunctive: huy|era,
~eras, ~era, ~éramos,
~erais, ~eran
huy|ese, ~eses, ~ese,
~ésemos, ~eseis, ~esen
Present participle: huyendo

[18] creer
Preterite: creí, creíste, creyó,
creímos, creísteis, creyeron
Imperfect subjunctive: crey|era,
~eras, ~era, ~éramos,
~erais, ~eran
crey|ese, ~eses, ~ese,
~ésemos, ~eseis, ~esen
Present participle: creyendo
Past participle: creído

[19] argüir
Present: arguyo, arguyes, arguye,
argüimos, argüís, arguyen
Preterite: argüí, argüiste, arguyó,
argüimos, argüisteis, arguyeron
Present subjunctive: arguy|a,
~as, ~a, ~amos, ~áis, ~an
Imperfect subjunctive: arguy|era,
~eras, ~era, ~éramos,
~erais, ~eran
arguy|ese, ~eses, ~ese,
~ésemos, ~eseis, ~esen
Present participle: arguyendo
Imperative: arguye, argüid

[20] vaciar
Present: vacío, vacías, vacía,
vaciamos, vaciáis, vacían
Present subjunctive: vacíe, vacíes,
vacíe, vaciemos, vaciéis, vacíen
Imperative: vacía, vaciad

[21] acentuar
Present: acentúo, acentúas,
acentúa, acentuamos,
acentuáis, acentúan

634

Present subjunctive: acentúe,
acentúes, acentúe, acentuemos,
acentuéis, acentúen
Imperative: acentúa, acentuad

[22] **ateñer, engullir**
Preterite: atañí, ~aste, ~ó,
~amos, ~asteis, ~eron
engullí ~iste, ~ó, ~imos,
~isteis, ~eron
Imperfect subjunctive: atañ‖era,
~eras, ~era, ~éramos,
~erais, ~eran
atañ‖ese, ~eses, ~ese,
~ésemos, ~eseis, ~esen
engull‖era, ~eras, ~era,
~éramos, ~erais, ~eran
engull‖ese, ~eses, ~ese,
~ésemos, ~eseis, ~esen
Present participle: atañendo
engullendo

[23] **aislar, aullar**
Present: aíslo, aíslas, aísla,
aislamos, aisláis, aíslan
aúllo, aúllas, aúlla, aullamos
aulláis, aúllan
Present subjunctive: aísle, aísles,
aísle, aislemos, aisléis, aíslen
aúlle, aúlles, aúlle, aullemos,
aulléis, aúllen
Imperative: aísla, aislad
aúlla, aullad

[24] **abolir, garantir**
Present: abolimos, abolís
garantimos, garantís
Present subjunctive: not used
Imperative: abolid
garantid

[25] **andar**
Preterite: anduv‖e, ~iste, ~o,
~imos, ~isteis, ~ieron
Imperfect subjunctive:
anduv‖iera, ~ieras, ~iera,
~iéramos, ~ierais, ~ieran
anduv‖iese, ~ieses, ~iese,
~iésemos, ~ieseis, ~iesen

[26] **dar**
Present: doy, das, da, damos, dais,
dan
Preterite: di, diste, dio, dimos
disteis, dieron
Present subjunctive: dé, des, dé,
demos, deis, den
Imperfect subjunctive: diera,
dieras, diera, diéramos, dierais,
dieran
diese, dieses, diese, diésemos,
dieseis, diesen

[27] **estar**
Present: estoy, estás, está,
estamos, estáis, están
Preterite: estuv‖e, ~iste, ~o,
~imos, ~isteis, ~ieron
Present subjunctive: esté, estés,
esté, estemos, estéis, estén
Imperfect subjunctive: estuv‖iera,
~ieras, ~iera, ~iéramos,
~ierais, ~ieran
estuv‖iese, ~ieses, ~iese,
~iésemos, ~ieseis, ~iesen
Imperative: está, estad

[28] **caber**
Present: quepo, cabes, cabe,
cabemos, cabéis, caben
Future: cabr‖é, ~ás, ~á, ~emos,
~éis, ~án
Preterite: cup‖e, ~iste, ~o,
~imos, ~isteis, ~ieron
Present subjunctive: quep‖a, ~as,
~a, ~amos, ~áis, ~an
Imperfect subjunctive: cup‖iera,
~ieras, ~iera, ~iéramos,
~ierais, ~ieran
cup‖iese, ~ieses, ~iese,
~iésemos, ~ieseis, ~iesen
Conditional: cabr‖ía, ~ías, ~ía,
~íamos, ~íais, ~ían

[29] **caer**
Present: caigo, caes, cae, caemos,
caéis, caen
Preterite: caí, caiste, cayó,
caímos, caísteis, cayeron

Present subjunctive: caig|a, ~as,
~a, ~amos, ~áis, ~an
Imperfect subjunctive: cay|era,
~eras, ~era, ~éramos,
~erais, ~eran
cay|ese, ~eses, ~ese,
~ésemos, ~eseis, ~esen
Present participle: cayendo
Past participle: caído

[30] **haber**
Present: he, has, ha, hemos,
habéis, han
Future: habr|é ~ás, ~á, ~emos,
~éis, ~án
Preterite: hub|e, ~iste, ~o,
~imos, ~isteis, ~ieron
Present subjunctive: hay|a, ~as,
~a, ~amos, ~áis, ~an
Imperfect subjunctive: hub|iera,
~ieras, ~iera, ~iéramos,
~ierais, ~ieran
hub|iese, ~ieses, ~iese,
~iésemos, ~ieseis, ~iesen
Conditional: habr|ía, ~ías, ~ía,
~íamos, ~íais, ~ían
Imperative: habe, habed

[31] **hacer**
Present: hago, haces, hace,
hacemos, hacéis, hacen
Future: har|é ~ás, ~á, ~emos,
~éis, ~án
Preterite: hice, hiciste, hizo,
hicimos, hicisteis, hicieron
Present subjunctive: hag|a, ~as,
~a, ~amos, ~áis, ~an
Imperfect subjunctive: hic|iera,
~ieras, ~iera, ~iéramos,
~ierais, ~ieran
hic|iese, ~ieses, ~iese,
~iésemos, ~ieseis, ~iesen
Conditional: har|ía, ~ías, ~ía,
~íamos, ~íais, ~ían
Past participle: hecho
Imperative: haz, haced

[32] **placer**
Preterite: plació/plugo

Present subjunctive: plazca
Imperfect subjunctive:
placiera/pluguiera
placiese/pluguiese

[33] **poder**
Present: puedo, puedes, puede,
podemos, podéis, pueden
Future: podr|é, ~ás, ~á, ~emos,
~éis, ~án
Preterite: pud|e, ~iste, ~o,
~imos, ~isteis, ~ieron
Present subjunctive: pueda,
puedas, pueda, podamos,
podáis, puedan
Imperfect subjunctive: pud|iera,
~ieras, ~iera, ~iéramos,
~ierais, ~ieran
pud|iese, ~ieses, ~iese,
~iésemos, ~ieseis, ~iesen
Conditional: podr|ía, ~ías, ~ía,
~íamos, ~íais, ~ían
Past participle: pudiendo

[34] **poner**
Present: pongo, pones, pone,
ponemos, ponéis, ponen
Future: pondr|é, ~ás, ~á,
~emos, ~éis, ~án
Preterite: pus|e, ~iste, ~o,
~imos, ~isteis, ~ieron
Present subjunctive: pong|a, ~as,
~a, ~amos, ~áis, ~an
Imperfect subjunctive: pus|iera,
~ieras, ~iera, ~iéramos,
~ierais, ~ieran
pus|iese, ~ieses, ~iese,
~iésemos, ~ieseis, ~iesen
Conditional: pondr|ía, ~ías, ~ía,
~íamos, ~íais, ~ían
Past participle: puesto
Imperative: pon, poned

[35] **querer**
Present: quiero, quieres, quiere,
queremos, queréis, quieren
Future: querr|é, ~ás, ~á,
~emos, ~éis, ~án

636

Preterite: quis|e, ~iste, ~o,
~imos, ~isteis, ~ieron
Present subjunctive: quiera,
quieras, quiera, queramos,
queráis, quieran
Imperfect subjunctive: quis|iera,
~ieras, ~iera, ~iéramos,
~ierais, ~ieran
quis|iese, ~ieses, ~iese,
~iésemos, ~ieseis, ~iesen
Conditional: querr|ía, ~ías, ~ía,
~íamos, ~íais, ~ían
Imperative: quiere, quered

[36] **raer**

Present: raigo/rayo, raes, rae,
raemos, raéis, raen
Preterite: raí, raíste, rayó, raímos,
raísteis, rayeron
Present subjunctive: raig|a, ~as,
~a, ~amos, ~áis, ~an
ray|a, ~as, ~a, ~amos, ~áis,
~an
Imperfect subjunctive: ray|era,
~eras, ~era, ~éramos,
~erais, ~eran
ray|ese, ~eses, ~ese,
~ésemos, ~eseis, ~esen
Present participle: rayendo
Past participle: raído

[37] **roer**

Present: roo/roigo/royo, roes,
roe, roemos, roéis, roen
Preterite: roí, roíste, royó, roímos,
roísteis, royeron
Present subjunctive:
roa/roiga/roya, roas, roa,
roamos, roáis, roan
Imperfect subjunctive: roy|era,
~eras, ~era, ~éramos,
~erais, ~eran
roy|ese, ~eses, ~ese,
~ésemos, ~eseis, ~esen
Present participle: royendo
Past participle: roído

[38] **saber**

Present: sé, sabes, sabe, sabemos,
sabéis, saben
Future: sabr|é, ~ás, ~á, ~emos,
~éis, ~án
Preterite: sup|e, ~iste, ~o,
~imos, ~isteis, ~ieron
Present subjunctive: sep|a, ~as,
~a, ~amos, ~áis, ~an
Imperfect subjunctive: sup|iera,
~ieras, ~iera, ~iéramos,
~ierais, ~ieran
sup|iese, ~ieses, ~iese,
~iésemos, ~ieseis, ~iesen
Conditional: sabr|ía, ~ías, ~ía,
~íamos, ~íais, ~ían

[39] **ser**

Present: soy, eres, es, somos, sois,
son
Imperfect: era, eras, era, éramos,
erais, eran
Preterite: fui, fuiste, fue, fuimos,
fuisteis, fueron
Present subjunctive: se|a, ~as,
~a, ~amos, ~áis, ~an
Imperfect subjunctive: fu|era,
~eras, ~era, ~éramos,
~erais, ~eran
fu|ese, ~eses, ~ese, ~ésemos,
~eseis, ~esen
Imperative: sé, sed

[40] **tener**

Present: tengo, tienes, tiene,
tenemos, tenéis, tienen
Future: tendr|é, ~ás, ~á,
~emos, ~éis, ~án
Preterite: tuv|e, ~iste, ~o,
~imos, ~isteis, ~ieron
Present subjunctive: teng|a, ~as,
~a, ~amos, ~áis, ~an
Imperfect subjunctive: tuv|iera,
~ieras, ~iera, ~iéramos,
~ierais, ~ieran
tuv|iese, ~ieses, ~iese,
~iésemos, ~ieseis, ~iesen

Conditional: tendría, ~ías, ~ía,
~íamos, ~íais, ~ían
Imperative: ten, tened

yazca, yazcamos, yazcáis,
yazcan
Imperative: yace/yaz, yaced

[41] traer

Present: traigo, traes, trae,
traemos, traéis, traen
Preterite: traje, ~iste, ~o,
~imos, ~isteis, ~eron
Present subjunctive: traiga, ~as,
~a, ~amos, ~áis, ~an
Imperfect subjunctive: trajera,
~eras, ~era, ~éramos,
~erais, ~eran
trajese, ~eses, ~ese,
~ésemos, ~eseis, ~esen
Present participle: trayendo
Past participle: traído

[42] valer

Present: valgo, vales, vale,
valemos, valéis, valen
Future: valdré, ~ás, ~á,
~emos, ~éis, ~án
Present subjunctive: valga, ~as,
~a, ~amos ~áis, ~an
Conditional: valdría, ~ías, ~ía,
~íamos, ~íais, ~ían
Imperative: val/vale, valed

[43] ver

Present: veo, ves, ve, vemos, véis,
ven
Imperfect: veía, ~ías, ~ía,
~íamos, ~íais, ~ían
Preterite: vi, viste, vio, vimos,
visteis, vieron
Present subjunctive: vea, ~as,
~a, ~amos, ~áis, ~an
Past participle: visto

[44] yacer

Present: yazco/yazgo/yago,
yaces, yave, yacemos, yacéis,
yacen
Present subjunctive:
yazca/yazga/yaga, yazcas,

[45] asir

Present: asgo, ases, ase, asimos,
asís, asen
Present subjunctive: asga, ~as,
~a, ~amos, ~áis, ~an

[46] decir

Present: digo, dices, dice,
decimos, decís, dicen
Future: diré, ~ás, ~á, ~emos,
~éis, ~án
Preterite: dije, ~iste, ~o,
~imos, ~isteis, ~eron
Present subjunctive: diga, ~as,
~a, ~amos, ~áis, ~an
Imperfect subjunctive: dijera,
~eras, ~era, ~éramos,
~erais, ~eran
dijese, ~eses, ~ese, ~ésemos,
~eseis, ~esen
Conditional: diría, ~ías, ~ía,
~íamos, ~íais, ~ían
Present participle: dicho
Imperative: di, decid

[47] reducir

Present: reduzco, reduces,
reduce, reducimos, reducís,
reducen
Preterite: reduje, ~iste, ~o,
~imos, ~isteis, ~eron
Present subjunctive: reduzca,
~as, ~a, ~amos, ~áis, ~an
Imperfect subjunctive: redujera,
~eras, ~era, ~éramos,
~erais, ~eran
redujese, ~eses, ~ese,
~ésemos, ~eseis, ~esen

[48] erguir

Present: irgo, irgues, irgue,
erguimos, erguís, irguen
yergo, yergues, yergue,
erguimos, erguís, yerguen

Preterite: erguí, erguiste, irguió, erguimos, erguisteis, irguieron
Present subjunctive: irg|a, ~as, ~a, ~amos, ~áis, ~an
yerg|a, ~as, ~a, ~amos, ~áis, ~an
Imperfect subjunctive: irgu|iera, ~ieras, ~iera, ~iéramos, ~ierais, ~ieran
irgu|iese, ~ieses, ~iese, ~iésemos, ~ieseis, ~iesen
Present participle: irguiendo
Imperative: irgue/yergue, erguid

[49] **ir**
Present: voy, vas, va, vamos, vais, van
Imperfect: iba, ibas, iba, íbamos, ibais, iban
Preterite: fui, fuiste, fue, fuimos, fuisteis, fueron
Present subjunctive: vay|a, ~as, ~a, ~amos, ~áis, ~an
Imperfect subjunctive: fu|era, ~eras, ~era, ~éramos, ~erais, ~eran
fu|ese, ~eses, ~ese, ~ésemos, ~eseis, ~esen
Present participle: yendo
Imperative: ve, id

[50] **oír**
Present: oigo, oyes, oye, oímos, oís, oyen
Preterite: oí, oíste, oyó, oímos, oísteis, oyeron
Present subjunctive: oig|a, ~as, ~a, ~amos, ~áis, ~an
Imperfect subjunctive: oy|era, ~eras, ~era, ~éramos, ~erais, ~eran
oy|ese, ~eses, ~ese, ~ésemos, ~eseis, ~esen

Present participle: oyendo
Past participle: oído
Imperative: oye, oíd

[51] **reír**
Present: río, ríes, ríe, reímos, reís, ríen
Preterite: reí, reíste, rió, reímos, reísteis, rieron
Present subjunctive: ría, rías, ría, riamos, riáis, rían
Present participle: riendo
Past participle: reído
Imperative: ríe, reíd

[52] **salir**
Present: salgo, sales, sale, salimos, salís, salen
Future: saldr|é, ~ás, ~á, ~emos, ~éis, ~án
Present subjunctive: salg|a, ~as, ~a, ~amos, ~áis, ~an
Conditional: saldr|ía, ~ías, ~ía, ~íamos, ~íais, ~ían
Imperative: sal, salid

[53] **venir**
Present: vengo, vienes, viene, venimos, venís, vienen
Future: vendr|é, ~ás, ~á, ~emos, ~éis, ~án
Preterite: vin|e, ~iste, ~o, ~imos, ~isteis, ~ieron
Present subjunctive: veng|a, ~as, ~a, ~amos, ~áis, ~an
Imperfect subjunctive: vin|iera, ~ieras, ~iera, ~iéramos, ~ierais, ~ieran
vin|iese, ~ieses, ~iese, ~iésemos, ~ieseis, ~iesen
Conditional: vendr|ía, ~ías, ~ía, ~íamos, ~íais, ~ían
Present participle: viniendo
Imperative: ven, venid

Verbos Irregulares Ingleses

Infinitivo	*Pretérito*	*Participio pasado*
arise	arose	arisen
awake	awoke	awoken
be	was	been
bear	bore	borne
beat	beat	beaten
become	became	become
befall	befell	befallen
beget	begot	begotten
begin	began	begun
behold	beheld	beheld
bend	bent	bent
beset	beset	beset
bet	bet, betted	bet, betted
bid	bade, bid	bidden, bid
bind	bound	bound
bite	bit	bitten
bleed	bled	bled
blow	blew	blown
break	broke	broken
breed	bred	bred
bring	brought	brought
broadcast	broadcast(ed)	broadcast
build	built	built
burn	burnt, burned	burnt, burned
burst	burst	burst
buy	bought	bought
cast	cast	cast
catch	caught	caught
choose	chose	chosen
cleave	clove, cleft, cleaved	cloven, cleft, cleaved
cling	clung	clung
clothe	clothed, clad	clothed, clad
come	came	come
cost	cost	cost
creep	crept	crept
crow	crowed, crew	crowed
cut	cut	cut
deal	dealt	dealt
dig	dug	dug
do	did	done
draw	drew	drawn
dream	dreamt, dreamed	dreamt, dreamed
drink	drank	drunk
drive	drove	driven
dwell	dwelt	dwelt

Infinitivo	*Pretérito*	*Participio pasado*
eat	ate	eaten
fall	fell	fallen
feed	fed	fed
feel	felt	felt
fight	fought	fought
find	found	found
flee	fled	fled
fling	flung	flung
fly	flew	flown
forbear	forbore	forborne
forbid	forbad(e)	forbidden
forecast	forecast(ed)	forecast(ed)
foresee	foresaw	foreseen
foretell	foretold	foretold
forget	forgot	forgotten
forgive	forgave	forgiven
forsake	forsook	forsaken
freeze	froze	frozen
gainsay	gainsaid	gainsaid
get	got	got
give	gave	given
go	went	gone
grind	ground	ground
grow	grew	grown
hang	hung, hanged	hung, hanged
have	had	had
hear	heard	heard
hew	hewed	hewn, hewed
hide	hid	hidden
hit	hit	hit
hold	held	held
hurt	hurt	hurt
inlay	inlaid	inlaid
keep	kept	kept
kneel	knelt	knelt
knit	knitted, knit	knitted, knit
know	knew	known
lay	laid	laid
lead	led	led
lean	leaned, leant	leaned, leant
leap	leaped, leapt	leaped, leapt
learn	learned, learnt	learned, learnt
leave	left	left
lend	lent	lent
let	let	let
lie	lay	lain
light	lit, lighted	lit, lighted
lose	lost	lost

Infinitivo	*Pretérito*	*Participio pasado*
make	made	made
mean	meant	meant
meet	met	met
mislay	mislaid	mislaid
mislead	misled	misled
misspell	misspelt	misspelt
mistake	mistook	mistaken
misunderstand	misunderstood	misunderstood
mow	mowed	mown
outbid	outbid	outbid
outdo	outdid	outdone
outgrow	outgrew	outgrown
overcome	overcame	overcome
overdo	overdid	overdone
overhang	overhung	overhung
overhear	overheard	overheard
override	overrode	overridden
overrun	overran	overrun
oversee	oversaw	overseen
overshoot	overshot	overshot
oversleep	overslept	overslept
overtake	overtook	overtaken
overthrow	overthrew	overthrown
partake	partook	partaken
pay	paid	paid
prove	proved	proved, proven
put	put	put
quit	quitted, quit	quitted, quit
read /ri:d/	read /red/	read /red/
rebuild	rebuilt	rebuilt
redo	redid	redone
rend	rent	rent
repay	repaid	repaid
rewrite	rewrote	rewritten
rid	rid	rid
ride	rode	ridden
ring	rang	rung
rise	rose	risen
run	ran	run
saw	sawed	sawn, sawed
say	said	said
see	saw	seen
seek	sought	sought
sell	sold	sold
send	sent	sent
set	set	set
sew	sewed	sewn, sewed
shake	shook	shaken

Infinitivo	Pretérito	Participio pasado
shear	sheared	shorn, sheared
shed	shed	shed
shine	shone	shone
shoe	shod	shod
shoot	shot	shot
show	showed	shown, showed
shrink	shrank	shrunk
shut	shut	shut
sing	sang	sung
sink	sank	sunk
sit	sat	sat
slay	slew	slain
sleep	slept	slept
slide	slid	slid
sling	slung	slung
slit	slit	slit
smell	smelt, smelled	smelt, smelled
smite	smote	smitten
sow	sowed	sown, sowed
speak	spoke	spoken
speed	speeded, sped	speeded, sped
spell	spelt, spelled	spelt, spelled
spend	spent	spent
spill	spilt, spilled	spilt, spilled
spin	spun	spun
spit	spat	spat
split	split	split
spoil	spoilt, spoiled	spoilt, spoiled
spread	spread	spread
spring	sprang	sprung
stand	stood	stood
steal	stole	stolen
stick	stuck	stuck
sting	stung	stung
stink	stank, stunk	stunk
strew	strewed	strewn, strewed
stride	strode	stridden
strike	struck	struck
string	strung	strung
strive	strove	striven
swear	swore	sworn
sweep	swept	swept
swell	swelled	swollen, swelled
swim	swam	swum
swing	swung	swung
take	took	taken
teach	taught	taught
tear	tore	torn

Infinitivo	*Pretérito*	*Participio pasado*
tell	told	told
think	thought	thought
thrive	thrived, throve	thrived, thriven
throw	threw	thrown
thrust	thrust	thrust
tread	trod	trodden, trod
unbend	unbent	unbent
undergo	underwent	undergone
understand	understood	understood
undertake	undertook	undertaken
undo	undid	undone
upset	upset	upset
wake	woke, waked	woken, waked
waylay	waylaid	waylaid
wear	wore	worn
weave	wove	woven
weep	wept	wept
win	won	won
wind	wound	wound
withdraw	withdrew	withdrawn
withhold	withheld	withheld
withstand	withstood	withstood
wring	wrung	wrung
write	wrote	written